D1165013

Short Story Criticism

Guide to Gale Literary Criticism Series

For criticism on	Consult these Gale series
Authors now living or who died after December 31, 1999	*CONTEMPORARY LITERARY CRITICISM (CLC)*
Authors who died between 1900 and 1999	*TWENTIETH-CENTURY LITERARY CRITICISM (TCLC)*
Authors who died between 1800 and 1899	*NINETEENTH-CENTURY LITERATURE CRITICISM (NCLC)*
Authors who died between 1400 and 1799	*LITERATURE CRITICISM FROM 1400 TO 1800 (LC)* *SHAKESPEAREAN CRITICISM (SC)*
Authors who died before 1400	*CLASSICAL AND MEDIEVAL LITERATURE CRITICISM (CMLC)*
Authors of books for children and young adults	*CHILDREN'S LITERATURE REVIEW (CLR)*
Dramatists	*DRAMA CRITICISM (DC)*
Poets	*POETRY CRITICISM (PC)*
Short story writers	*SHORT STORY CRITICISM (SSC)*
Literary topics and movements	*HARLEM RENAISSANCE: A GALE CRITICAL COMPANION (HR)* *THE BEAT GENERATION: A GALE CRITICAL COMPANION (BG)* *FEMINISM IN LITERATURE: A GALE CRITICAL COMPANION (FL)* *GOTHIC LITERATURE: A GALE CRITICAL COMPANION (GL)*
Asian American writers of the last two hundred years	*ASIAN AMERICAN LITERATURE (AAL)*
Black writers of the past two hundred years	*BLACK LITERATURE CRITICISM (BLC-1)* *BLACK LITERATURE CRITICISM SUPPLEMENT (BLCS)* *BLACK LITERATURE CRITICISM: CLASSIC AND EMERGING AUTHORS SINCE 1950 (BLC-2)*
Hispanic writers of the late nineteenth and twentieth centuries	*HISPANIC LITERATURE CRITICISM (HLC)* *HISPANIC LITERATURE CRITICISM SUPPLEMENT (HLCS)*
Native North American writers and orators of the eighteenth, nineteenth, and twentieth centuries	*NATIVE NORTH AMERICAN LITERATURE (NNAL)*
Major authors from the Renaissance to the present	*WORLD LITERATURE CRITICISM, 1500 TO THE PRESENT (WLC)* *WORLD LITERATURE CRITICISM SUPPLEMENT (WLCS)*

ISSN 0895-9439

Volume 125

Short Story Criticism

Criticism of the
Works of Short Fiction Writers

Jelena Krstović
Project Editor

Detroit • New York • San Francisco • New Haven, Conn • Waterville, Maine • London

Short Story Criticism, Vol. 125

Project Editor: Jelena O. Krstović

Editorial: Dana Ramel Barnes, Kathy D. Darrow, Kristen A. Dorsch, Jeffrey W. Hunter, Michelle Lee, Thomas J. Schoenberg, and Lawrence J. Trudeau

Content Conversion: Katrina D. Coach, Gwen Tucker

Indexing Services: Factiva®, a Dow Jones and Reuters Company

Rights and Acquisitions: Jennifer Altschul, Mardell Glinski-Schultz, Kelly Quin

Composition and Electronic Capture: Gary Leach

Manufacturing: Cynde Bishop

Associate Product Manager: Marc Cormier

For product information and technology assistance, contact us at **Gale Customer Support, 1-800-877-4253.** For permission to use material from this text or product, submit all requests online at **www.cengage.com/permissions.** Further permissions questions can be emailed to **permissionrequest@cengage.com**

Gale
27500 Drake Rd.
Farmington Hills, MI, 48331-3535

LIBRARY OF CONGRESS CATALOG CARD NUMBER 88-641014

ISBN-13: 978-1-4144-4204-4
ISBN-10: 1-4144-4204-1

ISSN 0895-9439

Printed in the United States of America
1 2 3 4 5 6 7 13 12 11 10 09

Contents

Preface vii

Acknowledgments xi

Literary Criticism Series Advisory Board xiii

Preface

S*hort Story Criticism* (*SSC*) presents significant criticism of the world's greatest short-story writers and provides supplementary biographical and bibliographical materials to guide the interested reader to a greater understanding of the authors of short fiction. This series was developed in response to suggestions from librarians serving high school, college, and public library patrons, who had noted a considerable number of requests for critical material on short-story writers. Although major short-story writers are covered in such Gale series as *Contemporary Literary Criticism* (*CLC*), *Twentieth-Century Literary Criticism* (*TCLC*), *Nineteenth-Century Literature Criticism* (*NCLC*), and *Literature Criticism from 1400 to 1800* (*LC*), librarians perceived the need for a series devoted solely to writers of the short-story genre.

Scope of the Series

SSC is designed to serve as an introduction to major short-story writers of all eras and nationalities. Since these authors have inspired a great deal of relevant critical material, *SSC* is necessarily selective, and the editors have chosen the most important published criticism to aid readers and students in their research.

Approximately three to six authors, works, or topics are included in each volume, and each entry presents a historical survey of the critical response to the work. The length of an entry is intended to reflect the amount of critical attention the author has received from critics writing in English and from foreign critics in translation. Every attempt has been made to identify and include the most significant essays on each author's work. In order to provide these important critical pieces, the editors sometimes reprint essays that have appeared elsewhere in Gale's Literary Criticism Series. Such duplication, however, never exceeds twenty percent of an *SSC* volume.

Organization of the Book

An *SSC* entry consists of the following elements:

- The **Author Heading** cites the name under which the author most commonly wrote, followed by birth and death dates. Also located here are any name variations under which an author wrote, including transliterated forms for authors whose native languages use nonroman alphabets. If the author wrote consistently under a pseudonym, the pseudonym will be listed in the author heading and the author's actual name given in parentheses on the first line of the biographical and critical introduction. Uncertain birth or death dates are indicated by question marks. Single-work entries are preceded by the title of the work and its date of publication.

- The **Introduction** contains background information that introduces the reader to the author and the critical debates surrounding his or her work.

- The list of **Principal Works** is ordered chronologically by date of first publication and lists the most important works by the author. The first section comprises short-story collections, novellas, and novella collections. The second section gives information on other major works by the author. For foreign authors, the editors have provided original foreign-language publication information and have selected what are considered the best and most complete English-language editions of their works.

- Reprinted **Criticism** is arranged chronologically in each entry to provide a useful perspective on changes in critical evaluation over time. All short-story, novella, and collection titles by the author featured in the entry are printed in boldface type. The critic's name and the date of composition or publication of the critical work are given at the beginning of each piece of criticism. Unsigned criticism is preceded by the title of the source in which it appeared. Footnotes are reprinted at the end of each essay or excerpt. In the case of excerpted criticism, only those footnotes that pertain to the excerpted texts are included.

- Critical essays are prefaced by brief **Annotations** explicating each piece.

- A complete **Bibliographical Citation** of the original essay or book precedes each piece of criticism. Source citations in the Literary Criticism Series follow University of Chicago Press style, as outlined in *The Chicago Manual of Style,* 15th ed. (Chicago: The University of Chicago Press, 2006).

- An annotated bibliography of **Further Reading** appears at the end of each entry and suggests resources for additional study. In some cases, significant essays for which the editors could not obtain reprint rights are included here. Boxed material following the further reading list provides references to other biographical and critical sources on the author in series published by Gale.

Indexes

A **Cumulative Author Index** lists all of the authors that appear in a wide variety of reference sources published by Gale, including *SSC*. A complete list of these sources is found facing the first page of the Author Index. The index also includes birth and death dates and cross references between pseudonyms and actual names.

A **Cumulative Nationality Index** lists all authors featured in *SSC* by nationality, followed by the number of the *SSC* volume in which their entry appears.

An alphabetical **Title Index** lists all short-story, novella, and collection titles contained in the *SSC* series. Titles of short-story collections, separately published novellas, and novella collections are printed in italics, while titles of individual short stories are printed in roman type with quotation marks. Each title is followed by the author's last name and corresponding volume and page numbers where commentary on the work is located. English-language translations of original foreign-language titles are cross-referenced to the foreign titles so that all references to discussion of a work are combined in one listing.

In response to numerous suggestions from librarians, Gale also produces an annual paperbound edition of the SSC cumulative title index. This annual cumulation, which alphabetically lists all titles reviewed in the series, is available to all customers. Additional copies of this index are available upon request. Librarians and patrons will welcome this separate index; it saves shelf space, is easy to use, and is recyclable upon receipt of the next edition.

Citing *Short Story Criticism*

When citing criticism reprinted in the Literary Criticism Series, students should provide complete bibliographic information so that the cited essay can be located in the original print or electronic source. Students who quote directly from reprinted criticism may use any accepted bibliographic format, such as University of Chicago Press style or Modern Language Association (MLA) style. Both the MLA and the University of Chicago formats are acceptable and recognized as being the current standards for citations. It is important, however, to choose one format for all citations; do not mix the two formats within a list of citations.

The examples below follow recommendations for preparing a bibliography set forth in *The Chicago Manual of Style,* 15th ed. (Chicago: The University of Chicago Press, 2006); the first example pertains to material drawn from periodicals, the second to material reprinted from books:

Morrison, Jago. "Narration and Unease in Ian McEwan's Later Fiction." *Critique* 42, no. 3 (spring 2001): 253-68. Reprinted in *Short Story Criticism.* Vol. 57, edited by Jelena Krstovic, 212-20. Detroit: Gale, 2003.

Brossard, Nicole. "Poetic Politics." In *The Politics of Poetic Form: Poetry and Public Policy,* edited by Charles Bernstein, 73-82. New York: Roof Books, 1990. Reprinted in *Short Story Criticism.* Vol. 57, edited by Jelena Krstovic, 3-8. Detroit: Gale, 2003.

The examples below follow recommendations for preparing a works cited list set forth in the *MLA Handbook for Writers of Research Papers,* 6th ed. (New York: The Modern Language Association of America, 2003); the first example pertains to material drawn from periodicals, the second to material reprinted from books:

Morrison, Jago. "Narration and Unease in Ian McEwan's Later Fiction." *Critique* 42.3 (spring 2001): 253-68. Reprinted in *Short Story Criticism.* Ed. Jelena Krstovic. Vol. 57. Detroit: Gale, 2003. 212-20.

Brossard, Nicole. "Poetic Politics." *The Politics of Poetic Form: Poetry and Public Policy.* Ed. Charles Bernstein. New York: Roof Books, 1990. 73-82. Reprinted in *Short Story Criticism.* Ed. Jelena Krstovic. Vol. 57. Detroit: Gale, 2003. 3-8.

Suggestions are Welcome

Readers who wish to suggest new features, topics, or authors to appear in future volumes, or who have other suggestions or comments are cordially invited to call, write, or fax the Associate Product Manager:

Associate Product Manager, Literary Criticism Series

Gale

27500 Drake Road

Farmington Hills, MI 48331-3535

1-800-347-4253 (GALE)

Fax: 248-699-8054

Acknowledgments

The editors wish to thank the copyright holders of the excerpted criticism included in this volume and the permissions managers of many book and magazine publishing companies for assisting us in securing reproduction rights. Following is a list of the copyright holders who have granted us permission to reproduce material in this volume of *SSC*. Every effort has been made to trace copyright, but if omissions have been made, please let us know.

COPYRIGHTED MATERIAL IN *SSC*, *VOLUME 125, WAS REPRODUCED FROM THE FOLLOWING PERIODICALS:*

All Things Considered, December 15, 1997 for "Best American Short Stories" by Tim Gautreaux, Robert Siegel, and Elizabeth Arnold. Reproduced by permission.—*The Atlanta Journal-Constitution,* November 28, 1999. Copyright © *The Atlanta Journal-Constitution.* Republished with permission of *The Atlanta Journal-Constitution,* conveyed through Copyright Clearance Center, Inc.—*Atlantic Online,* March 4, 1997 for "A Conversation with Tim Gautreaux" by Tim Gautreaux, Katie Bolick, and David Watta. Copyright © 1997 The Atlantic Monthly Company. All rights reserved. Reproduced by permission.—*The Carolina Quarterly,* June, 2005. Copyright © 2005 by The University of North Carolina Press. Reproduced by permission.—*Christianity and Literature,* v. 56, fall, 2006. Copyright © 2006 Conference on Christianity and Literature. Reproduced by permission.—*Commonweal,* November 8, 1996. Copyright © 1996 Commonweal Publishing Co., Inc. Reproduced by permission of Commonweal Foundation.—*Essays in Poetics,* v. 28, October, 2003. Copyright © 2003 by Joseph Sherman. Reproduced by permission.—*The Georgia Review,* v. LIV, winter, 2000. Copyright © 2000 by The University of Georgia. Reproduced by permission.—*Hispanic Journal,* v. 8, fall, 1986; v. 10, spring, 1989. Copyright © 1986, 1989 IUP Indiana University of Pennsylvania. Both reproduced by permission.—*Hispanofila,* January, 1989. Reproduced by permission.—*The Houston Chronicle,* December 19, 1999. Copyright © 1999 Houston Chronicle Publishing Company Divison. Reproduced by permission.—*Jewish Social Studies,* v. 7, January, 2001. Copyright © 2001 Indiana University Press. Reproduced by permission.—*Journal of Evolutionary Psychology,* v. 14, March, 1993. Reproduced by permission.—*Journal of Spanish Studies: Twentieth Century,* v. 1, winter, 1973; v. 6, 1978. Copyright © 1974, 1978 by the Journal of Spanish Studies. Both reproduced by permission of the publisher.—*Judaism,* v. 43, winter, 1994. Copyright © 1994 by the American Jewish Congress. Reproduced by permission.—*Logos,* v. 5, fall, 2002 for "A Sacramental Science Project in Tim Gautreaux's 'Resistance'" by L. Lamar Nisly. Reproduced by permission of the author.—*MACLAS: Latin American Essays,* v. 6, 1993. Copyright © 1993 by *MACLAS: Latin American Essays.* Reproduced by permission.—*Modern Language Studies,* v. 19, spring, 1989 for "Sholem Aleichem: Monologues of Mastery" by Ken Frieden. Copyright © 1989 Northeast Modern Language Association. Reproduced by permission of the publisher and the author.—*Monographic Review/Revista Monográphica,* v. 7, 1991. Copyright © Genaro J. Perez & Janet I. Perez. All rights reserved. Reproduced by permission.—*Prooftexts,* v. 21, winter, 2001. Copyright © 2001 Indiana University Press. Reproduced by permission.—*Review of Contemporary Fiction,* v. 18, summer, 1998. Copyright © 1998 *The Review of Contemporary Fiction.* Reproduced by permission.—*Revista Canadiense de Estudios Hispánicos,* v. 8, spring, 1984 for "'A Garden Inclosed': Fuentes' *Aura,* Hawthorne's and Paz's 'Rappaccini's Daughter,' and Uyeda's *Ugetsu Monogatari*" by Lois Parkinson Zamora. Reproduced by permission of the publisher and author.—*Sewanee Review,* v. 68, January-March, 1960. Copyright © 1960 by The University of the South. Copyright renewed 1988 by the University of the South. Reproduced with permission of the editor. —*Southern Literary Journal,* v. XXXVIII, fall, 2005. Copyright © 2005 by the University of North Carolina Press. Used by permission.—*The Tampa Tribune,* October 17, 1999. Copyright © 1999 The Tampa Tribune. Reproduced by permission.—*West Virginia University Philological Papers,* v. 42-43, 1997 for "Vengeance Is Mine: The Role of the Fantastic in Carlos Fuentes's *Los Días Enmascarados*" by Jeffrey C. Barnett. Reproduced by permission of the publisher and author.

COPYRIGHTED MATERIAL IN *SSC*, VOLUME 125, WAS REPRODUCED FROM THE FOLLOWING BOOKS:

Atkins, John. From *Six Novelists Look at Society: An Enquiry into the Social Views of Elizabeth Bowen, L. P. Hartley, Rosamund Lehman, Christopher Isherwood, Nancy Mitford, C. P. Snow.* John Calder, 1977. Copyright © 1977 John Atkins. Reproduced by permission.—deGuzman, Daniel. From *Carlos Fuentes.* Twayne Publishers, 1972. Copyright © 1972 by Twayne Publishers, Inc. Reproduced by permission of the author.—Ezrahi, Sidra DeKoven. From *Booking Passage:*

Gale Literature Product Advisory Board

The members of the Gale Literature Product Advisory Board—reference librarians from public and academic library systems—represent a cross-section of our customer base and offer a variety of informed perspectives on both the presentation and content of our literature products. Advisory board members assess and define such quality issues as the relevance, currency, and usefulness of the author coverage, critical content, and literary topics included in our series; evaluate the layout, presentation, and general quality of our printed volumes; provide feedback on the criteria used for selecting authors and topics covered in our series; provide suggestions for potential enhancements to our series; identify any gaps in our coverage of authors or literary topics, recommending authors or topics for inclusion; analyze the appropriateness of our content and presentation for various user audiences, such as high school students, undergraduates, graduate students, librarians, and educators; and offer feedback on any proposed changes/enhancements to our series. We wish to thank the following advisors for their advice throughout the year.

Sholom Aleichem
1859-1916

(Also transliterated as Sholem Aleykhem; pseudonym of Sholom Rabinovitch, surname also transliterated as Rabinovitsch, Rabinowitz, and Rabinovich; first name also transliterated as Sholem, Shalom, and Solomon; also known as A Litvak, Gamliel Ben Pdatsur, Baron Pipernoter [Baron Ogre], Ester, Shulamis, Salomon Bikherfreser [Solomon Bookeater], Salomon Esbikher, Der Yidisher Gazlen [The Robber Jew], and Terakh's an Eynikl [Terach's Grandson], among others.) Ukrainian short story writer, novelist, playwright, and essayist.

The following entry provides an overview of Aleichem's short fiction. For additional information on his life and career, see *SSC,* Vol. 33.

INTRODUCTION

Writing under the pseudonym Sholom Aleichem, a traditional Hebrew greeting meaning "Peace be unto you," Sholom Rabinovitch is considered one of the founding fathers of Yiddish literature. Using the common language of Eastern European Jews at a time when it was virtually unheard of for an intellectual to write in the vernacular, Aleichem became a tremendously popular Yiddish folk writer whose humorous short stories entertained readers worldwide. Most of his tales take the form of a monologue, with the pseudonymous Aleichem functioning as both listener and transcriber of tales told to him by everyday Ukrainian Jews, most of whom inhabit the Pale of Settlement—those areas of Russia to which Jews were restricted in the nineteenth century. Aleichem's stories often depict the resilience, optimism, and faith of these characters, in spite of the grim reality of tsarist anti-Semitism, cultural upheaval, violence, starvation, and poverty under which they live. One of his most popular and enduring characters is Tevye the Dairyman, whose metaphysical questioning of God evokes the beleaguered Biblical figure of Job and whose adaptation for the stage (in the form of the enormously successful 1964 Broadway musical *Fiddler on the Roof*) helped spark a renewed interest in Yiddish literature in the second half of the twentieth century.

BIOGRAPHICAL INFORMATION

Aleichem was born in Pereyaslav, in the province of Poltava, Ukraine, in 1859. As a young child he lived in the small town of Voronkov, which served as inspiration for many of his later stories, and attended the local, traditional Jewish school. Biographers describe him as a curious child, with a talent for quick-wittedness and mimicry and a love of storytelling and tales. In the early 1870s, his family, facing financial difficulties, moved back to Pereyaslav, where his father managed an inn. There, following the death of Aleichem's mother, his father remarried, to a punitive, harsh woman whose skill at cursing Aleichem claimed later to have used as a model for several of his fictional characters. Aleichem's early interest in and affinity for writing prompted his father to send him to the Russian government school rather than to the yeshiva, the traditional Jewish religious academy. Following graduation, Aleichem taught for a short time in a local village school. He then accepted a position as private tutor to the young daughter of a wealthy Jew in the Kiev province, but he was discharged of his duties three years later because of the father's displeasure over Aleichem's growing emotional attachment to his student.

In 1880 he became a certified rabbi of Louben, a government-appointed post, and around the same time began publishing articles in Hebrew and Russian on educational and liturgical reform. In 1883 he married his former pupil, Olga Loyeff, after her father eventually agreed to the marriage, and that same year published his first stories in the Yiddish magazine *Dos yidishe folksblat,* adopting the pseudonym Sholom Aleichem purportedly to spare embarrassment to his father and father-in-law, who were among many who strongly objected to the notion of a rabbi writing in the "uncultured" language of Yiddish. Though he immersed himself in investing in Kiev's emerging stock exchange, Aleichem became increasingly interested in writing, turning away from the moralizing and instructive tracts of fellow Jewish writers and moving instead toward humor. In 1885, independently wealthy after the death of his father-in-law, Aleichem endeavored to encourage the advancement of Yiddish literature by soliciting the works of other Yiddish writers for what would become the two-volume *Di yudishe folksbibliotek* (1889-90; "The Jewish Popular Library"). A few years later, in 1890, he became bankrupt as a result of a stock market crash and was forced to rely on his mother-in-law for the financial means to begin trading again. Throughout the 1890s he continued to write stories, most of which appeared in weekly Jewish literary supplements to newspapers. He began the immensely popular Tevye stories and Menakhem-Mendl stories during this period and achieved such financial success from them that by 1903 he was able to devote himself entirely to writing.

Two years later he fled Russia in the face of tsarist-sponsored pogroms—efforts whose purpose it was to eradicate Jews through organized massacres, forced immigrations, and starvation. He never again returned to his native country permanently. Instead, he gave readings and lectures throughout Europe and the United States, appearing each time to huge celebrations and overcrowded venues filled with audiences begging for more. He was forced to maintain a demanding speaking schedule in part due to increasing financial troubles—having sold his copyrights to unscrupulous publishers years before, he received no royalties from the sale of his works. Finally, in 1908, he collapsed from tuberculosis. For the next six years he convalesced first in Italy and then in several health resorts in Europe. Unable to pay his debts, he received assistance from friends who organized a twenty-fifth anniversary jubilee celebration of the publication of his first short story. They received donations from throughout the world and reclaimed the copyrights from his publishers. With his finances stabilized and his health seemingly restored by late 1914, Aleichem moved to New York, hoping to benefit from the support of the literary community there. News of his son's death from tuberculosis, however, coupled with reports of the relentless persecution of European Jews, taxed his health, and he died in New York City in 1916. It is estimated that over two hundred thousand mourners attended his funeral.

MAJOR WORKS OF SHORT FICTION

The bulk of Aleichem's hundreds of short stories center on the chaotic and despair-laden lives of turn-of-the-twentieth-century Ukrainian Jews, who are subjected to political, financial, and social oppression on a daily basis in the form of raids, violence, punitive economic policies, forced ghettoization, and barriers to higher education. Coupled with these hardships is their experience of the demise of their traditional, orthodox way of life—a result of the encroachment of technology, the increasing influence of European and Western societies, and the changing values of the younger generations, particularly their increasing secularization and disregard for tradition. Despite this overwhelming adversity, Aleichem maintained a tone of optimism and humor throughout the stories, many of which take place in the fictional Eastern European

shtetl of Kasrilevke. The residents of Kasrilevke tell their stories to Aleichem, a writer from the town of Yehupetz (a fictional Kiev), who in turn relates the tales to readers as he has heard them, with no authorial intervention. This strategy allows the storytellers to inadvertently reveal their attitudes and faults and contributes to Aleichem's overall emphasis on humanity and emotion as opposed to logic, a rigorous plotline, and a clear-cut ending.

Aleichem is most famous for three major characters—Tevye the Dairyman, Menakhem-Mendl, and Motl Peyse—all of whom appear in extended story sequences that were published in serial form over many years in the late nineteenth and early twentieth centuries. Written in pieces over two decades, the stories of Tevye are considered Aleichem's greatest. With his faith in God as his anchor, Tevye tells his life story as a poor, tradition-bound Jew whose dream for his many daughters is for each of them to marry rich, allowing him to rest and live in prosperity. A humble and sympathetic man, Tevye peppers his narrative with recitations and misquotes of ancient Hebrew Scripture and prayer books, questioning God's justice and His will throughout each of life's trials, including a daughter who marries a poor tailor against Tevye's wishes, another who marries a revolutionary whom she follows in exile to Siberia, another who converts to Christianity in order to marry a Russian, and still another who commits suicide after her lover is sent away by his disapproving mother. When yet another daughter attempts to ease Tevye's anguish and misery by marrying a wealthy man whom she does not love, Tevye's heart is broken by her suffering and her emotionally empty life. In the end Tevye, having already suffered the death of his wife, is forced by the Russian government to vacate his ancestral home. Though he ends up homeless and an aimless wanderer, his tales continually reflect his submission to divine authority and his unwavering faith in God.

The stories of the fast-talking and eternally optimistic Menakhem-Mendl are told in epistolary form, using letters exchanged between Mendl and his wife, Sheyne Shendl, detailing Mendl's travels throughout Europe and the United States as he seeks his fortune. Much of the humor derives from the contrast between Mendl's continually outrageous plans (despite his incessant failures) and Shendl's practicality and skepticism, reflected in part by her steadfast refusal to leave Kasrilevke. The son of Peyse the Cantor, who dies early on in the Motl sequence, Motl is a young Jewish boy whose stories Aleichem was still composing at the time of his death. Unique in part because of the absence of the middle figure of Aleichem (the stories are narrated by Motl himself), the almost forty episodes are considered the most affirming of Aleichem's writings, underscoring the enthusiasm and vitality of Jewish youth as opposed to the traditional portrayals of Jewish children as being urged into silence and hurried into adulthood by their elders. The stories are representative of the massive immigrant movement through European countries and into America during the late 1800s and into the 1900s, and convey the immigrant experience—including unrealistic expectations, exploitation, bigotry, tragedies, and triumphs—through the eyes of a child.

CRITICAL RECEPTION

Critics almost unanimously celebrate Aleichem as a highly skilled writer of humorous short tales, singling out his ability to fashion a restorative brand of humor founded upon empathy and compassion. Most scholars find Aleichem at his best when drawing characters whose identities are directly tied to their families, communities, and shared cultural history. He is often spoken of as a social historian, for his tales recreate the reality of the persecuted Russian Jew. Commentators call attention to his strict adherence to real-life details, claiming that he did not attempt to suppress or sugar-coat reality but to offer Jews what he perhaps believed were the only tools left for a powerless, despised, and poverty-ridden race: its ability to rise above despair by laughing at itself—and not in a self-deprecating way, but in a healing one based in acceptance, commonality, and resilience. Aleichem's characters talk a great deal in his stories, a facet that has elicited considerable acclaim. Critics praise Aleichem's ear for dialect and his ability to mimic the idiosyncrasies of Yiddish speech, and they underscore his skill at recreating the rhythms and tones of Yiddish speakers and accurately recording their mannerisms and gestures. Several scholars focus on Aleichem's use of the monologue, studying how the form reveals the inner nature of the narrators, and they speculate that Aleichem used the monologues to emphasize his characters' isolation and their separation from reality, almost to the point of insanity. Others find the form of the monologue intriguing because the bulk of the literary analysis resides with the reader himself, who must determine the reliability and integrity of the character on his own.

In other discussions Aleichem is acclaimed for being able to take a single, seemingly insignificant incident, and use it to symbolize the entire Jewish condition. Several critics, for example, see in the incessant and seemingly irrelevant chatter of the female protagonist of the famous "Dos tepl" (1905; "The Little Pot") a reflection of the grief and suffering of the entire Jewish race, claiming that the main character's constant talk masks her anxiety and desolation over her son's impending death. Other commentators focus on how the penname Aleichem functions in the narrative, examining the pseudonymous figure as a confidante or ghostwriter, one who provides the literary expertise for unlearned storytellers, or as a filter or a judge, controlling the reader's reaction based on how he tells a story and what details he includes. Still others concentrate on how the private identity of Rabinovitch was virtually swallowed up by his pseudonymous identity—a situation that intensified after Rabinovitch left Russia but continued to write of Russian Jews. Critics call attention to the disparity between Aleichem and the real-life Rabinovitch, who was an educated, semi-assimilated Russian-speaking member of the bourgeois Russian-Jewish community. This distancing from his subject matter increased significantly after 1909, when his separation from his homeland was exacerbated by illness, a sense of isolation, financial difficulties, and a lack of artistic inspiration. Some Aleichem scholars believe that the pseudonym, especially at that point in Rabinovitch's life, was vitally important as an intermediary to authenticate the work of a writer in exile.

Other areas of scholarly concern revolve around the character of Tevye, especially his constant uttering of malapropisms. Some critics view Tevye as a purely comic character, while others regard him as cunning and sharp, someone who deliberately intends his words to be read ironically in order to spark a reexamination of Jewish teachings. Additionally, some critics reflect on how the fate of Tevye and his family mirrors that of most turn-of-the-twentieth-century Russian Jews, while others oppose the traditionally positive responses to Tevye—who is typically viewed as a resilient and devout Jew—and instead see him as representing Jews as submissive and helpless in the face of persecution. Additional analyses revolve around Aleichem's literary debt to Sholem Yankev Abramovitch (penname Mendele the Book Peddler); how Aleichem's *Ayznban geshikhtes* (*The Railroad Stories*)—written from 1902 to around 1910—reflect the author's increasingly pessimistic feelings toward his own exile from Russia; and the fact that many of Aleichem's finest tales do not have well-defined endings—a fact that some critics claim reflects Aleichem's belief in the openness of life.

PRINCIPAL WORKS

Short Fiction

Di veltrayze: a gants sheyne mayse 1886
Dos meserl 1887

A bintl blumen 1888

A mayse on an ek: aroysgenumen fun an altn pinkes un baputst 1901

Sholem Aleykhems ale verk. 4 Vols. 1903

Dos tepl 1905

Hodl (a mayse fun Tevye dem milkhiger, vos hot zikh farlofn mit im nor in der letster tsayt) 1905

Oyf peysekh aheym: Fishl der melamed, a mayse 1905

Chava: Tevye dem milkhiker's 1909

*Menakhem-Mendl: Nyu-York—Varshe—Vin—Yehupets [The Further Adventures of Menachem-Mendl: New York—Warsaw—Vienna—Yehupetz] 1913

†Ale verk fun Sholem Aleykhem. 28 Vols. (short stories, novels, dramas, unfinished autobiography) [includes *Gants Tevye der milkhiker; Monologn,;* and *Ayznban geshikhtes: ksovim fun a komivoyazher*] 1917-23

‡Motl Peyse dem khazns. 2 Vols. [The Adventures of Mottel, the Cantor's Son] 1920

Stories for Jewish Children [*Mayses far yidishe kinder*] 1920

Collected Stories of Sholom Aleichem: The Old Country 1946

Dos naye Kasrilevke [*The New Kasrilevke*] 1948

Inside Kasrilevke 1948

Monologn 1948

Tevye's Daughters 1949

Stories and Satires 1959

Collected Stories of Sholom Aleichem. 2 Vols. 1965

Dos meserl 1983

‖Shir ha-shirim [The Song of Songs] (novella) 1987

The Jackpot 1989

A Treasury of Sholom Aleichem Children's Stories 1996

Other Major Works

Kindershpil (novel) 1887

Di yudishe folksbibliotek: a bukh far literatur, kritik un visnshaft. 2 vols. [editor and contributor] (anthology) [includes *Stempenyu* (novel) and *Yosele Solovey* (novel)] 1888-89

Reb Sender Blank un zayn fulgeshetste familye (novel) 1888

Shomers mishpet: oder der sud prisyazhne oyf ale romanen fun shomer (prose) 1888

Yaknehoyz: oder dos groyse berzn-shpil. A komedye in fir aktn (play) 1894

Der yidisher kongres in Bazl [*The Jewish Congress in Basel*] (essay) 1897

Meshiekhs tsaytn: a tsienistisher roman (novel) 1898

Oyf vos badarfn yidn a land [*Why Do the Jews Need a Land of Their Own?*] (essays) 1898

Hilf: a zamlbukh far literatur un kunst [editor and translator] (anthology) 1903

Tsezeyt un tseshpreyt (drama) 1905

Der mabl (novel) 1907; revised as *In shturem* 1918; revised version translated as *In the Storm* 1984

Samuel Pasternak (drama) 1907

Blondzhende shtern [*Wandering Star*] (novel) 1909-10

Shver tsu zayn a yid (drama) 1914

Dos groyse gevins (drama) 1916

Funem yarid: lebnsbashraybungen. 3 Vols. (unfinished autobiography) 1916-17; partially translated as *The Great Fair: Scenes from My Childhood* 1955; translated in its entirety as *From the Fair: The Autobiography of Sholom Aleichem* 1985

The Nightingale; or, The Saga of Yosele Solovey the Cantor (novel) 1985

The Bloody Hoax (novel) 1991

---

*The stories comprising *Menakhem-Mendl* were written between 1892 and 1913.

†Most of the stories contained in *Ayznban geshikhtes* were written between 1909 and around 1910. Aleichem actually wrote the stories in two segments: between 1902 and 1903, and between 1909 and about 1910.

‡Aleichem began writing the stories contained in *Motl Peyse dem khazns* in 1907 and continued writing them until his death. The version published in 1911 as part of the 16-volume *Ale verk: yubileum oysgabe,* therefore, is only a partial collection of the tales; the 2-volume edition published posthumously in 1920 contains all the *Motl* stories.

‖This novella was written between 1909 and 1911.

CRITICISM

Shmuel Niger (essay date 1926)

SOURCE: Niger, Shmuel. "The Humor of Sholom Aleichem," translated by Ruth Wisse. In *Voices from the Yiddish: Essays, Memoirs, Diaries,* edited by Irving Howe and Eliezer Greenberg, pp. 41-50. Ann Arbor: University of Michigan Press, 1972.

[In the following excerpt from an essay originally written in Yiddish in 1926, Niger finds the greatest expression of Aleichem's humor embodied in Tevye and the children of Aleichem's tales; the former endures his pain and suffering by considering them from the perspective of an empathetic and cheerful God-fearing man, while the latter enjoy a carefree and laughter-filled life free from the worries and anxieties of the adult Jew.]

The strength of Samson lay in his hair. There are writers whose greatness is similarly concentrated. Sholom Aleichem is one of these: his strength lies in his humor.

The humorist is not satisfied with the world, but he knows that his dissatisfaction is no more than a part of the world with which he is dissatisfied. The humorist is a child of the pessimist, but a smiling child who can smoothe out the wrinkles on the troubled face of his father. He tells him: "You take the world too seriously.

You believe in it, and demand from it more than it has to offer. Look at these trifles from a distance—from the proper distance that makes everything look insignificant—and you'll see that there is more cause for laughter than for tears. You are justified in your displeasure with the world, but even greater than justice is compassion. You are pessimistic because you are too much of an optimist. You think that the world deserves to be punished, whereas it deserves no more than forgiveness . . . " So concludes the consistent and therefore happy pessimist, laughing because he has made himself foolish in trying to make someone wiser. He laughs because he forgives his own foolish deeds as readily as those of another . . .

Forgiveness is both the bitterest root and the sweetest fruit of humor.

The most valuable, most human trait of Tevye the Dairyman, one of Sholom Aleichem's most wonderful characters, is precisely the ability of this common man to understand and forgive everything. To understand and forgive is a virtue of philosophers. And in every authentic humorist there is also something of the philosopher. Tevye the Dairyman is a philosopher, though of the heart, not the head, which is even better.

Though his head is the head of an ignorant and not overly sophisticated village Jew, he has the splendid philosophical ability to turn everything inside out, so as to discover the standpoint from which everything may be justified.

He tells, for example, of a conversation with his daughter, Tsaytl, about Lazar Wolf, the wealthy widower whose offer of marriage she is unwilling to accept: "So, my daughter, you weren't meant to fall into the lap of luxury and become mistress of a rich household, and we weren't meant to see a little happiness in our old age after all these years of work, I said, harnessed to the wheelbarrow day and night, knowing not a minute's peace, only poverty and misery and bad luck everywhere you turn . . . " He speaks to her softly, tenderly, and with his usual sympathy, but it almost seems as though he is offended and on the point of anger. Yet when he hears Tsaytl's tearful plea: "Papa, I'll hire myself out as a maid, I'll carry clay, I'll dig ditches"; when he hears this outburst of his daughter's, he understands *her* feelings too. A deeply human, fatherly compassion can be heard as he continues his story: "Why are you crying, silly girl, I said to her. Am I blaming you, silly child? Am I complaining about you? It's just that when things are bitter and gloomy I like to get them off my chest and have a talk with the Lord of the Universe about his treatment of me. I tell Him He's a Merciful Father, who takes pity

on me and lords it over me—may He not punish me for my words—He gives me all the joys that a father may expect, and go complain to the wall! So it is, and so it probably has to be. He is up there on high, and we are down here on the ground, deep, deep in the ground. We might as well admit that He is right and His Judgment is right, because if you want to look at it the other way around, aren't I a silly fool? Why am I shouting? Why am I raising a fuss? Who am I, but a tiny worm crawling around on earth? The slightest wind, if God wished it, could put an end to me in one blink of the eye. Who am I in my ignorance to give Him advice on how to run His world? If He wants it this way, it probably ought to be this way. Anyway, what good does it do to complain?"

In this delicate but penetrating irony of Tevye's, when the philosopher in him suddenly speaks out, we recognize not the pious but the knowing Jew, not the man of faith but the cheerful pessimist who knows that you can find an answer for everything if you want to, or no answer to anything if you want not to, so that it is better to pose no questions and admit no complaints against the Lord. "Anyway, what good does it do to complain?" Just be sure not to wallow like a fool in your own resentment; don't take it too seriously—which can be avoided if you set your own sufferings and joys before a higher authority than usual, and place yourself in the hands of fate, not because you doubt your own powers but because you set yourself above them.

The exceptional delicacy and complexity of feeling in Tevye—who is, after all, a simple, ordinary Jew—derive from his hidden store of humor, thanks to which he can transcend the pressure of immediate influences and surrender to life on terms that are not forced or slavish, but liberating. His liberating attitude of "taking it as it comes" creates a cloak of peace, tolerance, and submissiveness in which Tevye envelops his behavior, and which extends to his relations with other people.

At one point he is approached by Motl Kamzoyl, a young tailor from Anatevke. After a lengthy chat, filled with various insinuations, the tailor speaks out bluntly: "The story of the matter is as follows: your daughter Tsaytl and I gave each other our pledge over a year ago that we would get married." Tevye is angry, and even later, when he lets himself be won over, he still resents the outrage: "How could they give each other their pledge? What is the world coming to?" " . . . But when I looked at Motl, standing there with his head bowed like a sinner, perfectly serious, not wanting to take advantage of anyone, I reconsidered: If we look at it the other way around, what am I making such a fuss about? Who am I to put on airs?" And after considering it *the other way around,* everything seems right. Motl Kamzoyl now appears to be "quite a fine young man, a workingman who would provide for his wife, and an honest lad besides. So what do I have against him?—Tevye, I say to myself, don't make any lame excuses, and just give your blessing, as it says in the prayer, 'I have forgiven according to thy word'.—So, congratulations!"

This is Tevye's way of translating the sacred texts, and of "looking at things the other way around." He would be the unhappiest man in the world if he lacked this ability to smile down calmly on his own bitter fate; he would be another Job cursing the day of his birth were he not able to combine, as Ecclesiastes does, the ancient "vanity of vanities" with the later, wiser, and more pious verse, "Fear God, and keep his commandments."

"Whatever God ordains, His ways are best"—in this pious tone of "God giveth, God taketh," Tevye begins the sad story of his daughter Chava. But he immediately deepens the naive, common-prayerbook tone and says, "That is to say, His ways have to be best, because just try to be clever and improve on them! I tried to be smart, I tried twisting the verse this way and that, but when I saw it was of no use, I took my hand off my chest and said to myself: 'Tevye, you're a fool! You won't change the world. God has given us "the pain of bringing up children" which means, children will bring you trouble, but you had better make the best of it.'"

It is a mistake to think that the diaspora-Jew speaks through Tevye's mouth, or the *nebbish,* the humble man, the character whose formula is "this-too-is-for-the-best." Not at all. Tevye's healthy human instincts have been neither dulled nor weakened. He knows what is good in this world, and feels very keenly the misery of life. But since he cannot control it from the outside, he uses humor to sweeten it from the inside. Only in this delicate humorously-sarcastic sense does he put up with the "world as it is." Only after conquering it from within does he submit to it outwardly.

Here, for example, he is stopped on the road by his daughter, Chava, who has run off with Khvedke, a gentile writer from the local village. She wants to speak to Tevye, and a terrible inner struggle begins between the devout Jew and the devoted father. The insulted pride and stubborn determination of the God-fearing Jew gain ascendency for a minute, and Tevye drives his horse with wild vehemence, fleeing from his own flesh and blood. All the while we feel that "Tevye is not a woman," as might sometimes appear, but a man of firm character who, when occasion demands,

can be stronger than iron. Yet a moment later something occurs to him: "Tevye! You're taking too much on yourself! What harm would it do to stop for a while and listen to what she has to say? Maybe—who knows—maybe she is sorry, and wants to return? Maybe he has buried her six feet under and she needs your help to escape from hell? Maybe and maybe and a lot more maybes fly through my head, and I imagine her as a child and remember the passage—'As a father is merciful to his children'—to a father there is no bad child; I torment myself and accuse myself of being merciless and not worth the ground I walk on. What is at issue? What are you stewing about, you stubborn fool? What are you raising such a fuss over? Turn your wagon around, you brute, and make your peace with her. She is your child, not someone else's."

So Tevye argues with himself, wavering in his emotions, deeply moved, but not altogether ruled by them—neither their victor nor their victim. Even as his smile wrinkles into a deep crease of tragedy, he is illumined by the soft, elegiac shimmer of divinely inspired humor . . .

Although he is beset by one disaster after another we don't insult him with our small feelings of pity because we see that his troubles do not oppress or discourage him, but merely deepen his humanity.

Tevye has been seen by many as a representative of the old-fashioned, small-town Jewish masses; only the Jew in him was recognized. It seems to me, however, that precisely in the depiction of this simple villager Sholom Aleichem has also transcended that which is specifically Jewish. Tevye does have certain typical Jewish traits and mannerisms, including the characteristic Jewish ability to laugh out of one side of his mouth. Yet he also embodies something appreciably richer and fresher than the cold, angry, embittered Jewish irony, and he stands ten heads taller than the average ordinary small-town Jew.

If you see in this an idealization of Tevye, you must bear in mind that Sholom Aleichem himself idealized Tevye. He treats him quite differently from the other Kasrilevkites. Most of the men and women who people his stories are comic characters, objects of laughter, but Tevye is humorous. Sholom Aleichem stoops to the other characters in describing them, but Tevye he raises to his own level. He endows him with his own most beautiful talent—the ability to laugh. . . .

I have called Tevye Sholom Aleichem's beloved hero. I might have said his *most beloved hero.* Sholom Aleichem was not unfond of the other heroes of his novels, like Stempenyu, Yosele Solovey, Rafalesco of *Wandering Stars.* But whereas his love for them is of the "heroic" kind, his love for Tevye could be called simply "human." The above-mentioned and other romanticized heroes of Sholom Aleichem's works overshadow those around them because they are novelistic heroes—heroes by profession. God has blessed them with exceptional virtues and talents: one is a magnificent violinist, another a famous singer, the third an inspired actor. But Tevye is an everyday Jew, a common woodcarter, a simple villager. Thanks only to Sholom Aleichem's pen did Tevye become Tevye. When the heroes of the romances set out on their great adventures, when they soar to great heights and "speak poetry," it is no wonder; but Tevye had to be instructed by the author in what to say and what to think when he is alone with nature, or alone with himself. To Tevye the Dairyman the author entrusted his own role, the role of humorous story-teller, psychologist, portraitist, jokester, master of language—in short, the role of the writer. Consequently *Tevye the Dairyman* is not only the most moving and most likeable, but also the most intimate of Sholom Aleichem's books.

Tevye may have no match among the adults in Sholom Aleichem's cast of characters, but the children of Kasrilevke are portrayed with an equal measure of love and poetic tenderness. Like that great child, Tevye, the small children are poignant but never funny. And there is something else to be noted about them: Tevye, after all, is not utterly unique in Yiddish literature. No matter how refined his stories may be through humor, they are still sad, mournful stories; and sadness is the dominant mood of all Yiddish literature before Sholom Aleichem. Besides, if we really wanted to quibble, we could find several familiar traits in Tevye reminiscent of our old friend, Reb Mendele Mokher Sforim. With the children's stories, however, Sholom Aleichem brought an entirely new atmosphere into Yiddish fiction.

Who knows if we adults have not done an injustice by taking Sholom Aleichem away from the children? Who knows if he should not have written for them and no one else:

> -Pay attention, children, and I'll tell you a story about a pen-knife; not an imaginary story but a real story that actually happened to me. . . .

or:

> -Today, children, I'll play something for you on the fiddle. I don't think there is anything better or more beautiful than to be able to play the fiddle. . . .

or:

> -Children, guess which holiday is the best holiday of all? Hanukka! . . .

or:

> -Let me tell you a story about a flag. . . .

You have to have something of the child in you to be able to speak with children so simply and directly. You must still feel the boy in yourself in order to sense the profound difference between him and the adult Jew who has already taken upon himself the burden of the diaspora, the burdens of Torah and *mitzvas,* the pain of raising children and the worries of making a living; you must still keenly feel the boy you were to be able to set him up as a protest against the adult diaspora-Jew.

> -Why do you keep turning around like a corkscrew?— says my father as we all walk together to grandfather Meir's Purim feast, and I catch sight of the gang of masqueraders in the distance.
>
> -You're a grown boy already, praise God, can't you walk a little faster,—says my mother,—God willing, on the Sabbath before Passover you'll be eight years old, may you live to be a hundred and twenty.
>
> -Go on, go on!—Says my teacher, Reb Itzi, my angel of death, poking me from behind. . . .

Thus the old fashioned Jew trains his *eight-year-old* son, wanting to "make a man," that is, a little old Jew, out of him. But the little old Jew is not at all pleased at the prospect. He lowers his eyes to the mud on the ground, and keeps pace with the others, engrossed in miserable and gloomy thoughts: "Always with the grown-ups! Always with my teacher! . . . Morning, evening, Sabbath, and holidays! With Reb Itzi's big red tobacco nose, may it sink into the ground!" He isn't permitted to visit "the gang, King Ahasuerus— otherwise known as Kopel the Tailor wearing a golden crown." But the temptation is too great: when his childish heart, accustomed to yielding, can bear it no longer, he finally steals away from his grandfather's house and goes to join the masqueraders. He simply mounts a rebellion against the strict, boring regimen of the grown-ups. Nor is this the only rebellion.

"May my father in the world beyond forgive me," another of Sholom Aleichem's young boys tells us, "I could never understand what sort of a man he was. According to my mother he used to either study or pray all day long. In the first place, wasn't he ever tempted, as I am, to go outside on a summer morning before the sun is too strong, when it first begins to climb the sky? . . . What flavor can ordinary weekday prayers have on a glorious morning like that, can you tell me? Or sitting and studying in a dingy little room afterwards? . . . " The son cannot capture the feeling of his father's studying and praying because he lives in another world, without crowding or dinginess, without diaspora, and its heavy burden, without Jew and gentile. When cheder boys fight with the gentile boys (as in the story, **"Lag b'Omer"** it is only because the others, the gentiles, are "The Philistines," so they, "the Israelites," are obliged to wage war against them. How could it be otherwise? But elsewhere, Feitl plays very amicably with Fedka, and when spring comes they break out together into "God's great world, and taking each other by the hand they race towards the hill that beckons to them both: 'Come here, children!' They leap towards the sun that sends its greeting down to both: 'Come here, children!' And when they grow tired of running, they sit down on God's earth that knows no distinction between Jew and gentile, 'Come here, children, here to me!'" (*A Country Passover*). Let their fathers and mothers back there invent lies, blood libels, about one another; let them tremble in fear of one another; what does it have to do with them? The children, not having tasted the poisoned apples of the tree of knowledge, remain pure and healthy, as in the Garden of Eden. And if we grown-ups *are* poisoned by that knowledge, should we not desire at least the heart to feel and the eye to see again the innocence of children?

Sholom Aleichem is capable of childlike feeling and insight. When a gloomy Lithuanian rationalist, the nineteenth century writer, Moishe-Aaron Shatskes, described the Jewish Pre-Passover, he made of it a real tragedy, from which may Heaven preserve us! Whereas in Sholom Aleichem it appears as the **"Pre-Passover Emigration,"** one of his merriest, happiest stories. Why? Again, because the enlightened Shatskes, the unbeliever, ultimately looked at the world with the uneasy, weary, preoccupied, and argued-out eyes of the study-house-and-tenant-Jews, of the marketplace-and-kitchen women with their angry, haggard, overworked faces. He shared their attitudes, except that he was more critical. But Sholom Aleichem saw not only the father, the gloomy Jew who is angry at the forced emigration from alcove to kitchen and from kitchen to cellar and from cellar to attic, not only the mother, the Jewish housewife, frightfully absorbed in cleaning and preparing for Passover—he saw also the child, the schoolboy, the mischief-maker, for whom the pre-Passover migration is a great festivity, a real holiday.

As he says, "I would favor having Passover every week so that every week I could crawl up to the attic. First of all, the climb itself is an event. At any other time, even if I got down on my knees, would they let me climb up to the attic? And here I'm able to march up the steps, bold as you please. Down below my father follows my progress, and says, 'Slowly, take your time.' Why slowly? Why take my time? I feel as though I've sprouted wings, and can fly, fly!" A moment later, when he has an accident, and flies toward

the attic door and . . . "goes crashing head first down all the steps," the fall is not ominous either! "As you can see," he tells us, "I'm fine and well. May I never be any worse—except for this scar on my face [he concludes in Tevye's, or Sholom Aleichem's style] and some short-windedness that dates back from then, and this blinking of the eyes whenever I speak . . . " You can't help laughing when you read it, though the passage is quite sad. You feel that the Jew telling the story, were he still a boy, would go climbing up to the attic again, still marveling at his father who considers it a chore. Children pass so quickly from tears to laughter!

How precious a gift is this childish laughter for us chronic groaners. Not surprisingly it is Sholom Aleichem and no other who brings us this precious gift. The humorist and the child have one great virtue in common: their innermost carefreeness. The child *does not know* about life's cares, the humorist chooses to ignore them. That is why they understand each other so well, and why all humorists are writers for children.

It is interesting that with the exception of Tevye, Sholom Aleichem endowed only one of his other major characters with a humorous approach to life—Motl, Peysi the Cantor's Son.

In the book by that name, subtitled, ***Writings of an Orphan,*** most of the characters are comic or tragicomic. Only Motl is humorous; only he looks down upon the others with a gentle smile that suggests either simple childish innocence or a deep but rarified pain; he alone is set apart, at a slight distance from the others. We feel pity for the Kasrilevkites whose pain and suffering is described in these writings, but we feel nothing more than pity. Though Motl endures as much, if not more, than the others, we do not pity him at all. We love him. We love him because he doesn't need our help. In fact, with his bright and comforting smile, he may be able to help us in *our* need. His superb, calm humor enables him to tell us of many indescribable migrations, anxieties, and hardships, all in the tone of an idyll.

When Motl grows up he will become a Tevye. There is already something of Tevye in his nature, but for the time being he is still a boy, so his natural humor is not as overcast as that of Tevye, who is the father of children, with all the problems of raising them. Motl's humor is as yet much more innocent, pure, and bright than that of his close relative, Tevye. "I don't know," he says, "why mother cries so much over the children. The children seem very happy! When their mother begins to talk nonsense, they laugh aloud." And like all children, he too can laugh, not merely smile, as Tevye does.

Were we to ask ourselves whether Sholom Aleichem himself stood closer to Tevye or to Motl, we would say, to the latter. Like Motl, Sholom Aleichem cannot be satisfied with the tragic. Like Motl, he loves to laugh, simply and effortlessly. "Laughter is healthy; doctors prescribe laughter" is the motto of his writing.

The God of Laughter who reveals himself in H. D. Nomberg's Yiddish legend had two faces: one that laughed, and the other that grieved. There is of course a grieving face in Sholom Aleichem too, but it is hidden. Only the face that laughs and inspires laughter is revealed. Other writers have been able to tell happy tales; but no one else would take sad, often tiresome stories, and tell them for our pleasure, so that in our delight we might forget what is really going on, and like a child, ask no questions. Though his stories about Jewish life are almost always sad, they evoke not a sigh but a smile, and often a hearty laugh. He is always able to add something to the narrative that will ease our pain or dull it, or something to hide it from us so that we can forget. We thank Sholom Aleichem not because he awakens new ideas but to the contrary, because he is able for a moment to banish the thoughts that disturb our peace. We thank him for making the child his reader, but also for teaching his reader again to be a child.

Charles A. Madison (essay date 1968)

SOURCE: Madison, Charles A. "Sholom Aleichem: A Humorist of Veritable Greatness." In *Yiddish Literature: Its Scope and Major Writers,* pp. 61-98. New York: Frederick Ungar Publishing, 1968.

[*In the essay that follows, Madison presents an overview of Aleichem's life and fiction, finding a major theme to be Aleichem's personal experience of the tumultuous political and social environment of the turn-of-the-twentieth-century Ukrainian Jew, and asserting that Aleichem reached the pinnacle of his artistic achievement with his character sketches—particularly those of Reb Yosefel, Motel, Menachem Mendel, and Tevye the Dairyman.*]

"Sholom Aleichem" (peace be unto you) is a common expression of greeting among Hebrew or Yiddish speaking Jews. In the 20th century the phrase has also become synonymous with the pen name of Sholom Rabinovitch, the most beloved Yiddish author. The mere mention of this pseudonym exudes a delight quite excluding any other connotation.

Until recent years Sholom Aleichem's writings were little known to non-Yiddish readers. A genuine humorist, his style is intrinsically idiomatic and his subject-matter intimately and exotically Jewish, so that much of the allusion and gaiety of his stories inevitably evaporates in translation. In Eastern Europe some of his works have appeared in several languages, and more recently a good part of his writing has become available in English; although even the most successful translation has failed to overcome completely the barriers of complex idioms and an eccentric milieu, enough of his ebullient humor has percolated through to reveal his greatness as a writer.

Sholom Rabinovitch—his early years are depicted in *From the Fair* (1916; *The Great Fair,* in English, 1955) was born in March, 1859, in Pereyaslev, a town in the Poltava province. His father was "a tall man, with a forever-worried face, a broad-wrinkled forehead, a sparse finely formed beard. He was pious and sagacious, knew Hebrew, played chess, was a connoisseur of pearls and diamonds, and was considered the richest man in town." His mother, a frail little woman, was of the tribe of Amazons; she was "a fast worker and managed the general store." The family lived in Voronkov, a nearby village, during Sholom's childhood, and there he gained his first impressions of what later became the basis for much of his writing. Voronkov he later described as "very small" but with material for "many beautiful stories and legends."

From early youth an avid lover of tales, he was readily influenced by Shmielek, his story-concocting playmate, whom he paid with delicacies for yarns invented in the process of narration. Typical was the story of the Voronkov treasure, presumably hidden by the cruel kossak Bogdan Khmelnitski.

> Don't you know Khmelnitski? What a child you are! Khmelnitski was a bad man, a regular Haman even before Khmelnitski's time [a Yiddish saying exploited for its humor]; even a babe knows that! This Khmelnitski, this evil one, this Haman, had robbed the rich Poles and Jews of billions of rubles and brought them all to us, to Voronkov. Here he buried the treasure one night on the other side of the cemetery by the light of the moon, hid it so that no man should ever find it.

Sholom early developed a talent "to copy, to imitate, to mimic. . . . To grasp the ridiculous in everything and everyone: that was almost a disease with me." His mimicry amused bystanders and embarrassed his parents. Quick of mind and motion, charged with juvenile wit, blessed with a vivid imagination and a retentive memory, he soon knew the life of the townspeople to the minutest detail.

This blissful period of his childhood ended when his father became financially distressed owing to a partner's dishonesty. On the verge of bankruptcy, he moved the family back to Pereyaslev to operate an inn. Too young to be shaken by economic vicissitude, Sholom welcomed the change, which to him meant the conquest of a new world.

At the age of 12 he began to read current Hebrew writings. After perusal of Abraham Mapu's *Love of Zion,* he concocted a similar story and called it *The Daughters of Zion.* A little later, having read a Hebrew translation of *Robinson Crusoe,* he composed an account of a Jewish Crusoe. He was also beginning to feel the charm of feminine pulchritude, and a juvenile passion agitated him before he was 14.

The death of his frail mother and his father's remarriage to a shrewish woman from Berditchev, whose complaints and numerous curses he soon listed alphabetically with great relish, extending them to several pages, hastened his maturity. His father, pleased with his literary efforts, sent him to a government school, where he studied Russian and secular subjects. His curiosity was unappeasable, and he scrutinized and analyzed whatever he saw. He observed the numerous cantors and musicians who patronized his father's hostelry—attending their rehearsals, eavesdropping upon their talk and confidences. Later they furnished the themes of *Yosele Solovey* and *Stempenu,* two of his early novels.

Two years after his first infatuation he became enamored of the attractive daughter of a cantor, courting her with artless persistence. When he believed himself on the verge of success, the girl suddenly eloped with a Russian youth. The shame and shock aggravated a coincidental illness. When he finally recovered, he found himself a mature man.

At the age of 17 he obtained employment as a teacher in a nearby village, but a semester in the school yielded only aggravation and discontent. Soon, however, chance brought him a tutorship to the daughter of a wealthy provincial Jew. With this family he remained three years, a period of enjoyable self-advancement and personal gratification. His employer managed to free him from military service. Somewhat later, when the father discovered a growing affection between tutor and pupil, Sholom was abruptly dismissed. A brief sojourn in Kiev ended in the loss of his savings and forced deportation to his native Pereyaslev.

Several months later he became a government rabbi in Lubni, a nearby town, a position he kept until 1883. Having continued to write Hebrew prose while tutoring, he published his first piece in 1879 and several other sketches not long after. When he learned of the existence of Tzederboim's *Yiddish Folksblatt,* he decided to submit some recent compositions in Yiddish;

in 1883 this was still an act of daring on the part of an intellectual and a rabbi. Yet the urge to write in the language he knew best, and employed by his much-admired Mendele, was irresistible. He remembered how his father, surrounded by friends, had read a Yiddish story which made everyone laugh to tears, and he resolved to write similar humor for Yiddish readers. He rejected such criticism as that of the highly esteemed poet, I. L. Gordon, who as late as 1888 chastised him for favoring Yiddish: "It is a badge of shame of the driven wanderer, and I have always considered it as the duty of every educated Jew to see to it that the dialect should gradually disappear from our midst."

He was greatly encouraged when Tzederboim published his stories. To please his father and father-in-law, both of whom preferred that he write in Hebrew, he employed the pseudonym of Sholom Aleichem. S. Dubnow's praise of **"The Pocketknife"** elated him, Dubnow then being the forthright and highly regarded "Criticus." "Who knows?" he stated later. "If he had been critical, I might never have tried to write again." This story was indeed a special event in the rise of Yiddish literature. The feelings and reactions of a Jewish boy to his cherished possession was described with a simplicity of diction and humorous pathos never before seen in that commonly contemned "Jargon."

Somewhat earlier the father of his former pupil, realizing his daughter's persistent love for Sholom, had acquiesced in their marriage. Sholom engaged in business to make a living, but the urge to write remained irrepressible. In one letter he stated somewhat later: "Solomon Rabinovitch is for four hours a day a wheeler-dealer on the bourse, almost an ace, praised be His Name. But from about five in the afternoon until three or four in the morning I am Sholom Aleichem." He wrote a good deal, much of it satirical and moralistic. Yet he lacked the didactic impulse of most of his contemporaries, finding it more natural to be humorous. Later, still criticized for treating serious subjects lightly, he commented: "What shall I do when laughing is a kind of sickness with me since childhood?" To his friend Y. H. Ravnitsky he explained in 1886 that his forte was both to mock and amuse, but to mock lovingly, sympathetically.

His father-in-law's death in 1885 made him a man of wealth. He continued his activity on the Kiev bourse, but paid more attention to literary matters. He had started a correspondence, largely onesided, with Mendele, whom he greatly admired and addressed as "grandfather." In 1884, on Mendele's 25th anniversary as a writer, he informed the older man that he was "an admirer who works in the same field that you have plowed, and follows largely and deliberately in your traces, which you have left so sharply in the field of our Jargonic literature." In addition to doing much writing, completing *Sender Blank* and numerous shorter pieces of fiction, he was deeply interested in the work and condition of other Yiddish writers.

The popularity of Shomer and his imitators, whose lurid fiction Sholom Aleichem considered hurtful to the literary taste of their naive and uneducated readers, compelled him to condemn them in *Shomer on Trial* (1888). He was particularly critical of their emphasis on sensational and spurious plots and urged instead "portrayals familiar to us, of which we have an idea, which probably can happen in real life . . . not like Shomer's, which become fantastic, so that a poor teacher becomes a lord, a chimney sweep becomes a count, the dead come to life and the living die . . . diamonds worth millions lie in the sweepings." Most of all he wished to encourage better Yiddish writers by publishing their work at generous fees and thereby furthering the development of Yiddish literature.

In 1888 he arranged to publish his *Yiddish Folk Bibliotek,* an anthology of specimens from the best writers. He paid relatively high fees for contributions, among them Mendele's revised *The Magic Ring* and I. L. Peretz's "Monish." His own *Stempenu* was included, a sentimentally appealing story of Jewish musicians, treating sympathetically and with soft humor the haphazard and hard life of a fine violinist. In the same year his novel *Sender Blank,* a satirical portrayal of Jewish newly rich characterized by cultural emptiness and bourgeois greed, was serialized in *Yiddish Folksblatt.* A second volume of his anthology appeared in 1889 with a similar cast of contributors. It also included his novel, *Yosele Solovey,* which represented another phase of artistry within the Jewish milieu—singers who sweetened the synagogue services. Its rich humorous prose underlined the pathos of their often thwarted lives.

In 1890 the Kiev bourse relieved Sholom Aleichem of his wealth. In consequence of his bankruptcy he had to flee abroad to avoid imprisonment. To Dubnow he wrote: "Your broken friend . . . slipped and lost himself, lost to the world of gold and paper." When his affairs were settled through the aid of his mother-in-law, he returned to Russia and resided for a time in Odessa, where he sought to earn his living as a stock and insurance broker. While thus occupied he observed the numerous ne'er-do-wells who, much like himself, were building dream castles and going hungry. In 1892 he wrote **"London!"**—the first of the remarkable exchange of letters between Menachem Mendel, the luckless but irrepressible speculator, and his wife Shayne Shayndel, the earthy, commonsensical villager who considered the city a cesspool of iniquity.

In 1893 Sholom Aleichem returned to Kiev, where he began anew to seek his livelihood on the stock exchange. He remained primarily a writer, however, and by 1903 permanently forsook the marketplace. Writing became his whole life, and he worked at it with enthusiasm and great care. He wrote fast, but rewrote again and again, and so complete was his concentrated effort that he sometimes bit his nails until his fingers bled.

He soon became the central figure in the Jewish literary group of Kiev. Forced to depend upon his writing as a source of income, he fared badly materially, but his stories were highly popular and he was hailed everywhere as a folk hero and drawn into various Jewish affairs. Among other things, in 1903 he helped Maxim Gorki edit a Russian anthology of Yiddish writings—which the censor kept from publication. Young authors found him a generous friend and adviser. With them in mind, but no doubt thinking of himself as a conspicuous example, he complained that "not one of our writers earns his living from his pen." While avoiding dependence on the wealthy Jews of Kiev, he hoped in vain for a maecenas to relieve his poverty. When sick and in need, he wrote caustically about unethical publishers and the indifferent rich.

The massacres of 1905—he and his family had to hide to escape the Kiev *hooligans*—drove him from Russia. He sojourned in Switzerland, and visited London and New York. While in the United States he was urged to talk at meetings about the pogroms to accelerate collection of funds for victims, but he refused. "I read only my work . . . and the audience laughed heartily, lost a tear incidentally, and that was most important." On his return to Europe he gave similar readings in a number of the larger cities. While in Baronovici he became very ill, and doctors urged him to go to Nervi, Italy, to recuperate. Feeling downcast and without funds, he wrote to his friend M. Spector: "You can well imagine how I feel. At a time when there, in my beloved home, Jews are enjoying my holiday [his 25th anniversary as a writer was widely celebrated], I am here alone, sick, isolated, woebegone, and I weep. . . . " His frustrated dealings with grasping publishers and callous theatrical managers only added to his discouragement. Writing to I. Zevin of the New York *Tageblatt,* he deplored the vulgarity of the men who controlled the Yiddish theater: "At the moment I feel that the bargaining [over one of his plays] is like that concerning an ox. They want to buy an ox most cheaply, and they see to it that not only the meat, but the fat of the ox, and even the pelt alone, should be worth the price." His devoted friends finally arranged to repurchase the copyrights of his books, and issued a collected edition with himself as beneficiary.

From 1908 until 1914 he lived in Italy as often as he could in order to take advantage of the salubrious climate. He kept writing all the time, even when unable to leave his bed, and his warm and hearty humor was not in the least tinctured with the worries and suffering pressing upon him. Soon after the outbreak of World War I he managed to migrate to New York. The sudden death of his oldest son, and news of the dreadful fate of many Jews in the eastern war zones, proved too great a strain upon his delicate constitution, and on May 13, 1916, his heart gave way. To the last day of his life he continued to write *From the Fair,* reminiscences of his childhood, for serialization in a newspaper—a work that added to his total achievement.

Sholom Aleichem's writings are, to a greater degree than those of most authors, the literary expression of his personal experiences. However he may have dilated, enhanced, or elaborated his sense-data, he seldom let his imagination feed upon itself. All of his stories tell of some one, or of some phase, of the Jews he had observed and knew intimately; in every one of his characters he put something of himself or his own experience.

He drew his material from both the stagnant small town and the bustling city, although the former was the recipient of his warmer sympathy. The medieval religious outlook on life of the villagers, their usually meek and submissive deportment, and their pathetically meager existence appealed to him with greater immediacy than the precarious bustle and bluster of their urbanized brethren. Contemplating these various types of Jews (and they absorbed his waking thoughts), he could not but laugh at their foibles and flutter, but deep in his laughter lay the essence of his sympathetic sensibility.

The Jews he described were much the same as those depicted by Mendele—with this difference: they were already in the process of acclimating themselves to the hostilely strange ways of modern life. Most of them continued to feel the steely grip of poverty. This indigence, made acute by forced re-orientation coupled with further governmental restrictions, tended to quicken their conceits and lull their reason in the frantic hope of miraculous gain. Even those who remained in their native towns and clung to their orthodoxy were in some way affected by the invasion of contemporary inventions and technology. Sholom Aleichem saw them in this state of flux, and his stories reflected his humoristic view of their plight. How his conception of them differed from that of Mendele is evident in the very names of their composite towns. The older writer's Kabtzansk, literally Poorville, satirically connotes the dire economic condition of its inhabitants. Kaserilevke, the home of Sholom Aleichem's typical characters, has a similar significance, but with a disparity of nuance explained in the following passage:

The Jewish poor have many names. They have been called the needy, the impecunious, the indigent, the impoverished, beggars, mendicants, and dependents. Each name is uttered in pity or contempt. But they have another name: the Kaserilek. This name is pronounced in a wholly different tone. One says, for instance, "My, but I'm a Kaserilek!" A Kaserilek is not merely a starveling, a luckless fellow; he is, if you please, a poor man not downcast by his poverty. On the contrary, he makes a joke of it!

His Kaserilevke is situated in an obscure corner of the world, "orphaned, dreamy, hypnotized, interested only in itself." Nothing worldly matters at first to its inhabitants except as it concerns their immediate needs, although their curiosity is, from their peculiar point of view, as wide as the universe. They are insignificant yet conceited, poor yet jolly, naive yet charged with mother-wit. When one is asked how he earns his living, his reply is similar to that of Mendele's Jew, but more laconic: "How we earn our living? Just as you see, ha, ha! One lives. . . . " A few sketches of these Kaserilevkites will indicate how truly and vividly they are drawn:

Moishe was—but I cannot tell you what he was. He was a Jew. Whence his income was difficult to discover. He lived like many other thousands, tens of thousands of Jews in Kaserilevke: he kept himself near the local squire; that is, not near the squire himself but near the administrators of his estate, and not so much near these stewards as near the Jews who dealt with them. . . . But whether this brought him any income is a matter of speculation for the idle, as Moishe disliked to boast of his luck or bewail his misfortunes. He always appeared happy, with cheeks always red; one mustache was somewhat larger than the other, with his hat inclined to one side, and with his eyes always smiling and friendly. He was always in a hurry, and always, at any time, ready to walk ten miles to help friend and stranger alike.

Yoshe Heshel is an even finer specimen:

He is one of those Jews who are always in a hurry, ever on the go; who are always head over heels in business: a business consisting of only wind. Such as he live on wind. He conceives the world as a fair, to which one came sniffing, sniffing for some bargain. Void of any well-defined project, he would come to a county fair ready to price everything in sight, to buy and sell from hand to hand, regardless of profit or loss. A ruble more or less was inconsequential, so long as the transaction was honest. At the end of such a fair his enterprise left him penniless but undismayed. He only stroked his beard and said to himself, "Now that I have, praised be His Name, concluded the business of the fair, I must run somewhere to get a loan for traveling expenses."

Incapable of earning a living, Yoshel Heshel must depend upon his wife and grown daughter to provide the necessities of life by sewing shirts. But they seldom have sufficient work.

What do they do when there is no work? They suffer hunger; that is, they go to bed on an empty stomach and, with God's help, rise on the morrow to continue the fast. You may be certain no man will ever know this. Yoshe Heshel is not one to tell tales, to bewail his lot, to ask for help. . . . He would rather die! Yes, die! In short, Yoshe Heshel is one of the proud poor who suffer hunger on the quiet, without ceremony, without trumpetry. Not even the charitable know of his plight. It is fortunate that Yoshe Heshel is a Jew, and a very pious, honest Jew, who believes in God, who serves God, who loves God ardently, who loves God's spirit as a lover his bride. . . . Usually shy, dispirited, a worm for everyone to tread upon, he changes into a cheeky fellow once in the synagogue. There, in the house of God, he does not believe in riches, in aristocracy; he reduces everything to mere dust; he is convinced that all are equal before God. . . .

Although a pathetic character, Yoshe Heshel emerges as an object of mirth because Sholom Aleichem stressed not his adversity but his pliant acquiescence in it; not his hunger but his meek submission to the cudgels of fate. Yet the laughter he arouses is charged with sympathy and esteem.

Sholom Aleichem's humor plumbs the depths of sentiment in **"An Easy Fast,"** a sketch reminiscent of Peretz's "The Messenger." Here human life is shown yielding to the perseverance of poverty, a theme usually treated with pathos. Sholom Aleichem, however, divests it of all sentimentality. Khaim Khaikin is an elderly man no longer able to work and without means. The thought that he is wholly dependent on the meager earnings of his children grieves him terribly; he dislikes being a burden on anyone, even his own children. His heart feels cramped when he is forced to eat in their presence, acutely aware that every morsel he takes deprives them of that much food. To avoid this excruciating feeling he resorts to fasts. When there is no religious justification for abstaining from food he tries to avoid his solicitous children by lingering in the synagogue or taking a stroll at mealtimes. When they compel him to eat with them he secretly distributes his portion to the younger children. At the approach of a religious fast he feels more at ease; none dare ask him to eat on such a day! If possible, he prepares for the fast by abstaining from food on the previous day in order "to make it easier." On the day before the fast of the Ninth of Ab, commemorating the destruction of the Temple in Jerusalem, Khaim comes to the synagogue, sits down leisurely on an overturned bench, as was the custom on that occasion, and begins to read a religious book. Drowsiness gradually possesses him; hallucination soon follows.

> And Khaim Khaikin keeps his eyes shut, and he finds himself in a queer world, a new world, one which he has never, never yet seen. Angels hover before him. In observing them he recognizes his own children, all of

them, grown-up and babes. He wants to tell them something, but he cannot speak. . . . He wishes to apologize to them, to explain why he is not guilty. . . . Not he! . . . How can he, Khaim, be blamed because so many Jews have collected together in so small a place to crowd, oppress, and devour one another? How is he to blame if men force human beings to sweat, to bleed? How is he to blame if people have not yet reached the stage where one man would not exploit his fellow man as he would a horse, and where a horse too is to be pitied, being a creation of God, a living thing? . . . And Khaim Khaikin keeps his eyes shut and sees everything, the whole world, all worlds; and everything is clear and light, winding like smoke; and he feels that something is leaving his body, from within, from the heart, and rises, rises straight up, separating from his corporeal self; and he feels himself light, very, very light; and he emits a deep sigh, a very prolonged sigh. He feels relieved; then—nothing, absolutely nothing.

Here is another phase of Kaserilevke. Mordekhai Nosen, the wealthiest Jew in town by its own minuscule standards, is not at all like his indigent neighbors. In depicting him, Sholom Aleichem's sympathy grew cooler and his humor became less genial.

> Mordekhai Nosen is a tall man with long hands, thin and withered. His face, as square as that of a Chinaman because of protruding cheekbones, is covered with a sparse beard. He appears as if he is harboring some secret: his lips are always shut, his mouth slightly to one side; his mien is always serious, his forehead full of wrinkles; he never speaks loudly, never an extra word. But he becomes a changed man when in the presence of town officials. The wrinkles disappear, his face brightens, his lips unlock, his mouth straightens; he begins to talk: a truly different Mordekhai Nosen. Do you know why he acts so humbly before these officials? Solely for the love of eminence, out of pure vanity; only for the words, "Why, Reb Mordekhai Nosen, who is so esteemed by the officials as you?" uttered by a fellow Jew in need of some favor. Indeed for the word "esteemed" he would suffer all humiliation and expense! A peculiar man is Mordekhai Nosen.

Some of the wealthier Jews were in the habit of providing an annual feast for their townsmen. As was natural, the poorer the Jew the less was made of him on these occasions. **"Hannuka Pancakes"** describes such an event. Several tables are placed in the rear of the house for the poor, whom the family factotum treats with rude arrogance. Desiring the meal yet deeply humiliated, they devour the pancakes in haste and abasement. On the way home they let their fantasy have free play, and their humbleness is for the moment forgotten. The falling snow gives their fancy a new turn:

> How would it, for instance, incommode the Lord Almighty, if these snowflakes should suddenly turn into diamonds and saphires? We would then bend down, fill our pockets with handfuls, come home, and say to our wives: "Here, Esther, do with them as you please. If

you wish, turn them into money; if you wish, into jewelry for yourself; if you wish, into both; only leave me alone." We would then not need to depend upon the Steiners and their pancakes; as we say in our prayers, "Deliver me not into the hands of man!'"

Kaserilevke did not, of course, contain only poverty and its distressful consequences. Various idyllic aspects quickened its somber life. First there was the Sabbath, on which even the most wretched Jew became a self-respecting, leisurely human being, forgetful of weekday cares and anxieties. The serene atmosphere, ease of mind, and inner peace that pervaded the Jewish community on a Sabbath afternoon was one of its undeniable charms. At intervals there were long and joyous holidays, bringing in their wake exhilaration and pleasure. And if Sholom Aleichem was able to extract humor from the dross of life, he was truly exuberant when depicting its more cheerful occasions. Without the need of diverting pathos and pain, his humor assumed a carefree and natural mirthfulness.

The life of the small Kaserilevke boy provided him with another source of gay humor. Sholom Aleichem's several volumes of stories about him added a most attractive element to Yiddish literature. His boys love life: unlike the little Jews of other authors, they are irrepressible, mischief-loving urchins. S. Niger said of them:

> What a blessing was the healthy, naive humor of the child to the Jewish reader! No other writer was able to gather the scattered seeds of childish humor from among the Jews and plant them with so much art in his children portraits. In this achievement Sholom Aleichem is even more alone than in his creation of Tevieh, certain aspects of whom are found in other writers.

These children play games, run, jump, fall, get hurt, and do not mind it. They play pranks, are punished, and soon invent new ones, as is the way of normal boys. Every holiday, every season of the year, finds them eager to extract the most from the immediate moment. It is as if they have some intuitive foreboding of the cares and anxieties awaiting them in the years ahead, and are the more eager for mischief and fun while still children. Even in the midst of sorrow, when the faces of their elders are long and knit, they are most impressed by the, to them, amusing aspects. In story after story the principal theme concerns the boy anxious to act the child in opposition to parents, rabbis, and customs forcing him to behave like a little adult.

"The Pocket Knife," "The Violin," "The Watch," "The Flag," and similar stories concern boys prevented by poverty from owning these treasures, or by their fathers from using them. To possess a knife, for

instance, was considered unbecoming to a Jewish boy studying Hebrew lore. Yet every one of them secretly longed for one and usually managed to acquire something with a sharp edge. In **"The Pocket Knife"** the father finds his young son toying with a knife and exclaims: "A knife? What a child! What a lad! Can you not be with a book? A youth of eight years! I'll show you knives, you hoodlum! Knives all of a sudden! . . . The only plaything for a Jewish boy from his fifth birthday is a book; and not a children's story, but a religious tome!" Not that a Jewish father does not love his children enough—he loves them only too zealously; his strictures come from his concern for their future well-being. In this story the boy becomes seriously ill. When passing a crisis he hears his anxious father talking in so soothing a tone that he thinks: "If I were not ashamed, I should like to give him a hug and kiss, but hee, hee, hee, how can one kiss a father?" The ghetto child seldom kissed his father, even as the child in the Puritan family seldom kissed his.

Although Sholom Aleichem has written at length about boys, he hardly touched upon the Jewish girl. In this neglect may be seen how dependent he was on his sense-data. It was easy for him to write about boys because he only had to dip into his memory to do so. In his childhood, however, girls were a breed apart, and he was hardly aware of them until adolescence. Then his own emotional experience provided him with the lovely heroine for **"Song of Songs."** In this story he waxes truly poetical. Refreshing in theme, pure and biblical in style, it comes like the waft of a rose out of the Kaserilevke stench.

When Jews began to migrate into cities in the latter decades of the 19th century, some legally but mostly illegally, they made up a bizarre group. Without means, unskilled in any trade, unsophisticated, they became the hapless pawns of chance. In the desperate attempt to survive they took up any work that came their way. The Moishes and Yoshe Heshels, once in the city slums, became agents, brokers, salesmen, tradesmen; the less educated took up tailoring and other manual crafts. Few earned enough to keep body and soul together. The precariousness of their existence, more intensive than in their native towns, fired their fantasies and caused some of them to visualize substantial incomes, to conjure up suddenly acquired wealth. Undaunted by unfavorable conditions—there were too many after too little—these *luftmenschen* began to depend upon chance and pay homage to luck. In the process they landed in the realm of the grotesque, where the lottery appeared a solid and certain investment. It seemed so wonderful to win a fortune at a stroke! For a time Sholom Aleichem was one of them, though at an artistic remove, and observed them closely and compassionately.

Economic dreariness and failure were not their only besetting plight; government hostility aggravated their uncertain existence. Few Jews acquired the status of urban citizenship. Restriction after restriction was promulgated for the purpose of harrying the Jews undergoing social mutation. Efforts to avoid such unfair regulations as the draft, highly limited citizenship rights, the percentage norm in schools, and other handicaps resulted in many comic as well as cruel situations. Sholom Aleichem described these in a number of excellent stories and monologues. Two narratives, dealing with the same theme, illustrate the range, subtlety, and wholesomeness of his humor.

"The Lottery Winner" depicts the cleaving of the new generation from the old, and the aggravated results of educational restrictions. Benjamin, the son of a pious beadle, is a precocious child and the pet of the synagogue community. His poor father is justly proud of him and expects him to become "a light in Israel." When Benjamin learns in early adolescence of the world outside the synagogue, he conceives a great longing for a university education. Knowing his father's inimical attitude toward secular study, he secretly leaves home for the city. After much privation and intensive preparation he receives a high rating in the entrance examination—only to be excluded because of the percentage norm for Jews. In despair, he apostatizes and is at once welcomed by the university authorities. When news of Benjamin's recreancy reaches his father, the entire town is already agog at the unpardonable act. The shock to the pious beadle is severe. Shame and anguish paralyze his tongue and drive him from the sight of his synagogue cronies. In accord with Jewish custom he and his family consider Benjamin dead and sit down for the week of mourning. One of the bereaved man's friends comes to comfort him, but all his attempts are in vain.

> The visitor wishes to say something, but knows not what. After several efforts at vocalization speech finally comes; once started, he knows not how to stop, how to extricate himself without pain to the bereaved. . . . "Te," he addresses the beadle with the first words that come to mind, "everything is for the best. It is only, as we say, a trial of the Lord, because everything, you understand, comes from Him. Nothing may be done without His permission; a human being does not move his little finger here below before he is commanded to do so from above. . . . He is, what's the use of talking, a real Master. Oi, a Master! And He is being obeyed and very much obeyed, oi, oi, oi. . . . Therefore, you understand, everything is as it should be. The evidence for this comes from the fact that if things should have been different, they would have been so: for who can compel Him to have them thus and not otherwise? And if He should desire things to be different, could one have them otherwise? No! Then let things better be different, that is, let them better be thus and not otherwise. . . .

As in **"An Easy Fast,"** the situation is truly pathetic. What can be more calamitous to a pious Jew than the apostasy of a beloved and only son? Yet so unalloyed and adroit is Sholom Aleichem's art that the reader's attention is focused not on the grief of the father but on the manner in which he accepts and absorbs his sorrow. Had the beadle, for instance, been of Learian mold, the result would no doubt have been tragic; being a Kaserilevkite—a pious, reflective, submissive Jew, accepting his faith in God without question—he emerges as an object of pathetic humor.

Restrictive education is treated comically in **"Gymnasium,"** a popular monologue. The father in this story is a successful urbanized Jew. He is secure enough materially to think of things other than economic, and his aims are those that come with prosperity. His wife, as might be expected, is a social climber and wants her son to have a formal education: "he should at least be a doctor or lawyer." But the percentage clause—one Jewish student to ten Russian students—frustrates all their efforts, and the greater the endeavor the more futile the result. In the following early passage the father recounts his interview with the principal of a gymnasium:

> "What may be your wish?" he inquires, and asks me to be seated. So I say quietly into his ear: "Gracious sir," say I, "we," say I, "are not rich people; we have," say I, "a small establishment, and an extraordinary good son, who," say I, "wants to study, and I also want him to, but my wife especially desires it. . . . " But again he asks: "What is your wish?" So I move closer to him and repeat: "Dear sir," say I, "we," say I, "are not rich people, we have a small establishment, and an extraordinary good son, who," say I, "wants to study, and I also want him to, but my wife *especially* desires it. . . . " And I stress the "especially" he should understand me. But he, having the mind of a peasant, does not apprehend and now asks in anger, "What do you want?" So I slowly put my hand in my pocket, and slowly take it out, and tell him slowly: "Understand me, gracious sir, . . . " and I put my hand in his and squeeze it. . . . In short, it's done! He immediately grasps my meaning, takes out a little notebook, asks me my name, the name of my son, and in what class I should like to have him enter. At this I thought: "That's the way to talk!"

Here the circumstances are the reverse of those in **"The Lottery Winner."** The father does not experience true sorrow; he is only inconvenienced, at most frustrated. Though ostensibly veneered with urban sophistication, he very soon reveals his Kaserilevke origin. Speaking in the Russianized Yiddish of the city Jew, he arouses droll, contagious laughter with every phrase—Sholom Aleichem's sympathy with him being overshadowed by sheer amusement.

The wealthier Jews in the cities yield readily to the pleasures and frivolities of the newly rich: family discord, social jealousies, and gossip along with summer vacations, excursions to famous doctors, and similar luxuries. Sholom Aleichem perceived them as former Kaserilevkites divested of their piety, modesty, and geniality, and depicted them accordingly. **"Summer Life"** describes such a group on vacation. Written in letters between those in the resort and those in the city, it delineates their insincerities, pettiness, jealousies, and vanities with an irony bordering on caricature. His heart seemed to cool when dealing with bourgeois characters, and he observed them with his mocking eye only.

The revolutionary and Zionistic movements, with their di-divergent factions, were in the 1900's finding earnest and enthusiastic disciples among emancipated Jewish youth. Disintegrating conditions over the country, then being defeated in war and verging on revolution, aggravated by the 1903-1905 pogroms and the intensified oppression that followed, deeply affected these idealistic and zealous young men and women, as intense in their radicalism as was their fathers' faith in Jehovah. Sholom Aleichem recorded this social turbulence with his usual sensitivity and humor. In *The Deluge* the father is so engrossed in business that he tends to neglect his family. With the mother old-fashioned and indulgent, the children become the prey of their agitated environment. The elder son and daughter, entering maturity just prior to the upsurge of radicalism and tempted by their father's sudden wealth, yield to luxurious debauchery. The younger children, caught in the whirl of unrest, become fanatic revolutionists and Zionists. The brunt of this discord and disparity is borne by the parents. Although the theme has a serious content, Sholom Aleichem treated it with the obliqueness of his gentle mirth.

The pogroms beginning in 1903 made life in Russia more difficult and dreary than ever before for its millions of Jews. They began a mass migration to the United States, South Africa, Argentina, and other countries where they could gain ready entrance. With little or no means, and almost no knowledge of the world outside of their native towns, they set forth armed only with faith in God and the urgency to escape. Wandering westward through Austria and Germany, they met with innumerable obstacles and inconveniences, but their strong impetus to survive and settle drove them irresistibly to their destination. Sholom Aleichem was among them, both as victim and observer, sharing their experiences; nothing eluded his keen senses and deep sympathy.

Motel: Toward America is a veritable epic of Jewish life during the first decade of this century. Beginning with a description of the small town in which modern thought and inventions were getting a timorous welcome, Sholom Aleichem takes his characters through western Russia, across the border to Austria and Germany, through Belgium, into London, and finally to the ocean liner on its way to New York. He depicts this hegira of hapless and harried Jews, starting in the face of governmental restrictions, striking the protruding reefs of the border, surging past crest and trough across central Europe, riding the turbulent Atlantic, and landing on tear-drenched Ellis Island. In *Motel: In America* and *New Kaserilevke* Sholom Aleichem followed these immigrants to New York and described their efforts to establish themselves in a new and strange environment. With his quick eye and sharp ear he was aware of their every move, sensitive to their every mood; in writing about them he gave artistic form, embellished by sympathetic humor, to comic incidents and oblique behavior.

Successful as he was in creation of character, Sholom Aleichem was too much the humorist to write first-rate fiction. At the outset of his career, eager to wean the naive Jewish reader from the lurid Shomer romances, he wrote *Sender Blank, Stempenu,* and *Yosele Solovey,* authentic stories of Jewish life. To make them palatable he infused the action with elements of human interest. Yet the love displayed by his characters was the reticent and repressed emotion of the traditional Jew. In *Stempenu,* for instance, Rachel, though unhappy in her marriage, buries her love for the musician deep within her and resists strong temptation. As if apologetic of this, Sholom Aleichem, in the opening of one of the chapters, explains the absence of intrigue and passion:

> The reader must think to himself that he is being served a dull supper, he having been brought up on those "highly interesting" romances in which occur hangings and drownings, poisonings and shootings, or in which a rabbi becomes a count and a servant girl changes into a princess. . . . What shall I do, since we have no counts and princesses? We have only ordinary Jews, ordinary wives and daughters, and ordinary musicians.

Authentic and wholesome as was the life he depicted, it nevertheless lacked the depth and sustained insight of great fiction. This was equally true of his later novels—*The Deluge, Wandering Stars,* and *The Bloody Jest,* written as newspaper serials under trying circumstances. *The Wandering Star,* for example, describes the conditions obtaining at the birth of the Yiddish theater in Eastern Europe and in America. The atmosphere is presented realistically and humorously, but the injection of sentimental romance deprives the protagonists of artistic vitality. It was as if something of Shomer had infiltrated the action. His several plays likewise have the stamp of his warm humor, yet fail to measure up to his major works.

Although Sholom Aleichem's humor stresses the peculiarities and incongruities of a people undergoing radical transformation and oppressed by a hostile government and inimical social forces, he has achieved his best work in the creation of character. He has given Yiddish literature a number of fictional beings more real to his readers than the people around them; creations that grow, mature, and rise to imaginative heights. The following four major individuals embody his supreme artistic achievement.

When a well-known Jew became endeared to his townsmen, his name underwent expansion. Reb Yosef, the old rabbi of Kaserilevke, early came to be called Reb Yosefel. Not a soul in the town but adores the venerable man when he enters the pages of Sholom Aleichem's writings. He is indeed an idealized sage. The hero of numerous stories, he is portrayed as a revered octogenarian, blessed with good sense and actuated by the deepest altruism. Afflicted with loneliness, indigence, and illness, he retains his implicit faith in the goodness and rectitude of Jehovah. Considering himself but a speck in the ever-to-be-praised world of God, he is always modest and humble. With the phrase, "Vanity of vanities, all is vanity," he has succeeded in allaying his misery.

> He has reached the conviction that all the suffering and wretchedness with which the Lord visits him come from one of two ways: either it is a trial, a visitation from His beloved Name, a castigation while in this sinful, foolish world, or he really deserves the punishment; if not for his own sins, it is surely for those of his poor sinning brothers, the children of Israel, who are responsible for one another, and are due to suffer for each other. This is the conclusion Reb Yosefel arrived at, and he never complained even for a moment. He discarded this world with its vain pleasures, dismissed it with the smile of a philosopher.

Reb Yosefel was delineated as a noble leader of a medievally oriented Jewry—the rabbi who was disappearing together with the static culture he fostered. He was still the old patriarch, concerned for his flock not merely because they were his parishioners but also because they were human beings. Honest and sincere in all things, loving all living creatures, keeping soul and body in their respective places with rigorous piety, he succeeded in inspiring his fellow Jews with the reverence, awe, and poetry which went far to nullify the unsavory effects of their superstitious and blighting beliefs. Endowed by his Creator with the composite Jewish virtues, he was dedicated to the service of his people. And he found much to do! He went about Kaserilevke soothing the sore at heart, advising the perplexed, chastising the selfish, and collecting alms for the needy. In the process he talked, moved, and thought with unforgettable reality. The following two incidents are characteristic.

Reb Yosefel undertook to provide his beloved town with all essential improvements; not through his own

means, of course, since he was always penniless, but by soliciting contributions from the charitably inclined. When the need for an old folks home became urgent, he proceeded as usual to seek funds from those in a position to give. When a wealthy merchant came to town, Reb Yosefel at once went to see him about a contribution. Arriving at the inn, he was told the guest was not to be disturbed. Nevertheless he tapped at the man's door to announce his approach and entered the room. The wealthy stranger was so angered by this brazen mendicity and unwelcome familiarity of the quaint intruder that he lost his temper and gave the old man a cuff on the ear. The octogenarian only felt his face for blood and said mildly: "Well, so be it; this you gave *me,* so to say. What now, my good man, will you give for the decrepit sick, I mean for the old folks home?" When the rabbi left the short-tempered merchant, one side of his face was redder and shinier than the other, but he was in possession of a large enough contribution to begin building his pet project.

At another time he headed a delegation sent to a nearby city to collect money for the sufferers of a recent fire in Kaserilevke. While canvassing some of the wealthier Jews, he and his fellow townsmen were arrested for entering the city without passports. Through the intercession of one of the influential Jews they were soon released. Before letting them go the officer in charge, amused by the quaintness of these terrified rustics, asked who was the "chief rabbi" among them. The question put fear into their timorous hearts; their imagination at once assumed some dire punishment. Only the old rabbi was undaunted.

> "It is I," Reb Yosefel spoke up in a peculiar tone, and stepped forth courageously, as if ready to take the entire condemnation upon his own head, as if willing to sacrifice himself for his fellow Jews at a moment's notice. Handsome, very handsome was the octogenarian graybeard at that instant. A youthful fire was lit in his aged eyes; but his hands trembled and his shoulders shook. He waited for what was to be said to him, ready for everything, for the worst that evil people might be moved to do. Whom should this octogenarian fear? He placed one hand on the small of his back and looked at his inquisitor with such boldness and self-esteem that the death-fearing Kaserilevkites saw their rabbi in a new light.

"I can bet you any amount that no one in the whole world is so satisfied with the warm, sunny spring as I, Motel, the son of Payse the cantor, and the neighbor's calf, who is called Meny (it is I, Motel, who have named her so)." These childlike words open the first book bearing his name and bring the eight-year-old boy into being. Chief of Sholom Aleichem's boy creations, he is molded pretty much in the image of his own childhood. Motel represents the transitional generation in its youthful state: inheritor of Kaserilevke culture and destined exemplar of the urbanized Jew.

Motel and Meny come out on this first day of spring, and both enjoy it immensely. After describing his own pleasure, Motel continues:

> Meny, the neighbor's calf, first dug her black, wet chin into the dung, then kicked three times with her front hoof, lifted her tail, jumped on all fours, and issued a dull meh. The meh was so comical that it made me laugh, and I imitated exactly the same meh with the same intonation. This must have pleased Meny, for she soon repeated the same movements with the same jump and cry. I, naturally, imitated her to the minutest detail. Thus several times: I gave a jump and so the calf; the calf gave a meh, and I a meh.

This interpretative attitude in Motel is also shown toward his elders. Every word, every act, appears comical to him if it does not coincide with his preconceived idea of it. When his father becomes very ill and his mother is forced to sell the furniture piece by piece to pay the doctor and buy medicines, he thinks it amusing that she should conceal the truth from his father. It appears to him a violation of ethics for a mother to lie and a father to be fooled. But if concealing the truth is to him a laughable matter, the manner in which it is done is even more so. He thus describes it: "'What's the matter?' father asks from the sickroom. 'Nothing,' mother answers him as she wipes her eyes, and her lower lip and jaw tremble so that it is impossible not to burst into laughter."

His childish mind is amused because it is still unable to perceive the reason for his mother's equivocation; he feels superior to his father, who is fooled, while he is not. Unaware that his father is dying or of its effect on the family, he is excited by the depletion of his home's contents. It is only when his father is actually dead and the wailing of his mother brings him from his play into the house that the concrete manifestation of pain and grief produce in him similar emotions.

> My mother continues to weep and faint in turn while in the arms of my brother Elihu. And my brother Elihu, who does not cease crying himself, continues to reproach her: "Today is a holiday, mother, today is Pentecost, mother! Mother, it is forbidden to cry, mother!" And at once everything becomes clear. And I feel a cramp in my heart and a tug at my soul, and I want to cry, and I don't know what for. . . . And I pity my mother. . . . And I go up to her from behind, and tell her in the manner of my brother, as tears roll from my eyes, "Today is a holiday, mother, today is Pentecost, mother! Mother it is forbidden to cry, mother!"

Sorrow has loosened his mother's tear ducts. In his innocence he says: "Crying is as natural with her, for example, as eating or praying is with you. I don't understand how a person can have so many tears." But he develops rapidly and soon perceives the truth. "When Elihu began to scold her for her continuous crying, she told him, "What a foolish child you are! Do I force my tears? Tears come. . . ." And in what follows Motel discerns her state of mind with greater empathy than his older brother.

An instance of Sholom Aleichem's art in showing how a child's mind reacts to a tragic event is his telling how Motel learns the meaning of a pogrom from one of his older companions:

> "You don't know what a pogrom is? What a ninny you are! A pogrom is something that occurs everywhere. It begins almost out of nothing, but once it starts it continues for three days."
>
> "What is it, then?" I ask. "A fair?"
>
> "What fair? A nice fair! Windows are broken, furniture is broken! Pillows are torn! Feathers float down like snow."
>
> "What for?"
>
> "What do you mean what for? A pogrom is not against homes alone. A pogrom is also against stores. Stores are broken into, and their goods are thrown into the street, carried away, soaked with gasoline and burned."
>
> "Go on!"
>
> "What do you mean? Do you think I only imagine it? Later, as the robbing ends, they go through homes with axes, with irons and clubs, with the police in the rear. They sing and whistle and shout, 'Come on, fellows, kill the Jews!' And they beat and stab and kill. . . ."
>
> "Whom?"
>
> "What do you mean whom? Jews!"
>
> "What for?"
>
> "Some what for! It's a pogrom!"
>
> "And if it's a pogrom, so what?"
>
> "Go on, you're a calf. I don't want to talk to you about it."

Motel grows and develops with every related incident. If he seems too knowledgeable for his age, it is because, as a product of Kaserilevke, he too soon becomes a little adult. He reveals his inmost thoughts in a manner that stamps them indelibly upon the reader's mind. His impressions are charged with sensitiveness and humor. He describes everything and everybody as his senses perceive and his imagination interprets. Each narrative adds to the wholesomeness, simplicity, and fineness of the boy's spirit. Impressionable and pliant, he adjusts himself to every situation without a jolt or jar. His heart throbs with warm sympathy; his love of living things is quick and strong; his intuitive mind in time perceives the more delicate nuances of life. He is in truth a child philosopher, always eager to probe into the why of everything, and underlying his entire being is a rich vein of humor, gentle and refined.

In the preface to the second edition of *Menachem Mendel,* Sholom Aleichem declared:

> Menachem Mendel is no hero out of a novel, and especially no mere imaginary figure. He is a typical Jew with whom the author is intimately acquainted. Meeting in 1892 on the Odessa minor bourse, we went through, hand in hand, all the seven compartments of Gehenna. We speculated on the Yehupets [Kiev] stock exchange, "traveled" to Petersburg and Warsaw, withstood many crises, drifted from one enterprise to another, finding—oh, woe—not much in any, and were compelled to do in the end what most Jews do—immigrate to America.

Menachem Mendel is much more to the reader than these bare facts indicate: he is a citified Yoshe Heshel become the supreme *luftmensch,* a grotesque product of the 2000-year struggle of the Jews to survive under adverse and at times almost impossible conditions. Business, speculation, get-rich-quick schemes have become to him not merely a means of earning a livelihood but a passionate and irresistible end. He is fascinated not by wealth itself but by the idea of acquiring it suddenly and fortuitously. His repeated failures do not for a moment keep him from plunging into the first quixotic scheme that comes his way. In his excitement he often borders on paranoia; Dr. Eliashev, the first important Yiddish critic, interpreted him as "the Jewish insanity streak in the person of an insignificant Jewish businessman."

Menachem Mendel is married and the father of three children when he goes to Odessa to claim the remainder of his wife's dowry from a broker's office. For the first time in a bustling city, his fantasy begins to seethe with dreams of sudden riches. The bourse atmosphere obsesses him. The hearsay knowledge that a few speculators have amassed fortunes fires his fancy with the grandeur of doing likewise. He feels jubilantly optimistic and writes to his wife Shayne Shayndel that she will soon have a wealthy husband. Again to quote Eliashev:

> Thousands of plans, projects and deals fly about in his mind like spirits and demons. If he stops to think for a moment, it is a sign that to the thousands of schemes in his head is added a new and larger one. Menachem Mendel is in a constant fever. Each impression suggests ten possibilities; for he lives in a dream world, so that butter and leather, wheat and needles are all the same to him.

Having lost his capital, Menachem Mendel wishes he were dead. But only for a little while. When he receives the money his wife sends so that he can return home, he goes instead to Yehupets (Kiev). There he embarks on other wild-goose ventures, becomes enmeshed in the financial maze of the stock exchange, and suffers the repeated agonies of chronic failure.

Shayne Shayndel is of an earthy mold. A typical Kaserilevkite, encouraged by a mother who expresses her practical sense in common but apt aphorisms, she keeps urging her husband to drop his harebrained schemes, let the evil city burn to the ground, and return home to her and their children. "I don't understand, even if you behead me, what kind of stuff it is that one cannot see it! Is it a cat in a bag? . . . Listen to me, Mendel, I don't like it. I was never used to such airy dealings." And she adds that mother's comment on his enterprise is that "from air one catches cold." To another of his grandiose dreams she replies: "You can say what you will, but until I see with my own eyes I won't believe you; not because I think you're a liar, but because all that those fine Yehupets people tell you, you consider holy writ." When luck temporarily favors him and he is the ecstatic possessor of several hundred rubles, she tells him:

> What? You are jubilant, excited? "Stocks," "Transports," "Portfolios," indeed! You beguile yourself with the idea that one can become rich in the time it takes to say "Hear, O, Israel!" "A delusion," mother says, "is worse than a disease." Stupid! Why talk of fortunes, lucky breaks, stocks, dividends? Nonsense! They are all worth an egg-shell! One does not get rich empty handed.

Reproach can no longer discourage Menachem Mendel. He is so immersed in the exchange gossip and rumor that common sense has ceased to affect him. The thought that Brodsky, a prominent Jewish millionaire in Kiev, is a member of the stock exchange is unimpeachable evidence to his frenetic mind of the lucrativeness of speculation. In a postscript to one of his letters he adds:

> You must think, dearest wife, that I am the only one dealing in stocks. Brodsky also trades with them. The difference between us is: when I wish to place an order I must first figure out how much I can stomach; when Brodsky begins to buy, he orders 1000 shares, 5000 shares, 10,000 shares. Brodsky is no joke! When he rides through in his carriage, Kreschatik [Kiev's principal street] trembles, and all the Jews doff their hats, and I among them. It would be fine if I should some day become a Brodsky. With the help of God, little stupid. . . .

Bad news from Petersburg again wipes him out. Dazed, he cannot understand how and why it happened. Soon, however, his optimism surges forth and he is again the schemer. "Luckily," he tells his wife, "I have betimes thought of undertaking another means of livelihood, a respectable livelihood." He becomes an agent. "One need only be able to lie," he asserts, "and be insolent into the bargain, and one is already fit to be an agent." Able to do neither, he fails miserably. Subsequently he deals in sugar, real estate, forests, and oil; he even tries to be a marriage broker and to become a writer. "I now have a new occupation, a completely new one, somewhat nicer and easier. I've become a writer. I write. You will no doubt ask how I come to writing? It's from Heaven." In reply his wife quotes her mother: "A sick one will get well, a drunkard will become sober, a dark one will become light, but a fool remains a fool."

Menachem Mendel is essentially a comic character. A dreamer, mentally agile, earnestly eager, he is at the same time childishly naive and helpless in a world of hard and shrewd traders. He is at the mercy of an overexcited fantasy which leads him into absurd behavior. For Reb Yosefel and Tevieh religious faith was the mainspring of their existence; Menachem Mendel has no such solid anchor and is buffeted by the whims of chance. Consequently his every impulsive act and move, stimulated primarily by desperate hope of fortuitous gain, appears exaggerated and ludicrous, since inevitably each one fails. In describing his gullible enthusiasm over matters doomed to disappoint him, Sholom Aleichem makes clear that this behavior is not so much the result of a diseased imagination as of an inimical environment. Trained, as so many of his kind, in neither a trade nor a profession, without worldly sophistication, with his opportunities for earning a living greatly restricted by a hostile government, yet with a mind steeped in Hebrew lore and medieval ways, Menachem Mendel is depicted as more a victim of unfavorable circumstances than of his own inadequacy. No man is in full control of his intellect when in the grip of chronic starvation. Menachem Mendel's effort to free himself from penury, stimulated by his *luftmensch* upbringing, forces him to trust in luck and in his naive ingenuity until he becomes addicted to speculation. His implicit faith in his unrealistic and ridiculous schemes merely emphasizes the pathos of his misfortune. Because his conceit combined with gullibility make his behavior extreme and ludicrous, he appears an object of laughter; but the laugh takes not the form of ridicule but of compassion. One feels that he has not really deserved his repeated failure and despair.

Every major writer secretes his inmost self into at least one of his works. Sholom Aleichem was no exception. Although he has stamped his personality and art upon most of his writings, the stories of *Tevieh the Dairyman* best display his greatness. In this rustic, traditionally religious Jew he has embodied his highest humor, his truest philosophy of life; during the score of years in which he concerned himself with the character, he concentrated his utmost affection, warmest sympathy, and deepest spiritual probings upon this unfortunate milkman.

Tevieh differs conspicuously from Menachem Mendel in both attitude and behavior. Indeed, these two characters represent the polarization of nearly all of Sho-

lom Aleichem's creations: one verging on the pathological and the other being spiritually centripetal. Tevieh is a typical, if artistically heightened, product of orthodox Jewry: he adheres unquestionably to his faith in Jehovah, accepts the buffeting of fate as God's will, procures his bread with the proverbial sweat of his brow, and considers the idea of wealth a satanic temptation. Menachem Mendel is a Kaserilevkite in the process of urbanization, tossed about on the stormy waves of economic precariousness, with his fantasy rising rocket-like on imaginary gain and sinking to despair at the impact with hard reality.

The two are clearly contrasted in the only story in which both appear. Tevieh, a poor dairyman with several marriageable daughters, while in Yehupets on business is for once tempted by the sight of many valuables in store windows and thinks to himself:

> Dear God, if I owned even a tenth part of what this is worth—what would I then ask of God, and who would be like me? First I would marry off my eldest daughter, give her a dowry of 500 rubles in addition to wedding presents, clothing, and expenses; I would sell my horse and wagon, move to the city, buy a seat on the east wall of the synagogue, buy my wife, long may she live, some pearls, and hand out charity like the most generous of men.

Just then he sees Menachem Mendel, a distant relative, and before he realizes it is persuaded to invest his hard-earned savings—100 rubles in all—in a get-rich-quick stock. Inevitably his speculation results in complete loss and he feels robbed. Yet so innate is his understanding of human nature that he perceives the motive as readily as the result. Seeing Menachem Mendel's misery, he does not blame him for losing the money; aware that if he had not yielded to temptation he would still have his 100 rubles, he even comforts his tempter by telling him: "Money, brother, one must work for." Thus, while he reacts philosophically with an irony that saves him from grief, Menachem Mendel, having neither objectivity nor a true sense of values, becomes disconsolate—only to upsurge emotionally at the thought of a new scheme.

Tevieh enters these stories as a common drayman, working hard and suffering dire poverty. A lucky chance, causing him to bring two wealthy women who had lost their way in the woods to their grateful relatives, yields him a cow and enough cash gifts to enable him to set himself up as a dairyman. Life becomes easier for himself and his family, but he remains troubled about his dowryless daughters. Although he considers them attractive and accomplished, he knows that this means little without a marriage portion. He soon learns, much to his sorrow, that his daughters have minds of their own, and that in a world in social transition the lack of a dowry is the least of their disadvantages.

One day he is told that a wealthy butcher in the town wants to marry his eldest daughter. At first he recoils from the idea that his beautiful Tzaytel should become the wife of this coarse and commonplace widower, but he gradually acquiesces in the thought, knowing that the marriage would bring the girl material well-being. Tzaytel, however, has her own plans. She is already in love with a poor tailor of her own age and pleads with her father to grant his consent. Tevieh has no will to stop her from marrying the man of her choice and is sad to see her continue her indigent existence.

Hodel, his second daughter, decides to marry a zealous revolutionist. Tevieh is perplexed, finding it difficult to accept the idea that a young girl should become the betrothed of a strange youth without the consent and blessings of her parents. Confronted by this situation, however, he has not the heart to stop her from meeting with the brazen youth. In the end he consoles himself with the thought that she might have done worse, and gives his consent. Soon after, the young man is arrested and exiled to Siberia, and Hodel decides to accompany him to his desolate destination. No words of Tevieh can dissuade her. Again he accepts the infliction of fate, and although his heart almost breaks at the idea of her departure, he provides for her as best he can for the long and difficult trek. At the railroad station, very depressed, he relates, "I alone keep myself as cool as steel and iron; that is, as the saying goes, inwardly I seethe like a samovar, but to reveal my feelings—feh, Tevieh is no woman. . . ."

Tevieh next experiences the most agonizing adversity possible to an orthodox Jewish father. Eva, his third daughter, becomes enamored of a young Russian and accepts Christianity in order to marry him. This time he balks: the blow has struck at the very basis of his fundamental faith; unable to prevent it, he cannot submit to it. While the beadle in **"Te Lottery Winner"** is stunned by the calamity, Tevieh steels himself against reconciliation. One need only recall the scene in the forest where Eva runs after him to beg his forgiveness, and how he forces himself against his natural inclination "to jump off the wagon and embrace her," to realize the depth of his grief. Even when Eva seizes hold of the horse and exclaims, "Father, I shall die if you move. I beg you hear me first," he holds fast. "'So,' I think," he tells himself, "'Father dear,' eh; you want to take me by force? No, my soul! If so, then you don't know your father! . . . and I began to beat the horse as hard as I could. . . . Tevieh is no woman, Tevieh knows how to deal with Satan. . . . " He flees from her as from an evil spirit; and while his wound remains as wide as his heart, he simply cannot put God to shame!

This is not the end of his affliction. Shprintze, his fourth daughter, falls in love with a fickle youth, the son of a wealthy and haughty widow. On learning of the affair, which she scorns as beneath her station, the mother sends her son away to a distant city. The simple and trusting girl, deprived of her lover and already with child, drowns herself. Tevieh's grief is aggravated by the cruel arrogance of the youth's vulgar uncle. After this abuse, making mock of his self-respect, Tevieh says: "I approached my horse and wagon, put my face into it and—you won't laugh at me?—I cried and cried and cried. . . . " What depressed him most was the callous coarseness of these rich. "With God," said he, "I'll manage to get along—what troubles me are people, why people should be so bad when they could be good."

His next daughter, Golde, is as beautiful as her older sisters and has no difficulty in attracting suitors. But her mind dwells on her aged and unhappy father. Wishing to ease his remaining years, she marries a rich but vulgar businessman. At first Tevieh rejoices: at least one daughter is well married. But when he visits her one day and notes the unbreachable gap between his sensitive daughter and her coarse husband, her sacrifice becomes painfully obvious.

Tevieh's Job-like fate is climaxed by a government regulation driving him out of his village home, so that he has to seek a new abode in his old age. Still the homely philosopher, he addresses himself to his Maker:

> Ach, Creator of the world, dear God, why do you have to bother with such as Tevieh? Why don't you sometimes play a trick on, for instance, a Brodsky or a Rothschild? Why don't you teach them the chapter, "Get thee out of the country"? It would, it seems to me, suit them much better. . . . Let them also see that we have a mighty God!

Normally the events in Tevieh's life would hardly be a fit subject for the humorist. Yet the monologues of this unfortunate Jew, ostensibly related to their author, make one laugh much and often. In episode after episode Tevieh's character grows in stature. Yet he does not tower as a modern Job, or a tragic Lear cruelly treated not so much by his daughters as by harsh circumstances. The reason is that we are not for a moment permitted to forget his Kaserilevke origin; it affects his character like an oblique shaft of light in a dark room. In the midst of distress he manifests a pious fatalism, a wholesome artlessness, a habit of aptly misquoting and mistranslating Hebrew passages, a suppleness of spirit—elements woven into the fabric of his being with consummate skill. In combination they turn tragedy into mellow mirth. The highest humor results from the manner in which he meets and acquiesces in the buffeting of his fate. As he relates his misery, with a naive philosophical acceptance that reveals his inward distress, one laughs the more heartily to repress rising sympathy. For his woes are not only personal but also Jewish, and that gives them a ready universality. Thus, after the pathetic scene in the forest with his apostatized daughter, he tries to find solace in the fatalistic thought: "A man's a fool! A wise man must not set his heart upon his misery, and must understand that life is as it should be, because if it was to have been different it wouldn't be as it is." One smiles at this pious determinism as a form of idiosyncrasy and conveniently smothers the welling sympathetic sorrow.

Tevieh would, of course, have been disconsolate without his ability to accept his agony with a philosophical smile, and the conscious belief that it came to him as a trial of the Lord. If his mind tended to reflect, his heart was warm and expansive. He was naturally altruistic. Aware of the pettiness of life, he also knew of what depth of sorrow the heart was capable, the insignificance of everything else compared with that sorrow, and of the need to alleviate it as much as humanly possible. Hence his all-embracing sympathy, the more admirable because of his narrowly pious upbringing. For the good of others he was ready to rise above his innate prejudices, restrain selfish impulses, and yield whatever authority was still his. To arrive at such true humility and wisdom one must first reduce everything to fundamentals, strip all values to their essentials, expose all pomp and vanity to their relative futility. This perspicacious insight brought Tevieh a measure of relief when mere reflection was ineffectual. The reader, while laughing heartily at his foibles and fatalism, loves him for his mitigating altruism.

Humor, the noblest form of laughter, generates genial enjoyment combined with congenial sympathy. Humor sees the incongruities of life and seeks to lessen the poignancy arising from them. It essays to soften with mirth the unavoidable harshness of existence, to span with a smile the abyss that sometimes separates man from man. A humorist perceives human weaknesses with greater insight than the satirist, but seldom forgets that he too is not free from them. Unlike the satirist, he is never overwhelmed by human meanness or stupidity. To him the world is a puny microcosm, not to be scolded or scorned, but countenanced and smiled at. His precept is: smile while you may; sorrow may stop it soon enough.

Sholom Aleichem's generation of Jews was fertile with elements of humor. It was in the inevitable process of transition; harsh circumstances were relegating its medieval form of life to the irrevocable past, forcing each one to adapt himself to modern ways as best he could. Naive, quite gullible, wholly unprepared, these Jews were bewildered by the maze of urban modernity, confounded by their inability to tell the real from the apparent; necessity gave them no reprieve, compelling them to seek the means of subsistence hastily and haphazardly. For a time some of them unavoidably committed fantastic and ridiculous acts. To the casual observer, unaware of the genuine pathos motivating it, their behavior seemed highly comical. Sholom Aleichem knew this generation as well as Mendele knew his. Addressing himself to the reader in one of his stories, he said:

> I come, my dear friend, from Kaserilevke. There I was born, there I was brought up; there I was educated and there I was married. Afterward I sailed forth in my little bark on the great, wide, and powerful ocean called life, where waves cover the housetops. And although one is always being tossed and rocked on the raging surface, I have not for a moment forgotten my dear beloved home, Kaserilevke, long may it exist, nor my dear beloved brothers, the Kaserilevke Jews, may they thrive and increase. Whenever I hear of some misfortune, of a calamity, of a disaster, I think at once: what is going on *there,* in my native home.

He perceived the oblique direction of their transitional behavior and exposed the pathos of their altered status with compensating humor. In 1911 he stated in a letter: "I tell you it is an ugly and mean world and only to spite it one mustn't weep! If you want to know, that is the real source, the true cause of my constant good spirits, of my, as it is called, 'humor.' Not to cry out of spite! Only to laugh out of spite, *only to laugh!*"

He may truly be termed Kaserilevke's supreme achievement. His self was blended so successfully with the spirit of his people that in one sense his writings do not bear so much the stamp of individual authorship as that of genuine folklore, poetically interpreted. Had he lived in an earlier century, his stories would no doubt have circulated anonymously. As it was, his work became the literary expression of his generation to a greater degree than that of any other Yiddish writer. He had little of the self-consciousness of the modern artist, although he was too much Mendele's "grandson" not to rewrite and polish his stories many times. His senses seldom allowed him leisure for reflection; they crowded his consciousness with impressions and stimulated his imagination to incessant activity. The merest perception, the most casual observation, tended to excite his irrepressible humor.

As he was ever with and of the Jews of his time, he unwittingly became their literary chronicler, recording their deeds and aspirations, their misfortunes and tribulations, with the accuracy and sympathy of the intuitive writer. How truly the artist he was is evidenced in the following incident. While still a young man he visited his friend and mentor Mendele to have him read critically his latest story. "What is your purpose in writing it?" asked the older man. The query nonplussed him for the moment. Recalling it later, he said: "I confess that this was to me a new America discovered. It was then five years that I was writing, have written, praised be His name, so many things, and not once had I asked myself, 'What is my purpose?' What purpose can a writer have? A writer desires to write, for if he would not desire to write he would not be a writer. . . . "

Although he wrote primarily out of his own experiences, he made himself the artistic voice of his people. Little of his ego came to the surface. His literary self was chameleon-like in its happy blending with the characters he portrayed. His ear for authentic speech was unerring. His Jews talk naturally, with their own idiosyncrasies and peculiar idioms. Thus, most of his work is in the form of monologues or letters. His characters, at once unique and typical, are authentic representatives of the Ukrainian Jews at the turn of the century. They recalled a recent past imbued with nostalgic memories in the minds of many of his readers, and "something of Sholom Aleichem" became essential at Jewish gatherings and concerts.

For all the folkloric effect of his writings, he was ever the conscious and painstaking artist. Poverty and the conditions of newspaper serialization—the chief medium of publication in Yiddish—forced him to write regardless of his health or state of mind. Yet he never considered a work finished until he had revised and improved it to his heart's content. To a friend he wrote:

> A kind of Mephistopheles sits within me, and he laughs, mocks, pokes fun at my writings. Every time I write something and read it with enthusiasm, as is usual with an author, he only whistles through his lips and his eyes smile. If I could catch him I would choke him! It sometimes happens that he listens to me quite seriously and nods his head. This makes me think that he approves, and I send it to the printer—when he explodes with laughter—this Mephistopheles, may he burn!

Yet the urge to gain approval of his inner critic never slackened. Writing to the editor of *The Friend* to apologize for the delay in sending him the manuscript of *The Treasure* for serialization, he said: "Before I let anything out of my hands I must cut it apart at least five times, and then I must polish it, sharpen it—a misfortune! From a four-act comedy it was transformed into a one-act tragic-comedy with a prologue—sharply reducing the number of lines—isn't this insane?" And to the very end of his life he continued to choose his words and phrases as if he were matching pearls.

Dan Miron (essay date 1972)

SOURCE: Miron, Dan. "Sholem Aleykhem: Person, Persona, Presence." In *The Uriel Weinreich Memorial Lecture I: Sholem Aleykhem: Person, Persona, Presence,* pp. 3-45. New York: Yivo Institute for Jewish Research, 1972.

[*In the essay below, Miron focuses on Aleichem's use of his pseudonym, analyzing its origins and narrative function and exploring the relationship between the author's private identity and his fictional persona.*]

1. The pen-name, Sholem-Aleykhem (sometimes rendered in English in the spelling: Sholom Aleichem), made its first appearance in the year 1883, undersigning a short, biting satirical feuilleton published in *Dos yidishe folksblat,* then the only literary and news magazine in Yiddish. The feuilleton entitled **"Di vibores"** [**"The Elections"**][1] attacks the well-off leaders of a certain Jewish community in the Ukraine, whose efforts to prevent with threats, bribery, and chicanery the re-election of a young and popular *rabiner* (the official, government-authorized rabbi, to be distinguished from the traditional *rov,* the real religious authority) were frustrated by the spontaneous revolt of the poorer members of the congregation. The fact that the author, who by then had published quite a few Hebrew articles as well as one short romance in Yiddish under his real name—Sholem Rabinovitsh—saw fit this time to hide behind a rather bizarre pen-name, was perfectly understandable. His satire did not refer to its victims by name, and the provincial town where the elections took place was symbolically called *Finsternish* ('Darkness').[2] Yet nobody at all acquainted with the affair was meant to fail to identify either place or persons involved. Moreover, the re-elected *rabiner* was none other then Sholem Rabinovitsh himself, who at the time earned his living by holding this quasi-religious, actually administrative, position in the town of Lubny. In the characteristic *narodnik* mood of the contemporary young Russian intelligentsia he tried to improve the lot of the poor in the town, while his relations with the rich members of the community were strained. A pseudonym, which would confuse local identity hunters and make them lose scent, was needed. It is quite probable that it was conceived as nothing more than a temporary strategic device created for the particular purposes of a satire which, for all its legitimate social criticism, still smacked of a personal vendetta; a mask to be discarded once its immediate usefulness had been exhausted.

The mask, however, was not discarded. The publication of **"Di vibores"** more or less coincided with the young author's decision to give up his vocation as a Hebrew publicist and settle down to the career of a

Yiddish humorist, and that decision, as he himself confessed later in his life, once more made the concealment of his identity—at least for the time being—desirable, or even necessary.[3] That was why he stuck by his Sholem Aleykhem, and allotted him the authorship of a more ambitious and wide-ranging series of satirical sketches, **"Di ibergekhapte briv oyf der post"** [**"Letters Stolen from the Post Office"**], which he now began to publish in the *Folksblat*. This series can, for all practical purposes, be considered his real *debut* as a Yiddish writer. Why should a young writer, who was obviously trying to develop an impersonal, genuinely literary, and perfectly acceptable satire, find it necessary to conceal his identity? While to us this may indicate an excessive inclination to secretiveness, such behavior was, under the prevailing circumstances, understandable and quite common. It was not accidental that Leo Wiener, the Harvard instructor who in 1899 published, in English, the first survey of the history of Yiddish literature in the nineteenth century, had to add to his pioneering book a special appendix of pseudonyms and the real names they concealed.[4] Most Yiddish writers at the time felt, as some of them put it, that they had "to cover their nakedness" with a pseudonymous fig-leaf,[5] because, among other reasons, Yiddish was completely lacking in cultural status, despised as the "mixed" and deformed jargon of the "unenlightened" masses both by the purist Hebraists, the disciples of the Haskalah movement and its Hebrew literature, and by the newly assimilated, superficially Russified upper middle-class. It was extremely difficult for a writer, especially for one who had some reputation as a Hebraist at stake, to commit himself openly to the professional writing of Yiddish belles-lettres. Young Sholem Rabinovitsh knew only too well how disappointing such a commitment on his part would have been to his father, a genuine old-style lover of the holy tongue, who relished every Hebrew article his son managed to get published and expected him to become "a second Abraham Mapu." (Mapu, the most popular Hebrew novelist of the nineteenth century, was admired for the high idealism and the romantic intricacies of his fables as well as for his exquisitely polished pseudo-biblical style.) Sholem Rabinovitsh was also keenly aware of the contempt with which it would be regarded by members of the Jewish-Russified "plutocracy," with which he was now connecting himself through a marriage alliance. He decided, therefore, to keep it secret, as long as he could.[6]

These reasons for secrecy, however, soon became irrelevant. The status of Yiddish literature was rapidly improving during the 1880's. To its ever growing popularity with the masses was now added the goodwill of a part of the Jewish-Russian intelligentsia. For this group had been jolted from its illusion of emancipation and assimilation within the framework of a liberalized Russia and thrown into a fervent nationalistic mood by the 1881 pogroms. Under the influence of this new mood, Hebrew and Jewish-Russian intellectuals had second thoughts with regard to their derogatory attitude towards the manners and *mores* of traditional Jewish society, and started to discover in them inherent values. The Yiddish language was obviously one of these. Although it was still regarded by many influential intellectuals as unsuitable for cultural and literary use of lasting value—the newly created Zionism added to its other alleged deficiencies the stigma of *goles*, i.e., the stigma of being an exilic product—Yiddish, nevertheless, attracted well established Hebrew and Jewish-Russian writers, such as Y. L. Perets, D. Frishman, or S. Frug. Many of those started new careers as Yiddish writers without resorting to pen-names. Sholem-Aleykhem himself contributed enormously to this ascendancy to respectability of Yiddish literature by his creative writings, by his activity as a critic, and especially in his role as editor of *Di yidishe folksbiblyotek*, the literary almanac, which although short-lived, epitomized the new status of Yiddish. He appealed at the time both to the Yiddish-speaking masses and to such Jewish-Russian intellectuals of the new nationalist trend as Sh. Dubnov, who were praising the new Yiddish writing in the Jewish-Russian magazines. However, success breeds its own compulsions and constraints. As the popularity of his comic sketches grew, starting with the **"Ibergekhapte briv"** whose appeal to the readers of the *Folksblat* in a very short time made the name Sholem-Aleykhem a household word with them, the author must have realized that his pen-name was there to stay. For, of course, it immediately became more than a mere pen-name. It was regarded as a presence, with whom the reading public grew intimate, rather than as an indication of the name of an author. Sholem Rabinovitsh, who knew what an achievement such an intimacy was for a feuilletonist, was not going to spoil a good thing. On the contrary, he did everything in his power to make his Sholem-Aleykhem's grip on the public stronger and more widespread. As a matter of fact, he launched an elaborate public-relations campaign on behalf of his pseudonymous creation, which paradoxically made him come up with yet more and more pseudonyms. Under these he wrote various articles, feuilletons, and letters to the editor, attacking or praising the impudent Sholem-Aleykhem, alternately belittling him and his allegedly undeserved popularity, or wondering at his devilish cleverness, relishing his pranks.[7] This, by the way, was to become a recurrent pattern of behavior with him. His overpowering predilection for literary games of hide-and-seek prompted him to devise new pen-names, and it is quite conceivable that the list of twenty-three pseudonyms attached to his name in S. Chajes' lexicon of Hebrew and Yiddish pen-names is far from exhaustive.[8] He was, on the other hand, ever careful to employ them not as possible competitors of Sholem-Aleykhem, but rather as his foils. Clearly, he was determined to make the presence of Sholem-Aleykhem loom as large as possible in the consciousness of the widest readership accessible in Yiddish. He was certainly successful, perhaps even a little too successful. For such was the vitality and suggestiveness of this presence that Sholem-Aleykhem not only dispossessed the author's real name of its reputation (the name Rabinovitsh remaining hardly known outside a narrow circle of friends and literati), but also overwhelmed, to a certain extent, his private personality, blurring the dividing line between his public role, as the national comedian, and his private life. Moreover, one can sense how, more than one time along his career, the presence of Sholem-Aleykhem constrained the author, perhaps even prevented some possible developments in his literary art. This is seen most remarkably in the genre of the novel, where the constant intervention of Sholem-Aleykhem in the development of the plot, his loquacity and tendency to "sum up" the protagonists and send them about their business, often had disastrous results.[9] Here and there one can perhaps trace some well-concealed expressions of resentment against the omnipresence of this overpowering image. However, such resentment, even if it became fully conscious, came too late to have any effect either on the reading public or on the writer himself, who let his Sholem-Aleykhem share with his real name the authorship of the most personal and unfacetious of documents—his will.

2. The phenomenon of adopting a pen-name that has a life of its own, that somehow manages not only to take over the author's public image but also to make inroads into his private life, is, of course, not unprecedented. In fact, it has become quite a common phenomen in modern literature, especially following the Romantics in the early decades of the nineteenth century. The case of Beyle-Stendhal—that incorrigible masquer, who never tired of donning a new pseudonym nor of quoting nonexistent quotations from nonexistent authors—is perhaps the most prominent and interesting instance.[10] The uncomfortable co-existence of Mr. Samuel Langhorne Clemens and Mark Twain, as recently presented in Justin Kaplan's biography, is another fascinating instance of the autonomy a pen-name can assume, as well as of its sometimes obnoxious vitality.[11] Many will probably deem this instance more pertinent to our argument, since Sholem-Aleykhem's comic style and hold on a very large segment of the reading public have always been said to

resemble those of the American humorist. A score of other cases of prominent nineteenth-century writers, whose adoption of pen-names actually meant a redefinition of identity, comes to mind. They range from the romantic and exotic Novalis at the beginning of the century to that of the professedly "realistic" and down-to-earth Maxim Gorky (Gorky means 'bitter') at its end, not to mention those of famous women writers such as the two Georges—Sand and Eliot—whose masculine pen-names probably indicated more than sheer insistence upon equality in a man's world. The particular reasons that made this phenomenon a commonplace in nineteenth-century Yiddish literature have already been mentioned, and the precedent of Sh. Y. Abramovitsh, the central figure in this literature, is certainly significant in the present context. Abramovitsh's Mendele Moykher-Sforim ('Mendele the Book Peddler') was, like Sholem-Aleykhem, so omnipresent and overpowering that he almost obliterated from the consciousness of the reading public, as well as of the critics, the fact that he was a character, a dramatic creation, a part of the fictional reality of Abramovitsh's stories rather than their author. That this precedent directly influenced Sholem Rabinovitsh can not be doubted, since he regarded himself from the very start as Abramovitsh's disciple, tried to imitate his manner, and crowned him the "grandfather" of Yiddish literature—with the obvious intention of asserting his own right to occupy in it the position of the favorite grandson and the legitimate, dynastic heir. The precedent also influenced the Yiddish-reading public, whose intimate acquaintance with Mendele the Book Peddler made it take fancy pen-names such as Sholem-Aleykhem[12] for granted, and regard personae, narrators-characters, and other similar rhetorical constructions as a direct presentation of the author as an artist as well as a person.

All of us, to one degree or another, use the well-known literary pen-names as mere nominal replacements; that is, we use such names at Stendhal, Mark Twain, or George Eliot in the same way we use names such as Flaubert, Tolstoy, and Dickens. This usage may do for the purposes of current reference and is, indeed, unavoidable. It should not, however, be allowed, as it usually is, to dull our sense of the problematic and sometimes quite complicated relationship between an author, his pen-name, and his creative activity. Instead of taking pseudonyms for granted, we should be alerted and intrigued by most of them; for in almost every case where a serious artist adopted one, something of real significance both for the artist himself and for his artistic achievement, as such, has been attempted. This fact has recently been realized by many literary scholars whose intense interest in the function of the dramatic voice in the literary work made them pay more attention to the phenomenon. Once considered the domain of the lexicographer or, at most, the biographer, the pseudonym now holds interest not only for the psychologically-oriented critic, but also for the structuralist and formalist who regard it as a "device" or as part of the rhetorical structure of the text itself.

Of course, the phenomenon calls for a comprehensive explanation which will take all of its aspects into account—the social, psychological, historical, and personal, as well as the formal and rhetorical. Moreover, this explanation, based on a detailed comparison of the interrelated yet varied manifestations of the phenomenon in different times, national literatures, and genres,[13] should amount both to a history and a "theory" of the pen-name. This, however, is a subject for future research. The critical awareness of the pen-name as part of the work of art as well as a "mask" of the artist is, as was stated above, but a recent one. The scholar's hands are loaded with work both on individual cases and on the nature of the phenomenon as manifested in particular national literatures under particular historical circumstances. The example of nineteenth-century Yiddish literature and particularly that of Sholem-Aleykhem can serve as strong proof of the necessity of such cautious, inductive procedures. Clearly, the phenomenon of the pen-name-persona flourished in this literature under very special historical circumstances. A theorem defining the role the pen-name played in it would not be applicable to other literatures or even to the same literature in a different period.[14] It should also be apparent that even within this specific milieu the case of Sholem-Aleykhem, although it does not stand out in isolation, is rather markedly different from others (that of Mendele Moykher-Sforim, for instance). The history of Sholem-Aleykhem as a pen-name gives rise to a whole series of questions that bear directly on the analysis of the style and structure of the author's works, as well as on the understanding of his attitude towards his position as a Jewish artist and of the unique folk-hero status he achieved in his life-time and retained after death. It is the purpose of this paper to raise a few of these questions, and also, to a certain extent, attempt to answer them, or at least one of them: What are the particular functions and distinctive features of Sholem-Aleykhem as a rhetorical entity? The answer, needless to say, will consist of generalizations supported only by a tiny fraction of the extensive relevant evidence. It will also be a synchronic answer, i.e., it will treat different works from different phases in the author's career as belonging to one unified fictional continuum, and pay but little and sporadic attention to the fine changes the Sholem-Aleykhem persona underwent throughout its

thirty-three year progression from the **"Ibergekhapte briv"** to *Funem yarid* [Back from the Fair], the author's last major work, left incomplete when he died in 1916.

3. It is my contention, to put things bluntly, that the study of Sholem Rabinovitsh's work (as much as that of Sh. Y. Abramovitsh's), has been fundamentally flawed by insufficient differentiation between its author and his creation, Sholem-Aleykhem. When I say insufficient, I understate the case, since the name, Sholem-Aleykhem, has almost invariably been assumed to refer to the author as person and as artist. I do not mean, by this contention, to minimize the value of the great scholarly achievements, as well as of the interesting critical perspectives offered by some of the best Yiddish scholars and critics during the last sixty-four years.[15] Nor do I claim that the difference between Sholem Robinovitsh and Sholem-Aleykhem has never been noticed. It has, by one or two of the more sensitive interpreters, such as Y. Y. Trunk, who said: "It is simply difficult for us to match the quiet, humble name Sholem Rabinovitsh with the Sholem-Aleykhem-world, which is so full of color and fantasy and which rings with the sound of play."[16] But even with Trunk, this intuitive grasp of the incongruous element in the coupling of the author's everyday, shabby, middle-class name with his persona's colorful and fanciful one did not lead to a clear-cut dissociation of the historical author from the figment of his imagination, to the separation of the creator from his creation. It rather involved the critic in a lengthy psychological analysis, in which the difference between the two was treated as a change within the author's psyche, a biographical metamorphosis, which gradually mellowed the "gray" and "philistine" Rabinovitsh into the great "adventurer" Sholem-Aleykhem.[17] While a biographical-psychological approach to the Sholem-Aleykhem persona is perfectly legitimate, it can hardly carry one far when unassisted by a primary distinction between artist and artifice, and by a clear conception of the difference between the psychological development of the artist and the rhetorical development of his artifices—two processes, which are, of course, closely related, but the study of which call for totally different methodological procedures.

I submit, therefore, that the great achievements of the scholars and the critics should be re-examined on the basis of such distinctions. I also submit that the distinguishing or differentiating process should be carried to its logical consequences. It should cut deeper than the notion that the difference between Sholem Rabinovitsh and Sholem-Aleykhem merely separates the author in his authorial, public role from the author as a private person. This will not suffice, although the author himself sometimes thought along this line,[18] and despite the fact that in quite a few specific cases such separation more or less corresponds to the actual rhetorical structure of his works. The overall picture, to be correctly presented, calls for a deeper severance. What is needed is a perception of the ontological difference between author and persona, of the fact that they exist on totally different levels. True, Sholem-Aleykhem is always presented as an author, or at least as a person whose business involves him in reporting and publishing. This is how he introduces himself,[19] and this is how he is approached by the characters in the stories who seek his authorial advice: "Since you write so much, you must know everything, and only you can give me the right advice."[20] This is also how characters approach him who regard him—a man who writes for newspapers—as a source of information about international politics.[21] Sometimes they ask him to *bashrayb* ('describe') their personal enemies, thus making them the laughing stock of the whole Jewish world;[22] sometimes they fulminate against him, recognizing themselves in his caricatures.[23] Many of them count on him to publicize their own personalities, although they may express their wish not to be mentioned in the newspapers. Even Tevye the dairyman, who so often insists that he is telling the stories of his own and his daughters' misfortunes to Sholem-Aleykhem, as a personal friend and on a strictly confidential basis, counts on him to make these stories public, and intimates that a share of the honorarium is due him. He does it even as he goes on arguing that there is no "reason for the whole world to be suddenly informed that on the other side of Boyberik, not far from the *shtetl* Anatevke, there exists a Jew by the name of Tevye the dairyman."[24] This authorial aspect of Sholem-Aleykhem is certainly essential to his function in the stories. It should, however, be separated from the actual authorial activity of Sholem Rabinovitsh, even where it clearly reflects it, for this activity is part of Rabinovitsh's historical commitments, while the whole point of Sholem-Aleykhem's existence is his being dissociated from these very commitments and disencumbered from their burden.

This contention, I know, flies in the face of much of the Sholem-Aleykhem criticism, and, therefore, a demand at this point for some concrete illustration of its viability will be legitimate. Is the present attempt to contest a universally accepted assumption substantiated by any textual evidence? Do the works themselves supply us with the differentia between the historical author and the being indicated by his penname?

As a matter of fact, one can easily cull from the vast body of the author's work scores of illustrations that indicate not only the existence of such differentia, but also the author's own awareness of it. Indeed, they indicate the author's wish to share this awareness with at least some of his readers, the more perspicacious ones; for, of course, he could convey it only in cryptic or half-cryptic expressions. In these he actually was on the horns of a dilemma. On the one hand, he knew how valuable an asset the non-fictional "reality" of his Sholem-Aleykhem was both for the artistic and the non-artistic advancement of his career. By no means could he allow himself to undermine it and jeopardize the intimacy between a rather unsophisticated reading public and this useful image. On the other hand, he had some quite pressing reasons for making the fictional nature of this image perceptible at least to the more sophisticated part of his audience. His usual way of solving the dilemma, or rather of circumventing it, was that of the half-hidden joke, which could either be taken seriously, or be dismissed as a mere *jeu d'esprit,* or go totally unnoticed (by the simple-minded reader). The technique of the cryptic joke (which, incidentally, was also employed by Abramovitsh), was a safe compromise between two contradictory inclinations, and was, therefore, quite often resorted to. Here is a typical illustration of it.

In one of the early feuilletons Sholem-Aleykhem revisits his old hometown (not yet Kasrilevke, the quintessential East European *shtetl* of his later stories). The feuilleton is a simple, preliminary variation on the "you-can't-go-home-again" motif, which later on was to play an increasingly important role in the author's work, and it immediately strikes the note of estrangement. Sholem-Aleykhem finds himself on an altogether unfamiliar street with modern looking houses. "Be good enough to tell me who lives here, in this big brick house?" he asks a Jew who happens to hurry by. A characteristic conversation, to which, I am afraid, my translation hardly does justice, follows:

> "Oh yes, here lives. . . . Wait, wait, I'll remember presently. Oh yes. It seems that no lesser person than Monastiryov, Yakov Borisovitsh Monastiryov, lives here."
>
> "A Jew?"
>
> "A Jew."
>
> "Yakov Borisovitsh?"
>
> "The same!"
>
> "Wait a moment. Isn't he Yankl Bereles?"
>
> "Ask me another."
>
> "Isn't he the son of Berele Monastrishtsher?"
>
> "Why don't you ask him?"
>
> "Now don't be angry with me for asking. Do understand. This Yakov Borisovitsh was a school mate of mine. We studied in the same *kheyder,* and he was. . . ."

"But where do I come into all this?"

"But you must understand how important this is to me. After all, a friend. . . . I mean Yankl, Yankl Bereles was my friend . . . and suddenly Yakov Borisovitsh Monastiryov! What use does he have for this 'yov' of his! . . .'"

"No offense meant, but will you please leave me alone? What are you? A preacher? God's attorney? What do you want? What are you looking for?"

"God forbid! Have I said anything? Have I made any claim on anybody? I just talk to myself. For heaven's sake: Berele Monastrishtsher. A Jew learned in the Torah, a great philanthropist, comes of an elevated family of *rabonim* ['rabbis'] and *tsadikim* ['Hasidic spiritual leaders']. . . . —Suddenly he becomes a Borisovitsh Monastiryov! Yov! Do you see?—Yov!! . . ."

"What I see is that you are either an idler or somewhat of a crackpot, or both."[25]

And the impatient interlocutor flees. Obviously, Sholem-Aleykhem established himself in this conversation as a good, loyal Jew, who, although not necessarily an old-style fanatic, is flabbergasted by the total metamorphosis of his once *kheyder* friend. He finds it difficult to fathom the changes that the son of the rabbinical Berele Monastrishtsher must have undergone over the years in order to adopt such an ostentatiously Russified and Christianized name. (Monastiryov actually means 'of the monastery'.) As he resumes his walk along the modern street, he discovers—by the brass plaques on the brick and stone walls of the spacious houses—other *kheyder* classmates whose names underwent similar metamorphoses. Deciphering Russian names one by one and remembering his once very Jewish friends who now boast them, he encounters a name that is an especially disagreeable surprise to him:

> Solomon Naumovitsh: Who can this creature be? A-a-ah? Oh, it's you Sholemke; isn't it? Sholem Reb Nokhem Vevekes son. . . . Fine, fine, very fine indeed. I believe I still remember you when you walked in your little shoes and stockings and had quite a head for the *gemore*. I thought then that you would certainly end up as a *rov* of a small town, or at least as a *shoykhet,* a *moyel,* a *bal metsise,* and what do you know! Here you turn up a Solomon Naumovitsh, of all things. What does your uncle Pinye say to this? And Itsik?—Does he allow it? How come?[26]

Here, to be sure, the author is poking fun at himself. For the fictitious little Sholemke with his good *gemore-kepl* ('the sharp intellect needed for the apprehension of the niceties of the Talmudic text and its even subtler exegesis') and with prospects of becoming an impoverished *klekoydesh* in a small *shtetl,* who instead turned out to be a semi-as-similated gentleman bearing a Russian name and patronymic was, of course, none other than the real Sholem Rabinovitsh. Every reader

of his works, especially of *Funem yarid,* the great autobiographical work, will immediately perceive this; the few biographical details that Sholem-Aleykhem mentioned in order to emphasize the contrast between Sholemke's traditional Jewish childhood and his assimilatory adulthood, correspond perfectly to historical facts. One wonders how much of this was sensed by the readers when the feuilleton was published in 1889, long before the biographical development of the author became more or less publicly known. Some of the details could have been comprehended only by members of the author's family. Such, for instance, was the reference to uncle Pinye, a fanatic *khosid,* who had always suspected his brother Nokhem (hence the Russian "Naum") Rabinovitsh, with his reverence for Hebrew and its grammar, of being a *maskl* in his secret heart, and had therefore taken it upon himself to guard his nephews from sinning. He had been especially circumspect with the high-spirited Sholemke, about whose *yidishkeyt* ('Jewishness', 'commitment to the Jewish faith and way of life') he had always had the worst misgivings. As it turned out, his suspicions had been well-founded. The intention of the whole passage, however, was probably guessed by quite a few (although by no means the majority) of the readers, for whom the sight of the author satirizing himself certainly meant an additional source of enjoyment. But was it mere fun that the author was aiming at? Did he not indicate, by this little private joke, a deep critical self-awareness? Indeed, there was much in Sholem Rabinovitsh's way of life that invited satire, and nobody was more aware of this than he himself. It was not only the contrast between his childhood and adulthood that made for a satirical juxtaposition. An incongruity as glaring and more painful (and therefore rarely touched upon) resulted from his very position as the popular Yiddish artist, the champion of Yiddish literature, the favorite writer of the Yiddish-speaking masses, who conducted his own and his family's life according to the current etiquette of the assimilated Jewish upper middle class. This included, as a matter of fact, the speaking of Russian (not the best Russian at that), and the use of Russian literary culture as an obvious frame-of-reference. It is when we perceive this latent self-criticism, always present in the author's self-portraits, that we begin to understand not only how widely separate the rhetorical entity Sholem-Aleykhem was from the historical being of Sholem Rabinovitsh, but also how essential this separation was for the latter's functioning as an artist and critical observer of contemporary Jewish life. The radical separation of the historical author from his rhetorical representative was made obligatory by the schizophrenic socio-cultural circumstances under which Yiddish writers worked at the time. It is, therefore, no wonder that some symptoms of such a separation can be traced in the work and artistic development of almost every important figure in nineteenth-century Yiddish literature. The more prominent the figure, the more conscious and purposeful the separation seems to be. A serious Yiddish writer could not but feel the nature of his position as an artist addressing an audience to which, in a sense, he did not belong. He had then, by one way or another, to assume a mask, which instead of being a reflection of himself, often had to be a reflection on himself. The persona not only covered the real face; it also had to expose it.

The illustration I have quoted above should make this clear. It is not that Sholem-Aleykhem, as distinguished from the author, identifies himself in it with the old-style traditional, religious way of life, assuming the role, as his interlocutor says, of *a gots straptshe* ('God's attorney'). He does not; and he is perfectly free to cast a critical eye on traditional Jewish life, to expose its inherent absurdities as well as its deterioration and to make it, in general, the subject of comedy. However, he also does not have to identify with the way of life, with the cultural preferences that "Solomon Naumovitsh" adopted under the pressure of historical circumstances. He is perfectly free to find it absurd, to point out its inner contradictions, to make fun of it. He is not, in fact, bound by the "consequential" logic of a choice between conflicting possibilities. He is free to change his position, and this freedom of his, this ability to avoid the burden of choice between mutually exclusive options, is the essence of his being. While he is certainly an observer of history, he is hardly subject to historical limitations in the sense that all living people and most fictional characters are. Hence his wonderful mental agility and self-sufficiency, the source of the hilarity he radiates. This agility and self-sufficiency Sholem Rabinovitsh had, inevitably, forfeited.

Without an autonomous, an independent Sholem-Aleykhem, Sholem Rabinovitsh could then hardly have become the great humorist he became; nor could his works have attained that dimension of a total Jewish comedy we still sense in them. It was only through devising this free spirit, Sholem-Aleykhem, that the author could, in his best works, overcome his own historical limitations and create a comic world which is still relevant. Sholem-Aleykhem, although implicitly committed to the Jewish people, as such, and to Yiddish as their natural medium of communication is, within this very wide scope, restricted by nothing and beholden to nobody. His presence is exhilarating because it abounds with the *fluidum* of freedom. This, one suspects, was the main reason why the author, who stumbled throughout his life against so many hurdles, let it invade his personal being, or tried to throw himself into it even as one submerges oneself in an intoxicating element.

4. If not a pen-name, a mere nominal replacement of the author's real name, what then was Sholem-Aleykhem and how did he function in the author's works? Easy answers to these questions are readily available. An artistic creation rather than an artist or a creator, Sholem-Aleykhem must have been a fictional character, and his function obviously was that of the character-narrator, i.e., the fictional personality entrusted by the author with the task of narrating the stories and thus endowing them with the vivacity, warmth, and authenticity of his own dramatic being. This narrative procedure is an old and universally recognized one. It forms one of the major constructions of the so-called "rhetoric of fiction." It had been employed in modern Yiddish fiction before the appearance of Sholem-Aleykhem—most notably in the highly influential works of Sh. Y. Abramovitsh—and our author also had recourse to it many times throughout his career. Nevertheless, I submit that these answers, easy and comfortable as they are, neither account for the phenomenon nor, if you wish, for the "rhetoric" of Sholem-Aleykhem. To be sure, they are applicable to certain works, but on the whole they do not delineate correctly either the nature of Sholem-Aleykhem or his artistic function. Of the various reasons for this only the two most important ones will be mentioned here.

For one thing, the impression they give of defining the technical function of Sholem-Aleykhem within the structure of the author's works is misleading. Of the four major works—*Menakhem-Mendl, Tevye der milkhiker, Motl Peyse dem khazns [Motl, the Son of the Cantor Peyse]*, and *Funem yarid*—only the last one is a story narrated by Sholem-Aleykhem, who, however, appears in it in the capacity of an omniscient author, rather than in that of the character-narrator.[27] Two of the others are constructed as cycles of monologues spoken by the protagonists. In Tevye's monologues, Sholem-Aleykhem's presence is felt very strongly, but it is the presence of a hearer, a confidant, who provokes the protagonist's loquacity by his willingness to absorb, and not that of a narrator; for Tevye's stories are supposed to be verbatim reproductions of actual talks addressed to Sholem-Alekyhem.[28] Motl, unlike Tevye, is addressing his stories not to the second person singular, i.e., to an alleged confidant, but to a rather equivocal second person plural presumably representing us, the readers, in a direct way. Sholem-Aleykhem's presence is, therefore, supposedly missing from the stories, or is that of a mere scribe. Since Motl admits his illiteracy—he cannot write and he hardly reads[29]—it can be understood that Sholem-Aleykhem does the writing for him, although his presence is never mentioned. Actually, we are indirectly encouraged to suspect him of taking a more important part in the forming of Motl's monologues, which cannot be construed (as Tevye's and most of the author's other monologists' can) as a direct, verbatim reproduction of the protagonist's speech. For, while he was taking every possible advantage of the protagonist's naiveté and of the dramatic irony and unintentional comedy offered by his limited, childish consciousness, the author also allowed himself to disregard the limits prescribed by them. He put stories in Motl's mouth, which in content, structure, and vocabulary are clearly beyond the capacities of a nine-year old *shtetl*-boy, deprived of almost any education.[30] Thus, Sholem-Aleykhem can perhaps be said to function in *Motl Peyse dem khazns* in the capacity of a ghost-writer, or a *souffleur.*

In *Menakhem-Mendl* no narration, in the strict sense of the word, is done at all; the book presumably consists of letters exchanged by the protagonist and his wife at different times and from different places, not for purposes of narrating anything but rather for those of communication. The presence of Sholem-Aleykhem here is of a double nature. In the so-called "canonized" edition of *Menakhem-Mendl* it is the mere presence of an editor or of a piratical literary entrepreneur of sorts. He introduces himself as a long-time but hardly intimate acquaintance of the protagonist, who has somehow gained access to his personal correspondence. Having selected from it the parts he deems most interesting, he is now making them public, without bothering to ask for the permission of the protagonist, who at the time of publication is presumably seeking his fortune in that land of promise, the United States.[31] Readers familiar with the Menakhem-Mendl literature in its entirety, know that Sholem-Aleykhem is also present in it in the capacities of an addressee (Menakhem-Mendl wrote him no less than five long letters) and of a correspondent (he responds with one letter, advising Menakhem-Mendl to try his luck as a matchmaker).[32] These different modes of presence by no means exhaust the catalogue of the different rhetorical capacities in which the protean Sholem-Aleykhem functions as he emerges or vanishes, talks or is talked to, reports, is reported on, overhears, eavesdrops, steals letters, is interrogated, cursed, flattered, and declared nonexsistent along the extensive list of the author's work. They do, however, sufficiently illustrate my first reason for disqualifying a general description of Sholem-Aleykhem as a character-narrator.

My other reason is that even in the numerous works where Sholem-Aleykhem *is* responsible for the narration, and in which his direct presence is felt everywhere, he can hardly apply for the status of a full-fledged fictional character. I am aware of the fact that the term "character" is far from well-defined, and that it is stretched all the time to suit the particular purposes of one critic or another. Still, it seems to me that the term can hardly be stretched enough to cover Sholem-Aleykhem in most of his appearances. On the whole, Sholem-Aleykhem simply lacks the "materiality," the well-defined relations in terms of space and time and even in sheer behavioral continuity, which we have come to expect of a fictional character, whatever the definition of the term may be. He is too light, too airy to assume the attributes that even a minimalist definition would demand, minimalist in the sense that it does not require a high degree of psychological reality to pass for a full-fledged fictional character. As I have already suggested, lightness and spriteliness are not accidental or even secondary qualities in him, but rather his very essence.

Here a short comparison of Sholem-Aleykhem with Mendele the Book Peddler can be illuminating. Mendele functions in Abramovitsh's works in ways quite often resembling those of Sholem-Aleykhem: he describes, reports, overhears, is made a confidant, makes humorous comments, and most importantly, edits and publishes presumably authentic documents and stories even as Sholem-Aleykhem does in *Menakhem-Mendl* and *Tevye,* in the *Monologn* and in scores of other stories. It is, however, through his sheer "weight" as a fictional character that Mendele's figure differs from Sholem-Aleykhem, and the difference is decisive. True, Mendele is a static character devised to operate a certain narrative-structural apparatus, and is not allowed to develop much beyond the restricted range within which his technical task can be performed. Nevertheless, he is always psychologically real. Indeed, he is more so than all the other characters Abramovitsh created put together, and it is this instant and absolute reality of his that makes him the real starting point of modern Yiddish literature. He has his own uncanny ways of being equivocal, of mediating between the author, a modern European positivist, and the traditional, religious society he portrays; but he is nevertheless deeply and significantly anchored in history. His socio-economic "place" in the traditional Jewish world is clearly defined. His physical and mental idiosyncrasies, his ways of relating to other people, his specific ways of being cunning, his intentional bathos, his love of nature, his concepts of time, place, and causality are vividly conveyed by the author. Moreover, Mendele is always fully human in his vulnerability. He can be deeply offended (as in the case when an antisemitic policeman shaves off one of his sidelocks, in *Fishke der krumer* [Fishke the Lame]); he can be engaged (when his carriage collides with that of another Jewish book peddler, *ibid.*); fearful (when he loses his way in a forest, *ibid.*); and perplexed. He worries about his finances (as in the short story *Biyeme haraash* [In the Days of Tumult]), etc. All these attributes of reality are lacking in Sholem-Aleykhem, whose existence is almost never rendered in socio-historical terms. We know he is a writer who publishes in Yiddish newspapers, but his actual financial or social relationships with newspaper owners or with editors are never described. We know that he travels very frequently, that he is actually always on the move, but we do not know why. Above all else, we cannot think of him as a vulnerable and constrained human being. His freedom, equanimity, and good spirits are his trademarks. On the one or two very rare occasions that he loses them, he is not himself anymore, and we, the readers, are nonplussed; we feel that the very basis of his existence as a comforting presence has been undermined. Such, for instance, is the case in the monologue **"An eytse"** [**"A Piece of Advice"**], where Sholem-Aleykhem, instead of showing the young man who asks for his advice a way out of his perplexing dilemma, gets himself entangled in it, loses his temper, and physically attacks his interlocutor. But **"An eytse"** is, in more ways than one, an exception among the author's works. (It is also exceptional, for example, in its detailed description of Sholem-Aleykhem's physical environment: his study, desk, pens, bric-a-brac, etc., which endows his presence with an unusual "materiality.")[33] On the whole, however, Sholem-Aleykhem remains free, uncommitted, unrelated and unburdened. This does not mean that he is a less vivid creation than Mendele, but does indicate that his vividness is of a different order from that of the book peddler. This is clearly indicated by the very difference between the two names. While "Mendele the Book Peddler" includes both a definite personal name and the indication of a specific occupation, the name "Sholem-Aleykhem" is a spoof, a mere pun. Of course, it includes the first name, "Sholem," and thus, when used as a name it starts deceptively as the real thing. However, the added word "Aleykhem" undermines this impression of nominal "reality." Instead of qualifying the common first name by a surname, patronymic, placename, or an indication of an occupation, i.e., instead of making it more specific, it turns it into an idiomatic expression, as 'hello' or 'how-do-you-do'.

Here the comparison between "Sholem-Aleykhem" and "Mark Twain" suggests itself, for as we now know Clemens' pseudonym was as much of a joke as Rabinovitsh's was. Like "Sholem-Aleykhem," "Mark Twain" was not a name but rather an expression. The author's acquaintances (during his wild carousing days as editor of *The Territorial Enterprise* in Virginia City) interpreted "Mark Twain" as an appeal or a directive to friendly bartenders to mark two drinks to the author's account. In those days Clemens used to take his drinks two at a time, and being fresh from his long service on the Mississippi, he would drawl like a Mississippi leadsmen: "M-a-r-k twain!" instead of ordering the marking of two.[34] However, the difference between "Mark Twain" and "Sholem-Aleykhem" is more significant than the resemblance. The first was a private joke, intended to remain unknown to the general public. We know that when Clemens was asked to explain his pen-name later on, he tried his best to cover his own traces, pretending that it was "the *nom de plume* of one Captain Isaiah Sellers, who used to write river news over it for the New Orleans *Picayune*."[35] The greeting *sholem-aleykhem* was, of course used by every Yiddish-speaking Jew, and its incongruity as a name was, therefore, meant to be sensed and relished. "Mark Twain" sounded like a real name; "Sholem-Aleykhem" sounded like an intentional hoax.

5. A somewhat closer examination of this greeting may be worthwhile at this point. For it is perhaps the semantic contents of the name "Sholem-Aleykhem" that more than anything else can prove the clue to the nature of the mercurial being whose flights we are trying to trace. Of old Hebraic origin,[36] the greeting literally means 'peace be with you' (actually 'on you'), and it is answered with the same words in reverse order (*aleykhem-sholem*). Thus, greeting and reply form a symmetrical a b b a pattern.[37] In both of them the second person plural is used, indicating respect. All this goes to show how formal and ceremonious the *sholem-aleykhem* greeting basically was; a fact which is illustrated by its ritualistic use in the opening line of the hymn, with which the angels of peace were greeted by every Ashkenazic Jew upon his return from synagogue on Friday evening. These angels, according to old midrashic tradition, were escorting the holy Sabbath to every Jewish home and, of course, were to be greeted by the head of the family as the most welcome and venerated of guests. *Sholem-aleykhem* was then the formal greeting one offered an important personality (in the Talmud it is recommended as the greeting due a teacher from his disciples) and a welcome guest. A considerable residue of these formalistic and ceremonious qualities was retained even in its daily usage in Yiddish speech. It never degenerated into something as casual and automatic as 'hello' or 'how-do-you-do'. One would not waste it on a neighbor, an acquaintance, or a family member one sees daily or meets regularly. It is reserved for the special occasion of welcoming someone who has been long missed, or of getting to know a total stranger who has just happened to come to town, for according to traditional etiquette, the stranger, even when poor and undistinguished, is to be treated as an important and welcome

guest.[38] Of course, the actual degree of cordiality conveyed by the greeting, and by the handshake which as a rule follows it (to the extent that the expression *a sholem-aleykhem* may mean 'a handshake'), was determined by the real importance of the person greeted as well as by the good will and friendliness of the greeter. Hence the difference between a mere *sholem-aleykhem* and *a breyter sholem-aleykhem* (a 'hearty', literally a 'broad' one).[39] The expression was also used ironically, for formality and ceremony will always invite their reverse. Thus, *sholem-aleykhem,* uttered in a certain tone of voice, is a reaction to the unexpected appearance of something not exactly welcome, particularly to that of a person one would gladly do without.

These points are raised here not for the sake of ethnographic information, but because almost all of them were touched upon by the author in his use of the greeting as the name of his rhetorical representative.

(a) By choosing a formal greeting for a name, the author was first and foremost asserting the comic, prankish, and "contrary" nature of his persona. A being, whose very name consists in an incongruity or in a pun-like misuse of language, is bound to be "funny." Thus the name Sholem-Aleykhem, appearing under the title of a feuilleton or a story, conditions the reader's reading of the work and directs his expectations from it. As the name becomes popular and is frequently used, this primarily "funny," incongruous quality of it is, of course, in constant danger of erosion, even of complete obliteration. One suspects that most people who wrote on Yiddish literature became so familiar with the name Sholem-Aleykhem that they altogether lost the sense of its original absurdity. However, the author tried as hard as he could to keep the name's edge sharp. In order to recharge its waning comic potential and refresh the reader's perception of its preposterousness, he employed various gimmicks, such as that of comic misunderstanding, the semantic short-circuit created by the identity of a name and a greeting. Thus, Sholem-Aleykhem, met by strangers, is asked for his name. When he answers, he is understood as greeting his interlocutor. His greeting is, of course, accepted and reciprocated with the appropriate *aleykhem-sholem,* and then he is asked again, rather impatiently, to disclose his name, etc., etc. This simple little comedy of errors—which as a rule falls flat even in the best translation—is repeated again and again in different comic contexts. The most hilarious instance occurs in **Dos naye Kasrilevke** [**The New Kasrilevke**]. Here, Sholem-Aleykhem, on one of his "you-can't-go-home-again" visits to the town of his childhood, returns in the wee hours of the night to his hotel-room to encounter a gang of new-style *kasrilevker* housebreakers. Of course, they take whatever money he has,

which is very little, but after they are through with their paltry and not altogether convincing show of brutality, they start a more relaxed conversation with their victim and inquire, as every good Jew will, after his name. He answers, is misunderstood by them, etc.[40] The recurrent employment of such gimmicks should not be interpreted as a mere recourse to easy techniques of getting a laugh from an audience ready to laugh almost at anything, but rather as the author's persisting intention to protect the basic comic feature of his persona, which is the semantic absurdity of its name, from fading.

(b) As persistent as this, and in some way perhaps even more important, is his intention to evoke, by the use of the name Sholem-Aleykhem, the connotation of Jewish hospitality. Through this name the author was actually humanizing and Judaizing the technical procedure of publication. He was inviting the reader to consider the feuilleton or story not as so many words printed in a magazine, coming from far-off St. Petersburg (where the *Folksblat* was published), but rather as the spoken words of a human being, a guest, a talkative and friendly acquaintance one meets from time to time and greets, of course, with *a breyter sholem-aleykhem.* If we remember that Sholem-Aleykhem used to make his almost weekly appearances mostly on Fridays—Friday being the day on which the literary supplement of a Jewish newspaper is bound to appear—we can see how the author was linking the publication of his works with long and deep-rooted Jewish traditions. Was not his story or feuilleton an equivalent of the "guest for the Sabbath" without whom no Friday festive dinner could be considered complete? Moreover, as a welcome guest, who brought with him merriment and good-will, he was actually a companion of the Sabbath angels. As their name, *malakhe hashalom* ('angels of peace') indicated they were supposed to chase all the worries and irritations of weekly existence out of the Jewish home, and offer, instead, joviality, pleasure. and serenity. As a matter of fact, Sholem-Aleykhem's weekly appearance actually became for millions of East European Jews an almost institutionalized part of the Sabbath joviality. For it was on the Sabbath that the father of the family, or one of its other members, would read the new feuilleton or story, with proper comic intonation and mimicry, to the whole laughing family. Sholem-Aleykhem *was* a Sabbath guest in the actual sense of the words, and the author meant him to be one. In any case, he never missed an opportunity for drawing attention to this aspect of his being. After intervals in publication he would, for instance, start a new series of stories or humoresques with a scene of a hearty, if somewhat disorderly, meeting with a guest who had been missed for a long time. For example:

"A guest! A guest! Sholem-Aleykhem! A guest!"

"Aleykhem-sholem."

"Where are you coming from? Where have you been all this time? How are things? What's up with this, that, and the other, with us, with you, with . . . with . . . with . . .?"

"How can I answer all of you at once, good brothers? Let me catch my breath first, and then little by little every one of your questions will be answered. *Tishe yedesh—dalshe budesh* ['the quieter you ride, the further you will go']. Now, as for your first question."[41]

On other occasions, Sholem-Aleykhem, who is always supposed to be traveling, would break a long silence, caused allegedly by a particularly long journey, with a letter reassuring his readers that he had not forgotten them and that they were still going to have good times together. For example:

> Do confess, my dear sisters and brothers, loyal readers of the *Yidishes folksblat,* do confess that although I am not worthy of it some of you have already begun to miss me. . . .
>
> Confess, little sisters and brothers, that many of you have more than once looked for me down here on the ground floor [of the newspaper], where we once used to meet almost weekly. I even know that a few of my good friends have already begun to feel somewhat happy about it: "What's that? No more Sholem-Aleykhem?—Good riddance. . . ." Don't worry, little brothers, I am here! Don't you be too happy, dear friends; here I am![42]

(c) As the passage just quoted suggests, the author was not averse to evoking ironic or sarcastic connotations connected with the *sholem-aleykhem* greeting, i.e., to emphasizing the nuisance aspect of his persona. While he certainly wanted this persona to represent the welcome and merry guest, he also wanted it to call to mind the fellow who crops up where he is least expected or wanted; the rogue, who can always be counted on to play a trick, to set a trap and indulge in all sorts of light, not too painful mischief. In any case, he let the people who came into contact with Sholem-Aleykhem or read his works shower upon his head imprecations and abusive epithets such as *shlimazl* ('ne'er do well'), *a shlak* ('an insufferable nuisance'; literally—'a stroke'), a *farshlepte krenk* ('a dragged out, protracted disease'), *a meshumed* (literally, 'a converted Jew'; figuratively, 'a rascal, a miscreant'), *a meshulakhes* ('a plague', literally, 'visitation') and most often *a lets* or one of the *leytsim.* In order to appreciate the full thrust of this last epithet, which becomes Sholem-Aleykhem's nickname, one must take into account not only its present watered-down meaning, which is that of a buffoon or joker, but also its long history of semantic virulence. It begins with the Biblical warning not to sit in the seat of the scornful,

the scoffers (*leytsim*), and reaches its climax in popular demonology, which identifies the *leytsim* with a distinct order of minor demons. This last meaning is definitely what many characters have in mind when they refer to Sholem-Aleykhem as a *lets,* especially those characters whose secrets or personal correspondence was made public by him.[43] Sholem-Aleykhem himself hints, at least in his early appearances, at his devilry by introducing himself many times in Biblical Hebrew as coming *mishut boorets umihishaleykh bo* ('from going to and fro in the earth, from walking up and down in it'), i.e., by quoting Satan's reply to God's question ("From whence comest thou?") from the first chapters of the Book of Job.[44] The image conjured by this allusion is, of course, one of a devil at large who is both facetious and bent on mischief.

As a matter of fact, it was this aspect of the Sholem-Aleykhem persona that dominated **"Di vibores," "Di ibergekhapte briv,"** and other early works in which its basic features took form. It is also this aspect that indicates what was probably the origin both of the persona and of its name. At this early phase of the author's development, he was working within the framework of a "style" or a "tradition" in Yiddish comic and satirical writing, which although the historians have paid but little attention to it, was at the time highly influential. Its most celebrated representative was Y. Y. Linetski, whose savage but also hilarious anti-Hasidic satire *Dos poylishe yingl* [The Polish Boy] was the rage from the days of its first publication (1867) and throughout the 1870's. Linetski's speciality was the virulent satirical attack, unsophisticated and crude. Yet it was quite overwhelming by its combination of ferocious partisanship, tremendous verbal energy, and exaggerated caricature, which often sublimated a wildly distorted picture of historical reality into a grotesque vision. Linetski's persona (for like any other important Yiddish writer at the time, he consciously cultivated one) was modeled after the figure of the traditional *beyzer marshelik* ('wicked-tongued wedding jester'), who tells his captive audience the bitter truth about themselves and makes them swallow it, even enjoy it while being outraged by it, because he manages to make it funny, hilariously so. No Yiddish writer tended to present himself in terms of nuisance value more than did Linetski. His persona, *Eli Kotsin Hatskhakueli,* always paraded his awareness of his reader's willingness to tear him to pieces, as well as of their fear of his venomous pen. He developed the drama of his relationship with the readers around the image of the unexpected guest, whose visit amounts to a visitation. His best collection of *kartines* ('pictures, sketches'), *Dos meshulakhes* [The Visitation], which appeared in 1875 after a lull in his literary activity, was characteristically opened by a long chatty monologue entitled "Sholem-Aleykhem," which consisted of sarcastic apostrophes to the various categories of reader-victims, who are informed that the respite they were granted is over, and that it's now time to get ready for the flailing they richly deserve. Each of the apostrophes is opened with the *sholem-aleykhem* greeting and is developed by an ironic rhetoric of the hearty, noisy reunion of host and guest, who have been longing for each other, until it reaches a bathetic climax.[45] When Sholem Rabinovitsh started to write in Yiddish, he not only knew this collection but actually relished it. He was particularly taken (as he said in several letters)[46] with its final piece, which indeed was its *piece de resistance*. This was a little dramatic farce entitled "Di vibores," in which the efforts of the rich leaders of a certain Jewish community in the Ukraine to win an election with threats, bribery and chicanery were brilliantly exposed.[47] There is but little doubt that this was our author's starting point when he wrote his own **"Vibores,"** and there is a very strong probability that the pen-name he adopted for the publication of this Linetskian satire was suggested to him by Linetski's introductory monologue in *Dos meshulakhes*.

Sholem-Aleykhem's early career was directly influenced by Linetski's persona, much more than by the better-known Mendele Moykher-Sforim.[48] A residue of this influence was never to be completely obliterated, and the impudence of the irreverent truth-teller was to become an indispensible ingredient of the Sholem-Aleykhem flavor. However, from the very start the figure was devoid of Linetski's acerbity and verbal brutality, as well as alien to his overreaching anti-traditional bias. It was endowed instead with the rudiments of gentleness of carriage and melodiousness of phrase, traits which were to flourish in the mature works. Thus Sholem-Aleykhem presented from as early a work as the **"Ibergekhapte briv"** a metamorphosed version of the nuisance persona, a lighter and mellower image of a havoc-wrecker. Where Linetski's persona was cudgelling and trouncing, Sholem-Aleykhem dealt his lighter blows as part of a game. The former engaged in combat with his readers; his entrances and exits were martial, arranged as surprise attacks and strategic withdrawals. The latter played hide-and-seek with his readers, and his entrances and exits were those of a Puck-like sprite. What he left behind him was not seeping venom, but rather a breeze of playful mystery.

(d) It was mystery, indeed, although of the lightest brand, and devoid of any sinister aftertaste. As much as this may sound out of place in a description of a literary persona whose hallmark was convivial, chatty familiarity with the reading public, a persona through whom the author actually achieved unflagging rapport

with millions of readers, mystery or at least mystification was to remain an essential element in the Sholem-Aleykhem phenomenon. In fact, it was precisely the particular combination of familiarity and mystery that determined the nature of this phenomenon and made it an authentic part of the folklore. Sholem-Aleykhem was a kindred spirit, a reassuring guest, who could be counted on to relieve, for an hour, the dead weight of the terribly constrained existence of the contemporary Jew by his aura of freedom and vague promise of transcendence over all constraining circumstances. But in order to be reassuring in this way, in order to convey this promise, however vaguely, he also had to possess a guest's unfamiliarity, to be a stranger, a being free to assume new forms and able to evade any final, "placing" definition, which would immediately expose its limitations and strip it from any remnant of mystery. The mystery element in Sholem-Aleykhem was pronounced especially in the early works, but it lingered on in the late ones, informing the whole body of the author's works. One of the imaginary writers of the **"Stolen Letters"** reported:

> Yesterday evening I entered the house of a rich man where I found a large group of young people sitting around the table and reading our letter in the *Yidishes folksblat*. The laughter brought the house down. They invited me to join them so that I, too, would enjoy the feuilleton. Afterwards I asked them what they thought of **"The Stolen Letters"** and their answer was that Reb Velvele [who happens to be the writer of the present letter—D. M.] was crazy but not at all stupid. . . . One expressed the opinion that the whole thing was nothing but a fabrication by the correspondent, Sholem-Aleykhem, who had himself written the letters. Another said that this was impossible, since such a fabrication would amount to fraud, for which Sholem-Aleykhem could be sent to jail. A third person said that Sholem-Aleykhem was not afraid of being accused of fraud, for he, too, was a disembodied soul roaming in the *oylem-hatoyu* ('limbo'). [The addressee of this letter is allegedly a dead person who wanders in limbo. D. M.] The fourth one said that this was not possible either, because a person such as Tsederboym [the publisher and editor of the *Folksblat*—D. M.] would have nothing to do with either madmen or dead men. . . . The fifth one . . . but I am not going to tell what every one said, because it is not worth repeating.[49]

This obviously is a satire on the provincialism of contemporary Jewish society, but like many of our author's satirical thrusts it reaches deeper than facile social criticism. The reader of the feuilleton, who is wise enough to see through the fabrication of **"The Stolen Letters"** and to identify Sholem-Aleykhem as their writer, is not wholly in the right, while the naive reader who is superstitious enough to pronounce Sholem-Aleykhem a disembodied spirit, free from all human subordination, is not as wrong as he may seem. Sholem-Aleykhem, the persona, was actually meant to be taken as a comically mysterious being with fantastic mobility, who is everywhere and nowhere in particular, "going to and fro in the earth and walking up and down in it." He also was depicted as possessing an uncanny knack for unearthing secrets. How could he function otherwise in his capacity of a literary purveyor? How could he, for instance, publish the **"Stolen Letters"** allegedly exchanged between a man who had recently died and his friend, who since he had started to receive letters from the other world, had been pronounced insane? Mere journalistic indiscretion and a developed sense for sniffing out hidden documents could not suffice in such a case. A reporter had to establish connections with "sources" in higher circles and have his "channels of information" reach very far indeed![50] And how could Sholem-Aleykhem, without an uncanny power of penetration, rewrite the letters of Menakhem-Mendl and his wife. Menakhem-Mendl himself is utterly flabbergasted by this feat, as he confesses in this first letter to Sholem-Aleykhem. True, he concedes, Sholem-Aleykhem met him milling around the stock exchange quite often; still: "How remarkable! Every time I meet you it seems to me that while I see you, you never as much as notice me. Later, it turns out that you not only see *me,* but also see *through* me."[51]

6. Neither the author, nor a full-fledged fictional character, the Sholem-Aleykhem figure must then be referred to, as it has often been throughout this paper, as a presence. It is a presence informed by some immanent characteristics, but much too liable to metamorphosis and much too slight to pass for a character, and much too fanciful and free from biographical and historical commitments to be taken for the direct representation of the author. Assuming new faces and rhetorical functions as freely as a skilled and versatile actor, it nevertheless conditions the vast, variegated fictional world the author has created, unifies it and actually serves as an axis around which everything turns. It functions in different ways under different circumstances and for different purposes, but it is also one and indivisible. It represents many things, but it makes them look like different aspects or parts of a single, more comprehensive entity.

In some of his introductions to his major works, written late in his career, the author himself came as close as he could to a definition of this entity. In the introductory chapter to *Funem yarid,* he almost divulged his secret. There he explained the particular rhetorical structure of this autobiographical work written not as an autobiography, i.e., in the first person, but rather as a "biographical novel" narrated by an omniscient author: "It will turn out that I shall speak of myself as a third person, that is: I, *Sholem-Aleykhem the writer,* shall tell you the true biography of *Sholem-Aleykhem*

the person—as it would have been told, for instance, by an outsider, a total stranger who, however, had been everywhere with him, who together with him had been through the seven circles of hell."[52]

This, on the face of it, can be construed as nothing more than an elementary explanation of literary technicalities; an explanation intentionally simplified because offered to a reading public unacquainted with even the rudiments of literary-critical jargon (as, indeed, was the majority of our author's readership), and therefore in need of dramatic, situational renderings of such basic concepts as the omniscient author or the third-person narrative technique vs. the first-person one. However, it was meant not merely to serve as such an explanation, but also to go far beyond the elucidation of the particular formal or technical nature of *Funem yarid.* For one thing, the author went out of his way here to make even his most naive readers see that there was a difference between Sholem-Aleykhem the persona ("Sholem-Aleykhem the writer") and Sholem Rabinovitsh ("Sholem-Aleykhem the person"). But the intuition conveyed here was even more comprehensive than that. This one realizes by comparing the introduction to *Funem yarid* with other late perspective-opening introductions, such as the ironic prefatory note to the so-called "canonized" edition of **Menakhem-Mendl** (1910). The resemblance between the comments on the relationship between Sholem-Aleykhem the writer and the person, and those on the relationship between Sholem-Aleykhem and Menakhem-Mendl, is striking. Menakhem-Mendl, Sholem-Aleykhem says, is (not unlike the autobiographical hero of *Funem yarid*) a "true" and "uninvented" figure whom the author had known for years and followed along his pilgrimage from one stock-exchange to another. Like him he withstood many crises, went bankrupt, and finally emigrated to America. In short, he was his companion "through the seven circles of hell."[53] This, of course, was hardly a piece of bonafide biographical information. It was rather a metaphorical rendering of a relationship with more than one facet to it. On the one hand, the author clearly implied that there was more than a casual affinity between himself and the protagonist, who while being the butt of his satire was also his self-portrait. (One is reminded of Flaubert's dictum: "Madame Bovary—c'est moi.") On the other hand, he also implied that Sholem-Aleykhem's complete familiarity with Menakhem-Mendl, his inside knowledge of his life experience (which as we saw, Menakhem-Mendl himself could not comprehend), should never be understood as an identification with him. Sholem-Aleykhem, the persona, knows everything about Sholem Rabinovitsh and Menakhem-Mendl; he has followed them everywhere and seen them through imaginary successes and very real disasters, but he exits in a sphere totally different from theirs. The recurrence of the image of the journey through "the seven circles of hell" in both introductions is highly significant. It conveys the author's basic conception of direct experience, of "life" undistanced as a terrifying progression from one disaster to the other. Experience as such is infernal; the Jewish experience is doubly so. The vocation of Jewish art is to transform it, to endow it with some sense, to redeem its unbearable pain and absurdity. This can be done only by presenting it in comic terms, and this, in turn, can be achieved only by a free spirit, who while sharing this experience can also remain a "total stranger" to it. A Dantesque duality of protagonist (experience) and an accompanying presence (art, especially comic art) is therefore essential for a real presentation of "The Jewish Comedy." Thus Sholem-Aleykhem, a comic Vergil, shadowy, immaterial, a disembodied soul sees Menakhem-Mendl, Tevye, Motl, and scores of other protagonists, including Sholem Rabinovitsh, through the hell of existence in general and of Jewish existence in particular. He indicates, by his very existence, a possible road to freedom, perhaps the only road to it: the transforming path of art, the transcending trip of the comic spirit.

Notes

1. "Di vibores" in *Ale verk* [Complete Works], compiled and edited by N. Oyslender and A. Frumkin, I (Moscow, 1948), pp. 50-53. Hereafter this edition of *Ale verk* will be referred to as the "Soviet edition."

2. Sholem-Aleykhem was obviously imitating the well-known Hebrew and Yiddish fiction writers of the Haskalah ('Enlightenment') literature, such as P. Smolenskin, who had developed the plot of his major novel, *Hatoe bedarkhe hahayim* [Lost in the Paths of Life], in East European Jewish towns with names such as *Madmena* ('Dunghill', 'Bog'), *Mapelya* ('Darkness'), *Shakula* ('The Bereaved One'), etc., or Sh. Y. Abramovitsh with his *Tsvuashits* ('Town of Hypocrites'), *Glupsk* ('Town of Fools'), *Tuneyadevke* ('Town of Idlers'), etc.

3. See, for instance, the short autobiographical sketch the author wrote in 1908, translated from Russian into Yiddish in *Dos Sholem-Aleykhem-bukh* [The S.-A. Book], ed. Y. D. Berkovitsh (New York), pp. 3-4.

4. Leo Wiener, *The History of Yiddish Literature in the Nineteenth Century* (New York: Scribner's, 1899), pp. 383-384.

5. See Abramovitsh's well-known recollections of the psychological pressures he had to withstand when he began to write Yiddish (in 1863) in his *Reshimot letoldotay* (written in 1889), *Kol kitve*

Mendele Mokher-Sfarim (Tel-Aviv, 1947), p. 4. Abramovitsh refers here to those few Hebraists, who at the time (the 1860's) also wrote Yiddish, as philanderers visiting a despised mistress in the darkness of the night. They published their works either under pen-names or anonymously, "lest their nakedness be uncovered and their glory turned into shame."

6. See the autobiographical sketch mentioned in note no. 3.

7. These feuilletons, articles etc., published under such pen-names as *A Litvak, Gamliel Ben Pdatsur, Baron Pipernoter,* and *Menakhem-Mendl* (yes, here in 1887 the great Menakhem-Mendl made his first appearance in the author's works), as well as articles and letters written as a reaction to them, were collected in the first volume of Sholem-Aleykhem's *Ale verk,* Soviet edition, pp. 147-155, 487-514.

8. Saul Chajes, *Ozar beduye-hashem: Thesaurus Pseudonymorum quae in Litteratura Hebraica et Judaeo-Germanica Inveniuntur* (Vienna, 1933). See index, p. 46.

9. The tendency strongly influenced all of the author's novels but is particularly noticeable in the early ones. Preparing some of these for republication in his collected works, the author made an effort to diminish the part of Sholem-Aleykhem as the omniscient *raisoneur.* See, for instance, the long authorial musings he deleted from *Kindershpil* [Children's Game] and *Sender Blank* in the commentary section of the second volume of *Ale verk,* Soviet edition, pp. 289-337. What he left, however, was often more than enough.

10. An excellent exposition of Stendhal's case, of his philosophy of life as a masquerade, and of the distinction he made between "existence for oneself" and "existence for others," can be found in Jean Starobinski's article "Stendhal pseudonyme" in *L'oeil vivant* (Paris: Librairie Gallimard, 1961), pp. 191-244.

11. Justin Kaplan, *Mr. Clemens and Mark Twain* (New York: Simon & Schuster, 1966).

12. Many of the other pen-names adopted by Yiddish writers during the second half of the nineteenth century were fanciful and "funny." Some examples: *Shimshon-Bar-Yente* (S. Bernshteyn), *Eli Kotsin Hatskhakueli* (Y. Y. Linetski), *Meshugener Filosof, Khayim-Barburim* (M. Vintshevski), *Lamed-Vovnik* (M. Spektor), *Yankele-Khokhem* (M. Rombro, better known by his "European" pseudonym, *Philip Krantz*), Rabi Kotsin (Y. Kh. Ravnitski), *Simkhe-Sosn* (M. Freyd), *Lampenputser, Lutsifer, Lets fun der Redaktsye,* (Y. L. Perets).

Some of Sholem Rabinovitsh's "minor" pen-names were already mentioned in note no. 7. Here are some additional ones: *Ester, Shulamis, Salomon Bikherfreser, Salomon Esbikher, Der Yidisher Gazlen, Terakh's an Eynikl*, etc.

13. There can be no doubt that certain literary genres are more conducive than others to pseudonymity. The "humoristic" genres, for example, especially those of the comic or satirical feuilleton, always called for a thicker and more extensive pseudonymous cover. The traditions of "humoristic" writing, both in nineteenth-century American and in Yiddish literature, offer excellent instances of this phenomenon.

14. During the twentieth century, Yiddish literature completely liberated itself from its nineteenth-century "inferiority complex." Still, many of the central figures in it resorted to pen-names (a few examples: Der Nister and Y. Bashevis among the best-known fiction writers; Bal-makhshoves, and Sh. Niger among the most influential critics; A. Leyeles and L. Volf as founders of new, modernistic schools or "groups" in poetry). An explanation that will account for nineteenth-century Yiddish pseudonyms will have to undergo radical modifications when applied to these and many other twentieth-century ones.

15. It is generally agreed that it was the critic, Bal-makhshoves (pseud. of I. Eliashev), who launched the serious critical evaluation of Sholem-Aleykhem in his article "Sholem-Aleykhem," originally published in 1908. See Balmakhshoves, *Geklibene shriftn* [Collected Works], I (Warsaw, 1929), pp. 91-109.

16. Y. Y. Trunk, *Sholem-Aleykhem—zayn vezn un zayne verk* [Sholem-Aleykhem—His Essence and His Works], (Warsaw, 1937), p. 375.

17. *Ibid.*, pp. 375-443.

18. The author seems to have sanctified, with his own words, the fragmentation of his personality into authorial and personal sections. See the first chapter of *Funem yarid*, where "Sholem-Aleykhem the writer" is dissociated from "Sholem-Aleykhem the person," *Ale verk fun Sholem-Aleykhem* [Complete works of S.-A.] (New York: *S.-A. Folksfond oysgabe* [People's-Fund edition], 1917-1925), XXVI, p. 17. Also see below . . . .

19. Here is a characteristic self-introductory dialogue:

"What's your name?"

"Sholem-Aleykhem."

"Sholem-Aleykhem?—Then you certainly deserve *a sholem-aleykhem* [the greeting]."

"*Aleykhem veal beneykhem* [the continuation of the greeting]."

"What do you do for a living?"

"What should I do for a living? I write."

"What do you write?"

"What should one write? One writes what one observes."

"What do you get from your writing?"

"What should one get? One gets trouble, indigestion, heartache, disgrace, worries, cold sweat, vexation. . . . "

"And that's all?"

"What else did you expect?"

("Sholem-Aleykhem," in *Yidishe shrayber* [Jewish Writers], *Ale verk*, Folksfond edition, V, pp. 9-10)

For the exact meaning of the greeting and its reply see below, . . . and note no. 37.

20. From the monologue "An eytse" [A Piece of Advice], *Monologn*, in *Ale verk*, Folksfond edition, XXI, p. 75. For characteristic advice-seeking see also Menakhem-Mendl's letter to Sholem-Aleykhem entitled "Vos tut men?" [What's to be Done?], originally published in *Der yid* (1900) and recently republished in *Sovetish heymland* IX (1969), no. 2, pp. 73-75.

21. That happens very often in the early feuilletons. See, for instance, the description of Reb Khayim, the innkeeper (who has an interest in the intricate politics of the Balkans), in the series "Bilder fun der barditshever gas" [Pictures from Barditshev Street], *Ale verk*, Soviet edition, I, pp. 458-463.

22. See, for instance, the chapter "Di lezer fun der doziker gas" [The Readers of This Very Street] in the same series; *ibid.*, pp. 463-469. Here is how one of the readers addresses Sholem-Aleykhem (p. 467):

Dear, beloved Sholem-Aleykhem! I beg you! Do it for my sake, and describe in the magazines that roughneck, that bankrupt, who robs the shirt off my back, sending his impudent servants from every corner to attract my customers! Since he became my tenant. . . . He should have rather become a corpse, the dirty bastard! I beg you, Sholem-Aleykhem, you have a knack for it, describe him precisely, so that every one will know that it's he, the Motyukhe, who plays cards all night long! And you write whatever you want about him; it will be nothing but the truth, so help me God, as much as he has helped me until now, for heaven's sake!—You write in the magazines anyway; what difference will it make to you if you describe him, too?

23. *Ibid.*, pp. 464-465.

24. See Tevye's letter to Sholem-Aleykhem, "Kotonti" [I am not Worthy of . . .], *Gants Tevye der milkhiker, Ale verk*, Folksfond edition, V, pp. 10-11.

25. S.-A., "Di gas" [The Street], in "Bilder fun der zhitomirer gas" [Pictures of Zhitomir Street], in *Ale verk,* Soviet edition, I., pp. 476-477.

26. *Ibid.,* p. 478: *rov*—'rabbi'; *shoykhet*—'ritual slaughterer'; *moyel*—'circumciser'; *bal metsise*—'functionary at a circumcision ceremony'.

Sholem-Aleykhem obviously expected Sholemke, whom he remembered wearing the characteristically Hasidic low shoes and white cotton stockings, to become one of the *klekoydesh,* the clerical elite of the Jewish congregation, but in a very small, perhaps grotesquely miserable way. He did not forsee him as achieving a rabbinical reputation and proving a "success" in his clerical vocation.

27. That is his function in most of the author's novels proper, such as *Stempenyu, Yosele Solovyey* [Yosele the Nightingale], *Der mabl* [The Deluge] (the novel was also entitled *In shturem* [In the Storm]), *Blondzhnde shtern* [Wandering Stars], *Der blutiker shpas* [The Tragic Joke], etc., on different levels of authorial conspicuousness. It was perhaps only in the very early novel *Kindershpil* [Children's Game] that the author made his Sholem-Aleykhem play the role of the character-narrator, for there he introduces him as a classmate of the two friends-turned enemies, the fathers in this comic-melodramatic version of a Jewish *Romeo and Juliet.* However, even in this novel the technique of the character-narrator is not sustained, and Sholem-Aleykhem too often lapses into the role of the omniscient author.

28. The full title of Tevye's first monologue, as it originally appeared in 1895, reads:

Tevye the Dairyman

A marvelous story of how Tevye, a poor Jew and father of many children suddenly made good by dint of a strange coincidence worth describing in a book; as told by Tevye himself and transmitted word for word

by Sholem-Aleykhem (*Hoyzfraynt,* vol. IV, p. 63)

29. See *Motl Peyse dem khazns,* first part, "Fun der heym keyn Amerike" [From Home to America], *Ale verk,* Folksfond edition, XVIII, pp. 225, 241. Motl's illiteracy, by the way, strangely contradicts the work's subtitle: "Ksovim fun a yingl a yosem" [Writings of an Orphan-Boy]. The "rhetoric" of Motl, for all its apparent simplicity, is a most tricky one.

30. The opening pages of Motl's first story abound with instances of this methodical inconsistency, which most commentators seem unable to detect. Motl talks here as an ardent reader of Goethe and Schiller (expressions such as *dankbarkeyt tsu der natur* 'thankfulness to nature', etc.) rather than as a boy who has hardly mastered the alphabet. The different linguistic and rhetorical levels of Motl's monologues call for a detailed analysis.

31. See Sholem-Aleykhem's introductory note to the "canonized" (second) edition of *Menakhem-Mendl,* in *Ale verk,* Folksfond edition, X, pp. 10-11.

32. Menakhem-Mendl's letters to Sholem-Aleykhem were originally published in *Der yid* (1900) and *Der fraynd* (1903/4). All of them were recently republished in *Sovetish heymland,* IX (1969), no. 2, pp. 73-94. This republication also includes Sholem-Aleykhem's only letter to Menakhem-Mendl, *ibid.,* pp. 76-78 (originally published in *Der yid,* 1900). The idea that was to be fully developed in the "Es fidlt nisht" [No Luck] section of *Menakhem-Mendl* germinated in this letter.

33. Y. Y. Trunk sensitively pointed out some of the peculiarities of this monologue. See his *Sholem-Aleykhem—zayn vezn un zayne verk,* pp. 199-207.

34. Paul Fatout, "Mark Twain's Nom de Plume" in *Mark Twain—a Profile,* ed. Justin Kaplan (New York: Hill & Wang, 1967), pp. 161-168; also Fatout, "Enter Mark Twain" in *Mark Twain in Virginia City* (Bloomington: Indiana University Press, 1964), pp. 34-49.

35. From an open letter of Clemens to J. A. McPherson (1877). See Fatout's article in Kaplan's collection, *op. cit.,* p. 161.

36. The preposition *al* ('on') follows the noun *shalom* ('peace') in the context of a greeting or wish but twice in the Bible and in an identical form: *shalom al yisrael* 'peace shall be upon Israel' (Authorized Version, Psalms 125,5, 128,6). The regular Biblical greeting connects *shalom* with the prepositional prefix *le* ('to'). However, in post-Biblical Hebrew *shalom al* became the normative form of greeting. (See, as a Talmudic instance, *Berakhot* 27b and Rashi *ad. loc.*)

37. The greeting could be replied to, on special occasions, with the Biblical *aleykhem veal beneykhem* (Psalms 115, 14: 'on you and your children'): See a characteristic example of modern Yiddish use of this elaboration in note no. 19.

38. See, for instance, the opening passages of Yisroel Aksenfeld's *Dos shterntikhl* [The Headband], the first modern Yiddish novel, where the narrator jocosely delineates the differences between a *kleyn shtetl,* a *shtot,* and a *groyse shtot* in the Russian-Jewish Pale during the first half of the nineteenth century. The differentiating feature of the "big town," as he puts it, is that *do barimt zikh itlekher,*

az er hot eynem fun der ander gas gegebn sholem-aleykhem vayl er hot im gehaltn far a fremder ('here everyone boasts of having greeted someone from the other street with a *sholem-aleykhem,* mistaking him for a stranger'), Aksenfeld, *op. cit.,* ed. M. Viner (Moscow, 1938), p. 52.

39. Significantly, Tevye the dairyman uses this expression (along with other elaborations of the conventional greeting) only in his last monologues, allegedly heard by Sholem-Alekyhem after twenty years of an acquaintance that developed into a real intimacy. Most markedly, the monologue "Lekh lekho" [Get Thee Out (after Genesis 12,1)] written in 1914, after five years during which Tevye had not seen Sholem-Aleykhem, is opened with the greeting in its most elaborate form: *a sheyner, a guter, a breyter sholem-aleykhem oyf aykh, pani Sholem-Aleykhem! Aleykhem ve'al beneykhem! Ikh kuk shoyn oyf aykh lang aroys* ('A fine, good, hearty *sholem-aleykhem* to you, Mr. Sholem-Aleykhem! *Aleykhem veal beneykhem!* I have been looking forward to seeing you for a long time'), *Gants Tevye* in *Ale verk,* Folksfond edition, V. p. 199.

40. See the chapter "Kasrilevker banditn" [The Bandits of Kasrilevke], in the story "Dos naye Kasrilevke" [The New Kasrilevke], in *Alt-nay Kasrilevke* [Kasrilevke—Old and New], *Ale verk,* Folksfond edition, XIII, pp. 120-125. By the way, in this scene of "robbery" Sholem-Aleykhem does not for a moment lose his equanimity, his attitude of an amused observer. It is an excellent instance of his invulnerability. The fact that he is poor, and that whatever money he has is being taken from him, is not presented as a threat either to his physical or spiritual autonomy.

41. From "Kurtse antvortn oyf lange fragn" [Short Replies to Long Questions] *Ale verk,* Soviet edition, vol. I, p. 470. See a similar opening in the feuilleton "Stantsye Mazepevke" [Mazepevke Station], where Sholem-Aleykhem is "attacked," the moment he gets off the train, by a crowd of impatient readers: "*Aleykhem-sholem,* Reb Sholem-Aleykhem, a guest, a guest! How are you? How are the wife and the kids? What's new? Where are you coming from, and what brings you here?" (*Hoyzfraynt,* III, 1893, p. 157.)

42. "Funem veg" [From the Road], *Ale verk,* Soviet edition, II, p. 208.

43. The "Ibergekhapte briv," for instance, are full of such epithets: *Ale verk,* Soviet edition, I, pp. 68-69, 79, 82, 122, etc.

44. See, for example, the opening paragraphs of the first letter in "An ibershraybung tsvishn tsvey alte khaveyrim" [A Correspondence Between Two Old Friends], *Ale verk,* Soviet edition, I, p. 165; the chapter "Di simkhe" [The Celebration] in *Bilder fun der barditshever gas, ibid.,* p. 438; "Kurtse antvortn oyf lange fragn," *ibid.,* p. 470.

45. Eli Kotsin Hatskhakueli, *Dos meshulakhes* (Zhitomir, 1875), pp. 3-10.

46. See his letters to Linetski of March 19/20 and 27, 1888, in *Sholem-Aleykhem—zamlung fun kritishe artikeln un materyaln* (Kiev, 1940), pp. 234-235.

47. *Dos meshulakhes,* pp. 58-71.

48. Linetski's influence over Sholem-Aleykhem has not yet been recognized by most Yiddish scholars outside the Soviet Union, and has not been properly studied. For the fullest account now available, see H. Reminik's "Linetski un Sholem-Aleykhem," *Shtern,* XV (1939), no. 9, pp. 80-90.

49. From Letter VI of the "Ibergekhapte briv," *Ale verk,* Soviet edition, I, p. 105.

50. The author was using the correspondence of the madman and dead man to present his readers with a comprehensive satirical view of contemporary Jewish society "in its true colors," i.e., from the vantage point of absolute, objective truth as revealed to the soul after death in the other world, which both in Hebrew and Yiddish is referred to as "the world of truth." The other vantage point, that of the relative, subjective, but still revolutionary truth of the madman, or the man society pronounces mad for breaking away from the net of accepted lies in which all "normal" people are caught likewise is presented. There was nothing new about the author's choice of this satirical technique. Both the dead and the allegedly insane as truth-tellers are as old a convention as satire itself. Anti-traditional satire in nineteenth-century Yiddish and Hebrew literature employed these conventional figures *ad nauseam* (A. Volfson, T. Feder, Y. Erter, Y. L. Levinzon, Sh. Y. Abramovitsh, Y. Y. Linetski, A. B. Gotlober, M. L. Lilyenblum, et al.). In many ways the "Ibergekhapte briv" were a mere continuation of the satirical literature of the *Haskalah* movement. What was new about it, however, was the softening of the anti-traditional line, and more importantly, the role the *lets,* Sholem-Aleykhem, played in stealing and publishing the letters. The "supernatural" machinery of this specific satirical convention enabled the author to develop the characteristics of his persona.

51. From "Vos tut men?" [What's to be Done?], *Sovetish heymland,* IX (1969), no. 2, p. 73.

52. See note no. 18.

53. See note no. 31.

Ruth R. Wisse (essay date 1979)

SOURCE: Wisse, Ruth R. "Sholem Aleichem and the Art of Communication." In *Sholem Aleichem and the Art of Communication,* pp. 1-31. Syracuse, N.Y.: Syracuse University Press, 1979.

[*In the following essay, Wisse addresses how Aleichem used conversations and monologues in his short fiction to address the unique social and political situation of Eastern European Jews at the turn of the twentieth century, including such themes as assaults on orthodox religious tenets, severed relations between parents and their more modernized children, and the confusion and bewilderment of socially and politically powerless Jews attempting to survive in foreign urban settings.*]

Voices, the sounds of recognizable human speech, are heard in the pages of Sholem Aleichem with such liveliness and authority that they won for him the ultimate literary compliment of being taken for real. One of his admirers, the Hebrew writer, Y. Ch. Brenner, said that Sholem Aleichem was not a folk writer, nor even *the* folk writer; he had transcended all literary genres to become "the living essence of the folk itself."[1] A generation later, the Soviet Yiddish critic, I. Dobrushin, wrote with much the same enthusiasm that Sholem Aleichem's works were actually "life itself; his works transgress the boundaries separating literature from life."[2] Sholem Aleichem's characters have been accurate embodiments of the typical Jew and enduring images of the "eternal Jewish fate."[3] The truth-to-life of those characters who speak in their own voices and are their own story-tellers has almost obscured the author who created them.[4]

It is true, of course, that Tevye the dairyman, Menakhem-Mendl the speculator, and Motl the cantor's son are surprisingly "real," as are all the innumerable spell-binders of Sholem Aleichem's repertoire. The authentic vivacity of their speech is one of the main reasons that his characters have remained so popular—even in translation. But the emphasis on their expressive realism has obscured other interesting aspects of the work in which they figure. Sholem Aleichem's stories, filled as they are with monologuists and talkers, have also much to say about the delicate art of communication. Not all speakers are as effective as they are entertaining, and even the juiciest vernacular can be applied to wicked ends. There is no automatic correlation between the quality of a person's discourse and its appropriateness, or its ability to realize its own intended aims.

Sholem Aleichem—or Sholem Rabinovitch, the author who created his fictional counterpart, Sholem Aleichem—was writing during an exceptionally turbulent period of Jewish history. While the idiomatic richness of his speakers conveys the brilliant flavor of East European Jewish civilization, their frequent problems of communication, of understanding others and being understood in turn, suggests the break-up of that civilization, sometimes in gentle stages, sometimes with catastrophic suddenness. To shift our focus from the "folk-voice" of Sholem Aleichem's characters where it has so often rested, to the effectiveness of that folk-voice in its various manifestations, is to appreciate the full artistry of the author, and the cultural complexities of the society he describes.

Whenever there is a speaker there should also be a listener, if only the implied reader, who has to determine the reliability of the narrative.[5] This is done, in literature as in life, by assessing the storyteller's character and credibility. Within a cohesive community, where people literally and figuratively "speak the same language," this proper identification depends on good judgment in distinguishing rogues from fools, saints from sinners, those who talk to reveal from those who talk to conceal. In a changing or mobile society, in which people cannot be presumed to share the same assumptions or cultural idiom, identifying the quality of a speaker is considerably more complicated. It is necessary first to understand the social, cultural, and even geographic origins and affiliation of the person before one can properly assess his words. In Sholem Aleichem's world, for example, a Russian speaking Russian to a Jew (because it would have been most natural for him to do so) would be quite different from a Jew speaking Russian to a Jew (because it would have been unnatural for him to do so). Character and motive, in such situations, lies hidden within the folds of social and cultural identity.

The nature of identification is still more critical when actual danger is involved. As in the animal kingdom, there are moments when discovering the nature of the intruder is not merely a matter of interest, but of ultimate importance, requiring an instinct of self-preservation. The sheep had better know whether it is addressing one of its own kind or a wolf in its own kind of clothing.

The literary world of Sholem Aleichem moves through each of these spheres, the benign, the indeterminate, and the malign. Characters and readers are repeatedly invited to participate in the popular literary sport of recognition, whose aim is the identification—as quickly and accurately as possible—of the real nature of the speaker and his intentions. For the reader it is a matter of fun: the sooner he breaks the code, the longer he can delight in the dramatic irony of his privileged angle of insight and savor the anticipated outcome. For the character in the story, however, it is usually a more serious game. His happiness, prosperity, his sanity, and occasionally his life may depend on his skill in deciphering the signs, the semiotic language. There are clues to be found in physical appearance and dress. But since Sholem Aleichem's characters are known primarily through their voices, it is necessary, above all, to listen.

In the Benign World

Sholem Aleichem's work was thought to represent an intimate linguistic community whose flavorful Yiddish draws vertically from the deep intellectual and folk traditions, and extends horizontally to simulate a quasi-national Jewish territory.[6] Much of Sholem Aleichem's fiction does indeed reinforce the notion of cultural continuity and cohesion. The monologues of Tevye, to bring but the most obvious example, show a simple *folksmentsh,* a Jewish villager,[7] who barely worked himself up to the status of dairyman, entertaining a sophisticated urban writer on many successive occasions. The very first words Tevye is seen to address to Pani Sholem Aleichem, when he learns that the author has "written up" his story, refer to their shared language, and to the oddity of direct communication between two such disparate Jews:

> "I am not worthy!"—This is what I should tell you in the language that our patriarch, Jacob, uses in the portion, *Vayishlokh,* when he sets out against Esau . . . but in case I haven't got it quite right, please forgive me, Pani Sholem Aleichem, because I am just a simple being—you certainly know more than I do—no question about it! In a village you grow coarse; who has the time to look into a book, to study a portion of the Torah with Rashi's commentaries. . . .[8]

Drawing attention to his ignorance, Tevye nonetheless uses and creatively misuses all the more accessible Jewish sources—prayers, psalms, parts of the Bible that are read during the year in synagogue, homiletic books and midrashic stories. Tevye's extraordinary verbal agility, the degree to which he has integrated the full spirit, if only the broken letter of Jewish tradition, stands, as we shall see, against the many social and political forces that are ranged against him. The presence of "Pani Sholem Aleichem" as Tevye's appreciative listener throughout the various Tevye episodes confirms the common culture that these two men share despite the social chasm that divides them.

Of course, even within this cohesive Jewish world of the author's where everyone "speaks the same language," communication sometimes breaks down. When Tevye, for example, is summoned by the well-to-do butcher, Leyzer Wolf, to discuss an important matter, Tevye enters the conversation on the assumption that they are talking about his cow, whereas the butcher is actually in pursuit of Tevye's daughter. This kind of lapse in mutual understanding is a staple of comedy, used here to underscore the different priorities of the two characters.

Sometimes, however, the joke is not quite so funny. Sholem Aleichem has a short story called **"Tsugenumen"** (**"Taken"**) that describes several Jews coming together in a railway compartment. Two of the men are discussing how many young Jews were "taken" in their particular towns, when a third man breaks in with the remarkable news that in his little town of Pereshtshepene eighteen Jews had recently been taken. The conversation is spirited and homey until, inevitably, they discover what the good reader has known all along; that though they appear to be addressing the same topic, they are sadly estranged. The first two men are hopeful that their children will be among those "taken" into the local *gymnasium* despite the quotas that disciminated harshly against Jews; the third man is mourning his son's forced conscription into the tsarist army. The story ends in mutual shame:

> It was remarkable how these three men suddenly turned into utter strangers. Not only do they not say a word to one another, they don't even look one another in the eye, as though they had committed an ugly crime. . . .[9]

Meeting as Jews, and therefore presumable equals, as their shared language entitles them to do in an otherwise unfriendly train, they are embarrassed to discover that they are not, after all, equal. While the first two are aspiring to social advancement, the third man has already lost his hopes. Against the tsarist repression they are indeed intimately united, but within their subject community, some remain far better off than others.

Here the increasing mobility of the Jews, represented by the train that has taken them out of their respective *shtetlakh,* becomes a source of internal divisiveness. The sense of wrongdoing which concludes the story derives from their unspoken awareness that the outside world with its lures of advancement has begun to encroach on their erstwhile unity.

If the train is a sign of Jews on the move, Sholem Aleichem's fictional *shtetl* of Kasrilevke, which means something like "town of jovial paupers," seems to be a charmingly self-contained unit, soundly fixed in its values and traditions, and unshaken by the unfriendliness and evil that lurk all around it. In many stories it assumes just this role of cultural haven that withstands outside dangers and threats. Yet according to Sholem Aleichem's subtle vision, it is also possible to be *too* self-contained. The author himself spent most of his life at a considerable remove from the small Jewish towns in which he had been raised, and though he delights in recreating them as wholesome strongholds of faith, he also admits a note of anxiety about their insularity. A community may feed too securely upon itself, drawing back into an ever-narrowing circle. This kind of danger finds its literary representation in his famous monologues.

The monologues are the most admired instances of Sholem Aleichem's juicy "flavorful" Yiddish. They are also, less obviously, examples of total self-isolation. In **"The Pot,"** a housewife comes to the rabbi to ask him a question, ostensibly about the kosher status of her meat pot into which a drop of milk may have fallen. But so caught up is she in the tangle of her problems that she doubles back into her story again and again, telling a story within a story, until the poor rabbi faints from the onslaught. In a second monologue, a woman sets out to tell a story; she becomes so caught up in the description of who she is and what she does for a living that we never get to hear the story behind the introduction. In a third monologue, a young man comes to the author, Sholem Aleichem, to ask his advice: should he stay with his wife, despite the fact that she appears to be infatuated with the local doctor, or should he leave his wife, despite the fact that he wants her and has no other place to go? No sooner does the author propose one solution than the young man protests Sholem Aleichem's inability to understand the other side of the case. The see-saw continues until the author attempts to strangle the young man in exasperation.[10]

A study of these monologues has described them as solipsistic vehicles, "a way of talking about oneself to oneself, the verbal epitome of isolation."[11] The monologuists are trapped within their own, self-referring consciousness, oblivious to the reaction of the listener with whom they are supposedly making contact. Here the vigor of the speaker's Yiddish does not testify solely to the wholesome vitality of *shtetl* culture, but to a subjectivity so extreme that it becomes a form of assault. The comedy of these monologues has its basis in their isolation from the reality they are presumably addressing. Individuals and communities can be too confined; they may indeed stave off the unwelcome influences of the outside, but in doing so they may sink totally into themselves, almost to the point of madness.

IN THE INDETERMINATE WORLD

The history of modern fiction has its roots in the breakdown of feudal society, when new possibilities of individual mobility were created in a changing social order. The same holds generally true for Yiddish fiction, though at a much later date, and in clearly modified

circumstances. Without here attempting an analytic comparison between European and Yiddish fiction, one point of difference is immediately apparent. In an English or French novel, when an Oliver Twist or Julien Sorel tries to find his desired niche in society, the many levels of society within which he moves are all English, or French, respectively. Accents and manners may change from one rung of the ladder to the next, but the component properties of nationality remain constant.

This was not the case in East European Jewish society of the late nineteenth and early twentieth centuries. Social mobility for the Jew demanded and elicited modifications of language, cultural affiliation, and often religious conversion. Though there was also a good deal of change going on internally, within the Jewish society,—as enlightenment spread new secular ideas, as the towns emptied into the cities, as the economic consequences of industrialization widened the gulf between the Jewish rich and poor—behind these relatively minor changes lay the more decisive choice between Jewish and Gentile identity. This awareness of the ultimate implications of "mobility" permeates modern Yiddish writing, and always lies very close to the surface of Sholem Aleichem's work.

Returning once again to the Tevye stories, Sholem Aleichem's best known and probably greatest work, we recognize in the nature of communication between the father and his daughters their increasing alienation from his traditionalism, and his mounting opposition to their defection.

With Tsaytl, the eldest daughter, Tevye engages in full-bodied discussions of their differences. Motl, the tailor, her choice over Leyzer-Wolf, the butcher, introduces the language of Russian Positivism with its emphasis on direct production of goods and idealization of manual labor. At first Tevye tries to impose his own traditional Jewish ideals of status, but when he gives way, he argues himself down in the very same words that the young couple had used against him. "So maybe Motl is only a tailor, but at the same time he is a good man, a worker, he'll be able to make a living. And besides, he's honest, too. So what have I got against him?" The fact that Tevye has no semantic difficulty in understanding this daughter is a sign of their relative cultural proximity.

But with Hodl, the second daughter, the cultural distance grows. From Tevye's first encounter with Feferl, the revolutionary on the road, to the final leave-taking from Hodl when she goes off to join her husband in Siberian exile, there is a gap of understanding that no amount of affection can bridge:

I talked to her about Feferl, and she answered me with the "cause of humanity" and "workers" and other such talk. "What good is your humanity and your workers," I say, "if it's all a secret? There is a proverb: where there are secrets, there is knavery. But tell me the truth now. Where did he go and why?"

"I'll tell you anything," she says, "but not that. Better don't ask. Believe me, you'll find out yourself in good time. You'll hear the news— . . . maybe soon—and good news at that."

"Amen," I say, "from your mouth into God's ears! But may our enemies understand as little about it as I do."

"That," says she, "is the whole trouble. You'll never understand."

"Why not?" say I. "Is it so complicated? It seems to me that I can understand even more difficult things."

"These things you can't understand with your brain alone," she says, "you have to feel them, you have to feel them in your heart."[12]

Tevye is certainly not without empathy, but Hodl knows she has moved beyond her father's range of options. No wonder there is such pathos in their leave-taking from one another. It is final not only because father and daughter may not see one another again, but because they no longer bear primary allegiance to a common community or set of values.

The pathos increases in ratio to the threat that each daughter poses. With the third daughter, Chava, all communication is severed. Chava's decision to marry a non-Jew necessitates her conversion to Christianity. At this point, the very act of speaking to his daughter would imply a measure of acceptance that would undermine Tevye's essential being. When he sees his daughter on the road, wanting to explain herself, Tevye, one of the greatest talkers in literature, elects to keep silent as the only possible means of self-preservation.

Throughout these and the later Tevye stories, though the father's communication with his children is increasingly flawed, his own narrative ability is both the instrument and symbol of his authentic resilience.

In dozens of other stories, Sholem Aleichem plays variations on this same theme. Sometimes traditional Jewishness triumphs over its defectors; at other times it falters; at still other moments it fails. Every time a parent finds it hard to understand his child, the humor is a warning of cultural danger. In the story, **"Keyver-oves" ("Parental Graves")**, a father does not understand his daughter's interest in Artzybashev. The only Artse-Bashe's he knows, a local teacher who was blind, has long since died. But the same process of estrangement that causes this mirthful mistake leads to the daughter's suicide. Permeated by the pessimism of the Russian writer, Artsybashev, and unable to sever herself from her parents (because her love for her Russian tutor would "kill" them) she kills herself instead. Her Yiddish suicide note is the sign of her utter resignation to a world she was powerless to leave though unwilling to join.[13]

Elsewhere in Sholem Aleichem's fiction, an indigent father places all his hopes in his brilliant son whom he dubs his "Lottery Ticket." By the time the boy goes off to yeshiva he has already surpassed his father, who cannot even write properly, and must appeal to a more learned neighbour to send his letters. As the son becomes progressively estranged from the *shtetl* he left behind, the communication between father and son grows clumsier and more opaque. Finally word is sent—in Russian, to the local constabulary—to strike the son's name off the local Jewish rolls. The son's letter explaining his conversion is so ambiguous that the father needs help in deciphering its message. He is literally the last to know. Ultimately, of course, comprehension dawns: the message is death. The father sits *shiva* and becomes as silent as he was once garrulous and boastful.[14]

The parents who can no longer understand or be understood by their children are only one small symptom of an entire Jewish world in this state of violent transition. In Sholem Aleichem's stories, characters are often on the move, and as they leave the confines of their comprehensible *shtetl*, they make mistakes of identification. They are like the proverbial country bumpkins, an easy prey for swindlers who use the common idiom of "fellow Jews" to lull them into a false sense of security. The family of Motl, Peysi the cantor's son, is taken in by a woman with a bright red wig, an advertisement of her supposed piety.[15] Sholem Aleichem "himself" is almost picked clean by a jovial Jew sharing his train compartment who tries to lure him into a game of cards by telling him of all the occasions on which *he* was fleeced.[16] These skilled conmen and women flash the signals of piety and propriety in order to disarm their victims, using the disorientation of Jews in a changing world to ply their ancient, unchanging trade.

In the Malign World

Oddly enough, in semiotics, the language of signs, the most direct threats are the easiest to identify and to confront. At least so it is in the world of Sholem Aleichem. The anti-semite with his edicts, insults, and pogroms, declares himself hostile, and it only remains to try to outwit or escape him. In the final episode of the Tevye stories, when the neighbors come to throw him off his land, Tevye confounds the peasants with the unpronounceable word, "vekholaklakoys," which he takes, with characteristic appropriateness, from Psalm XXXV, one of the psalms of distress, that inveighs against the enemy, "Let their way be dark and *slippery*." Unable to pronounce this word is a challenge that Tevye throws them, his would-be persecutors must let him pack up, undisturbed. This is almost a magical use of language to confound one's foes: because of this verbal victory, Tevye seems to be leaving his village on his own "terms."

The anti-semite is not a pleasant presence, but the threat he poses has the advantage of being utterly clear. There is a priest in the story, **"The Miracle of Hoshano Rabo"** who refuses to recognize the real identity of the Jew, Berl Esigmakher, calling him "Moshke" and "Yudke" and other stereotypic Jewish names, and denying him his own. While Berl and the priest are exposed to physical danger, there is no dangerous ambiguity in their relations, and Berl is able to turn the tables on his oppressor.[17] Sholem Aleichem's major work is less an account of action than of action filtered through speech. Thus acts of interpretation and verbal mastery take precedence over the drama of actual events. In this kind of literary atmosphere the Jew has an even chance, if not the advantage. In Sholem Aleichem's work, Jews repeatedly "win" the situation they were historically losing in fact.

The atmospheres I have here separated into three degrees, benign, indeterminate, and malign, of course coexisted, both in Sholem Aleichem's society, and in his work. Because the process of modernization occurred so rapidly, transitions that would normally have taken place over several generations were here compressed into one; because these changes were accelerated by the repressive measures of the tsarist regime, that had as its goal the virtual elimination of the Jews from Russia, they affected an exceptionally large portion of the population, and affected them deeply. The *shtetlakh* in which the author grew up were still rooted in a system of order and law that was as firm as it was comprehensive. More than any other writer of his time, Sholem Aleichem appreciated the quality of this civilization that Jews had created on what they were now being made to feel was foreign soil. But his affection made him all the more aware of its precariousness. His characteristic theme is the encounter of the traditional Jew, rich in the language of his culture, with the varying forces that were demanding of him new accommodations and a new posture.

The story, **"Oylem Habe"** (**"Eternal Life"**), based on an incident in the author's life, provides a piercing— and very funny—picture of the Jew setting out into the world. In this work, we see only the faint beginnings of the process. The hero is still a sheltered young man who does not go all that far from his original

point of departure. Yet in his brief adventure, and particularly in the changing forms of his communication with those around him, we trace the full range and intensity of his required adaptation.[18]

This is an initiation story in which a young Jew sets out on his first journey and achieves maturity by painfully mastering a system of languages and signs. Noah, the protagonist of this tale, moves from innocence to experience, learning how to understand each successive aspect of the surrounding world and how (not) to deal with it.

The adult narrator, looking back at his *voyage de passage,* tells us of the trip from Zwihil to Radomishli that marked his transition to manhood. The occasion for this adventure was a summons to register in his home town of Radomishli for the draft, or for deferment if he could show cause. Noah, who had been selected as a bridegroom by his mother-in-law, and was being maintained according to the dowry system of *kest* at his in-laws' home, sets out on this first independent journey in a sled, propped up by three cushions, and accompanied by his mother-in-law's warning that the trip was ill-fated.

The first stretch of the story leads through a forest— the literal forest that often separated towns from one another, and the literary forest, primitive and ominous, where the natural man is unmasked and the flaws of civilization revealed. Noah's driver is a suitable version of the "natural man," a singularly taciturn gentile who responds to his eager attempts at conversation with a dry negative "ba-nee" or affirmative "ehe". Noah wishes he were in more familiar company, with a Jew, *lehavdil*:

> He'd have told me not only where the inn was, but who was the owner, what he was called, how many children he had, how much he had paid for the inn, how much he earned by it, how long he's been there, and whom he had bought it from—he'd have recited me an epic. A strange people. Our Jews, I mean, God bless them.

Afraid of the forest, chilled by the cold and the silence, Noah dreams of at least a touch of the familiar, a wayside inn with a Jew and a samovar. When he comes upon it, however, he gets rather more than he had anticipated. A bereaved innkeeper and his weeping orphans ask Noah to help them bring the dead wife to proper Jewish burial, appealing to his nascent manhood and to the Jewish values they share. In sharpest contrast to the stillness of the sleighride, the torrential pleading of the innkeeper has a jarring and uncomfortable effect: "What should I do? What should I do? And what's to be done?" His repeated wails, and promise of "Eternal Life! As I am a Jew, you will win

Eternal Life!" sweep up the young man to a dangerous pitch of daring. The cushioned, over-protected, and wholly inexperienced boy undertakes to become a hero, a savior, "ready to move mountains, overturn the world."

In this, the enchantment scene of many a forest tale, the innkeeper-magician works a rhetorical spell over the boy and sends him out on his mission, to bring the dead woman with a message of instruction to the Burial Society of the nearest *shtetl.* The innkeeper also gives him what is equivalent to a magic formula of safekeeping, namely the dead woman's full Jewish name, Chava-Nechama, daughter of Raphael-Michel. When Noah resumes his wintry journey he repeats the incantation, but as his heroism gives way to panic he begins to garble the terms. He has been distracted from his original, modest goal by an appeal to the noblest of missions, the mythical quest for immortality, in its domesticated Jewish version of eternal life. But as the magical spell of the heightened Jewish rhetoric wears off, the young man turns back into the inexperienced provincial that he is.

The midwinter forest journey reaches its climax in a heavy snowstorm in which the horse loses its way, the driver his temper, and the boy his last ounce of courage. When horse and driver finally do come through the storm, and discern in the distance a glimmer of light, Noah is overcome with affection for the gentile driver whose every "ehe" and "ba-nee" are now as dear to him as his life. For the first time he asks after the driver's name, and repeats it warmly. The storm in the forest, exposing everyone to the same creature level of existence, has shown the similarity of Jew and gentile, forging a human bond of mutual acceptance. No longer is the driver's taciturnity a hindrance to communication and interaction; its simplicity now connotes qualities of strength and endurance that exert over Noah a special charm.

And then they are in town. This is merely another Jewish *shtetl,* but since the young hero has just passed through a chastening experience, he sees the familiar in a different light. When Noah is refused help by the first Jew to whom he turns, he feels ashamed before the gentile beside him:

> "What," I asked myself, "must he be thinking in that head of his about us Jews? How must we look—we the merciful and sons of the merciful—to peasants like this, coarse and boorish, when one Jew shuts the door against another and won't even let him in to warm himself on a freezing night?" It seemed to me then that our fate, the fate of the Jews, made sense after all. I began to blame every one of us, as usually happens when one Jew is wronged by another. No outsider can find more withering things to say of us than we ourselves.

You can hear bitter epithets among us a thousand time a day. "You want to change the character of a Jew?" "Only a Jew can play such a trick." "You can't trifle with a Jew." And other such expressions. I wonder how it is among the gentiles. When they have a falling out, do they curse the whole tribe?"

The code of the forest, where all men have just been proven brothers, comes into conflict with the code of his own people, leaving Noah in a crisis of doubt. He questions both the nature of group loyalty and its absence. Noah's sympathy for the gentile places him in a more critical relation to his own culture.

As Noah meets one after another of the leading citizens of the "Sodom" among *shtetlakh,* his anger grows. The good Jews are generous with their solicitude, but offer no assistance. They are particularly unresponsive to Noah's promise of eternal life, which he is prepared to share with them. Instead, since he cannot even remember the woman's name (the formula that would have granted him safety) he is blackmailed by the community into paying heavily for the good deed of burial that was to have brought him such spiritual reward.

Ironically, the strongest contempt for the promise of eternal life comes from the most devout Jew of all, Reb Shepsel, whom Noah interrupts at prayer. When he first sees Reb Shepsel, wrapped in his prayer shawl and with tears of fervour in his eyes, Noah is delighted by this show of religious ecstacy. As in the case of Mikita, the driver, he is taken in by false appearances. Reb Shepsel's conversation, like Mikita's, is curt and halting, but here it is the studied counterfeit of holiness, not the simple reticence of a holy man. In order not to interrupt his prayers, he motions to Noah and grunts, "I-yo; nu-o?" This broken language, supposedly a means of sustaining the purity of a spiritual moment, is actually a perfect vehicle for hypocritical posturing. Behind the mask of piety, Reb Shepsel's pickings are more plentiful. He who only pays "lip service" to eternal life may plow more fertilely the resources of this life.

Penetrating the unfamiliar in the first stage of the journey, Noah recognized the universal language of a common humanity. In this second stage, behind the familiar assumptions, he recognizes the imperfections of his own community, particularly of those who merely pretend to be acting for the sake of heaven.

But the social education of an East European Jew could not be complete without exposure to the source of power and authority—the Chief of Police, or local representative of tsarist might. Here the problems of communication are menacingly direct. By the time the elders of the Burial Society agree to bury the corpse for a fee, word has gotten around that a rich young stranger is interring his mother-in-law (the subconscious has evidently made *its* statement) and the crowd of beggars accompanying the funeral procession strips the boy of his last penny. It also attracts the attention of the police and Noah is hauled in for questioning.

The encounter between Noah and authority is predictably disastrous. The form it takes, of abrupt question and defensive answer, is the clearest verbal manifestation of power challenging powerlessness:

"Your name?"

"Moishe."

"Your father's name?"

"Itzko."

"Age?"

"Nineteen."

"Single?"

"Married."

"Children?"

"Children."

"Occupation?"

"Merchant."

"Who is the corpse?"

"My mother-in-law."

"Her name?"

"Yente."

"Her father?"

"Gershon."

"Her age?"

"Forty."

"Cause of death?"

"Fright."

"A fright?"

"Yes, a fright."

"What sort of a fright?" he said, putting down his pen, smoking his cigarette, and glaring at me from head to foot.

Weaving his network of lies, Noah finally stumbles over the truth; he is dying of fright. But there is no room for truth in the strained, unequal relation between the Chief of Police and the Jew, and a single hopelessly honest word triggers his downfall.

When Noah lands in prison, the author sends in an ironic *deus ex machina,* the boy's mother-in-law, to bail him out. As Sholem Aleichem has so often explained, he does not like unhappy endings. Though this twist of the plot saves the hero, it does not affect the predicament of the story. In the final analysis, the Russian Jew finds himself in a world he is unable to negotiate because no level of language, no system of signs is effective when one party has the power to impose or change them at will.

Having passed then, through the three major stages of instruction, the speaker resolutely concludes, "From then on, when anyone mentions Eternal Life, I run."

The appeal to "heroism" is just too inflated for the psychological reality of a little man like Noah, or for the socio-political reality of the *shtetl,* threatened by overt aggression and imperfect in itself. Better a limited approach to survival than aspirations that soar too high and flop too low. The story exposes hypocrisy within the *shtetl* as a calculated cynicism about its own stated ideals. Noah's flight from "eternal life" is a flight from rhetorical hyperbole to a lower, ironic usage that accepts the gap between human aspirations and human potential. His comedy of quixotic idealism ends with a narrator who "knows his proper place."

This story contains a certain biographical strain. When the young Sholem Rabinovitch brought his wealthy father-in-law to the neighboring town for burial, he was forced to pay a heavy extortion tax to the local Burial Society before he could see the duty through. No doubt some of the story's fire was fueled by that unpleasant memory. It is also likely that the author's travels through Russia in 1904, the year the story was written, dictate its wintry tone and landscape. In the wake of terrible pogroms, and in the grip of great impoverishment, Russian Jewry was then at a bleak impasse, not unlike the hopelessness of Noah through most of the story.

In testing the possibilities of human interaction, Noah, the young hero, ultimately adopts a level of irony that is somewhere between Reb Shepsel's cynical self-interest and his own early inflated idealism. The voice of the adult narrator, who begins his story by admitting, "If I were clever, wouldn't I be rich?"—finds in this self-deprecating humor the perfect balance between goodness that is unattainable and evil that in inadmissible. This is a way of committing oneself to communicating with the world while shielding oneself from its worst blows. The adult speaker's voice in the story bears an unmistakable resemblance to the literary voice of "Sholem Aleichem" himself.

Sholem Aleichem's will, published immediately after his death in the local Yiddish and English New York newspapers, is often quoted for its democratic sentiment and generosity.[19] Sholem Aleichem asked to be buried among the poor and common folk so that their graves should brighten one another's. Instead of the formal *Kaddish* of remembrance, he allowed his children and grandchildren to read among themselves one of his stories in whatever language they best understood. He particularly enjoined his children to look after one another, and he left part of his royalties to a fund for his fellow Yiddish writers. But there is also a less frequently remembered clause in the will. While allowing his children whatever religious convictions they may or may not hold, he bids them remain Jews. "Those of my children who cut themselves free from their roots and cross over to another faith have thereby severed themselves from their roots and from their family, and erased themselves from my will, and they shall have no share or portion among their brothers."

Here Sholem Rabinovitch, the celebrated author, places himself within the tradition of his own characters. Having shown himself capable of infinite adjustments, adaptable to geographic, social, economic, political, and cultural upheavals, and able to forge an artistic language that recognizes the common human denominator within arbitrary national distinctions, he stops short, like all the many fathers of his stories, at the point of "conversion," of becoming not a Jew. The process of Jewish modernization, which he so brilliantly interpreted, had, according to his judgment, a distinct cultural limit. Within the process of change, Sholem Aleichem appreciated and developed the art of communication as no Yiddish writer before him or since. This art has an almost infinite range of adjustment, but also recognizes a very finite boundary: in learning how to address others, it is nevertheless necessary to remain oneself.

Notes

1. Y. Ch. Brenner, "For Sholem Aleichem" (in Hebrew).

2. I. Dobrushin, "Reading Sholem Aleichem" (in Yiddish), *Sovetish,* 12 (1941) 72-94.

3. I. I. Trunk, *Tevye un menakhem mendl in yidishn velt-goyrl* (Tevye and Menakhem Mendl as Expressions of Eternal Jewish Fate) (New York, 1944).

4. Dan Miron, *Sholem Aleykhem: Person, Persona, Presence* (New York, YIVO Institute for Jewish Research, 1972). In tracing the development of the Sholem Aleichem pseudonym, Miron analyses its exact origins and literary functions.

5. A full discussion of the problem of narrative reliability was introduced by Wayne C. Booth in *The Rhetoric of Fiction* (Chicago, 1961). My discussion here deals, for the most part, with problems of communication and reliability within the narrative itself, among the characters and the social roles they represent; the reader's role in deciphering the trustworthiness of the narrative is only implied.

6. Borukh Rivkin, *Gruntshtrikhn fun der yidisher literatur in amerike* (Characteristics of Yiddish Literature in America) (New York, 1948), p. 15.

7. Tevye is not a shtetl Jew, as is often mistakenly assumed, but a villager, farther removed from the centre of Jewish communal culture.

8. Sholem Aleichem, "Kotonti" (I am not worthy), in *Gants tevye der milkhiker* (The Complete Tevye the Dairyman) in *Ale verk fun S. A.* (All Works of S. A.) (New York, 1917-1925). 28 volumes. All references are to volumes in this edition.

9. ———, *"Tsugemumen"* (Taken) in *Ayzenban geshikhtes* (Train Stories), *Ale verk.*

10. ———, *Monologn* (Monologues), *Ale verk.* English translation of "The Pot" by Sacvan Bercovitch in *The Best of Sholem Aleichem,* ed. Irving Howe and Ruth R. Wisse (Washington, 1979), pp. 71-81.

11. Victor Erlich, "A Note on the Monologue as a Literary Form: Sholem Aleichem's '*Monologn*'—a Test Case," *For Max Weinreich on his Seventieth Birthday* (The Hague, 1964), pp. 44-50.

12. Sholem Aleichem, "Hodl" in *Gants tevye, op. cit.* English translation by Frances Butwin, *Tevye's Daughters* (New York, 1949) pp. 63-64. Most of the Tevye stories, though not all, are included in this volume.

13. ———, *"Keyver oves"* (Parental Graves) in *Ayzenban-geshikhtes, op. cit.* English translation (A Daughter's Grave) by Julius and Frances Butwin, *The Old Country* (London, 1958), pp. 287-296.

14. ———, "A vigrishne bilet" (The Lottery Ticket) in *Oreme un freylekhe* (The Poor and Jolly), vol. II, *Ale verk.* English translation by Julius and Frances Butwin, *The Old Country,* pp. 239-259.

15. ———, *Motl peysi dem khazns* (Motl the Cantor's Son), *Ale verk.* English translation (*Adventures of Mottel the Cantor's Son*) by Tamara Kahana (New York, 1953).

16. ———, "A zeks un zekhtsik" (A Sixty-Six; Game of Cards) in *Ayzenban geshikhtes, op. cit.*

17. ———, "Der nes fun hoshano rabo" (The Miracle of Hoshano Rabo) in *Ayzenban geshikhtes, op cit.* English translation by Julius and Frances Butwin, *The Old Country,* pp. 260-269.

18. ———, "Oylem Habe" (Eternal Life) in *Oreme un freylekhe,* vol. I. English translation by Saul Bellow in *A Treasury of Yiddish Stories,* ed. Irving Howe and Eliezer Greenberg (New York, 1954). I have relied on Bellow's translation except where it abbreviates the original.

19. ———, Last will, dated September 19, 1915, New York (in Yiddish). Reprinted in *Tsum ondenk fun Sholem Aleykhem* (In Memory of Sholem Aleichem), ed. Sh. Niger and Y. Tsinberg, (Petersburg, 1918), pp. 13-15.

Hillel Halkin (essay date 1986)

SOURCE: Halkin, Hillel. Introduction to *Tevye the Dairyman and The Railroad Stories,* by Sholem Aleichem, translated by Hillel Halkin, pp. ix-xli. New York: Schocken Books, 1987.

[*In this essay, written in 1986, Halkin presents an overview of the social, political, and economic situation of Russian Jews around the turn of the twentieth century; discusses the tone, thematic content, and literary form of the "Tevye" stories and* The Railroad Stories*; and notes some difficulties of translating Yiddish into English.*]

1

A little over a century ago, in 1883, an aspiring writer of comic talents named Sholem Rabinovich, who was then serving as a "crown rabbi," a state-appointed clerical functionary in a small Jewish community in the Ukraine, published a satirical account of local politics in the St. Petersburg *Yiddishe Folksblat* and playfully signed it "Sholem Aleichem"—that is to say, "Hello There!" It was not his first alias. He already had, and would continue to assemble, a precocious collection of pseudonyms, including such curiosities as "Solomon Bikherfresser" (Solomon Bookeater), "Baron Pipernoter" (Baron Ogre), "Terakhs an Eynikl" (Terach's Grandson), and "Der Yiddisher Gazlen" (The Robber Jew). Compared with these titles, however, which had at best a slapstick humor, the ancient Hebrew salutation first employed in the *Folksblat* (its Arabic cognate of *salaam aleykum* can be heard today throughout the Middle East) was a prescient choice. Meaning literally "peace be upon you," the phrase is used in Yiddish not as an everyday greeting but as a more emphatic one that is reserved for either old acquaintances long unmet or new ones just introduced; thus, besides encoding in the form of a pun Rabinovich's own name of "Sholem," it pithily anticipated the career of an author who, over the next three decades, was to come and go in the Yiddish press from one newspaper and magazine to another, delighting an ever-growing audience with his unpredictable appearances before vanishing again until the next time. Gradually he used the new pen name more and more. It did not replace its rivals all at once, but by 1894, the year in which the first chapter of what is possibly the greatest of all Jewish novels, *Tevye the Dairyman,* appeared in the pages of the Warsaw yearbook *Der Hoyzfraynt,* it had become an exclusive trademark recognized by Yiddish readers everywhere. Eventually his own friends and intimates took to calling him by it too. Whereas Sholem Aleichem had once been Sholem Rabinovich, Sholem Rabinovich was now Sholem Aleichem, the private man subsumed in the public identity of the world's most famous Yiddish writer.

Yet if comedy seems to imply a sufficient degree of well-being to make laughter possible, the debut of Sholem Aleichem as a comic Jewish writer did not come at an auspicious time. Indeed, coinciding as it did with the drastic deterioration in the Jewish situation in Russia that began in 1881 with the assassination of Alexander II and the bloody pogroms that followed, it could hardly have come at a worse one. Today, it is true, when modern Jewish history is read backwards in the monstrous light of the Holocaust, it is difficult to be as shocked as contemporaries were by the plight of Russian Jewry in the last decades of the Czarist Empire, during which the number of Jews murdered by Christian mob violence did not exceed several hundred. But in the context of its own time and place, the era of 1881-1917 in Russia was an exceedingly black period, the most savage experienced by Jews anywhere since the terrible massacres of Khmelnitsky's Cossacks in the Ukraine in 1648-1649. Moreover, not only were the pogroms that took place under Alexander III and his successor, Nicholas II, actually incited and approved by the Russian government, they were part of an official policy of anti-Semitism calculated to render life so intolerable for the country's Jewish inhabitants that, in the notorious words of Alexander III's adviser Constantine Pobyedonostzev, a third of them would be forced to emigrate, a third to convert, and a third to perish from hunger. One has to go back to the Spanish Inquisition and Expulsion of 1492 to find a previous instance of a European government setting out on a deliberate course of first terrorizing and then eliminating its Jewish population.

Such were the times that Sholem Aleichem wrote about—and that, remarkably for a humorist, he wrote about without either ridiculing or rose-tinting, neither saying to his reader, "Laugh and be above it," nor telling him, "Come, it's not as bad as you think; let me show you the brighter side." On the contrary: it was consistently his method, for all the near-manic exuberance of his prose, to confront the reader with reality in its full harshness, laughter being for him the explosive with which he systematically mined all escape routes away from the truth. Despite the exaggeration that is an ingredient of all humor, he had a reportorial passion for fact; more than one of his stories actually came from reading the morning newspaper. In the absence of other sources, one could infer much of the history and sociology of the Russian Jewry of his time from his work alone. And because, before one can fully appreciate this work's universal dimensions (of which he himself was well aware) one must read it as the specific anatomy of Russian Jewish existence that it was, a few more words about the latter may be helpful.

Russia did not develop a Jewish problem; it swallowed one whole. Unlike other European countries, whose Jewish populations were built up in medieval times by a slow process of migration, often initially encouraged by rulers wishing to benefit from Jewish commercial skills and contacts, the Russian state, which had traditionally barred Jews entirely, suddenly acquired large numbers of them, and without any desire to do so, by virtue of the three partitions of Poland in 1772, 1793, and 1795, and the revisions of them made by the Congress of Vienna in 1815. Overnight, as it were, the Jewish communities of eastern and central Poland, Lithuania, Latvia, Byelorussia, and the Ukraine found themselves on annexed Russian soil—beyond whose boundaries, however, the Czarist regime in St. Petersburg had no intention of letting them spread. And so by the end of the eighteenth century, there had come into being the human enclosure of the Pale of Settlement, that vast ghetto of western and southwestern Russia to which millions of Jews were confined by a jumble of confusing laws. Although it ran roughly along the lines of the new territories, the Pale as an entity was never clearly defined; its exact borders kept shifting as different parts of it were declared in or out of bounds according to the whims of bureaucrats, the outward pressure of the Jews bottled up inside it, and the counterpressure of anti-Jewish officials and Russian merchants fearing Jewish competition. Thus, for instance, the Ukrainian capital of Kiev, the "Yehupetz" of Sholem Aleichem's fiction and the city in which he lived for many years, was first opened to Jews (1794), then barred to them (1835), then put back on limits for temporary visits only (1862), then gradually reopened to Jewish residence by special permit, which depended on the petitioner's profession and the connections he happened to have. Even more filled with reversals was the history of Jewish residential rights in the Pale's rural villages, as opposed to its cities and towns. Originally left to the discretion of the local nobility in 1797, rural resi-

dence for Jews was denied in 1804, temporarily restored in 1807, redenied that same year, restored again in 1808, partially revoked once more in 1823, and so back and forth until 1910, when a final wave of rural expulsions began. Not all the restrictions on the books, of course, were always put into practice; yet even when they were not, the everpresent anxiety that they might be was enough to make a nightmare of the lives of great numbers of Jews who, generally for reasons of economic opportunity, were domiciled illegally.

Confinement to the Pale of Settlement, however, was not the worst of Russian Jewry's problems. Far more onerous was the fact that within the Pale itself, where most Jews lived in grinding poverty, they were discriminated against at every turn by an imperial administration that, lacking Pobyedonostzev's inclusive vision, could never quite make up its mind whether it wished to starve them or assimilate them, and so alternated between the most oppressive features of both approaches. Jews were excluded from local councils and trade guilds, even in towns where they formed a majority of the inhabitants. They were made to pay special and frequently humiliating taxes—a head tax, a property tax, a tax on the slaughter of kosher meat, a tax on Sabbath candles, a tax on the right to wear their traditional clothes. They were barred at different times and places from a wide range of occupations—law, agriculture, tavern keeping, the production and sale of liquor, the retailing of manufactured articles, the employment of their wives as market vendors. They were harassed in the education of their children, now forced to send them to Russianizing schools and now confronted with a system of quotas that made a Russian schooling almost impossible. And they were subjected to especially harsh draft laws, being inducted into the army in higher percentages and for longer terms of service than other sectors of the population. This last affliction reached a horrendous extreme in the reign of Nicholas I, who decreed in 1827 that an annual number of Jewish boys aged twelve and up should be taken to the army for premilitary training until they turned eighteen, at which time they were to be drafted for twenty-five years. These "cantonists," as the unfortunate children were called, rarely saw their homes again, and until its abolition by Alexander II in 1856, the institution of juvenile conscription struck terror into the hearts of Jewish families. Extortionate bribery, child snatching, and the physical mutilation of one's sons were some of the measures employed to ensure that the boy taken to the army was not one's own.

Under Alexander II, whose liberalizing tendencies were most prominently expressed by his emancipation of the Russian serfs, the condition of the Jews improved too; some of the discriminatory legislation against them was relaxed, and a more thorough removal of the rest was contemplated. Yet even before Alexander's assassination in 1881 by a bomb-throwing revolutionary, further progress had become mired in a welter of indecisive commissions of inquiry, and with the succession of his son, Alexander III, the anti-Jewish outlook of former years was revived with fresh vigor. There was now, moreover, a new factor that made this policy more brutal than ever: the desire to blame the Jews for the growing revolutionary movement, thus simultaneously discrediting the revolutionaries by painting them as Jewish conspirators, and deflecting the grievances of the Russian peasantry and working class from the government to the Jews. For the first time, government persecution of the Jews ceased to be a simple matter of social and economic containment and became a political tool. An idea of the cynical cruelty with which this tool was wielded can be gained even from an abbreviated chronology of the rash of anti-Semitic decrees and outbreaks that followed in the next several years:

1881/ Government-incited pogroms in Yelisavetograd, Kiev, and elsewhere in the Ukraine, as well as in Warsaw; the government officially blames them on Jewish economic exploitation of the masses, which have been driven to exact their just revenge.

1882/ Jews are again forbidden to settle in any of the rural sections of the Pale of Settlement (that is, in ninety percent of its area) or to buy property there. Jews already living in the villages are made subject to expulsion if they do not own their homes, if they move from village to village, or if they are absent from the village they live in for even a few days.

1883/ Pogroms in Rostov-on-Don; thousands of Jews living illegally in St. Petersburg are rounded up by the police and expelled.

1884/ Pogrom in Nizhni-Novgorod.

1887/ All high schools and universities within the Pale of Settlement (where Jews, though roughly a tenth of the inhabitants, form a majority of the literate population) are limited to a Jewish quota of ten percent of their student bodies.

1890/ Numerous towns in the Pale are reclassified as villages, from which Jews are therefore expelled; Jews are disqualified throughout the Pale of Settlement from voting for deputies in local elections.

1891/ Twenty thousand Jews are expelled from Moscow.

1894/ Jews are forbidden to change their names to non-Jewish ones; Jewish identity passes are marked with the word "Jew."

1899-1900/ More pogroms in the Ukraine; in Vilna a Jew is put on trial on the atavistic charge of attempting to murder a Christian girl in order to bake Passover matsoh from her blood. (This medieval "blood libel" was to be repeated in 1911 in the more famous case of Mendel Beilis, which attracted worldwide attention.)

1903/ The worst pogrom yet in Kishinev; forty-five Jews killed, eighty-six severely wounded, fifteen hundred Jewish houses and stores looted and demolished. Pogrom in Homel; when Jews try for the first time to defend themselves with arms, thirty-six are indicted for attacking Christians.

1904/ Outbreak of the Russo-Japanese war; Jews are called up in disproportionate numbers; the number of Jewish soldiers sent to the front is also disproportionately large.

Even the popular-backed Revolution of 1905, which broke out in the aftermath of Russia's defeat by Japan and led Nicholas II to grant a short-lived liberal constitution that aroused, among other things, extravagant hopes of a new age for Russia's Jews, only ended in the further shedding of Jewish blood: the ink on the constitutional manifesto had hardly dried when gangs of counter-revolutionary thugs known as "the Black Hundreds," organized with the complicity of the Czarist police, attacked Jewish neighborhoods all over Russia under the cover of nationalist slogans holding the Jews responsible for the country's troubles and accusing them of subverting the authority of the Czar in order to seize power themselves. The worst of these pogroms took place in Odessa, where over three hundred Jews were killed, thousands injured, and tens of thousands left homeless. Another that occurred in Kiev was witnessed by Sholem Aleichem himself from the window of the hotel in which he had taken refuge with his family. Soon afterward he left Russia, never to return again except for brief visits until his death in New York in 1916.

In taking his departure, of course, Sholem Aleichem was joining a flood of Jews heading westward; it is estimated that between 1881 and 1914, when World War I shut the gates of emigration, nearly three million Jews left the Russian Empire, mostly for the United States. This mass flight, however, only partially relieved congestion within the Pale itself, both because of a high birthrate and because economic pressures and the rural expulsions led to an internal migration of Jews to the crowded quarters of the larger towns, where mass proletarization took place. Despairing of a future under the Czarist regime, many young Jews turned to the revolutionary movement. If at the time of Alexander II's assassination the specter of Jewish insurrectionism had been largely a red herring, by the first decade of the twentieth century it was an unassailable fact. Jews were active in large numbers in the two major underground parties, the Social Revolutionaries and the Social Democrats, and in 1897 they formed a clandestine Marxist organization of their own, the League of Jewish Workingmen, or "Bund." Jewish youth that was not politically active was becoming modernized too, so that a yawning gap developed between an older generation that still clung to the traditional ways and a younger one that was rapidly forsaking them. Russian began to displace Yiddish in daily speech (it is an astounding symptom of the times that Sholem Aleichem himself spoke Russian to his wife and children!) and the medieval culture of Orthodox Judaism that had remained intact for centuries was in the process of crumbling. Everywhere, battered from without and eroded from within, Jewish life was in a state of flux, disarray, decomposition.

It has been commonly remarked that while in most humor the self, be it individual or collective, laughs at that which is unlike it and with which it does not identify, thereby proclaiming its own superiority, in Jewish humor it laughs at itself—the explanation for this presumably being that among a people with so long a history of persecution, the most pressing task of humor has been to neutralize the hostility of the outside world, first by internalizing it ("Why should I care what the world thinks of me, when I think even less of myself?") and then by detonating it through a joke ("Nevertheless, the world doesn't know what it's talking about, because in fact I am much cleverer than it is—the proof being that it has no idea how funny I am, and I do!"). There is doubtless much truth in this, provided one realizes that the type of humor in question is not historically very Jewish at all and first makes its appearance in Jewish literature in the course of the nineteenth century, especially in the second half. Before that, Jews reacted to hatred and oppression in a variety of ways—with defiance, with scorn, with anger, with bitterness, with vengefulness, with lamentation, with (and perhaps here the seeds of modern Jewish humor were first sown) copious self-accusation—but never, as far as can be determined from the literary sources, with laughter directed at themselves. This is strictly a latter-day method of coping (one prompted perhaps by the loss of the religious faith that had given meaning to Jewish tribulations in the past), and Sholem Aleichem is one of its great developers and practitioners.

The fact that the inner dialectic of such humor (which, despite its defensive function, can easily undermine the ego from within) became in the hands of Sholem Aleichem a therapeutic force of the first order is one of his most extraordinary achievements. It is a matter of record that the Jews of his time who read his work, or heard him read it himself at the many public performances that he gave, not only laughed until their ribs ached at his unsparing portrayals of their perversity, ingenuity, anxiety, tenacity, mendacity, humanity, unplumbable pain, and invincible hopefulness, they emerged feeling immeasurably better about themselves and their fate as Jews. His appearance in a Russian shtetl on one of his tours was a festive event: banquets were given in his honor, lecture halls were filled to overflowing, pleas for favorite stories were shouted at him from the audience, encores were demanded endlessly, crowds accompanied him to the railroad station to get a last glimpse of him before he went. Besides being a sensitive performer—contemporary accounts describe him as reading his stories aloud with great restraint and simplicity, never overacting or burlesquing them—he clearly touched his listeners in a place where nothing else, except perhaps their ancient prayers and rituals, was able to. He gave them a feeling of transcendence.

This feeling, as has been stated, had nothing to do with the sense of being "above it all," with that comforting assurance given us by a great deal of comic literature that life is ultimately so silly a business that there is no point in taking it too seriously. Quite the opposite: Sholem Aleichem's humor demanded of its readers that they take life seriously indeed—nor, in any case, with pogroms and hunger often at the door, were they in any position not to. His comedy did not lift them *above* the suffering world that they were part of; it lifted them *together with it*. The laughter his work evoked was not that of contempt, or of embarrassment, or of relief, or even of sympathy, but rather of identification and acceptance. "You who have been through all this," it said, "and who know that such are our lives and that no amount of self-delusion can make them less so—you who have experienced fear, and humiliation, and despair, and defeat, and are aware that there is more yet to come—you to whom all this has happened and who still have been able to laugh—you, my friends, need no consolation, because you have already prevailed." Those who rose at the end of such an evening to give him a standing ovation were also paying tribute to themselves.

2

Readers of **Tevye the Dairyman** who are familiar with the play or movie *Fiddler on the Roof* will notice that, in more ways than one, there is scant resemblance between Sholem Aleichem's novel and the charming musical based on it. (Indeed, this is true even of the musical's name, which does not come from the work of Sholem Aleichem at all but from the art of Marc Chagall with its recurrent motif of a sad-gay Jewish fiddler playing upon the rooftops of a Russian village.) To begin with, there is the tone: unlike *Fiddler* which, whether sad or gay, keeps within the range of the safely sentimental, *Tevye* has a giddy energy, a recklessness of language and emotion, a dizzy oscillation of wildly funny and wrenchingly painful scenes that come one on top of another without letup. In addition, the dramatic plot of *Fiddler on the Roof* is culled from just four of the eight *Tevye* episodes, the third, fourth, fifth, and eighth, so that Chapters 1, 2, 6, and 7 have no bearing on it. Lastly, in *Fiddler* Tevye has only three daughters, Tsaytl, Hodl, and Chava, whereas in *Tevye* . . . but how many daughters Tevye has in *Tevye* is a question we will come to in a moment. Suffice it to say first that, quite apart from the pointlessness of comparing two such different treatments simply because one derives from the other, similar departures from the text of *Tevye* (except for its being set to music) were made in 1914 by Sholem Aleichem himself for a dramatized version of the book that had a long stage life of its own. In fact, his cannibalization of the novel was even more extreme than the musical's: essentially it utilized only Chapters 5 and 8, and Tevye's daughters were reduced to two, Tsaytl and Chava, the plot revolving entirely around Chava and her marriage to and ultimate break-up with Chvedka, the Ukrainian villager, leaving Tsaytl in a mere supporting role. In sentimentality, too, Sholem Aleichem's play, written as it clearly was with one eye on the box office of the highly commercial Yiddish theater, is every bit the equal of *Fiddler on the Roof,* which is without a doubt the more stage-worthy of the two.

But how many daughters *does* the original Tevye have? As Professor Khone Shmeruk has shown in an absorbing study, the uncertain answer to this question casts considerable light on the composition of the book as a whole. In its opening episode, **"Tevye Strikes It Rich,"** which first appeared in 1894 and was revised in 1897, the number of Tevye's daughters is given as seven. In Chapter 2, **"Tevye Blows a Small Fortune,"** and Chapter 3, **"Today's Children,"** which is about Tsaytl, Tevye's oldest daughter (both were published 1899), no count is given at all. In **"Hodl"** and **"Chava"** (1904 and 1905) we again read of seven girls—yet in Chapter 6, **"Shprintze"** (1907), there are only six, the two youngest of whom are Beilke and Teibl, while in Chapters 7 and 8 (1909 and 1914) Teibl has vanished and only Beilke remains. What can be concluded from this? Clearly, it would seem, that Sholem Aleichem planned *Tevye* in several stages, each representing a modification of his previous conception. Indeed, the first episode, which was based on his acquaintance with an actual milkman whom he befriended one summer in the resort town of Boyarka near Kiev (the "Boiberik" of the novel), was no doubt written as an independent story with little or no thought of a sequel, its figure of seven nameless daughters being no more than a way of saying "many." Also probably meant to stand by itself was the second episode, in which Tevye meets Menachem Mendl, who was already the comic hero of another, epistolary work of fiction that Sholem Aleichem was working on at the time. By the third, or at the latest, fourth chapter, on the other hand, Sholem Aleichem had evidently de-

cided to write a series about Tevye's daughters, which meant producing seven more stories, one for each of them; yet in Chapter 6, either tiring of the subject or feeling he was running out of material, he reduced their number to six, and in Chapter 7, he cut it again to five. This chapter, in fact, was evidently intended to conclude the Tevye cycle with Tevye's departure for Palestine, since in 1911, with Sholem Aleichem's authorization, it was printed together with the first six episodes as a book called *Tevye the Dairyman*—the first time such a title was used for the series as a whole. The eighth and last episode, added several years later, was apparently written as an afterthought (one motive, Shmeruk conjectures, being the desire to return Chava to the bosom of her family). Having written it, however, Sholem Aleichem must have planned at least one further installment, because he did not give this story, **"Lekh-Lekho,"** a coda-like ending, as he did Chapter 7, and only subsequently sought to make up for the omission by adding a brief fragment that was published shortly before his death.[1]

Can a work of fiction begun with no overall plan, written in installments over a twenty-year period, and ending more than once, be called (as it has been here) a novel at all? There are critics whose answer is no. The noted Sholem Aleichem scholar Dan Miron, for instance, has written that the structure of *Tevye* is more "mythic" than novelistic, each of its episodes consisting of a pattern of rise, fall, and recovery that can repeat itself endlessly; Sholem Aleichem, Miron argues, could have brought *Tevye* to a close after its seventh chapter or gone on to write a tenth and eleventh—in terms of the book's form and thematic contents, it would hardly have mattered. But though it certainly is true that each episode of *Tevye* can be read as a story in itself (which is undoubtedly how some of its original readers, not all of whom were familiar with what came before, did read it), and true too that each shares basic patterns with the others, it is equally clear that each builds on the previous installments and that there is a definite development from one chapter to the next. Indeed, if what perhaps most characterizes the novel as a literary form is the flow of time in it, the fact that more than in any other artistic medium we see human beings exposed to time, shaped by time, worn by time, then *Tevye* is a novel *par excellence,* perhaps the only one ever written in real time, that is, according to a scale on which time for the author and time for his characters are absolutely equivalent. Sholem Aleichem and Tevye age together: a year in the life of one is a year in the life of the other, and twenty years in the life of one is twenty years in the life of the other. Even as Sholem Aleichem sits at his desk writing down Tevye's stories, Tevye continues to grow older by the amount of time that writing takes.

It is in part this aspect of Tevye that makes him so real a character, for despite the great misfortunes that befall him and his extraordinary resilience in confronting them, the years affect him much as they do most men: slowly, subtly, almost imperceptibly in the course of any one of the book's episodes—in which, as in the short story generally, time is not a significant factor—but enormously when regarded over the whole span of them. *Le plus ça change, le plus ça reste la même chose* is only one side of Tevye and of us all; *le plus ça reste la même chose, le plus ça change* is the other. He is, as Miron says, always Tevye; but who, meeting him in 1894 and again in 1914, would not be shocked by the difference—and not only because of the gray hairs? Tevye has changed internally—and with these changes, the novel's three internal levels of meaning all reach a climax too. Let us consider them.

The first of these is the story of Tevye and his family as a paradigm of the fate of Russian Jewry. It is a measure of Sholem Aleichem's great artistry that Tevye, Golde, and their daughters—and with what a bare minimum of strokes these last are sketched!—are all wonderfully alive and individualized human beings who never strike us as being anything but themselves. Yet this should not obscure the perception that they are also, like most of the other characters in the book, representative types of Russian Jewish life who, taken together, tell the tale of its destruction. Indeed, each of Tevye's daughters falls in love with and/or marries a man who can be said to embody a distinct historical force or mood, and if Tevye himself is the very incarnation of the traditional culture of the shtetl, then beginning with the novel's second chapter, every one of its episodes illustrates another phase of this culture's helpless disintegration. In **"Tevye Blows a Small Fortune,"** for example, we see in the person of Menachem Mendl the economic collapse of a community that has been driven by the unnatural conditions imposed on it to seek its livelihood in the most pathetic kinds of nonproductive speculation. In **"Today's Children"** we read of that undermining of parental authority which, though still relatively mild in Tsaytl's case, will eventually bring Tevye's world crashing down on him. **"Hodl"** deals with the defection of Jewish youth to the revolutionary movement, and **"Chava"** with its loss to intermarriage. Shprintze's suicide is the outcome of a situation that at first resembles Tsaytl's and her other sisters', i.e., she has fallen in love with a young man whom Tevye originally disapproves of as a match for her—but precisely because of this parallel, the difference between Tsaytl's and Motl's behavior, on the one hand, and Shprintze's and Ahronchik's, on the other, shows how dramatically the lines of communication between generations have broken down in the space of a few years. In Beilke's story, **"Tevye Leaves for the Land of Israel,"** we meet yet another new Jewish type, the contractor Podhotzur, a vulgar nouveau-riche assimilationist ruthlessly intent on climbing the social and economic ladder of a society making the transition from rural feudalism to urban capitalism. And finally, in **"Lekh-Lekho,"** what is left of Tevye's life literally falls apart: expelled from the village in which he and his ancestors have lived since time immemorial, he is forced to become a homeless wanderer. Coming in the final chapter of the novel, this expulsion is the ultimate concretization of the ruin of an entire world.

In all this, Tevye's role is essentially passive; he schemes, he fantasizes, he makes a great fuss over things (although less so as the years go by and he grows more aware of his powerlessness)—yet each time the events, like his own unruly horse, simply run away with him, leaving him aghast and uncomprehending. And yet, as the Yiddish critic Y. Y. Trunk has perceptively observed, what makes him a genuinely tragic figure and not just the comic victim of a world beyond his control is that in every case it is he himself who brings about his downfall—a theme that comprises the second level of the book, that encompassing the relationships in Tevye's family, especially between him and his daughters. With his wife Golde, all in all, Tevye's relations are simple: they might be defined as those of a harmonious conjugal antagonism, a common enough modus vivendi among East European Jews that is composed on Tevye's side of equal parts genial misogyny and husbandly loyalty to hearth and home. This misogyny, however, runs only skin-deep, because, despite his protestations to the contrary (it is when he protests, in fact, that he most reveals his true feelings, a more direct expression of affection not being in his vocabulary), Tevye clearly loves his daughters to distraction. Nor does he just adore them; he admires and respects them with that unconventionally unsnobbish openness, that basic inclination to judge everyone on, and only on, his merits, which, beneath his facade of patriarchal autocracy and middle-class pretensions, is one of his most endearing traits. It is just this openness and capacity for love, however, that prove his undoing, for without his quite grasping the fact, these are the qualities that, absorbed from him by his daughters, make them act as they do in the face of his own apprehensions and objections. As is so often the case with parents and children, Tevye's daughters are much more like him than he is willing to admit; they are, in fact, the actors-out of the fantasies and values that he has transmitted to them. Does Tsaytl, disappointing her father, refuse to marry the rich Layzer Wolf and choose the poor Motl Komzoyl instead? But Tevye cannot stand Layzer Wolf, he truly likes Motl, and he himself has told Sholem Aleichem:

"Money is a lot of baloney . . . what matters is for a man to be a man!" Is Tevye devastated because Hodl has linked her life with the young revolutionary, Pertchik? But besides having brought Pertchik into his home (for which, it is true, he blames himself—he just does not go beyond this), who if not Tevye has sat on his front stoop imagining what it would be like to trade places with the rich Jews of Yehupetz, living in their dachas while they bring him milk and cheese each day! Has Chava done the unthinkable, married a goy? Why, Tevye himself has wondered in the solitude of the forest, "What does being a Jew or not a Jew matter?" It is Tevye who in his fondness for Ahronchik has introduced him to Shprintze, and Tevye who, in his anger at Beilke for selling her soul to marry wealth, forgets that this is exactly the arrangement that he planned for Tsaytl long ago. Tevye knows that Beilke has sacrificed herself for his sake—yet it does not occur to him that she has done so because of the vision of magical riches that he himself has handed down to her.

In short, whether he is simply a natural democrat, or whether, staunchly traditional Jew though he is, he has unknowingly been affected by the liberal winds blowing in Russia, Tevye has fathered the daughters of his deepest dreams. Trunk puts it well when he writes of the man and his children, "Though consciously they have different outlooks on life, unconsciously they share the same sense of it." It is only in the novel's penultimate chapter, the story of Beilke, however, that Tevye achieves a belated insight concerning this fact, for then, seeing Beilke's unhappiness in her stultifyingly opulent surroundings and recalling the vivacious child who lived with him in semipoverty, he articulates at last what at heart he has always known, namely, that all that really matters in life is human love, warmth, and intelligence, thus realizing the pitifulness of his one great conscious obsession: to have a rich daughter. Fate, he tragically learns, not only mocks a man by withholding his desires, but also—and sometimes most of all—by granting them. And like any tragic hero's, Tevye's fate, as Trunk reminds us, is his character.

But what a disproportion between the two! What a character and what a fate! Surely no man, and most surely none as good as Tevye, deserves to see his daughters stricken, as he says, by a curse worse than any in the Bible . . . and this conviction of injustice, the subject of Tevye's running debate with God, forms the novel's third and most profound level of all. Sholem Aleichem, it is true, is not often thought of as a religious writer. Religious observance, though constantly referred to in his work as part of the everyday fabric of Jewish life, does not play an especially important role in it, and genuinely spiritual figures are

rare there. Indeed, this was one of the reasons that Y. L. Peretz, his leading rival among the Yiddish writers of the day and the author of much edifying fiction, dismissed Sholem Aleichem as a basically lowbrow figure who never grappled with ultimate Jewish issues. Humor in general, though by no means an illegitimate medium for serious religious expression, is not commonly put to that purpose. Yet having said all this, I would submit that *Tevye the Dairyman,* the comitragic historical account of the death of an ancient culture and psychological analysis of a father's unhappy love for his daughters, is also one of the most extraordinary Jewish religious texts of our own, and perhaps of any, time.

Tevye is a God-arguer: as such he belongs in a long Jewish tradition that starts with Abraham and runs prominently on through Moses, through Job, through the Tannaitic rabbi Yehoshua ben Levi (who refused to accept a heaven-backed interpretation of Scripture even though it was supported by divine miracles), through Levi Yitzchak of Berdichev, the saintly Hasidic master who is said to have held a trial at which God was the absentee defendant, accused of having inflicted undeserved suffering on His people. Other religions may have their folktales about men who debate with and even rebuke God, but only in Jewish tradition, I believe, are such stories taken with high seriousness, the behavior in question being regarded— provided, of course that it comes from a spiritually ripe individual—as the highest form of religious service. Though it is Job's friends who keep telling him to accept God's judgment and Job who insists that he will not because that judgment is unjust, God Himself, after finally speaking to Job from the whirlwind, turns to his friends and says, "My wrath is kindled against you . . . for you have not spoken of Me what was right, as My servant Job has." And what is right, apparently, is to hold God to the highest standards of a man's conscience, even if He does not seem to behave by them.

It is worth considering this for a moment, for it presents an oddly paradoxical alternative, and by no means the main one adopted by Judaism either, to what have commonly been the standard responses of advanced cultures to the problem of innocent suffering in the world. Basically there have been three of these:

> 1. God exists, is good, and is all-powerful; what appears to us His injustice is either a legitimate testing of our character, a just retribution for our sins, or an illusion created by our inability to understand the workings of the Divinity.

> 2. God exists, is good, but is not all-powerful; beside Him are other, evil forces that contend with and sometimes best Him, thus gaining power over the world.

3. God does not exist and suffering is the result either of blind chance or of immutable laws working themselves out in the lives of men.

The first of these answers has been the one most often given by the major monotheistic religions; the second by Manichaeism, Gnosticism, Zoroastrianism, and various other dualistic beliefs; the third by modern science and, essentially, by Buddhism.

But there is also, as we have seen, a fourth possible response: God exists; He is good; He is all-powerful; therefore He must be just; but He is not just; therefore He owes man an explanation and man must demand it from Him.

This is Job's response. And it is also Tevye's.

Job is not one of the religious texts that Tevye is always quoting from, nor would it be likely to be. On the whole it was not a part of Scripture widely read by East European Jews, both because it was not linked to specific prayers, rituals, or holidays like other books in the Bible, and because its Hebrew is extremely difficult. But Tevye knows its story and, in **"Shprintze,"** on his way home from his humiliating meeting with Ahronchik's uncle, when it seems to him that nothing worse can happen (little does he know that he is soon to receive the most terrible blow of all), his identification with it emerges. And yet though his suffering is truly Jobian, as is his reaction to it, how much more lonely and isolated a figure he is than Job! Job has his three friends, who despite their aggravating piety are a comfort merely by their presence, and he has his God, who finally speaks to him in a blazing epiphany that rewards him for all his anguish; Tevye, however, has no one. Alone in his village, without a Jew to speak to, without a synagogue to go to, without a God to be spoken to by, he must carry on the dialogue of Job all by himself, now being Tevye demanding to know what he has been punished for, now being his comforters patiently explaining that whatever God does is for the best, and now being God Himself threatening to blow him, little Tevye, away with a puff of His breath if he does not stop his tiresome complaining. All around him the world is as silent as the forest in which he has his deepest thoughts. There is not a consoling word. Man says nothing. God says nothing. The Messiah is a policeman with an eviction notice. And Tevye, who will not take nothing for an answer, goes on arguing with them all!

Did Sholem Aleichem think of this side of Tevye in more than just comic terms? Of course he did. Listen to what his son-in-law Y. D. Berkovits has to say about him at the time he was writing **"Shprintze"**:

> It goes without saying that none of these externals [Berkovits has been discussing Sholem Aleichem's attitude toward Jewish religious observance] had very

much to do with the inner religious feelings that existed in him and that frequently stirred him greatly. For that Sholem Aleichem had in his own way a most religiously sensitive personality—of this I have not the slightest doubt. On the table by his bed always lay a small, open Bible that he would read now and then, especially at night when he had trouble sleeping. I suspected that he was mainly reading the Book of Job, and once indeed, when he began to test me on my knowledge of it, I was astounded by his familiarity with it, especially when I thought of how hard we had found it in the schoolroom when we were young.

One more word on the subject.

Not long ago I gave a talk on *Tevye the Dairyman* to a small audience in the town in Israel where I live. A lively discussion ensued, during which one of the participants, a professor of the history of science, exclaimed angrily, "But Tevye is a fool! Instead of realizing once and for all that there is no God, and that his own life is the best proof of it, he goes on wasting his energy on a God who doesn't exist." It was a perfectly natural comment and it led to an even more animated exchange, but as that went on, I kept asking myself, where have I heard those words before? And then it came to me: Job's wife! "And then his wife said to him, 'Do you still hold fast to your integrity? Curse God, and die!'"

For Job—and for Tevye—to curse God *is* to die, because neither can live in a world without Him. Even if God never answers, even if He never will, Tevye must go on debating with Him, for the minute he stops, his life has lost its meaning. And besides, who is to say when God answers and when He does not? In Job's case, you say, it was obvious: "And then the Lord answered Job out of the whirlwind." Yes: but had you or I been present in that whirlwind, would we have heard anything but wind? "So the Lord blessed the latter end of Job more than the beginning: for he had fourteen thousand sheep, and six thousand camels, and a thousand yoke of oxen, and a thousand she-asses. And he also had seven sons and three daughters." Tevye has exile and the road beneath his feet—and the daughter he loves most, Chava, restored to him from the dead. The Lord giveth and the Lord taketh away. And what shall Tevye call that which sometimes giveth again?

Tevye's habit of peppering his Yiddish speech with endless quotations from sacred Hebrew sources is his most distinctive verbal quirk and, on the whole, the thorniest problem he presents to the translator. It does not, however, make him unique. The tendency liberally to cite Scripture and liturgy was widespread among speakers of Yiddish, as it must always have been among observant Jews everywhere, who, merely in the course of their daily prayers and their weekly and yearly rituals, commit to memory an enormous number of texts. It was and is not unusual, for example, for a simple, uneducated Jew to know by heart the three daily Hebrew prayers, which even recited at breakneck speed would take a good half hour to get through, plus various other devotions, blessings, and bits of the Bible. In the work of Sholem Aleichem, too, Tevye is by no means the only chronic quoter, even if he is an extreme case for whom chapter and verse, depending on the situation and the person he is talking to, can serve any conceivable purpose: to impress, to inform, to amuse, to intimidate, to comfort, to scold, to ridicule, to show off, to avoid, to put down, to stake a claim of equality or create a mood of intimacy, and so on. He has, as his daughter Chava says, a quote for everything, and sometimes one quote for several things, for his stock is ultimately limited and he has to make the most of it.

In traditional Jewish terms, that is, Tevye is not nearly so erudite as the uninformed reader, or some of his own unversed acquaintances, may think. (Of course, such things are relative; there are not a few American Jewish congregations today in which he would have to be considered a highly learned Jew, second only—and not even always that—to the rabbi.) An analysis of his quotations shows that nearly all of them come from four basic sources, each read and heard year in and year out by the average Orthodox Jew: the daily and holiday prayer book; the Bible (especially the Pentateuch, portions of which are read every Sabbath; the Book of Esther, which is chanted on Purim; and Psalms, which observant Jews often recite as a paternoster when troubled or in their spare time); the Passover Haggadah; and *Pirkey Avot* or "The Ethics of the Fathers," a short Mishnaic tractate of rabbinic sayings that is printed in the Sabbath section of the prayer book. Of the rest of the Mishnah and of the Talmud, to say nothing of the many commentaries upon them— the real bread and butter, as it were, of a higher Jewish education—he appears to know next to nothing. Indeed, when he wishes to quote a line of Talmud to Layzer Wolf, he has to make it up out of whole cloth.

Yet if Tevye is no scholar, neither is he the Yiddish Mr. Malaprop that others, overly aware of these limitations, have taken him to be. To be sure, he does occasionally clown, deliberately inventing, confusing, or misattributing a quote in order to mock an ignoramus who will never know the difference, thus scoring a little private triumph of which he himself is the sole witness. On the whole, however—and certainly when directly addressing Sholem Aleichem, who is his superior in Jewish knowledge and whose approval he desires—his quotations are accurate, apropos, and show an understanding of the meaning of the Hebrew words, if not always of their exact grammar. Sometimes they

are even witty, taking an ancient verse or phrase and deliberately wrenching it out of context to fit the situation he is talking about, as when, at the beginning of **"Hodl,"** in discussing how hard it is for a Jewish youngster to be accepted by a Russian school, Tevye says, *"Al tishlakh yodkho:*[2] they guard their schools from us like a bowl of cream from a cat." The words *al tishlakh yodkho* mean "lay not thine hand" and are found in the story of the sacrifice of Isaac in Chapter 22 of Genesis, in which, at the last second, just as Abraham is about to slaughter his son, an intervening angel cries out, "Lay not thine hand upon the lad, neither do thou anything unto him; for now I know that thou fearest God, seeing thou has not withheld thy son, thine only son, from Me." Tevye knows perfectly well where the phrase he is quoting comes from (the highly dramatic chapter is not only read once a year on the Sabbath like the rest of the Pentateuch, it is chanted a second time as a special selection for Rosh Hashanah)—but this does not keep him from putting it in the mouths of Czarist officials telling Jewish applicants to keep their hands off Russian schools!

Here too, it must be stressed, there is nothing particularly original about his method: Jews have been "deconstructing" biblical texts in this way practically since the Bible was written, and the vast corpus of rabbinical exegesis known as the midrash is based precisely on the enterprise of pouring new wine into old Scriptural bottles. Though these reinterpretations are not generally humorous, there is definitely a creative playfulness in the activity of midrash *per se,* which was, one might say, the ancient rabbis' chief form of recreation—and to this day, if one has the good luck to be among a group of knowledgeable Jews who are in a "midrashic" mood, one can witness this fascinating interplay of encyclopedic recall and wit in which biblical and rabbinic texts are caromed around and off each other as though they were billiard balls. Tevye is not quite in this league, but it is one he aspires to, for a religiously educated Jew in the traditional culture of Eastern Europe belonged to a universally recognized aristocracy of the spirit, regardless of his economic status. The riches Tevye dreams of are a mirage; yet the opportunity to rise above his station by a vigorous display of a body of knowledge that, while not large, he is in total command of, is a subjective and objective reality that he exploits to the utmost, and sometimes a bit beyond.

How, though, can this reality be translated into English? Theoretically, the translator has four choices:

> 1. He can give Tevye's quotations in English instead of in Hebrew.

> 2. He can give them both in English and in Hebrew, the latter transliterated into Latin characters.

3. He can give them only in Hebrew (as in the original Yiddish text).

4. He can omit them entirely.

I have in fact utilized all these approaches [in *Tevye the Dairyman and The Railroad Stories*]. In some places, where a quotation of Tevye's is neither especially striking nor crucial, and where leaving it out does not adversely affect the tone or the significance of his remarks, I have done so. At a few points in the text I have translated his quotes into English, sometimes retaining the Hebrew as well and sometimes deleting it. In the great majority of cases, however, I have chosen Option 3 and, like the Yiddish text, given only Tevye's Hebrew, translations of which will be found in the glossary and notes at the back of [*Tevye the Dairyman and The Railroad Stories*]. Though this may be the solution that seems at first glance to be the most inconvenient for the English reader, I preferred it for several reasons.

The first of these is that many of Sholem Aleichem's Yiddish readers also failed to understand some or all of Tevye's quotes. Sholem Aleichem had a mass audience, much of it composed of working men and women with little or no religious education, and if they did not mind being stumped by Tevye's Hebrew, neither need the English reader today.

Secondly, most of the characters in *Tevye the Dairyman*—in fact, nearly all of them—are simple Jews themselves who complain that they can't follow Tevye's quotations, from which they keep begging him to desist. For the English reader to be told what these mean at the same time that Tevye's family and acquaintances are baffled by them would create a rather odd effect.

Thirdly, translating Tevye's Hebrew in the text itself almost always results in the wrong tone, since the biblical and rabbinic passages that he cites have an archaic sound in English, which is not at all the case in the original. On the contrary, even when a Yiddish speaker did not know the meaning of a Hebrew verse, the feeling it suggested to him was generally the warm, homey one of religious rituals and synagogue services that he knew well.

Finally, as far as Jewish readers are concerned, modern Jewish history has ironically reversed the composition of Sholem Aleichem's public. Once he was read by Jews who knew more Yiddish than Hebrew; today he is mostly read by those who, if they know any Jewish language at all, know more Hebrew than Yiddish. It is my hope that many such readers who cannot read Sholem Aleichem in the original will nevertheless be able to enjoy Tevye's Hebrew wordplay in this English translation [of *Tevye the Dairyman and The Railroad Stories*].

For those who cannot, there are two consolations. One is the glossary, which the reader is free to consult not only for the meaning and pronunciation of Tevye's Hebrew quotes, but also for explanations of historical references and Jewish customs that may elude him. The other is the fact that there is no need to skip over the Hebrew quotations just because one does not understand them. Read them aloud; savor them; try saying them as Tevye did. There is no way to reproduce in print the exact sights, smells, and tastes of Tevye's world, but a bit of the sound of it is in these pages.

3

Though there is only one Tevye, there was also only one Sholem Aleichem, and, as readers of the twenty *Railroad Stories* will notice, as prolifically creative as he was (the first posthumous, incomplete edition of his work ran to twenty-eight volumes!)—indeed, it would seem, as a prerequisite for such productivity—there are in his work certain basic themes and situations that occur again and again. Thus, one is reminded by the story **"Eighteen from Pereshchepena"** of the comic scene between Tevye and Layzer Wolf in which the two carry on a single conversation that each thinks is about something else; by the narrator's attitude toward women in **"High School"** of Tevye's antifemale posturing; by Berl Vinegar's fast-talking of the priest in **"The Miracle of Hoshana Rabbah"** of Tevye's handling of Ivan Paparilo in the pogrom scene of **"Lekh-Lekho,"** etc. Even Tevye's rampant quotationism has its parallel in the narrator of **"Burned Out"**—who, however, is even less of a "scholar" than Tevye and wildly throws Hebrew phrases about without always knowing what they mean. Such recurrent elements served Sholem Aleichem as modular blocks out of which he was able to construct an amazing variety of characters and plots.

Although *The Railroad Stories,* first assembled in book form in 1911, are contemporary with the *Tevye* episodes, their composition was not widely spaced like that of *Tevye* but rather concentrated in two intense bursts of activity, one in 1902 and one in 1909-1910. In the first period were written **"High School,"** **"The Automatic Exemption,"** **"Burned Out,"** **"Fated for Misfortune,"** and, though it was later slightly revised to form the collection's closing story, **"Third Class."** With the exception of **"It Doesn't Pay to Be Good,"** which dates from 1903, all the other stories belong to the second period. It was only then, indeed, that Sholem Aleichem decided to write a book of tales all told to or overheard by a traveling salesman on a train, which explains a fundamental difference between the 1902-1903 series and the 1909-1910 one; for in the latter group trains and train rides are generally intrinsic, whereas in the former they are not.

The 1902-1903 stories, in other words, were not originally written with railroads in mind, to which they were adapted after the fact by the simple device of adding a brief descriptive opening paragraph placing them on a train. As for the order of the stories in the book, it was determined by Sholem Aleichem himself. While it does not strictly reflect the sequence in which they were written, it does have a chronological basis, the first eleven tales dating from 1909-1910, the next five from 1902-1903, and the next three from 1909-1910 again.

Like *Tevye,* nearly all *The Railroad Stories* are monologues; this was Sholem Aleichem's favorite form and one he repeatedly returned to. At first glance it may seem that the traveling salesman who records them is a more active party than the Sholem Aleichem who merely listens to Tevye, since he describes what he sees and occasionally participates in the conversation—yet this is but one side of the coin. Though Sholem Aleichem never speaks to Tevye, Tevye is always conscious of speaking to Sholem Aleichem; his idea of the educated, cultured, sophisticated author he is talking to colors all that he says, and more than once he insists that he would never confide such things to anyone else. The commercial traveler of *The Railroad Stories,* on the other hand, is simply someone to whom his fellow passengers can tell their tale, at times revealing to the book's readers aspects of themselves that he himself is naïvely unaware of. (Such as the fact, for example, that the **"Man from Buenos Aires"** is really a rich pimp engaged in the white slave trade, the shanghaiing of girls to Argentina to work as prostitutes there.) Who he is does not interest them in the least. A Jew meets another Jew on the train and straightaway begins to talk about himself.

Nevertheless, though the notion of trains running through Russia with almost no one in their third-class cars but Jews who tell each other stories may seem like an artificial literary convention, this is actually not the case. The Russia of Sholem Aleichem's day, especially in the provincial Pale of Settlement, had a relatively small Christian middle and lower-middle class. The great bulk of the population belonged to either the peasantry or the landed aristocracy, and of the two groups, the first rarely traveled, and the second never traveled third class. Jews were often merchants, but mostly petty ones who preferred to travel as cheaply as they could—and the fact that Jews, when traveling, tend even today to talk nonstop to each other is something that can be vouched for by anyone who has ever taken a crowded flight to Israel.

Nor is this the only example in *The Railroad Stories* of the way in which our distance from the times may mislead us into thinking that Sholem Aleichem was deliberately exaggerating for literary or comic purposes. Take, for instance, the seemingly surrealistic plot of **"The Automatic Exemption,"** in which a father must run endlessly from draft board to draft board because a son who died in infancy still appears in the population registry; "the [Russian] government," writes the Jewish historian Simon Dubnow, "refused [in drafting Jews] to consider the fact that, owing to inaccurate registration, the conscription lists often carried the names of persons who had long since died, or who had left the country to emigrate abroad"; even the three hundred rubles that a lawyer tells the distraught father he will have to pay as a fine was the exact sum stipulated by Russian law for such cases! Or take the apparently farcical section of the story **"High School"** in which a Jew must get a Christian drunk so that he will agree to send his son, at the Jew's expense, to a commercial school together with the Jew's son. Here is Dubnow again:

> In the commercial schools maintained by the commercial associations Jewish children were admitted only in proportion to the contributions of the Jewish merchants toward the upkeep of the particular school. In private commercial schools, however, percentages of all kinds, varying from ten to fifty percent, were fixed in the case of Jewish pupils. This provision had the effect that Jewish parents were vitally interested in securing the entrance of as many Christian children as possible in order to increase thereby the number of Jewish vacancies. Occasionally, a Jewish father, in the hope of creating a vacancy for his son, would induce a Christian to send his boy to a commercial school—though the latter, as a rule, offered little attraction for the Christian population—by undertaking to defray all expenses connected with his education.

This is not to say that there are not elements of farce in these stories, but they lie far more in the reaction of the characters than in the situation itself. Always a stickler for getting the details right (even the fabulous Brodsky of *Tevye* and **"Go Climb a Tree if You Don't Like It"** was a real Jewish sugar magnate of that name who lived in Kiev), Sholem Aleichem became even more so after leaving Russia in 1906, for he was afraid of being thought out of touch with the world he continued to write about. The Soviet Jewish critic Max Erik quotes a revealing letter written by him to an acquaintance in the White Russian town of Homel at the time that he was working on these tales:

> Perhaps you would consider doing something for me: I would like you to send me raw material from Homel, from Vitebsk, from Bialystok, from wherever you care to, as long as it is subject matter that I can use in my **"Railroad Stories."** I have in mind characters, encounters, anecdotes, comic and tragic histories, events, love affairs, weddings, divorces, fateful dreams, bankruptcies, family celebrations, even funerals—in a word, anything you see and hear about, have seen and heard about, or will see and hear about, in Homel or any-

where else. Please keep one thing in mind, though: I don't want anything imaginary, just facts, the more the better!

Two more examples of such (on our part) unsuspected factuality in these stories are of particular interest.

One concerns a matter of language. In the first of *The Railroad Stories,* **"Competitors,"** we are presented with a woman train vendor who, when her tongue is unleashed, turns out to be a stupendous curser—and by no means a rote one, but a talented improviser who can match every phrase she utters with an appropriate imprecation. One of a kind, no? No. In a chapter devoted to curses in his *The World of Sholom Aleichem,* Maurice Samuel writes of what he calls the "apposite or apropos" curse in the Yiddish of Eastern Europe:

> The apposite or apropos curse is a sort of "catch," or linked phrase; it is hooked on to the last word uttered by the object of the curse. Thus, if he wanted to eat, and said so, the response would be: "Eat? May worms eat you, dear God!" Or: "Drink? May leeches drink your blood!" "Sew a button on for you? I'll sew cerements for you!" If the person addressed does not supply the lead, the curser does it for herself. "There runs Chaim Shemeral! May the life run out of him!" . . . "Are you still sitting? May you sit on open sores! Are you silent? May you be silent forever! Are you yelling? May you yell for your teeth! Are you playing? May the Angel of Death play with you! Are you going? May you go on crutches."

Indeed, in his autobiography *From the Fair,* Sholem Aleichem describes his stepmother as being just such an "apropos curser" and confesses to having modeled several characters on her—one of whom is no doubt the woman vendor from **"Competitors."**

Finally, there is the story **"Elul,"** whose ending, if we do not know what lies behind it, must strike us as rather forced. After all, it does not seem quite credible for an apparently normal girl, even if her father is a smirking bully, suddenly to kill herself just because a jilted and possibly pregnant friend has done the same. But there is a clue here, and that is Mikhail Artsybashev's novel *Sanine,* which the two girls have been reading in secret. All but forgotten today, *Sanine* was a literary sensation when it appeared in 1907 (the shopboy Berl's "summary" of it, of course, is a hilariously garbled version of the story). Written during the period of Czarist reaction that followed the abortive Revolution of 1905 by an author who was himself a professed anarchist, the novel, with its curious combination of (for then) daring erotica, world-weary cynicism, and obsession with death, led to a wave of youthful suicides in Russia, comparable to that caused in Europe by *The Sorrows of Young Werther* over a century before. The times were ripe for it; they were

what Tevye's youngest daughter calls the disillusioned "Age of Beilke" as opposed to the idealistic "Age of Hodl"; and Etke, the daughter of the narrator, was patterned on cases of actual youngsters swept up in an adolescent death cult.

Apart from the fact that they are all monologues, *The Railroad Stories* do not fit into any one mold. Some, like **"The Miracle of Hoshana Rabbah"** and **"Tallis Koton,"** are sheer hijinks; others, like **"High School,"** have an aspect of social satire; still others, like **"The Man from Buenos Aires," "A Game of Sixty-Six," "It Doesn't Pay to Be Good,"** and **"Fated for Misfortune,"** belong to that ironic genre of gradual exposure wherein the reader comes to realize that the speaker is not the kind of man he is pretending to be. **"The Automatic Exemption," "Burned Out,"** and **"Go Climb a Tree If You Don't Like It"** are comic studies in hysteria and mania; **"The Happiest Man in All Kodny"** is a piece of pure pathos with few comic lines in it; and yet another story, **"The Tenth Man,"** is a single brilliant joke whose punch line is withheld till the last moment. Indeed, there are perhaps only two things that all these narrators have in common: each has his distinctive verbal tic or tics, one or more favorite expressions that keep recurring as a kind of nervous identification tag, and each has an obsessive, an uncontrollable, an insatiable, an almost maniacal need to talk.

4

This obsessive garrulousness is common in Sholem Aleichem and is in effect a precondition of the monologue, which can hardly be based on taciturn types. The speakers of his stories talk when they have something specific to say and they talk when they do not; in his famous monologue **"The Pot,"** for example, a woman, whose nagging voice is all we ever hear, comes to see a rabbi about some minor matter of Jewish law, chatters on and on about one unrelated subject after another without ever coming to the point, and stops only when the rabbi, still not having gotten a word in edgewise, finally faints from exhaustion. . . . There is something of this pot woman in many of Sholem Aleichem's characters, who seem to be saying, "I talk, therefore I exist." Nothing frightens them so much as silence—most of all, their own.

Jews have perhaps always been a highly verbal people, certainly since the time when their religion became centered on a growing number of sacred texts and the constant exposition and reexposition of them; the vast "sea of the Talmud" itself, as it is called in Hebrew, is but the edited record of endless oral discussions and debates among the early rabbis, and for centuries, down to the yeshivas and synagogues of Sholem Aleichem's Eastern Europe, the most common method of studying the Law was to talk about it aloud in groups of twos and threes and fours. Here the spoken word is still a functional tool of analysis and communication. In Sholem Aleichem's world, however, it has become something else—or rather, many things: a club, a cloud, a twitch, a labyrinth, a smokescreen, a magic wand, a madly waved paper fan, a perpetual motion machine, a breastwork against chaos, the very voice of chaos itself. . . . His characters chute on torrents of words and seek to drag others into the current with them. And succeed. When the storyteller in **"Baranovitch Station"** breaks off his unfinished tale because it is time for him to change trains, his fellow passengers cannot believe that a Jew like themselves would rather stop talking in the middle of a sentence than miss his connection.

No one understood better than Sholem Aleichem that this astonishing verbosity, this virtuoso command of and abuse of language, was at once the greatest strength and the ultimate pathology of East European Jewish life. Reviled, ghettoized, impoverished, powerless, his Jews have only one weapon: the power of speech. And because it is a weapon that has come down to them honed by the expert use of ages, they wield it with the skill of trained samurai, men, women, and children. (One of Sholem Aleichem's most wonderful long monologues, the picaresque *Motl, Peysi the Cantor's Son,* is narrated by a ten- or eleven-year-old boy.) What can a Jew not accomplish with his tongue? He can outsmart a goy, bury an enemy, crush a wife or husband, conjure up a fortune, turn black into white, turn white into black . . . and believe it all has happened, so that the very sense of reality becomes distorted and defeat turns into victory, humiliation into triumph, grimy wretchedness into winged flight. Don Quixote would have felt at home in Kasrilevke and Anatevka. He might even have learned a few tricks there.

Yet can we be so sure that this defiant quixotism, when all is said and done, does not represent a real triumph of sorts? In a discussion of Sholem Aleichem's story **"Dreyfus in Kasrilevke"** (in which, being told by a fellow Kasrilevkite, who has just read it in the newspaper, that Dreyfus was found guilty, the town's Jews refuse to believe it), Professor Ruth Wisse writes:

> Here, too, the oppressed replace the world's reality with the reality of their argumentative concern. But the Sholem Aleichem story equates the Jews' far-sightedness with faith. . . . Dreyfus in Kasrilevke is judged by God's law; and is God's truth to be sacrificed for journalism?

And she quotes the final lines of the story:

> "Paper!" cried Kasrilevke. "Paper! And if you stood here with one foot in heaven and one foot on earth, we

still wouldn't believe you. Such things cannot be! No, this cannot be! It cannot be! It cannot be!"

Well, and who was right?

"It cannot be": such is the true human voice of Sholem Aleichem's world and the only one he really cared about. For a great writer, he was in some ways oddly limited: he rarely wrote more than cursory descriptions of people, places, and things and was not outstandingly good at them; abstract ideas did not interest him; and even his dialogue reverts quickly to monologue or peters out in misunderstandings and cross-purposes. As a consequence, those of his novels that are not monologic do not rank with the best of his work, and, when their comic thrust fails, they often lapse into sentimentality. (As all cynics are said to be wounded idealists, are not all humorists wounded sentimentalists?) The solo voice was his specialty: he had an uncanny ability to mimic it, to catch its rhythms and intonations, to study it as the mask and revelation of inner self. (Y. D. Berkovits relates how, upon emigrating westward in 1906 and first stopping in Austrian Galicia, whose Yiddish was quite different from that of Russia, Sholem Aleichem imitated the natives so well that soon they could not tell him from a local!) This voice is indomitable. It keeps on talking. It will not be stilled. "It cannot be!" is what it says, and in one way or another it is right.

Human speech, of which nearly all the fiction in this volume is composed, is both the easiest and the hardest language to translate: the easiest because it is usually syntactically so simple, the hardest because it carries the greatest freight of those localisms and culture-bound words of a community that can never have a true equivalent in other languages. And this is especially so of Yiddish, that Jewish tongue woven on a base of middle high German and richly embroidered with Hebrew and Slavic, whose syntax is far simpler than German's but which is culturally more remote from the languages of Christian Europe than any of them are from each other. True, one needn't exaggerate the difficulties: professional translators are used to insoluble problems, and they generally manage to solve them. There are, however, two aspects of Yiddish speech that, because they have no real parallel in English and cannot be satisfactorily approximated in it, deserve to be mentioned.

The first has to do with formulas for avoiding the evil eye. Superstition and the fear of provoking or attracting the attention of hostile forces, or simply of causing offense, are of course universal; but in Yiddish (perhaps because it was the language of a culture in which aggression, given little external outlet, was always felt to be threateningly close to the surface) this anxiety is so extreme that it dictates the use of a wide variety of appeasing expressions in daily speech. Thus, one should not mention a dead person one has known without adding *olov hasholom,* "may he rest in peace"; one does not boast of or express satisfaction with anything unless one says *kinnehoro,* "no evil eye" (i.e., touch or knock wood); if one mentions a misfortune to someone, one tells him *nisht do gedakht* or *nisht far aykh gedakht,* "it shouldn't happen here" or "it shouldn't happen to you"; if one makes a remark critical of somebody, one prefaces it with *zol er mir moykhl zayn,* "may he forgive me"; if the criticism is aimed at Providence, one says *zol mir got nisht shtrofn far di reyd,* "may God not punish me for my words." Moreover, such expressions cover only the specific case; if a person is talking about a deceased relative, for example, and mentions him ten times, it is good form to say *olov hasholom* after each. The result is that one or several sentences of spoken Yiddish can contain a whole series of such phrases that break the speech up into a sequence of fragments punctuated by anxious qualifications. The translator can and should retain some of these, but being overly faithful to them makes the English tiresome, and I have left quite a few out. Wherever the reader sees one such expression in the English, he can assume there may be more in the Yiddish.

Secondly, there is the widespread use in Yiddish of Hebrew, not in the form of quotations, as with Tevye, but of idioms that have become rooted in popular speech, commonly transplanted there from religious texts and prayers. These occupy an ambivalent position: on the one hand, they are understood and used even by uneducated speakers, yet on the other, their Hebrew etymology continues to be recognized and their sacral origins are not obscured, so that they often produce ironic or comic effects. For example, when the arsonist who narrates **"Burned Out"** relates his neighbors' suspicions of him, he does not say that they accuse him of "setting fire" to his house and store, but rather of "making *boyrey me'oyrey ho'eysh.*" Literally these Hebrew words mean "He Who creates the light of fire," but they belong to a blessing ("Blessed art Thou O Lord our God, King of the Universe, Who creates the light of fire") that is said every week in the *havdalah,* the ritual of ending the Sabbath on Saturday night, part of which involves lighting a candle (an act forbidden on the Sabbath itself) and holding one's hand up to the flame. What can the translator do with such untranslatabilities, which are not uncommon in Yiddish, and especially not in a comic Yiddish like Sholem Aleichem's? Shut his eyes and hope to think of something! And in this case I did, because suddenly I remembered a snatch of a comic ditty that I knew as a boy in New York about a Jew who burns down his

store for the "inshurinks," just like the narrator of **"Burned Out."** It was sung in a Yiddish accent to the tune of the Zionist anthem *Hatikvah,* and one stanza of it went:

> Vans I hed a kendy store, business it vas bed,
> Along came a friend of mine, vat you tink he said?
> "I hear you got a kendy store vat you don't vant no more;
> Take a metch, give a skretch, no more kendy store!"

And so "to make *borey me'oyrey ho'eysh*" became "to give the match a scratch"—not an ideal solution perhaps, but certainly a passable one. One does the best one can. Sometimes it's a matter of luck.

I have been translating fiction for many years, but from Hebrew, not from Yiddish, and this volume [*Tevye the Dairyman and The Railroad Stories*] is the first full-scale Yiddish translation I have attempted. I wish, therefore, to express my deepest thanks to the editor of this series, Ruth Wisse, both for trusting and encouraging me to undertake this translation and for going over it with a fine-tooth comb. She was the safety net above which I felt free to be as acrobatic as I liked, knowing I would always be caught if I fell. This book is hers too.

I also wish to thank Michael Stern of Washington, D.C., for kindly letting me use an unpublished paper tracing the sources of Tevye's Hebrew quotations, thus sparing me much arduous spadework; and my sister, Miriam Halkin Och, of Haifa University Library, for her generous help in obtaining bibliographical materials.

Notes

1. This fragment, which was given the tongue-twisting Hebrew name of *Vekhalaklakoys,* after the verse in Psalms 35:6, *Yehi darkom khoyshekh vekhalaklakoys,* "Let their path be dark and slippery," was written in 1914, the same year as "Lekh-Lekho," but not published until two years later. Though it seems to have been begun as a genuine sequel to "Lekh-Lekho," that is, as a ninth episode of *Tevye,* it is less than a third of the average length of the other stories, repeats much of the material in Chapter 8 without adding anything essentially new, and has a rather tired quality that contrasts with the sparkle of the rest of the book. Still, one cannot call it unfinished; on the contrary, it contains precisely the "finale" that Chapter 8 lacks. In the absence of explanatory biographical material, of which there appears to be none, one can only speculate what this fragment represents. My own guess is as follows: while Sholem Aleichem indeed intended to write a full-length sequel to "Lekh-Lekho" and began it immediately

after finishing the latter, he soon, whether because of failing health or because he realized that the book had reached its natural conclusion and had nowhere else to go, gave it up—though not before hastening to write a proper end for it, his main concern being that *Tevye* should have one. Unhappy with the results, however, he refrained from publishing this, possibly hoping to revise and expand it; yet ultimately, seeing this was not to be, he consented to its publication in the days before his death. Subsequently, in all the Yiddish editions of *Tevye* printed after Sholem Aleichem's death, the *Vekhalaklakoys* fragment has appeared as its last chapter.

As the translator of *Tevye,* I was in a dilemma. On the one hand, *Vekhalaklakoys* was published by Sholem Aleichem himself in his lifetime, and without it *Tevye* has no real end; yet on the other hand, apart from its last page, not only does it add nothing to the remainder of the work, it qualitatively detracts from it. What was one to do? In the end I decided to follow the example of Frances Butwin's 1948 English translation of *Tevye* and to omit most of the fragment, some six pages of Yiddish text in all, retaining only the final coda, which I spliced on to the end of "Lekh-Lekho," adding several lines of my own to make the transition smoother. Though taking such a liberty in translating a classic of world literature may seem presumptuous to some readers, I would like to think that Sholem Aleichem might have welcomed it. Besides always being open to criticism of his work, frequently revising it as a result, he encouraged his Russian and Hebrew translators, whom he personally helped and advised, to be extremely free in their renditions. Anyone comparing his Yiddish with the Hebrew translations by his son-in-law Y. D. Berkovits, for example, and especially with Berkovits' translation of *Tevye,* in which Sholem Aleichem was an active collaborator, will be struck by the enormous differences between them. (Berkovits himself omitted the *Vekhalaklakoys* fragment entirely in his complete Hebrew edition of the novel, which he ended with "Lekh-Lekho," but this was apparently his own decision, made after Sholem Aleichem's death.) There will no doubt come a time for variorum editions of *Tevye* in which the full text of *Vekhalaklakoys* can appear alongside whatever ending the translator cares to give the book.

Apart from this fragment, I have departed (as did Berkovits) from the standard Yiddish text of *Tevye* in one other place. When the first episode of the book, "Tevye Strikes It Rich," was published in 1894, it was accompanied by a brief preface, purporting to be a letter written by Tevye to Sholem Aleichem, the literary purpose of which was to in-

troduce Tevye to the reader. Though this preface was later republished as part of the novel as a whole, it was clearly written for "Tevye Strikes It Rich" alone, makes no reference to any of the stories that come after it, and cannot possibly be construed as applying to them. I have therefore omitted it.

2. Tevye's Hebrew is transliterated here, as it is throughout, according to the Ashkenazic pronunciation of Eastern Europe, which is quite different from the way Hebrew is pronounced in Israel and by most Jews today.

Ken Frieden (essay date spring 1989)

SOURCE: Frieden, Ken. "Sholem Aleichem: Monologues of Mastery." *Modern Language Studies* 19, no. 2 (spring 1989): 25-37.

[*In the essay that follows, Frieden shows how Aleichem's "monologues of mastery"—stories narrated by educated and prosperous males—are examples of social satire, for despite the fact that the narrators can dominate and manipulate readers, they are ultimately undermined by their own narrative unreliability.*]

Sholem Aleichem's monologues give voice to a diverse cast of characters. Sholem Aleichem is best known as an author who speaks for the common people, or *folkstipn,* because his digressive, free-associative style is most effective when attributed to untrained narrators.[1] A vastly different situation arises, however, when relatively educated monologists narrate and manipulate events; I refer to monologues of this manipulative kind as "monologues of mastery." These monologues preclude an affectionate or even a neutral response, and raise questions concerning the moral content of satire. In two particular cases, when Sholem Aleichem represents the voices of bourgeois characters, he stages an unusual drama of social criticism.

Previous writers have touched on the social and political implications of Sholem Aleichem's work. In a seminal essay entitled, "The Social Roots of Sholem Aleichem's Humor," for example, Meir Viner disputes the claim that Sholem Aleichem did not criticize the Jewish plutocracy of Kiev.[2] Viner refers to the first period of Sholem Aleichem's creativity, from 1890 to 1895, arguing that he *did* stray from the "path of mercy" onto the "path of judgment." Yet Viner only mentions the "years of reaction" (from 1905 to 1907), and does not analyze the later stories written during these years. A recent article by Hana Wirth-Nesher, "Voices of Ambivalence in Sholem Aleichem's Monologues," continues where Viner left off. Paraphrasing

Viner, Wirth-Nesher concludes that Sholem Aleichem strives to preserve neutrality: "the linguistic disguises which Sholem Aleichem has draped around his speakers . . . permit the writer to escape from making the moral choices that his mutually contradictory and eclectic petit bourgeois social views would have eventually necessitated."[3] I will dispute this conclusion: while many of the monologues do express basic ambivalences, others convey Sholem Aleichem's sympathies and (especially) antipathies. In short, Sholem Aleichem employs monologues to enact a subtle form of social satire.

Interpreters of Sholem Aleichem's monologues have concentrated on a few major figures.[4] As a result, critical and popular awareness hardly extend beyond **"The Pot," "Advice," "Geese,"** and the Tevye stories. Reader reception has suppressed or overlooked another, potentially threatening world of Sholem Aleichem's work, which is epitomized by the monologues of mastery. The elements that comprise this mock genre may be found elsewhere, but they are particularly evident in the stories **"Yoysef," "Three Widows,"** and **"A Story of a Greenhorn."** Rather than attempt a comprehensive discussion of Sholem Aleichem's monologues, I will interpret two of these relatively unknown and atypical tales.

The monologues of mastery are narrated by men whose wealth and education enable them to carry out sinister schemes. They often claim to be impotent or indecisive; unlike Sholem Aleichem's impoverished speakers, however, these narrators are in a position to dominate events, both in their fictional worlds and in their acts of narration. As they address their monologues to Sholem Rabinovitsh's persona, Sholem Aleichem, we search for a clue as to how we should react. But the listener betrays no emotions, except in his occasional, ambiguous smiles. The author's implicit stance lies deeper, beneath the surface of the narrative situation.

"Yoysef" (1905) carries the subtitle: **"Narrative of a 'Gentleman.'"**[5] This epithet at first appears as Sholem Aleichem's ironic designation, yet it also comes from within the story: "'The gentleman'—I had no other name," the narrator explains, among the revolutionaries he knows. Throughout, the speaker describes himself and the other characters roughly, in accordance with their differences in status. The ensuing rivalry between two men resonates with political overtones.

The story is simple enough: the gentleman admires and desires a poor girl who is the waitress in her mother's restaurant. She, however, is attracted to Yoysef, one of the social revolutionaries who frequent the res-

taurant. Hence the drama centers around the question: Who exerts greater power (that is, of attraction), and by what means? Whereas the gentleman is primarily concerned with powers that vie for a woman's love, Yoysef occupies himself with revolutionary ideas.

The narrator evasively describes the girl who motivates the story: "You yourself probably understand that I will *not* tell *who* she is and *what* she is, and *where* she comes from. She is a woman, a girl, indeed a beautiful girl, and poor."[6] Despite his evasiveness, the gentleman quickly reveals what he considers to be the essential facts: she is beautiful and poor. He wishes to possess her, but finds that she is not as helpless as her financial and social position lead him to expect. That the gentleman views his beloved girl in capital terms is clear from his glowing account of her laughter, "which alone is worth all the money" one pays to eat in her mother's restaurant. In short, he wants to purchase her on the strength of his financial holdings, and is thwarted when her affections are unmoved by monetary concerns.

The gentleman initially defies the hearer of his tale: "You can laugh at me, you can make a *feuilleton* out of me, even a book, if you wish—I'm not afraid of you" (107). Aware of Sholem Aleichem's usual, satiric practices, the monologist asserts his independence. Nevertheless, the final lines of the story undermine this initial bravado: "Give me your hand that everything I have told you here will remain between the two of us" (133).[7] From start to finish, the narrator is aware of power struggles, and is especially sensitive to those associated with speech. While he tells a story of his efforts to manipulate others, he strives to manipulate the fictional hearer of his tale, simultaneously manipulating the reader of Sholem Aleichem's story. But by writing the account which his character has supposedly asked him to keep secret, Sholem Aleichem hints at a betrayal of his fictional speaker.

The narrator boasts that women constantly fall in love with him and that matchmakers always chase him. His self-description is, however, unconvincing:

> *Ikh bin a yungerman a hayntiger, un a sheyner yung, a gezunter, mit a shtikel nomen, un a hibsher fardiener, un a kerbel iz bay mir blote.*

> I am a modern, handsome young man, healthy, with a bit of a name, and a fine breadwinner, so that a ruble is nothing to me.

(108)

The gentleman resorts to this self-portrait in order to authenticate his status, and it becomes a kind of nervous reflex, but his oft-repeated refrain only unsettles the identity it is intended to secure.[8] Rather than respect his position, we come to see it as a joke: he turns himself into a caricature of the up-to-date gentleman. Whenever he encounters a difficulty, an awkward pause, or a threat to his presumed power, he comically sketches out his profile. Although he claims to have "a bit of a name," in his own story he never receives one, and despite all his efforts, only his rival's name, Yoysef, will be remembered.

For the narrator who is so conscious of his image, class relations are clearly marked by styles of dress. The socialist "Yankelekh" (generic "Jacobs") frequent his favored restaurant wearing long hair and black shirts. In contrast, the narrator wears a smoking jacket with a white vest. The tension between speaker and hearer intensifies with the remark that "you yourself, it seems, wear long hair and a black shirt, and if you think it handsome, excuse me, but you're wrong" (111). This assault places the fictional hearer, implicitly Sholem Aleichem (the fictional persona, not the author Sholem Rabinovitsh) at odds with the speaker and closer to the revolutionary intellectuals.[9] Language becomes a medium of aggression, and the reader may well feel uneasy about the narrator's attacks and feints.

Language also becomes an issue in connection with the Marxist terminology which is so popular among the "Yankelekh." The speaker says that he has nothing against honest talk, but

> *Ikh hob nor faynt, az me zogt mir, az ikh bin a "bourgeois." Ikh, far'n vort "bourgeois," kon geben a fohrarayn in bak arayn!*
>
> I simply dislike it, when someone tells me that I am a "bourgeois." For the word "bourgeois" I can deliver a slap in the cheek!
>
> (112)[10]

The monologist is familiar with Marxist terminology, and he uses it to approach Yoysef and his circle. On occasion he even resorts to their key words: "proletariat," "Marx," "Bebel," "react" *(reagiren),* and "conspiratorial" (114, 123, 124, 126, 130). For the gentleman, however, these words merely form the mask by means of which he hopes to attain his ends.

Although the narrator boasts of his good name, he discovers that another name is far better, in the usage of his beloved: "She speaks the name 'Yoysef' with an odd sort of sing-song. Only a bride uses such a sing-song, when she speaks the name of her groom" (110). Impoverished, the desired girl asserts her freedom from the narrator by means of a word, one of her only words which he records: "Yoysef." This word presents such an obstacle that it structures the narrative and provides its title. Like a spell against Satan, the name of the beloved keeps the narrator at a distance. Since

the mildly satanic gentleman cannot become Yoysef in order to correspond to her longings, he wonders how he can eliminate the rival.

The relationship between power and language is explicit in one central scene, when the gentleman attends a revolutionary meeting. While Yoysef speaks, the narrator observes his success as an orator; he is especially struck by Yoysef's sway over *her*:

> That minute I envied him, not so much for the force of his speaking, not for the honor and the applause which he received afterward, when he finished speaking—not for these things was I so envious of him, as for the way *she* looked at him! For such a look of hers, I would give away—I myself don't know what!
>
> (117-18)

The narrator decides to eliminate his adversary, whom he credits with rhetorical skill: *me darf zayner poter veren* (120). Having determined that Yoysef's power resides in his language, the narrator resolves to fight him on this ground: "I'll have a chat with him alone" (ibid.). When they meet, the gentleman begins by showing off all the Marxist vocabulary he knows. Then he transforms *reagiren* from a political term into a description of bourgeois emotions, to explain that he is not accustomed to "reacting" to a girl in this way. It remains unclear whether the speaker says anything more threatening to Yoysef. We merely see that, in contrast to the gentleman, Yoysef has concerns other than amorous pursuit.

The next we hear, Yoysef is in trouble with the authorities. Given the political environment of early 1905, one must assume that his trial turns out badly; he is presumably hanged or exiled. The gentleman's obstacle appears to have been overcome. He then makes a ruthless attempt to ambush his beloved's heart in a moment of weakness, but without success. He tells her that she need not *reagiren* (again this word!) so strongly to what has happened; she should forget it all. Although he is momentarily surprised by his power of speech, his efforts fail (130). Soon afterward the girl, her mother, and their restaurant disappear. All inquiries are in vain; their memory is like a dream. The gentleman can only tell the tale of a girl who revealed to him the limits of his power.

The narrator strives to manipulate the hearer of the story at the same time that he pretends to be weak and a failure (108). Yet he evidently plays an active role at some points in his account, and we may wonder whether there is any connection between the narrator's schemes and Yoysef's demise. This question is unanswerable, since it lies beyond the limits of the story. Nevertheless, a passing comment may hint that the gentleman contributed to Yoysef's arrest. He explains that he keeps a record of the conspiratorial activity he observes: "I wrote it out in a notebook" *(ikh hob es farshriben bay zikh in bikhel)* (115). Sholem Aleichem employs irony when he has the narrator add: "Whether it will be of use, or not, I don't know, but certainly it doesn't hurt" (ibid.). Of course, certain kinds of notes can have deleterious effects, though perhaps not on their author. Again, language is the medium in which power exerts itself; writing can be an act of aggression.

Without yet drawing conclusions, I turn to a more intricate version of this basic plot, Sholem Aleichem's **"Three Widows"** (**"Dray almonos"**; 1907).[11] The narrator of this monologue is similarly wealthy and literate, but the subtitle emphasizes an ungentlemanly characteristic: this is "a story of an old bachelor, an irascible man *[bal kasan]*." Anger is central to the story, in part because the speaker continually provokes the listener, implicitly Sholem Aleichem.

"Three Widows" is the longest of Sholem Aleichem's *Monologn*.[12] The narrator's tense, belligerent relationship to his audience helps hold together the three sections of the narrative. His opening words immediately create a dramatic situation, following something the interlocutor has supposedly said: "You are wrong, my lord. Not all old maids are unhappy, not all old bachelors are egoists. Sitting there in your study with a cigar in your mouth and a book in your hand, you imagine you already know everything!" (165). The reader is drawn into an aggressive scene for the duration of the narrative.[13] Similarly, the second part begins: "why have I made you wait so long?—Because I wanted to. When I tell a story, I do it when I wish, not when *you* wish" (190). The speaker insists that the hearer sit silently in an uncomfortable chair; and he sets the time and place of their meeting. After he concludes the second section, he tells the listener that to hear the rest of "the story about my 'widow number three,' you should trouble yourself to come to my home. If not—as you wish! I won't drag you by the coattails." He taunts, "You'll come by yourself" *(ihr vet aleyn kumen)* (199). Sholem Aleichem displaces the three sections of his story (originally serialized in more than three installments) onto three separate scenes within the fictional world.

The plot of **"Three Widows"** parallels the earlier **"Yoysef,"** although the irascible speaker's account borders on absurdity. The monologist begins his story by narrating the death of an acquaintance. He helps the bereaved widow and her daughter Roza, who is born a few months later. Although infatuated by the widow, he explains that indecisiveness prevents him from satisfying his desire to marry her. Meanwhile, as

Roza matures, the narrator's infatuation shifts from mother to daughter. Again, however, he never goes so far as to propose marriage. Roza eventually marries a bookkeeper who promptly poisons himself after a business failure. She subsequently gives birth to Feygele, and the earlier pattern recurs. The narrator delays his marriage proposal to the daughter for so long that he finally transfers his attentions to the granddaughter. (In structure, if not in tone, this repetition of events *ad absurdum* associates the story with some of Sholem Aleichem's more familiar, comic tales.) Insensitive to his charms, Feygele marries a chemist who, like Yoysef, is soon arrested for conspiratorial activities and hanged. The speaker continues his close associations with the three widows, and twice interrupts his story to dine with them. As the story ends, he anticipates spending the night at their home. This narrative combines dark humor, perversity, and the absurd, in multiple layers of satire.[14]

One early digression on buttons, revolving around a failure to marry, prepares for the events of the story:

> What is a button? A button, dear friend, with one of us, with a bachelor, is an important thing! An entire world! Over a button a nasty story once occurred: a bachelor came to look at a girl, and someone pointed out to him with a laugh that he was missing a button; he went away and hanged himself.
>
> (168)

According to his account, the bachelor narrator is a master of buttons, of reserve, to the extent that he never seems to undress or to have a lewd thought.

Our speaker shows all the twists and turns of an unreliable narrator. His claim to speak "from the heart, without tricks" only arouses suspicions. He is evasive, self-contradictory, and at odds with established ethical norms: he withholds details (e.g., 166, 177-78), contradicts himself (e.g., 167/180-81/201), and repeatedly mocks social conventions (e.g. 185). Like the narrator of **"Yoysef,"** he is an individualist and an outsider.[15] He even predicts that the hearer will label him "an old bachelor, an irascible man," anticipating the criticism he knows he provokes. Still, the success of this fiction derives from the problematic (rather than entirely and obviously reprehensible) position of its speaker.[16]

As he speaks, the narrator taunts the hearer: "I don't ask your opinion!" (167); "I won't enter into discussion with you" (172); "What does it matter to me what you think?" (173). He has only harsh words to say about "your writers" (197). The first widow's daughter grew and blossomed "like a delicate rose," he says, alluding to her name and mimicking "the language of your novelists, who know as much about the blossoming of a rose as a Turk knows about the *rabonan kadesh* [the prayer for the masters and disciples of the law]" (171).[17] Later, he refuses to narrate sentimental details, which "the novelists employ in order to squeeze out a tear from the foolish reader" (189; cp. 195). In particular, he rejects the word "love," which "your writers" have spoiled by indiscriminate use (197; cp. 210). These polemics cover up his cool reactions to the lives of his loves and to the deaths of his rivals.

The speaker carefully monitors the hearer's reactions to his story. This is one result of the story's unusual tone, which is closer to black humor than is usual in Sholem Aleichem's work. To offset this atmosphere, the gentleman narrators befriend women whose infectious laughter brings light to an otherwise dark universe: "She laughs, and everything laughs.. . . The table laughs, the benches laugh, and the walls laugh—all of life laughs" (109-10). The grim mood of **"Three Widows"** is lightened by laughter for, when beset by difficulties, "they laugh": "With them everything is laughter! All of life is laughter" (183; cp. 191).[18] The redeeming laughter of the three widows differs sharply from the potentially critical or ironic smiles of the hearer. Hence even this silent reaction is unacceptable: "I dislike it when one smiles. You can laugh as much as you wish, but not smile" (200; cp. 168, 187; 107). In this case, most of the laughter occurs within the story rather than on the part of the reader. Somewhat proud of his education, the irascible man explains why, as guardian of the three widows, he receives the name "Cerberus": "They gave me the name 'Cerberus,' a dog, that is, that stands at the entrance to paradise" (176). Inadvertently reversing the classical myth, possibly because for him the widows' home is a paradise, he betrays the fact that he has turned it into a hell for all other suitors.[19]

"Three Widows" ends in a situation of charged ambiguity. The irascible narrator often refers to his inability to fulfill his desires, saying that despite his infatuation for the first widow, "I had no courage to tell her" (181). There is no way to test his honesty, because the fictional world exists only in the story he tells. Yet internal inconsistencies unsettle the surface effects. The monologist claims never to satisfy his longings for those he calls "my three widows," but he manages to completely dominate their lives, apparently spending most of his days and even some nights with them. This is the conclusion of the story:

> You're ready to go? Come, I'll go with you. I have to be with my three widows. Just a moment, I want to arrange to have the cat fed, because sometimes I can sit there until morning [*ikh kon mikh dort farzitsen biz tog oykh amol*]. We play Yerulash, sometimes Preference. We play for money. And you should see how everyone wants to win! And when someone makes a bad play,

> one doesn't show any mercy, neither they toward me nor I toward them. With me, if someone makes a bad play in cards, I'm capable of trampling on them, tearing them to pieces! What does your smile mean, for example? I know what you think now. I know you through and through and laugh at your grandma! You're thinking about me now: "An old bachelor, an irascible man."

> (212)

In the context of his confessional love story, the hostile relationship between the narrator and his three widows has never before been so evident. It cannot be purely coincidental that one of their card games is called "Preference." The narrator claims that he has never been able to express or enjoy his preferences. Why, then, does he haunt the widows' house, deep into the night?[20]

There is no basis for further speculation on what "actually" happens between the narrator and his widows. He tells us that he has wasted his life—as a result of his timidity with regard to women. And yet in another sense he has victimized the three widows, constantly hovering nearby, a bourgeois Cerberus, always on the verge of proposing marriage and always delaying. The questionable nature of the irascible man's attentions becomes clear, from the standpoint of the first widow, when she once asserts that she has wasted her life because of him (178). Although the narrator is a master in the ethereal world of chess strategy, he claims to suffer defeat in real life (177-78). Even this resignation may be a guise which conceals a deeper strategy. Instead of choosing one of the three widows, he possesses all three, both as a sinister benefactor and as their narrative inventor. No amount of scrutiny can fully penetrate the story's layers of deceit, but the speaker himself alludes to Bismarck, saying: "Words were given to us in order to mask our thoughts" (196).

"A Story of a Greenhorn" (1916), which closes the volume of *Monologn,* intensifies the earlier voices of mastery. On one level, it epitomizes Sholem Aleichem's scathing critique of America, and (more specifically) of business practices on the Lower East Side. But this monologue also reworks the narratives of manipulation by the gentleman and by the old bachelor. The subtitle of this satire informs us that in it "Mr. Baraban, business broker, tells how he taught a lesson to a greenhorn, who married for the sake of business" (251).[21] This narrator, whose name means "drum," pounds out a self-righteous account of his wrongdoings. Whereas the gentleman and irascible man have a somewhat ambiguous moral standing, Mr. Baraban has no positive features. This one-sidedness produces a more straightforward and less subtle effect of social criticism.

Like **"Yoysef"** and **"Three Widows,"** **"A Story of a Greenhorn"** opens in reaction to the interlocutor: "You say: America is a land of business—nevermind. It has to be like this" (*Ihr zogt: Amerike iz a land fun biznes—nevermind. Es darf azoi tsu zayn*) (253). But where **"Three Widows"** initially attacks psychological theories, this monologue refers to the practices of newcomers and states a moral:

> After all, to go and marry and sell oneself for the sake of business—that is really, excuse me, swinishness. I don't preach morality, but I'm telling you, it's a fact that ninety-nine percent of greenhorns among us marry for the sake of business. That vexes me, and when I catch such a greenhorn, he doesn't get away from me in one piece.
>
> (Ibid.)

By beginning with a relatively uncontroversial moral judgment (i.e., one should not marry for money), the speaker forestalls our recognition of his own immorality. Mr. Baraban tells a tale of his unethical actions, under the mask of self-righteous criticism. This dual presentation produces the strained irony of the story, which the narrator calls a "comedy" (255). As in the other monologues of mastery, the drama centers around a desired woman, and recounts the elimination of a competing man.

An unsuspecting newcomer visits Mr. Baraban, the business broker, together with his wife. They ask for assistance in opening a stationery store. Because Mr. Baraban happens to have a laundry up for sale, he convinces the greenhorn to go into the laundry business. What most impresses the monologist is the greenhorn's well-favored marriage to a beautiful girl with a fine dowry.

Although the girl is a passive observer of the ensuing spectacle, she is the source of its drama. Mr. Baraban describes her enthusiastically, as he first sees her: "with him a woman—what shall I tell you?—blood and milk. Beautiful as the day and fresh as an apple, just off the tree" (253). His outrage against the greenhorn flares up when he compares their assets:

> The bastard has only a few hundred dollars in his pocket and a woman at his side—fine gold! Why does he deserve it? Mr. Baraban, the biggest business broker of the East Side, has to have a wife, excuse me, a monster and what's more a Xantippe; and God has to send such a jewel to the greenhorn.
>
> (257)

In **"Yoysef,"** the gentleman monologist learns the limits of his wealth, since his beloved is attracted to a poor intellectual. Mr. Baraban refuses to acknowledge forces greater than capital; in Sholem Aleichem's fiction, the American milieu tends to confirm this view.

By a series of swindles, the business broker succeeds in completely bankrupting the greenhorn who, like the other monologists' competitors, is imprisoned. As the story closes,

> I picked a lawyer for his wife who demands from him, on her account, three things: 1) her money, the thousand-dollar dowry; 2) a divorce; and 3) until she receives a divorce from him, he shall support her in accordance with the laws of the country.
>
> (259)

Radicalizing the leanings of other wealthy speakers, this last monologist embodies the triumph of evil. Mr. Baraban unabashedly eliminates his opposition and takes control of the woman's affairs, through the mediation of a lawyer. Financial power yields personal power, and a self-assurance that blinds the caricatured speaker to the possibility of seeing his actions in a negative light. The story ends *in medias res,* since we do not know what may ensue between the usurper and the woman whose life he dominates.

After perpetrating a violent scheme, Mr. Baraban narrates his misdeeds complacently and even moralistically. His language is as violent as the actions he relates; this violence is directed both against people and against language itself. Specifically, the business broker wrecks the Yiddish language by slipping in English words at every turn. This perversion of Yiddish reaches such proportions that the volume of *Monologn* includes an extensive dictionary of *farenglishte* words. Sholem Aleichem's monological narrators betray themselves in the language of their narrations.

Despite the power of the master monologists, we finally resist their attempted domination. Like the implied hearer of these stories, the Sholem Aleichem persona, we leave their narrators with a grimace. This happens in part because we question their actions, and also because they undermine themselves through inconsistencies and questionable language. Each of the bourgeois speakers puts on airs and presumes to know more than he does. They boast of their knowledge, but garble Marxist jargon, place Cerberus at the gates of paradise, and (in **"A Story of a Greenhorn"**) do obvious violence to the Yiddish language.

Monologue is an appropriate form for these stories, whose speakers live monologically. Dialogue hardly enters into their experience, for they never exchange words or thoughts. We seldom hear a dialogue; the desired women appear almost entirely mute. The monologists are wont to impose their wills, not to suit their actions to others' needs. They are openly hostile to whatever the captive audience may say, preferring to do all the talking themselves, without interruption.

In the erotic realm that is both suppressed and decisive in these stories, the monologists present themselves as voyeurs. They desire beautiful women from afar, but never seem to get beyond appearances. Ultimately, they desire only their own desire, in a fantasy that cannot be disturbed by any opposing will. Thus these monologists never procreate; their only offspring are words, words, words. They never escape the limits of the mastery they desire.

Although it is tempting to interpret Sholem Aleichem's monologues of mastery on the mimetic plane, with an eye to clues of unreliability, even the unreliable narrator is only a fictional persona. Sholem Aleichem directs a wide range of narrative strategies toward irony at the expense of his monologists. When they are "low" characters, this irony achieves the effect of light comedy or humor. But when the speakers are more imposing personalities, the irony cuts deeper, challenging the social contexts that empower them. In the monologues of mastery, monologue has become a luxury—and a delusion—of the rich.[22] Their wealth is no extraneous detail; it buys greater freedom from constraints and power to manipulate events. But these monologues are invariably unsettled by discrepancies. Allied with perversions of desire, the monologists are overthrown by their forced dependence on others.

Social criticism in literature often depicts corruption in one form or another. Sholem Aleichem's "monologues of mastery" employ a subtler means: in these stories the depiction itself is corrupt. There is no distance between the narrative voice and the world that is described. The monologists inadvertently turn their words against themselves, uncovering bourgeois foibles from within. Monologue, when it is a luxury of the rich, acts as a double-edged sword.

Notes

The Lady Davis Fellowship Trust, the American Council of Learned Societies, and the Memorial Foundation for Jewish Culture generously supported the research leading to completion of this essay. The author also thanks Dan Miron and Avrom Novershtern for conversations that influenced the writing of this paper. An earlier draft was read at the Eighteenth Annual Conference of the Association for Jewish Studies, on 15 December 1986. Transliterations of quoted passages follow the original Yiddish texts, even where spellings do not conform to current standards set by the YIVO Institute for Jewish Research.

1. Compare Dan Miron, *A Traveler Disguised: A Study in the Rise of Modern Yiddish Fiction in the Nineteenth Century* (New York: Schocken, 1973), p. 179. The monologists' personae should not be confused with the Sholem Aleichem persona, which Dan Miron discusses in "Sholem Aleykhem: Person, Persona, Presence," *The Uriel Weinrich Memorial Lecture,* 1 (New York: YIVO, 1972).

2. M. Viner, "Di sotsiale vortseln fun Sholem Aleykhem's humor," in *Tsu der geshikhte fun der yidisher literatur in 19tn yorhundert* (1931; rpt. New York: Yidishe kultur farband, 1946), pp. 235-37.

3. Hana Wirth-Nesher, "Voices of Ambivalence in Sholem Aleichem's Monologues," *Prooftexts,* 1 (1981), p. 170.

4. See, for example, I. J. Trunk, *Sholem Aleykhem: zayn vezn un zayne verk* (Warsaw: Kultur-lige, 1937), pp. 161-224, and Victor Erlich, "A Note on the Monologue as a Literary Form: Sholem Aleichem's 'Monologn'—A Test Case," in *For Max Weinrich on his Seventieth Birthday* (The Hague: Mouton, 1964), pp. 44-50.

5. "Yoysef" was first serialized in *Der veg,* September 22, 24, 25, 1905, and in *Dos yidishe togeblat,* October 5, 6, 8, 10, 11, 1905. Without substantial changes, the story was reprinted in Sholem Aleichem's *Nayeste verk* (Warsaw: Progress Edition, 1909), vol. 1, pp. 21-41. These earlier printings bear lengthier subtitles than the Folksfond edition, and do not place "Gentleman" in quotation marks. In *Der veg* and the Progress edition, the subtitle reads: "Narrative of a Gentleman and Retold Word for Word by Sholem Aleichem." *Dos yidishe togeblat* presumably chose its own punning title: "Narrative of a Gentleman and Retold Incidentally in 'Veg' [Underway] by Sholem Aleichem." In a letter to Sholem Aleichem of September 7 (August 25), 1905, Bal Makhshoves mentions having received a copy of this story from him.

6. Sholem Aleichem, "Yoysef," in *Ale verk fun Sholem Aleichem* (New York: Folksfond edition, 1917-25), vol. 21, p. 108. Further references to this volume of *Monologn* are by page alone. I am not aware of any translation of "Yoysef" into English.

7. Despite the narrator's hasty claim to autonomy, he admits that he broke off his studies and married a girl after being threatened by her brother (107). The gentleman tells us that he suffered for three years with her before regaining his freedom. From start to finish, in fact, he is aware of power struggles, and is especially sensitive to those associated with speech; even Yoysef's powers appear to him primarily rhetorical (in the original sense of the word). On the relevant, yet problematic, concept of the unreliable narrator, see Wayne Booth, *The Rhetoric of Fiction* (Chicago: Univer-

sity of Chicago Press, 1961). Booth defines the unreliable narrator as one who does not speak or act "in accordance with the norms of the work (which is to say, the implied author's norms)" (p. 158). Unreliability need not be confined to matters of mimetic detail, but can extend to moral views, judgments, and standards of character.

8. Compare 109, 112, 115, 118, 122, 123, 128, 130, 132.

9. In his essay on "The Social Roots of Sholem Aleichem's Humor," Viner refers to a letter in which Sholem Rabinovitsh discusses his malaise within his own social circle, consisting of wealthy people "who value my finances much higher than my literary talent" (op. cit., p. 242). See *Dos Sholem Aleykhem bukh,* ed. I. D. Berkovitsh (New York, 1926), p. 287. Of course, Sholem Rabinovitsh's situation should not be uncritically identified with the fictional situations of Sholem Aleichem.

10. Compare Hana Wirth-Nesher, op. cit., p. 169.

11. "Dray almonos" was first serialized in *Dos yidishe togeblat,* June 2-17, 1907 and in *Der fraynd,* June 14-July 7, 1907. Collected in Sholem Aleichem's *Nayeste Verk* (Warsaw: Progress Edition, 1909), vol. 2, pp. 65-102. A translation of "Three Widows" is contained in *Stories and Satires by Sholem Aleichem,* trans. Curt Leviant (New York: Thomas Yoseloff, 1959), pp. 182-213. For the purposes of this analysis, I have retranslated all quotations in an effort to approximate more closely the tone of the original.

12. Agreeing with Dan Miron's *Sholem Aleichem: Pirkey masa* (Ramat Gan: Massada, 1970), pp. 58-9, note 76, I reject I. J. Trunk's overly general definition of Sholem Aleichem's "autobiographical monologue" and "written monologue." See I. J. Trunk, op. cit., p. 166.

13. At the same time, Sholem Aleichem employs irony against himself when he has a fictional character criticize his own paper-thin conception of the world. In effect, this critique may grant a greater illusion of reality to the provoking speaker, who pretends to understand the real world better than does his creator.

14. At every turn, the present scene of narration is relevant to the events narrated. From the start, the speaker challenges his hearer to grasp the paradoxical tale he will relate; psychology, he says, is incapable of explaining such hard realities: "Why are you telling me about psychology? If you want to know the true psychology, you should sit down and listen carefully to what I tell you" (165). Only after listening to the tale, the speaker claims, may the hearer express an opinion on the origins of

sadness and egoism, or concerning the character of old maids and bachelors.

The narrator demands freedom to narrate without interruptions, almost as if he were outlining the rules for Freud's talking cure. Sholem Aleichem knew little or nothing about Freud in 1907, but from our contemporary standpoint, the scene of monologue in some ways resembles a psychoanalytic interview. At several points, in fact, the narrator toys with the prospect that he is *meshuge* (166, 171, 178-79, 181, 185, 191, 208). He directs the hearer to trade places with him, so that while he narrates he may recline in a rocking-chair; "by the way, it's better for you right there, you won't fall asleep" (166; cp. 186). Moreover, the speaker says: "I'm speaking out my heart to you, and with you I want to analyze, to find out: where is the worm?" (185). The hearer's brief reactions are not recorded, however, but only implied by the monologist's words. Thus the burden—and power—of interpretation rests with the reader, which gives the story a large measure of its interest.

15. He also makes slurs against the Jewish people (172, 187), unlike the gentleman narrator who admits in passing that he is, in spite of everything, a Jew (120).

16. In the narrator's telling of his tale, one early point of contention is his relationship to the first widow's husband: "I was acquainted with her husband. Not only acquainted, but friendly (*bafraynt*). That is, I don't say that we were friends. I say that we were friendly" (167). Later in the story, the narrator refers back to this "friend" (169, 180-81, 201); his relationship to the widow makes this a potentially sensitive point.

Similar to Sholem Aleichem's other monologists, the irascible man digresses frequently and employs a linguistic catchword to bring himself back to the main thread. His rather Germanic reflex is the connective adverb, "alzo" (e.g., 166, 167, 169, 171, 172, 173, 176, 177, 182, 184, 185, 190, 201, 203). By means of this word the speaker indicates that he is returning to the earlier narrative line, but his digressions remain apparent.

17. Compare "Yoysef," 110, 120.

18. In these monologues, laughter also occurs at the expense of their narrators, within the stories they tell. See, for example, the mother's play on the word *farzorgt,* in "Yoysef" (110). These stories are neither humorous nor comic in the usual senses, because we do not laugh heartily *with* or *at* their speakers. (In *Sholem Aleykhem: zayne vikhtigste verk, zayn humor un zayn ort in der yidisher literatur* [New York: Yidisher Kultur, 1928],

Shmuel Niger differentiates between laughter *with* humorous characters and *at* comic characters [pp. 102-4].) Wealthy rather than poor, the domineering speakers do not represent *folkstipn* with whom we laugh in order not to cry. Nor do they make the best of an imperfect world; they add to the world's imperfections. They have the means to overcome most obstacles to the fulfillment of their desires. In fact, Sholem Aleichem's fictions depend on the power of these speakers to impose their narrative wills. The gentleman, the irascible man, and the business broker are authors, not only of their monologues, but of devious plots within their narratives. Hence these monologists enable Sholem Aleichem to exercise his mastery of form by transferring the burden of mastery to them. We may, in consequence, admire the compositions while disliking their fictional inventors.

19. To the extent that the narrator is obviously manipulative, his efforts fail to achieve their desired effect. We end the story with a critical smile on our lips, and with an uneasy awareness that we have been had. This conclusion is analogous to that of a "A zekhs-un-zekhtsig," in *Ale Verk fun Sholem Aleichem* (New York: Folksfond Edition, 1917-25), vol. 28: *Ayzenbahn-geshikhtes*, p. 171.

20. Curt Leviant's translation perhaps aims to spare innocent readers when it mistranslates the words that contribute most to our recognition of the speaker's unreliability. It translates "ikh kon mikh dort farzitsen biz tog oykh amol" (212) by "I'm liable to spend the whole day there" (*Stories and Satires,* op. cit., p. 213). Granted: given the narrator's equivocations, day is night and night is day. But "biz tog" does mean "until dawn." "Farzitsen" here means "to sit," although (especially when applied to women) it can also mean "to remain unmarried." This is exactly what the narrator does, summed up in a phrase: he stays with the widows night and day, and remains unmarried.

21. "A mayse mit a grinhorn" was first published in *Di varhayt,* January 16, 1916, with a long subtitle that was probably not written by Sholem Aleichem. An English rendition is contained in Sholem Aleichem, *Some Laughter, Some Tears: Tales from the Old World and the New,* trans. Curt Leviant (New York: G. P. Putnam's Sons, 1968), pp. 243-48. Again, I retranslate all quotations.

22. Compare my *Genius and Monologue* (Ithaca: Cornell University Press, 1985), p. 178.

Naomi B. Sokoloff (essay date 1992)

SOURCE: Sokoloff, Naomi B. "Sholem Aleichem—*Mottel, the Cantor's Son.*" In *Imagining the Child in Modern Jewish Fiction,* pp. 43-63. Baltimore, Md.: Johns Hopkins University Press, 1992.

[*In the essay below, Sokoloff analyzes how the child narrator of* Mottel, the Cantor's Son *provided Aleichem with the perspective of an innocent and exuberant outsider through whom the author could observe, interpret, recontextualize, and filter a Jewish adult world at the turn of the twentieth century.*]

> *God has pity on kindergarten children.*
> *He has less pity on schoolchildren,*
> *And on grown-ups he has no pity at all.*
>
> —Yehuda Amihai, "God Has Pity on Kindergarten Children"

The conventional Haskalah portrayal of the *heder* boy as a miniature adult, old before his time, often relied on an opposition between the world of books and the world of nature. The little Jew, immersed in holy writ, was seen as having been deprived the delights of the outdoors and so denied a child's fundamental need for play. In his autobiographical narrative from the turn of the century, *Of Bygone Days,* S. Y. Abramovitch (known by his pen name, Mendele the Bookseller) moves a step toward liberating the child from the study hall. Speaking on behalf of the boy he once was, the narrator voices the sensibility and perceptions of childhood long silenced by religious tradition. Significantly, the decisive moment of self-assertion and self-definition for the child protagonist is that time when, leaving the *heder* behind, he suddenly and belatedly discovers nature. The text remarks that as he ran barefoot one day in a spring storm, "that was the day when my eyes were opened and I was revealed to myself as I really am."[1] This experience brings with it, much as in Bialik's "The Pool" ("Habrekha," 1905), a new language, one more appropriate than sacred writ for the expression of youthful vitality and exuberance:[2]

> That was the moment I first came to know myself, God, and his world. All these things were revealed to me in thunder and lightning, and human intelligence came to me in the storm. That great vision is engraved on my heart and I can never forget it. In my heart—the heart of a naive child—I comprehended the vision before me, and I understood the language of nature round about. I knew the speech of the plants and the garden vegetables, the song of the running waters, and the frog's croak, as he lay up to his neck in the fetid marsh staring upward with gray eyes—all this I understood well and answered in the same voice, croaking with joy.

(269)

Sholem Aleichem, like Mendele, Y. L. Peretz, and others, also at times lamented the early maturity imposed on Jewish children.[3] However, he went far beyond Mendele's efforts to present the child's outlook on the world. Not unlike Charles Dickens and Mark Twain, authors with whom he has often been compared, Sholem Aleichem devoted a considerable portion of his *oeuvre* to the treatment of childhood. This was so partly because, like Dickens and Twain, he composed popular fiction, suitable for family entertainment and designed to appeal to youngsters (particularly his festival stories). Partly, too, he was attracted to childhood as a theme that accented a mixture of mischief and nostalgia. His interest in child characters also coincided with and enhanced his purposes as a humorist and a satirist, for his young creations, like himself, often exhibit a lighthearted disrespect for accepted custom. His most sustained narrative of childhood, ***Mottel, the Cantor's Son,*** emerges out of the literary tradition that protests restrictive *heder* instruction, but the text then puts the main character to a variety of purposes that include satiric humor and, above all, an expression of hope for the continuing vigor of the Jewish people at a time of persecution and cultural upheaval.

The narrative takes as its point of departure a scene that conforms closely to many of the features in the passage just cited from *Of Bygone Days*. The tale opens with an account of a little boy's foray into the outdoors at springtime, accompanied by his favored playmate, the neighbor's calf. This initial scene combines emphasis on nature with self-expression, as Mottel avoids his school lessons, discards traditional language, and replaces it with his own. At odds with his predecessor, though, Sholem Aleichem's interests are less with nature than Mendele's, and more with human nature.[4] This passage contrasts with the lines from *Of Bygone Days* as it shifts emphasis notably from the "speech of plants" and the "song of the running waters" to the child's voice, his interpretation of the landscape, and his irreverence toward authority.

> After we climbed out into God's free and sunny world, both of us, Menie and I, out of thankfulness to nature began to display our joy [and] from my swelling breast a kind of song burst forth—much finer than those I sang with father on holidays at the altar, a song without words, without music, without melody—a kind of nature-song, a song of waterfalls, of running waves, a song of songs: "Oh papa, oh father, oh everlasting God!"
>
> (3-4)[5]

Here, as Mottel gladly exchanges the chanting of *shul* for his own song, the author further emphasizes the substitution of youthful high spirits for traditional language by engaging this character in a dialogue with the calf. Menie says, "meeeeh," the boy mimics the cow, and, enormously pleased with themselves, they continue to imitate each other and converse "*in dem-selben nusaḥ*." This rather ordinary phrase in Yiddish,

signifying *in the same way,* recalls the sacred meaning of *nusaḥ,* the musical formulation or version in which the prayers are chanted in the synagogue. Drained as it is of religious connotations, "*nusaḥ*" here parallels Mottel's own effacing of traditional meaning and his substituting of his own, secular expression for the discourse of the synagogue.

The child functions throughout the narrative to undermine the old ways. To examine his role it is crucial to point out that this stance is not a narrowly personal one nor merely an instance of childish disrespect. At issue is a moment of collective transition from tradition to modernity. *Mottel* recounts the life of a small shtetl child whose society as a whole is disintegrating due to economic hardship, pogroms, and the deterioration of religious authority. There begins a mass emigration to America, and the narrative follows the boy's adventures on both sides of the ocean. Early on in the plot action the protagonist's father dies, leaving him an orphan by the reckoning of his society; soon the entire world of his parents will find itself in irreversible decline and its patriarchal order threatened. All these matters, however, are filtered through the prism of the youngster's perception, and Mottel is renowned for putting a comic twist on events. With his famous pronouncement, "Hoorah, I'm an orphan," Mottel welcomes the special indulgence that his misfortune has brought him. He revels in no longer being expected to behave himself or attend school. As a result, debates about the book have centered on the degree to which Sholem Aleichem emphasizes tragedy and how much the child's mitigating presence serves as comic rejoinder to dire circumstance.[6] Mottel's views have decisive impact, because this text does not only orient itself to a child's perspective, it also adopts Mottel himself as a narrative persona. The long-established typology of the child as suppressed voice in Jewish life thus ostensibly gives way to representation of that very voice itself. The thematic stress on the child as source of novel vision and expression coincides with exploration of the child as narratorial figure and the artistic experimentation attendant on that possibility.

As Dan Miron has pointed out in a detailed article about Mottel, this head-on confrontation with the formal complexities inherent in representing a child's voice proves highly problematic.[7] Sholem Aleichem does not sustain a childish style, but also does not refrain from it. At times the narrative avails itself of short sentences, simple speech patterns—and, it could be added, rhymes, a bandying about of nicknames, the recounting of childish jokes and verbal games. All of these properly belong in the category of mimetic impulses that indicate a young speaker. At other times, though, the narrator waxes poetic, turns to complex syntax, or indulges in sentimental abstractions entirely inappropriate to a child's speech. The opening paragraph, portions of which were quoted above, provides a case in point. (It is telling that in some early versions of the text this scene is presented in the third person, through an implied narrator, without pretense of using a child's voice.)[8] Further incongruities riddle the text as well. While Mottel sometimes fails to grasp the metaphorical nature of idioms, at other times he himself produces elaborate metaphoric language and alliteration of his own. His performance, moreover, divides itself erratically between features of oral delivery and written composition. The narrative was at times subtitled *"ksovim fun a yingl a yosm"* (writings of an orphan boy), but on any number of occasions Mottel announces that he is illiterate. The writerly qualities that do pervade the narrative reveal quite openly that this work has not been created by a child. Mottel, for instance, shares the author's concern with serialization and takes care to summarize preceding episodes at the beginning of each new chapter. Though assuming intimacy with his audience and addressing them as if in conversation, Mottel's text does not make sense as a dramatic monologue, for it is not situated in concrete dramatic circumstances that might provide the character clear motivation for speaking.

On top of all these peculiarities, Mottel very often speaks in the present tense. He does not acquire mature awareness, and he does not develop either in the narrated events or in the narration. (His age is indeterminate; Sholem Aleichem variously designated his character to be five, seven, or nine years old on different occasions. Mottel does not progress in anything resembling plausibly sequential fashion from one stage of life to another.)[9] If for no other reason than these temporal oddities, his language would remain highly inconsistent with that of any natural speaker. Miron therefore concludes that Mottel's speech abides by only one law, "the law of energy, of constant crackling, sparkling movement" (179). This quality is symptomatic of the central thematic thrust of the narrative as a whole. Mottel's effervescence and vitality, in response to the ossification of tradition and the loss of shtetl culture, turn the child into a symbol of newness and an endorsement of optimism. As he dispenses with mourning over a moribund European past, this character enthusiastically embraces the New World. The nondeveloping figure in this way conveys a most acute feeling for historical change and its significance, and so the author turns to advantage the vestiges of childishness in his character, even while employing them "as elements of a larger conception which is removed from any intention of the fictional creation of a child character" (145).

Miron's astute analysis should not obscure the fact that the adoption of the child's voice, problematic as it is from the standpoint of mimetic force, bears a series of additional artistic benefits. It is possible to extend critical discussion on Mottel by considering interanimations of language that result from the focus on the child's perspective. Lending itself to comedy and the celebration of vitality, this narrative persona also bears exceptional dialogic capacities, in the Bakhtinian sense that Mottel selectively appropriates, reinterprets, speculates on, and, in the process, challenges the authority and privilege of adult idiom. The ways in which the language of the child comes in contact with, transforms, or recasts adult expression reflect the instability of his setting. His words, consequently, also emphasize the dynamic shifts and upheavals of his society. In this capacity Mottel allows for variation on the polyphonic qualities that are such a fundamental part of Sholem Aleichem's art. This is a writer known for introducing into his fiction a plethora of garrulous characters intent on talking their way out of disaster or disappointment.[10] The child has a special role in this scheme of things, for his naive incomprehension affects the way he filters, apprehends, and interprets the words of others. He is instrumental in admitting adult voices to the text or excluding them from it, allowing them to articulate their views or preventing them from doing so.

For example, Mottel fulfills an important function as a narrator by overhearing and recording conversations around him. Bakhtin has drawn analytic attention to the importance of reported speech in narrative. Of recurrent interest for his literary readings are the transmission and assessment of what others say, the rebuttals and responses that one character brings to the comments of fellow characters.[11] Because Mottel is a child, incapable of understanding many things, he becomes an ideal foil for presenting what Bakhtin considers the fundamental component of novelistic art: attention to the speaking person and spoken words. Reporting much without being fully a party to it or absorbing it, the young protagonist easily allows extra voices to be heard alongside his own. Since he does not truly assimilate their words into his personal conceptual system, he remains an outsider, but at the same time he facilitates the orchestration of multiple speakers within the narrative. Benefits to plot action brought in this way are evident. The child focalizer/narrator permits Sholem Aleichem tremendous flexibility over what to disclose and what to omit. In addition, this approach can foster a panoramic view. Like the Sholem Aleichem persona itself, Mottel enjoys mobility and a highly useful capacity to engage with and disengage from a variety of scenes and verbal exchanges. He can come and go as necessary to present events in a way congruent with the comic tone set by the author.[12]

Consider, as a case in point, the scene in which he first has active contact with adults. The boy hears grown-ups arguing but only partially incorporates their words into his own thinking. The child in effect filters out the harsher aspects of their discussion, and so the naiveté of his perspective makes for a sweeter assessment of social upheaval. The exchange is reported immediately following Mottel's introductory romp with the calf, when brother Elye comes to fetch him and announces that their father is lying ill, approaching death.

> The swarthy doctor comes to see him; he's a stout man with black whiskers and laughing eyes—a jolly doctor. He calls me *Belly button* and flips my belly with his finger. Every time he comes he tells mother not to stuff me with potatoes and to give the sick man bouillon and milk, milk and bouillon. Mother listens to him silently and after he leaves hides her face in her apron and her shoulders quiver. Then she dries her eyes, calls my brother Eliahu aside and they whisper secrets. What they talk about, I don't know, but it sounds to me as if they quarrel. Mother keeps urging Eliahu to go somewhere, but he doesn't want to go. He says to her,
>
> "I'd rather sink through the ground than turn to them. I'd rather die this very day."
>
> (5)

Here, as elsewhere in the novel, the reader may appreciate the bitterness of the family's travails through the grown-ups' arguments. The older figures often complain of their straitened circumstances. At the same time the child, through his lack of response, stands in opposition to the adults' grief. As the patriarch agonizes, as the house is dismantled and family possessions are sold off one by one, Mottel's glee increases. His joy does not seem grotesque, thanks to his incomprehensions. In this particular passage, that impression is brought about as the prose runs the gamut of possibilities that Brian McHale has described to classify representations of speech in fiction.[13] The variety of speech acts enables Mottel to emphasize, accentuate, and deaccentuate certain issues. These lines, for instance, include "diegetic summary," that is, the bare report that a speech event has occurred. Mother calls Eliahu aside, "and they whisper secrets." This minimal report deemphasizes or obscures the grim content of what they are saying. There follows a somewhat more specific summary, which comes closer to naming the topic of conversation: "What they talk about I don't know, but it sounds like they quarrel." Indirect content paraphrase, which disregards the style or form of the original utterance, occurs as Mottel reports, "Mother keeps urging Eliahu to go somewhere, but he doesn't want to go."

In varying degrees each of these pronouncements keeps the grownups' concerns secondary, not explicit or foregrounded. This approach subsequently gives way to indirect discourse as the doctor prescribes for the sick man "bouillon and milk, milk and bouillon." The upbeat prescription, the jolly, reassuring words of the physician, more nearly approach citation and so are brought closer to the surface of the text than are the upsetting words between Mother and Eliahu. Similarly, direct discourse clearly set off by quotation marks comes only with a happier exchange: the doctor's cheerful, teasing appellation of the child as *"pupik,"* that is, belly button. The final line of the paragraph, the direct quote from Eliahu, also contributes to lightheartedness as it turns the passage to a satiric, jesting focus. Eliahu makes a buffoon of himself by spouting empty threats; he would prefer to die rather than compromise his pride by asking someone for financial help. In actuality he is in no danger of death, while his father truly is. Already the older brother is taking on the traits of inflated self-importance and pride that make him a laughingstock throughout the book. Altogether, the child's role as observer accomplishes a reversal of figure and ground. In the midst of a crisis comedy becomes more prominent and genuinely scary matters recede into the distance. The grievousness of the family's situation is conveyed to the reader, yet the child essentially remains aloof from their conflicts, mourning, and hardship.

Mottel more actively appropriates adult language through his interpretations of idiomatic phrases. These he often defamiliarizes by taking them in an overly literal way. For example, after Eliahu marries the daughter of a rich man, Mother remarks that her son has fallen into a *"shmaltsgrub,"* a mine of fat. More familiarly, in English, he has hit upon a gold mine. Mottel wonders if his brother has fallen in a mine literally filled with *"schmalts,"* and the ludicrous image that emerges is an appropriate challenge to his mother's self-satisfaction. The baker/father-in-law soon loses his money, and Eliahu, stuck now with a petulant, disagreeable wife, must return to his old poverty. As it turns out, the mine was bankrupt and Mottel, divesting the idiomatic expression of its usual richness, turns out to have forewarned the reader of this eventuality. His misreading savvily suggested that it would be dangerous to put too much stock in the assumptions of the older generation. In comparable fashion, as Mottel muses on his own wedding day he notes, "Mother caresses me and says that a lot of water will flow under the bridge until that day arrives. Meanwhile her eyes grow wet. I don't understand why so much water has to flow until I get married and why one must cry about it" (48; in Yiddish, 38). The metaphorical water, coming to be associated with and dramatized by Mother's tears, is part of the adult speech that the child dismisses. Both represent a sorrowful outlook that he rejects, even as he thwarts the referential force of the phrases Mother proffers. These literalizations, like many other examples from the text, are not merely cute, but form part and parcel of his distancing from adult understandings.[14]

Certainly, Mottel's observations may seem cloyingly sweet or overly contrived. His innocent misappropriations of sayings are often, at best, innocuous and frequently less resonant than, for example, Tevye's misquotations of scripture. That character turns intertextualities to highly ironic commentary on the shtetl life in decline. Nonetheless, it should be noted that Mottel's is a humor that sets him apart from other Sholem Aleichem characters. The success or failure of incomprehension as a narrative strategy in this text must be gauged in relation to the fact that the main character is conceived as a child. Underestimating the seriousness of things seems natural for a child, and so Mottel serves as a pretext that allows the text to embrace a carefree attitude. This point distinguishes this protagonist not only from Tevye but also from Menachem Mendel. The boy's optimism is not immediately invalidated by the satire that Menachem Mendel's antics invite; pranks, misunderstandings, and an inability to become sobered by defeat are acceptable in a very young person where they would not be in an adult, much as Mottel's substituting mooing sounds for liturgy can be read less as a boorish disregard for sanctity than as an invigorating liberation from a deteriorating world of tradition.[15]

In a move that shows Mottel refusing to be drawn into adult frames of meaning, the character also shakes words free from their usual semantic burdens. The narrative often uses the child to call attention to language per se and to question its denotative powers. Take, for instance, the following scene in which the emigrants have arrived in Cracow. Another little boy explains to Mottel that his family left home because of a pogrom:

> I ask him what a pogrom is. All the emigrants keep talking about "pogroms" but I don't know what they are. Koppel says,
>
> "Don't you know what a pogrom is? Then you're just a baby. A pogrom is something that's everywhere nowadays. It starts out of nothing and once it starts it lasts for three days."
>
> I say, "What kind of thing is it? A fair?"
>
> "Some fair! They break windows, they bust up furniture, rip pillows, feathers fly like snow . . . "
>
> "What for?"
>
> "What for? For fun! But pogroms aren't made only on houses. They're made on shops, too. They break them up, throw all the wares out into the street, scatter them about, pour kerosene on them, set fire to them, and they burn . . . "

> "Go on!"
>
> "What, do you think I'm kidding? Next when there's nothing left to break, they go from house to house with axes, irons, and sticks, and the police walk after them. They sing, whistle and yell, 'Hey fellows, let's beat up the Jews!' And they beat and kill and murder."
>
> "Who?"
>
> "What do you mean, who? the Jews."
>
> "What for?"
>
> "What a question! It's a pogrom, isn't it?"
>
> "And so it's a pogrom. What's that?"
>
> "Go away, you're a fool. It's like talking to a calf."
>
> (147-48)

The passage juxtaposes naiveté with horror, underscoring the hatefulness of the anti-Semitic violence. (In this, as David Roskies has pointed out, *Mottel* exemplifies a stance that might be designated as a child's chronicle of destruction; allowing for play between innocence and awareness, Sholem Aleichem provided a narrative model for other writers, importantly Itzik Kipnis in his tale "Of Months and Days," 1926.)[16] The grim humor, however, also defuses pathos and even makes for a conundrum or riddle game that mocks referentiality. That is, not having experienced a pogrom, Mottel does not share Koppel's framework of understanding. Consequently, he reacts with an apparent thick-headedness that unsettles the usual frightful connotations of the word "pogrom." The other boy cannot define it, because none of Koppel's talk makes sense to Mottel. The child's incomprehension signals the incomprehensibility of the disaster, and the entire conversation thereby remarks on the senselessness of pogroms. Sholem Aleichem does not make light of suffering, but he does cast the whole issue in a less lugubrious light as the child's pliant optimism refuses to come to terms with bereavement. The text insists on the primacy of an imagination that cannot be co-opted into the values of a brutal world. Significantly, Koppel calls Mottel a calf, reinscribing in the text that same image of innocence with which the novel opened. Here, that designation has taken on insulting intentions from Koppel's perspective, but for the reader the word can only be apprehended in association with the context of the earlier scene. It acquires the redemptive, creative connotations of a rejuvenating new language and a new vision.

It should be remembered that the entire chapter in which this scene appears, **"Mit die emigranten,"** was omitted from some editions of *Mottel*—notably, those versions aimed at young audiences. Sholem Aleichem felt that the attention to pogroms was too grotesque and too weighty a matter to fit in with the overall tone of Mottel's frivolity.[17] This decision may serve as a measure of the dialogic quality afforded by the passage just cited. The presence of different voices and mutually unsettling outlooks made the text richer as an adult literary work but inappropriate for children's reading. Accordingly, it gave way to a more homogenized, less multivoiced prose. In lieu of the conversation with Koppel, the author later retained only Mottel's assertion, in a different chapter, that whenever he hears the word "pogrom" he runs away. As the protagonist explains, he prefers stories (*"mayses"*) to talk of calamity. Evading the issue of anti-Semitism, his narrative is transformed into a more uniform prose that deletes contrapuntal combinations of voices and thereby regains its composure and confidence at the price of complexity and layeredness.

Chapter 13, **"We Steal across the Border,"** merits close reading as it introduces in microcosm the intersections of voice and the recontextualizations that inform the text as a whole. Here, once again, the plot revolves about adult speech as it penetrates into the consciousness of the child, and once again the narrative emphasizes that the child figure only partly absorbs adult meanings, refusing to endorse them fully. As Mottel challenges the usual semantic force of particular words, he puts into relief the whole problem of context and referentiality, drawing attention to language per se.

The chapter opens as the family has just left home on their way to America. In the first line Mottel notes that riding on a train is heavenly, a *"gan eydn"* (Garden of Eden). This comment, recalling earlier shifting definitions of that phrase, immediately introduces into the chapter an attention to reinterpretation and reaccentuations of words. According to Mother, Father is in heaven—that is, dead; according to Mottel's uncle, *"gan eydn"* is a steambath. Mottel himself reassigns meaning to the phrase by using it to refer to his own pastime, filching apples from the neighbor's garden. The paradisiacal locomotive in chapter 13 is an extension of this last meaning. Undermining the sacred connotations of *"gan eydn,"* Mottel gaily welcomes novel experience as the Old World crumbles. By the same token, much as at the beginning he expressed his joy by singing a song without words, on the train Mottel finds himself so filled with wonder as to be speechless. He is wedged tightly into an overcrowded railroad car, but remarks,

> And me, don't you worry about me. I'm all right. I'm fine. I'm almost flattened out, but I'm standing near a window. What I see I'm sure you never have. Past me there fly houses, mileposts, streets, people, woods, fields . . . indescribable! How the train speeds! How it rumbles, squeaks, groans, whistles, squeals . . .
>
> (117)

Ordinary expression is simply not commensurate with the unfamiliar marvels the boy experiences (the world is indescribable, *"nit tsu bashraybn"*), and the onomatopoeia indicating the noise of the wheels (*"fayft," "trasket," "kvitshet"*) recalls the opening "meeeeh" of Menie's lowing. Like that animal sound, exceeding the old vocabulary, these sounds better convey the little boy's gladness.

Mottel's challenge to conventional language is made more explicit when the family arrives at the border. The grown-ups have begun to speak frequently about the frontier as a forbidding hurdle to overcome, and they trade stories with their fellow travelers about border crossings. The child asserts, "I thought a 'frontier' was something with horns" (120; *"Di grenets hob ich gemeynt iz mit herner,"* 99). His literalizing, as it comically personifies the border, making it seem strange, prefaces a more thorough undoing of assumptions. Providing a series of circumstances that alter the impact and implications of the word *"ganvenen"* (to steal), the text puts into question the values of the old social order. First, Mother warns her child not to wander about the market in the border town, for fear someone may kidnap him. Next, the agent they engage to assist them, a piously dressed woman, ends up fleecing them of their possessions and reneging on her promise to lead them across the border. Once on their way, they fall into the clutches of robbers who hold them at knifepoint. These varieties of thievery prove that appearances and traditional criteria for judging goodness, such as wearing a wig and praying, are not trustworthy or reliable measures of virtue.

These same events also raise questions about whether or not the immigrants themselves are engaged in transgression. In this connection Mottel brings the semiotic issue, the question of instability in meaning, clearly to the fore: "I don't understand what stealing the border means. Are we thieves then?" (120; *"Ikh farshtey nisht, vos heyst dos ganvenen di grenets. Mir zenen den ganovim?"* 99). Naturally, the author directs the reader toward sympathy with the family's illegal border crossing. The word *"ganvenen"* in this context is divested of its negative connotations. This turn of events stands in direct contrast to an earlier episode in which thievery was presented as anathema. In that episode, to Mother's horror, Eliahu angrily called Mottel a thief. The younger boy had eaten a roll, uninvited, at the father-in-law's bakery, and the mother at that time defended Mottel indignantly. She excused his behavior on the grounds that he was an orphan, and she insisted haughtily on the honesty and respectability of the family. By chapter 13 the valuations placed on the notion of stealing have been altered to resemble Mottel's association of *"gan eydn"* with filching apples. Illegality here is cast as mischief, relegated to the category of a carnivalesque renunciation of propriety, which turns ordinary rules topsy-turvy.[18]

Attention to the whole issue of transgression elsewhere in the chapter invests these variations on *"ganvenen"* with increased polyvalence. On the way to the train station, for instance, the family had hired a wagon whose surly driver Mottel described as a *"gazlen."* Literally meaning "like a bandit," *gazlen* here signifies that this man had a murderous temper. Playing further on the same set of nuances and the opposition of honesty and vice, the driver is presented as a virtuous man who suffers only one fault, *"eyn aveyre"* (literally a sin or transgression). He leaves the family without delivering their beggage at the proper place, and a rowdy brawl ensues. These reevaluations and colorations of the notion of transgression reinforce uncertainty about degrees of right and wrong. The driver's ill temper, which is cast in rather severe terms, does not compare to the genuine evil of the robbery later encountered. At the same time, the act construed as a small fault leads to considerable upheaval. It is against this background of definitional turmoil that Mottel asks, *"vos heyst dos ganvenen di grenets?"*

Significantly, in this quandary Mottel feels no one has an answer to his question. No one can fill him in due to the instability of his world. Patriarchal authority has broken down, and he cannot ask the women, for, the boy concludes, "what do women know?" (98). Brother Elye, for his part, cannot be consulted, since he assumes pretentious airs of authority and insists that children should not interfere with grown-ups' discussions. Elye, furthermore, is not merely inaccessible. He has also disqualified himself as a paternal figure through his misadventures at earning a living: flooding the world with ink, selling adulterated *kvass,* and starting a plague of sneezes. Therefore, for all his pomposity, he has proven himself hilariously inept at taking over Father's functions as breadwinner and head of the family. Pinney, likewise, despite his posturing as a worldly-wise adventurer, is also fundamentally ignorant about the reality of travel and of America. Together with the rest of them he faces a highly uncertain future.

The impression of defenselessness in these characters is subsequently reinforced as the group finally crosses the frontier. Shots ring out, the robbers flee, and Mother shouts, "Run, children!" To be sure, she is the matriarch, a generation older than her companions, and so has the right to call them children. Her use of the word *"kinder,"* however, also underscores that the whole group, like Mottel, finds itself in a crisis without leaders and without the support of stable custom. Mottel's incomprehensions, then (here, most prominently, his attempt to figure out whether or not the

family has turned into thieves), become an emblem of the adults' own unknowing and naiveté. All are taking on a new world, and the child narrative persona serves as a synecdoche of their unpreparedness. He is the narrative agent for pointing out a vulnerability his elders are sometimes loath to admit.

Mottel's function as the outsider who records others' words also takes on heightened importance in this connection. Consider, for example, the scene at the border, where the agent, Chaimova, gives the travelers elaborate instructions on how to escape. Sholem Aleichem has Mottel quote her at great length, repeating her directions verbatim:

> When it's midnight, she says, we should go out behind the city. There, she says, there's a hill. She says we should go past the hill and turn left.
>
> (121)

This pattern of narration continues, and the phrase *"zogt zi"* recurs ten times in the space of one paragraph.[19] Reiterated over and over, it demonstrates insistently that Chaimova's words stand in woeful contrast to actuality. No one, finally, waits for the family at the inn, no one guides them to safety, and, again contrary to the account given to them by the agent, their goods are never returned to them. Reported by Mottel, a figure consistently oriented less to referential objects than to someone else's speech, this passage makes clear that the whole family is not only attentive to, but entirely dependent on, the words of others. They rely on the agent's good will, much as they also hang on the stories they have heard about America: about streets paved with gold and all the rest of the myth of an easy life. They do not have the experience necessary to judge the veracity of this discourse vital to their own survival. Such decisive imbalance in their relation to words and referential reliability leaves ample room for deception or for gaps between dreams and their realization. Later, by noting that initially things worked out just as Chaimova had foretold (*"azoy vi di yidine hot nevies* [prophecies] *gezogt"*), Mottel underscores the family's gullibility. To be sure, there is a hill behind the city, and after that there are woods and an inn as Chaimova had predicted. The crucial fact that no one awaits them there, however, becomes all the more distressing because the party had believed so strongly at first in a false prophet. This treatment of unrealistic expectations takes on added resonance in the context of the author's personal life. The *Mottel* narratives were begun shortly after Sholem Aleichem returned to Europe from New York. The pogroms of 1905 had convinced him to seek a better future in America, but, once there, he met with significant financial and professional disappointments.[20] The child character, Mottel, introduces humorous treatment of emigrants' hopes and dreams, and, as a personification of optimism, reflects the author's own hopefulness. At the same time, reflecting Sholem Aleichem's own difficulties, his chronicle also admits serious undertones and cognizance of the uncertainties faced by families fleeing the Old World.

Altogether, thanks to the superimposition of a child's voice and an adult perspective in chapter 13, the reader receives vacillating impressions of the fictional world. If, as Mottel first suspected, the border is not something that has horns, still, it did prove most dangerous. His interpretation therefore unsettles that of the grown-ups; he makes the whole episode out to be something of a lark. Subsequently, his view is also unsettled, this time by the menacing appearance of the thieves and the rifle shots. The result is a double-edged irony. The co-presence of tragedy and comedy is readily expressed and even fomented by the necessarily dual, mature/immature stance inherent in the use of the child focalizer. In short, Mottel's monologue serves propitiously as a locus of dialogue as conceived by Bakhtin.[21]

Related inversions of expectations and the upsetting of preconceptions continue once the family arrives on the other side of the border. They discover that they are safe, because they happen upon a Jew leading a goat by a rope. Costumed somewhat differently than they, speaking Yiddish with a slightly unfamiliar pronunciation, this man is nonetheless clearly one of their own and not a threat. When they ask after their whereabouts, he informs them they are nowhere near the frontier. This means that the border with its imagined horns is behind them and the goat, presumably with real horns, is not scary at all. Appropriately, after this reversal of danger, the small band of travelers bursts into *"moyredike gelekhter."* Their terror has turned to laughter, and the very word *"moyre"* (fear), which appeared a number of times earlier in the chapter (96, 97), has been drained of its threatening force. Here it indicates not terror, but rather an outcome of events that is *terribly* funny. Once again context has transformed the accentuations of the word.

The transitions of this fictional world, constantly yielding new frames of reference and new understandings, also involve the crossing of different social strata and so give rise to a host of additional dialogic encounters. Travel increasingly confronts the provincial group with different kinds of speech. Within chapter 13, for instance, the family is presented for the first time as coming in extended contact with non-Jews. (Later they pass through Cracow, Vienna, Amsterdam, and London, among other places, en route to America, and meet up with all sorts of people.) The new situations, as they arise, call attention to a variety of ethnic or na-

tional clashes and to the multilingual milieu in which the narrated events take place. Accordingly, various techniques of representing alien words begin to surface in the prose of the text. For example, in **"We Steal across the Border,"** an exchange with a non-Jewish porter at the train station is presented both in transliterated Russian and in Yiddish (115). This incident illustrates direct citation of foreign language.[22] By contrast, in the following passage a kind of intermittent quotation serves as a mimetic synecdoche of Pinney's utterances. Mottel remarks,

> With the stationmaster Pinney uses an altogether different vocabulary. He doesn't use such strong expressions, but he does gesticulate a lot. He uses strange words which I've never heard before: "Columbus . . . Civilization . . . Alexander von Humboldt . . . Slonimsky . . . Mathematics . . .
>
> (117)

The conversation is recorded only in bits and pieces, for the child does not understand the Germanized Yiddish nor the abstractions Pinney invokes. The use of the child to convey overheard conversation makes this kind of procedure in representing speech seem persuasively natural and appropriate. The technique has the advantage of maintaining an element of quotational fidelity while also remaining concise. Here, recreating in very abbreviated form Pinney's attempt to regale the stationmaster with a massive shower of words, the prose suggests both his comically grandiose, idealistic notions about what it means to be an immigrant and his underestimation of the power of authority. The family and their friends want to keep all their baggage with them, but Pinney's effort on their behalf is to no practical avail; the stationmaster is unconvinced, and the passengers have to relinquish their precious bedding. In the final scenes of the chapter the text invokes another alien voice, this time through discussion in one language about another.[23] Calling attention to the oddity and newness of their surroundings, Mottel comments on the difference between his own Yiddish and the Yiddish of the man on the other side of the border, which is the same but full of broad a's, *"mit pasakhn"* (102).

Illustrative of Bakhtin's contention that language is dynamic and plural, the presentation of variegated speech communities in this chapter also combines with emphasis on distinctions of social class to show how the emigrants, in a world of flux, must deal with shifting meanings. Two incidents demonstrate how different groups color the connotations of particular words. First, when the guard at the station says to the family that they are carrying too much, he warns that they will not be allowed on the train with so many rags. In parenthesis, indicating a shift in context and expectations, Mottel expresses shock at this man's disrespect for their possessions.

He means, apparently, the quilts. A little bit tattered and that already for him means rags!

(117)

Once more, there appears the phrase *"heyst dos,"* commented on already in connection with Mottel's queries about crossing the border. This indicator of reaccentuation is mentioned frequently throughout the remaining portions of **Mottel**. Repeatdly signaling differences of views about a single event, *dos heyst* comes to function virtually as a refrain of redefinition.[24]

A subsequent incident alerts the reader to heteroglossia, that is, the collision of conflicting social forces within a specific word, and so further documents the upheavals of this world in motion. Once inside the railroad car the family is scattered, for all the seats have already been taken. Mother, afraid that her son might fall out a window, calls to him, "Mottel, Mottel" (99). A non-Jew, mimicking her to the merriment of the Christian crowd, repeats, "Mottel, Mottel" (*"Un epes eyner a poritsl mit bloye briln krimt ir iber un zogt ir nokh mitn eygenen nign, motl? motl? ale kristn lakhn,"* 99). The interethnic tensions present in the car convey themselves here neatly in the repetition of a single word that, changing in context, changes in implications. Overladen with the intentions of others, the boy's name turns from an expression of motherly concern to antagonistic mockery. Mottel himself, of course, as narrator, has the power to reinscribe that discourse within his own and so to redefine the attack not as power but as cruelty, less as superior self-confidence than as inferior hatefulness. He accomplishes this reversal by calling the Gentile a *"poritsl"*; the diminutive of the word for lord or wealthy man implies that this character, in the third-class compartment, has put on airs and deluded himself with a laughable self-importance. In this way the speakers modify one another's statements, but Mottel's perspective retains a certain privilege and claim on the reader's sympathy. To the extent that the child is a naive recorder of speech acts and does not dominate or reinterpret the words he hears, the prose does admit several refractions of one character's words in those of another. At the same time, at stake here is not fiction that radically decenters authorial point of view by exalting the thought and opinions of a spectrum of characters. Sholem Aleichem both creates multiple voices and also firmly controls his focalization, combining conflicting aspirations well within the bounds of a single consciousness, which he constructs as a child narrator.

All these passages that feature the appropriation of one individual's language by another are, aptly enough, associated in chapter 13 with the particle *iber*. It appears repeatedly in this section of narrative where

the action revolves about varieties of transformation, passages to a new life, reinterpretations of the world, and contact with new views and new modes of speaking. Transport, transfer, transitions, translations, and transactions between varied social groups are pervasive concerns here. *Iber* captures the shifting of circumstance and of social stances at play. Mottel, for example, announces he will first give Eliahu's dialogue with the guard in Russian (*"ibergebn"*), and then that he will translate (*"ibersetsn"*) into Yiddish. The family tries to win a porter over to their side (*"iberbetn"*) as he passes the baggage over to its proper place (*"ibertrogn"*). In the train the family must traverse social and spatial distances in order to talk (they are scattered *"ibern gantsn vagon"*), and this sparks the mimicry of the *poritsl* (*"iberkrimn"*) that also traverses difference. Altogether, in stealing across the border, the family continually puts into relief the borders of their own discourse as it comes in contact with others. Showing the multiple stratifications of their language milieu, this chapter also shows how they have come to challenge the parameters of their own past life, at times making old, accepted definitions more fluid or more susceptible to reformulation or rejoinder.

As an uncomprehending outsider who playfully disregards society's rules, Mottel to some extent resembles that classic novelesque figure, the picaroon. Like the picaresque novel, Sholem Aleichem's narrative concerns ingenious struggles for livelihood and getting by in a world without a center. Thematically, Mottel most resembles the prototypical Lazarillo in his service to different masters: an apprenticeship to a mean-spirited cantor with a crippled daughter, a stay with a madman named Luria, his assistance in brother Elye's ill-conceived plans to get rich quick. More essentially, for discussion of the dialogic imagination in fiction, the status of the child as someone on the margins of adult activity recalls the marginality of the picaroon (who also often starts out on adventures at an early age, and whose naiveté or incomprehension helps him cast social convention in an unfamiliar light). Mottel fulfills comparable functions of undermining established values and ways of speaking. By quoting adult words and transforming them into his own, the boy allows for a highly ironic view of the foibles and moral unsoundness in his society. (Chaimova's deceptions and Pinney's impracticality are but two examples.) It should be noted, however, that the childhood angle of this narrative allows a more affectionate, less bitter satire of society than is characteristic of the picaresque novel proper. All incidents are cast finally in a light-hearted mold.

This phenomenon may be explained in accord with Ruth Wisse's assessment of Sholem Aleichem and his reaction to a discredited Haskalah. The Yiddish and Hebrew writers of the Enlightenment leveled severe criticism at Jewish society and urged self-improvement and measures of assimilation in order for the Jews to be accepted into European society. Such acceptance, of course, turned out not to be forthcoming. Sholem Aleichem, aware of Jewish shortcomings but even more aware of anti-Semitism and the hardships imposed on the Jews by others, was disinclined to view his own people too harshly. For these reasons, Wisse concludes, the only fictional characters in his work who successfully challenge tradition are children:

> The boy who would rather play with a calf than sit in the house of study, or the boy who would rather play the fiddle than adjust to the machinery of shtetl stratification, are the sole vehicles through whom the evils of shtetl life may safely be criticized. And only because they stand against all and any society, because they are more "unrealistic" than even their elders, and better still at denying the tyrannical crucible in which their tortured destiny is being forged.[25]

Mottel is just such a figure who, in rebellion against social strictures, does not abandon his community. He turns first to nature and then, in defiance of previous norms, to art (pledging to become a cartoonist). His innocence, though, takes the criminal edge off his own roguishness and mischief, even as it takes the harsh satirical bite off his portrayal of problems around him. In short, the dialogic capacities of the narrative persona in *Mottel* are used less to berate Jewish society than to register changes and uncertainties at a time of flux and mass emigrations.

Mottel does adhere to the model of the picaroon in a further way. The picaroon's recasting of the world generally entails no internal agony of consciousness, and this point distinguishes the picaresque from the Bildungsroman as a genre. Appearing as "a fixed personality who never substantially alters during the course of his varied experiences," the picaroon learns but does not change.[26] That is to say, the protagonist wises up, figures out how to play the game and to survive as a self uprooted and alone, but does not develop into a figure of complex psychological interiority. At issue is not discovery of self but thirst for experience and variety. Delighting in his adventures, such a character provides a panoramic view of changing circumstance. This lack of inwardness parallels or coincides with that of Mottel, who, more than a believable child, is a "typological amalgam" of childishness and maturity that serves the author's rhetorical purposes.[27] Certainly, he is distant even from the psychological depth explored in others of Sholem Aleichem's tales about children, such as **"The Penknife"** and **"The Fiddle."** Mottel, in his mischievousness, is detached from stable collective definitions of propriety

and, refusing to be defined by the existing social system, is a figure who defines himself. His uncertain status, like that of the picaresque hero, makes him a suitable symbol for freedom from community. Associated with the artist and with individual expression, he is an ideal embodiment of the impulse to break loose from the old order. All the same, the deemphasis on depth and interiority in his characterization suggests that he is, finally, a narrative construct that gauges changing collective values, not a complex individual in his own right. Above all he consists of an intersection of discourses, and he resists being swallowed up in any one of them.

It seems only appropriate that in this narrative the artifice of imagined child language and the imagining of the child's imagination serve to depict transformations of communal circumstance more than to explore the inner dimensions of childhood. In Sholem Aleichem's text the orphan cut adrift from his father's past is not alone. The whole family and their entourage are part of a *"faryosemt"* folk, collectively orphaned in feeling cut off from the past and beset with a new beginning.[28] The novelty of the child's perspective reinforces this point clearly, as it shows adult assumptions to be unstable. Not only does Mottel confuse destruction and recovery, as Miron has argued. This narrative also dismantles the very opposition child/adult which in the traditional world decisively subordinated youngsters to their elders. Demonstrating the flux of changing circumstance and the breakdown of previous meanings, *Mottel* shows adults are childlike in their unpreparedness and vulnerability, even as childish resilience and disregard for tragedy come to signify an all-important vitality.

If, as has been argued,[29] the virtue of powerlessness, the sanctity of the insulted and the injured, constitutes the great theme of Yiddish literature, Mottel in his innocence represents a cheerful variation on the figure of the little man, long-suffering and antiheroic but able to bear up thanks to his own redeeming perceptions of the world. Moving beyond the earlier established portrayal of the child as little adult in Jewish literature, Mottel functions aptly as an example of *"dos kleyne mentschele."* Sholem Aleichem's creation of a young narrator/protagonist makes only a very partial move toward exploring the consciousness of children in Jewish literature, but it yields an experiment that is at once innovative and an integral part of the wider concerns in this author's *oeuvre,* particularly in its treatment of Jewish accommodation to modernity.

Notes

1. Abramovitch, *Of Bygone Days* [S. Y. Abramovitch (Mendele the Bookseller), *Of Bygone Days*, 1894-1911], 268.

2. Alan Mintz [*Banished from Their Father's Table: Loss of Faith and Hebrew Autobiography* (Bloomington: Indiana University Press, 1989)] comments on the invention of a new language, *"safah aḥeret,"* in Bialik's "Habrekha" ("The Pool") and in M. Z. Feierberg's "Whither"; see "Mordechai Ze'ev Feierberg."

3. For example, Peretz's "Lag B'omer" and Sholem Aleichem's *Yosele Solovey.* S. Niger discusses these matters in his study of Sholem Aleichem, in *Geklibene Shriftn* (New York: Idischer Kultur Farlang, 1928), 77-89.

4. Niger, 88, contrasts the treatment of nature by these two authors.

5. *Motl Peyse dem khazns.* All quotations here are taken from the Yiddishe Buchfarlag edition (Warsaw, 1953). An English translation exists as *Adventures of Mottel the Cantor's Son,* done by Tamara Kahana (New York: H. Schuman, 1953). My quotations draw on this version but significantly modify it at times.

6. For example, Niger insists on Mottel's carefree innocence as it stands in sharp opposition to the woe and travails of his elders. In contrast, Maurice Samuel insists on a consonance between Mottel and his elders; his book, *The World of Sholem Aleichem* (New York: Knopf, 1943), argues that Mottel is a perfect little Kasrilevker, i.e., one who only has to "see the world in the proper way and all is well" (191). Whether or not they see Mottel as an unusually optimistic character or one who is typically so, both see the breakdown of the shtetl as a tragedy. Dan Miron's study of Mottel, discussed below, suggests that the narrative has quite a different emphasis, a celebratory farewell to the old and welcome of the new.

7. Dan Miron, "Bouncing Back: Destruction and Recovery in Sholem Aleykhem's *Motl Peyse dem khazns,"* *YIVO Annual of Jewish Social Science* 17 (1978): 119-84. Miron also provides a review of earlier scholarship (by M. Viner, Y. Y. Trunk, and S. Niger), pointing out that previous criticism failed to address in depth such matters as composition, structuring, and stylistics.

8. Khone Shmeruk documents the evolution of the text through its various versions in "Sippurei Mottl ben haḥazan leShalom Aleikhem: hasituatisiah ha'epit vetoldotav shel hasefer," *Siman Kri'ah* 12/13 (1981): 310-26.

9. See ibid., 314.

10. In "Dekonstruktsiah shel dibur: Shalom Aleikhem vehasemiotika shel hafolklor hayehudi," the afterword to *Tevye hehalban umonologim* (Tel Aviv:

Simon Kri'ah and Hakibbutz Hameuchad, 1983), 195-212, H. Benyamin (Benjamin Hrushovsky) comments on the representation of spoken discourse in Sholem Aleichem's art, which in some ways resembles the fiction of Dostoevsky. Much as that novelist introduces varied voices through ideological harangues, Sholem Aleichem admits multiple speakers through the conversations of his garrulous characters. Both writers are intensely concerned with the transmission and assessment of the speech of others. Consequently, the issue of reported discourse surfaces here as in Dostoevsky's fiction, which stimulated and has been illuminated by one of Bakhtin's major works, *Problems of Dostoevsky's Poetics,* available in English translation by Caryl Emerson (Minneapolis: University of Minnesota Press, 1984). Any number of critics have commented on the talkativeness of Sholem Aleichem's characters. See, e.g. Ruth Wisse, *Sholem Aleichem and the Art of Communication* (Syracuse: Syracuse University Press, 1979). For commentary on the cacophony of voices that Sholem Aleichem creates in reaction to disaster, see Roskies, *Against the Apocalypse* [Harvard University Press, 1984], 163-94.

11. [Mikhail] Bakhtin, *The Dialogic Imagination,* [Austin: University of Texas Press, 1981] 332.

12. Miron, "Bouncing Back," 178. Miron examines the function of the Sholem Aleichem narrator at length in "Sholem Aleykhem: Person, Persona, Presence" (Uriel Weinreich Memorial Lecture 1, New York: YIVO, 1972). Related discussion of Abramovitch's adoption of the Mendele persona is presented in Miron's *A Traveler Disguised: A Study in the Rise of Modern Yiddish Fiction in the Nineteenth Century* (New York: Schocken Books, 1973).

13. [Brian] McHale, "Free Indirect Discourse." [*Poetics and Theory of literature* 3 (1978): 249-87]

14. For discussion of this kind of humor with relation to other double entendres in Sholem Aleichem, see Rhoda S. Kachuk, "Sholom Aleichem's Humor in English Translation," *YIVO Annual of Jewish Social Science* 11 (1956/57): 39-81. My contention is that this sort of humor is not simply meant to raise a smile but is also fully integrated thematically into the chapter.

15. On Mottel as a diminutive but less grotesque Menachem Mendel, see Y. Trunk, *Sholem Aleykhem—zayn vezn un zayne verk* (Warsaw, 1937), 313-71.

16. Roskies, *Against the Apocalypse,* 176, 182-84. Though the narrator in Kipnis's text is twenty-two years old, he exhibits a childlike incredulity. Closer to Mottel's story would be Bialik's "Ha-

ḥatsotsra nitbaysha." See the detailed analysis by Gershon Shaked in *'Al arba'a sippurim: perakim bisodot hasippur* (Jerusalem: Jewish Agency, 1963), 94-121. Mottel's innocent reactions to catastrophe make him a precursor also of child characters in fictional treatment of the Holocaust, such as in Appelfeld's *The Age of Wonders* and Grossman's *See Under: Love.* A narrative more contemporaneous with *Mottel,* and one that focuses more specifically on catastrophes of special impact for children in Eastern Europe, is Yehuda Steinberg's *In Those Days* (*Bayamim hahem,* 1905). This text details a boy's conscription into the Russian army and the pain of his separation from family and Jewish custom. The child's naiveté there is cultivated more for purposes of pathos, as a contrast with brutality, than as a way to defuse pathos.

17. Shmeruk, "Sippurei Mottl," 317.

18. Bakhtin's well-known discussion of language as a subversive, carnivalesque force can be found in *Rabelais and His World* (Bloomington: Indiana University Press, 1984).

19. For more on such verbal exchanges, see Benyamin, "Dekonstruktsiah shel dibur."

20. For a biographical sketch, see Joseph Butwin and Frances Butwin, *Sholem Aleichem* (Boston: G. K. Hall, 1977).

21. This view is compatible with, but extends beyond, Dov Sadan's early observation that Sholem Aleichem's monologues often serve as frames for the typology of a large family. Sadan notes that, often, one individual speaks but focuses attention more on his surrounding milieu than on himself. See "Three Foundations [Sholem Aleichem and the Yiddish Literary Tradition]," trans. David G. Roskies, *Prooftexts* 6 (January 1986): 52-64. (Special issue on Sholem Aleichem, ed. Roskies.) Miron's argument, that *Mottel* does not present genuine monologue, is made on the grounds that the narrator's words are not dramatically situated as authentic child speech in a concrete, believable circumstance. At issue, for my point, is less the verisimilitude of Mottel's utterances than the underlying structural propensity of the text (thanks to the child figure) to admit oscillating perspectives.

22. In "Polylingualism as Reality," Meir Sternberg [*Poetics Today* 2, no. 4 (1981): 221-39] labels this technique "selective reproduction," as opposed to "vehicular matching," which cites a foreign language at length.

23. Sternberg calls this technique "explicit attribution."

24. Functioning similarly to relativize signification is the phrase "*er meynt*" or "*dos meynt*"; for instance, on pages 121, 122, 127.

25. Ruth Wisse, *The Schlemiel as Modern Hero* (Chicago: University of Chicago Press, 1971), 43. Art and nature as positive, shaping forces of the imagination are discussed by David Roskies in connection with *Mottel,* Sholem Aleichem's autobiographical *Funem Yorid* (*From the Fair*), and Mendele's *Shloyme reb khayims* (*Of Bygone Days*) in an essay called "Unfinished Business: Sholom Aleichem's *From the Fair*," *Prooftexts* 6 (January 1986): 65-78.

26. Robert Alter, *Rogue's Progress: Studies in the Picaresque Novel* (Cambridge, Mass.: Harvard University Press, 1961).

27. Miron, "Bouncing Back," 148.

28. Butwin and Butwin (*Sholem Aleichem*) discuss the role of orphanhood in connection with the Bildungsroman tradition and Sholem Aleichem's writing.

29. Irving Howe and Eliezer Greenberg, "Introduction" to *A Treasury of Yiddish Stories* (New York: Viking Press, 1974), 1-71.

Aviva Weintraub (essay date March 1993)

SOURCE: Weintraub, Aviva. "Talking Cure/Talking Curse: Death and the Storyteller in Sholem Aleichem's 'Dos tepl.'" *Journal of Evolutionary Psychology* 14, nos. 1-2 (March 1993): 37-40.

[*In this essay, Weintraub finds that what lies underneath the stated motive for the widow's encounter with the rabbi in "Dos tepl" is her frantic fear over her son's impending death.*]

Yente, the monologist in Sholem Aleichem's **"Dos tepl" ("The Pot")**[1] approaches her rabbi with a technical religious question concerning a pot: she is afraid it may no longer be kosher. It soon becomes clear, however, that Yente is not about to state the problem succinctly and wait for the rabbi to make his ruling. When Yente launches into her monologue, the result is not merely the story of a pot embellished with infinite circumlocutory elaborations, and in fact the details about the pot itself are saved for near the end. These seeming digressions themselves form another complete story. And the subject of this second, emergent monologue is—death.

Death assumes two forms in the monologue. The first concerns actual, past deaths. Names of deceased persons and the circumstances of their death punctuate the monologue at frequent intervals. The most important of these is the death of Yente's husband Moishe Ben Zion. Within the very first paragraph we learn that Yente is a widow: "Of course, if my husband (may he rest in peace) was with me now, in the flesh . . . " (71). In the second paragraph we learn the circumstances of his death, that he died young and had a chronic cough.

From Moishe's cough Yente travels verbally through doctors, garlic, and toothaches to yet another death, that of Yockel's (a fellow townsman) sister Pearl. This death is mentioned in passing to refer to Yockel himself who was spared from death. Still the opportunity is not missed to elaborate on Pearl's death: "Poor thing, her luck left her . . . in childbirth . . ." (72).

The second form that death takes in this monologue is in the likely imminent death of Dovidel,[2] Yente's only son. The possibility of this death, while almost never spoken of directly, suffuses all of Yente's words and pervades the mood of her entire speech.

Once the reader establishes the obvious connection between the son's illness and the father's same illness and early death, it becomes clear that it is Dovidel's impending death that is the true subject of Yente's tirade.

Indeed Yente herself touches upon the disturbing similarity between father and son:

> You should see him, my Dovidel (may he live a long life)—the image of his father, exactly Moishe Ben Zion, even the same height. And that face! Just like *his* (may he rest in peace)—yellowish, exhausted, skin-and-bones, and *weak* weak and worn out, poor thing . . .
>
> (75)

But before she lets herself verbalize her immediate fear for her son's life, Yente digresses and describes a commonplace conversation between Dovidel and herself. Just at the moment of supreme tension, when an outright connection between the two deaths seems about to surface, the monologue veers off in another related, but less threatening direction.

The thought of Yente's husband's death and the idea of her son's approaching death seem to engage in a ghastly dance, taunting, teasing, threatening to embrace. The closest these ideas come to being united is when Yente says, "And meanwhile I can't keep my eyes off him, Dovidel, I mean. Just like *him* (may he rest in peace). Even the cough's the same, woe is me" (75). The connection having been expressed, the dancers retreat and the stream of Yente's speech turns from Dovidel's impending death to how hard Yente has had to work to keep her son alive and how she has saved him from a variety of diseases.

Yente reveals herself as someone who is on intimate terms with death. She saw her husband succumb and she tries to protect her son from death, even as it breathes over her shoulder. As a monologist, she incorporates death into the narrative and lets it suffuse her speech.[3] In this sense, Yente fulfills an important criterion for Walter Benjamin's concept of a storyteller. Benjamin writes, "Death is the sanction of everything that the storyteller can tell. He has borrowed his authority from death."[4]

Yente's storytelling authority comes from her various encounters with death, firstly the death of her husband. She criticizes townsman Yosi Moishe Avram's for falling apart when his wife dies, clearly seeing herself as an example in opposition: " . . . he just let go and gave up, body and soul. 'Reb Yosi,' I said to him, 'God help you! All right, your wife died. What's there to do? That's God's business. The Lord gives and the Lord takes away . . . '" (75). This statement also places Yente on rather intimate terms with the death process as an act of God.

Yente carries this relation a step further when she asserts that she saved her son's life when he was "scared to death" by a man in a white fur coat (76): "I made deals with all the angels! I bargained for him a hundred time over, and pulled him back out of the jaws of death!" (76). She pleaded with God that he might punish her in any way but not take away her son.

Interestingly, Yente comments on Dovidel's near brush with death by saying, "How I survived is a miracle from Heaven" (76). This statement does more than indicate that Yente's emotional survival is contingent upon her son's physical survival: it also illustrates how Yente herself encounters and battles with death through her son's illness, and how she in turn uses this relationship with death to sanction her story.

Part of Yente's attempt at her intervention on her son's behalf involves her giving him another name, Khaim, which means life. While this was a usual custom in time of grave illness,[5] Yente's choice of the name-changing strategy attests to her belief, on some level, in the power and efficacy of words. Perhaps the most intriguing quality of *her* words in the way they reveal so much about her and her desperate concern for her son's life without actually addressing the subject directly ("in so many words").

Yente's seeming avoidance of direct reference to her son's impending death may seem like a lack of acknowledgement on her part. However, her manner of speaking or recounting reveals a reluctance to concretize her worst fears in words. She relates that when the doctor asked her how old her husband was when he died and of what he died, she replied, "He died of death. His years ran out, see, and he died. What kind of comparison is that to this?" (77). Yet we know that Yente does not really believe that her husband's years ran out: she has already declared that he "died young." It is reasonable to assume that Yente has already made the appropriate connections in her mind and does not want to be forced into assimilating them further by hearing the doctor speak the words.

At the time Yente stands before the rabbi, she has not only acknowledged her son's illness and its resemblance to her late husband's but she has also recognized the utter hopelessness of the situation. So complete is her realization and understanding of the situation that she does not even bother asking the rabbi for a blessing for her son. Realizing that that would be futile, she tries instead to buy time, if only for herself and her grasp on sanity, simply by talking. What she says to the rabbi is, at this point, not of primary importance: she is Scheherezada trying to prolong life by maintaining (in this case) an assaultive and unrelenting stream of words.

Yente is, however, at a total impasse, and she is frighteningly aware of it. Even in the case of the pot, which she probably knows to be unacceptable according to Jewish dietary laws, she still goes to the rabbi, knowing that it is a lost cause. By spinning a web of words, Yente prevents the rabbi from giving her the negative answer she does not want to hear.

And her impact upon the rabbi is such that he feels Yente's on position in extremis so strongly that he takes ill and comes to the verge of fainting. The rabbi, inundated with words and suffocated by the impossibility of Yente's situation, experiences the same feelings of "no exit" that Yente does, and takes his "exit" by physically blacking out.

Notes

1. Sholem Aleichem, "The Pot," trans. Sacvan Bercovitch, in *The Best of Sholom Aleichem,* ed. Irving Howe and Ruth R. Wisse (Washington, D.C.: New Republic Books: Philadelphia: Jewish Publication Society of America, 1979), 71-81.

2. Dovidel is the diminutive form for the name Dovid (David) in Yiddish.

3. Compare Walter Benjamin's comment on the presence of death in Johann Peter Hebel's "Unexpected Reunion": "Death appears in it with the same regularity as the Reaper does in the processions that pass around the cathedral clock at noon" (Walter Benjamin, "The Storyteller," in *Illuminations,* Hannah Arendt, ed., New York: Schocken Books, 1969, p. 95).

4. Benjamin, "The Storyteller," p. 94.

5. According to Joshua Trachtenberg, the Talmud (book of Jewish tradition) lists change of name as a healing device: "Moses of Coucy plainly explained that the one who changes his name as much as declares to the angel looking for him, 'I am not the person you are seeking.'" (Trachtenberg, *Jewish Magic and Superstition: A Study in Folk Religion,* New York: Atheneum, 1987). Indeed, in some Jewish communities, this custom is still practiced.

Emanuel S. Goldsmith (essay date 1993)

SOURCE: Goldsmith, Emanuel S. "Sholom Aleichem's Humor of Affirmation and Survival." In *Semites and Stereotypes: Characteristics of Jewish Humor,* edited by Avner Ziv and Anat Zajdman, pp. 13-27. Westport, Conn.: Greenwood Press, 1993.

[*In the essay below, Goldsmith locates the source for Aleichem's humor in such human qualities as optimism, compassion, kindness, religious faith, and playfulness, and discusses the enormous impact his humor had on Jewish readers.*]

The humor of Sholom Aleichem (1859-1916) is a unique phenomenon in the history of Jewish culture and a surprising mutation in the evolution of the Jewish spirit. When one takes into account that for many centuries nonreligious literature was viewed as alien by Jews and especially by Ashkenazi Jewry (92 percent of world Jewry in 1939) and that the reading of such literature was considered a sin (*bittul Torah*), his achievement becomes even more remarkable. While scattered examples of wit and humor may be found in the Bible, the Talmud, the Midrash, and medieval Hebrew writings, the higher reaches of humor are almost completely absent from Jewish literature before Sholom Aleichem's appearance. Still, his work too must be viewed within the context of the evolution of Judaism and the history of the Jewish people. Biblical monotheism discovered God's presence in history and the purpose of human life in ethical behavior. It held the immorality and meaninglessness of human life in paganism up to ridicule and created a context of optimism which fostered confidence and hope.

In the middle of the eighteenth century, two revolutionary movements in Jewish thought prepared the ground for the flowering of Jewish humor a century later. Hasidism or Jewish Pietism, in fostering joy as the proper mood for religious life and worship, criticized the strictness and rigidity of traditional Jewish religion. It viewed the religious leadership and accepted standards of piety with contempt. It could not help but make fun of conventional religious standards and values. The Haskalah or Jewish Enlightenment movement, on the other hand, held both the Hasidim and their opponents up to rational scrutiny and found them wanting. Haskalah gave birth to a relatively large body of satirical writing in Hebrew and Yiddish that sought to wean Jews away from the excesses of religious tradition and the narrowness of isolation and exclusivism.

Sholom Aleichem's appearance on the stage of Jewish history is best understood in terms of particular trends in the Jewish Enlightenment movement as well as general developments in Russian political and intellectual life in the second half of the nineteenth century. Eastern European Jewish Haskalah was based on the eighteenth-century German-Jewish Haskalah of Moses Mendelssohn (1729-1786), which had been influenced by rationalism and Deism. Later, romanticism entered modern Jewish thought and contributed to the emergence of the Science of Judaism (*Wissenschaft des Judentums*) with its historical approach to Jewish studies. What all of this meant was the weakening of the traditional theological rationale for Jewish existence and its replacement with historical and cultural approaches to Jewish survival. Nachman Krochmal (1785-1840) in his philosophical work, *Guide for the Modern Perplexed,* shifted the center of gravity in Jewish thinking from God to the Jewish people, that is, from theology to history. His disciple, the father of the Haskalah movement in Russia, Isaac Baer Levinsohn (1788-1860), proclaimed that "there is no greater sin than that of the man who causes the disappearance of his nation from the world" (Levinsohn, 1901, p. 84). The Hebrew journalist Peretz Smolenskin (1845-1885) popularized these ideas in his essays and novels, underscoring the national significance of the Jewish religion and emphasizing Jewish unity, the Hebrew language, and the hope for national redemption as the basic elements of modern Jewish consciousness. In Russia, the populist approach of the Russian intellectuals, who preached a return to the folk for authenticity and spiritual nourishment, strengthened similar "folkist" and proto-nationalist trends among Jewish intellectuals. Early Jewish socialism and Zionism as well as the Yiddish and Hebrew language and culture movements were founded on these nationalist and social stirrings among the Jewish intellectuals of Eastern Europe (Goldsmith, 1987, p. 259).

The emergence of modern Jewish humor is thus coincident with the proliferation of ideological diversity in Eastern European Jewish society and with the triumph of the Yiddish language as a major written as well as oral medium of Jewish culture. It is inextricably linked to the traditional Jewish way of life with its inter-weaving of poverty, ritualism, intellectualism, and wit, and has been described as the spiritual laughter of a people who laughed in order not to always have to cry. Modern Jewish humor is related to the historical experience of the Jewish people. Its primary characteristic, adumbrated in the Psalms and the Prophets, is the ridicule of idolatry and all man-made gods. Other characteristic elements are the love of Torah and learning generally, the consequent opposition to ignorance, and a deep sense of justice that refuses to recognize differences between rich and poor. The source of a good deal of Jewish humor is the eternal Jewish complaint voiced frequently by Sholom Aleichem's character Tevye: Where is God and where is justice? For the authentic Jew, God, justice, and equality are inseparable (Zeitlin, 1980, p. 178).

The humor of Sholom Aleichem has been characterized as a gracious way to overcome an unpleasant situation in which one finds oneself through no fault of one's own. Without self-respect, purity of the spirit, and wisdom of the heart, no such humor is possible. It soothes the pain of a perplexing or degrading situation with inner spiritual power derived from faith in the dignity of man and in the ultimate victory of justice. Even in the most hopeless of situations, such humor playfully feigns victory in order to emphasize the meaninglessness, evil, and unnaturalness of our predicament. It protests sarcastically and gives oneself and others the courage to endure (Wiener, 1946, p. 287). To students of literature and philosophy, such humor is familiar as positive or divine laughter and as divine comedy or humor.

Sholom Aleichem's humor is the highest expression of divine comedy. "I wasn't worried about God so much," says Tevye. "I could come to terms with Him one way or another. What bothered me was people. Why should people be so cruel when they could be so kind? Why should human beings bring suffering to one another as well as to themselves, when they could all live together in peace and good will?" (Sholom Aleichem, 1949, p. 160). Sholom Aleichem's laughter is philosophical, creative, affirmative, and healthful. It is provoked primarily by the discrepancy and the distance between what is and what ought to be. It helps to rationally and realistically evaluate the world and encourages improvement. It triumphs over pain and hardship in loyalty to an ideal, and brings happiness, truth, and beauty into a dark world. It inculcates love for the Jewish people and its heritage of history, culture, and religion. On the day before Yom Kippur, Sholom Aleichem tells us, we would hardly recognize Noah-Wolf the butcher. "He stops fighting with the other butchers, becomes soft as butter toward his customers, is considerate to the servant girls, becomes so unctuous you could almost spread him over a boil." He puts on his holiday garment, goes from house to house, to all his customers and neighbors, to ask for pardon for the sins he may have committed during the past year. "If anything I have said offended you, I want to apologize, and wish you a happy New Year." "The same to you, Noah-Wolf," they respond. "May God pardon us all" (Sholom Aleichem, 1946, p. 321).

Where Dante's *Divine Comedy* describes Hell, Purgatory, and Paradise, Sholom Aleichem describes God's dwelling in the midst of the Jewish people and participating in the daily tragicomedy of their life. Sholom Aleichem's humor opens a window on the enduring values and traditions of the Jewish people. It possesses broad humanity and profound faith in man's unconquerable spirit. In trying times, it sweetened the bitterness of a difficult existence. During the Holocaust, it brought comfort to the Jews locked in ghettos and annihilation camps.

The primary characters of Sholom Aleichem's three major works—*Tevye the Dairyman, Menahem-Mendl,* and *Motl, Son of Peysi the Cantor*—are variations on the theme of the indefatigable optimism of the Jewish people. Motl's motif is "Hurray for me! I'm an orphan!" Menahem-Mendl refuses to permit his constant failures at earning a livelihood to dissuade him from trying something new. Tevye, like Job of old, refuses to permit adversity to turn him from the path of faith. Unlike Job, however, Tevye is able to transcend tribulation through humor as well as religion. "I say that the main thing is faith," proclaims Tevye. "A Jew must hope. What if we work ourselves to the bone? That's why we're Jews. . . . As you know, I'm a great believer. I never have any complaints against the Almighty. Whatever he does is good. As Scripture says, 'Trust in the Lord'—Put your faith in God and he'll see to it that you lie six feet under, bake bagels and still thank him. . . . I say that we have a great God and a good God but nevertheless, I say, I would like a blessing for every time God does something the likes of which should happen to our enemies" (quoted in Trunk, 1944, p. 31).

Tevye the Dairyman, Menahem-Mendl, and *Motl, Son of Peysi the Cantor* are Sholom Aleichem's masterpieces. Not novels in the formal sense, they are rather cycles of episodes about these three seminal characters. In the first episode of each cycle, the character is already fully developed. Subsequent episodes serve merely to confirm what we already know about Tevye's indefatigable optimism, Menahem-Mendl's daydreaming, and Motl's precocious sense of humor. Each of the three characters is symbolic of one or another aspect of Sholom Aleichem's own personality and experience (tradition-rooted Jewish father, unsuccessful stockbroker, and prototypical *luftmentsh,* eter-

nal child and prankster). Moreover, each character is an archetype (i.e., different from both the traditional hero, who is completely individuated, and the stereotype, who represents a specific group or class of people) (Miron, 1970). Tevye, Menaham-Mendl, and Motl are each representative of the Jewish people as a whole. Each represents, albeit from different angles, the psychology, characteristics, and aspirations of the Jews as Sholom Aleichem saw them. In a sense, these works are his own versions of the biblical books of Job, Ecclesiastes, and the Song of Songs, respectively.

Tevye the Dairyman harks back to the traditions of the medieval Yiddish folktales and the Hasidic legends of the righteous man who is able to transcend his sufferings and whose faith is ultimately vindicated. The various episodes also reflect the particular problems and circumstances of Russian Jewry at the beginning of the twentieth century. Tevye's misinterpretations of biblical and Talmudic quotations are a literary tour de force. They frequently came closer than any literal rendering could to the inner meaning of the texts as they were perceived by *shtetl* Jews.

Menahem-Mendl parodies the popular Yiddish letter-writing guides (*brivnshtelers*) with their stilted vocabularies, openings, and closings. The epistolary technique is especially appropriate to the character of Menaham-Mendl, who on one level symbolizes the Jew who has been overwhelmed by the lures of modern civilization and who completely succumbs to the hustle and bustle, noise, confusion, and rootlessness of urban living. The garrulous monologue, on another level, enhances the elements of tradition-rootedness in *Tevye* and the childish playfulness in *Motl.*

Motl, Son of Peysi the Cantor is an epic of Jewish childhood and a spiritual history of the great transition of Jewish life from Eastern Europe to the United States in the last two decades of the nineteenth century and the first two decades of the twentieth century. It is a hymn to the Jewish people's ability to withstand and overcome whatever obstacles would thwart its survival, growth, and continuing contribution to the human spirit.

Sholom Aleichem's humor is actually the kind of divine gift and stratagem for personal and national survival that may yet save mankind from itself. The kind of laughter Sholom Aleichem evokes—the laughter of acceptance, friendship, sympathy, and contentment—is essential to human dignity and sanity. Laughter is, in fact, a tactic for human survival. Sholom Aleichem's laughter is the kind "born out of the pure joy of living, the spontaneous expression of health and energy—the sweet laughter of the child . . . the warm laughter of the kindly soul which heartens the discouraged, gives health to the sick and comfort to the dying" (Boodin, 1934, p. 212). In the Bible, Abraham is willing to sacrifice the beloved son of his old age in order to demonstrate his faith. In a Sholom Aleichem story, the "happiest man" in Kodno is the poor man who risks his life to save his dying son by throwing himself before the carriage of the physician who may be able to save him. "I would have liked to take a picture of him," writes Sholom Aleichem, "to let the whole world see what a really happy man looked like, the happiest man in Kodno" (1949, p. 77).

Joy, the higher pleasure of comedy, can be obtained only from an author in whom we sense joy's opposite, since "the comic dramatist's starting point is misery; the joy at his destination is a superb and thrilling transcendence" (Bentley, 1964, p. 302). Sholom Aleichem concludes his travelogue of the town of Kasrilevka with a description of its two cemeteries—the old and the new. "The new one is old enough and rich enough in graves. Soon there will be no place to put anyone, especially if a pogrom should break out or any of the other misfortunes which befall us in these times." The Kasrilevkites take special pride in the old cemetery both because famous people are buried in it and because it is "the only piece of land of which they are the masters, the only bit of earth they own where a blade of grass can sprout and a tree can grow and the air is fresh and one can breathe freely" (Sholom Aleichem, 1946, p. 6).

Five years before Sholom Aleichem's death, in a letter of consolation to friends mourning the death of a child, he revealed the deepest secret of his humor. "It's an ugly, evil world," he wrote. "I say to you that just to spite the world one must not cry. If you want to know, this is the true source, the real reason for my usually good mood, for my 'humor,' as they call it. Just to spite the world—don't cry! Just to spite the world—only laugh, only laugh!" (Berkowitz, 1966, p. 168). It took many years of privation, hardship, and artistic struggle for Sholom Aleichem to come to that realization. The little boy who delighted in mimicking his elders and whose first literary work was an alphabetical glossary of his stepmother's curses developed his understanding of the function of laughter and the nature of humor gradually. Slowly he overcame the natural tendency to provoke laughter by telling jokes and pointing out the grotesque and incongruous, and instead explored the healing powers of understanding, acceptance, and compassion. By that time he had become the Columbus of Jewish laughter and the discoverer of the power of the Jewish smile. He became the physician with an effective balm for his people's wounds, the engineer capable of tapping its hidden wellsprings of joy and comfort.

The tremendous adulation that Sholom Aleichem achieved from all segments of Yiddish-speaking Jewry during his lifetime, which continued unabated until the Holocaust, is one of the truly remarkable phenomena in the history of Jewish culture. Once during a reading tour in Warsaw a pious young man ran up to Sholom Aleichem on the street and kissed his hand. Although he belonged to that sector of Jewry for which the reading of secular literature was absolutely forbidden, he could not help saying to Sholom Aleichem: "You are our comfort. You sweeten for us the bitterness of exile" (Berkowitz, 1958, p. 355). Even before the critics took to Sholom Aleichem, he was well known in almost every Jewish home. S. Niger, a literary critic who took many years to warm up to Sholom Aleichem, eventually admitted that no one thing in Jewish life affected the modern Jew in Eastern Europe so much as Sholom Aleichem's stories. Just as pogroms brought to the surface the Jew's repressed fears and tears, so Sholom Aleichem evoked his less profound but equally suppressed laughter (Niger, 1946).

To be properly understood, Sholom Aleichem's popularity must also be viewed in terms of the position he attained relatively early in his career as the "grandchild" of Mendele Mocher Seforim and the colleague and contemporary of Yitzchok Leybush Peretz. These three writers, the founding fathers of Yiddish literature, all of whom died between 1915 and 1917, played a crucial role in the emergence of modern Jewish culture and self-consciousness. They wrote when the great masses of Eastern European Jewry were emerging from their medieval status as a segregated pariah people, leaving their traditional little towns or *shtetls* and becoming part of Western culture. Mendele, Sholom Aleichem, and Peretz belonged to those small circles of *maskilim* or idealistic intellectuals who were at once committed to both the modernization of Jewry and the conscious preservation and furtherance of Jewish distinctiveness and identity. As the east European Jews moved into the large cities of Europe and America, they took with them feelings of inadequacy that stemmed from their lack of familiarity with Gentile languages and culture and from the inferior role that Jews had traditionally been forced to play in Christian mythology. The founding fathers of Yiddish literature urged their people to step proudly into the modern world as heirs of a great culture that had much to contribute to modern civilization. While repudiating Jewish isolationism and cultural backwardness, they pointed with pride to the humanistic impulses of the Jewish tradition and the superiority of Jewish ethical standards. For them the solidarity and spiritual unity of Jewry were inviolate and to be preserved at all costs. These concerns, popularly referred to since the early days of the Hasidic movement as *ahavat Yisrael* or love of the Jewish people, in fact constituted a modern, nontheological version of the doctrine of Jewish chosenness, albeit without overtones of chauvinism or exclusiveness.

As several modern scholars have pointed out, the chosen people idea of Judaism, despite some of the narrow interpretations to which it was subjected over the course of the centuries, originated not in feelings of superiority but as an expression of humility. Whereas some peoples of the ancient world saw themselves as divine or semi-divine beings and others as barbarians, the ancient Israelites intuited the unity of the human race. Israel was not divine or superior; it was only God's chosen people—chosen to bear witness to its God and spread the truth of His existence throughout the earth (Kahler, 1967). Through the ages, this doctrine comforted the beleaguered Jewish people and compensated psychologically for the suffering and malice that were its lot in history. It helped forge the character, conscience, and strong sense of solidarity of the Jewish people.

The maintenance of group identity or we-feeling even as Jews merged with the outside world was consciously fostered by the founding fathers of Yiddish literature even when other, more immediate concerns dominated their writings. Mendele, Sholom Aleichem, and Peretz became culture heroes who actually had a greater impact on the lives of their readers than any of the characters they created in their fiction. Mendele was the wise, knowledgeable Jew rooted in the tradition who was also aware of new winds blowing in the Jewish community. Sholom Aleichem was the happy-go-lucky storyteller who made his readers marvel at the poor but cheerful characters of his tales and take pride in their traditional values and ideals. Peretz was the voice of Jewish humanism and the modern teacher of national ethics and Hasidic idealism.

Sholom Aleichem seems to have rediscovered two insights of the biblical Book of Proverbs: "A joyful heart makes for good health; despondency dries up the bones" (17:22) and "If there is anxiety in a man's mind let him quash it and turn it into joy with a good word" (12:25). The traditional rendering of the last verse is "If there is anxiety in a man's mind let him talk it out of his mind." An awareness of the powers of laughter and speech was Sholom Aleichem's most important contribution to Jewish literature. But Sholom Aleichem modified these two insights in the light of East European Jewish life. Laughter was not to mock or scoff but to fondle and encourage, and speech had to include movements, facial expressions, and vocal intonations. In his writings Sholom Aleichem includes comically detailed descriptions of facial movements and physical gestures. This technique, which he learned from Mendele Mocher Seforim, Charles Dickens, and some of the Russian masters, was a major new departure in Jewish writing.

Verbal play with logic is another characteristic of Sholom Aleichem's humor. His characters often sacrifice the rules of sound reasoning to considerations of humanity and kindness. They even find it impossible to conceive of their persecutors as impervious to the cause of justice and the cry of the oppressed. Sholom Aleichem's "little people" take things for granted. They count their chickens before they are hatched. They commit regularly every fallacy of logic. Rules do not appeal to them because they are creatures of the heart (Roback, 1959).

Laughter has been described not only as an expression of life but also as a revelation of life. Sholom Aleichem's writings took the Jewish world by storm. They did indeed seem to have the authority and power of a new revelation. His biblically inspired notion that "laughter is healthy; physicians bid us laugh," despite its ironic overtones, had the impact of a religious edict permitting laughter. It opened the floodgates of merriment and joy for the Jewish people.

"If I were Goethe," Sholom Aleichem tells us,

> I would not describe the sorrows of young Werther, I would describe the sorrows of a poor Jewish lad who was madly in love with the cantor's daughter. If I were Heine, I would not sing of Florentine nights; I would sing of the night of *Simchat Torah,* when Jews make the rounds of *Hakafot* and when young women and pretty girls mingle with the men in the synagogue—the one night when this is permitted. The women kiss the Scroll of the Law. They jump up and down squeaking in every key. "Long life to you!" The answer is "Same to you, same to you!" . . . One felt proud—this was the night of the Rejoicing of the Law! Above was the sky and God was there—your God, your heaven, your holiday!
>
> (Sholom Aleichem, 1955, p. 295)

Sholom Aleichem's artistic purpose was to portray the ordinary Jew, who may have been outwardly crushed by depressing conditions but who glowed inwardly with a majestic sense of his people's past and future. On *Simchat Torah,* Sholom Aleichem writes, even the grouchy Jew who disapproves of everything and is critical of everything is proud of his heritage. Though he be a man whom nothing can satisfy and no one can please, on this festival he too feels that it is good to be a Jew. Joyously he shouts: "Friends! I want to know, is there anything better than to be a Jew? I ask you one thing: What can be finer than to be a Jew on *Simchat Torah*?" (1949, p. 170). To laugh with Sholom Aleichem is to experience the joy of Jewishness.

Sholom Aleichem's writings demonstrate that the truly humanistic and universal elements of literature are firmly imbedded in the specific and particular. The natural breeding ground for responsible behavior and loyalty to mankind is indeed the civilization and tradition into which one is born. The great comic writers have often combined literary realism, philosophical rationalism, and cultural nationalism so that their works might reflect and advance their national cultures. The contradictions that Sholom Aleichem points out and utilizes to make us laugh are the contradictions inherent in Jewish life. At a time when Jewish continuity seemed threatened because of immigration, religious and cultural erosion, and other factors, Sholom Aleichem's writings, which reached more Jews than those of any other author, gave a sense of reality and concreteness to a community in transition. "Is there a Jewish people in the world?" asked Y. H. Brenner, an important Hebrew writer, in 1905. "Is there a specific character to these transports which come and go? Do these wandering groups possess an approach of their own to the world? Can they laugh and cry about life in their own way? Has the Jewish street any vital strengths, any talent for living at all? Yes indeed! The answer is affirmative because there is a Sholom Aleichem!" (Brenner, 1967, p. 106).

One of Sholom Aleichem's major contributions to Yiddish literature was thus his conferment of an "illusion of territoriality" on the homeless Jewish people. His characters are presented in universal dimensions and bear resemblance to the non-Jewish characters of "normal" nations one finds in world literature. This legitimized Yiddish creative writing for a people that had hitherto sought hidden, esoteric meanings—religious, ethical, mystical, didactic, tendentious—in its writings. Reading Sholom Aleichem, Jews began to look at themselves with a sympathetic, understanding smile as if viewing themselves from afar. They could laugh through tears at their own misfortunes. This was the highest achievement of belles lettres: a liberation and redemption effecting complete transcendence (Rivkin, 1948).

The roots of Sholom Aleichem's unique humor must also be sought in the traditional *Purim-shpielers,* who regaled the Jewish community with plays, songs, and entertainments on the Purim festival, and in the *badkhonim* or wedding jesters, who improvised their own humorous rhymes at wedding feasts. The itinerant preachers (*maggidim*) often spiced their discourses with witty remarks and concocted parables and stories within stories to illustrate their moral preachments. The proverbs, witticisms, anecdotes, riddles, and jokes of Jewish folklore and the oral parodies of schoolboys and yeshiva students who jested good-naturedly about biblical verses, Talmudic disputes, religious hypocrisy,

outdated laws and customs, and so on, also contributed to Sholom Aleichem's humor. Tales of religious saints (both Hasidic and non-Hasidic) and their wondrous adventures were often parodied by the skeptical. Haskalah devotees often laughed at the credulousness of the benighted traditionalists with their provincial outlooks.

In the middle of the nineteenth century Yiddish and Hebrew writing erupted with parodies, satires, comedies, and collections of jokes and humorous stories. Most significant of all for Sholom Aleichem's development were the early Yiddish writings of Sholom Jacob Abramovich or Mendele Mocher Seforim, which had begun to appear in the 1860s. Mendele's works were rich in humor as well as satire. He taught Sholom Aleichem how to utilize jokes, parody, and wordplay. Sholom Aleichem actually dedicated one of his early novels, *Stempenyu,* to Mendele. Mendele had written to Sholom Aleichem that Jewish novels should be different from those of other peoples. "Your words impressed me deeply," said Sholom Aleichem. "I began to understand that a Jewish novel had to be very different because Jewish life and the conditions under which a Jew can fall n love are unlike those of other peoples. In addition, the Jewish people have a character and spirit of their own; unique customs and habits unlike those of other nations. Our national characteristics, always deeply Jewish, must appear in a Jewish novel if it is to be true to life" (Sholom Aleichem, 1927a, p. 123). Mendele also taught Sholom Aleichem to constantly revise and rewrite his works. Literature was not the sin of *bittul Torah* but a serious matter that deserved one's best efforts. Moreover, literature had to inform as well as amuse. It had to educate and inspire as well as entertain.

Sholom Aleichem drew freely on the writings of Mendele for plots, characters, and ambience. He succeeded, however, in transcending the predominantly critical approach to Jewish life in many of Mendele's works by translating the latter's satire and irony into the language of joy and laughter. He replaced the latter's sadness and seriousness with compassion and humor. Mendele had spoken of his writings as expressing the very core of a Jew "who, even when he does sing a merry tune, sounds from afar as if he were sobbing and weeping" (Mendele, 1960, p. 13). His view of life was trenchantly conveyed in the names he chose for the three towns in which his major stories take place: Idlersville, Foolstown, and Paupersville. Sholom Aleichem, on the other hand, described the *shtetl* whose little people refused to allow poverty to depress them. The name of the town became a synonym for people who are "poor but cheerful." It was called Kasri-levka—a derivative of the Hebrew name Kasriel, meaning "crown of God" (Sholom Aleichem, 1946, p. 1).

There is a direct line from the Yiddish folktales of the "wise men" of Chelm through Mendele's Kabtzansk or Paupersville to Sholom Aleichem's Kasrilevka or Cheerfultown. In the Chelm tales wit dominates; in the Kabtzansk stories, satire reigns; in the Kasrilevka adventures, pathos and humor have the day. "The town into which I shall now take you, dear reader," writes Sholom Aleichem, "is exactly in the middle of that blessed Pale [of Settlement] into which Jews have been packed as closely as herring in a barrel and told to increase and multiply. The name of the town is Kasrilevka." The Pale of Settlement, the restricted are of czarist Russia in which Jews were permitted to live, was a symbol of Jewish degradation and oppression and could hardly be called blessed. Yet although Jews there were packed as tightly as herring in a barrel, they managed to reproduce themselves like fish in water as if they had been commanded to do so by their enemies, who instituted the Pale of Settlement and promulgated other decrees against them. Or was the act of proliferation perhaps the *shtetl*-dwellers' only way of getting back at their oppressors? It is signifi-cant that the town's name is Kasrilevka—a happy name, a joyous name. "A *kasrilik* is not just an ordi-nary pauper, a failure in life. On the contrary, he is a man who has not allowed poverty to degrade him. He laughs at it. He is poor, but cheerful."

When a *kasrilik* finally reaches Paris and manages to visit a famous fellow Jew, he convinces Rothschild that he has brought with him something the latter can't buy in Paris for any amount of money: eternal life. Upon hearing how much eternal life will cost him, Rothschild says no more, but counts out three hundred rubles one by one. The Kasrilevkite slips the money into his pocket, and says to Rothschild: "If you want to live forever, my advice to you is to leave this noisy, busy Paris and move to our town of Kasrilevka. There you can never die, because since Kasrilevka has been a town, no rich man has ever died there" (Sholom Aleichem, 1946, p. 4).

Sholom Aleichem also writes of the Kasrilevka *melamed* or schoolteacher who fantasizes about what he would do if he were Rothschild. "This is the life! No more worries about making a living. No more headaches about where the money for the Sabbath is coming from. My daughters are all married off—a load is gone from my shoulders." After taking care of the needs of his family and his town, the *melamed* ex-tends his philanthropic efforts to his brothers and sis-ters all over the world. In his daydreams, he brings an

end to the persecution of his people and to wars throughout the earth.

> Do you understand what I've done? I have not only put over a business deal, but people have stopped killing each other in vain, like oxen. And since there will be no more war, what do we need weapons for? The an-swer is that we don't. And if there are no more weap-ons and armies and bands and other trappings of war, there will be no more envy, no more hatred, no Turks, no Englishmen, no Frenchmen, no Gypsies, and no Jews. The face of the earth will be changed. As it is written: "Deliverance will come—" The Messiah will have arrived.
>
> (Sholom Aleichem, 1949, p. 19)

Sholom Aleichem never completed his autobiography, *From the Fair,* but the last chapter he wrote tells of his decision as a young man to become a modern rabbi (Sholom Aleichem, 1927b, pp. 259-69). In czarist Rus-sia, modern rabbis were public officials in the employ of the government. The institution of "crown rabbi," "government rabbi," or "authorized rabbi" was gener-ally looked upon unfavorably by the Jewish masses, who correctly understood that the government's inten-tions were not only to modernize them but to wean them away from their ancestral faith. Because of the proliferation of anti-Jewish decrees in the 1880s, many Jews who had finished secondary school were unable to go on to higher education or find employment in their professions. Many were thus ready to fall back on the post of authorized rabbi as a source of liveli-hood. As a result, many who took the position were secondary school graduates, doctors, veterinarians, pharmacists, jurists, engineeers, and so on (Shohet, 1975).

When Sholom Aleichem lost his position as the tutor of the young daughter of a wealthy Jew because his student fell in love with him (he subsequently married her), he found himself without employment and de-cided to run for the position of crown rabbi in the small town of Lubin. Having won the position, the young *rabbiner* decided to return home to visit his family while he awaited government confirmation of the election. In his home town he was dismayed when his good friends and neighbors suddenly treated him with coolness and distance. At last a good friend blurted out the collective sentiment of the town: "All crown rabbis are hypocrites and fakers. They are merely sycophants of the rich. Worse, they are toadies to the authorities." Dejected, Sholom Aleichem asked himself why a government rabbi need be a hypocrite, faker, sychophant, and toadie. He vowed that he would not become an authorized rabbi of that kind. He would first and always be a *mensch,* a man of absolute integ-rity.

Rabbi Solomon Rabinovich (Sholom Aleichem's real name) who had come into the rabbinate with idealism and hope, soon discovered that his efforts were not dispelling the heavy plague of benightedness in the community he served. There had to be another way to help it. He decided to turn to the written word (Chiel, 1974, p. 27). As a writer, Sholom Aleichem sought to fulfill the task he had wanted to assume as a modern rabbi—to dispel his people's ignorance of the modern world while at the same time helping to preserve and advance its character and identity, its heritage of culture and religion.

In a memoir of Sholom Aleichem, his son-in-law, Yiddish journalist B. Z. Goldberg, recalls the great humorist walking to the synagogue on the Sabbath in New York. In the noisy, busy city streets, he looked like "a bit of Jewish Sabbath in a top hat, in a world which did not want to know about the Sabbath." He did not notice the people who stared at him on the street because he was too deeply engrossed in the mood of the Sabbath. What was it that motivated Sholom Aleichem to attend synagogue despite the fact that he was not outwardly pious in the accepted fashion? He did not, for example, keep the Sabbath or observe the dietary laws in the orthodox way. He did not don phylacteries or observe the religious fasts. Nevertheless, he had "a certain religiosity" not unlike that of other great Jewish artists of his time such as Mendele and Haim Nahman Bialik. He observed the aesthetic and emotional parts of Jewish ritual and on intimate occasions called upon the name of God (Goldberg, 1951).

Sholom Aleichem's writings possess a strong spiritual dimension which qualifies them to be considered part of the Torah tradition of the Jewish people. Kierkegaard spoke of religious faith beginning with a sense of the discrepancy between the infinite and the finite, and felt that the religious individual is the discoverer of the comical in the largest measure (Sypher, 1980, pp. 196f., 234). In his autobiography, Sholom Aleichem describes his Uncle Pinney as an extremely observant Jew for whom

> another person's business, anything that smacked of communal affairs, everything that constituted helping a fellow Jew took precedence . . . he would hurry off to arrange the wedding of a poor orphan and dance all night with her poor relatives—here surely was an opportunity to be kindly which did not often present itself. . . . The poorer the wedding, the greater the merrymaking. That is, the poorer the bride, the wilder Uncle Pinney danced. . . . Uncle Pinney would throw his coat off, pull his *tallit katan* [ritual garment] out, roll up his sleeves, his trousers tucked into his boots, his feet barely grazing the ground, his head thrown back and his eyes shut. Ecstasy and inspiration would illuminate his face as at prayer. The musicians would play a Jewish tune; everybody would clap to the rhythm; the circle would gradually widen; and the

> dancer, balancing among the burning lights, became more ecstatic and more inspired as he proceeded. . . . It was not dancing. Rather it was a kind of divine service, a holy rite.

> (Sholom Aleichem, 1955, p. 61)

Sholom Aleichem's humor was, like his Uncle Pinney's dancing, a divine service and a holy rite. Association with others is as necessary for laughter as it is for worship. If joke-telling requires a teller, subject matter, and an audience, Sholom Aleichem's humor also requires awareness of the presence of the God of Israel, who is the subjective and objective representation of the spirit of the Jewish people. "The tragic arc is only birth: struggle: death. . . . Comedy is essentially a Carrying Away of Death, a triumph over mortality by some absurd faith in rebirth, restoration, and salvation" (Sypher, 1980, p. 220). In his will Sholom Aleichem warned his descendants not to forsake their people or their faith and commanded them to bear with honor his hard-earned Jewish name. In the dedication of his autobiography to his children, he wrote: "Read it from time to time. Perhaps you or your children will learn something from it—to love our people and to appreciate their spiritual treasures which lie scattered in all the corners of our great Exile, in this great world." Sholom Aleichem's humor was suffused with a deep love for his people, committed to the alleviation of their suffering, and determined to record for posterity the radiance of a way of life based on humanity and kindness. In Sholom Aleichem's legacy of divine laughter the Jewish people lives. In his affirmative humor it confronts itself and, getting to know itself and its heritage with a spoonful of sugar, is forever reborn with a chuckle and a smile.

References

Bentley, E. (1964) *The Life of Drama.* New York: Simon and Schuster.

Berkowitz, I. D. (1958) *Dos Sholom Aleichem Bukh.* 2nd ed. New York: YKUF Farlag.

———. (1966) *Underzere Rishoynim.* Vol. 4. Tel Aviv: Farlag Hamenorah.

Boodin, J. E. (1934) *God: A Cosmic Philosophy of Religion.* New York: Macmillan.

Brenner, Y. H. (1967) *Kol Kitvey Y. H. Brenner.* Vol. 3. Tel Aviv: Hotza'at Hakibbutz Hame'uhad.

Chiel, A. (1974) "When Sholom Aleichem Was a Rabbi." *Jewish Frontier,* February.

Goldberg, B. Z. (1951) "Sholom Aleichem in Amerike inem Letstn Yor fun Zayn Lebn." *Yidishe Kultur,* May.

Goldsmith, E. S. (1987) *Modern Yiddish Culture: The Story of the Yiddish Language Movement.* New York: Shapolsky.

Kahler, E. (1967) *The Jews among the Nations.* New York: Frederick Ungar.

Levinsohn, I. B. (1901) *Zerubavel.* Vol. 1. Warsaw: B. Z. Sheynfinkel.

Mendele Mocher Seforim. (1960) *Fishke the Lame.* Translated by G. Stillman. New York: Thomas Yosseloff.

Miron, D. (1970) *Sholom Aleichem: Pirkey Masah.* Ramat Gan: Masada.

Niger, S. (1946) "The Gift of Sholom Aleichem." *Commentary,* August.

Rivkin, B. (1948) *Grunt-Tendentsn fun der Yidisher Literatur in Amerike.* New York: YKUF Farlag.

Roback, A. A. (1959) "Sholom Aleichem's Humor." *Congress Bi-Weekly* 26, no. 6: 16 March.

Shohet, A. (1975) *Mosad Harabanut Mita'am Be-Rusya.* Haifa: University of Haifa Press.

Sholom Aleichem. (1927a) *Yidishe Romanen.* New York: Sholom Aleichem Folksfond Oysgabe.

———. (1927b) *Funem Yarid.* New York: Sholom Aleichem Folksfond Oysgabe.

———. (1946) *The Old Country.* Translated by J. Butwin and F. Butwin. New York: Crown.

———. (1949) *Tevye's Daughters.* Translated by F. Butwin. New York: Crown.

———. (1955) *The Great Fair.* Translated by T. Kahana. New York: Noonday Press.

Sypher, W. (1980) "The Meanings of Comedy." In *Comedy.* Edited by W. Sypher. Baltimore: Johns Hopkins University Press.

Trunk, I. I. (1944) *Tevye un Menakhem-Mendl in Yidishn Velt-Goyrl.* New York: Cyco Bikher-Farlag.

Wiener, M. (1946) *Tsu der Geshikhte fun der Yidisher Literatur in Nayntsntn Yorhundert.* Vol. 2. New York: YKUF Farlag.

Zeitlin, A. (1980) *Literarishe un Filosofishe Eseyen.* New York: Alveltlekher Yidisher Kultur Kongres.

Joseph Sherman (essay date winter 1994)

SOURCE: Sherman, Joseph. "Holding Fast to Integrity: Shalom Rabinovich, Sholem Aleichem, and Tevye the Dairyman." *Judaism* 43, no. 1 (winter 1994): 6-18.

[*In this essay, Sherman examines Aleichem's narrative strategy in the "Tevye" stories, focusing on his use of Tevye's recitation of passages from Jewish holy books to force a serious reexamination of orthodox Jewish teaching and dogmas.*]

Written as they were over a period of twenty years, between 1894 and 1914, the nine stories and brief prologue which recount the life of Tevye the Dairyman have long been recognised as presenting a character who is simultaneously part and paradigm of that traditional Jewish life in Eastern Europe which was destroyed by violent socio-political and economic pressures at the turn of the last century. The concomitant tendency among today's general readers, both in the Diaspora and in Israel, is to regard these stories as period pieces, reflecting an ugly—and mercifully vanished—*goles* in which Jew-hatred was endured by Jew-helplessness. Hence, Tevye, while now accepted, like *lokshn,* as part of Jewish folk culture, tends to be treated with an affectionate condescension little better than contempt. *Ḥaluzim, Irguniks* and Entebbe raiders have long since replaced him as modern Jewish role models, while the forceful Zionist thrust of modern Jewish education, with its glorification of aggressive independence and technological mastery, has impatiently discarded the Yiddish language and its literature. If Tevye is known at all by young people today, it is as Topol's caricature in the musical, *Fiddler on the Roof.* The literary standing of Tevye's creator, Shalom Rabinovich, has diminished proportionately. Popular taste now generally perceives him as an old-fashioned purveyor of *heymisher* jokes. He is rarely regarded as a serious thinker whose mastery of narrative techniques raises his work to the level achieved by Gogol and Chekhov, those Russian masters whom he most admired.

On the other hand, those who do recognise the writer's achievement perhaps weigh the balance too heavily on the other side. Among other giants, for instance, Tevye has been likened to Job, because, facing an increasing succession of personal tragedies, he questions God's justice. Like Job, he challenges Judaism's traditional answer to the problem of innocent suffering, which is steadfastly to maintain—as Job's comforters do—that undeserved punishment does not come upon the righteous. Affliction is always God's just retribution for sins, or a test of individual moral character, or simply an illusion created by the limitations of mortal perception. Tevye, however, like Job before him, refuses to accept this. Believing that God exists and is all-powerful, Tevye insists that He must also be all-just, and since, in Tevye's bitter personal experience, He is not, He owes man an explanation and man must demand it from Him.[1] So Tevye persists in seeking that which never comes. Of course, no real explanation ever comes to Job either: God's answer out of the whirlwind, by intensifying Job's awareness of his personal ignorance, enables him to renew that faith which he has always held, and gains him a double reward for his fidelity. For Tevye, however, there is neither tentative answer nor even half a reward. If, despite all the odds, Tevye continues to profess faith, it is because without such a profession hope dies, the meaning of Jewish existence vanishes, and the burden of Divine election becomes unbearable.

But behind Tevye and his interrogations of Divine Justice lies Tevye's creator, Shalom Rabinovich, who formulates the questions and forms the characters who ask them. Tevye may respond to his unanswered questions with resignation; we need not, nor did his creator necessarily intend that we should. In reading Tevye, it is a grave error to identify the character with his creator and, hence, to assume that Tevye speaks for Rabinovich. On the contrary, Rabinovich's fiction achieves its complexity through a carefully crafted narrative strategy which filters the garrulous monologues of a variety of Jewish persons to us through the *persona* of a fictional construct called Sholem Aleichem. This construct is either an ever-present listener through whose ears we hear what is being said, or he is a narrative voice who reports to us what has been said to him. In either case, the narrative is mediated in such a way as to place upon it a double or even a triple perspective. In this way, the questions which the narrative raises about itself tend to multiply alarmingly. We are continually challenged to ask: Who is saying this, and why? Who is reporting to us what is being said, and how reliable is this reporter? And, in any case, why are we always made to hear conversations at second- or third-hand anyway?

To illustrate the radically deconstructive effect of this kind of narrative strategy, it is worth pursuing a little further the tempting analogy between Tevye and Job. In defiance of his wife's despairing demand, "Dost thou still hold fast thine integrity? Blaspheme God and die" (Job 2:9), Job insists to the end on averring, "Till I die I will not put away mine integrity from me" (Job 27:5). So it may seem with Tevye. For him, as for Job, to blaspheme God may, indeed, be to die, for then the world, devoid of comprehensible meaning as it is for him, will then be devoid also of hope that it may not be so. But, for all their surface similarities, Tevye is not another Job. Good, generous, tender-hearted and conventionally pious he may be, but he has not so adamant a sense of his own moral integrity that he dares to demand an accounting from God Himself. Neither rich nor influential, neither profoundly learned nor tormentedly deep-thinking, Tevye is not, as Job is, *ish tam v'yashar,* a man whole-hearted and upright. Rather, he is placed in a moral condition *vis-à-vis* Job to which we could apply one of his own favourite definitions: *bemokoym she'eyn ish iz a hering a fish,*[2] "in a place where there are no men [of moral stature], even a herring passes for fish." Tevye is someone like ourselves, not someone morally, intel-

lectually and spiritually far above us. Thus, while Tevye's questions might be our own, the answers which satisfy him might not satisfy us. We, too, may find that there is no escape from the burden of Chosenness, but we may not find it easier to bear, as Tevye does, through patient acceptance of the formulations of traditional theology, endlessly repeated in the daily, weekly and yearly liturgy. Fully aware of this—indeed, determined to challenge us on this very ground—this is precisely the area from which Rabinovich selects his material for that sharp interrogation of tradition which he puts into Tevye's mouth.

Tevye's most characteristic and endearing habit is to quote repeatedly from the holy books for a variety of purposes. As his daughter Hava tells him impatiently, *"ayn antik! oyf altsding host du a posek!"* "It's beyond belief! You've got a verse for everything!"[3] It is commonly recognised, of course, that Tevye's stock of knowledge is by no means as vast as he likes to pretend. Most of his quotations are drawn from sources with which every *shul*-going Jew is familiar—from the daily liturgy, the weekly *parshah,* the annual services for Festivals and High Holy Days, and from *Pirkei Avot,* the tractate of the Mishnah traditionally read on Sabbath afternoons in the summer and included in the *Siddur.* Tevye's knowledge of the Talmud and Commentaries, the *kleyne oysyes* ("little letters") that he venerates, is confined to a few rabbinical phrases which have passed into idiomatic daily speech. In a moment of necessity, in the presence of an *amorets* (ignorant person) whom he wishes to deflate, Tevye has no hesitation in fabricating his own imaginary Talmudic quotation from an assortment of Russian and Yiddish words onto which he tacks Aramaic endings. The most resounding putdown of this type is one he concocts for his daughter Beylke's husband, the *nouveau-riche* vulgarian, Podhodzur— *miznavto deḥazirto loy makhent shtraymilto, dos heyst* (i.e.), *fun a ḥazershn ek kon men keyn shtrayml nisht makhen,* "you can't make a *shtraymil* out of a pig's tail."[4] Ironically, though, if we compare Tevye's humble ordinariness to the towering individuality of Job, this snub becomes an observation on Tevye himself. Such a devastating piece of fictional deconstruction is but one example of how carefully Rabinovich manipulates the multiple ironies essential to his purpose.

From the time of his first appearance, readers more learned than Tevye have hastened to point out his scholarly shortcomings, ultimately more to shine a spotlight on themselves than to illuminate the meaning of what Rabinovich is doing. Why, after all, does Tevye's creator—whose own knowledge was extensive—choose to limit himself only to these areas of Jewish learning? It is quite valid to point to realistic characterisation as one reason. In the degree to which Tevye is a simple Jew, his sources of learning are simple as well. But this is not the only, nor even the chief reason. Rabinovich, through the mediation of Sholem Aleichem, aims chiefly to subject traditional Jewish teachings to a thoroughgoing examination of their validity. The most effective way to challenge the thinking of ordinary folk is to confront them with instantly-recognisable formulaic responses which, torn from familiar contexts and placed in unconventional ones, demand re-evaluation. The disintegrating situations in which Tevye finds himself cry out for answers to questions which Rabinovich wishes to ask. The quotations with which Tevye encounters them offer the stock responses of orthodox theology. But their incompleteness, inappropriateness or irrelevance merely accentuate their essential inadequacy. So, while both Tevye, the created, and Rabinovich, the creator, may "hold fast to integrity," that integrity is by no means the same. The interrogation process that is instituted through the frequent repetition of texts, with which all of Tevye's readers are familiar, is a process that simultaneously interrogates not only these traditional responses themselves, but our individual preparedness to accept them. Tevye may find his answer—or at least his consolation. Can we? Do we? Should we? These are finally the questions that Tevye's recital of sorrows is designed to raise in us.

The way this process of interrogation operates is seen by examining one liturgical source of quotations to which Tevye most often has recourse—the *Hallel,* a prayer of praise made up of Psalms 113-118. In theory it is recited on festivals of jubilation. However, on several such occasions it is either omitted or not recited in full. On Purim, *kri'at ha'Megillah* takes its place; on Pesaḥ, according to Midrashic tradition, God forbade His angels from rejoicing at the destruction of the Egyptians. Even on *Rosh Ḥodesh* (the beginning of the "New Month") it is abridged.[5] Though the chief intention of the *Hallel* is to thank God for His great mercies to His people, Israel, the relative infrequency of its full recitation might suggest to troubled minds that these mercies have seldom been unequivocally evident. The ordinary worshipper might be pardoned for finding it easier to remember when *Hallel* is *not* recited, than when it is. It should come as no surprise, therefore, that every time Tevye quotes from the *Hallel,* the effect of his quotation is to challenge the existence of the mercies that it celebrates in the everyday experience of ordinary folk like himself.

We first meet this kind of interrogation in **"Hayntiker Kinder"** (**"Today's Children"**), the story of Tevye's eldest daughter, Tsaytl.[6] Returning from Boiberik, where he has just received the congratulations of the whole town on what he believes to be Tsaytl's forth-coming marriage to the rich butcher, Leyzer-Volf, and slightly tipsy from the drinks he has bought all round to celebrate, Tevye joyously gives himself over to song. Since Tevye's music is always taken from that of the synagogue, *Hallel* not only becomes an automatic choice but also provides an opportunity for serious reflection:

> I look up there, into the heavens, but my thoughts are all muddled up down here, on the earth. "The heavens are the heavens," they are for God, but the Earth, it seems to me, He's given away to the children of men, so they should bang their heads against the wall, tear themselves to pieces like cats fighting for the cream, beating each other up for the prestige of sitting at the head of the synagogue, for the honour of being called up to the Reading of the Law . . . "The dead cannot praise the Lord," the dead understand afflictions, they understand how they ought to praise God for all the good things He does for them, but we, poor creatures, if we have one good day, we thank God and we praise God, and we say, "I love God" because He listens carefully to my voice and my prayer, He lends His ear to what I have to say. At the very moment when "I am encircled," I'm surrounded on all sides by poverty, trouble, miserable afflictions: one day a cow drops dead in broad daylight; another day a real stroke of luck brings to light a loose fish of a relative, a certain Menahem-Mendl from Yehupetz who grabs my last farthing, and I think "in my haste," enough already, the world has fallen in, "all men are deceitful," there's no truth in the world. What does God do? He puts it into Leyzer-Volf's head to take my Tsaytl; therefore, I say not once but twice, "I thank thee," I will praise you, dear Lord, because You've looked round and spotted Tevye and come to my help, so that at last I should have a bit of pleasure from my child.

> ("**Hayntiker Kinder,**" pp. 78-9)

Exactly at this moment, Tevye's horse breaks into a gallop, overturning the wagon, upsetting all the milk cans, and leaving Tevye flat on his back underneath it all. The situational irony explicitly reinforces the same spiritual irony to which Tevye had called attention earlier, in his disastrous encounter with Menaḥem-Mendl, through an interpretation of Proverbs 27:1: *al tis'haleyl beyoym moḥor—a mentsh trakht un got lakht,* "a man plans and God laughs."[7] Tsaytl's independence of spirit upsets all of her parents' carefully-laid plans and shatters their fondest dreams. She wants the poor tailor, Motl Komzoyl, not the rich butcher, Leyzer-Volf; she insists on marrying for love and not for money. Whatever thanks man may fleetingly imagine are due to God are ironically undercut by the consequences of human choice.

Tevye does not fail to reognise the irony inherent in the statement of Psalm 115:16-17: *hashomayim shomayim laShem, veho'orets nosan livney odom,* "The Heaven is the Lord's heaven, but the earth He has given to mankind." God sits in solitary glory in His heaven, leaving the world to the envy and strife bred by petty human ambition; *loy hameysim yehallelu Yoh,* "the dead cannot praise the Lord"—not because death has silenced their power of speech, but because, having experienced nothing but affliction, they can perceive no reason for gratitude. Only *anaḥnu,* we who are alive and can speak, must offer praise—for the irreconcilable disparity between the ideal and the real, between what we have been taught joyfully to anticipate, and what we are forced bitterly to endure. The only principle governing God's Providence that Tevye can perceive is that whirligig which he repeatedly defines as *oylim veyordim:* sudden and inexplicable ascent followed by equally sudden and even more inexplicable descent.

The context from which Tevye tears this conviction of the random operation of human life is, in orthodox terms, disturbingly deconstructive. The phrase is taken from Genesis 28, describing how, in a dream, Jacob beheld a ladder, *sulam muẓav arẓah, v'rosho magiya ha'shamayim, v'hiney malakhey Elohim olim veyordim,* a ladder "set up on the earth, and the top of it reached to heaven; and behold the angels of God ascending and descending on it" (Genesis 28:12). The angels perform God's will and sing His praises, assured of the beneficence of His purposes; they precede the appearance of God Himself to promise Jacob that *ha'areẓ asher atah shokhev aleha, lekha etnenaḥ u'le'zarekha . . . ve'nivrekhu bekha kol-mishpekhot ha'adamah u've'zarekha,* "The land whereon thou liest, to thee will I give it and to thy seed . . . And in thee and in thy seed shall all the families of the earth be blessed" (Genesis 28:13-24). These ancient promises can now only be taken on trust by Tevye and the Jews of his generation. In their daily experience they sound like a hollow mockery, because the comings and goings of men, unlike those of God's angels, are arbitrary and inconclusive, presumably the result of culpable individual choices. These, tradition insists, collectively add up to *avoynoseynu harabim,* our many sins, on account of which we have been deprived of our homeland and punished with dispersion. But how are these "many sins" to be quantified in terms of God's justice? How can they justly be described as "sins" at all, born as they are of sociopolitical circumstances over which Jews as a people exercise no control whatever?

Intertwined with this question of free choice is obviously the more central question of God's plan for the world, specifically for the Chosen Jewish part of it. If Tsaytl, in choosing unwisely, brings poverty and hardship upon herself, her children and, ultimately, upon her father and mother, how can God be held responsible? Yet, if God, omniscient and omnipotent, rules over the world with justice and mercy, and is ever mindful of His promises to our forefathers, how are His purposes to be understood by those like Tevye, who suffer the consequences of that freedom of choice that God has granted to His creatures? How is Tevye to come to terms with Hodl's decision to follow Pertchik, the revolutionary, to the ends of the Russian earth, abandoning father and mother never to see them again? Scripture teaches one lesson, the experience of life another, and Tevye—like Job, but much more like each of us—cannot reconcile them. How must he cope with Hava's determination to convert and marry a Gentile? The only response he is able to make publicly—although his private feelings are different—is the one prescribed by *Halakhah:*

> So I arrive home and find my Golde lying in bed, rolled up tightly like a black ball, and she has no more tears left to cry. So I call out to her, "Get up, my wife, and take off your shoes," I say, "and let's sit on the floor for the seven days of mourning, as God has commanded. 'The Lord gave and Lord has taken away'— we're not the first, we won't be the last . . . " I speak from my heart, and I feel the tears choking me, sticking like a bone in my throat. But Tevye's not a woman, Tevye can control himself! . . . How could I control myself when I'd lost a child like that, alive and well? . . . At one time we used to sit up whole nights over her; many times we called her back, literally called her back from death, breathed life back into her, as you breathe life into a tiny crushed chick, because, if God wishes, He calls the dead back to life, as we say in *Hallel:* "I shall not die, but live"—if you're not fated to die, you don't die . . . In short, it's not for nothing that our holy books tell us, "Regardless of your will, you live"—a person doesn't take his own life. There's no wound in the world that doesn't heal, and there's no sorrow that you can't forget. What I mean is, you don't really forget, but what can you do? "Man is like the beast that perishes"—a person needs to toil, to drudge, to blacken his days and get torn to pieces for the sake of his bit of bread.

> (**"Hava,"** pp. 133-5)

In this moment of his most extreme anguish, Tevye turns to the palliatives offered by convention, and finds them far from soothing. On one of few occasions, he quotes directly the words of Job 1:21, which tradition and the Law have long incorporated into the Burial Service. Providing no answer, they merely demand acceptance. But though Tevye tries to be obedient, his questions break out more movingly here than elsewhere. He utters one of the consolations of the *Hallel—loy omus ki eḥyeh,* "I shall not die but live"—but he significantly truncates the verse (Psalm 118:17). He concludes, not with its jubilant assertion, *ve'asapeyr ma'aseh Yah,* "[but live] to recount the deeds of the Lord," but rather with the numb fatalism of a mortally wounded creature, *az s'iz nit bashert shtarbn, shtarbt men nit.* "If one is not fated to die, one is forced to live on to endure even more of the unendurable."

Tevye gropes for guidance among the most fatalistic observations of the rabbis—*be'al korkhekho atoh ḥay,* "regardless of your will, you live" (*Avot* 4:29), stumbling towards the bleak recognition that *odom kiveheymoh nidmeh,* "man is like the beasts that perish." Rabinovich once again makes Tevye truncate and reshape this quotation from Psalm 49:20. The original asserts that *adam bikar ve'lo yavin nimshal ka'behemot nidmu,* "man that lives in honour and does not understand is like the beasts that perish." Lacking both honour and understanding, all Tevye can now recognise is the similarity between dumb men and dumb beasts. The world view propagated by centuries of tradition is subjected here to one of its starkest and least comforting interrogations.

Questioning God's justice as he does, Tevye, it has been argued, should perceive that, unlike Job, he has to a large extent been the author of his own misfortunes.[8] He himself brought Pertchik to his house and encouraged his visits. In doing so, however, he acted with the best intentions and in fulfilment of the *miẓvah* of hospitality. Does he receive the just reward such *mentshlekhkayt* deserves? And how can Tevye be held responsible for the fact that Hava elopes with a Christian? Only after he has broken-heartedly rejected her appeal to speak with him does Tevye challenge the basis on which God has ordered the world:

> What's the meaning of Jew and non-Jew? . . . and why did God create Jews and non-Jews? . . . and if God did create Jews and non-Jews, for what purpose should they be segregated one from another, and are not even allowed to look at one another, as if one was created by God, and the other was not?
>
> ("**Hava,**" p. 138)

However much this interrogation may disregard Covenantal impositions attendant upon Divine Chosenness, every one of the countless times it recurs in the experience of individual Jews, it unambiguously calls to mind the very reason given in the Midrash for not reciting *Hallel* on Pesaḥ. God's world, as Tevye encounters it, operates exclusively within the parameters of shattering irony.

Tevye's greatest wish—to have his daughters marry rich men and allow him to live in ease—is fulfilled when his youngest girl, Beylke, sacrifices herself to the boorish Podhodzur. Yet, he finds her living in an emotionless void which, more concretely than the experiences of his other daughters, symbolizes the futility of all human aspirations:

> Meanwhile a personage arrives in huge white gloves and says that the snack is already on the table, and all three of us get up, and we go into a room that's solid oak: the tables are oak, and the benches are oak, the walls are oak and the ceiling's oak, and everything's carved and varnished and painted and dolled up, and on the table—a feast for a king: tea and coffee and chocolate, with butter-pastries, and fine cognac, and the best pickled herring, and every other kind of eating pleasure, with so many different kinds of fruit that although I'm ashamed to admit it, I'm afraid my Beylke never ever even saw such things on her father's table. Well, they pour me a glass, and then another glass, and I drink good health to everyone, and I look over at her, at my Beylke, and I think, "Tevye's daughter, have you really lived to experience what we say in *Hallel*: "He raises the poor out of the dust"—when God helps a poor man—"he lifts the needy out of the dunghill"—so high that you can't even recognise him anymore. And I think—it's Beylke, and, yet it's not Beylke.
>
> ("**Tevye Fort Keyen Erez Yisroel,**" p. 180)

For Tevye, the expectations encouraged by prescribed formulas detailing God's mercies are all realised in bitter reversal. Yet again, *Hallel* is subjected to critical reappraisal. The fulfilment of its assurance that God "raises the poor out of the dust, and lifts the needy out of the dunghill" (Psalm 113:7) transforms Beylke into a frozen study of unhappiness; it seeks to send Tevye to the Holy Land, not to fulfil a *miẓveh,* but to prevent him from embarrassing his *parvenu* son-in-law. In Tevye's experience, what that assurance actually delivers is not what it appeared to promise.

If, Job-like, Tevye argues with God, Golde certainly does not play the role of Job's wife. Her own sufferings from the consequences of her daughters' actions are even greater than Tevye's, since she has never shared those of his dreams which they act out. On the contrary, with feet planted firmly on the ground and rooted deep in reality, she opposes them with vehemence, only to be treated in return with patronising disparagement by her husband. In Tevye's oftenrepeated view, she is merely a *nekeyve,* a female, from whom nothing more can be expected. Consequently, she is made a double victim. Because she expects so much less from life, because she is preoccupied with domestic cares and lacks both time and capacity for philosophical introspection, she unquestioningly accepts conventional pieties as truths which are as much above challenge as they are unrelated to her day-today experience. She dumbly bears her burden, even when she is dying:

> "So tell me," she says, "what've I got to live for in this world, when very soon I won't have child or chattel in the house? Why, even a cow, excuse the comparison," she says, "longs for her calf when you wean it away from her." . . . And while she was saying this to me, my Golde, she shed bitter tears. And I could see the poor woman pining away from day to day, going out like a candle, and I probably spoke my heart out to her for compassion, and I said this to her," . . . We have," I said, "a great God, and a good God, and a mighty

God." I said, "although in that respect," I said, "I wish I could have a blessing for every time the Master of the Universe . . . does such a piece of work for us that my enemies should only have a whole year of it." . . . But my wife, may she forgive me for saying so, was only a female, so all she says to me is, "It's a sin to speak like that, Tevye, . . . You shouldn't sin." "There you go again," I said. "Did I say anything wrong, then? . . . Did I do anything, perish the thought, against God's will? . . . If it comes to that, . . . if He created His little world so beautifully, . . . that children are not children, . . . and parents are no better than dirt under the feet, . . . I suppose He knew exactly what He was doing . . . "

(Ibid., p. 169)

Behind this ambiguous exchange, Rabinovich interrogates the attitudes and values of both husband and wife. Golde is *a Yidene a proste, on ḥokhmes,* "a simple [Jewish] woman without deep thoughts," but her unquestioning acceptance not only leaves the ways of the world unchallenged—it perhaps even encourages them to get worse. At the same time, for all of Tevye's partly-informed challenge to God's justice, he can do as little as his wife to change the way things turn out. Moreover, his complaints against God hover only on the outskirts of defiance. In the face of God's rebuke, he backs down and backs away, muttering from behind the fence of conventional teaching which, however inadequate, is the only protection he has. It is chiefly to us, however, that Rabinovich has thrown the challenge, and we must meet it—or reject it—as our individual capacities permit.

In the penultimate chapter of his history, Tevye confronts the latter-day equivalent of God's command to Abraham: *lekh lekha me'arzekha umi'moladetekha umi'bet avikha el ha'arez asher areka,* "get thee out of thy country, and from thy kindred, and from thy father's house, unto the land that I will show thee" (Genesis 12:1). Facing the dreadful reality of a pogrom, Tevye longs with all his heart for the immediate appearance of the Messiah; raising his eyes, he does, indeed, behold a white horse whose rider dismounts at his door. But this is another of God's little ironies: *az me kukt aroys oyf moshiaḥ, kumt der oratnik,* "when one anticipates the messiah, the policeman arrives."[9] Tevye's command comes not from God but from the Tsar: *for-for nakh Barditshev,* "fly away to Berdichev."[10] Where is the fulfilment of God's promise now? In the face of human persecution and Divine absence, Tevye is helpless either to resist or to understand:

"What are we? What is our life?"—what am I today, and who am I? A half-man, a shattered vessel, a broken shard! For pity's sake, Master of the Universe, dear God!—I thought—Why have You deliberately picked on poor Tevye? For a change, why don't you play a

trick or two on a Brodsky, for example, or on a Rothschild? Why doesn't someone teach *them* the Torah lesson, "Get thee out"? Wouldn't it have done them more good than me, I wonder? In the first place, they would've tasted the real flavour of what it means to be a Jew. In the second place, let them also see that we have a mighty God. . . . In short, it's all empty words. You can't argue things out with God, and you can't give Him any advice on how to run the world. If He says, "The heavens are Mine and the earth is Mine,"—it's quite clear that He's the boss, and we have to follow Him. What He says, goes!

(**"Lekh Lekha,"** p. 212)

Defenceless, Tevye must accept what cannot be altered. So he "gets him out" to become a despoiled wanderer upon the face of the earth. We meet him chatting with Sholem Aleichem for the last time on a train, modern history's most enduring symbol of Jewish dispossession. Face to face in old age with a condition of permanent homelessness, Tevye can only take refuge in the pieties of orthodoxy which Rabinovich has by now rendered utterly platitudinous:

. . . as we say every day in the morning prayers—"Happy are they that dwell"—it's all good and well for those that can dwell. . . . "Happy art thou, O Israel"—it's lucky for me that I was born a Jew, because I know the taste of exile and of dragging myself around among all the nations of the earth, and of "sojourning and encamping"—wherever I spend the day, I don't spend the night, because on account of my sins they've taught me the Torah lesson, "Get thee out" . . . Tevye doesn't ask any questions. They told him to get out—so he goes. . . . Today I've met up with you, Mr. Sholem Aleichem, on the train here—tomorrow it could carry us away to Yehupets. In a year's time it could dump us in Odessa, or in Warsaw, or even in America—unless the All-Highest were to look round Him and say: "You know what, children? I actually want to send the Messiah down to you!" Let's hope He does it for us just out of spite, that old Master of the Universe! Meanwhile keep well, travel safely, send regards to all our little Jews, and tell them out there that they shouldn't worry—our old God is still alive!

(**"Vekhalaklakoys,"** pp. 229-230)[11]

These, the last words we hear Tevye speak, are far from comforting, His exclamation of seeming fidelity, *"unzer alter Got lebt,"* coupled as it is with an encoded imprecation in the exclamation, *"der alter Reboyne Sheloylem!"* are whistlings in the wind. Jews are left wandering without meaning in a dispersion as unrelated to individual transgression as it is sundered from any sense of Providential mercy. If *goles* is a punishment for sins, how long must it take before these sins are atoned for? And if it is not, then how are we to reconcile what appears to be malicious caprice with orthodox teachings about Divine beneficence?

Rabinovich died in 1916, in the middle of the Great War. He was not to know that those interminable train journeys, on which Tevye finally joined the endless stream of Jewish scatterlings who babbled their lives away to Sholem Aleichem, would ultimately reach their destination in the Nazi death-camps. But the interrogations of orthodox pieties which he put into Tevye's mouth become, with a hindsight born of the appalling experience of our own times, even more pertinent today. Tevye sees all around him the erosion of traditional faith, custom, order, and meaning in Jewish existence and, believing unbelievingly, he clings to them because there is no other spar in the wreckage around him.

To what shall we in the Diaspora cling today, when the trains have carried us neither to Berdichev nor to Odessa, but to Auschwitz? To the restored State of Israel, Zionists insist. For them, Tevye's world was passively complicit with the forces which murdered it. For the sins of Tevye's castrated people, the virility of those reborn has atoned. In 1991, in response to the seventy-fifth anniversary of Rabinovich's death, the Israeli novelist, David Grossman, could see no link binding Tevye's painful past to his own children's contented present:

> When I was eight years old, my father gave me a set of books by Sholem Aleichem. It was his way of linking me to his childhood in Poland . . . In the heroic Israel of that day, I felt that I was the only one who knew that sad, vulnerable world. Now, I have a son who is a year older than I was when I was given Sholem Aleichem. It is strange that I never thought of giving it to him. I don't know how today my son could bridge the gap between his life and the wretched, passive *galut*.[12]

The well-fed, well-housed, thoroughly assimilated Diaspora concurs in the smug voice of the Canadian writer, Mordechai Richler:

> I remember having Sholem Aleichem stories read aloud to me—mother read them to me. I enjoyed them. And—occasionally—they were read to her groups of ladies; that was part of growing up in Montreal in the early '40s. I myself, I've read him exclusively in English. He was enjoyable, but I haven't read his stories in a long time. It's part of a tradition. His stories came out of a different part of the world. It's part of our heritage, but not part of my experience.[13]

Richler might as easily have said the same about the Exodus. Such a comment may tell us something about this writer's personal indifference; it says nothing about the meaning of being Jewish today.

To those who seek such meaning, however, the interrogations of Rabinovich, informing each of Tevye's utterances, will not go away. They are not answered merely because the questions are no longer asked, either by unconcerned secularists or by obedient traditionalists. Predictably, only among the doctrinaire leaders of the latter is the force of Rabinovich's scrutiny fully perceived. In the ultra-Orthodox communities of Bnei Brak and Brooklyn, the only places where the Yiddish language is still alive in the mouths of contemporary Jews, there is no place for Rabinovich, Sholom Aleichem or Tevye. According to one instructor of girls in Bnei Brak, Yiddish has today replaced Hebrew as *loshn-koydesh* (the "holy tongue"). Therefore, it must purge itself of all inquiring matter:

> Since the Emancipation, when Jews were allowed to participate in Gentile society, speaking Yiddish has become an ideology. It has been seen as a "fence" against assimilation, and in the Land of Israel as a way of "closing off" from the Zionists who were anti-religious. . . . It is felt that even those secular writers not openly opposed to *Yidishkayt* belittle it, and can be more dangerous.[14]

Such Jews believe that they are holding fast to the integrity of their faith by excluding questions in favour of repeating pat answers. For these faithful, questions belittle and endanger a *"Yiddishkayt"* which knows nothing of doubt or diversity. Our Sages, by contrast, insisted that only through questions can truth be discovered; that an unexamined faith, like an unexamined life, is an exercise in vanity. This way was also the way of Rabinovich.

Today, a century after he began to write about Tevye, Rabinovich continues to hold fast to his own integrity, and to challenge ours by insisting, with Job, that it cannot consist of slavish adherence to uninvestigated dogma. To demonstrate that such interrogations are vital to the experience of us all, Rabinovich puts them in the mouth of a Jew like ourselves. There is, perhaps, greater depth in the fact that Tevye is a *milkhiker* than is commonly recognised. The English translation, "dairyman," accurate enough up to its limited point, is incapable of suggesting to the reader who is not Jewish the word's connotations in respect of the central distinction on which Jewish dietary laws are based—the separation of what is *milkhik* from what is *fleyshik*. In the context of these narratives, if we read this word not simply as a literal description of Tevye's vocation, but as a figurative description—a metaphor—of his avocation, then the distinction that Rabinovich is drawing between Tevye and Job immediately becomes both recognisable and resonant. In the profundity and perseverance of his search for truth, Job is a *fleyshiker*; in the humility and uncertainty of his doubts, Tevye is a *milkhiker*. The more he protests, in the moments of his greatest grief, that *Tevye iz nisht keyn Yidene* ("Tevya is not a [simple] Jewish woman"), the more we recognise that tenderness of heart which he feels it is unbecoming to show in the artificial role that he is trying to play. The more we see through his unconvincing bluff, the more do his misgivings become our own. He may not articulate them with the *fleyshiker* voice of Job, but his *milkhiker* spirit, however humble, is equally indomitable. Behind all his tentative interrogations, and supporting all his patient acceptance, we hear clearly the eternal human cry of incomprehension at undeserved suffering which, in challenging pious cliches, echoes in a poignantly minor key the majestic demand of Job:

> *ke'da'atkhem yadati gam ani*
> *lo nofel anoḥi mikem:*
> *ulam ani el Shaddai adaber*
> *vehokheyaḥ el Eyl eḥpaz.*
> What ye know, do I know also;
> I am not inferior to you.
> Notwithstanding, I would speak to the Almighty,
> And I desire to reason with God

(Job 13)

Notes

1. This argument is advanced by Hillel Halkin in the Introduction to his recent new English translation. See *Tevye the Dairyman and The Railroad Stories* (New York: Schocken, 1987), pp. xxiv-xxvii.

2. Tevye first makes this remark, "*vi di Gemore zogt,*" "as the Gemara says," in "*Dos Groyse Gevins*" (1895), p. 31. All quotations from the Yiddish text are made from Sholem Aleichem, *Gants Tevye der Milkhiker,* Vol. 5 of *Ale Verk fun Sholem Aleykhem* (Vilne-Varshe: Farlag B. Kletskin, 1925). In my romanisation of Aleichem's Yiddish, I generally follow the YIVO system of morpho-phonemic transcription, which indicates pronunciation rather than the original Yiddish orthography. I transliterate Tevye's Hebrew quotations according to the Ashkenazi pronunciation of the Eastern Europe of his day; all other quotations in Hebrew are transliterated according to the Sephardi pronunciation in modern use.

3. "*Ḥava*" (1906), p. 125.

4. "*Tevye Fort Keyn Erez Yisroel*" (1909), p. 185.

5. See Phillip Birnbaum (ed.), *Daily Prayer Book,* 1949, pp. 565-574.

6. "*Hayntiker Kinder*" (1899), pp. 67-91. Page references to specific passages subsequently quoted are cited parenthetically after the text.

7. "*A Boydem*" (1899), p. 62.

8. This is what Hillel Halkin suggests in his Introduction, p. xxiii.

9. "*Lekh-Lekho*" (1914), p. 209.

10. Ibid., (1914), p. 211.

11. "*Vekhlaklakoys*" (1914-1916), pp. 223-230.

12. Quoted in the *Jerusalem Report,* 23 May 1991, p. 9.

13. Ibid.

14. Ibid., p. 13.

Sidra DeKoven Ezrahi (essay date 2000)

SOURCE: Ezrahi, Sidra DeKoven. "By Train, by Ship, by Subway: Sholem Aleichem and the American Voyage of Self-Invention." In *Booking Passage: Exile and Homecoming in the Modern Jewish Imagination,* pp. 103-30. Berkeley: University of California Press, 2000.

[*In the essay that follows, Ezrahi analyzes the theme of migration in the "Tevye" narratives,* The Railroad Stories, *and the "Motl" tales, demonstrating how the first two show the negative connotations of Jewish mobility, while the third celebrates the possibility of personal reinvention.*]

The Jewish journey, as we've traced it from the end of the nineteenth century, assumes two alternative and dialectically related poetic forms. When the primary epic is articulated as a pattern of "return" (*shivat Zion*), its reference is to the earliest, sacred memory-places and pilgrimage narratives and to a vision of their reinscription in "political time"—a downscaled version of messianic time. Its parody, the picaresque voyage, though ostensibly linear, is episodic in form and circular in direction. Mired in the stagnancy of *galut* culture, but propelled by the skepticism of a return to the profane point of departure and the reflexive aesthetic of the romance, it issues in an implicit rejection of any utopian or epic resolution.

Mass migration westward from the homelands of Eastern Europe issued in another paradigm. As a kind of sanguine rewrite of both the epic, utopian and the anti-epic, satiric narrative of Israel's sojourn among the nations, it constitutes a third, *non*-epic model. The quotidian in this model is neither redeemed nor purgatorial time, but simply the time of our lives; neither time fulfilled nor time suspended, but time spent; neither Zion nor Galut but Diaspora. Although examples of the journey to (and in) America abound, and many of the writers from the "other Europe" have celebrated the haven they found there over a century of mass immigration,[1] it is Sholem Aleichem's last, unfinished novel, *Motl Peyse dem Khazns* [*Motl the Cantor's Son*], that comes from the same workshop as and therefore furnishes the best commentary on Abramovitsh's anti-epic; from our perspective, it can also furnish an "innocent" and therefore subversive commentary on Agnon's epic. The story of the journey to

America is the most affirmative of Sholem Aleichem's writings and in many ways the most mobile and open-ended of the fictions of his generation. It comes at the end of his series of travel narratives, which we will examine briefly; their cumulative effect is to reinvent and finally to relinquish the world of the shtetl as the Jewish imaginary.

KASRILEVKE: A MOVABLE FEAST?

Dov Sadan argued in 1959 that Sholem Aleichem (b. Shalom Rabinowitz, 1859; d. 1916) had not received the critical attention he deserved, an oversight attributable to his position as the middle element in the "classic triad" that also included Mendele (S. Y. Abramovitsh) and I. L. Peretz; Sadan then went on to assert that Sholem Aleichem had achieved in his work a true measure of mobility while the other two remained essentially chained to the society that nourished their nostalgia as well as their disdain. The "travels" of Benjamin the Third are predicated on imagining remote places and are enacted within the narrow confines of a few versts in the Pale of Settlement, creating a "satire of the desire to transform Jewish destiny" through movement. I. L. Peretz extends the time line of the Jewish spirit while remaining within the physical bounds of Poland and its environs. Though Sholem Aleichem's narratives are time bound, many of them move spatially along "the most dynamic lines of Jewish existence during the past generations, namely, along the routes of Jewish migration." Rooted in the Ukraine, his fictions reach out to the most remote lands of the European and even as far as the American Diaspora: "The Jewish migratory course throughout time and place is the very essence of Yiddish prose, but anyone desiring to find its outline in the works of the classic triad will be led only to Sholem Aleichem. The fact that none of them ever set eyes on Jerusalem, the oldest among them dying in Odessa, the next in line in Warsaw, and the youngest in New York, is more than mere biographical data."[2]

Jerusalem, the place on which "none of them ever set eyes," will remain a protean reference, the motherland that beckons her children home and also impedes their arrival, making other itineraries possible. Sholem Aleichem, the one who died in New York, had in the last of his narratives incorporated the American city into a viable extension of Jewish geography; these fictions initiated a process that substitutes mobility as a Jewish opportunity for wandering as a Jewish curse. In each of the stories I will consider, distancing from the point of origin is a function both of a specific form of mobility and of the narrative's implicit recipient or addressee, a subtle acknowledgment of the global village as a Jewish echo chamber for the Yiddish storyteller.

The epistolary travelogue of **Menakhem-Mendl** (1892-1913) expresses both the wanderlust and the essentially domesticated orientation of the shlemiel. As traveler and would-be entrepreneur in the affairs of an indifferent and exploitative world, Menakhem Mendl ventures as far away as New York, only to return. Even as he leaves the shtetl behind for the metropolises of Europe and America, his wife Sheyne Shendl remains the lodestone that draws him back to the fictive Ukrainian town of Kasrilevke; within the rubric of Jewish exile, once again, it is the wife at home, the wife *as* home, that allows the male to wander.[3] By contrast, the narratives that constitute the cycle of **Tevye der milkhiker** [**Tevye the Dairyman**], written between 1894 and 1916, maintain Kasrilevke as their proving ground and Tevye-in-Kasrilevke as center of gravity; Tevye's agon is primarily with his Creator,[4] and even Kasrilevke is large enough to accommodate dramas enacted on the vertical plane.

The majority of the stories that came to be known as **Ayznban geshikhtes: ksovim fun a komivoyazher** [**The Railroad Stories: Tales of a Commercial Traveler**] were written between 1909 and 1911,[5] when Sholem Aleichem himself was on the road in Eastern Europe, giving readings to adoring crowds but already ill with the tuberculosis that would shorten his life. He had essentially been en route since 1905, when his first attempt at settling in and transplanting his literary center to America (1906-1907) had ended in defeat. (His second attempt, in 1914, was more successful—or at least irreversible; he died and was buried in New York in 1916.) **The Railroad Stories** are confined to a space that is both a microcosm of the shtetl and the site of its deconstruction; the oral exchanges in the railway cars that progress sluggishly from one nondestination to another do not even gesture toward incorporating the romantic or skeptical act of return.

The serial novel **Motl** overlaps in part with the composition of the **Railroad Stories,** as it was begun in 1907 and was still being written on the author's deathbed in 1916. The forward thrust that distances the characters from Kasrilevke, their point of departure, also allows them to incorporate it as portable luggage in this narrative. Here there are no personal, geographical, or even linguistic impediments to the assimilation of the wonders of the New World.

TEVYE: DEFERRING THE LAST JOURNEY

Neither interior spaces nor vast outdoor panoramas contain the saga of Tevye the dairyman and his daughters; the country roads, the courtyards, and the forests provide the settings for his ongoing monologue with/at God. But in his dotage a new geographical possibility seems to unfold before him. The final chapters of **Tevye** *der milkhiker* plot what is meant to be Tevye's last journey—to the Land of Israel. A scheme by the petit-bourgeois husband of Tevye's youngest daughter Bey-lke to be rid of his impoverished father-in-law focuses on sending the old man to the farthest corner of the world; as he explains unabashedly, "With a business like mine, a reputation like mine, a public position like mine, I can't afford to have a cheesemonger for a father-in-law. . . . How about Palestine? *Isn't that where all the old Jews like you go to die?* . . . You take the express train to Odessa . . . and from there a ship sails to Jaffa" (emphasis mine).[6] Tevye recounts this episode to his interlocutor, Sholem Aleichem, adding: "don't ask me what I'll do in the Land of Israel if I get there safely, God willing." In attempting to answer the (unasked) question, he reveals that like his son-in-law, he views the Land of Israel on a par with Heaven itself, where the dead (including his own wife) spend their time interceding for the living.[7] The only thing he knows "for sure" at the end of the story titled **"Tevye Leaves for the Land of Israel"** (1909) is that as soon as he arrives, "right off, I plan to visit Mother Rachel in her grave. I'll pray there for the daughters I'll probably never see again" (E [English] [*Tevye the Dairyman*] 116; Y [Yiddish] [*Gants Tevye der milkhiker*] 195). Despite all the intervening years and changing sensibilities, it is a dream not unlike Yehuda Halevi's death-saturated vision of worship at ancestral shrines.

Sholem Aleichem's relationship with Tevye was described by his son-in-law as an intensely empathic one. In reminiscences of the author's last years, Y. D. Berkovitz relates that Sholem Aleichem had taken to writing a new installment of the Tevye saga each year; during the nearly two decades in which his story unfolded, Tevye aged and changed along with his creator. **"Tevye Leaves for the Land of Israel"** was written while Sholem Aleichem was recovering from a serious bout of tuberculosis. The writer, who remained a Zionist in principle throughout his life, had been informed by Zionists in Kiev that they were close to realizing their plan to build a house for him in Palestine: a delegation leaving for Jaffa to buy agricultural land would include some property for him in their purchase. In anticipation of this, explains Berkovitz disarmingly, "he would dispatch Tevye the dairyman ahead of him to Palestine, and if he should follow him and settle there, Tevye could be his mouthpiece and intercessor." Berkovitz assures us that whenever Sholem Aleichem returned to writing Tevye, he did so with great gaiety; while the actual work of composition exhausted him, he positively shone with the joy of creation.[8] Holding on for a moment to the charming conceit of Tevye as his creator's fellow traveler, I want to argue that the decision to "send" Tevye to the Holy Land, corresponding with Sholem Aleichem's own battle with the Angel of Death, is more complex than it at first appears.

The next and penultimate story in the final version of the *Tevye* cycle, **"Lekh-Lekha,"** is dated 1914; written in America, it follows the thread that had been introduced in the previous story but weaves it into a very different tapestry. **"Lekh-Lekha,"** the biblical account of the divine summons to Abraham to leave his fatherland and travel to the land of promise, and Abraham's alacritous response (Gen. 12), comes near the beginning of the annual lectionary cycle and constitutes the most fundamental reference for the theodicy of exile and homecoming. The actual effect of the intertext here, however, is not to inspire Tevye to settle in Palestine as part of either an ancient religious injunction or a modern historical-political strategy for changing Jewish fate. On the contrary, it reinforces *wandering* as mythic Jewish behavior grounded in the ancient sources and the vision of the Land of Israel as the "other side": "I had one foot on the *other side* (*yener zayt*), that is, in the Holy Land" (E 117; Y 200).[9] Tevye gives Sholem Aleichem a lesson based on his own inimitable, and proprietary, reading of the Bible:

> *Lekh-lekho*—get thee out, Tevye—*meyartsekho*—from your land—*umimoyladetkho*—and from the village you were born in and lived in your whole life—*el ha'orets asher arekko*—to wherever your legs will carry you. . . . And when did it occur to the powers-that-be to tell me that? Not a minute before I'm so old, weak and lonely that I'm a real *al tashlikheynu le'eys ziknoh*, as it says in the Rosh Hashanah prayer. . . . Only I'm getting ahead of myself, because I was telling you about my trip and what's new in the Land of Israel. Well, what should be new there, my dear friend? It's a land flowing with milk and honey—if you don't believe me, you can read up on it in the Bible. There's only one thing the matter with it, which is that it's there and I'm here . . . and not only am I still here in Russia, I'm still a schlimazel in Russia, and a schlimazel I'll be till I die![10]

> (E 117; Y 200)

What was it that subverted this scheme at (as) the very last moment? Why is it that Sholem Aleichem, old and ailing in America, deprived his equally aged and frail Tevye of the moment of arrival in the Land of Israel? Why, in 1914, is there no "news" from the Old/New Land? Why is the historical option, tentatively entertained in **"Tevye Leaves for the Land of Israel,"** superseded by a resounding return to the sanctuary of the *text*? Is it an interrogative, reflexive gesture similar to that which released Benjamin the Third both from the czarist army and from his fantasies of rescue and redemption in the Holy Land?

At the level of the *fabula,* the scheming son-in-law goes bankrupt and flees to America; another son-in-law dies suddenly and his widow Tsaytl and their children move in with Tevye: "How could I even think of a pilgrimage to the Holy Land when I had a house full of little pilgrims myself?" (E 118; Y 201).[11] At this point the true meaning of *lekh-lekho* reveals itself: the authorities prepare a little "pogrom" for the Jewish townspeople (in which they are invited to smash their own windows) and then expel them. Finally, Chava, the beloved daughter excommunicated for having married out of the faith, is reunited with her family and elects to share their fate. The structural function of this reconciliation as closure for the family saga is revealed by Tevye himself, who interrupts his tale at the moment Chava appears in order to assure his interlocutor that "it was just like in one of your books" (E 129; Y 219).[12] But however self-reflexive or contrived its presentation, this is only a provisional ending, which is inevitably undermined by the biblical scaffolding that authorizes the narrative and demands a resolution of a different order. I am proposing that we shift our attention from the romantic theme, which is certainly dominant throughout all the stories, to the migration theme and examine its relation to forms of narration and closure.

In the context of the pogrom that is a cameo version of the original scenario of banishment and exile, Tevye once more cites the injunction to Abraham, this time explaining it to Tsaytl as a decree devolving on him and "all the Jews": "*lekh-lekho meyartsekho,* get thee out of thy land, did Abraham ask Him where to? God told him exactly where to, *el ha'orets asher arekko*—which means in plain language, hit the road! We'll go where all the other Jews go—that is, where our two feet take us" (E 126; Y 213).

So making his "trip to Israel" turns out to be nothing more—nor less—than divesting himself of all forms of private aggrandizement (even the old horse has been sold) and preparing for the proverbial crossing to the Other Side. But since Sholem Aleichem in his infinite mercy will not allow Tevye to die, he cannot admit him to the Holy Land; foreclosing Tevye's *'aliyah* to the Holy Land is, in a way, foreclosing closure itself, endowing him with the eternal life that guarantees the continuation of his narrative and a complicating or doubling of exile as the primary condition of Jewish storytelling.[13] In the chapter published just before Sholem Aleichem's death (1916), which provides the coda for the entire Tevye cycle, "arrival" is relegated to the messianic future; every practical option for the Jewish journey is entertained except that which would bring the journey itself to an end:

> "You see, ever since I was given that lesson in Lekh-Lekho, I've been on the go; there hasn't been a place I could point to and say, 'Tevye, we're here; now sit

down and relax.' But Tevye asks no questions; if he's told to keep moving, he does. Today, Pani Sholem Aleichem, we met on the train, but tomorrow may find us in Yehupetz, and next year in Odessa, or in Warsaw, or maybe even in America . . . unless, that is, the Almighty looks down on us and says, 'Guess what, children! I've decided to send you my Messiah!' I don't even care if He does it just to spite us, as long as He's quick about it, that old God of ours! And in the meantime, be well and have a good trip."[14]

(E 131)

Tevye takes up his staff and goes off into an undetermined afterlife. The Land of Israel reverts to a place in a text, a place identified with the arrival that is death—with the shrines to the dead patriarchs or with one's own death or messianic high drama. When it comes to living, and making a living (meager as it is), one stays here, on this side, in Yehupetz or Odessa or even . . . America.

The Railroad Stories: Getting Nowhere, Slowly

Admittedly, it seems rather perverse to argue that just a few decades before the mass extermination of the Jews of Europe and the establishment of the State of Israel, Odessa or Warsaw retains a position in the Jewish imagination as the place of the living and Jerusalem as the domain of death; as early as 1907, after all, writers like S. Y. Agnon were referring to the shtetl as *'ir ha-metim* (city of the dead).[15] I am nonetheless arguing here for the value of a self-consciously naive reading, especially of the *Railroad Stories.* Trains shuttled Jews back and forth in the Pale of Settlement and provided the locus for their stories and jokes for several decades before becoming the metonymy of their collective doom. For the post-Holocaust reader, spending even a few moments cooped up with these third-class passengers without reference to their extratextual fate is a self-limiting gesture, an act of resistance to the "backshadowing" or anachronism that inevitably informs belated encounters.[16] Not only does such a strategy help reconstruct the "presentness of the past," but it also preserves the profiles of those characters for whom the trains were crowded enough without adding ghostly presences from the future. As we saw, the last story in the *Tevye* cycle is recited in the train. If wandering is reaffirmed here as Jewish destiny, it is in the *Railroad Stories* and finally in *Motl the Cantor's Son* that the journey itself becomes primary.

The train, the most palpable and ubiquitous embodiment of the industrial revolution, has informed the imagination of every society through which it has passed.[17] The forms of complex pastoralism that characterize both the American and the European reception of the railroad are, for the most part, represented in late-nineteenth-and early-twentieth-century art and literature by views of the serene landscape marked (or pockmarked, as the case may be) by the steam engine and its snaky appendage. The view we get of the train in many Yiddish and Hebrew fictions is not the gaze from the outside, the gaze of a society *in charge of* its natural environment, but the nervous report from within the overpopulated third-class compartment. Such compartments become, in their literary representations, the cultural compensation for a kind of mobile proletariat in a state of profound socioeconomic alienation. Reflecting the absence of a proprietary relationship to the surroundings, the view *from the inside* reinforces both the intimacy and the hermetic quality of this space; the train stories by Yiddish and Hebrew writers in fact constitute a uniquely intermediate imaginary space at the turn of the century.[18]

In his reconstruction of "everyday" spaces for the "ordinary man," Michel de Certeau invokes the immobility of both inner and outer spaces that is belied by the *experience* of railway travel between two points. The "order" within the railway car is at once fixed and provisional, based on the anonymity and randomness of the encounters:

> There is something at once incarcerational and navigational about railroad travel. . . . Between the immobility of the inside and that of the outside a certain *quid pro quo* is introduced, a slender blade that inverts their stability. The chiasm is produced by the windowpane and the rail. . . . The windowpane is what allows us to *see,* and the rail, what allows us to *move through.* The first creates the spectator's distance: You shall not touch; the more you see, the less you hold—a dispossession of the hand in favor of a greater trajectory for the eye. The second inscribes, indefinitely, the injunction to pass on; it is its order written in a single but endless line: go, leave, this is not your country, and neither is that—an imperative of separation which obliges one to pay for an abstract ocular domination of space by leaving behind any proper place, by losing one's footing.[19]

Lekh-lekho. Go, leave, this is not your country. . . . We might argue that unlike one who is rooted to a place and observes from a stable position on the outside a train cutting through the landscape—or, for that matter, a *picture* of a train slicing the landscape[20]—the traveler enacts the "imperative of separation" from the land she or he traverses. This separation, experienced through the agency of the machine, mimics for the duration of the journey the essential condition of the *golus* Jew whose cultural ambassador is the storyteller. The "silence of these things put at a distance," of "object[s] without discourse" beyond the windowpane that in de Certeau's scheme separates interior from exterior space, "makes our memories speak or draws out of the shadows the dreams of our secrets."[21] It thus becomes the perfect venue for telling stories. Silence holds the pageant enacted on the outside; speech is inside. The speech-intoxicated Jews hardly have time to look out the window at scenery to which they can never lay claim anyway. These stories rarely have any relation to the landscapes through which the train travels, except for occasional references to stations that function as terminals or watering holes. The coach promotes the illusion both of being away from home and of having a "roof over your head" (E [*The Railroad Stories*] 143; Y [*Ayznban-Geshikhtes*] 25)—an interior space whose physical boundaries are the dimensions of the railway car, but whose cultural boundaries are defined by the Yiddish speech within and the goyish landscape without.[22]

S. Y. Abramovitsh's Hebrew story "Shem and Japheth on the Train" (1890) moves between stations in a railway coach filled with Jews whose destinations seem determined by the exigencies of their hungry stomachs. Jewish exile is confirmed here as an inexorable pattern of the universe; even the comets (Japheth as Polish cobbler) that stray into this (third-class) galaxy learn to conform to its physical laws.[23] Such narratives, which tease their passengers with a whiff of westward, forward motion, are but journeys into the recesses of the Pale of Settlement. As mobile echo chambers for storytelling, trains will also furnish Sholem Aleichem with the perfect venue for practicing his craft.

The absence of destination in Sholem Aleichem's narrative cycle defines the aimless movement of Jews through a space measured only as the distance between neighboring stations. Even the pretense of direction offered in Abramovitsh's tales has been relinquished in the ***Railroad Stories*** in favor of the narratological function of local stations as the terminal points of a story. One of the lines, the Slowpoke Express (*Der leydikgeyer*), moves so slowly that "you needn't ever worry about missing it: whenever you arrive at the station, it's still there" (E 184; Y 105). What verbal compensations are there for such sluggish movement through space? The Jews confined in crowded railway cars consider the same subjects that were aired in that other claustrophobic place, the bathhouse, in *Benjamin the Third*—but with a keener edge: the discussion of the "recent harvest" gives way to a heated negotiation of the war with Japan, the Revolution of 1905, the Constitution, the "pogroms, the massacres of Jews, the new anti-Semitic legislation, the expulsion from the villages, the mass flight to America . . . " (**"Baranovich Station,"** E 152; Y 41-42). (The causal connection between the pogroms and the mass migration to America was elevated to the status of theodicy in Sholem Aleichem's writing as early as

1906; we will see later how it became an animating force in *Motl*.)

The *Railroad Stories* are vignettes of life in the shtetl as captured from a distance without preserving them for future reference in the formaldehyde of nostalgia, as did Sholem Aleichem's more popular fiction, but instead recording the moment of the breakup of the society—the economic, social, and psychological upheaval that is a response to threats from within and without. Dan Miron argues persuasively that they are *not*, as Y. Y. Trunk suggested, "Kasrilevke on wheels,"[24] but rather a gesture of *distancing* from the shtetl as the matrix of an innocent, pristine existence and point of reference for the alienated traveler. Miron goes so far as to define these stories as "anti-Kasrilevke" and sees in their deviation from what had come to be understood and adored as Sholem Aleichem's style the reason for the relative lack of critical attention paid them. But the more popular Kasrilevke stories have, after all, been filtered through the roseate lenses of their American reception and Sholem Aleichem's benedictory presence in them. The railroad stories lack the unifying "comic-pathetic" narrative voice of a folk hero such as Tevye or Menakhem Mendl or Motl, or the mediating presence of a "Sholem Aleichem," and thus the words are a more flimsy barrier against the destructive forces undermining shtetl life from the outside. The motifs of "immigration, displacement, separation and alienation," which run throughout Sholem Aleichem's fiction, appear here without the "grace and the innocence" of the small-town context; it is, Miron argues, the story of the road as opposed to the home, of the transitory as opposed to the permanent, of passing as opposed to ongoing human encounters, of cognitive dissonance or systematic misunderstandings in place of the subtle mutuality of intimates, of the anonymity that provides not only a context for the revelation of sordid human behavior but also a smoke screen against the consequences of such revelations.[25] On this reading, the crowded third-class coach imposes the forced, ephemeral intimacy of strangers who convene as a "community" only for the purpose of hearing a story: "My three Jews had parted company," says the narrator after relating a tale of mutual misunderstanding between a storyteller and his listeners; "the brief friendship was over. . . . It was curious how the three had become total strangers" (**"Eighteen from Pereshchepena,"** E 166; Y 68).[26]

This is one of the moments in which the modern representation of exile as alienation and anomie adds an entirely new existential layer to the inherited meanings of *golus*. True to the monologic form (in a sense its very distillation, produced in the laboratory of a railway coach), nothing really happens in narrative time except for *narration itself*; granted, people eat and

sleep and pray, and a few peddlers even manage to peddle their wares . . . but mostly what people do in these coaches is to tell stories. Many of their stories are narrated acts of suicide, extortion, and embezzlement and assorted reports of hard-heartedness. They are stories from which the softness of Sholem Aleichem's benevolent and gentle sensitivity has been withdrawn—and it is not coincidental that he "himself" does not appear as either the narrator or addressee of the stories. That this is perhaps the most sinister of Sholem Aleichem's fictions is evidenced by the absence of the compassionate intervention of the narrator-qua-author. Instead, the mediating voice is that of an anonymous self-styled "commercial traveler" (*komi-voyazher*)—not exactly a writer and most certainly not Sholem Aleichem. The passengers are in some profound sense truly lost, abandoned even by the gently chiding humor of their creator, who joins Stephen Dedalus's God-as-artist—refined out of existence, indifferent, paring his fingernails.

And yet something urgently personal or even self-consciously autobiographical in these stories is paradoxically signified by the author's withdrawal as persona; on the road since 1905, Sholem Aleichem refers to himself in correspondence from the sanatorium as a "reizender, a komi-voyazher be-khol tefutzot Yisrael" (a voyager, a commercial traveler in all the diasporas of Israel).[27] The stories are artifacts from the shtetl as well as evidence of its disintegration and of the author's remove from it. The circumstances of their composition, as related by Berkovitz, add another dimension to the narratives themselves and to the representation of the life of the author as fellow traveler in his constructed universe. By his own account, Sholem Aleichem was "incarcerated" in the sanatorium at St. Blasien in the company of the moribund ("hatzi-metim," in Berkovitz's words); on one of his regular walks in the rain-drenched Schwartzwald, his encounter with a young yeshiva student who had come there expressly to meet the great writer produced a unique "collaboration" that issued in four of the *Railroad Stories*. The student was, naturally, curious to hear stories from the mouth of the literary eminence— but Sholem Aleichem was interested only in listening to the "facts" his interlocutor had to convey from his backwater shtetl in Podolia. It is the same appeal that the ailing writer makes in the above-mentioned letter, asking a journalist friend in White Russia for "raw material from Homel, from Vitebsk, from Bialystok, from wherever you care to, as long as it is subject matter that I can use in my *Railroad Stories*. . . . Please keep one thing in mind, though," he adds: "I don't want anything imaginary, just facts, the more the better!"[28]

Of particular interest here is the emphasis Sholem Aleichem places on "factuality," insisting that both the student and his correspondent relay true and not invented stories.[29] Berkovitz points out that his father-in-law, on the road for some time, was separated from the sources of his creativity and languishing among the sick and dying; a healthy young man full of stories from the homeland acted as a catalyst for his imagination. It is tempting to argue, nevertheless, that Sholem Aleichem is concerned with something far more subtle and consequential than mere accuracy in transmitting these stories—though they do reproduce the diction of the region and other local colors, the raw material has clearly gone through the alchemy of Sholem Aleichem's pen. The very insistence on facts is not only a well-worn literary convention for authorizing flights of the literary imagination but also a refusal of the digressions from the press of history that Sholem Aleichem's humor had provided in the stories that had endeared him to his readers; at the same time, it marks his distance from the source. The author here makes a testimonial or conservationist gesture vis-à-vis an endangered culture not unlike that which motivated Agnon or Buber or Berdichevski, each fashioning a specific form of intertextual or "documentary" response to the passing traditions whose very passing they had encouraged. David Roskies argues that storytelling filled the vacuum created in the process of transition, becoming a kind of "politics of rescue"—a form of displacement or "creative betrayal" by which the culture could reincorporate its own oral traditions.[30]

The storytelling performed on a train follows certain external constraints peculiar to its context. Sholem Aleichem, writing from St. Blasien, creates a third-class, claustrophobic version of the sanatoria, spas, hotels, and inns that so frequently provide the venues for random encounters in twentieth-century fiction. But what is most striking in these mobile talking chambers is that their destination is absent or insignificant except as a structural element. Unlike *Benjamin the Third,* the train stories do not trace a skeptical pattern of return. Where there is no teleological orientation, there is also no antiteleological or dystopic disorientation. The Jews may not be going anywhere on the train, but they're not going back to the shtetl either (except for a visit or to "buy" a kosher wife).[31]

The ultimate consolation for the breakdown of social cohesion is the perfection of form. The short story is as protective of its parts as the train is of its cars; when it reaches the station, the "terminal" that signals that the story has ended and history has begun—halting the "incarceration-vacation," the "Robinson Crusoe adventure of the travelling noble soul that could believe itself *intact* because it was surrounded by glass

and iron"—then narrative must end and "history begin again."[32] The generic advantage of the short story, which can capture the life it tells in a frozen cross-section, is doubled here within the context of the railroad. Virtually all of these stories are structured by the intervals between stations, marking the entrances and exits of the players; a few of them, like **"Baranovich Station,"** which tells an excruciating tale of extortion practiced by a villager who had been saved by his fellow townspeople from a flogging, are abruptly discontinued when the train reaches the storyteller's point of disembarkation: "Hey there! You can't do this to us! We won't let you go. You have to tell us the end of the story!" (E 163; Y 58)

Many of the other stories do reach closure—but it is the provisional closure of life captured in a moment, *in medias res,* between stations. In **"Happiest Man in All Kodny,"** a storyteller accompanies a medical specialist to his home to examine his tubercular son; the story relates the father's successful adventure in persuading the good doctor to pay the poor Jew a house call. He is indeed the "happiest man"—enjoying temporary respite in what is sure to unfold *beyond the confines of the train and the story* as a tragedy.

The reader and Sholem Aleichem "himself" do not belong inside the railway coach; like distant relatives or curious onlookers, they are relegated to the other side of the window, peering in. The pane of glass that separates the voyagers from the reader is an alienating device that is utterly shattered in *Motl.* That novel directly addresses a large second-person audience, as the young narrator brings with him to America not only all the inhabitants of the shtetl but all of its readers as well.

AMERICA: DETOXIFYING THE EUROPEAN STORY

That the most affirmative of Sholem Aleichem's writings is a narrative of the journey to (and in) America can be understood largely in terms of a common thread binding a host of European writers and their American readers. The perennial rediscovery of America as an inherently optimistic construct illuminates some of the darkest corners of the European imagination. As unlikely as the comparison between Sholem Aleichem and Franz Kafka may appear at first,[33] even Kafka's *Amerika* can reveal the transformative power of the ethos of immigration.

In the American cartography of Europe, both Sholem Aleichem and Kafka are identified with remote places: the small Jewish towns of Eastern Europe and the urban remnants of the Austro-Hungarian Empire. Each of these writers was imported into America as the expression of a different aspect of the European imagination and Jewish fate: the one representing innocuous Jewish humor (identified eventually with fiddlers on roofs), the other a sense of the absurd and the alienated (associated ultimately with Jews in gas chambers). But in the European cartography of America, neither would be viewed as a creator or recorder of American landscapes. It is true that whereas Sholem Aleichem spent the last years of his life in New York and was buried there, Kafka, who hardly ever ventured outside Prague, seems barely to have dreamed of America.[34]

Yet Motl's New York has the same pride of place in the Yiddish narrative as Karl's "Nature Theatre of Oklahoma" in the German. Both *Motl Peyse dem Khazns* and *Amerika,* written during the same years and left unfinished at the time of their authors' deaths,[35] represent not only versions of the American immigrant saga, and the story of childhood or youth whose innocence is assaulted but never completely undermined, but also a major recasting of the topos and telos of the Jewish journey—as the curse of wandering yields to the blessings of mobility.

Kafka's America, the target not of celebration but of mild scorn, would nonetheless become the place where his imagination could play with relative safety: where the innocent are exploited *but not killed*;[36] where wide open spaces replace the confinement of the "European prison";[37] where aphasia replaces the burden of knowledge and memory;[38] where modern technology and architecture are restricting and possibly enslaving but not lethal;[39] where the insidious forces that stalk their victims everywhere in this godless universe are somehow *interrupted* in their work;[40] and where, finally, tinsel and apocalypse come together to produce a version of Hollywood's never-never land as directed from Prague.

It was the darker side of Kafka's imagination that was imported to America in the 1940s when the American mind needed a European language to speak of European forms of alienation and finally of European atrocities;[41] *Amerika,* the sunniest of Kafka's long fictions, never quite received the attention lavished on *The Castle* or *The Trial.* To be sure, one can overstate the sunny disposition of this narrative. Some among Kafka's readers offer powerful counterarguments that from the very first glimpse of the teeming immigrants on the boat and Miss Liberty with a sword in place of a torch, *Amerika* is a scathing indictment of *Zivilization* without *Kultur,* a transposition onto the American imaginary of Kafka's "Mitteleuropa decadence"—or even that it is the quintessential modern representation of the Jewish condition of exile.[42] Nevertheless, in America the elements of Kafka's imaginative universe undergo detoxification. In the case of Sholem Aleichem, as I will show, the journey to and arrival in

America are more akin to alchemy—not so much dispelling the fear as transforming the dross of one's European baggage into the gold of American opportunity. The writings of both are related to the American discovery narrative and the primary myth of self-invention. "In its simplest, archetypal form, the myth affirms that Europeans experience a regeneration in the New World," observes Leo Marx. "They become new, better, happier men—they are reborn."[43]

Rebirth is predicated on a forgetting and an "oceanic feeling" that in Kafka's and Sholem Aleichem's narratives are initiated by crossing the ocean itself. *Motl Peyse dem Khazns* moves deliberately from the invented town of Kasrilevke through several of the stations that make up the actual geography of the European migration (Brod, Cracow, Lemberg, Vienna, Antwerp, London), with New York as its terminus. They describe a tangent that brushes and then moves resolutely away from the circular geometry of the Pale of Settlement, away from the stations of the train that, laden with Jewish passengers in its third-class compartments, snaked its way aimlessly through the Eastern European landscape. This story is narrated in the first person by Motl, the young son of the ailing Cantor Peyse. The father's illness and death precipitate the divestment that ends in the family's emigration to and settlement in America.

When first published as a whole, posthumously, in 1920, the narrative was divided into two volumes: the first brings the group of *emigrants* to England, the site of embarkation for America; the stories of the second, which remains unfinished, are located onboard the ocean liner, on Ellis Island, and finally in the streets and tenements of New York. Consistent with their theme, the publishing history of these stories also embraces the entire range of Jewish geography; the first story was published in *Der Amerikaner* in New York in May 1907; others appeared in Yiddish journals in Vilna and Petersburg as well as New York. The earliest story of the second part appeared in 1914, but the outbreak of World War I postponed until 1916 the publication of the other "American" chapters.[44]

Serialization was common in contemporary Yiddish and Hebrew fiction; but the publication of this text as a series of relatively autonomous narratives distributed over time and space becomes significant as thematically and even formally emblematic of its expansive spatial purchase. Although the first story, published as an occasional piece in honor of Shavuoth, does not give any indication of a larger conceptual framework, the open-ended narrative, read as structurally inherent rather than as a defect, elides questions of artistic intent and control as well as closure. The open-ended story also proves functional in generating interpretive communities.[45] Discussing immigrant journalism in the United States at the turn of the century, Werner Sollors argues that "serialized fiction intensified the sense of community between writer and audience as well as among the readers themselves."[46] Still, there is something quite extraordinary in the ingathering of Sholem Aleichem's readers, scattered as they are over the globe. His status as a storyteller was reinforced in the public readings he gave during the decade of his peregrinations in Europe—and his funeral, attended by as many as a quarter of a million people, was a public rite testifying not only to the affection with which he was regarded but also to the value accorded to both the storyteller's performance of literature and the audience's act of witnessing.[47]

And yet by giving both the **Train Stories** and **Motl** the label *ksovim* (writings), Sholem Aleichem may be acknowledging another direction in which this storytelling tradition is moving. The presumed transition from "oral" to "written" culture implies the very mobility that is being enacted in his narrative. The act of writing is a form of *editing* reality, and "reality" includes the orally transmitted folk wisdom no less than the events being related. The cozy boundaries of the storytelling circle are canceled here, as Motl in his monologue appeals directly to an explicit but nonspecific, extratextual reader without the mediation of "Sholem Aleichem" or the crowd of familiar strangers of the sort that traveled through the train stories. The second-person formal pronoun, which incorporates both singular and plural addressees, is as essential to the progress of the narrative as it is undefined: "I spend the whole day at the river fishing and swimming. I learned how to fish all by myself. If you wish (*az ir vilt*), I can teach you. You take your shirt off . . . "; "Before I start telling you (*eyder ikh gey aykh dertseyln*) how one makes a living in the new country . . . "[48] It is as if Sholem Aleichem en route to and in America had opened his storehouse to an unbounded world of readers; by taking his (expandable) audience with him, he manages to leave his native ground without relinquishing his ties to posterity.

Many critics have noted the contrast between the events of the first, "European," part of **Motl,** encoded in the adult mind as a series of catastrophes, and their redefinition in the child's narrative; Motl's "forgetting," or inappropriate response, one might say, takes on the weight of a radical reformulation of cultural, social, and eventually linguistic categories. The boy as tabula rasa is the site of negotiable realities. Other consciousnesses, recorded faithfully by Motl, mediate the related events: that of "our friend Pini," the local prophet and know-it-all; that of "our brother Eliahu," the bane of Motl's young existence; those of the teary-eyed mother and her multiple-chinned friend Pessie.

But Motl's voice is not only the most persistent; it is also the loudest and most outrageous. The first chapters, located in Kasrilevke, narrate the process by which the family's chattel is sold to purchase medication for Motl's sick father—a dispossession celebrated by the nine-year-old son as a form of liberation.[49] Orphanhood signals the initial deliverance from authority; "Mir iz gut—ikh bin a yosem!" (It's grand to be an orphan) (E [*Adventures of Mottel the Cantor's Son*] 23; Y [*Motl Peyse dem Khazns*] 1:33) are the words by which he announces to his readers that his father has died.[50]

The chapters located in the shtetl and on the journey itself are thus under the sign of a massive negation, a rewriting of the world. Dan Miron reads *Motl* as a mythic story of death and regeneration, in which "death is not only a convenient point of departure, but a necessary one. Implied is that one cannot begin a new life without laying the old one to rest." Death is the place where "comedy and tragedy fuse: the myth of the old father, king or god, who dies in order to fertilize a wasteland for its eventual flowering under the spirit of the young divinity."[51]

Insistence on the primordial, and therefore inexorable, nature of the myth holds particular comfort for those of us who survey, from the end of this bloody century, the waves of immigrants who left their "fatherlands" to embrace a new order in Palestine or in America (each a world of sons and daughters) and reflect on the great conflagration that utterly consumed what was left of the "world of the fathers." *Motl,* however, conceived at the more innocent end of our century, reconstructs this myth out of local, more lightweight materials: the American theater of self-invention provides the stage and the narrative privilege of Purim furnishes the script by which Jewish worlds are abandoned and then reinvented.

PURIM: CASTING OF LOTS AND RECASTING OF PLOTS

The acts of exaggeration or masking and of repression or transformation are transparently connected in this narrative with theatricality or the carnivalesque and with language as a medium for restructuring reality.[52] Though the holiday that Jews celebrate is explicitly referred to as an instance of self-empowerment and deliverance, the Purim principle of inversion or *nahafokh-hu* is manifest in this narrative more as a series of compositional strategies. Cognitive dissonance marks Motl's monologues, as we have seen ("It's grand to be an orphan"); systematic misunderstanding marks his dialogues. In exchanges between Motl and Kopl, another young emigrant traveling from Kasrilevke to London, the inevitable subject of pogroms arises:

I ask him what is a pogrom? All the emigrants keep talking about "pogroms" but I don't know what they are. Kopl says, "Don't you know what a pogrom is? Then you're just a baby! A pogrom is something that you find everywhere nowadays. It starts out of nothing, and once it starts it lasts for three days."

"Is it like a fair?"

"A fair? Some fair! They break windows, they bust up furniture, rip pillows, feathers fly like snow. . . . And they beat and kill and murder."

"Whom?"

"What do you mean, *whom*? The Jews!"

"What for?"

"What a question! It's a pogrom, isn't it?"

"And so it's a pogrom. What's that?"

"Go away, you're a fool. It's like talking to a calf."

(E 147-18; Y 1:213-14)

The circular reasoning that loops back on the initial question keeps the threat contained—but also exposes the sinister underpinnings of Yiddish idioms in which a fair (*yarid*) can yield up its original meaning to signify a pogrom. The next time the subject comes up, Motl is ready with a more aggressive form of defense that self-consciously edits out the gloomier aspects of Jewish memory: "Once upon a time, when I heard people tell about pogroms, I was all eyes and ears," admits Motl. "Now, when I hear the word *pogrom,* I run. I prefer jolly stories."[53] Compare the epistemological effects of such denial here with Isaac Babel's short Russian story "The Story of My Dovecot" (1925), in which the slow evolution of a child's consciousness of evil culminates in the invocation of the sinister word. By the time he can admit the term "pogrom" into his own lexicon, Babel's young narrator has endured a rite de passage into the adult world where evil and violence prevail.[54] Motl's passage is to a world that refuses to accommodate evil—or, for that matter, adults.

In a universe perceived as having been created with an answer for every conundrum, a balm for every plague, a cure for every disease, America is represented as the remedy prepared in anticipation of the pogroms that would drive the Jews there. In the chapters written in and about America, composed shortly before the author's death, this is an article of faith enunciated by "our friend" Pini with all the pomposity of one who has just passed the Statue of Liberty: "You forget that God created America in order to shelter and protect the meek and the poor, the offended and the persecuted, and the ones who are hounded from all parts of the world" (E 252; Y 2:64).[55]

Patterned after such a divine model, the license to rewrite a sinister plot can be an invitation to a Purim carnival; Miecke Bal has pointed to the analogous acts

of casting lots (*purim*) and recasting *p*lots.[56] Motl's "revisionism" becomes a form of masquerade that borders on the grotesque. In the leave-taking passage, as his family departs for America, the egregious deformities of each of the characters serve to undermine the conventional pathos of the situation by suggesting to the unsentimental narrator a form of *teater* (theater); as players in a melodrama, they act their roles to the hilt: "All of a sudden everybody starts to sniff and to cry. Mother cries harder than anyone. She falls into Pessie's arms, wailing, 'You've been a sister to me! You've been more than a sister!' Our neighbor Pessie doesn't cry, but her triple chin trembles and tears, as large as peas, roll down her fat glistening cheeks. Everybody has done his share of kissing except Pini. To see Pini kiss is a spectacle (*zen Pinyen kushn zikh— darf men nisht keyn teater*). He kisses the middle of somebody's beard, the tip of somebody's nose, or else he bumps into somebody's forehead" (E 112; Y 1:163). The significance of Motl's chosen "vocation" as cartoonist is nowhere more pronounced than in this scene.[57] His métier takes the place of satire, which he is too young and nonreflective to enact, serving as a distancing device from the culture of origin. The connection between caricature, theater, and the masking or rewriting of reality is maintained as long as it is functional and necessary—that is, through the shtetl chapters and the voyage to America.

The journey itself, fraught with the terrors of the unknown, exacts extraordinary editorial feats. The escape from Europe and the ocean voyage are recorded and edited with Puccini-like realism so that the intolerable lies fully disclosed—a corpse on the stage about which Motl tiptoes in madcap denial. Mama's tears wash over the narrative like a tidal wave over an ocean liner, leaving the threat of both maudlin sentimentalism and trachoma in their wake. Seasickness, bedbugs, the inequities of the immigrant aid societies, missing luggage, and missing persons submit, one by one, to the spirit of Purim.

The Purim spirit is an inebriated state in which one confuses the saintly Mordecai with the villainous Haman. It is a ritual reenactment of the effect of a contravening narrative on the "original" story of genocide, a performative interpretation of a royal decree that empowered the would-be victims to commit preemptive acts of self-defense against the edict that had authorized their murder. The "revision" converts the outcome from a funeral into a masked ball. Recent studies of Purim as exemplifying the "cultural poetics of Judaism" stress the acts of writing and reading that are central to the scroll of Esther itself and the observance of the holiday, the inherently "diasporic" nature of the event and of the forms of its commemoration, and the more obvious principles of inversion and masquerade.[58] The sinister aspects of the holiday as licensing vengeance, which have also been explored in the less-apologetic historiography of the late twentieth century,[59] reveal the desperate undercurrents that run through a chronically disabled culture. In *Motl,* these undercurrents are suppressed by the abiding presence of the child who keeps the tale within the safe precincts and innocence of make-believe. The acts of violence transfigured through magical writing can include even the "killing" of the father at the beginning of the narrative (and the "killing off" of the whole community at the end, as we will see below).[60] Defined as a defense against the fear of annihilation in the Esther story, a defense against the fear of the death of the father and the journey to the unknown in *Motl,* the act of writing becomes utterly consequential.[61]

AMERICA IS FOR CHILDREN

Purim is for children, and so is America. At the beginning of the century, the idea of America as a place of rebirth meant, symbolically, that it was a place for the young. "Amerike—a naye velt far yiddishe *kinder,"* wrote Sholem Aleichem in a letter to Bialik and in Motl's monologue—a comment that can be loosely paraphrased, with a nod to Yeats, as "that is no country for old people."[62] The romantic and midrashic notions of the child who comes into the world trailing clouds of glory, close to the source but amnesiac, represent the American moment captured in this narrative. Motl's redefinition of old-world reality is a very active form of amnesia. The inconsistencies of presenting as the author of "writings" a boy who, as it turns out, is preliterate, who has the literalizing mind of a child but the vocabulary and occasionally the syntax of a sophisticated adult, who does not grow up or mature over the nine years in which the chapters of his journey are being composed and disseminated, render this story something other than a historical novel or bildungsroman.[63]

Though Motl doesn't grow, he *moves,* ultimately acting out his capacious dreams in New York's streets. In the economy of this narrative, change is located not in time or character development but in geographic venues, each with a different social value. The first chapter is marked by emergence from the darkness of winter, the cellar, and the lugubrious sickroom where Peyse the Cantor lies dying; the second celebrates the space gained when the furniture is sold to buy medicine and food for the sick man; the middle chapters are laid out across the expanse of the voyage; and the final chapters chart urban and domestic spaces in America. But space in urban America is not empty; discarding the old creates room for acquisition, for grounding in the world of *things.* The child as site of a Purim sensibility and as a miniature shlemiel, editor of

an intolerable reality, performs what may be the ultimate act of alchemy in modern Jewish letters. But no less significant, though seldom remarked, is that it is followed by its antithesis: the embrace of an alternative reality, of America as the space of unlimited possibility. Preoccupied with the child's redefinition of reality, critics often fail to note that this principle is no longer operative in the second section of the novel: American reality as configured in these chapters does not require a radical act of rewriting in order to fit Motl's yea-saying disposition.

The Purim privilege is renounced as superfluous in a country in which every day is Purim. As the gang who once swarmed over the dirt paths of the shtetl in the hopelessness of their poverty populate the streets of New York in the first flush of their success, Motl's friend Hershl, who had been nicknamed "Vashti" in Kasrilevke (after the unfortunate first wife of King Ahasuerus in the Book of Esther), is renamed "Harry":

> This is Vashti, who in the old country never saw a coin, even in a dream. Except on Purim in return for delivering Purim sweets for others. But Purim comes only once a year—while here, every weekday is Purim for Vashti. He earns money every single day.
>
> "Columbus, who can compare with you!" our friend Pini is moved to exclaim when he strolls along Rivington Street and with his own eyes sees Vashti working at the stand. He goes up to him, buys three cents' worth of carobs, and gives Vashti one cent, *na tshayock,* or a "tip," as they say here, in America.[64] (Words appearing in English in the original are underscored here.)

With the help of Pini's ideological slogans, we can trace the process by which the world of the shtetl is replaced by the world of America: "Vashti" is exchanged for "Harry" and Purim for Columbus, the coinage of Russian poverty for American capitalism and Yiddish for English.

Granted, a sweatshop is not a textile factory, and Brother Eliyahu's salary doesn't quite match Rothschild's; but role-playing is so much a function of the fluidity of the American economy that every day is carnival day. Like a quick-change artist, Eliyahu moves from sweatshop to entrepreneurship as waiter, as "collector," and ultimately as petty businessman with a newspaper stand. America has become the incarnation of Motl's optimism, rendering it unnecessary to recast the world in language. If conditions are bad, if the "fumes of gas in the pressers' shop are so strong that it weakens the workers, and many of them even faint," then the remedy is not a verbal rewrite but remedial action: "No, this can't go on any longer. We'll have to call a strike," writes the young capitalist with a socialist consciousness (E 284; Y 2:113).

The reality of America is affirmed as the realia of America penetrate the language of the narrator with an abandon that precludes the need for further acts of magical thinking. Although Motl begins his life in the Golden Land with the desire to turn a somersault, he acts less to turn the world over than to explicitly renounce such *luftgesheftn*; he celebrates the ground beneath his feet in a chapter titled **"With Both Feet on the Ground"** or **"Down to Earth"** (E 244; Y 2:57). Even the items in the family's little stand are enumerated with a celebration of their *thingness* that is the antithesis of the process of *divestment* and creation of empty spaces in the first part of the novel: "One sells cigarettes, writing implements, candy and soda water. And newspapers too. . . . We sell ice cream in sandwiches . . . [and] 'cider.' . . . People who have tasted champagne wine say it tastes like real champagne. And even though cider is an American drink, who do you suppose manufactures it? My brother Eli! . . . Later on, in mid-summer, when watermelons appear on the market, we make even better business" (E 322-25; Y 2:173-77).

While the language is not altogether different from that of Menakhem Mendl in his business ventures, or even from the get-rich-quick schemes of Motl and his brother in Kasrilevke, in the American chapters words do not invert but only exaggerate reality. Seeking, like so many city people before and after him, to be absorbed into what Philip Fisher defines as the "magical life of . . . things, the vitality of objects in the city [and] what Walter Benjamin called the 'sex-appeal' of objects," Motl remains undeveloped and revels in the projection of his desires onto the object world that surrounds him in New York. Like characters in Zola or Dickens, he lacks the consciousness of a private self and discovers instead the "maps for the empire of the self within the city."[65]

In addition to the public areas of the street, the train station, the subway, and the candy stand, there are new interior spaces—such as the "kitchen" (in English in the original) or the bedroom—that signify the private forum of the family and the self. In the shtetl stories the interiors were represented either as too confining for dialogues with one's Creator, in the case of Tevye, or as too undifferentiated, serving simultaneously as sites of cooking, sleeping, and (in the case of Motl's father) dying; but here they are affirmed as part of the differentiation of space that allows for exploration of "new" worlds. This process is of a piece both with the comic view that reconstitutes the material fragments of a world in dissolution and with the modernist view that embraces profane space as the site of primary encounters.[66]

THE ALCHEMY OF WORDS

In Motl's world the borders of language become as porous as the physical boundaries. For even if move-

ment through space seems to be the primary form of mobility and the physical environment more definitive than the linguistic, the acoustic aspects of this narrative are no less salient here than elsewhere in Sholem Aleichem. But the narrative privilege that defines the world of the shlemiel, caught as he is in *discourse* itself,[67] culminates in this, the last of Sholem Aleichem's narratives—and then self-destructs in the wide-open spaces of America. Language has not lost its magical properties nor the Diaspora its narrative privilege; but America emerges as a world in which *words* come into alignment with the *object world*.

The presence of foreign phrases in the Yiddish of Sholem Aleichem is one of the most striking components of his polyphonic universe. Miron presents the linguistic corruption in the ***Railroad Stories*** as emblematic of the existential condition of the travelers themselves, arguing that the frequency of words and phrases in Russian, Ukrainian, and Polish marks the decline or "twilight" of the culture and a deviation from Sholem Aleichem's own former standards of authenticity. The babel of languages reflects, in this instance, "a socio-linguistic reality of people who are no longer within their intimate world of the community of origin. . . . They go so far as to introduce the linguistic estrangement into their souls. . . . These are people whose fortified boundaries of their cultural territory have been infiltrated. . . . The language confusion . . . reflects the larger collective condition of spiritual and cultural confusion."[68]

Miron sees both the more sinister manifestations of that process in the ***Railroad Stories*** and its more humorous manifestations in ***Motl*** as part of the evolution of an aesthetics of cacophony or disharmony. I am arguing here that the fragmentation of language that signals the cultural breakdown in one text may signal cultural formation in another. In ***Motl*** the increasing porousness of the Yiddish in the "American" section (nearly every chapter title contains an English word)[69] is made more conspicuous by the absence of the scriptural or liturgical intertexts that pepper Tevye's speech. Motl has very few texts in his head; the rare allusions to holiday liturgy or to the *parshat ha-shavu'a* biblical readings represent the limited repertory of a child of the Eastern European shtetl. Their presence or absence relates to the authorizing forces behind the novel, reflecting how the concept of narrative itself is changing: rather than proceeding as commentary on another text, it becomes a self-authorizing process. The source of authority is no longer hermeneutic but experiential. Motl doesn't read; he exists, he observes, he listens. What he hears and experiences does not refer to other worlds, to private or collective memory. This form of retrenchment serves the trope of rebirth and signals the oceanic feeling that will become, in the next generation, the pervasive amnesia of a transplanted culture lost in the embrace of its host.

If the **Railroad Stories** can be said to have been written by the last rays of a culture's twilight, it was by the dawn's early light over a new continent that **Motl** was composed. In the former, the confusion of languages is a function of profound levels of miscommunication and dispossession; in the latter it is a celebration of new forms of aggrandizement—spatial, material, linguistic. The porousness at the borders of language signals an aesthetics of fragmentation that is fundamentally compatible with American democratic aesthetics.[70]

The parallel processes of a massive forgetting and a massive recall of Scriptures that unfold simultaneously on two continents are anticipated in the respective monologues of Motl and Tevye. Y. D. Berkovitz suggests that when Tevye "arrives" in Palestine, he'll find "a whole new world with new *pesukim* [biblical quotations] and midrashim—the real *pesukim* that float there wherever you turn."[71] Since he lives by the book, as it were, transporting him to the place of that book's original enactment would realign Tevye with the very ground of his being. Like that of Benjamin the Third, Tevye's shtetl world is a self-enclosed, hermetic reality, reflected in a textual prism; Motl's world, in contrast, is full of objects undergoing constant interrogation and renaming. The Holy Land as the place where "original" speech can be reactivated, the place where ancient memory animates the present, is the alternative to America as the land of amnesia and self-recreation.

As I have already noted, however, Tevye never made it to the Holy Land, an arrival that would have been equivalent to his being transported to the Other Side. One might say that as the locus of a true diaspora, America is not a place for the dead; Motl's mother puts it best, with a sigh and a backward glance at her dear departed husband; "he who lives, comes; he who lies in the ground, comes not" (*ver es lebt, der kumt. Kumen kumt nit nor der, vos ligt in der erd*; Y 2:58).[72] The last chapter that Sholem Aleichem was working on at the time of his own death was called, appropriately enough, **"Mir mufn"** [**"We Move"**]—leaving open the possibility of another chapter and another station, of movement itself as the principle of this new universe. Sholem Aleichem's final act of grace is to grant Motl, Tevye, and himself the option of moving on to keep the story going and to resist the seductions of the Other Side.

The tendency to regard the final words that are squeezed from a dying writer's pen as his last literary will and testament is reinforced in this final novel by

the polemic culture that informed Hebrew and Yiddish literature and that defined Jewish life as a set of specific alternatives. Somehow Sholem Aleichem managed to embrace *all* of the three possible routes followed by Jews that nearly every other writer found mutually exclusive: the "old home," Zion, *and* America. Although the manifestations changed over the years, *golus* remained largely a positive but increasingly remote reference; Zion was an ideal but not an existential imperative. Unlike Abramovitsh, Sholem Aleichem ideologically embraced Hibat Zion and then Herzlian political Zionism. In his polemical writing he argued that "the Jews need a land of their own."[73] But it remained for him and his characters, as for so many of the writers of the preceding eight centuries, the Other Side, the place of ultimate arrival—and death.

Sholem Aleichem's global reach and his irrepressible mobility are ironically underscored by his fate after death. Though he was buried with great fanfare in New York, the family had planned to remove his body and give it permanent burial in Kiev, Russia; even though he lived his last years and died in America, he continued to be regarded as a Russian writer. And he remained in the minds of his Yiddish readers always the storyteller from the shtetl.[74] In 1912, in the New York Yiddish paper *Dos yidishes tageblatt*, Sholem Aleichem had written: "The power of 'home'! Time doesn't weaken it. The ocean can't obliterate it. Freedom won't make you forget it. On the contrary—the further away you are, the more you want to know what's going on over there in our unfortunate home. How are our unlucky brothers and sisters doing? How are they managing to bear the yoke of exile? What makes them laugh, what makes them cry, and what do their writers have to tell us?"[75]

He seems to be implying that the "yoke of exile" does not extend to America. The paradoxes of Jewish life in the early twentieth century are highlighted when we recognize that the American Diaspora is the place to which the Jews of Eastern Europe are *self-exiled* from their home in *golus*. As a voluntary condition, the American exile will provide the launching pad for imaginary rearticulations of the European *golus* in the second half of the century in the fictions of such writers as I. B. Singer and Philip Roth. Notwithstanding all his—and his readers'—emphasis on the "factuality" of his portraits of the shtetl Jews, Sholem Aleichem evokes a "home" that is captured entirely in the imagination, embalmed in accessible forms later mined by other writers in the years of devastation and partial recovery. Burning Kasrilevke near the end of Motl's story dramatically enacts the effacement of the past that is the fundamental premise of this forward-looking narrative.[76]

This is not the only fictional narrative of its time in which the Jewish town is burned as a sign of its moribund, anachronistic state—or of its future reference as a ruined shrine; Sholem Aleichem's own story, **"Hanisrafim shel Kasrilevke" ["Kasrilevke in Flames"]** and Abramovitsh's "Hanisrafim" [Burned Out] partake of the mock-epic paradigm that is difficult for post-Holocaust readers to approach without, once again, superimposing the epic dimensions forced by historical hindsight.[77] In 1943, when Maurice Samuel published his whimsical *World of Sholem Aleichem,* he introduced the book as "a sort of pilgrimage among the cities and inhabitants of a world which only yesterday—as history goes—harboured the grandfathers and grandmothers of some millions of American citizens. As a pilgrimage it is an act of piety; on the other hand it is an exercise in necromancy, or calling up of the dead. . . . For that world is no more. . . . Fragments of it remain *in situ*; other fragments, still recognizable but slowly losing their shape in the wastage of time, are lodged in America."[78] Unable to fully anticipate, from his vantage point in the midst of the war, either the extent of the destruction then occurring or the acts of pilgrimage to and "necromancy" in the burned cities, towns, and concentration camps that would follow several decades later, Samuel nevertheless provided an early model for the forms of return and sentimental reappropriation of the shtetl through the writings of Sholem Aleichem and then through fragments of its physical culture.

The figure of the shlemiel in general and Motl in particular presented a challenge that postwar Israeli culture would resist in subtle ways. In Palestine in 1945, Hebrew poet Natan Alterman wrote an elegy to the Jews of Europe in the form of a last letter from Menakhem Mendl to his wife Sheyne Shendl; moribund himself, Menakhem Mendl uses his last breath to describe the death of all the inhabitants of Sholem Aleichem's house of fiction, including Motl.[79] This poetic eulogy acts as a form of compassionate exclusion, effectively preempting any acts of the imagination that would bring Motl and his fellows closer to the shores of Palestine. For that very reason, perhaps, the nine-year-old child continues to haunt the recesses of Hebrew memory, reappearing some forty years later in a radical rewrite of the history of catastrophe, David Grossman's novel *'Ayen 'erekh: ahava* [See Under: Love] (1986). Living in Israel in the 1950s among Holocaust survivors, the child narrator, Momik, begins reading Sholem Aleichem and eventually finds in Motl a companion and kindred spirit. What explains Momik's fascination with Motl is the latter's unqualified success in rewriting unacceptable scenarios. Momik's revisionist attempt to glorify obscure figures like

"Sonder from the Commando" as the head of a fighting unit in Europe can be seen as a latter-day version of "It's grand to be an orphan."

Motl's naïveté and negative capability are his passport into an American future, whereas those very same qualities lead Momik in Israel to a form of madness: the difference has everything to do with the time and place of telling and the consequentiality of speech acts. After World War I, Walter Benjamin proclaimed the loss of the capacity to tell stories: "the art of storytelling is coming to an end. . . . A generation that had gone to school on a horse-drawn streetcar now stood under the open sky in a countryside in which nothing remained unchanged but the clouds, and beneath these clouds, in a field of force of destructive torrents and explosions, was the tiny, fragile human body."[80] Whatever remained of the revising potential of the fictive imagination after World War I barely survived Auschwitz; even Momik's youthful inventions cannot release him from his parents' untold story. But by engaging in a major act of reinventing the past, Momik reassumes some of the prerogative and burden of the Diaspora and challenges the limits of narrative as they had developed in Hebrew literature.[81] As we will see below [in *Booking Passage: Exile and Homecoming in the Modern Jewish Imagination*], it is post-Holocaust writers from Europe such as Dan Pagis and Aharon Appelfeld who introduce new centrifugal forces into Israeli culture.

Celebrating the theatricality of everyday life, the richness and variety of the object world, and the street as the venue of urban experience, Motl is one of the first of a series of Jewish Walkers in the City. As Jews acquire new spaces in their journeys across the globe, the distinctions between the appropriation of object space in Palestine and in America will go through numerous transformations before the century is out. At the same time it was being slowly and then brutally divested of its tenancy in Europe, the Jewish imagination was becoming intoxicated with ownership and realia in two alternative dimensions: as sacred, original space in Zion, signified by the reclaiming of "territory" and acts reifying and realizing the text culture of Exile; and as a fascination with the material world in America, with "real" estate, and with the *thingness* that signifies not original but duplicatable space—and, eventually, with its mechanical reproductions and simulacra.

Notes

1. From Mary Antin's *From Plonsk to Boston* (New York: M. Wiener, 1986), originally published in 1899, to Eva Hoffman's *Lost in Translation: A Life in a New Language* (London: Heinemann,

1989), Jewish journeys to America have been well documented over the last century. Writers from the Other Europe is a Penguin series launched by Philip Roth that features writers from Estern Europe who were relatively unknown in the West.

2. Dov Sadan, "Three Foundations: Sholem Aleichem and the Yiddish Literary Tradition" (1959), tr. David G. Roskies, *Prooftexts* 6, no. 1 (January 1986): 57 (translated from *Avnei miftan: masot 'al sofrei yidish* [Corner Stones: Essays on Yiddish Writers] [Tel Aviv: Y. L. Peretz, 1961], vol. 1, pp. 45-54). Critical interest in Sholem Aleichem has increased dramatically since Sadan wrote those words, as witnessed by the very issue of *Prooftexts* that reproduced this essay.

3. See [Ezrahi, Sidra DeKoven. *Booking Passage,* Berkeley: University of California Press, 2000], chapters 2 and 3. In the original version of the epistolary narrative, the shtetl to which Sheyne Shendl was attached was Mazepfke, not Kasrilevke.

We might note Natan Alterman's 1945 Hebrew "elegy" to the Jews of Eastern Europe, written in Palestine as the "last" letter from Menakhem Mendl to his wife, Sheyne Shendl; Menakhem Mendl remains in the Hebrew imagination as the quintessential Wandering Jew, as his wife remains "in the shtetl" even after it has been destroyed. (This poem is discussed later in this [essay] and in chapter 8 [of Ezrahi, *Booking Passage*].)

For an interesting Marxist critique of *Menakhem-Mendl,* written in the mid-1930s, see Max Erik, who maintains that while Menakhem Mendl, the irrepressible traveler and petty businessman, is intoxicated with the metropolis (Odessa, Yehupetz [Kiev]), Sheyne Shendl remains "frozen and immobile, contentedly stuck in the Kasrilevke mire." Erik equates the "faith" she exhibits in the status quo and in divine providence with the "precapitalist [but also pre-*modernist*] fantasies" that characterized Benjamin's position in *The Travels of Benjamin the Third.* Erik, "*Menakhem-Mendl*" (1935), tr. David G. Roskies, *Prooftexts* 6, no. 1 (January 1986): 36-38.

4. Hillel Halkin calls Tevye a "God-arguer." Introduction to Sholem Aleichem, *Tevye the Dairyman and the Railroad Stories,* ed. and tr. Hillel Halkin (New York: Schocken Books, 1987), p. xxiv.

5. The cycle was originally called simply "Ksovim fun a komi-voyazher." A few of the stories that Sholem Aleichem adapted and appended to the text when he reworked it from 1910 to 1911 had been written between 1902 and 1903.

6. Sholem Aleichem, "Tevye Leaves for the Land of Israel," in *Tevye the Dairyman,* pp. 108, 110, 111;

from the Yiddish original, *Gants Tevye der milkhiker,* in *Ale verk fun Sholem Aleykhem* (New York: Sholem-Aleykhem Folksfond oysgabe, 1927), vols. 1-2, pp. 183, 185, 187. All subsequent page references to these stories, made parenthetically in the text, are to these Yiddish and English editions (designated Y and E). Halkin added "go to die," which is a gloss on the more allusive Yiddish that translates literally as "all old Jews go to Eretz Yisroel."

7. When he reported on his wife Golde's death, Tevye had told Sholem Aleichem that "I only hope she puts in a good word for her daughters where she is, because the Lord knows she went through enough for them" (E 98; Y 168). Here, in a departure from the convention of woman as/at home, it is Tevye who stays put while his women move: Golda to Heaven ("Zion") and the daughters to (and beyond) the geographical and existential borders of the Pale of Settlement.

8. Y. D. Berkovitz, "Tuvya ha-holev nose'a le-eretz Yisrael," in *Ha-rishonim ki-vnei adam: sipurei zikhronot 'al Shalom 'Aleichem u-vnei doro* [The Founders as Human Beings: Memories of Sholem Aleichem and His Generation], vol. 8 of *Kitvei Y. D. Berkovitz* [The Writing of Y. D. Berkovitz] (Tel Aviv: Dvir, 1954), pp. 192-94.

9. I have emended Halkin's translation somewhat here.

10. Dov Sadan, Dan Miron, Benjamin Harshav, and Ruth Wisse, among other contemporary scholars, have debated the nature and function of Tevye's malapropisms, misquotes, and misprisions. Michael Stern takes the discussion one step further by closely examining some of the biblical and liturgical intertexts in his essay "Tevye's Art of Quotation," *Prooftexts* 6, no. 1 (January 1986): 79-96. The significant shift in meaning that takes place in this and other passages between the biblical phrase "el ha-aretz asher areka" (to the land that I will show thee) and Tevye's "wherever your eyes will take you" (which Halkin changes in the English translation to "wherever your legs will carry you") could, he says, be a gloss on the difference between Abraham's mission, "assured of God's watchful protection," and Tevye's, enacted in its absence (p. 94). But it can also mark the shift from directed to aimless movement, as discussed later in this [essay].

11. As with "I'm a real *al tashlikheynu le'eys ziknoh*" in the passage above, Halkin's liberal translations always maintain the spirit of the original; here, the translation also tends to accentuate the tension between the explicit textual references to a physical return to the Holy Land and Tevye's interpretive

strategies that reinforce exile as the normative condition of the Jew.

12. "Tevye fort kein eretz-yisroel" was the final story in the cycle as it appeared in the 1911 edition; because that story ended with the death of Golda, and because the romantic theme had been exhausted with the marriages of Tevye's daughters, it would be fitting, argues Chone Shmeruk, to take leave of Tevye as he departs for the Holy Land. He further maintains that the impetus behind the story "Lekh-lekho" relates to the author's own unrest at having facilitated, through Chava's marriage to a non-Jew, the ultimate boundary crossing. So he "returns" Tevye to his village, stages a little pogrom, and brings Chava back into the fold. Written around the time of the Beiliss trial, "Lekh-lekho" also reflects, in its subtheme of persecution and banishment, Sholem Aleichem's concern with actual events. On the composition of the *Tevye* stories and the conflicts that are revealed through revisions appearing in the various editions, see Shmeruk, "Tevye der milkhiker—toldoteha shel yetzira" [The History of "Tevye the Dairyman"], *Ha-sifrut* 7, no. 26, (April 1978): 26-38. Shmeruk is clearly dissatisfied with the 1918 edition, which was edited by Berkovitz and appeared after the author's death as *Gantz Tevye der milkhiker* [The Complete Tevye the Dairyman]; Shmeruk reveals his own ideological (and aesthetic) position by insisting that "Tevye's departure for Eretz Yisrael would have been more convincing not in the context of Beylke but especially after the banishment from the village and the return of Chava. But with the text of *Gantz tevye der milkhiker* before us, we cannot but contemplate the unrealized potential for a great work (*yetzirat mofet*)" (pp. 37-38).

13. "Oh, God likes to play games with us, He does. He's got a favorite game He plays with Tevye called *Oylim Veyordim,* which means in plain language Upsy-Daisy—now you're up, and now you're pushing daisies" (E 119; Y 202-3). Hillel Halkin, who finds a wonderful equivalent in daisies for the double entendre of the language of Fortuna (*yordim* as those who are down-at-the-mouth), nevertheless is therefore forced to omit the allusion in this passage to the pioneering language of *'aliyah* (ascent) to and *yerida* (descent) from the Land of Israel.

14. There is some disagreement among critics about the status of the final chapter, "Vekhalaklakoys." In his translation of the last few *Tevye* stories, Hillel Halkin spliced the final passages from "Vekhalaklakoys" onto the penultimate chapter, "Lekh-Lekho," with the result that the return to the Land of Israel, reinforced by the biblical resonances from Genesis 12 in the title and in Tevye's

supposed destination, is effectively subverted by the final paragraph. Halkin justifies his editorial practice by citing the inferior quality of this last story, published a short time before Sholem Aleichem's death and written two years previously; he does not, however, dwell on the ideological import of adding to the natural conclusion of the Tevye cycle (the reconciliation of Tevye and his beloved daughter Chava) a chapter whose primary purpose seems to be to affirm the nature of Jewish wandering and preclude other "resolutions" to the homeless condition of the Jews. It is hardly surprising that in his Hebrew translation of the text, Sholem Aleichem's son-in-law Y. D. Berkovitz left out this chapter altogether.

For discussions of closure in this and other of Sholem Aleichem's fictions, see Shmeruk, "'Tevye der milkhiker,'" pp. 34-37; David Neal Miller, "Don't Force Me to Tell You the Ending: Closure in the Short Fiction of Sh. Rabinovitsch (Sholem-Aleykhem)," *Neophilologus* 66 (1982): 102-10; David G. Roskies, *A Bridge of Longing: The Lost Art of Yiddish Storytelling* (Cambridge, Mass.: Harvard University Press, 1995), pp. 176-88.

15. While still an adolescent, Agnon published "City of the Dead" as a feuilleton in Buczacz; see Arnold Band, *Nostalgia and Nightmare: A Study in the Fiction of S. Y. Agnon* (Berkeley: University of California Press, 1968), pp. 37-38.

16. See chapter 7 [of Ezrahi, *Booking Passage*] for a discussion of Michael André Bernstein's notion in *Foregone Conclusions: Against Apocalyptic History* (Berkeley: University of California Press, 1994) of "backshadowing" and "sideshadowing" as compositional and critical strategies. An example of the inevitable backshadowing that prevails in post-Holocaust readings of the texts before us can be found in David Roskies's argument that because many of the pogromists of the 1880s were either train workers or transported to the *shtetlakh* by train, "the train was already being transformed in Sholem Aleichem's fiction from a vehicle of dislocation to a vehicle of death." Roskies, "Sholem Aleichem and Others: Laughing Off the Trauma of History," *Prooftexts* 2, no. 1 (January 1982): 63. (It is worth noting that these stories contain as many tales of miraculous rescue as of danger on the train.)

The train had become so identified as a context for Jewish stories that it survived as one of the artifacts of the fragmented postwar poetic imagination. For one of the most radical expressions of this, see the long poem "Footprints" by Dan Pagis ("'Akevot," in *Kol ha-shirim; 'Abba' (pirkei proza)* [Collected Poems and "Father" (prose passages)], ed. Hanan Hever and T. Carmi [Jerusalem: Hakibbutz ha-me'uhad and Bialik Institute, 1991], pp. 141-46), and my discussion of it in chapter 6 [of Ezrahi,*Booking Passage*].

17. See Leo Marx, *The Machine in the Garden: Technology and the Pastoral Ideal in America* (London: Oxford University Press, 1964). Marx's pathbreaking study of the forms of American cultural response to technology in general and to the railroad in particular generated many subsequent studies, and he himself reconsidered the subject in the mid-1980s. See Marx, "Pastoralism in America," in *Ideology and Classic American Literature,* ed. Sacvan Bercovitch and Myra Jehlen (Cambridge: Cambridge University Press, 1986), pp. 36-69.

18. To be sure, Jewish literature is not unique in recording the train from the inside; from Agatha Christie's *Murder on the Orient Express* to Italo Calvino's "Adventure of a Soldier," many dramas have been enacted on trains in fiction and in film. Yet peculiar to the Yiddish and Hebrew literature is both the report on life viewed from within the third-class coaches and the absence of the view from the outside. The "commercial traveler" who narrates Sholem Aleichem's train stories concludes his tales by admonishing the reader to "avoid going first or second class. . . . What can be the point, I ask you, of a Jew traveling in total solitude without a living soul to speak to?" (E 279; Yiddish original is from *Ayznban-Geshikhtes* in *Ale verk fun Sholem-Aleykhem,* vols. 25-26, p. 296). Halkin claims that "though the notion of trains running through Russia with almost no one in their third-class cars but Jews who tell each other stories may seem like an artificial literary convention, this is actually not the case"; because of the social structure of the society, Jews as petty merchants were far more mobile than the peasants who rarely traveled and were more garrulous than the aristocracy who never traveled third-class (introduction to *Tevye the Dairyman,* p. xxxiii). The class consciousness presented in these stories is, nonetheless, more proletarian than petit-bourgeois.

19. Michel de Certeau, *The Practice of Everyday Life,* tr. Steven F. Rendall (Berkeley: University of California Press, 1984), pp. 1, 112-13.

20. The famous lithograph by Fanny Palmer that became a Currier and Ives print in 1868, *Across the Continent: "Westward the Course of Empire Takes Its Way,"* incorporates all the icons of the Westward Movement: Native Americans and white settlers, covered wagons and the new schoolhouse, mountains and plains—bisected and foregrounded by the steam locomotive and cars headed west. For a new evaluation of these images, see Henry Nash Smith, "Symbol and Idea in *Virgin Land,"* in

Bercovitch and Jehlen, *Ideology and Classic American Literature,* pp. 21-35.

21. De Certeau, *The Practice of Everyday Life,* p. 112.

22. The commercial traveler who narrates Sholem Aleichem's railroad stories demonstrates the narratological principle governing this perspective in a prefatory note "To the Reader," which in English translation reads as follows: "Since we travelers often spend whole days on end sitting and looking out the window until we want to bang our heads against the wall, one day I had an idea: I went and bought myself a pencil and notebook and began jotting down everything I saw and heard on my trips" (E 135; Y 7). But it is the translator who adds "looking out the window"—as if it were obvious that that is what a passenger on a train does; the original Yiddish is a *domestic* image connoting indolence, "having nothing to get one's hands wet for" (*nisht tsu tun keyn hant in kalt vaser*). "Everything that [he] saw and heard" as related in the subsequent stories is confined to the pageants inside the railway cars, an internal discourse with virtually no reference to what might have been seen had the narrator *really* been looking out the window. Rare references to life or to the weather outside are part of the minimal circumstantial framing of the stories.

23. Mendele, who narrates the story, admits regretfully to having relinquished the freedom of the open-air horse and buggy for the incarceration of the crowded railway coach: "All this business of a railway journey is new to me. . . . In the train there is no feeling of independence. One is like a prisoner, without a moment's respite." S. Y. Abramovitsh, "Shem and Japheth in the Train," in *Modern Hebrew Literature,* ed. Robert Alter (New York: Berman House, 1975), pp. 20-21 (for the Hebrew, see "Shem Ve-yefet ba-'agala," in *Kol Kitvei Mendele mokher sforim* [The Complete Works of Mendele Mokher Sfarim] [Tel Aviv: Dvir, 1957], pp. 399-405).

Traveling in the open air had allowed Mendele to be a free spirit, having an affinity with but a non-proprietary relationship to the world through which he passed. Along with his former mode of conveyance, Mendele has, by his own report, abdicated his position as semidetached Jew and now appears beside his characters in the guise of a fellow traveler; the irony that we identified in *Benjamin the Third* as inhering in the distance between Mendele and the subject of his narrative seems to be replaced here, willy-nilly, by acts of empathy and identification. But something has also been gained: the third-class compartment in a train is the perfectly enclosed environment for an exchange of stories, and each family or personal unit is a tale waiting to be told.

Mendele's traveling companions in "Shem and Japheth" are generic samples of the human race, such as it has become since the Flood; it is not so much their story but their companionship that piques Mendele's interest. In joining the ranks of the Jewish beggars, a Polish cobbler who is traveling third class is reported to have "converted"—not to Jewish faith but to Jewish destiny: "Stay a Christian as you have always been," he is told, "but . . . come to master the Jewish art of living, and cleave to that, if you are to preserve yourself and carry the yoke of exile" (pp. 35-36). "Shem" in his earlier incarnation had struggled to leave the confines of his tent and travel in the footsteps of the world's great adventurers and liberators; now he ends up by bringing "Japheth" into his own quarters. But along with the acts of empathy and incorporation is a deep satire on the death-in-life of the shtetl Jew and a kind of proto-socialist solidarity among the hungry of the earth.

24. Trunk refers specifically to the "slowpoke express" (*Der leydik-geyer*) as "Kasrilevke on wheels." Y. Y. Trunk, *Sholem Aleykhem: zein vezen un zeine verk* [Sholem Aleichem: His Being and His Work] (Warsaw: Kulturlige, 1937), p. 218.

25. Dan Miron, afterword to Sholem Aleichem, *Sipurei rakevet* [The Railroad Stories], ed. and tr. Dan Miron (Tel Aviv: Zmora Bitan, 1989), pp. 246, 243, 236, 247, 244, 263, 298. This long essay traces the publishing history of the stories and, in addition to arguing for their unique status collectively as a cultural watershed, analyzes many of them in detail.

Each of the critical positions Miron alludes to reflects, naturally, the ideological agenda to which the respective critics were responding. That Y. D. Berkovitz, Sholem Aleichem's son-in-law, literary confidant, and official Hebrew translator and mediator for generations of Israeli readers, did not translate more than a few of these stories into Hebrew may well be related to his decisions not to translate the last chapter of *Tevye* and to eliminate, as we will see later, many of the "American" chapters from *Motl.* All of these sections are affirmations of the phenomenon we have been probing in the fiction of Abramovitsh and Sholem Aleichem: the connection of wandering and mobility in a nonepic, nonteleological scheme. The translations by Aryeh Aharoni (1986) and Dan Miron (1989) of these stories into Hebrew and by Hillel Halkin (1987) into English make them available in those languages for the first time as a whole. Halkin's interpretation of these stories, as reflected in his translations, is not as sombre as Miron's.

26. Compare this to the instant sexual intimacy created between two complete strangers, a soldier and a "widow," who never exchange one word as they engage in their erotic encounter in Italo Calvino's "Adventure of a Soldier," in *Difficult Loves,* tr. William Weaver, Archibald Colquhoun, Peggy Wright (London: Picador, 1983), pp. 185-96.

27. From Sholem Aleichem's letter to Noach Zablodovski, reproduced in the *Sholem Aleykhem-Bukh* [Sholem Aleichem Book], ed. Y. D. Berkovitz (New York: n.p., 1926), p. 295.

28. Quoted by Halkin in his introduction to *Tevye the Dairyman,* p. xxxiv, and by Miron in his afterword to *Sipurei Rakevet,* pp. 231-32.

29. Berkovitz quotes Sholem Aleichem as saying to the yeshiva student (in his own Hebrew translation): "Likhtov—zohi melakhti. Ata tzarikh lidaber. Ve-lo dimyonot—uvdot tisaper!" (Writing is my craft. You have only to speak. And nothing imaginary—only relate the facts!) (in *Kitvei Y. D. Berkovitz,* vol. 8, p. 257).

30. Roskies, *A Bridge of Longing,* p. 173.

31. Such is the intention of "the man from Buenos Aires" who, in the story of that title, returns from white slave trading in South America to his hometown of Soshmakin to marry a "hometown girl" (E 175; Y 86).

32. De Certeau, *The Practice of Everyday Life,* p. 114.

33. See, for example, the distinction Ruth Wisse draws between the two: "Kafka's heroes are themselves a part of the universal horror confronting them. Sholem Aleichem's heroes are confronted by horror, but within a universe of meaning." *The Schlemiel as Modern Hero* (Chicago: University of Chicago Press, 1971), p. 53.

34. Kafka's dreams of escape or refuge did project, as we know, as far as Palestine—imagined as an ideal pastoral or cultural construct by his sister Ottla and by such friends as Max Brod, Martin Buber, Gershom Sholem, and, finally, Dora Dymant.

35. *Amerika,* Kafka's first full-length novel, was begun in 1912. The first chapter, "The Stoker—A Fragment," published separately by Kurt Wolff in 1913 (*Der Jungste Tag*), remained the only section to be published during Kafka's lifetime; *Amerika, roman,* as reconstructed and edited by Max Brod, was published posthumously (Munich: K. Wolff, [1927]).

36. Perhaps the most salient sign of this is the dog image that recurs in Kafka's fiction and that will resonate throughout the narratives of subjugation

in the twentieth century, from Agnon to Günter Grass. Joseph K. dies like a dog; the condemned man in *The Penal Colony* submits like a dog. However, when Karl's unsavory traveling companion, Robinson, explains that "if you're always treated like a dog, you begin to think you actually are one," and invokes the same paradigm, Karl *resists,* neutralizing the threat. *America* in *The Penguin Complete Novels of Franz Kafka,* tr. Willa and Edwin Muir (Harmondsworth: Penguin, 1983), p. 592.

37. The phrase comes from a diary entry where Kafka records that he has started a novel in which two brothers (based evidently on two cousins) quarreled—the one went to America, while the other remained behind in a "European prison." Quoted in Ernst Pawel, *Nightmare of Reason: A Life of Franz Kafka* (New York: Farrar, Straus, and Giroux, 1984), p. 254.

38. Amerika is *not* Combray. When Karl loses the photograph of his parents, he seems to lose the parents themselves—and the past itself—as a reference (*America,* pp. 507, 530). We receive one or two more glimpses of them later, but memory is not an organizing or enabling principle in the narrative or in the character's existential development.

39. In some ways, the machine that functions—or malfunctions—in so much of Kafka's fiction reaches a level of ultimate, Chaplinesque, American (not Prussian) efficiency in *Amerika.* In the first chapter, "The Stoker," the boiler room is a piece of machinery; the desk in the uncle's home is an invention of great intricacy. The social machine is configured with the individuals appearing as cogs and gears—in the hotel, in Uncle Jacob's office, in the political demonstrations that run with "machine-like regularity" (*America,* p. 606; see also pp. 570, 573, 471). In the final chapter, Karl declares his desire to be an engineer—though he is subsequently lowered to the status of "technician" in the Nature Theatre (pp. 628-29). Gilles Deleuze and Félix Guattari maintain that every enumeration is a manifestation of a machine and follows sets of rules and procedures; each statement "constitutes the real instructions for the machine." *Kafka: Toward a Minor Literature,* tr. Dana Polan (Minneapolis: University of Minnesota Press, 1986), p. 82.

On America as the context for "technological optimism," see Yaron Ezrahi, *The Descent of Icarus: Science and the Transformation of Contemporary Democracy* (Cambridge, Mass.: Harvard University Press, 1990).

40. It is true that Karl gets himself evicted from every safe refuge—his uncle's house, the hotel where he lands a job—and that he is taken in and mistreated by his traveling companions. But, just as inevitably, in the following chapter he finds himself by some miraculous narrative means—or by the sheer corruption of the text—out of danger.

41. Hannah Arendt is generally credited with having introduced Kafka to America. Although there were some earlier translations of Kafka into English, Arendt, as the first director of the newly established American branch of Schocken Press, bought the rights to all of his works and oversaw the translations. "Arendt had the unfortunate intuition that America needed Kafka, and people who lived quite comfortably in the world he had scorned, assured each other gleefully that they were living in a Kafkaesque world," writes Henry Pachter; "perhaps it was meant to épatez les bourgeois, but it only tickled them." Pachter, "On Being an Exile," in *The Legacy of the German Refugee Intellectuals,* ed. Robert Boyers (New York: Schocken Books, 1969), pp. 27, 43. For a less cynical view, see Walter Kaufmann, "The Reception of Existentialism in the United States," in ibid., p. 85.

Kafka remains, of course, the brooding presence in this study, as in nearly every cultural enterprise in the twentieth century. It is Kafka who is credited with inventing the modern language of exile and Kafka who is hailed as the prototype of the nomadic imagination; see [Ezrahi, *Booking Passage*], chapter 1.

42. See Pawel, *Nightmare of Reason,* pp. 254-57; Michael Löwy, *Redemption and Utopia: Jewish Libertarian Thought in Central Europe, a Study in Elective Affinity,* tr. Hope Heaney (London: Athlone Press, 1992), pp. 71-94; Gershon Shaked, *The Shadows Within: Essays on Modern Jewish Writers* (Philadelphia: Jewish Publication Society, 1987), pp. 9-10.

43. Marx, *The Machine in the Garden,* p. 228. The American myth, Marx adds, is a "variant of the primal myth described by Joseph Campbell: 'a separation from the world, a penetration to some source of power, and a life-enhancing return.'"

44. The first story of the second section, "Vasershtub" [The Floating House], was revised and renamed "Mazl tov! mir zenen shoyn in amerike!" [Hurrah, We're in America!] before appearing in the book. Three of the stories were still unpublished at the time of Sholem Aleichem's death; one of them, "Mir mufn" [We Move] was unfinished. For the publishing history of *Motl* as well as a critical evaluation of its fate at the hands of Sholem Aleichem's official literary executor and Hebrew translator, Y. D. Berkovitz, see Chone Shmeruk, "Sipurei Motl ben he-hazan le-Shalom Aleichem:

ha-situatzia ha-epit ve-toldotav shel ha-sefer" [The Tales of Motl the Cantor's Son by Sholem Aleichem: The Epic Situation and the History of the Text], *Siman Kri'a,* nos. 12/13 (February 1981): 310-26. See also Chone Shmeruk, "Nokhvort" [Afterword], in Sholem-Aleykhem, *Motl Peyse dem Khazns* (Jerusalem: Magnes Press, 1996), pp. vii-viii.

45. There is good reason to assume that when Sholem Aleichem published the first of the *Motl* stories, called "Haynt is yomtev—me tor nisht veynen" [Today Is a Holiday: It Is Forbidden to Cry] and "related" by Sholem Aleichem "in honor of Shavuoth," he had at best a vague conception of the shape of the narrative as a story of immigration to and settlement in America. Each of the stories had autonomy even as each was governed by the voice of the first-person child narrator and by a loose geographical and chronological structure. "Ein mukdam u-me'uhar" (there is no chronological order), writes the author in a letter to Yiddish critic S. Niger, adopting the Talmudic code for sacred narrative as justification of whatever anachronisms appear in the text (quoted in Shmeruk, "Sipurei Motl," pp. 312, 315-16). A Russian version of the first part of *Motl* presented as a consecutive narrative appeared a year before the first Yiddish version of 1911.

Dan Miron discusses the author's concern with the problem of serialization that brought him to accommodate an "undefined mass of readers." On this and other issues related to the publication history of the text, see "Bouncing Back: Destruction and Recovery in Sholem Aleykhem's *Motl Peyse dem khazns,*" *YIVO Annual of Jewish Social Science* 17 (1978): 136-37.

46. Werner Sollors, "Immigrants and Other Americans," in *Columbia Literary History of the United States,* general ed. Emory Elliott (New York: Columbia University Press, 1988), p. 588.

47. For a description of the funeral of Sholem Aleichem, attended by a crowd estimated at somewhere between 100,000 and 250,000 people, see Ellen D. Kellman, "Sholem Aleichem's Funeral (New York, 1916): The Making of a National Pageant," *YIVO Annual* 20 (1991): 277-304. Examining it as a public performance and rite of social cohesion and as the largest funeral New York had seen up to that time, Kellman notes that the path traced by the funeral cortege, which covered the city from the Bronx to Brooklyn, was orchestrated in such a way that the "hundred thousand or more mourners were laying claim to New York as their turf in a physical as well as a political sense" (p. 289).

The funeral itself, Jeffrey Shandler points out, takes on symbolic power not unlike the ritual of reading Sholem Aleichem as a form of "'geyn af keyver-oves' (visiting the graves of one's parents or ancestors), a substitute for visiting the inaccessible and later effaced graveyards of one's actual relatives." Shandler, "Reading Sholem Aleichem from Left to Right," *YIVO Annual* 20 (1991): 327.

48. Sholem Aleichem, *Adventures of Mottel the Cantor's Son,* tr. Tamara Kahana (New York: Henry Schuman, 1953), pp. 25, 293; *Motl Peyse dem Khazns,* vol. 1, p. 35; vol. 2, p. 129. Subsequent references to these editions, E and Y, will be made parenthetically in the text.

49. Motl's age ranges from five to nine in the different (not necessarily chronological) stories and versions. What is important, as we will consider at greater length in a moment, is that he does not grow.

50. The different translations of this sentence—which literally means "it is well with me—I am an orphan"—will largely reveal the interpretive strategies for translating all the inversions to come.

51. Miron, "Sholem Aleykhem's *Motl Peyse dem khazns,*" p. 180.

52. The work of Mikhail Bakhtin on the carnivalesque, the comic, and the grotesque informs much of the discussion below. The cultural implications of the Jewish celebration of Purim and its modern transformations provide fertile material for his theories.

53. "Haynt, az ikh derher dos vort pogrom, antloyf ikh. Ikh hob beser lib freylekhe mayses" (E 190; Y 1:269). In the earlier passage, I have incorporated Naomi Sokoloff's translation, which is more accurate than Kahana's. Sokoloff develops the idea of the denial of threatening reality in Sholem Aleichem's fictions that was defined by David Roskies as "laughing off the trauma of history." The "grim humor" in this passage, she writes, "also defuses pathos and even makes for a conundrum or riddle game that mocks referentiality." Sokoloff, *Imagining the Child in Modern Jewish Fiction* (Baltimore: Johns Hopkins University Press, 1992), pp. 51-52. The referents are, however, encoded in the Yiddish idioms themselves; Sholem Aleichem's "autobiography" was ambiguously titled *Funem Yarid* [From the Fair] (New York: Warheit, 1917).

In some versions of this story, explicitly intended for children, Sholem Aleichem himself deleted the first pogrom passage. On this see Shmeruk, "Sipurei Motl," pp. 316-17, and Sokoloff, *Imagining the Child,* p. 50.

54. Isaac Babel, "The Dovecot," in *Collected Stories,* ed. and tr. Walter Morison (New York: Meridian Books, 1955), p. 165.

55. See Chone Shmeruk, "Sholem-Aleykhem un Amerike" [Sholem Aleichem and America], *Di Goldene Keyt,* no. 121 (1987): 58-59.

56. Miecke Bal, "Lots of Writing," *Poetics Today* 15, no. 1 (spring 1994): 101 and passim.

In the passage from *Motl* just cited, Pini invokes Purim just before his reference to America; his comment ("Purim nokhn kaltn kugl") is translated into English as "sheer idiocy!" (E 252; Y 2:64).

57. In tracing the evolution of Motl from a promising musician into a cartoonist, Miron evokes the real-life model, a painter-cartoonist whom Sholem Aleichem met on his way back to Europe after his first failed visit to America ("Sholem Aleykhem's *Motl Peyse dem khazns,* pp. 120-21, 169).

58. The textual nature of the holiday and the cultural sensibilities it promotes are explored in two very different directions by Harold Fisch and Miecke Bal in the special volume of *Poetics Today,* "Purim and the Cultural Poetics of Judaism," edited by Daniel Boyarin. Fisch's study of the "semiotics of Purim" is a fascinating inquiry into the process by which the "sign" mediates between history and theology. "Reading and Carnival: On the Semiotics of Purim," *Poetics Today* 15, no. 1 (spring 1994): 55-74. Bal emphasizes the destabilizing effects of *writing itself,* which she sees as central to the Esther narrative; the writing which begins as official kingly edict moves to the word of Esther as a "fully realized agent, or subject" ("Lots of Writing," pp. 89-114).

59. Some studies in the 1990s have traced the sinister implications of the holiday not only in its "tropic" or performative but also in its behavioral dimensions—and have examined the dilemmas they posed for the more apologetically minded Jewish historians in the nineteenth century and their intimidated counterparts in Hitler's Germany. See Elliott Horowitz, "The Rite to be Reckless: On the Perpetration and Interpretation of Purim Violence," *Poetics Today* 15, no. 1 (spring 1994): 9-54. It is commendable that such an essay is included in the issue, given the editor's declared commitment to a diasporic sensibility and to Purim as the quintessential diasporic holiday; the evidence of Purim-related acts of anti-Christian violence beginning in the early medieval period and renewed in the early modern era complicates a reading of Diaspora as a disempowered and inherently nonviolent cultural form.

60. Mikhail Bakhtin has shown that the world of the comic and the grotesque incorporates death "in close relationship with the birth of new life and—simultaneously—with laughter." Death is "something that occurs 'just in passing,' without ever overemphasizing its importance"; it is, then, "an unavoidable aspect of life itself," part of the "temporal series of life that always marches forward." *The Dialogic Imagination: Four Essays,* ed. Michael Holquist, tr. Caryl Emerson and Michael Holquist (Austin: University of Texas Press, 1981), pp. 198, 194, 193.

61. Natalie Zemon Davis has made a strong case for the presence in Rabelais's *Gargantua* and *Pantagruel* of a Purim sensibility, suggesting an immanent and not just a generic connection between the Rabelaisian chronotope and the *Purimshpiel.* It becomes a "writing against fear"—in the case of Rabelais, the fear of censorship. "Rabelais among the Censors," *Representations,* no. 32 (fall 1990): 21.

62. The letter from Sholem Aleichem to Bialik is quoted in Shmeruk, "Sipurei Motl," p. 313. The statement appears slightly altered in *Motl* (E 258; Y 2:76).

63. Miron attributes these and other inconsistencies in the story of this Jewish Peter Pan to what may be the most "elaborate stylistic paradox" in Sholem Aleichem's works—namely, that we have neither the language of a "genuine child nor . . . the sustained style of an adult narrator recapitulating his childhood" ("Sholem Aleykhem's *Motl Peyse dem khazns,*" pp. 136-37). This is hardly a paradox, however, but rather a rhetorical tension not uncommon in European literature. Elsewhere Miron suggests that the absence of "Sholem Aleichem" as either narrator or interlocutor implies that he has become a "ghost writer" for Motl, since the "writings" of an illiterate boy would demand such mediation. *Sholem Aleykhem: Person, Persona, Presence* (New York: Yivo Institute for Jewish Research, 1972), pp. 24-25. Sokoloff argues that the absence of growth makes the novel more of a picaresque narrative than a bildungsroman (*Imagining the Child,* pp. 60-63). Roskies claims that the child's voice recovers the "unadulterated experience" (*A Bridge of Longing,* p. 172). And Shmeruk extends the discussion to consider the *reader* as child, arguing that although the targeted reader in the Yiddish original was not meant to be a child, since children's literature in Yiddish hardly existed at the time, the author talked to Bialik and Ravnitzky about making it a series for children when negotiating the translation of the stories into Hebrew ("Sipurei Motl," p. 319). So it remains until this day; the paratext in both the Hebrew and the English translations, as well as the illustrations and cover graphics, clearly designates

it for the children's shelf. On the issue of translations and targeted audiences, see also Shandler,
"Reading Sholem Aleichem from Left to Right,"
and Rhoda S. Kachuck, "Sholom Aleichem's Humor in English Translation," *YIVO Annual of Jewish Social Science* 11 (1956-57): 39-81.

All of these discussions acknowledge that the
child is a pivotal figure in this moment of transition from traditional to more modern forms of
Jewish life. Mine goes beyond the intratextual in
the direction of the *con*textual by incorporating
the contradictory narrative signs into a grammar
of socialization.

64. Sholem Aleichem, "Di Khaliastre oyf der arbeit"
(E 266-67; Y 2:86-87). I have modified the translation somewhat.

65. Philip Fisher, *Hard Facts: Setting and Form in
the American Novel* (Oxford: Oxford University
Press, 1987), pp. 134-35. He adds: "For a man inside the city his self is not inside his body but
around him, outside the body" (p. 134).

66. As Stephen Kern points out, "'profane' means
'outside the temple,'" and many artists and intellectuals of this century found themselves not only
outside but without a temple, facing a post-
Nietzschean void; yet many "learned to love their
fate in the face of the void. If there are no holy
temples, any place can become sacred; if there are
no consecrated materials, then ordinary sticks and
stones must do." *The Culture of Time and Space,
1880-1918* (Cambridge, Mass.: Harvard University Press, 1983), p. 179. On the loss of the sense
of eternity that goes along with the modernist enactment of life's scenarios in the spatial plane, see
also Frederick Hoffman, *The Mortal No: Death
and the Modern Imagination* (Princeton: Princeton
University Press, 1964).

67. Here I am suggesting a different emphasis from
that of Sokoloff, who argues on the basis of the
polyphonic nature of the novel that Motl is, "finally, a narrative construct that gauges changing
collective values, not a complex individual in his
own right [and that] in 'stealing across the border'
[the title of one of the chapters], the family continually puts into relief the borders of their own
discourse as it comes in contact with others"
(*Imagining the Child,* pp. 60, 62). Although that is
largely true of Motl's family, who are more instances of language 'talking,' I am arguing that
the fact that Motl is not a 'complex individual'
does not make him a 'narrative construct'—at least
not once he arrives in America.

68. Miron, afterword to Sholem Aleichem, *Sipurei
rakevet,* pp. 292-94.

69. Examples include "In new-york oyf der *street*" (In
the streets of New York), "Mir zukhn a *djob*" (We
look for a job), "Mir *straykn!*" (We strike), "Mir
kolektn" (We collect), "Mir geyen in *biznes*" (We
open a business), "Mir *mufn*" (We move); empha-
ses mine.

70. On democratic aesthetics, see Yaron Ezrahi, *The
Descent of Icarus,* p. 290. This is an American
sensibility that is shared, conceptually at least,
with a number of European modernisms, including those adapted by Jewish writers. See Chana
Kronfeld, *On the Margins of Modernism: Decentering Literary Dynamics* (Berkeley: University of
California Press, 1996).

71. Berkovitz, "Tuvye ha-holev nose'a le-eretz Yisrael," p. 192.

72. I have substantially altered the English translation
(E 245).

73. "More than eighteen hundred years we have been
dragging around as tenants from one house to another. Have we ever tried thinking seriously—how
long? How much longer? What will be the end of
it?" Sholem Aleichem, "Why Do the Jews Need a
Land of Their Own?" the title essay in a collection of his writings on Zionism (1890-1913), edited and translated by Joseph Leftwich and Mordecai S. Chertoff ([New York: Herzl Press, 1984],
p. 49). This is a populist interpretation of well-
defined Zionist ideas.

74. All of the eulogies at the funeral presented Sholem
Aleichem as the quintessential "goles Jew"; the
funeral itself was described by one contemporary
journalist as "the ingathering of the exiles, like a
meeting-place of the children of the entire Diaspora." "Traversing the Jewish turf of their
adopted city," Kellman writes, "they mourned the
Yiddish writer as one vast community of the uprooted" ("Sholem Aleichem's Funeral," pp. 291-
97). Shandler cites the Smithsonian Institution's
1979 exhibition titled *Abroad in America: Visitors
to the New Nation, 1776-1914,* which included
portraits of prominent visitors to America from
Alexis de Tocqueville to . . . Sholem Rabinowitz.
He justifies the definition of Sholem Aleichem's
status as that of sojourner rather than immigrant
to America, even though he died there ("Reading
Sholem Aleichem from Left to Right," p. 305).

75. Reprinted in Sholem Aleichem, *Geklibene verk*
[Selected Work] (New York: Dos yidishes tageb-
lat, 1912), vol. 1, unpaginated preface; quoted in
Kellman, "Sholem Aleichem's Funeral," pp. 280-
81.

76. What is important is that for all intents and purposes, Kasrilevke has already moved to New York:
"All Kasrilovka has moved to America. They tell

us that after we had left the old country, a commotion started there, a real exodus. They tell us that a terrible pogrom broke out—slaughter and fire. The whole town went up in flames" (E 293; Y 2:129). Yet no one from the "known world" died in the pogrom; the others made it to New York, and the moral and human *communitas* of the shtetl was preserved.

77. See again Bernstein, *Foregone Conclusions,* and the discussion of its implications for post-Holocaust representations in chapter 7 of this volume [Ezrahi, *Booking Passage*].

Discussing the image of the shtetl in classical Yiddish and Hebrew fiction, Dan Miron argues that in editing his collected works late in life, Sholem Aleichem accentuated the "Kasrilevke" factor, making it appear even more ubiquitous in an ongoing sequence of narratives that underscored its hermetic, economically non-viable (feudal), but socially intimate character. As historical anachronism and as the personal point of reference relegated to the sphere of childhood—i.e., ephemeral—memories, it becomes a candidate for extinction and nostalgia, according to this reading. The shtetl's destruction by conflagration or pogrom in the writing of Sholem Aleichem, Abramovitsh, and others takes on the mythical status of a *hurbn,* complementing myths of origin. Miron, "The Literary Image of the Shtetl," *Jewish Social Studies* 1, no. 3 (spring 1995): 1-43 (originally published in Hebrew as a five-part article, "Ha-dimui ha-sifruti ha-klasi shel ha-'ayara," *Hadoar* 55 [1976] and 56 [1977], and in Yiddish as *Der imazh fun Shtetl: dray literatishe shtudiye* [Tel Aviv: Y. L. Peretz, 1981]). And see [Ezrahi, *Booking Passage*], chapter 2.

78. Maurice Samuel, *The World of Sholem Aleichem* (1943; reprint, New York: Schocken Books, 1965), p. 3.

79. Natan Alterman, "Mikhtav shel Menakhem Mendl" [Letter from Menakhem Mendl], *Davar,* March 9, 1945; reprinted in *Ha-tur ha-shvi'i* [The Seventh Column] (Tel Aviv: Ha-kibbutz ha-me'uhad, 1977), vol. 1, pp. 12-14; discussed more fully in chapter 8 [of Ezrahi, *Booking Passage*].

80. Walter Benjamin, "The Storyteller," in *Illuminations,* ed. Hannah Arendt, tr. Harry Zohn (New York: Schocken Books, 1969), p. 84.

81. See David Grossman, *See Under: Love,* tr. Betsy Rosenberg (New York: Farrar Straus, and Giroux, 1989). "When I was eight years old," writes Grossman in an essay,

> my father gave me the stories of *Mottel, the Son of Peyse the Cantor* to read. . . . That was my Sholem Aleichem year. Incessantly I dug my tun-

nel to the Diaspora. . . . The strange thing about it was that all that time (about a year and a half) I believed that the other world existed parallel to mine . . . carrying on somewhere according to its laws and its mystery and its various institutions and its special language. When I was about nine and a half, in the middle of the Holocaust Day ceremony . . . suddenly, it pierced me: the six million, the slain martyrs . . . they were my people. They were my secret world. The six million were Mottel and Tevye and . . . Chava . . . and Stempenyu. . . . On the blazing asphalt of the Beit Hakerem schoolyard, I felt as if I was literally disappearing, shriveling and dissolving. . . . Where had their army been? Why didn't their air force or their paratroopers fight? Above all, I was panic-stricken because I imagined that I might now be the only child . . . whose responsibility it was to remember all those people. . . . The first part of *See Under: Love* is about a child called Momik . . . who tries to understand the Diaspora in Israeli terms [or, as I have been arguing, Israel in diasporic terms].

> "My Sholem Aleichem," *Modern Hebrew Literature,* no. 14 (spring/summer 1995): pp. 4-5

Bibliography

Abramovitsh, S. Y. [Mendele Mokher Sfarim]. *Ale verk fun Mendele moykher sforim (S. Y. Abramovitsh)* [The Complete Works of Mendele Moykher Sforim (S. Y. Abramovitsh); Yiddish]. Cracow: Farlag Mendele, 1911.

―――. *Kol kitvei Mendele mokher sfarim* [The Complete Works of Mendele Mokher Sfarim]. Tel Aviv: Dvir, 1957.

Alter, Robert, ed. *Modern Hebrew Literature.* New York: Berman House, 1975.

Alterman, Natan. "Mikhtav shel Menakhem-Mendl" [Letter from Menakhem Mendl]. *Davar,* March 9, 1945. Reprinted in *Ha-tur ha-shivi'i* [The Seventh Column], vol. 1 (Tel Aviv: Ha-kibbutz ha-me'uhad, 1977).

Antin, Mary. *From Plonsk to Boston.* 1899. Reprint, New York: M. Wiener, 1986.

Babel, Isaac. 1955. *Collected Stories.* Ed. and tr. Walter Morison. New York: Meridian Books.

Bakhtin, M. M. *The Dialogic Imagination: Four Essays.* Ed. Michael Holquist, tr. Caryl Emerson and Michael Holquist. Austin: University of Texas Press, 1981.

Bal, Mieccke. "Lots of Writing." *Poetics Today* 15, no. 1 (spring 1994): 89-114.

Band, Arnold. *Nostalgia and Nightmare: A Study in the Fiction of S. Y. Agnon.* Berkeley: University of California Press, 1968.

Benjamin, Walter. *Illuminations.* Ed. Hannah Arendt, tr. Harry Zohn. New York: Schocken Books, 1969.

Berkovitz, Y. D. *Kitvei Y. D. Berkovitz* [The Writing of Y. D. Berkovitz]. 2 vols. Tel Aviv: Dvir, 1959.

Bernstein, Michael André. *Foregone Conclusions: Against Apocalyptic History.* Berkeley: University of California Press, 1994.

Calvino, Italo. "The Adventure of a Soldier." In *Difficult Loves.* Tr. William Weaver, Archibald Colquhoun, and Peggy Wright. London: Picador, 1983.

Certeau, Michel de. *The Practice of Everyday Life.* Tr. Steven F. Rendall. Berkeley: University of California Press, 1984.

Davis, Natalie Zemon. "Rabelais among the Censors." *Representations,* no. 32 (fall 1990): 1-32.

Deleuze, Gilles, and Félix Guattari. *Kafka: Toward a Minor Literature.* Tr. Dana Polan. Minneapolis: University of Minnesota Press, 1986.

Erik, Max. "Menakhem-Mendl" (1935). Translated in *Prooftexts* 6, no. 1 (January 1986): 23-39.

Ezrahi, Yaron. *The Descent of Icarus: Science and the Transformation of Contemporary Democracy.* Cambridge: Mass.: Harvard University Press, 1990.

Fisch, Harold. "Reading and Carnival: On the Semiotics of Purim." *Poetics Today* 15, no. 1 (spring 1994): 55-74.

Fisher, Philip. *Hard Facts: Setting and Form in the American Novel.* Oxford: Oxford University Press, 1987.

Grossman, David. "My Sholem Aleichem." *Modern Hebrew Literature,* no. 14 (spring/summer 1995): pp. 4-5.

———. *See Under: Love.* Tr. Betsy Rosenberg. New York: Farrar, Straus, and Giroux, 1989.

Hoffman, Eva. *Lost in Translation: A Life in a New Language.* London: Heinemann, 1989.

Hoffman, Frederick. *The Mortal No: Death and the Modern Imagination.* Princeton: Princeton University Press, 1964.

Horowitz, Elliott. "The Rite to Be Reckless: On the Perpetration and Interpretation of Purim Violence." *Poetics Today* 15, no. 1 (spring 1994): 9-54.

Kachuck, Rhoda S. "Sholom Aleichem's Humor in English Translation." *YIVO Annual of Jewish Social Science* 11 (1956-57): 39-81.

Kafka, Franz. *The Penguin Complete Novels of Franz Kafka.* Tr. Willa and Edwin Muir. Harmondsworth: Penguin, 1983.

Kaufmann, Walter. "The Reception of Existentialism in the United States." In *The Legacy of the German Refugee Intellectuals,* ed. Robert Boyers. New York: Schocken Books, 1969.

Kellman, Ellen D. "Sholem Aleichem's Funeral (New York, 1916): The Making of a National Pageant." *YIVO Annual* 20 (1991): 277-304.

Kern, Stephen. *The Culture of Time and Space, 1880-1918.* Cambridge, Mass.: Harvard University Press, 1983.

Kronfeld, Chana. *On the Margins of Modernism: Decentering Literary Dynamics.* Berkeley: University of California Press, 1996.

Löwy, Michael. *Redemption and Utopia: Jewish Libertarian Thought in Central Europe, a Study in Elective Affinity.* Tr. Hope Heaney. London: Athlone, Press, 1992.

Marx, Leo. *The Machine in the Garden: Technology and the Pastoral Ideal in America.* London: Oxford University Press, 1964.

———. "Pastoralism in America." In *Ideology and Classic American Literature,* ed. Sacvan Bercovitch and Myra Jehlen. Cambridge: Cambridge University Press, 1986.

Miller, David Neal. "Don't Force Me to Tell You the Ending: Closure in the Short Fiction of Sh. Rabinovitsch (Sholem-Aleykhem)." *Neophilologus* 66 (1982): 102-10.

Miron, Dan. "Bouncing Back: Destruction and Recovery in Sholem Aleykhem's *Motl Peyse dem khazns.*" *YIVO Annual of Jewish Social Science* 17 (1978): 119-84.

———. "The Literary Image of the Shtetl." *Jewish Social Studies* 1, no. 3 (spring 1995): 1-43. Originally published in Hebrew as a five-part article, "Ha-dimui ha-sifruti ha-klasi shel ha-'ayara," *Ha-do'ar* 55 (1976) and 56 (1977), and then in Yiddish as *Der imazh fun Shtetl: dray literatishe shtudiyes* (Tel Aviv: I. L. Peretz, 1981).

———. *Sholem Aleykhem: Person, Persona, Presence.* New York: Yivo Institute for Jewish Research, 1972.

Pachter, Henry. "On Being an Exile." In *The Legacy of the German Refugee Intellectuals,* ed. Robert Boyers. New York: Schocken Books, 1969.

Pagis, Dan. *Kol ha-shirim; 'Abba' (pirkei proza)* [Collected Poems and "Father" (prose passages)]. Ed. Hanan Hever and T. Carmi. Jerusalem: Ha-kibbutz hame'uhad and Bialik Institute, 1991.

Pawel, Ernst. *Nightmare of Reason: A Life of Franz Kafka.* New York: Farrar, Straus, and Giroux, 1984.

Roskies, David. *A Bridge of Longing: The Lost Art of Yiddish Storytelling.* Cambridge, Mass.: Harvard University Press, 1995.

———. "Sholem Aleichem and Others: Laughing Off the Trauma of History." *Prooftexts* 2, no. 1 (January 1982): 53-77.

Sadan, Dov. '*Al Shai Agnon* [On S. Y. Agnon]. Tel Aviv: Ha-kibbutz ha-me'uhad, 1959.

———. *Avnei bedek* [Foundation Stones]. Tel Aviv: Ha-kibbutz ha-me'uhad, 1962.

———. *Avnei miftan: masot 'al sofrei yidish* [Corner Stones: Essays on Yiddish Writers]. 3 vols. Tel Aviv: Y. L. Peretz, 1961.

———. "Three Foundations: Sholem Aleichem and the Yiddish Literary Tradition" (1959), tr. David G. Roskies. *Prooftexts* 6, no. 1 (January 1986): 55-64.

Samuel, Maurice. *The World of Sholem Aleichem.* 1943. Reprint, New York: Schocken Books, 1965.

Shaked, Gershon. *The Shadows Within: Essays on Modern Jewish Writers.* Philadelphia: Jewish Publication Society, 1987.

Shandler, Jeffrey. "Reading Sholem Aleichem from Left to Right." *YIVO Annual* 20 (1991): 305-32.

Shmeruk, Chone. "Nokhvort." In Sholem-Aleykhem, *Motl Peyse dem Khazns* [Motl the Cantor Peyse's Son], vol. 2. Jerusalem: Magnes Press, 1996.

———. "Sholem-Aleykhem un Amerike" [Sholem Aleichem and America]. *Di Goldene Keyt,* no. 121 (1987): 55-77.

———. "Sipurei Motl ben he-hazan le-Shalom Aleichem: ha-situatzia ha-epit vetoldotav shel ha-sefer" [The Tales of Motl the Cantor's Son by Sholem Aleichem: The Epic Situation and the History of the Text]. *Siman Kria,* nos. 12/13 (February 1981): 310-26.

———. "Tevye der milkhiker—toldoteha shel yetzira" [The History of "Tevye the Dairyman"]. *Ha-sifrut* 7, no. 26 (April 1978): 26-38.

Sholem Aleichem. *Adventures of Mottel the Cantor's Son.* Tr. Tamara Kahana, illustr. Ilya Schor. New York: Henry Schuman, 1953.

———. *Ale verk fun Sholem Aleykhem* [Sholem Aleichem: The Collected Work]. 28 vols. New York: Sholem-Aleykhem Folksfond oysgabe, 1927.

———. *Funem Yarid* [From the Fair]. New York: Warheit, 1917.

———. *Sholem Aleykhem-Bukh* [Sholem Aleichem Book]. Ed. Y. D. Berkovitz. New York: n.p., 1926.

———. *Sipurei rakevet* [The Railroad Stories]. Ed. and tr. Dan Miron. Tel Aviv: Zmora Bitan, 1989.

———. *Tevye the Dairyman and the Railroad Stories.* Ed. and tr. Hillel Halkin. New York: Schocken Books, 1987.

———. *Why Do the Jews Need a Land of Their Own?* Ed. and tr. Joseph Leftwich and Mordecai S. Chertoff. New York: Herzl Press, 1984.

Sholem-Aleykhem [Sholem Aleichem]. *Motl Peyse dem Khazns* [Motl the Cantor Peyse's Son]. 2 vols. New York: Sholem Aleichem Folksfand Oysgabe, 1927.

Smith, Henry Nash. "Symbol and Idea in *Virgin Land.*" In *Ideology and Classic American Literature,* ed. Sacvan Bercovitch and Myra Jehlen. Cambridge: Cambridge University Press, 1986.

Sokoloff, Naomi B. 1992. *Imagining the Child in Modern Jewish Fiction.* Baltimore: Johns Hopkins University Press.

Sollors, Werner. "Immigrants and Other Americans." In *Columbia Literary History of the United States,* general ed. Emory Elliott. New York: Columbia University Press, 1988.

Stern, Michael. "Tevye's Art of Quotation." *Prooftexts* 6, no. 1 (January 1986): 79-96.

Trunk, Y. Y. *Sholem Aleykhem: zein vezen un zeine verk* [Sholem Aleichem: His Being and His Work]. Warsaw: Kulturlige, 1937.

Wisse, Ruth. *The Schlemiel as Modern Hero.* Chicago: University of Chicago Press, 1971.

Ruth R. Wisse (essay date 2000)

SOURCE: Wisse, Ruth R. "The Comedy of Endurance: Sholem Aleichem." In *The Modern Jewish Canon: A Journey through Language and Culture,* pp. 31-64. New York: Free Press, 2000.

[*In this essay, Wisse centers on Tevye's use of language—his propensity to quote Hebrew sources, his love of storytelling, and his verbal interactions with his daughters and his wife—as it reflects his unyielding faith in God.*]

Such a one is a natural philosopher.

Shakespeare, *As You Like It*

Literary heroism implies the possibility of meaningful action, action that can determine the outcome of personal or national destiny. Nineteenth-century European literature had already pronounced its skepticism about such possibilities when Jewish literature was just beginning its search for them: as Fabrice del Dongo roams the Napoleonic battlefield in *Charterhouse of Parma* (1839) determined to prove himself a real soldier, the narrator lets us know that he "could not understand in the least what was happening." Raskolnikov (1867) decides to test his philosophy of exceptionalism by murdering a useless old woman and ends by confessing his crime to the police and to God. Yet creators of the failed or anti-hero still enjoy the benefits of the tradition they depose. These bids for heroism may be unmasked by their authors as comically and tragically misguided, but the young men still go into battle, still wield their axes. The narratives remain charged with tension and dramatic action that feed off the inherited models of heroism.

Writers of the Yiddish and Hebrew renaissance at the end of the nineteenth century inherited no such tradition of literature. The politically dependent Jews found it difficult to acclaim the man of action as their authentic Jewish hero. Most Jewish writers had not spent their youth in political action like Stendhal or in the political opposition like Dostoyevsky but rather breaking out of *yeshivas* to gain a secular education. The man of learning, who defined the Jewish image of masculinity, was not the best candidate for literary heroism. There were Jews who mastered the culture of the Gentiles and made their mark as intellectuals in Western Europe. But here language and cultural orientation became a problem: what kind of hero could Moses Mendelssohn or Heinrich Heine be to the writer in a *Jewish* language, whose culture was predicated on the perpetuation of *Jewish* civilization? Writers of Jewish pulp fiction created improbable saviors of damsels in danger, but their adventures and even their costumes lacked credibility. It seemed that the more Jewish the main character was, the less heroic he appeared to be and the more heroic, the less Jewish.

Sholem Aleichem was the first to break through this impasse. The anchoring work of the modern Jewish canon—***Tevye the Dairyman***—is the transcribed repertoire of the first Jewish stand-up comedian who was also in the process of creating his audience. The comic hero is something of a compromise, to be sure: his words speak louder than his actions. Still, let us not fail to note that he manages to assist women in distress.

TEVYE THE DAIRYMAN: THE MAKING OF A COMIC HERO

In 1894, when he was thirty-five years old, Sholem Aleichem created a character named Tevye, a village Jew with a number of unmarried daughters, as in the Yiddish proverb "*Zibn tekhter iz nisht kayn gelekhter* [seven daughters are no laughing matter]." The maxim makes fun of what it says is no laughing matter, and on that same contradictory premise Tevye would turn the problems of his life into humor. Sholem Aleichem had just returned to Kiev from his customary summer vacation in nearby Boyarka, and as he wrote to his good friend Mordecai Spector, he intended to convey

some of that holiday experience in the forthcoming volume of Spector's *Hoyzfraynd* [Home Companion]:

> The story will be called ***Tevye der milkhiker,*** composed in Boyarka, that is to say, I heard the story from Tevye himself as he stood in front of my *dacha* with his horse and cart, weighing out our butter and cheese. The story is interesting, but Tevye himself a thousand times more interesting! I convey the story in his own words, and am spared the effort of describing him since he describes himself.[1]

Like an impresario who knows that he has just landed his meal ticket, Sholem Aleichem negotiated with Spector over every detail of spelling, layout, typeset, and the quality of paper on which the Tevye story was to be printed.[2] Before long, everyone was in on the game. Members of Sholem Aleichem's family and critics familiar with the region confirmed that there was, indeed, such a Jew named Tevye, and when a local dairyman protested that he did not have any daughters, it seemed only to reinforce the notion that a new literary talent had been discovered.[3]

Yiddish literature was still young and untried when Sholem Aleichem began writing. Just as Samuel Richardson and Daniel Defoe used "discovered" diaries and letters, pseudobiography, editorial footnotes, and other such authenticating artifices to win the trust of new English readers by insisting that their books delivered other people's words, so too did Sholem Aleichem often present himself as the intermediary between his characters and his readers to attest to the actuality of his creations. A decade earlier, after he had begun to publish in the *Di yidishe folksblat* [The Jewish People's Paper], then the only Yiddish newspaper in the Russian empire, he had turned his name into the most common greeting in the language. That is, by keeping his first name, Sholem, and changing his patronymic, Rabinovitch, he formed the phrase one might address to an old friend when meeting him in the street: "Sholem Aleichem [how are you doing]?" Behind this friendly pseudonym—really only half a disguise, since the fictive author shared the vital statistics of his creator—Sholem Aleichem gave the impression of being one of the people, intermingling with his fellow Jews wherever they happened to be.[4]

In this he had adapted the practice of the man he called *zeyde,* the "grandfather" or shaping genius of modern Yiddish and Hebrew literature, Sholem Yankev Abramovitch, who assumed the literary disguise of Mendele Moykher-Sforim (Mendele the book peddler) when he began to write Yiddish fiction in 1864. Mendele Moykher-Sforim took on such an independent reality as the agent and publisher of the stories he brought to the public that he eclipsed his creator and became known as the author of his works. The Mendele narrator seemed not only to unite but virtually to create a community of readers as he traveled through the Jewish Pale of Settlement, between cities, towns, and villages, among the learned and the simple Jews, bringing fresh reading material to men and women, old and young. By carrying both religious and secular material—amulets to ward off the evil eye and the new kind of novels—he implicitly appealed to a modern audience that included old-fashioned Jews. Rabinovitch's Sholem Aleichem was even more peripatetic and democratic than Mendele in that he figured as the listener or the amanuensis of a people, providing what many assumed was "the life of the people in its authentic form."[5] Tevye, whom the critic Meir Viner called Mendele's younger brother, was homier still. Both characters enjoy quoting Jewish sources, but undereducated Tevye feels freer to play around with them, inviting perpetual uncertainty over how much of his humor is involuntary and how much is willed. Both peddlers offer merchandise to the public, but Mendele retains the rights to everything he brings to market and has to persuade his potential customers of the value of each new book. A creature of the Jewish Enlightenment, Mendele assumes that literature must prove its worth by bettering the life of its readers. Tevye offers food and entertainment, and according to Sholem Aleichem, the very best of both. His merchandise purports to be just good, not good *for* you. And unlike Mendele, who kept mum about his private life, Tevye enjoys sharing confidences about himself and the family.

At first Sholem Aleichem went to elaborate lengths to establish the distnce between Tevye and himself, the implied author of the work. In the first installment that appeared in *Hoyzfraynd* he describes a big-boned, hirsute Jew, one of those healthy village specimens who eats dumplings with cheese "and spends his ninety years on earth without the help of glasses, false teeth, hemorrhoids, and other such Jewish pains and troubles."[6] In a letter to the author, Tevye declares himself flattered by the attention of the author from Yehupetz (Sholem Aleichem's fictional rendition of Kiev) who now promises to bring *his* story to the reading public. Citing Genesis 32:11, Tevye protests, "*Kotoynti [I am not worthy]!*"—echoing Jacob's exclamation ("I am not worthy of all the mercies and of all the truth, which Thou has shown Thy servant") as he flees his vengeful brother Esau. Jacob is reminding God of their special relationship while admitting that he does not deserve His help, and with the same mixture of humility and *chutzpa* Tevye tells Sholem Aleichem where to send the money he is owed, presumably for royalties. But by the time Tevye reappeared in a second chapter a few years later, he was brought on stage without preamble, like a performer so famous he needs

no introduction.[7] Sholem Aleichem realized that he had discovered in Tevye the Jew through whom he could tell the story of his time, and he brought him back again and again over the next twenty years at critical moments in his own and the nation's life.

The first monologue, **"Tevye Strikes It Rich,"** is exceptionally cheerful. Nine or ten years after the events in question (time enough for the narrative to have ripened), he recalls how once on his way home from Boiberik (the fictional Boyarka) after a long day of hauling logs, having earned not nearly enough to feed his abundant family, he was startled out of his late afternoon prayers by the sudden appearance of two creatures in the woods. First he fears robbers, then, seeing that they are female, demons. They turn out to be simply a Jewish mother and daughter who had lost their way in the woods that morning. Tevye is slow to understand his heroic potential in guiding these women out of the forest, and they are mildly contemptuous of the *schlimazl,* the hapless bumbler, who has to serve as their savior. But at their urging, he agrees to turn his horse and wagon around and to transport them back to their dacha in Boiberik. There he is rewarded beyond his wildest fantasies. For bringing the women home, the head of the family, a traditional Jew like himself, showers Tevye with more money than he has the temerity to ask for and invites all the other members of the family to contribute something from their own pockets as well. The bounty Tevye receives that day allows him and his wife to set up a home dairy, producing cheese and butter products they had never before been able to afford.

Tevye tells this story at his leisure in Boiberik, the charming summer retreat. The literary scholar Frank Kermode argues that Ben Jonson and William Shakespeare were attracted by the pastoral genre at a time of exceptionally poignant social transformation in England: when London was developing a "distinctively metropolitan ethos" and traditionally rural citizens had to adjust to the new social standing of the commercial classes and the growth of wealth based on new values.[8] Using Nature as its background, Elizabethan drama reestablished a common humanity among people otherwise estranged. Similarly, Sholem Aleichem conjured up the perpetually summery Boiberik-Boyarka in a period of significant upheaval among Russian Jews. The infamous May Laws, imposed after the assassination of Alexander II in 1881, had prohibited Jews from settling or buying property outside their towns, or *shtetlakh,* and forbade them to open their markets to peasants on Sundays and Christian holidays. "Poor!" I. L. Peretz had exclaimed in a story of the previous year. "It's hard to imagine how poor!

Ten grain dealers throw themselves on every measure of rye that a peasant brings . . . one hundred tailors for one pair of overalls, fifty shoemakers for one small repair."[9]

The government not only failed to protect its Jewish subjects from the violence of pogroms but conducted what the historian Simon Dubnow called "legislative pogroms" through its policies of economic harassment.[10] Such solidarity as might have been created among Jews in reaction to these punitive measures was undermined by a policy of exceptions that allowed certain categories of Jewish merchants, professionals, artists, students, and craftsmen to live in cities outside the Pale. By distinguishing between wealthy and poor Jews, educated and ignorant Jews, the Russian government drove a wedge into the Jewish body politic, rewarding those who were able to distance themselves from the masses. Sholem Aleichem's readers would have known that while the summer vacationers enjoyed the privilege of residence in Yehupetz, a Jew like Tevye could not legally stay in the city overnight.

Anti-tsarism contributed to the problem. Opposed to the government's oppressive policies in all other respects, Jewish nihilists shared the tsar's interest in exacerbating the tension between richer and poorer Jews in order to replace Jewish loyalties by loyalties to class. Already in the 1870s, Jews in the revolutionary movement had repudiated national allegiance in favor of class solidarity. "You know very well that I detest Judaism just as I hate all other . . . isms," wrote Aaron Lieberman, the founder of the first Jewish socialist organization, who claimed to fight only for the oppressed Jews, "the suffering masses among them and those who intend to join us."[11] While only a minority of revolutionaries actually welcomed the anti-Jewish pogroms of 1881 as a preparatory stage for the revolt of the masses, socialism substituted the brotherhood of class for the communal discipline of the Jews and encouraged Jews to express the kind of hostility toward the rich that could never be openly voiced against the *goyim* (people of other religions and nationalities).

Against this background of repression and divisiveness, Tevye tells of bridging the extremes of poverty and wealth. The chapter title **"Dos groyse gevins"** [**"The Big Win"**] refers literally to winning the lottery, but had Tevye won such a jackpot, the miracle would have been his alone, insulating one more Jew from his impoverished coreligionists. Instead, Tevye's windfall is the result of a Jewish exchange of services very much like the interaction between him and the author in the frame of the story. Just as Tevye makes a living off Sholem Aleichem, so the vacationing author intends to milk the milkman, turning Tevye's stories

into literature and then bringing them to market. Neither commercial exploitation nor charity, theirs is a mutually beneficial transaction. As such, Tevye *earns* his reward from the rich man's family through his own generous act, just as he earns his author's gratitude for his humor and his cheese.

Tevye's narrative is set at the beginning of summer—the high season of literary comedy. He is returning from a long day's work and, in the way that an epic narrator might call upon his muse, is reciting the *shimenesre* (Eighteen Benedictions of the afternoon service) when his horse suddenly breaks away on a "pleasure jaunt":

> In a word, there I was running behind the wagon and singing the *shimenesre,* forgive the comparison, like a cantor at the pulpit: *Mekhalkeyl khayim bekhesed,* Who provideth life with His bounty, *Umekayeym emunosoy lisheyney ofor,* Who keepeth faith with them who slumber in earth—even with those who already lie in the ground baking bagels. With my troubles I was six feet underground already! Oh, do we suffer! Not like those rich Yehupetz Jews sitting all summer long in their dachas in Boiberik, eating and drinking and swimming in luxury! Master of the Universe, what have I done to deserve all this? Am I or am I not a Jew like any other? Help! . . .*Re'ey-no be'onyeynu,* See us in our affliction—take a good look at us poor folk slaving away and do something about it, because if You don't, just who do You think will?[12]

Running away with texts is as much a part of Jewish tradition as prayer itself, but the dialectical tension of Tevye's argument is new. The reader trained in paradox may note that Tevye's prayer triggers the revolt against it: praising the Lord for His bounty reminds him of his want, the Hebrew affirmation prompting his Yiddish commentary in perpetual point counterpoint. What the verbs promise—a God "Who provideth" and "keepeth faith"—Tevye desires for himself. Remove the liturgical text, and you have the slogans of the emerging revolution. The then-Marxist critic I. I. Trunk took this theological independence to mean that "for all his Jewish belief, Tevye doesn't have the least confidence in God."[13] But one can as readily cite Tevye's interpolations as proofs of his investment in God. After all, who but Tevye out there in Nature cared whether or not he recited his prayers? Without the liturgy's repeated promises of justice Tevye would have no occasion to take his human lot so seriously, no context for expecting any more than he has. The Covenant is the source of his self-confidence, inviting him to expect fair judgment and to appreciate his worth.

Tevye's eagerness to show off prompted some critics to accuse him of overreaching, as though he were the Mrs. Malaprop of Yiddish letters. Richard Sheridan's memorable character says things like "Forget this fellow: illiterate him from your memory" and "I'm sorry my affluence over my niece is very small," mistakes that expose her ignorance at the very moment that she is trying to impress us with her expanded vocabulary. Sholem Aleichem's translator Frances Butwin thought that Tevye's interpolations were similarly "completely cockeyed": "The juxtaposition of a lofty phrase in Hebrew or Aramaic with a homely Yiddish phrase which is supposed to explain it but has no bearing on it whatever—that is the gist of Tevye's humor. Tevye, of course, has no idea that he is funny."[14] But this is like saying that Sholem Aleichem himself has no idea that he is being funny. Tevye's delight in mangling and appropriating quotations is the entertainer's delight in amusing his public. Not only does his play with the Hebrew sources confirm his psychological adaptiveness, but it also shows off the culture's strategy for coping with adversity, since much of his routine was already drawn from the Yiddish idiom. By making Tevye a more traditional Jew than himself, Sholem Aleichem could turn him into an exegetical humorist, a comical Rashi,[15] rewarding those readers who were familiar with the sources by inviting them to enjoy his distortions.

Tevye's comedy accepts the ontological disparity between what is possible and what is necessary, refusing to homogenize the competing claims of hope and skepticism. Tevye stood Hegelian ambition on its head, in the sense of denying that there can be any *development* in the tension between thesis and antithesis, since the finite human being can never attain what he must continue to struggle for. Tevye's humor follows the pattern of those Yiddish proverbs that simultaneously credit and subvert the quotations from which they derive: "*Ato bokhartonu* [*Thou has chosen us* from among the nations]: why did you have to pick on the Jews?" "*Avodim hoyinu* [*we were slaves* in the land of Egypt]: that's reason enough for being Jews in the world!" (How, you may ask, can slavery make it worth being a Jew? Because the preeminence of the Jew is rooted in this history of slavery, which also became the basis for Jewish moral imperatives ["because you were slaves in the land of Egypt"]. The heights of Jewish national fortunes—the Exodus and the granting of the Law at Sinai—begin at the lowest point of Jewish degradation in Egypt; that is, the history of Jewish humiliation is also the ground of Jewish pride.)

It is legitimate to place Tevye, as Hillel Halkin does, in the long tradition of God-arguers that "starts with Abraham and runs prominently on through Moses, through Job . . . [to] Levi Yitzchak of Berdichev, the saintly Hasidic master who is said to have held a trial at which God was the absentee defendant, accused of having inflicted undeserved suffering on His people."[16] Yet in realistic fiction, justice can only be effected

through human agency. While most intellectuals and writers of his day expected a kindlier solidarity to replace a society founded on religion, Sholem Aleichem recognized the likelier possibility that without fealty to a common God, Jews would have no further claim on one another's loyalty. Hence, Tevye's negotiations with the *gvir* (the wealthy Jew) are a testier version of his exchange with the Almighty:

> "A little brandy?" I say. "Who can refuse a little brandy? What does it say in the books: *Eyze 'lekhayim' ve'eyze lemoves,* who shall live and who shall die, or as Rashi comments, God is God and brandy is brandy. *Lekhayim!*" And I emptied the glass in one gulp. "God should only help you to stay rich and happy," I said, "and may Jews always remain Jews; God give them health and strength to overcome their troubles."
>
> "What name do you go by?" asked the man of the house, a fine-looking Jew with a skullcap. "Where do you hail from? Where do you live now? What's your work? Do you have a wife? Children? How many?"
>
> "Children?" I say. "I cannot complain. If each child of mine were worth a million rubles, as my Golde tries convincing me they are, I'd be richer than anyone in Yehupetz. The only trouble is that poor isn't rich and a mountain's no ditch. As it says in the prayer book, *Hamavdil beyn koydesh lekhoyl*—some make hay while others toil. The Brodskys have money and I have daughters. . . . But you'll have to excuse me for carrying on like this. There is nothing straighter than a crooked ladder and nothing as crooked as an honest word, especially as I've gone and made the blessing over brandy on an empty stomach."[17]

Nervous and nervy, Tevye tells the rich Jew what he told the Almighty, that even the greatest spiritual inheritance is no substitute for a square meal. Offered a drink, Tevye tucks his toast "to life [*Lekhayim*]!" into the liturgy's ominous forecast of "who shall live and who shall die." Hence, the blessing he proffers ("God should only help you to stay rich and happy") hints broadly at the alternative. Comparing himself to the Brodskys, the Jewish sugar magnates who were Russia's version of the Rothschilds, Tevye both accepts God's arrangement and objects to having another Jew arranged on top of him. He is not quite as aggressive as that beggar of the Jewish joke who protests when informed that his benefactor has gone bankrupt, "So if his business is bad, why should I suffer?" That wit risks everything on a strategy of confrontation, claiming his right *ahead* of his benefactor's. Tevye merely confirms that Jews are responsible for one another; hence his wish that Jews may remain Jews so that he can tap into that obligation. Similarly, Sholem Aleichem knew that his career, like Tevye's reward, depended materially and morally on Jews who still felt bound by the traditions in which they had been raised.

In the humor anthology edited by Sholem Aleichem's close friend Y. Kh. Ravnitski, we find the following joke: A group of Jewish merchants in a restaurant are being harassed by a peddler who will not take no for an answer. Time and again he invites them to buy his handkerchiefs, wallets, haberdashery. Finally, one of the merchants says, "Watch me. I'll play a trick on him that he won't soon forget." The next time the peddler comes over to their table, he asks, "How much for these suspenders?" The peddler, still praising his merchandise to the skies, quotes a price of two rubles. Without a word, the merchant hands over the sum, and the peddler walks off in confusion. "How do you like the trick I played on him?" asked the merchant. "Now he'll be kicking himself all day for not having asked three rubles."[18]

When Tevye is asked how much he is owed for having brought the women home, each party wants the other to name his price:

> "No," they say, "we want you to tell us, Reb Tevye. You needn't be afraid. We won't chop your head off."
>
> Now what? I asked myself. I was really in a pretty pickle. It would be a crime to ask for one ruble when they might agree to two. On the other hand, if I asked for two they might think I was mad. *Two* rubles for one little wagon ride?
>
> "Three rubles!" The words were out of my mouth before I could stop them.
>
> Everyone began to laugh so hard that I could have crawled into a hole in the ground.[19]

While Ravnitski's version perfectly illustrates Freud's interpretation of tendentious jokes as instruments of aggression, Tevye invites us to experience the disjunction between dreams of profit and fears of loss. The sum he is embarrassed to ask for amuses his benefactors by its modesty. The merchant springs the surprise of the joke by subordinating his economic interests to his pychological victory, drawing attention to the competitive element in buying and selling that goes far beyond the incentive for profit. As the joke's point of view shifts from merchant to peddler, it reveals the human cost that the joke was designed to mask. The host in the Tevye version intervenes to put a stop to the merriment, chiding the insensitivity of those newly raised in wealth. The humorist wins his reward by making himself the *sentient* target rather than the butt of the joke.

Often mistaken for a typical *shtetl* Jew,[20] Tevye is actually distinguished by the fact that he is a villager, the antithesis of those "*kleyne mentshelekh mit kleyne hasoges* [little people with little ideas]," the far too many salesfolk and tradesfolk chasing after too few potential customers in Sholem Aleichem's stories about the *shtetl*. Not unlike his author, Tevye manages both the means of production and the distribution of his wares, standing somewhat apart from the Jewish society he serves. He only visits Anatevka, the local Jewish market town, twice a year, when he needs a *minyan* (the quorum of ten Jews required for communal worship) to say *Kaddish,* the memorial prayer on the anniversary of his parents' deaths. To emphasize this independence of the *shtetl* is no mere quibble. For although it has been noted that Sholem Aleichem creates a Jewish "quasi territory" in his writing—a network of fictional Jewish towns, villages, and cities with nary a church steeple in sight—the virtual island of discourse inhabited by Tevye and Sholem Aleichem is the first genuinely autonomous Jewish territory to appear in modern Yiddish literature, not coincidentally at the very moment that Zionism became a mass movement. Though obviously rooted in Ukrainian soil and still negotiating a generally hostile Christian world, Tevye and Sholem Aleichem are culturally autonomous and economically interdependent, serving their Christian neighbors out of superfluity, not necessity. As arguments began to appear in the Jewish press over the prospects of Jewish agricultural initiatives in Palestine, Sholem Aleichem, who was in sympathy with these efforts, created an adumbrated, comically miniature land of *milk* and honey in this opening episode of the Tevye saga.[21]

SHOLEM ALEICHEM: THE AUTHOR BEHIND THE CHARACTER

Autobiography, the most popular form of Jewish literature in the nineteenth century, usually claims that the first-person singular guarantees the truthfulness of the disclosure. But Tevye is a character twice removed from the author by the presence of the fictional Sholem Aleichem. Sholem Rabinovitch was a sophisticated literary man who spoke Russian to his children. How could the Kiev householder with the golden watch chain across his vest be mistaken for a dairyman who thinks two cows constitute a fortune? Yet, differences notwithstanding, Sholem Rabinovitch consigned to Tevye the most significant aspects of his life, beginning with the all-important matter of his talent and extending to the size of his household. Twice before, Rabinovitch had tried to compose a novel about an artist—the eponymous Stempenyu, a gifted fiddler, and Yosele Solovey, a golden-voiced cantor—who must either realize his ambitions by going out into the world or suffer the tragic consequence of staying home among the Jews.[22] But in Tevye he had a performer whose skill actually depended on a Jewish audience.

The humorist's instrument is his language. Sholem Rabinovitch's creative pleasure and anxieties as a Yiddish writer are transposed into Tevye's delight in racontage and fear of a breakdown in communication with his children. Among artists, the humorist was destined not to be taken with ultimate seriousness because of his delight in disinhibition, his ability to be "unashamedly childish."[23] Hence, *kotoynti*, Tevye's artful modesty, embodies his creator's admission that he excels at the disdained literary form of humor rather than the epic novel to which he aspired. Tevye *der milkhiker* meant not simply Tevye the dairyman but a man of milky disposition.[24] In Russian, milquetoasts were sometimes called *molokanye,* or milk-drinkers, after the sect of Russian pacifists who abjured meat, and, of course, the Jewish dietary laws that proscribe the mixing of dairy with meat had produced a typology of *milkhik* (milky) and *fleyshik* (meaty) personalities. Sholem Rabinovitch endowed Tevye with his own sweet male temper that used humor to parry aggression it could not oppose in kind.

The author's life had been transformed by a lucky break very much like Tevye's.[25] He was born in 1859 in Pereyaslav, Ukraine, and spent his childhood in the smaller Voronkov, where he attended a traditional *cheder* until a sudden business reversal forced his father to bring the family back to his native city under reduced circumstances, and with a sense of having come down in the world. His mother's early death further unsettled the boy and saddled him with a punitive, unfriendly stepmother. His father, who was interested in the new Hebrew literature and the Jewish Enlightenment, supervised his son's Hebrew education and, recognizing his intellectual gifts, sent him to the local Russian *gymnasium,* from which he graduated with distinction. Then, at seventeen, like hundreds of other young men without economic prospects, Sholem tried to support himself by tutoring. He left home, hoping to find a job as secretary or bookkeeper to one of the newly minted Russian Jewish entrepreneurs. Through a serendipitous encounter, he was hired by Elimelekh Loyev, a rich Jewish landowner in the Kiev province, to become the tutor of his only daughter. The Cinderella romance that developed between teacher and pupil angered Loyev when he first discovered it, more out of pique at the secrecy of the young couple than because he objected to his future son-in-law, but he was reconciled to their marriage, which occurred in 1883. Two years later Loyev died, leaving Sholem Rabinovitch in charge of a household of females that included his wife, her younger cousin, and his mother-in-law, who lived with them thereafter. The atmosphere of Loyev's welcoming wealth permeates the opening monologue of *Tevye the Dairyman.*

Rabinovitch's most productive years were 1883-1890, when he lived in Kiev as a speculator in the double sense, investing on the newly opened stock exchange and in a new high-level Yiddish literature, paying the highest royalties ever for Yiddish writing. He adopted the Yiddish pen name Sholem Aleichem so as "not to embarrass [his] father," who expected him to write in Hebrew, and waged literary battles against the trashy romances that he felt were corrupting Yiddish literature. But he overreached and went bankrupt, and until his family paid off his debts he was forced to wander for several years to Odessa, Paris, Vienna, and Czernowitz.

The second Tevye monologue, **"The Bubble Bursts"** (1899), is all about overreaching. Here it is as if Shakespeare had brought together Hamlet and Othello in a single work, pitting the hesitancy of the first against the impulsiveness of the second, for Tevye encounters Menakhem-Mendl, the frenetic speculator whom Sholem Aleichem had introduced to readers in 1892. Menakhem-Mendl figured in his own comic series as the male half of an epistolary exchange with his *shtetl*-bound wife Sheyne-Sheyndl.[26] Having left his small-town family to seek his fortune in the big city, he is the prototype of the *luftmentsh,* the man who lives on air, and of the philosophic optimist, the Jew who lives on faith. Each series of letters is organized around another of Menakhem-Mendl's ventures—into stocks, bonds, brokerage, and so forth—and each sequence repeats the same pattern: the husband writes home to his wife about the new investments that are bound to bring him a fortune, he enjoys the first dizzying returns, the market crashes, he rebounds. Sheyne-Sheyndl's (losing) argument is also the same, reinforced by her mother's proverbs, such as "*Kreplakh* [dumplings] in a dream are not *kreplakh* but a dream." "The worm lies in horseradish and finds it sweet." Her barbs puncture her son-in-law's airy schemes, but the longer the comedy continues, the more certain it is that Menakhem-Mendl will never return to the *shtetl.*

If Tevye's first monologue fulfilled the promise of Psalm 113—"He lifts the poor man from the dust, from dirt he raises the beggar"—his metamorphosis into a small entrepreneur now situates him among the potential benefactors rather than the petitioners, with a corresponding shift of economic and social responsibility. Having previously demonstrated the benefit that Jews could bring one another through a minor redistribution of resources, this late-autumn episode explores the opposite proposition, the destabilizing effect of economic temptation. Inevitably, it is in the big city Yehupetz that Tevye falls prey to temptation. Looking at a shopwindow display of silver, gold, and banknotes and dreaming of the things he could do with but a tithe of that money, Tevye is tapped on the shoulder by a bedraggled Menakhem-Mendl, who introduces himself as a relative by marriage twice removed and explains that he is slinking around the city without a residence permit, eluding the police. Tevye invites the hungry man to join him for a day in the country. There Golde fills Menakhem-Mendl's stomach, and

Menakhem-Mendl fills Tevye's head with get-rich-quick schemes. Neither man can resist what the other offers.

In this fateful encounter between his two major protagonists and the two sides of his own personality, the dependable father and the irresponsible child, Sholem Aleichem gives Tevye pride of place. Menakhem-Mendl figures in Tevye's monologue—not vice versa—as the *schlimazl* who gave him "the itch to be rich."[27] To be sure, Menakhem-Mendl may well signify Sholem Aleichem's unfettered creative impulse, the necessary condition for art. But nothing is as characteristic of Sholem Aleichem's opus as the regretful subordination of the messianist to the qualified optimist, and the contrast between the two men as husbands may clarify what is at stake. Menakhem-Mendl resists domestication with near-fatal abandon; no matter how desperate the news from his wife, neither duty nor practical self-interest can lure him home. Even as he enjoys his relatives' bounty, he does not hesitate to put it at risk. For his part, Tevye will not celebrate striking it rich until he has first fed his horse. He cries when he sees his daughters wolfing down their first abundant meal, and he cannot live without the approval of the wife whom he mocks as his inferior.

And so after losing all his savings on what came to be known in Yiddish parlance as a Menakhem-Mendl scheme, Tevye seesaws to equilibrium:

> And that, Pani Sholem Aleichem, is how I blew all my money. But if you think I've been eating my heart out about it, you have another guess coming. You know the Bible's opinion: *li hakesef veli hazohov*—money is muck! What matters is the man who has it—I mean, what matters is for a man to be a man. Do you know what I still can't get over though? Losing my dream! If only you knew how badly, oh Lord, how really badly I wanted to be a rich Jew, if only for a while! But go be smarter than life. Doesn't it say *be'al korkhekho atoh khai*—nobody asks if you want to be born or if you want your last pair of boots to be torn. "Instead of dreaming, Tevye," God was trying to tell me, "you should have stuck to your cheese and butter." Does that mean I've lost faith and stopped hoping for better times? Don't you believe it! The more troubles, the more faith, the bigger the beggar, the greater his hopes.[28]

The supportive quotation from the prophet Haggai (2:18), *"The silver is mine and the gold is mine,* saith the Lord of Hosts,"* delivers God's promise to Israel that the glory of the rebuilt Temple will surpass the one that was destroyed. Tevye rebounds with gratitude to the challenge of his loss the way the Jews have been doing since at least the Babylonian exile, with an appreciation of paradox grown suppler over the centuries. Acknowledging God's grandeur, Tevye briefly downplays the importance of his own material assets,

but then, having recovered his optimism, he regrets not having the money after all. The cycle starts again with Tevye's favorite quotation from *Ethics of the Fathers:* "Regardless of thy will thou art conceived, and regardless of thy will thou art born, and *regardless of thy will thou livest,* and regardless of thy will thou diest." No sooner does he reconcile himself to mortal finitude than he begins to hope for better times. Tevye never simply quotes but rather subjects all authority to his own interpretation, so that even God seems merely to confirm a conclusion he has reached on his own.[29] Resignation is no sooner denied than readmitted: the expulsion from Eden triggers the yearning for redemption; the authority of texts can only be demonstrated when individuals freely adapt them; the Covenant with God invites man to stand up against Him; in the surrender to nature is born the instinct for life. Chastened by the blowout that follows hitting the jackpot, Tevye henceforth tries to hold on to what he has.

THE DAUGHTERS

How many daughters had Tevye? In asking this question, the literary scholar Chone Shmeruk highlights a discrepancy that emerged in Sholem Aleichem's masterpiece as a result of its having been written in real time, over a span of twenty years.[30] In the opening monologue (1895) Tevye is worried about having to feed seven hungry daughters; by the sixth chapter (1907) he mentions only six girls, and by the seventh (1909) he is left with five. Clearly, the author did not know when he wrote his first Tevye monologue that he would go on to develop a family saga, but as he himself had four daughters of six children, superabundant paternity was one of his biographical connections with Tevye. He developed the stories of the daughters—Tsaytl, Hodl, Chava, Shprintse, and Beilke—one at a time, never knowing from one episode to the next when or how he would continue. But why, then, didn't Sholem Aleichem redact his text to provide internal consistency? Did he balk at retroactively "killing off" the excess children out of some sense that they had been his own? Was he still hoping to continue the series when death cut it short?

More intriguing than the number of his daughters is that in contradistinction to most contemporary European literature, Sholem Aleichem wrote his masterwork about generational conflict from the *parent's* point of view. From the moment that Bazarov appeared in Turgenev's *Fathers and Sons,* he involved all literate Russia in an argument over whether he was the villain or hero of the emerging new age. Dostoyevsky created a rogues' gallery of revolutionaries that warned Russia long before the Bolsheviks took power of the social threat posed by young people who stood free of God. Leo Tolstoy cast Levin and Anna Karenina as the happy and the unhappy face of Russia, as the psychological and moral alternatives in a land where the educated young were forcing a new society into being. From Samuel Butler's *The Way of All Flesh* to D. H. Lawrence's *Sons and Lovers* and throughout most Yiddish and Hebrew literature, authors presented the clash between parents and children from the dynamic perspective of the rebels, and in his formal novels Sholem Aleichem did exactly the same.

Yet Sholem Aleichem had an overriding artistic reason for creating a Yiddish narrator of the older generation. By the late nineteenth century, Yiddish may have been as fully formed and culturally productive as most other European languages, but every youngster who quit his or her traditional home to attend *gymnasium* or to foment revolution or to move to America or to a settlement in Palestine felt the need to adopt a language other than Yiddish as a consequence of the change. Yiddish may have been spoken by the vast majority of Jews in the Russian Empire—indeed, by more Jews than had ever before simultaneously spoken a common language—but as the repository of Jewish religious civilization, Yiddish would not suffice for Jews who no longer wanted to remain exclusively within its bounds. Sholem Aleichem had often alluded to this problem:

> Once, about ten years ago, Morris Silverman was called "Meir," and his mother Golde Reb Meir's still calls him "Meir'l" to this day. But since civilization began to appear among our brethren, we bolted in fear of her, and quickly began to adjust our clothing and our names: the satin *kapote* and the round *shtreiml* were traded in for a short jacket and top hat, and yesterday's Meir Berl's, Zerakh Naphtali's, and Kalman Reb Velvele's suddenly became Morris Borisovitch, Zachary Pantelemonovitch, and Clementi Vladimirovitch . . .[31]

Morris Silverman in *Taybele,* this early work of Sholem Aleichem's, anticipates Ahronchik, the mama's boy who will break Shprintse's heart in the sixth chapter of **Tevye the Dairyman.** But the broken heart at issue here was the author's: Sholem Aleichem knew that he could not hope to satisfy the new Morrises and Zacharys and Clementis, because he himself was speaking and writing Russian to his children. So that they might have access to everything emancipation had to offer, he weaned them from the language to which he was devoting his creative genius. Tevye is the expression of this tragic paradox. The father knows that in addition to letting his children go, he will abet their defection so that they might enjoy a better life.

Sholem Aleichem may have absorbed a great deal from his beloved Nikolai Gogol, but there is nothing in his writing remotely like *Taras Bulba,* the all-out struggle between the dashing Andrey, who abandons his people for the love of a woman, and the Cossack father who is obliged to kill his renegade son. In the oedipal conflicts of the "Jewish Gogol," the prepubescent child already assumes responsibility for what his father is too weak to protect: a boy in Sholem Aleichem's maiden story, **"The Penknife,"** sacrifices his desire to own a penknife in deference to his sickly father.[32] The narrator renounces the forbidden temptation and redirects his libidinous energy into telling the story of his parentification. Should the long-overdue critical biography of Sholem Rabinovitch ever be written, it may connect this theme of renunciation with his becoming "merely" a humorist, whose measure of the human is the capacity for accommodation.

Freud might have had Sholem Aleichem in mind when he wrote, "Is there any sense in saying that [the humorist] is treating himself like a child and is at the same time playing the part of the superior adult in relation to this child?" Freud suggested that through the agency of humor, the superego tries to comfort the ego and to protect it from suffering, as if saying, "Look here! This is all that this seemingly dangerous world amounts to. Child's play—the very thing to jest about!"[33] Tevye was this mature child. Whether Sholem Aleichem kept his characters within bonds because the nature of Yiddish seemed to require it or adored Yiddish because it flourished within filial bonds, he recognized an uncanny congruence between his natural talent and the fate of his language.

TSAYTL

Tevye's attempt to arrange a proper match for his eldest daughter, Tsaytl, in the **"Modern Children"** episode begins in the slapstick tradition. Tevye's encounter with the butcher Leyzer Wolf turns on the classic misunderstanding over what the two men have come to barter—here, daughter or cow—and from behind the hilarity of their confusion emerges criticism of arranged marriages in which women may be treated like *beheymes* (domestic animals). According to the East European concept of *yikhes,* the hierarchy of Jewish social standing, no one was lower than the artisan. Tsaytl's preference for the lowly patchwork tailor Motl Kamzoyl over a wealthy butcher signals the protest that was common to positivists and revolutionaries against a system that undervalued productivity and equal rights. The seed of revolt is sown by the daughter who follows her heart into marriage.

Today, with feminism once again in ascendance, one can appreciate how the rebellion of daughters rather than sons both softened and sharpened the theme of generational conflict. While the absence of overt competition cushioned the force of female rebellion, Jewish women could attack the tradition more forcefully since they had no stake in its intellectual heritage. Tevye's pride in his ability to quote from the traditional sources does nothing to shore up his authority among the womenfolk. "Spare us your Bible!" says Golde, impatient with the impractical drift of Tevye's thought. Her sarcasm grows heavier with the years: "My *milkhik* borsht is more fundamental than all your fundamentals!"[34] Hodl and Chava have no trouble out-arguing their father—precisely because they talk right to the point without any need for prooftexts. Tevye knows that his power is invested in his speech and that it, like Samson's hair, can be cut off by women. The decline of his authority is manifest in the collapse of communication from one daughter to the next.

From Tsaytl's 1899 romance Tevye still emerges unscathed. Having betrothed her to the wrong man, he not only undoes the damage and accepts the proposal of the tailor Motl Kamzoyl, but dreams up a scheme to reconcile his wife to the inferior match: "'You know what, Motl?' I said to my future son-in-law. 'You go home and leave the rest of it to me. . . . As it says in the Book of Esther, *vehashtiyah kedos*—everything has to be thought through.'"[35] Minutes after yielding to the boy, Tevye casts himself majestically as King Ahasuerus through the quotation "And the king [Ahasuerus] made a feast . . . *and the drinking was according to custom,*" thus assuring the couple by means of a pun on the word *kedos* that they will be married *kedos moshe veyisroel,* that is, according to the laws of Moses and Israel (part of the marriage vow), and that they can count on him to do right by them with a merry celebration. At the end of this episode Tevye is shaking with laughter.

HODL

By contrast, Tevye's communication with his second daughter and Perchik in the next episode, **"Hodl"** (1904), is frayed by dramatic irony. On some level, Tevye must have wanted this Marxist firebrand for a son-in-law, since the very first time he meets him on the road, he parodies a bride-groom being called up to the reading of the Torah: "*Yaamoyd hakhosn reb yokl ben flekl* [Let the bridegroom Yokel son of Jokel rise]!" He brings him into his household of daughters: "We crowned him with the name 'Feferl' [Peppercorn], transposing Perchik into Yiddish, and you could say that we began to love him as one of our own."[36] But whereas Tevye's meager investment in the social hierarchy had made it relatively easy for him to accept a tailor for a son-in-law, he knows that the revolutionary's plotting against tsarist authority is also directed in some measure against himself. Feferl and Hodl are secretive by design, and assuming that Tevye cannot grasp their ideas, they don't bother to explain their conspiratorial work. "I can't tell you that, it's confi-

dential," says Feferl when Tevye asks him why he must leave his new wife so soon after their marriage. "The trouble is, you don't understand," says Hodl when Tevye asks what the young couple is up to. The phrase from the Book of Esther that Tevye repeatedly associates with her—"*Eyn ester magedes,*" from "*And Esther spoke not* of her nativity or her people"—refers to the way Esther concealed her Jewishness from the other girls when she was in the harem of Ahasuerus, hence to the way Hodl conceals her *non-Jewish* behavior from her father here. The correspondence between Esther, who is ordered by her cousin Mordecai to say nothing (in order that she might benefit the Jews in the long run), and Hodl, who is told by Perchik to say nothing (in order that they might advance the Russian Revolution), casts Tevye once again as King Ahasuerus, only here as the foolish authority who is duped into compliance.

Sholem Aleichem compressed his contradictory feelings about the revolutionary movement in this, Tevye's most ambivalent story. Perchik the revolutionary is attractive and lethal in just the way Menakhem-Mendl was, promising great things but stealing away a treasure. Perchik steals a beloved daughter, just as Menakhem-Mendl stole Tevye's accumulated fortune. Had Sholem Aleichem wanted to promote Marxism among Jews, he could have cast Perchik as a member of the Jewish Socialist Bund, which was organizing Jewish workers in Yiddish. Instead, Perchik's fellow revolutionary is "dressed like a *sheygetz* [Gentile], if you will forgive me," and the gang goes off to propagandize among the "real" Russians in the north. The socialist sympathies of this story, so admired by like-minded critics, are greatly complicated by the mutual distrust between the skeptical father and the children who think they know ever so much more than he does. Tevye suspects when he says good-bye to Hodl that he will never see her again. He ends his wrenching monologue with what was to become his most famous tag line: "You know what, Pani Sholem Aleichem? Let's talk about something more cheerful: Have you heard any news of the cholera in Odessa?"[37] "More cheerful" is Tevye's theory of relativity.

CHAVA

"Chava goes beyond Hodl, but is not simply a repetition," Sholem Aleichem wrote to his friend Y. Kh. Ravnitski when he was on the point of finishing the story **"Chava"** in 1906.[38] This was an understatement, for although this episode follows almost exactly the narrative pattern of its predecessors, Tevye's third daughter takes the romantic impulse to its logical conclusion: if a girl may follow her heart into marriage, why should she be prevented from marrying a Christian? In tsarist Russia, unlike America, exogamy required conversion to the dominant religion. The implications of love as the arbiter of destiny are made explicit as Chava converts to Christianity to marry Chvedka Galagan, the Ukrainian village scribe whom she considers "a second Gorky." Her romance therefore involves Tevye in negotiations with the local priest and marks the first time that his rhetorical strategies come up against the religion of the state. What begins as a friendly discussion between Tevye and the village priest about "your God and my God" escalates into the priest's insistence "that his God had it over on mine." Tevye trades quotations with his usual flair, but just as he is giving his adversary a piece of his mind, he notices the priest laughing and combing out his beard. "I tell you, there's nothing more aggravating in all the world than being treated to silence by the person you've just reduced to dirt."[39] The priest can afford his smug silence, knowing that Tevye's daughter Chava is in love with a Christian and that standing behind *his* religion is the power of the tsar.

Chava is the first of Tevye's daughters to present her own case to her father without the mediation of a boyfriend:

> "It's beyond belief," she says, "how you have a verse from the Bible for everything! Maybe you also have one that explains why human beings have to be divided into Jews and Christians, masters and slaves, beggars and millionaires. . . . "
>
> "Why, bless my soul," I say, "if you don't seem to think, my daughter, that the millennium has arrived." And I tried explaining to her that the way things are now is the way they've been since Day One.
>
> "But why are they that way?" she asks.
>
> "Because that's how God made them," I say.
>
> "Well, why did He make them like that?"
>
> "Look here," I say, "if you're going to ask why, why, why all the time, we'll just keep going around in circles."
>
> "But what did God give us brains for if we're not supposed to use them?" she asks.
>
> "You know," I say, "we Jews have an old custom that when a hen begins to crow like a rooster, off to the slaughterer she goes. That's why we say in the morning prayer, *hanoyseyn lasekhvi binoh*—not only did God give us brains, He gave some of us more of them than others."[40]

Rescued from this losing argument by Golde's call to supper, Tevye offers not a single reason for why Jews should remain a people apart. Never mind that he cannot quote Maimonides; he does not even quote some Hasidic master or express appreciation for Jewish practices such as the Sabbath, which is said to preserve the Jews more than the Jews preserve it. Tevye's tradi-

tionalism obscures the fact that, apart from his contentious praying, he is never seen observing any Jewish ritual, unless eating blintzes on Shavuos can be termed a religious act. For all his implicit observance, he resembles, in what we see of him, many another modern Jew who wants to keep his child Jewish just because she *is* his child. The verse that he cites from the morning prayers to clinch the debate with Chava—"Blessed are Thou, O Lord God, King of the Universe, *Who giveth the rooster knowledge* to tell the dawn from the night"—exposes his desperation, for had he been better able to parry her universalist ideals, he would not have had to threaten his errant daughter with the example of the hen that is slaughtered for imagining herself a rooster. Unable to win the argument, he tries to resort to the priest's strategy of flaunting his power. But this merely betrays his helplessness, for the priest's power is precisely what he lacks.

The reader should not be surprised by how much intelligent sympathy is invested in Chava's passion for the "second Gorky." Following the Kishinev pogrom of 1903, Sholem Aleichem himself paid a call on the actual Maxim Gorky to enlist his support for the victims and the families of the dead. In letters to his children he gushed over the warmth of the reception he had received at the hands of the man he called "the icon of our age."[41] It is this naive hope of his own for Jewish rapprochement with the Russian intelligentsia that Sholem Aleichem here imaginatively ascribes to Tevye's third daughter, deputizing her to speak for the humanism of his day.

To remain a Jew, Tevye has to play the tyrant, repudiating not just his daughter but his own *milkhik* nature. The metaphoric hen that he brings to the slaughterer is the tender part of his soul. Ultimately, however, he gains the moral advantage. Once the priest has Chava in his house, preparing her for conversion, Tevye is not even allowed to see his daughter, lest he persuade her to change her mind! The juxtaposition of Tevye's discussions with his daughter and with the priest shows up the cruelty of what is supposed to be the "religion of love." Chava's high-minded humanism translates into a victory of the priest over her father and not, as she would have it, into a kindlier tolerance. Tevye reaches the limits of accommodation when on the day after her defection Chava tries to intercept her father at nearly the same spot on the road where he had given in to Tsaytl and Motl Kamzoyl in Episode Three and picked up the revolutionary Perchik in Episode Four. In narrative terms, Chava appeals to her father's tenderness at the very place where he has so often proven it. But Tevye is transformed from a passive into an active hero when he refuses to speak to his Christian daughter on the forest road. He commands his family to sit *shiva,* that is, to repudiate Chava's apostasy by mourning her as dead.

Tevye understands—even if his daughter pretends not to—the essential weakness of the Jew in Christian society, and he is furious with Chava for exposing his impotence. But he also admits that her argument emanates from his own enlarged sympathies, for he, too, wonders why being or not being a Jew should matter. "Why did God have to create both? And if He did, why put such walls between them, so that neither would look at the other even though both were His creatures?"[42] Ultimately, he is humbled by one of his favorite quotations from Psalms: *kerakheym ov al bonim, "Like as a father pitieth his children"* [so the Lord pitieth them that fear Him]. Just a few pages earlier he had tweaked a phrase from this quotation to his own male advantage: "Why doesn't it also say *kerakheym eym al bonim*—as a mother loves her own child—too? Because a mother isn't a father. A father speaks to his children differently."[43] But now he is haunted by quite another image of paternity: "Could there be anywhere a child so bad that a father couldn't still love it?"[44] Far from denying his love for Chava to make his task easier, Tevye admits that she is the most deeply "baked into his heart," having been sickly in childhood and exceptionally sweet as a girl. In Sholem Aleichem's version, the Jew who so often stands accused of authoritarian rectitude is just the opposite—a father who barely has it in him to defend his Jewishness.[45]

As Tevye describes to Sholem Aleichem an imaginary visit to Chava, a strange thing happens in the text: Tevye is told by the station agent when he tries to buy a ticket for Yehupetz that he has never heard of such a place, reminding readers that Tevye has been inhabiting an imaginary Jewish location within a Gentile society that has no objective correspondence on the Russian map. Simultaneously, Tevye worries for the first time about having become the butt rather than the purveyor of his humor. The priest's derision can now be heard reverberating inside himself. The conversion of Chava has pushed the humor over the edge, and whenever Sholem Aleichem reaches such a point, he is in the habit of exploding the fiction he has hitherto presented as real.[46] Tevye asks for anonymity when he takes his leave from Sholem Aleichem in this episode, putting a reverse twist on the biblical reference to Joseph, *"Vayishkokheyhu"* [And the Chief Butler did not remember Joseph] *and he forgot him* (Gen. 40:23). As a result of the Chief Butler's neglect, Joseph languishes unjustly in prison, but Tevye *asks* to be ignored, at least for the moment, because the humorist-hero doesn't want to be seen stripped of his daughter and his art.

SHPRINTSE AND BEILKE

Sholem Aleichem would celebrate the completion of each new Tevye episode by gathering his family for a preview performance. They knew that Tevye best expressed their father's "philosophy of life, his attitudes toward God and other human beings."[47] The family custom must have acquired new urgency following the abortive Russian Revolution of 1905. During the Easter pogrom in Kiev, the Rabinovitch household was forced into hiding for three days while their housekeeper protected their apartment by convincing the pogromists that she was in the service of Christians. As the tsar's long-awaited constitution became the catalyst for unprecedented violence against the Jews, Sholem Aleichem saw no further point in pretending that Russia could be his home. Along with hundreds of thousands of his fellow Jews, he made plans to leave his native land, and by the time he wrote **"Chava,"** in the spring of 1906, he was already in Lemberg en route to America. The mourning period for Chava expressed Sholem Aleichem's grieving for the liberal illusion of Russian-Jewish brotherhood.

Coming as they do after the dramatic climax of Chava, Tevye's stories about his fourth and fifth daughters almost sink under their historical weight. When Tevye meets Sholem Aleichem at the beginning of **"Shprintse"** (1907), he notes how much has happened since their last encounter—"Kishinev, a Constantution, pogroms, riots, and troubles"—dating their previous meeting about 1902, before the Kishinev pogroms, or, in terms of the narrative, before the fatal downturn in Jewish political fortunes. Although he had written the Chava episode only one year earlier, Sholem Aleichem situated it retroactively during the high tide of idealism, while setting the story of Shprintse in the dark days that followed. From this point onward, the narrative darkens, too. Writing from "exile" in western Europe and America, Sholem Aleichem confronted Tevye with a collapsing world as if to test how much adversity his humor could absorb.

Shprintse's story reverses Tevye's lucky break. As he had once rescued the Jewish women in the forest, Tevye tries to help out one of his customers, a wealthy widow, whose only son, Ahronchik, is itching for a father's authority. He invites the young man into his home as he had done with Perchik, and once Ahronchik begins showing an interest in Shprintse, Tevye dreams that a union may result in another mutually beneficial exchange between the Jewish haves and have-nots. Instead, having insisted that he wanted to marry Shprintse, Ahronchik abandons her without a word, and his uncle comes down from St. Petersburg to extricate his nephew from the affair. The uncle accuses Tevye of being a shadier kind of "uncle," of having set up his daughter, "assuming that that really is your daughter," in order to ensnare a wealthy boy. Tevye is rendered speechless by this cynicism of a fellow Jew, and is reduced to tears once he is safely out of sight. "What did poor Job ever do to You, dear Lord, to make You hound him day and night?"[48] Shprintse takes her cue from her father. She voices no protest either but drowns herself, "like a candle flickering out."

The succeeding episode is an even more stunning parody of Tevye's dreams. Tevye meets Sholem Aleichem on a train looking very prosperous in new clothes. He explains that following the death of Golde, his youngest daughter Beilke had married a rich man, playing out at last his fantasy of the ideal match. But the social climbing son-in-law was so embarrassed to have a Jewish dairyman for a father-in-law that he determined to ship him out of the country! When he suggested America, Tevye held out for Palestine ("Isn't that where all the old Jews go?"), acceding to the proposal because his daughter's marriage had anyhow failed to provide him with a home. Whereas Tevye wanted to be rich so that he could be a better Jew, his son-in-law Podhotsur (a biblical name here hinting of *putz,* Yiddish for penis) wants to be rich so that he can cease being a Jew. Thus, Tevye takes "never judge by appearances" for his parting theme: *"Al tistakeyl bakankan"* [Rabbi Yehuda Hanasi said, *Look not at the storage jar* but at what it stores]. Now that Tevye looks like the man he thought he wanted to be, he feels he is being driven through the gauntlet.

The title of this seventh episode, **"Tevye Leaves for the Land of Israel"** (1909), hints at historical changes on a larger scale. Sholem Aleichem's son-in-law I. D. Berkowitz says that when some of the author's admirers promised to set him up in Eretz Israel, he thought of shipping Tevye off there in advance of his own departure.[49] Under doctors' care at the time in Nervi, Italy, Sholem Aleichem wept tears of joy when he read of the ovations that greeted Haim Nahman Bialik upon his arrival for a visit in Palestine, envying him not the reception itself but "the honor" of having reached the Land of Israel.[50] But since Sholem Aleichem did not make it to Palestine, the title of the story remained a tease. Once again, he expressed through Tevye his unfulfilled longings, his disappointed dreams.

Idealism in the early episodes was conveyed by the notion that love conquers all, so when Tevye yields to the wishes of his daughters, he feels his sympathies are enlarged by their ideas of progress. Shprintse and Beilke are the victims of a morally altered atmosphere of crude material striving. "Don't go comparing me to Hodl," says Beilke whenever her father invokes the sister who went off to Siberia. "In Hodl's day the world was on the brink. There was going to be a revolution and everyone cared about everyone. Now the world is its own self again, and it's everyone for his own self again, too."[51] Indeed, Tevye's lingering and unresolved admiration for Russian radicalism makes it that much harder for his youngest daughter to adjust to what she considers her duty. But in Tevye's telling, her pragmatism threatens his poised faith no less than, and perhaps even more than, the rebellions of his other children, which had at least some aspiration, some goal, in common with Tevye's reach for godliness. Beilke's well-intentioned material calculations destroy the home they were intended to protect.

"GET THEE OUT": TURNING HISTORY INTO HUMOR

After the Beilke chapter, five years elapsed before Sholem Aleichem returned to his favorite character, the longest time that had ever passed between episodes. The impulse for revisiting Tevye seems to have been the worsening situation of Jews in Russia.[52] The incredible 1911 case of Mendel Beilis, charged in Kiev with murdering a Christian boy to secure ritual blood for Passover matzos, heralded a new and more lethal government-sponsored antisemitism. Using the potential for Jewish disloyalty as its excuse, the tsarist government forced evictions of Jews from border villages and gave local authorities the right to change the status of town to village for that express purpose. An eviction of this kind is precisely what sends Tevye packing in **"Get Thee Out,"** the eighth Tevye episode, which captures the full anxiety of the time in which it was written.

Greeting his old friend Sholem Aleichem after their long separation, Tevye for the first time attributes his deteriorated appearance only partly to his private sorrows—"God forgive me for putting myself first!"—and the rest to the collective sorrows of the Jewish people. Having given up his dairy business, Tevye says he has become "just a Jew, a plain ordinary Jew," about to be evicted from his home. His wife is dead, Hodl lost to the Revolution, Chava to Christianity, Shprintse to the river. Beilke and her husband have escaped their creditors by fleeing to America—which explains why Tevye can no longer be supported by his son-in-law in Eretz Israel and must instead return to his homestead. But although the last chapter recounts Tevye's expulsion from what had for so long been the land of his fathers, nothing about his narrative is ever linear or final. Since Tsaytl and her children became Tevye's charges when Motl died, Tevye is once again responsible for sustaining a family. And at the point of his leaving, Chava comes home. The exodus from Russia is the beginning of national reunification.

Sholem Aleichem was not quite accurate when he once wrote that Tevye remained unchanged throughout his cycle of stories. The man who gave us his first running commentary on prayers as he was chasing his horse now takes possession of the biblical text with the authority of a *darshan,* a homespun preacher.

> In a word, what Bible reading are you up to in the synagogue this week, the first chapter of Leviticus? [This would situate the monologue about the end of March, a couple of weeks before Passover.] Well, I'm on another chapter, on *Lekh lekho. Lekh lekho*—get thee out, Tevye, I was told—*meyartsekho*—from your land—*umimoyladitkho*—and from the village you were born in and lived your whole life—*el ha'orets asher arekho*—to wherever your legs will carry you! . . . And when did it occur to the authorities to read Tevye that passage? At the very moment when he is old and weak and lonely, as we say in the Rosh Hashanah prayers: *al tashlikheynu le'eys ziknoh!*
>
> [*Cast us not away,* O Lord, *in our old age.*][53]

If we think of the English expression "to pull out all the stops," having in mind the organist who releases the foreshortening hammers, we may appreciate Tevye's gloss on the emergence of the modern Jewish people. Just as God told Abraham to leave everything behind (at the beginning of Genesis 12), so too do the Russian authorities tell this to the Jews, but though God promised Abraham that He would show him a new land, "make of thee a mighty nation," "bless thee, and make thy name great," Tevye hears himself being told to "go wherever your legs will carry you." The irony doesn't make him feel Abraham is inferior or threaten the terms of the ancient Covenant. Tevye's helplessness at the hands of the political powers-that-be may call into question God's ability to secure him, but his intimacy with God calls into question the ultimate authority over him of the powers-that-be. Moreover, as he conflates Abraham's situation with the heart-stopping plea of the penitential prayers (don't cast us out in our old age), he domesticates the image of the solitary Abraham and takes the patriarch under his wing as a fellow aging Jew. All the while that Tevye adds his Yiddish gloss to the Hebrew quotation, he is slipping from the domain of sanctity into the profane, undercutting the biblical promise with evidence that it has not been fulfilled. This legacy of eternal postponement reconnects him to his biblical ancestors, who were promised a security that still eludes their descendants.

There are two main events in this chapter, the expulsion order and the return of Chava, and Tevye asks us to attend carefully to the order in which they occur.

> But before we get to *Lekh-lekho,* suppose we have a look, if you don't mind, at the chapter on Balak [Numbers 22-25]. I know that the way things have always been done in this world, *Lekh-lekho* comes before Balak, but in my case the lesson of Balak came first and *Lekh-lekho* after. And I suggest that you listen to the lesson they taught me, because it may come in useful some day.[54]

The Yiddish idiom *lernen Balak,* meaning to teach someone a harsh lesson, suits Tevye's context particularly well, since it invokes the attempt of the Moabite king to frighten the Jews with a false prophecy. When his Ukrainian neighbors, from the village elder to the shepherd, come to perpetrate a pogrom against him, Tevye asks them (as if teaching *them* the chapter of Balak) whether they are certain that the God who stands above the tsar is on their side or his. The concession he wins from them is that instead of roughing him up and destroying his house, they merely break his windows.

In a second, weaker, version of the expulsion story that Sholem Aleichem wrote two years later, Tevye challenges the Ukrainians to repeat a Hebrew word that he will "randomly" choose at the place where his psalter opens. The book opens at Psalm 35, the prayer of a virtuous man under oppression who asks God to confound those who would plot his downfall, to make their way dark and slippery (*vekhalaklakoys*). Of course, the Ukrainians slip up on this word, just as Tevye intended, and he concludes from this sport that at least in verbal matters "there's no getting around the fact that we Jews are the best and smartest people." Twice before in his monologues, Tevye had manufactured quotations to expose the ignorance of Leyzer Wolf the butcher and Podhotsur the purveyor, but here his life is at stake. The humor that has always been Tevye's salvation is now his only protection.

Yet Sholem Aleichem holds out at least one consolation for Tevye. The trajectory of loss that cuts through the monologues—from the debacle of Menakhem-Mendl's scheme, through the rebellions of the daughters, to his humiliations at the hands of his fellow Jews—stops when Chava returns to her father at the very moment that he is driven from his home. Sholem Aleichem may have regretted letting Chava convert in the first place (the only such instance of intermarriage in his oeuvre) and was now trying to reverse the deed. Chone Shmeruk wonders "whether the expulsion from the village is the crux of the issue, or merely the rationale and background for Chava's penitent return (*khazara bitshuvah*)."[55] Since Chava does not figure at all in the second expulsion story, it might be more accurate to say that Sholem Aleichem provided Tevye with not one but two psychological-rhetorical rejoinders to the humiliations heaped upon him—an outlet for his anger in the *vekhalaklakoys* monologue and recompense for his steadfastness with Chava's return.

In trying to eliminate the Jewish presence, the Christians inadvertently return some Jews to their people. Chava's homecoming rewards Tevye for his earlier resistance to her intermarriage by a belated expression of the loyalty that his own Jewish loyalties have bred in her.[56]

POLITICAL OPPOSITION TO TEVYE

Sholem Aleichem paid a price for telling the story of "progress" from a conservative perspective. Between his two comic heroes, Tevye and Menakhem-Mendl, almost the entire Jewish intelligentsia preferred the radical over the balanced ironist. The Marxist literary historian Max Erik, writing in Moscow in the mid-1930s, cherished Mehakhem-Mendl, as the caricature of capitalism run amok, over Tevye, the sorry embodiment of the falsely idealized petit bourgeoisie.[57] With subtler appreciation for the psychology of these two archetypes, I. I. Trunk in Warsaw interpreted Menakhem-Mendl and Tevye as the vying forces of messianism and ironic resignation that govern Jewish history. But in 1939 when Trunk had to flee the Nazis, the very sanity he had admired in Tevye proved insufficient to counteract the madness of Europe, while Menakhem-Mendl's credulity seemed reliable precisely because it was not subject to rational or experiential disproof.[58] Even the American Yiddish modernist Jacob Glatstein, who was untouched by Marxist influence, singled out Menakhem-Mendl from among Sholem Aleichem's characters for the *poetry* of his Yiddish.[59] Glatstein explained that his generation had considered Sholem Aleichem too old-fashioned for its taste and had to pass through a chastening lifetime before it "did penance" for its artistic oversight. Tevye was to Menakhem-Mendl as Sholem Aleichem was to the Jewish intelligenstia—the conservative impulse in a time of revolution.

The Yiddish literary elites disdained the "harmonious nature" of Tevye, because they understood the conservative roots of his humor. The team that adapted Tevye to the American stage and screen in *Fiddler on the Roof*—lyricist Sheldon Harnick, composer Jerry Bock, and writer Joseph Stein—simply changed Tevye into the character they wanted without acknowledging that they had done him any violence at all. In two interpolated scenes, they recast the Ukrainian who marries Chava as a liberal savior of the Jews while presenting Tevye's desire to remain Jewish as a form of prejudice. Fyedka (their version of Chvedka) is first seen protecting Chava from some of his friends, who have ambushed her, and when she still refuses his advances after he has saved her, he asks, "Do you feel about me the way they feel about you?" This parity between aggression against the Jew and Jewish self-affirmation is reinforced in the closing sequence when the Jews are expelled from their villages and Tevye is packing up to leave. The film shows Chava and her husband Fyedka passing by his house as part of the stream of refugees.

CHAVA:

> Papa, we came to say good-bye. We are also leaving this place. We're going to Cracow.

FYEDKA:

> We cannot stay among people who could do such things to others.

CHAVA:

> We wanted you to know that.[60]

Leaving aside the historical improbability that a Ukrainian writer would join his wife in Polish exile, this resolution means that Chava can never come home to her father or to her people, because she would be betraying the assimilationism that has become—and here remains—her creed. Seth Wolitz claims that the writers of *Fiddler* created a paradox in their Americanization of Tevye, maintaining Tevye's wavering ambivalence toward Chava yet legitimizing her mixed marriage.[61] But the American version is not ambivalent at all. When Tevye continues to ignore the couple, Fyedka chides, "Some are driven away by edicts; others by silence." According to the stage directions, Tevye, who has been trying to ignore the couple as he packs his wagon, now says under his breath, "And God be with you," thereby invoking the Almighty's blessing on the daughter who has converted. The Ukrainian son-in-law has become Tevye's moral instructor! Drawing a parallel between the tsar's edict of expulsion and Tevye's wish to have his daughter remain a Jew, Fyedka accuses the Jew of bigotry for wishing to remain a people apart. Tevye is made to apologize for holding firm as a Jew by the Ukrainian who appears as the spokesman for tolerance.

It should be said that the interpretation of Chvedka or Fedya-Fyedka, was always the most changeable feature of the dramatic version of the Tevye stories. In one of Sholem Aleichem's unpublished drafts of the play, Chava says she left her husband because he joked about Jews needing Christian blood for Passover. Berkowitz, who reworked the play after Sholem Aleichem's death (and after an estimated one hundred thousand Jews had been killed in the Ukrainian massacres of 1918-19), "dipped Fedya into hot tar" and turned him into an overt antisemite.[62] More usually, Yiddish and Hebrew productions did not attribute antisemitism to Fedya, if for no other reason than it would have undermined Chava's credibility as a character to have married a Jew-hating Gentile. In Sholem Aleichem's own final version of the play, Chvedka's only fault is that he failed to tell Chava about the impending expulsion of Jews from the village. All these modifications to the character of the husband did not affect, however, the basic action of Chava's return to her father. The American version was the first to champion mixed marriage and the liberal ideal of an undifferentiated humankind.

Adaptation is part of the tradition of theater, and *Fiddler* is in many respects an adaptation of genius, perfectly attuned to the liberal ethos of America and the integrationist theme that was then at its height. The production was mounted in 1964, when second and third generations of American Jews were enjoying as never before the benefits of a genuinely democratic society, and popular culture was touting the advantages of youth, individual self-expression, and choices of the heart. The American civil rights movement was on the march, with rabbis joining Black leaders to enfranchise Americans "irrespective of color, race, or creed." While the promise of emancipation on the European continent was always being discredited by thuggish antisemitism, just the way Chava's humanism is mocked by the pogromists who chase her family off its land, America had never reneged on its promise to respect religious pluralism. It must have felt perfectly innocent to change a Jewish classic into a liberal classic, making the team of Chava and Fyedka, rather than Tevye, the moral anchors of the play. But if a Jewish work can only enter American culture by forfeiting its moral authority and its commitment to group survival, one has to wonder about the bargain that destroys the Jews with its applause.

The transformation of Sholem Aleichem's **Tevye the Dairyman** into *Fiddler on the Roof* goes to the very heart of this book about the Jewish canon [*The Modern Jewish Canon: A Journey through Language and Culture*]. Part of the impulse of modernity that gave birth to modern Jewish literature was the need to interact with the world at large. The end result of such interaction was often the wish to join that world as an undifferentiated member. Writers starting down that open road did not always see where it led, but none could pretend to ignore the fork when they reached it. Liberalism may take the sting out of conversion by seeming to ignore the relevance of distinctions among peoples and religions in favor of the human sympathies that draw them together. But when liberalism *requires* merging as the price of its tolerance, it denies the pluralism it pretends to uphold. No artistic creation that ignores this immanent conflict can qualify as a Jewish work, or as a great and truthful work.

What was King Lear's expectation of Cordelia as compared with Tevye's of Chava? Lear's whim was no more than a matter of pride, yet Shakespeare builds his greatest tragedy on a daughter's refusal to give exaggerated protestations of her love. By contrast, Chava's conversion assaults Tevye's very being: his God, his way of life, his idea of family, the source of his language, not to mention his *Jewish* pride before the antisemitic representative of the Church. In effect, she is substituting the "religion of Love" for Judaism and asking him to dissolve his religious civilization in her favor. Tevye's nature is so contrary to Lear's that he is tempted to sacrifice all this for the sake of his daughter. He is therefore faced with the opposite set of challenges—to stand firm where Lear should yield, to insist on his Jewish integrity where Lear should acknowledge the limits of his power.

Tevye became the first hero of modern Jewish literature when he contained his impulse of leniency, the milkiness of his nature. His humor knew better than to leave its Jewish sources, because it would have failed him at the point of letting go. His trilingual play with the Hebrew sources, Gentile folk sayings, and his Yiddish vernacular gives the impression of being impossible to translate, yet when students are asked to describe an incident in their lives "in the style of Tevye," the daughter of Korean immigrants and the Puerto Rican freshman know just how to approximate his irony with folk quotations from their native languages. In Sholem Aleichem's comedy the father tries to realize his freedom and to grant his children freedom without sacrificing the model of peoplehood that created his model of freedom. At the same historical moment that Theodor Herzl created *Altneuland* (Old-New Land), the utopian fantasy of a people trying to regain its sovereignty, Tevye provided one man's comic experience of auto-emancipation.

Notes

*Author's note: Transliterated Hebrew phrases with translations are in italics within quotation marks. That part of the phrase that appears in roman type and square brackets is the fuller expansion of the text in which the translated phrase is embedded.

1. Letter to M. Spector in Warsaw, dated Kiev, 21 September 1894, and, according to the Hebrew calendar, the Fast of Gedalya (between Rosh Hashanah and Yom Kippur), 5655. The story's progress is discussed in letters of 26 September and 20 October. On November 4, Sholem Aleichem writes that he is still following the advice of his mentor, Mendele Moykher-Sforim, to "file, file, file" (to refine the writing by paring it down); three days later he sent off the first half of the story and on the 10th he announced that "Reb Tevye is done!" See *Briv fun sholem-aleykhem 1879-1916,* ed. Abraham Lis (Tel Aviv: Beit

Sholem Aleichem and I. L. Peretz Farlag, 1995): 295 ff. For studies of Tevye's publication history, see Chone Shmeruk, "'Tevye der milkhiker': History of the Work" [in Hebrew] *Hasifrut* 26 (1978): 29-38; Ken Frieden, *A Century in the Life of Sholem Aleichem's Tevye,* The B. G. Rudolph Lectures in Judaic Studies, New Series, I (Syracuse, N.Y.: University of Syracuse Press, 1993-94).

2. See, especially, letter to the typesetters of *Hoyzfraynd* [Home Companion], 7 November 1894, *Briv*: 298.

3. Marie Waife-Goldberg, *My Father Sholem Aleichem* (New York: Simon & Schuster, 1968): 144-47. Nachman Meisel says that when he was in Boyarka in 1911, the local dairyman named Tevye told everyone he was famous, thanks to Sholem Aleichem. See *Our Sholem Aleichem* [in Yiddish] (Warsaw: Yiddish bukh, 1959): 57.

4. For an analysis of the persona in the works of these authors, see Dan Miron, *A Traveler Disguised: The Rise of Modern Yiddish Fiction in the Nineteenth Century,* 2nd ed. (Syracuse, N.Y.: Syracuse University Press, 1996); Miron, *Sholem Aleykhem: Person, Persona, Presence* (New York: YIVO, 1972).

5. Yosef Haim Brenner, "On Sholem Aleichem," from an essay written on Sholem Aleichem's death in 1916, *Kol kitvey Y. H. Brenner* [The Complete Works], vol. 3 (Tel Aviv, 1967): 106-8. Translated in *Prooftexts* 6: 1 (January 1986), quotation on p. 18.

6. *Hoyzfraynd* 4, (1895): 67.

7. Sholem Aleichem dropped the description of Tevye, along with Tevye's two-page "Letter to the Author," from the first collection of Tevye stories that he issued in 1903. The posthumous Folksfund edition of Sholem Aleichem's work, which became the model for all subsequent collected editions, restored Tevye's letter to the text, but neither the Hebrew translator I. D. Berkovitch nor the English translator Hillel Halkin included it.

8. Frank Kermode, *English Pastoral Poetry from the Beginnings to Marvell* (London: 1952): 37.

9. I. L. Peretz, "In the Mail Coach" (1893), trans. Golda Werman, in *The I. L. Peretz Reader,* ed. Ruth R. Wisse (New York: Schocken Books, 1990): 114.

10. Quoted by John D. Klier and Shlomo Lambroza, eds, *Pogroms: Anti-Jewish Violence in Modern Russian History* (Cambridge: Cambridge University Press, 1992): 41.

11. Aaron Lieberman, letter dated 23 November 1876, in *The Letters of Aaron Lieberman* [in Yiddish], with an introduction and notes by Kalman Marmor (New York: YIVO, 1950): 80.

12. Sholem Aleichem, *Gants tevye der milkhiker* in *Ale verk* [Selected Works] (New York: Tog-Morgn Zhurnal Edition on the Centenary of Sholem Aleichem, 1959), 1: 19. In the following notes, this Yiddish version is referred to as *Gants tevye*. For the English equivalent see Sholem Aleichem, *Tevye the Dairyman and The Railroad Stories,* trans. with an introduction by Hillel Halkin (New York: Schocken Books, 1987): 6, which is referred to in the following notes as *Tevye*. I occasionally slightly modify the translation to make it more literally faithful to the original.

13. I. I. Trunk, *Tevye and Menakhem Mendl as Expressions of Eternal Jewish Fate* [in Yiddish] (New York: Central Yiddish Culture Organization 1944): 38.

14. Frances Butwin, "Introduction" in *Tevye's Daughters* (New York: Crown, 1949): xv. Butwin later modified this notion of Tevye: her book, coauthored with her son, contends that "[each] of Tevye's locutions is controlled by his recognition of the paradoxical place of suffering in Jewish history." See Joseph Butwin and Frances Butwin, *Sholem Aleichem* (Boston: Twayne, 1977): 92. Tevye is funny the way musicians may be spontaneously musical. For a rich analysis of his verbal skill, see Michael Stern, "Tevye's Art of Quotation," *Prooftexts* 6 (1986): 79-96.

15. Rashi (1040-1105), called after the initial letters of his name *Rabbi Shlomo Yitzhaki,* is the foremost French exegete whose commentaries on the Bible and the Talmud are regularly printed together with the text.

16. Halkin, Introduction: xxiv-xxv.

17. *Gants tevye*: 30; *Tevye*: 14.

18. Y. Kh. Ravnitski, ed., *Yidishe vitsn* [Jewish Jokes], 2nd edition (Berlin: Moriah, 1923): 7-8.

19. *Gants tevye*: 32; *Tevye*: 15.

20. Sol Gittelman, *From Shtetl to Suburbia: The Family in Jewish Literary Imagination* (Boston: Beacon, 1978): 58.

21. A selection of Sholem Aleichem's Zionist writings appear in *Why Do the Jews Need a Land?*, translated from the Yiddish and Hebrew by Joseph Leftwich and Mordecai S. Chertof (New York: Cornwall Books, 1984).

22. *Stempenyu* (1888), trans. Joachim Neugroschel in *The Shtetl: A Creative Anthology of Jewish Life in Eastern Europe* (New York: Richard Marek, 1979): 287-375. *Yosele Solovey* (1889), trans. Aliza Shevrin as *The Nightingale, or The Saga of Yosele Solovey the Cantor* (New York: Putnam, 1985).

23. Harvey Mindess, *Laughter and Liberation* (Los Angeles: Nash, 1971): 23. Mindess considers Sholem Aleichem the most convincing exponent of "compassionate irony."

24. The Yiddish term for dairyman is *pakhter,* and as far as I can ascertain, Sholem Aleichem was the first to suggest *milkhiker* in its stead.

25. For biography see Chone Shmeruk, *Sholem Aleichem: His Life and Literary Work* [in Hebrew] (Tel Aviv: Porter Institute for Poetics and Semiotics, 1980); entry by Dan Miron in *Encyclopedia Judaica,* Vol. 14 (Jerusalem: Keter, 1971): 1271-1286; I. D. Berkowitz, *Our Pioneers: Memoiristic Stories About Sholem Aleichem and His Generation* [in Yiddish], 5 vols. (Tel Aviv: Hamenorah, 1966).

26. For a first-rate study of the development of *Menakhem-Mendl,* see Abraham Novershtern, "'Menakhem-Mendl' to Sholem Aleichem: From Textual History to Structural Analysis" [in Hebrew], *Tarbiz,* 54 (1985): 105-146.

27. Hillel Halkin's felicitous translation, *Tevye*: 27.

28. *Gants tevye*: 63; *Tevye*: 34-35.

29. Benjamin Harshav offers an analysis and diagramed study of Tevye's "chain of associations" in *The Meaning of Yiddish* (Berkeley: University of California Press, 1990): 102-107.

30. Shmeruk: 29.

31. Sholem Aleichem, "Taybele," in *Ale verk,* 23: 14. My translation.

32. Sholem Aleichem, *Dos meserl,* ed. Chone Shmeruk (Jerusalem: 1983). Translated as "The Penknife," in *Some Laughter, Some Tears,* ed. Curt Leviant (New York: G. P. Putnam, 1968): 113-128. For other similar motifs see, e.g., "The Fiddle" (a boy gives up his instrument) in Sholem Aleichem, *Selected Stories,* intro. Alfred Kazin (New York, Modern Library, 1956): 307-323; "Visiting with King Ahasuerus" (a boy gives up acting with Purim players) in *Old Country Tales* trans. Curt Leviant (New York: Paragon Books, 1966): 51-64; "A Ruined Passover" (a boy's clothes are ordered oversized so he can grow into them) in *Holiday Tales,* trans. Aliza Shevrin (New York: Charles Scribner's Sons, 1979): 45-68.

33. Sigmund Freud, "Humour," in *Collected Papers,* vol. 5, ed. James Strachey (New York: Basic Books, 1959): 218-220. Hegel appears to be making a similar point in his distinction between tragedy and comedy: "In tragedy the individuals destroy themselves through the one-sidedness of their otherwise solid will and character, or they must resignedly accept what they had opposed even in a serious way. In comedy there comes before our contemplation, in the laughter in which the characters dissolve everything, including themselves, the victory of their own subjective personality which nevertheless persists self-assured." See G. W. F. Hegel, *Aesthetics: Lectures on Fine Art,* trans. T. M. Knox, II (Oxford, U.K.: Clarendon Press, 1974): 1199.

34. Halkin's translation reads, "Better my borscht without the universe than the universe without my borscht." *Tevye*: 73.

35. *Gants tevye*: 87; *Tevye:* 50.

36. *Gants tevye*: 98; *Tevye*: 55. The greeting by Tevye is translated by Halkin: "Hurry up or you'll be late for the wedding!"

37. *Gants tevye*: 118; *Teyve*: 69.

38. Letter to Y. Kh. Ravnitski, dated Lemberg, 16 April 1906, *Briv*: 453.

39. *Gants tevye*: 123-4; *Tevye*: 71.

40. *Gants tevye*: 126; *Tevye*: 72-73.

41. Letter to the children, dated St. Petersburg, 15 November 1904, *Briv*: 40.

42. *Gants tevye*: 138; *Tevye*: 81.

43. *Gants tevye*: 131; *Tevye*: 76.

44. *Gants tevye*: 138; *Tevye*: 81.

45. In this context, nothing is more ironic than Tevye's repeated protestation, whenever sentiment gets the better of him, that "Tevye is not a woman." Tevye's actual abiding concern, confided to Sholem Aleichem, is whether he has it in him to "be a man." "I'd give a lot to know if all males *[ale mansbiln]* are like me or if I'm the only madman of my kind. Once, for example . . . but do you promise not to laugh at me? Because I'm afraid you'll laugh . . . " *Gants tevye*: 139; *Tevye*: 82.

46. See, e.g., "Der fakishefter shnayder [The Haunted Tailor]," trans. Hillel Halkin, in *The Best of Sholem Aleichem,* ed. Irving Howe and Ruth R. Wisse (Washington, D.C.: New Republic Books, 1979): 2-36.

47. Waife-Goldberg, *My Father Sholem Aleichem*: 147.

48. *Gants tevye*: 160; *Tevye,* 95.

49. I. D. Berkowitz, *Our Pioneers*: 3: 199.

50. Letter to M. Ben Ami (Rabinovitz), dated Nervi, 21 March 1909, in *Briv*: 497.

51. *Gants tevye*: 175; *Tevye*: 103.

52. In the winter of 1914, Sholem Aleichem also wrote a dramatic version of the Tevye stories, hoping that it would be a vehicle for the German actor Rudolph Schildkraut or for Jacob Adler of the American Yiddish stage. See Letters to David Pinski and Jacob Adler, *Briv*: 584-587.

53. *Gants tevye*: 200; *Tevye*: 116.

54. *Gants tevye*: 204; *Tevye*: 120.

55. Shmeruk: 37.

56. In the five years after the tsarist ukase of 17 April 1905, permitting converts to the Orthodox Church to return to their original faiths, 476 Jews returned to Judaism. See the discussion on East European Jewish converts in T. M. Endelman, "Memories of Jewishness," in *Jewish History and Jewish Memory: Essays in Honor of Yosef Hayim Yerushalmi*, ed. Elisheva Carlbach et al. (Hanover, N.H.: Brandeis University Press, 1998): 322-325.

57. Max Erik, "Menahem-Mendl: Character and Method" [in Yiddish], in *Shtern* [Star] (1935), 5-6: 180-202; 8: 82-90. This quotation is from a translation by David G. Roskies in *Prooftexts* 6: 1 (January 1986): 24-25.

58. Trunk, *Tevye and Menakhem-Mendl:* 82.

59. Jacob Glatstein, "Menakhem Mendl," in *In toykh genumen* [Sum and Substance] (New York: Farlag Matones, 1947): 483.

60. *Fiddler on the Roof* (New York: Limelight Editions, 1992): 150-51.

61. See Seth L. Wolitz, "The Americanization of Tevye or Boarding the Jewish *Mayflower*," *American Quarterly* 40 (1988): 514-36.

62. Jacob Weitzner, *Sholem Aleichem in the Theatre* (Madison, N.J.: Fairleigh Dickinson University Press, 1994): 83. See discussion of its performance history, pp. 74-110.

David G. Roskies (essay date winter 2001)

SOURCE: Roskies, David G. "Inside Sholem Shachnah's Hat." *Prooftexts* 21, no. 1 (winter 2001): 39-56.

[*In the following essay, Roskies comments on "On Account of a Hat" in the original Yiddish, finding a rich polyphony of voices and a thematic complexity he had failed to notice when he read the tale in translation.*]

In 1954, when Irving Howe and Eliezer Greenberg showcased **"On Account of a Hat"** in the landmark *Treasury of Yiddish Stories,* they rescued it from a grab bag of holiday-related tales that cover the yearly cycle, *From Pesach to Pesach.*[1] Such was Howe's enthusiasm for this neglected work that he chose it to introduce Sholem Aleichem as one of the three "Fathers"—a term that would later signify the entire usable past of American Jewry. Why this story before all others? Because, to quote Howe, it displayed Sholem Aleichem's "gift for making a seemingly innocent anecdote into a remarkably shrewd and poignant evocation of the whole social position—the constant burden of peril—of the Jews" (74-75). Even if we allow that in the early fifties, few Americans were as yet preoccupied with "the constant burden of peril—of the Jews" and that it would take another thirty years for this peril, which culminated in Hitler's nearly victorious war against the Jews, to become absorbed into the national, nay, even international, master narrative; and whether or not his intended readers accepted Howe's global view of Yiddish as the culture of powerlessness, or identified Sholem Shachnah Rattlebrain as a species of the "kleyne mentshele"—these caveats notwithstanding, Howe undoubtedly put forward a reading so "strong," so morally compelling, that all subsequent readings of this, as of other works by Sholem Aleichem, would follow suit. With his selection and placement of Sholem Aleichem's **"On Account of a Hat,"** Howe launched an ongoing search for socio-psychological verities about the Jewish condition that lay buried beneath the surface of this hilarious tale of a scatterbrain who loses his head when he loses his hat. And should any of us have missed the story the first time around, we found it anthologized, somewhat improbably, in Howe's *Jewish-American Stories* (1977); yet again, in *The Best of Sholom Aleichem* (1979), edited by Howe and Wisse; and from there, with a great cartoon, as a lead act in Novak and Waldoks's *Big Book of Jewish Humor* (1981).

It was a brilliant choice, and an equally brilliant choice of translator: Howe's friend, the critic and novelist Isaac Rosenfeld. Indeed, much in the story fairly cried out for a modernist reading, provided that the focus of one's attention was on the character of Sholem Shachnah himself: his feeble negotiation with a rapidly changing world; his somewhat bolder attempt to respond to tsarist tyranny and antisemitism; his crisis of identity when failing to recognize the face in the mirror as his own; his object lesson in human fate and frailty delivered at story's end by his furious wife. In my own first sortie into the field, published in these pages nineteen years ago, I might have enshrined Sholem Shachnah within the pantheon of fictional Jews who tried to "laugh off the trauma of history," only there were so many worthier contenders: Tevye, Motl, Menakhem-Mendl, the merchant from Heissin, Yankl Yunever.[2] Other critics, meanwhile, were struck by the affinities between Sholem Shachnah and his illustrious precursor, Nikolai Gogol's Akakiy Akakievich, the lowly collegiate assessor who left for the office so triumphantly in his new overcoat, only to have it stolen. "Le chapeau fait-il le Juif?" asked Delphine Bechtel. In more ways, she concluded, than Gogol's overcoat made the hapless bureaucrat Russian.[3] Subjecting both stories to a very close reading, and writing against the backdrop of apartheid, Joseph Sherman concluded that both Sholem Shachnah and the small-time stationer who narrates the tale are morally discredited for dealing with the Gentiles as stereotypes rather than as individuals. Sholem Aleichem, then, like Gogol, purports to defend the underdog, while at the same time unmasks his moral and imaginative failings.[4] Rachel Adler, taking an explicitly "sociopsychological look" at the story, noted another hidden connection: between Sholem Shachnah and Sholem Aleichem, both of them consigned to a life in exile, as their shared first name suggests. Both of them, according to Adler, harbored unconscious desires of living free of the hat that stigmatized them as Jews.[5] In short, the professional class of readers agreed with Howe that this story provides an unusually stark portrait of the modern Jew *in extremis,* and, as such, Sholem Shachnah is the father of us all.

This overriding concern with character, at the expense of so many other tantalizing elements in the story, bespeaks a very modernist agenda. It also reveals the virtue of necessity—the necessity of reading Sholem Aleichem in translation. Through most of my teaching career, it is time for me to admit, I have done the same thing. Like my Anglo-American and French fellows, I routinely cut to the existential quick. Once, in a moment of inspired pedagogy, I even compared myself to Sholem Shachnah, thrust into a mini-crisis of identity on account of a new hat.[6] I do not disavow these modernist readings, but I view them now as woefully inadequate—indeed, as patronizing and apologetic. Patronizing, for in trying to bridge the gap between the story's past significance and present meaning, these ingenious interpretations place the critic-reader far above the author and his intended audience. Apologetic, because by applying terms and concepts that are utterly foreign to Sholem Aleichem's time and place, they aim to remove the stigma of provincialism from what appears to be, after all, merely a droll Yiddish *mayse.*

Out of a droll Russian *mayse,* however, the aforementioned tale by Nikolai Gogol, there later sprang the school of literary interpretation known as Formalism, which in turn spawned the school of prosaics associated with Bakhtin.[7] Together with Donald Fanger's brilliant book on Gogol, they provided me with a mandate to revisit Sholem Aleichem in the Yiddish original.[8] Rereading Sholem Aleichem in Yiddish and under the tutelage of the Slavicists was a lesson in polyphony, the complex interplay of voices at work in this story, each with its own diction and direction. It trained me to listen for tag lines, speech rhythms, double-voicedness, stylization, parody, the comic and connotative meaning of sounds, multilingualism, diglossia, and other stylistic features that I had never heard of before. To be sure, neither had Sholem Aleichem, but rather than push the text in a centrifugal direction toward an ever more "universal" reading, these analytic concepts and theoretical constructs opened up the varied mental curriculum that underlies his seemingly most innocent tales. To access the "world of Sholem Aleichem," I needed to look no further than the inside of Sholem Shachnah's hat, which meant that Howe had been right after all, but for reasons he either dimly perceived or was unable to hear.

Lesson One was to retrieve the multifacetedness of Sholem Aleichem himself. In my research on "the lost art of Yiddish storytelling," I found a writer who was always much more than just a writer.[9] When he started out "on the road," as Mr. How-Do-You-Do, he fast became the favorite traveling companion of Jewish merchants crisscrossing the Russian Pale in search of a ruble; then, with the mass immigration westward, he became an intimate in Yiddish-speaking homes on both sides of the Atlantic; still later, with the rise of modern schools, he supplied Jewish children the world over with their main source of classroom entertainment. My own experience was fairly typical: the high point of sixth grade was performing in a Hebrew adaptation of **"The Penknife"**; in seventh grade, when Lerer Dunsky became our home-room teacher, the reward for good behavior were those Friday mornings when, after a boring class on the siddur, he read aloud from *Mayses far yidishe kinder.*

For Solomon Rabinovitsh, therefore, the invention of an all-purpose persona went hand-in-glove with the creation of multiple literary contexts, which in turn governed where, when, and how each text was read and received. From 1899 onward, each new narrative was identified, often in précis form, as belonging to one or another of his open story cycles: ***Menakhem-Mendl, Tevye the Dairyman, Monologues, Holiday Tales, Tales for Jewish Children, The Little People with Little Minds, Railroad Stories,*** and so on.[10] Take, for example:

"On Account of a Hat"

A tale in honor of Pesach, recounted by a Jew from Kasrilevke, who deals in *obryezkes* and smokes thin cigarettes, retold exactly in his own words.

Here, up front, was everything the Yiddish reader could need in order to situate the story that follows within a recognizable literary context. Should the story be read as a Holiday Tale, it will partake of a familial landscape governed by the cycles of the Jewish festivals. Pesach, of course, is the most popular, for show me a Jew who doesn't turn heaven and earth to be "home for Passover." No matter that other than to heighten suspense, the plot has nothing to do with Pesach; it might just as well be happening on the eve of the Sabbath. What's important is the holiday marker itself, which signals to every seasoned reader that the story will end badly. Nine times out of ten, the holiday stories track the feverish preparations attending the given festival, but end in disillusion.[11] Neither is the "Kasrilevke" marker any guarantee of a happy end. Most of these communal narratives tell of "happy paupers," an oxymoron by any other name. They are bittersweet tales of dissolution. More telling is that the story is narrated by a native son who deals in something called *obryezkes,* glossed in the opening paragraph as "pieces of paper," and chainsmokes. He's traveling by train on his way home for Pesach when he bumps into the famous Sholem Aleichem, who dutifully transcribes the story word for word, and, except for an early digression, lets his informant do all the talking.

So the Yiddish reader is offered an embarrassment of riches, a variety of generic clues—Pesach, Kasrilevke, the monologue—to guide a proper reading of the story. And just in case someone happens to recognize a certain affinity between the story that follows and a well-known joke about mistaken identities, "Sholem Aleichem" throws in an authorial disclaimer.

> I must confess that this true story, which he related to me, does indeed sound like a concocted one, and for a long time I couldn't make up my mind whether or not I should pass it on to you. But I thought it over and decided that if a respectable merchant and dignitary of Kasrilevke, who deals in stationery and is surely no *littérateur*—if he vouches for a story, it must be true. What would he be doing with fiction? Here it is in his own words. I had nothing to do with it.

"Surely no *littérateur, iz nit shayekh tsu literatur un geher zikh klal nisht on mit keyn sforim,*" i.e., though he has no truck either with secular or religious books, our stationery dealer is no illiterate, either. This man, who remains anonymous, is a loyal reader of Sholem Aleichem and not only recognizes his illustrious traveling companion straightaway, but also has literary pretensions of his own, as when he ends his first digression on the vagaries of train travel with a trilingual joke, inspired by his reading of *Tevye the Dairyman.* This tells us, despite Sholem Aleichem's protestations to the contrary, that the stationery dealer has probably embellished his tale in other ways as well.[12]

Whichever of these manifold clues the Yiddish reader follows—whether Pesach, Kasrilevke, the monologue, the "anecdote," or the train—will determine whether or to what extent the story of Sholem Shachnah's hat can be domesticated. At first, it does appear that Sholem Aleichem is up to his old tricks. Sholem Shachnah tells a story to his *landsman,* who tells it to "Sholem Aleichem," who transcribes it for us. This is akin to Berl Vinegar retelling his "Miracle of Hoshana Rabba" to the traveling salesman who records it for us; or better yet, to Reb Nissl Shapiro telling the story of Kivke the stool pigeon to his grandson, the Jew from Kaminka, who performs it in front of a group of third-class passengers on the train, among whom is the traveling salesman, who records it for us (**"Baranovitsh Station,"** 1909).

As in the best of Sholem Aleichem's *oeuvre,* **"On Account of a Hat"** is based on a well-known joke. In two versions told to me, one by Yehudah Elberg, the other by David Weiss-Halivni, the butt of the joke arrives in the dead of night either at an inn (Elberg) or at a cheap hostel attached to a train station (Halivni), falls asleep next to an Eastern Orthodox priest, is rudely awakened when the time comes, and in his confusion exchanges his *kapote,* or gaberdine, for a *reverentke,* a priestly habit. When the Jew washes his face in the water barrel (Elberg) or walks by a mirror on the wall (Halivni), he stops dead and exclaims, "That idiot! I asked him to wake me up, and what does he do? He wakes the priest up instead!"

Like all good jokes, this one has a nervous edge. It flirts with the unthinkable: behold a Jew parading as a priest. Because that divide is unbridgeable, the underlying message is deeply conservative, and the joke is on the nincompoop who cannot separate the clothing from the man. But consider what happens when instead of a gaberdine, the article of clothing is the ubiquitous Jewish hat, and instead of a priest, the Jew falls asleep next to a tsarist official, then mistakenly dons his military cap with a red band and visor. At the very least, the story now flirts with a different kind of danger zone, one that separates the victim from the victimizer, the powerless Jew from the Russian overlord. The Yiddish reader, who is in on the (old) joke, is therefore pulled in two directions. There is some consolation in recognizing the story's plot line and knowing that we've been here before. Contrariwise, there is something very depressing about the pattern of eternal return. Here we are traveling by train, under the benevolent rule of the tsar, in a seemingly civil society, yet the divide between the haves and have-nots is still so great that the very thought of switching roles gives rise to the most extreme cognitive dissonance. By thoroughly secularizing the joke, Sholem Aleichem renders it more potentially subversive.

Sure enough, the story has everything to do with the perils of train travel, with the vagaries of schedules and refuelings that conspire against every attempt to live by the Jewish calendar. The narrator may be no more than a petty merchant himself, but he is savvy when it comes to a good story, his audience-of-one, and the modern industrial landscape. The main action occurs in the purgatorial train station of Zlodievke ("Roguesville"), located between two poles of desire: the big world of business and the safe haven of Kasrilevke. Once the generic road map veers away from the Holiday Tale and moves decisively toward the cycle of **Railroad Stories,** it signals a focus far removed from the traditional, communal realm, and situates the story instead amid the corrosive, technological forces that wreak havoc with the lives of one's fellow Jews.[13] Read from the inside, and following the tracks that the author has provided, the Yiddish reader might indeed have uncovered "the whole social position—the constant burden of peril—of the Jews," beginning with the telltale signs of poverty (one petty merchant narrating a tale of marginal existence about another; the perils of doing business far away from home); the telltale signs of political antisemitism (a rigid hierarchy, with drunken peasants at the bottom, impoverished Jews in the middle, and tsarist officials on top; a tyrannical rule so reductionist that its Jews can be treated like human beings only if they're dreaming or have been mistaken for someone else); not to speak of the eternal battle of the sexes, between the men, so full of bravado and so inept, and their womenfolk, raised in the school of hard knocks, so pragmatic and fatalistic. No wonder Sholem Shachnah spends most of the story balancing between sheer exhaustion, utter confusion, and mortal terror. In the story's denouement, which returns both him and us to native ground, Sholem Shachnah is put down, first by his wife, and then by all the children of Kasrilevke, even while he tries to save face by denying the whole story, thus holding out some hope that the terrors of modernity can be held at bay, so long as the prodigal son returns to the fold still wearing his own hat. This was a Passover message that Sholem Aleichem's readers in that terrible year of 1913 desperately needed to hear, what with the infamous Beilis trial still dragging on in Kiev, and Purishkevitsh rallying his Black Hundreds from his seat in the Saint Petersburg Duma.[14]

Because the story is made up of so many heterogeneous elements—Pesach, Kasrilevke, train travel, politics, henpecked husbands, all in the context of an old joke retold in so lively a fashion that it remains a perennial howler—it defies a sustained reading along any single generic route. One reader's pablum is another's existential parable. It is a story, moreover—like the best of Sholem Aleichem's stories—without

an end. The artful artificiality of the ending underscores what Bakhtin has called the "unfinalizability" of life. Why, from the very start of the journey we were told that this is but one choice tidbit from among a whole repertoire of stories told about the local wonder, Sholem Shachnah Rattlebrain. Should God grant us life, we may someday hear more, wherever our own travels—or hapless business pursuits—may take us.

What is lost in translation is not the plot line or punch line, not the story's manifold interpretive possibilities, from pious to postmodern, each locatable within a different contextual-generic map, but the story's orality. "Iber a hitl" is a written transcript of several dialogically linked, spoken narratives. At least five such narratives can be heard *simultaneously,* each with its own diction and direction.

(1) In the central voice chamber, resonating outward, is recounted Sholem Shachnah's nightmare. Although mediated, like everything else in this story, by someone's else's voice, it alone preserves Sholem Shachnah's personal style and sensibility. His defenses are at their low point. He is exhausted after two sleepless nights and has just secured a pitiful place for himself on the bench, right next to "Buttons," some high-ranking tsarist official with a military cap with a red band and a visor. Enacted in this dream sequence is the return of the repressed. Because Sholem Shachnah is being driven home in a horse-drawn buggy, as opposed to the train he is about to board, and because none other than Ivan "Zlodi" (The Rogue) is in charge, the dream gets played out not in Yiddish but in *Ukrainian,* a language that in the semiotics of Jewish culture is deemed to be "Low Goyish."[15] No sooner does Sholem Shachnah urge on the lazy son of a bitch, who couldn't care less that Passover is near, then the Goy, as if out of spite, starts driving out of control, and our hero is suddenly un-Jewed: his hat flies off his head. Realizing, with horror, that he cannot pull into town hatless, he pleads with Ivan to stop, all the while agonizing (*un klogt zikh*) that he has lost his hat. So what has brought on this terrifying fantasy of abandoning his Jewishness? Was it precipitated by his earlier "success" clinching a real-estate deal, which deal was comically capped by Sholem Shachnah sending home a victory telegram in High Goyish, i.e., Russian? Perhaps, as Rachel Adler argued, the dream expresses his fear of success. Certainly it is a premonition of failure, in the symbolic language of dreams. Sholem Aleichem is flirting with the supernatural here, creating a liminal moment of utter confusion that is grounded in the psychological reality of his protagonist:

> Time? What time? Sholem Shachnah is all confused.
> He wakes up, rubs his eyes, and is all set to step out of

the wagon when he realizes he has lost his hat. Is he dreaming or not?

Later, when standing in front of the mirror in the first-class train compartment, Sholem Shachnah will be asking himself the same question: Is this a dream or a nightmare?

(2) If the story's ambiguities are staged in so folksy a fashion, and its supernatural elements are so easily conjured away, it is surely because the story has already become part of the communal narrative, a mock-heroic tale about a local boy who thought he could pass himself off as a tsarist official. This folktale quality is underscored both structurally and linguistically. Like all Indo-European folktales, it partakes of a tri-partite structure: (A) the hero leaves home and clinches a deal; (B) there follows a confrontation on alien ground between him and Buttons, an ogre-like figure whom he tries to vanquish by inadvertently stealing his hat, the military cap that is the source of his magical powers; then (C) everything goes wrong, for instead of returning home in triumph, our hero is undone by his newfound powers and fails to return home in time for the seder.

More subtle are the linguistic-stylistic means that suggest a folk narrative. To the Yiddish ear, folksiness is synonymous with the Slavic component of the language, which is here played for all its worth, beginning with "the military cap with the red band and a visor; *a VOYENE hitl mit a roytn OKOLESHOK un mit a KOKARDE*," where every third word is an unmerged Slavicism, especially the comic-sounding KOKARDE, and ending with "Your Excellency," the honorific title with which Sholem Shachnah, now miraculously transformed into a tsarist official, is greeted by the ticket agent and the conductor, one using the High Goyish (= Russian) form, BLOGODARNIE, and the other using the Low Goyish (= Ukrainian) form, BLAHO-DARNIE. Needless to say, the children of Kasrilevke adore the sound of this word, and they mercilessly taunt our hero with it in the story's final lines. Indeed, if Sholem Shachnah didn't exist, the folk would have to invent him, for his double name is a dead giveaway of his utter provincialism (cf. the names of Sholem Aleichem's most celebrated provincials, the husband-and-wife team of Menakhem-Mendl and Sheyne-Sheyndl). Thus the communal narrative, in ways both substantive and stylistic, is the most consoling, for it delivers a conservative message. Sholem Shachnah gets his just deserts. He is punished for being such a scatterbrain and for sleeping next to a Goy.

(3) Performing this communal tale for the benefit of his illustrious traveling companion is the anonymous stationer from Kasrilevke, whose incessant tag line,

"*ir horkht, tsi neyn,* do you [using the formal form of address] hear what I say?" perfectly complements his chain-smoking. Intent upon grabbing—and maintaining—Sholem Aleichem's rapt attention, he repeats his tag line twenty-nine times. This he alternates with a second tag line, "*Sholem-Shakhne heyst es,* Sholem Shachnah, that is," which is more playful, because by emphasizing (eighteen times) the subject of this bizarre tale, the stationer directly challenges our credulity: believe this, if you dare, that a lowly shtetl Jew actually pulled off such a caper![16]

Once he has "Panie Sholem-Aleykhem" hooked, the stationer proceeds to establish his own credentials by launching into a lengthy, and brilliant, digression about the mixed blessings of train travel, which, with its rich peppering of Russian terms, demonstrates his technical expertise, and with its climactic, trilingual punch line, demonstrates his literary expertise:

> When the wise men of Kasrilevke quote the passage from the Holy Book, "*Tov shem mishemen tov*" [Eccles. 7:11], they know what they're doing. Now how would your Tevye explain it? "*Svami dobre, a bez vas lutshe*" [which, in Ukrainian, means "When I'm alone I'm happy, but without you—I'm even happier"]. In other words, we were better off without the train.

Like Tevye, whose word games he is here mimicking, the stationer delights in the presence of a learned listener, and therefore uses every opportunity to show off his Hebraic knowledge, his mastery of what Max Weinreich called "the language of the way of the SHaS."[17] These learned and mock-learned phrases—*teyln zikh mitn rakhash, iz . . . gevorn . . . a vayitsaku, borekh shepotrani, odn beyfokdekho, vi baym tatn in vayngortn*—are used ironically throughout, to undercut his subject and his heroic pretensions. They are the main source of double-voicedness in this twice-told tale, because they preserve Sholem Shachnah's version of things even as they subject it to comic scrunity. The game begins with the stationer's put-down of Sholem Shachnah's one and only accomplishment, clinching his first real-estate deal:

> One day God took pity on Sholem Shachnah, and for the first time in his career as a real-estate broker—are you listening?—he actually worked out a deal. That is to say, the work itself, as you can imagine, was done by others, and when the time came to collect the fee, the big rattler turned out to be not Sholem Shachnah Rattlebrain, but Drobkin, a Jew from Minsk province, a great big fearsome rattler, a real-estate broker from way back—he and his two brothers, also brokers and also big rattlers.

While Rosenfeld wonderfully mimics the parodic syntax, with its manic repetitiveness, no translation can capture the comic interplay of the Slavic "*imenyes,* estates," repeated ten times in the course of two paragraphs—which suggests that Sholem Shachnah merely mastered the terminology, but not the practical side, of doing business in the Slavic outback—with the very Yiddish epithet "*dreyer,* rattler," used contrapuntally both as a noun and a verb, but the face-off between the Rattlebrain and the real rattlers is rendered null and void by the strategic placement of the mock-learned phrase "*az s'iz gekumen tsum teyln zikh mitn rakhash,* when the time came to collect the fee," *rakhash* meaning, in context, the salary that the community (or an individual) pays to hire a Rabbi, KHazn, and SHames. So what does our hero do? The only thing a Sholem Aleichem character *can* do: he yells and screams, "*iz . . . gevorn . . . a vayitsaku,*" until Drobkin and Co. can't take it any more, and they give Sholem Shachnah his cut, just to shut him up, and "*borekh shepotrani,* good riddance it was, too." Once a shtetl Jew, always a shtetl Jew.

The whole of the stationer's monologue is cast in this mock-hermeneutical mold, even though "Sholem Aleichem" had sized him up earlier as having no truck either with secular books or *sforim,* and, as a dealer in *obryezkes,* pieces of paper, he can't be making much of a living, either. It takes one to know one, the stationer's real forte lying in his gift of gab, more wickedly clever, more persuasive, than Sholem Shachnah's, but gab nonetheless.

The stationer's core narrative, analogous to Sholem Shachnah's nightmare, is the confrontation with Buttons. Here the narrator pulls out all the stops, using both his tag lines obsessively, setting the stage in the Zlodievke train station as "*ongeroykhert, ongeshpign, fintster, khoyshekh,* the walls of the station were covered with soot, the floor was covered with spit. It was dark, it was terrible"; the hero prepared "*laydn khibet-hakeyver,* to bear the blandishments of purgatory." The rhythm of this section is extremely choppy; the rhetoric is at high pitch, every phrase ending either with a question or an exclamation, the better to render Sholem Shachnah's fierce mental struggle: dare he sit next to Buttons or not? Is there room for a Jew in this world or is there not? Once again, the key—untranslatable—moment is both elevated and deflated by the use of learned language. "*Mi yoydeya,* who knows?" the stationer asks, paraphrasing what is racing through Sholem Shachnah's mind as he contemplates the tsarist official lying on the only available bench in the station, "*vos far a knepl, vos far an odn beyfokdekho dos iz,* what kind of a Buttons, or high official, this might be." The key phrase, taken from the penitential prayers before Rosh Hashanah, where it means, "Lord, in Your bringing to account," had entered into folk speech long before Sholem Aleichem as an ironic epithet for a *macher* very much of this world. (In folk parlance, the difficult, medieval Hebrew locution is often pronounced *odn beyfokdokh.*) Through constant recourse to the language of Jewish learning, then, the stationer could also be trying, unconsciously, to keep the madness at bay, to establish a source of authority and truth that lies outside the danger zone of Roguesville and Goysville.

Be that as it may, the tension between the logic of learning and the absurdity of the situation reaches its climax when Sholem Shachnah faces himself down in front of the mirror. In this moment of radical self-confrontation, when everything hangs in the balance—Sholem Shachnah's newfound self-confidence, the efficacy of his plan to enlist Yeremei's help, the dreamlike quality of his miraculous transformation—our hero experiences total cognitive dissonance. Savoring the punch line, the stationer delivers it in Sholem Shachnah's own, spicy, words:

> All my bad dreams on Yeremei's head and on his hands and feet, that lug! Twenty times I tell him to wake me and I even give him a tip, and what does he do, that dumb ox, may he catch cholera in his face, but wake up the official instead! And me he leaves asleep on the bench! Tough luck, Sholem Shachnah old boy, but this year you'll spend Passover in Zlodievke, not at home.

This last touch, of having Sholem Shachnah address himself in the third person, is particularly rich, because it is both a folk reflex and a measure of the split between the actor and his setting, the man and his life.

The stationer reserves the super-punch line for himself, describing in luxurious detail how Sholem Shachnah actually jumps off the train, carpetbag and all, to wake his "real" self up. And there is more to come, a denouement reserved for men's delectation alone:

> First of all, he has a wife—Sholem Shachnah, that is—and his wife—how shall I describe her to you? *I* have a wife, *you* have wife, we all have wives, we've had a taste of Paradise, we know what it means to be married. All I can say about Sholem Shachnah's wife is that she's a Number One. And did she give him a royal welcome! Did she lay into him!

This is locker-room talk, of a piece with the traditional misogyny of world folklore. It reveals something new about the stationer's story—the extent to which it is a gendered narrative—and something new about the stationer himself—that there are ironies and ambiguities at work here that escape even his all-seeing eye. For what enrages Sholem Shachnah's wife is not so much his failure to make it home in time for the seder as the telegram he sent her from the road,

> And not so much the telegram—you hear what I say?—as the one short phrase, *without fail.* Was he trying to make the telegraph company rich? And besides, how dare a human being say "without fail" in the first place?

The stationer's jocular tone suggests that he doesn't get it. The reader understands what he does not: that Sholem Shachnah was punished for his hubris, for testing fate, for believing in human assurances, while the stationer reads her put-down as yet another voice in the Kasrilevke choir, albeit the voice of a Number One emasculator, who knew all along that her *shlimazl* of a husband should sell and come right home.

(4) So who does get it? "Sholem Aleichem," the loyal scribe and responsible folk writer, who admitted straightaway that the story was pure invention by playfully protesting its absolute truthfulness. Jews, he said in so many words, we're all in on this joke together. His language, to judge from the story's preamble, is the most balanced, as befits someone whose name is EveryJew, the favorite Yiddish author, who offers his loyal readers a piece of local lore in honor of their favorite holiday, the world traveler who joins his brethren each year in their Passover journey home. What is the moral of his story? That technology has made it harder, not easier, for a Jew to make it home in time for the holiday. Jews, like all of humankind, are still at the mercy of inscrutable forces—but especially Jews, who live in Russian exile.

Lately, however, after living abroad for so many years, and with the winds of reaction gaining strength everywhere, Sholem Aleichem is growing despondent, his humor is becoming ever darker, and the very act of writing a Passover parable now strikes him as bordering on the absurd. From his exilic perspective, the story of a Jew, whose worst nightmare is returning home without his hat, and therefore grabs the first available hat upon awakening, is a dead-end. The logic of this story dictates that Sholem Shachnah is not rewarded for his fealty, but punished for it. His story only flirts with the possibility of becoming a Goy, for other than the dumb Goyim in the Zlodievke train station, no one is taken in by the disguise. Why else does Sholem Shachnah remain all alone in the first-class compartment? He could never have pulled off such a hoax among his own kind. Rather, his is the story of an ordinary Jew who cannot possibly live as a Jew. Either he can make it home in time for the seder, but without his hat, or he can retrieve his hat, and miss the seder.

(5) Not so, for Solomon Rabinovitsh, who speaks Russian at home to his children, and wears many hats—top hats, fedoras, straw hats, but never, never a "Jewish" cap, except in the minds of his many admirers.[18] This man can deconstruct and reconstruct any Jewish narrative at will. For Solomon Rabinovitsh, this frightening parable about "the constant burden of peril . . . of the Jews" that emanates as much from within Jewish life as without cannot possibly be the last word,

for if it were, he would not have invented Sholem Aleichem in the first place, and not have made him into the grand ventriloquist of a tale-within-a-tale-within-a-tale-within-a-tale-within-a-tale, each one narrated by another speaker of another subdialect of Yiddish. He would not have seduced us, hatless, rootless cosmopolitans that we are, to eavesdrop on two Jews shooting the breeze on a train heading home for the seder. He would not have made us laugh at the utter absurdity of the Jewish condition—including our own. He would not have orchestrated each of his five voices to speak to and through each other, no one speaker speaking exclusively for the author. And he would not have turned Yiddish into the consummate language of polyphony.

When Alan Mintz and I launched *Prooftexts* twenty years ago, our goal was to rescue Jewish literature from its paraphrasers, plagiarizers, and panderers. And so, I entered the fray, donning the hat of a lit-critical maverick, something akin to a military cap with a red band and a visor. Among other labors, I tried to raise Sholem Shachnah Rattlebrain onto a high literary pedestal, by focusing on his character, and by reading his story with and against the contextual grain. What I—and other professional critics—unwittingly sacrificed was nothing less than the Yiddish original. For it turned out, upon close reinspection, that the science of solitary reading could not uncover the story's modernism and multivalence. To that end, one had to relearn the communal, cacophonous, art of listening. The search for the "real" Sholem Aleichem, moreover, revealed a man who, by restoring the multi-lingualism, diglossia, stylistic and parodic registers of an ideal Yiddish folkspeech, was able to turn the unredeemable facts of Jewish life in exile into a celebration of life's open-endedness, a five-ring, Yiddish circus. The writer we had been reading for so long in translation turned out to be Sholem Aleichem parading around in someone else's hat.

Notes

1. Sholem Aleichem, "On Account of a Hat," trans. Isaac Rosenfeld, in *A Treasury of Yiddish Stories,* ed. Irving Howe and Eliezer Greenberg (New York: Viking, 1954), 111-18; "Iber a hitl," in *Fun peysekh biz peysekh, Ale verk fun Sholem-Aleykhem* (New York: Folksfond, 1917-1925), 2:241-54.

2. David G. Roskies, "Sholem Aleichem and Others: Laughing Off the Trauma of History," *Prooftexts* 2 (1982): 53-77; later revised as chapter 7 of *Against the Apocalypse: Responses to Catastrophe in Modern Jewish Culture* (Cambridge, Mass.: Harvard University Press, 1984).

3. Delphine Bechtel, "Le chapeau fait-il le Juif? Aspects de la poétique de Sholem Aleykhem," *Yod,*

no. 31-32 (1990): 67-79. Less convincing is Bech-tel's claim—borne out neither textually nor bio-graphically—that "On Account of a Hat" should be read as a deliberate parody of Dostoevsky's *Poor Folks.* Howe, too, had noted Sholem Ale-ichem's debt to Gogol, in the story "Eternal Life." See *Treasury,* 75.

4. Joseph Sherman, "'God and the Tsar': Ironic Am-biguity and Restorative Laughter in Gogol's 'Overcoat' and Sholem Aleichem's 'On Account of a Hat,'" unpublished manuscript.

5. Rachel Adler, "Mabat sotsio-psikhologi shel sipuro shel Shalom Aleichem 'Beshel kova,'" *Hado'ar* 65, no. 15 (1986): 15-17 and 16:18-19.

6. David G. Roskies, "On Account of Two Hats," in *The Seminary at 100: Reflections on the Jewish Theological Seminary and the Conservative Move-ment,* ed. Nina Beth Cardin and David Wolf Sil-verman (New York: The Rabbinical Assembly and the Jewish Theological Seminary of America, 1987), 239-49.

7. I am thinking of Dmitry Merezhkovsky, "Gogol and the Devil" (1906), and such classics of the Russian Formalist school as Boris Eichenbaum, "How Gogol's 'Overcoat' is Made" (1919); Alex-ander Slonimsky, "The Technique of the Comic in Gogol" (1923); Dmitry Chizhevsky, "About Gogol's 'Overcoat'" (1938), in *Gogol in the Twen-tieth Century,* ed. and trans. Robert A. Maguire (Princeton: Princeton University Press, 1974); and V. V. Gippius, *Gogol* (1924), ed. and trans. Robert A. Maguire (Ann Arbor: Ardis, 1981).

8. Donald Fanger, *The Creation of Nikolai Gogol* (Cambridge, Mass.: Harvard University Press, 1979).

9. David G. Roskies, *A Bridge of Longing: The Lost Art of Yiddish Storytelling* (Cambridge, Mass.: Harvard University Press, 1995), chap. 5.

10. Kh[one] Sh[meruk], "Sholem-Aleykhem," *Le-ksikon fun der nayer yidisher literatur* 8 (1981): 681, 689.

11. Roskies, *A Bridge of Longing,* 167-74.

12. Cf. other late monologues such as "Gitl Purish-kevitsh" and "Yoysef," in which the speaker, ad-dressing the reknowned writer Sholem Aleichem, allows the author to revel in the games that fiction plays and to reveal the serious role of the writer.

13. See Dan Miron, "Masa' be'eizor hadimdumim," afterword to his Hebrew translation of Sholem Aleichem, *Sippurei rakevet* (Tel Aviv: Dvir, 1989), 227-300.

14. To establish a link to these current events, Purish-kevitsh gets dishonorable mention in the story it-self. For more on the historicity of the railroad

stories, see Hillel Halkin's introduction to Sholem Aleichem, *Tevye the Dairyman and the Railroad Stories* (New York: Schocken, 1987), xxxii-xxxvi.

15. For a fuller discussion, see my *Against the Apoca-lypse,* 163-72.

16. I owe this analysis of the tag lines to Joseph Sher-man's unpublished manuscript.

17. Max Weinreich, *History of the Yiddish Language,* trans. Shlomo Noble (Chicago and London: Uni-versity of Chicago Press, 1980), chap. 3.

18. For the striking evidence, see *Shalom-Aleichem: His Life in Pictures,* ed. Abraham Lis (Tel Aviv: Dvir, 1988), to which may be added the huge statue of him recently erected in Kiev, where he is captured doffing his hat to all passers-by. Most of the famous drawings and caricatures, in other words, render an imaginary, folksy, "Sholem Ale-ichem," not the urbane and meticulously dressed Solomon Rabinovitsh.

Leah Garrett (essay date January 2001)

SOURCE: Garrett, Leah. "Trains and Train Travel in Modern Yiddish Literature." *Jewish Social Studies* 7, no. 2 (January 2001): 67-88.

[*In the excerpt that follows, Garrett contends that the majority of tales in* The Railroad Stories *present train travel negatively, emphasizing the loss of the protective* shtetl *community and the increasing despair and suffer-ing of the Jewish people; only two stories, the "Slow-poke Express" tales, counterbalance this dark correla-tion, according to the critic, by portraying Jews as mastering modern technology while remaining faithful to God.*]

AYZNBAN-GESHIKHTES

Sholem Aleichem's *Ayznban-geshikhtes* is a collec-tion of tales[1] by a self-described traveling salesman re-counting his encounters with fellow passengers on a third-class train car.[2] The stories are important, within both Sholem Aleichem's corpus and the development of Yiddish literature, for the groundbreaking way in which they offer a critique of Jewish communal life at the turn of the century.

At a time of profound personal dislocation for the au-thor and the Jews he was describing, the railroad car became a setting for telling stories.[3] The salesman-narrator seeks to make the stories heard in the car into *peklekh* (sob stories) that he can sell (matching Sholem Aleichem's original intent for the collection), whereas the collection as a whole functions as, David Roskies writes, "a vast panorama of dissolution" reflecting Sholem Aleichem's mature and dark vision after his own personal exile. The reader is put in the uncomfortable position of both being "entertained" by the tragic tales, much like fellow passengers in the train car, and feeling compassion toward the characters.

A train would seem to be the ideal locale for storytelling: a group setting, disconnected from a grounded location, and representing the archetypal Jewish "community." Yet the train is also a symbol of the encroachment of the machine onto rural spaces. It is thus a space in which to enact stories that reflect the ascendancy of industry, with its concomitant breakdown of the rural, enclosed, isolated shtetl. The path of the train matches the decline of the shtetl and the erosion of the ideal Jewish community. The stories told to the salesman thus reflect the hard times associated with urbanization and the decline of the shtetl.

The salesman-narrator conceives of the stories he has collected as his "story merchandise." The wrenching stories are not only entertainment but also something to exploit by turning them into a type of goods he will later sell. He reflects a notion of literature as merchandise that is bought and sold. In the era Sholem Aleichem is describing, little is given freely, and individual needs often override communal ones. Help is given in exchange for goods; one listens to a fellow Jew's stories to be entertained rather than to be empathetic. Although the passengers telling the stories seek out a community of listeners who will sympathize with and support them, their fellow passengers listen to the tales as brief, exciting respites from the boredom—in contrast to the real compassion in *Shem un Yefes in a vogn,* when Mendele feels so deeply for the poor family's suffering.

The over-packed train car increases the opportunities to be entertained and becomes the reason why the salesman suggests that the best form of train travel is in the third-class car—versus first class, where there is only bourgeois silence.[4] Whereas the "bourgeois" space is segregated and polite, the third class, the locale of the masses, offers "continuous communication."[5]

In the final section of the collection "Third Class," the salesman-narrator recounts a few other reasons why the third-class cars are preferable: although it is loud and crowded, it is also friendlier and a good place to conduct business. And if you need anything, the others can provide it for you. However, the assistance of fellow Jewish travelers is not based on communal friendship and the free giving of help but on the barter system (which, it seems, is the central type of business in this Jewish space). The interactions with strangers are motivated by a mutual desire to exchange something, unlike in first class, where it is assumed the talk will be conversational rather than as a means of business. Moreover, many of the stories in *Ayznban-geshikhtes* are about the oppressive nature of public discourse, be it bureaucratic or otherwise, and how removed the communication of the current time is from idealistic communal storytelling.

In the third-class car, one can gain valuable advice and folk cures from fellow travelers. However, this positive notion is subverted when the salesman recounts how one of the folk cures he learned of on the train nearly killed him. At the very least, by riding in the third-class car one can gather information from locals on where to stay in their towns. But, again, this also has its dark side, because those who offer to help may be thieves.

At first reading, the folksy tone of the salesman seduces the reader into believing that third class is the only place Jewish travelers can feel at home, whereas only self-hating, assimilated Jews could like the first- and second-class cars. On a closer reading, it is clear that each positive aspect is undermined by a negative: instead of a home, this is a business setting where every assistance is in exchange for something else; instead of good information, the advice could be dangerous; instead of safety, there is the constant possibility of being robbed. There is no community in the positive sense of mutual support. The Jewish community has become a community only in the negative sense of the word. To be sure, in the third-class car you may be entertained, but the narrative suggests that the price is too dear: so many of the stories are fraught with profound suffering that only a sadist, or someone seeking to utilize them in some way, could "enjoy" them. Thus we have the salesman-narrator, who wants to sell the stories as merchandise for a modern readership that finds them to be a form of entertainment, rather than expressions of the communal will.

Ayznban-geshikhtes portrays a distressing picture of Jewish life at the turn of the century, where the desperate plots of the story-telling passengers are matched by the cynical standpoints of the listeners. As Dan Miron has asserted, the "selection of the railroad coach as the setting of the cycle symbolizes the end of the intimacy of *shtetl* literature."[6] Thus, the collection of stories "does not continue the shtetl experience, but rather undermines it."[7] Moreover:

> The small fraternity of the train compartment is rife with ambiguities and unexpected negative attitudes. As much as the travelers would like to treat each other as brothers, the cold winds of suspicion and mistrust have already swept them and influenced the behavior of

most. This is the reason that many of the *Railroad Stories* deal with ambiguous connections, with irregular communication, with dual meaning messages, with discoveries that are in fact cover-ups, [and] with truth that is also a lie.[8]

Whereas, according to Schivelbusch, rail travel is "experienced as participation in an industrial process,"[9] for Jews in turn-of-the-century Yiddish literature the train setting is symbolic of the new industrial age and the collapse of any community.

Instead of throwing away all the stories he has collected, the salesman has decided to "publish them in a book or newspaper." However, he chooses to remain anonymous and to disassociate himself from all that an author represents.[10] The traveling salesman's purported plan is to "record" the encounters he has with fellow passengers. The train is a choice setting for narratives relying on chance encounters with strangers. The stories he hears represent a collective image of Jewish life in a state of ever worsening suffering, where families are struggling day in and day out to take care of their children while battling anti-Jewish governmental edicts.

Within *Ayznban-geshikhtes,* however, a pair of tales does offer respite from the suffering described in the other stories. These are the **"Leydikgeyer"** (**"Slowpoke Express"**) train tales. The Slowpoke Express connects isolated shtetls and is part of the rural landscape. Its stories, following the logic of *Ayznban-geshikhtes,* are more uplifting because they are enacted in a landscape where the destructive forces of modernization have not yet led to the breakdown of the shtetl.

The first story about the Slowpoke Express, **"The Miracle of Hoshana Rabba,"** is a comic tale about an adventure of a Jew and a priest, and it also gives the naive Jewish reader a solid grounding in steam mechanics. The plot is the adventure of Berl Vinegar and the local priest and antisemite, and the story is set when "the train was still new" and locals would come to watch this strange machine. Berl, the Jewish character, strolls up and down the platform focusing his attention on the train while the priest focuses his attention on the Jew. One underlying critique, then, is that Jewish energy is well spent on learning new things but Christian energy is wasted on harassing Jews.

Berl explains to the priest that this new machine is so wondrous because it is so simple: by merely flipping a few switches, the train starts. The priest is incredulous and cannot believe a Jew could possibly know how this huge machine works. Berl, and the story, will prove the priest wrong by showing that a Jew is ca-

pable of understanding fairly complicated steam mechanics, whereas a priest is completely ignorant about them. Berl thus tells the priest to get on the train and he will show him that he knows his stuff.

Not only does Berl get the train to move, but he gets it to run quicker than it ever has. Berl, the Jew, has used his brains to get the massive machine to run more efficiently, in contrast to the regular train crew, who are nothing but lazy, ignorant drunks. The real fault for the train's slowness is not the train itself but the inefficient way it is used.

Berl's mastery of the machine soon ends when he is unable to get it to stop, and he imagines the horrible impending crash. However, Berl then remembers the other facet of a steam machine—the brake—and reaches out to pull it, only to be stopped by the antisemitic priest, who is still too filled with hate to acknowledge that a Jew may in fact be more capable than he is.

Although the Jew may have a higher moral outlook and may be the intellectual victor, the real control of the situation is still with the priest. Berl can certainly hold his own verbally and outwit the priest, but there is nothing he can do physically with a non-Jew who refuses to allow him to pull the brake. In the end, a crash is averted, not by pulling the brake but by the train running out of coal.

The train is seemingly on the side of the Jews because it has stopped before an accident can occur and is a setting for a Jew to morally surpass an antisemite. In reality the train merely follows the same machinery logic that Berl had deduced earlier. Yet Berl, the believer, puts a spiritual spin on the logic of the machine by declaring it is God's will that the train stops and spares their lives (194). This tale is told not by Berl himself or by the traveling salesman but by a passenger who heard of it from someone else. Its structure takes on aspects of a folk legend.[11] It is a comforting, miraculous folktale for the Jews by having a character able to show up an antisemite and to keep his faith while mastering the modern world.

In the second tale about the Slowpoke Express, **"The Wedding That Came without Its Band,"** the train again "miraculously" helps the Jewish characters. In this tale, as well, the theme of escaping from antisemites is central as the train "saves" the Jews from "a horrible fate." This story, like the previous one, is in the framework of a folktale told by the same traveler to the salesman about an event "back in the days of the Constitution" when pogroms were continuously occurring.

As the speaker describes it, pogroms were breaking out all over, though none took place in his shtetl. Soon enough, however, a local decided it was time to start one and sent off for outsiders to assist him. In response, the Jews attempted to get a Russian prefect to help them. In return for a large payment, or bribe, the prefect ordered "a company of Cossacks from Tulchin" to protect the Jews from the pogromists. The speaker is aware of the irony of Jews getting help from Cossacks.

The Jews, aware of the catastrophe that awaits them, beg the prefect to at least have his police force meet the train. In like measure, the local magnate-residents, whom the speaker sarcastically calls "our local patriots" (because they are leaving the dirty work to others), also head off to meet the train. The imminent arrival of the train and the Cossacks transforms the train platform into a multiethnic gathering.[12] There are the Jews, fearfully awaiting a pogrom; Ukrainian pogromists on the train; Polish magnate-residents on the platform gleefully awaiting a pogrom; a Russian prefect bribed to keep the peace; and Cossack hired thugs arriving by horse. It is a multilingual hodgepodge, tragicomically gathered together to await or to enact a pogrom.

With the platform packed, the train pulls into the station. As the train's driver steps down, the tragicomic moment reaches it peak as the onlookers realize he has forgotten all the passenger cars! There will be no pogrom.

As in the previous tale, trains are machines that follow their own machinery logic and are on the side of whoever can master them. The stupidity of non-Jews has again led to the Jews being saved. Both tales suggest that Jews in the current age need to balance their faith with awareness of the machinery of the new age. To reject the new invention will make them as shortsighted and ignorant as the anti-semitic priest.

The Leydikgeyer stories show the means to balance faith and science through characters such as Berl, who offers spiritual interpretations to mechanical occurrences. In these tales, the train becomes "Judaized," whereas in the rest of *Ayznban-geshikhtes* the train is a symbol of a host of negatives related to the advent of modernization and the breakdown of shtetl life.

Berl stands in stark contrast to the salesman-narrator of the collection, who represents the current times. The salesman feels no real empathy with or connection to his fellow passengers. Instead, he seeks to be entertained or to exploit the suffering of others. In place of a deep spirituality, we have a figure who again and again is taken in by surface appearances. Instead

of Berl, with his ability to start a train by making a logical leap, we have a character of marked naivete. Yet, unlike the salesman, who comes across as a real character, Berl exists only within a folk legend where the wondrous can occur and where good always wins out in the end.

In the Leydikgeyer tales, the train becomes a comic Jewish machine that delivers great punch lines: running out of steam, and arriving without the pogromists. In these stories, unlike those in the rest of the collection, the train is not the setting for stories told by Jews about their lives. Instead, the train is the story: a Jewish story of how oppressors are outwitted through comedy. In the end, however, these stories are merely comic relief from the majority of the tales in which the train is a negative symbol containing a negative Jewish community whose dark stories match the dark times. . . .

Notes

1. Both Max Erik and Dan Miron have traced the publication history of the stories. See Max Erik, "Vegn Sholem Aleykhems 'Ksovim fun-a-komivoyazhor,'" *Visnshaft un revolutsye* (Kiev) 3-4 (1934): 161, and Dan Miron, "Journey to the Twilight Zone," trans. Mark Miller, in Miron, *The Image of the Shtetl and Other Studies of Modern Jewish Literary Imagination* (Syracuse, N.Y., 2000). The Hebrew original is "Masa be-eyzor ha-dimdumim." This is the afterword to Miron's Hebrew translation of *Ayznban-geshikhtes* entitled *Sipurei rakevet* (Tel Aviv, 1989).

2. For the Yiddish original, I am using *Ale verk fun Sholem-Aleykhem,* vol. 6 (New York, 1923). The English translation is in *Tevye the Dairyman and the Railroad Stories,* trans. Hillel Halkin (New York, 1987), 135-284. For a thorough discussion of the biographical background of *Ayznban-geshikhtes,* see Miron, "Journey to the Twilight Zone," 1-12.

3. David G. Roskies, *A Bridge of Longing: The Lost Art of Yiddish Storytelling* (Cambridge, Mass., 1995), 177.

4. [Wolfgang] Schivelbusch, [The] *Railway Journey* [: *The Industrialization of Time and Space in the 19th Century* (Berkeley, 1986)], 66-67.

5. Ibid.

6. Miron, "Journey to the Twilight Zone," 27.

7. Ibid., 29.

8. Ibid., 30-31.

9. Schivelbusch, *Railway Journey,* 72.

10. For the classic essay on the meaning of author status (which the salesman-narrator avoids), see M. Foucault, "What Is an Author?" in *Textual Strategies: Perspectives in Post-Structuralist Criticism,* Josue Harari, ed. (New York, 1979), 141-60.

11. David G. Roskies, *Against the Apocalypse: Responses to Catastrophe in Modern Jewish Culture* (Cambridge, Mass., 1984), 173.

12. For a thorough analysis of the role of non-Jews in the works of Sholem Aleichem and how they reflected the real ethnic makeup of the region, see Israel Bartal, "Dmut ha-lo-yehudim ve-hevratam bi-yetsirat Shalom-Aleichem," *Ha-sifrut* 26 (1978): 39-71.

Joseph Sherman (lecture date September 2002)

SOURCE: Sherman, Joseph. "The Non-Reflecting Mirror: Gogol's Influence on Sholem Aleichem." *Essays in Poetics* 28 (autumn 2003): 101-23.

[*In this essay, originally delivered as a lecture in September 2002, Sherman contrasts how Aleichem in "On Account of a Hat" and Nikolai Gogol in* The Overcoat *(1842) responded to human suffering under a repressive tsarist regime.*]

1.

Nikolai I's disingenuous assertion, 'I do not rule Russia; ten thousand clerks do,' in seeming to shift responsibility for daily pettifogging persecutions on to the State's vast bureaucratic apparatus, betrays a smug pride in Peter the Great's system of civil, military and ecclesiastical administration which his successors refined into a near-sacred ritual of rank. The mystique of absolutism, so expertly buttressed by the public service, ensured that the deference paid in strict taxonomic degree to every one of those ten thousand clerks steadily aggregated into total obedience to the tsar himself.[1] Conferring Divine Right on its secular head, Russian Orthodox Christianity upheld an ideology of unquestioning submission to established authority, coming, after the eighteenth century, to share with the secular machinery of the State the common aim of eliminating those who resisted tsarist despotism.[2] To survive, such a system had self-evidently to deny human considerations such as compassion and empathy with human weakness—the very qualities which, summed up in the Yiddish word *mentshlekhkayt,* are the cornerstones of Judaism's spiritual profession. Predictably, therefore, in the last quarter of the nineteenth century, the Jews, perhaps even more than the liberals and socialists whose zeal for human rights recalled the imperatives of the Jewish Prophets, suffered the hatred

of such fanatical supporters of traditional paternalism as Pobedonostsev and Purishkevich. For observant Russian Jews, theologically locked into a conception of history as a fully-revealed cycle, and economically trapped in debilitating poverty by repressive ghettoization, it was not the tsar but God to whom absolute obedience was owing; it was not the *ukaz* of the emperor, but the commandment of the Everlasting that was sacrosanct.

Some of the most brilliant literary responses to tsarist autocracy came from two writers whom a mischievous destiny placed at diametrically opposed religious and social polarities, yet caused to be born and brought up in the identical area of a Russian Empire that was holy to one and hostile to the other. Nikolai Gogol, the violently conservative, Jew-hating traditionalist, died in Moscow seven years before the *shtetl* Jew Sholem Yankev Rabinovitsh—who wrote in the *persona* of Sholem Aleichem—was born in Gogol's home province of Poltava in the Ukraine.

Gogol's work, especially its formalistic techniques of comic grotesque, remained a lifelong influence on that of Rabinovitsh. So greatly did the Yiddish writer admire his Russian predecessor that, as a young man, he even cultivated a resemblance to Gogol in the way he styled his hair and moustache. In an early photograph, Rabinovitsh self-consciously poses before a portrait of Gogol to call attention to their similitude. This youthful *jeu d'esprit* obviously proclaims that, as with their physical likeness, Rabinovitsh also intends to mirror aspects of Gogol's work in his own. Given the unbridgeable socio-cultural gulf that separated these two writers, however, that mirror could only be non-reflecting, since the world each of them displayed in it, though superficially similar, was nevertheless fundamentally distinct. Gogol was a Christian Russian with entrée into Imperial Russia's highest social circles, while Rabinovitsh was a Jewish victim of that same Russia's social and legislative discrimination. Gogol negates the worth of individuals, however publicly exalted, where Rabinovitsh asserts their value, however communally despised. While Jews appear frequently in Gogol's stories, they are always shadowy figures of contempt hovering on the margins of the scene. As a Jew writing for other Jews, Rabinovitsh naturally moves Jews to the centre of his stage.

This paper seeks to illustrate how this oxymoronic 'non-reflecting' mirror functions. Both Gogol and Rabinovitsh responded to the plight of human beings under tsarism with equivocal humour, so that for years it was commonplace to speak of Gogol's art as presenting 'laughter through tears.' Of his own work, Rabinovitsh also once observed in a letter:

> I tell you it is an ugly and mean world and only to spite it one mustn't weep! If you want to know, that is

the real source, the true cause of my constant good spirits, of my, as it is called, 'humor.' Not to cry out of spite! Only to laugh out of spite, only to laugh![3]

Each conceived the function of both laughter and tears very differently, though. The stock formula applied to Gogol's work obscures the more telling recognition that in sacrificing individualism to absolutism, Gogol's laughter is essentially rebarbative.[4] For Rabinovitsh, by contrast, laughter is restorative: by 'spiting' the world, it seeks to confer identity upon individual Jews, and to validate their survival.

To focus on the complexity of Rabinovitsh's art, as exemplified in his short story **"Iber a hitl"** (**"On Account of a Hat,"** 1909), it is useful by way of comparison to glance at Gogol's *Overcoat* (1842). Both stories scrutinize 'little men' ostensibly crushed by tsarism. At first glance, Akakii Akakievich seems to be a downtrodden lackey whom a bureaucratic juggernaut has entirely depersonalised. But closer examination exposes him as more an object of contempt than of compassion. Having made the copying of documents his *raison d'être,* he can see nothing before him except his own handwriting, and when he is ludicrously jolted back into the real world by bumping into a horse, 'only then did he realise that he was not in the middle of a sentence, but in the middle of the street.'[5] Gogol presents him as a man deprived more of emotional than of financial resources, an obsessive cut off, by choice and without sense of loss, from any life-promoting contact with community or individuals. His acquisition of a new overcoat becomes, fleetingly, the acquisition of a new potential for happiness, but given his desiccated personality, when he is robbed of his overcoat on the first night on which he wears it, to go for the first time in his life to a party in the fashionable, brightly-lit suburb he has never visited before, he is effectively deprived of something which can never really be his own.[6] His spectral return is to reclaim the overcoat of the Important Person—in short, to take back that which never was, and never could be, his, but which he is exposed as having always coveted. Akakii Akakievich ends up asking not for sympathy but for status; he does not seek the overthrow of established authority, but a greater share of its privileges. Consequently Gogol's ending mocks not only his readers but also Akakii Akakievich himself. The perfect social system requires requital for one who has been unjustly treated, not because justice is owing to the individual by right, but because the public credibility of tsarism demands it. Gogol's laughter destroys Akakii Akakievich in order to destroy sentimentality.[7]

Under no illusions about tsarism's menace to Jewish survival, Rabinovitsh also lays bare the wounds tsarist autocracy inflicts, but he applies laughter as balm.[8]

"On Account of a Hat" also examines an individual under the dead weight of tsarism, but from the perspective of a Jew, the persecuted deviator from Christian norms, balanced precariously between two sociocultural extremes.[9] The plot of Rabinovitsh's tale can be briefly summarized. Sholem Shachnah, one of those innumerable impoverished inhabitants of an Eastern European *shtetl* who, having no visible means of support, was known in Yiddish as a *luftmentsh,* has made some money in a business deal, and is hurrying home to wife and family in his home town of Kasrilevke in time for the annual celebration of the Passover. Weary after three nights without sleep, he decides to doze on a station platform, and bribes a porter to wake him in time to catch his train. Startled out of sleep by this train's arrival, he hastily snatches up a hat he takes to be his own, but which is actually the red-banded cap of a Russian officer seated next to him. Going to board his train, he is dumbfounded when the station porter insists on carrying his bags and seating him in a first-class compartment. Catching sight of himself in a mirror, Sholem Shachnah sees on his head the Russian officer's cap, and instantly concludes that he has been cheated by the lying porter, who has woken not him but the officer, for how else is it possible for a Jew in Imperial Russia to be seated in a first-class compartment? From this anecdotal material, Rabinovitsh polishes the surface of his Gogolian mirror.

The image it reflects, however, is not the one Gogol saw. Sholem Shachnah is distinguished from Akakii Akakievich by having a mutually enriching relationship with the two interdependent functions of collective Jewish identity, community and family. Despised and discriminated against he may be in the world of greater Russia into which he periodically makes forays, but he always returns to a cultural, spiritual and emotional matrix that defines and dignifies him. From the outset of each tale, the reader's attitude to its central figure is carefully preconditioned by the names their creators give them. Even when he is made the butt of the whole town's raillery, Rabinovitsh's little man is addressed in the formal Yiddish manner as *Reb* Sholem Shachnah. Fellow Jews mock the absurdity of his claims, not his dignity as a human being. By contrast, the rigmarole through which Gogol takes us before settling on the name of his chief character, and that name itself, are primarily designed to mock through degradation. Identifying the vulgar word for excrement, *kak,* in the name of Akakii Akakievich carries considerably more conviction than acknowledging tendentiously pious correspondences that have been suggested with the holy life of St Akakii. Chekhov clearly understood this when he rewrote Gogol in his own sketch, *Death of a Civil Servant* (1883). There he derives the name of his chief character, Cherviakov, from *cherviak,* the Russian word for worm. Both Gogol and Chekhov dehumanise their characters in the names they give them; by contrast, Rabinovitsh's Jew, through all his fantastic misadventures, remains an empathetic fellow creature.

2.

Authoritarianism breeds a reductive society that degrades individuals into stereotypes, and diminishes empathy to stock response. Both Russian and Yiddish literature repeatedly show how tsarism benumbs the popular mind: for Russians, all Jews are thievish, cowardly and alien; for Jews, all Russians are violent, drunken and antisemitic. In different ways, and for different purposes, both Gogol and Rabinovitsh develop narrative strategies that jolt readers into shocked awareness of cant of this kind. *The Overcoat* has tricked generations of readers into revering Akakii Akakievich as the paradigm of suffering humanity. That Gogol takes considerable pains to encourage the sentimental response he intends to explode is evident in a famous passage often quoted to illustrate the tale's putative noble purpose. When he can bear no more of the cruel teasing of his colleagues, Akakii Akakievich reproaches them with one standard, doleful remark which, uttered one day in the presence of a potential new tormentor, effects on the latter—we are expected to believe—an almost mystical conversion:

> . . . for a long time afterwards, even during the gayest moment, [the new clerk] would see that stooping figure with a bald patch in front, muttering pathetically: 'Leave me alone, why do you have to torment me?' And in those piercing words he could hear the sound of others: 'I am your brother.' The poor young man would bury his face in his hands and many times later in life shuddered at the thought of how brutal men could be and how the most refined manners and breeding often concealed the most savage coarseness, even, dear God, in someone universally recognized for his honesty and uprightness . . .
>
> (74)

This extravagant moralising colours into mawkishness by juxtaposition with the very next sentence, in which the narrative voice assures readers that Akakii Akakievich 'worked *with love*' (Gogol's emphasis): that contrary to what fanciful idealism would have us believe, his life's whole purpose and pleasure lies in mechanical copying. Offered a reward for his long service in the form of 'the preparation of a report for another department from a completed file' which entailed 'altering the title page and changing a few verbs from the first to the third person,' he suffers a complete paralysis of capacity, and begs fervently to be allowed to stick to his old work (75). The gullible reader is lured further away from recognising this as persi-

flage by Gogol's hyperbolical presentation of Akakii Akakievich as not only an automaton but also as a pauper, inhabiting a single room in a squalid boarding house, rapidly eating without tasting whatever is set before him (including unnoticed flies), in order to return as soon as possible to that monomaniacal transcription which is his reason for existence:

> After he had copied to his heart's content he would go to bed, smiling in anticipation of the next day and what God would send him to copy. So passed the uneventful life of a man quite content with his four hundred roubles a year . . .
>
> (77)

The predispositions of the liberal reader, determined to see powerful social criticism here, are reinforced at the very moment that they are maliciously undercut. Having first solicited acceptance of Akakii Akakievich as the embodiment of humiliated penury, the narrative then makes it impossible for the attentive reader to understand the cause of this devastating indigence. Akakii Akakievich has no dependants, no indulgences and no recreations. Tracing his character's terror and despair when faced with the appalling prospect of finding eighty roubles for a new overcoat, Gogol, having dragged us through a heart-rending catalogue of all the other necessities Akakii Akakievich cannot afford, then delivers an arithmetical body blow to conventional sentimentalism by briskly informing us how half the required sum has already been saved:

> For every rouble he spent, Akakiy Akakiyevitch would put half a kopeck away in a small box, which had a little slot in the lid for dropping money through, and which was kept locked. Every six months he would tot up his savings and change them into silver. He had been doing this for a long time, and over several years had amassed more than forty roubles.
>
> (85)

By calculating strictly according to Akakii Akakievich's own scrupulous regimen, this represents the startling gross expenditure of eight thousand roubles. Even conceding that this scrimping has gone on for twenty years, what all that money has been spent on remains inexplicable, since Akakii Akakievich has no clothes, no shoes, no linen, and his meagre board and lodging cannot possibly have consumed his entire annual income.[10] Yet Gogol now makes Akakii Akakievich practise mortifying austerities in order to scrape together the rest of the money, an agonizingly comic process which devastatingly transforms the quest for a new overcoat into an unmistakable metaphor for the acquisition of enhanced social status. When the tailor finally delivers the new overcoat to him,

> . . . without doubt it was the most triumphant day in Akakiy Akakiyevitch's whole life . . . [he] continued on his way to the office in the most festive mood. Not

one second passed without his being conscious of the new overcoat on his shoulders, and several times he even smiled from inward pleasure. And really the overcoat's advantages were two-fold: firstly, it was warm; secondly, it made him feel good.

(87-89)

These undercutting narrative devices have, by the end of the tale, demonstrated to readers how they themselves, as much as Akakii Akakievich, have become the object of that sardonic joke upon which *The Overcoat* builds an enduring claim to mastery.

Rabinovitsh similarly sets up persons and situations for which he subtly invites acceptance at face value, before knocking them down to show bemused readers how far they have fooled themselves. The chief narrative device he deploys is that of multiple narrators. On yet another station platform, Sholem Shachnah's misfortunes are related to that well-known itinerant raconteur, Sholem Aleichem, who then purveys them, at third hand, to the reader. The petty dealer recounting the trials of a luckless fellow townsman to Sholem Aleichem soon reveals himself as a man who deals with stereotypes rather than with individuals. To him, Sholem Shachnah is always incompetent, his misadventures always comic, his traumas always overblown. He presents as a one-dimensional view of a stock character what gradually emerges as the complex experience of a defenceless human being whose vulnerabilities are intensified by being a Jew in a Jew-hating world.

In the process of laying bare the depths of this *angst,* however, Rabinovitsh, with ongoing ironic ambiguity, also reveals that Sholem Shachnah is himself as much in the grip of bigotry as everyone around him. In his dream, he typecasts Ivan Zlodi (Ivan 'Thief') as a boorish Gentile peasant, *a goyisher kop,* fit only to be alternately cursed and cajoled in the same way as he himself is daily type-cast as a sub-human alien fit only to travel in the third class. A discriminatory society is shown to warp the humanity of all alike. Confronting the unimaginable in the mirror of his first-class compartment, Sholem Shachnah jumps to the biased conclusion that Yeremei, the station porter, has—true to stereotypical form—cheated him by taking a tip in exchange for a promise to wake him, and then reneged. Yet we know that Yeremei has, ironically, proved as honest as Sholem Shachnah, just as ironically, has genuinely been seated in a first-class compartment. The stock constructs of human existence under tsarism are shown to deconstruct themselves in the process of actual lived experience, in direct proportion as the narrative techniques of Gogol and Rabinovitsh deconstruct the stereotypes they superficially appear to underprop.

3.

The way hats can define status and identity, or the lack of both, has unforgettably been illustrated in our own time by the bowlers of Charlie Chaplin and his eminent progeny, Beckett's tramps Vladimir and Estragon. Rabinovitsh's manipulation of this classic circus device counterpoises two cultural, social and ethical systems between which the *shtetl* Jew must struggle to maintain his balance. Fellow Jews recognise in a man wearing a hat one who is fulfilling the injunction of the *Halakhah,* the religious laws of Judaism, to cover his head as an expression of *yires shoma'yim,* awe for God who dwells above him. Gentiles in tsarist Russia recognize under that hat merely a *zhid,* denied the salvation of the Church and the protection of the Emperor who is its guardian. Thus ironically, what in spiritual terms is made for Jews a symbol of awe before the Almighty, is, in social terms, made for Russians a sign of abasement before the tsar. Where the Jew covers his head to show respect for God, the Gentile uncovers it to show respect for man; where for a Jew a hat imposes the equality of spiritual humility, for the Gentile it confers the superiority of social rank. In this tale, confusing the hats of a Jew and a Russian officer therefore becomes a confusion of identities on several profoundly existential levels.[11] In tsarist Russia, it transforms *zhid,* despised object, into *vashe blagorodie,* respected person, and so contrasts the spiritual definition Jews give themselves with the social denigration imposed on them by others. When he sees himself in the mirror, wearing the alien headgear, Sholem Shachnah experiences what Camus has called 'the divorce between man and his life, the actor and his setting.'[12] His response, within the parameters of this 'absurd' situation, is wholly logical. Since spiritual and social sundering in Russia has been rendered too absolute for a Jew not only ever to be an official, but also ever to be treated with respect, the Jewish response is to divide experience, to live physically under the rule of the tsar, but spiritually under the rule of God.

The artificiality of such a division is pointed in the irony of Rabinovitsh's style. When Sholem Shachnah first sees the officer, he wonders ' . . . mi yodeye vos far a knepl, vos far an odn befokdekh dos iz?' (Y [Yiddish] [**"Iber a Hitl"**] 247) ([Literally] 'Who knows what sort of a button [official], what sort of a lord in his bringing to account this is?')

By making Sholem Shachnah open his deliberations with the Hebrew, rather than the Yiddish, formulation of the question 'Who knows?' Rabinovitsh gives particular weight to the problem being pondered, since Hebrew, as the language of the Revealed Law, is the idiom in which spiritual questions are posed. Sholem

Shachnah then describes the officer's exalted rank with the Hebrew phrase *odn befokdekh,* or literally, 'Lord in your bringing to account.' In the Penitential Prayers recited on the Eve of *Rosh Hashanah,* from which this phrase is drawn, it is the opening of a plea for God, who brings all men to account, to temper with mercy the severity of Absolute Justice.[13] In everyday Yiddish usage it is a form of litotes, calculated, like the metonym *knepl,* button, applied to any man in uniform, to deflate the pretensions of 'man, proud man / Dress'd in a little brief authority.' In Sholem Shachnah's social situation, however, the irony rebounds on itself. The official, as a functionary of the tsar, is truly a 'lord who brings to account.' While Jews may believe that the decrees of Heaven set at naught the legislations of the world, they are in day-to-day experience more victims of the latter than beneficiaries of the former. Since human identity is derived not only from how we define ourselves, but from the roles in which others cast us, Sholem Shachnah's dream of making vast profits out of *imeniyes,* real-estate 'transactions', can never be anything but a delusion in a Gentile world of which he simultaneously is, and is not, a part. His contemplation of the Russian official complacently taking his ease on the station bench offers the bitter alternative to the old wry acceptance of being Jewish, 's'iz shver tsu zayn a yid' ('It's hard to be a Jew'): 'tsu zayn a goy un nokh a knepl dertsu iz, aponim, take gornisht shlekht'. (Y246-47) ('It's not such a bad life to be a Gentile, and an official one at that, with buttons . . . ') (E [English] [**"On Account of a Hat"**] 113)

It is the Russian official, not the Jew, who stretches himself out 'vi baym tatn in vayngorten' ('as if in his father's vineyard'). In the tsar's Russia, the prophetic promise of Isaiah (Isaiah 65: 21-22) seems to have been fulfilled for the Gentile and denied to the Jew.

4.

Because an 'absurd' existence continually displaces the boundaries of possibility, the tale's narrative strategy keeps reality and fantasy in ironic suspension through the device of three overlapping narrative voices. The central comic disaster befalls one whose nickname has been earned through a lifetime of misadventures, and who is thus established as both a *luftmentsh* and a *shlimazl,* a chronic hard-luck case. Although his trials are reported in the minutest detail, suggesting that he has himself divulged them, Sholem Shachnah's ambiguous position at the centre of 'whole crates full of stories and anecdotes' (E111) throws doubt upon the credibility of what is related. The misadventures of the permanently luckless are often exaggerated for the sake of a good yarn. Moreover, the present purveyor of the latest Sholem Shachnah joke

is presented reductively as 'a Kasrilevke merchant, a dealer in stationery, that is to say, snips of paper' (E111). This garrulous conversationalist is purportedly a substantial businessman, yet like Chaucer's Sergeant of the Lawe, he too 'semed bisier than he was.' His tale is offered on seemingly unimpeachable authority to a willing listener who vouches for its truth in terms that radically undermine it:

> I must confess that this true story, which he related to me, does indeed sound like a concocted one, and for a long time I couldn't make up my mind whether or not I should pass it on to you. But I thought it over and decided that if a respectable merchant and dignitary of Kasrilevke, who deals in stationery and is surely no *littérateur* [A kasrilevker yid a soykher, vos handelt mit obriyezkes, iz nit shayekh tsu literatur un geher zikh klal nit on mit keyn sforim]—if he vouches for a story, it must be true; and so I repeat this tale to you in his own words, not adding even a single word of my own.
>
> (E112; Y244)

At the same moment that the littérateur Sholem Aleichem blandly invites us to believe that only literary people, corrupted by fiction, tell lies, he explicitly establishes that what he relates is a story told by one *luftmentsh* about another. If one can believe that, his two separate strategies of disverification imply, one can believe anything.

Rabinovitsh then inserts into the stationer's narrative what, by virtue of endless repetition, become two choric refrains that further undercut the veracity of what is being reported. The first is a regular assurance—'sholem-shakhne heyst es' ('Sholem Shachnah, that is')—that Sholem Shachnah is really the subject of the bizarre events described. This repetition, because it is directly meant to challenge credulity, goes far beyond the necessity often demanded in Yiddish speech-narration to remove ambiguity about which of two persons spoken about is specifically meant. The second common Yiddish speech-narrative device, a frequent call for rapt attention to maintain a listener's suspense—'ir horkht tsi neyn?' ('Are you listening or not?')—comes, when read in this context, to demand, 'Believe, if you dare, that a *shtetl* Jew is treated with respect by tsarist authority-worshippers who treat all Jews with scorn, and all officials with servility'. What reduces all this to 'absurdity' for the Jew is that stock respect is accorded to an outward sign through which Christian officials render unto Caesar what for Jews is due unto God.

This use of multiple narrators forces the reader carefully to distinguish between whose views of events are actually being offered, and consequently to puzzle over where the truth of what is related actually lies. The stationer recounts Sholem Shachnah's misadventures with heavy irony, not only for sport but also for self-aggrandizement. In effect, however, his style ends up undercutting him as much as his subject. He classifies Sholem Shachnah as a *dreyer,* a word that, like Rosenfeld's English equivalent 'rattler', can denote both competence and incompetence. The deal from which Sholem Shachnah benefits was actually clinched by a professional man of affairs, Drobkin, 'a groyse, a moyrediker dreyer' ('a great big fearsome rattler, a real-estate broker from way back') (Y244-45; E112). Sholem Shachnah, on the other hand, is a hopeless amateur: according to his itinerant biographer he is not a 'rattler' but a 'rattlebrain', not a *dreyer* but a *drey-zikh.* The double edge of this irony becomes apparent when the reader recognises that it is, after all, to one who himself deals merely in snips of paper that the bumbling Sholem Shachnah appears irremediably provincial. Pretending to possess far greater worldly wisdom than Sholem Shachnah, the butt of his jest, this petty trader in *obriyezkes* ridicules the naïveté of applying traditional Jewish processes of reasoning to situations in the Gentile world where these have no validity. Yet only one brought up to ponder life's problems in the same way could make Sholem Shachnah inwardly debate his petrifying confrontation with the Russian officer in the dialectic of a *yeshive bokher,* a rabbinical student, and choose a course of action according to a pious conviction that God does not suffer injustice to prevail in the world: 'tsi iz dos take a yoysher, az dos gantse bisl oylem-hoze zol arraynfaln tsu eynem, un dem andern gornit?' (Y247) ('So is this Justice, that all the pleasures of the Present World [*oylem-hoze,* as opposed to *oylem-habe,* the World to Come] should be given to one, and nothing to another?') (author's translation)

Playing Gentile games by Jewish rules is rendered even more farcical by Sholem Shachnah's effort to persuade the porter in *gemore-loshn,* the legal language of the Talmud's disquisitions:

> heyoys azoy vi er, sholem-shakhne heyst es, vet zikh tsushparn a bisl ot do oyf eyn ek bank, vu der odn ligt, un heyoys azoy vi er, sholem-shakhne'n heyst es, shoyn di drite nakht, az er hot keyn oyg nisht tsugemakht, hot er moyre, er zol, kholile vekhas, nisht farshpetikn dem poyezd, alkeyn zol er, yareme heyst es, lemenashem, tomer shloft er, im oyfvekn, sholem-shakhne'n heyst es, vorum morgn oyf der nakht hobn mir yontev, peysekh . . .

(Y247-48)

(Whereas it will transpire that he, Sholem Shachnah of that name, will repose himself for a short while even here on a corner of that bench upon which the lord reclines, and inasmuch as it has befallen that it is now the third night that he, the Sholem Shachnah aforesaid, has not closed an eye, and he is in great fear lest he, may the Almighty forbid and avert it, might delay and hence take nothing by his motion to board the steam car, therefore on that account let him, Yeremei of that name, for the sake of the Holy One Blessed be He, be sure to awaken him, the Sholem Shachnah aforesaid, lest he be asleep, for wherefore on the morrow at night do we celebrate the Festival of Passover . . .)

(author's translation)

Giving Sholem Shachnah high-flown Talmudic legal language at this critical juncture enables the second narrator to deride him as a *shtetl* innocent abroad. But in the act of mocking the small-time Jew for trying to control the big-time Russian bureaucracy, we are moved to recognise the incapacity of the life experience of all Jews in tsarist Russia.

Hence the culminating irony of the tale is that, for the *shtetl* of Kasrilevke, the ultimate falsehood is not Sholem Shachnah's dream of financial success, but his experience of obsequious treatment on a railway station. Importantly, the jeering of children, so soon themselves to be Jewish adults in a Jew-hating world, suggests that, for one glorious moment, they themselves indulge a wish-fulfilment fantasy that becomes real in direct proportion to the gusto with which they reject it. At the same time as their mocking use of Russian titles of respect satirize Imperial Russia's obsession with rank, it also suggests how good it must feel to be so addressed, and how impossible that is for Russian Jews:

> But where from a big business deal? Where from a forest? It was all horsefeathers! They held their sides with laughter! They pointed at him with their fingers! Others asked him: 'How did you feel, Reb Sholem Shachnah, to wear a cap with a red band and a visor?' Others wanted to know whether it was really as good to travel first-class as the whole world claimed? And as for the naughty children, whole gangs of them ran after him— you hear what I say—and shouted out after him, 'Vashe blagorodie! Vashe visoka blagorodie! Vashe visoka visoka blagorodie!'

> —You think it's so easy to put one over on Kasrilevke?

(E118)

Though Kasrilevke steadfastly refuses to believe either of Sholem Shachnah's stories, both are, ironically enough, perfectly true. In his ineffectual way, Sholem Shachnah did make a small commission as a distant middleman. In all its grotesquerie he did indeed also don the wrong hat and received the deference demanded by rank. But incapable of believing that a Jew can possibly have any identity outside the confines of his own *shtetl* world, Sholem Shachnah himself insists on falsifying both truths, and is doubly victimised for his pains. By denying both reality and fantasy, the people of Kasrilevke, as much as Sholem Shachnah himself, unwittingly interrogate the nature of reality for Jews under tsarism. Try as they will, they cannot live simultaneously inside and outside the profane values of the secular world. Within their *shtetl,* they may attempt to define a meaningful identity for themselves, but that *shtetl* is unavoidably part of the Russian Empire, which defines, through intensifying government persecution, the precariousness of both identity and existence. Their self-chosen division of experience can never be complete: balanced against their own *modus vivendi* is another, which insists on redefining their identity to the extent of erasing it altogether.

5.

The narrative makes the dimensions of this abstract problem concrete through depicting recurrent journeys that become metaphors of rootlessness, whether undertaken in the wagons of peasants, or in that terrifying destroyer of all boundaries and distinctions—the train.[14] The paper-dealer's condemnation of the train is given, through the connotative varieties of the different registers in which he voices it, the force of an extra-textual digression which pinpoints the principal source of Jewish dispossession:

> pruvt akorsht, zayt moykhl, gebn a for-aroys oyf a tsikavest tsu undz, keyn kasrilevke heyst es, mit der nayer ban, vos me hot undz a toyve geton un tsugefirt, vet ir filn a tam gan-eydn! ir vet shoyn farzogn kindskinder! vorum biz ir kumt keyn zlodievke, veyst ir nokh, as ir fort, un az ir kumt keyn zlodievke, hot ir a *peresadka,* dos heyst, ir darft zikh iberzetsn oyf der nayer ban, vos me hot undz a toyve geton un tsugefirt keyn kasrilevke. badarft ir koydem blaybn shteyn oyf etlekhe sho loyt der *raspisanije,* oyb me farshpetikt nit, un ven? akurat nokh halbe nakht, ven s'iz gut mlosne oyfn hartsn un es vilt zikh gut shlofn, un s'iz nishto afilo vu dem kop tsutsushparn - nisht umzist zogn undzere kasrilevker khakhomim un fartaytshn, vi ayer tevye taytsht: *tov shem meshemon tov - s vami dobre, a bez vas lutzhe.* der pshat iz: az on der ban is geven a sakh beser, vi mit der ban.

(Y245-46)

(Pardon me, just try taking a quick ride out our way on the new train and see how fast you'll arrive. Ah, what a pleasure! Did they do us a favor! I tell you, Mr Sholom Aleichem, for a taste of Paradise such as this you'd gladly forsake your own grandchildren! You see how it is: until you get to Zlodievka there isn't much you can do about it, so you just lean back and ride. But at Zlodievka the fun begins, because that's where you have to change, to get onto the new train, which they did us such a favour by running out to Kasrilevke. But not so fast. First, there's the little matter of several hours' wait, exactly as announced in the schedule—provided, of course, that you don't pull in after the Kasrilevke train has left. And at what time of night may you look forward to this treat? The very middle, thank you, when you're dead tired and disgusted, without a friend in the world except sleep—and there's not one single place in the whole station where you can lay your head, not

one. Not for nothing do the learned men of Kasrilevke explain the matter, as your Tevye explains them, with a quotation from the Holy Book, *'Tov shem meshemon tov,'* and add *'s vami dobre, a bez vas lutzhe'*. The plain, simple meaning is: We were better off without the train.)

(E113)

To place them squarely within the purviews of the ubiquitous tsarist bureaucracy, the mechanical functioning of a railway service like a change of trains (*peresadka*) and a schedule (*raspisanije*), or often the train itself (*poyezd*), are referred to in Russian. But the most devastating verbal indictment against the fragmentation caused by this supposed 'progress' appears in the quotation from Ecclesiastes 7:1, cited first in Hebrew, then reinterpreted with a Russian proverb, and finally paraphrased in plain Yiddish. The generalised moral observation, by virtue of being restated in three languages, each of which carries specific existential connotations for Jews, is thus transformed into a kind of syllogism of reduction. Its first term, the Scriptural teaching that 'a good name is better than precious ointment,' insists on rigorously separating the spiritual from the material, and giving exclusive weight to the former. Its second term, a common Russian proverb, 'With you it's good, and without you it's better,' coarsely acknowledges material benefits, the cost of which ultimately outweighs any advantages gained. The dichotomy thus presented is neatly united and reduced by the Yiddish conclusion, 'We were much better off without the train'. With their mobility curtailed, cut off from contaminating contact with the Gentile world, traditionally observant Jews could indulge the illusion that they lived in daily and holy expectation of the coming of the Messiah. Now, however, the train scatters them about in the void of the outside world, and bursts Jew-hatred violently in upon them. All too often, in Rabinovitsh's work, the train as rapidly separates families forever as it brings carloads of pogromists to raze whole *shtetlekh* where they stand. This is why the station platform appears to Sholem Shachnah a vision of death and the torments of Gehenna:

> bekitzur, gekumen mit tshemodandl keyn zlodievke, hot undzer sholem-shakhne, ir horkht tsi neyn, vos iz shoyn frier tsvey nekht nisht geshlofn, zikh tsugegreyt layden khibut ha'keyver, dos heyst, opvartn a nakht— vos zol me ton?—un genumen zukhn an ort oyf tsutsuzetsn zikh. ver? vos?—nishto! ongeroykhert, ongeshpign, fintster, khoyshekh.

(Y246)

(To make a long story short, when our Sholem Shachnah arrived in Zlodievka with his carpetbag he was half dead; he had already spent two nights without sleep. But that was nothing at all to what was facing him—he still had to spend the whole night waiting in

157

the station. What shall he do? Naturally he looked around for a place to sit down. Whoever heard of such a thing? Nowhere. Nothing. No place to sit. The walls of the station were covered with soot, the floor was covered with spit. It was dark, it was terrible.)

(E113)

Rosenfeld's otherwise sound English version does not fully convey the apocalyptic connotations of the Hebrew words deliberately employed in this description. Sholem Shachnah comes to the station prepared to endure 'khibut ha'keyver', the punishment of the wicked after death; the smoke-filled grime that surrounds him is not only murk, but *khoyshekh,* recalling the 'khoshekh al p'nei t'hom' or 'darkness which was upon the face of the deep' before Divine Light brought the world out of chaos. Subconscious terror that for Jews, too, 'the centre cannot hold; / Mere anarchy is loosed upon the world' racks the dream which disturbs his exhausted sleep by vividly bodying forth 'a gants farplontenish', 'a total derangement' of self and station which Jews suffer outside the confines of *shtetl* and community.[15] Once again he finds himself a passenger in a Gentile conveyance, this time hastening to impose order on an aggregatingly chaotic existence by observing the ritual of the Passover *Seder.* In the wagon of the *orl,* the uncircumcised one, Sholem Shachnah's ability to perform his religious obligations as a member of the Covenant is made dependent on the goodwill of one who is specifically placed outside that Covenant. The Festival of Freedom must ironically still be celebrated in Egypt, where the alternative to being painfully dragged thither is being hurtled along at a breakneck speed which, in tearing off his hat, threatens. to obliterate him both spiritually and physically: 'nokh a minut—un er vert tseshotn' ('another moment and he'd be scattered [to pieces]') (Y249). Sholem Shachnah's instinctive reaction emblematises his desperation to preserve his selfhood: ' . . . [er] khapt zikh mit beyde hent baym kop un klogt zikh, az er hot farloyren dos hitl'. (Y249) ('He seized his head with both hands and bewailed the fact that he had lost his hat.') (author's translation)

Agonized over the loss of his entire identity as a Jew that hatlessness emblematises, Sholem Shachnah endures the fearsome climax of his terror fantasy when the wagon suddenly stops dead still in the middle of an open field where, hatless and homeless, he must confront an existence utterly deprived of defining parameters. At this precise moment, he is abruptly awakened from a dream to a reality which actualises his worst fears—in the hurly-burly of a railway station, he unwittingly not only loses his own hat but puts on that of the official; not only sheds his identity as a Jew, but assumes that of a Gentile; not only discards his lowliness as one of the oppressed, but gains the status of

one of the oppressors. Dream and reality merge: 'di mashmoes, az der kholem iz nit keyn kholem' (Y249) ('the probability is that the dream is not a dream'). He awakens from identitilessness in the middle of an imaginary open field, into identitilessness in an all-too-real 'field of [Gentile] folk.'

6.

This tale, which appears in a volume of Rabinovitsh's stories posthumously entitled *Fun peysekh biz peysekh (From Passover to Passover)*, is set on the eve of *z'man kheyruteynu*, 'the time of our freedom', that Festival which celebrates God's redemption of His Chosen People from bondage. This Festival's significance informs both the frame narration and the story proper. The paper-dealer regrets that Sholem Aleichem is in a hurry to get home because it is once again *erev peysekh* (Y243), the same necessity that was the source of all Sholem Shachnah's misfortunes. In the Diaspora, the Passover *Seder* recalls the promise of redemption in its concluding prayer, 'Next year in Jerusalem'. The pain of this unfulfilled wish is intensified for Sholem Shachnah personally when he is compelled to spend 'both *Seders* among strangers in the house of a Jew in Zlodievka' (E117). True Jewish belonging is shown to depend upon individual families and personal dwelling-places. Sholem Shachnah's concern, having made a little money, is to send it home immediately to provide his family with the means of celebrating the Festival with the dignity it simultaneously demands, and in turn bestows on its celebrants (Y245; E112).

In egging on the Ivan Zlodi of his dream, Sholem Shachnah urges his need to be home in time for *paska nasha yevreiska*, 'our Jewish Easter', hoping to wrest respect for his own religious observances by equating them with those of the Christian. The Ukrainian waggoner can only be encouraged to do Jews a favour by a false correspondence between his religion and theirs, just as Russian station officials can only be prevailed upon to treat a Jew with dignity when they falsely take him for one of themselves. To survive in Exile, this tale suggests, a Jew can only survive through guile. Ironically, however, Sholem Shachnah has no conscious intention to deceive. He knows there is no similarity between *Peysekh* and Easter with the same conviction that he knows it is not he but the Russian official who has been awakened and put into a first-class compartment. Yet we know, as clearly as does Rabinovitsh who writes the tale, that there is indeed a direct connection between *Peysekh* and Easter, just as we know that Sholem Shachnah is indeed wearing an alien hat. The deliberate juxtaposition of *Peysekh* and Easter, like the confusion of signifying hats, invites the ambivalent recognition that in the tsar's Russia, both Jews and Christian annually celebrate a festival of spiritual redemption under conditions that testify only to temporal subjugation.

In its widest implications, this confusion of real with ideal touches the nerve centre of Jewish identity in the Russian *goles*, Exile. Jews are, theologically speaking, God's Chosen People singled out for a particular spiritual mission, just as they are, politically speaking, the tsar's rejected subjects, singled out for specific persecution. Viewing the prospects of their long-term survival, they must cling to faith in a God who gives no evident sign of his benevolent intentions, in despite of terror at a tsar whose malign purposes are daily apparent. In such an ambiguous state of being, human assurance cannot exist. Hence Sholem Shachnah's wife is above all enraged by the import of his telegram:

> zi hot zikh a nem gegebn tsu im gants raiyel. zi hot tsu im nisht gehat keyn taynes nit defar, vos er iz nit gekumen oyf yontev aheym, un nisht far'n roytn okoleshok mit der kokarde—neyn! dos alts iz zi im dervayl moykhl; derfar vet zi zikh shoyn mit im shpeter rekhenen;—a tayne tsu im hot zi gehat nor far der depesh. un nit azoy far der depesh, ir horkht tsi neyn, vi far'n vort '*bezpremyenno*'. velkher gute yor hot im getrogn, er zol raykh makhn kazna: '*bezpremyenno yedu paska domoi*'? un bekhlal vi kon a lebediker mentsh zogn '*bezpremyenno*'? . . .

(Y253)

> (And did she give him a royal welcome! Did she lay into him! Mind you, she didn't complain about his spending the holiday away from home, and she said nothing about the red band and the visor. She let that stand for the time being; she'd take it up with him later. The only thing she complained about was—the telegram! And not so much the telegram—you hear what I say?—as the one short phrase, 'without fail'. What possessed him to put that into the wire: Arriving home Passover 'without fail'? Was he trying to make the telegraph company rich? And besides, how dare a human being say 'without fail' in the first place?)

(E117)

For her, the waste of money is aggravated by its open defiance of a Scriptural teaching: 'Boast not thyself of tomorrow; for thou knowest not what a day may bring forth' (Proverbs 27:1). Her more immediate awareness, however, is that in tsarist Russia no Jew can ever consider himself safe, as the fact that the telegram had to be written in the Russian language makes clear. Her rage is therefore provoked both by an unshakable conviction that in the mortal world, under God, no human being can determine his future, and that in the Russian world, under the tsar, no Jew can ever be safe. Her impotent fury is thus chiefly directed, through the absurd plight of her unfortunate husband, against a condition of human and particularly of Jewish existence that appears unalterable. The accident that so radically altered it for Sholem Shachnah, even briefly, underscores the appalling disparity between things as they could be, and thing as they are.[16]

7.

While both Gogol and Rabinovitsh maintain the *status quo* of their respective worlds, the former preserves it as inherently beneficent, and the latter as irremediably to be endured. Where Gogol's humour upholds tsarism by making it, however grotesquely, the instrument of restored justice, Rabinovitsh upholds human values, and the Jewish faith that informs them, in the teeth of Gentile persecution. Akakii Akakievich's ghostly visitation makes an insecure and self-important blusterer into a better administrator for the tsar, while he himself receives from his exalted superiors in spirit what was denied him in flesh:

> The encounter had made a deep impression on [the Important Person]. From that time onwards he would seldom say, 'How dare you! Do you realise who is standing before you?' to his subordinates. And if he did have occasion to say this, it was never without first hearing what the accused had to say. But what was more surprising than anything else, the ghostly clerk disappeared completely. Obviously the general's coat was a perfect fit.

(107)

Gogol, perceiving in tsarism not mortal wounds to the condition of being human but rather blemishes on the perfect face of absolutism, burns them off with derision. Rabinovitsh, recognising his powerlessness to heal these wounds, uses laughter to soothe them.[17] Sholem Shachnah is restored from identitiless terror to the bosom of home and family, where even the tirade of his wife and the ridicule of his townsfolk are redemptive, because they reassert, in wholeheartedly human terms, those relationships which confer and receive meaning from his existence. The difference, after all, between a *luftmentsh* and a ghost is finally the difference between being alive and being dead.

Notes

1. See, for instance, H. Iswolsky, *Christ in Russia: The History, Tradition and Life of the Russian Church,* Kingswood, Bruce, 1962, pp. 110-21.

2. See James H. Billington, *The Icon and the Axe: An Interpretive History of Russian Culture,* New York, Vintage, 1970, pp. 290-6.

3. Quoted in Charles Madison, *Yiddish Literature: Its Scope and Major Writers,* New York: Schocken, 1971, p. 96.

4. Richard Peace, *The Enigma of Gogol,* Cambridge, Cambridge University Press, 1981, pp. 9-10.

5. N. V. Gogol, *The Overcoat* in *Diary of a Madman and Other Stories,* in Ronald Wilks, trans. and ed., Harmondsworth, Penguin, 1982, p. 76. All quotations and page references from *The Overcoat* are from this translation.

6. Richard Peace, *The Enigma of Gogol,* p. 143.

7. Of the destination to which Gogol's tortured humour led him, James Billington observes: 'Gogol . . . could find no guiding road except one which led to destruction—first of his later works and then of the frail body which had linked him with the world. The caricatured figures of *Dead Souls* . . . reveal Gogol's fascination with human disfigurement . . . But there is no bearer of salvation, nothing as compelling as the images of evil and blight.' James H. Billington, *The Icon and the Axe,* p. 339.

8. Rabinovitsh's response to tsarist tyranny is also explored by David G. Roskies, *Against the Apocalypse: Responses to Catastrophe in Modern Jewish Culture,* Cambridge, Mass., Harvard University Press, 1984, pp. 163-92.

9. S. Y. Rabinovitsh, pseud. Sholem Aleichem, 'Iber a Hitl' in *Ale verk fun Sholem Aleichem,* II, *Fun peysekh biz peysekh,* Vilna, Kletskin, 1925, pp. 243-54. English version, "On Account of a Hat," translated by Isaac Rosenfeld, in Irving Howe and Eliezer Greenberg, eds., *A Treasury of Yiddish Stories,* New York, Schocken, 1973, pp. 111-18. All quotations and page references from the Yiddish original are incorporated into the text between parentheses after the letter Y, and from the English translation after the letter E. In places I have rephrased the published English version where it lacks important nuances.

10. Richard Peace, *The Enigma of Gogol,* p. 142, p. 325n. Peace persuasively re-reads *The Overcoat* simply by making this elementary calculation—something that appears obvious, but which the majority of readers rarely do.

11. The significance of his hat to Sholem Shachnah has been noted by Murray Baumgarten, 'Clothing and Character' in David Neal Miller, ed., *Discovering the Canon: Essays on Isaac Bashevis Singer,* Leiden, Brill, 1986, pp. 89-91. I do not share Baumgarten's implication on p. 90 that since 'Sholem Shachnah cannot accept the good fortune of even momentarily being someone he isn't', he really wants to be accepted by the Gentile world.

12. Albert Camus, *The Myth of Sisyphus,* quoted in Martin Esslin, *The Theatre of the Absurd,* Harmondsworth, Penguin, 1968, p. 23.

13. The liturgical sentence in Hebrew, from which this phrase is taken, reads, 'adon b'fokdakh enosh lab'korim b'mitzui ha-din al timtakh', literally, 'O Lord, in Your bringing [of man] to account every morning, do not be over-strict in Your judgement'. See *Seder slikhot l'erev rosh ha-shanah,* Vilna, 1855, p. 57.

14. The arrival of railroads aroused similar consternation in Russians as well. Railroads provoked a 'sense of confusion and bitterness'; and 'brought the first massive intrusion of mechanical force into the timeless, vegetating world of rural Russia, and a great increase in social and thus class mobility throughout the empire.' See James H. Billington, *The Icon and the Axe,* pp. 382-5.

15. David Roskies notes: 'The dream sequence . . . is the storyteller's shorthand for the hero's psychic state. It is also the pivotal point in the story, where reality gives way to hallucination. For once Sholem Shachnah awakens, he no longer knows what world he's in. Which brings us to the central theme of the story—the crisis of identity.' David G. Roskies, 'On Account of Two Hats' in N. B. Cardin and D. W. Silverman, eds., *The Seminary at 100,* New York, Jewish Theological Seminary of America, 1987, p. 245.

16. The complexities of this story have been summarised by Ruth Wisse: 'The kernel 'story' of "On Account of a Hat" . . . was once told to me as a regional Jewish joke, in about ten seconds. Out of this insubstantial matter, Sholem Aleichem has woven a masterpiece with a dozen interpretations: it is the plight of the Diaspora Jew, an exposure of rootlessness, a mockery of tyranny, the comic quest for identity, a Marxist critique of capitalism, and, of course, an ironic self-referential study of literary sleight of hand . . . It is easy to mock the highfalutin readings this story has received, but those who catch its serious import are not wrong either.' Irving Howe and Ruth R. Wisse, eds., *The Best of Sholom Aleichem,* London, Weidenfeld and Nicolson, 1979, p. xxvi.

17. Gogol's influence on Rabinovitsh is undoubted, but critics dispute the nature of that influence. In a review in *The New Republic,* 9 November 1987, p. 39, cols. 1-2, David Roskies argues that 'what is most prized today in Sholem Aleichem's work owed its inspiration to Gogol.' However, the *mentshlekhkayt* characteristic of Rabinovitsh, even in the darkest stories of his last period, seems to me entirely absent from Gogol, whose sardonic mockery precludes either compassion or hope.

Howard Stern (essay date 2002)

SOURCE: Stern, Howard. "Shprintze, or Metathesis: On the Rhetoric of the Fathers in Sholem Aleichem's *Tevye the Dairyman.*" In *Literary Paternity, Literary Friendship: Essays in Honor of Stanley Corngold,* edited by Gerhard Richter, pp. 337-44. Chapel Hill: University of North Carolina Press, 2002.

[In the essay that follows, Stern attempts a rhetorical analysis of four of the father-daughter pairs in Tevye

the Dairyman, *fitting each daughter's particular situation into a tropological system consisting of the ignoramus, the righteous, the intermediate, and the wicked.*]

It would be hard to think of a novel more intensely concerned with the joys and sorrows of fatherhood than Sholem Aleichem's *Tevye the Dairyman.* In four of the novel's five central chapters, Tevye loses a daughter in marriage—whether hopefully, resignedly, reluctantly, or kicking and screaming—and in the fifth he loses a daughter to suicide when the engagement is broken. Needless to say, pathos abounds—more than enough for a relatively short novel; indeed, more than enough for a novel, stage play, musical, and movie. But the father-daughter relation is of tropological as well as thematic interest. Sholem Aleichem assigns to each daughter (more precisely: to each daughter's ambit) a characteristic figure of thought that derives from the limited repertory of Tevye's paternal discourse and that turns out to control, with astonishing rigor, the political and social the-matics of that daughter's chapter. Thus *Tevye the Dairyman* combines features of the tearjerker and the handbook of rhetoric; it organizes a welter of highly charged material according to a grid of systematic tropes. To describe the novel in this way is to suggest affinities with other classics of the early twentieth century: Joyce's *Ulysses,* for example, or Berg's *Wozzeck.* One goal of the present paper is to confirm Benjamin Harshav's thesis that the virtuoso display of premodern modes of discourse in Sholem Aleichem paradoxically establishes a unique Yiddish variant of European modernism.[1]

It will have to suffice here to demonstrate the tropological system at its most explicit moment, the chapter **"Shprintze"**, ["Hope"] and then to adumbrate connections with the rest of the novel. We begin with a rather puzzling conversation between Tevye and the happy-go-lucky Ahronchik, who has quietly been courting the eldest available daughter, Shprintze:

"A good evening!" I said to him.

"And to you, too," he replied. He stood there a little awkwardly with a blade of grass in his mouth, stroking his horse's mane; then he said, "Reb Tevye, I have an offer to make you. Let's you and I swap horses."

"Don't you have anyone better to make fun of?" I asked him.

"But I mean it," he says.

"Do you now?" I say. "Do you have any idea what this horse of yours is worth?"

"What would you price him at?" he asks.

"He's worth three hundred rubles if a cent," I say, "and maybe even a little bit more."

Well, Ahronchik laughed, told me his horse had cost over three times that amount, and said, "How about it, then? Is it a deal?"

I tell you, I didn't like it one bit: what kind of business was it to trade such a horse for my gluepot? And so I told him to keep his offer for another day and joked that I hoped he hadn't come just for that, since I hated to see him waste his time. . . .

"As a matter of fact," he says to me, as serious as can be, "I came to see you about something else. If it's not too much to ask of you, perhaps the two of us could take a little walk."[2]

What is the rationale of this proposed exchange, which is never mentioned again? One could certainly answer that there needn't be any rationale, since Ahronchik has already been richly characterized as the initiator of many acts of capricious or whimsical generosity—bestowing a fistful of money upon a beggar, taking a brand-new jacket off his back to thrust it upon a perfect stranger, and so on. Still the horse trade seems to be featured as especially pointless, and it leads directly (the "little walk") to Ahronchik's asking for the hand of Shprintze in marriage. The key to this scene is not Ahronchik's casual generosity—the disproportion of what he bestows on others—but the very principle of exchange: I take what you have and you take what I have. Only in a world governed by the principle of exchange can social relations be understood as reversible enough to permit the marriage of a millionaire's son and a milkman's daughter. As Tevye himself puts it, Ahronchik's mother would have no "reason to be ashamed of me . . . because if I wasn't a millionaire myself, I would at least have an in-law who was, while the only in-law she'd have would be a poor beggar of a dairyman; I ask you, then, whose connections [*yikhes*] would be better, mine or hers?" (92). Such a reading of the horse trade may seem extravagant at first, but it is supported by the text on every level from the narrative down to the phonological. It will be remembered that **"Shprintze"** begins with a discussion of Russia's liberal constitution of 1905, which triggered a series of pogroms and persecutions in the Pale of Settlement. The rich Jews of Yehupetz (Kiev) have abandoned their dachas in Boiberik and fled to other parts; Tevye's dairy business, however, has continued to blossom because rich Jews from other parts have been flocking to Boiberik: "But why, you ask, are they all running here? For the same reason, I tell you, that we're all running there! It's an old Jewish custom to pick up and go elsewhere at the first mention of a pogrom. How does the Bible put it? *Vayisu vayakhanu, vayakhanu vayisu*—or in plain language, if you come hide in my house, I'd better go hide in yours" (83). The Hebrew words quoted here ("and they journeyed and they camped, and they camped and they journeyed") are not to be found in the Bible in this configuration; the chiasmus that expresses reversibility here is directly attributable to the liberal constitution, which Tevye cannot pronounce and persists in fracturing as *kosnitutsye*—that is to say, chiasmus as a figure of words derives from metathesis as a figure of sound (ns/sn). The tragedy of **"Shprintze"** can thus be summarized as follows: a brief hope-dream of social mobility inspired rhetorically by a metathetic liberal constitution reveals itself as deceptive, and the world returns to its customary state of irreversible relations—which state is then explored in the following chapter, **"Tevye Leaves for the Land of Israel."**[3]

Since Tevye seems unable to discuss any issue for more than two sentences without quoting Biblical, rabbinic, or liturgical support—*vayisu vayakhanu* being only a slender pseudoquotation—it seems reasonable to expect the rhetorical system uncovered here to be anchored in some genuine holy-tongue material; and so it is. Late one evening Tevye is summoned to the dacha of Ahronchik's mother in Boiberik, and he speculates on the reason: "What can be so urgent, I wondered as I drove there. If they want to shake hands on it and have a proper betrothal, it's they who should come to me, because I'm the bride's father . . . only that was such a preposterous thought that it made me laugh out loud: who ever heard of a rich man going to a poor one for a betrothal? Did I think that the world had already come to an end . . . and that the tycoon and the beggar were now equals, *sheli shelkho* and *shelkho sheli*—you take what's mine, I take what's yours, and the Devil take the hindmost?" (92-93). The Hebrew here is taken from the (for our purposes marvelously titled) Mishnaic tract *Pirkey Avot* ("Ethics, or better: Sayings of the Fathers"). Chapter V, verse 10 reads as follows: "There are four qualities in a human being: he who says, what's mine is mine and what's yours is yours, that is the intermediate quality. And some say, that is the quality of Sodom. What's mine is yours and what's yours is mine—an ignoramus. What's mine is yours and what's yours is yours—a righteous man. What's yours is mine and what's mine is mine—a wicked man." How appropriate that Tevye associates Ahronchik, subconsciously perhaps, with the quality of an ignoramus! But the important reason for quoting this compass-rose of the Mishnaic fathers in its entirety is that each of the four quadrants plays a role in the novel: each designates in traditional Jewish terms the governing trope of a daughter (again, more precisely, of a daughter's ambit). There are four quadrants and five daughters because the youngest daughter, Beilke, repeats the story of the eldest, Tsaytl, with an alternative (tragic) outcome. It remains now to sketch these connections.

In the case of Hodl, who marries a communist and follows him into Siberian exile, "what's mine is yours and what's yours is yours"—the communist Peppercorn (Yiddish: Feferl) is memorably figured as a righteous man. Hodl maintains of him and his revolutionary comrades that "they were the best, the finest, the most honorable young people in the world, and that they lived their whole lives for others, never giving a fig for their own skins" (63). "Her husband, she swore, was as clean as the driven snow. 'Why,' she said, 'he's a person who never thinks of his own self! His whole life is for others, for the good of the world'" (68). (The key phrases in Yiddish here are *nor fun yenems vegn* and *yenems toyve*.) Many years later, in telling the story of Beilke (**"Tevye Leaves for the Land of Israel"**), Tevye actually brings himself to concur in this assessment: "At least that Peppercorn of hers is a human being—in fact, too much of one, because he never thinks of himself, only of others" (109). (*Er aleyn iz bay zikh hefker, un der gantser iker iz di velt.*) It must be admitted that the crucial formulation of righteousness from *Pirkey Avot* is not explicitly present in **"Hodl"**—whether because Sholem Aleichem preferred to submerge the tropological scheme in a wealth of figurative variations, or possibly because the explicit rabbinic theme of those variations did not occur to him until a later stage in the serial publication of the novel—but the structure is evident, given the explicit citation in **"Shprintze"** and the constant informing presence of "Sayings of the Fathers" throughout the novel.

To confirm our reading of **"Shprintze"** and **"Hodl,"** we turn to Beilke's chapter, which invokes both of them, thematically as well as rhetorically. Beilke, the youngest daughter, has sacrificed her own happiness by marrying a very rich middle-aged vulgarian in order to make life easier for her father (this is the sacrifice that Tsaytl, the eldest daughter, was ultimately saved from making in **"Today's Children"**; hence the tropological congruence of these two chapters). Tevye attempts to forestall the sacrifice by pointing out that "'money is a lot of hooey, anyway, just like the Bible says. Why, look at your sister Hodl! She hasn't a penny to her name, she lives in a hole in the wall at the far end of nowhere—and yet she keeps writing us how happy she is with her schlimazel of a Peppercorn.' Shall I give you three guesses what my Beilke answered me? 'Don't go comparing me to Hodl,' she says. 'In Hodl's day the world was on the brink. There was going to be a revolution and everyone cared about everyone. Now the world is its own self again, and it's everyone for his own self again, too.' That's what she said, my Beilke—just go figure out what she meant" (103). The Yiddish here is more accurate in describing the condition of the world in Hodl's day: *hot men zikh gezorgt far der velt, un zikh hot men fargesn*—not "everyone cared for everyone" (reciprocity or revers-ibility = ignorance), but "one cared about the world and forgot oneself" (righteousness). Beilke often speaks as though her world were the exact opposite of Hodl's, and this move is understandable since Hodl was her father's choice of counter-example. Actually, though, Beilke's insistence on self-identity and social rigidity proves that "what's mine is mine and what's yours is yours"—her world is the exact opposite of Shprintze's (which of course had no stability).[4]

It must be admitted that this moment in the text achieves a maximum of tropological density and even ambiguity—partly because the story of Beilke not only revises the story of Tsaytl and rejects the story of Hodl, but also serves as a bravura recapitulation of all the previous episodes.[5] Nevertheless, we can adduce another powerful piece of evidence for the deep analysis according to four quadrants. Podhotzur, the rich vulgarian, who is naturally impervious to Tevye's theory of in-law reversibility (or *yikhes* relativity) as developed in **"Shprintze,"** demands that his father-in-law either give up the dairy business or, better still, remove himself to either America or Palestine. Since Tevye has always wanted to see the Holy Land any-way (more precisely, to inhabit the five books of Moses), Palestine is decided upon. Later, mortified by her complicity in this attempted erasure of the father, Beilke bursts into tears and Tevye begins to comfort her: "'Have you forgotten that God is still in His heaven and your father is still a young man? Why, it's child's play for me to travel to Palestine and back again, just like it says in the Bible: *vayisu vaya-khanu*—and the Children of Israel knew not if they were coming or going. . . . ' Yet the words were no sooner out of my mouth than I thought, Tevye, that's a big fat lie! You're off to the Land of Israel for good— it's bye-bye Tevye forever" (112). Here the spatial and social reversibility of **"Shprintze"** is reinterpreted temporally, and the point is: it's no longer available (if it ever was). At the end of a series of tropological in-ventions on the theme of confusing mine and thine, everything is what it is. Such was already the condi-tion of the world in Tsaytl's day; but at least it fol-lowed then as a consequence that people could be who *they* were: Tsaytl did not have to sacrifice herself by marrying the rich middle-aged vulgarian (the butcher Layzer Wolf), but could start a life of penurious felic-ity with her dreamboat of a tailor boy, Motl Komzoyl. Beilke is not so lucky: Podhotzur "has businesses ev-erywhere. He spends more on telegrams in a single day than it would cost us to live on for a year. But what good does all that do me if I can't be myself?" (113). Now another saying from "Sayings of the Fa-thers" returns to govern the world as a spectral double of "what's mine is mine and what's yours is yours," namely, Hillel's famous "*im eyn ani li mi li?*" (113)— "If I am not for myself, who will be?"

It remains only to discuss the case of "what's mine is mine and what's yours is mine—a wicked man." The daughter in question here is obviously Chava, who marries the Christian scribe of the village, Chvedka Galagan, and is disowned by her father. It must be ad-mitted that the evidence here is at its least explicit; what we find is a series of encroachments, subsump-tions, misappropriations. Thus, for example, the vil-lage priest turns out to have knowledge of Hebrew— insisting, to Tevye's amusement and horror, that "he knew our Scriptures better than I did and even reciting a few lines of them in a Hebrew that sounded like a Frenchman talking Greek" (71). The Christian sub-sumes the Jew—both his religion and his authority. The priest claims to "think a great deal of you Jews. It just pains me to see how stubbornly you refuse to re-alize that we Christians have your good in mind" (74). Chava is in his "charge," his "custody" (*rshus, hazhgokhe*). Naturally, Tevye is outraged: "I demanded to know . . . what he thought of a man who barged uninvited into another man's house and turned it up-side down—the benches, the tables, the beds, every-thing" (77). As in the diametrically opposite case of Hodl, there is no distinction between mine and thine— Chava denies that "human beings have to be divided into Jews and Christians, masters and slaves, beggars and millionaires" (72). Tevye can only respond that such distinctions will not disappear until the Messiah comes; "but he already has come," says the priest (74). Everything is already "theirs."

This completes our sketch of the tropological system. It would be illuminating now to delve more deeply into the texture of the Yiddish. Our remarks on met-athesis in **"Shprintze"** (*kosnitutsye* for "constitution") would have to be supplemented by aphaeresis in **"To-day's Children"** (*stikratn* for "aristocrats"), prosthesis in **"Tevye Leaves for the Land of Israel"** (*natalye* for "Italy"), syncope in **"Hodl"** (*khlire* for "cholera"), and various types of ellipsis in **"Chava."** But space prohibits. A detailed rhetorical analysis of *Tevye the Dairyman* in Yiddish will be presented to Stanley Corngold—most generous of readers and writers!—on the occasion of his 120th birthday (*biz hundertuntsvantsik!*); or perhaps before.

Notes

The author gratefully acknowledges the assistance of Anita Gallers and Susanne Fusso in developing the ideas and working out the details of the present paper. He thanks David Katz for allowing him to discuss a version of the material with his eager and perceptive students at Yale University. Quotations from Sholem Aleichem refer to *Tevye the Dairyman and the Railroad Stories,* trans. Hillel Halkin (New York: Schocken, 1987).

1. Benjamin Harshav, *The Meaning of Yiddish* (Berkeley: University of California Press, 1990) 98-107.

2. *Tevye,* 88-89. Subsequent references in parentheses.

3. Halkin's "Constantution" misses the point. In general, his translation is funny, ingenious, idiomatic, and a pleasure to read—highly recommendable. Nevertheless, it introduces a number of small errors that tend to obscure the tropological structure of the novel. For example, Halkin dubiously adds the name of Peppercorn to the passage about *vayse khevrenikes* (93). On the other hand, his hilarious metatheses on the name of Podhotzur (Hodputzer, Hodderputz), while not in the Yiddish, are attractive additions to "Tevye Leaves for the Land of Israel" and can be motivated by Tevye's nostalgic preference for the metathetic days of Shprintze.

4. In "Today's Children" the operative rabbinic expression is *"Odom koroyv le'atsmoy*—charity begins at home" (39)—literally: "A man is closest to his own self." Money, of course, is normally understood as a medium of *exchange*; but not exchange in the sense of "Shprintze." According to the tropology of *Tevye the Dairyman,* the world of commerce is governed not by easy exchange but by obstinate hoarding.

5. Two examples of recapitulation: Efrayim the Matchmaker returns from "Hodl" (but recalls Motl Komzoyl—"the matchmaker, the father-in-law, and the groom all rolled into one" (48) from "Today's Children"); and the misunderstanding with Efrayim (101) recalls a similar scene of double entendre with Layzer Wolf (37-8), also in "Today's Children."

FURTHER READING

Criticism

Aarons, Victoria. *Author as Character in the Works of Sholom Aleichem.* New York: Edwin Mellen Press, 1985, 176 p.

Analyzes Aleichem's narrative techniques, rhetorical strategies, and use of humor in his short fiction in light of the political, cultural, and economic upheavals in Eastern Europe around the turn of the twentieth century.

Booth, David. "The Role of the Storyteller—Sholem Aleichem and Elie Wiesel." *Judaism* 42, no. 3 (summer 1993): 298-312.

Focuses on each author's literary response to Jewish despair and suffering, arguing that both favor telling stories, which offer readers a feeling of transcendence, kinship within a living Jewish community, and a shared identity.

Brenner, Rachel Feldhay. "Sholem Aleichem's *Shir ha-shirim*: The Portrait of a Self-Conscious Artist." *Yiddish* 9, no. 2 (1994): 12-29.

Analyzes the intricate narrative structure of *Shir ha-shirim* as it relates to Aleichem's self-examination, vulnerability and loneliness, his maturity as an artist and as an individual, his search for artistic inspiration, and his inability to resolve the tension between a lingering emotional connection with his traditional Jewish past and a sense of alienation from the modern world.

Butwin, Joseph, and Frances Butwin. "The Speaking Voice." In *Sholom Aleichem,* pp. 95-124. Boston: Twayne Publishers, 1977.

Centers on Aleichem's use of *skaz* in his short fiction, emphasizing the nature of the tales as spoken communication.

Frieden, Ken. "Tevye the Dairyman and His Daughters' Rebellion." In *Classic Yiddish Fiction: Abramovitsh, Sholem Aleichem, and Peretz,* pp. 159-82. Albany: State University of New York Press, 1995.

Maintains that by allowing Tevye to quote, misquote, or misappropriate scriptural verses, Aleichem was able to draw attention to ancient Jewish history and tradition in a world undergoing drastic social changes.

Gittleman, Sol. "Stories for Jewish Children." In *Sholom Aleichem: A Non-Critical Introduction,* pp. 143-60. The Hague, The Netherlands: Mouton, 1974.

Examination of the figure of the son in Aleichem's stories about children, discussing it in relation to domineering mothers, subjection to physical abuse, emphasis on learning, and enthusiastic participation in adventures.

Halberstam-Rubin, Anna. "Internal Divisions." In *Sholom Aleichem: The Writer as Social Historian,* pp. 85-98. New York: Peter Lang, 1989.

Discusses Aleichem's portrayal of class divisions within the Jewish community in his plays and short fiction, pointing out that—whether political, economic, or social—conflicts are characterized by antagonism and friction and fraught with bigotry, alienation, greed, exploitation, and resentment.

Samuel, Maurice. "The Children's World." In *The World of Sholom Aleichem,* pp. 286-98. New York: Alfred A. Knopf, 1962.

Reflects on young persons in Aleichem's stories about children, calling them "not simply human beings growing up . . . [but], throughout, Jews, Kasrielevkites, in the making."

Additional coverage of Aleichem's life and career is contained in the following sources published by Gale: *Contemporary Authors,* **Vol. 104 (Brief Entry);** *Dictionary of Literary Biography,* **Vol. 333;** *Literature Resource Center*; *Short Story Criticism,* **Vol. 33;** *Twayne's World Authors*; **and** *Twentieth-Century Literary Criticism,* **Vols. 1, 35.**

Carlos Fuentes
1928-

Mexican novelist, short story writer, playwright, screenwriter, critic, and essayist.

The following entry provides an overview of Fuentes's short fiction. For additional information on Fuentes's life and works, see *SSC,* Vol. 24.

INTRODUCTION

A novelist, short story writer, commentator, and political activist, Fuentes is recognized worldwide as a foremost Latin American writer. Achieving international attention in the late 1950s and early 1960s as an important contributor to the "boom" in Latin American literature, Fuentes is best known for epic novels that revolve around the cultural individuality of Mexico. In his novels as well as in his short fiction he delves into Mexico's past, combining reality with myth in his investigations into its political and power struggles. Of primary interest to him is the complex legacy of Spanish settlement in the New World and the consequent diversity produced in Latin America through war, colonization, and miscegenation. He also focuses on the idea that the true Mexican identity is hidden behind the mask of contemporary society, partially the result of the tremendous power of European and U.S. influence. His short stories, though less popular than his novels, are characterized by unusual treatments of time as well as by surprise endings that often feature an ironic twist. In addition, they frequently emphasize the fantastic and the supernatural.

BIOGRAPHICAL INFORMATION

Fuentes was born in Panama City, Panama, to Berta Macías Rivas and Rafael Fuentes Boettiger, a diplomat who at the time of Fuentes's birth was employed as an attaché for the Mexican government in Panama. Because of his father's work, Fuentes spent much of his childhood in foreign countries; by the time he entered law school in the mid 1940s, he had lived in such cities as Rio de Janeiro, Washington D.C., Santiago, Chile, and Buenos Aires. He earned his LL.B. from the National University of Mexico in 1948, then undertook graduate studies in international diplomacy and law at the Institut des Hautes Études Internation-

ales, in Geneva, Switzerland. In the early 1950s he became Secretary of the Mexican delegation to the International Labor Organization in Geneva, then served an appointment to Mexico's Ministry of Foreign Affairs. Around this same time he began an affiliation with the National University of Mexico, beginning in the Bureau of Cultural Diffusion and becoming head of the department of cultural relations in 1957, a position he held for two years. By this time he had already resolved to become a writer, having published his first story, the experimental "Pastel rancio," in 1949 and the horror tale "Pantera en jazz," about a hysterical man who is convinced a ferocious beast lives in his bathroom, in 1954. That same year Fuentes published his first short story collection, *Los días enmascarados* ("The Masked Days"), which, though it failed to attract much critical or public attention, did secure his entry into the sphere of Mexican letters.

By 1956 he was writing for periodicals and had cofounded the *Revista mexicana de literatura* ("Mexican Review of Literature"). He published his first novel, the experimental *La región más transparente (Where the Air Is Clear)*, in 1958 and gained fame four years later with his third novel, *La muerte de Artemio Cruz* (1962), which achieved worldwide recognition upon its English translation as *The Death of Artemio Cruz* in 1964. Fuentes served as his country's ambassador to France from 1975 to 1977. From 1977 on, in addition to his writing, he has served as lecturer or professor at a number of universities, including Columbia, Harvard, the University of Oklahoma, the University of Concepción in Chile, Cambridge, and the University of Paris. He is also the recipient of several honorary degrees and awards, including the Miguel de Cervantes Prize in 1987 from the Spanish Ministry of Culture; the National Prize in Literature—the highest literary award in Mexico—in 1984; and the first Latin Civilization Award.

MAJOR WORKS OF SHORT FICTION

Among the major themes of Fuentes's short fiction is how the indigenous history of Mexico shapes the Mexican character; the author often uses the ghosts of the country's past—such as Aztec or Mayan gods, or historical figures—to explore how the past informs the collective unconscious of Mexico's citizens, who Fuentes believes to have lost a sense of national identity. He links this loss with the ongoing battle over political control of Mexico, begun with the Spanish conquistadors and continuing into the post-Revolution years. These power struggles are mirrored in Fuentes's fiction through such ruptures as divisions within the father-son relationship, a metaphorical reference to the idea of Mexico as an "orphan," the result of the invasion of the "Other." This notion of the "orphan" is often depicted in the form of an unbalanced character (usually unmarried) who is unable to perceive the world clearly because of a lack of emotional, mental, or physical support. This individual often becomes isolated and uncommunicative, ultimately succumbing to a brutal end due to his or her blindness toward reality. The six stories of *Los días enmascarados* are a blend of irony, allegory, fantasy, satire, surrealism, and magic realism and revolve around the idea of a corrupt and cruel modern world that destroys those who may possess some good. The present and the past intermix as the ghosts and spirits of times past infiltrate and hold the present captive. One of the most discussed tales in the collection is "Chac Mool," considered one of Fuentes's finest and a classic of Mexican literature. Told in large part through the diary entries of its male protagonist, "Chac Mool" centers on middle-aged antiquities collector Filiberto, whose statue of Chac Mool, the rain god of the Mayans, seems to come to life in Filiberto's basement. Attempting to escape his imprisonment under the now-emboldened Chac Mool, Filiberto drowns off the coast of Acapulco under suspicious circumstances. Fuentes leaves the ending ambiguous, as a friend who initially doubts the veracity of Filiberto's account encounters an elderly Indian apparition—apparently the pre-Columbian deity—upon returning Filiberto's body to his home. In "Tlactocatzine, del jardín de Flandes" (translated as either "Tlactocatzine, in the Garden of Flanders" or "In a Flemish Garden"), the young male caretaker of a Mexican mansion is lured into eternal imprisonment by the mad phantom of Carlota, the nineteenth-century Mexican Empress who believes the narrator is her late husband, the Emperor Maximilian I of Mexico, who was executed in 1867. In "Por boca de los dioses" ("Through the Mouth of the Gods"), Oliverio cuts out the lips from a painting of an Indian in a museum. As the lips come to life, mythical Aztec gods pursue Oliverio and he is coerced into confronting his own death by the goddess Tlazol, who stabs him after deriding his manhood.

Recognized as belonging to the tradition of Latin American magic realism, the novella *Aura* (1962) centers on teacher and doctoral student Felipe Montero, who becomes a secretary to an old woman who lives with her young niece, Aura. Felipe and Aura become

lovers but, in the end, the old woman and Aura seem to be one person, and Felipe comes to believe that he is some kind of reincarnation of the old woman's deceased husband, a former Mexican military leader. Revolving around the notion of eternity and the idea of the double, the narrative offers an ambiguous ending: as the account can be viewed as either the supernatural possession of the inner being and intellect of Felipe, or as the tale of the psychologically unstable state of the main character, who in the end becomes a helpless victim of Consuelo, the aunt. Fuentes's second major collection of short fiction, *Cantar de ciegos* ("Songs of the Blind"; 1964), shifts attention away from the supernatural and Mexico's past and toward detailed character studies of individuals in modern society. "La muñeca reina" ("The Doll Queen") centers on a young man's quest to find Amilamia, a female friend from his youth whom he idealizes as embodying all the joy, innocence, and spiritual richness of his childhood. Upon paying a visit to her home he finds her parents holding a perpetual and monstrous funereal remembrance of their daughter (using a doll in a coffin), while they confine and abuse Amilamia, who has grown into a disabled and deformed woman. Revolving around the theme of fantasy/illusion versus reality, the tale questions whether or not the couple is really hideously evil or whether their portrayal in the story, related through the eyes of Carlos, simply reflects Carlos's reaction to them based on his own limited emotional development. Another tale in the collection, "Un alma pura," revolves around the incestuous feelings between a weak brother, Juan Luis, and his assertive, domineering sister. In the story, Juan Luis transfers these forbidden feelings onto his Swiss girlfriend, Claire, whose despair over the abortion he advises her to undergo and over her role as victim in the brother-sister relationship leads to her suicide—an act which is followed in kind by Juan Luis himself.

Fuentes's 1993 collection, *El naranjo, o los círculos del tiempo* (*The Orange Tree*), offers five novellas whose subjects span several centuries, each connected by the image of the orange. For Fuentes, the orange tree signifies the possibilities of beauty, sustenance, transplantation, and rejuvenation. Its seeds were introduced in Spain by Roman and Moorish invaders and reached the New World with the conquistadors. Fuentes illustrates various manifestations of violence, deception, and suffering by recounting episodes from the conquest of Roman Iberia and Mexico, a contemporary corporate takeover, and the death wish of an American actor. In *La frontera de cristal* (*The Crystal Frontier*; 1995), Fuentes turned his attention to the notion of crossing boundaries, in this case mostly internal conflicts that plague and confine his characters. Through nine linked stories, *The Crystal Frontier* considers such barriers as racial bigotry and class discrimination and examines conflicts between the present and the past, colonizer and colonized, youth and the elderly, and the wealth and materialism of the north and the impoverished and indigenous culture of the south. Set in the northern part of the Mexico-U.S. border, the tales express anger over the covetousness and cruelty found in both Mexico and the United States and reveal the internal conflict of the author, who desires the preservation of Mexican culture yet also wishes to erase cultural boundaries. In 2004 Fuentes published a gothic short story collection, *Inquieta compañia* ("Uneasy Company"). In this book he explores Mexico's place in the geopolitical environment and especially the alienation and fear in its people's lives. Two years later he released *Todas las familias felices* (2006), which in 2008 was translated into English as *Happy Families.*

CRITICAL RECEPTION

Though his short fiction has generally received less critical attention than his novels, Fuentes is celebrated as a clever and gifted storyteller. A central line of discussion revolves around how Fuentes's stories relate to his political views. Many of them, especially "Chac Mool," are viewed as blending the fantastic with a social message—that the indigenous Mexican past is still alive and will haunt Mexico until it is recognized as the true identity of the Mexican. This identity, according to how a number of critics read Fuentes's stories, is hidden behind a mask whose goal it is to hide the "backwardness" of Mexico's native culture, which is primarily agricultural and poor. Critical discussion in this vein revolves around how Fuentes's tales reflect Mexico's efforts to destroy or reject its own past, begun during the Conquest and continued into the present through greed and avarice and through acculturation to European or American power. Toward the end of the twentieth century various scholars began reading Fuentes's stories not simply as social or historical, revolving around the wretchedness and violence of real-life Mexico, but as strictly literary pieces, analyzing them with regard to such aspects as their use of myths or symbols, their success as fantasies, their approaches to narration, and their experimental rendering of spacial and temporal elements. Others, however, continue to emphasize the relationship between Fuentes's literary oeuvre and his social and political views, with several commentators pointing out how his short fiction reflects Fuentes's paradoxical belief in the need to preserve a Mexican national identity as well as well as to embrace modernity and its emphasis on multiculturalism and multinationalism.

PRINCIPAL WORKS

Short Fiction

"Pastel rancio" 1949

Los días enmascarados 1954

"Pantera en jazz" 1954

"El muñeco" 1956

"Trigo errante" 1956

Aura [*Aura*] (novella) 1962

Cantar de ciegos (short stories and novellas) 1964

**Dos cuentos mexicanos* 1969

Cuerpos y ofrendas 1972

†*Chac Mool y otros cuentos* 1973

†*Agua quemada: cuarteto narrativo* [*Burnt Water*] 1981

Constancia y otras novelas para vírgenes [*Constancia and Other Stories for Virgins*] (novellas) 1989

El naranjo, o los círculos del tiempo [*The Orange Tree*] 1993

La frontera de cristal: Una novela en nueve cuentos [*The Crystal Frontier: A Novel in Nine Stories*] 1995

Inquieta compañia 2004

Todas las familias felices [*Happy Families: Stories*] 2006

Other Major Works

La región más transparente [*Where the Air Is Clear*] (novel) 1958

Las buenas conciencias [*The Good Conscience*] (novel) 1959

La muerte de Artemio Cruz [*The Death of Artemio Cruz*] (novel) 1962

The Argument of Latin America: Words for North Americans (nonfiction) 1963

Pedro Paramo (screenplay) 1966

Tiempo de morir (screenplay) 1966

Cambio de piel [*A Change of Skin*] (novel) 1967

Los caifanes (screenplay) 1967

Zona sagrada [*Holy Place*] (novel) 1967

Paris: La revolución de mayo (essays) 1968

Cumpleaños (novel) 1969

El mundo de José Luis Cuevas [bilingual edition] (essays) 1969

La nueva novela hispanoamericana (essays) 1969

Casa con dos puertas (essays) 1970

Todos los gatos son pardos (play) 1970; revised and enlarged edition published as *Ceremonias del alba* 1991

El tuerto es rey (play) 1970

‡*Los reinos originarios: Teatro hispano-mexicano* (plays) 1971

Tiempo mexicano (essays) 1971

Terra nostra (novel) 1975; English translation published as *Terra Nostra* 1976

Cervantes, o la crítica de la lectura [*Don Quixote; or, The Critique of Reading*] (essays) 1976

La cabeza de la hidra [*The Hydra Head*] (novel) 1978

Orquídeas a la luz de la luna: comedia mexicana [Orchids in the Moonlight] (play) 1978

Una familia lejana [Distant Relations] (novel) 1980

High Noon in Latin America (nonfiction) 1983

On Human Rights: A Speech (speech) 1984

El gringo viejo [The Old Gringo] (novel) 1985

Latin America: At War with the Past (nonfiction) 1985

Cristóbal nonato [Christopher Unborn] (novel) 1987

Gabriel García Marquez and the Invention of America (criticism) 1987

Myself with Others: Selected Essays (essays) 1988

La campaña [The Campaign] (novel) 1990

Valiente mundo nuevo: Épica, utopía y mito en la novela hispanoamericana (essays) 1990

El espejo enterrado [The Buried Mirror: Reflections on Spain and the New World] (essays) 1992

Geografía de la novela (essays) 1993

Tres discursos para dos aldeas (essays) 1993

Diana, o la cazadora solitaria [Diana, or the Goddess Who Hunts Alone] (novel) 1994

Neuvo tiempo mexicano [A New Time for Mexico] (essays) 1994

Los años con Laura Diaz [The Years with Laura Diaz] (novel) 1999

Instinto de Inez [Inez] (novel) 2001

En esto creo [This I Believe: An A to Z of a Life] (essays) 2002

La silla del águila [The Eagle's Throne: A Novel] (novel) 2002

Carlos Fuentes: viendo visions (nonfiction) 2003

Contra Bush (nonfiction) 2004

Los 68: París-Praga-México (essays) 2005

La voluntad y la fortuna (novel) 2008

*This volume is made up of two stories originally published in *Cantar de ciegos.*

†These collections contain stories published in previous volumes.

‡This volume contains *Todos los gatos son pardos* and *El tuerto es rey.*

CRITICISM

Daniel de Guzmán (essay date 1972)

SOURCE: de Guzmán, Daniel. "The Short Stories." In *Carlos Fuentes,* pp. 72-90. New York: Twayne Publishers, 1972.

[*In the essay that follows, de Guzmán combines a discussion of the individual tales in* Los días enmascarados *and* Cantar de ciegos *with an analysis of Fuentes's development as a writer, covering such aspects as his style, technique, language, tone, and presentation.*]

To trace the course of human development since the Renaissance is to catalogue the steps which have led us in our day to the dehumanitazion of man. John Updike summarizes it most succinctly:

> First went supernatural faith, then faith in kings, then faith in reason, then faith in nature, then faith in science, and, most lately, faith in the subconscious.

The next step is the loss of faith in human nature and this perhaps final step is, it seems, already epidemic in our society. The course of development in the arts has been parallel; as Updike says, "The texture of prose and the art of narration have changed to fit the case"; and, in passing, he points out that "indeed, since *Don Quixote* fiction has to some extent thrived on disillusion." But the process has gone far beyond disillusion, of course, and

> . . . in this century the minimal presupposition of human significance . . . seems too much to be assumed. [All this] renders obsolete the interconnectedness of action that comprises "plot" and the trust in communication that gives a narration voice and pulse. Formless tales blankly told may be the end result . . .[1]

We have not only reached the point he indicates but are already passing it. Much of contemporary literature is already pointing out the void and many of the "characters" in this "literature" are already more humanoid than human.[2] Formless tales blankly told are already the norm in certain little magazines. This is the logical end of the extreme materialist position, the inevitable conclusion of the behaviorist assertion that human nature is after all nothing but a series of mechanical conditioned reflexes. The squirming caused in the artist as he tries despairingly to reconcile this logic to his own desire for self-expression is what produces much of our current tortured prose.

Carlos Fuentes, resting on the Objectivist ledge, taking refuge in his version of the *nouveau roman,* has only recently reached the perilous point he is at in his current development. When he first started writing seriously in the 1950's, he had not yet foreseen the logical end of his beginning, and his first productions were frankly experimental. However, even then, the selectivity which must operate in any artist had already inclined him toward a certain type of experiment rather than another. The literature he was exposed to and his own choice of reading influenced his own first efforts and we can easily see traces of Poe, Rimbaud, and Horacio Quiroga in his early short stories which have been characterized as "clearly a tour-de-force by a young writer."[3]

I *LOS DÍAS ENMASCARADOS* ("THE MASKED DAYS")

His first collection was published in 1954 with the title ***Los días enmascarados* ("The Masked Days")**, not yet translated into English. It presents six short stories "fantastic in theme and ironic in style."[4] The fantasy of the themes shifts from the macabre to the heavily playful, and the irony of the style from the subtle to the labored. A young writer, at the beginning of his career, rarely has a developed style and tends to fluctuate between a simple, direct narrative and too much involution. We can see this clearly in these six tales.

The titles of the six stories are: 1. **"Chac Mool,"** 2. **"En defensa de la Trigolibia"** (**"In Defense of Trigolibia"**), 3. **"Tlactocatzine, del jardin de Flandes"** (**"Tlactocatzine, the One from the Flemish Garden"**), 4. **"Letanía de la orquídea"** (**"Litany of the Orchid"**). 5. **"Por boca de los Dioses"** (**"The Gods Speak"**), and 6. **"El que inventó la pólvora"** (**"The Man Who Invented Gunpowder"**). The first and fifth are tales that show young Fuentes' horrified fascination with the primitive deities of his country. The second and sixth express his interest in manipulating language and his rejection of capitalist technology. The third is a forerunner of his novelette, *Aura*— concerned with age and myth. The fourth, in Freudian terms, is an anal-erotic fantasy on the medieval punishment for sodomy—impalement. A Freudian exegesis could be applied to all these stories, since they are all preoccupied with what is evidently young Fuentes' reaction to theories of the unconscious and its expression by Surrealism.

The unconscious, in fact, is the theme that connects them all. In Fuentes' view, as expressed here, the primitive deities of Mexico are forms of projection of the unconscious, symbolizing horrible instincts of the human heart, mostly cannibalistic and self-devouring. Filiberto in **"Chac Mool,"** Oliverio in **"Por boca de los Dioses,"** are both quite mad and wander in panic through a distorted world that is the fantasied embodiment of their own fears. Oliverio is the more developed of the two characters, he participates more in the self-devouring process, he kills a little old bore who has annoyed him (cf. the "old man" in Poe's story, "The Tell-tale Heart"); he steals a pair of lips off a painting, which in turn pursue him and run from him like dreadful incarnate blobs of living flesh; he visits the underworld, in the bowels of his hotel, into which he is plunged by a reluctant elevator, and where he is almost torn to pieces by the howling pantheon of Mexico that now resides there. Finally he is destroyed in the erotic embrace of the incarnate female deity, Tlazol, just as Filiberto is pursued and destroyed, even to Acapulco, by the animate statue of the Chac Mool. The stories are told with flashes of irony and macabre humor, by juxtaposing idiocies of modern life with idiocies of primitive life. Both stories are a child's nightmare dressed in the Surrealist trappings of a modern Red Riding Hood. The Wolf is the horrible deities that still reign in the human heart and lay in wait for us in the jungle-like woods of the human soul. Grandmother is the myth which suddenly throws off its disguise, its mask, to reveal the gleaming fangs, the writhing lips that lure, that pursue, that devour. The child wakes screaming, but it is a sophisticated child who sees the night-light and accepts the comfort of outward reality although it is not too sure in its heart that the old inner fear, evoked, monster-like, in its dream may not be the real reality, lurking just outside the door, waiting to pounce as soon as the eyes are closed.

These stories are forceful, effective, and semiconvincing. They convince us when the mood of horror is sustained and then simultaneously destroy the conviction when some idiotic irrelevancy is imposed on the horror. Is this technique—a conscious attempt to portray the unconscious—or is it the talent of a young writer, still not entirely sure of what he can do? Perhaps a combination of both: the technique not yet fully mastered; the talent, not yet sure of the direction it is to take. In any case, these stories are interesting because of the new setting for old themes (the city of Mexico) and new vestments of old themes (the primitive gods of Mexico). Also, let us admit it, Fuentes has the sovereign ability that all writers must have—he is able to tell a tale, to "spin a yarn," to weave the spell—an ability without which no writer can succeed. It is not simply technique, although much of it is (apt metaphors, smooth transitions, psychologically acceptable associations). It is that quality that seems to be innate in good writers and that is the despair of critics because it is almost impossible to define. Artistic perception, intuitive awareness—call it what you will—it is undoubtedly an innate quality, what makes a man a writer rather than a tailor. Part of it is a preoccupation with words, which is well expressed in the playful second story.

In **"En defensa de la Trigolibia"** the author, drunk with the power to manipulate words, displays a virtuosity that can be compared to that of a young violinist showing off with one of Paganini's more difficult caprices. The setting, what the story is about, the excuse for this coruscation, is a tiny satire in the "plague on both your houses" vein; the Nusitanios, who represent the United States, after proclaiming a Declaration of the Trigolibios of Man, in which the inalienable right of all men to free trigolibing is set forth, find themselves at odds in their interpretation and application of these inalienable rights with Tundriusa, representing the U.S.S.R. The latter points out dialectically that true trigolibing can exist only under certain conditions which, naturally, are to be found only in Tundriusa. The dialectical form lends itself admirably to this sophomoric exercise in satire, which any smart undergraduate could dash off for the school paper in half an hour. It is hardly worthwhile to mention the George Orwell influence. It is more interesting to observe that Fuentes seems to be expressing disillusion with Russia. That he is also expressing disillusion with the United States is simply a form of conventionality—it is practically obligatory in certain intellectual circles abroad to talk of the United States, if at all, with jesting disdain. But that, in the early 1950's, a young writer should publicly poke fun at the Soviet Union was not so conventional. Historically, it is interesting to observe the attitudes taken in turn by the young intellectuals who metamorphose from angry young men to disillusioned young men to cynical young men. In the process of growing up, they occasionally leave interesting artifacts behind them. And that is just about what " . . . **Trigolibia**" is.

"**El que inventó la pólvora**" is also a satire, somewhat less sophomoric this time, on technological obsolescence. The usefulness of a spoon, for example, is reduced from an indefinite period to a week, then to seventy-two hours, at which time it turns into gelatin. Very soon the revolt of the "things" extends to toothbrushes, writing desks, shoes, and soon becomes universal—all manufactured articles turn into heaps of trash until finally this "new Industrial Revolution," or technological malady, attacks man and nothing is left but the narrator, who starts over by rubbing two sticks together. A slight effort, perhaps a little better than " . . . **Trigolibia**," since it is is Huxley rather than Orwell from whom it derives.

"**Letanía de la orquídea**" is told with more control and with more artistic pretension; the language is more selective and the figures of speech more apt. However, it too is a finger exercise. In all these tales (excepting possibly the third), Fuentes is "performing," practicing at the keyboard, amusing himself by producing variations on themes. This is a perfectly legitimate pastime for a young artist and may even provide half-an-hour's entertainment for the idle reader. But we need not take these *études* too seriously—they are slight and are of interest chiefly for the indications they give of Fuentes' interests, attitudes, external preoccupations, and trends. As we shall see in his second volume of short stories, some of his themes are repeated, developed, and more expertly handled.

In this fourth story, a small ironic study of inversion, we see again, a little more subtly arranged, the juxtaposition of incongruities, and adherence to realism of presentation (enhancing the fantasy of content), the deliberate selection of detail to emphasize the point of view. Here there seems to be more mastery of technique than in " . . . **Trigolibia**"—the writer is surer of himself, virtuosity is no longer necessary. There are even experiments with stylistic syncopation that foreshadow the influence of Dos Passos in the first novel. Again, the story itself is almost beside the point. In Panama (the humidity, rain, heat: the tropical atmosphere), Muriel, a young female impersonator (the exotic, the unusual), finds a luxuriant orchid sprouting from his coccyx. Cutting a hole in his trousers so that this gorgeous flower may freely wave, he goes to his mulatto dance hall and is a great success (the outlandish, the hilariously pathetic). Back in his room at the end of the evening, he cuts off the flower at the root, planning to sell it (the double switch: perversion of a perversion), but from the stump now grows a splintery stake that turns inward and impales him/her. The "realism" of the next-to-last paragraph is calculated to make the reader gasp. It may be dismissed as an example of the fallacy of intention, as well as further evidence of the writer's youthfulness— what reader gasps anymore, what writer tries to make him do so?

We have left until last the best story of the collection, "**Tlactocatzine, del jardín de Flandes**." This is a subtle evocation of a mood, the mood of nostalgia, in a setting of vaguely eerie circumstances. There are metaphysical changes of time and even of place, as though H. G. Wells had decided to write a story in the style of Henry James. The mood is Jamesian, perhaps, but the style is still too Wellsian, too abrupt, too chronological. Two well-known critics have pointed out that " . . . the pattern of poetry resides primarily in its arrangement of language, and the pattern of prose fiction primarily in its arrangement of action." Action, of course, is simply "a progression from one position or one point of awareness to another."[5] But the progression need not be chronological; as a matter of fact, loss of subtlety is precisely the result of such a straightforward progression. In a short story of only ten pages, however, there is no room for too much subtlety and the writer must, as indirectly but as economically as possible, proceed to create his effect. This is done by a description, artfully presented, of the old house, built during the period of the French Intervention, with its faded elegances, its great salon, its tapestried library—all this is transferred to the young narrator, who falls under the spell of the house—and the ambience is prepared for the apparition. First, the garden, which opens only off the library, is not a Mexican garden, the tones are too muted, there is no sun. The young man ventures into the garden and meets the faded apparition of a mad old lady, and the odor of death and the unearthly rain are all about. In the end he cannot escape from the garden and he is a prisoner forever of the mad ghost who is Carlota, Empress of Mexico.

This story is, on the whole, well done; the transitions, the deepening of the mood, are handled skillfully, the language changes, as we penetrate more deeply into the action, from colloquial to poetic, and, finally, we are moved by the capturing of the pathos of age and madness. The fact that the ghost in the story is none other than Carlota is partially an indication of a romantic interest on the part of the author. This whole episode of the French Intervention in Mexico has been of great romantic interest to several Mexican writers, and one may almost gauge their real social attitude toward being Mexican by their treatment of the Carlota legend, acceptance of the pathos from a romantic sentimentality, or rejection of the whole legend from an almost historical indignation. Actually, we need not read too much into the author's intention here, since it has little actual bearing on his performance (except, of course, to inspire it), but it is a point to bear in mind, since it ties in with some of the information in the previous chapter [of Daniel deGuzman, *Carlos Fuentes,* New York: Twayne, 1972] and must be amplified slightly in the last chapter. Of more importance is the fact that this story is a rehearsal, we might say, for the novelette, *Aura,* which is considered in the next chapter [of *Carlos Fuentes*]. Let us keep in mind therefore the performance here to see how the fuller orchestration is handled later.

Parenthetically, we should say that in case any reader is feeling querulous about the critical judgments made on these stories of the first collection, he might prefer to read over the first few pages of the last chapter [of *Carlos Fuentes*], in which we state, as far as is possible or necessary for an essay of this type, what critical norms have been used as guidelines for evaluation of the whole corpus of Fuentes' work.

To sum up on this first collection. In **"Chac Mool"** and **"Por boca de los Dioses,"** the author's preoccupation is with the impact—the *residual* impact—of the primitive gods on the subconscious mind (his own, primarily) of a man who was born of Mexican heritage and who must, therefore, come to terms with that heritage. The presentation in both cases is ironic, fantastical, Surrealistic. It is as though a young, modern writer feels somehow obliged to deal with this aspect of his heritage but resents having to do so and therefore mocks it. There may indeed be some artistic acceptance of the Jungian theory of the collective unconscious, a theory which, as we all know, has had much influence on writers ever since it was proposed. These primitive gods, being monstrous and annihilative, must be rejected, after having been used as part of a Surrealistic setting. The fact that they kill the two protagonists in the stories is part of the rejection, since these protagonists, in their weak-mindedness, are also aspects of the personality which must be destroyed.

Part of this feeling seems to come briefly into play in **"Tlactocatzine. . . . ,"** since Carlota calls Maximilian by the name the Mexicans gave him, in their language, and furthermore the last four words of her closing monologue (or ravings) are in the language of the Aztec. This presumably was meant to show that somehow the Aztec gods were responsible for Carlota's madness or possession. This is entirely fantastical on the part of the author, since there is no evidence that her madness had any "Aztec" overtones at all. There are innumerable facets to the author's preoccupation with these aspects of the subconscious and its partial intrusion into the third story. Unfortunately we cannot take the space here to investigate them further, although they are well worth thinking about in themselves, in connection with contemporary Mexican literature as a whole and Fuentes' work in particular.

Perhaps we have dealt a little harshly with " . . . **Trigolibia"** and " . . . **Pólvora."** They are of contributory importance since it is precisely through work of this sort, of little value in itself, that a young writer develops his talent and explores attitudes. Young writers who are exploring the world as well as attitudes also occasionally feel the need to deal with themes that in themselves have no particular attraction for them—in a way, this too is a developmental exercise since all themes, all human passions, are grist in the writer's mill. This may account for the tale about the orchidaceous Muriel, although it is worth-while noting that the same theme, in a much more straightforward fashion, is again dealt with in the second collection, which we shall consider shortly.

And there we have the first public bow—a slight collection and one which did not stir up either much fuss or much interest when it was first published. The date of the publication of a collection has little to do with the importance of the stories in it for the development of the writer, since in most cases the stories were written long before publication date, probably reworked and rewritten before finally being collected, and published only when the author's reputation is wide enough to warrant the hope that there may be some profit in offering such a collection to the public at that time. We must not forget, in our concern for literary values, that publishing is a business and commercial values often override aesthetic ones. Chronologically, Fuentes' next work is his first novel, *Where the Air Is Clear,* but from a point of view of genre, it is more to our purpose to continue here with a consideration of the short stories and to take up next, therefore, the second collection.

II *CANTAR DE CIEGOS* ("SONGS OF THE BLIND")

First published in 1964, **Cantar de ciegos ("Songs of the Blind")** is an assortment of seven tales, all far superior in depth of penetration and in technique to the first group we have just considered. In the ten years between the two collections, the development of the writer as an artist is formidable and exciting. Of course, by 1964 he had already produced two novels, both of which, being experimental in direction, served to further his development enormously. The stories have been produced concomitantly and not always originally as stories since during this period Fuentes was interested in and working actively with the cinematographic circles in the Mexican capital. In a relatively small artistic milieu, such as is inevitable in a compact country like England or in a centralized country like Mexico (or like France, for that matter), there is a great deal of commingling of arts and artists, everyone knows everyone else, everyone knows what so-and-so is up to, not only professionally but in his private life as well, and Bohemia meets regularly in the same places and for the same occasions, so it is the most natural thing in the world for a director or an actress to suggest casually to a promising writer that he might find it interesting to try his hand at a scenario or a script. Quite often it turns out that a novelist is unable to adjust to the demands of the theatre (and the movies are a form of theatre) in that he is unable to work with a team since he is used to solitary creativity. Or, for aesthetic or social reasons, he finds the movies crass, vulgar, unsatisfactory. Fuentes himself has always insisted that "the rebuilding of the movies in Mexico is not a technical problem but one that is essentially human and social."[6] He feels that the themes of an authentic cinematographic art in Mexico should be drawn from the collective life of Mexicans, of their present-day collective life, a life which he feels is infinitely diversified. In other words, he recognizes that Mexico, within its own framework, has joined the great world in direction and interest. And he feels that the youth of Mexico (of which he is, of course, a part) is carrying to completion that psychological revolution which its grandparents started, but in a manner much more honest and much more direct than that of the older generation.

So, in spite of the fact that Fuentes himself disclaims in these stories any intent at "writing for the cinema,"[7] it is most likely that there was a close connection between the actual script-work he was doing at the time and the conception of some of these tales. Compartmentalization would be strange in anyone with such a zest for living totally as Fuentes has shown—it is no more possible for him to separate the creative segments of his personality than it would be for him to subdivide his personal life. Whatever else he may be, he is not a schizophrenic. And yet the whole question of his creative life is infinitely complicated by the fact that he is also an intellectual. So much so that occa-

sionally it gets in his way, in the sense that the intellectual of his sort is more prone than other men to rationalization. This makes him untrustworthy as a sociologist or as an explainer of his own motivations, although it may make him a very good novelist. This intellectual subtlety in reasoning (in Fuentes it seems to be almost an Italian trait), deviousness perhaps, may be expressed in apparently quite straightforward language in conversation or in interviews, giving the impression of a sincere man groping honestly toward reasonable answers. Such an impression can be most deceptive and it will be discussed further, in Chapter 10 [of *Carlos Fuentes*]. We must not allow it to lead us astray.

The attitude common to these stories is that modern society is decadent, rotten, and that the few "decent" individuals encountered are destroyed by it. Fuentes has not yet become an Objectivist, so he does not simply present this corruption but implies a moral position, an implicit condemnation. It is loss of innocence that is the common theme on the psychological level in these stories. But what kind of innocence can be lost in this modern world where nothing is innocent anymore, and who can be the loser? That is the subtlety that has been noted. Despite the general decadence and rottenness surrounding us in all areas, there is still possible in some areas an innocence which may be, actually, no more than naiveté or ignorance of the world, but which leads in any event, no matter what it is at bottom, to destruction of the innocent. This is almost the old metaphysical idea of sin, differently stated. But let us not get too subtle ourselves, or be beguiled by the intellectual's pastime of "reading into" a work of art possibly more than is actually there. Let us look at the works themselves for enlightenment.

It is difficult to say, on any meaningful level, which is the best of these stories. Usually in a collection of this sort, if the author has any interest in the matter at all, he will prefer to put the story he likes best at the beginning. Liking a certain story best does not mean that it *is* best, however; but in such a matter of taste, what test could be applied except that of the total effectiveness of the story—its impact, so to speak? But again, one man's impact may be another man's cushion. We can only state which of these stories seemed most effective, without then trying to rationalize this impression into a statement that tries to convince others. With stories of this calibre, so much superior to the first group, it is every man his own critic and no need to argue. So, let us take them in the order in which they are presented.

The first story, **"Las dos Elenas"** (**"The Two Helens"**), is a subtle study in scarlet, the scarlet of amorality. It is a triple character sketch built around a young wife, the first Helen, her husband Victor, and her mother, the second Helen. The wife, a very modern young woman, is trying to persuade her husband of the theoretical acceptability of the *menage-à-trois* as a way of life. Guy de Maupassant presented this idea long ago. What is new here is that the husband is already carrying on an affair with his mother-in-law, the second Helen. The tale depends for its full effectiveness on the "punch" ending à la O. Henry, when it is revealed that the man's mistress is in effect his wife's mother. The fact that the impact depends on this final revelation actually weakens the effect. Again, it is the implied moralistic attitude that the idea is somehow shocking which, in fact, destroys the shock. There is a remnant here of the old Marxist puritanism in the effect sought. The true decadent element is that the wife, the first Helen, is naively honest in *her* approach to the problem of marital boredom while her husband and her mother are playing the old game of adultery behind closed doors, in the old dishonest and traditional way. So the deepest level, it would seem, is the author's intent to show that modern so-called amorality may actually be the most innocent sort of naiveté when compared to the age-old dishonesty of the real serpent. Who is more immoral, Helen in her amorality, or Victor in his hidden adultery? And what about the mother? The fact that she is from the tropics— Veracruz—is brought out several times. Is this supposed to suggest a reason for *her* deception of her own husband and her daughter? If so, it is a deliberate cliché: women from the tropics are notoriously of easy virtue. Or is it simply "atmosphere"? There is no need for that sort of atmosphere in a story that takes place entirely in the highlands of Mexico City. It cannot be just an extraneous detail tossed in by the author. Selectivity here is high on his part and each detail contributes to the total effect. Perhaps it is an attempt to give a touch of morbidity to the story. This is more likely, since the tropical woman is still an effective stereotype of adulterous femininity.

Fuentes' style and method of presentation here is almost completely developed: the use of dialogue, the *art-nouveau* descriptions (like an Aubrey Beardsley illustration in prose), the incongruous realism (Helen matter-of-factly munches a sandwich as she discusses her visit to a brothel), the use of synesthesia—all elements of Fuentes' style, which he employs with great dexterity to contribute, independently and in combination, to produce the effect of naturalness. Again, one gets the impression of the sincere, straightforward, honest observer of life presenting a most subtle, devious tale that is effective and convincing. It is a *tour-de-force,* of course; but when a clever trick becomes habitual it is no longer simply a clever trick but becomes mastery. It is all very well to call the first col-

lection by a young writer such a name, but that is no longer enough here. And this may be one of the reasons for the controversy around Fuentes—he is like a disarming child who runs up with an intricate artifice he has made and presents it for our attention. The first reaction is amazement and then suspicion—what is this seemingly straightforward man up to? And the first thing that becomes apparent is that he is not so straightforward as he seems. We have been taken in. Many readers (and critics) are annoyed by this, they feel it is insincere writing (see the last chapter [of *Carlos Fuentes*] for the reaction of Keith Botsford), but once we have caught on, there is no need to be annoyed, we can relax, admire the cleverness of the child, this *enfant terrible,* and enjoy the product he has contrived.

So subtle is the weaving of this story that there is even an alternate idea: all the way through the narrative Helen, the wife, uses the epithet *Nibelungo* as a pet name for her husband. He, Victor, who is the narrator, confesses he does not know why his wife calls him that. But we all know who the Nibelungs were, a race of demonic beings. Are we therefore supposed to infer that Helen knows that her husband's nature is demonic? Nothing would delight Fuentes more than to think that he has his reader so *enredado* (involved and confused), and what compounds the pleasure of this mischievous writer is that the more careful the reader the more *enredado* he will be. Just as Fuentes has developed a technique for the writing of these stories, so one must develop a technique for reading them. It is the same technique that must be used in regarding a contemporary painting or listening to a piece of modern music—one must not *seek* meanings, which are multiple and on many levels, rather one must simply be "open" to them, receptive. Perhaps in a way this is what the Objectivists originally had in mind when they spoke of "participation" and before they elaborated the thought into a dogma.

"La muñeca reina" ("The Doll Queen"), the second story, is an approach again to the *Aura* theme. The *Aura* theme, as in **"Tlactocatzine . . . "** in the first collection, and as in the novelette *Aura* itself, is that of the reality of illusion, of hallucination. In **"Tlactocatzine . . . "** only one aspect of the idea is developed: the old enchantress who is really dead but who nevertheless draws the helpless young man into her spell, as her victim. In *Aura* this is further developed so that the aged enchantress has her complimentary aspect as a radiant young woman—this incarnation of the witch ensnares the hapless youth who, when he is about to possess his love finds he is embracing the old witch. In **"La muñeca reina"** the poetic and romantic young man, lost in the cold rain of the modern world, seeks again the innocent maiden who captivated him when he was an adolescent. He finds her but now she is a dreadful, vulgar invalid in a wheelchair, the captive of two sadistic parents who pretend that their beautiful little daughter Amilamia, whom the young man seeks, is dead. Thus they are free to victimize the monster that the real Amilamia has become. They have even gone so far as to keep their "dead" daughter's bedroom "as she left it," with a large doll dressed in her clothes on the bed, while the real Amilamia, paralyzed, cigarette smoking, hopelessly ordinary, is confined to her wheelchair in the back of the house. Again a variation on a theme: Coppelia, Pygmalion; but again with the "new twist," the modern touch—the combination of realism of presentation and fantastical horror of content, all skillfully evoked and displayed for our inspection, rather like a vampire bat found mounted among the gorgeous butterflies of a crazy lepidopterists's collection. The tale starts off with all the nostalgic loveliness of a child's fairy tale and suddenly it turns into a child's nightmare, and no longer a child's but an adult's. It is this element of horror that is hidden, hinted at, of the serpent behind the mask, that gives Fuentes' retelling of an old theme its immediacy. This sort of "switch" can be traced back to medieval ballads, and many writers have dressed old themes in new vestments. So let us not analyze this too thoroughly at the moment; it will be more appropriate in the discussion of *Aura,* in the next chapter [of *Carlos Fuentes*].

The third story, **"Fortuna lo que ha querido"** (**"What Fortune Brought"**), presents a character sketch of an artist, a painter, and his preoccupation with sex which, although he does not realize it, seriously interferes with his ability to paint. Impressed by the single-minded dedication of great artists to their art, Fuentes seems to be telling himself (as much as us) that promiscuity inevitably dilutes art to say nothing of affecting the artist's vision of others: if they are objects of sexual satisfaction they are rarely also objects of art. **"Fortuna . . ."** is a slight story but is interesting because it illustrates in capsule form much of the style and attitude that Fuentes was to use in *Where the Air Is Clear.* The novel was published before the collection, but this particular story antedates the novel. Fuentes is not a prolific writer; his writing seems to require maximum utilization of all materials, which he reworks and reuses, and his inventiveness is more one of presentation than of themes. Even so, he seems always able to invest even reused material with a fresh appeal and interest so that one does not mind having met the idea before.

"Vieja Moralidad" (**"The Old Morality"**), the fourth story, may be considered the "best" of the collection. It is again the theme of loss of innocence, as in **"Las dos Elenas,"** but it is presented much more effectively because there is no doubt about the point of view and the narrator is the "victim" himself, rather than the double-dealing adulterer. In other words, there is more inner consistency and no attempt to mystify the reader by too many implications. This time the presentation is truly more straightforward and amorality is again seen to be more "innocent," more honest, than the "old morality" of the title. Although now the old morality is not presented as decadent (implied in the adultery of Victor and his mother-in-law) so much as a form of ignorance—psychological ignorance, tortured into perversion and incestuous outlet because of an unreasoning adherence to the old hypocritical, priest-ridden "ethics" of Mexican Catholicism.

The attack on the priests and their hypocrisy, as a matter of fact, is the very keynote of the story. It is stated at once, with the opening words: ¡*Zopilotes negros*! ¡*Cuervos devoradores*! (Black buzzards! Ruinous crows!). Thus the old grandfather, shaking his cane angrily, insults the seminarians who pass his house, threatening to set the dogs on them. Of course, grandfather does all this theatrically, with his arm around his young concubine, Micaela, with whom he lives openly and whom he flaunts in the priests' faces. The narrator is a boy of thirteen who lives with his grandfather and Micaela and worships the old man in his uncompromising honesty. But the boy's aunts, who live nearby in the city (Morelia), are scandalized by the exposure of this youngster to the demoralizing influence of such a household. This environment, which the aunts see as vicious, is presented skillfully from the boy's point of view as one of bucolic innocence, of farm activities, vastly to the liking of the boy who is not in the least troubled by the situation that so disturbs his aunts. It is a hearty life, full of good food and play, undisturbed sleep, and no complications about sex.

Inevitably the aunts arrive, with a writ from the court that has jurisdiction over minors, to "rescue" Alberto, the boy, from the moral squalor in which he lives. The interview between the grandfather and the aunts is in Fuentes' best style, rapid, deadly, deeply ironic. In a paragraph we "see" the three aunts, one with a tic of the eye, the second with a wig that slips, and the third, the unmarried aunt, Benedicta, always dabbing at her nose with her black-lace hankie. The dialogue is economical but most effective—the three aunts firing off their condemnations like hysterical old pea-shooters, brandishing their writ. They win, and carry off Alberto to be "properly" brought up in the house of Aunt Benedicta.

Fuentes presents her in a not unkindly fashion. She is the real victim of the old morality because it is her character that has been twisted and warped by this hysterical adherence to a hypocritical creed. She is not even aware herself of the primitive physical, biologic forces that propel her to seduce her nephew. She is thirty-four, he is now fourteen, a juicy young man who by his very presence, his propinquity, his physical animality, actually seduces her, although he is not aware of this either. It is part of Fuentes' art that he presents all this to the reader indirectly, subtly, through the actions and reactions of the two protagonists who act out their inevitable comedy in the big, old-fashioned house. Speaking of Micaela, the grandfather's cook-concubine, Alberto repeats what his grandfather has said: "Naturally, they sleep together. Grandfather says that a man should never sleep alone or he'll dry up, and a woman the same."[8] This statement upsets the aunt out of all proportion and she stops bothering the boy for the rest of the day. All is not unrelieved psychological sordidness, however. Fuentes develops the boy's character skillfully showing, through his changing interests, how he, the boy, is changing from an unaware thirteen-year-old into a pubescent, sexually ready fourteen-year-old, still with some little-boy reactions, not yet a man—the incident of the captured lizard, which he gives to his aunt with all a little-boy's eagerness, and which becomes subtly symbolic of the boy himself as the palpitating body of the little reptile fills her hand. The whole story is consistently and convincingly presented from the boy's point of view, from the sequence of the mutual seduction to the end, at which point the boy is his aunt's little lover. He is, naturally, somewhat confused at the end and he somehow feels that back at the ranch, with his grandfather, there was *más moralidad* (more morality).

This is a delicate theme to handle and even more delicate to present without slipping into bathos. At the end he almost does, but Fuentes avoids it because all the way through the story the boy's character and its development have been consistent and convincing. He is an innocent child even though he has accepted a conventionally shocking solution to the aunt's problem. Again, this is a fairy tale seen through the horrifying glass: Tom Sawyer gone wrong with a lecherous Aunt Polly. But it is not pornographic, unless sensuality itself, the innocent sensuality of a young animal, or even the smothered, hysterical sensuality of an aging virgin, be so considered.

On the basis of our analyses so far, we can say that it is clear that Carlos Fuentes as a writer is more interested in character and character development than in any other aspect of the novelistic art. When we have done with our total view of his work, we shall see that he is not really interested in plot in any sense of the word. "Plot," even in the modern view of it as a "progression," in Fuentes is simply contributory to the pre-

sentation of a fascinating character. The situation in which the character develops may be realistic or fantastical, but it is essential only to the unfolding of the observed figure as such. Fuentes is a people-watcher and he populates his books and his tales with existential, even Surrealistic, characters who react convincingly in the situations, largely naturalistic, that he contrives for them.

The three remaining stories of this collection do not merit such close attention as the one we have just discussed. The fifth, **"El costo de la vida,"** with its ironic title (**"The Cost of Life"**), is one of the author's sociological comments on life. A young schoolteacher, trying to make his union an effective and truly representative instrument for bettering the conditions of life for himself and for his fellow teachers, is cynically murdered by the local union bosses who prefer to keep the instrument in their own hands as a source of income and power. Once more the "innocent," who naively thought he could do something against the age-old forces (in this case disguised as union leaders and not as Aztec gods) of evil and corruption, is destroyed. Prometheus never wins, not because he is not really Prometheus, not even because he is a naive little fool, but because by the very nature of things he cannot win. This pessimistic despair is by and large only an aesthetic attitude on Fuentes' part, not an innate world view. In his own life he betrays little of this aesthetic despair which he eliminates by projecting it into his work.

"Un alma pura" (**"A Pure Soul"**), the sixth story, is a touching tale of star-crossed lovers, lost through the complications of their own neuroses rather than through any circumstantial forces inimical to the fulfillment of their love. It is fulfilled and ends in disillusion and ennui, a variation on the French idea that the opposite of love is not hate but indifference. The story is ably told and we are sorry for the lovers but we do not feel really involved in their inevitable misfortune since it is obvious almost from the beginning that their creator intends to destroy them. The fact that their love ends in death is also incidental since, in any case, the heart must die before the body, and once the heart has stopped the rest is unimportant. Fuentes is very skillful in his handling of the presentation—the international ambience, the vocabulary evocative of mood, the nostalgic air—but the characters in this case do not really live, he has lost them in the clouds of fantasy which surround them. One might say that there is a quality of lyrical unreality that invests the whole story, but somehow it does not quite come off. Juan Luis never really touches us, Claire is too misty to be real.

The seventh and last tale, **"A la víbora de la mar"** (**"To the Sea Serpent"**), is an unrelieved study in evil, in which two homosexuals, partners, fleece women on transatlantic liners by pretending to be in love with them until they get their money. Isabel, the victim, is the innocent, aging (thirty-seven-year-old) virgin who, in her ignorance of the world (again that Fuentian combination), is driven to suicide when she accidentally discovers the relationship of her "husband" with his lover. The whole company of the ship, from the bartender to the passengers, is evil—not a ship of fools but of devils—and Isabel moves among them condemned to destruction from the beginning. The story is depressing and one seeks diversion in the details: the name of the "husband," Harrison Beatle (with mischievous humor, Fuentes makes him a Philadelphian); the fact that this evil ship is British; the young adventurer is a Seventh-day Adventist. The story is, in fact, so heavy that one is inclined to think that Fuentes cannot be serious; he has written it with his tongue in his cheek. But if so, he spoofs everything, even himself, since after all he *is* telling the story. We cannot even take Isabel's suicide seriously. Nobody can be that naive. He is putting us on, pulling the reader's leg, providing a tale of unrelieved evil for the titillation of the bourgeoisie. He must be aware that most of his readers will "catch on." This story illustrates, perhaps better than any other, what may be called, for lack of a better adjective, the mischievous element in Fuentes. An occasional spoof may be allowed him—in general he has given good value in this collection.

We have said enough about the short stories to whet the appetite for a consideration of the more important genre in the work of Carlos Fuentes. First and last he is a novelist, he thinks like a novelist, he writes like one—. . . .

Notes

1. *The New Yorker,* Jan. 7, 1967, p. 91.

2. We must keep in mind the difference between humanoid and subhuman, of course; the difference between, say, the characters of a Dostoevski and a William S. Burroughs.

3. Robert G. Mead, Jr., "Carlos Fuentes, Mexico's Angry Novelist," in *Books Abroad,* Autumn 1964, pp. 380-82.

4. *Ibid.,* p. 381.

5. Both quotes are from Bacon (Wallace A.) & Breen (Robt. S.), *Literature as Experience* (New York, 1959), p. 215.

6. From an article Fuentes wrote on the cinema in Mexico for *Siempre!,* No. 632, August 4, 1965, VII.

7. *Ibid.*

8. *Cantar de ciegos* (Mexico, 1966), 2nd ed., p. 83.

Selected Bibliography

<small>PRIMARY SOURCES</small>

1. WORKS BY CARLOS FUENTES

The name, publisher, place, and date of the first Spanish edition will be given first. If there has been an English translation, the data for that publication will be given second (if there has been no translation, only a rendering of the title in English will be given).

The Short Stories

1. *Los días enmascarados* (Mexico: Los Presentes, 1954). (Los Presentes was a publishing house, of short duration, founded by Juan José Arreola especially for young writers. There was also a Studium edition published the same year.) ("The Masked Days").

2. *Cantar de ciegos* (Mexico: Editorial Joaquín Mortiz, S. A., 1964). ("Song of the Blind").

The Novels

La región más transparente (Mexico: Fondo de Cultura Económica, 1958). (*Where the Air is Clear* [New York: Ivan Obolensky, Inc., 1960]).

Aura [Mexico: Era (Alacena), 1962]. (*Aura*).

The Other Writings

To try to make anything like a complete listing of Fuentes' articles, political essays, topical reviews, script work, etc., would be little short of impossible, since he has written and published such work all over Europe and the Western Hemisphere, from Russia to Chile, Argentina, Cuba, Central America, the United States, and most, of course, in Mexico. The Spanish-speaking reader is referred especially to the catalogue and collection in the Hemeroteca Nacional in Mexico City, and to such publications as those of the Universidad Autónoma de México, *Siempre!, Política* (before 1962), *Life en Español, etc.* The English-speaking reader will find Fuentes' work in *Holiday, Show, The Nation, Monthly Review,* and other current periodicals. He has written and published scores, if not hundreds, of articles of varying length on almost every conceivable subject.

<small>SECONDARY SOURCES</small>

Mead, Robert J., Jr. "Carlos Fuentes, Mexico's Angry Novelist," *Books Abroad,* XXXVIII, No. 4 (Autumn, 1964), 380-82. An estimate of Fuentes' work up to the year 1964.

Anthony Julio Ciccone (essay date winter 1973)

SOURCE: Ciccone, Anthony Julio. "The Artistic Depiction of Fantasy-Reality in the Uncollected Short Stories

(1949-57) of Carlos Fuentes." *Journal of Spanish Studies: Twentieth Century* 1, no. 3 (winter 1973): 127-39.

[*In this essay, Ciccone contends that four uncollected short stories—"Trigo errante," "Pantera en jazz," "El muñeco," and "Pastel rancio"—demonstrate Fuentes's early attempts at experimenting with spacial and temporal elements as well as with modes of narration—strategies he used to help convey a distorted and fantastic sense of reality, and which he further refined as he continued writing fiction.*]

The world-wide literary fame of Carlos Fuentes is founded upon his accomplishments as a novelist, a dramatist and as a short story writer. From 1949-64 he wrote seventeen shorter narratives. In addition to his two collections, *Los días enmascarados* (1954) and *Cantar de ciegos* (1964), he has four uncollected short stories to his credit: **"Pastel rancio," "Pantera en jazz," "El muñeco,"** and **"Trigo errante."** They were written in the period 1949-57, the era before *Los días enmascarados* (1954) and that preceding *La región más transparente* (1958), and have never been incorporated into a book. Although their artistic merit is less than that of the two published collections they are important because they reveal certain thematic tendencies and literary techniques which were employed in some of Fuentes' later works. These stories, then, represent a literary experiment by the Mexican author. The more successful topics and features of these uncollected stories will reappear, in more complex form, in his later short narratives and novels. Essentially, they help us see a segment of Fuentes' art which predates his first published work by five years and which influences the scope of subsequent publications.

In the course of the article significant attention will be accorded to the importance of the artistic techniques of point of view, time and space in evoking the desired ambience of fantasy-reality in these stories. Since the element of irreality-reality is a recurrent literary concern in much of Fuentes' art, a consideration of it in these four naratives provides an insight into this aspect of his work. Brief indications will also be made, in this study, as to the relative simplicity of these early stories in comparison with the author's later literary creations.

The first of the four tales was published on November 26, 1949[1] in the newspaper, *Mañana,* under the title of **"Pastel rancio."** This two-page story is that of a German-Jewish immigrant, Sarah Goldbaum, who had been separated from her son, Hans, for thirteen years. One day she learns that her son is due to arrive in New York City on a German ship. Sarah goes to meet Hans at the pier, but he arrives accompanied by two German girls and disowns her. He maintains that she

is his family's old Jewish maid who mistakenly believes that she is his mother. Sarah, rejected by her son, returns home.

Of foremost importance are the time and the narrative person of this story. The third-person, omniscient mode is interrupted at the story's end by the narrator directly addressing Sarah Goldbaum. This brief experiment in narration is actually the germinal point for the complex narrative innovations found in *La muerte de Artemio Cruz* (1962), in *Aura* (1962) and in *Cambio de piel* (1967). In the first, we notice a mode of narration: " . . . a kind of voice of conscience that addresses the protagonist in the second person and the future tense, a disembodied accusative . . . "[2] *Aura,* similiarly, is narrated exclusively in the second-person, singular *tú* form thereby providing a multi-faceted role for Felipe Montero, the narrator-protagonist-spectator. Finally, the narrator of *Cambio de piel* not only continually addresses the novel's four protagonists but ultimately emerges as their author/creator.[3]

Time, in **"Pastel rancio,"** is treated in two distinct ways. In the first, the author relates, in a chronological manner, the events prior to Sarah's departure for the pier. In contrast to this linear elaboration is the flashback which portrays her reaction after her rejection by her son in which Sarah recalls the moment before she left to meet Hans. By dwelling upon that moment she assuages her pain and fantasizes that her son's rebuff never occurred. The temporal inversion which Fuentes introduces here is expanded into a most intricate form in *La muerte de Artemio Cruz* in which the abbreviated temporal scale of the protagonist's final hours gains breadth through continual references to previous epochs.

Although **"Pastel rancio"** has not gained literary recognition, it contains some of the techniques for subsequent works and the thematic basis for *Cantar de ciegos* (1964) and *Zona sagrada* (1967). In the latter, Fuentes chose to explore, in greater depth, the complex bond unifying Claudia Nervo and her son, Guillermo. In three of the seven narratives of *Cantar de ciegos*; **"Vieja moralidad," "Las dos Elenas,"** and **"Un alma pura,"** we find a mature, intricate elaboration of the theme of **"Pastel rancio,"** self-delusion and its relation to familial discord. This story is also significant because it presents Fuentes' use of the Jew as a protagonist. The simple description of Sarah Goldbaum prefigures the Biblical character, Lazarus, in **"Trigo errante,"** (1956) and the multi-faceted Elizabeth/Isabel (the Jewess) in *Cambio de piel.* Furthermore, the inclusion of Yiddish phrases in **"Pastel rancio"** serves as a precursor to the tendency to insert entire sentences in different languages in later works. Three possible examples are; the sentences in Nahautl in *Los días enmascarados* in **"Tlactocatzine, del jardín de Flandes,"** to suggest the persistence of the pre-Hispanic past in modern-day Mexico, the use of French in *Aura,* to depict the omnipresence of the nineteenth century era, and the brief phrases in English in **"A la víbora de la mar,"** from *Cantar de ciegos,* to accentuate the protagonist's sense of alienation from the unfamiliar atmosphere which surrounds her.

Fuentes' second story, **"Pantera en jazz,"** published six months before *Los días enmascarados,*[4] wholly different from **"Pastel rancio,"** presents a retiring, alienated bachelor protagonist who complements his uneventful and hostile existence with fantasy. The title suggests the existence of a fantastic beast, a panther, in an oneiric form (a jazz-like dream); both elements therefore infer the protagonist's instability.

In this particular work a bachelor, while eating breakfast, reads an account of an escaped panther. A moment later he imagines that he hears a growl in his bathroom. That night, upon returning home with a woman he has met in a bar, he hears the same sound. The woman's questions regarding the mysterious animal noises anger the protagonist and he forces her out of his apartment. After he has lived with the panther in his bath for two weeks, he decides to resign from his job and to take solace in the nearest bar. Upon returning home one evening he concludes that the panther's hunger would be satiated by feeding it the girl who lives in the apartment below. The story's conclusion depicts the protagonist's metamorphosis into a panther awaiting its next human victim.

The similiarity between the plight of the anonymous protagonist of this tale and that of Kafka's *Metamorphosis,* is readily apparent. In both instances the young men perceive that their human form has been transformed into a bestial semblance. Further, both are bachelors beset by difficult conditions which contribute to their nightmarish situations.

The third-person narrative mode of **"Pantera en jazz"** functions as a contrasting source of verosimilitude to the protagonist's infered insanity and unreliability of perception. The first hint of his possible derangement is furnished by the acute sense of alienation which he feels towards his modern, impersonal, urban environment. The marked degree of estrangement which this male personage senses is manifested in his conception of his co-workers at the office:

> (La oficina pedaleaba un fandango espontáneo y crujiente de apuntadores Remington y escenario de cemento y vidrio. Tronaban puertas y abofetaban máquinas, y mascaban chicle y bebían agua en en-

> debles copitas de papel y daban órdenes y las recibían y estornudaban y pedían permiso y bajaban las persianas y las volvían a subir y leían novelas de crimen (¿quién lo hizo?) escondidas tras de un parapeto de papel amarillo e importante (. . .) bajaban las persianas otra vez y tictacqueaban un poco y siesteaban otro y se arreglaban las medias y regían las corbatas y salían a la avenida zumbante llenos de espíritu y felices de estar ocupados, de trabajar, de poseer escritorio propio.[5]

The senselessness and superfluousness of his job is intensified by his vapid social life, devoid of any form of human warmth or acceptance. In order to counter these debilitating circumstances, the protagonist decorates his apartment in a manner intended to create an atmosphere of impeccable neatness and tranquility. The apartment thus represents a haven of serenity which assuages the abrasive quality of his existence; it also shields him from an imminently threatening outer reality:

> ¿Cómo puede algo o alguien introducirse en mi baño? Este lugar tan seguro, pagaba un poco más de lo normal por él, y estaba situado en el barrio más selecto: por lo menos eso era lo que él pensaba y lo que el anuncio decía. De manera que si algo, o alguien, estaba en su cuarto de baño—destruyendo sus lociones, babeando su pasta dental—no había seguridad, y lo único que él anhelaba después de un día de trabajo, era confort, confort y seguridad, y no un baño lleno de bichos molestos y ruidosos y sin respeto hacia la vida privada de los ciudadanos.

> (p. 120)

Thus, the inexplicable presence of a panther within the sanctuary of his apartment represents the incursion of the uncontrollable and unpredictable in a structured, ordered realm. The protagonist, totally unable to cope with this fantastic phenomenon, develops an aversion to his apartment and progressively passes more of his leisure time drinking in bars. In effect, he chooses to escape an unacceptable reality through the fantasizing which alcohol makes possible. The altered state of perception, which continual inebriation provides, assists the protagonist of this story in formulating a convincing explanation for the fantastic event:

> . . . tiene que pensar un poco: el ruido en el baño. No hay manera de entrar ahí, como no sea llegando por la puerta principal. No hay ventanas en el baño. La cosa necesita haber entrado por la planta baja, subido la escalera, abierto la puerta del apartamento. Debe haberse arrastrado por la sala hasta llegar a la puerta del baño; abrió, se introdujo en el cuartito y cerró la puerta. Pero entonces él estaba en la regadera alrededor de las siete cuarenta y cinco, lo cual significaba que la cosa no se había colocado durante la noche, lo natural; en consecuencia debe suponerse que entró mientras el hombre preparaba el desayuno en la cocina. Esta era la única explicación posible, la única explicación posible.

> (p. 122)

The explanation is significant because it reestablishes in his mind the ordered atmosphere of his home. That is, what the character finds most unnerving is not the panther's presence in his apartment but its inexplicable entry. Once he has established a basis for its appearance he may then grant it a parity of existence with all the other constituents in his home. Nevertheless, his estrangement from society is highlighted by the feeling of confusion which accompanies the realization that the panther actually exists for him: "No puede encontrar una salida ya. No hay donde ir, huyendo de este monstruo invisible. Sólo queda el apartamento sucio, y se abraza a la pared junto a la puerta del baño y siente el corazón latir y la cabeza nadar, mientras los arañazos truenan en sus orejas empapadas de sangre martillan allí, sin piedad. Ningún lugar, ni bar, ni oficina. Nada, sólo la niñita tocando escalas y cantando rimas un piso abajo" (p. 122).

Essentially, he perceives himself as encarcerated with the panther within the cage-like confines of his apartment, whose disordered appearance is an attempt to re-create a more primitive habitat which was characteristic of man's earlier stages of evolution: "Entonces olfateó un sueño hediondo, y escuchó el gemido del animal, temblando significadamente mientras toda aquella existencia enervante rondaba con su fetidez enjaulada hasta el último poro del hombre, o mueble. Nada podía ocurrir, sólo que él, el hombre, se tornara en bestia también, bestia capaz de cohabitar con la otra, siempre invisible, bestia en el baño" (p. 124).

Thus, his fantasy not only succeeds in convincing the protagonist of the panther's presence in his home, but ultimately causes him to perceive himself as metamorphosed into a beast thoroughly devoid of human features: "La pantera hambrienta comenzó a lamentarse de nuevo y a rondar y a rugir alrededor del baño. Entonces el hombre arañó la pared, arañó su cuerpo y sintió su brazo desnudo, grueso y aterciopelado y sus uñas convirtiéndose en garras de clavo y algo como caucho ardiente tostando su nariz y todo su cuerpo, un torso desnudo, trémulo y peludo como el del animal, y sus piernas acortándose al reptar sobre el tapete para arañar las almohadas y destrozarlas y entonces esperar y esperar, mientras, sin duda, pisadas cautelosas ascendían la escalera con el propósito de tocar su puerta" (p. 124).

The temporal elaboration of **"Pantera en jazz"** is not as important as its depiction of space in evoking the suggested fantasy. The temporal element recounts the events which occurred from the day the protagonist read the newspaper account to the final moment, two weeks thereafter, in which he perceives himself as fantastically transformed into a panther resembling the one which inhabits his bath. As such, the time indi-

cated progresses in a linear, conventional manner and does not evidence any of the flashbacks or other techniques found in Fuentes' later works.

The spatial element has two components in **"Pantera en jazz."** The first one describes the apartment as a limited, hermetically enclosed area which is the site for fantastic events. In this respect, it is a forerunner to the designation of place as a *zona sagrada* in later works. By a *zona sagrada,* we understand, a location in which the supernatural is nurtured and is allowed to flourish. These particular spatial zones are found in three stories in *Los días enmascarados*; "Chac Mool," "Por boca de los dioses" "Tlactocatzine, del jardín de Flandes" and in *Aura.* In the spaces described in these four works the Mexican historical past coexists with the present and eventually displaces it. The second spatial aspect found in **"Pantera en jazz"** is that of unrealistic space engendered by fantasy. Two examples of this irreality are the panther and the character's perceived metamorphosis. In opposition to the actual dimensions of the apartment and the physical attributes of the man are those which are attributed to them by the protagonist's imaginative powers. The latter qualities are fantastic because they are products of the personage's mania while lacking any substance in reality. Essentially, the apartment is a metaphor representing the protagonist's mind. His rigid thought patterns, which ultimately convince him that his form is bestial likewise compel him to see his surroundings in an alien, jungle motif.

In Fuentes' later production we find another instance of unrealistic space engendered by fantasy, that depicted in *Los días enmascarados* in **"Letanía de la orquídea."** Muriel, the Panamanian protagonist of this work, mistakenly believes that an expensive orchid has grown from his *rabadilla.* Upon severing the phenomenal growth he precipitates his death by self-mutilation.

"Pantera en jazz" also presents a particular type of literary personage who will become progressively more important in the author's total work, namely, the unmarried protagonist whose emotional and sexual unfulfillment produces psychological instability, unreliability of perception and an inclination towards fantasy. We find this type of protagonist portrayed in *Los días enmascarados* and in *Aura.* The personages of; **"Chac Mool," "Tlactocatzine, del jardín de Flandes" "Por boca de los dioses," "El que inventó la pólvora,"** as well as Felipe Montero, in *Aura,* are all representatives of this particular type of personality. Their psychological maladjustment and imaginative complicity are instrumental in precipitating the occurrence of fantastic phenomena. The unmarried, frustrated, fantasy prone individual is also integral to the thematic scope of *Cantar de ciegos*. The protagonists of: **"La muñeca reina,"** **"Un alma pura,"** **"Fortuna lo que ha querido,"** **"A la víbora de la mar"** and **"Vieja moralidad"** are alike in their adoption of self-induced blindness which obscures the horror of their actual existence.

Unlike **"Pastel rancio"** and **"Pantera en jazz,"** Fuentes' third uncollected work, **"El muñeco,"** is concerned with the nineteenth century Mexican past. It is a two-page story which was published in the *Revista de la Universidad de México* in March 1956.⁶ In some respects it resembles Rodolfo Usigli's *Corona de sombra* (1943). Both works portray Carlota as the ambitious and insane survivor of the Mexican Empire. As in *Corona de sombra,* this story's scenes alternate between Europe and Mexico.

We learn, in the course of the story, that before Carlota left Mexico for the Vatican she entrusted a message for her husband with Abbot Fischer. Maximilian, upon reading the note, discovered that Carlota wished the Empire preserved at any cost. His subsequent decision not to abdicate resulted in his death. Maximilian's remains, which are compared to a *muñeco,* were sent via Veracruz to Trieste. Carlota, unaware of the turn of events, travelled from the Vatican to her brother's castle in Laeken. In the course of her European journey she was assailed by intense feelings of guilt and by a strong sense of persecution. Fearing that she was to be poisoned, she decided to subsist on shelled nuts and fountain water. The nuts, she came to believe, also contained *muñecos* who would be magically transformed, at the appropriate moment, into attendants who would render her homage.

"El muñeco" is recounted in the third-person omniscient-narrator form. In contrast to this narrative mode, which serves to portray reality, are Carlota's interior monologues which reveal her derangement.

The first indication of Carlota's insanity is evidenced in her instructions to her servant: "—Agua que corre, la que nadie puede apresar. Y nueces silvestres, duras, donde ningún veneno penetra. Nueces de corazón protegido. Silvestres, duras."⁷ Her fears of being poisoned compel her to believe that nuts are the only safe source of nourishment. Their structure symbolizes to Carlota an impenetrable citadel: the hard outer surface shelters the inner fruit. In much the same way, Carlota attempts to duplicate the protective insularity which the shell affords by imagining that she is enmeshed in the confines of a mirror: " . . . pero ya estamos dentro del espejo, para siempre, dios mío, para siempre, pasan los demás y no nos ven; queremos gritarles y de nuestros labios sale vidrio, dócil y duro. Estamos dentro

del espejo, comiendo ávidamente nueces y bebiendo agua en la fuente pública. Aquí no nos ven, no nos tocan" (p. 7). (The use of small letters at the beginning of these sentences shows Fuentes' early attempt to artistically portray the interior monologue form.)

Carlota's worsening state of derangement brings her to the conclusion that not only is she within the mirror but that once inside it she may penetrate further within its depths and thus progressively separate herself from a reality she deems harshly unacceptable: "Voy hacia dentro, cada vez más; me perderé en la llanura del espejo? no me percibo ya; sólo sueño, el espejo es el sueño" (p. 7).

Once removed from the reality she believes alien, vindictive and disagreeable, Carlota constructs an alternate realm of fantasy in which her husband survives and in which their Empire functions unimpaired. The continuance of this fantastic creation is contingent upon Carlota's sustained effort: " . . . sólo yo sueño, lo sueño a él, sueño el imperio, porque yo sueño vive él, vive el imperio, vive la tierra alfombrada de fieles. (. . .) debo soñar con los ojos abiertos frente al espejo para que mi sueño no muera; si duermo la liga de la vida se rompe, si duermo termina el sueño, . . . " (p. 7).

Carlota begins to see actual transformations in her physical surroundings. Thus, while viewing Europe from a train window she notices that the terrain suddenly and miraculously acquires the semblance of the Mexican countryside: "Carlota pegó la cara al vidrio, y el paisaje se transformó: una sábana de tierra cocida apareció en lugar del río, y las riberas se fueron poblando de casitas bajas y descascaradas, de fronteras de nopal y de niños desnudos, barrigones y de mujeres morenas, impávidas, envueltas en rebozos" (p. 8).

Essentially, Carlota has succeeded in emancipating herself from Europe by reproducing there the physical setting of Mexico. She must further rely upon her fantasy to complete this creation by duplicating the image of her husband and their attendants at court. This she accomplishes in accordance with Abbot Fischer's description of Maximilian: "Es tan hermoso nuestro Emperador! Un Dios Sol, se diría de lejos—desde donde conviene que se le vea. Pero allí en la recámara, desnudo de toda pompa, de cerca, se vuelve entrañable: el Dios es un muñeco . . . " (p. 7). For Carlota the royal court's attendants, must possess the same physical attributes and stature of her husband. In her fantastic conception she believes that they, too, when divested of their elaborate regalia and accoutrements will resemble *muñecos*. Then, in their diminuitive forms they could inconspicuously remain within the shell of a nut and reveal themselves at the appropriate instance. Their appearance would attest to the efficacy of Carlota's fantasy of re-creating a bygone epoch:

Sí, allí está, como siempre, escondido entre la carne del fruto. Extrae un diminuto muñeco rubio, lo contempla y vuelve a encerrarlo en la cáscara. (. . .) Después, ya sin expectación, dirige sus pasos hacia el castillo, no sin premura, pues la noche va a caer, poblada de remordimientos; no sin alivio, pues sabe que los muñecos—olvidados o presentes, pero siempre cercanos, listos a saltar de sus mágicas cajitas: el príncipe, el barón, el apuesto húsar—la visitarán en unas cuantas horas más, después de que escriba la carta al Emperador, y le darán conversación, respetuosa y lejana, como conviene a una Emperatriz"

(p. 8)

The spatial and temporal elements of **"El muñeco"** are as important as the narrative mode in portraying the desired fantasy. The space presented here manifests a dual basis. The first plane is composed of those places in Mexico and in Europe which are the sites for the events which occur during and after the epoch of Carlota and Maximilian. In a "cinematic" manner, more expertly developed in *La región más transparente,* the spatial scenes alternately encompass the environs of the Vatican, Orizaba, the Rhine Valley, Querétano, Metz and Belgium. Carlota, through her fantasy, creates the second facet of this story's space. Although she is safe within the protective confines of Europe her conscious recall of her residence in Mexico succeeds in making her oblivious to her surroundings and colors them with the essence of her previous Mexican milieu. Thus, her fantasy allows Carlota to survive in Europe while dwelling in the receptive and gracious atmosphere of Mexico.

The time depicted also possesses a dual foci. The first temporal plane contains all the events from the demise of the Hapsburg Empire in Mexico to the Franco-Prussian War. Its progression is linear and in accordance with calendar or historical time. The second aspect is represented by Carlota who is removed from this orderly flow and lives exclusively in the past. Through her fantasy she escapes from the present, which signifies her husband's death and the loss of an empire, to a previous epoch in which she was respected by her subjects and royally attended.

"El muñeco" is significant in terms of Fuentes' subsequent artistic endeavors in several repects. The use of parallel forms of narration to suggest unreliability of perception, which is first seen in this story, is employed, in a more complex fashion, in *Los días enmascarados* in **"Chac Mool"** and in **"Las dos Elenas,"** from *Cantar de ciegos*. In the former, Fuentes deftly employs a narrative mode involving two first-person accounts; sections of the protagonist's diary and the narrator who furnishes his impressions of those entries. **"Las dos Elenas,"** evincing an even more complex form of narration, is recounted in the first-person by Victor, its protagonist. In conjunction with Victor's subjective accounts of two female personages, are the interior monologues which portray the latters' conversations. Moreover, **"El muñeco"** is concerned with the Mexican past of the nineteenth century. As such, it serves as the thematic precursor to the treatment of the same epoch in **"Tlactocatzine, del jardín de Flandes"** and in *Aura.*

In September 1956, six months after **"El muñeco,"** Fuentes published his fourth uncollected work, **"Trigo errante."**[8] This work deals with the Arab-Israeli conflict in Palestine in 1948. The protagonist is the Biblical character, Lazarus, who after his resurrection by Christ, achieves immortality.

"Trigo errante" is recounted in a third-person narration which alternates with interior monologues. In this way an omniscient account is contrasted with the subjective thoughts of the protagonist. Although this technique was first used in **"El muñeco,"** its repetition in this story ensures the adoption of this narrative form in **"Las dos Elenas."**

The spatial element of this tale is hardly functional in evoking the depicted literary fantasy. Its time is however presented as cyclical and thereby anticipates the theme of reincarnation and the temporally fantastic present in *Los días enmascarados* in; **"Chac Mool," "Por boca de los dioses,"** and **"Tlactocatzine, del jardín de Flandes,"** in *Aura,* and in *Cumpleaños* (1969). Immortality, Fuentes suggests in **"Trigo errante,"** is actually an unmitigatingly harsh punishment as it compels the individual to witness fantastically the same human mistakes repeated *ad infinitum.* Thus, Lazarus, the protagonist of this story, being immortal lives to witness a recent war between Israel and its Arab neighbors.

In conclusion then, **"Pastel rancio," "El muñeco," "Pantera en jazz,"** and **"Trigo errante,"** do not represent a collection of organically unified stories. Each one is rather a separate and significant attempt by Fuentes to explore different thematic and technical material. Hence, the four uncollected works, published between 1949-57, are representative of his experimental period. Essentially, they form the unsophisticated basis for much of his later and more complex work. Their unifying element is the preponderant role display of fantasy as self-deception, as a distorted mode of perception and as supernatural occurrence. **"Pastel rancio"** presents the theme of self-delusion related to family discord, a subject which will be of paramount importance in *Cantar de ciegos*. **"Pantera en jazz"** and **"El muñeco"** center around a type who becomes progressively more significant in this author's total production, namely, the unmarried protagonist whose emotional and sexual unfulfillment engenders psychological instability, unreliability of perception and an inclination towards fantasy; lastly, the supernatural fantasy of cyclical time and re-incarnation found in **"Trigo errante"** is a topic which will be of some concern to Fuentes in *Los días enmascarados* and in *Aura* and of prominent interest in *Cumpleaños*.

The techniques of narrative person, time and space found in these texts are relatively uncomplicated in comparison to those of subsequent works. In **"Pastel rancio"** we see the initial stage of the complex narrative innovations implemented in *La muerte de Artemio Cruz,* in *Aura* and in *Cambio de piel*. Too, the use of temporal flashback presented in this tale is vital to the time scheme employed in *La muerte de Artemio Cruz*.

"Pantera en jazz" presents two spatial designations which are significant with respect to Fuentes' later literary creations: the use of space as a *zona sagrada,* for the depiction of supernatural occurrences, in *Los días enmascarados* and in *Aura* and the description of unrealistic space engendered by fantasy found in **"Letanía de la orquídea."**

Lastly, **"El muñeco"** is important in the scope of this author's art in several ways. Firstly, it employs the technique of parallel modes of narration to suggest unreliability of perception. This narrative form is employed in stories in both of Fuentes' published collections. The use of different spatial locations, described in this tale, serves as a precursor to the panorama of places presented in *La región más transparente*. This story also introduces a topic which will continue to command the Mexican author's literary attention in later years: the simultaneous existence of divergent historical eras in his country. He will later treat the persistence of the Hapsburg past in **"Tlactocatzine, del jardín de Flandes,"** and in *Aura*.

Thus, this experimental period presents a number of literary techniques and some of the thematic material which will reappear in a more complex form in Fuentes' art. More importantly though, this initial phase of his career presents a constant which he will explore in later periods of his artistic development: the individual in a situational crisis which forces him to adopt a fantasy mode of perceiving reality.

Notes

1. Carlos Fuentes, "Pastel rancio," *Mañana,* XXVI, 326 (26 de noviembre de 1949), pp. 226-27.

2. Luis Harss and Barbara Dohmann, *Into the Mainstream: Conversations with Latin American Writers* (New York: Harper & Row, 1967), p. 301.

3. Sharon Spencer, *Space, Time and Structure in the Modern Novel* (New York: New York University Press, 1971), p. 66.

4. Carlos Fuentes, "Pantera en jazz," *Ideas en México,* 1, 3 (enerofebrero de 1954), 119-24. (All references are to this edition).

5. *Ibid.,* p. 120.

6. Carlos Fuentes, "El muñeco," *Revista de la Universidad de México,* X, 7 (marzo de 1956), 7-8. (All references are to this edition).

7. *Ibid.,* p. 7.

8. Carlos Fuentes, "Trigo errante," *Revista de la Universidad de México,* XI, 1 (septiembre de 1956), 8-10.

Shirley A. Williams (essay date spring 1978)

SOURCE: Williams, Shirley A. "Prisoners of the Past: Three Fuentes Short Stories from *Los días enmascarados*." *Journal of Spanish Studies: Twentieth Century* 6, no. 1 (spring 1978): 39-52.

[*In the essay below, Williams considers how in "Chac Mool," "Tlactocatzine, del jardín de Flandes," and "Por boca de los dioses" Fuentes focused on the past, crafting fantasies that center around the notion that the ghosts and apparitions of Mexico's past permeate and haunt the collective Mexican psyche.*]

The six short stories contained in Carlos Fuentes' first published work, *Los días enmascarados* (1954), represent an impressive *tour de force* by the young artist. Although as a collection, the stories are uneven in style and reveal many of the technical inconsistencies characteristic of first works, three of the stories in particular merit close analysis. In these three stories: **"Chac Mool," "Tlactocatzine, del jardín de Flandes,"** and **"Por boca de los dioses,"** Fuentes traces several basic themes which he will continue to explore in greater depth as a maturing artist.

As Octavio Paz has noted, the title of the collection itself prefigures the direction of much of Fuentes' later work. With reference to the title Paz states:

> Alude a los cinco días finales del año azteca, los *nemontani*: "cinco enmascarados/con pencas de maguey", había dicho el poeta Tablada. Cinco días sin nombre, días vacíos durante los cuales se suspendía toda actividad—frágil puente entre el fin de un año y el comienzo

de otro—. En el espíritu de Fuentes, sin duda, la expresión tiene además un sentido de interrogación y de escarnio: ¿qué hay detrás de las máscaras?[1]

Although Paz does not cite his own work as a possible source for Fuentes' title, it seems clear that Paz's *Laberinto de la soledad* (1950) exercised a tremendous influence on the youthful Fuentes. Indeed, Fuentes' title may be a literary acknowledgement of his intellectual debt to Paz and his philosophical exploration of the concept of "la máscara mexicana"—the mask which both disguises the Mexican's true identity and separates him from the rest of society.

Fuentes himself admits to being fascinated by the "second reality" which he sees beneath the mask of surface appearances:

> El mundo de la segunda realidad siempre me ha apasionado aunque a veces logre ocultarlo. . . . Siempre he tratado de percibir detrás de la apariencia fantasmagórica de las cosas una realidad más tangible, más maciza que la realidad evidente de todos los días. Esa preocupación es producto de mis lecturas infantiles, muy dadas a gustar autores como Robert Louis Stevenson y Edgar Allen Poe.[2]

But the other reality Fuentes sees beneath the surface of contemporary life is quite different from that perceived by Poe and Stevenson. It is a uniquely Mexican reality, a reality peopled by ghosts and phantasma from Mexico's past—a past that refuses to die, that remains eternally a part of the present. "'No hay progreso histórico—dice Fuentes—, hay un simple presente perpetuo, la repetición de una serie de actos rituales.'"[3] Thus for Fuentes, an exploration of the reality-behind-the-mask leads unavoidably to the past. The past becomes a source of phantoms that Fuentes draws upon to create fantasy tales in which several levels of historical reality intermingle, and ghosts from the past take possession of the present.

The idea for **"Chac Mool,"** the first story contained in **Los días enmascarados,** came to Fuentes, by his own account, after reading a newspaper article concerning an exposition of Mexican art which toured Europe in 1952.[4] The exposition included a statue of the Mayan rain god, Chac Mool. Wherever the figure was exhibited, violent storms followed. The European peasant farmers began placing offerings before the god in an attempt to bring rains to drought stricken areas. This anecdote provided Fuentes with the theme for **"Chac Mool"** which, he says, is based on the perception of:

> . . . un hecho muy evidente para todos los mexicanos: hasta qué grado siguen vivas las formas cosmológicas de un México perdido para siempre y que, sin embargo, se resiste a morir y se manifiesta, de tarde en tarde, a través de un misterio, una aparición, un reflejo. La anécdota gira en torno a la persistencia de nuestras viejas formas de vida.[5]

In Fuentes' story, Filiberto, a collector of pre-Colombian artifacts, buys a statue of Chac Mool at the Lagunilla flea market. He lodges the new statue in his basement. During the course of the next several months, Chac Mool gradually comes to life and takes control of both the house and life of his hapless owner. Filiberto flees to Acapulco where he is drowned under mysterious circumstances. When a friend returns the body, he is met at Filiberto's home by an old Indian who orders him to take Filiberto's body to the basement.

The story is presented from two contrasting points of view: that of Filiberto and that of the friend who recovers his body. Filiberto's viewpoint is conveyed by means of notations he had written in a diary which his friend discovers among his other personal belongings. These diary entries, interspersed with the friend's narrations, form the bulk of the story. Filiberto's diary records his acquisition of and ultimate possession by Chac Mool. Due to the unlikely nature of the events Filiberto records, the reader is inclined to regard his account as fantasy, or at least as the product of an unbalanced mind. Filiberto's friend too tends toward this interpretation and attempts to find a rational explanation for Filiberto's delusions, thus reinforcing the reader's tendency toward scepticism. A dichotomy is thus established in which Filiberto's narrative is accepted as fantasy while his friend's interpretation represents reality. The story builds to a climax as both Filiberto's friend and the reader come to the progressive realization that Filiberto's story, which they assumed to be fantasy, is in fact reality.

Fuentes prepares his reader carefully for this final reversal of fantasy-reality. The friend's narration, which begins the tale, contains several clues which, in light of Filiberto's later diary notations, become highly significant and attest to the reality of his experiences: Filiberto drowned under suspicious circumstances at midnight; he had appeared on the verge of physical collapse; he bought a one-way ticket to Acapulco, although he supposedly went there only for a short vacation. And most significantly, the diary which the friend begins to read gives off an overpowering odor.

The diary records Filiberto's purchase of the Chac Mool idol and the subsequent "tragedias acuáticas" which plagued his house. Once Chac is installed in the basement, the plumbing begins to malfunction and municipal drain pipes back up into the basement for the first time. The excess of moisture causes Chac to become covered with slime. The idol begins to soften and his stone takes on a flesh-like texture. Filiberto notes with dismay that Chac's arms are growing hair. At this point, the friend observes that Filiberto's handwriting changes dramatically. The next diary entry three days later reveals Filiberto's confused state of mind and the radical change that has taken place in his life:

> Hasta hace tres días, mi realidad lo era al grado de haberse borrado hoy: era movimiento, reflejo, rutina, memoria, cartapacio. Y luego, como la tierra que un día tiembla para que recordemos su poder o la muerte que llegará, recriminando mi olvido de toda la vida, se presenta otra realidad que sabíamos estaba allí, mostrenca, y que debe sacudirnos para hacerse viva y presente.[6]

Chac Mool, who represents "la segunda realidad," the reality behind the mask, has come to life.

After reading this entry, the friend notes that it was shortly after this date that Filiberto was fired from his office job. Still looking for a rational explanation he notes:

> No supe qué explicación darme. Pensé que las lluvias excepcionalmente fuertes, de este verano, lo habían enervado. O que alguna depresión moral debía producir la vida en aquel caserón antiguo. . . .
>
> (p. 24)

Filiberto's notes continue. At first Chac returns to the basement to sleep, then appropriates Filiberto's bed. At last Filiberto admits "Debo reconocerlo, soy su prisionero" (p. 26). He also notes significantly that the horrible smell emanating from Chac has permeated the entire house (p. 26). Filiberto notices that Chac is becoming more civilized and demonstrates an affection for silk dressing gowns, soap, and after shave lotion. At the same time, his yellowed face appears to be aging. Filiberto's diary ends with his decision to flee to Acapulco, leaving the house to Chac Mool.

After finishing the diary, Filiberto's friend still finds himself unable to believe the events Filiberto has recorded. But when he delivers Filiberto's body, he is met by an apparition which is calculated to convince him of the reality of his friend's tale:

> Antes de que pudiera introducir la llave en la cerradura, la puerta se abrió. Apareció un indio amarillo, en bata de casa, con bufanda. Su aspecto no podía ser más repulsivo; despedía un olor a loción barata; su cara, polveada, quería cubrir las arrugas; tenía la boca embarrada de lápiz labial mal aplicado, y el pelo daba la impresión de estar teñido.
>
> —Perdone . . . , no sabía que Filiberto hubiera . . .
>
> —No importa; lo sé todo. Dígale a los hombres que lleven el cadáver al sótano.
>
> (pp. 28-29)

Here the story ends. The two perspectives have merged; what appeared to be fantasy is revealed as reality.

The reality-fantasy dichotomy in **"Chac Mool"** is paralleled by a dichotomy of present and past time levels which, like the reality-fantasy perspectives, merge at the story's end. Chac Mool obviously represents the indigenous past which, donning the mask of civilization, penetrates and ultimately takes possession of the present. But Fuentes explores the theme of the past in several other contexts in **"Chac Mool,"** thus enabling the reader to view the past's domination of the present from several different perspectives, both individual and collective. Filiberto's first notation records his visit to a café which he had frequented in his youth. Here he feels the weight of time's passage and realizes he has been molded by his own past in ways he is unable to comprehend:

> Desfilaron los años de las grandes ilusiones, de los pronósticos felices, y, también todas las omisiones que impidieron su realización. Sentí la angustia de no poder meter los dedos en el pasado y pegar los trozos de algún rompecabezas abandonado. . . .
>
> (p. 18)

Filiberto's recognition of the past's domination of his own life is followed, in the next notation, by an anecdote which underlines the past's domination of the collective Mexican life. One of Filiberto's friends, Pepe, who has a passion for theorizing, concludes:

> . . . si no fuera mexicano, no adoraría a Cristo. . . . El cristianismo, en su sentido cálido, sangriento, de sacrificio y liturgia, se vuelve una prolongación natural y novedosa de la religión indígena.
>
> (pp. 18-19)

Mexico's indigenous past thus predetermines the national character in the same way that an individual's past inscrutably influences his present and future.

The theme of the eternal presence of the past which Fuentes explores in **"Chac Mool"** is further elaborated in **"Tlactocatzine, del jardín de Flandes."** In **"Tlactocatzine"** a wealthy lawyer buys a mansion built during the French Intervention. The lawyer does not want to live there himself, but persuades a young friend to move in as caretaker. Almost immediately the friend feels the influence of strange forces, particularly in the garden. An ancient woman mysteriously appears. On several succeeding nights, the woman reappears, leaving enigmatic notes. Her final correspondence reveals her true identity: she is the mad empress Carlota. The young man, whom she believes to be her dead husband Maximilian, realizes that he must remain forever in the old mansion. Like Filiberto, he has become a prisoner, held captive by the past.

Throughout **"Tlactocatzine"** Fuentes intermingles a variety of time levels both historic and mythic. The story builds to a climax as its protagonist moves from contemporary historical reality into a world outside the dimensions of historical time. Like **"Chac Mool,"** **"Tlactocatzine"** is narrated by means of diary entries, but here we view the events only from the narrator-protagonist's point of view. There is no "friend" reading the diary and offering a different viewpoint or interpretation of the events in question.

The commentary begins on September 19, as the narrator records the lawyer's invitation to live in the unoccupied mansion and his initial impressions of the house. This first day's notes establish an inherently historical time perspective. As the narrator inventories the nearly empty house, he catalogues its architectural features and art works, placing each neatly into its appropriate historical niche. He obviously sees all of these things as belonging to historical epochs that are infinitely remote from the present. Even on the first day, however, the narrator feels special forces emanating from the garden. It seems clear that the garden represents a world outside of historical reality—an eternal world dominated significantly by the perfume of "siemprevivas."

The next day's entry records the narrator's changing perspective as he begins to pass from his historical world into the timeless world of the garden. Gone are the historical references of the previous day. Instead he notes:

> Aquí se está lejos de los 'males parasitarios' de México. Menos de veinticuatro horas entre estos muros, que son de una sensibilidad, de un fluir que corresponden a otros litorales, me han inducido a un reposo lúcido, a un sentimiento de las inminencias. . . .

> (p. 43)

He begins to develop an almost primitive sensitivity to nature and the eternal round of seasons:

> Entre los remaches de la ciudad, ¿cuándo he sentido el cambio de las estaciones? Más: no lo sentimos en México; una estación se diluye en otra sin cambiar de paso, 'primavera inmortal y sus indicios'; y las estaciones pierden su carácter de novedad reiterada, de casilleros con ritmos, ritos y goces propios, de fronteras a las que enlazar nostalgias y proyectos, de señas que nutran y cuajen la conciencia. Mañana es el equinoccio. Hoy, aquí, sí he vuelto a experimentar, con un dejo nórdico, la llegada del otoño.

> (p. 44)

Once he has undergone this transformation, he is prepared to make contact with the ancient woman. He begins to sense her presence: " . . . casi podría decirse que se escuchan pasos, lentos, con peso de respiración, entre las hojas caídas" (p. 44).

The next day the narrator moves a step closer to understanding the garden, as he realizes that it seems to occupy a different time-space plane than the surrounding city. He first compares the garden to landscapes he had seen in Memling's paintings, and then realizes suddenly:

> Era un paisaje ficticio, inventado. El jardín no estaba en México . . . , y la lluviecilla . . . Entré corriendo a la casa, atravesé el pasillo, penetré al salón y pegué la nariz a la ventana: en la Avenida del Puente de Alvarado, rugían las sinfonolas, los tranvías y el sol, sol monótono, Dios-Sol sin matices ni efigies en sus rayos, Sol-piedra estacionario, sol de los siglos breves. Regresé a la biblioteca: la llovizna del jardín persistía, vieja, encapotada.

> (p. 45)

While gazing at the garden that afternoon, he senses a "ruido sordo" and for the first time sees the ancient woman, perceived only as a "pequeño bulto, negro y encorvado" (p. 46). It is important to note that the old woman appears only after the narrator has begun to enter the mysterious world of the garden. His perceptions of the woman will become clearer on successive encounters as he enters more fully into her world, until at last his recognition of her true identity is accompanied by his realization that he has definitely left the world of historical time. The narrator becomes progressively disoriented as he feels himself moving into the strange garden-realm. This disorientation is reflected in his increasing use of synasthesia ("ruido sordo") to express his experiences. His encounters with the old woman are almost invariably preceded by a sense of other-worldliness which he can only express by means of the incongruous imagery of synasthesia.

On September 22, the narrator wonders why he has no desire to leave the house ("i . . . por qué no puedo arrancarme de esta casa, diría mejor, de mi puesto en la ventana que mira al jardín?" [p. 46]). As he continues his lonely vigil, the woman returns. This time, he observes her clearly:

> Era una viejecita . . . , tendría ochenta años, cuando menos . . . delgada, seca, vestía de negro . . . de perfil, sus facciones de halcón, sus mejillas hundidas, vibraban con los ángulos de la guadaña.

> (pp. 46-47)

But a mysterious pathway seems to open leading from the garden, and the woman vanishes.

The next night, Sept. 23 according to the diary's chronology, the narrator locks himself in his bedroom in an effort to avoid another encounter with his mysterious visitor. But the old woman appears nevertheless and slips a message bearing a single word—"Tlactocatzine"—under the door. Although at this point the narrator does not realize its significance, this message both identifies the woman and mandates the narrator's fated relationship to her.[7]

The narrator's sense of historical, chronological time now breaks down completely, symbolically indicating his passage into the timeless world he now shares with "la anciana." His loss of chronological time sense is clearly revealed by the next two diary entries which continue to be dated September 23, although they clearly refer to the day following his receipt of the first message. As the narrator leaves chronological time behind, his sense of disorientation is reflected once more by his use of synasthesia ("luz parda," "luz blanca" [p. 49]).

The last entry records the narrator's realization that he is now a prisoner, forever doomed to re-enact the role of the dead Maximilian for the eternally mad Carlota:

> Esa noche escuché a mis espaldas—no sabía que lo iba a escuchar por siempre—el roce de las faldas sobre el piso; camina con una nueva alegría extraviada, sus ademanes son reiterativos y delatan satisfacción. Satisfacción de soledades compartidas. Era su voz de nuevo, acercándose, sus labios junto a mi oreja, su aliento fabricado de espuma y tierra sepultada:
>
> ' . . . desde ahora, no más cartas, ya estamos juntos para siempre; nunca saldremos; nunca dejaremos entrar a nadie . . . Oh, Max, contesta, las siemprevivas, las que te llevo en las tardes a la cripta de los capuchinos, ¿no saben frescas? Son como las que te ofrendaron cuando llegamos aquí, tú, Tlactocatzine. . . . '
>
> (pp. 50-51)

Thus the narrator of **"Tlactocatzine, del jardín de Flandes"** becomes a prisoner of the past. But the "past" here is much more complex than the past represented by Chac Mool. Chac Mool clearly symbolized the persistence of an indigenous past—a remote but nevertheless essentially historical past. The past embodied in the ancient Carlota, on the other hand, is both historical and archetypal.

Fuentes' letters to Gloria Durán reveal that the author's preoccupation with "la segunda realidad" frequently manifests itself as an obsessive fascination with themes of witchcraft and sorcery. And even more significantly, he reveals that:

> 'Esa obsesión nació en mí cuando tenía siete años y después de visitar el castillo de Chapultepec y ver el cuadro de la joven Carlota de Bélgica, encontré en el Archivo Casasola la fotografía de esa misma mujer, ahora vieja, muerta, adornada con una cofia de niña, la Carlota que murió loca en un castillo el mismo año en que yo nací, las dos Carlotas: Aura y Consuelo.'[8]

Aura and Consuelo are characters from Fuentes' later novel, *Aura.* The ancient Consuelo, a sorceress, is able to appear at will as her younger manifestation,

the lovely Aura. The author's statement seems to indicate that even as a boy he associated the figure of Carlota with the theme of witchcraft.

Gloria Durán has interpreted the figure of the witch or "bruja" in Fuentes as merely one aspect of the *anima,* an integral manifestation of the Jungian collective unconscious. Basing her observations on a careful study of the works of Robert Graves (*The White Goddess*) and various etymological derivations of the word *bruja* in Spanish, Durán concludes that the figure of Carlota in **"Tlactocatzine"** does indeed manifest many of the characteristics of the Jungian *anima*: Carlota is associated with the house and the wood (the traditional symbols of the *bruja -anima*); her physical description matches that given in the oldest etymologies of *bruja* ("tiene el pico corvo como ave de rapiña"), and she appears with the coming of night. All of these correspondences seem to support Durán's conclusion that in **"Tlactocatzine"** Carlota represents not only the historical personage, but the archetypal *bruja* or *Madre Terrible* as well.

This interpretation would, of course, explain the timeless aspect of the garden and "la anciana." For Jung affirms that the *ánima* exists outside of the bounds of time. Under the spell of the *ánima* man is able to abolish chronological time and, like the narrator of **"Tlactocatzine,"** enter the timeless realm of the eternal present.

The relationship of the past to the Jungian collective unconscious is seen once again in **"Por boca de los dioses."** In his very Jungian interpretation of Mexican history, Octavio Paz notes that phantoms from the past form part of the collective Mexican unconscious. As a people Mexicans:

> . . . struggle with imaginary entities, with vestiges of the past or self-engendered phantasms. These vestiges and phantasms are real, at least to us. Their reality is of a subtle and cruel order, because it is a phantasmagoric reality. They are impalpable and invincible because they are not outside us, but within us. On the struggle which our will-to-be carries on against them, they are supported by a secret and powerful ally, our fear of being. Everything that makes up the present-day Mexican . . . can be reduced to this: the Mexican does not dare to be himself.
>
> In many instances these phantasms are vestiges of past realities. Their origins are in the Conquest, the Colonial period, the Independence period or the wars fought against the United States and France. Others reflect our current problems, but in an indirect manner, concealing or distorting their true nature.[9]

"Por boca de los dioses" can be seen as Fuentes' fictional rendering of the theme of the Mexican's struggle with the ghosts of his collective unconscious. As the tale begins, the narrator, Oliverio, is fearfully awaiting the arrival of phantoms from the past:

Cuando el reloj se abraza a sí mismo, al reguirse y apretarse las dos piernas del tiempo en la medianoche, sé que no tardarán las visitas indeseadas; están, silenciosas, en la antesala de mi olvido, hasta que los pies les punzan con un ritmo obscuro; sé que el repiqueteo de la puerta, el aullar de las gargantas peludas cantando en silencio a su plexo, el falso balumboyó tropical, su tántara-ranta-tantán en las paredes, es un disfraz, un disimulo cortés, una invitación al chocolate de los canónigos con ojos de serpiente, envenenado de dolor y latente de coágulos; y rasguean sin cesar, miles de guitarras, como si sus dedos mismos fueran cuerdas. ¿Qué traen en sus manos y en sus cerebros, detrás de la sonrisa y el cachondeo de los abrazos inevitables? Una noche quisieron introducirse como mariachis. . . .

(p. 64)

This initial narrative establishes several ideas which are crucial to the story's development. The phantasms that haunt the narrator belong to the realm of the unconscious ("están en la antesala de mi olvido"), and represent a typically Mexican reality, a reality linked to the indigenous past. As the narrative continues, the references to the Aztec past become more obvious:

La suya [la mitología] sigue viva, sus monstruos de jade y embolias siguen gravitando como máscaras daltónicas que sin color se pierden en el polvo y el drenaje, que corretean subterráneas para asomar sus fauces de tarde en tarde, que cabalgan por el aire secando sus montes y moviendo los puñales de obsidiana.

(pp. 64-65)

The ancient mythology survives, penetrating and threatening the present, but like Chac Mool, the old gods have put on the mask of contemporary reality and are thus not immediately recognizable. We note in the preceding quotation how they attempt to enter the narrator's room under the guise of modern mariachis. Having established these ideas by means of Oliverio's surrealistic introductory meditation, Fuentes moves on with his story.

Oliverio tells of his visit to an art museum. There he meets don Diego, an old acquaintance whom he finds vaguely repulsive. They argue over the art works on display, don Diego preferring works of the colonial period, Oliverio preferring modern art. Their argument centers around a portrait by Tamayo. Don Diego insists that the mouth is poorly done, looking more like an ear than a mouth. As they argue in front of the painting, the mouth begins to take on a three dimensional character and appears to be laughing. Oliverio tears the mouth from the portrait. When don Diego protests the mutilation of the work, Oliverio throws him from a window to his death and escapes with the mouth, which he refers to as "mi presa," securely stashed in a bucket.

After an intermediate stop at a department store, Oliverio returns to his hotel room (whose number significantly happens to be 1519—the date of the conquest of Aztec Mexico). In the hall he meets Tlazol, the Aztec goddess of carnal love, who reproaches him for his handling of Don Diego's death, implying that he should have killed the old man as part of the traditional collective sacrifice ("¿ . . . por qué lo mataste de esta manera, para tu goce personal, sin tolerar el contacto de todos . . .?" [p. 71]).

At midnight, phantasms from the past group themselves outside the door, but are unable to enter the room. After their departure, Oliverio leaves, taking the captive mouth with him. The mouth escapes and Oliverio chases the lips thinking: "Ya no era cuestión de tenerlos o admirarlos, sino de hacerles sentir el peso de mi voluntad . . . " (p. 73). Once he recaptures the mouth, however, it takes possession of him. He realizes with horror:

. . . mi boca seguía hablando, retorciéndose, diciendo lo que no pensaba. Corrí a mi cuarto. . . . Me detuve frente al espejo. Estaba triste, y lancé una carcajada. Mi aliento sabía a calcinación antiquísima. Mis labios se movieron.—Eres mi prisionero, Oliverio. Tú piensas, pero yo hablo.

(p. 74)

The mouth takes its captive on a tour of his usual clubs—"en todas partes aullando, insultando, escupiendo odio y sangre" (p. 75), and warning of the impending destruction of the present by the past:

'Disfraces de Galilea, disfraces de Keyes, disfraces de Comte, disfraces de Fath y de Marx; todos los trituraremos, todos quedarán desnudos, y no habrá más ropa que la piedra y escama verde, la de pluma sangrienta y ópalo de nervios . . . '

(p. 76)

Once more contemporary civilization is seen as a mask which disguises reality. The reality-behind-the-mask is the true Mexican reality, and this reality is linked to the Aztec past.

Upon returning to the hotel, the mouth commands the elevator operator to push the last button, sending the elevator to the basement. There Oliverio is met by a pantheon of Aztec gods who reign once more in the city in the middle of the lake. The elevator operator is dragged out and sacrificed, but as the gods return for Oliverio, he escapes. His escape, however, is short lived. Tlazol pursues him to his room, and asks him to open the door. When Oliverio refuses, Tlazol taunts " . . . yo creí que eras muy macho" (p. 78). The Mexican gauntlet has been dropped, and Oliverio reacts to this threat to his manhood in a typically Mexican way by throwing open the door to meet Tlazol. He then describes his own death:

Tlazol cerró la puerta con llave, sus labios se acercaron a los míos, y a mordiscos arrancó su carne. En la mano de la Diosa brillaba un puñal opaco; lenta, lenta, lo acercó a mi corazón.

(p. 78)

Oliverio dies a sacrificial death, and the Goddess reclaims the lips which the reader now realizes had always been her own. The symbolic message is clear. Once again Fuentes denies historical progress and affirms an eternal present. Or in the words of Ixca Cienfuegos, a character from *La región más transparente*:

> . . . el origen. Todo lo demás son disfraces. Allá, en el origen, está todavía México, lo que es, nunca lo que puede ser. México es algo fijado para siempre, incapaz de evolución.[10]

Fuentes will continue to explore the theme of the past in most of his later works. Indeed, like the protagonists of the three short stories we have just examined, Fuentes himself can be said to be a prisoner of the past. Like Filiberto of **"Chac Mool,"** Fuentes feels " . . . la angustia de no poder meter los dedos en el pasado y pegar los trozos de algún rompecabezas abandonado" (p. 18), and returns obsessively to the past, doggedly rearranging its fragments in an effort to understand completely the resulting configuration that is the Mexican present. Fuentes' exploration of the past in *Los días enmascarados* is a mere foreshadowing of the deeper exploration of all aspects of the past—individual and collective, historical and archetypal—which the author will later undertake in his major novels: *La región más transparente, Cambio de piel, La muerte de Artemio Cruz,* and most recently *Terra nostra.*

The theme of "la segunda realidad," with its emphasis on phantoms, witchcraft and sorcery will also be amply developed in later works. As Fuentes himself has noted, **Aura** is in many aspects only a deeper exploration of the *bruja* figure which the author first traces in **"Tlactocatzine."** The theme of sorcery will be further elaborated in *Zona sagrada* and *Cumpleaños.* Even the figure of the mad Carlota will reappear in a later work, *Cuerpos y ofrendas.* Thus, because of the thematic trajectory they establish, a careful reading of these early short stories is an important introduction to the study of Fuentes' later works.

Notes

1. Octavio Paz, "La máscara y la transparencia," in *Homenaje a Carlos Fuentes,* ed. Helmy F. Giacoman (New York: Las Américas, 1971), p. 17.

2. Emmanuel Carballo, *El cuento mexicano del siglo XX* (México: Empresas Editoriales, 1964), p. 77.

3. Claude Fell, "Mito y realidad en Carlos Fuentes," in *Homenaje a Carlos Fuentes,* ed. Helmy F. Giacoman (New York: Las Américas, 1971), p. 376.

4. Carballo, *El cuento,* p. 77.

5. Carballo, p. 77.

6. Carlos Fuentes, *"Los días enmascarados"* (México: Organización Editorial Novaro, 1966), p. 23. All succeeding page references are made to this edition.

7. Tlactocatzine: title the Aztecs used to refer to Maximilian.

8. Gloria Durán, "La bruja de Carlos Fuentes," in *Homenaje a Carlos Fuentes,* ed. Helmy F. Giacoman (New York: Las Américas, 1971), p. 249.

9. Octavio Paz, *The Labyrinth of Solitude,* trans. Lysander Kemp (New York: Grove Press, 1961), pp. 72-73.

10. Carlos Fuentes, *La región más transparente* (México: Fondo de Cultura Económica), p. 128.

Jason Weiss and Carlos Fuentes (interview date December 1981)

SOURCE: Weiss, Jason, and Carlos Fuentes. "Carlos Fuentes." In *Writing at Risk: Interviews in Paris with Uncommon Writers,* pp. 108-24. Iowa City: University of Iowa Press, 1991.

[*In the interview below, conducted in December 1981, Fuentes elaborates on subjects including the definition of history (particularly Latin American history); the cultural identities of Latin America and the United States; ways in which his political concerns inform his fiction; and the realm of the supernatural in American fiction.*]

History, civilizations, and the complex cultural identity of Mexico have been the stuff from which Carlos Fuentes' twenty books are made. The open adventure of his novelistic structures is indicative of the new language wrought by recent generations of Latin American writers, many of whom he has helped to get their work read beyond their own borders. A keen interpreter of politics, a sincere advocate of culture and thought, Fuentes is above all a man of conscience. Mexican ambassador to France from 1975 to 1977, he resigned his post in protest when former president Gustavo Díaz Ordaz, responsible for the massacre of hundreds of students by police at Tlatelolco in 1968, was appointed ambassador to post-Franco Spain.

For the French publication of his latest novel, Distant Relations, *Fuentes was back in Paris again, where this interview was conducted in the offices of his publisher, Gallimard, in late December 1981. We began by discussing his massive novel of 1976,* Terra Nostra, *which Gabriel García Márquez has said requires a one-year fellowship to read.*

[Weiss]: *In reading* Terra Nostra *it is surprising how much turns out to be factual. So that discovering more about the history, one discovers more about the book.*

[Fuentes]: Yes, certainly. After all, history is only what we remember of history. What is fact in history? The novel asks this question. We made history. But history doesn't exist if we don't remember it. That is, if we don't imagine it, finally.

Did you have a specific sense of where fact and fiction diverge while writing Terra Nostra?

Well, I have another book, it's an anti—*Terra Nostra* in the sense that it's so short: **Aura,** a novella. And the protagonist of **Aura,** who is caught by this sort of witch in this house in Mexico City, says, "Well, I'm here to work and make enough money so that I can write what I've been imagining all my life I could write. A great opus of the Renaissance world, of the discovery of the New World, of the conquest of the Americas, the colonization." I mean, this is a historian who would like to deal with fact. But of course he is caught in a world of pure fiction, a surreal world. So, I guess that from this mold, from this matrix, came *Terra Nostra.* It is written by the protagonist of **Aura,** who is a man caught between life and death, between youth and old age, between reality and surreality, so he writes *Terra Nostra.* But it's not the book he wanted to write, it's not the history book he wanted to write, it's a book in which he has to imagine history, that is, to reinvent history. That is, to write history, really.

How long did you spend researching the book?

All my life. I never consulted a note when I was writing *Terra Nostra.* Because this is something I've carried with me all my life, this is my whole heritage. As a Mexican, as a Latin American, as a man of the Caribbean basin, of the Gulf of Mexico, of the Mediterranean, all the things I am are there. So I never had to consult, I just had to imagine my history and kill a few characters, because of psychological reasons, create or resuscitate others, that's it. But, basically, as a writer and as a man of political preoccupations at the same time, I've always been very impressed by the writings of Vico, in the eighteenth century. Because Vico's probably the first philosopher who says *we* create history. Men and women, we create history, it is *our* creation, it is not the creation of God. But this throws a certain burden on us. Since we made history, we have to imagine history. We have to imagine the past. Nobody lived in the past, nobody present lived in

the past. So we have to imagine the past. And I've always had that as a sort of credo. And for *Terra Nostra,* of course, that is essential, to imagine the past.

And then there is the notion of history as of people, rather than history of leaders.

But here of course there is an element, in *Terra Nostra,* which one could call madness in high places. Something Americans know a great deal about in recent times. Because in societies that have always been pyramidal and authoritarian, as the Hispanic societies—Queen Joan of Spain, Philip II—they count a lot in our lives. When Franco died, Juan Goytisolo wrote a very beautiful piece called, "In Memoriam Francisco Franco." Of course he was in opposition to Franco all his life, but he said, "Why have you died on me? What can I do without you? I was born when you came to power, you told me what I could read, what movies I could see, what I should be taught in school, how I should make love, how I should pray to God, you taught me everything. Suddenly I'm an orphan without you. Here I am at forty, an orphan because you have left us."

What brought about your latest novel, Distant Relations? *What was the seed of that?*

So many things. It's difficult to pinpoint one origin. Because, of course, by now I have managed to understand more or less what I am writing and how it all fits in. So this is part, really, of *one* novel I am writing, a novel I have imagined with twenty titles—most of which are written, by the way—and twelve different sections. And one of these sections is three novels that deal with another reality, with a parallel contiguous reality, and they are **Aura, Cumpleaños,** which is a novel that has never been translated, and *Distant Relations.* And it has to do with *Terra Nostra* also.

But it has to do with writing, above all, it has to do with fiction. Although on the surface you would say, "Okay, it's a novel about these contacts that have taken place throughout history between France and Spanish America." There's a lot of stuff about this, about this quantity of poets and politicians and musicians of Latin American origin that have had a prominent role in French life. Lafargue, who was the son-in-law of Karl Marx, and the poets Heredia and Lautréamont and Supervielle and Laforgue, and the musician Reynaldo Hahn, who was so close to Proust, came from Caracas, etcetera. At one level, it is that, but then it is about a family called the Heredias, who have a homonymic counterpart in France, a French Heredia family, and a person who is narrating the story, a French count, Branly, who through the contact of the two Heredias discovers in a way the past he himself had forgotten, as the past of the Heredias is recovered basically through the encounters of two children, whom we are at difficulty to define or to understand the nature of their relationships. Finally, there is a delving into the family tree of the Heredias, but one discovers as one reads that genealogy is very much like fiction. You cannot know all the story. I think the clue to *Distant Relations* is the final phrase, which says, "No one remembers the whole story." No one knows the whole story of the Heredia family and therefore no one can tell the whole story. But this can be said of all fiction. It is a fiction to say that fiction can end, that it has a beginning and an end. Because there is a reader. If you are an active reader, you will not let the author finish the story, you want to finish it yourself.

About halfway through the book, French Heredia says, "The new world was the last opportunity for a European universalism: it was also its tomb. It was never possible to be universal after the century of the discoveries and conquests. The new world turned out to be too wide, on a different scale." What does that mean for you?

It means that America was invented by Europe, that America is an invention of the European mind. As the Mexican historian Edmundo Gorman has said, America was discovered because it was designed, and it was designed because it was needed by Europe. Europe wanted a place to regenerate history, to regenerate man. It wanted to find the golden age and the good savage. It came over and it burned the golden age, razed it to the ground, and it enslaved the noble savage. So that the utopia on which the New World is premised was promptly corrupted by the epic of the colonization and the universality of the utopia broke up into the particular histories, the balkanization of the different epics that took place.

The dream was killed, yet the dream remains alive. Latin America wants to be utopia, wants to be utopia desperately. And so does the United States. Therefore, we cannot have tragedies, which I think is a tragedy. That Latin America cannot give anything to the very great need of restoring tragic values in this terrible world of ours in which instead of tragedy we have crimes. Because we have not been capable of understanding the conflict between good and good. We have only the Manichean vision of good and bad, of good guys and bad guys, white hats and black hats, this sort of very Ronald Reagan vision of the world. But the only tragedian, I think, of the New World is Faulkner. There's no other writer who really understands the nature of the tragic and he extracts it from the South, from the defeat of the South, and tells it in baroque terms. Which is something we should have done in Latin America. But we can only tell our great mock

epics, our very funny mock epics, like *A Hundred Years of Solitude,* which resembles *Don Quixote* so much, in that it is not a tragedy, it is a grandiose hyperbolic mock epic of sorts.

What do you think accounts for the urge to want to embrace everything, among many Latin American writers, which doesn't particularly exist in North American writers?

Well, I'm thinking of Thomas Pynchon, who raises it a great deal. And John Barth, in many of his works. You do have that sort of writer also.

But it doesn't seem to be as prevailing. For instance, in your book-length essay on the new Latin American novel, La nueva novela hispanoamericana, *you talk about how the New World was too wide. But that has many different results between Latin America and North America, which is also a very wide country, if not as wild in a sense.*

It was big and vast, but it was empty. There was hardly anything in the North American continent. There were many obstacles in Mexico and Latin America, the first of them were civilizations that had to be destroyed. Of course, the North Americans destroyed civilizations also, they killed Indians. But the colonization of the United States doesn't have an epic like the *Chronicle of the Conquest of New Spain* by Bernal Díaz, which is really the foundation of our literary life, of our novel. It's an epic, as of the world it has discovered. Read the chapters when he enters Tenochtitlán, it's fantastic, it's like entering a story in the Arabian nights. And then he is forced to destroy this, his dream has to become a nightmare, and yet he wants to love what he has destroyed. And then he has to remember what he has destroyed fifty years after the events, when he writes the book, which is like Proust, *A la recherche du temps perdu.* So you have all these very complicated cultural facts which were not present in the colonization of what was to become the United States. It's a very different cultural program and cultural perspective when you have killed a civilization.

How much, when we speak of this, do you think we can talk about Latin America and how much does it apply specifically to Mexico?

I'm talking about Mexico mostly. Of course in Peru, maybe, in the Quechua empire. And the Aztec empire. It certainly doesn't apply to Argentina or Chile, although the Araucanos gave a lot of resistance in Chile, but in Argentina the tribes were decimated and finally really killed by the republican presidents of the nineteenth century, very similar to what happened in the United States. So the sense of a cultural genocide is much stronger in Mexico and in Peru, but it's also very strong in the Caribbean because really there the population disappeared completely, completely. Not a single Caribe Indian was left.

Your books talk a lot about a sense of identity. What do you sense as a kind of identity that comes out of the North American experience, which is very different and in a way is more confused because it has so many more elements?

Well, I see a lot more homogeneity in the United States than I do in any Latin American country.

Yes, but it's not a homogeneity of the peoples in it. It's a homogeneity of the dominant class.

Of the dominant class, what it offers, what it gives as entertainment, what it gives as styles of living, architecture, eating. That is tremendously homogeneous and terrible. It destroys variety a great deal.

And it's only been within the last twenty years that people are paying more attention to the cultural heritage as well as the cultural contribution in present tense.

The great effort is of course to absorb people into the mainstream, to absorb blacks into the mainstream. I think the great challenge is going to come from the Hispanics, because they're much less assimilable than anybody else, for the simple reason that they have their cultures right over the border or in an island fifty miles away or whatever. They do not give up their culture so easily or their language. So it's very different when you have come from Sweden or Poland or Italy, or even from Africa, to assimilate into the mainstream. It's much more difficult for the Hispanics.

How much, in Mexico, has there been a reconciling of the Indian cultures and the Spanish?

Well, Mexico is probably the only country in Latin America that has made heroes of the defeated and not of the conquerors. In Lima you have the statue of Pizarro in the central square. In Mexico you have the statue of Cuauhtémoc, and there is no statue of Cortés, which is a mistake I think. Because we are the descendants of Cortés also and of Spain and of its culture. But, Mexico has always made the decision to sing the eulogy of the defeated, of the Indians. Is this only rhetoric? Well, if it's rhetoric, we're all educated in that rhetoric. Mexicans are educated in the rhetoric of respect for the fallen Indian civilizations and respect for the Revolution. So, this is the only real form of checks and balances we have in our country, that generation after generation of Mexicans are educated in

liberal ideas. And they go into society and they are formed by these ideas. So, the problem there is not that we have not recognized the heritage, we have done so. You go to the anthropology museum in Mexico City, and you see that it is mostly children who go there. You see children and students. It means that generation after generation of Mexicans are being educated in the respect and understanding of the old civilizations. Now, the Indians that exist in Mexico today are part of another social and economic structure. There are about four million Indians and they, many of them, like to live in their communities and protect their values and their sense of the sacred and things that have little to do with the modern world. Then there is a double problem, there is a problem of respect to these values and the integrity of these communities, which is sometimes achieved, sometimes it is not. They are exploited, they are corrupted, and that is where a lot of work has to be done.

How much of the snobbish pride for the pure-blood Spanish ancestry is there in Mexico?

Very little, because there are so few pure whites in Mexico. Very, very few pure whites. If it's three, four percent of the population . . . We're all mestizos. I'll tell you, I have forebears that are Spanish, Moorish, Jewish, German, and Yaqui Indian. And I'm a typical Mexican in that sense, I have a total mixture of ancestry. There are very few people who came to be pure Caucasian. You have only to look at us: where are they? I don't think it's a racist country. It's a country that has many social and economic injustices, but racism is not among the injustices of Mexico, I think. Besides, whom would you discriminate against?

And that's part of the central difference between Mexico and the United States, in that in Mexico the Spanish not only conquered the Indians but they bred with them.

The great difference, of course, is that the United States, in spite of the melting pot, has tended to nurture, as we say, a homogeneous culture. The ruling classes in the United States tend to believe that it is in uniformization, and then atomization within the uniformization, that you have power. In Mexico we're very conscious that we coexist with many cultures and many times. It's a country of many historical times, of many different cultures coexisting. This is the nature of the country, and it is a value. I think it is a great value and it has to be protected. And Mexico is a country that has been very isolated. First, because of its geography. It's a country of deserts and mountains, chasms, canyons. Very difficult, the communication in Mexico. When Charles V asked Cortés to describe the country to him, Cortés picked up a very stiff piece of parchment from the table of the emperor and crushed it like this and put it on the table and said, "That's Mexico, that's the country I've conquered."

And I imagine a very moving thing that happened to me, visiting a part of Jalisco, the country of the Huichol Indians, with the president, Echeverría, at that time. And a strip was made in one of the Huichol towns for us to land. The plane landed there, and the Indian chiefs were there in their attire, very beautiful, and said hello to the president. This little village was situated next to a gorge, an enormous canyon, the canyon of the Santiago River which is as deep as the canyon of the Colorado River in the United States. The president said, "What can I do for you?" etcetera, and the Indian chief said, "Something very simple, look over the canyon at those people waving at us from the other side. They are our brothers but we have never been able to touch hands with them. Never, never, never, for thousands of years. So would you take us in your great white bird to the other side of the canyon so we can finally embrace and touch hands?" Well, this is a great image of the isolation of Mexico.

You know, the Mexican Revolution had one great success, its cultural success, especially in the sense that it destroyed that isolation to a great degree. The sense of all these great cavalry charges, of Villa from the north, Zapata from the south, means that Mexicans were moving for the first time and meeting each other and learning to cry together and sing together and what their names were and what they talk about, etcetera. So there is a breakdown of this lack of communication. But not only in an internal sense, also in the international sense. Traditionally, Mexico has been like a cat who was burned with hot water: too many invasions, all contacts with foreigners have been terrible, we lost half our territory to the United States, we were invaded by Napoleon III, we were invaded by Pershing, the Marines took Vera Cruz, don't have anything to do with foreign countries, we got into trouble. In the last decade, during the governments of Echeverría and López Portillo—and oil had to do with this but also a cultural image of ourselves—we have come out much more into the world. In contact with other Third World nations, in contact with countries that offer us an opportunity to diversify support—political, economical, cultural—as is the case today with the Mitterrand government in France, there's a very close relationship between the two governments.

Mexico also serves as a sort of crossroads between the rest of Latin America and the United States.

Well, yes, the United States has the great, great advantage, the great boon, of having friends on its borders, Mexico and Canada, and not satellites. And friends are not yes-men. People who go around saying yes are false friends, they prove to be false; they're good for our ego, for a couple of days probably, but no more. So, Mexico, a country that has a long experience in the Central American—Caribbean area, tells the truth to the United States. Sometimes a harsh truth, a truth the Americans don't like but we do tell it. Because they might avoid making some of the mistakes they have made traditionally, which cost everybody a lot of suffering.

How have you, as a writer and intellectual, managed to reconcile your literary interests and political concerns? How do you find to best express and act upon your political beliefs?

Let me say several things about this. First, my writing is not political in the sense that it's pamphletary writing or anything of the sort. It's not even popular writing. It's rather elite writing, it takes a lot to get into my books and to win readers for my books. I like to win readers, not to have ready-made readers, I don't care for that. I prefer to have more readers by the year 2000 than to have fewer readers by the year 2000 than I have today. And that is in a sense of the integrity of the work, I think, it has something to do with that. But I do think that there is a political element in literature always, because we are political beings, because we live in a society. Now, the thing is not to write pamphlets certainly, because that is paving the sidewalks of hell with good intentions. We've had too many novels and poems in Latin America that pretend to be political but do not serve either literature or the revolution. They're just bad writing, they don't serve anybody, it's useless. So, what I aim at, I hope to, because these are great models—my God, I'm not comparing myself to them—is what you find in Balzac or Dostoyevsky. And that is that the political reality you find in *La comédie humaine* or in *The Possessed* is in constant tension with what Balzac would call the search for the absolute or the metaphysical urge in Dostoyevsky. And this extraordinary tension between what is most passing and brittle, which is the political reality, and something that should be lasting and permanent creates the marvelous tension of these novels. In that sense I would like to write political novels, like *The Possessed* or like *Lost Illusions*. But who knows?

Anyway, writing's a rather solitary activity, an extremely solitary activity, and I am a gregarious man. I am not a solitary man and I suffer greatly from spending eight or nine or ten hours a day sitting alone, hunched, drawing a hump, and scribbling little fly's feet on white paper. This can drive you nuts, absolutely. It's a form of torture and it is against nature. If there's anything against nature, it is writing. So, my political preoccupation—which is authentic—is also a way of getting together with people, of establishing contact with people. But I try to do it mostly as a citizen than as a writer. Or as a writer who writes journalism. Because I love journalism, I love writing in papers, and I love friendship and contact and conversations with journalists. So it is at that level of journalism and teaching and lecturing that I try to have a certain political bearing on things.

But as far as your political concerns, does that seem to be a main thread in the Latin American cultural identity?

Yes, yes, yes. Because I'm very conscious . . . you know, a lot has been said about the ideological nature of Latin American writers, and I disagree with this, on the level of the greatest writers. I mean, of Pablo Neruda, or Vallejo, or Octavio Paz, Cortázar, García Márquez, Carpentier. We're not dealing with ideology. We are dealing with writers who are restoring our civilization, the facts of our civilization, who are creating our cultural identity. This is not the same as offering ideological ghosts for political consumption, it is *not* the same, it is very different. And I think, yes, we are all in the same boat of trying to reconstruct, in order to construct for the future, the house of our civilization.

It's interesting to hear you say "reconstruct" with a writer like Cortázar. In his work most often it's less a sense of history than a sense of what is behind the door that you didn't bother to open.

Yes, exactly. But that can be history too, what is behind the door. When you recognize yourself in the little axolotl, when the house is being taken over, you are understanding that behind the appearances of reality, of everyday reality, in the world but also in Latin America, there is another reality. Which is basically what García Márquez and Carpentier and the poets are saying also. Because that is our problem, discovering the true reality. And in trying to discover it, adding to that reality, adding something new. Not reproducing reality, but adding something to it.

Which seems, again, a certain divergence between the realism of the North American writers and the heightened realism and the fantastic of the Latin American writers.

Well, there is a great tradition of the supernatural in American fiction. And I, for one, have learned a great lesson from the literature of the United States. There's a very famous page where Nathaniel Hawthorne asks himself if North Americans can write books of romance and gothic fiction, since they do not have the romantic décor, they don't have the castles, the moats, the dungeons, all that goes with it. He says, "Well, but

I prefer the blessed, sunlit, prosperous tranquility of my native land to all the gloomy gothic backgrounds of Europe." Well, of course, he wrote supernatural stories. And so did Edgar Allan Poe. That's a fictional gothic world, the House of Usher doesn't exist really. But Poe discovers something marvelous for all of us in the New World. He discovers that the heart of fiction, of the supernatural, is really the telltale heart. That it's not in the décor, it is in your heart and your mind. Then James brings the ghosts out at noon, they don't know they're ghosts. Their life goes by waiting for an event and the event doesn't happen, and it proves they are spectral.

So I think with these three illustrious North American antecedents, one cannot talk about a lack of the supernatural dimension in North American fiction. And then I think Faulkner has decidedly a flavor of the spectral in him. There are lots of ghosts and the fact that all his novels are novels in which you remember the past, but you remember it in the present, and the past only takes place in the present or as he said, "The present began ten thousand years ago," he says in *Intruder in the Dust.* Well, this has a lot to do with us. We're facing a lot of common problems in the New World, be it Anglo-Saxon or Iberian. But, of course, there are a lot of differences also because the social and economic conditions of the two worlds are very different.

Though there seems to be more of a sense of the autobiographical in North American writers.

Yes, perhaps the autobiography is more collective in Latin America in a way. But, in another way, we need very much books of memoirs, we don't have this. We don't have the personal recollection. The Donoso book (*The Boom in Spanish American Literature, a Personal History*) is very interesting in this sense, it's a wonderful book which I hope will start a trend. Or Guillermo Cabrera Infante, the Cuban writer, with his *La Habana para un infante difunto,* which is a marvelous book of his memoirs as a child in Havana. But when I think of books like *Sophie's Choice,* or *The Ghost Writer,* or even *The Executioner's Song,* I find that we are facing a mutation in North American letters, in which we are coming together a lot more than is perceptible to the naked eye. Styron is recreating the forces of a civilization as it destroys itself, as it meets its opposites, its parallels, Poland and the South in the United States, Stingo in Brooklyn and a Catholic Polish woman at Auschwitz. The extraordinary play on history that Philip Roth offers us in *The Ghost Writer.* Or the transformation of reality and naturalism through the sheer exercise of language in Norman Mailer, in *The Executioner's Song,* where you are creating a world with language even if you know the story of Gary Gilmore. It is a different world because

Mailer has written it. And besides, the language of the West appears and appears and appears in that novel and suddenly takes over the novel, and it is not the same language of the East. It is finally the language of a different civilization, of a cultural component that is different. So here we are dealing with civilizations, with cultures, with societies, which were not the great preoccupations of most psychological or realistic writers in the past, in the United States. You have a much broader canvas in the works of any of these three writers I have mentioned.

Do you have a sense of North American writers being influenced by Latin American writers?

Well, I hate the word "influences" but I think that we all form part of a tradition, and if you mean that we recognize more and more, north and south in the Americas, that we belong to a tradition and that there are many common points in that tradition, that is right. Allen Tate once called William Faulkner, I guess with a pejorative intention, a Dixie Góngorist. Well, I don't find anything pejorative about being compared with the greatest European poet of the seventeenth century. But the fact is that without the previous poetic experience of Góngora, probably the North American and the southern writer Faulkner could not have written his novels. And without the novels of Faulkner, many of us would not have written our novels. It is in this sense that the health of literature is the openness of its tradition, the openness of its several streams. Who is not influenced, of course! Books are the products of other books, certainly.

What are you working on now?

I'm in the middle of a novel. I think at this stage of my life and my career, I know more or less how many novels I carry in myself. Basically, three big novels I want to write. And I hope I have time to write them. I couldn't write them before because I didn't know how to write them. I've carried them with me since I was twenty. Now I know how.

There's something in The Death of Artemio Cruz, *where he talks about how he could never see things in black and white like the North Americans. First, is that a statement representative more or less of your own attitude, and also do you think that North Americans can ever learn to see those colors and shades of gray?*

Yes, I think you do not understand the world in its shadings. We were talking about the Manichean perspective, the black and white thing, a while ago. And this has a lot to do with success. Rome tended to see the world in black and white, so does the United States. And I think it's only through the experience of

failure that you understand the shadings of the world. And the experience of failure is a rather universal experience, it's much more universal than success. So I think that in the measure that the United States meets failure—and it has met it in the last fifteen or twenty years, God knows it's met it—it will become really a more civilized nation. A nation more capable of these shadings, of which its intelligentsia is capable. Because this way you understand you are part of the human race. You have a better chance of saving yourself if you know you are human than if you think you are superior to the rest.

In some of your books, the accumulative awareness of one's past and of a nation's past becomes an identity. Then, what about the history that isn't written or isn't remembered, but is there just the same? Does that then become part of the identity that is always discovered?

This has for me a very important literary dimension. To take it by parts: when I hear your question, I think of Kafka. Imagine, of all things. I think of several things in Kafka. One of the impulses of the modern novel as conceived basically by the English writers of the eighteenth century, by Defoe and Richardson and Fielding, and certainly by Madame de LaFayette in France, is the characterization process. The process of differentiation of characters. So that they not be allegorical characters, as they were in some of the medieval writing. And this I think is taken to its very culmination by writers such as Balzac and Dickens. In Dickens it is by differentiation that you know the characters. They're so peculiarly characterized in the way they speak, they dress, they move, their names, everything, Micawber, Uriah Heep, etcetera. Flaubert makes us understand that the characters are the product of the writing, of their names, and that their actions are verbs. I was talking to Susan Sontag the other day and she says, "How difficult it became to write after Flaubert." Because you are self-conscious, because you're conscious of every adjective, of every verb, of every noun, every single thing you write. It is no longer innocent after Flaubert, and it's certainly not innocent after Proust, who I think takes psychological writing to its very culmination. There's very little you can do after that in the investigation of the self, of the individual, of his internal characterization.

And then we have a man without a face, who is the man of Kafka. I ask myself, when I read Kafka, this man has no face, K. has no face. But then, because he has no face, should I guillotine him, should I chop his head off? Or can I give another kind of face to him? And I realize that Kafka is writing stories at the same time which are about forgotten myths, myths he finds in the basements of history and of the mind, things that had been forgotten, precisely as you say, and then recreates them. And he says so, he declares, "I only want to rewrite the old German and Jewish myths and fairy tales, that's all I want to do in this life." But of course in rewriting them, he writes a new myth, a new fairy tale, through the appropriation of the forgotten, of the old memory, the forgotten memory. And in this double creation of the new character, this devastatingly solitary and faceless man who becomes a bug, Samsa, in the writing of his fable, we suddenly come upon the meaning of all the opportunities of modern fiction, I think. Kafka said a wonderful thing, "There shall be much hope, but not for us." And he's offering a sacrifice of literature and himself for the future, which I find very very moving.

And through this understanding of Kafka, I understand a lot of what we're trying to do in Latin America, which is not to create psychological characters in the Flaubert sense or differentiate characters in the Dickens sense, but to discover something new which I couldn't name for you. Which perhaps we could call figures. I support myself a great deal on archetypes, especially the great archetypes of Spain: Don Juan, and La Celestina, and Don Quixote. But these are archetypes and I'm interested in figures. I'm interested in three young men thrown on a beach with no identification and no memory. So as to surprise them in the moment in which their character is totally unconstituted and see where we can go from there and how we can construct a new character, a new personality, a new identity, through a more intimate relationship with the facts of our civilization, of our culture.

But is there, in the end, with Kafka or elsewhere, anything that can differentiate the resonances of a story that is fable-like or myth-like as opposed to one that is a new version?

Of course. The old myth disappears in a way. What you get is a story called "The Judgment," or "The Metamorphosis," or "In the Penal Colony." And the original myth is lost. Sometimes in his little, little fables and versions of Prometheus and of Ulysses, he lets you take a look at the way he goes about it. "Did Ulysses hear the sirens or not? Did he plug his ears or did they know that he would have his ears plugged, because he is wily, and therefore that time they didn't sing?" And what happened to Prometheus? And finally how bored and how tired we are of Prometheus, and the eagle, and the liver, everybody's tired of the tragedy. These things he lets you perceive, but when he goes into his major works you don't perceive them, you are right.

Are there particular writers you like to read?

Well, I've already mentioned the novelists of the present, I think that fills in the picture quite well. But, in the past, I'm a great reader of Cervantes. That is one book I read every year, I can't live without that book. There's a Guatemalan author who lives in Mexico, Tito Monterroso, who has a volume of *Don Quixote* open in every room in his house, at a different page. And he goes from room to room reading this, he always has *Don Quixote* open. I would like to imitate him. That's one book I can't live without.

Bibliography of World in English

CARLOS FUENTES

Where the Air Is Clear. Translated by Sam Hileman. New York: Ivan Obolensky, 1960.

The Good Conscience. Translated by Sam Hileman. New York: Ivan Obolensky, 1961.

Aura. Translated by Lysander Kemp. New York: Farrar Straus & Giroux, 1964.

The Death of Artemio Cruz. Translated by Sam Hileman. New York: Farrar Straus & Giroux, 1964.

A Change of Skin. Translated by Sam Hileman. New York: Farrar Straus & Giroux, 1968.

Holy Place. Translated by Suzanne Jill Levine (in *Triple Cross*). New York: Dutton, 1972.

Terra Nostra. Translated by Margaret Sayers Peden. New York: Farrar Straus & Giroux, 1976.

The Hydra Head. Translated by Margaret Sayers Peden. New York: Farrar Straus & Giroux, 1978.

Burnt Water. Translated by Margaret Sayers Peden. New York: Farrar Straus & Giroux, 1980.

Distant Relations. Translated by Margaret Sayers Peden. New York: Farrar Straus & Giroux, 1982.

The Old Gringo. Translated by Margaret Sayers Peden and the author. New York: Farrar Straus & Giroux, 1985.

Myself with Others: Selected Essays. New York: Farrar Straus & Giroux, 1988.

Christopher Unborn. Translated by Alfred Mac Adam and the author. New York: Farrar Straus & Giroux, 1989.

Constancia and Other Stories for Virgins. Translated by Thomas Christensen. New York: Farrar Straus & Giroux, 1990.

Lois Parkinson Zamora (essay date spring 1984)

SOURCE: Zamora, Lois Parkinson. "'A Garden Inclosed': Fuentes's *Aura*, Hawthorne's and Paz's 'Rappaccini's Daughter,' and Uyeda's *Ugetsu Monogatari*." *Revista Canadiense de Estudios Hispánicos* 8, no. 3 (spring 1984): 321-34.

[In the essay that follows, Zamora views the 1844 Nathaniel Hawthorne short story "Rappaccini's Daughter," Octavio Paz's 1956 stage adaptation of "Rappac-

cini," and the 1953 Japanese film Ugetsu Monogatari *as literary forerunners to* Aura, *stressing that all four works feature an enclosed or walled-off setting whose metaphorical significance includes associations with paradise, imprisonment, surreal time and space incongruities, and isolation.*]

> A garden inclosed is my sister, my spouse; a spring shut up, a fountain sealed.
>
> Awake, O north wind; and come thou south; blow upon my garden, that the spices there may flow out. Let my beloved come into his garden, and eat his pleasant fruits.
>
> *(Song of Songs,* 4: 12,16)

Aura (1962), by Carlos Fuentes, has provoked a remarkable variety of comparative commentary. The novella has been discussed in terms of Faulkner's "A Rose for Emily," James' "The Aspern Papers," Pushkin's "The Queen of Spades," Reyes' "La Cena," Michelet's *La Sorcière,* Castiglioni's *Encantamiento y magia,* Edgar Allan Poe and the Gothic novel tradition, as well as the mythic material of Jungian psychological archetypes. Fuentes himself has proposed comparative links to Donoso's *Coronación,* Bianco's *Sombra suele vestir,* and Miss Havisham in Dickens' *Great Expectations.*[1] Such an outpouring of comparative criticism is explained in part by the cultural range of the creator of *Aura,* but also, and perhaps more directly, by the nature of the work itself, with its generalized psychological and metaphysical concerns.[2] Although many distant relations have already been visited and many literary genealogies traced and charted, I want to propose two more literary kinships. Both are suggested by extra-textual evidence and both will further illuminate, I hope, the dark house of words which is ***Aura.***

The first comparative connection which I propose to explore is the short prose romance, "Rappaccini's Daughter," written in 1844 by Nathaniel Hawthorne, and translated by Octavio Paz into poetic drama in 1956 for the Mexican stage.[3] The stage production was the second of the series of performances known collectively as *Poesía en voz alta,* presented by some of Mexico's most talented writers, musicians, graphic artists and directors, at the *Teatro del Caballito* in Mexico City, in a building which has since been torn down.[4] In Paz's *La hija de Rappaccini,* Juan José Arreola played the part of Rappaccini and a young and relatively unknown writer named Carlos Fuentes wrote the program notes.

Aura and "Rappaccini's Daughter" are similar in their plot structures and in their symbolic use of setting. Both portray an act of creation which is effected by unusual or unnatural means, a character who is ob-

sessed by the product of that creative act, and the consequent transformation of the obsessed character, although the transformations are very different in nature and outcome. Both stories take place in realms which are sealed off from the daylight world of rational experience, realms created and inhabited by aged characters—Consuelo and Rappaccini—who exert extraordinary power over the other characters and over time and nature as well. The scientist Rappaccini cultivates in his Paduan garden sumptuous flowers which are as deadly as they are beautiful; some are said to creep "serpent-like" along the ground, others use "whatever means of ascent was offered them" (594). The most beautiful creation in his garden—its most exotic blossom—is his daughter, Beatrice; because she has inhaled from infancy the garden's poisonous perfumes, her own breath has become deadly to all who approach her. Her dependence upon the enclosure of the garden, and upon its creator, is absolute, just as Aura's very being resides in Consuelo and in the dark old mansion in Mexico City. If either were to leave her walled garden, she would cease to exist.

Into these enclosed worlds venture young men, Giovanni in Hawthorne's story and Felipe in Fuentes', lured by a combination of love and horror, passionate attraction and repulsion. Giovanni (like Dante, to whom he is compared), is accompanied into an infernal region by Beatrice, but through her he has the opportunity as well to behold undreamed of wonders. Similarly, Felipe follows Aura to his room, guided by the rustle of her taffeta skirt, then by the candelabra which she holds up against the dark, an aura of light seeming to emanate from the character herself. Whereas Felipe yields to his obsession, embracing Consuelo's dark world as he embraces Aura sexually, Giovanni resists looking at Beatrice because he knows that to do so is to "put himself . . . within the influence of an unintelligible power . . . " (598). He refuses to embrace Beatrice, but aims rather to remove her from the garden, to save her from her father, as Felipe had initially thought to save Aura from Consuelo. So Giovanni attempts to bring her "rigidly and systematically within the limits of ordinary experience" (598), but Rappaccini's powers are far greater than the young man's, and he is brought into the garden against his will. Giovanni gives Beatrice an antidote supplied by Baglioni, a scientist and rival of Rappaccini's, in order to counteract the force of the poison in her system, but he compounds it instead, and she dies of its effects. So he becomes the agent of Beatrice's fate, as she has unwittingly become the agent of his.

The creations of Rappaccini and Consuelo are similar in their isolated irreality, their combination of beauty and horror, but the motives and methods of the creators are very different indeed. Rappaccini's creative act is scientific, his tool "perverted wisdom." The demonic nature of his artistry is constantly suggested by Hawthorne's narrator: he is motivated by his desire for control over time and nature in general, and he exerts his power on one innocent being in particular. When Beatrice, as she is dying, accuses her father of cruelty, he defends his actions, saying that he wished only to make her powerful too by making her capable of evil. Indeed, he implies that in so doing, he has given her the means to transcend her very status as woman: he asks her, "Wouldst thou, then, have preferred the condition of a weak woman, exposed to all evil and capable of none" (605)? Of course Beatrice despairs not because she is weak but because she is separated from the true source of her feminine power, which she knows is not evil but love. Giovanni does recognize "the delicate and benign power of her feminine nature" in the passionate outpourings of her heart (604), but he is too weak, too selfish to understand or respond appropriately. The irony of Beatrice's situation is thus invisible to Rappaccini and incomprehensible to Giovanni, but fully intended by Hawthorne, who alone among North American writers before Henry James created complex female characters, and who six years after this story created perhaps *the* great female character in all of our literature. Hawthorne fully develops in *The Scarlet Letter,* in Hester Prynne, what he suggests in Beatrice, that, like Eve, to whom he often refers in his fiction, women represent a tragic involvement with sin but also the consequent possibility of regeneration.[5]

Unlike the rapacious Rappaccini, Consuelo's creative act is spiritual; she uses her feminine powers to create in the figure of her youth the child she never had. Her nature is dual—both creative and life-threatening—as critics have already amply noted;[6] but the novella ends by emphasizing her powers of regeneration and, as her name suggests, consolation. Inspiring and then directing Felipe's love for Aura, Consuelo creates a realm which enables them both to see beyond ordinary experience, to perceive something perhaps eternal. Rappaccini, on the other hand, has the power to make Beatrice terribly poisonous, but not to save or recreate her. Whereas Aura will return by the power of Consuelo, Beatrice will never return: Felipe has his *consuelo,* Giovanni has nothing. "Rappaccini's Daughter" is a tale of paradise lost, *Aura,* of paradise regained.

If the plots of *Aura* and "Rappaccini's Daughter" are conceptual mirror-images of the myth of paradise, their symbolic settings also depend upon the concept of paradise, a word etymologically rooted in the Persian word for "walled garden." The walled gardens of Fuentes and Hawthorne are at once traditional and original: clearly both authors accept the challenge of

working with a metaphor so conventional and yet so intrinsically poetic, and both choose the metaphor of the garden for the manifold ways in which it links passion and idealism, the material and the spiritual, the profane and the sacred, the temporal and the eternal. In the metaphor of the garden inheres the very ambiguity of human existence—a potentially divine yet mortally corrupt nature—which Hawthorne explores in all his work, and which is also consonant with Fuentes' dialectical turn of mind, as Wendy Faris suggests in her analysis of Fuentes' propensity for structural and syntactical chiasmus.[7] Both gardens contain elements which are at once demonic and divine, attractive and repulsive, regenerative and deadly, and the stories are, to varying degrees, products of these conflicting elements. Thus Aura is described in terms of the plants in the garden, her smile combining "the taste of honey and the taste of gall."[8] And Beatrice's story builds with a litany of contradictions to its culmination in a chiasmus of paired opposites: "To Beatrice . . . as poison had been life, so the powerful antidote was death" (605). For Giovanni, it is precisely the "lurid intermixture" of light and dark in Rappaccini's garden that "produces the illuminating blaze of the infernal regions" (598). The metaphor of the garden comprehends the internal contradictions of life and language, the duplicity as well as the duality of which both Hawthorne and Fuentes are so acutely aware.

If bringing together incompatible tendencies is the primary function of the gardens in these stories, claustrophobia is their primary characteristic. They are enclosures within enclosures, as much prisons as paradise. Now it may be that paradise inevitably has something of the prisonhouse about it, as Milton's Adam—and Milton—sensed uneasily. Similarly, nineteenth-century North American authors, with patriotic propaganda about the boundless west ringing in their ears, wrote obsessively about enclosure: Poe imagined casket-like rooms without windows, without a world beyond them; Melville created sealed enclosures with sails to wander the world in, a literal coffin for the sole survivor of the *Pequod*; and more recently Faulkner, in *Absalom, Absalom!,* places Quentin Compson in an "icebox room" at Harvard and charges him to decipher the world outside. In contemporary Latin American literature we well, enclosure and the fear of it is not merely a formal theme but a poignant image for the self: one thinks immediately of the inheritors of Quentin's artistic burden, the succession of Aurelianos who enclose themselves in Melquíades' room, where it is always March and always Monday; or Horacio Oliveira, in the asylum at the end of *Rayuela,* his illusory spatial freedom revealed to be just that, illusion; or again Roberto Michel at the end of "Las babas del diablo," straing at (not through) the window of his room, realizing that it is not an opening onto the world but an unreal landscape, an artifice of the mind. A concern for the metaphysics of space seems to come with the American territory, where our immense continents hold out great promise but where the self finds no commensurate freedom, where indeed many of our fictional characters seem unable to batter free of the enclosures of their own minds.

When Felipe enters Consuelo's old house, he is aware of the gulf separating the inside from the outside and of the irreversibility of his passage. He tries to retain an image of the outside world, but it slips away from him; later, when he wishes to return to his apartment to retrieve some papers, Aura wonders reproachfully why he would want to go out. Darkness characterizes the enclosure of the house and reinforces its separation from the world outside. Even the dim light from the candelabra is confined by a larger circle of darkness: Felipe observes "el círculo de luz compacta que arroja el candelabro . . . , el círculo mayor, de sombra, que rodea al primero" (42). When he asks Consuelo if he can go into the garden, she responds by referring to the buildings which enclose the house; the windows have been blocked by exterior construction, hermetically sealing Consuelo's garden within. It is after Felipe has made love to a woman whom he cannot see but who smells "en su pelo el perfume de las plantas del patio" that he enters the interior garden. It is precisely this heady, even narcotic perfume which draws him to it. By lighting matches, which burn his fingers, he can see dimly what he has only sensed: "las hierbas olvidadas que crecen olorosas, adormiladas: las hojas anchas, largas, hendidas, vellosas del beleño: el tallo sarmentado de flores amarillas por fuera, rojas por dentro; las hojas acorazonadas y agudas de la dulcamara; la pelusa cenicienta del gordolobo, sus flores espigadas; el arbusto ramoso del evónimo y las flores blanquecinas; la belladona" (100, 102). As Felipe's burned fingers and the nature of the plants suggest, the garden is dangerous; it is also the source of Consuelo's creative power. In his diary, Consuelo's husband, general Llorente, writes that even as a relatively young woman, Consuelo insists on growing herbs in her garden. He recounts a morning in which he found her walking in a delirium: "No me detengas—dijo—; voy hacia mi juventud, mi juventud viene hacia mí. Entra ya, está en el jardín, y llega" (132). And at the moment when Felipe realizes that he *is* General Llorente, he smells damp, fragrant plants. Thus Aura's apparition is conceptually linked to the garden and particularly to its perfumes; indeed the word "aura" comes from the Greek, meaning a breath of air.

Just after his visit to the enclosed garden, Felipe goes to Aura's bedroom, where he describes their union by saying, "Aura opens up like an altar" (109); the metaphor is above all spatial, rather than religious or sexual, as most critics have assumed, although of course it combines all of these elements. As Aura comes progressively to represent an opening up, a liberation from the strictures of rational consciousness, so the enclosed garden progressively expands, becoming by the end of Fuentes' novella a metaphor for the creative imagination itself. Aura *is* the belladonna, *la bella donna,* the beautiful and necessarily dangerous woman of Consuelo's imaginative cultivation.

The spatial confinement of Rappaccini's garden is not reversed or transcended as it is in ***Aura***: Hawthorne's worst indictment of Giovanni is made on precisely this ground. If Aura is conceptually linked to the garden's perfumes, Beatrice is linked to a shattered marble fountain from which gushes forth water, like "an immortal spirit, that sung its song unceasingly and without heeding the vicissitudes around it . . . " (594). So Beatrice's spirit also sings when it is temporarily freed by the love she feels for Giovanni. Giovanni later recalls "many a holy and passionate outgush of her heart, when the pure fountain had been unsealed from its depths . . . " (604). The young man has not, however, the power to estimate such spirituality, such transcendence. Rappaccini's garden closes in rather than opens up; the fountain is sealed forever.

In "Rappaccini's Daughter," structural enclosure reiterates the thematic enclosure of the garden, for the story is itself framed by windows which might open out onto the world but which are, like Consuelo's windows, blocked off.[9] At the beginning of the story, Giovanni looks downward from his window onto the garden below, and it is through this window that Beatrice first beholds the beautiful young man, whom she contemplates as if he were a framed work of art. The promise of liberating love which Giovanni represents to Beatrice, a promise of which the open window is emblematic, is, as we know, subverted during the course of the story. This subversion also finds emblematic representation in the window, for the story concludes ironically with Baglioni's visage filling the window frame. The scientist who has provided the deadly antidote looks down on the garden, comments rudely upon Beatrice's fate, confirming the triumph of destructive reason. Whereas the blocked windows of Consuelo's mansion direct the anima inward and downward toward fruition in her interior garden, Rappaccini's blocked windows prevent the anima from moving outward and upward, stifling, and ultimately, suffocating her.

In addition to its particular spatial characteristics, the walled garden, whether paradise or prison, has its special temporal nature, which may be eternal, or interminable.[10] Felipe, the historian, discards his watch as he enters Consuelo's realm, and when Consuelo prays for the end of this world, her prayer is above all a plea for a timeless realm, a world where time shall cease, as St. John of Patmos explicitly promises in his apocalyptic vision of the end of the world, the New Jerusalem, which concludes the New Testament. Consuelo's longing for an eternal, that is, an atemporal realm, where past and present, age and youth are meaningless distinctions, would seem to be fulfilled in the figure of Aura.[11] Rappaccini's garden, on the contrary, ends as it began, a time-bound prison. The possibility of an eternal paradise is not, however, abandoned: Hawthorne's narrator says that Beatrice will pass "across the borders of Time—she must bathe her hurts in some fount of paradise, and forget her grief in the light of immortality, and *there* be well" (605). Hawthorne cannot concede, as Fuentes does, a boundless mythic realm based on sexual love and the creative imagination within this world, but he cannot let go the vision either.

Fuentes' epigraph, from the romantic historian, Jules Michelet, is instructive with regard to the temporal nature of Consuelo's garden. For Michelet, the aim of historiography was, to use Michelet's own word, "resurrection," by which he meant the restoration to "forgotten voices" their power to speak to living men, the penetration of the deepest recesses of past lives in order to reconstitute them in all their strangeness and mystery as once vital forces.[12] Fuentes has often spoken in similar terms, referring to a mythical time, "a present which is accreting, which is constantly enriching the moment, the instant. The past is never condemned to the past in a mythical system."[13] Hawthorne too was deeply concerned about the relation of the past to present, particularly the Puritan past of North America, where he set much of his fiction. In his longer works, which are properly termed romances rather than novels, action often involves the acceptance of the burden of inheritance, a coming to terms with a history-laden environment, in short, a movement from innocence to experience.

Octavio Paz's surrealistic poetic drama, which may have been the mediating work between Hawthorne's "Rappaccini's Daughter" and Fuentes' *Aura,* begins by addressing the theme of limitation, both spatial and temporal. The play opens with a character called El Mensajero, who is, Paz tells us in the stage directions, "un personaje hermafrodita vestido como las figuras del Tarot, pero sin copiar a ninguna en particular" (4). In a lyrical soliloquy which rises to a level of vatic intensity, the messenger presents himself as transcending precisely the limitations with which Hawthorne's, and now Paz's, characters struggle: "Espacio, puro espa-

cio, nulo y vacío! Estoy aquí, pero también estoy allá; todo es aquí, todo es allá. Estoy en cualquier punto eléctrico del espacio y en cualquier fragmento imantado del tiempo: ayer es hoy; mañana, hoy; todo lo que fué, todo lo que será, está siendo ahora mismo, aquí en la tierra o allá, en la estrella" (4). Such mythic ubiquity collides head on with the story of incarceration which follows, exacerbating by contrast the sense of the characters' bondage. The messenger's prologue continues with the enumeration of the figures of the Tarot deck—implicit analogues to the characters in the play: la Reina nocturna, el Rey de este mundo, el Ermitaño, el Juglar, "y la última carta: los Amantes. Son dos figuras, una color del día, otra color de noche. Son dos caminos. El amor es elección: la muerte o la vida" (5)? So Paz begins by emphasizing, like his predecessor Hawthorne and his successor Fuentes, the enclosure and the duality of the garden, this "paraíso envenenado."

If dichotomies are proposed by Paz, however, they are proposed in order to be transcended. Paz, like Hawthorne and Fuentes, has a radically dialectical turn of mind, but his concern in this play, like Fuentes' in *Aura,* is not so much chiasmus *per se* as its conceptual resolution. The play concerns the union which may proceed from separation, which in fact depends upon separation. The phrase "uniones y separaciones" becomes a kind of refrain throughout, and even Rappaccini plays with digits until they are integers. Paz's Rappaccini, with a comprehensiveness of vision unknown to Hawthorne's character, proposes a chiasmus which in fact unifies rather than divides: "Cuando nacemos, nuestro cuerpo empieza a morir; cuando morimos, empieza a vivir . . . Venenos y antídotos: una y la misma cosa . . . basta un pequeño cambio, una leve alteración, y el veneno se transforma en elíxir de vida. Muerte y vida: nombres, nombres" (8)! And again, emphasizing the garden as the site of unification, Paz's Rappaccini says, "Sólo vemos la mitad de la esfera. Pero la esfera está hecha de muerte y vida . . . Jardín de fuego, jardín donde la vida y la muerte se abrazan para cambiarse sus secretos" (9)! Although Rappaccini's motives are still misguided in Paz's play, his aim, like that of Fuentes' Consuelo, is to unify life and death, that is, to transcend the limitations, the dichotomies, of time and space.

In addition to Paz's Rappaccini, other characters in the play also seem more closely related to Fuentes' characters, serving perhaps as intermediaries between Hawthorne and Fuentes. Paz's Juan is more expansive, adventurous, poetic, than Hawthorne's Giovanni; he is far from the Giovanni who keeps talking about the limits of ordinary experience. Paz's Beatriz, like Hawthorne's Beatrice, is both victim and victimizer, but she too is more energetic than her model, more rebellious, expressing early on her wish to escape her incarceration, rejecting her role in the cold pastoral which her father has created. Her doubleness as spirit and flesh, past figment and present reality, is suggested by mirrors, as is Aura's. The walled garden becomes in Paz's play a labyrinthine city of glass, suggesting the timeless New Jerusalem at this world's end, for which Consuelo prays in **Aura**. The messenger addresses Beatriz directly before the fourth act: "marchas por una ciudad labrada en cristal de roca. Tienes sed y la sed engendra delirios geométricos. Perdido en los corredores transparentes, recorres plazas circulares, esplanadas donde obeliscos melancólicos custodian fuentes de mercurio, calles que desembocan en la misma calle. Las paredes de cristal se cierran y te aprisionan; tu imagen se repite mil veces en mil espejos que se repiten mil veces en otros mil espejos"(11). The "delirios geométricos" become "galerías transparentes," "corredores infinitos que se cruzan y enlazan." That Paz's messenger should, for his primal metaphor of enclosure, transform the walled garden into a self-reflexive labyrinth is, of course, not at all surprising.

There is in the play's metaphoric structure one image taken from Hawthorne which Paz does not transform but instead heightens by repetition and variation. That is the image of breath. In Hawthorne's story, Beatrice's poisonous breath is primarily an element of plot; in Paz's play, however, breath becomes a metaphor for the soul, with which it has been traditionally identified: the etymological link between respiration and inspiration is revivified. In a cluster of images of air, wind, perfume, Paz's Beatriz becomes the anima, a word which itself means air or breath; she is perhaps as well the inspiration for Fuentes' Aura, which, as I have said, also means breath.

I proposed at the outset of this article to refer to two of Aura's distant literary relations. I have concentrated my attention on "Rappaccini's Daughter," but I want to mention briefly the other, which was brought to my attention in a conversation with Carlos Fuentes last year.[14] Fuentes said that on the night in Paris in 1961 when he began to write **Aura,** he had gone to see a Japanese film called *Ugetsu Monogatari,* directed in 1953 by Kenji Mizoguchi (1898-1956), and based on stories by Uyeda Akinari, written in the eighteenth century. The film, which is set in the sixteenth century in rural Japan, tells of two peasant neighbors who dream of bettering themselves financially and socially. The first becomes a samurai, but it is the second who interests us here, because he clearly suggests Felipe. Genjuro is a potter who risks his life crossing the besieged countryside in order to take his pottery to the city where he can sell it for a better price. In the city, a beautiful young woman, accompanied by an ancient female companion, approaches him, buys a great deal of his work, and tells him to deliver the work to the Katsuki family mansion, which is outside the city. When he does so, the old woman encourages him to come in. The young woman, who seems somehow otherworldly in her beauty and her manner, praises his artistry, telling him that he must deepen and enrich his talent. When he asks how, the old woman, as if she had been expecting his question, says that he should marry the beautiful Lady Wakasa, which he does, despite the fact that he has a wife and child in his village. He leaves the mansion briefly to go back to the city, and when he returns, the old woman says that he should not go out any more. The three characters listen to unearthly sounds which prove to be the voice of the young woman's father, calling from the grave. The old woman then explains that Lady Wakasa had died without a proper love, so she has brought her back from the grave and that her existence depends upon them. The peasant is aghast; he picks up a sword and starts to slash at the women, in the process falling out of the house onto the ground in a faint. When he awakes, he is surrounded by men who ask him where he has stolen the ancient and precious sword. He explains that he got it from the Katsuki mansion, at which the men laugh and point to its crumbling ruins. Genjuro then remembers a song which the Lady Wakasa sang: "The best of silk of choicest hue, / May change and fade away, / As would my life beloved, / If thou should prove untrue." He understands that the women have disappeared because he ceased to allow them their existence in his imagination.

Mizoguchi creates haunting scenes of misty landscapes and dim interiors which heighten the story's distanced irreality. Environment is essential to the psychological portrayal of characters in all of Mizoguchi's films, and the characters' spiritual and social crises, the pathos with which so many of those films are imbued, are reiterated and reinforced by the spatial composition of their cinematic world. Mizoguchi composes his black and white images self-consciously and symmetrically, using the lines created by shadows, paper panelling, sloping eaves, and he breaks up those compositions with lamps, candles, translucent screens. Like Japanese houses, Mizoguchi's sets are often a visual play of horizontals and verticals, patterns which intersect, parallel, repeat.[15] But Mizoguchi, who was uneducated and early apprenticed to a kimono maker, also integrates into his sets floral motifs and backgrounds. The initial title and list of credits of *Ugetsu* are run against a sumptuous brocade of chrysanthemums, dahlias, blossoming trees; flowers often serve as compositional or symbolic elements in a scene. [A] photograph of Masayuki Mori and Machiko Kyo as the bewitched lovers in the Katsuki mansion shows this combination of the geometrical and the floral, of the simple and the ornamental, the modern and the baroque. It is a combination which suggests both Hawthorne's Italian garden and Paz's crystalline labyrinth, an aesthetic synthesis of the two works which I am proposing as direct precursors of *Aura.* It is a synthesis which Fuentes must have sensed when, after seeing *Ugetsu,* he returned to his room to begin writing *Aura.*

In many of Mizoguchi's movies, as in Japanese houses and buildings, the distinction between interior and exterior space is blurred, the separation between inside and outside not at all absolute. Rooms are often connected by covered outdoor walkways upon which they open through sliding doors of translucent paper. Characters often move between the enclosure of an interior room and an equally enclosed and composed garden, which is nonetheless outside rather than inside. [A still] from *The Life of Oharu* (1952), illustrates the proximity of interior and exterior in a typical Mizoguchi set: in the enclosed garden behind the characters, Oharu compromises herself, faints, and is immediately carried by her illicit lover to a room which opens on the garden, where she is shown lying and where she will be discovered and disgraced. In *Ugetsu,* the Katsuki mansion is thus a notable exception in Mizoguchi's work, for it does not permit easy egress, nor do the characters leave the rooms once the peasant returns from his visit to the town (where he perceives the gulf separating the mansion from the world which surrounds it). The hermeticism of the house is emphasized by the cuts from scenes inside the house to scenes of the war-torn countryside where we see the peasant's wife killed and his friend's wife brutally raped. The juxtaposition of the sealed interior realm to the open spaces of the countryside is meant to impugn the peasant for having left his wife unprotected and without enclosing shelter, to suggest as well the unnatural remove of the house from temporal and spatial reality, and thus to foreshadow the eventual disappearance of the house and its ghostly inhabitants.

The movie is based on the gothic tales of Uyeda Akinari, which are also entitled *Ugetsu Monogatari,* and are translated as *Tales of Moonlight and Rain: Japanese Gothic Tales*; the movie is taken from the first two stories, "Homecoming" and "Bewitched."[16] These tales of the supernatural, which were first published in woodblock print in 1776, present mystical experiences in a dreamlike world which is inhabited by wraiths, spectres, and monsters—a world altogether consonant with that created by Fuentes in *Aura.* The women's house, as it is first envisioned in the peasant's dream and then in apparent reality, is distinguished by its shutters and bamboo blinds—that is, by enclosure and separation from all which is external to it; and the enchanting young woman who invites him inside is described in terms of a "spring zephyr." Like Aura, she

seems to be the breath of life. When the peasant awakens to find the house in a state of desolation and decay, he returns to the once lavish interior garden, now parched by "spectral winds," where his sense of loss is confirmed. Although Fuentes had perhaps not read these tales, Mizoguchi of course had, and his film reiterates visually Uyeda's symbolic settings, the bewitching house with its interior garden, and its ghostly currents of air. Thus, it is tempting to speculate that the women of Mizoguchi's film and Uyeda's tale may be forebears in Consuelo's Aura's complex literary lineage and, to speculate more generally, as I have, that Uyeda's eighteenth-century Japanese gothic tales, Hawthorne's nineteenth-century North American romance, and Paz's twentieth-century Latin American surrealistic drama are confluent in that lineage. Indeed, their abstract personages, idealized locations, and symbolic interplays of light and dark suggest a kinship to the magic realism (that combination of gothic, romantic, and surrealistic elements) which characterizes not only *Aura* but much of contemporary Latin American fiction as well.

In his most recent novel, *Una familia lejana* (1980), published in English under the title, *Distant Relations,* Fuentes uses genealogical imagery to explore the multiple origins and offspring of the self and literature. Speaking of both, one of Fuentes' characters says that the generations are infinite, that we are all fathers of the fathers and sons of the sons.[17] Surely my discussion of *Aura* corroborates this statement, though I am tempted in this case to change the gender of the continuum. In another context, Fuentes' has said, "No hay literatura huérfana."[18] I would add further that distant relations are likely to become close relations in Fuentes' synthesizing artistic vision.

Notes

1. Listed in the order in which they are mentioned in the text, the studies are: Ricardo López Landeira, "Aura, 'The Aspern Papers,' 'A Rose for Emily': A Literary Relationship," *Journal of Spanish Studies: Twentieth Century,* 3 (1976), 125-43: Djelal Kadir, "Another Sense of the Past: Henry James' 'The Aspern Papers' and Carlos Fuentes' *Aura,*" *Revue de Littérature Comparée,* 50 (1976), 448-54; Gloria Durán, "El problema de la imitación y la inspiración en *La Dama de Espadas, Los papeles de Aspern y Aura* (unpublished manuscript); Gerald W. Peterson, "A Literary Parallel: 'La Cena' by Alfonso Reyes and *Aura* by Carlos Fuentes," *Romance Notes,* 12 (1970), 41-44; Ana María Albán de Viqueira, "Estudio de las fuentes de *Aura* de Carlos Fuentes," *Comunidad,* 28 (Aug. 1967), 396-402; Joseph Sommers, *After the Storm: Landmarks of the Modern Mexican* Novel (Albuquerque, N.M., 1968), 181; Richard J. Cal-

lan, "The Jungian Basis of Carlos Fuentes' *Aura,*" *Kentucky Romance Quarterly,* 18 (1971), 65-75; Carlos Fuentes, in a letter to Gloria Durán on December 8, 1968, *La magia y las brujas en la obra de Carlos Fuentes* (México, 1976), 209-210.

2. Gloria Durán develops this point: "Esto es cierto porque al tratar de fantasías de esta clase los detalles de carácter son insignificantes. Estos relatos no tratan de individuos como tales sino más bien de fuerzas dominadoras en la psiquis humana que son esencialmente las mismas en todos. Su inspiración es filosófica o religiosa y tiene poco que ver con los antojos de la personalidad individual," (*La magia y las brujas en la obra de Carlos Fuentes,* 42).

3. Nathaniel Hawthorne, "Rappaccini's Daughter," originally published in *The Democratic Review* (December, 1844); revised by the author for the second edition of *Mosses from an Old Manse* (Boston, 1854); rpt. in *American Poetry and Prose,* eds. Norman Foerster *et al.* (Boston, 1970), 970. Subsequent page references are to this edition and are cited parenthetically in the text.

Hawthorne's story was preceded when it was first published by a whimsical preface surveying his own literary production. Referring to himself as Monsieur Aubépine ("hawthorn" in French), the author gently chides himself for his "inveterate love of allegory which is apt to invest his plots and characters with the aspect of scenery and people in the clouds." The fiction of Monsieur Aubépine, Hawthorne laments self-mockingly, is "too remote, too shadowy and insubstantial;" his stories are "sometimes historical, sometimes of the present day, and sometimes, so far as can be discovered, have little or no reference either to time or space." Hawthorne was very aware of his departure from the prevailing tenets of nineteenth-century realism, of his propensity for romance. This preface is reprinted in *The Norton Anthology of American Literature,* eds. Ronald Gottesman et al., 2 vols. (New York, 1979), I, 947. The classic treatment of nineteenth-century American romance is Richard Chase, *The American Novel and its Tradition* (Garden City, N.Y., 1957).

Hawthorne's own source is suggested in his notebooks. He refers to a story by Sir Thomas Browne: "A story there passeth of an Indian king that sent unto Alexander a fair women fed with aconites and other poisons, with this intent, either by converse or copulation complexionally to destroy him." *American Poetry and Prose,* 593. Hawthorne's story, like Fuentes', has rich comparative resonances: it alludes to or evokes a broad Christian literary tradition—Dante, Bunyon, Spenser and Milton—and has been compared to the story

of Jason and Medea, "The Sandman" by E. T. A. Hoffman, and Keats' *Lamia.* See Roy R. Male, *Hawthorne's Tragic Vision* (New York, 1957), and Don Parry Norford, "Rappaccini's Garden of Allegory," *American Literature,* 50, 2 (1978), 167-86; Octavio Paz, *La hija de Rappaccini,* in *Revista mexicana de literatura,* 7 (Sept.-Oct., 1956), 3-26.

4. Manuel Calvillo, "Poesía en voz alta," *Revista mexicana de literatura,* 7 (Sept.-Oct., 1956), 104-106.

5. Roy R. Male, "The ambiguity of Beatrice," in *Hawthorne's Tragic Vision,* 54-70.

6. Richard J. Callan, "The Jungian Basis of Carlos Fuentes' *Aura,*" Kentucky *Romance Quarterly,* 18 (1971), 65-75; Gloria Durán, *La magia y las brujas en la obra de Carlos Fuentes,* 39-73.

7. Wendy B. Faris, *Carlos Fuentes* (New York, 1983).

8. Carlos Fuentes, *Aura,* trans. Lysander Kemp (New York, 1965), 105. This is a bilingual edition, so both English and Spanish cites are from this text.

9. Roy R. Male notes the "antique sculptured portal" through which Beatrice passes, and connects that image to the windows in the story. *Hawthorne's Tragic Vision,* 69-70.

10. In the Judeo-Christian tradition, visions of paradise, whether the pastoral Eden of Genesis before time begins or the urban New Jerusalem of Revelations after time ends, are above all atemporal realms, cognate in their changeless perfection. For explicit examples of the peculiar temporality of prison narrations, see Abram Tertz (Andrei Sinyavsky), *A Voice from the Chorus,* trans. Kyril Fitzlyon and Max Hayward (New York, 1976), and Christopher Burney, *Solitary Confinement* (London, 1952).

11. See Manuel Durán, *Tríptico mexicano: Juan Rulfo, Carlos Fuentes, Salvado Elizondo* (México, 1973), 112.

12. Hayden White, *Tropics of Discourse: Essays in Cultural Criticism* (Baltimore, 1978), 256.

13. Fuentes in an interview with Jonathan Tittler, *Diacritics* (Sept. 1980), 49.

14. A conversation with Carlos Fuentes at the University of Texas at Dallas, December 1981.

15. For my observations on Mizoguchi's film style, I am indebted to my colleague, Phillip Lopate, who is a sensitive interpreter of Mizoguchi's art, and to the Museum of Fine Arts, Houston, for presenting a major retrospective of Mizoguchi's films in the spring of 1982.

16. Uyeda Akinari, *Tales of Moonlight and Rain: Japanese Gothic Tales,* trans. Kengi Hamada (New York, 1972). These tales have also been translated into French and Spanish: Ueda Akinari, *Contes de pluie et de lune,* trans. René Sieffert (Paris, 1956); *Cuentos de lluvia y de luna,* trans. Kazuya Sakai (México, D.F., 1969). Fuentes referred to the French title during our conversation.

17. For a discussion of the issue of literary relations in *Una familia lejana,* see Wendy B. Faris, *Carlos Fuentes.*

18. Gloria Durán, *La magia y las brujas en la obra de Carlos Fuentes,* 210.

Cynthia Duncan (essay date fall 1986)

SOURCE: Duncan, Cynthia. "Carlos Fuentes's 'Chac Mool' and Todorov's Theory of the Fantastic: A Case for the Twentieth Century." *Hispanic Journal* 8, no. 1 (fall 1986): 125-33.

[*In the following essay, Duncan contends that "Chac Mool" fulfills Tzvetan Todorov's criteria for fantastic literature, including the need for the reader to reject a symbolic reading of the tale in favor of accepting the reality of the characters' existence, and the hesitation on the part of the reader to fully accept the actuality of the events as they are presented.*]

Tzvetan Todorov, in his landmark study *The Fantastic: A Structural Approach to a Literary Genre,* offers one of the most restrictive definitions of the fantastic to date. Unlike some others who have bandied this term about and contributed to a vague and ambiguous usage of it, Todorov insists on limiting the type of literature which can properly be called fantastic.[1] Perhaps for this reason, his interpretation has met with great favor among today's scholars and his conception of the fantastic has become the model against which many works of fiction are judged. It is somewhat ironical to note, however, that in an age when fantastic literature is appreciated and studied as an art form by greater numbers than ever before, Todorov claims that it no longer exists as a genre. According to this structuralist critic, the fantastic is confined to a specific moment in historical time: it existed only from the end of the eighteenth century through the end of the nineteenth. As he puts it, "literature of the Fantastic is nothing but the bad conscience of this positivist era" (p. 168).

Contemporary readers can, of course, enjoy and even identify with characters and situations out of the past, but in order for the fantastic to be most effective, it must recreate the world of the reader as faithfully as possible. The fantastic is the irruption of the unreal, the inexplicable, into the real world which is governed by certain laws of nature and logic. When these laws are violated, leaving no rational explanation for what has occurred, the fantastic comes into being. Todorov sees this condition as "the very heart of the fantastic" (p. 25). He states:

> In a world which is indeed our world, the one we know, a world without devils, sylphides, or vampires, there occurs an event which cannot be explained by the laws of this same familiar world. The person who experiences the event must opt for one of two possible solutions: either he is the victim of an illusion of the senses, of a product of the imagination—and the laws of the world remain what they are; or else the event has indeed taken place, it is an integral part of reality—but then this reality is controlled by laws unknown to us.
>
> (p. 25)

Clearly, the fantastic event would give rise to greater doubt and hesitation in the reader if it were to occur in a contemporary setting rather than in a musty nineteenth century drawing room where literary convention leads us to expect ghosts and goblins. According to Todorov, the reader's vacillation between rejection and acceptance of the inexplicable as part of reality is the *sine qua non* of the fantastic. Therefore, it stands to reason that the twentieth century should be capable of producing some of the best fantastic literature, since it would call into question the reader's own world rather than that of past generations.

Todorov's claim that the fantastic is a dead genre overlooks the abundance of fiction that has emerged in recent decades in Latin America, where the fantastic is undeniably alive and flourishing. Writers such as Jorge Luis Borges, Julio Cortázar, and Adolfo Bioy Casares have achieved universal recognition as masters of this genre. In Mexico, the fantastic has never had the immense popularity it has enjoyed in the River Plate region, yet it is an important vehicle of self-criticism and self-examination for the Mexican writer who challenges the narrow conception of reality that has come to characterize our century. It is not merely a literary game, but an alternative view of the world. Carlos Fuentes, who is today one of Mexico's most famous and prolific authors, began his career as a writer of fantastic tales in this vein. Of them, **"Chac Mool,"** has become a classic in Mexican literature. It is also a classic example of the fantastic as defined by Todorov and clear proof that the genre is still cultivated by talented writers in our century.

Todorov sums up his conception of the fantastic by stating:

> First, the text must oblige the reader to consider the world of the characters as a world of living persons and to hesitate between a natural and supernatural ex-

planation of the events described. Second, this hesitation may also be experienced by a character; thus the reader's role is so to speak entrusted to a character, and at the same time the hesitation is represented, it becomes one of the themes of the work—in the case of naive reading, the actual leader identifies himself with the character. Third, the reader must adopt a certain attitude with regard to the text: he will reject allegorical as well as 'poetic' interpretations. These three requirements do not have an equal value. The first and third actually constitute the genre; the second may not be fulfilled. Nonetheless, most examples satisfy all three conditions.

(p. 33)

A close examination of **"Chac Mool"** will reveal how the story meets these three fundamental requirements.

Fuentes's tale is set in modern-day Mexico City and features as its protagonist a seemingly ordinary inhabitant of the capital who blends in with the thousands of educated, middle class Mexicans who are his neighbors there. One finds passing references to immediately recognizable, real places, such as the "Lagunilla," a famous flea market in Mexico City, and to other cities such as Acapulco, Tlaxcala and Teotihuacan. The daily routine of Filiberto, the lonely middleaged bureaucrat who is the central character and narrator during most of the story, is described in detail. His unrewarding office job, his nightly outings to cafes where he searches for companionship but rarely finds it, his petty interests and preoccupations, and his solitary existence in a spacious but shabby old house are outlined for the reader in Filiberto's diary. Like most fantastic stories, **"Chac Mool,"** begins with the complete absense of fantastic elements but, once Filiberto's character has been clearly drawn and an appropriate setting has been created, inexplicable events begin to occur.

Filiberto is an avid collector of indigenous Mexican art and one day he is delighted to find a life-size replica of Chac Mool, a pre-Colombian rain god, in the marketplace. He is able to buy it at a modest price because it appears to be a modern reproduction. He humorously records in his diary that the vendor had anointed the stomach of the god with tomato catsup "para convencer a los turistas de la autenticidad sangrienta de la escultura" (p. 14). Filiberto installs the statue in the basement of his home, but it seems to bring him bad luck. The plumbing in the house stops working, the pipes constantly break, and the basement is always flooded. The idol quickly becomes covered with mildew and mold, which gives him an uncanny human look. Filiberto begins to experience the first subconscious tremors induced by the incursion of the fantastic when he writes "Le da un aspecto grotesco, porque toda la masa de la escultura parece padecer de una erisipela verde . . . " (p. 16). Thus, Todorov's conditions for the fantastic are met when the central character begins to experience hesitation about the nature of events portrayed in the tale, and the reader shares this feeling. Because the story is set in the recognizable world, poetical and allegorical interpretations do not influence the reader's attitude, and he is able to experience the full impact of the fantastic.

Fantastic elements gradually enter the story, creating a mood of doubt and tension for both the main character and the reader. For example, Filiberto's diary slowly changes tone and style after the acquisition of Chac Mool. Previously, he had dwelled on anecdotes about his daily life, and the passages tended to be long, elegantly written, and marked by strong currents of loneliness and nostalgia for the past. After Chac Mool comes into his possession, Filiberto begins to feel uneasy, and the entries in his diary are characterized by short, choppy sentences which hint at strange happenings but, at the same time, attempt to explain them rationally. Filiberto becomes increasingly divided: intellectually he rejects the possibility that a statue can come to life, but emotionally, he fears that such a thing could happen. The style of his diary reflects his state of mind as he tries to deal with this internal conflict. For example, Filiberto first describes Chac Mool as a lifeless statue, but as the narrative progresses, he attributes more and more human qualities to the idol until, finally, he is convinced that the rain god actually lives. In the beginning, he relates that he collects "ciertas formas del arte indigena mexicano" (p. 12) and that he spends his free time searching for "estatuillas, idolos, cachorros" (p. 12). He has a possessive attitude toward Chac Mool and the other pieces in his collection: he calls them "trofeos" and speaks of the rain god as "mi Chac Mool" (p. 14). He considers all of his belongings in the same light; when the basement floods, Filiberto records: "El Chac Mool resiste la humedad, pero mis maletas sufrieron . . . " (p. 14), as if these items had equal importance to him. Filiberto calls Chac Mool "una pieza preciosa" (p. 13), a "simple bulto agónico" and "una figura" (p. 14), all inanimate terms, but he also begins to see human characteristics in the statue as soon as he installs him in his home. He writes, after he has placed the statue in the basement, "su mueca parece reprocharme que le niegue la luz" (p. 14). The verb *parecer,* commonly used throughout the first part of the narrative, is important. As long as Filiberto believes that Chac Mool cannot possibly come to life, he is hesitant to commit himself in writing by using a more concrete and definite verb. Rather than stating emphatically that an event *did* happen, Filiberto says that it "seemed" to have happened. He continues to think of Chac Mool as "la escultura" (p. 16) while at the same time he visualizes the stone as skin: "parece padecer de una eri-sipela verde" (p. 16). He is confronted with daily indications that the statue of Chac Mool is coming to life, yet the stronger the proof, the more inclined he is to deny it. He states, "No quiero escribirlo: hay en el torso algo de la textura de la carne, lo aprieto como goma, siento que algo corre por esa figura recostada . . ." (p. 17).

When Filiberto begins to hear strange noises in the night, he dismisses them as fantasy, but his diary entry reveals nervous strain: "Desperté a la una: habia escuchado un quejido terrible. Pensé en ladrones. Pura imaginación" (p. 15). When rain-water floods his house, he writes, "Es la primera vez que el agua de las lluvias no obedece a las coladeras y viene a dar en mi sótano. Los quejidos han cesado: vaya una cosa por otra" (p. 16). The water motif, which always accompanies Chac Mool in the text, appears in various forms throughout Filiberto's narrative and provides clues for the reader that something inexplicable is taking place: Filiberto mentions the broken water pipes, the rain, the water he carries from a near-by fountain, and finally, the ocean, which is the scene of his death. Most of the water images are related to Filiberto's growing doubt and hesitation. For example, he covers the statue with rags to protect it from water damage, but a short time later, he discovers, "Los trapos están en el suelo" (p. 17). His only comment is "Increíble" (p. 17), which shows his reluctance to reach a decision about the nature of events he is witnessing. Nevertheless, his perception of Chac Mool has changed. He is no longer a statue—he has become a god: "Chac Mool blando y elegante, había cambiado de color en una noche; amarillo, casi dorado, parecía indicarme que era un Dios, por ahora laxo, con las rodillas menos tensas que antes, con la sonrisa más benévola" (p. 20).

As Todorov points out, the hesitation induced by the emergence of the fantastic is usually of a limited duration. Once the doubt is resolved in the narrative, it moves into a neighboring category: if there is a logical explanation for the phenomena described, it belongs to the uncanny, and if the phenomena is accepted as a natural occurrence, it belongs to the marvelous. In **"Chac Mool,"** Filiberto attempts to explain events with rational arguments, but they fail to resolve his doubts. Eventually, he must admit that the seemingly impossible has come to pass. He writes, "No cabe duda: el Chac Mool tiene vello en los brazos" (p. 18). This is the first time Filiberto does not preface his remarks with the verb *parecer.* Significantly, this same night, Filiberto awakens to find a living Chac Mool hovering over him. The scene is reminiscent of one from a gothic horror tale. The senses are on edge, sharpened by fear, and doom seems to hover in the air. However, the scene ends not with death, but with a sudden rain storm, which temporarily dissolves the spell of the fantastic:

> El cuarto olía a horror, a incienso y sangre. Con la mirada negra, recorrí la recámara, hasta detenerse en dos orificios de luz parpadeante, en dos flámulas crueles y amarillas.
>
> Casi sin aliento encendí la luz.
>
> Allí estaba Chac Mool, erguido, sonriente, ocre, con su barriga encarnada. Me paralizaban los dos ojillos, casi bizcos, muy pegados a la nariz triangular. Los dientes inferiores, mordiendo el labio superior, inmóviles; sólo el brillo del casquetón cuadrado sobre la cabeza anormalmente voluminosa, delataba vida. Chac Mool avanzó hacia la cama; entonces empezó a llover.

> (pp. 20-21)

This is a turning point in the story, for the reader must now come to a conclusion that will account for Filiberto's experience and, once a conclusion is reached, the story is no longer fantastic. The reader may choose to believe that Filiberto is mad, that he has imagined the episode, or that it is some kind of fantasy, but the story is not structured to allow the reader to believe, for more than an instant, that Chac Mool has indeed come to life. Parenthetical statements, made at the beginning and the end of this entry in the diary by a second narrator, encourage the reader not to trust Filiberto. This other, seemingly objective narrator voice offers a temporary refuge of sanity and calm and allows the narrative tension, which Filiberto's revelation had created, to dissipate. The reader grows wary of Filiberto's remarks and the remainder of the story is understood to be the product of Filiberto's imagination.

The narrative moves into the marvelous when Filiberto overcomes his terror and accepts Chac Mool as a companion. He notes, "Chac Mool puede ser simpático cuando quiere . . ." (p. 22), yet Filiberto comes to resent the rain god's interference in his life. He neglects his work and is dismissed from his post, he loses contact with his friends, and he becomes the prisoner of Chac Mool when a role reversal takes place and Filiberto is forced to act as a servant in his own home. When an opportunity arises to escape the watchful eye of the rain god, Filiberto runs away to Acapulco. where he drowns. His diary ends a few days before his death, and one of the last entries contains a reference to a threat made by Chac Mool to kill him should he try to flee.

If Filiberto were the only narrator in the story, the fantastic would cease to exist when Chac Mool comes to life, since this supernatural event is portrayed without further doubt and hesitation on the part of the main character. At the same time, the reader's uncertainty comes to an end when he is confronted with Filiberto's startling revelation. The tension, which had been steadily building in the narrative, is diffused by the marvelous descriptions of the living rain god and his relationship with the hapless Filiberto. However, there is a second narrative voice introduced into the story when a nameless friend travels to Acapulco to collect Filiberto's body and discovers the diary. Through this new narrator, the reader is exposed to a series of logical explanations that counterbalance Filiberto's allegations, and a new feeling of doubt and hesitation arises as the story once again wavers between a natural and supernatural explanation of the events described in the diary. In this way, Todorov's three conditions for the fantastic are met a second time in the story, although tension is purposely kept at a minimum now so that the reader will be off guard when the story reaches its true climax.

As the friend reads Filiberto's diary, his reactions mirror the process which Filiberto had undergone when confronted with the fantastic. At first, he tries to analyze the situation logically: "No supe qué explicación darme; pensé que las lluvias excepcionalmente fuertes, de ese verano, lo habían crispado. O que alguna depresión moral debía producir la vida en aquel caserón antiguo, con la mitad de los cuartos bajo llave y empolvados, sin criados ni vida de familia" (p. 21). Because there is no clear explanation, he dismisses the problem—"No quise volver a pensar en su relato" (p. 27)—but he becomes obsessed with what he does not understand. This narrator, more so than Filiberto, is characterized by a detached, logical attitude toward life. He raises a number of questions about Filiberto which make the reader hesitant to believe anything written in the diary, but confident in the friend's ability to sort out the truth. Excerpts from Filiberto's diary reveal that he lost his grip on reality, but the second narrator's comment remain cool and analytical. He notes: "La entrada de 25 de agosto, parecía escrita por otra persona. A veces como niño, separando trabajosamente cada letra; otras, nerviosa, hasta diluírse en lo ininteligible" (p. 18). This narrator assumes the task of putting Filiberto's story in proper perspective. He says, "Pretendí dar coherencia al escrito, relacionarlo con exceso de trabajo, con algún motivo psicológico" (p. 27), but despite his efforts, he fails: "Aun no podía concebir la locura de mi amigo" (p. 27).

Unlike Filiberto, who gradually came to accept the inexplicable as part of reality, the second narrator leads the story toward the realm of the uncanny by explaining the fantastic events described in the diary as "madness." Indeed, this explanation would be perfectly acceptable to the reader, as well, and the fantastic could be dismissed were it not for the final, unexpected scene of the story, where the second narrator comes face to face with a character who may or may not be Chac Mool. When the friend arrives at Filiberto's house with the corpse, he is greeted at the door by a stranger. Doubtlessly, this stranger closely resembles the description of Chac Mool in the diary, yet the final image is vague and ambiguous. The narrator is taken aback by him: "Su aspecto no podía ser más repulsivo; despedía un olor a loción barata; su cara, polveada, quería cubrir las arrugas; tenía la boca embarrada de lápiz labial mal aplicado, y el pelo daba la impresión de estar teñido" (p. 28). This scene differs markedly from the one in which Filiberto discovered Chac Mool leering at him in his bedroom in the middle of the night. There is less overt horror, but much greater hesitation on the part of the character and the reader. The concluding lines of the story are highly suggestive, but open to various interpretations: "Perdone . . . no sabía que Filiberto hubiera . . . " / "No importa; lo sé todo. Dígales a los hombres que llevan el cadáver al sótano" (p. 28). Thus, the reader is left to form his own opinion about this final turn of events, but he will undoubtedly experience hesitation between natural and supernatural explanations; as long as he hesitates, he is in the presence of the fantastic.

In Latin America, where fiction is often judged by its social content rather than its form, the fantastic has sometimes been criticized as "escapist" literature because it is not always grounded in socio-political issues. **"Chac Mool,"** however, is part of an important new trend that began around mid-twentieth century: it is a fantastic story with a clear social message. For Fuentes and others, the fantastic is not a way of escaping reality but, rather, of penetrating it and uncovering new dimensions.[2] **"Chac Mool,"** for example, reminds the Mexican that the past is not dead, that indigenous Mexico has not been smothered and buried under the mask of European culture and that it will come back to haunt him until he confronts it and learns to deal with it in a more direct and honest way.

Chac Mool is portrayed by Filiberto as a character who is bitterly resentful of the present. He was once a god, a highly respected deity but, in the intervening centuries, he has been desecrated and forgotten. He resents the attitude of modern Mexicans who have abandoned their nation's indigenous heritage and are ignorant of their cultural history. Filiberto is guilty of this crime: he has purchased Chac Mool as a curiosity piece, and has treated him irreverently. He has no real knowledge of the culture that Chac Mool represents and he feels no spiritual bond to him. Ironically, as Chac Mool gains vitality and becomes a living being, he loses the immortality he had as a statue and grows old and corrupt. He loses his dignity and divine poise, and develops bourgeois tastes. The humanization process is one of corruption, for when Chac Mool gave up his ancient ways and adapted to the twentieth century, he lost his identity. At the end of the story, he is a culturally hybrid character who, rather than benefitting from the blend of two heritages, adopts and maintains the worst characteristics of both. He is treacherous, despotic and fickle, a pathetic imitation of something totally alien to his essential being.

"Chac Mool" is not an allegory, but it does have a symbolic interpretation. The rain god of the story's title can be seen as the representative of many contemporary Mexicans. Like them, he turns his back on his indigenous heritage, and comes to have the same values as those he earlier criticized for disparaging the importance of native cultures. The transformation which Chac Mool undergoes is not unlike the change millions of Mexicans have experienced since the Conquest: it is an act of self-deception and self-denial which has crippled the Mexican psyche and blocked the emergence of an authentic national identity.

The fantastic clearly does exist in the twentieth century, but it has changed to meet the needs and tastes of a modern society. Today's reader, who is familiar with the literary conventions and cliches of earlier fantastic tales, must be caught off guard if he is to experience hesitation between the natural and supernatural. Therefore, the fantastic has developed into a more subtle, more sophisticated art form, and has acquired more symbolic and metaphysical implications. For many writers like Fuentes, it is also an excellent vehicle for expression of social concerns and an effective tool with which to reshape Latin American reality.

Notes

1. For other critical approaches to the fantastic, see Thomas C. Meehan's "Bibliografía de y sobre la literatura fantástica," *Revista iberoamericana,* 46, 110-111 (1980), 243-56.

2. Some other Mexican stories in this same vein are: "Por boca de los Dioses" by Carlos Fuentes (in *Los días enmascarados*); "La culpa es de los tlaxcaltecas" by Elena Garro (in *La semana de colores*); and "La fiesta brava" by José Emilio Pacheco (in *El principio del placer*). "Tlactocatzine, del jardín de Flandes" by Fuentes (also in *Los días enmascarados*) and "Tenga para que se entretenga" by Pachaco (also in *El principio del placer*) deal with a very similar theme. In these stories, a contemporary Mexican character comes into contact with Carlotta and Maximilian, respectively, who ruled the short-lived Mexican Empire from 1864-1867. This attempt at European domination is seen by many Mexicans as a repetition of the original Spanish Conquest, and the figures of the Emperor and Empress in these two tales come back to haunt the contemporary Mexican and remind him of the dangers of using foreign cultures as a role model.

Works Cited

Fuentes, Carlos. "Chac Mool." *Los días enmascarados.* México: Los Presentes, 1954, 7-28.

Todorov, Tzvetan. *The Fantastic: A Structural Approach to a Literary Genre.* Trans. Richard Howard, Ithaca, N.Y.: Cornell University Press, 1975.

Becky Boling (essay date January 1989)

SOURCE: Boling, Becky. "Parricide and Revolution: Fuentes's 'El día de las madres' and *Gringo viejo.*" *Hispanofila,* no. 95 (January 1989): 73-81.

[*In the essay below, Boling contends that in "El día de las madres" and* The Old Gringo *Fuentes used the structure of the family saga to comment on the political structure of Mexico from the Revolution to the modern era, exploring such aspects as patriarchal authority, violence, alienation, power, independence, and the victimization of women.*]

As in Octavio Paz's essay, *El laberinto de la soledad,* Carlos Fuentes sees the Mexican character as resulting from a historical trauma, embedded in a psycho-historical scenario of father-son rivalry, the battle for authenticity, the overthrow of the father and his internalization. However, again like Paz, Fuentes senses that the primal act has never been successfully worked out. Paz traces Mexican alienation or *orfandad* to pre-Cortesian Mexico: the rupture of society by the Conquest, the abandonment of the Indians by the gods, the struggle with a new racial segment of colonial Mexico. Fuentes finds parallel concerns in the more recent past, i.e., the Revolution. In this event, Fuentes discerns in the birth trauma of a nation the mythic struggle for authenticity and the reconfirmation of *orfandad* that Paz associates with the national character.

Since his earliest writings, Fuentes has been intrigued by Mexican history, in particular, the Revolution. This latter event has afforded the author the socio-historical foundation upon which he has erected the face or mask of modern Mexico. Prominent is *La región más transparente* with its kaleidoscopic view of Mexico City, "el ombligo del mundo," which has failed to bury its pre-Columbian world, but rather consecrates it anew in repeated bloody sacrifices such as that of the Revolution or, in miniature, that of Norma by Ixca. In *La muerte de Artemio Cruz,* the Revolution and its aftermath unfold in the deterioration, physical, psychological, and moral, of the prototypical revolutionary of the title. Many of the same themes emerge and converge in subsequent narratives. In *Agua quemada* and *Gringo viejo,* Fuentes again questions the Revolution, in this case, modeling the narratives on the paradigm of the family.

Fuentes portrays the Mexican as desirous of a past, determined by key historical events, which he is unable to control: the pre-Columbian past in *La región más transparente,* the epoch of French colonialism in *Aura,* the Revolution in *La muerte de Artemio Cruz,* and the discovery and conquest of America in *Terra nostra.* Fuentes's narratives retrace the history of Mexico and, as Luis Leal has stated, reinterpret history:

> to present a new version of its development, a version reflected by a mind keenly conscious of the significance of past events in the shaping of the contemporary course of human events. In most of his novels he has gone one step further, to the recreation of history by the combination of realistic and mythical structures.
>
> (Leal 3)

A peculiarly Mexican stance toward alienation characterizes Fuentes's narratives. Octavio Paz poetically conceives of the mestizo as orphan, offspring of a rape of the land perpetrated by the Other, the invader (Paz 76-78). This sense of *orfandad* in terms of the family creates a mythology peculiar to Mexico and determines the people's history (Cassirer 5).

Mexico "es un clan de amorosos parientes que se roban los unos a los otros" (Poniatowska 34). In this way, the Mexican novelist and essayist, Elena Poniatowska points out how Fuentes deals with the underlying contradictions to Mexico in his fiction. In *Cambio de piel,* Fuentes sets the dilemma within the family scenario: "¿Qué sería de México sin un padre supremo, abstracto, disfrazado en nombre de todos, para que los demás no tengamos que mostrar nuestra cara verdadera?" (Poniatowska 34). Obviously the image of the family extends to the arena of politics. Fuentes's most recent fictions, *Agua quemada* and *Gringo viejo,* are literary responses to the rhetoric of politics in Mexico. Leopoldo Zea's study of Mexican positivism reveals that its roots are paternalistic. Judith Hellman proves that the same structures of power exist today in PRI's political families: "the 'family' exists of those men whom the president feels constrained to consult on major policy-making decisions" (56). Fuentes critiques the politics of patriarchy: "El paternalismo, signo fehaciente de desconfianza en el pueblo, es hoy tan sistemático, aunque más sutil, que en tiempos de Porfirio Díaz" (*Tiempo* [*Tiempo mexicano*] 70).

Fuentes unmasks the rhetoric of the patriarchy by casting the political events of this century within a repetitive family scenario. The reiteration of historical movements suggests the existence of an unrecognized substructure. As Eliade shows, "The gesture acquires meaning, solely to the extent to which it repeats the primordial act" (5). The primordial act is that of the identification and subsequent rejection of the father (dictator) by the children *(pueblo).* Although this paradigm excludes the woman (as mother or wife), Fuentes's inclusion of the woman in his narratives constitutes a critique of the model. Since Mexico is a patriarchy that subordinates the feminine, the mother becomes the figure least specified and yet most sought. Fuentes's narrative recognizes the victimization and absence of the mother and her impact upon the struggle between law (the father) and Revolution (the children). She is never quite regained, but her role is significant.

The first story in *Agua quemada,* **"El día de las madres,"** deals with the absent mother. It is Plutarco Vergara's retrospective on his family life. In the story, the family—all male—becomes the metaphor for Mexico's history. Three generations represent past (Revolution), present (the economic development of post-Revolutionary Mexico), and future. The Abuelo is the Mexican Revolution. His history is that of vague ideals, rapid changes of loyalty, and glorification of violence: "Se le veía acompañando a todos los caudillos de la revolución, pues anduvo con todos y a todos sirvió por turnos" (15-16).

This past becomes the spectrum through which Plutarco judges Mexico and his own identity. In **"El día de las madres,"** the young Plutarco recalls a previous political hero: "Tu padrino, chamaco. Míralo, el día que te bautizó, el día de la unidad nacional, cuando mi general Calles regresó del destierro" (**"Día"** [**"El día de las madres"**] 17). Plutarco also perpetuates the climate of the Revolution through his infatuation with his Abuelo, and their closeness would suggest a sympathy and likeness between the generations. To Plutarco, the Abuelo is a romantic figure. The young man wishes to have fought like his Abuelo in the age of the heroes. Plutarco's enthusiasm for the Revolution divorces the movement from its consequences and leaves only an exaggerated machismo: "no me han interesado nunca los negocios ni la política, ¿qué riesgo comparaba a lo que antes vivió mi abuelo, las cosas que sí me interesaban?" (22). However, the narrative slowly discloses the ideological implications of that age.

In fact, the Abuelo is also the image of the patriarchy. Vicente Vergara, the Abuelo, chose to emulate the "fathers" of the Revolution. His room is a shrine, walls covered by photographs from the days "cuando los hombres eran hombres" (11). He is seen with a series of leaders, "muy protegido por la figura patriarcal y distante de don Venustiano Carranza, el primer jefe de la revolución." This is the family to which the Vergara clan owes fealty: "esa [foto] parecía casi foto de familia, un padre justo pero severo y un hijo respetuoso y bien encarrilado" (16). Not surprisingly the Abuelo, too, is a strict father, one who devours his children figuratively, as is only clear toward the end of the story when Agustín, Plutarco's father, denounces him:

> él es nuestro eterno don Porfirio, ¿no ves?, a ver si nos atrevemos a demostrarle que no nos hace falta, que podemos vivir sin sus recuerdos, sus herencias, sus tiranías sentimentales . . . el general Vicente Vergara es nuestro mero padre, estamos obligado a quererlo y a emularlo.
>
> (41)

Agustín, however, is incapable of defeating or superseding the ethos his father represents.

Plutarco's father represents the economic miracle of Mexico, the rise of the middle class, the institutionalization of U.S.-Mexican trade dependence, the abandonment of Mexico's resources to foreign exploitation. The Abuelo (Revolution) had left Agustín "la riqueza de la tierra . . . la única riqueza segura," whereas the next generation has built its fortune on "un imperio de saliva" (28): "Fuentes es testigo del llamado 'despegue' económico y del 'milagro' mexicano. El país se industrializa, se vuelve sujeto de crédito" (Poniatowska 11). Agustín's wealth comes not from the land but from heroin traffic with the U.S. The Pedregal, "ese cementerio involuntario que se levanta al sur de la Ciudad de México," comes to symbolize the deterioration of post-Revolutionary Mexico (Fuentes, "Día" 36). The ethos arising from the Revolution is steeped in the rape of the nation. We discern this violence once we consider the role of the mother in the story.

The lack of women in the narrative is significant. After all, the title clues the reader to this absence: "Mother's Day" never comes in a way; its celebration is a homage to the dead/absent women of the Vergara clan. The Abuelo dedicates an entire wall of his room to photographs of his dead wife, Clotilde. Agustín's room stands in sharp contrast: "Allí no hay ningún recuerdo, ni siquiera una foto de mi madre" (25). The only woman represented in the Vergara world is "la Victoria de Samotracia . . . una diosa guardiana de nuestro hogar" (27). Nevertheless the women are essential in understanding the rivalry between the generations. In fact, the feminine holds a special place in Mexican mythologie. In Octavio Paz's essay, the conquest is the rape of the Indians. They are imaged in the guise of the feminine, the opened self, vulnerable, the defeated, the *chingada* (77). In Fuentes's short story, modern Mexico City, too, is associated with the femi-

nine. The narrator describes the Pedregal as a woman putting on garish make-up: "el Pedregal . . . se pintó los labios de acrilita, se incrustó de mosaicos las mejillas . . . Puertas cerradas como cinturones de castidad . . . flores abiertas como heridas genitales, como el coño de la puta Judith" (36-37). In this male world of the Vergara, what Jane Gallop describes as the "exchange of women between men" leads to a "mediated form of homosexuality," a community dependent upon a "sexuality of sames, of identities, excluding otherness" (84). Therefore, the journey from Revolution to modern Mexico is metaphorically portrayed as the necessary violation, exchange, and murder of the mother.

The family saga affords a microcosmic view of Mexican history, the forces of conquerors and conquered, the repetition of past events. The pattern Fuentes tinkers with are as inherent as growth and separation of children from their parents. Dramatically the process is seen as the overthrow of the father and often implies (Oedipally) the possession of the mother: "Mas lo característico del mexicano reside . . . en la violenta, sarcástica humillación de la Madre y en la no menos violenta afirmación del Padre" (Paz 72). In Mexico, this family scenario suggests the revolution against Porfirio Díaz (the grand patriarch, Oedipus's father, Chronos, or simply "big daddy"). The repressed element in the family drama and in history is the voice of the victim. The missing figure that ties the father to the son is also the victim, the mother.

"El día de las madres" reveals her. But who is she? She is saintly Clotilde, a war victim, seized and forced into a loveless marriage by the Abuelo. She is also Evangelina, the Malinche, the one who gives her love willingly and who, therefore, must be abjured. Plutarco's voyage through the city is the journey to find his mother, Evangelina. The odyssey is a mock Revolution in which Plutarco seizes and humiliates a prostitute that he associates with his mother. This act is figured in terms of war—"la victoria era sólo para mí y nadie más" (35)—and, indeed is analogous to his Abuelo's adventure in the Revolution when he met Clotilde: "Recogí a una huerfanita que hubiera aceptado al primer hombre que le ofrecía protegerla" (22). Whereas Clotilde was "parte de su botín de guerra, por más que quisiera disfrazarlo," Agustín explains how Evangelina, Plutarco's mother, differs: "en cambio Evangelina me escogió a mí" (40). Unlike the passive Clotilde, Evangelina desired, and her desire labeled her a pariah within the mausoleum in which the Abuelo reigned. Both men are complicit in her death: "—El parte médico dijo que tu mamá había muerto atragantada con un pedazo de carne. . . . Esas cosas se arreglan fáciles. Le amarramos tu abuelo y yo una mascada muy bonita al cuello, para el velorio" (42). In a patriarchal scenario, the man guarantees his power by suppressing the woman. Because she challenges the patriarchy's exclusive right to power or desire, the woman may exist only in effigy (the photographs of Clotilde) or in the abstract (the Virgin or the statue of Victory). Paz indicates the tragedy of such a paradigm: "Al repudiar a la Malinche . . . el mexicano rompe sus ligas con el pasado, reniega de su origen y se adentra solo en la vida histórica" (78). This is the source of alienation that Paz and Fuentes, in **"El día de las madres,"** attribute to the modern Mexican, an alienation inherent to a patriarchal structure.

In *Gringo viejo,* several family scenarios intervene and merge. The plot is simple. It rests on the symbolic reconstitution of the family paradigm in order to understand power and regain independence. On a microcosmic scale the plot analyzes the transition of power within society: 1) Power, in this paradigm, is isolated and defined (father), whereas during the Mexican Revolution power was decentralized, dispersed among several key contenders for control of the nation's future. 2) The family paradigm associates legitimacy with authenticity and power. In the novel, the characters develop a sense of identity in reaction to the paternal figure. This tension (between child and father) gives Harriet Winslow and Tomás Arroyo meaning. Harriet Winslow's sense of mission in Mexico is determined by the lessons she learned from her father (*Gringo* [*Gringo Viejo*] 94, 101). Her role in the course of the novel is changed when she selects the Gringo as her new "father." At this point, her mission is to save the Gringo from Arroyo: "—¿No sabes que quise salvarte [Gringo] para salvar a mi propio padre de una segunda muerte?" (140). 3) The children, once aware of their own identity, must depose their father in order to attain autonomy.

The family that exists within the novel is invented. Each character, the Gringo, Harriet Winslow, and Tomás Arroyo, have escaped their biological parents. This break occurred for the Gringo during the Civil War and is ritualistically reenacted during the battles in the desert:

> él [Gringo] sólo sabía que los padres se les aparecen a los hijos de noche y a caballo montados encima de una peña, militando en el bando contrario y pidiéndoles a los hijos:
>
> "—Cumplan con su deber. Disparen contra los padres."
>
> (79)

The Gringo came to Mexico, just as his father had before him, to witness his autonomy confirmed through the Revolution. The drama he expects to see is "el drama revolucionario del hijo contra el padre" (58).

He initiates the creation of the family paradigm with Winslow and Arroyo: "estaba mirando de lejos a un hijo y una hija, él opaco, ella transparente, pero ambos nacidos del semen de la imaginación que se llama poesía y amor" (63).

Harriet Winslow and Tomás Arroyo are orphans, too. The figure of the father is absent or dead in the case of Winslow and Arroyo (136). However, in both cases the absence of the father has not empowered them. On the contrary, Winslow and Arroyo are "illegitimate." Arroyo, the illegitimate son of the Miranda family, is "el hijo de la parranda, el hijo del ayer y la desgracia" (65). He failed to confront his father: "lo espiaba bebiendo y fornicando. Se me escapó" (136). Winslow, although born to a respectable family, suffers alienation within her society for many reasons. A spinster, she is unprotected by a man. To remain a member of society, she and her mother live a lie: "Mi padre no murió ni se perdió en combate. Se aburrió de nosotras y se quedó a vivir con una negra en Cuba. Pero nosotras lo dimos por muerto y cobramos la pensión para vivir" (141). The lie itself is not significant; the abandonment is. But the father exercises his control from the void. Winslow has no way of breaking from this ghostlike presence, the empty grave in Arlington. In addition, Winslow must occupy a subordinate position and will only have indirect access to power because of her sex. The roots of patriarchy are exemplified in the Christian vision of the deity as male. La Luna's denunciation of Christianity's suppression of the body of woman for the body of Christ, "el cuerpo de un hombre que compartía su divinidad con dos hombres más," explains how woman is forced to remain in an undeveloped state, never allowed to attain autonomy. The father, the husband assure "que una permaneciera siendo la niña novia" (151). Thus, Winslow, as a woman, parallels the marginalized mestizo, Arroyo.

At the same time that the Gringo is imagining Arroyo as his son and Winslow as his daughter, these are recreating their parental images in one another. As Winslow dances with Arroyo, she recalls her father's mistress: "olió a sexo erizado y velludo de una negra." Arroyo is internalizing the mother: "detrás de una puerta de espejos salió Tomás Arroyo un niño a bailar con su madre, su madre la esposa legítima de su padre, la madre la señora limpia y derecha" (106). Similarly, the violence of the Revolution has disrupted the normal paths and ties within society (the loss of the original parents), and the participants in the conflict are forced to network, to establish connections within the extant society of the military unit.

In concert, Arroyo and Winslow adopt the Gringo as the image of the father. His existence and survival link the two lovers. Harriet understands that to save the Gringo's life, whose image merges into that of her father, "en ese sueño su padre no había muerto," she must make love to Arroyo, who, in turn, desires her "como deseo que mi madre resucite" (109). The sexual bargain struck between the woman and the general symbolically revives the parental figures. It also creates a field in which power must be disputed and eventually assigned.

The narrative discloses the ambivalence of the father figure. He not only legitimizes his offspring, but he also holds the power of life and death. As long as the father exists, the children are vulnerable to his wrath. This, indeed, is the novel's insight into power. In the guise of protection, those who have power may abuse their wards. Arroyo states that "el peor patrón era el que decía quererlos como un padre" (146). The Revolution initially responded to this problem. The Gringo reveals the paternalistic nature of pre-Revolutionary Mexican government: "Díaz era un tirano, pero era el padre de su pueblo, un pueblo débil que necesitaba un padre estricto, decía Hearst" (79). However, does Mexico escape the paradigm of power that the Gringo discerns?

The answer is apparent in the conclusion to the novel. Arroyo does destroy the father symbolically, by murdering the Gringo: "y ahora los dos [Winslow and Arroyo] estaban de nuevo solos, huérfanos, mirándose con odio" (165). Nevertheless there is a continual recuperation of the paradigm. The Revolution becomes the new family: "la revolución es una gran familia, todos andamos juntos, lo importante es seguir adelante, yo [Arroyo] dependo de Villa como si fuera mi padre y dependo de ustedes como si fueran mi familia" (147). Hence, Arroyo is trapped within the paradigm where the father also destroys his offspring. Villa orders him executed (167-168). The violence continues on a national scale:

> Qué impalpable . . . es la información que un padre hereda de todos sus padres y transmite a todos sus hijos . . . lo [Gringo] habían acusado de parricidio imaginario, pero no al nivel de un pueblo entero que vivía su historia como una serie de asesinatos de los padres viejos, ahora inservibles.
>
> (79)

In the novel the mother is silent. She is the land itself: "vio una tierra donde los frutos escasos tenían que nacer del vientre muerto, como un niño que seguía viviendo y pugnaba por nacer en la entraña muerta de su madre" (64). Or she is the Revolution: "¿Por qué han de escapar sus hijos al destino de su madre la revolución?" (81). There is no help from the mother; the children must confront their fathers alone.

Fuentes's recent fictions continue to coincide with Octavio Paz's analysis of the Mexican character. However, the novelist enrichs this perception by turning to classical myths, archetypal narratives such as the journey in which the hero seeks knowledge. Plutarco's descent into Mexico City and Arroyo's attempt to return to the Miranda estate are quests in the classical sense. Arroyo "había regresado al hogar, revivía uno de los más viejos mitos de la humanidad, el regreso al lar, a la tibia casa de nuestros orígenes" (*Gringo* 124). The classical dramatizations of the myths of Medea, Agamemnon, Oedipus, etc. are firmly based upon the family as the structure in which desire and power are unmediated. The family, existing within the private and the public spheres, facilitates the study of human will, social structures, and hierarchy. In much the same way that the classical stories centering upon the great families of mythology constitute an artistic representation of power and its use in a historical time, Fuentes's narratives reveal the political realities of 20th century Mexico.

Works Cited

Cassirer, Ernest. *Mythological Thought*. Vol. 2 of *The Philosophy of Symbolic Forms*. New Haven: Yale University Press, 1955.

Eliade, Mircea. *The Myth of the Eternal Return or, Cosmos and History*. Princeton: Princeton University Press, 1971.

Fuentes, Carlos. *Agua quemada*. México: Fondo de Cultura Económica, 1981.

———. *Gringo viejo*. México: Fondo de Cultura Económica, 1981.

———. *Tiempo mexicano*. México: Joaquín Mortiz, 1971.

Gallop, Jane. "Impertinent Questions." In *The Daughter's Seduction: Feminism and Psychoanalysis*. Ithaca: Cornell University Press, 1982: 80-91.

Hellman, Judith Adler. *Mexico in Crisis*. 2nd Ed. New York: Holmes & Meier Publishers, 1983.

Leal, Luis. "History and Myth in the Narrative of Carlos Fuentes." *Carlos Fuentes*. Eds. Robert Brody and Charles Rossman. Austin: University of Texas Press, 1982.

Paz, Octavio. *El laberinto de la soledad*. México: Fondo de Cultura Económica, 1959.

Poniatowska, Elena. *¡Ay vida, no me mereces!* México: Joaquín Mortiz, 1985.

Zea, Leopoldo. *El positivismo en México*. México: El Colegio de México, Fondo de Cultura Económica, 1943.

Joseph Tyler (essay date spring 1989)

SOURCE: Tyler, Joseph. "'Chac-Mool': A Journey into the Fantastic." *Hispanic Journal* 10, no. 2 (spring 1989): 177-83.

[*In this essay, Tyler identifies several literary precursors to "Chac Mool," singling out Fuentes's indebtedness to Jorge Luis Borges, then discussing how Fuentes ultimately crafted a humorous tale through the use of elements common to fantasy, including suspense, the coming to life of an inanimate object, and a surprise ending.*]

> "The fantastic is defined as a special perception of uncanny events . . . "
>
> Tzvetan Todorov[1]

An approach to the universe of the supernatural quite often requires an explanation delineating the pre-existing barriers between two deceptively similar worlds: the marvelous and the fantastic. Roger Caillois in his *Anthologie de fantastique (Anthology of the Fantastic),* one of the earlier and better known books on the subject, distinguishes succinctly, but categorically, between what is considered marvelous and what is thought as fantastic in literature. Thus he explains,

> Le féerique est un univers merveilleux qui s'ajoute au monde réel sans lui porter atteinte ni en détruire la cohérence. Le fantastique, au contraire, manifeste un scandale, une déchirure, une irruption insolite, presque insupportable dans le monde réel[2]
>
> (The world of the fairy-tale is a marvelous universe which adheres to the real world without harming it or destroying its coherence. The fantastic, on the other hand, manifests a scandal, a tear, an unusual invasion, almost unbearable in the real world.)

Naturally, the marvelous world of the fairy-tale was almost non-existent in the American continent until the importation of European tales. On the other hand, the history of the fantastic in oral literature is a long and ancient one. Adolfo Bioy Casares, writing on the subject, says, "Ancient as fear itself, fantastic fiction makes its début long before written literature appears. All literatures are populated by ghosts: they show up in the *Zend-Avesta,* the Bible, in Homer, and in *The 1001 Nights.* It's quite plausible that the first specialists in this genre were the Chinese."[3] To these texts one should add those of pre-Columbian origin.

This particular kind of narrative defines and establishes itself in the literature written in English during the XIX century, but among the many forerunners, we are able to recognize the names of the Infante Don Juan Manuel and Quevedo. Both are the unchallenged initiators of the fantastic in Spain.

In Spanish-America, on the other hand, the writers who most frequently appear associated with the supernatural in literature are Jorge Luis Borges, Julio Cortázar, and Juan Rulfo among others. They are joined by Carlos Fuentes with the publication of his **"Chac-Mool"** and other supernatural tales he has authored.

It is essential that before moving on to discuss the many aspects of the *récit* in this story, we pause to indicate some of the very obvious affinities between this narrative and others which we consider its predecessors. Included in what we would call literary forerunners of **"Chac-Mool"** we find the influential force of German Romanticism (the tales of Hoffmann and, at least, one of Rilke's narratives) and that of later literature, such as the works by Franz Kafka (the theme of the unbalanced individual and the many idiosyncrasies caused in him by the bureaucratic system) and even "Santelices,"[4] the short story by the Chilean José Donoso.

The making of this story, **"Chac-Mool,"** also owes much to Mary Shelley's *Frankenstein* and to *El golem (Der Golem)* of Jorge Luis Borges and others who have written about the same tale. Fuentes' literary debt to Borges grows even greater when we find and recognize, within his short story, a well-known excerpt from "La flor de Coleridge,"[5] ("The Flower of Coleridge") in which we read the following commentary: "If a man could pass through Paradise in a dream, and have a flower presented to him as a pledge that his soul had really been there, and if he found that flower in his hand when he awoke—Ay!—and what then?"[6] This quotation, taken *verbatim* from *Otras inquisiciones (Other Inquisitions),* is indispensable in Carlos Fuentes' text because it allows him to make us think about the final possibilities of his story. Let us now move on to its textual commentary.

The initial narrative mechanism in **"Chac-Mool"** is similar to the one Fuentes employs in another of his short stories; we are thinking, for example, in **"Un alma pura" ("A Pure Soul").** In both of these short stories the narrators share a common objective: to retrieve a body. In **"Chac-Mool,"** however, it is not a sister (Antigone?) who goes out to claim the fallen body of a brother to return it eventually to the Fatherland (in Spanish, "La madre patria") but a dear friend, who not only brings the body of the main protagonist back, but who, also, informs us, though succinctly, of the who, when, and where mechanism of the plot. His function in the story is not only to open and close it, but to explicate some of the important narrative developments within it. The final enigma, as is often the case with this type of stories, will be to determine the reason (why?) for the uncanny *dénouement* of the story.

We are told, in the beginning, that Filiberto, author of the diary that reveals most of what happens in the story, has recently drowned during Semana Santa (Holy Week) in Acapulco—sacred time spent in profane places. These details of the who, where, and how represent the structural elements of the *récit*, which, at an elementary level, satisfy the initial curiosity of the most demanding of readers, even when he or she may not necessarily formulate such querries. The third phrase in the first paragraph of the story seems to be charged with abundant information; in it we read that Filiberto is an ex-bureaucrat who has been fired from his position in the government agency where the main narrator also works. Until now, everything that we have been told is void of fantastic elements. It is simply a realist narrative. But from this moment on, we cross the borders of realism and venture, almost unknowingly, into the universe of the fantastic. Consequently, the plot begins to thicken, and our interest in the work grows as well. Among the few belongings of the deceased, the narrator finds, as you can very well imagine, a diary. In this peculiar diary, Filiberto had been faithfully recording his afflictions. His notes reveal, furthermore, an emotional state, which ultimately provokes his total imbalance and finally leads him to suicide. The first entry in his diary also reveals his discomfort, the fragmented state in which he finds himself, and his perennial frustration. We know he is a man of forty years of age and in process of physical and mental deterioration. We are able to perceive that much when we read about his visit to the soda fountain, where he finds his former schoolmates. Their physical presence brings back unfortunate memories within him. That is why he says," . . . Some who seemed to have the most promise got stuck somewhere along the way, cut down in some extracurricular activity, isolated by an invisible chasm from those who'd triumphed and those who'd gone nowhere at all."[7] His pessimism and frustration grow even more intensely when he bitterly points out that the majority of his schoolmates, now more prosperous than he is, ignore him or do not even recognize him. His everlasting inferiority complex seems to increase when he writes, "Between us stretched the eighteen holes of the Country Club." (***Burnt Water,*** p. 5) Subsequent entries in the diary show that Filiberto is very fond of collecting pre-Columbian figurines and that he is possessed by a growing desire to acquire one in particular, but of full human-size. This is the Chac-Mool which his friend Pepe, the main narrator, has recommended that he buy at one of the common markets in Mexico City.

Chac-Mool, like the Golem of Hebraic tradition, is a clay figure with human dimensions, but which, in this case, represents a pedestrian reproduction of an original model.

As soon as Chac-Mool comes into Filiberto's possession, he begins to experience all kinds of aquatic mishaps, one after the other. The first of a series of accidents occurs when one of the water pipes bursts, then he cannot find a plummer to repair it, and, finally, because of his oversight, the water runs all night, flooding the basement where he keeps the Chac-Mool. Very deeply concerned with solving all these domestic problems, Filiberto, without realizing it, neglects his professional duties. At the same time that all these small catastrophes are taking place, the Chac-Mool starts to show signs of a very peculiar transformation. Clearly affected by the dampness in the basement, *the statue* is completely covered with moss. Slowly we can feel the action coming to its climax, for this is one of the many intense moments in the story. It is at this point that Filiberto is very close to losing contact with reality. One night, past twelve o'clock, he suddenly awakes when he "hears" a terrible moan. His first reaction is not unusual, and he thinks it might be burglars trying to break in. But soon dismisses these thoughts and concludes that the moans he hears are *purely imaginary*. The nocturnal moans continue to be heard with the same synchronic frequency as the problems with the water reoccur. The Chac-Mool, meanwhile, acquires a grotesque appearance, and Filiberto is forced to use a trowel to scrape off its growth, and thus restore it to its original state. In spite of all the restoration efforts by Filiberto, the Chac-Mool's complete metamorphosis coincides with another series of mishaps which the protagonist suffers at work. His instability is more noticeable in the following lines:

> I don't want to write this: the testure of the torso feels a little like flesh; . . . No doubt about it: the Chac-Mool has hair on its arms . . . This kind of thing has never happened to me before. I fouled up my work in the office: I sent out a payment that hadn't been authorized, and the director had to call it to my attention. I think I may even have been rude to my coworkers.
>
> (***B.W.*** [Carlos Fuentes, ***Burnt Water*** trans. Margaret Sayers Peden, New York: Farrar, Straus and Giroux, 1980], pp. 8-9)

His mental imbalance is of such magnitude that he doesn't realize it and blames his troubles on the statue. This is the way he describes his feelings: "I'm going to have to see a doctor, find out whether it's my imagination, whether I'm delirious, or what . . . and get rid of that damned Chac-Mool." (***B.W.,*** p.9)

By the end of this last paragraph, quoted above, a noticeable change begins to take place—a probable sign of the character's psychosis. This pecularity is quickly observed by the main narrator, who is of course telling the story based on Filiberto's diary: "The entry for August 25 seemed to have been written by a different person. At times it was the writing of a child, each letter laboriously separated; other times, nervous, trailing into illegibility . . . " (**B.W.,** p. 9) From this moment on—a central point for all connections of the *récit*—we find a few contradictions in the written statements which Filiberto has left. At the same time that he leaves proof of having lost contact with reality, he also shows his lucid reasoning. This is the moment the author utilizes to make his character conjecture about what is real and imaginary. Therefore, Filiberto is programmed to say, "It's all so natural, though normally we believe only in what's real . . . but this is real, more real than anything I've ever known . . . An ephemeral smoke ring is real, a grotesque image in a funhouse mirror is real; aren't all deaths, present and forgotten, real . . .?" (**B.W.,** p. 9) And in order to support his thesis, the author cleverly manipulates his character, so he can insert within his text the already mentioned quotation taken from "The Flower of Coleridge." Conveniently, we have a text within a text, within another text.

At first, the Chac-Mool's presence merely serves to illustrate nightmares, those produced by Filiberto's feverish mind; but later, it reappears, within his private and imaginary world, as a true (flesh and blood) human being—someone who shares past experiences (historias fantásticas) and peaceful moments, but someone who can be demanding and dominating, a real slave driver who demands ambivalent aquatic and meaty tributes. The Chac-Mool's final sin is that he is turning decadent; he "is falling into human temptations."

Since all fantastic literature must have an element of suspense, the author is very resourceful at controlling this narrative mechanism. He uses narrative counterpoint throughout his tale, alternating both narratives, and thus delegating the telling of the story to the main narrator. This narrator's personal commentary serves to slow down the course of the action in the diary and also to inform the reader of the clinical state in which he finds the main protagonist. But let us get back to our main concern.

The growing fear, on the part of Filiberto, that the Chac-Mool might turn completely human, forces him to escape to Acapulco. He leaves holding on to an illusion, hoping that the situation might get back to "normal," since without his support, the Chac-Mool will have no other recourse than to return to its original state.

As we have mentioned in the beginning, the main function of the primary narrator is to open and close the story; therefore, the synthesis he makes at the end of his narrative serves to explain, what from the very

first moment we suspected, the neurosis of the main character. But even then, the story holds in store a surprise ending. When the main narrator returns to Mexico City, bringing with him Filiberto's body, he is met by a strange, repulsive "character" who, well informed of everything, orders to place the coffin in the basement. The narrator, at this time, is completely bewildered and surprised, for this individual closely resembles an incarnate Chac-Mool: "A yellow-skinned Indian in a smoking jacket and ascot . . . he smelled of cheap cologne; he'd tried to cover his wrinkles with thick powder, his mouth was clumsily smeared with lipstick, and his hair appeared to be dyed." (**B.W.,** p. 14) And thus the story ends leaving the reader to draw his or her own conclusions.

Well then, let us now make an evaluation of this short story in general terms. First of all, we have before us an unmistakable catalogue of elements taken from various tales of the fantastic genre, some of which we already have mentioned in the beginning of this study. In the second place, **"Chac-Mool"** is an exceptional adaptation of a fantastic theme and an application of several elements of extraordinary type. Filiberto, in some way, resembles, in his neurotic character, the personage created by Rainer Maria Rilke for his *Die Aufzeichnungen des Malte Laurids Brigge (The Notebooks of Malte Laurids Brigge).* The following element of its composition is what we would call *The Prague Connection,* for it turns out that Rilke, like Kafka, was born in Prague: both writers are Czech. And when we speak of transformations in literature of the neurotic kind, we immediately think of Kafka's *Metamorphosis.* The remaining "purely" German elements of the short story are represented by a secondary character: Frau Müller, who owns the boarding house where Filiberto stayed during his holidays, and who, now, refuses to allow a wake for her former paying guest. All these details are fully charged with irony; one only needs to reread, carefully and unceremoniously, that first paragraph to which we have already referred.

Whereas in regarding Chac-Mool, we do not need to insist that he represents mythical values for the peoples of old Mexico; but having selected a cheap reproduction of the archetypal rain god, the Chac-Mool reveals the playful intentions of the author. Nevertheless, this particular decision to use a full-size statue of Chac-Mool for his story proves to be a sensible choice. As Roger Caillois, and most recently Tzvetan Todorov, has remarked, "la statue, le mannequin, l'armure, l'automate qui soudain s'animent et acquièrent un redoutable indépendance" ("the statue, the mannequin, the armor, the automaton which suddenly comes alive and acquires a formidable independence") are truly the main ingredients of any genuine fantastic narrative.[8]

Of course, the animated statue of Chac-Mool is only a creature formed in the imagination of a character who has written something similar to *The Diary of a Madman.*

In conclusion, we would like to insist, once again, on the influential effect which Borges has on Carlos Fuentes. The Mexican writer, emulating the Argentine master, has learned his lesson well and thus, he has been able to create literature out of literature. The "mythical" element represented by the rain god, Chac-Mool, the Mexican surroundings, and the personal problems of a neurotic character are only a vehicle to lead us to the realization of a jocular exercise. This is something which permeates the texture of a certain text entitled **"Chac-Mool."**

Notes

1. Tzvetan Todorov, *The Fantastic: A Structural Approach to a Literary Genre* trans. Richard Howard (Ithaca, New York: Cornell University Press, 1975), pp. 24-57.

2. Roger Caillois, *Anthologie du fantastique* Tome I (Paris: Gallimard, 1966), p. 8.

3. Jorge Luis Borges, Silvina Ocampo y Adolfo Biou Casares, *Antologia de la literatura fantástica* (Buenos Aires: Editorial Sudamericana, 1967), p. 7.

4. José Donoso, "Santelices," en *Cinco maestros* ed. Alexander Coleman (New York: Harcourt, Brace and World, Inc., 1969), pp 194-217.

5. Jorge Luis Borges, *Otras inquisiciones* (Buenos Aires: Emecé editores, 1966) p. 20.

6. *Borges: A reader* Ed. Emir Rodríguez Monegal and Alastair Reid (New York: E. P. Dutton, 1981), p. 164.

7. Carlos Fuentes, *Burnt Water* trans. Margaret Sayers Peden (New York: Farrar, Straus and Giroux, 1980), pp. 4-5. All future references belong to this edition and they appear within the text in abbreviated form as, *B.W.* and the number of the corresponding page.

8. See Caillois, p. 20 and Todorov, pp. 43-44.

Gracia R. Goncalves (essay date 1991)

SOURCE: Goncalves, Gracia R. "The Myth of Helen and Her Two Husbands: Ferreira and Fuentes Mirroring Their Selves." *Monographic Review/Revista Monográfica* 7 (1991): 315-24.

[*In the essay below, Goncalves centers on the portrayals of the female protagonists of Fuentes's "Las dos Elenas" and Vergilio Ferreira's 1974 novel* Rápida, a Sombra, *claiming that, from a feminist point of view, the former is more successful than the latter in terms of the author's distinct narrative approach and depiction of sexual desire.*]

This essay is an attempt at comparison of the female figure in two contemporary writers: Carlos Fuentes' short story **"Las dos Elenas"** (1973) and Vergilio Ferreira's novel *Rápida, a Sombra* (1974).[1] I intend to comment on the representation of the female figure under the perspective of a male heterosexual narrator. I believe that both works present a "self-conscious, self-contradictory, self-undermining" writing, in tune with postmodernist insight (Hutcheon: *Politics,* 1-2).[2] Although the past is gendered and bias-shaped, I intend to point out to what extent Fuentes' work succeeds better than Ferreira's in providing feminists a more fulfilling approach. The main reason lies in the way each one lets inscribed narrative intention and erotic desire interact with each other: Fuentes' narrator foregrounds erotic desire to conceal his narrative intentions.[3] At first sight, he is just a man burning inside for a woman; then one notices that there is really no woman, but Woman, a much more free and ambivalent subject, something in between the real and the virtual, which neither he or anybody else can ever grasp. Ferreira's narrator, on the other hand, foregrounds his metafictional tendency, parodies and makes fun of conventional love, but ends up being caught by an explicitly erotic, voyeuristic desire.

To establish this relationship, I rely on two apparently disparate works: Linda Hutcheon's *Narcissistic Narrative: The Metafictional Paradox* and Wendy Lesser's *His Other Half: Men Looking at Women Through Art.* The latter criticizes the Freudian-Lacanian perspective of the "Narcissistic" figure, and replaces the myth of the acquisition of self by another one: Aristophanes' version of Genesis in Plato's *Symposium.* Hutcheon emphasizes that there should be no derogatory connotation in recognition of the term "narcissistic" as standing for any "self-representational" art; her work concerns one metaphor suitable for the analysis of a literary phenomenon (Hutcheon, 17-8). Lesser probes deeper into the psychoanalytical aspect, in terms of self-identity, and rejects Lacan for Winnicott, who never recognizes such a term. I think that "the psychoanalitic (Winnicott-based) underpinnings" of Lesser's work, which concern the interaction between the "writing self" and "written-about self" (as a relationship of mutual response rather than possession), better fits Fuentes' story. The latter illustrates the assumption that the narcissistic eye loves "what he once was" or "someone who was once part of himself," rather than "himself" or "what he would like to be", as Freudian-Lacanians would advocate (Lesser, 17-8). Both texts are "constructions"; the narrator in *Rapida, a Sombra does look* for a centre, in spite of denying it, whereas the narrator of **"Las dos Elenas"** deliberately chooses "splitting images" which expose a lack, an indetermination which is really his determination not to arrive at closure. The more responsive relationship between both parts, narrator's gaze and object, like the child and mother's image, instead of the cold surface which Lesser so much dislikes, better exemplifies the kind of relationship that one feels between the narrator of **'Las dos Elenas"** and his feminine characters.

Ferreira' text can be tackled for several reasons under the perspective of "metafiction": it can classified as what Hutcheon terms "overt narcissistic narrative," revealing "its self-awareness in explicit thematizations or allegorizations of its diegetic or linguistic identity within itself" (Hutcheon, 5). It presents elements such as parody and "mise en abyme" proper to the former category which puts more emphasis on the diegetic, i.e. on its own structure. Given its circularity, the Ferreiras text may be considered a type of "self-begetting" narrative (cf. Steven G. Keller, "The Fiction of Self-Begetting"). Kellen defines as such any first-person narrative where "the final line . . . returns to the beginning . . . " and which recounts the creation of a work very much like itself, but also paints the portrait of a fictive artist being born (7).[4]

The circularity of *Rapida, a Sombra* is evident in the fact that Julio Neves, its narrator, believes his wife has left him by "writing" him a brief note, which begets the story: an ordinary triangle of husband, wife and younger lover, who interact in an interior monologue situation. From that point on Julio mixes memories of his own infidelities with suspicions of having also been betrayed, as he also analyses his failure as a writer. In spite of the fact that the reader is not directly addressed by the narrator, he/she is alluded in the person of Julio's daughter, with whom we identify ourselves as critics. At the end his wife returns (actually she had never left him) and he begins another book.

A formalistic approach to the names (or nicknames) becomes irresistible: Julio calls his son-in-law, whom he ignores for being a weak character, Tulio. But equating his own name to his son-in-law's, Julio Neves practically effaces himself. He points to the artificiality of his daughter friend's name, Elia, which should be spelled with an "H". He simply endows her with one, so that the referent can match the interpretant, while, at the same time, he makes fun of theory: "Althusser, Barthes, Derrida, Bachelard . . . o código. Assim a produção do texto . . . " (*RS* [*Rapida, a Sombra*], 53). Only a post-Saussurean background would call attention to such a slide of signifiers.

Fuentes' narrator is not identified by name, but several nicknames that his wife gives him, of whose meaning he is unaware: Nibelungo, Ni Ve Lungo ("Can't See Further"), Niebla or Nibble etc.; it does not seem to matter at all to him. He never complains of anything; on the contrary, he simply informs the reader how always busy with an appointment, with someone or something else his wife is. And how she becomes even more interesting exactly because of that. There is no real plot, except for a long dinner when an amalgam of Elena's character through members of her family's opinions, especially his mother-in-law's, as well as her own, is composed. Nibelungo is an engineer, an architect, someone always surrounded with papers and "projects". He only lives for her and his plans. In both stories, the wives are Helens: Elena and Helena. I am not suggesting a kind of intertextuality so much as of an "interhistoricity:" life and art, two husbands and an old myth. History and myth go hand in hand.

Nibelungo is not suspicious of his mythical learned denomination and there remains the greatest irony. In the legend Siegfried refuses love for power, but he finally falls into a trap and is beaten by Brunhilde, "the strong woman." It seems there is an intentional obliteration of the male characters' presences through their names, so that the female characters become bold. This can be seen as a reversal of Lacan's "Name/Law of the Father."

Still focusing on the female characters' names, one notices that, in order to make bolder the figure of Elena, she has a foil, her mother, another Elena. Elena-mother talks with Nibelungo about a past which she herself can no longer remember; Elena-daughter in turn lives in the future: "Pensé que Elena podría tener razón en el futuro" (12). Both move along time, even though they rarely meet each other. Like memory and imagination on the same foggy route. Julio's attention is also divided between his wife, Helena, and his daughter's friend, Helia. Helena, Helia; the mythical and the mythological together. History is thus equated with fiction, becoming but another construction.

It could be argued that the explicitly embedded narrative of Elena-mother turns the text into an overt "mise-en-abime" type. As Hutcheon remarks, the categories she presents are not rigid; however, another aspect seems even more relevant to the present study: "the erotic" mode, as a way of tantalizing the reader, or a variation of the detective plot, turned into an "adultery plot" better defines such process of story telling. Its subtlety lies in presenting a narrator who plays both the naive victim and the wise detective who manipulates the facts and peoples' narratives, producing a special kind of metafiction. The reader, always in pursuit of Elena, is caught in a "hermeneutic act of reading" that classifies the covert narcissist narrative (Narcissistic, 10). "Can't-See-Further" leads the reader without recognizing it; it is a form of self-reflexive, but not self-conscious writing. At the end, there is no evidence whatsoever, nor is there supposed to be. The concealed search, or the process of composing the image of "Helen" goes on over and over.

My superficial gaze now pierces deeper into the text to inquire about eroticism, the power of seduction of both figures over their two beholders. Since I have recognized that one seems to be more "absorbed" in the picture of Helen, whereas the other is overtly "framing" her, I wonder why this feeling that such reversal occurs: at a certain point Julio's desire and his creation itself will overlap, and one will see Nibelungo actually giving plasticity to attributes he once considered just lively. The relationship with Lesser's text can be then established. A brief summary of the version of Genesis recited by Aristophanes in Plato's *Symposium,* presented and interpreted by Lesser follows: in the beginning there was no notion of separate sexes but "four-legged, two-headed people" that Zeus decided to split in order to "enfeeble their strength" (10). As soon as this happened there began the search for the other half. By starting with male-female pairs, Lesser dares to advance in her binary analysis which she classifies as "impressionistic, audience-based criticism" (20), and extends it to other selves which search for completion in each other. She relates them:

> the onlooker and the participant: the *writing self and the written-about self,* the willed creature of mind and the less conscious sould of being; they were the public character, located in history, and the private character, defined psychologically and individually; they were, moreover the high arts and the popular arts.
>
> (10)

Lesser suggests that despite the fact that we are indeed defined by "lack" and "death," as opposed to "life" and "eternity," that does not necessarily mean that we share the same connotation of negativity. One should cope with the idea "that to be a 'whole' individual inevitably entails division, separation, and unappeasable longing" (19). This recalls Bataille's theory according to which "What we desire is to bring into a world founded on discontinuity all the continuity such a world can sustain" (Bataille, 19).

Lesser posits a dynamic relationship between creator and art work where one seems to lose himself/herself in the other

> there was something both compelling and moving, I felt, in the way certain male artists portrayed women: a kind of longing that was not just an expression of the erotic . . .; a desire to *be* the other as well as to view her, and at the same time an acknowledgement of irrevocable separation.
>
> (10)

The more the reader shares the narrator's longing, the less phallocratic, the less voyeuristic, the text sounds; because it denotes a strong attempt to project oneself in the hope of completion, not domination; because it recognizes oneself as part of a process, never just an outsider. Ferreira, despite his intentions of dissemination of sense, of deconstructing truth, of not controlling "his other half" is more a viewer focusing from one single side than he seems to admit. He speaks through the mouth of a conventional lover, but just to *sound* satyrical. Utterances like "mon amour" and "my love" permeate the text. This would be a self-undermining statement, open to its own deconstruction, but he actually betrays himself. He cannot hide his tendency to describe "poses" rather than actual responses of a body in movement, in *any* movement. Women appear like sculptures; he stands for their eternal beholder.

As an instance of how such use of parody does not suffice to cover his phallocentric tendencies one can analyze the passage where he describes Helena and Helia at the moment they were introduced. He revives the myth of Venus as portrayed by Boticcelli, Courbet and others:

> "Entao *ela* lavanta-se-*me* ao extremo do areal, nua, aérea, . . . ressurges-*me* de entre as ondas,
>
> —Vem do fundo do mar?
>
> o breve calção descaído, a transparència da camiseta . . . (emphasis added)
>
> (*She stands up in front of me* at the end of the beach, naked, . . . comes out to *me* in the middle of the waves, the tiny bikini, the transparency of the T-shirt . . . do you come from the bottom of the sea?)
>
> (My translation)

The "fisher" line, "Vem do fundo do mar?" becomes a leit-motiv within the book, with Helena's image, as the young girl he met, and Helia's, interchanging positions in the narrator's memory.

The nude in art history traditionally required a context either mythological or historical, to become acceptable. The parody would be convincing, if he himself did not seem so drowned in the waves. The expressions "levanta-se-*me*", "Ressurges-*me*" are good enough examples: the ostensible barrier of objectivity is undermined by the narrator's pointing out "Look' it is just an art work," to stand like an ordinary beholder in explicit delectation. Like Michelangelo in love with his Moses, he seems to expect a physical, personal response. Not only "parla," but "parla con me." Ferreira plays with this awareness of the artifact against the real: "E inclinado *avanco,* tu, *hierática.* Solene. Linda pura branca. De plástico? Até que, inverossímil, na fina evaporacao de mim, imaterializado sucinto, breve afloro no apice do desejo . . . " (159) (Emphasis added). So far, so unreal; the plastic, unbelievable woman gets shape not *in* but rather *from* his imagination, his aura, his breath. She is made out of his desire to compose her; out of his matter, like Eve. She mirrors what "he is" or "what he would like to be."

In his struggle between problematizing desire, or accepting the fact of letting it go, Julio Neves alternates spontaneity with a sense of measure and aesthetic judgement, somehow preserving the feminine image of goddess: if he objectively sees her hand as "feía," he compliments her gesture; he see her neck skin as a turkey's, he compensates with the adjective "solene." Emphasis should be placed on the use of "avanco" and "hieratica." Lucien Dallenbach in his *Mirrors and After: Five Essays on Literary Criticism,* expands the Gidean definition of the "mise en abyme" from the repetition of "the subject" on the "level of the characters" to "any sign having as its referent a pertinent continuous aspect of the narrative (fiction, text or narrative code, enonciation ["enonciation] which it represents on the diegetic level" (Dallenbach, 10). It seems there is a sequence of mirrorings along both narratives: Julio's wife's note that she would leave him spurs him to write the story of his infidelities, which will lead her to leave him, and so on. There is also the inscription of Helena in a classical landscape and her substitution for Helia, who nevertheless reflects Helena's image as young. Something similar will occur with Elena-mother, who looks like Elena-daughter, or vice-verse. But whereas the obsession for preserving youth is in *Rapida a Sombra* more centered in the narrator's expectations, in **"Las dos Elenas"** it remains in the sphere of the other characters themselves.

Were Ferreira a bad writer, as the narrator admits that his daughter says he is, she would not have been given the power to criticize; he would not be able to construct, by deconstructing page by page, a novel about the uselessness of fiction, rescuing it at the very end. The narrator begins by listening to a song "Amanhecer," and finishes by stating the title of the book that he "is going" to write: *Anoitecer,*" whereas the readers know it is already written. He could not so well play in this sliding field of irony. His persona would not age, nor would Helia so realistically reject him for another lover:

—Helia! Voce nao gosta de homens?

— . . .

Tenho um amigo.

(161)

Another apparent difference between a wife's or a lover's infidelity, the text suggests, is that the latter does not threaten the Name/Law of the Father that seemed

to have been deconstructed. Fortunately, the real wife who had left at the beginning, ends by returning home, thereby removing the inverted commas of the word "story;" no history any more, only fiction. She appears just in time to save his reputation, in this case not so much of a writer, as of a husband.

By contrast, Fuentes' narrator Nibelungo has never been anxious about questions of domination. He describes and seems to accept Elena as an image that she herself constructs, or that others construct about her, providing a quilt of peoples' remarks—her father's, her mother's; she is shown less for the thighs, for example, than for the green extravagant stockings she wears, outlined rather for what she does than how she looks. This is achieved through a process of association with her mother's image, recalling the latter's same naive and seductive gestures. When describing Elena's mother, differently from Ferreira, the narrator gives special emphasis to her movements rather than her body itself: the movement of her hands making little balls out of bread; her gaze which he pursues: "seguí sui nueva mirada" (18). Her slips tell more about her power of seduction than her presence. In the embedded narrative sequence when she remembers her past, as she tenderly caresses the pieces of bread, she decreases her age: "Me casé . . . " (the first time she says that she was twenty-one; the second time, that she was eighteen, 20-1).

This sequence presents an interesting, unconventional situation: Nibelungo plays the mother so that Elena-daughter can sleep on his knees like a cat. Elena-mother plays the sensual woman: "cruzó una pierna y se arregló la falda sobre las rodillas" (20). Then, as if she were giving him her hand to dive in the time tunnel, she leads him to the warm and humid interiors of the tropics, like a return trip to the uterus of earth: "En cada cuarto había un ropero y las criadas tenían la costumbre de colocar hojas de laurel y orégano entre la ropa. Además, el sol nunca secaba bien algunos rincones" (21). If woman can write "with her body", as Irigaray would say, Nibelungo may not be able to see further, but he can definitely see "deeper."

When Nibelungo returns to the present, like a newborn who looks for light he calls attention to the outside asking if those memories came to her as a result of the new spotlight as the end of the lot. There are no closures however: he does not wait for the answer. He awakes Elena-daughter and continues playing the double role of the maternal husband. The recurrent image of Elena leaning against his legs reverses the image of the "pietá" and her son, "the one that I once was," and "who once was part of me." It is as if "the said, the spoken, is to be heard and discounted, the unsaid, the unspoken, is unheard but counted" (Hutcheon, *Splitting,* 98).

In the last scene, after having left Elena, he drives for a while just to return her "image": her skin and also her "infinitos proyectos" (51). Once more she has no time for him, and he verbalizes his desire thus: "y pensar que soy feliz al lado de una mujer tan vivaz, tan moderna, que . . . que me . . . que me complementa tanto" (51). The dots say more than the sentences, calling attention to the gap, which shows either a linguistic lack of competence, or a witty device inviting the reader to think it over. Such a slip debunks a desire so overtly admitted and hides an irony: of the one who knows enough to know that he does not know. By shaping Elena through others' point of view, the narrator avoids the uncomfortable position of "taking sides"; by stating the wants to keep her "image," he denounces his worship, but also reveals she is a vanishing point in his life. The splitting ironies of the text—to listen and not to hear, to tell and not to say, to have and not to possess, to look and not to see—point to the conclusion that no conclusion is possible. The passive, undesirable voyeur may have been nurturing himself, while also offering the reader the fruit from another dimension: the dimension of fiction. In this twilight zone he knows how questionable it is "to know" a Woman; and that makes him wise enough.

Notes

1. I will refer from this point on to both works through their abbreviation, respectively DS and RS.

2. For a further discussion on the subject see also Creed, Flax, and Hutcheon.

3. By intentionality I mean inscribed in the text itself, rather than authorship.

4. I owe credit for this approach to my colleague Euridice Silva for his discussion on the subject "Identidade e Metaficcao em *Rápida a Sombra*."

Bibliography

Bataille, Georges. *Erotism: Death and Sensuality.* San Francisco: City Light Books. 1986.

Creed, Barbara. "From Here to Modernity: Feminism and Postmodernism." *Screen.* 28.2 (1987): 50-61.

Dallenbach, Lucien. *"Mirrors and After: Five Essays on Literary Theory and Criticism.* New York: The Graduate School City University of New York. 1985.

Ferreira, Vergílio. *Rápida, a Sombra.* Póvoa de Varzim: Tipografia Cameos. 1975.

Flax, Jane. *Thinking Fragments: Psychoanalisis, Feminism and Postmodernism in The Contemporary West.* Berkeley: University of California Press. 1990.

Fuentes, Carlos. "Las Dos Elenas." *Cantar de Ciegos.* Mexico: Editorial Joaquín Mortiz. 1964. Salvat Editores, S.A. 1973. 11-24.

Hutcheon, Linda: *The Politics of Postmodernism.* London: Routledge. 1989.

———. *Narcissistic Narrative: The Metafictional Paradox.* Waterloo: Wilfrid Laurier University Press. 1980.

———. *Splitting Images.* Toronto: Oxford University Press. 1991.

Irigaray, Luce. *Speculum of the Other Woman.* Trans. Gillian C. Gill. New York: Cornell University Press. 1985.

Jardine, Alice. *Gynesis: Configurations of Woman and Modernity.* Ithaca: Cornell University Press, 1990.

Linger, Kate: "Eluding Definition," *Artforum* (New York): December 1984, 61-7.

John Incledon (essay date April 1992)

SOURCE: Incledon, John. "Fiction into Film: *¿No oyes ladrar los perros?* by Carlos Fuentes." *Maclas: Latin American Essays* 6 (1993): 147-52.

[*In the essay below, originally presented in April 1992, Incledon considers how Fuentes, in his film adaptation of Juan Rulfo's short story "¿No oyes ladrar los perros?," changed the father-son relationship from a bitter one into a loving and hopeful bond—a modification the critic considers a response to the conflicted father-son relationship in Fuentes's novel* The Death of Artemio Cruz.]

Master and servant, king and citizen, conqueror and conquered, authoritarian dictator and oppressed masses—the history of Spanish and Latin American civilization is a story of ruling power and the subversive forces that challenge that power. It is a struggle of fathers and sons. Juan Rulfo's short story, "No oyes ladrar los perros" is just such a tale. And Carlos Fuentes' storyline for the film adaptation of this story pushes that theme in several interesting and original directions.

Adapting literature to film is often an impoverishing exercise. So many things can go wrong. There is always the danger that a film will be poorly made and unable to stand on its own. *Tune in Tomorrow,* for example, the film adaptation of *La tí Julia y el escribidor* by Vargas Llosa, is at best a mediocre film. Another oft-seen problem is the difficulty of adapting sizeable literary works. The recently-released *Mambo Kings,* for example, treats only the first part of the Oscar Hijuelos novel. And some attempts, while fine films, are uninspired adaptations. Hector Babenco's *Kiss of the Spider Woman,* while a very well-made film, is arguably unoriginal and uninspired by being so faithful to the novel by Manuel Puig. Such, too, is the case of the filmscript Carlos Fuentes wrote, along with Carlos Velo and Manuel Barbachano, for the 1966 adaptation of Rulfo's *Pedro Páramo*. (A complete filmography on Juan Rulfo is available in the appendix to *El gallo de oro*.)

But some of the richest and most interesting adaptations are of short works of fiction which have been turned into full-length feature films. In 1970, Bernardo Bertolucci made a very fine film, *The Spider's Stratagem*, based on "tema del traidor y del héroe" by Jorge Luis Borges. Bertolucci changes the locale from Ireland to fascist Italy in the 1930's and adds several interesting touches—most notably the scene at the railroad station at the end of the film—that enhance the questions of the circularity of time and the confusion of history and fiction, which are central to Borges' story. But one of the most interesting film adaptations of a Latin American literary work is Michelangelo Antonioni's *Blowup*, based on "Las babas del diablo" by Julio Cortázar. While the basic premise of the story is retained—a man photographs a couple in a park and, upon blowing them up, makes a startling discovery—Antonioni and his scriptwriter, Tonino Guerra, take a free hand in making the film their own. Not only are the locale, several of the characters, the mystery in the park—indeed the whole ambience of the film, which is set in the "mod" London of the mid-60's—different from the story, but Antonioni and Guerra also add an existential dimension which would seem to sharply diverge from the aura of the fantastic and the interplay of reality and illusion that are present in Cortázar's story. In spite of all this, Cortázar, as he said in an interview with Rita Guibert, felt that Antonioni "was winking at me, and that we were meeting above or below our differences" (Peavler, 893).

François Reichenbach's *¿No oyes ladrar los perros?*, with a storyline developed by Carlos Fuentes, is another example of a short work of fiction being expanded and developed into a full-length feature film. If Fuentes's script for *Pedro Páramo* is uninspired, his storyline for *¿No oyes ladrar los perros?* is interesting in a number of ways. Not only does Fuentes make some significant changes to the story itself, but in order to transform a five-page short story into a ninety-minute feature film, he adds a significant amount of new material to Rulfo's plot. And in so doing he re-explores some of the important themes of his own work, especially the relationship of fathers and sons.

The basic premise of *¿No oyes ladrar los perros?* is identical with that of the story: a man carries his son, who is ill, in search of a doctor. Some differences, however, are immediately apparent. In the story, for example, the son is older—a young man—while the

son in the film is a boy of ten or eleven years. Fuentes has also given his characters an Indian identity. They are members of the Chamula tribe. And late in the film, he draws a striking parallel between Ignacio's suffering and the agony of Christ. More importantly the relationship between the boy, Ignacio, and his father is completely different. In the story, there is a deeply-rooted bitterness between father and son. "Para mí usted ya no es mi hijo," his father tells him. "He maldecido la sangre que usted tiene de mí (115). Ignacio is a thief and murderer, and has killed Tranquilino, one of his father's *compadres*. Ignacio's illness is the result of a wound he has received during a holdup. His father helps him only because of the love his dead wife had for the boy. The story is saturated with bitterness, rancor, and hopelessness. After an exhausting journey, the father arrives in Tonaya—the town with a doctor—only to find that his son has died on his back.

In the film, on the other hand, there is a loving relationship between father and son. Ignacio's illness results from his failure to receive a free inoculation along with the other members of his *pueblo*. But, unlike the story, the film displays a sense of hope emanating from the loving relationship of father and son. This difference can be seen even in the two titles. Throughout both the story and the film Ignacio's father asks him if he can hear the dogs barking. It is a way of knowing if his son is still alive. The story's title, however, is a statement rather than a question— "No oyes ladrar los perros." (The title of the translation by George Schade reflects this, too—"No Dogs Bark.") The title of Rulfo's story tells us—though we do not realize it until the end—that Ignacio no longer hears the dogs bark, that he is dead. The question in Fuentes' title—*¿No oyes ladrar los perros?*—besides being a way to distinguish itself from the story, leaves open a ray of hope. Perhaps Ignacio will survive.

Indeed, this loving relationship between father and son in the film opens the way for Fuentes to add material to the film. In order to pass time during their journey in search of a doctor and, more importantly, to help Ignacio hold on in his fight for life, his father imagines scenes in his son's future, picturing the happiness and success he will achieve—marriage, leadership in the pueblo, raising a family. It is this imagined future—technically, these scenes are the opposite of flashbacks—that turn the five-page short story into a ninety-minute feature film. In fact, these projected images of the future are not all of the father's making. Engaging himself in their content, Ignacio questions his father regarding them and even creates some of his own. Some reflect Ignacio's own fears and, in some cases, they are bizarre and surrealistic ([i.e. . . .] man bathing in an enormous bowl of soup). They are his fever talking, the result of his delirium, as can be seen in the dream sequences. (The image of Ignacio stepping out of his body in one of these sequences alludes to the famous scene in Buñuel's *Los olvidados*.) In short, *¿No oyes ladrar los perros?* becomes a vehicle for Fuentes to explore a whole range of questions important to him—fathers and sons, nature *versus* culture, country *versus* city, Indian culture *versus* European culture, and so on. In the film, Fuentes explores the alienation of the Indian from modern, Western life in the city.

While most of these themes are original to the film, the relationship of father and son is carefully contrasted with the story. It is curious and, I believe, significant that Fuentes changes the negative father/son relationship in the story to a positive one in the film. The relationship is in some ways the opposite of and an answer to that of Artemio Cruz and his son, Lorenzo, in Fuentes' novel, *La muerte de Artemio Cruz,* published some twelve years earlier. Like "No oyes ladrar los perros," *La muerte de Artemio Cruz,* too, has a refrain that is repeated over and over throughout the novel—"Esa mañana lo esperaba con alegría. Cruzamos el río a caballo" (12)—a refrain which relates to the day, years before, when Lorenzo told his father he was leaving to fight on the Republican side in the Spanish Civil War. It was a moral decision of a kind Artemio himself was never able to make, selling out instead to be on the winning side and to serve his own self-interest. Artemio spends his last hours in the hospital thinking back on the twelve most important days in his life, trying to make spiritual contact with his son, who went on to die in the Civil War, and with himself at that point in the past when his ideals were still intact and he had not yet betrayed the values inculcated by his teacher, Sebastián.

Fuentes' adaptation of Rulfo's story is, I would suggest, an answer of a kind to *Artemio Cruz*. Artemio, in his dying hours, tries to make contact with his son, who serves as a reflection of himself as a young man: "tajo de tu memoria, . . . la fruta tiene dos mitades: hoy volverán a unirse: recordarás la mitad que dejaste atrás: el destino te encontrará" (17). In his adaptation of the Rulfo story, however, Fuentes portrays the father/son relationship as strong right up until the end. The two are closely united, even in death, as can be seen in the final scene in the film, when his father says: "Tú vivirás, hijo mío. Porque un padre sin su hijo no es nada. Tú y yo juntos. Tú y yo juntos somos un sólo hombre. ¿Verdad que sí, Ignacio?" In the case of Artemio Cruz, however, it is only many years later, on his own deathbed, that he is able to reconcile himself with his son's death.

In sum, Fuentes uses his expanded adaptation of Rulfo's "Oyes ladrar los perros" to re-explore a theme—the relationship of fathers and sons—which is present in earlier works, such as *La muerte de Artemio Cruz,* and which would reappear in later works, such as *Terra Nostra* and *El gringo viejo*.

References

Fuentes, Carlos. 1962. *La muerte de Artemio Cruz.* México, D.F.: Fondo de Cultura Económica, 1970.

Peavler, Terry. "*Blow-Up*: A Reconsideration of Antonioni's Infidelity to Cortázar." *PMLA* [*Publications of the Modern Language Association of America*]. 94.5 (1979): 887-893.

Reichenbach, François, director. *¿No oyes ladrar los perros? / N'entends-tu pas les chiens aloyer?* Storyline by Carlos Fuentes. Script by Jacqueline Lefebvre, Noel Howard, and François Reichenbach. Conacine, Cinematográfica Marco Polo, and Les Films du Prism ORTF, 1974. Based on Juan Rulfo's "No oyes ladrar los perros."

Rulfo, Juan. *The Burning Plain and Other Stories.* Tr. with an intro. by George D. Schade. Austin: University of Texas Press, 1973.

———. *El gallo de oro.* México, D.F.: Era, 1980.

———. *El llano en llamas.* 1953. México, D.F.: Fondo de Cultura Económica, 1978.

Jeffrey C. Barnett (lecture date September 1993)

SOURCE: Barnett, Jeffrey C. "Vengeance Is Mine: The Role of the Fantastic in Carlos Fuentes's *Los días enmascarados.*" *West Virginia University Philological Papers* 42-43 (1997): 68-73.

[*In the essay below, originally delivered as a lecture in September 1993, Barnett analyzes how Fuentes fused elements of the fantastic with social commentary in the stories in* Los días enmascarados, *outlining an overall structure to the volume based on Mexico's past, ongoing, and future attempts to reject its indigenous roots.*]

Throughout the second half of this century, critics have generally attempted to categorize Latin American fiction in two principal groupings: namely, magic realism or social realism. Both salient characteristics are found throughout Carlos Fuentes's novels and short fiction, ranging from the social or exterior concern, in *La muerte de Artemio Cruz,* to the interior or fantastic nature of writings such as **Aura**. Nevertheless, while much of his fiction can be readily identified either as a work of the fantastic or as one of social thesis, Fuentes's first published volume of fiction defies rigid categorization. In the collection of short stories **Los días enmascarados** (1954) Fuentes initiates his vision of the fantastic as a destructive force which both controls the character's destiny and, in turn, serves to elicit a social reading of the text.[1] This becomes apparent when we view the role of the fantastic in isolated stories; however, upon examining the volume as a whole, one finds a shared structural relationship among the stories which affords the fantastic even greater significance as a driving force of conflict from the past, within the present, and extending into the future. Thus, this study examines how the stories relate to one another, and specifically how the fantastic is a driving force throughout the volume.

Several critics have called attention to the prevalent use of the fantastic throughout the collection.[2] For example, John S. Brushwood suggests that "fantasy probably establishes itself, by the time these [first] four stories are read, as the primary characteristic in common."[3] Cynthia Duncan also acknowledges the fantastic as a unifying characteristic of the volume and goes on further to say that the first story of the collection, **"Chac Mool,"** meets the criteria for the restricted definition of the fantastic as set forth by Tzvetan Todorov.[4] Based on this understanding, Duncan approaches the story with two important premises: first, the reader must hesitate when confronted with elements which defy both a natural and supernatural explanation; and second, the reader must reject an allegorical or poetic interpretation of the text. Unlike Duncan's restrictive use of the term, Daniel de Guzmán and Wendy Ferris view the fantastic nature of the collection in a broader sense, combining terms excluded from Todorov's definition. For example, de Guzmán describes the author's presentation of the stories as "ironic, fantastical, Surrealistic."[5] Likewise, Ferris alludes to the allegorical nature of the stories and further points out that "Because they contain eruptions of the fantastic into everyday life, these early stories can be included in the general category of magic realism."[6] Terms such as surrealism, magic realism, irony, and allegory may lead some to question whether the work in fact fits into the realm of the fantastic, especially if one holds a very restrictive use of the term such as Duncan explicates in relation to Todorov's ideas. In my view, and as I use the term here, the fantastic suggests the recognized intrusion of a force which defies explanation from the character's perspective of the physical world.

With this understanding of the fantastic in mind, a structural relationship becomes evident throughout *Los días enmascarados* delineated as follows: the conflict in each story centers around a fantastic force envisioned in my reading as a god, albeit a pre-Columbian deity, an allegorical figure, or symbolic entity; the protagonist fails to acknowledge the supreme power properly or even rejects the force; and,

ultimately, the consequence of the character's actions results in his demise. Moreover, when we examine the stories with this structure in mind, an alternative ordering of the stories becomes apparent based on a temporal grouping. In the first, third, and fifth stories (**"Chac Mool," "Tlactocatzine, del Jardín de Flandes,"** and **"Por boca de los dioses"**) the fantastic forces derive from Mexico's past. The second and fourth selections—**"En defensa de la Trigolibia"** and **"Letanía de la orquídea"**—entail fantastic elements that corrspond to the present. And in the final selection of the work, **"El que inventó la pólvora,"** the fantastic extends to the future.

To illustrate the structural relationship, let me first offer a brief description of the stories that relate to a fantastic god from the past which visits and intrudes upon the present-day character. The most discussed and sophisticated story of the collection, **"Chac Mool,"** presents the tale of a modern-day collector of indigenous artifacts, who purchases a cheap replica of the Toltec-Mayan rain god Chac Mool. As the outer-frame narrator studies Filiberto's diary, the reader comes to find how he has purchased the statue, how seemingly it has come to life and taken control of his entire existence, leading him to flee to Acapulco where he drowns. Ultimately, when the narrator returns with Filiberto's body, he is greeted at the door by an enigmatic figure, a repulsive "indio amarillo," whom we are to assume is now the anthropomorphic pre-Columbian god.[7]

Similarly, **"Por boca de los dioses"** involves a pantheon of Aztec mythological deities who come to life after the protagonist removes a pair of lips from a Tamayo painting. The gods who run amuck on the streets of Mexico City eventually entrap the protagonist in the symbolic muddy basement of his hotel where Tlazol—the goddess of excrement, filth, and forgiveness—performs her duty of expiation and sacrifice: "Tlazol me abrazó en un espasmo sin suspiros. El puñal quedó allí en mi centro, como un pivote loco" (72).

Finally, **"Tlactocatzine, del Jardín de Flandes"** also conjures up a spirit from the past. Unlike the stories involving pre-Columbian gods, however, this time the past is more immediate: the indigenous name Tlactocatzine refers to the Hapsburg emperor of Mexico, Maximillian. In this instance, a modern-day character inhabits a once grandiose mansion where he is haunted by an eerie presence, presumably that of Carlotta. As in the other two previous stories, the confrontation between the real-life, modern-day protagonist and the unreal spirit from the past culminates in the demise of the character when he is imprisoned forever within the walls of the mansion's courtyard.

Although very distinct in some ways, the stories that I have identified with fantastic forces from the past share similar qualities, in particular the nature of the gods, their relationship with the characters, and the ensuing consequences. In **"Chac Mool"** fantasy intrudes upon reality when Filiberto is confronted with the fact that a replica of a statue has come to life and, more importantly, he is in the presence of a god whom he has openly defiled. By smearing it with ketchup to make it look more lifelike, he has reduced the god to an object intended for display not unlike a piece of furniture. Thus, his failure to pay appropriate homage and to recognize Chac's power constitute his sin. He must acknowledge his atavistic pre-Columbian nature, Fuentes suggests, or be destroyed. Yet Filiberto's singular actions are of course emblematic of Mexico as a nation. As with Filiberto's fate, Mexico must pay the price for having attempted in the past as well as in the present to destroy its historical legacies which seemingly defy the physical and contemporary reality.

Such is the case too in **"Por boca de los dioses"** where the character's denigration of his past leads to his demise in the present. Again emblematic of all Mexico, the character shares the blame for the conquest even in the present since it is an ongoing process. For example, the number of his hotel room, 1519, is an obvious reminder of the year in which Cortés began the conquest, but more importantly it signals the extent to which Mexico's historical past is subtly incorporated into the modern setting.

Similarly, in **"Tlactocatzine, del Jardín de Flandes"** Mexico must pay for its sin of having killed another element of its past, Maximillian. In this case, the avenging force is that of the empress Carlotta, who wanders about in the old mansion as a soul in torment. Moreover, if we understand as is suggested by the narrator that the new owner intended to demolish the mansion, again we find the same analogy as before: an attempt to destroy or reject the past. Although the wrath of the gods in **"Chac Mool"** and **"Por boca de los dioses"** differs in intensity from the vengeance enacted by Carlotta, the result is the same. The young man who has fallen under the spell of the ghostly being is entrapped forever, just as Mexico has been entrapped by its past gods. In short, in these three stories characters confront a fantastic deity or spirit, fail to acknowledge the force properly, and thus incur the wrath of the supernatural antagonist.

If the collection were to end here, we could conclude that Fuentes's purpose is to address the social message of Mexico's plight of having turned its back on its past; yet the remaining three stories lead us to consider the entire volume from a temporal point of view, similar to the tripartite structure of the past, present,

and future in *La muerte de Artemio Cruz*. Thus, moving to the present we find in **"Letanía de la orquídea"** that the fantastic erupts, or better stated protrudes, when a female impersonator awakens one morning to find that an orchid has sprouted from his coccyx. The seemingly absurd association between the orchid and Muriel's condition makes sense when one recalls that the etymology of "orchid" is testicle (f. Greek, *orxi-*; Latin, *orchis*). Instead of being alarmed and trying to remedy the fantastic element, Muriel decides to let nature run its course and take advantage of the situation by growing and selling the costly flowers. In the end however the symbol is subverted or, more literally, inverted. The orchids cease to sprout outwardly; instead the root transforms into a splintery stake which now turns inward and impales him, suggesting an ancient punishment for sodomy.

From the very beginning of the story the reader probably identifies the setting as Panama, yet only gradually are we led to understand through allusions to impersonation, prostitution, and political symbols that the fantastic has transformed into the allegorical. Muriel in fact is Panama, and the orchid represents the Panama Canal. At one and the same time, the once seemingly attractive and viably economic venture of the orchid/canal brings death. Just as the orchid/stake has severed Muriel in two, the canal similarly has cut a gash through Panama. Moreover, although in his role as female impersonator, what Muriel does implies that the effect is death and the agent is the canal, the true cause is prostitution, or rather the prostitution of Panama. Just as Panama has acted as a nation, Muriel's greed and betrayal to self and his culture have led to the vengeful wrath of the present-day gods.

In addition to **"Letanía de la orquídea,"** the second piece of the collection—**"En defensa de la Trigolibia"**—also corresponds temporally to the present; however, the two-page "story" contains few if any characteristics of fiction and instead is more akin to a political commentary disguised in clever double-speak through which Fuentes expresses his contempt for the Cold War setting of the 1950s. Brushwood, however, notes the value of the work as a means of creating a "seesaw experience" since the text is intercalated between **"Chac Mool"** and **"Tlactocatzine, del Jardín de Flandes,"** thus producing a shock effect given the ordering of the stories (21). As a playful exercise based on the neologism "Trigolibia" and its derivatives, the short commentary ridicules the struggle for superiority by two global superpowers. Thus, the absurdity of the neologisms corresponds to the senseless rhetoric voiced by the United States and the former Soviet Union. More importantly, despite the light-hearted tone of the language, the extended allegory serves to warn the reader of the impending doom of a global holocaust. In this respect the contemporary referent of **"En defensa de la Trigolibia"** now serves to frame the last story in the collection, **"El que inventó la pólvora,"** which leads us to a futuristic manifestation of the fantastic.

One of the most common trends within recent Mexican narrative is the theme of the consumer consumed within the cult of materialism.[8] Analogous to the sacrifice demanded by pre-Columbian gods, the idolater of consumerism and sacrificial victim are one and the same. **"El que inventó la pólvora"** seemingly presages this trend through its satirical description of a futuristic society where consumer goods such as spoons, shoes, and toothbrushes come to life and turn against their creator. The description in this instance of the rebellion of inanimate objects bears a strong resemblance to a similar passage in the Mayan *Popol Vuh* in which water jars, tortilla griddles, plates, and grinding stones are empowered by the gods to seek vengeance against the *muñecos,* or Man, and destroy him because of his disobedience and abuse.[9] As the various types of inanimate objects come to life and speak, they each exact a punishment corresponding to the treatment they have received from Man: the grinding stone pounds and grinds his flesh; the cooking pots and griddles burn and crush his face (31). Although it seems very likely that this particular passage from the *Popol Vuh* may have influenced Fuentes or even served as the inspiration for **"El que inventó la pólvora,"** the difference lies in that Fuentes moves away from the mystic or supernatural found in the creationary myth to the fantastic as a means of social commentary against materialism. More specifically, the revolt of the masses becomes the revolt of the mass-produced items. However, unlike the vindictive and triumphant animate objects of the *Popol Vuh,* the material goods in **"El que inventó la pólvora"** ultimately enter a stage of atrophy and return to dust, a meltdown so to speak of a material holocaust. Their revolution has come full circle, as nothing remains except for the narrator, who ends the story while rubbing two sticks together on a solitary beach.

Brushwood points out that the story "ends the book on a rather strange note," yet he adds that "One might, of course, note the intensification of destruction, followed by a new beginning" (25). Indeed the idea of apocalypse followed by regeneration is evident not only in Fuentes's works but throughout much of contemporary Mexican fiction. More importantly, the idea of complete annihilation in this case serves as an appropriate ending, especially if we consider the significance of "pólvora" and one other final image, that of "un hongo azul." First, "pólvora" symbolically conjures up images of primitivism and reinforces the idea that the material items are progressively reverting to

an organic state of dust; yet we should remember that as signifier it explicitly denotes gunpowder. Thus with one symbol Fuentes subtly hints at cause and effect. Could we not take "pólvora" here to imply the cause of atrophy, meaning that gunpowder or warfare lies at the root of the problem? At first this seems unconvincing within the frame of the story, but when we consider the symbolic reference to the "hongo azul," the duality of primitivism and warfare again comes to mind. As the narrator sits alone in his basement, before the world is begun again, he indicates that "un hongo azul con penachos de sombra me ahoga" (84). In a freely associative way, the blue mushroom evokes the image of the atomic cloud, and with good reason if we remember that the work was published in the mid 1950s. Furthermore, the image is also identified with primitivism or at least a regression to the past if we associate "hongo azul" with *huitlacoche,* the Aztec culinary delicacy described as a blue fungus.

As a final consideration, we come full circle to the title of the work, "los días enmascarados" or the *nemontani,* the five atemporal days in Aztec cosmology when all was motionless as society awaited the outcome of the cosmic battle between darkness and light, a time which in itself suggests the fantastic since this period alone defied the rigid Aztec calendar. In effect, the *nemontani* were accumulated days when one cycle of the universe ended and another began, much the same as within **"El que inventó la pólvora."** Moreover, the reference to the *nemontani* underscores the social message woven throughout the collection by the fantastic: the Latin American quest for identity is not solely about the past. Instead, just as the "masked days" suggest a sense of spiraling time, the past must be contemplated in relation to the present and future. For this reason, Fuentes has juxtaposed fantasy with social reality to comment upon the Latin American, who has rejected his indigenous legacies (in **"Chac Mool"** and **"Por boca de los dioses"**); has betrayed Hispanic culture in favor of European or North American imperialism (in **"Tlactocatzine"** and **"Letanía"**); and has surrendered to the vicissitudes of a non-Hispanic, modernized, and mechanized world (in **"En defensa de la Trigolibia"** and **"El que inventó la pólvora"**).

In short, in *Los días enmascarados* the reader finds a tenuous link on the one hand between a credible world invaded by elements of the fantastic, and on the other a fantastic world which embraces commonly accepted traits of reality. It is this tenuous link which affords the author the aesthetic discourse to go beyond the mere didacticism of social thesis and, instead, to combine the social concern of cultural betrayal with the aesthetic concern of fantasy as a god that ultimately can claim "vengeance is mine."

Notes

1. Lanin Gyurko points out a similar destructive usage of the fantastic in Cortázar's works. Gyurko asserts that Cortázar presents the fantastic as an initial means of emancipation, a freedom or escape; yet, the creative potential of the fantastic inverts to a "tyrannical" force when the same medium which has offered the character emancipation now entraps him. (See Lanin Gyurko, "La fantasía como emancipación y como tiranía en tres cuentos de Cortázar," *RI* [*Revista Iberoamericana*] 41 [1975]: 219-36.)

2. Although some critical attention has been given to individual stories in the collection—in particular "Chac Mool" and "Tlactocatzine, del Jardín de Flandes"—to my knowledge few studies have addressed the volume as a whole, as I do, with the exception of those cited below by Brushwood, Duncan, de Guzmán, and Ferris.

3. "*Los días enmascarados* and *Cantar de ciegos*: Reading the Stories and Reading the Books," *Carlos Fuentes: A Critical View,* ed. Robert Brody and Charles Rossman (Austin: U of Texas P, 1982) 23.

4. "Carlos Fuentes' 'Chac Mool' and Todorov's Theory of the Fantastic: A Case for the Twentieth Century," *HisJ* [*Hispanic Journal*] 8 (1986): 125-33.

5. *Carlos Fuentes,* Twayne's World Authors Series 151 (New York: Twayne, 1972) 79.

6. *Carlos Fuentes* (New York: Frederick Ungar, 1983) 93.

7. (Mexico City: Biblioteca Era, 1954) 27.

8. Cynthia Steele, *Politics, Gender, and the Mexican Novel, 1968-1988* (Austin: U of Texas P, 1992) 88-109.

9. In the creationary beliefs of the Mayans, the gods created Man in various experimental stages or forms, one being that of a *muñeco,* meaning in this context a manikin or woodcarving. Since the manikins were incapable of speech and, thus, unable to return praise to their creators, the gods became dissatisfied and destroyed them. *Popol Vuh,* ed. Adrián Recinos, (México: Fondo de Cultura Económica, 1981) 30-32.

Kent D. Wolf (review date summer 1998)

SOURCE: Wolf, Kent D. Review of *The Crystal Frontier,* by Carlos Fuentes. *Review of Contemporary Fiction* 18, no. 2 (summer 1998): 229-30.

[*In the following review, Wolf provides a brief overview of the tone, thematic concerns, and plotlines of the stories in* The Crystal Frontier.]

Originally written in Spanish in the aftermath of California's Proposition 187, *The Crystal Frontier,* as the title suggests, adopts as its theme the paradoxical barrier—reflective, deformative, and transparent—separating the United States and Mexico. Here, Fuentes takes aim at the greed and callousness of both cultures from American CEOs to lecherous assemblyline foremen to racist border guards.

Composed of nine interconnected stories, *The Crystal Frontier* has as its central figure Leonardo Barroso, a powerful businessman with strong economic ties to the United States. Of the myriad characters, all are in one way or another linked to the enigmatic Don Leonardo. Throughout the novel we see underpaid women toil away in his *maquiladoras;* a Mexican medical student receives a scholarship from Barroso to study at Cornell; a once wealthy young man finds himself reduced to cleaning office windows as part of Barroso's migrant workforce; Don Leonardo's long-forgotten brother, after having suffered a stroke, is abandoned by his family on a lonely highway.

Fate has dealt many of these people a cruel hand, and given the circumstances under which the novel came into being (Mexicans were just dealt the inevitable blind-sided slap from NAFTA [North American Free Trade Agreement]), one can sense the anger in these pages. However, *The Crystal Frontier*'s most powerful moments lie in its humor, as Fuentes uncovers the comic absurdity in Mexican-American cultural differences. This humor is most prevalent in **"The Spoils,"** a riotously funny critique of American cuisine and our missing sense of moderation, which also serves as a homage to large women before it ends in Don Quixote fashion as two men escape from the plasticity of San Diego and flee, naked, to their *patria.*

Ultimately, *The Crystal Frontier* is a novel about identity as it addresses the timely issue of multiculturalism. Fuentes occupies a rather tenuous position between the wish to surpass cultural differences and the desire to preserve them, as he recognizes the impossibility of finding answers in a world of migrations and crossings.

Carlos Fuentes (essay date 2001)

SOURCE: Fuentes, Carlos. "Decalogue for a Young Writer," translated by Margaret Sayers Peden. In *Mexican Writers on Writing,* edited by Margaret Sayers Peden, pp. 72-83. San Antonio, Tex.: Trinity University Press, 2007.

[*In this essay, which first appeared in 2001, Fuentes outlines his views on writing in the form of a list of ten commandments for young writers.*]

Carlos Fuentes. Ambassador extraordinaire. For Mexico. For Mexican literature. Fuentes is the son of diplomats and was himself Mexico's ambassador to France from 1975 to 1977. It is often suggested that had he not been born in Panama City, he would by now have been president of Mexico.

As a writer, Fuentes stands as a monolith in Mexico's literature: her greatest innovator, her most brilliant cultural and social analyst, her most visible representative abroad. He is one of the standard quartet of novelists—the others being Gabriel García Márquez, Julio Cortázar, and Mario Vargas Llosa—who personify the Latin American Boom, a phenomenon of literary creation and disruption.

Fuentes has won major prizes and taught in universities across three continents. Eloquent, witty, self-assured, and gifted with a penetrating mind, he has earned his place in the pantheon of Latin America's great writers. He has been quoted as saying that Spanish "is the language that with the greatest eloquence and beauty offers the broadest spectrum of the human soul." He also once told a translator that English is supposed to be the most "malleable language," so obviously it should not be difficult to recreate his novels and short stories in English. He explained to an interviewer who, after listening to a lecture Fuentes gave in flawless English, asked why he doesn't write in English. "I dream, count, curse, and make love in Spanish," he replied. "Therefore, I write in Spanish."

Like many Mexican writers before him, Fuentes has consistently explored the theme of *Mexicanidad,* the question of identity that has haunted Mexican intellectuals since the time of the Conquest. From the union between Cortéz and the Malinche was born the first Mexican mestizo, the bastard child of an Indian woman who gave herself to a conquering white god. In *Todos los gatos son pardos* (All Cats Are Gray) Fuentes explores the many facets of that symbolic betrayal.

In an interview on National Public Radio, Fuentes commented, "You have an absolute freedom in Mexican writing today, in which you don't necessarily have to deal with the Mexican identity. You know why? Because we *have* an identity. We know who we are. We know what it means to be a Mexican." And one might interject that this is in large part due to Fuentes himself. "Now the problem is to discover difference—not identity but difference: sexual difference, religious difference, political difference, moral differences, esthetic differences. . . . "

In his hundreds of lectures and scores of university courses, Fuentes has often been asked for advice and insights on writing. In "Decalogue for a Young Writer," he refines and condenses those views. That these commandments have been well tested may be seen in major novels such as *Where the Air Is Clear, The Death of Artemio Cruz, Terra Nostra, The Old Gringo, A Change of Skin,* and *The Days of Laura Díaz.*

COMMANDMENT NUMBER ONE: DISCIPLINE

Books do not write themselves. Neither are they cooked in committee. To write is a solitary act, sometimes a frightening one. It is like entering a tunnel without knowing if there will be a light at the end, even if there will be an end at all.

I remember having spent many weekends, as a very young man, in the Mexican tropical town of Cuernavaca with the writer Alfonso Reyes, whom Borges called the greatest prose writer in the Spanish language during the twentieth century. Reyes was nearly seventy, I was seventeen, and sometimes I came in from a *parranda* at five in the morning and saw the light in Reyes's study shining and Don Alfonso himself bent over his writing table like a magical shoemaker gnome.

He calmed my astonishment—let's say my envy, my desire to emulate him—with a sentence by Goethe, another early riser. "The writer must take the cream off the top of the day." So that after writing from five to eight, Goethe could go on to spend the day collecting stones, inventing a theory of light, counseling the court at Weimar, and chasing after chambermaids.

In any case, Alfonso Reyes taught me that discipline is the daily name of creation, and Oscar Wilde that literary talent is 10 percent inspiration and 90 percent perspiration.

But if this is the logical part of literary creation, there is another, both mysterious and unfathomable, that I do not relate to the vagueness of inspiration, a word often used as a pretext for postponing work while waiting for Godot—something, in olden days, called The Muses.

That mysterious part of creativity is dreaming.

I can plan, the night before, the next morning's work and go to bed peacefully though impatient to get up and renew my writing. But when I sit down the next morning, the plan outlined by my literary logic goes off on a tangent, suffers too many exceptions, and is invaded by the totally unforeseen.

What has happened?

It happens that I have dreamed. And it so happens that the dreams I remember are repetitive, commonplace, and useless. I cannot but think, then, that the creative hand that is guiding my own the next morning is the hand of the dreams that I do not remember, dreams doing their invisible chore: displacing, condensing, re-elaborating, and anticipating, in the dreamwork, the literary work.

Now, each one of us has his or her own way of swatting flies, and mine is to get up at six in the morning, write from seven to twelve, exercise for one hour, go out and buy the newspapers (what they have to say always seems older than my imagination), have lunch with my wife Silvia, read for three hours in the afternoon—from three to six—and then go out to the movies, the theater, the opera, friends.

This is possible—I hastily add—in my literary fortress in London, a well-organized city. In Mexico City things are different. You have so-called political breakfasts—rituals of power brokering, trading information, destroying reputations, advancing others—from eight to ten-thirty. The eating is heavy, as if there were no politics without *pozole*. Lunch is from three to six under the ironic eyes of the Aztec goddess Coatlicue, assuring that digestion will be a difficult task. And then there are the Exterminating Angel dinners from ten at night until two in the morning.

If I manage to write an Op Ed piece under these conditions, I feel well served.

But Mexico—my friends, my family, my marvelous, courteous, tender people, my strangled, asphyxiating city where the air is no longer clear, the territory of my memory and a political life in which reality constantly surpasses fiction—does fill my vessels of communication and renew my creative juices with a fiery diet of tequila and enchiladas.

I can then return to London and be thankful for the bad climate, the awful food, and the cold courtesy of the islanders, without losing my nostalgia for nine hundred varieties of chilis and seven types of *mole*, and treasuring in my ears the two constant sounds of Mexico that are like the daily applause of my country: the hands of our women shaping corn tortillas and the hugs of our men slapping each other's backs.

COMMANDMENT NUMBER TWO: READ

Read a lot, read it all, voraciously. Fernando Benítez, an old friend, the great chronicler of the Indian cultures of Mexico, had calling cards that simply said: *Fernando Benítez, Reader of Novels.*

My generation in Mexico, and throughout the Latin world (including Italy, France, Portugal, and Spain) was probably the last one to feed its imagination reading the marvelous books that transported us to other worlds, the universe of childhood dreams. They were central to us, but unknown in the Anglo-American world. Emilio Salgari and the tales of Sandokan, the Tiger of Malaysia; Paul Feval and the hunchback Lagardere; the swashbuckling tales of the Pardaillans that permitted us to sport capes and swords instead of overalls and marbles; or the sentimental *Cuore* by the Italian Edmondo d'Amicis that authorized us to cry without shame.

These were the initial books of Latin childhoods, from Rome to Buenos Aires and from Paris and Madrid to Mexico City. But then we added the books we shared with the Anglo-America world, notably Dickens, Stevenson, and Mark Twain, and two giants of the universal imagination, Dumas and Jules Verne. But we were as ignorant of Nancy Drew and the Hardy Boys as gringo kids were of Salgari and the Black Pirate.

Are any of these authors read today, or do children spend all of their time playing Nintendo? I don't know, but I don't believe that is so. My British publisher takes me to the corner of her library in London and from her window shows me a queue, four blocks long, of kids from seven to eleven with ten pounds in their fists, waiting to buy the latest Harry Potter volume. Initial printing: a million and a half books. Expected printing: six million copies.

And a modern version of a Norse epic poem of the seventh century, *Beowulf,* has in the luminous translation by Seamus Heaney become a best seller throughout the English-speaking world.

In Latin America, all through my life, it was a sign of identity and proof of social advancement in the working, student, and middle classes to read Neruda and Lorca, García Márquez and Cortázar, Rulfo and Paz.

The writer is the pioneer of reading, the protector of books, the insistent gadfly: the price of a book must not be an obstacle to the reading of a book in poorer countries or poor classes. Let there be public libraries, open to all. Let young people know that if they lack money to buy books, there are public libraries where they can read books.

This, I am aware, is a lesson well learned in the United States. It has yet to be implemented in Latin America.

Which takes me to my third consideration.

COMMANDMENT NUMBER THREE: TRADITION AND CREATION

I join them because I profoundly believe that there is no new literary creation without the support of the previous literary tradition, in the same way that there is no tradition that survives without the juices of new creation. There is no T. S. Eliot without John Donne—but from now on, there is no John Donne without T. S. Eliot. Yesterday's writer thus becomes today's author, and the present-day writer is tomorrow's author. And this is so because the reader knows something that the author ignores: the reader knows the future, and the next reader of *Don Quixote* will always be the first reader of *Don Quixote.*

The bridge between creation and tradition lies in my fourth proposition.

COMMANDMENT NUMBER FOUR: IMAGINATION

Imagination is the madwoman of the house, said the Spanish novelist Pérez Galdós. A madwoman who does not stay in the attic as she does in Victorian fiction but opens wide all the windows, respects the vampires sleeping in the basement, but flies out and raises roofs in Madrid, Mexico, or Manhattan to see what truly goes on in bedchambers and chambers of state.

Imagination flies and its wings are the writer's eyes. The imagination sees, and its eyes are the memory and the prophecy of the writer. For the imagination is the union of our liberated sensations, the sheaf that joins together the disperse, the nature of the symbols that permit us to cross jungles—Dante's *selva selvaggia*—more savage today, perhaps, in cities than in the jungle itself.

To imagine is to transcend, or at least to give some sense to, experience.

To imagine is to transform experience into destiny and to save destiny from mere fatalism.

There is no nature—*natura*—without the bucolic imagination of *Daphnis and Chloe* by Longus, of Montemayor's *Diana* or Spenser's *Shepherd,* all of them pleasant forms that contrast with the terrible, untamable nature of Melville's *Moby Dick* or the desolate urban nature of Eliot's *The Waste Land.*

But the character of literary nature consists, not only of reminding us that the worlds surrounding us can be agreeable or cruel, friendly or unfriendly, but in creating, through the imagination, a second literary reality from which the first, physical, reality can no longer divorce itself.

COMMANDMENT NUMBER FIVE: LITERARY REALITY

Which means that literary reality is not limited to a servile reflection of objective reality. It adds to objective reality something that was not there before. It en-

riches and boosts primary reality. Imagine—try to imagine—the world without *Hamlet* or *Don Quixote.* We would not tarry in understanding that the Prince of Denmark and the Knight of the Sorrowful Countenance have as much or more "reality" than many of our neighbors.

So literature creates reality yet cannot divorce itself from the historical environment—physical, chronological, geographical, imaginative—in which it takes place. That is why it is important to distinguish literature from history given the premise that follows: History belongs, strange as it may seem, to the world of logic, that is, the zone of the univocal: the Napoleonic invasion of Russia took place in 1812. Literary creation, on the contrary, belongs to the poetic universe of the plurivocal: What contradictory passions agitated the souls of Natasha Rostova and Andrei Volkinski in Tolstoy's novel?

Literary works—a poem or a novel—shoot out in many directions. They do not demand a singular, unique explanation or, much less, a precise chronology.

Let us read the excellent Russian historians of the nineteenth century, but let us try to imagine that same century without Tolstoy or Dostoyevsky, without Gogol or Turgenev. That is, *War and Peace* does not happen only in 1812. It is reborn on all the battlefields of the war of time; it happens in the reader's mind and there it inscribes itself as a fact of the literary imagination, which, in turn, determines the relationship of the work to time, through the event we call language.

COMMANDMENT NUMBER SIX: LITERATURE AND TIME

Literature transforms history—what happened on the battlefield of Waterloo or what happened in the bridal chamber of Natasha Rostova and Pierre Bezhukov—into poetry and fiction.

Literature sees history, and history subordinates itself to literature because history is incapable of seeing itself without language.

The Iliad, according to the Italian philosopher Benedetto Croce, is the proof of the original identity between literature and history. It is, he wrote, the work of *un popolo intero poetante,* a whole poetizing people.

That unity has been lost. Modernity is fragmented; it is individualistic. It has not tolerated anonymous collective poetry (or painting or architecture) since Montaigne said, "To be known is not enough; now we must also be renown." The poetic and collective anonymity of Homer did not require this. Victor Hugo does not require it for, according to Jean Cocteau, Victor Hugo was simply a madman who thought he was Victor Hugo.

The epic universe of antiquity is like Gogol's Petersburg, a gigantic animal broken into a thousand pieces. The unity of Homeric language is lost. Hector and Achilles, in *The Iliad,* speak the same language. After *Don Quixote,* one can speak of language only in the plural. Cervantes overcomes lost unity by discovering plurality. Don Quixote speaks an epic language; Sancho Panza, the language of the picaresque—that is, the anti-epic. Ulysses and Penelope can understand each other. Madame Bovary and Anna Karenina cannot understand or be understood by their husbands. They speak different languages.

The breakup of unity thus becomes the unity of ruptures. There is no communication without diversification, and there is no diversification without admitting the existence of The Other—he or she who is not like you or me.

Language thus translates into levels of language, and literature into a re-elaboration of hybrid, migrating, *mestizo* languages in which the writer uses his language to throw light on other languages. So proceeds Juan Goytisolo in Spain, contaminating the purity of the Castilian language with a revival of Jewish and Arab roots, or Gunter Grass in Germany, bringing sense and truth back to a language debased by the Third Reich, or the mere multicultural hyphenation of the English language in the United States, as employed by the Afro-American Toni Morrison, the Sino-American Amy Tan, the Mexican-American Sandra Cisneros, the Cuban-American Cristina García, the Puerto Rican-American Rosario Ferré, or the Native-American Louise Erdrich.

God takes his sabbatical before Nietzsche declares him dead, and in his place—God's, not Nietzsche's—appears Don Quixote. That is, the novel appears, no longer as an illustration of well-known truths, but as a search for unknown truths. No longer as the bearer of the antiquity of the past but of the novelty of the past.

I come back to the idea that the next reader of *Don Quixote* shall always be the first reader of *Don Quixote.* The past of literature becomes the future of literature. But also the eternal language of literature.

The language of the original myth that roots us in the lands of our births.

The epic language that pushes us out of the land we know to the worlds we ignore.

The tragic language of the return to our home and the family wounded and divided by passion and by history.

Literature, finally, restores the lost community, the *polis* that demands our political words and actions; the *civitas* that needs our voice as an act of civilization so that we may learn the art of living together, coming closer, loving one another, supporting one another in spite of the cruelty, the intolerance, and the bloodshed that have never abandoned the shadows of a human mind illuminated, in spite of everything, by the light of justice.

Literature gives to the city the unwritten part of the world and becomes a meeting place—that is, a common ground—not only of character and plots, but of civilizations (Thomas Mann), languages (James Joyce), social classes (Balzac), historical eras (Hermann Broch), or *imaginary* eras, as the Cuban writer Lezama Lima called them.

Literary language, in this sense, is a language of languages. It is language regarding itself because it is capable of regarding the languages of others.

COMMANDMENT NUMBER SEVEN: TRUE CRITICISM

Once published, the literary work ceases to belong to the writer to become the property of the reader. It also becomes an object of criticism. And when I say "criticism," I speak of an art neither superior nor inferior to the work under consideration, but rather its equivalent. A critique at the same height as the work criticized. A dialogue between the work and its critique.

For this reason, the best literary critics are the best literary creators. The critical co-respondence, say, between Baudelaire and Poe, Sartre and Faulkner, Georges Bataille and Emily Brontë, transforms the critique into the equivalent of the literary creation. But the great professional critic—as different from an author writing about another author—reaches the same co-respondent relationship: Michel Foucault and Borges, Donald Fanger and Gogol, Bakhtin and Rabelais, Leavis and Lawrence, Barthes and Proust, Van Wyck Brooks and Hawthorne, are but a few examples of this fruitful corespondence between critic and book.

Thus I distinguish true criticism from mere reviewing—the majority of opinions one reads in the press—or even from undercover criticism—the critic who reads only the cover of the book and then proceeds to authoritatively destroy it.

I recommend that the young writer not occupy or preoccupy him- or herself excessively with newspaper reviews. But let's not be hypocritical about this. We are grateful for praise. We deplore negative opinion, and we admire Susan Sontag because she does not read good or bad reviews. But to subject oneself to either is a mistake. They fade like a whistle. Or, as we say in Mexico, "Le hacen lo que el aire a Juárez." Put in American terms, that would mean that Washington could not be dissuaded from crossing the Delaware.

Let the writers console themselves by remembering that there is no statue, anywhere in the world, honoring a literary critic.

Furthermore, an activity that can be noble and necessary is sometimes diminished by those who practice it while moved by envy or frustration. But the paradox—or, if you prefer, the dilemma—stands. Only in literature is the work of art identical to the instrument of its criticism: language.

Neither the plastic arts, nor music, nor film suffer from this incestuous relationship between creative word and critical word. Not even theater, which is an art of live, but distanced, representation.

COMMANDMENT NUMBER EIGHT: BE LOYAL TO YOURSELF

This is my recommendation for the young writer. Do not let yourself be seduced by immediate success or by the illusion of immortality. The majority of seasonal best sellers soon lose themselves in the sands of oblivion, and today's bad seller can be tomorrow's long seller. Stendhal is a good example of the second case. *Anthony Adverse,* super best seller of the year 1933, of the first case. That same year Faulkner published a nonseller that became a long seller: *Light in August.*

Well, eternity, said William Blake, is in love with the works of time. Works of time are *Don Quixote* and *One Hundred Years of Solitude,* and eternity fell in love with them from the very start. But Stendhal's *Charterhouse of Parma* gained only a handful of readers when it first appeared, and that thanks to Balzac's generous praise for a work considered strange and difficult in its time. Destined, originally, for "the happy few," today it enjoys the eternal and renewed glory of generations of readers.

The lesson: Be loyal to yourselves, listen to the deep voice of your vocation, take on the risks of being both classical and experimental, and remember that there are no longer any dogmas for either tradition or renovation.

There is no vanguard because art conceived as the companion to novelty has ceased to be news, because novelty, in its turn, was the companion of progress, and progress has ceased to progress. The twentieth century left us with a stricken, deeply wounded sense of progress. Today we are aware that scientific and technical achievements do not assure the absence of moral and political barbarism.

The artistic response to the political and economic crisis of the modern has been a practically unlimited freedom of style that permits the artist to write in the style he or she prefers. But on one condition: that freedom never forget what it owes to tradition, and that tradition never forget what it owes to creation.

COMMANDMENT NUMBER NINE: CONSCIOUSNESS OF TRADITION AND CREATION

I come back to the beginning of my Decalogue with this commandment: the consciousness the young writer must have of both tradition and creation. T. S. Eliot, of course, has written the definitive essay on this subject.

Let me distinguish, nevertheless, two slopes. One is the social position of the writer placed between past and future in a present that does not permit escaping the political climate. I do not say this in the manner of the obligatory Sartrean *engagement.* I say it in the name of a citizen's free option.

The writer complies with his social obligation by keeping both imagination and language alive in his writing. Even if the writer has no political opinions, he contributes to the life of the city—the *polis*—thanks to the flight of imagination and the root of language. There are no free societies without writers, and it is not fortuitous that totalitarian regimes immediately try to silence them.

And yet, standing in the public square, alone with his notebooks and his pen (as is my case), or with their PCs (as most today), the writer is giving life, circumstance, flesh, and voice to the big, eternal questions of men and women in our brief passage through earth.

What is the relationship between freedom and fate?

In what measure can we shape our own destiny?

What part of our lives is adaptable to change and which to permanence?

And finally, why do we identify ourselves by the ignorance of what we are—a union of body and soul? We cannot answer. But we go on being exactly what we do not understand.

So, literature is an education of the senses, an indispensable school of intelligence and sensibility through the medium that most distinguishes us from and in nature: the Word.

COMMANDMENT NUMBER TEN

The tenth commandment, therefore, is that I leave in the hands of each and every one of you your imagination, your word, and your freedom.

Lanin A. Gyurko (essay date 2007)

SOURCE: Gyurko, Lanin A. "Mortality and Double Standards: *Cantar de ciegos.*" In *Lifting the Obsidian Mask: The Artistic Vision of Carlos Fuentes,* pp. 78-94. Potomac, Md.: Scripta Humanistica, 2007.

[*In the following essay, Gyurko concentrates on the compulsive idealism of the male protagonists of "La muñeca reina" and "Un alma pura," maintaining that this inability (or refusal) to face reality ultimately results in their deaths—whether symbolic, as in "La muñeca reina," or actual, as in "Un alma pura."*]

In the stories from the collection *Cantar de ciegos* ("Songs of the Blind"), many of the characters suffer from psychological and moral blindness. Often this is the blindness of rampant egotism, as self-indulgent characters fail to view objectively either the world or themselves. Some stories exemplify the blindness of extreme naiveté, of insensitivity, and of self-delusion. In "Las dos Elenas," for example, a wife who flirts with the idea of a *ménage a trois* becomes so caught up in her delusion of being a liberated woman that she does not suspect that her seemingly resigned and docile husband, far from being willing to play the role of cuckold, is carrying on an affair with her own mother. In "A la víbora del mar" ("To the Viper of the Sea"), another story of ingenuousness and betrayal, the dowdy heroine is duped into marriage by a smooth-talking gigolo and then deceived again by the amorous advances of his scheming accomplice, until finally she is driven to suicide. "La muñeca reina" ("The Doll Queen") and "Un alma pura" ("A Pure Soul"), the two stories discussed extensively in this [essay], exemplify the tragic consequences of the blindness of misguided idealists. In their single-minded devotion to imaginative or social ideals, these characters refuse to confront reality. They inadvertently dehumanize and even destroy the lives of those with whom they come into contact.

The narrator of "La muñeca reina," rebelling against the tedium and hollowness of his present life, wishes to return to his past in an attempt to find the creative, spiritual center that his life is missing. The symbol of this lost and forever unattainable world is the girl Amilamia, whom he had rejected as a youth but whom he now idealizes as he goes back to the scene of his encounters with her. Yet instead of finding an adult Amilamia to match his expectations, he is stunned by the deformed child-woman, crippled and confined to a wheel chair, whom the once lithe and irrepressible girl has become. Yet so tenaciously does he cling to his nostalgic ideal, that he cannot relate to the real Amilamia. The monstrous parody of the idealism of Carlos is found in the behavior of the parents of the stricken Amilamia. Cherishing the illusion that their daughter has died, they perversely channel their devotion and their sorrow upon a mere doll that symbolizes for them the only Amilamia they are willing to accept—one who is forever young and forever beautiful. Worshipping the doll, they treat their living daughter as an animal, keeping her locked up and beating her. Yet they take refuge behind a facade of sanctimoniousness that protects them from any feelings of guilt over their inhuman treatment of their daughter.

Like the narrator of "La muñeca reina," Juan Luis, one of the main characters in "Un alma pura," is another searcher for the ideal. He chafes at the intellectual and social constrictions on his life in his native Mexico:

> Just wanting to *live* makes you a potential traitor; here you're obliged to serve, to take a position; it's a Country that won't let you be yourself. I don't want to be respectable. I don't want to be courteous, a liar, *muy macho,* an ass-kisser, refined and clever.[1]

He departs for Switzerland in pursuit of freedom and of the opportunity to construct an authentic self. Yet the naive Juan Luis fails to realize that although he has succeeded in breaking out of a social tyranny, he is under the sway of a far more insidious psychological domination—his incestuous feelings for his sister Claudia, a love which he has repressed. His ingenuousness and his idealism act to shield him from the recognition of this forbidden love. What he subsequently believes is his genuine love for the Swiss girl Claire is but the transference of his lifelong devotion to his sister, whom he is possessing vicariously. The blindness of Juan Luis results in the emotional collapse and, finally, in the physical destruction of Claire, who commits suicide when she comprehends that she has been a mere pawn of both brother and sister.

Like Juan Luis, Carlos in "La muñeca reina" is discontent with his bourgeois life—with the constant striving for professional status, the stultifying routine, and the superficial social relationships. Opening the books untouched since the days of his adolescence, Carlos turns to explore an imaginative realm, in search of relief from the pressures of the outside world: "I met surprise after surprise . . . the edges of the leaves were grainy, and a mixture of old dust and grayish scale fell on my open palm . . . " (27). The object that catalyzes his longings for spiritual fulfillment is the white card he finds, with its scrawled message from Amilamia: *"Amilamia wil not forget her good friend—com see me here wher I draw it"* (27).

Long forgotten, the white card now becomes a treasure map for the alienated Carlos. It is the intriguing stimulus that leads him on a quest not only for Amilamia but for the essence of his own lost innocence and youth. He seeks self-renewal through his persistent attempts to resurrect a past that he has now consecrated through his poetic imagination. Significantly, in both adolescence and in adulthood, Carlos is portrayed as an introspective, dreaming person. He remembers himself merely imagining adventures rather than acting them out. Outside of Amilamia, the friends of his adolescence that he now recalls are all fantasy characters: "After all, Michel Strogoff and Huckleberry Finn, Milady de Winter and Geneviève de Brabant were born, lived, and died here: in a little garden surrounded by mossy iron railings" (119). As an adolescent he had projected himself into a world of mythical women, perhaps fashioning himself as the hero who would one day claim these glorious creatures of fantasy:

> Then I dreamed about the women in my books, about the quintessential female—the word disturbed me— who assumed the disguise of Queen to buy the necklace in secret, about the imagined beings of mythology—half recognizable, half white-breasted, damp-bellied salamanders—who awaited monarchs in their beds.
>
> (118)

Yet Carlos's subsequent real-life experiences with women have not matched his adolescent expectations. Thus he is now drawn back once more into the fantasy kingdom of his youth—with the significant difference that instead of the thrilling and mysterious "women in my books," Amilamia is now the object of his romantic fantasies.

In his youth Carlos had responded ambivalently to Amilamia, seeing her as both an attraction and an annoyance. The adolescent Carlos, then twice the girl's age, was preoccupied with the painful process of maturation—with self-discovery and self-definition. Amilamia had originally represented temptation for him, the enticement to cast off the solemn and perplexing struggle to enter the adult world and to return instead to the carefree and joyous world of innocent youth. Yet he had finally rejected the girl, whom he had perceived as a reflection of that part of himself which he was attempting to suppress—his childishness and his irresponsibility. Now, fifteen years later, without fully realizing it, Carlos has abstracted the girl into the

quintessence of life as joy, exuberance, and wonder. She is poeticized as "a point of fluctuating shadow and sunshine" (117). In his revery, Amilamia is evoked as a frolicsome sprite in constant motion. The buoyant vitality of the girl is captured by the style of the narrative, with its crescendo of phrases:

> Amilamia in the thousand postures she affected around my bench, hanging upside down, her bloomers billowing; sitting on the gravel with her legs crossed and her chin resting on her fist; lying on the grass, baring her belly button to the sun; weaving tree branches . . .
>
> (117)

But Carlos will never find the Amilamia he seeks, because this poetic spirit never existed to the great degree he remembers. She is much more the creation of his adult hopes and dreams than the memory of a real-life person. The negative outcome of his quest is foreshadowed from the very beginning of the narrative, when Carlos himself emphasizes the failure of experience ever to match the magic realm of dreams: "certain bodies glimpsed first in dreams and later in deceptive reality of the first ballet performance to which we're taken." (115).

Yet Carlos is obstinate in his desire to impose his idealized vision of Amilamia upon present reality. At first he is markedly disillusioned as he returns to the setting of his youthful encounters with the girl and finds it inferior to his memory of it:

> adorned by a concrete bench painted to look like wood which forces me to think that my beautiful wrought-iron green bench never existed, or was part of my ordered, retrospective delirium.
>
> (119)

What he has glorified as a hill where he had romped with the girl is in reality but a mound of earth; the garden that in his romantic imagination is idealized into almost a garden of Eden is small and unimpressive. But Carlos refuses to become discouraged. He continues to perceive the present world only in terms of the past, hoping to see his dream girl come to life among the children whom he does sight:

> I stop a moment to watch them, with the sensation, as fleeting, that Amilamia must be among these groups of children, immodestly exhibiting her flowered panties, hanging by her knees from some balcony, still fond of acrobatic excesses her apron pocket filled with white petals.
>
> (120)

But as the narrator continues his search, there is a greater and greater discrepancy between his illusions and the depressing world that he confronts. The neighborhood in which Amilamia lives has drastically deteriorated. The past is grotesquely suspended within the present. The girl's blue-checked apron, which Carlos sights hanging stiffly on a clothesline, ominously foreshadows the paralyzed state of Amilamia. The garment hangs between an iron bar and a nail; these metallic images suggest obduracy and cruelty and symbolize the parents of Amilamia.

"La muñeca reina" has begun with images of openness, as the narrator with gusto extends his life imaginatively back into the past, allowing his fantasy free reign. Now, in reality, there is emphasis on closed, constricted life. The narrator reaches his first obstacle to his reunion with Amilamia her bleak house with its tightly closed shutters that seems more like a mausoleum. Previously he had exalted Amilamia from pesky imp to princess; now he goes to the opposite extreme and transmogrifies the parents, viewing them as ogres from out of his childhood stories. Carlos's real-life experience thus is constantly distorted by him to make it coincide with the world of his childhood fairy tales, a realm of excitement, adventure, and mystery, that he wishes to live out: "Do I bestow a gratuitous strangeness on my reluctant hostess? If so, I'll only take greater pleasure in the labyrinths of my own invention." (127)

At the very beginning of his narrative, he had recalled his bewilderment after reading stories in which children were the innocent victims of preying adults, and now he seems to fashion himself the hero who will thwart their designs:

> Children who are ungrateful to their parents; maidens kidnapped by splendid horsemen and returned home in shame . . . old men who in exchange for an overdue mortgage demand the hand of the sweetest, most long-suffering daughter of the threatened family.
>
> (116-117)

Frustrated and angered at the obstacle which the recalcitrant and threatening father presents to the completion of his search, Carlos strikes back in the only way he can—through his imagination. He animalizes the man, whom he describes as "this asthmatic old bear" (128), with "The neck of an ancient turtle" (127). The inhumanity of the parents is graphically conveyed through their reduction to a mineral state: "every pore of that flesh seems fabricated of brittle rubber, of painted, peeling oilcloth," (128); "their faces of wax and rubber" (18). There is a continued emphasis on life that has been physically choked off. The old man has "a distant, choking voice" (128); his breathing is labored and constricted: "as if every breath must breach a floodgate of phlegm, irritation, and abuse" (127). This physical constriction symbolizes an emotional suppression—the parents' total denial of sympathy and love to Amilamia.

Carlos himself seems to realize how much he is under the sway of his overactive fantasies when he utters the magic word "Amilamia" to the parents. The word brings about a dramatic transformation in their appearance and attitude, changing them in his eyes from predators to victims:

> Suddenly the two ogres of my imagination are two solitary, abandoned, wounded, old people, scarcely able to console themselves in this shuddering clasp of hands that fills me with shame.
>
> (128)

Just as the word, the handwriting of Amilamia, has awakened the expectations of the narrator, so now does the name of the girl infuse the crabbed parents with new life, unlocking their stifled emotion. It almost seems to resurrect their daughter for them. Although initially suspicious and hostile toward Carlos, they now cling to him as the sole link between themselves and the Amilamia of the past for whom they too are searching. Ironically, instead of finding out the truth about the girl from the parents, Carlos himself is importuned to provide them with information about what their daughter was like: "What was she like, what was she like?" (130). Yet in response to their anguished pleading, he does not give them a factual recounting of his past experience with Amilamia but instead continues to idealize the girl. He submerges himself once more in a private, poetic universe that has no meaning for the grief-stricken parents, who continue with their pleas:

> Now I see her, coming down the hill. No. It isn't true that it was a scarcely elevated patch of stubble . . . It was a hill, with grass, and Amilamia's comings and goings had traced a path, and she waved to me from the top before she started down, accompanied by the music, yes, the music I saw, the painting I smelled, the tastes I heard, the odors I touched . . . my hallucination . . . Do they hear me?
>
> (129)

Significantly, Carlos shuts his eyes as he is led up the stairs by the parents. He again struggles to blot out the adverse reality of the external world that continually threatens to dissolve his spiritualized Amilamia. Despite his professed desire to penetrate the mystery surrounding the girl, he does not seem to want to ever know the truth.

Carlos makes a clumsy, short-lived attempt to deceive the parents when he poses as a representative of the owner of their house in order to gain access without having to confess his true motive. This deception is more than matched by the theatrics of the parents themselves, as they perpetuate the misconception that their daughter has died. They bring Carlos to the childhood room of Amilamia which they have converted into a grotesque funeral parlor. Here they hold a perpetual funeral over a coffin containing a beautiful doll. In this chamber, death seems to live. In contrast with the delicate white flowers that Carlos remembers Amilamia wearing and which have come to symbolize her beauty, grace, and fragility, are the funeral flowers with their mephitic smell that becomes almost tangible, emphasized by the narrator's pyramiding of similes of concreteness. The odor overpowers everything else: "it routs the other senses, it takes its seat like a yellow *Mongol* upon the throne of my hallucination, heavy as a coffin, insinuating as the slither of draped silk, ornamented as a Turkish scepter, opaque as a deep, lost vein of ore, brilliant as a dead star" (130).

In **"La muñeca reina"** there is a grotesque inversion of human, animal, vegetable, and mineral realms. On the one hand, human beings are degraded by being linked with the animal and the inanimate, while on the other the hideous flowers, "the sweetness of the jasmine, the nausea of the lilies, the tomb of the tuberose, the temple of the gardenia" (130), achieve a weird life: "they seem to take on the quality of living flesh" (130). Within this monstrous sanctuary, the doll is elevated to the level of the human and even of the divine, while Amilamia herself is dehumanized. The perversion of religious devotion by the mother, dressed in mourning black, is symbolized by the rosary that she has placed around the neck of the doll as a sign of consecration, but that Carlos sees as strangling the doll—just as Amilamia's existence has been suffocated. The physical deformation of the girl is far exceeded by the moral deformation of her parents; they emerge as the true monsters of the story.

Childhood that at the beginning of the narrative had been evoked as a realm of freedom, beauty, and joy now appears as a junkyard of broken and worn-out toys. The mound of toys provides another example of the dead past that remains grotesquely suspended in the present:

> the plethora of used toys: the colored hoops and wrinkled balloons, cherries dried to transparency, wooden horses with scraggly manes, the scooter, blind hairless dolls, bears spilling their sawdust, punctured oilcloth ducks, moth-eaten dogs, frayed jumping ropes
>
> (131)

The mutilated toys also signify the broken life of Amilamia as well as the shattered illusions of Carlos. There are ironic parallels between the protagonist and the parents. All three remain mesmerized by the ideal. The doll, the parents' idealized conception of their daughter, both mocks the spiritualized Amilamia cherished

by the narrator and yet seems in an ironic way to be the youthful girl that he is seeking: "cheeks as healthy as in the park days. Serious red lips, set almost to an angry pout that Amilamia feigned so I would come to play" (131). In his initial mood of nostalgia, Carlos has wished to fix in time the image of the mercurial girl: "I must remember her fixed forever in time, as in a photograph album" (117). Ironically, this is just what the parents have done in a perverted way, in their fanatic worship of the doll. The monstrousness of their death cult is indicated as the narrator touches the skin of the perfect and lifelike doll that has first captivated him—and then recoils in repulsion: "I withdraw my fingers from the sham cadaver. Traces of my fingerprints remain where I touched the skin of the doll" (132)

Yet although Carlos is shocked, his experience does not obliterate his romantic conception of his childhood friend. Nine months later he returns once more to the house of Amilamia with his illusions forcefully intact:

> The real Amilamia has returned to my memory and I have felt, if not content, sane again: the park, the living child, my hours of adolescent reading, have triumphed over the specters of a sick cult. The image of life is more powerful. I tell myself I shall live forever with my real Amilamia, the conqueror of the caricature of death.
>
> (132)

Naively overconfident in the power of his imagination to triumph over a bitter reality, he wishes to impose a happily-ever-after ending on both his narrative and on his real-life experience. He embarks on an errand of mercy: he wishes to give to the parents the white card that had originally sparked his quest, the card that now acquires the value of a relic. The parents have also become idealized within Carlos's fantasy—they are evoked as bereaved victims. But Carlos is finally forced to confront the grotesque antithesis of the poetic Amilamia in whom he has so devoutly believed and whom he has sought to immortalize. As Dauster states:

> The web of illusion that Carlos has constructed is definitively broken and he remains surrounded by the truth underneath . . . there is a double plot: Carlos visits the house twice; he sees Amilamia two times, two times he is advised not to return. But the first time everything is an invented reality, contrived by her parents, of an Amilamia who has died many years ago and is now venerated. The second time, Carlos sees the truth of a girl who is humpbacked and abused and constantly beaten, as much a simulacrum of the child Amilamia as is the false dead girl.[2]

At first the optimistic, Carlos has evoked the rain as a magic, restorative power, one that will bring new life to the earth, just as he has resurrected Amilamia. The rain also symbolizes his own spiritual regeneration, which he self-deludedly believes he has at last achieved:

> Rain is beginning to fall in large isolated drops, bringing out of the earth with magical immediacy the odor of dewy benediction that stirs the humus and quickens all that lives with its roots in the dust.
>
> (133)

Yet when Carlos finally comes face to face with Amilamia, the rain symbolizes his grief. The horrible irony is that he has found his Amilamia still preserved in the past, yet not as an eternal child but as a retarded child-woman. She is still dressed in the blue-checked apron and in a dress that has now become a *trapo blanco*. Only her gray eyes remain as testimony of the Amilamia whom Carlos has been fervently seeking

> The little woman extracts a pack of cigarettes from her apron pocket and quickly lights a cigarette, staining the end with orange-painted lips. The smoke causes the beautiful gray eyes to squint.
>
> (133)

At the end, the narrator can only stand stunned as the father threateningly approaches in order to drive Amilamia back into the house which is her prison, the coffin for her death-in-life state. Carlos cannot rescue his princess from the ogre; his shock and now permanent disillusionment preclude any response except that of unabashed tears. He cannot cope at all with the living Amilamia. His final helplessness has been adumbrated from the start, when he mentioned his childhood response to the fairy tale stories that bewildered him because they did not end happily-ever-after: "a series of more or less truculent exemplary tales which had the virtue of precipitating us onto our elders' knees to ask them, over and over again: Why?" (115).

The one person in **"La muñeca reina"** who has no illusions either about self or world and who, therefore, is extremely perceptive to outer reality is Amilamia. She is the true heroine of the story. Although her body is warped, she constitutes a spiritual center that has been untouched by time and by affliction. Her devotion to Carlos and her concern for his welfare remain constant throughout her life. It is her cry that saves Carlos from being run down by the traffic to which he, in his single-minded preoccupation with the ideal, has been characteristically inadvertent. Despite her deep desire for reunion with Carlos, who now more than ever represents her salvation, Amilamia is sensitive enough to realize the impossibility of their relationship. Seeming to know that he has come back searching for the exuberant and beguiling Amilamia of the past, she herself warns him never to return. She wants

him to remain with the romantic image of herself, rather than force him to endure the painful collapse of his dream world. In her spirit of empathy and self-sacrifice, Amilamia does constitute an ideal, but one which will pass unnoticed by the crushed narrator.

"La muñeca reina" is a narrative of the impossibility of love. The only constant, genuine love is that of Amilamia for Carlos, but this love will never be fulfilled. What the parents self-deludedly regard as their love and devotion to their "true daughter" is really only idolatry and self-pity. They grieve and pray not for Amilamia's state but for their own loss. The narrator himself seems capable of loving only the romantic illusion of the girl. The narrative is really one of death—the repulsive cult of death by the parents, the death-in-life of Amilamia, and the final death of the illusions of Carlos.

Both **"La muñeca reina"** and **"Un alma pura"** are stories of mystery. Carlos assumes the role of amateur detective in his attempts to solve the mystery of Amilamia. He finds strange clues that indicate a childlike presence in the house—the comic book scrawled on with crayon, the teeth indentations on the plastic fruit, the tread marks on the rug that seem to be those of a child's tricycle. In this narrative, the mystery is finally solved—Amilamia has never transcended the mentality of a young child. But **"Un alma pura"** holds deeper mysteries that can never be fully explicated. The true nature of the relationship between brother and sister never becomes clear. Benedetti gives the following analysis:

> Halfway between extreme purity and incest, the attraction which unites (and separates) Juan Luis and Claudia causes that Juan Luis seeks desperately an illusion, in this case the substitute for his sister, the substitute who is irremediably condemned. Juan Luis, who has fled from Mexico and also from something else, moves to Switzerland, sees how the lake reflects the Alps, transforming them into a vast cathedral that is submerged and he writes to Claudia again and again, throwing himself into the water in order to dive in search of the mountains. But Claire appears, and Juan Luis believes that he is once more encountering Claudia, and he submerges himself in her, he dives into her in search of his sister.[3]

The narrative is replete with ambiguities. Claudia, from whose point of view the story unfolds, seems to be addressing her brother in silent soliloquy. It is not until the story is two-thirds over that we learn that Juan Luis is dead. Claudia retreats into a false piousness as a means of covering up both her passion and her guilt. She refers to her relationship with her brother as "our secret, that mystery" (74). Refusing to acknowledge the illicitness of her desire, she depicts their adolescence in terms that are deliberately vague:

But we were friends again the next year, going every-where together, no longer picking up shells or invent-ing adventures, but seeking now to prolong a day that began to seem too short and a night forbidden to us, a night that became our temptation, symbol of the new possibilities in a recently discovered, recently begun life.

(74)

Theirs is a secret love, of unconfessed desires, of si-lence that is cherished because it protects them from the uncomfortableness and shame of having to articu-late or to confront the true nature of their feelings. Claudia's physical desire for her brother is only al-luded to, through the sensuousness of the imagery in which she depicts their walks together on the beach at Acapulco:

> but that had to do with the warm sand beneath our bare feet, with the silence of the sea at night, with the brush-ing of our thighs as we walked together, you in your new long, tailored white pants, I in my new full red skirt.

(75)

The strong-willed Claudia is always the more aggres-sive one in the relationship. She repeatedly desires to de-emphasize the blood bond between them in order to make it easier for the reluctant Juan Luis to confide in her about his heterosexual relationships, through which she lives vicariously: "Juan Luis, hadn't we been best friends before we were brother and sister?" (79-80). To protect himself from his attraction toward his sister, the adolescent Juan Luis keeps himself aloof, talking with her only in the more formal setting of the University rather than at home. Significantly, the one place where they do speak to one another is in the "Facultad de Mascarones," the Drama School. The lit-eral meaning of "mascarón" is "large, grotesque mask." The allusion is to the mask of reserve and re-straint that both brother and sister are compelled to wear throughout their lives.

Another mystery is provided by the letter that the jeal-ous and vindictive Claudia sends to Claire. Perhaps it reveals to Claire the truth about the real love of Juan Luis, or the reasons why Juan Luis had compelled Claire to get an abortion rather than marrying her. Whatever the contents of this crucial letter, which are never revealed, it contains a confession damaging enough to drive the distraught Claire to commit sui-cide. The third mystery, which also will never be solved, is the motive for the suicide of Juan Luis. Per-haps it is his inconsolable grief or his feelings of guilt as he blames himself for having caused Claire's death. Perhaps it is the result of his shock at finally being forced to confront his incestuous feelings for the sister whom he has idolized. In any case, the mysterious let-ter of Claudia to Claire, later found on Juan Luis's pil-low, seems to have precipitated two suicides.

Like the warped parents of Amilamia, Claudia also sustains herself on death. She regards the suicide of Juan Luis not as a tragedy but as an act that has fi-nally united them. The parting words of Claudia to her brother before he left for Switzerland are now ironi-cally fulfilled: "Think about me a lot. Find a way to be with me always" (77). She implies that her broth-er's suicide had little to do with Claire but rather was the means of remaining faithful to his childhood pact with her. The extremely vain sister evokes Juan Luis as a disconsolate lover who has given up his life as a sacrificial offering to her as the only way of consum-mating their incestuous love and at the same time re-taining his innocence:

> I shall always believe it was a private act, that you didn't do it because . . . I don't know why I'm think-ing these things. I don't have the right to explain any-thing in your name. Nor, perhaps, in mine either. How will I ever know, Juan Luis? Do you think I am going to insult our memories by affirming or denying that perhaps, at such and such a moment, or over a long pe-riod of time—I don't know how or when you decided, possibly when you were a child, why not?—you were motivated by dejection, or sadness, or nostalgia, or hope?

(71-72)

The title **"Un alma pura"** applies, in different senses, to all three of the main characters. Claire quotes from Raymond Radiguet's *Le Bal du Comte d'Orgel,* a quo-tation also used as the epigraph to the story, when she states to Juan Luis: "Let's not make plans. I believe as Radiguet does that the unconscious maneuvers of a pure soul are even more singular than all the possible combinations of vice" (81). The sensitive Claire is the true "alma pura" of the story. She originally cites the words to affirm spontaneity and freedom in both life and love. She is genuinely devoted to Juan Luis and willing to follow him in either a prolonged affair or in marriage. But the words of Radiguet apply to the be-havior of Juan Luis in a far different sense from that intended by Claire. The idealistic yet terribly ingenu-ous Juan Luis is also an "alma pura," the pure heart who acts in apparent innocence but who without real-izing it is exploiting and destroying Claire. The culmi-nating irony is that the self-righteous Claudia also seems to fashion herself an "alma pura," even though she is a treacherous and monstrously cruel person whose machinations result in the deaths of two per-sons.

Both **"La muñeca reina"** and **"Un alma pura"** ex-emplify the primacy of the past. Both are developed from the point of view of an introspective character who is reliving the past, vivified through being con-veyed in the present tense. In both narratives a child-hood game becomes highly significant because it establishes the pattern of adult relationships. In **"Un alma pura,"** Claudia becomes the passive center of an imaginative world created around her and for her by her devoted brother. In their childhood game, Juan Luis plays the role of the hero who rescues his sister, the princess, from imaginary dragons:

> To accompany your actions you hummed background music invented at that very moment: dramatic, a perpetual climax. Captain Blood, Sandokan, Ivanhoe: *your* personality changed with every adventure: I was always the princess besieged, nameless, indistinguishable from her nebulous prototype.
>
> (74)

Ironically, although the creative Juan Luis is successful in his childhood drama, he cannot in his adulthood rescue his real-life princess Claire. In a situation where the true heroism of decisiveness and courage is required, he remains helpless. When Claire becomes pregnant as a result of his carelessness and looks to him for the decision that would resolve the future of their relationship, Juan Luis retreats anti-heroically from the crisis, taking refuge in crossword puzzles. Claire's pregnancy is the brutal reality that intrudes upon Juan Luis's romantic idyll and smashes his delusions of independence and self-affirmation. Juan Luis is both unwilling and unable to cope with the crisis because he cannot love nor even understand Claire. His relationship with her is but a simulacrum; he can see her only to the extent that she reflects Claudia:

> She looks at me. Do you know how, Claudia? As *you* looked at me, high on the rocks at the beach, waiting for me to save you from the orge. You had to pretend you didn't know whether I was coming to save you or to kill you in the name of your jailer.
>
> (86)

For Juan Luis, as for the introspective Carlos, the present and future are but pallid imitations of the past that he is seeking to regain. Juan Luis achieves but a glimmer of self-knowledge, insufficient to make him understand how he is hurting Claire:

> I stretched my perception, my prophecies, the whole trauma of the present, like a bow, so as to shoot into the future, which wounded, would be revealed. The arrow flew from the bow, but there was no bull's eye, Claudia, there was nothing in the future. and all that painful internal construction—my hands felt numb from the effort—tumbled down like sand castles at the first assault of the waves, not lost, but returning to that ocean we call memory; to my childhood, to our games, our beach, to a joy and warmth that everything that followed could only imitate, try to prolong, fuse with projects for the future and reproduce with present surprise.
>
> (87)

Just as Claudia is the unconscious center of Juan Luis's existence, so also is the brother throughout his life and even after his death the center of Claudia's life. From childhood the more solemn, reserved sister derives emotional and spiritual fulfillment by seeing the world through the eyes of the excited Juan Luis. In his celebration of life as breathless wonder, he is similar to the young Amilamia. He acts as the idealistic soul of the partnership:

> Look at the kites, Claudia; look, Claudia, thousands of birds in the trees; look, Claudia, silver bracelets, fancy sombreros, lemon ice, green statues; come on, Claudia, let's try the wheel of fortune.
>
> (73)

Along with freedom, Juan Luis also searches for an ideal love. He wishes to avoid the debasement of love found in his native land, where love becomes a composite of puerile *machismo* and the double standard according to which women are treated as either saints or whores but never accepted as equals to the male: "I don't want to go from brothel to brothel. When you do that, then all your life you are forced to treat women with a kind of brutal, domineering sentimentality because you never learned to really understand them" (76). In Switzerland, Juan Luis enters into a number of affairs, all of which are shortlived and inconsequential, like the escapade with the exuberant, artistic Amazon Doris:

> She says she makes love to stimulate her subconscious, and she leaps out of bed to paint her gouaches with the white peaks of the Jungfrau before her. She opens the windows and takes deep breaths and paints in the nude while I tremble with cold.
>
> (78)

Yet, ironically, although he becomes involved with a bevy of "liberated" women, Juan Luis never achieves an understanding of a woman as an individual, as is proved by his pathetic response to Claire's desperate plea for help in defining their relationship.

Claudia views his early escapades as entertaining. The libertine life of her brother seems to afford her a means of vicarious compensation for her own staid and loveless existence in Mexico. Yet when he develops a prolonged, serious relationship with Claire that he does not parade before his sister as he has all the others, the jealousy and extreme possessiveness of Claudia are awakened: "I wanted to know everything. I demanded to know everything." She makes the preposterous demand that Juan Luis write down his conversations with Claire verbatim to which the extremely ingenuous brother complies. The sustained interest of Juan Luis in Claire is the result of his unconscious perception of her as the compensatory, physical and intellectual double of his sister. Claire's blond hair, her literary sensitivity, and even her name underscore her similarity to Claudia. In his letters to his sister, Juan

Luis transcribes his words to Claire in the second person and in the present tense, thereby granting them both an immediacy and an intimacy. Only the name "Claire" itself needs to be changed in order to convert the missive into a love letter to Claudia: "Claire, Claire—you wrote me—you have understood everything. I have what I always had. Now I can possess it. I've found you again, Claire." (81). Through the letters, the forbidden love of brother and sister is consummated vicariously:

> Claire, as I turn back the sheet, I forget the places you have warmed through the night and I ask myself if this isn't what we always wanted, from the beginning, when we played and walked in silence, holding hands. We had to sleep beneath the same roof, in our own house, isn't that true? Why don't you write me, Claudia? I love you, Juan Luis.
>
> (82)

At first Claudia also seems to be looking for a substitute Juan Luis. Her boy friend Federico is reduced to a mere sounding board for Claudia's rapt portrayals of her brother's life in Switzerland: "Yesterday I was telling Federico everything you're doing and seeing and reading and hearing" (81). Yet, although Juan Luis can channel his devotion for Claudia onto another person, the sister finds it impossible to do the same with Federico. She first plans an excursion with him to Acapulco but later cancels the invitation and finally excludes him from her life altogether. The setting of her childhood interludes with her brother becomes for Claudia *zona sagrada,* a sacred realm that must not be contaminated by any outside presence.

The vacillating Juan Luis goes from a period of confessional intimacy with his sister to one of complete silence. Perhaps feeling threatened by the officiousness of Claudia's correspondence, he does not write her for a year and a half. In the face of this setback, Claudia cuts herself off almost entirely from the outside world. During Juan Luis's lifetime, she never travels to Switzerland to visit her brother. Perhaps she is afraid of confronting her rival Claire and of having to accept the humiliating role of second-place status in her brother's life. By remaining in Mexico and retreating into solitude and into the world of literature, Claudia can preserve the illusion of being the center of Juan Luis's life, as she was during their childhood. As compensation for the loss of Juan Luis, she nourishes herself on the praise received from her professors, whom she intimidates by her intelligence. For Claudia, literature and life coincide. After receiving Juan Luis's letter in which he alludes to his intentions of marriage, Claudia cites Garcilaso's famous "Soneto X." Not only her shock and despair but also the passionate depth of her love for her brother are echoed by the

theme of the sonnet, that emphasizes the inconsolable grief of the lover over the irrevocable loss of his beloved

> Sweet souvenirs of love now sadly pondered, yes, sweet they seemed when God did so assign, in memory joined and bound, mine not to sunder, with memory, too, they work my death's design.
>
> (85)

The literary text, like the letters of Juan Luis to Claudia, comes to represent another spiritual transmutation of forbidden love. Ironically, although the lover portrayed in the sonnet is deprived of his beloved by death, death is the only means by which Claudia's beloved can be restored to her.

In order to subvert and destroy the relationship between Juan Luis and Claire, the wily Claudia uses a most effective weapon—idealism, the force that most easily sways Juan Luis into remaining single, free from the marriage that the sister depicts as asphyxiating:

> But we must remain united in what matters most, we mustn't concede anything to demands that we be anything other (do you remember?) than love and intelligence and youth and silence. They want to maim us, to make us like themselves; they can't tolerate us.
>
> (88)

She stresses his moral responsibility to her intellectual and spiritual growth which she implies that he is defaulting on by his capitulation to bourgeois standards: "You mustn't betray yourself, please, you know that I depend on you, on your growing with me, I can't go ahead without you" (88). Ironically, although Claudia poses as the guardian of Juan Luis's welfare and pays lip-service to the values of independence and self-integrity, she is really using these ideals to tyrannize over her brother. Although she insistently reproaches him for his betrayal of their youthful idealism, she herself is a traitor. In her letter she upholds the value of silence, yet she violates the confidentiality of her brother's confessions to her by informing their parents of his crisis with Claire. Although she poses as an advocate of a life unfettered by conventional morality, Claudia is in fact an inflexible adherent to the middle-class standards that she has so vehemently condemned. The ruthless sister plays off her own parents against Juan Luis. She exacerbates the delicate heart condition of their mother by showing her the letter in which Juan Luis discusses Claire's illicit pregnancy. Then she uses the illness of the mother to increase the guilt feelings of her brother, deflecting the blame on him: "I had to show your letter to our parents. Mama got very sick. High blood pressure. She's in the cardiac ward. I hope not to have to give you bad news in my next letter."(88).

It is Claudia's letter that impels the indecisive Juan Luis to go through with plans for the abortion. He announces the abortion in a letter to Claudia but sends a different letter to his parents, lying to them by stating that he and Claire are going to be married. Claudia informs them of the truth, thereby showing a callous disregard for her mother's precarious health. Having instigated the abortion, Claudia needs to purge her own conscience of any possible guilt, which she does by conveying the parents' condemnation to Juan Luis, who thus once more becomes the scapegoat: "I told our parents the truth. I showed them your last letter. They were stunned for a moment and then Papa said he would never allow you in the house again. He shouted that you were a criminal" (89). The perverted idealism of Claudia is matched by the misguided and ineffectual idealism of her brother. At first his quest for self-actualization is all-consuming. His poetic evocation of the natural world of Switzerland provides an indication of the intense spiritual nature of his search:

> You wrote me that in the summer the lake is the eye of the Alps: it reflects them, but it also transforms them into a vast submerged cathedral, and you said that when you plunged into the water you were diving in search of the mountains.
>
> (73)

The vast cathedral into which Juan Luis plunges suggests his striving for redemptive grace. It is extremely ironic that the lake in which he symbolically seeks the ideal at the end becomes the setting of his death. Claudia sardonically describes the ill-fated quest of Juan Luis as a "mirage." Literally this mirage applies to the summit of the Alps, the idealistic pinnacle which Juan Luis pursues only in its illusory, reflected form, as an image in the water. So also is his quest for self-transcendence and for genuine love only a false ideal, a self-delusion. Juan Luis is at heart not the rebellious individualist that he fashions himself to be. His youthful ideals, although strongly voiced, are but shallow ones; he readily abandons them as he adapts to the role of pampered, well-fed, and indolent bourgeois that as a youth he had rebelled against. He becomes but the continuation of his father, falling into the same stultified role in Switzerland that he would have assumed had he remained in Mexico. It is thus ironic that in his initial letters to Claudia, Juan Luis celebrated the independence that he believed he had gained in Geneva, "a city of transients and exiles." Juan Luis cannot really handle freedom; he is a weak, dependent person who in moments of crisis lets himself be guided by the inexorable will of his domineering sister. Claudia mocks her impetuous brother for having embarked on a foolish and futile search:

> I laugh when I think how you left the order of our home in Mexico for the disorder of your freedom in

Switzerland. Do you understand? From security in the land of bloody daggers to anarchy in the land of the cuckoo clock.

> (72)

Significantly, the one outburst of emotion by Claudia is not of grief but of sardonic laughter. She feels no remorse over the deaths of Claire and Juan Luis. Instead, at the end, she calmly confronts the father of Claire and shreds the incriminating letter that he returns to her—the one she had spitefully sent to Claire. The pitiless restraint with which Claudia thinks and acts as she brings her dead brother back to Mexico, and back under her control, gives the narrative a dark, chilling quality.

In both **"Un alma pura"** and **"La muñeca reina,"** the past, paradoxically, represents both the salvation and the destruction of the characters. The trip of Carlos to Amilamia's house and the journey of Juan Luis to Switzerland are journeys both in space and back into time. Both male protagonists attempt, either consciously or unconsciously, to impose a past upon the present. Both strive to actualize an idealistic vision of the world as innocence, wonder, and freedom, that they have cherished from childhood. Yet the spiritual quests of these cowardly and ineffectual dreamers are doomed to failure. When their ideals turn out to be mere self-delusions that are all finally swept away, the sordid, brutal reality underneath crushes the sensitive Carlos and Juan Luis. At the end of **"La muñeca reina,"** Carlos remains emotionally paralyzed. Finally forced to confront the true nature of his feelings toward his sister and the way he has abused the innocent Claire, who like him has been blind to the malevolence of Claudia, Juan Luis continues the pattern of escapism that has characterized his whole life by committing suicide. Narratives which begin as an exuberant affirmation of imaginative and social idealism end by exemplifying the destructive consequences of the moral blindness to which such obsessive idealism has led.

Notes

1. Carlos Fuentes, *Cantar de ciegos* (México: Joaquín Mortiz, 1964), p. 76. Subsequent references are included in the text. The translations are from *Burnt Water* (New York: Farrar, Straus and Giroux, 1980) translated by Margaret Sayers Peden.

2. Frank Dauster, "La transposición de la realidad en las obras cortas de Carlos Fuentes," *Kentucky Romance Quarterly, XIX,* 3 (Fall, 1972), pp. 310-311.

3. Mario Benedetti, *Letras del continente mestizo* (Montevideo: Area, 1967), pp. 168-169.

Selected Bibliography

PRIMARY WORKS

NOVELLAS AND SHORT STORIES

Los días enmascarados. Mexico City: Los Presentes, 1954.

Aura. Mexico City: Ediciones Era, 1962.

Cantar de ciegos. Mexico City: Joaquín Mortiz, 1964.

Agua quemada. Mexico City: Fondo de Cultura Económica, 1981.

TRANSLATIONS TO ENGLISH

Aura. Translated by Lysander Kemp. New York: Farrar, Straus and Giroux, 1968.

Burnt Water. Translated by Margaret Sayers Peden. New York: Farrar, Straus and Giroux, 1980. [Contains stories from *Los días enmascarados, Cantar de ciegos, Agua quemada*]

Lanin A. Gyurko (essay date 2007)

SOURCE: Gyurko, Lanin A. "Crossing Physical, Metaphysical and Linguistic Frontiers: *La frontera de cristal.*" In *Lifting the Obsidian Mask: The Artistic Vision of Carlos Fuentes,* pp. 351-78. Potomac, Md.: Scripta Humanistica, 2007.

[*In the essay that follows, Gyurko examines the predominant theme of crossing boundaries in* The Crystal Frontier, *emphasizing Fuentes's treatment of both actual and metaphorical divides in the work.*]

The title of this compelling work captures both the transparency and the fragility of the vast geographical frontier between the United States and Mexico. Like Fuentes himself, this engaging novel incessantly crosses boundaries, even on the structural level. *La frontera* is a unique novel in that it contains nine stories. The encapsulation of the characters within these short stories symbolizes their imprisonment within the confines of self, of their anxieties, fears, prejudices, all of which must be transcended in order to break through the "crystal frontier" that is both internal and external. In *The Old Gringo,* Fuentes evokes Mexico's northern border with the United States as a deep wound, as a scar that will not heal. He returns to this complex, fascinating geographic area in *The Crystal Frontier,* depicting it as a borderland whose socioeconomic importance has vastly increased in the last twenty years. As Leonardo Barroso, the exploitive owner of a *maquiladora* in Ciudad Juárez and a plutocrat in the mold of Artemio Cruz, exuberantly ex-

claims, Mexico in 1965 had zero *maquiladoras,* on the border and in 1994 had one hundred thirty-five thousand and even this immense number is ceaselessly expanding. This growth is transforming Mexico, severely altering its population patterns as economically impoverished Mexicans from southern regions like Veracruz migrate to the borderlands in quest of an ever-elusive paradise, a phenomenon depicted by the film director Gregory Nava through the characters of the Guatemalan youths Enrique and Rosa who cross both the Guatemalan and the Mexican borders to find only an ironic paradise in the United States, in his masterful border film, *El Norte.*

The Crystal Frontier[1] is a highly readable work because of both its border theme and its deft and convincing creation of a host of impoverished characters on both sides of the border—Mexicans and gringos, impoverished Chicanos who are exploited and oppressive owners of *maquiladoras* who emulate businessmen in the United States; Mexicans like Juan Zamora, who crosses the border to study medicine at Cornell University, and the *Malintzin de las maquiladoras,* the young girl Marina, who crosses the border from Ciudad Juárez to El Paso to rendezvous with her lover; and fictional characters and historical personages like Benito Juárez, Sam Houston, Stephen Austin, and even the Secretary of the Treasury in the Bill Clinton presidency, Reuben. *The Crystal Frontier,* like almost all of Fuentes's writings, but in this case much more directly, is addressed to a North American audience; the author constantly contrasts national characters and customs, political ideologies, social stratification, and even the great difference between Mexican and United States cuisine, as he lambastes the United States for the sterility of its cuisine, its overwhelming emphasis on fast food, as opposed to the immense variety and richness of Mexican cuisine.

Fuentes offers a critique of the gringo for the prevalence of racial prejudice, seen in the extremely supercilious and racist characters like the widowed Miss Amy, who treats her servants with contempt and incessantly seeks to find defects in her patient and loyal Mexican maid Josefina. Nonetheless, Fuentes does not present a facile dichotomy between the wealthy and prejudiced gringos and aggressive North American business interests who partner with Barroso, such as the shadowy gringo Murchison, and who exploit Mexico for financial gain, and the ever downtrodden submissive Mexicans. Indeed, Fuentes's criticism in this work as in *La muerte de Artemio Cruz,* is much more harshly directed toward his fellow countrymen. The imperious character Leonardo Barroso, like Artemio Cruz, who laments the fact that he was born on "the other side" of the border, wants desperately to be accepted as an equal by his North American financiers, wants them to call him "Len," but on the other hand has little but contempt for his workers and for the city, Ciudad Juárez, that has made him a multimillionaire. Instead, he characterizes this immense city sardonically as a defiled mother, seated atop chaos.

As in *The Death of Artemio Cruz,* the gringos in *The Crystal Frontier* most often appear as background figures—the materialistic Wingate family who board Juan Zamora in Ithaca but who become uneasy because of his homosexuality; the silent partner Murchison, whom Leonardo Barroso slavishly courts, sanctimoniously presenting himself as the savior of the New Mexican Woman to whom he is providing employment and the professional opportunity to liberate themselves from domestic incarceration. In the story **"Las amigas,"** **"The Friends,"** the house servant Josefina works to pay the legal expenses of her husband, victimized by fellow Mexicans. Josefina's husband is jailed because members of the Mexican community have falsely accused him of murdering a fellow Mexican. Josefina sees her husband's accusers as highly resentful of their own countrymen who have but recently arrived in the United States. In this narrative which avoids a Manichean dichotomy between oppressed Mexicans and greedy gringos, the North American is evoked positively. Miss Amy's nephew, the lawyer Archibaldo, not only defends Josefina's husband but teaches him about the law so that he can defend himself, and at the end the reclusive and embittered Miss Amy crosses the harsh border of social class and racial prejudice, which has led her to condemning Josefina as an indolent thief, and achieves reconciliation and even friendship with her Mexican companion.

The story **"La pena"** crosses many borders: between heterosexuality and homosexuality, between lower and upper classes, between reality and dream. Although it is written in a clear, direct, persuasive style, Fuentes develops one of his most enigmatic characters, Juan Zamora, the recipient of a scholarship from the boss of his father, Leonardo Barroso, who falls in love with the upper-class North American, Jim Rowlands. Rowlands is referred to as "Lord Jim" not only to indicate the class superiority of the gringo but also to underscore that he is dominant in the relationship—maintaining it or, abruptly, severing it when he learns about Zamora's lower class origins. After the breakup, the extremely sensitive Juan Zamora is devastated and takes refuge in a recurrent dream in which he and Lord Jim commit suicide together, jumping from the Triphammer Bridge in Ithaca into Fall Creek Gorge. This is a dream of only ironic unity, achieved only through self-obliteration. In *The Crystal Frontier,* as throughout Fuentes's work, one of the most difficult of

all the boundaries for Fuentes's many times fated characters to cross is that of the Self; interpersonal relationships are seldom, if ever, successful.

The same is true of the affair depicted in the short story, **"Malintzin de las maquilas."** Its title alludes to the fated Malintzin/La Malinche, the mistress of Cortés, whom he never married but in return for her service and loyalty abruptly abandoned her to marry into Spanish royalty. Marina, whose greatest desire is to escape the confinement of her desert existence and journey to the sea, as if to fulfil the symbolism of her name, is betrayed by her Don Juan lover Rolando, whom she visits in El Paso only to find him in bed with his gringa lover. Like Juan Zamora, like Félix Maldonado in *The Hydra Head* and Felipe Montero in *Aura,* like Elizabeth and Isabel in *A Change of Skin,* Marina finds not love but only permanent disillusionment, evident even in her characterization as "Malintzin." It is not love but death that predominates, both in this chapter and at the end, in both **"The Bet"** and **"Río Grande, Río Bravo."**

Dinorah, one of Barroso's many female employees, laments the lack of adequate day-care facilities and leaves her young son alone at home, tied up. The son dies accidentally, hanging himself, but Barroso's only concern is to raze the slums where she lives, purchasing the land for a pittance and then developing it with the assistance of North American capital and expanding his empire, on the model of Federico Robles and Artemio Cruz. The narrative ends tragically—Barroso crosses the final border, the one between life and death, when he is gunned down on the international bridge between Juárez and El Paso. And he is assassinated by another Mexican, by the bandit Serafín Romero, who on the model of Pancho Villa rustling cattle in the United States, steals appliances from one of Barroso's factories and smuggles them into Mexico. The border at the end of *The Crystal Frontier* is one of both violence and liberation. And the violence engulfs both oppressors and oppressed, in this case a group of viscious skinheads, who gun down a group of illegals attempting to cross the border into the United States. Yet, ironically, *The Crystal Frontier* crosses another boundary, that between one work of Fuentes and another. The fate of Barroso is changed; in Fuentes', *La Silla del Águila,* he is resurrected; he has not been killed but merely wounded, and he is forced into a paralytic existence that makes him the double of his paralyzed brother Emiliano Barroso in *The Crystal Frontier.* And Leonardo Barroso's mistress, Michelina, also crosses fictional boundaries in *The Eagle's Throne;* she appears as the mother of the future President of Mexico, Nicolás Valdivia.

Most of the time, however, boundaries are never crossed. Although Juan Zamora, now a medical doctor on both sides of the border, attempts to save the life of Barroso, it is too late, and Zamora never even recognizes the person whom he is attending as his former benefactor. The image of the crystal frontier is repeated, in various manners, throughout the work. It first appears in the opening story, **"La Capitalina,"** **"A Capital Girl,"** depicting Michelina, the impoverished but haughty descendant of Porfirian aristocrats who has nothing but disdain for the Mexican side of the border, and regards the border town Campazas as culturally vacuous. She views contemptuously the town's unique baroque architecture, lovingly fixing her gaze on the gleaming glass skyscrapers on the United States side of the border.

Here Fuentes's attitude toward the borderlands is a continuation of that seen in Mexican authors like Martín Luis Guzmán at the beginning of the twentieth century. In *El águila y la serpiente,* Guzmán draws a marked contrast between the prosperous and dynamic town of Nogales, Arizona, one which is thrown into a frenzy of commercial activity catering to Mexicans who need war supplies, and the lethargic and impoverished Nogales, Sonora. The contrast is even more pronounced in Guzmán's evocation of Ciudad Juárez, as Guzmán, like Michelina a *capitalino,* journeys from Mexico City to the border town for a personal interview with the rebel commander Pancho Villa. Ciudad Juárez is evoked as a primitive region where sidewalks rapidly disappear and the houses loom as replicas of those in ancient Mesopotamia. Guzmán, both the narrator and a character in *The Eagle and the Serpent,* dual functions performed by Fuentes in *The Crystal Frontier,* presents Pancho Villa as an emanation of borderland barbarism, as more animal than human, as a jaguar in his lair, recumbent but deadly.

The crystal frontier again appears in the huge one-way mirror, the walls of plate glass that separate Barroso from his workers on whom he can spy at will, as he looks out for the slightest signs of union organizing. It is evoked again, in dramatic close-up, in the story by the same name, which treats the abortive romantic interlude between the gringa office worker Audrey, and the Mexican window washer one who like many of Fuentes's characters has experienced a fall in socioeconomic class and is forced to become one of Barroso's pawns, Lisandro Chávez. The ever opportunistic, wily Barroso, who maintains that Mexico's greatest export is not oil or agricultural products but human labor, devises a scheme to legitimize border crossings by Mexicans into the United States to work. He flies Mexican workers into New York City just for the weekend to clean the windows of the skyscrapers. Audrey, divorced from her husband and longing for romance, remains separated from Lisandro, her exotic new acquaintance on the other side of the immense

"crystal frontier" which for reasons left ambiguous cannot be crossed. Audrey writes her name on the glass but Chávez, out of shame, or a sense of inferiority like Juan Zamora, or the deep-seated realization of the impossibility of their relationship, writes only his nationality on the other side of the glass before disappearing.

Barroso crosses the border between morality and immortality, as does Michelina, who agrees to marry the son of Barroso, the maladroit and reclusive Marianito, in order to mask the real relationship—Michelina as Barroso's mistress and constant companion. In general, Fuentes's shorter narratives are far more fatalistic than his huge, open, epic narratives like *Cristóbal nonato.* **"The Bet"** is the tragic story of the Mexican Leandro Reyes and his lover from Spain, Encarnación. Discontent with his existence as a tourist guide in Mexico, Reyes longs to escape to the United States. In a style that becomes darkly poetic, Reyes evokes the socioeconomic determinism of his country:

> Stone country. Stone language. Stone blood and memory. If you don't escape from here, you're going to turn to stone. Get out quick, cross the border, shake off that stone
>
> (191)

Yet mirroring Reyes's fated life is the fact that he travels from one country of stone to another. Spain, where he seemingly is going to construct a new life, as chauffeur of Leonardo Barroso and husband to Encarnación, is depicted as but another country of fated stone, from the perspective of Paquito, the village idiot:

> He feels terrible pains in his head. If he closes his eyes, the sun will die. He opens them and looks at the stone. Stone plaza. If you don't heave here, you will turn to stone.
>
> (193)

The determinism on Reyes's existence is complex. Much of it comes from his father, whom Reyes condemns as a petty man with a servile profession as waiter who wanted his son not to be something greater but to be a carbon copy of his father. The few opportunities that do arise for Leandro are thwarted by his own father. Seeming to sense the possibility that his son will be more successful than he has been, the despotic and cruel father resents his own son and acts to frustrate his ambitions. The extremely bitter Reyes broadens his scathing attack against the father who has suffocated his identity to encompass the whole of Mexico:

> what he was servile, submissive, a slave, like almost everybody else in this country. A few people can do

everything, very few; the majority is fucked over forever and can't do anything. A handful of fuckers en-
slave millions of servile jerks, that's how it's always
been.

(198)

The violence present in Mexico is reflected in Spain,
in the public beating of the village idiot by a group of
gang members. The irate and vengeful father in retrib-
tution challenges the gang with a bet—to race through
a tunnel in their cars, in opposite directions, to see
which group, the father or the gang, is the braver. As
what often happens, neither side of those waging the
bet loses but it is the innocent Reyes, driving through
the tunnel at the same time the opposing cars are hurl-
ing through it, who dies. Crossing boundaries in this
narrative is sometimes positive as in the case of Baco
Rangel, and at the end, the poet José Francisco, the
portavoz of Fuentes himself. But most often to cross
boundaries is a negative experience, a when Paquito
dares to look at the members of the gang who shield
themselves behind an elaborate facade of machismo.
For daring to look, for crossing a forbidden boundary,
Paquito is almost beaten to death:

> You and your friends also didn't look at one another
> . . . They were afraid of offending one another with a
> glance. Eye contact was worse, more dangerous than
> the contact of hands, sexes, or skin. It had to be
> avoided. All of you were manly because you never
> looked at one another; you walked the street of the
> town staring at the tips of your shoes and always you
> gave other people ugly looks, disdainful, challenging,
> mocking, or insecure. But Paquito did look at you,
> looked directly at you, frightened to death but direct
> and you never forgave him that—that's why you beat
> him up.

(211)

Fuentes's ambivalent, love-hate relationship with
Mexico, is captured in his exuberant depiction of one
of his most joyous, talented characters, Baco Rangel,
who paralleling Fuentes as an artist achieves instant
and enduring success in the United States as a culinary expert. His full name, Dionisio "Baco" Rangel,
expresses his *joie de vivre* attitude. But Baco, even
though enjoying acceptance and enormous fame in the
United States, finally abandons it, ecstatically tearing
off his clothes as he rushes back across the border into
his homeland, tossing into the air all of the material
possessions he has acquired in the United States, as if
to be naked signifies his rebirth. Through Baco, Fuentes once again reveals his extreme class sensitivity.
For him, Mexico has a rigid class structure unlike that
of the United States, but here Fuentes admires and
even exalts that aristocratic culture, to which he himself belongs:

> A good Mexican, Dionisio conceded all the power in
> the world to the gringos except that of an aristocratic
> culture: Mexico had one, paying the price, it was true,

with abysmal, perhaps insurmountable inequality and
injustice. Mexicans also had courteous manners, tastes,
subtleties that conformed her aristocratic culture

(65)

Yet ever ambivalent, Fuentes undercuts his own glorification of Mexican aristocracy by evoking the perni-
cious influence of the United States on the cultured
life he so cherishes:

> an island of tradition increasingly whipped and some-
> times flooded, though, by storms of vulgarity and styles
> of commercialism that were worse, because grosser,
> cheaper, more disgusting, than those of North America

(165)

Baco perhaps parallels Fuentes's own disenchantment
with the United States, which he has visited less and
less frequently as he spends part of his time in England and the other part in Mexico. Baco becomes a
liberator, taking with him back to Mexico a fellow
countryman who has spent his life asleep in a shopping mall, hired to depict the stereotype of the indolent Mexican, and rejoices that he has left "the land
that has everything" to return joyfully to "the land that
has nothing" (88).

At times the crystal frontier is vast and limitless, at
times it is shriveled to but a fluorescent line on the
floor which Emiliano Barroso, confined to his wheelchair, cannot cross, in the episode entitled **"The Line
of Oblivion."** This is one of the most heart-rending of
the short stories. It depicts the other brother, isolated
and alienated and despised by his countrymen, even
by his own family for urging Mexicans to remain in
Mexico. His own family almost worships the other
brother, the successful one, the emperor of the frontier, Leonardo. Attacked by a group of border guards
and crippled, the whole of Barroso's tortured account
is conveyed through his monologue. Again the image
of the crystal frontier appears, in a negative manner,
symbolic of incarceration:

> And I howl. Like an animal. I scream as if I were im-
> prisoned in a fragile crystal glass and my screaming
> could shatter it. The sky is my glass.

(93)

In contrast with the contempt that his fellow Mexicans
show for Emiliano, even though he has risked his life
to defend them, is their veneration of Leonardo, who
achieves a godlike aura, again reminiscent of the
"mummy of Coyoacán," Artemio Cruz:

> It's your brother who moves the world. He's the owner
> of the whole line from sea to sea. He creates wealth.
> He draws water from stones. He makes the desert
> bloom. He makes bread from sand. He can change the
> world. Not you, you poor devil . . . You aren't your
> brother. You have no name.

(98)

Emiliano is *ninguneado,* reduced to a nonbeing, by his own people. Emiliano's own family bitterly rejects him. Once more, he symbolizes the idealist in Fuentes's world who is constantly defeated. Emiliano's own family embrace the heady materialism of the United States and condemn their own country:

> They laughed at me. It's worse on the other side: Mexico's the enemy. On the Mexican side, there's more injustice, more corruption, more lies, more poverty. Be thankful we're gringos.
>
> (101)

The narrative itself constantly crosses borders as it captures the point of view first of the martyred Emiliano then of his *pocho* children: "Pochos, I called them, denaturalized Mexicans, worst of the worst," as Fuentes deftly captures the many divisions within the Mexican community itself. Another rigid boundary that Fuentes crosses is the sharp division between youth and old age. Emiliano finds himself condemned, confined to the Other Side of the age barrier:

> I feel surrounded by a world—North and South, both sides—that venerates the young. Before my eyes pass advertisements, images, offers, temptations, window displays, magazines, television—all promoting young people, seducing young people, prolonging youth, disdaining old age, discarding old people, to the point that age seems a crime, a sickness, a misery that cancels you out as a human being.
>
> (102)

In contrast to the many dynamic figures in the narrative, Baco Rangel and José Francisco, Leonardo Barroso and Michelina, are the static, paralyzed characters like Emiliano. Here the frontier that must be crossed is that between being and nothingness, between self-assertion and self-effacement: "I don't remember who I am. I should make an effort to remember my face, I just realized something absurd: I've never seen my own face. I should invent a name for myself" (90).

As he does so strikingly in *La región más transparente,* Fuentes satirizes the pretentiousness of the "Lords of the Frontier" like Leonardo Barroso, who like Federico Robles apes foreign models of architecture and artistic design. Agrarian, impoverished, indigenous Mexico is seen by Fuentes as donning a series of foreign masks and foreign ideology and suppressing its autochthonous identity. Thus Barroso masks his Mexicanness behind the facade of an English gentleman. In the midst of the intensely hot Northern desert of Mexico, Barroso constructs for himself a medieval castle:

> The Barroso's house was Tudor Norman, with a double roof of blue slate, exposed timbers and leaded glass windows everywhere. The only things missing were the Avon River in the garden and Anne Boleyn's head in some trunk
>
> (10)

In gesture of self-mockery, Barroso himself refers to reconstructed Campazas as "Disneyland." It is a weird combination of Tudor England, Hollywood, and Las Vegas. The building materials that are native to the region, such as adobe, are scorned. Indigenous Mexico serves only as a plaything for the wealthy Northerners, who have at their orgies a naked Indian boy for their delight. Once more Fuentes attacks the decadence and corruption of the *nouveaux riches:*

> walled mansions, each one half fortress, half mausoleum, mansions with Greek capitals, columns and svelt statues of gods wearing fig leaves; Arabian mosques with little fountains and plaster minarets; reproductions of Tara, with its neoclassical portico
>
> (10)

Based on the model of the impoverished Porfirian aristocrat Pimpinela de Ovando, who dedicates her life to restoring the social prominence and wealth that the De Ovandos had lost as a result of the Revolution, trading "Class for Cash," Michelina rapidly deserts her boyfriend in Mexico City to become Barroso's mistress and to marry the son by whom she is repulsed. Michelina is filled with complexes. She never wants to cross the boundary between youth and adulthood: "I always want to be a girl, Blessed Virgin, help me. Don't turn me into a woman." Perhaps it is this perpetual child-woman who so attracts Barroso. Steeped in the past, she even wears crinoline skirts and wants to enter a colonial convent.

Fuentes has always been fond of inversions, as he is in *The Orange Tree,* in which the lead story, **"Las dos orillas," "The Two Shores,"** tells of the counter invasion of Spain by a force of two thousand Mayan Indians who invade Cadiz. In *The Crystal Frontier* he emphasizes that the first "wetbacks," the first persons to cross the Rio Bravo illegally and to occupy the territory of another nation, were North Americans: Sam Houston and Stephen Austin and the nameless *tejanos* who eventually took possession of what was originally the northern half of Mexico. Fuentes in his always balanced view of contraries, sees this North Americanization of Mexico as being countered by the Mexicanization of the United States, as myriad emigrants cross over the border bringing their food and customs and values to the United States.

Indeed Fuentes is an eloquent advocate of open boundaries between the two nations, both in *La frontera* and in his essay *Nuevo tiempo mexicano (A New Time for Mexico;* 1995). Here he indicates his support for NAFTA, the North American Free Trade Agreement, despite its controversial reception in Mexico, where critics complain of its devastating effect on local Mexican industries. The ending of *The Crystal Frontier* seeks reconciliation between the two countries, again expressive of Fuentes's great diplomatic skills. At the end, he takes a bitter, cynical proverb from the nineteenth century, "pobre México, tan lejos de Dios, tan cerca de los Estados Unidos," "poor Mexico, so far from God and so close to the United States," and transforms it to link the two countries, who emerge not as antagonists but as sharing a common plight, a common destiny, and a need to resolve international problems: "poor Mexico, poor United States, so far from God, so close to one another" (266).

The image of the crystal frontier, both external and internal, repeated throughout the narrative, grants unity to this highly diversified work. At times the gleaming crystal frontier appears as temptation, but at other times it is a gleaming prison, like the manner in which Barroso's television assembly plant is evoked: "a mirage of glass and shining steel, like a bubble of crystalline air," and the prison of glass in which the anguished Emiliano Barroso sees himself confined and longs to break out of. The mirage-like nature of the television plant underscores its false promise of a new, prosperous existence for its female employees. Leonardo Barroso becomes pompous in his self-righteous exaltation as a national savior, on the model of Federico Robles. Barroso poses as the savior of Mexican women when in fact he is ruthlessly exploiting them. He employs a bevy of women because they are far more docile than male workers. He refuses to better their working conditions or to grant them benefits and is content to deal with an ever shifting labor supply, as his employees move on to other jobs. And Barroso will say anything, including mouthing an adherence to democracy, to gain the favor of his North American partners:

> the plants liberated women from farming, prostitution, even from machismo itself, because working women soon became the breadwinners in the family. Female heads of household acquired a dignity and strength that made them free, made them independent, made them modern women. And that, too, was democracy—didn't his partners agree?

(127)

A key figure in *The Crystal Frontier,* one who appears at the very end and reinforces the optimism of Fuentes regarding the future of the frontier, is the iconoclastic José Francisco, the spokesperson for Fuentes himself, who as a border person defines himself as neither Mexican nor gringo but Chicano. Articulate, philosophical, creative, José Francisco makes an eloquent plea for understanding and mutual harmony. Riding his motorcycle back and forth, across the border, suspected of dealing in contraband when he deals only in the interchange of literary texts, José Francisco delivers Chicano writings to Mexico and Mexican writings back to Texas. José uses the *we* form, signifying brotherhood, in his advocacy of international understanding, in his dynamic quest for the form that is absent from the solipsistic narrative of *Aura* and present only sparingly in the introspective, alienated narrative of Artemio Cruz. The mission of the irrepressible José Francisco parallels that of Fuentes, who on several occasions has referred to himself as a *Chicano* writer.

In the concluding segments of *The Crystal Frontier,* Fuentes crosses the most dramatic of structural and stylistic boundaries, as he creates a vast, expansive monologue, a pyramiding epic discourse, as he flashes back thirty thousand years to evoke the beginnings of the frontier region, in a segment entitled "**Rio Bravo, Rio Grande.**" Fuentes adroitly develops concluding segments that repeatedly cross the frontiers between prose and poetry and which create an epic, mythopoetic vision of the frontier that parallels the great *Canto General* of the extraordinary Chilean poet, Pablo Neruda.

The one genre that Fuentes has not cultivated *per se* is poetry yet he is a masterful poet nonetheless. Herman Melville, the great North American novelist of the nineteenth century and author of the epic novel *Moby Dick,* was a master of poetic prose, and in his sweeping, intensely lyrical prose monologues, Fuentes's poetry can also be found. The prime example of this is the dense, tumultuous, all-encompassing monologue in *Where the Air is Clear,* delivered by the impassioned Ixca Cienfuegos. This marvellous technique is repeated at the end of *The Crystal Frontier,* as Fuentes's all-encompassing, multitemporal and multispatial *monólogo totalizante* flashes back, to focus on the first, anonymous indigenous inhabitants of the border region, then moves rapidly forward in time to trace the invasion and settlement of this territory by first the Spanish and then the North Americans. In the course of this convoluted monologue, Fuentes evokes Francisco Vázquez de Coronado and his futile search in Coahuila and Chihuahua for the Cities of Gold, focuses on Cortés and Pizarro and De Soto as frontier personalities even in their native Spain, in Extremadura, comes down to the nineteenth century to evoke Santa Anna and Benito Juárez, and repeatedly crosses the magic frontier between reality and fantasy, history and myth and legend, as he expertly and compactly and dynamically fuses all epochs of border history just as he does all epochs of Mexican history as a whole at the end of *Where the Air is Clear,* a text which has so profoundly influenced *The Crystal Frontier* on the levels of both characterization and style.

The superb climax to *The Crystal Frontier* constitutes an ode to the beauty and majesty of the Border Region. Unlike Ixca's thundering monologue which continues uninterruptedly, the concluding chapter of *The Crystal Frontier* alternates between remote past and narrative present, between epic poetry and dialogue of border inhabitants in the twentieth century, incessantly crossing borders, so that the novel itself becomes a dramatic exposition of its major thesis—free and open borders, in both directions. The realistic portion of the concluding segment focuses on the border agent Dan Polonsky, himself the son of Polish immigrants to the United States, but who becomes fanatic in his crackdown on illegal Mexican entrants to his country. Polonsky is developed as a caricature of the immigration official; he is so proud of his whiteness that he even refuses to acquire a tan when he goes on vacation.

Fuentes caricatures the United States, referring to it as the United States of Amnesia, to indicate the little importance that North Americans give to history. Dan Polonsky exemplifies this amnesia, although his ancestors were repeatedly discriminated against and denied opportunities because of their lower class European origin, Polonsky refuses to grant Mexicans the very opportunities that his own ancestors were repeatedly denied. He fails to learn from the past, and exemplifies the dictum that those who forget the past are condemned to repeat it. Polonsky becomes another example of the convert to a cause being more radical than the initial adherents to that cause. He is the son of immigrants yet he becomes a super-American, glorying in America's territorial acquisitions. He and the Mexican illegals whom he persecutes are Self and Double:

> They gave their lives in two world wars and also in Korea and Vietnam. They almost equaled the sacrifices of the Anglo-Saxon generations of the previous century, the conquerors of the West. Why didn't anyone ever say so? Why did they still feel shame at having an immigrant past?
>
> (228)

Polonsky is a hypocrite in that he exploits the illegals to provide care for his children inexpensively. And he both condemns them and yet expresses his desperate need for them in order to confirm and sustain his existence:

> He distrusts the illegals. But he adored and needed them. Without them, damn it, there would be no budget for helicopters, radar, powerful infrared flight lights, rocket launchers, pistols . . . Let them keep coming by the millions, he begs, to give meaning to my life.
>
> (227-228)

In contrast with the racist Polonsky is the Mexican American patrol officer Mario Islas, who dares to defy his superior Polonsky. When an illegal crosses the Río

Grande and runs right into Mario and embraces him, Fuentes symbolizes the Self and Double theme which appears so often in his art. The illegal identifies himself as Eloíno, the godson of Mario, thereby confirming the unity of Patrol officer and illegal. Once more there is a crossing of borders; the barrier of self-isolation and superiority so often assumed by Fuentes's characters such as Miss Amy and Michelina, is broken. Ironically the blood relationship that Eloíno claims with Mario is fictitious, but he is allowed to escape and to remain in the United States. Here is a rare moment of unity, as the two Mexicans embrace one another. Although Mario's own desire is for division: "he wished the whole Río Grande, Río Bravo really were divided by an iron curtain, a deep, deep ditch" (240) yet, as in **"Las amigas,"** the two adversaries at least momentarily become friends:

> He laughed again and again hugged Mario, the way only two Mexicans know how to hug each other, because the border guard couldn't resist the current of tenderness, affiliation, machismo, confidence and even trust that there was in a good hug between men in Mexico, especially if they were related . . .
>
> (242)

As opposed to the highly negative evocation of ancient indigenous Mexico in *La región más transparente* is the positive, mythopoetic, celebratory evocation of the indigenous inhabitants of the border region: Indian culture is linked with an incessant, transcendental metamorphosis, and is consecrated by Fuentes, in contrast with the brutal government imposed on the Indians by the Spanish conquistadores. Fuentes evokes Indian culture in biblical terms. The sections of epic monologue are italicized, to underscore their spiritual, redemptive nature:

> *the world has sprung forth from the invisible springs of the desert waters: the underground rivers, the Indians say, are the music of God, thanks to them the corn grows, the bean, squash, and cotton, and each time a plant grows and yields its fruits, the Indian is transformed, the Indian becomes a star, oblivion, bird, mesquite, pot, membrane, arrow, incense, rain, smell of rain, earth, earthquake, extinguished fire, whistle in the mountain, secret kiss, the Indian becomes all this when the seed dies, becomes child and grandfather of the child, memory, bark, scorpion, buzzard, cloud, and table, broken vessel of birth, repentant tunic of death*
>
> (223)

At the ending of *La frontera,* Fuentes returns to the beginnings, to a Genesis of the frontier region, a depiction of the moment in which God created it. In *La región más transparente,* the return to the origins is not redeeming but fatalistic, the ancient Aztec gods re-emerge in modern Mexico seeking blood vengeance. But in *La frontera* the anonymous indigenous civilization is evoked in a highly positive, mythopoetic manner. Indeed, the tumultuous concluding monologue becomes rhapsodic. Here is a marked contrast with the expository and delineative prose that characterizes most of **La frontera de cristal,** as Fuentes combines a declamatory with an epic tone, blending the dramatic with the celebratory. Here is the grandest of the boundaries crossed by Fuentes, as he moves from the mundane to the spiritual and consecrates the origins of the Río Bravo/Río Grande border:

> *the valley drops anchor between the pine and the cypress until a flight of doves raises it again, carrying the river up to the steep tower from which the earth broke off the very first day, under the hand of God*
>
> (216)

The crystal frontier is transmuted into a "mirror of air" that underscores its magical aura. The beauty and the majesty and the profound spiritual characteristics of the border are all caught by Fuentes in his intense poetic prose:

> *Now God, every day, gives a hand to the río grande, río bravo, so that it may rise to his balcony once more and roll along the carpets of his waiting room before opening the doors to the next chamber, the stop that brings the waters, if they manage to scale the enormous ravine, back to the roofs of the world, where each plateau has its own faithful cloud that accompanies it and reproduces it like a mirror of air*
>
> (216)

Structurally and stylistically, there is at the end an incessant crossing and recrossing of boundaries, as Fuentes does not present an uninterrupted monologue as he does in the epic ruminations of Ixca Cienfuegos, but continually moves from elegiac and epic mythopoetry to discursive prose, from remote past to the present day, and from divine creation to the violence and murder that mar the borderland in the twentieth century. The incessant fragmentation of the narrative also underscores the extreme fragmentation of the lives of the characters, very few of whom ever gain transcendental unity with others, so that those who do succeed in crossing the boundary of individual self-interest to attain a redemptive unity with another culture, with another race, like Miss Amy and José Francisco, stand out. Together with individual characterization, there is often a focus on communal character, which is spiritualized, as Fuentes evokes the band of nameless immigrants who raise their hands in the form of the cross, to suggest their martyrdom.

As so often in the magical world of Fuentes, dream precedes reality. The narrative crosses the border between reality and dream, as Fuentes identifying with the ancient indigenous cultures who descry a blood-stained and horrifying future under the domination of the invading conquistadores and their descendants:

> *the Indian dreams and his dream becomes a prophecy, all the dreams of the Indians become reality, incarnate, tell them they are right, fill them with fear and for that reason make them suspicious, arrogant, jealous, proud but horrified of always knowing the fixture, suspicious that the only things that become reality is that which should be a nightmare: the white man, the horse, the firearm*
>
> (223-224)

Fuentes in the twenty-first century becomes a successor to Fray Bartolomé de las Casas, the Dominican who in his *Brevísima relación de la destrucción de las Indias* condemned the horrors of the Conquest as a New World genocide. And Fuentes is influenced as well by a contemporary Latin American poet, Pablo Neruda, who in his vast, epic poem *Canto General,* evokes the Latin American continent throughout the centuries. In **La frontera de cristal,** the evocation of the enormous devastation of the Conquest is evoked in dramatic and poetic terms that echo the *Canto General:*

> *Steel and gunpowder came*
> *the bloodhounds came*
> *death came: fifty-four million*
> *men and women lived in the vast*
> *continent of the migrations, from*
> *the Yukon to Tierra del Fuego,*
> *and four million north of the*
> *río grande, río bravo,*
> *when the Spaniards came fifty years later,*
> *only four million lived*
> *on the whole continent*
>
> (224)

Now the Southwest frontier has vastly expanded, as Fuentes leaps to encompass the whole of Latin America, breaking down all boundaries as he evokes a Conquest of holocaust proportions. In this titanic ending, Fuentes uses of intertextuality, always present in his art, to include many of the Hispanic authors of the Conquest, from Ercilla's *Araucana* in Chile to the *Letters* of Hernán Cortés to the *Historia verdadera de la conquista de la Nueva España* of Bernal Díaz to the *Naufragios y Comentarios* of Cabeza de Vaca. Once again, in Fuentes's evocation of the New World Conquistador who chronicles not victory by incarceration by the indigenous peoples, Fuentes evokes another crystal frontier, this time an inner, existential one, the possibility of fulfilling the Indian other present with the Spanish nobleman Cabeza de Vaca:

> *and tries to see himself reflected there as the hidalgo he was, the Spanish gentleman he no longer is; the only mirror of his person are the Indians he finds, he has become identical to them, but he misses the chance to be one of them, he is equal to them but does not understand the opportunity he has to be the only Spaniard who could understand the Indians and translate their souls into Spanish.*
>
> (233)

And Cabeza de Vaca becomes the historic double or mirror self of Fuentes himself, who unlike the Spanish *cronista* does succeed in translating the indigenous soul into Spanish.

Fuentes's depiction of Cabeza de Vaca is one of the most haunting of his literary portraits; he evokes the spectre of an adventurer who crosses physical frontiers but is unable to cross cultural and psychological ones, truly to become the Other. In his collection of short stories *El naranjo, o los círculos del tiempo,* Fuentes evokes Gonzalo Guerrero, the Spanish explorer who does cross the line, who marries an indigenous woman in the Yucatán and paints his face and when Cortés arrives is unwilling to leave his newfound family to join the *conquistador.* In contrast to Gonzalo Guerrero whom Fuentes re-creates as the captain who will lead a group of Mayans to conquer the Old World, Cabeza de Vaca seeks desperately to retain his original self:

> in reality he fights, horrified, against the loss, layer by layer, of the skin and clothes of his European soul, he clings to it, pays no need to the advice of his internal voice: God brought us naked to know men identical to ourselves in their nakedness . . .

> (234)

In his capital work *This I Believe,* Fuentes has affirmed that Bernal Díaz was the first Mexican writer. In *La frontera de cristal,* Cabeza de Vaca becomes the first Mexican-American *fabulator,* as he deliberately propagates the myth of the borderland as a realm of untold riches that makes it the rival of Mexico and Peru:

> they heard word of the incalculable wealth of Quivira, they propagate they illusion of El dorado, another Mexico, another Peru, beyond the río grande, río bravo

> the immortal dream of wealth, power, gold, happiness that compensates for all our sufferings, for the thirst, the hunger, and the shipwrecks and the Indian attacks

> (235)

The frontier region again becomes one of mere mirages; the Spanish never found the Seven Cities of Cíbola in lands that were rugged and desolate. Ironically, the border regions do become a land of limitless wealth, but only centuries later, when oil is discovered in the Texas deserts and the volume of trade increases exponentially as well as the rapid development of the *maquiladoras* which convert men like Leonardo Barroso into *nuevos conquistadores* in the twentieth century.

The final conquistador to be evoked is Juan de Oñate, who has inherited from his father silver mines in Mexico but who leaves wealth and privilege and comfort behind to submerge himself in a life of adventure and conquest. Oñate, like all of the characters in this tightly constructed narrative, has a dual identity, in his case both colonial and contemporary. He emerges as the prototype of the economic entrepreneur; he is dedicated not to finding more gold and silver but to the exploitation of the land, and thus becomes a predecessor of Leonardo Barroso. In his evocation in grandiose, godlike terms, Oñate becomes a frontier personage not only in his domestication of the borderlands but his being a bridge figure between the avarice of Pizarro and the shrewdness and gigantic egotism of Barroso:

> he founds El Paso del Norte and claims Spanish dominion over all things, from the leaves on the trees to the rocks and sand in the rivers, nothing stops him, the founding of El Paso is merely the springboard for his grand imperial dream.

> (238)

Delineated as well in a contemporary manner as "a private contractor, a businessman" (238), Juan de Oñate is evoked in terms that apply equally to the domineering Leonardo Barroso and that serve to underscore the fatalism of the narrative. In dramatic contrast with the efforts of those like Baco Rangel and José Francisco to break through the prison of the crystal frontier and assert an equality are the megalomanic dreams of Oñate:

> this is a matter of founding, in truth, a new order, where Juan de Oñate rules as he pleases, capriciously, not owing anyone anything, intent on losing everything as long as he's infinitely free to impose his will, to be his own king and perhaps his own creator

> (239)

Fuentes contrasts the iron certainty of the United States, evinced in its nineteenth century policy of Manifest Destiny, with the tentativeness and the uncertainty of Mexico, in the twentieth century as in the nineteenth, ever since its liberation from its colonial status in the War of Independence, for an identity:

> looted country, sacked country, mocked, painful, cursed, precious country of marvelous people who have not found their word, their face, their own destiny, not manifest but uncertain human destiny

> (255)

With heavy fatalism Fuentes depicts the arrival of the North Americans to his homeland: "*and the first gringos arrive: the territories were lost before they were won,*" alluding to the desperate attempts of the Mexican government to populate the vast arid territories to the North, including California, New Mexico, Utah, Colorado, Arizona, and Texas, previously regarded by Mexico as but a barbarous wasteland. The Mexican government even invites families from the Canary Islands to settle these territories, all lost forever as a result of Mexico's defeat under General Santa Anna in what is known as the Mexican-American War in the 1840s, in which Generals Scott and Taylor occupied Mexico City, in what Fuentes sees as an ignominious defeat for his country, which nevertheless continues to cede land to the United States, this time selling it, the Gadsden Purchase, and more of what is now Texas. Ironically, at first the gringos, under the leadership of Austin, are depicted by Fuentes as the first wetbacks, as they swim over the Río Grande into Mexico and at first are welcomed by the Mexican government, who regard them as a mirror, as a double of Mexico, as also independent and democratic. Once again Fuentes is ambivalent in his evocation of the gringos; Austin, for example, is seen as both invader and energetic carrier of the North American values of freedom, due process of law, and juries of peers instead of authoritarianism. Austin's implorative voice is heard as he is evoked in a positive manner:

> let them enter, even illegally, crossing the Sabinas River, wetting their backs, sending the border to hell, says another energetic young man, thin, small, disciplined, introspective, honorable, calm, judicious, who knows how to play the flute: exactly the opposite of a Spanish hildalgo
>
> (247)

Presenting Houston as a tall, patient conquistador, Fuentes portrays his Mexican adversary, Santa Anna as a caricature, once again demonstrating his ambivalence to his country. The plain, utilitarian clothing of Houston contrasts with the overdressed, vainglorious Mexican dictator:

> Houston, almost six feet tall, wearing a coonskin cap, a leopard vest, patiently whittling any stick he finds nearby, Santa Anna wearing epaulets and a three-cornered hat, sleeping his siesta in San Jacinto while Mexico loses Texas: what Houston is really carving is the future wooden leg of the picturesque, frivolous, incompetent Mexican dictator
>
> (248)

Here Fuentes refers to the amputation of Santa Anna's leg, which the general had buried with full military honors.

From descriptive, explanatory and interpretive, as Fuentes traces the incessant incursions of the North Americans into Mexico and the willingness of the government under Porfirio Díaz, characterized cynically as "madre de los extranjeros y madrasta de los mexicanos," "mother of foreigners and stepmother of Mexicans," then suddenly changes its skin as the style becomes poetic and surrealistic. This is now vibrant and exalting imagery as Fuentes dramatically conveys both the promise and the suffering of his homeland:

> They didn't see the Mexicans who wanted to see Mexico whole, wounded, dark, stained with silver, and cloaked in mud, her belly petrified like that of some prehistoric animal, her bells as fragile as glass, her mountains chained to one another in a vast orographic
>
> prison, her memory tremulous: Mexico
> her smile facing the firing squad: Mexico
> her genealogy of smoke: Mexico
> her fruit bursting like stars
> her songs breaking apart like piñatas
>
> (261-262)

As at the end of *La región más transparente,* Fuentes at the conclusion of **La frontera** crosses boundaries between present-day and ancient, indigenous Mexico. Yet there is a dramatic difference: instead of the threatening blood-seeking, vengeful lxca there is now an ebullient and consecrating evocation of Mexico's pre-Columbian past as the magical papers of José Francisco become transformed into featherwork, an allusion to the exquisite feather craftsmanship of the Aztecs, art that was not understood and was destroyed by the Spanish invaders. Fuentes's vision encompasses both the United States and Mexico as he repeats the refrain:

> to the north of the río grande
> to the south of the río bravo
>
> (266)

Just as *La región más transparente* ends on a note of resignation and stubborn endurance, as the same characters, the superhuman and the human, Ixca Cienfuegos and Gladys García, are present at both the outset and the end of the narrative: "Here we bide. What are we going to do about it. Where the air is clear." (376), so too at the end of **La frontera** there is a note of shared fatalism:

> poor Mexico,
> poor United States,
> so far from God,
> so near to each other
>
> (266)

In this ending, which fuses national pride and national identity as well as postulating a shared identity between the United States and Mexico, Fuentes adds to the national symbols of his homeland—to the Eagle and the Serpent he adds the Feathers as symbols of grace, dignity, artistic achievement, and spiritual redemption. In the concluding pages of the work, the italicized monologue that has previously encompassed the whole of the borderlands throughout the ages now focuses specifically on the characters in the contemporary period, and the style becomes exhortatory:

> toss the papers as if they were feathers, ornaments, tattoos to defend them from the inclemency of the weather,

clan markings, stone collars, bone, conch, diadems of
the race, waist and leg adornments, feathers that speak,
José Francisco

(266)

feathers emblematic of each deed, each battle, each
name, each memory, each defeat, each triumph, each
color

(266)

The ambivalence so characteristic of Fuentes's art is
also seen in his evocation of the past. On the one
hand, there is a negative power of the past as seen in
the contemporary bandit, Serafín Romero, who steals
appliances from the factory of Leonardo Barroso and
ships them to Mexico, and who is depicted in terms of
Pancho Villa, who rustled cattle in the United States to
pay for his weapons: "And Serafín Romero thought,
leaving the stopped train behind, that the only thing
missing for him to be a hero was a whinnying stallion
. . ." (237).

Small issues resonante deeply; Lord Jim is surprised
to learn that the same building that housed the first
medical school in Mexico was initially the headquar-
ters of the Inquisition. He cannot comprehend this fusion of two, contradictory times, one of persecution
and death and the other of the assertion of life, and
this unsettling phenomenon starts the rift in his relationship with Juan Zamora that will quickly lead to its
dissolution. When Encarnación visits Mexico and
views the magnificent murals of Diego Rivera that
now adorn a previously despotic structure, the Palace
of Cortés in Cuernavaca where even before the Spanish conquistador, the ancient Aztec Emperor Mocte-
zuma had his palace, once again there is an ambivalence toward the past and its meaning for the present.
Fuentes is one of the very few Mexicans, along with
Vasconcelos, to advocate the recognition by Mexicans
of Hernán Cortés as the founder of the nation, Fuentes
who even advocates openly the erection of a statue to
Cortés, officially condemned by the post-Revolutionary
Mexican government as a symbol of the Spanish invasion and conquering of country. This attitude of recognizing the contributions of Spain is continued in *La
frontera de cristal* as the audacious Fuentes crosses
another border, that between the *madre patria* and her
Mexican colony, that between *gachupín* and *mestizo,*
that between blind Mexican nationalists who exalt the
ancient indigenous past and vilify the Spanish invaders, to attempt to establish a balanced viewpoint. When
Leandro praises the ancient Indians and laments the
destruction of their civilization, and he and the Spanish Encarnación view Rivera's mural which underscores the contribution of Mexico to Europe: "chocolate, corn, tomatoes, chiles," Encarnación retorts
defiantly, echoing the pro-Spanish sentiments of Fu-

entes: "Hold it right there," . . . "If he's put everything Mexico owes Europe, all the walls in this palace
wouldn't be enough." (197).

Another of the boundaries that Fuentes crosses not
only in *La frontera de cristal* but throughout his work,
is that between the present and the historical past.
Mexico is depicted as forced to remember the past because it was victimized and still suffers the consequences of that past. In contrast, the United States,
victorious in its wars of Manifest Destiny, its incessant
desire for more and more land, is oblivious to that
past because it is not compelled to keep remembering
it. The major part of the United States which still has
reverence for the past and continues to celebrate it
with passion is the Deep South, which lost the Civil
War and was subject to the invasion of the carpetbag-
gers and to the anguish of Reconstruction:

> The generosity of Mexico, Dionisio would habitually
> say, shows in its not holding a grudge for that terrible
> despoiling, although the memory lingered on, while the
> gringos didn't even remember that war, much less know
> its unfairness.

(57)

Yet Fuentes, always even-handed, blames Mexico itself for the loss of its gigantic territories, more than
half the nation, "through abandonment, indifference
and a sparse population" (57).

Unlike many Mexican intellectuals, who see the Revolution of 1910 as the most significant event in Mexican history, for Fuentes that defining event is not the
Revolution, which he regards as but a transient moment of national self-transcendence before Mexico's
lapsing again into corruption and authoritarianism, but
the Conquest. As we have seen, Fuentes believes that
the Conquest changed the face of Mexico forever. In
tribute to the enormity and to the complexity of the
Conquest, Fuentes has one of the characters in *The
Years with Laura Díaz* admit that Diego Rivera not
only attacked the stunning Spanish conquistadors as
he portrays in his stunning mural at Cuernavaca a
dwarf, syphilitic Cortés with a prognathous jaw, but
also emphasizes the whiteness of the horse of the
Spanish conquistadores as ennobling these foreign invaders.

Fuentes's ambivalence toward the Revolution can in
part be explained in that his upper class Veracruz ancestors were ruined by it—in *Los años con Laura Díaz,*
Fuentes evokes the invasion of the coffee plantation of
Laura's grandfather by campesinos from Veracruz. Yet
Fuentes's family recovered rapidly from the Revolutionary chaos and destruction; he records in *This I Believe* that his maternal grandmother, Emilia Rivas Gil,

was a childhood friend of Alvaro Obregón in Sonora and was appointed inspector of schools in the Revolutionary government of Obregón. Fuentes's father, initially sent by Huerta as one of the cadets defending Mexico against the United States occupation of Mexico by Wilson, was appointed by the Revolutionary government at age twenty-five as a lawyer for the Mexican and American Mixed Claims Commission. Perhaps one of the reasons why Fuentes, now nearing eighty, is still so rabidly dedicated to his profession and so prolific a writer is that he remembers how his father's retiring from the diplomatic service that he so loved killed him spiritually, as Fuentes states in *This I Believe:*

> Back in Mexico, he yearned for his driver, his reports, his daily diplomatic agenda, all the essential elements of his life, and slowly faded away, disconcerted, wearing a poignant expression of absence and nostalgia.
>
> (89)

As in *La región más transparente,* Fuentes in *La frontera* runs the gamut of social classes in Mexico, from the upper class Michelina, whose antecedent is Pimpinela de Ovando in *La región más transparente,* both families Porfiristas ruined economically by the Revolution yet frantically, obsessively seeking to restore their wealth and power, as Michelina does by marrying into the Barroso family, to the lower classes, in his stark evocation of Serafín Romero:

> growing up surrounded by the mountains of garbage in Chalco, dedicated since childhood to digging around in the disfigured mass of rotten meat, vomited beans, rags, dead cats, scraps of unrecognizable existence, giving thanks when something kept its form—a bottle, a condom—and could be brought home.
>
> (235)

La frontera de cristal in its hybrid form, a combination of novel and short story, anticipates Fuentes's *Todas las familias felices,* a narrative composed of sixteen short stories united in their focus on dysfunctional families, disintegrating, afflicted by inconsolable loss. Instead of one vast concluding monologue, *Todas las familias felices* contains what Fuentes refers to as a *coro* after each segment that dramatically changes style, from expository to demonstrative and poetic.

La frontera de cristal, like *Todas las familias felices,* is a work of primarily abortive relationships. Juan Zamora permanently loses his beloved Jim; Michelina loses Barroso when he is assassinated on the border; she never consummates her matrimony with Mariano, whom she finds repulsive; the marriage between Leonardo Barroso and his socially pretentious wife Lucila is but a facade, like his opulent Norman mansion; Leandro succeeds in crossing boundaries, this time be-

tween Mexico and Spain, but finds only death; Malintzin de las malquilas, Marina, even though knowing that Rolando is a Don Juan and content to share him with others, will never reach the sea of which she dreams and which she envisions as a liberation from her barren, desert existence.

On the one hand, *La frontera de cristal,* is a stark, realistic work, punctuated with crisp and battling dialogue, delving into the daily lives, most often seen as an accumulation of frustrations, of its characters. Yet this unique novel is always on the verge of dream, and in the case of the eccentric Baco Rangel as he dines in the American Grill and under the powers of the magic genie in the bottle of hot sauce sees appearing before him a woman metamorphosed out of each of the dishes he is served. Here there glimmers the comedic talent of Fuentes, a humor not often seen in his somber narrative:

> And it was not cleared away by the arrival of dessert, a lemon meringue pie whose female counterpart Baco was afraid to see, especially because at the beginning of this adventure he'd watched the fat women pass by, desiring them platonically. He was right to be afraid. Seated opposite him, he saw when the noise of the *charro's* shot had faded, was a monstrous woman who weighed 650 if she weighed a pound. Her pink sweatshirt announced her cause: FLM, the Fat Liberation Movement.
>
> (82)

Fuentes parodies the tale of the genie in the lamp, the magic spirit who appears once the lamp is rubbed. Instead of this device, it is a bottle of jalapeño chile sauce that Dionisio inadvertently rubs, releasing the genie inside who is immensely grateful to Baco for his sudden liberation: "No gringo would open me up. Thank you! Your wish is my command" (73). This is the most humorous, most imaginative crossing of boundaries, that between reality and the supernatural. And once more the theme of the double appears: the genie complete with Zapata-like moustache and pistol is the alter ego of the Europeanized, suave, sophisticated Baco:

> The charro genie his kitschy alter ego, that bastard, that picturesque asshole, that skirt chaser, that total opposite of his Symbolist, Baudelarian, French alter ego, was also his double, his brother, but the little guy was Mexican and was always pulling a fast one, teasing him, offering him the moon but handing him shit, devaluing his life, his love, his desire . . . his other Aztec ego, his pocketsized Huitzilopochtli, his national minimoctezuma.
>
> (85)

In *La frontera,* the spirt of the Aztec gods once again appears, but not as in *La región más transparente* menacing and destructive, but this time satirical, as

Baco Rangel is compelled to engage in a ritual canni-
balism—never being allowed to possess any of the
women by whom he is suddenly confronted because
they are only temporary incarnations of the dishes he
is devouring: "the genie didn't tell him that when he
ate a steak or a shrimp cocktail or a lemon meringue
pie he was also eating the woman who was the incarnation of each dish, and here he was, delirious, going
mad" (85). Fuentes in depicting Baco is also depicting
himself, his complex, contradictory persona, the one
who soars to metaphysical heights and demonstrates
his dedication to Nietzsche and Schopenhauer and his
vast erudition that encompasses European, North
American, and Oriental literature, and on the other
hand the Fuentes who as a youth had visited brothels
and who continues to be entranced by the underworld
of Mexico. From polished and witty cosmopolitan
gentleman, Fuentes can move to the incorporation of
the "sleeping tiger" that he has always seen as charac-
terizing Mexico.

Baco Rangel emerges as the exuberant and iconoclastic opposite of Leonardo Barroso. Although both men
are privileged, and both are in control of the border,
both able to cross and recross it at ease, the overwhelming appeal of the cities on the other side of the
border for the ambitious Barroso and the materialistic
Michelina is meaningless for Baco Rangel. Baco bur-
lesques American materialism just as he has inveighed
against the fast food diet that causes obesity throughout North America, in contrast with the diet of chiles,
beans, and flour tortillas in Mexico that Fuentes sees
as healthful and slenderizing. Another, much more
somber definition of the border, one which has been
influenced by Gloria Anzaldúa, is given by the anguished Juan Zamora. As in so many of Fuentes's
works, the reader must put together all the diverse perspectives on the border evoked fragmentarily in this
narrative and compose a mosaic of these cubistic and
contradictory interpretations:

> He dreamed about the border and saw it as an enor-
> mous bloody wound, a sick body, mute in the face of
> its ills, on the point of shouting, torn by its loyalties,
> and beaten, finally, by political callousness, demagogu-
> ery, and corruption.
>
> (244)

Yet the opposite of this pessimistic viewpoint is expressed by the irreverent José Francisco at the end of
the work, who incarnates himself the fusion of two
nations, Mexico and the United States, to produce the
New Man, the Chicano. At the end, the double
achieves a positive, redeeming expression, in the marvelous doubling of José Francisco, who is a figure,
like Fuentes of synthesis and of fusion of contraries,
who is the most exuberant and articulate voice in the
novel:

What belongs here and also there but where is here and
where is there? Isn't the Mexican side his own here
and there? Isn't it the same on the gringo side? Doesn't
every land have its own invisible double, its alien
shadow that walks at our side the same way each of us
walks accompanied by a second "I" we don't know?

(250)

Continuity is provided to the narrative by the fact that
José Francisco's family are from Zacatecas, living on
land that once belonged to Oñate. José Francisco refuses to Anglicize his name to "Joe Frank" because
for him it would mean the loss of his identity, "I'd be
mute, bro." He writes, again as the interior double of
Fuentes himself, of the Mexican Americans and their
families "that was the wealth of the border world, the
quantity of unburied stories that refused to die, that
wandered about like ghosts from California to Texas"
(281).

Like Fuentes himself, who as a young writer faced the
dilemma of which language to write in, the language
of his birth or the language which he had acquired
through his schooling in Washington, D.C., José Francisco is also faced with the choice of what idiom to
use to convey his message:

> when he began to write, at the age of nineteen, he was
> asked, and asked himself, in which language, English
> or in Spanish? And first he said in something new, the
> Chicano language, and it was then he realized what he
> was, neither Mexican nor gringo but Chicano, the lan-
> guage revealed it to him, he began to write in Spanish
> the parts that came out of his Mexican soul, in English
> the parts that imposed themselves on him in a Yankee
> rhythm
>
> (252)

For José Francisco, the border is crystalline not in the
sense it has conveyed throughout the narrative, that of
a glass prison, but crystalline because it does not exist; for José Francisco as for Fuentes himself, one day
in Mexico, the next week in Barcelona or London, the
next week in the United States, there are no external
frontiers. [. . .] He chooses to write in Spanish, because, as he has stated the English and North American novel have been richly defined the Latin American
novel was waiting for its voice. Yet Fuentes more and
more has been writing directly into English, and has
also assisted in the translations from Spanish to English of his work. Fuentes has declared, in an interview with the author of this study [*Lifting the Obsidian Mask: The Artistic Vision of Carlos Fuentes*], that
in the construction of *Cristóbal nonato* he would write
a chapter first in Spanish, and then do an English translation, which in turn would lead him back to amplify-
ing or emending the original Spanish. Here is depicted
a fascinating exercise in crossing linguistic bound-

aries, which Fuentes does so well, offering courses to undergraduate and graduate students in English and delivering lectures, such as the Commencement Address at Harvard University, in English.

The texts that José Francisco joyfully, ecstatically tosses into the air do not fall to earth but cross borders. Through the power of the word the Mexican side of the border and the United States side are fused into a single whole. Here is depicted an aesthetic journey across physical and cultural boundaries. The flying texts of José Francisco/Fuentes mark a movement that at the end, in contrast to the downward spiraling of Juan Zamora's dream of the gorge in Ithaca is upward, soaring, liberating, affirming the power of the word to forge a new culture. Instead of resisting the border guards who search him for contraband, José Francisco helps them disperse the papers:

> And José Francisco happily helped the guards, tossing manuscripts into the air, to the river, to the moon, to the frontiers, convinced that the words would fly until they found their destination their readers, their readers, their tongues, their eyes . . .
>
> (253)

Throughout his work, Fuentes has repeatedly crossed the boundary into intertextuality. At the end of *La frontera* Fuentes incorporates contemporary Chicano literature into his exhilarating vision:

> They simply went flying from the bridge into the gringo sky, from the bridge to the Mexican sky, Ríos's poem, Cisneros's story, Nercio's essay, Siler's pages . . . Aluristas's butterflies, Denise Chávez's thrushes, Carlos Nicolás Flores's sparrows, Rogelio Gómez's bees, Cornejo's millennia, Federico Campbell's *fronteras*
>
> (253)

The Chicano and Chicana authors are thus made co-authors of Fuentes's text.

Some of the characters of *La frontera* are extensively developed, such as Leonardo Barroso, some are incarcerated in but a single segment, such as his martyred brother Emiliano, some are encapsulated in brief but unforgettable vignettes such as the hundred-year old grandmother of Dinorah, who is evoked as she returns from the funeral of her grandson back to the United States. She is presented as a sad but venerable and consecrated figure: "*an unreadable old woman under a palimpsest of infinite wrinkles that cross her face like the map of a country lost forever*" (264). In her advancing age, she is forgetting her native Spanish and never has learned to speak English. She is a feeble, isolated figure whom Fuentes creates as a symbol of both alienation and stoic endurance. And she is crossing the one frontier left for her to cross, that between reality and dream. Her inner world is conveyed through an italicized narrative that underscores its spiritual nature:

> *she can't communicate with anyone (except with time, except with the night, except with oblivion, except with mongrels and parrots, except with the payas she touches in the market and the coyotes that visit her at dawn, except with the dreams she can't tell anyone*
>
> (264)

Again and again in this paradoxical narrative, characters separated and even, like Michelina and Marianito never consummating their relationship, are united only ironically in dream. In the case of Michelina, the paramour who paradoxically dreams of being a nun, the extreme guilt that Michelina experiences for failing to remain faithful to her desire to enter a convent is dramatized through her nightmare:

> Michelina tried to escape from her dream, whose space was identical to that of the convent, but all the nuns, crowded in front of the altar, blocked her way. The black maids tore the habits off the sisters, stripping them naked to the waist, and then the nuns screamed imploringly for the whip to suppress the devil in the flesh and to give an example to Sister Michelina
>
> (22)

Marianito too is devastated by dreams. And the painfully fearful Mariano is also echoed in the religious devotion of the young Jaime Ceballos of *Las buenas conciencias* who even seeks to exculpate the sins of his family by adopting the role of the crucified Christ in a local pageant. Marianito is the extreme of the young Ceballos, who like Michelina also combines religious fervor with eroticism. Marianito even desires to commit suicide, and in his self-imposed isolation on Leonardo's ranch, his only company the Pacuache Indians who are characterized as "erased Indians," ironic doubles of the self-erased Marianito, who achieves the monastery-like isolation longed for by Michelina:

> Others lay next to the prostrate, bleeding, wounded, thorn-pierced Christs, and here Michelina's dream in Mexico City fused with Marianito's in the lightless bedroom in Campazas. The boy, too, dreamed of one of those dolorous Christs in Mexican churches, more dolorous than their Virgin Mothers, the Son laid out in a crystal coffin surrounded by dusty flowers, He Himself turning to dust, disappearing on His homeward journey to the spirit, leaving only the evidence of a few nails, a lance, a crown of thorns, a rag dipped in vinegar . . . how he longed to leave behind the miseries of this ephemeral body!
>
> (22)

Evoked as a shining glass building symbolic of Michelina's desire for rapid acquisition, the crystal frontier metamorphosizes into a glass coffin, and, it its most dramatic and gargantuan form, the immense crystal skyscraper in which Audrey has her office. Once again, Fuentes caricatures a glass object. He prefers the baroque church in Campazas so disdained by Michelina; his evocation of the immense glass masterpiece in New York is filled with sarcasm:

> an immense music box made of mirrors, unified by its own chrome-covered, nickel-plated glass, a place like a crystal deck of cards, a toy of quicksilver labyrinths.
>
> (179)

Audrey is depicted not as master inhabitant but as prisoner of this transparent building:

> she went to the top floor without looking at anyone, like a bird who confuses its cage for freedom. She walked through the corridor on the fortieth floor—glass walls, glass doors, they lived suspended in midair; even the floors were made of opaque glass, the tyrant of an architect having forbidden carpeting in his crystal masterpiece.
>
> (182)

Note

1. Carlos Fuentes, *La frontera de cristal: una novela en nueve cuentos* (México: Alfaguara, 1996). References are to *The Crystal Frontier: A Novel in Nine Stories,* (New York: Farrar, Straus and Giroux, 1997) translated by Alfred J. MacAdam, and are included parenthetically in the text.

Selected Bibliography

PRIMARY WORKS

NOVELS

La región más transparente. Mexico City: Fondo de Cultura Económica, 1958.

Las buenas conciencias. Mexico City: Fondo de Cultura Económica, 1959.

La muerte de Artemio Cruz. Mexico City: Fondo de Cultura Económica, 1962.

Cambio de piel. Mexico City: Joaquín Mortiz, 1967.

La cabeza de la hidra. Barcelona: Argos, 1978.

Gringo viejo. Mexico City: Fondo de Cultura Económica, 1985.

Cristóbal nonato. Mexico City: Fondo de Cultura Económica, 1987.

La frontera de cristal: Una novela en nueve cuentos. Mexico City: Alfaguara, 1996.

Los años con Laura Díaz. Mexico City: Alfaguara, 1999.

La Silla del Águila. Mexico City: Alfaguara, 2003.

NOVELLAS AND SHORT STORIES

Aura. Mexico City: Ediciones Era, 1962.

El naranjo, o los círculos del tiempo. Mexico City: Alfaguara, 1993.

Todas las familias felices. Mexico City: Alfaguara, 2006.

ESSAYS

Nuevo tiempo mexicano. Mexico City: Aguilar, 1995.

En esto creo. Barcelona: Seix Barral, 2002.

TRANSLATIONS TO ENGLISH

Aura. Translated by Lysander Kemp. New York: Farrar, Straus and Giroux, 1968.

A Change of Skin. Translated by Sam Hileman. New York: Farrar, Straus and Giroux, 1991.

Christopher Unborn. Translated by Alfred J. Mac Adam and Carlos Fuentes. New York: Farrar, Straus and Giroux, 1991.

The Crystal Frontier: A Novel in Nine Stories. Translated by Alfred J. Mac Adam. New York: Farrar, Straus and Giroux, 1997.

The Death of Artemio Cruz. Translated by Sam Hileman. New York: Farrar, Straus and Giroux, 1964. Retranslated by Alfred J. Mac Adam. New York: Farrar, Straus and Giroux, 1991.

The Eagle's Throne. Translated by Kristina Cordero. New York: Random House, 2006.

The Good Conscience. Translated by Sam Hileman. New York: Farrar, Straus and Giroux, 1961.

The Hydra Head. Translated by Margaret Sayers Peden. New York: Farrar, Straus and Giroux, 1978.

A New Time for Mexico. Translated by Marina Gutman Castañeda and Carlos Fuentes. New York: Farrar, Straus and Giroux, 1996.

The Old Gringo. Translated by Margaret Sayers Peden and Carlos Fuentes. New York: Farrar, Straus and Giroux, 1985.

The Orange Tree. Translated by Aldred J. Mac Adam. New York: Farrar, Straus and Giroux, 1994.

This I Believe. Translated by Kristina Cordero. New York: Random House, 2005.

The Years with Laura Díaz. Translated by Alfred J. Mac Adam. New York: Farrar, Straus and Giroux, 2000.

FURTHER READING

Criticism

Brody, Robert, and Charles Rossman, eds. *Carlos Fuentes: A Critical View.* Austin: University of Texas Press, 1982, 221 p.

Collection of critical essays on Fuentes by such contributors as Lanin A. Gyurko, Margaret Sayers Peden, Richard Reeve, Gloria Durán, Manuel Durán, and Roberto González Echevarría.

Durán, Gloria B. *The Archetypes of Carlos Fuentes: From Witch to Androgyne.* Hamden, Conn.: Archon Books, 1980, 240 p.

Examines Fuentes's fiction from the point of view of myth, focusing on his depictions of such figures as witches and hermaphrodites and his use of such symbols as labyrinths, numbers, and the mandala. Though primarily focused on Fuentes's novels, covers *Aura* as well as *Los días enmascarados.*

Larson, Ross. "Archetypal Patterns in Carlos Fuentes's 'La muñeca reina.'" *Mester* 11, no. 1 (1982): 41-6.

Elucidates how "La muñeca reina" embodies the theme of the archetypal heroic quest, finding the tale appealing to modern audiences because it allows readers to partake with its antihero in an imaginative and, at times, dangerous, type of detective story.

Reeve, Richard M. "Fuentes's 'Chac Mool': Its Ancestors and Progeny." *Mester* 11, no. 1 (1982): 67-74.

Delineates Fuentes's literary precursors to "Chac Mool" and emphasizes how the tale's motif—the avenging Mexican past—influenced his later works as well as those of other Latin American and Mexican authors.

van Delden, Maarten. *Carlos Fuentes, Mexico, and Modernity.* Nashville, Tenn.: Vanderbilt University Press, 1998, 262 p.

Using Fuentes's fiction and nonfiction works, including journalistic pieces and essays, analyzes his development as a leading Latin American intellectual against the backdrop of the Mexican political, literary, and cultural landscape.

Tim Gautreaux
1947-

American novelist and short story writer.

INTRODUCTION

Since the publication of his story "Same Place, Same Things" in *The Atlantic Monthly* in 1991, Gautreaux has been recognized as a fine storyteller whose writings about rural Louisiana combine humor and pathos to express hope amidst poverty and failure. The tales in his two short-story collections, *Same Place, Same Things* (1997) and *Welding with Children* (2000), are populated with down-on-their-luck characters in strange and difficult circumstances. Questions of morality pervade these ironic tales, as do themes of miscommunication, failure, and redemption. The protagonists of Gautreaux's stories are often losers who suffer numerous indignities but manage to find their own quiet salvation. A retired professor of English and creative writing at Southeastern Louisiana University, Gautreaux has given numerous interviews in which he discusses the craft of short-story writing. Critics, comparing his short fiction to that of Flannery O'Connor and Garrison Keillor, admire Gautreaux's tightly controlled prose, gently humorous portrayal of life in the rural South, and complex depiction of human frailty.

BIOGRAPHICAL INFORMATION

Gautreaux was born in Morgan City, Louisiana—"Cajun country"—in 1947. His father, Minos Gautreaux, was a tugboat captain and his grandfather a steamboat engineer. Gautreaux grew up in Morgan City, which he has described as a "tough oil-patch town," before moving to Hammond, Louisiana. He received his undergraduate degree from Nicholls State University in Thibodaux, Louisiana, in 1969. In interviews he has joked that he intended to be a business major, but when someone stole his accounting books he switched to English. After receiving his undergraduate degree he entered the University of South Carolina, where he studied under the novelist and poet James Dickey. In South Carolina Gautreaux met and married Winborne Howell, who was studying for her master's degree in American literature. The couple returned to Louisiana in 1972 and, with a Ph.D. in English in hand, Gautreaux began teaching English at Southeastern

Louisiana University in Hammond. In 1992, his short story "Same Place, Same Things," after appearing the previous year in *The Atlantic Monthly,* was included in *Best American Short Stories.* Thereafter his work began to be published in more and more prestigious literary magazines. In the fall of 1996 he was the John and Renee Grisham Visiting Southern Writer-in-Residence at the University of Mississippi. The following year he completed his first book, a collection of stories previously published in small journals. In 1998 he was awarded the National Magazine Award for Fiction, and the following year received a National Endowment for the Arts Fellowship. In addition to his two collections of short fiction, Gautreaux has published three novels. He remained a professor of English and a writer-in-residence at Southeastern Louisiana University until his retirement in 2002. In 2005 Gautreaux received the John Dos Passos Prize, which is awarded annually to the best under-recognized American writer in the middle of his or her career. He continues to live in Hammond with his wife and two sons.

MAJOR WORKS

Almost all of Gautreax's stories take place in the rural Louisiana of his childhood. *Same Place, Same Things* depicts a small world populated by all manner of losers who seem to find themselves in most unusual predicaments and trying circumstances. These stories about working-class characters also involve a lot of machines, and as one critic has pointed out, the collection "contains the most detailed writing about workplace accidents ever found outside of an OSHA report." In "Same Place, Same Things" a water pump repairman is pursued by a beautiful young widow who electrocuted her last husband. "Waiting for the Evening News" is about a malcontented, drunken train engineer who derails a train and then flees the scene of the accident, leaving untold tragedy in his wake. "The Courtship of Merlin LeBlanc" is about a farmer who must raise his granddaughter after his own daughter dies, and realizes this is a second chance to be the father he never was to his own children. Several of Gautreaux's stories touch on his long experience in academia, as in "Navigators of Thought," about several former English teachers who must take on blue-collar jobs after being denied tenure at their universities.

Gautreaux's interest in failed lives continues in *Welding with Children,* a collection of eleven tales that deal with the problems of communication—between old and young, educated and uneducated, haves and have-nots. In "Easy Pickings" a Texan convict steals a car and drives to Louisiana, where he tries to rob an eccentric eighty-five-year-old widow who spends her day cooking spicy gumbos. Their miscommunication (he talks about robbing and killing her while she talks about stew) drives the action and humor of the story. The title story, "Welding with Children," centers on Bruton, a grandfather who babysits the children of his four unmarried daughters. When he learns that his neighbors call his car the "bastardmobile," he resolves to do better by his grandchildren, and is rewarded when the youngest child speaks his first word. "Dancing with the One-Armed Gal," another satirical look at academia, is about a hitchhiking women's studies professor, a "crippled black woman and gay feminist," who loses her job to a "gay black female double amputee from Ghana."

CRITICAL RECEPTION

Gautreaux began teaching creative writing in 1972, when he was just twenty-five, but it would be almost two decades before his own writing would reach a wide audience. His big break came with the inclusion of "Same Place, Same Things" in the 1992 edition of *Best American Short Stories;* this opened the door to publication of his other short fiction in such well-regarded magazines as *Harpers, GQ,* and *Story.* Gautreaux's first short fiction collection, *Same Place, Same Things,* met with immediate acclaim, and critics, praising his character-driven narratives about blue-collar Southerners wrestling with moral dilemmas, compared him to O'Connor. Gautreaux's second volume of stories garnered equally strong reviews. Commentators noted especially the careful crafting of his prose to express a particular Southern sensibility without resorting to sentimentality or satire. Although most critical commentary on Gautreaux's short fiction is in the form of book reviews, a few critics have written more detailed analyses of his stories. These scholars have discussed, among other things, the author's fascination with machinery, his literary influences, and the impact of his Cajun identity on his work. Like other reviewers, they have also noted the bleak situations of Gautreaux's characters and have praised his unromantic depiction of rural life in Louisiana. Commentators have paid particular attention to the affinities between Gautreaux's stories and those of O'Connor because of their Southern Gothic sensibility, use of dark humor, and portrayal of redemption in the most unlikely of situations.

PRINCIPAL WORKS

Major Works of Short Fiction

Same Place, Same Things 1997
Welding with Children 2000

Other Major Works

The Next Step in the Dance (novel) 1999
The Clearing (novel) 2003
The Missing (novel) 2009

CRITICISM

Rand Richards Cooper (review date 8 November 1996)

SOURCE: Cooper, Rand Richards. "Local Color." *Commonweal* (8 November 1996): 24-5.

[*In the following review of* Same Place, Same Things, *Cooper focuses on the rural Louisiana setting of Gautreaux's stories and notes that the author presents his characters and their circumstances—including poverty, under-education, and alcoholism—with sympathy and humor.*]

To judge by Tim Gautreaux's fiction, Thoreau's famous dictum had it half wrong: true, the mass of men do lead lives of desperation; but they are hardly quiet about it. Consider this from **"License to Steal,"** in which an unemployed, hard-drinking workingman wakes one morning to discover that his wife has gone, taking the car—and her paycheck—with her:

> Curtis put on his brown vinyl bedroom slippers and walked down to the corner to use the pay phone outside the Mudbug Café to call his son, Nookey, who worked at a sausage plant in Pochatoula.
>
> "What do you want?" Nookey yelled over the whir of a dozen grinders. "I got a pig to do here about the size of a Oldsmobile."

There's nothing hidden about the miseries on display in *Same Place, Same Things,* a collection of stories set in the rural South. A locomotive engineer named Jesse guzzles a half pint of whisky, then drives a hundred cars of propane and vinyl chloride through the Louisiana night. A stoical well-pump repairman discovers a farmer dead by a freak accident and a bored and flirtatious wife who ominously doesn't much seem to care. A widowed strawberry farmer left to raise his infant granddaughter when the girl's mother dies in a plane crash gives her shotgun shells to play with as toys.

It's hard to know whether to find such doubtful men and dire predicaments funny, scary, or pathetic. These are lives harshly circumscribed by poverty, under-education, and alcohol, and Gautreaux inspects them sympathetically, but with a rueful, hardscrabble humor. When Leblanc, the strawberry farmer, needing help with the baby, undertakes to head out to a bar woman-hunting, he showers, shaves, and reaches for a green bottle on the bathroom shelf, only to slap his face with foot liniment his late wife bought years before. Gautreaux's antiheroes prove magnificently adept at failure.

Theirs is a world in which work—when it can be found—alternates petty humiliations with spectacular mishaps. *Same Place, Same Things* contains the most detailed writing about workplace accidents ever found outside of an OSHA report; it's a chilling study of how vehicles and heavy machinery get converted into lethal weapons. Tugboats sink; gravel trucks race downhill toward stopped schoolbuses; the train carrying deadly chemicals leaps off the track, igniting a whole town.

Carelessness and hard drinking feature prominently in these wrecks, along with a paradoxical sense of invulnerability. Habituated to irrelevance, unable to imagine being able to make a dent in the world, Gautreaux's protagonists have been made dangerous by their own deep impotence. "The sense of being invisible made Jesse think he could not be taken seriously, which was why he never voted, hardly ever renewed his driver's license, and paid attention in church only once a year at revival time." These stories shrewdly trace the roots of irresponsibility, not to a heedless assertion of self, but rather its opposite, a literal lack of self-image. With special acuteness Gautreaux captures the stunned disbelief of little men as they are precipitated, horribly and against their own wishes, into mattering.

Tim Gautreaux's prose strikes few notes, but strikes them true and clear. There's the terse descriptive vigor of **"Died and Gone to Vegas,"** a Stephen Crane-like fable of liars' poker on a dredging ship anchored in the Mississippi:

> The steel door next to the starboard triple-expansion engine opened, letting in a wash of frigid air around the day-fireman, pilot, deckhand, and welder who came into the big room cursing and clapping the cold out of their clothes. Through the door the angry whitecaps of Southwest Pass raced down the Mississippi, bucking into the tarnished Gulf sky.

More often, the order of the day is rueful humor. Boisterous farm idioms serve his characters' steady habit of lamentation ("We didn't know no more about raising children than a goat knows about flying"). One hears tones of Flannery O'Connor; but Gautreaux is a little less mordant, his humor more doleful than baleful.

> . . . His grandson was living with him again, complaining of the evils of capitalism, eating his food, using all the hot water in the mornings. . . . Lenny would never hold a job because he suffered from inborn disrespect for anybody engaged in business. Everybody was stupid. All businessmen were crooks. At twenty-five his grandson had the economic sense of a sixty-year-old Russian peasant.

Unlike O'Connor, Gautreaux doesn't make you feel his characters necessarily deserve their lot in life; it's enough that they're stuck with it.

These hefty portions of rural working class life are served up with a distinct Cajun spice. The men in *Same Place, Same Things* have names like Robichaux and Lejeune; they sit around all night playing *bourre,* then wake in the morning for two links of *boudin* and a pot of grits; when something is creepy they get *les frissons.* In bars on their way to the plant to look for work they stop to snack on pickled eggs and pigs lips. Living hell is getting the car radio stuck on a public radio station, where the soprano, one remarks, "sounds like a tomcat hung up in a fan belt." Armadillos forage in the kitchen. It feels like a foreign country—one steeped in haplessness, where even the towns, places like Gumwood and Grand Crapaud, sound like insults—and the inhabitants know it. Curtis's son Nookey explains why his mother left: "Said she was tired of living in Louisiana with somebody didn't bring home no money. Said she wanted to move to the United States."

Once upon a time, regionalism wasn't merely an aspect of American culture; it was our culture. It is now beating a rapid retreat, driven relentlessly by Walmart, video megachains, the O.J. trial, and a host of other forces which exert a profoundly homogenizing influence on our literal and imaginative landscapes, and on our language, too. "I ain't heard nobody around here talk like you in a while," says a woman in one of Gautreaux's stories, to a man all the way from distant Missouri. Robustly local in its settings, speech, and folkways, *Same Place, Same Things* creates a vividly realized milieu. To the characters busy making a mess of their lives there, Tim Gautreaux offers neither transcendence nor escape, merely the comforts of home—sloppy sinners, yes, but sinners in their own world. For the rest of us, these stories make for welcome relief from the blandness of McWorld; they bring reassuring evidence of the continuing existence of places away from the big place where, increasingly, we all live.

Tim Gautreaux with Katie Bolick and David Watta (interview date 14 March 1997)

SOURCE: Gautreaux, Tim, Katie Bolick, and David Watta. "A Conversation with Tim Gautreaux." *Atlantic Unbound* (14 March 1997): n.p.

[*In the following interview, Gautreaux discusses location in his short fiction and his status as a "Southern" writer.*]

In a world characterized by increased transience, Tim Gautreaux is a writer with a strong sense of place. His accurate prose, both visual—"a yellow butterfly playing in a clump of pigweed"—and vernacular—"Whoo. Grendaddy can bust a move"—is culled from a lifetime spent keenly observing the South, beyond the anesthesia of cultural homogeneity.

"*Welding with Children*" (March, 1997, *Atlantic*), is Gautreaux's third *Atlantic* story. His fiction has appeared in, among other journals, *Harper's, GQ,* and *Story,* and been selected for publication in *New Stories From the South* and *Best American Short Stories.* The recipient of a National Endowment for the Arts fellowship and the National Magazine Award for Fiction, Gautreaux has directed the creative writing program at Southern Louisiana University for more than two decades. St. Martin's Press has recently published his book of short stories, **Same Place, Same Things** (1996), and will issue his novel, *Machinery of Dreams,* early next year.

Gautreaux recently spoke with Atlantic Unbound's Katie Bolick and David Watta.

[*Bolick and Watta*]: *The majority of your writing is based in Southern Louisiana, where you have spent a great deal of your life. Although location never overwhelms your characters, it certainly determines some, if not all, of who they are and will be. Does the same hold for you as well?*

[Gautreaux]: I think every writer is limited by where he's from, particularly someone who has spent his entire life in one region. This is, of course, a mixed blessing. You get to know a place very well but you don't know others at all. A writer who has lived only in Nebraska, for example, has to write about Nebraska. This is not a problem to be lamented but it is a determiner of who your characters will be.

What would you say the differences are, if any, between the preoccupations of a "Southern" writer and other American writers? And how do you feel your work fits into the Southern tradition?

I don't really understand what a "Southern" writer is. Writers just tend to write about their environment. If the South tends to be more poverty stricken, or has a less-educated population, or the politicians seem more arrogant, or there's a more intense devotion to religion, that's just the way it is.

Perhaps the only difference I can perceive between a "Southern" writer and a non-Southern writer is that maybe the "Southern" writer loves where he lives more than other writers. When you read Eudora Welty or Walker Percy you sense they really enjoy the details of where they live, warts and all. This quality doesn't seem to surface as much with non-Southern writers.

I would rather be classified in the *Frontier* tradition than the "Southern" tradition, because I can see elements of the old tall tale and frontier humor in my writing. Much of my early reading was devoted to folklore and the likes of Mark Twain. Tall tales, with their hyperbole and outlandish plots, seem to have had an effect on my writing.

I hearken back to the days when television was a minimal presence in American life. People used to sit around and tell tales, particularly the older relatives who would come over and entertain with stories. This is something that Earnest Gaines writes about—he used memories of his aunts sitting on the porch and telling stories to provide the rhythms for his characters' dialogue. For me, it was a little different: I listened to retired tug-boat captains and oil-field workers try to outdo each others in stories.

The themes you choose to write about seem to rise from regional roots to encompass universal concerns. Which come first, the characters or the themes?

Themes rise out of character organically. A writer who sits down and thinks "I'm going to deal with a theme," rather than "I'm going to tell a story," is not a fiction writer but an essayist in disguise. I think no matter what character a writer chooses he's going to write about the same themes, because a writer's favorite thematic concerns arise no matter what the story line is, no matter what characters are chosen. I just set a couple characters against each other on the first page, and next thing I know, the story is "about" some idea that interests me—and that is the theme.

Your characters are so real and so vividly rendered that they seem to live on long after the story is finished. How do you approach characterization?

When people say, "Your characters are memorable," they are remembering what the characters say and how they say it. For description, as far as characters are concerned, I try to use unique details rather than a bland inventory of a character's experience. I like to do that in a very minimalist fashion—two or three carefully chosen details that quickly give the reader an idea of what this character is about. I pay a lot of attention to little body movements: the way people move their hands, position their feet, what they do with a cigarette. Movement becomes a language unto itself.

The names you use are interesting—Moonbeam, Nu-Nu, Pig, Bullfinch, Fernest, to name but a few. How and why do you choose the names you do?

I have no particular method in mind when I choose names. Striking names are hard for a reader to forget. But the names that appear in my stories are the types of names found in rural Louisiana.

Most of your stories seem to pivot on moral questions. Could you talk about moral weight as an aspect of fiction, and its importance in your work?

I consider myself to be a Catholic writer in the tradition of Walker Percy. If a story does not deal with a moral question, I don't think it's much of a story.

You have been both a professor and editor while continuing to write. How do these different roles inform your fiction? How justified do you feel about asking others to revise and how do you feel about changes that are suggested to you?

When you teach creative writing, you're always telling people what to do, and this constant discussion of technique has an effect on your own writing. When you're an editor, you're micro-managing other people's manuscripts, and it's similar to being a teacher. What you end up telling the person whose manuscript you're looking at is something you're basically teaching or telling yourself. It's a learning process both ways.

As far as feeling justified about asking others to revise, my take is, "How can I help this person to make a better manuscript?" That's the sole thought I have in my head when I read others people's work. With regard to recommendations about my own work, I generally always follow them. If a writer or editor takes the time to make a recommendation, he must care about my work and want to make it better. If someone tells me to cut 1,000 words, I'll do it in a heart beat. It's okay for story writing to be a collaborative art.

How would you describe your writing habits?

I'm very erratic in the way I write. I have no particular schedule I adhere to. I simply write whenever the urge hits. I compose on a word processor, print out a first draft, and read for sentence structure. After edits I show it to someone (generally my wife or a graduate student I've worked with), and then I make five additional passes—each pass lasting about two and a half hours—before the manuscript is sent out for publication. On the first pass, I concentrate solely on language—vocabulary and authenticity, that is. The second pass consists of looking for all the tropes, metaphors, and similes in order to make sure they're integral to the story. Then, after letting it age a few days, I go through a third time and check all the punctuation and thin out anything extraneous. In the fourth pass I expand on the material still there. The final pass is an edit of anything that has been added. The process is a bit mechanical but very effective; it produces a clean manuscript.

You once wrote, about teaching fiction: "I'm big on telling students to incorporate their own fascinations into the fabric of their writing, whether it's mounting butterflies or collecting toilet bowls. I've also taught them that they should write about what goes on in their own back yards." What's your approach to the teaching of fiction?

What I do with students is try to put them in touch with where they're from. Everybody's heard the cliché, "Write what you know," and as is the case with most clichés, there's a great deal of truth in it. One of my big problems with beginning writers is that they act like they're all from Los Angeles or New York, and that's because they've been bombarded by everything from MTV to Burger King ads to Hollywood stereotypes, all originally from those two places. My job is to tell them that no, this way of thinking is inaccurate. They've been given a little piece of territory all their own, consisting of their family and neighborhood. If they're going to write, they've got to write about characters based on people they know: aunts, uncles, the eccentric guy down the block, and they've got to write using the unique language patterns of that landscape they own. Once I get them to use their own culture, everything starts to gel: the way people talk, the way things look, the way people value things.

Tim Gautreaux with Robert Siegel and Elizabeth Arnold (interview date 15 December 1997)

SOURCE: Gautreaux, Tim, Robert Siegel, and Elizabeth Arnold. "Best American Short Stories." *NPR, All Things Considered* (15 December 1997): n.p.

[In the following interview, which originally aired on National Public Radio, Gautreaux discusses the discipline, balance, and control required of the short story form.]

[Siegel]: This is ALL THINGS CONSIDERED. I'm Robert Siegel.

[Arnold]: And I'm Elizabeth Arnold.

A consistent top seller during the holiday season is the Best American Short Stories. *Every year since 1915, it's provided a roundup of the best short fiction to have appeared in print the previous 12 months.*

About 100 stories make the first cut, then they are passed on to a guest editor. This year it was writer E. Annie Proulx). Among the 21 stories she chose for the 1997 anthology is **"Little Frogs in a Ditch"** *by Tim Gautreaux.*

Gautreaux has taught creative writing at Southeastern Louisiana University for the last 25 years and is recognized as a master of the short story.

[Gautreaux]: I think something that gets out of the box pretty quickly is one thing I try to produce; something that grabs the reader. Russ Tills said that every story starts with something called moving action, something out of the ordinary happening in a person's life. And that point is where many great artists, down through literary history, start.

Shakespeare, for example, starts *in medias res*. And that's what I like to do, start right with that change in a character's life, that out-of-the- ordinary thing that happens to a person.

[Arnold]: Although it seems attractive at the outset, I would think that the short story would actually be a difficult literary form, requiring more in the way of discipline and balance and control than a longer work.

Well, this is true. Every line, every sentence has to have some sort of a connection with what you're trying to do in the way of theme or in the way of the narrative.

A short story—I like to tell students that a short story is like an automobile engine. There are no redundant parts. If you lift up your hood and you look at your car, you don't find extra spark plugs scotch-taped to the side of the engine . . .

(LAUGHTER)

. . . with a note from someone at the factory saying, "we just found this on the floor. Thought you'd like to have it."

(LAUGHTER)

Everything in the story has to have some kind of a function. And this means that what determines a good story is not so much what's in it, but what's not in it. It's important to know what to cut.

[Arnold]: You know, you must look at a lot of students' work. In the introduction to this collection that E. Annie Proulx writes, she talks about the stories that didn't make it into the collection.

And she writes, "some were weak anecdotes, not stories at all. Not a few were written in chatty, slangy, conversational style, a kind of TV dialogue-like jabber, characterized by short, hard little sentences with the rhythm of a woodpecker in a dead tree."

Does this sound familiar to you?

Yes. It's hard to turn students on to authentic dialogue, to make them pay attention to the way people around them actually speak—their aunts and their uncles and the people in their neighborhood—and to make them realize that people in Minneapolis do have a slightly different way of speaking than people in any other place, even in the Midwest.

But students have absorbed so many—really tens of thousands of hours of television script dialogue by the time they're 18 years old that this is embedded in them, the fact that everybody talks the way Hollywood script writers had them talk.

[Arnold]: Hmm.

And they don't really listen to the people they grow up with.

[Arnold]: How do you approach a story? I mean, let's talk about the one in this collection, **"Little Frogs in a Ditch."** *Where did that come from?*

Stories very often are found things. That one came to me entire while I was overhearing a radio broadcast. I listen to a lot of local talk radio.

[Arnold]: Un-huh.

And one morning the subject was the meanest trick you ever played on anyone as a kid. And this fella called up and said that he actually took an ad out in the local newspaper saying that he could sell homing pigeons, instructions included, $10.

And what he was doing is actually just getting ordinary pigeons off somebody's shed roof and selling them as homing pigeons with this incredibly difficult regimen of how to train the bird. It took two weeks.

Well, by the time the person bought the bird and made a fool out of himself by doing this, they wouldn't bring it back, complaining. And of course, when they turned the pigeon loose, it would never show up again. It would disappear.

I thought, "what an incredibly mean thing to do. And what would it be like to have someone like that in your family?" And that was the beginning of that story. It was totally found. And many of my stories are like that.

[*Arnold*]: *What do you tell students who are struggling with the short story form?*

That it takes a lot of practice. It takes a long time to learn the trade. And it's an art form, just like ice skating or painting. You don't get good overnight.

It takes a long time. It takes a lot of rejection. And I try to teach them that they should thrive on rejection.

[*Arnold*]: *One last question. How do you write? I mean, are you disciplined? Are you lazy and sporadic? Are you—do you sit down in the morning? How do you write?*

I write a lot late at night. And basically, my method is rewriting. I'll come out with a first draft and, of course, I'll go over it and then cut it. Everything that's extraneous goes.

And then I'll go over it, sentence by sentence, looking for structure of each individual sentence. Then I'll put it aside and go over it, looking at all the tropes—the metaphors, the similes, everything in the way of figurative language—to make sure everything is right there.

And then, of course, I send it—I give it to my wife. And she reads it and tells me what she thinks of it. And several people see it.

And then I set it aside and let it age like a cheese or something and then a month later look at it. And what I thought was ready to send off to my agent still has a lot of problems. And I'll go over it again.

And that's kind of, really, a brief version of what I do to a story. I make—I mean, I make specialized passes. I—and it—the myopia of it helps me really make a story take on a certain type of polish.

That's one thing—students think they can very often turn out an excellent story on one pass, but that's not the case with me, anyway.

[*Arnold*]: *Tim Gautreaux, thanks so much for talking with us.*

You're very welcome.

[*Arnold*]: *Tim Gautreaux is a writer who lives in Hammond, Louisiana. His stories appear in numerous literary collections, including this year's* Best American Short Stories.

He joined us from WEZB in New Orleans.

The Tampa Tribune (review date 17 October 1999)

SOURCE: Review of *Welding with Children. The Tampa Tribune* (17 October 1999): 4.

[*In the following review, the anonymous critic praises Gautreaux's light touch in his stories in* Welding with Children *and admires the author's ability to offer an intimate and honest description of rural Louisiana culture.*]

Tim Gautreaux has assembled a delightful collection of short stories about outlaws and inlaws and families and strangers and small communities in his latest book, **Welding with Children.** Set in the backwoods of south Louisiana, where he lives, the stories describe a culture that exists at times separately from the rest of the world. Here the family names are Boudreaux and Barrilleaux and LeBlanc, and the characters drive old John Deere tractors and speak Cajun French to their chickens. Here everyone knows everyone else's business, and they know better than to come in to a bourree game with the jack dry.

Gautreaux's stories are full of the Southern charm of his previous novel, *The Next Step in the Dance,* but they lack the occasional heavy-handedness that showed up in that novel's plot. In fact, these plots are stitched together with the grace of a storyteller who can combine a variety of elements and then add just the right detail or just the right dialect at just the right moment.

In **"Easy Pickings,"** an ex-con from Texas drives into a remote part of a south Louisiana parish (or county) in his stolen car and preys on little old ladies, using a Bowie knife. "His name was Marvin, but he called himself Big Blade because the name made him feel other than what he was: small, petty, and dull." Somewhere near Grand Crapaud—to the south is marsh and alligators, to the north, rice fields—Big Blade encounters the widowed 85-year-old Doris Landreneaux.

Listen to Landreneaux address Big Blade: "You with the crawfish drew on you throat, you trying to scare me wit' a knife? Like I ain't use to death? I break a chicken neck three time a week and my brother, he got shot dead next to me at the St. Landry Parish fair in 1936 and all my husband's brother got killed in that German war and that Lodrigue boy died with his head in my apron the day the tractor run over him, course he was putting on the plow with the damn thing in gear and even the priest said it wasn't too bright to get plowed under by your own plow. . . ."

Landreneaux and her bourree-playing friends just down the road give this story a twist that recalls the outcome of O. Henry's "The Ransom of Red Chief."

In **"Good for the Soul,"** a brandy-tippling Father Ledet is called one evening to hear the confession of a man dying of emphysema who has never actually entered his church. On his way to Clyde Arceneaux's hospital room, Ledet plows his car into Mamie Barrilleaux's at an intersection and gets a DWI. Eventually he loses his driver's license in traffic court. Meanwhile, Arceneaux is feeling remorse for stealing a car from his brother-in-law 10 years ago. He confesses to the crime and admits he wants to return the car—but he doesn't want his brother-in-law to know who stole it. Arceneaux asks Ledet to drive the stolen car back to his brother-in-law for him. Father Ledet discovers that he cannot always make forgiveness happen, but sometimes he can save a soul.

"Sorry Blood" is a poignant story about a man who's losing his memory to old age. Etienne LeBlanc, a retired farmer from St. Mary's Parish, emerges from a Wal-Mart one day only to forget where he is and what his car looks like. A strange man named Andy poses as his son and calls him "Ted." Andy drives off with a confused Etienne and forces him to dig a ditch in Andy's backyard.

"Had his memory come back," writes Gautreaux of LeBlanc, "he would have known he was too old for this work. He leaned on the polished wood of the shovel handle and looked at his straight line, almost remembering something, dimly aware that where he was, he had not been before. His memory was like a long novel left open and ruffled by a breeze to a different chapter further along."

LeBlanc tries to reconstruct his memory through sight, sound, touch. Even in his lost state, he knows that his "son" is a sorry human being and that the woman who's married to the man is capable of murder. He remembers love as a sensation. When he gets a splinter caught in his hand, a light goes on: "Paper, the old man thought. Shelf paper. His wife would have never put anything in a cabinet without first putting down fresh paper over the wood, and then something came back like images on an out-of-focus movie screen

when the audience claps and whistles and roars and the projectionist wakes up and gives his machine a twist, and life, movement, and color unite in a razory picture, and at once he had remembered his wife and his children and the venerable Oldsmobile he had driven to the discount store."

In **"The Piano Tuner,"** Michelle Placervent is the end of the line for her old rich family of sugar farmers, "Creole planters who always had just enough money and influence to make themselves disliked in a poor community." The piano tuner, Claude, pities this depressed middle-aged woman living alone in her falling-down house and helps her get a job playing piano in a lounge. But Placervent is capable of mood swings and unpredictable behaviors that strike Claude—and others—as bizarre. The story's turning point is a moment of unbelievable hilarity and surprise that combines all the elements of Placervent's mysterious character and strange circumstances. You don't know whether to laugh or cry.

"Welding with Children" is the story of a man, an underemployed welder, whose life of neglect has come back to haunt him. While babysitting his four grandchildren—the children of his unmarried daughters—he overhears an acquaintance call his car the "bastardmobile." He's determined to do better by his grandchildren, though, and he begins by unplugging the television and reading to them. An astonishing thing happens when the baby utters his first word.

Like Flannery O'Connor, Gautreaux knows how to portray, faithfully, these good country people. He speaks in the manner of a south Louisianian, and he knows his way around their homes and their kitchens and their churches and their communities. And whether he's taking on the alcoholic parish priest or the failed grandfather or the elderly ladies anteing up at the card table, his stories celebrate, with great humor, human strengths and weaknesses and our everlasting capacity for hope.

Hal Jacobs (review date 18 November 1999)

SOURCE: Jacobs, Hal. Review of *Welding with Children,* by Tim Gautreaux. *The Atlanta Journal-Constitution* (18 November 1999): K13.

[*In the following review of* Welding with Children, *Jacobs likens Gautreaux's style to that of the Midwestern humorist Garrison Keillor, but notes that Gautreaux's stories are more edgy.*]

The verdict: Pitch-perfect stories in a minor key.

Move Garrison Keillor's Lake Wobegon stories to Louisiana, add heat and Tabasco, and the result would be Tim Gautreaux's *Welding with Children.*

These stories have all the Keillor ingredients: humor, warmth, irony, suspense and endings that are either uplifting or poignant but never bleak or indifferent. These are stories about good, working-class folks going about their business and stumbling over situations that life hasn't prepared them for. If Gautreaux (*Same Place, Same Things, The Next Step in the Dance*) has more edge to his stories, one explanation is that his Cajuns must deal with three opposing forces: their individual codes of ethics, the law of physics that says natural objects follow the path of least resistance, and the long, stupefying hot days and nights of a Louisiana summer.

In the title story, Bruton, a welder and shade-tree mechanic with four daughters who are in the habit of regularly dropping off his four grandchildren, decides to get his act together after he drives up to the Pak-a-Sak with his grandkids and overhears two geezers call his Chevrolet Caprice a "bastardmobile." He realizes that it's too late to change his daughters, "four dirty blondes with weak chins from St. Helena Parish (who) thought they lived in a Hollywood soap opera." So he sits under the tree of knowledge at the courthouse, talks with one of the village elders and receives the following words of wisdom: Join the Methodists, keep the grandchildren with you as much as possible and clean up your yard.

In other words, Bruton learns, "Everything worth doing hurts like hell."

And he's not the only one who receives that message. So does the parish priest in **"Good for the Soul."** He reluctantly honors a dying man's last request, which involves returning an eight-cylinder Toronado with no muffler that the man stole from a neighbor more than 10 years ago. So does the retired maintenance foreman in **"Resistance"**—he helps the emotionally battered girl living next door with her science project on resistors. Anybody who ever prayed for last-minute help with a science project is guaranteed a lump in the throat after reading this one.

In **"Misuse of Light"** a camera store clerk buys a '50s-era Rolleiflex from a young woman, develops a roll of film he finds inside and becomes intrigued by the image of a beautiful woman leaning against a ship railing. His interests lead him to unraveling a family tragedy that involves the camera and the last shot of the woman on the roll of film.

In **"The Piano Tuner,"** a woman from a family of Creole planters, the last of the line, depends on the kindness of a piano tuner to leave her house and take her place in the world, which turns out to be a piano player in a motel lounge.

History of small places. That's the minor key these stories are written in. When time moves slow, memory looms large. And if you lose your memory, you may wander around a Wal-Mart parking lot until a driver slouched behind the wheel of a parked Ford sedan notices you and hisses, "What's wrong with you, gramps?" That's what happens to retired farmer Etienne LeBlanc in **"Sorry Blood."**

"'Do you know me?' the old man asked in a voice that was soft and lost.

"The driver looked at him a long time, his eyes moving down his body as though he were a column of figures. 'Yeah, Dad,' he said at last. 'Don't you remember me?' He put an unfiltered cigarette in his mouth and lit it with a kitchen match. 'I'm your son.'"

What happens next should be added to the subgenre of Southern fiction titled **"What Happens When Nice People Meet Sorry White Trash."** On a scale of 1 to 10, with James Dickey's "Deliverance" being 10 and Flannery O'Connor's collected works coming in at 7, **"Sorry Blood"** deserves a solid 5. The lesson for LeBlanc is simple: A life without memories is a life of nightmares and strangers.

Some of these stories by Gautreaux, a native of Louisiana who teaches creates writing at Southeastern Louisiana University, first appeared in *The Atlantic Monthly, Harper's, Ploughshares* and *Georgia Review.* One story that hasn't been published elsewhere, and should get big laughs from creative writing seminar attendees on both sides of the table is **"The Black Cat Writers' Conference."** It's a jaundiced look at the backwaters of the publishing ecosystem, but, even here, Gautreaux can't avoid leaving behind a poignant message.

"What makes good writing?" asks aspiring writer Brad Sandle, "a neat, tanned little man who'd always wanted to write something more significant than contracts and briefs."

The answer is: "God or hard work."

In this collection of short stories, Gautreaux's hard work is obvious, and God is never far away.

Harvey Grossinger (review date 19 December 1999)

SOURCE: Grossinger, Harvey. Review of *Welding with Children. The Houston Chronicle* (19 December 1999): 14.

[*In the following review, Grossinger praises the stories in* Welding with Children *and calls Gautreaux a master of idiom and tone.*]

With the publication of this second collection of stories, we can put Tim Gautreaux at the top of a growing list of gifted short-story writers at work in America today. The hope here is that his fiction will reach a wider audience.

Acoustics are at the center of Gautreaux's aesthetics. He is a master of idiom and tone, his sundry, clashing voices a yoking of frivolous vulgarity with the modulated and irresolute desires of the innermost self.

The circumference of his chosen landscape embraces the back roads and cypress swamps of Louisiana, a grimy topography of ramshackle properties and contrary souls where dilapidated car engines, bald truck tires and rusted-out zinc washing machines hang from dead willow-oak branches.

The brilliant title story maps this messy geography in unflinching detail. An addled grandfather named Bruton is charged with caring for his four wild grandchildren. The young children have names such as Nu-Nu and Tammynette.

Each belongs to one of Bruton's four unmarried daughters, the oldest of whom has also dropped off a broken bed rail she wants her father to weld. Bruton wonders, "Now, what the hell you can do in a bed that'll cause the end of a iron rail to break off is beyond me."

Working with the children underfoot proves impossible, so Bruton drives them down to the Pak-a-Sak for Icees. As his car rolls to a stop, he hears Mr. Fordlyson, a geezer older than himself, say, "Here comes Bruton and his bastardmobile."

The incident stings Bruton to the quick and leaves him feeling depressed and isolated. He thinks of the inbred nature and intolerance of his community and imagines that his family must be the object of much cruel gossip. He feels he must do something to educate and civilize his grandchildren, since he clearly failed with his daughters.

"The girls grew up watching cable and videos every night, and that's where they got their view of the world," Bruton concludes, "and that's why four dirty blondes with weak chins from St. Helena Parish thought they lived in a Hollywood soap opera."

He forces himself to try reading the Bible to the youngsters, all about Adam and Eve and the Garden of Eden and then the story of Abraham and Isaac. When Bruton asks them what it all means, Tammynette yells that Abraham is just like O. J. Simpson.

Glum and out of patience, Bruton contemplates packing the kids up and heading west to start over. He finally manages to calm them down by reading from a storybook bought 20 years ago for one of his daughters.

> But while I was reading, this blue feeling got me. I was thinking, What's the use? I'm just one old man with a little brown book of Bible stories and doggy-hero book. How can that compete with daily MTV, kids' programs that make big people look like fools, the Playboy Channel, the shiny magazines their mammas and their boyfriends leave around the house, magazines like Me, and Self, and Love Guides, and rental movies where people kill one another with no more thought than it would take to swat a fly, nothing at all like what Abraham suffered before he raised that knife?

When he sees old Fordlyson again, he makes sure the old buzzard knows that what he said was mean.

Bruton tells him he's already raised his own kids, and now he needs help with those grandchildren, not spite and meanness. Fordlyson orders him to make sure those kids go to a decent church, and he further directs Bruton to clean up his shameful yard.

When Bruton says he doesn't know what that has to do with it, Fordlyson says, "It's got everything to do with everything. . . . Everything worth doing hurts like hell." This counsel incites an expunging of filth of near-allegorical dimension.

There are other pearls in this collection. In **"Sorry Blood,"** the frail and disoriented Etienne LeBlanc loses his way in a crowded Wal-Mart parking lot. Unable to recognize his car, he roams around, "aimless as a string of smoke."

He is abducted by a shifty loafer who calls himself Andy and who convinces the older man that he isn't Etienne but Ted Williams (yes, the Ted Williams) and Andy's father.

Andy steals Etienne's wallet, drives him back to his shabby property and convinces him to dig a long drainage ditch while Andy drinks margaritas and dozes under the shade trees.

Even in his fog, Etienne knows something is very wrong. The story takes on a keener moral edge as the bewildered Etienne studies Andy more closely and grows to despise the slovenly excuse for a son he must have raised.

Etienne validates his false patrimony with an act that ultimately enables him to recover his real family.

"Easy Pickings" concerns a collection of Cajun retirees who manage to thwart the assault and kidnapping of a neighbor, eccentric 85-year-old Doris Landreneaux, who spends her days cooking spicy gumbos and stews.

The robber is a bungling, small-time Houston hustler who calls himself Big Blade. He is outfoxed by his prey, who warns him: "Like I ain't use to death? I break a chicken neck three times a week."

That's all the foreshadowing a careful reader requires to discern what will befall pinheaded Big Blade. The fierce energy of this story comes from its vivid details and its pungent Cajun repartee.

"The Piano Tuner" is the most carefully restrained story in the collection, a masterpiece of delicate shading and mood that ponders the psychic incongruities and limitations of change.

Michelle Placervent, a Creole recluse, asks Claude, the parish piano tuner, to come out and tune her George Steck upright.

Michelle lives in a big, decaying house hidden in the grubby cane fields south of town. Claude doesn't understand why a good-looking woman in her 30s who has a little money to spend chooses to live like a hermit in a 150-year-old house. He remembers that "Michelle was the end of the line for the Placervents, Creole planters who always had just enough money and influence to make themselves disliked in a poor community."

Claude knows Michelle graduated from college with a music degree years ago, came home to care for her dying mother and alcoholic father, and never left the house after that.

Claude is a kind and generous man, and he is moved when he hears Michelle play the piano. He is "the kind of person who hated for anything to go to waste and thought the saddest thing in the world was a fine instrument that nobody ever touched."

He takes it upon himself to ferry Michelle back into the world. Their odd friendship forms the wide-ranging heart of this multitextured story. But Gautreaux is too astute an artist simply to leaven his tale with human need and empathy—life is more complicated than that.

The piano tuner convinces a friend to give Michelle a job in the dim cocktail lounge of a Lafayette motel. She bewilders the weary drinkers with dreamy renditions of Patsy Cline, Scott Joplin and Franz Liszt, and Claude wonders whether he's "done the right thing by turning a Creole queen into a motel lounge pianist."

You'll have to read this marvelous collection to find out.

Erin McGraw (review date winter 2000)

SOURCE: McGraw, Erin. "Book Reviews." *The Georgia Review* 65, no. 4 (winter 2000): 727-37.

[*In the following excerpt, McGraw reviews* Welding with Children, *admiring especially its dark humor and tightly controlled language.*]

Welding with Children is Tim Gautreaux's second book of stories, following the well-received ***Same Place, Same Things.*** In that first collection, which chronicles hard, shabby, often raucous working-class lives in southern Louisiana, Gautreaux established himself as a writer with impressive range, able to depict scenes of cold violence and of broad, howling humor with equal skill.

If anything, the darkness is darker and the humor quite a bit broader in ***Welding with Children.*** Gautreaux has claimed his material, and his sense of ownership shows. Characters move with clear motivation; although there's plenty of unhappiness, there isn't a scrap of existential indecision in these pages. Even the drifters, the disappointed, the addled and unemployed and one-armed, know where they think they're going and how they aim to get there, so their narratives move with considerable purpose. A Tim Gautreaux story is very hard to put down.

One of the reasons is Gautreaux's vigorous prose. **"Rodeo Parole"** begins,

> Four inmates walked out into the hot, powdery dirt of the corral to sit in folding chairs at a neon-orange card table. Where they dragged their boots, the soil smoked. Jimmy, the burglar, was the youngest, a tall, bent rail of a man with scrambled-egg hair and a barbecued, narrow face. He didn't want to sit at the table under the blowtorch sun with his palms down on the flimsy surface, waiting for the pain, but the others had told him that if he stayed with them longest, if they all could just sit there with their hands on the table while it happened, they could win, and the reporters would put their pictures in the statewide paper, where the parole board would see what good Joes they were, brave competitors, winners. Two members of last year's winning team were free already.

In just five sentences Gautreaux establishes the idea of a convict rodeo (resembling the annual event at the Louisiana state penitentiary in Angola), introduces his main character, sets the scene, and begins the story's action. But none of these essential tasks is as engaging as Gautreaux's writing. The smoking soil, Jimmy's barbecued face, the paragraph's long penultimate sentence set off by the punchy final one—all of these combine to give the scene a terrific sharpness.

Gautreaux rarely misses an opportunity for fresh, sometimes brilliant phrases that he tosses off with the deftness of a juggler. The porch of a neglected house is "sagging into a long frown," summer air in Louisiana is a "sopping, buggy, overheated funk," the sound of a shovel hitting a woman's head forms "a white scar" in an observer's brain. Such consistently rich language is tonic, if often shocking. Even when the action is violent, the clarity of the prose urges a reader to continue.

In the collection's best pieces, Gautreaux uses his high-octane language to fuel interactions that are stark and surprising, usually centering on that well-known Southern preoccupation, human behavior—what Flannery O'Connor called "manners." He writes about how people should act, and how people really do act. The gap is wide.

"Sorry Blood" (the title also recalls O'Connor) begins with an old man walking out of a Wal-Mart and finding himself unable to remember the look or location of his car, what he was doing, or his name. Tales from the point of view of Alzheimer's sufferers are not uncommon, but the action of "Sorry Blood" is extraordinary, as the man is caught up by a sharp-eyed opportunist named Andy who sees in this confused old man an ideal yard boy. Andy just happens to have a ditch at home that needs digging. The plot links moral outrage to wild, angry humor, every bit the equal of O'Connor's in the depravity of its characters. And like O'Connor's, Gautreaux's vision doesn't flinch.

His control is not so perfect in every story. "Easy Pickings," as its title foretells, descends to mere slapstick after an uncharacteristically flat-footed description of its main character: "His name was Marvin, but he called himself Big Blade because the name made him feel other than what he was: small, petty, and dull." The action that follows does not challenge this judgment, as Marvin, thinking to make an uncontested robbery, is trapped by eighty-five-year-old Mrs. Landreneaux and her bourée-playing partners. And the movement of "Good for the Soul," in which an alcoholic priest finds himself compelled by his weakness and his profession to commit larger and larger misdemeanors, trades genuine characterization for broad, dumbed-down comedy: fiction that begins like Graham Greene's ends like Fannie Flagg's.

But these stories are exceptions, and even they are fun to read. Most of *Welding with Children* is marked by a supercharged prose matched by a highly engaged vision. Characters here battle with all their strength over issues of moral substance. At the end of "Sorry Blood" the main character feels his memory swim back to him as he remembers his car, his grandson Etienne asleep behind its wheel, the woman he's just seen murdered. Through the car's open window, he leans over Etienne:

He knew him, and his mind closed like a fist on this grandson and everything else, even his wife fading in his arms, even the stunned scowl of the copper-headed woman as she was hammered into the gravel. As if memory could be a decision, he accepted it all, knowing now that the only thing worse than reliving nightmares until the day he died was enduring a life full of strangers. He closed his eyes and called on the old farm in his head to stay where it was, remembered its cypress house, its flat and misty lake of sugarcane keeping the impressions of a morning wind.

The image is an apt one for this accomplished book: the tough stalks bending to hold a new and distinct shape.

L. Lamar Nisly (essay date fall 2002)

SOURCE: Nisly, L. Lamar. "A Sacramental Science Project in Tim Gautreaux's 'Resistance.'" *Logos* 5, no. 4 (fall 2002): 135-51.

[*In the following essay, Nisly examines some recurring themes—including machines, academia, and small-town life—in Gautreaux's* The Next Step in the Dance *and two collections of short stories.*]

> *The action of grace changes a character. Grace can't be experienced in itself. An example: when you go to Communion, you receive grace but you experience nothing; or if you do experience something, what you experience is not the grace but an emotion caused by it. Therefore in a story all you can do with grace is to show that it is changing the character.*
>
> Flannery O'Connor[1]

Louisiana author Tim Gautreaux claims that he inadvertently became an English major when he was in college. His plans of majoring in business were short-circuited, he says, when someone stole five accounting books that he had purchased. "I went to see my adviser," he reports, "and told him to put me in something where nobody would steal my books. He put me in English."[2] While the veracity of this account may be uncertain—Gautreaux admits that he is drawn to storytelling because "I liked to make up stuff and lie"[3]—what seems more telling than the factual quality is the understated and slightly surprising humor that comes through this account. For the wonder of Gautreaux's stories is that in the midst of accounts filled with less than remarkable, sometimes downright unlikable, small-town characters, Gautreaux is able with memorable dialogue, pithy descriptions, and—often—a touch of the divine to help us see the humanity, growth, and grace in these characters. As occurs in much of his best fiction, Gautreaux's story "Resistance" reveals an unlikely hero, Mr. Boudreaux, quietly offering assistance to Carmine, the plain girl next door. While they work together on a science project—and even more clearly when he reconstructs the work after Carmine's father has destroyed the first project—Mr. Boudreaux becomes an agent of grace to this lonely girl. Emphasizing the mysterious quality of sacramental action, however, Gautreaux refuses to reveal if this offered grace has been received.

At a glance, Gautreaux would seem to be easy to label a Southern Catholic writer, but he resists at least a part of that designation. A professor at Southeastern Louisiana University since 1972 and a native of Louisiana, Gautreaux nevertheless argues that the title of "Southern writer" tends to confuse more than it clarifies:

> I don't really understand what a "Southern" writer is. Writers just tend to write about their environment. If the South tends to be more poverty stricken, or has a less-educated population, or the politicians seem more arrogant, or there's a more intense devotion to religion, that's just the way it is. Perhaps the only difference I can perceive between a "Southern" writer and a non-Southern writer is that maybe the "Southern" writer loves where he lives more than other writers.[4]

Instead of this category, Gautreaux identifies more closely with the Frontier tradition, with its mix of tall tale and humor.[5] On the other hand, Gautreaux accepts the weight of identification as a "Catholic writer." On a basic level, Gautreaux says he could not write about South Louisiana culture without encountering the Church because Catholicism so permeates all of life.[6] However, Gautreaux's commitment to portraying Catholicism is much more than cultural: he switched from writing poetry to fiction after taking a seminar with Walker Percy, and he describes himself as "a Catholic writer in the tradition of Walker Percy. If a story does not deal with a moral question, I don't think it's much of a story."[7] He self-deprecatingly acknowledges, though, "I'm not a philosopher like Walker Percy. . . . I'm just a Catholic from the bayou. But it's one of the rhythms of life."[8] And from his stories, it would appear that this rhythm is an important element in how Gautreaux understands the world around him. In fact, he suggests that themes of moral dilemmas and redemption develop largely subconsciously in his stories: "Each of us has a type of ingrained, almost instinctual interest in a theme. . . . No matter what story you write, no matter what plot you choose, that theme is going to be in there."[9] In his stories, even though there is considerable pain, he resists suggesting that such darkness is the final answer: "there's a lot of depressing stuff in my fiction, but personally I don't believe that you have to constantly remind people that life sucks, then you die, because everybody knows that."[10] Such commitments become clear in Gautreaux's stories as his characters are often significantly challenged but usually have some suggestion of hope, of redemption, by the story's close.

Some patterns of interest emerge in Gautreaux's stories. Machines, particularly old steam engines, figure prominently in his stories. The son of a tugboat captain and grandson of a steamboat engineer, Gautreaux is a collector of antique machinery, having old John Deere tractors, antique railroad lanterns, and steamboat whistles on his several acres of property.[11] This love of machinery plays a prominent role in his stories, whether the characters are pump repairmen, tugboat crew members, or machinists. Often Gautreaux's life in the academic world seems far from the small-town locale of his stories, since by his own admission he is drawn to the less formally educated people around him. He finds there is "still a rich creative metaphorical magic alive, and it's in the mouths of uneducated people. Educated people tend to speak a standard English which is not creative and is not conducive to storytelling or bullshitting or any verbal color at all. . . . People who are uneducated basically have to make up an idiom as they go along. These are the people I like to listen to, because they're very acrobatic with the way they use the language."[12] Besides the sounds of these characters, Gautreaux likes the ways that in these communities, "everyone knew everyone else, everyone was Catholic, I like the fact that everyone eats the same things. They share a common heritage so they make all sorts of assumptions about each other."[13] It is in these small towns with their shared understandings that Gautreaux often sets his humorous and enlightening tales.

In Gautreaux's three published volumes—one novel, *The Next Step in the Dance* (1998), and two short story collections, ***Same Place, Same Things*** (1996) and ***Welding with Children*** (1999)—several thematic commonalities emerge. Although it is not a large category, Gautreaux does have several stories that deal with the academic life. **"Navigators of Thought"** (in *Same Place, Same Things*) and **"The Pine Oil Writers' Conference"** and **"Dancing with the One-Armed Gal"** (in *Welding with Children*) are skillful and sometimes hilarious commentaries on academics. In **"Navigators of Thought,"** five out-of-work professors try to navigate a tugboat; Gautreaux's ironic skill is well in place as he describes one of these crew as "a true academic, very intelligent, but so educated that he was unable to compose two coherent paragraphs in a row."[14] Likewise, in **"Dancing with the One-Armed Gal,"** a professor who describes herself as a "crippled black woman and a gay feminist" loses her job to a "gay black female double amputee from Ghana."[15] There is substance along with this humor in these stories, but these tales involving academics do not seem Gautreaux's strongest.

More common—and more compelling—are Gautreaux's stories about the sordid lives of small-town folk. These accounts focus on such characters as a drunk train engineer, whose derailment while carrying hazardous chemicals causes a massively destructive fire; he runs away from the fire, is astonished to see a portrayal of himself that he cannot recognize on the evening news, but eventually seems to come to some recognition of his guilt. Or at times these tales have a surprise in them seeming worthy of Flannery O'Connor, as in the title story **"Same Place, Same Things,"** when a pump repairman encounters a widow whose sole desire seems to be to leave her too familiar farm. Occasionally Gautreaux's stories end with little possibility of hope, but more common is the ending of **"Same Place, Same Things,"** when the decent repairman, waking after being slugged on the head by the widow who then stole his truck, realizes, "It didn't matter. She was a woman who would never get where she wanted to go. He was always where he was going."[16] In two sentences, Gautreaux is able to suggest the kind of rootedness, the sense of who he is, that allows the repairman to be able to right himself after his encounter with this rootless and ruthless woman.

In this Louisiana small-town world that Gautreaux presents, the most common theme is the presentation of an unlikely person serving as a help, even an agent of grace, to someone in need. At times these are service people—a piano tuner, an exterminator—who come into people's homes and end up offering more than what was requested. Gautreaux acknowledges that he enjoys writing "about service persons who visit our homes and get just a little entangled in our lives."[17] Often, though, the characters who help others find their way are part of a shared community—older relatives, elders of a community—who serve as guides to those who are lost. Part of what makes Gautreaux's stories so compelling, though, is that frequently it is these guides themselves who demonstrate a human fallibility even as they offer a gracious hand to another. For instance, in the hilarious yet poignant title story, **"Welding with Children,"** the first-person narrator Bruton is stung when he overhears an older man in town call his car a "bastardmobile" on seeing Bruton pull up to the Pak-a-Sak with his four grandchildren, offspring of his four unwed daughters.[18] From this snide comment, Bruton recognizes his own culpability in the upbringing of his daughters and begins to work to clean up the mess of his family's life. In describing Bruton's efforts, though, Gautreaux creates some of the most humorous passages since Flannery O'Connor's stories, especially when he is describing Bruton's attempt to introduce these children to Bible stories. While it certainly has humorous passages, Gautreaux's novel *The Next Step in the Dance* is a somewhat more serious look at a similar theme. Colette Thibodeaux leaves her town and her husband,

largely because, as she complains, "Everybody aims so low" in her town.[19] Colette wants to find more "glittering" dreams, so she moves to California;[20] her husband Paul, who is a solid but not driven man, follows her. Gautreaux explores the manner in which each of them needs to learn, and by having them return to their hometown, shows how the larger community nurtures them while urging them back together. Particularly striking in the novel is the role of Paul's grandfather, an old man who seems initially to be nearly forgotten amid the daily rhythms of life, but who ends up playing a pivotal supporting role in their healing relationship. The list of Gautreaux's compelling stories that work within this broad category could go on for some time, for I find these kinds of tales his strongest in their mix of humor, community, and redemption.

"Resistance" (in *Welding with Children*) seems to fit within this rubric, but as he often does, Gautreaux pushes the theme in a slightly new direction. In this case, the story is set in a subdivision rather than a small town, with Mr. Alvin Boudreaux feeling left behind by his changing neighborhood, as the opening lines of the story quickly suggests:

> Alvin Boudreaux had outlived his neighbors. His asbestossided house was part of a tiny subdivision built in the 1950s, when everybody had children, a single-lane driveway, a rotating TV antenna, and a picnic table out back. Nowadays, he sat on his little porch and watched the next wave of families occupy the neighborhood, each taking over the old houses, driving up in their pairs of bug-shaped cars, one for each spouse to drive to work.[21]

He feels isolated and worthless, with "no movement on his street that had consequence for him" (121). More than just seeing a new set of people whom he does not know, Mr. Boudreaux is realizing how much patterns of life have changed since he had a young family. At times he thinks back to memories of his own father and of his wife, who has been dead for eight years. And even though he has tried to make small talk with the new family next door, he has gotten only slight responses from the woman, who runs an electric coffee-grinding machine for six hours a day. In this context, Mr. Boudreaux is contemplating replacing his fifteen-year-old Buick: "Maybe it was time to trade it off for something that would fit in"—something like a Japanese-made compact (124). Mr. Boudreaux's thoughts here suggest more than a change in automobile; they imply that he is reconsidering his approach to those around him. Rather than resist the impersonality of his neighborhood, he seems to be thinking, perhaps he should simply accept the changed interactions between people; perhaps he should simply hole up in his house, live with his television and his memories, and allow the people around him to go on with their anonymous lives.

The new people next door embody the worst of this new generation. The wife is "a young, blond woman, overweight, with thin hair and raw, nervous eyes. The husband was small and mean, sat in a lawn chair in the backyard as though he was at the beach, and drank without stopping, every weekend. They had one ten-year-old, a plain, slow-moving daughter" (122). Mr. Boudreaux is bothered by their lack of care for the rose bushes they inherit when they move in, watching them wither away and die. He laments their leaving the garbage cans by the road until the grass dies under them. One afternoon, he overhears that the daughter needs to construct a science project, a project that the father angrily refuses to take on and that the mother insists is beyond her abilities. When Mr. Boudreaux next sees the girl Carmine, he wants to avoid any involvement in her problems, telling himself, "Don't look. But at his front steps, he felt a little electrical tug at his neck muscles, a blank moment of indecision," and he turns to the girl (124). Against his own better judgment, he talks to her mother and offers to help.

Although Carmine gives evidence in several ways of her intelligence, she remains largely uncommunicative as Mr. Boudreaux undertakes this project with her. Carmine has designed a project dealing with electricity to study how resistors work. Her ability with things mechanical and electrical becomes clear as she works with Mr. Boudreaux, a former maintenance foreman and veteran of his own children's science projects, to put her project into place. She also shows a kind of street smarts, as she mentions in passing how she and her mother need to act on Sundays to avoid the wrath of her drunken father. Yet even though Mr. Boudreaux keeps a pleasant stream of conversation, the girl says very little: "Carmine was mechanical, earnest, and as communicative as a very old pet dog" (127). Gautreaux's development of Carmine adds to the depth and plausibility of the story. Her bland appearance and uncommunicative nature keep the reader guessing about what is going in on her mind. We wonder if she has been bludgeoned into silence by her mind-numbing parents; we worry that perhaps the close attention that she is getting from Mr. Boudreaux is so unusual that she does not know how to assimilate it; we get only the briefest hints—a glint in the eye, one clap of the hands—to indicate that she is enjoying working with Mr. Boudreaux. At the same time, Gautreaux's presentation of this unresponsive girl gives the story a level of believability and offers a helpful corrective to the too-common sentimentality found in stories: not every child who is helped by a caring adult is cute, articulate, and immediately rewarding. In fact, Gautreaux's

portrayal of Carmine seems to be his way of suggesting that children—indeed everyone—intrinsically are worthy of caring attention, not only the beautiful ones who make their way into Hallmark movies.

Feeling a sense of satisfaction, Mr. Boudreaux and Carmine work late on Saturday evening to finish up the project. Although the seventy-eight-year-old Mr. Boudreaux is feeling weary and achy, he experiences a renewed sense of purpose in his work. On his way home from Mass the next day, he reflects with satisfaction on the completed science project, believing that "he had completed something important and that he and the girl had learned something" (133). In fact, he is feeling so energized that he considers again getting a new car, not so much now as a way of fitting in, I believe, but as an indication that he has connected with the contemporary world. This feeling that all is right with the world lasts only until that afternoon when Mr. Boudreaux, while washing his car, sees Carmine's father destroying the science project in a drunken rage; on being told to leave the work alone by Mr. Boudreaux, the man turns on him and shoves him to the ground.

That evening, Mr. Boudreaux is restless, unable to settle into any of his usual routines. Finally, he begins to take apart his TV, his stereo, his power tools, stealing wire and bulbs and resistors to recreate the project. "Though the workshop windows showed a trace of dawn, and though Mr. Boudreaux's legs felt as though someone had shot them full of arrows, he allowed himself a faint smile" as he finished the project (137). After the girl's father leaves for work, Mr. Boudreaux loads the project in his car and follows Carmine's bus to school. She takes the project from him, her face showing nothing. After a few technical questions about the switches, "He watched her waddle off among her classmates, bearing her load, then he turned for his car. She could have called after him, smiled, and said thank you, but she didn't" (139).

A central question in the story, often implied, occasionally articulated, is why Mr. Boudreaux goes to such an extreme, pushing his old body well beyond its limits, to carry out this task. As he admits to himself, a portion of his motivation is to get back at the girl's father for destroying the previous project and pushing him around. But it becomes clear in the story that revenge or one-upmanship is not his primary motivation. At one point in the story, the narrator mentions that Carmine said the name of her science project, Resistance, "as though it had another meaning" (126). This other meaning becomes a central concern of the story, as Mr. Boudreaux begins to resist the mindset of the neighbors around him, people who seem to find little to value or invest in deeply. When Mr. Boudreaux tells Carmine that he had two daughters, she is surprised, asking, "What would anybody need with two girls?" (128) Carmine has integrated the attitude from her parents, suggesting that there is little utilitarian use for a child, especially not two. In response, Mr. Boudreaux's self-giving actions underline the intrinsic value of each child. During the long night of Mr. Boudreaux's work on the second project, the narrator makes clear the connection that Mr. Boudreaux feels to the emotionally abandoned children around him: "At four o'clock, he had to stop to take aspirin for his back, and from the kitchen window, he looked across through the blue moonlight to the dark house next door, thinking maybe of all the dark houses in town where children endured the lack of light, fidgeting toward dawn" (137). In his own physical pain, Mr. Boudreaux identifies with the emotional pain of those around him, showing through his actions that it is possible, even necessary, to care deeply about the least of these. The reconstructed science project then becomes a visible symbol of Mr. Boudreaux's resistance to anonymity and insistence on celebrating each individual.

Mr. Boudreaux's action is also connected to a memory of his own father. While he is working with Carmine on the project, he tells her about one time during his school years that he had forgotten until late one evening to complete a project related to *Great Expectations*. Seeing his son's concern over the expected bad grade, Mr. Boudreaux's father asked him about the novel and sent him to bed. The next morning, he found a beautifully constructed and painted boat waiting for him. Mr. Boudreaux muses, "The old man was like that. . . . He never asked me if I liked the boat, and I never said anything to him about it, even when I brought home a good grade for the project" (132). By mentioning this memory of his father, Mr. Boudreaux implies that his actions in a sense pay homage to his father's earlier night of work. In this reading of the story, Gautreaux is showing us a trail of goodness, that helpful patterns as well as hurtful ones can be passed from one generation to the next—and this memory offers a hopeful suggestion that Carmine may also remember his action and share it with another. Further, the parallel between his own lack of thanks to his father and Carmine's uncommunicative silence suggests also that Mr. Boudreaux may be able to understand that her lack of verbalized thanks does not indicate ingratitude so much as an inability to put into words what she is thinking. Gautreaux reiterates the connection between Mr. Boudreaux's father's actions and his own by the final movement of the story. After dropping off the newly constructed project at school, Mr. Boudreaux considers shopping to replace his ruined appliances or to look for his long-contemplated new car. Instead, he goes to a department store, buys some plastic jonquils, and takes them to his father's gravesite, honoring his father's influence in his life.

While each of these explanations seems accurate and helpful for an understanding of the story, none seems fully to exhaust Mr. Boudreaux's motivations. Certainly a part of the sense that there is an "overplus of meaning"[22] in the story is attributable to Gautreaux's technical skills as a writer, as he refuses to allow an easy interpretation of an action. But one senses that there is something more, that the "overplus" may be related to the hint of the numinous that is present in the story. More than a reiteration of the intrinsic worth of each person or a son's tribute to his father—important though each of these motivations is—Mr. Boudreaux's actions suggest a divine movement, an action of grace. In the offering up of his achy back and his tired legs for this forgotten girl next door, Mr. Boudreaux seems to function as a conduit of God's love to the world. A hint of this anagogical level in the story occurs when Carmine's father, grumbling about Mr. Boudreaux's interference in their lives, complains, "I don't know why you think you got to do this" (128). Her father's comment is very believable: he cannot understand what could motivate anyone to go out of his way to help another; it makes no earthly sense to him. Mr. Boudreaux's response, when Carmine later repeats the question, is a telling indication that Mr. Boudreaux himself could not adequately explain why he felt drawn to help her. He answers Carmine, "It just needed doing" (131). In my view, as Mr. Boudreaux sacrifices his own privacy and comfort to help Carmine, his actions become a sacramental offering of grace. As Katherine Vaz writes in *Signatures of Grace: Catholic Writers on the Sacraments,* "Sacramental rites wait to be replicated in our quotidian lives: simple grace. Unlofty eucharists."[23] Similarly, Richard McBrien notes:

> Everything is, in principle, capable of embodying and communicating the divine. There is no finite instrument that God cannot put to use. On the other hand, we humans have nothing else apart from finite instruments to express our own response to God's self-communication. Just as the divine reaches us through the finite, so we reach the divine through the finite. The point at which this "divine commerce" occurs is the point of *sacramental encounter.*[24]

Mr. Boudreaux's actions in working with Carmine on the science project, and perhaps even more in struggling to replicate the work, take on a sacramental quality when seen in this light. He has become an instrument offering grace to Carmine, and in the encounter it seems that he has experienced God's grace as well.

At first glance, Carmine's lack of response to Mr. Boudreaux's gracious act may seem to push against this reading of the story. Yet, as the *Catechism of the*

Catholic Church explains, "Since it belongs to the supernatural order, grace *escapes our experience* and cannot be known except by faith."[25] By his actions, Mr. Boudreaux does offer a sign of God's love to Carmine, but to what extent she has responded to it remains in the mysterious realm. Augustine says, "A good person receives the sacrament and the reality of the sacrament, but a bad person receives only the sacrament and not the reality."[26] Obviously, Carmine has received the physical "sacrament" of the science project; what remains unarticulated is how it has affected her. The Church has taught that people have free choice, so they can choose whether or not to accept God's offered grace. There has been, however, a strong emphasis on God's work within people, helping move them toward that acceptance. As Aquinas explains, even though people do have freedom to choose, God "so infuses the gift of justifying grace that at the same time He moves free choice to accept the gift of grace, in such as are capable of being moved thus."[27] Given that emphasis, and given the model Mr. Boudreaux has himself provided in his late appreciation of his father's own act of love, it seems plausible to see Mr. Boudreaux's sacramental action being received in Carmine's life. Yet, perhaps that question is less central to the story than the model that Mr. Boudreaux has offered in extending a gracious hand.

More obvious than the effect on Carmine is the impact that this encounter has had on Mr. Boundreaux. The ending of the story, when Mr. Boudreaux goes to the cemetery to place flowers at his father's grave, suggests that through his engagement with a vulnerable child of God, Mr. Boudreaux has transcended the narrow confines of his life to commune with the divine:

> He drove to the old city graveyard, and after walking among the brick tombs and carefully made marble angels, he placed a colorful pot on the sun-washed slab of his father's grave. His back pained him as he put down the flowers, and when he straightened up, the bone-white tombs hurt his eyes, but still he turned completely around to look at this place where no one would say the things that could have been said, and that was all right with him.
>
> (139)

The mention of the angels and the blinding whiteness calls to mind a sense of holiness, a quality of otherworldliness. Mr. Boundreaux, in his satisfaction with the silence of the dead around him—and of Carmine's silence—seems to have found a new dimension in his life. No longer is he merely fretting over his neighborhood going to ruin; he has found a new ability to live deeply in this world and in so doing to encounter another reality as well. Michael and Kenneth Himes, describing their understanding of a Catholic public theology, write, "Put simply, there are not seven sacraments,

seven sacred rites, in a profane world but seven events which presume and seek to evoke awareness of the sacredness of all reality. Catholicism's sacramental vision, founded upon its theology of grace, teaches that God's gracious self-communication (grace) is always mediated."[28] The final passage of the story suggests that Mr. Boudreaux has glimpsed this sacredness of all reality; he is able to live contentedly in the present because he has sensed a brush with the numinous.

In his own reflection on being a writer, Gautreaux says, "One of the most important reasons I write is the feeling that I can write. People tell me that I do it well, and I actually believe it would be evil for me to not do what I can do well. Whatever you can do well is a gift, and if you don't exercise it, then you're doing something wrong."[29] In the story, Mr. Boudreaux seems to have learned just this lesson: it is through fulfilling those things that "needed doing" that he encounters the divine. As such, the science project at the heart of this story serves wonderfully on various levels to suggest the themes that are developed in the story. Not only does Mr. Boudreaux offer resistance to the destruction of Carmine's sense of self; the very concept of electricity functions metaphorically to underline the central theme of the story: just as electricity is present in wires even though it is invisible, grace is offered in the story even though we cannot see it.

Notes

1. Flannery O'Connor, *The Habit of Being,* ed. Sally Fitzgerald (New York: Farrar, Straus & Giroux, 1979), 275.

2. Sheila Stroup, "He's Got the Right Stuff," *Times-Picayune,* 26 January 1993. Lexis-Nexis Academic Universe (20 June 2001), printout p. 1.

3. Tim Gautreaux interview with Christina Masciere, "Tim Gautreaux Takes 'the Next Step,'" *New Orleans Magazine,* March 1998. *Proquest* (20 June 2001), printout p. 3.

4. Tim Gautreaux interview with Katie Bolick and David Watta, "A Conversation with Tim Gautreaux," *The Atlantic Unbound,* 14 March 1997. www.theatlantic.com/unbound/factfict/gautreau/tgautr.htm (20 June 2001), printout p. 2.

5. Gautreaux interview with Bolick and Watta, 2-3.

6. Gautreaux interview with Masciere, 1.

7. Gautreaux interview with Bolick and Watta, 4.

8. Susan Larson, "Pelican Briefs," *Times-Picayune,* 15 September 1996. Lexis-Nexis Academic Universe (20 June 2001), printout p. 2.

9. Gautreaux interview with Masciere, 1-2.

10. Ibid., 3.

11. Larson, "Pelican Briefs," 1.

12. Gautreaux interview with Masciere, 2-3.

13. Susan Larson, "The Writer Next Door," *Times-Picayune,* 15 March 1998. Lexis-Nexis Academic Universe (20 June 2001), printout pp. 1-2.

14. Tim Gautreaux, *Same Place, Same Things,* (New York: Picador USA, 1996), 78.

15. Tim Gautreaux, *Welding with Children* (New York: Picador USA, 1999), 199 and 192.

16. Gautreaux, *Same Place, Same Things,* 17.

17. Irene Wanner, "An Imaginative Teller of Tales," *The Seattle Times,* 10 October 1999. Lexis-Nexis Academic Universe (20 June 2001), printout p. 2.

18. Gautreaux describes the genesis of this story: "I found that one at Wal-Mart. Basically I was there buying motor oil one day, and on the next aisle was a gentleman lamenting the fact that his daughters were not getting married but they were having children and leaving the children with him. And it was a peculiar type of sadness in his voice—not rage or anger or anything—but a type of sadness and a quality of being flabbergasted—whatever that is. He just didn't understand what was happening to this generation that he had brought up. All I heard was his voice. I didn't look at him. And that's all I needed for the story. And the story is told in his voice." (Greg Langley, "Gautreaux Doesn't Need a Label Other than 'Writer,'" *The Advocate ONLINE,* 10 October 1999. www.theadvocate.com/enter/story.asp?StoryID=1768 [20 June 2001], printout p. 2.)

19. Tim Gautreaux, *The Next Step in the Dance* (New York: Picador USA, 1998), 23.

20. Gautreaux, *The Next Step in the Dance,* 105.

21. Gautreaux, *Welding with Children,* 121. All future references to this story will be noted parenthetically in the text.

22. Rudolf Otto, *The Idea of the Holy,* trans. John W. Harvey (New York: Oxford University Press, 1950), 5.

23. Katherine Vaz, "Baptism," *Signatures of Grace: Catholic Writers on the Sacraments,* eds. Thomas Grady and Paula Huston (New York: Dutton, 2000), 25.

24. Richard P. McBrien, *Catholicism* (New York: HarperSanFrancisco, 1994), 787.

25. *Catechism of the Catholic Church,* 2d edition (Washington, D.C.: United States Catholic Conference, 2000), 486.

26. McBrien, *Catholicism,* 794.

27. Thomas Aquinas, *Basic Writings of Saint Thomas Aquinas,* ed. Anton C. Pegis, vol. 2 (New York: Random House, 1945), 1024.

28. Michael J. Himes and Kenneth R. Himes, *Fullness of Faith: The Public Significance of Theology* (New York: Paulist Press, 1993), 85.

29. Gautreaux interview with Masciere, 3.

Bibliography

Aquinas, Thomas. *Basic Writings of Saint Thomas Aquinas.* Vol. 2. Ed. Anton C. Pegis. New York: Random House, 1945.

Catechism of the Catholic Church. 2nd edition. Washington, D.C.: United States Catholic Conference, 2000.

Gautreaux, Tim. "A Conversation with Tim Gautreaux." *The Atlantic Unbound.* By Katie Bolick and David Watta, 14 March 1997. www.theatlantic.com/unbound/factfict/gautreau/tgautr.htm (20 June 2001), printout pp. 1-5.

———. *The Next Step in the Dance.* New York: Picador USA, 1998.

———. *Same Place, Same Things.* New York: Picador USA, 1996.

———. "Tim Gautreaux Takes 'the Next Step.'" *New Orleans Magazine.* Interview with Christina Masciere, March 1998. *Proquest* (20 June 2001) Printout pp. 1-4.

———. *Welding with Children.* New York: Picador USA, 1999.

Himes, Michael J. and Kenneth R. Himes. *Fullness of Faith: The Public Significance of Theology.* New York: Paulist Press, 1993.

Langley, Greg. "Gautreaux Doesn't Need a Label Other than 'Writer.'" *The Advocate ONLINE,* 10 October 1999. www.theadvocate.com/enter/story.asp?StoryID=1768 (20 June 2001), printout pp. 1-3.

Larson, Susan. "Pelican Briefs." *Times-Picayune* 15 September 1996. Lexis-Nexis Academic Universe (20 June 2001), printout pp. 1-2.

———. "The Writer Next Door." *Times-Picayune* 15 March 1998. Lexis-Nexis Academic Universe (20 June 2001), printout pp. 1-3.

McBrien, Richard P. *Catholicism.* New York: HarperSanFrancisco, 1994.

O'Connor, Flannery. *The Habit of Being.* Ed. Sally Fitzgerald. New York: Farrar, Straus & Giroux, 1979.

Otto, Rudolf. *The Idea of the Holy.* Trans. John W. Harvey. New York: Oxford University Press, 1950.

Stroup, Sheila. "He's Got the Right Stuff." *Times-Picayune* 26 January 1993. Lexis-Nexis Academic Universe (20 June 2001), printout pp. 1-2.

Vaz, Katherine. "Baptism." *Signatures of Grace: Catholic Writers on the Sacraments.* Eds. Thomas Grady and Paula Huston. New York: Dutton, 2000.

Wanner, Irene. "An Imaginative Teller of Tales." *The Seattle Times* 10 October 1999. Lexis-Nexis Academic Universe. (20 June 2001), printout pp. 1-2.

Tim Gautreaux with Maria Hebert-Leiter (interview date June 2005)

SOURCE: Gautreaux, Tim, and Maria Hebert-Leiter. "An Interview with Tim Gautreaux." *The Carolina Quarterly* (June 2005): 66-74.

[*In the following interview, Gautreaux discusses his literary influences, including Ernest Gaines and Walker Percy, before reflecting on why he writes and describing his Cajun cultural identity and its effect on his art.*]

Tim Gautreaux is the author of the short story collections **Same Place, Same Things** (1996) and **Welding with Children** (1999), and of the novels *The Next Step in the Dance* (1998) and *The Clearing* (2003). Born and raised in Morgan City, Louisiana, he grew up among blue-collar Cajuns. From this past experience, Gautreaux creates a fictional world that relates the everyday lives and cultural ways of south Louisiana Cajuns. In 1972, he received his Ph. D. from the University of South Carolina, Columbia, where he wrote his creative dissertation under the direction of James Dickey. He taught at Southeastern Louisiana University for thirty years before retiring in 2002. On October 15, 2004, I interviewed Tim Gautreaux by phone. We discussed his literary influences, his Cajun identity, and his motivation for writing.

[*Hebert-Leher*]: *Like Faulkner and Gaines, you write about your postage stamp of land, which you call Tiger Island and which Louisianians recognize as Morgan City. How much have these two authors influenced your work?*

[Gautreaux]: Ernest Gaines, of course, is a great influence particularly in the way he treats language. Gaines has an excellent ear, and when I was attending a conference one time, Gaines gave a reading. It was the first time I had heard him. It was many years ago. And in his reading I could hear that he was working with the cadences and the grammar of individual speakers in such a way as to really give a vivid and accurate representation of their language. Now you don't pick that up exactly or as much when you're at home reading his books, something like *A Gathering of Old Men* or *A Lesson Before Dying*. But what that reading did for me is make me go back and read all of Gaines again and to see what he was doing with dialogue. And how important that was to a feeling of authenticity for the readers. And so when I began to work on my own dialogue, I always kept what Gaines was doing in the back of my mind.

A sense of place was always very important to me. Gaines created his entire fictional universe out of a single gravel lane in Point Coupée parish, but a place he moved away from when he was about sixteen. He lived a very long time in other places and would try to create a fiction out of these non-Louisiana locales, but it just didn't work very well for him. However, whenever he set something in Louisiana in an imaginary landscape that was similar to where he grew up, well, he was very successful. And that of course told me something that is pretty obvious from the beginning of any writer's career—that is that a writer . . . owns a certain literary territory. It's the place of his birth, where he grew up, the language that he listened to, the values that were implied, and the everyday commerce of his life. And this is something that the writer has to remember and pay attention to.

Even though Gaines's origins are very humble and he grew up with what you might consider unimportant people, he made great literature out of it. And that was kind of an archetype for me. You can say what Gaines does forms a pattern that I noted when I started to write fiction.

Interesting because I did hear Gaines read A Lesson Before Dying *twice, and it is a very different feel when he reads it to you than when read it in your head. There is very much an oral quality in his writing that I do think you are picking up on in your own. And that these Cajuns are talking in your fiction.*

You have to pay attention while reading Gaines . . . the one thing I learned from Gaines and other sources, too, [is] how important it was to listen to the people around you and to remember as accurately as you can how people spoke when you were younger.

So Gaines obviously has had a strong influence on your work. I think that any Louisiana writer today couldn't ignore him. Who else has most influenced your work?

Probably Walker Percy from the standpoint of ideas. . . . What was interesting to Percy is not that people did things but why people did things. That carried over to his teaching of fiction. He would lead us in class to think not how we wrote, but why we wrote. There was always this moral foundation to whatever he wrote. And he was never didactic or preachy. He was always asking us, his readers, to think about why we did things. And when he taught me (a novel writing course in 1977, at Loyola), he was not very opinionated as to what we should write about, but he was very adamant in letting us know that we're all on some kind of a quest. The writer is always looking for something, the characters are always looking for something. It's an exploration. An exploration of what? Well, for Percy, it was, at least in part, always spiritual.

We are looking for what makes us happy, and the characters are looking for what makes them happy. And for Percy it wasn't money, and it wasn't fame. So what was it? Well, he never really told us, but you could guess.

How did you come to take that class? I read that you were one of the students in I think it was Patrick Samway's biography of Walker Percy.

The fact that the class was going to be taught was actually in the paper, I believe. And people were invited, writers were invited to submit samples of their work. That's how we got in to the class, based on samples of our writing. And there were ten of us chosen, as I remember. And one of them was Valerie Martin, who is a successful novelist. Another one was Walter Isaacson. . . . And so, it was an interesting class.

Is there anyone else, besides Percy and Gaines, or are those your biggest influences?

Well, naturally an influence on just about everybody writing in the South was Flannery O' Connor. She's probably the country's premier short story writer. If you analyze her stories you see she was working with tragedy, and humor, and irony. And putting all of these elements together in a technically perfect way, and that was because she really took to heart what the instructors at Iowa gave her in the way of how to put a story together. She was *very* expert in the way she assembled her story structure. Also, you know, she was Catholic, and I can relate to that because I'm Catholic.

So you obviously have Louisiana literary ancestors with Gaines. Do you recognize yourself as a Louisiana writer? And do you recognize yourself as a Cajun writer?

Well, the short answer is no. Because if you think of yourself as a particular kind of writer, you limit yourself and you also lead others to define everything you do by some labels. And I think that's a bad thing. And also you tend to begin to rely on stereotypes and cliches if you think of yourself as a Midwestern writer, or an Indian writer, of an Amish writer, if there is one,

or a Polish writer. You limit yourself, I think, by doing that. I just prefer to think of myself as a writer who just happens to live in the South.

You know, I sometimes ask myself what I would be writing if I were raised in Chicago. I would be writing about that city, using the same technique, and the same type of wit, and the same structure that I use now. The stories would just be about a different part of the country. Sometimes I meet writers who identify strongly with a region, they might call themselves an Alabama writer, or they might call themselves a western writer, and they sometimes get trapped in this notion that they have to use details from their region that people from other regions expect. And that's dangerous for a fiction writer. A writer shouldn't write what others expect of him. Now if I use a character named Boudreaux and he's eating plate of crawfish *etoufee* in a restaurant, it's because I was . . . that's my territory. I was born and raised in a place where people ate heavy stews everyday. But I'm not using such details because people *expect* it of me. There's a difference between paying attention to details of a region for the sake of authenticity, and using details for some cornball notion of being entertaining.

When did you know you wanted to be a writer?

Well, writing is something like singing or tapdancing, it's born talent. If somebody has a good singing voice, he'll sing in the choir, he'll sing in the shower. Even if he's not commercial about it, he'll utilize his talent in some fashion. So it's something I always fiddled around with. This business about when did you know you were going to be a writer, it's something that happens over an entire lifetime. It's not as though lightbulb comes on at any one moment when you say, "oh, boy, I can be a writer." I don't even consider myself a writer. I'm just a retired school teacher.

A better question might be, "*Why* did you write?" And one reason for that was to give myself credibility in the classroom. If I was going to teach three and four sections of creative writing during the year, I had to have some justification for my comperence. So I always wanted to be published in good places, in order to tell students, "See, this is how it's done."

If Cajun still, to some degree, means a somewhat rural person with somewhat limited outside experience, can Cajuns write about educated Cajuns while still capturing Cajun culture in their fiction or is it just in writing about more rural Cajuns who have not gone very far from home that represents a true, more complex picture of Cajun life?

Someone asked me one time, "well why don't you write about doctors and lawyers?" [I do not write about them] because they're not very interesting, culturally at least. Someday I might write about doctors and lawyers, Cajun doctors and lawyers. [It goes] back to my raising again, and my territory, because the people I knew were blue-collar people. They were rural people. They were fisherman. They were mechanics. They were dredge-boat operators and tugboat captains and railroad engineers. They weren't doctors and lawyers. So that's probably the main reason I deal with those types of people. That's my territory.

And, like Gaines, very often when I stray out of that territory I don't do as well. In my first novel, *The Next Step in the Dance,* people tell me that the California section is by the least interesting part. I do have some experience in California. I used to spend summers out there with my sister who lived in Los Angeles. And I still couldn't put into it anything that was really first rate, that is writing about California. When I got back to the territory that I was raised in, I could do a lot better.

Do you think that education removes Cajuns from a traditional way of Cajun life in such a way that perhaps that's why doctors and lawyers don't make as interesting characters?

Yeah, I think so. Because, and that's the way with just about anybody who is raised [among] the lower-middle class or blue-collar people and becomes educated, begins making money, begins to prosper, begins to move in the popular culture. [You] begin to feel that your plainer beginnings are something you should leave behind. And I think that's sad. You begin to lose all sense of history and all sense of the past, and then you lose the sense of the importance of present things. For example, when I was a kid, I was the one who was always sent out to paint the family graves on All Saints' Day, actually on All Souls' Day is when we used to do it. And that was a very important thing, to maintain the memory of your ancestors. And over the years, especially the three years I was not living in Morgan City, I sort of lost track of that, the importance of maintaining the family tradition of painting the graves. And now I'm even further away from it. I mean I'm closer to the traditions of south Louisiana in some ways, but in that way, I'm not. And it's kind of sad because nobody maintains the graves now. Sometimes they get in sad shape. Maybe some day I'll go down and do it again in my older age.

Is that why in The Next Step in the Dance, *when Colette's parents die, you have a passage where Abadie says that when somebody dies, the younger generation turns on the television set. Does that passage come from your own experience?*

The more you get caught up in making money and in a busier, modern, non-rural lifestyle, the more you are insulated from the things that count. And that's true not only in Cajun culture, but in any culture.

How has your education affected your Cajun identification and your writing of Cajun culture in fiction?

I try not to think about it too much. You see things have changed a lot [over the last fifty years]. I was born in '47, however old that makes me, and people from my age bracket didn't think about being Cajuns when we were growing up in the fifties. It just didn't occur to us. If you would have asked me when I was twelve years old, "Are you a Cajun?" I would say, "I don't know." It was when I moved away to South Carolina when I was maybe 21, 22 years old (for graduate school), that I found myself in a different culture at that point, and realized how different Louisiana was, south Louisiana in particular, from the rest of the country. When I moved to South Carolina, the food was totally different, and the religion was different, the politics was different, everything was different. Attitudes were different. At that point it began to be clear to me what being Cajun was. And it had to do with attitudes, the value of food, the value of religion, and things of that nature. And it's sort of an attitude about life. The attitude that though people think they're better than you, you know different.

I guess it was kind of a generational thing. Now it has become this academic study.

Yeah. I think a lot of it started in the 1960s and 70s. In Lafayette there were several people [who] realized that this traditional Cajun accordion music was sort of passing away from the scene. So they began to put together Festival Acadienne, for example, and several other festivals in Lafayette that showcased local music. Well, people from away started to come to those festivals, and certain record companies started to put out cds, well they didn't have cds in those days, but tapes of Nathan Abshire, who was at that point a watchman in a garbage dump, but he was recorded. And they began to tape the Balfa brothers and other musicians, and Cajun music began to be kind of a regional thing. It began to spread out of the area, of southwest Louisiana. And by the early 80s, you start to hear a little Cajun music even in New Orleans, for God's sake. Now, you never heard accordion music east of the Atchafalaya River. It just didn't exist. Starting in the 70s and 80s, you began to see more and more Cajun music in barrooms, in nightclubs, in dancehalls, and also in restaurants in New Orleans. It began to be more and more popular. People began to understand that it was . . . was immanently danceable. [This interest in Cajun music] led to a heightened interest in Cajun food.

You couldn't get a lot of Cajun food in New Orleans until, oh, the 1980s. It was all French cuisine or just standard New Orleans Creole fare, like Shrimp Creole and stuff like that. But as far as a lot of gumbo, particularly *etoufees* and stews, or white beans or anything of that nature, you never saw that in New Orleans till the 80s. So the Cajun influence sort of followed the music out of Acadiana. And then, there were a couple of bad movies made. [. . .] And several companies started exporting Cajun spices and Cajun hot sauce. . . . There's Paul Prudhomme and the blackened fish stuff, and Justin Wilson, all these cooks had nationally-syndicated cooking shows and would mention Cajun foods and derivations of Cajun foods. And all of this made local people think better about the culture. To grow up in the 80s as a Cajun was a thing to be proud of.

My father spoke French, but I guess I thought everybody's father spoke French in the United States. And my favorite thing to eat would be, you know, shrimp okra gumbo, and I thought shrimp okra gumbo was served in every restaurant in the United States until I left and found out otherwise.

You can now find it, though, in most states if you look hard enough. It's been that exported. And now there are even international bands. There are bands in Australia and Great Britain who play Cajun music.

Cajun bands tour, too.

Times have changed. So, what do you think of the state of contemporary Cajun culture?

It's hard to generalize. It's hard to put your finger on it. But, you know the music is still going strong, and the food will always be there. And, as far as people speaking French, that's dying off because it's hard when there's no practical application for a language, it's hard to utilize it daily. There are school programs. The CODOFIL program [Council for the Development of French in Louisiana] down here in southwest Louisiana. And there are some young French bands, [made up] of very young people, who are singing songs in French and even learning French. They speak better French than the old people. So there's a limited maintenance, I guess you might call it, of French speaking that is still going on in the Lafayette region.

A lot of Cajun culture flies below radar. And if you want to experience Cajun culture you have to go to Breaux Bridge, St. Martinville, Henderson, or Whiskey River Landing and dance on Sunday afternoon. It's not in books. Well, it's not in many books. And I tried in *The Next Step in the Dance* to record the culture as it was in the 1980s. There are also elements of the 70s, and 60s, and 50s in that story, particularly all the fist-fighting scenes. Because I found that if I didn't

nobody else would. There aren't many people down there writing "literary" fiction about blue-collar Cajun culture.

It seems that Cajun literature is trying to deal with tensions we've been feeling between identifying yourself as American and taking pride in Cajun culture and its differences. I do recognize this tension in your Cajun characters. Especially among your women who leave their husbands. For instance, Colette who goes to Los Angeles because she wants something more or better. How do you feel about this tension? Do you feel it yourself? Why is it especially your women who embody this tension in your fiction?

Someone told me one time that they thought Colette was kind of mean. Women I was raised around were just like Colette. I'm not quite sure why Colette is the way she is. I'm going to go at [the topic of women's lives] from a south Louisiana perspective. Life then was very hard for women in the 1950s, in that Louisiana was a poor state. It's always been a very poor state, and very often women had to work at jobs in addition to raising a family. Particularly if you were a fisherman's wife or a trapper's wife, you helped. And even if you were the wife of a sugarcane farmer, you sewed, you raised chickens, or you worked as a secretary in town. And this is true of many cultures, I guess, where the common denominator is poverty. But Louisiana and Mississippi have always been the poorest states in the union. The women had to be very tough, and they also had to assert their dominance in the family. . . . The Cajun mother was very influential and strong. She had to keep her husband in line. . . . And if she was a push over, she had a miserable life. So she had to run the finances, so to speak, of the family and keep her husband in line. She couldn't be a sweetcakes, you know. Sometimes she had to be pretty rough with her husband to get him to behave. This attitude, I think, was passed on to the daughters, because I remember even on the playground the girls were pretty darn mean. They would throw rocks at you. If some girl was especially interested in you, she would throw a big rock at you.

So what do you think about films like The Big Easy *and* The Waterboy?

[. . .] Hollywood is very superficial. So unless you're watching a documentary, you're not going to get any type of serious treatment of culture out of Hollywood. They just don't understand culture. And the directors and the studios in Hollywood more or less believe that every place in the United States is like every other place. If there's a Burger King and a record store in a town in northern Alabama, it's just like New York. . . . Well, [they think] it's all the same. They

actually believe that popular culture has totally conquered everything in the way of culture in this world
and in this country. And really nothing could be further from the truth. There's still a lot of ethnic diversity in this country. It tends to stay regional, and media moguls tend not to think much about it. . . . .
Hollywood just doesn't seem to know how to make
use of Mexican polka festivals, for example.

*Do you find yourself writing in response to the Holly-
wood depictions?*

No. Hollywood is not on my radar screen.

*Ken Wells defines Cajun sayings and gives pronuncia-
tion keys in a glossary at the end of each of his novels.
You do not define your characters' Cajun French when
they do speak it. For instance, I know in* The Next Step
in the Dance, *you don't. I find it interesting that you do
not because of Cajun loss of Cajun French usage. Why
don't you translate your Cajuns' French phrases?*

Well, for one, in context, you ought to be able to figure out what they're saying. [. . .] Two, . . . you
know, I don't believe that a reader should be made to
understand every molecule of what's going on in the
story. I might mention a certain type of wrench, and
you might not know what that wrench looks like. Well,
do I have to sit there and explain it to get an effect.
No, that would be tedious. What do I do, not mention
it? Well then that robs the story of a certain authenticity and texture. If I mention a certain machine. You
don't know what it looks like. But does that mean I
shouldn't write about it? If you actually look through
an average novel, there's lots of stuff you don't understand. That doesn't mean [the author] has to explain
what it is or anything. . . . This is . . . a complaint
that people make against Cormac McCarthy, that he
uses Spanish phrases in his novels. But you can figure
out from the context what the phrases mean. . . . .
And even if you don't understand one speck of Spanish, you're not going to miss anything in the novel. So
Spanish is put in there for authenticity, for texture. . . . I think it's insulting to a reader's intelligence, turning a fictional work into a manual.

*Marcia Gaudet wrote in 1989 that "there has not yet
been an accurate portrayal of Cajun culture by a major
American literary figure." And this statement is part of
a larger argument that Cajun literary representation is
more a misrepresentation than anything else. I believe
that you answer her call for accuracy. How do you feel
about her statement, and have you ever consciously
written in response to such statements?*

I think that she's right. It's really almost impossible to
understand a culture unless you live in it. And literature can, I think, go a long way towards letting you

know what a culture is like, but you still won't totally
understand it unless you live among the people. Unless you see and smell where they live. Literature can
only do so much. Now, of course, Marcia's statement
that it's not been well represented is true, and that's
why I wrote *The Next Step in the Dance*. Some people
read the novel and ask, "Well, what's the point?" And
I think they don't see it as an archetype, a tribute to a
culture that could be imitated.

*That completely answers my question, because that's
how I feel whenever I read it. It's certainly more accurate and more sincere. It's very much . . .*

[People who] read it and say what's the point, those
are people who don't think there is any type of culture
in America at all. That it's just a mall rat culture. That
there's nothing else. . . . They just don't understand
how intense and cherished many different cultures in
the United States are.

*So you wrote it to celebrate this Cajun culture or these
cultural ways that don't just disappear when a Dillard's moves into your neighborhood?*

That's right. Recently, I was in a little town in Michigan and they were having a Dutch festival, and people
demonstrating Dutch folk dancing . . . That kind of
stuff goes on all over the United States, and most
Americans don't know about it.

What is your next project?

I'm working on a novel set in the same period as *The
Clearing*. It begins in Louisiana, in New Orleans and
takes place on a boat on the Mississippi River. I'm in
the early stages of writing it, so we'll see where it
goes. It might wind up in Chicago!

Ed Piacentino (essay date fall 2005)

SOURCE: Piacentino, Ed. "Second Chances: Patterns
of Failure and Redemption in Tim Gautreaux's *Same
Place, Same Things*." *Southern Literary Journal* 38, no.
1 (fall 2005): 115-33.

[*In the following essay, Piacentino discusses the influence of the southern Louisiana Cajun cultural milieu on
the stories in* Same Place, Same Things.]

In a contemporary review of Tim Gautreaux's first
book ***Same Place, Same Things*** (1996), a collection
of short fiction, Suzanne Berne perceptively observes
that "most of the characters . . . live in a swamp of
repetitive mistakes and disappointments." These characters, whom she classifies as "emotionally stagnant

people," become involved in situations where the "dramatic tension centers on whether they'll seize a last chance to inch out of their particular quagmires" (16). Focusing principally on blue-collar whites, usually southern Louisiana Cajuns, these stories feature characters whose lives, Rand Richards Cooper points out, are "harshly circumscribed by poverty, under-education, and alcohol" and whose "world in which work—when it can be found—alternates petty humiliations with spectacular mishaps" (24). Moreover, Gautreaux's Louisiana is "rough around the edges . . . a tough place, where it's hard to make a living" (Larson, "Writer Tim Gautreaux," D-1).

Gautreaux, born in Morgan City, Louisiana, has been a life-long resident of the state, except for his years as a graduate student at the University of South Carolina at Columbia, where he received his Ph.D., and a brief stint as writer-in-residence at the University of Mississippi. A self-proclaimed advocate that "a writer has a duty to get in touch with his culture" (qtd. in Masciere 47), Gautreaux, in all his principal works—the stories of *Same Place, Same Things* and of *Welding With Children* (1999) and his two novels, *The Next Step in the Dance* (1998) and *The Clearing* (2003)—uses southern Louisiana as his fictional domain, particularly the society of blue-collar Cajuns, many of whom are devout Roman Catholics with strong family ties. In fact, on several occasions, he has proudly pointed out his own family's working-class background: his father, a tugboat captain; his grandfather, a steamboat chief engineer; and his great-uncle, a master mechanic (Masciere 31).

Concerning Cajun culture and its durability, Gautreaux confesses, "I am amazed by it. The lack of cynicism—I don't know, maybe it's the Catholicism or the sense of family among Cajuns. Acadian emigrants showed up in Louisiana between 1765 and 1785, and they clumped together and remained an ethnic entity where many other groups lost their identities" (qtd. in Levasseur and Rabalais 33). Therefore, it seems quite natural that Gautreaux in his fiction has principally portrayed a class and ethnic group he knows personally and intimately.

Though in a number of ways Gautreaux has, through his education and personal experiences, transcended his Cajun working-class roots, he has always drawn on and, by his own admission, will continue to mine the rich lode of subject matter, character types, colorful dialect, and the lively storytelling tradition associated with the south Louisiana Cajun cultural milieu that has shaped him and that continues to hold his interest. While many of the characters in *Same Place, Same Things* are misfits, Gautreaux treats them sympathetically. Perhaps such compassion may in part be

attributable to his Catholic background and the Catholic dominance in southern Louisiana. In an interview with Katie Bolick and David Watta in 1997, Gautreaux acknowledged that he viewed himself "to be a Catholic writer in the tradition of Walker Percy" as well as a moralist, asserting that "if a story does not deal with a moral question, I don't think it's much of a story" (4). In another interview in 1998 he further explained, while acknowledging writers "h[ave] a type of ingrained, almost instinctual interest in a theme," that in his own fiction "[themes of moral dilemmas and redemption] come out more or less subconsciously" (qtd. in Masciere 31). And indeed, as we will see, his short fiction addresses issues involving moral decisions and their consequences.

In the title story, **"Same Place, Same Things,"** for example, Harry Lintel, a widower with grown children who enjoys the freedom of mobility to follow droughts and who prides himself in having the ability and confidence to "fix any irrigation pump or engine ever made" (3), is self-absorbed and standoffish. Harry has been summoned to Ada and her husband's drought-afflicted, run-down strawberry farm to repair their broken down irrigation pump; the farm reflects Ada's lament of entanglement in a place where she does not want to be. Desperate, bored, and restricted, admitting that she "was kept back in that patch and never came in to drink or dance or nothing" (10), Ada is apparently responsible for electrocuting her husband as he attempted to fix the pump. With her third husband conveniently out of the way, she regards Harry as her chance to escape. A man who "could figure out any machine on earth, but with women, he wished for an instruction manual" (8), Harry, though he seems physically attracted to Ada, also seems certain that she has murdered her husband, which creates moral and legal complications the pump repairman desires to avoid. Moreover, seeking consolation in the past, in memories of his then young wife and three young children, Harry, though feeling sorry for Ada, rationalizes his inability to help her, admitting that "he didn't know what to do for her" (13), a response relieving him of any responsibility for her. Such a rationalization, coupled with the likelihood that Ada has murdered her husband, gives Harry sufficient reason to avoid her. Once the rains begin and Harry leaves the area to seek out new drought-afflicted farms in need of his repair skills, he discovers that Ada is hiding in his truck. When she says to him, "You can go somewheres. I can't" (15), Harry begins to realize that Ada does not really care about him; instead, she only envies his freedom and mobility. In fact, her eyes, Harry notices, "seemed already to be looking ahead, looking at the whole world passing by a truck window" (15). When Harry rejects her plea to go away with him, Ada accuses the pump repairman of insensitivity, and when he offers her money to buy a train ticket home, she hits him on the head with a wrench and then exclaims, "I've never met a man I could put up with for long. . . . I'm glad I got shut of all of mine" (16).

At the end of the story, while Ada seems uncertain what she wants and where she wants to go, Harry, emerging from semi-consciousness, turns his thoughts to "tomorrow's big repair job, waiting" (17). Not only do both characters fail to connect but also the prospect for meaningful connections with others in the future seems unlikely. And though he seems unaware of it, Harry's next "big repair job," Suzanne Berne perceptively points out, "will need to be himself" (16). Both Harry and Ada find themselves in an interminable cycle, figuratively still in the "same place, [doing] the same things." As Gautreaux succinctly puts it, "She was a woman who would never get where she wanted to go. He was always where he was going" (17).

"Waiting for the Evening News" focuses on another failure, Jesse McNeil, a malcontent who destroys any opportunity for a second chance to redirect his life from a calamitous course in which he is moving. Recognizing that "he had been guilty of many mistakes" (31), Jesse is an engineer on a chemical train (called by engineers the "rolling bomb"), his only reason for working being to escape his wife "who was always after him to paint or fix something" (21). As a personal act of rebellion, Jesse desires to "do something wild and woolly" to celebrate his fiftieth birthday (19). Inebriated and compelled to drive the locomotive at a dangerously high speed, Jesse derails the train, causing a major disaster and then running away from the consequences of his irresponsible and reckless action. According to the media reports, the long-term effects of the train wreck are catastrophic: "a white cloud of escaped chemical had rolled over a chicken farm and killed ten thousand hens"; "three firemen were seriously injured when the wind shifted and they were overtaken by a toxic blanket" (28); the chemicals spilled near the town where the train wreck happened were so noxious that it "could never be inhabited again"; and "all the soil for one square mile would have to be removed down to six feet, treated, and hauled off to a toxic-waste pit at a cost of tens of millions" (34).

Having been a nonentity for his entire life, Jesse acquires media notoriety, television sensationalizing what he has done so that "now his name had sailed out into the region like parts of his exploded train" (23). Jesse's past life, characterized by a sameness that he himself had hardly noticed, has been uneventful, so uneventful that "sometimes he imagined himself an unseen part of this faded, repetitive background" (25). In fact, because he feels unnoticed and unimportant, he has come to regard himself as "invisible," a person "not [to] be taken seriously," and for this reason, "he never voted, hardly ever renewed his driver's license, and paid attention in church only once a year at revival time" (25). Now Jesse P. McNeil of Gumwood, Louisiana, has become known, but for the wrong reasons, a situation that he wishes he could obliterate. Describing the effect of this unwanted publicity on Jesse's guilt-ridden and troubled character, Gautreaux points out that the fugitive engineer realizes that he should not have fled the scene of the wreck because his "absence" has caused the complications surrounding the incident to mushroom to astronomical proportions, at least from the perspective of watching the television news accounts of the disaster.

In an effort to show Jesse's gnawing despair and uneasiness in discovering his recently acquired notoriety via television's brazen rendering of the train wreck and its aftermath, Gautreaux vividly captures Jesse's sense of his personal culpability using a series of storm metaphors to accentuate the engineer's disbelief of and anxiety over what he has done—caused "one of the largest ecological and industrial disasters the country has ever known" (35): "In his absence, what he had done was growing like a thunderstorm, feeding on hot air and invisible moisture, or bigger, like a tropical storm, spinning out of control, created by TV people because it was good business. He could not for the life imagine how drinking a half-point of whiskey could generate such a hurricane of interest in who he was" (29). At the time of Jesse's capture when a policeman inquires if he is Jesse McNeil, Jesse feebly responds: "I feel like I'm two different people," an indication not only of his personal identity crisis and the confusion in his mind associated with this but also of his apparent unwillingness to accept the monstrous specimen of humanity he has become (35).

Another story where recklessness and failure prevail, **"Navigators of Thought,"** focuses on several former college English teachers, all denied tenure because they proved incapable of meeting the demands and expectations of academic life and of necessity were forced to seek blue-collar employment. Now tugboat crewmen who seem out of place, they hope to be able to publish something of significance in their respective literary fields, facilely believing this may be their ticket to return to higher academe. Yet in this new profession they likewise prove incompetent and inept. As Bert Davenport, the captain of the tugboat, succinctly tells one of his fellow English professors now turned tugboatman: "Sometimes I think we think too much" (78). In fact, as a consequence of their pensiveness, they often prove careless and destructive in attempting to manage the practical responsibilities on the boat. In a recent mishap Davenport and the captain of a new tugboat who had been at the controls had lost an attached barge because his crew of college professors had failed to secure it properly; the barge had "charged the dock at an angle, hammering two pilings into kindling" (74). Dixon, their employer who laments the expense their carelessness and accidents have cost him, also seems to delight secretly in their failures.

Reassigned by Dixon to an old spare tug, the *Phoenix Three,* this neophyte crew of intellectuals botches their second chance to prove their capability. While in pursuit of a runaway barge, a formidable but practical challenge, Bert and his crew, though exhibiting a noble and heroic effort, fail again, their tug capsizing and sinking and one of the men losing his life and the manuscript he hoped, if published, would create the opportunity for him to return to the academy. Afterwards when Dixon asks why the drowned man, Max Renault, did not escape with the rest of the crew, the cook Dr. Grieg replies, "I guess he got trapped" (85). Grieg's comment figuratively expresses the collective dilemma of these former academics, all of whom in their displacement from their college English teaching positions are "trapped" by a web of circumstances they do not comprehend. Unable to return to the rarified environment of higher education and now facing inevitable termination as tugboatmen, Bert Davenport and his fellow "navigators of thought" are indeed entrapped with nowhere to go.

In contrast to Bert and his crew in **"Navigators of Thought,"** the recklessness in **"People on the Empty Road"** stems from youthful immaturity, impatience, and irresponsibility, all of which may have negative consequences. Twenty-four-year-old Wesley McBride, the story's central character who has wrecked and blown engines in more than his share of cars and who hauls gravel at break-neck speeds for a gravel company in Pine Oil, Louisiana, "used his recklessness like a tool to get the job done" (89). Attempting to justify his fast and reckless driving, Wesley pragmatically explains to his concerned father, "The construction folks want the rock quick. If we can't get it to them when they need it, someone else gets the contract" (89). In fact, Wesley has become so proficient at making fast deliveries from the gravel plant to the casino construction site in New Orleans that his boss has come to rely on him. Interestingly, Wesley's recklessness extends to his life after the job as well:

> After every twelve-hour day, he would tear out of the gravel pit in his rusty Thunderbird, spinning his wheels in a diminishing shriek for half a mile. The road turned through worthless sand bottoms and stunted growths of pine, and the car would surge into the curves like electricity, Wesley pushing over the blacktop as if he were teaching the road a lesson, straightening it out with his wheels. When he would charge off the asphalt at eighty onto a gravel road, he would force the low sedan over a rolling cloud of dust and exploding rock as though he were not in danger at every wheel skid and shimmy of slamming into a big pine like a cannonball. For Wesley, driving possessed the reality of a video game.

> (90)

Moreover, an environment of wreckage surrounds Wesley, who inhabits a "dented sea-green mobile home parked in an abandoned gravel pit" (90) and who observes "an abandoned locomotive, its wheels sunk into the sand" and "shards of machinery and cable" (91), both emblematic reminders of his carelessness and self-destructiveness.

Because Wesley nearly collides with a stopped school bus full of children on one of his breakneck runs to deliver gravel, he decides to reform, seeking out a local radio talk-show host Janie Wiggins to advise and teach him self-control and patience. With Janie as his mentor (and a romantic interest as well), Wesley sees the possibility for correcting the destructive course of his life; however, this second chance is never carried to fruition. Realizing that Janie "could give advice . . . , but she couldn't follow it," Wesley discovers that she is not what she has appeared to be; instead of being even-tempered, easy going, controlled, she proves to Wesley as well as to her radio listeners who call her for advice that she is moody, irrational, and impulsive (106). When Raynelle Bullfinch, the president of a motorcycle club, calls Janie during her show to defend not putting mufflers on their cycles, Janie loses control, angrily lashing out at Raynelle and then abruptly quitting her job right in the middle of the broadcast. Wesley McBride, who loses Janie and who becomes disillusioned by her hypocrisy, loses something much more significant—his chance for viable change and personal fulfillment. Consequently, he reluctantly resigns himself to working for his father as a meat cutter, a lackluster, dead-end job, offering the young man little hope for renewal.

Another young man whose life is on "an empty road" going nowhere, Lenny Fontenot in **"Little Frogs in a Ditch,"** has just been fired from a laundry, the latest of numerous jobs he has held and subsequently has lost. Expressing cynicism, finding fault everywhere he looks, and "suffer[ing] from inborn disrespect for anybody engaged in business," believing as he does that "everybody is stupid" and that "all businessmen were crooks," Lenny lives with his grandfather who constantly berates him for his negativity, immaturity, and disreputable behavior (128). A deadbeat and ne'er-do-well, Lenny was rejected by his parents, "who frowned on [their son's] efforts to manage the country's only Cajun punk salsa band" and his "selling cracked birdseed to grammar school kids as something he called 'predope,' or 'pot lite'" and who sold their house and purchased a Winnebago in order to travel and get away from him (130). Living in an environment not only where he is estranged from his parents, who have given up on him, but also where "useless household junk" and broken things abound, including his grandfather's rundown Ford, Lenny turns to a new scheme or rather scam with the intent of making enough money to repair his grandfather's car for his own personal use.

Lenny successfully manages to deceive people, selling them pigeons he has caught and making them believe they can train the birds to become homing pigeons. Disgusted with his grandson's deceit and dishonesty and regarding him as a "crook," Mr. Fontenot throws Lenny out of the house and later tries to persuade his grandson to see a priest and confess this sin: "Remember what Sister Florita told you one time in catechism class? If you close your eyes before you go to confession, your sins will make a noise. . . . They'll cry out like little frogs in a ditch at sundown" (140-141). Feeling no genuine guilt, no remorse of conscience, Lenny responds, "Well, I don't hear nothing. . . . What's the point of me confessing if I don't hear nothing" (141). Nor does he do anything of consequence to make reparation to the victims of his scam, losing any chance to correct the disgraceful course he has been following.

Of essentially the same mold as Lenny Fontenot, fifty-two-year-old Curtis Lado in **"License to Steal"** represents the kind of character that an older Lenny would likely become if he does not change. Uneducated, debt-ridden, currently unemployed, lacking marketable skills, having no stable employment record, and a drunk with slim prospects of obtaining a job, Curtis has been rejected by his wife who has recently left him and told their son Nookey that "she was tired of living in Louisiana with somebody didn't bring home no money" (151). Forced by circumstances to seek employment, Curtis goes to a metal casting company, and when the personnel director, smelling alcohol on Curtis's breath, inquires if he drinks, he humorously responds in a self-deprecating manner: "Not so it affects my working, no ma'am—just a few to wash down my meals, and at night with my podnuhs down in Hammond, but I seldom ever pop a top before breakfast" (154).

Curtis's dysfunctional life and adamant attitude toward constructive change, which both disgust and amuse, prevent him from finding gainful employment. Interestingly, his incorrigibility, Gautreaux suggests, is comparable to his truck's radio, the tuning dial on it having become stuck on a National Public Radio station where the highbrow musical sounds tantalize Cur-

tis and clash with his narrow and provincial cultural tastes. In reacting, "he tried the buttons and the tuning knob, but the radio was forever jammed on violins and cellos" (156). Later when his son Nookey turns on the truck radio and hears a "passionate voice of a soprano shrill[ing] from the speaker," he exclaims in exasperation, "Sounds like a tomcat hung up in the fan belt" (158).

Following in the path of the antebellum South's humorists, Gautreaux generates a ludicrous, hyperbolic effect not only in Nookey's exaggerated reaction to the radio but also more importantly in his descriptions of Curtis Lado. Employing stark incongruous comparisons by yoking of the human and the animate, Gautreaux captures suggestively the disorder and defectiveness reflected in Curtis's character. Rejected for a job at a metalworking shop because he could not read blueprints and lacked sufficient math skills, Curtis "cocked his head like a feisty rooster observing a big yard dog" and confidently told the owner that he could cut the iron so long as he could have someone else draw the lines (156). Later when he returned home and discovered that his electric power had been cut off and the meter removed, "he felt nauseated, his eyes hurt, and his heart knocked away like a big woodpecker in a hollow tree" (157).

Like the drunken engineer in **"Waiting for the Evening News"** and the tugboat crew in **"Navigators of Thought,"** Curtis seems primed for a downfall, his principal action in **"License to Steal"** culminating in devastation resulting from his recklessness. And like these other characters, his impetuous, irresponsible behavior defines his inability to refashion his life into a positive and constructive channel. Having been rejected for a possible job at a sawmill because the owner doesn't "hire old drunks," the inebriated Curtis mounts a steam-powered carriage, a machine used for pushing a log against a saw blade to be cut into boards. In so doing, he wrecks the carriage by crashing it through a wall of the building and likewise flattens a late model Cadillac. When he tries to escape the scene of the devastation and his truck will not start, "his heart fluttered like an engine running out of gas" (163), and when in his frustration and defeat he reclines on the front seat and turns on the radio, the knob still jammed on an NPR station, he feels overwhelmed by "somber, incomprehensible music" (164) as he awaits the legal consequences of his impulsive action.

In contrast to the previously examined stories from *Same Place, Same Things,* **"Died and Gone to Vegas,"** one of Gautreaux's most popular and amusing works of short fiction, features Raynelle Bulfinch, also a minor character in **"People on the Empty Road."** In this story, however, Raynelle, who is a cook on a government steam dredge, actually gains a second opportunity by sheer luck, winning the pot in a card game of bourrée. Called a "Cajun *Canterbury Tales*," because each of the seven crew members takes his or her turn as a storyteller, **"Died and Gone to Vegas,"** like several of the other stories in *Same Place, Same Things,* draws on the oral storytelling tradition, particularly of the variety principally associated with southern backwoods humor. Each of the outlandish tales, characterized by what Gautreaux terms an "energetic hyperbole," and employing a "spontaneous inter-narration," becomes an invented lie, part of a competitive process in which the yarn spinners swap tales in an attempt to outlie one another (qtd. in Levasseur and Rabalais 22, 23). Such narrative strategies Gautreaux attributes both to his reading of tall tales and frontier humor and as a child to listening to "retired tug-boat captains and oil-field workers try[ing] to outdo each others [sic] in stories" (qtd. in Bolick and Watta).

Raynelle, the only woman in the group, not only holds her own in the storytelling competition but also wins the card game. The latter she perceives as her ticket to transcend the limitations of her working-class background, getting out of Louisiana and finding a more exciting and more glamorous existence. With her winnings, the most money she has ever possessed, Raynelle boasts to her fellow crew members, "I'm gonna buy me a silver lamé dress and one of those cheap tickets to Las Vegas, where I can do some high-class gambling. No more of this penny-ante stuff with old men and worms. . . . I'm gonna gamble with gentlemen. Rancher, not cow farmer, either" (54-55). Yet the prospects of Raynelle achieving success as a big-time gambler in Vegas are slim. Though she has been lucky once, odds are that she will not be successful for a second time, especially in Vegas. And if this occurs, as Nick, the young oiler and Raynelle's fellow crew member on the dredge, confidently predicts, the future for Raynelle looks bleak and unpromising. And if Nick's dour imaginings come true, Raynelle will fail in her new venture, likely ending up back in Louisiana and in her failure also "might not live to get out" of the "desert" of her defeat:

> He imagined her wearing a Sears gown in a casino full of tourists dressed in shorts and sneakers. She would be drinking too much and eating too much, and the gown would look like it was crammed with rising dough. She would get in a fight with a blackjack dealer after she'd lost all her money, and then she would be thrown out on the street. After selling her plane ticket, she would be back at the slot machines until she was completely broke, and then she would be out on a neon-infested boulevard, her tiny silver purse hanging from her shoulder on a long spaghetti strap, one heel broken off a silver shoe. He saw her at last walking across the desert through the waves of heat . . . , until she sobered up and began to hitch, picked up by a carload of

Jehovah's Witnesses driving to a convention in Baton Rouge in an unair-conditioned compact stuck in second gear.

(55)

Unlike the previous stories featuring misfits whose lives seem headed for inevitable ruin and/or who seem inclined to destructive behavior, **"The Bug Man,"** a transitional piece, treats the affable and compassionate Felix Robichaux, an exterminator who eagerly attempts to connect with the lives of some of his clients, hoping to alleviate or at least to lessen the emptiness that afflicts them. Having tried unsuccessfully for their entire married life to have children, Felix and his wife Clarisse have a void of their own. Despite his personal disappointment, the well-intentioned Felix does not become self-absorbed. Nor does he attempt to lose himself in his job, devoting his attention exclusively to taking care of clients' home insect problems. Instead, having an uncanny intuition, "seeing into private lives like the eye of God, invisible and judging," and exhibiting a compassionate sensibility, Felix is insightfully in tune with the personal deficiencies of others (118). For instance, he perceives in one of his regular customers, Mrs. Malone, a former beauty queen and childless widow of four years, an underlying disenchantment stemming from loneliness. Though "he thought it a waste for such a fine woman to live an empty life" (110), Felix "knew most people were isolated and uncomfortable around those not exactly like themselves [and] he also believed that there was a reason why people like Mrs. Malone opened the doors in their lives just a crack by telling him things" (111).

Regarding it as his mission to bring joy and fulfillment to people like Mrs. Malone, Felix manages through his routine monthly visits to bring the widow and single attorney Dave McCall together, initiating a match between the two. Felix's elation in effecting this connection gives him the self-satisfaction equivalent, Gautreaux notes, to the "anticipation and hope a farmer feels after he has put in a crop, a patient desire for a green future" (118). Yet this apparently promising relationship does not last. When McCall gets Mrs. Malone pregnant, he promptly rejects her, indicating that he does not want to see her again. Empathizing with Mrs. Malone's hurt, Felix kindly offers that he and his wife would be glad to take the baby should she decide to put it up for adoption, an offer she coldly rejects. In fact, she not only informs him that she plans to have an abortion but also questions what he would do with a baby who would be nothing like his wife or himself, a cruel and smug remark that prompts him to ponder the "meanness of the world and how for the first time he was unable to deal with it" (122).

Though Felix clearly realizes providing a good home for Mrs. Malone's yet-to-be-born baby is the morally right and humane thing to do, she allows her class prejudice to influence her decision. Ten years later, Felix's exterminator business having expanded and prospered, chance circumstances give him the opportunity to visit Mrs. Malone's home once again. While there, he encounters a young boy, the product of the pregnancy that she had originally intended to abort. Suspicious of Felix, since his mother has told him not to let anyone into the house he did not know, the boy thwarts the exterminator's well-intentioned effort to connect. Though attempting to reassure Mrs. Malone's son that he is the **"Bug Man"** and that he need not fear him, Felix experiences rejection a second time, this occasion with terminal effects of painful alienation and with the realization that he had stolen only "one glance" of the child he had once hoped to make his son. Disillusioned and defeated, his identity still defined only by his occupation as an exterminator, his desire for reciprocation remaining elusive, Felix Robichaux reluctantly must resign himself to his defeat, a victim of "missed connections" (125).

In contrast to Felix Robichaux, the "veteran of missed connections," Elaine Campbell in **"Returnings"** briefly connects with and helps to effect a successful outcome for a young Asian American helicopter pilot who is trying to pass the final test in his training to be a pilot. Elaine, whose son had died from encephalitis and whose temporarily disabled husband cannot work their farm, feels a lingering sense of loss she cannot dispel. When the young pilot lands at her farm and asks Elaine for directions back to the airbase, the practicum of his solo flight exam, she readily assists him. From the perspective of the helicopter, however, everything below appears different, and she feels "like a child lost in a thousand acres of razor-leafed cane" (188). Still, Elaine's keen perception of and genuine concern for Le Ton, the pilot, seem almost maternal, an attachment in which Le Ton becomes her newfound surrogate son whom she can guide and nurture, albeit only temporarily, to fill the void left by the death of her own biological son. "The more she looked at him," Gautreaux writes, "the younger he appeared, some mother's favorite, she guessed, noticing something in his eyes" (187).

This motherly connection is reinforced when Elaine, perplexed because she cannot find recognizable landmarks so as to be able to guide Le Ton back to the base, must ask assistance from a local resident who lives in the vicinity, "someone," she remarks, "who won't call a newspaper" (189). She finds such a person in Mary Bankston, an African American tenant farmer who, like Elaine, empathizes as much as Elaine with Le Ton's plight. After listening to Le Ton relate his humble rural background and express the likelihood that he will be sent to Vietnam as a foot soldier

should he fail his training flight, Mary casts a "long mother's look to Elaine, the expression a woman owns at night when she sits up listening to a child cough and rattle, knowing there is nothing she can do but act out of her best feelings" (191). Before Elaine and Le Ton continue their mission to locate the airfield, Le Ton, Gautreaux writes, "glanced back to the tenant house, where Mary Bankston was probably watching him as she would a young child crossing the street," yet another indication of Mary's maternal attachment and instinct (192). When Le Ton takes Elaine back to her farm before proceeding to the airfield, she asks him to call and let her know if he passed his flight test. While this gesture may appear obligatory, it represents much more than that; Elaine's actions are actually emblematic of her pluralistic sensibility and her desire to show maternal nurturing. The connection that she has established with the Vietnamese pilot, a young man who represents a surrogate son to her, has given her a second chance to be a mother. The temporary respite from the work of the farm and the bonding with Le Ton have given Elaine Campbell a new perspective of life, a renewed belief of who she is, and a stronger relationship with her own husband. At the story's close, with news that the young pilot has successfully passed his flight test and that she has helped him, Elaine can comfortably depart for town with her husband, knowing as they drive down the road that her nurturing instincts extend beyond "the land around her [that] would [soon] bear cornstalks growing like children" (194).

An even better example of a reaffirmation and strengthening of family bonds, of a second chance for reinforcing and restoring family harmony and solidarity, is **"Floyd's Girl,"** a story in which Gautreaux, much in the same manner as Ernest Gaines in "Just Like a Tree" and *A Gathering of Old Men* (1983), skillfully employs multiple points of view to accentuate the strength and cohesion of the rural Cajun community. Floyd Bergeron, a Cajun farmer whose free-spirited wife has run away with a man from Texas, receives the assistance of extended family and friends in the Cajun community of Grand Crapaud to rescue his daughter Lizette from her mother's boyfriend who has traveled there to kidnap her. A devout Roman Catholic, Floyd unquestionably accepts the traditional belief that marriage is forever, even though his wife, "a LeBlanc gone bad," violates her nuptial vows (170). Steadfast and audacious, Floyd, though a dedicated and caring father but neither large in stature nor physically strong, must rely on the intervention of friends and family to derail the Texan's attempt to kidnap Lizette. One such ally is T-Jean's grandmother, who in her motherly way worries what will happen to Lizette in Texas removed from traditional Cajun foods to which she has grown accustomed. Moreover, it is T-Jean's grandmother, elderly and physically handicapped, who ably retaliates after the Texan has easily overpowered Floyd and his cousin René Badeux.

Defying the stereotypes associated with age and disability, the grandmother proves herself a formidable and effective opponent, "lower[ing] her head and work[ing] her walker ahead of her like some sort of field machine." Then coming upon the "Texas man [who] was still down on one knee, she raised the aluminum frame and poked one of its small rubber feet an inch into his eye socket" (177). Then she verbally lacerates him in a stinging tirade, and in the process proudly recalls and celebrates scions in the family heritage and their pioneering spirit: "You don't come to Grand Crapaud and take no Bergeron child to drag off to no place," she scolded, threatening him with the walker. . . . "This child belongs with her papa. She got LeBlanc in her, and Cancienne way back, and before that, Thibodeaux . . ." (178). Physical reinforcements arrive in the Larousse twins, Victor and Vincent, hulking physical specimens who drive up in a truck carrying two portable cutting torch rigs. Cajun friends of Floyd and still notorious as "bad boys over in Tiger Island" (179), the twins use their acetylene torches and make quick work of demolishing the Texan's truck beyond recognition, reducing it to scraps of metal so "all that was left on the side of the road was a puddle of oil and a patch of singed glass" (179). Moreover, they blatantly threaten him, indicating that if he ever returns to Grand Crapaud, Louisiana, Floyd will call them. For Floyd and his dedicated collaborators, the rescue of Lizette becomes a second chance to reenergize and reinforce the bonds of the Cajun community and to reaffirm the strong family values that the Cajuns have embraced. Summing up the attributes of **"Floyd's Girl,"** Susan Larson perceives the story as an effective amalgamation of the "broad comedy of a tall tale, the heartbreak of a family fearing a terrible loss, and the resounding and satisfying triumph of ties of place and kinship" (Larson, "First, You Make a Roux . . ." E-7).

"The Courtship of Merlin LeBlanc" represents another redemptive transformation in character, a story centering around the death in a plane crash in the Gulf of Mexico of farmer Merlin LeBlanc's thirty-four-year-old daughter Lucy. Lucy "had been married twice, abandoned by both husbands, had been an alcoholic, a drug abuser, had been detoxified twice, and . . . had a seven-month-old daughter by a Belgian tourist she had met at a bar in New Orleans" (59). Now as the sole self-appointed guardian and caretaker of Susie, Lucy's infant daughter, Merlin is given a second chance to be the father he never had been to his own three children, all of whom died prematurely. As he recalls his negli-

gence as a father to his biological children, Merlin is haunted by the thought that "his wife had tended the children just as he had tended the pigs they used to have in back of the tractor shed. He wondered if what went wrong was that he had treated his children like animals" (61). When his children were growing up, Merlin equated them with animals that reacted instinctively in satisfying their basic needs. In short, he neither communicated meaningfully or caringly to his children nor did he ever attempt to offer them useful advice or guidance. In rationalizing his past failures with his own children, Merlin muses to himself, "Why do you have to tell children things? Why don't they do what's logical?" (61). Merlin's attitude here creates a clear impression of his shallow and naïve view of child rearing and pathetic evasion of his fatherly responsibilities.

In his daughter's death, however, Merlin discovers a second opportunity to correct his past deficiencies in parenthood. Interestingly, his father Etienne and his grandfather Octave provide a mature perspective to induce Merlin to redress the imbalance of his former life. Both men berate him sharply and unsparingly. As he gazes nostalgically at a photograph of his three children and his wife, Merlin is touched with a feeling of guilt as he wonders what went wrong with his children. His reaction is defensive as he exclaims aloud so his father Etienne can hear him: "I was never mean to them." His father's rejoinder, "Maybe you should have been. . . . At least that would've been something" (66), not only reinforces Merlin's failures as a father but fuels his already active self-guilt as well. Later in the story Octave, his grandfather, accentuates Etienne's scathing condemnation, chastising Merlin for failing to advise his daughter not to ride in an airplane: "Didn't you teach her nothing?'"—to which Merlin reacts, "shudder[ing] like a beef cow hit with the flat side of an ax" (67). Once again, Gautreaux's use of an incongruous comparison to create comic hyperbole, a device similar to that employed by the South's antebellum humorists, accentuates a stark contrast which tends to counteract and mellow the criticism of Octave's accusation.

Still entertaining the patriarchal notion that the care of children should be a woman's responsibility, Merlin goes to a local bar, hoping to find a desirable single woman who will marry him for this purpose, but his search proves unsuccessful. Again, it is Octave who scorns his courting methods, derisively remarking, "Merlin in a damn barroom lookin' for a woman like a pork chop. . . . Looking for a woman like a damn toaster he can bring home and take in the kitchen and plug in. Plug in and forget it" (68-69).

When Merlin resigns himself to the fact that he must be the principal caregiver to baby Susie, clearly a role he has never had to play before, he is ready for the new transition in his life. His new life will require that he relinquish thinking of himself first, his strawberries, and his tractor. Having married young and having never exhibited any genuine feelings for his three children, who, as his father humorously puts it, "didn't know no more about raising children than a goat knows about flying," Merlin LeBlanc now possesses the right mindset, now seems ready mentally and emotionally to follow the right path of making family his priority and raise his granddaughter in the proper manner (70). In fact, **"The Courtship of Merlin LeBlanc"** concludes with Octave demanding of and receiving from Merlin the promise that he will raise Susan (and Merlin's grandfather insists that she be called Susan, not Susie) in a manner a child should be raised. As a positive reaffirmation that Merlin has been enlightened and has recovered, discovering for the first time latent feelings he has always previously suppressed, he quickly descends the steps to assist his father Etienne who, the moment before, "sat back in his chair so hard he lost his balance and tumbled off the porch onto the grass . . ." (70).

In contrast to **"Floyd's Girl"** and **"The Courtship of Merlin LeBlanc,"** which emphasized second chances through the strengthening of family ties and reaffirmation of family values, **"Deputy Sid's Gift,"** the final story in *Same Place, Same Things,* presents a new dimension in Gautreaux's handing of the redemption theme. In this first-person confessional narrative Bobby Simoneaux, a former oil field worker who at present is employed in a nursing home, retrospectively recounts, or rather confesses, to a priest, a series of disruptive events involving his confrontations with Fernest Bezue, a destitute black man, social misfit, and chronic alcoholic who has repeatedly stolen Simoneaux's 1962 Chevrolet pickup truck to use as a makeshift home. A disreputable character, easy to loathe, the invasive Fernest, as a reviewer in the *Kirkus Reviews,* astutely recognized, "rescue[s] . . . [Bobby] from his own meanness."(991). In an interview with Jennifer Levasseur and Kevin Rabelais, Gautreaux admitted that "racism is very painful to write about [and] 'Deputy Sid's Gift' is as close as I can come to dealing with it" (33).

For a long time, Bobby seems angry and unsympathetic with Fernest, demonstrating his contempt through derisive hyperbolic comments. The first time he and a local African American sheriff's deputy, Sid Touchard, find Bobby's truck with Fernest in it, sleeping off his most recent bout of drunkenness, Bobby flippantly and disparagingly remarks that "Deputy Sid tugged Fernest out into the sunlight, slow, like he was an old cow he was pulling out a tangle of fence" (198). Afterwards, when Bobby and Deputy Sid take Fernest

home to his mother (Sid has convinced Bobby not to file charges against him), Bobby employs striking derisive imagery, creating an unflattering point of reference, one reflecting his impersonal impression not only of Fernest but of Fernest's mother as well. As his mother comes from inside the ramshackled and delapidated house, Bobby flippantly describes her as "look-[ing] like a licorice stick" as she stands before them "dressed in some old limp dress," and on a later occasion, after she suffers a stroke and is admitted to the nursing home where Bobby works, he perceives her as "all dried up like beef jerky" (204). Nor does there seem to be any genuine filial attachment between Fernest and his mother. When he confronts her after Deputy Sid pleads with Bobby to let Fernest stay with his mother rather than to be sent to jail for stealing the truck, Fernest "stared at her like maybe she was a tractor or a cloud" (198,199). Bobby's insensitivity is captured in Gautreaux's selection of humorous and deflating metaphors.

The title of the story—**"Deputy Sid's Gift"**—relates to Bobby Simoneaux's partial conversion in his attitude toward the physically and psychologically troubled chronic drunkard Fernest Bezue. Though Bobby initially resists, staunchly adamant to the idea of doing anything to assist Fernest, even admitting to the priest that while "other people deserve my help . . . , Fernest didn't deserve nothing," Bobby 's temperament mellows (204). Plagued by Deputy Sid's worthy example in trying to help Fernest (he buys him a sandwich to eat and drives him to the edge of town), Bobby is motivated to action after being plagued by his conscience and by Mrs. Bezue's singling him out as "the one" to save her son. Sid's gift is his repeated insistence that Fernest needs outside help, and ultimately, as Perry Glasser accurately observes, his "understanding the nature of true charity" (43). In other words, Sid becomes the principal catalyst in making Bobby realize that his role is to be his brother's keeper, doing so by suppressing his anger and disabling his impatience with Fernest and instead extending to him sympathetic understanding and kindness. As evidence of Bobby's transformation, he dreams about Fernest when he goes to sleep at night and even during his waking hours. As he puts it, "[W]hen I went to sleep, there he was in my head. When I read a newspaper, there he was in a group picture" (204). Moreover, Bobby finds himself persistently haunted by thoughts of Mrs. Bezue's ever-present "pointing finger," reminding him that he is "the one."

The defining moment for Bobby occurs after Fernest steals the old truck a final time. When Deputy Sid is able to find Fernest, Bobby, as he recounts to the priest, uneasily concocts several false excuses, which he shares with Sid, for deciding this time to help

Fernest. After Sid and Bobby reach the barn, where Fernest is sleeping in a feed trough, the aftermath of his most recent intoxication, Fernest inquires what Bobby wants with him. Though Bobby lies, but for a good reason, in saying that Deputy Sid bought the truck and is giving it to Fernest as a gift so that "he could stay in it sometime" (207), the real benefactor is Bobby himself. In response to Sid's query concerning why he said this, Bobby, who seems to have undergone only a partial alteration in his attitude toward Fernest at this point, his spirit of magnanimity not entirely genuine, remarks: "I didn't want nothing for what I did" (207). After all, as the guilt-ridden Bobby tells the priest, who, as Gautreaux has explained, serves as the "sounding board for the narrator's conscience" (qtd. in Levasseur and Rabelais 33), his true purpose in giving Fernest the truck was "to make myself feel good, not to help Fernest Bezue." Yet the priest absolves Bobby's guilt-ridden anxiety spawned by his selfishness, consoling him by disclosing, "there's only one thing worse than what I did . . . not doing it" (207).

The fruition of Bobby Simoneaux's redemption occurs several months later when Deputy Sid phones to inform him that he found Fernest Bezue dead in the truck Bobby gave to him. Though Bobby admits sorrow in hearing this news, Sid offers a conciliatory observation to accentuate the good that he and Bobby accomplished before Fernest's death: "we couldn't do nothing for him but we did it anyway" (208).

Same Place, Same Things has rightly been lauded as reminiscent of the "early work of Flannery O'Connor" (*Kirkus Reviews* 991), a compliment which places Tim Gautreaux's debut story collection in distinguished company. Some of the tales comprising this collection feature miscreants, some of whom, like Jesse McNeil in **"Waiting for the Evening News,"** Wesley McBride in **"People on the Empty Road,"** and Curtis Lado in **"License to Steal,"** are despicable and at the same time amusing specimens of humanity, characters for whom we feel compassion and scorn simultaneously. Plagued by recklessness and irresponsibility and, in the case of Jesse and Curtis, alcoholism as well, these characters, each of whom is a grotesque, follow a track of inevitable failure and destruction. The sense of being in a rut, of being unable to break out of their stagnant, dead-end existences, afflicts many of these same characters who consistently fail to take advantage of opportunities to reconstruct their misshapen lives. Ada, the strawberry farmer's wife who has never been a hundred miles from home, expresses accurately the general malaise and gnawing despair that not only afflicts her but most of Gautreaux's other lost souls as well, who, like Ada, cannot seem to turn around the direction of their meaningless, lost lives. As she com-

plains to Henry Lintel, the traveling irrigation pump repairman, "Sometimes I think it's staying in the same place, doing the same things, day in, day out, that gets me down. . . . Same place, same things, all my life" (12-13). Typically, these very same characters cannot make meaningful connections outside themselves, a possible corrective to fill the void of their empty and unfulfilling lives. Still, Gautreaux achieves a healthy and hopeful balance, showcasing in some of the stories the essential goodness of humanity and the capacity for personal improvement and transformation of flawed characters. Like fellow Catholic writer O'Connor, Gautreaux's stories feature several promising moral reformations wherein characters are offered second chances to turn their meaningless and restricted lives around. Merlin LeBlanc in **"The Courtship of Merlin LeBlanc,"** Floyd in **"Floyd's Girl,"** Elaine Campbell in **"Returnings,"** and Bobby Simoneaux in **"Deputy Sid's Gift"**—all seize the opportunity and successfully gain new perspectives and leases on their lives by doing so. In fine, the stories of *Same Place, Same Things*—but most particularly this latter group of narratives—"are imbued," Susan Larson keenly points out, "with the rich roux of family, place, race, and religion that is the base of all good Southern fiction" (Larson, "First, You Make a Roux . . ." E-7).

Works Cited

Berne, Suzanne. "Swamped." Rev. of *Same Place, Same Things,* by Tim Gautreaux. *New York Times Book Review* 22 Sept. 1996: 16.

Bolick, Katie, and David Watta. "A Conversation with Tim Gautreaux." *The Atlantic Online.* 14 Mar. 1997. 20 June 2003. <http:www.theatlantic.com/unbound/fact/fict/gautreaux/tgautr.htm>.

Cooper, Rand Richards. Rev. of *Same Place, Same Things,* by Tim Gautreaux. *Commonweal* 8 Nov. 1996: 24-25.

Gautreaux, Tim. *Same Place, Same Things.* New York: Picador USA, 1996.

Glasser, Perry. Rev. of *Same Place, Same Things,* by Tim Gautreaux, *North American Review* Mar.-Apr. 1997: 43.

Larson, Susan. "First, You Make a Roux . . ." Rev. of *Same Place, Same Things,* by Tim Gautreaux. New Orleans *Times-Picayune.* 15 Sept. 1996: E 7.

———. "Writer Tim Gautreaux Sets His Short Stories in a Louisiana That's Rough Around the Edges." New Orleans *Times-Picayune* 15 Sept. 1996: D 1, D 6.

Levasseur, Jennifer, and Kevin Rabelais. "Interview with Tim Gautreaux." *Mississippi Review* 27.3 (1999): 19-40.

Masciere, Christina. Interview. "Novel Approach: Tim Gautreaux Takes the Next Step." *New Orleans Magazine* Mar. 1998: 31, 35, 47.

Rev. of *Same Place, Same Things,* by Tim Gautreaux. *Kirkus Reviews* 11 Sept. 1996: 991.

L. Lamar Nisly (essay date fall 2006)

SOURCE: Nisly, L. Lamar. "Wingless Chickens or Catholics from the Bayou: Conceptions of Audience in O'Connor and Gautreaux." *Christianity and Literature* 56, no. 1 (fall 2006): 63-85.

[*In the following essay, Nisly compares Gautreaux's writings with those of another Southern Catholic humorist, Flannery O'Connor, noting that Gautreaux's stories do not share the sense of prophetic urgency that is a hallmark of O'Connor's work.*]

The critical receptions of Flannery O'Connor and Tim Gautreaux are at very different points, with O'Connor's stories clearly seen as canonical and Gautreaux still in the midst of his writing career. Yet they also have obvious connections, as Gautreaux, who lives in southern Louisiana, makes apparent in interviews:

> Well, naturally an influence on just about everybody writing in the South was Flannery O'Connor. She's probably the country's premier short story writer. If you analyze her stories you see she was working with tragedy, and humor, and irony. And putting all of these elements together in a technically perfect way. . . . Also, you know, she was Catholic, and I can relate to that because I'm Catholic.
>
> (Gautreaux, Hebert-Leiter interview 3)

More succinctly, he writes, "When I feel I'm losing my sense of humor, or that I'm becoming sentimental, I read an O'Connor story and her prose adjusts my perceptions" ("Behind the Great Stories" 1). Gautreaux's stated appreciation of O'Connor rings true when one reads his fiction, for particularly in his stories, his mix of humor and serious intent calls to mind O'Connor's best fiction.

Yet even though the two authors do share essential commonalities, a salient difference emerges within their fiction: *their sense of audience.* As I will explain, O'Connor presents a very clear vision of her audience—her "hostile audience," as she says in many of her essays—that she imagines herself addressing. It is an audience with a secular perspective that is uncomprehending and likely antagonistic to her Catholic vision, an audience prone to be confused and put off by her fiction. In contrast, Gautreaux has a very different conception of his audience. Gautreaux describes his audience in terms that sound warm, friendly, companionable. He imagines a broad range of readers, all of whom can connect with what he is writing. I argue that because of these divergent understandings of audience, O'Connor and Gautreaux develop strikingly different tones in their fiction, particularly through their treatment of characters. Finally, as I will show by analyzing "A Good Man Is Hard To Find," O'Connor's prophetic stance to her unbelieving audience leads her, at times, to create characters as acted parables, characters who perform disturbing actions so that O'Connor can confront her reader. In contrast, **"Welding with Children"** reveals that Gautreaux's "audience as companion" position allows him to present an early crisis in the story and then guide his character to embrace the moral position he knew all along was right.

In his highly influential book *The Rhetoric of Fiction,* first published in 1961, Wayne Booth argues that critics have assumed for too long that "True artists . . . take no thought of their readers. They write for themselves" (89). Booth insists, to the contrary, that the audience always plays a role in literature: "nothing the writer does can be finally understood in isolation from his effort to make it all accessible to someone else—his peers, himself as imagined reader, his audience" (397). Booth in particular stresses the importance that shared beliefs play in this interaction between writer and reader, insisting that "literature is radically dependent on the concurrence of beliefs of authors and readers" (140). Yet Booth remains primarily concerned about the way a text creates a reader, considering the way the implied author addresses the implied or postulated audience (422).

Peter Rabinowitz creates a more complicated analysis of readers, working to sort out the various levels of audience addressed by an author. Rabinowitz argues that there are the actual, authorial, and narrative audiences. The actual audience "consists of the flesh-and-blood people who read the book. This is the audience that booksellers are most concerned with—but it happens to be the audience over which an author has no guaranteed control" (*Before Reading* 20). In contrast,

> Both the authorial and narrative audiences are abstractions, but they are abstractions in radically different senses. The authorial audience is a hypothetical construction of what the author expects his or her readers to be like; the narrative audience, on the other hand, is an imaginative creation by the author—something he or she hopes to convince the readers to pretend to become.
>
> (Rabinowitz, "Where We Are When We Read" 23)

Of most interest for my purposes is Rabinowitz's authorial audience; no writer can know with certainty who will make up his or her actual audience, but "no author can make any rhetorical decisions (conscious or unconscious) without relying on prior assumptions about precisely what values, experiences, habits, and familiarity with artistic conventions his or her readers will bring to the text" (Rabinowitz, "Where We Are When We Read" 5). While Rabinowitz acknowledges the role of the author in constructing the authorial audience, his primary concern is the role of readers in taking on the characteristics of the authorial audience, for "To the extent that we do not, our reading experience will be more or less seriously flawed" (Rabinowitz, "Where We Are When We Read" 5). He particularly notes that no authorial audience is pristine, free from presuppositions; instead, "you need to ask what sort of *corrupted* reader this particular author wrote for: what were that reader's beliefs, engagements, commitments, prejudices, and stampedings of pity and terror?" (*Before Reading* 26). Rabinowitz presents a compelling case that authors envision a particular, "corrupted" audience as they are writing.

WINGLESS CHICKENS

Certainly Rabinowitz's argument rings true for O'Connor, as becomes clear in her letters and essays. She writes in her first letter to Elizabeth Hester, who became an extremely important correspondent (identified in *The Habit of Being* only as "A"),

> the moral sense has been bread out of certain sections of the population, like wings have been bred off certain chickens to produce more white meat on them. This is a generation of wingless chickens, which I suppose is what Nietzsche meant when he said God was dead.
>
> (*The Habit of Being* 90)

O'Connor is very aware of these "wingless chickens," for she sees herself as writing her fiction for them. As she further explains in her next letter to Hester,

> One of the awful things about writing when you are a Christian is that for you the ultimate reality is the Incarnation, the present reality is the Incarnation, and nobody believes in the Incarnation; that is, nobody in your audience. My audience are the people who think God is dead. At least these are the people I am conscious of writing for.
>
> (*The Habit of Being* 92)

In response to her perceived hostile audience, O'Connor embraces a stance as prophet in her writing, a position she makes clear in letters, essays, and interviews. Insisting that she has "to push as hard as the age that pushes against" her (*The Habit of Being* 229), she explains that the fiction writer should be characterized with "prophetic vision," a "realism which does not hesitate to distort appearances in order to show a hidden truth" (*Mystery* 179). O'Connor intends for her fiction to confront and persuade her readers, to con-

vince them that they should turn from a modern skepticism of belief to an encounter with the Divine. Her Catholic outlook so directs her understanding of life that she feels compelled, as one of her literary group colleagues explains, "to hurl protests, as loud and vehement as she could make them, against the two-fold assumption that 'God is dead,' and 'Man is God'; i.e., modern man is now beyond the God of the Bible, and he doesn't need the God of orthodox Christianity" (Kirkland 160).

As she speaks about her audience, O'Connor makes clear for whom she is writing—and who is outside of her focus. O'Connor explicitly rejects writing for a Catholic audience, joking that the audience is too small (*Conversations* 14). However, apart from this practical consideration, I believe she also feels compelled to speak to a secular audience as a means of spreading the good news of the gospel. In one of her most famous statements about her audience, O'Connor provides a vision of a hulking reader unable to understand her fiction. Yet she asserts,

> I know that I must never let him affect my vision, must never let him gain control over my thinking, must never listen to his demands unless they accord with my conscience; yet I feel I must make him see what I have to show, even if my means of making him see have to be extreme.
>
> (qtd. in Feeley 45)

Particularly striking in this quotation is O'Connor's evident fear that her audience cannot comprehend her writing coupled with her own belief that she must only write what grows out of her faith. At the same time, the last phrases indicate that O'Connor is willing to pursue even "extreme" approaches to communicate her message.

Because O'Connor is so aware of writing for an unbelieving audience, she recognizes that her fiction is directly affected by her sense of her audience, particularly lamenting what is not understood by her audience:

> The problem of the novelist who wishes to write about a man's encounter with this God is how he shall make the experience—which is both natural and supernatural—understandable, and credible, to his reader. In any age this would be a problem, but in our own, it is a well-nigh insurmountable one. Today's audience is one in which religious feeling has become, if not atrophied, at least vaporous and sentimental.
>
> (*Mystery* 161)

Attempting to communicate with her audience, then, leads O'Connor to her shocking approach. The fiction that she writes is a response to this unbelieving world, a rejoinder that O'Connor insists on writing even if it is not understood. As Robert Brinkmeyer explains,

"That her fiction was often misunderstood and occasionally viciously attacked in reviews reinforced
O'Connor's view that she stood far outside the intellectual establishment" (11). Nevertheless, she continued to forge ahead, for, as she insists, "You have to
push as hard as the age that pushes against you" (*The
Habit of Being* 229).

Although O'Connor frequently alludes in her letters to
her lecture tours being solely motivated by the need to
pay bills, Jean Cash, in her biography, asserts that
"O'Connor, by lecturing so widely, created her own
pulpit, one from which she could and did use both
clarity and humor to enlighten her listeners to the
theological intention of her work" (263). Her willingness to "explain" her stories, as she frequently does in
her letters and lectures, shows her intense desire for
the reader to understand the theological dimensions of
her stories.[1] Paul Giles is certainly correct that
O'Connor's stories often have "potential ambiguity
and excess of signification" which prevent them from
"being mere diagrammatic expositions of Catholic
principles" (362). Yet O'Connor keenly wants to communicate her core beliefs. She feels compelled to
present to her unbelieving readers the "central Christian mystery: that [life] has, for all its horror, been
found by God to be worth dying for" (*Mystery* 146).
One way to describe her prophetic approach is to say
that her message derives from her Catholic faith, but
the directness of her method grows from fundamental-
ist preaching (Brinkmeyer 8). Because O'Connor believed so intensely her core convictions, she put on
the mantle of prophet to reach her unbelieving audience.

Catholics from the Bayou

Unlike the collected essays and interviews available
from O'Connor, Gautreaux's non-fiction materials are
limited to a few brief essays and a series of uncollected—yet very helpful—interviews. From this material, though, it is readily apparent that Gautreaux's
perception of his audience is radically different than
O'Connor's sense of a hostile reader, as he seeks to
appeal to a friendly audience.

Gautreaux was an English professor at Southeastern
Louisiana University for thirty years until his retirement in 2002, yet he retains a strong affection for
blue-collar, less formally educated people. As he often
explains, Gautreaux comes from a blue-collar family;
his father was a tugboat captain and his grandfather a
steamboat engineer. Even in his self description, he
downplays his career as an academic, describing himself as a retired schoolteacher rather than a writer because calling himself a writer "strikes me as being
pretentious" (Gautreaux, Scanlan interview 4). Al-

though he sees himself writing in the same Catholic
tradition as Walker Percy, he explains, "I'm not a philosopher like Walker Percy. . . . I'm just a Catholic
from the bayou. But it's one of the rhythms of life"
(qtd. in Larson 2). Gautreaux's stories seem to appeal
both to people within his Cajun culture, these Catholics from the Bayou, as well as those from outside
southern Louisiana. Similarly, he also hopes to engage
an audience that has a widely varied socio-economic
and educational background:

> I pride myself in writing a "broad-spectrum" fiction,
> fiction that appeals to both intellectuals and blue-collar
> types. Many times I've heard stories of people who
> don't read short stories, or people who have technical
> jobs, who like my fiction. . . . My nephew, who in-
> stalls wiring harnesses on oil rigs, was out on one last
> year, and he saw a man with his legs dangling over the
> Gulf, reading a paperback, and he walked up to see
> what he was reading, and it was my first collection of
> short stories. And I hear tales over and over about blue-
> collar types sitting around somewhere reading a Tim
> Gautreaux book. This is the crossover aspect, the broad-
> spectrum aspect, that I'm talking about, that I like about
> what I do.
>
> (Gautreaux, Kane interview 140)

Gautreaux imagines a very diverse audience, all of
whom can connect with his tales.

Gautreaux's perception of audience seems clearly
shaped by his experience growing up in southern Louisiana, for the shared values that Gautreaux encountered as a child have allowed him to imagine an audience that connects with many of his most firmly held
beliefs. Themes of moral decisions and the possibility
of grace have been ingrained in Gautreaux, allowing
them to emerge naturally in his writing: "It comes
from just living in Louisiana in the 1950s. Louisiana
is one of those places that has a very strong spiritual
presence, even though it's a place where people like
to drink and fight" (Gautreaux, Meyering interview 8).
He has experienced a solidity of common understandings, and his fiction reveals a conversation with a companion who shares similar beliefs. Gautreaux's goal is
not to convert his reader since he already sees the
reader as a companion along the way. Indeed, his understandings become clear when he speaks of his years
of teaching modern poetry:

> After a while, I saw students struggling so hard to deal
> with *The Waste Land,* and I started to think, "Why am
> I making these people suffer so much?" It was so hard
> to deal with Eliot's early poems—the theme of which
> was, basically, life sucks—and my ultimate response
> was "What was your first clue?" . . . That's one of the
> reasons I like blue-collar people. With all their short-
> comings and biases and pent-up angers, most of them
> understand the value of being good-natured and having
> a good time. You'd never catch a welder reading *The
> Waste Land,* thank God.
>
> (Gautreaux, Levasseur and Rabalais interview 31)

Thus, even though Gautreaux is not afraid to take on difficult subjects, his cordial relationship with his audience leads him to a gentler tone, a conversational approach with his readers. Unlike O'Connor, who feels compelled to confront her hostile audience, Gautreaux sees his audience as made up of fellow travelers. Gautreaux's imagined audience, it seems, consists of people who recognize the difficulties in life but, because of their Christian faith, do not see the world as finally brutal and hopeless. What he imagines his audience relating to are the moral questions that he finds compelling. These grounded questions are at the heart of Gautreaux's conception of his audience: "the business about value—what do you do with children, why do you do *anything* in life?—is always behind my fiction" (Gautreaux, Kane interview 135). Gautreaux's stories are not arguments about the right thing to do. Rather, they are tales that embody moral questions and dilemmas, pushing his readers toward decisions that, on some level, Gautreaux seems to believe, they already know are right.

Because of his conception of audience, Gautreaux's fiction embodies the values of Catholicism, community, and family. With a gentleness to his characters and frequently a deft use of humor, Gautreaux creates striking fiction that invites the reader into an individual's struggle with doing what is right. In this effort to choose the good, the character is often supported and confronted by a supportive community and extended family.

Characters in Acted Parables

In O'Connor's story "Revelation," Ruby Turpin amuses herself by considering what type of person she would choose to be if she were not herself. If the reader of fiction were approached by the god of all literature and asked what fictive character he or she would like to become, a reasonable response might be, "Nobody from an O'Connor story!" Life tends to be difficult for O'Connor's characters, a fact often noted by O'Connor's critics. Martha Stephens complains, "what is oppressive about the O'Connor work as a whole, what is sometimes intolerable, is her stubborn refusal to see any good, any beauty or dignity or meaning, in ordinary human life on earth" (9). Joanne McMullen laments, "Impersonality in her treatment of character types forces O'Connor's audience away from any concern for the fates of her characters and often reduces to a ridiculing humor the vagaries of their souls" (21). Even more harshly—although eloquently—Laurence Enjolras insists, "we do not confront human beings; we encounter monsters who assail us either with their defects, with their impairments, or with their clownishness, caught as they are—fierce, violent, pathetic creatures—in the gruesome show of

the puppet life through which they totter" (7).[2] In response to these critiques, other critics attempt to show that O'Connor loved some or all of her characters. For instance, Bill Oliver believes that O'Connor had sympathy for characters such as Mr. Head ("The Artificial Nigger"), Tanner ("Judgment Day"), Parker ("Parker's Back"), and the twelve-year-old girl ("A Temple of the Holy Ghost") because, "despite their limitations, they have the capacity to respond with childlike wonder to the mystery of things. They differ radically from most of O'Connor's characters, who fear and try to suppress what they cannot grasp immediately through reason" (9). Sarah Gordon presents a somewhat different list:

> Surely one could argue that such strong and memorable characters as the grandmother, Mrs. McIntyre, and even General Sash, Hazel Motes, and the great-uncle and nephew Tarwater in a sense become lovable to us as readers through the extent to which we invest in their struggles and identify with them. We might surmise these characters were lovable to O'Connor in that sense as well.
>
> (227)

More broadly, Richard Giannone argues that love is at the core of all O'Connor fiction, with the surprising and violent endings reflecting "the overwhelming boldness of divine love invading human life" (*Love* 6).

Given the shock of O'Connor's treatment of her characters along with her explicitly enunciated theology, these wildly divergent responses should perhaps be expected. Characters are gored by a bull, shot by a son, blinded, drowned, raped, stuffed through a banister, wiped out on a family vacation, smashed against a rock, hanged in an attic, and driven over by a tractor. That list does not include the "milder" offenses, such as having a wooden leg stolen, being beaten by a broom, or having a woods burned. Yet my argument is that all of this discussion about whether or not O'Connor had compassion for her characters to some extent misses the point. Focusing on O'Connor's prophetic stance may help us know how to think about her characters.

It is important at the outset to insist that O'Connor was a writer not an allegorist, so her characters function as characters, not as representations. Sarah Fodor rightly points out that her characters "must be believable before they can stand for something else" (112). However, given her self-understood role as a prophet—what Giannone calls "a one-woman war against the age's moral blindness" (*Hermit* 6)—we may be led astray if we focus too heavily on the particulars of what happens to her characters. For I believe that, in the tradition of the Old Testament prophets, O'Connor was less concerned about her characters than she was about her *audience,* an audience, as we have seen, that she perceived as hostile to her message.[3]

O'Connor was certainly very familiar with the prophets, for she peppered her fiction with references to them and read books that focus on them. For instance, when Parker in "Parker's Back" is thrown out of the pool hall, "a calm descended on the pool hall as nerve shattering as if the long barn-like room were the ship from which Jonah had been cast into the sea" (*Collected Works* 672). O. E. Parker's name, when he finally utters it, is also revealed to combine an Old Testament prophet's name, Obadiah, with Elihue, meaning "He is God." In "The Lame Shall Enter First," Rufus Johnson chews up and swallows a page from the Bible and exclaims, "I've eaten it like Ezekiel and it was honey to my mouth!" (*Collected Works* 628). *The Violent Bear It Away* contains several references to biblical prophets. At the moment that old Tarwater figures out that Rayber had written an article about him, "His eyeballs swerved from side to side as if he were pinned in a strait jacket again. Jonah, Ezekiel, Daniel, he was at that moment all of them—the swallowed, the lowered, the enclosed" (*Collected Works* 378). Young Tarwater's arrival at Rayber's house sparks another prophetic reference, since "His whole body felt hollow as if he had been lifted like Habakkuk by the hair of his head, borne swiftly through the night and set down in the place of his mission" (*Collected Works* 385). And as Tarwater drifts in and out of sleep while remembering his struggle to drown Bishop, "His pale face twitched and grimaced. He might have been Jonah clinging wildly to the whale's tongue" (*Collected Works* 462).

Besides her own reading of the Bible, O'Connor's knowledge about the prophets was increased through books that she read to review. She praises J. C. Chaine's *God's Heralds* (1955) as an "invaluable aid in deepening appreciation of prophetic revelation and the conditions under which this was given to the world" (*Presence of Grace* 41). She is even more appreciative of Bruce Vawter's *The Conscience of Israel* (1961) for placing the prophets in their historical context. She notes, "In this setting alone it is possible to understand an Isaiah walking naked as a warning to Egypt, and [sic] Hosea agonizing over his prostitute wife or an Ezekiel baking his bread over dung to symbolize the destruction to come" (*Presence of Grace* 141).[4] Through these references and books that she read, it becomes clear that O'Connor was well familiar with the Old Testament prophets.

Indeed, O'Connor's comment about Vawter's study points toward the way that I understand O'Connor's characters: just as God had the prophets perform odd, even disturbing, actions as a way of communicating

God's message to the Israelites, so O'Connor causes distressing outcomes for her characters as a means of reaching her hostile audience. The litany of Old Testament "acted parables," as Curt Kuhl identifies them, is as bizarre as it is lengthy. Besides his walking around naked and barefoot (Isa. 20:2-3), Isaiah is also directed to give his sons such odd names as "a remnant shall return" (Isa. 7:3, 8:3-4). Jeremiah must walk around wearing a yoke (Jer. 27:2) and is ordered to buy land when it appears that all is lost (Jer. 32:25). Ezekiel, the prophet with the longest list of acted parables, is directed in astonishing ways: to be tied hand and foot while unable to speak (Ezek. 3:25); to lie on his left side for 390 days and then on his right for 40 more days (Ezek. 4:4-6); to bake with human dung—although he receives an exemption to use animal dung (Ezek. 4:12-15); to shave, weigh, and burn his hair (Ezek. 5:1-2); to put aside any grieving for his dead wife (Ezek. 24:14, 18); to be unable to speak (Ezek. 33:22-3). Though Hosea's directions are not as numerous, his assignment is astonishing: to marry an unchaste woman, sometimes identified as a prostitute (Hos. 1:3). Even after she leaves him to chase other men, God directs Hosea to bring her back, although he is not to have sexual relations with her for a time (Hos. 3:1-3). In each of these instances, the word comes to the prophet to carry out this task, apparently with no concern for the prophet's own comfort, embarrassment, or welfare. What is foremost for God and the prophets is communicating a message from the divine to the people. As Kuhl dryly notes, "Ordinary standards of normality are not, of course, to be applied to a prophet . . ." (123). More substantively, E. W. Heaton explains,

> The prophets were violent, because they lived in a society where honesty and decency were being violated everyday. They could not profess a vocation from the Lord, the God of righteousness, and stand aloof when disgusting luxury was being purchased at the price of the blood of the defenceless poor.
>
> (60)

Following God's command and warning the people were foremost for the prophets, not a concern about the individual prophet's well-being. Nothing could come in the way of presenting the message as dramatically as possible, for "Prophets are first and foremost 'proclaimers'" (Sawyer 1).

To read O'Connor's fiction as prophetic utterances, then, changes the way we see the stories. They are realistic in a sense, since they are peopled with real, if odd, characters, typically in a rural Georgia setting. But they cannot be read as fully realistic because our focus, if we are considering them as prophetic speech, needs to be on the effect these characters and their outcomes have on the audience rather than any deep sympathy for the individual character. Seeing characters as taking part in an acted parable becomes perhaps most clear when we examine O'Connor's most shockingly famous story, "A Good Man Is Hard To Find" (1953), a story that O'Connor often read aloud and one that many readers find compelling and disgusting, often all at the same time.[5] Indeed, in her comments about this story, O'Connor implies a reading such as I am suggesting, although she did not, of course, use the term "acted parable." In an introduction to her reading of this story, O'Connor tries to signal her audience how to understand her fiction: "in this story you should be on the lookout for such things as the action of grace in the Grandmother's soul, and not for the dead bodies" (*Mystery* 113). Similarly, in an interview response on the issue of brutality in her stories, O'Connor says,

> There really isn't much brutality. It always amuses me when people say "brutality." People keep referring to the brutality in the stories, but even "A Good Man Is Hard To Find" is, in a way, a comic, stylized thing. It is not naturalistic writing and so you can't really call it brutal.

> (*Conversations* 58)

Given the list of violent actions I mentioned earlier, O'Connor's response may initially seem somewhat disingenuous. Granted, it does appear to stretch credulity to say that there is no brutality in her fiction, but O'Connor's comment does helpfully point us away from fully naturalistic writing and toward a view of acted parables, with characters' action more important for its contribution to the total effect of the story rather than the outcome of an individual character.

"A Good Man Is Hard To Find" certainly performs O'Connor's common seduction of the reader with its comic ordinariness, as we become introduced to a bickering family preparing for a summer vacation. The humor of the pretentious grandmother's seeing herself as a lady, the familiar complaint of the father's seat kicked by the children in the backseat, the description of the redneck Red Sammy Butts's barbecue stand all draw in the audience and encourage us to lower our guard. The bizarre turn occurs when the grandmother's cat springs free from her basket, claws the father Bailey, and causes an accident. Shortly thereafter, the Misfit and his henchmen arrive on the scene, and the mood shifts from humorous to darkly disturbing. In small groups, the family is invited into the woods to be shot while the grandmother, hoping to distract him long enough to let her live, keeps up a running conversation with the Misfit. Finally, after a prolonged discussion about Jesus and the effect of his coming to earth, the grandmother suddenly reaches out her hand and touches the Misfit, exclaiming, "Why you're one of my babies. You're one of my own children!" (*Collected Works* 152). In response, the Misfit shoots her.

Given the startling nature of this story, it is easy to become overwhelmed in the details of destruction. But just as the people of Israel were to remain focused on God's call to redemption rather than on Isaiah's nakedness or Ezekiel's sore side, reading O'Connor's stories as prophetic literature reminds us to focus on the effect on the reader rather than the harm done her characters. As such, the story works in at least two directions. First, the grandmother has been shown to operate entirely on the surface, being concerned about wearing proper clothing so that in case of an accident—which, of course, did occur—people would know she is lady. But beyond her prattling chatter, the grandmother appears never to have deeply connected with others, never seen beyond whether or not someone has the proper upbringing to be a "good man"— nor ever realistically examined her own soul. Almost in spite of herself, in the midst of what is for her a meaningless conversation about the most important questions (in O'Connor's view) of how we respond to Christ's life and sacrificial death, the grandmother's "head cleared for an instant" and she acknowledges her deep kinship to the Misfit (*Collected Works* 152). O'Connor uses this acknowledgement to show the centrality of a deep love and compassion for others, insisting that we must embrace their and our own sinfulness as part of our fallen humanness. The grandmother's revelation at the very end of her life leads to the Misfit's wonderful line, "She would have been a good woman if it had been somebody there to shoot her every minute of her life" (*Collected Works* 153). Through the grandmother's change and violent death, O'Connor hopes to force the reader to examine his or her own soul as well.[6]

Part of the power of this story, of course, derives from the second punch that the ending packs, for O'Connor's acted parable includes not only the grandmother but also the Misfit. The Misfit has been shown to be a rationalist, insisting that he recognizes the potential impact of what Jesus claims to have done but, because of scant evidence, he cannot be certain of the truth of Christ's supposed actions. With his glasses, his professorial manner, and his carefully considered skepticism, one can almost imagine him with a coffee cup rather than a gun in his hand, lecturing to a group of college students. In what I trust is an aberration from professors, though, he informs the grandmother that he has determined that given the uncertainty of what is true, the only approach that makes sense is to "enjoy the few minutes you got left the best way you can—by killing somebody or burning down his house or doing some other meanness to him. No pleasure but meanness" (*Collected Works* 152). After his encounter with the grandmother, when the Misfit's companions return from their murders, one of them says, "Some fun!" The Misfit responds, "It's no real pleasure in life" (*Collected Works* 153). Though we are left with no narrative direction to know what will happen in the Misfit's life, it is clear from this response that the grandmother's action of graciously reaching out to him has affected his calm rejection of belief. Again, in seeing this gesture as part of an acted parable, we can see that the central issue is not exactly how the Misfit might eventually respond but rather how the audience is moved by the grandmother's sacramental act.[7] Will this astonishing gift of a recognized common humanity move the reader as it has unsettled the Misfit? Will the reader follow the Misfit's lead and move from a position of settled disbelief to being a seeker? If so, O'Connor's prophetic story will have found success.

EVERYTHING WORTH DOING HURTS LIKE HELL

"Welding with Children," the title story in Gautreaux's second volume of stories, serves well as an example of his fiction, for it embodies many of Gautreaux's best attributes. Although Catholicism is sometimes overtly a part of his fiction, in this story none of the characters is Catholic—and, in fact, the only mention of Catholicism is a passing satiric comment that some Catholics contribute only a dollar each week, "but there's so many of them, and the church has so many services a weekend, the priests can run the place on volume like Wal-Mart" (15). Nevertheless, the story's humor, gentleness to characters, and distinctly moral tone serve as a delightful entrée into Gautreaux's fiction.

One of only a few first-person narratives in Gautreaux's oeuvre, Gautreaux explains the origin of the story:

> I was in Wal-Mart one day, in the compressed-air driven tools, sandpaper, Bondo, and auto paint aisle, when I heard a phlegm-filled smoker's voice float over the racks from the motor oil section. It was a middle-aged man talking to a friend he'd bumped into. He was complaining about his three daughters, who kept having children out of wedlock and then bringing them over to his house for him and his wife to take care of. The old guy had a great voice, southern, smart, and full of humor. But it was full of hurt too. His blue-collar salary was being eaten up by Cokes and diapers, and his blue-collar heart was smashed flat by children who were running their lives like a drunk runs a truck with bald tires downhill in a rainstorm.

> (*Best Stories* 289)

From that starting point, Gautreaux could have written a sad or bitter story—or his tale could have been a mere send-up of this unfortunate grandfather. Instead,

Gautreaux has created a story with plenty of humor, but also a warmth and care for Bruton, this grandfather blessed with four squabbling grandchildren to watch.

To draw in the reader, Gautreaux infuses the story with some of the funniest lines written since O'Connor was at the height of fictional prowess. Bruton describes his brief experience as a student at Louisiana State University. He imagines that the Pakistani composition instructor sent their portfolios "back to Pakistan for his relatives to use as stove wood." In the chemistry class, with a professor who heated Campbell's soup over a Bunsen burner, he sat "way in the back." "Time or two, when I could see the blackboard off on the horizon, I almost got the hang of something, and I was glad of that" (3). His daughters drop off the grandchildren, Nu-Nu, Moonbeam, Tammynette, and Freddie, and his assignment is to weld his oldest daughter's bedrail.

> Now, what the hell you can do in bed that'll cause the end of a iron rail to break off is beyond me, but she can't afford another one on her burger-flipping salary, she said, so I got to fix it with four little kids hanging on my coveralls.

> (1)

With little for the children to do, they begin using an engine hanging from a tree as a swing: "Tammynette and Moonbeam gave the engine a long shove, got distracted by a yellow butterfly playing in a clump of pig-weed, and that nine-hundred pound V-8 kind of ironed them out on the backswing" (3-4). Bruton tries, amidst hilarious interruptions from the children, to talk to them about the Bible, a process that has little success because "the Bible was turning into one big adventure film" for them (10). Bruton appears at a loss to know how to deal with these four children who have been foisted upon him, particularly because he was not especially involved as a parent with his own children. Yet Gautreaux refuses to allow the humor to take over the story, instead using the comedy to invite the reader along for a closer consideration of Bruton and his difficult situation. As Liam Callanan writes in the *New York Times Book Review,* "Despite the laughter, the writing never entirely succumbs to the humor, and by the end Gautreaux is able to wrestle out a few moral lessons that even Tammynette can appreciate" (31). With his humor, Gautreaux creates a light tone, entices the reader, and creates space for a conversation about the deadly serious questions raised in the story.

These sober concerns circle around the prominent overlapping themes evident in much of Gautreaux's fiction. As often occurs, the larger community plays an important role. In two other stories in the ***Welding*** *with Children* collection, for instance, members of the community—almost against their own intentions—find themselves connecting with a vulnerable person: in **"The Piano Tuner,"** Claude helps a lonely woman find work as a lounge pianist; in **"Resistance,"** elderly Mr. Boudreaux assists the neglected girl next door with a science project. As a humorous twist on this theme in **"Welding with Children,"** the impetus that moves Bruton to try to change is old Mr. Fordlyson's muttered comment of "bastardmobile" when Bruton arrives at the grocery store with his grandchildren in tow. Bruton later seeks out Mr. Fordlyson, recognizing that for all his nastiness, he has managed to raise his children well. The narrative provides clues that Fordlyson can provide needed wisdom for Bruton, for as he and his grandchildren are reading through the illustrated Bible, Moonbeam points out that Fordlyson looks like God (9). Bruton meets Fordlyson under a pecan tree called by the locals the "Tree of Knowledge," and Gautreaux insists on the Garden of Eden connection by Fordlyson's stopping Bruton from eating, with a command, "Don't eat that green pecan—it'll make you sick" (15). Fordlyson emphasizes a point typically important in Gautreaux's stories: the worth of children and the effort that relatives (commonly in his fiction, grandparents) must expend to help their children do what is right. Specifically, Fordlyson gives Bruton a list of duties:

> He pulled down one finger on his right hand with the forefinger of the left. "Go join the Methodists." Another finger went down and he told me, "Every Sunday, bring them children to church." A third finger, and he said, "And keep 'em with you as much as you can."
>
> I shook my head. "I already raised my kids."
>
> Fordlyson looked at me hard and didn't have to say what he was thinking. He glanced down at the ground between his smooth-toe lace-ups. "And clean up your yard."

(16)

Though put in the mouth of an annoying character, this advice that Fordlyson gives connects to a core value that Gautreaux enunciates. He argues,

> You know, you don't give somebody values when they're fourteen or fifteen—you give them when they're two and three and four. Then when they're seven and they reach the age of reason, you've got to hit them real hard. [Others] would say, 'Well, I'll let my kids—when they grow up and when they're 21 they can decide whether or not they'll believe in God.' I think they're taking a gigantic risk. I don't particularly believe in that.

(Gautreaux, Meyering interview 11)

This concern emerges in many of Gautreaux's stories, including **"The Courtship of Merlin LeBlanc"** and **"Little Frogs in a Ditch"** (both in *Same Place, Same Things*). It is just such an engaged parenting role that Bruton is beginning to embrace by the end of the story.

The moral choices characters make are central to Gautreaux's fiction. As Erin McGraw points out, he focuses on what O'Connor refers to as manners: "He writes about how people should act, and how people really do act. The gap is wide" (736). While they share common concern with what people do and how they behave, Gautreaux differs significantly from O'Connor in his treatment of his characters. Rather than O'Connor's prophetic model of using her characters to make a point with her readers, Gautreaux tends to be kinder to his characters, treating them with respect and allowing them to change within the course of a story. As Ed Piacentino points out, growing from his Catholic perspective, Gautreaux treats even his misfit characters sympathetically and with compassion (1). Again, to draw a specific comparison to O'Connor's "A Good Man Is Hard To Find," Bruton, just like the grandmother, has a crisis that causes him to change, to enlarge his vision of his responsibility and connections. But rather than learning this insight at the end of a gun, Bruton's crisis occurs with hearing his car called a "bastardmobile," an incident that takes place on the story's fourth page. Bruton has the rest of the story to learn and begin to change in response to this crisis.

Bruton's transformation begins with an acknowledgement of his guilt and responsibility. "I started thinking about my four daughters. None of them has any religion to speak of. I thought they'd pick it up from their mamma, like I did from mine, but LaNelle always worked so much, she just had time to cook, clean, transport, and fuss" (*Welding* 7). Recognizing his mistakes but still immersed in a sense of helplessness, he says, "I guess a lot of what's wrong with my girls is my fault, but I don't know what I could've done different" (7). As he acknowledges the squalor of their lives, exemplified by the junk in his yard, "I formed a little fantasy about gathering all these kids into my Caprice and heading out northwest to start over, away from their mammas, TVs, mildew, their casino-mad grandmother, and Louisiana in general" (12). Yet, in a sign of his growing self-understanding, he "realized we couldn't drive away from ourselves. We couldn't escape in the bastardmobile" (12). One can almost hear echoes of the Harrison Ford character in the movie *Six Days, Seven Nights,* deriding the idea of people seeking to find happiness on a tropical paradise island: "It's an island, babe. If you don't bring it here, you won't find it here." Bruton accepts that whatever good will happen with his grandchildren will have to happen here, amidst the mess and distractions of their lives—but he decides that he can act to provide these children with more support than he gave their mothers.

Because she sees her audience as hostile, O'Connor's central point is to provide a shocking conclusion, hoping to jolt her readers into a confrontation with Christianity. Because he sees his audience as companions, Gautreaux follows his characters past their crisis, allowing his readers to experience changes that they themselves may need to make. Both approaches carry with them some risks, for O'Connor's readers may simply be put off by her extreme treatment of characters and turn away from her fiction. In contrast, Gautreaux's readers may too easily encounter Bruton's growth without feeling ethically challenged. Yet when most effective, each approach allows the author to connect with her or his imagined audience, pushing the reader to consider ultimate concerns.

In significant measure, Bruton does not need to experience a conversion, more a gentle nudge—or, perhaps more fittingly, a kick in the behind—to turn him back to what, on some level, he already knew he should do. Yet these changes, in Gautreaux's fiction or in life, are never cheap or easy. After Fordlyson offers his new four commandments, he smiles a mean smile and says, "Bruton, everything worth doing hurts like hell" (16). The final movement of the story shows Bruton embracing this pain and hard work. He cleans up his yard, hauling out "four derelict cars, six engines, four washing machines, ten broken lawn mowers, and two and one-quarter tons of scrap iron" (16). He cuts the grass, paints the shop and the house. He welcomes his grandchildren to stay at his house. As the story closes, Bruton and the children are planning to hang a tire swing from a tree and the youngest child has just said his first words:

> The baby brought me in focus, somebody's blue eyes looking at me hard. He blew spit over his tongue and cried out, "Da-da," and I put him on my knee, facing away toward the cool green branches of my biggest willow oak.

> (19)

Bruton has learned in the course of the story, has accepted that raising children is what he must do. The baby's gurgled words identifying him as a father suggest that he is taking on a role that he failed earlier with his own children, embracing the morally correct position that he needed to re-learn from his community. And Gautreaux makes this point quietly and with humor to his friendly audience.

CONCLUSION

O'Connor's focus on her audience seems to have served as a central driving force behind her writing. Frequently in her essays and her letters, she referred to her sense of her audience and her prophetic desire to influence them. In describing the role of a Hebrew prophet, Jewish theologian Abraham Heschel writes in 1962,

> To a person endowed with prophetic sight, everyone else appears blind; to a person whose ear perceives God's voice, everyone else appears deaf. No one is just; no knowing is strong enough, no trust complete enough. The prophet hates the approximate, he shuns the middle of the road. . . . Carried away by the challenge, the demand to straighten out man's ways, the prophet is strange, one-sided, an unbearable extremist.

> (16)

In the context of O'Connor's work, Heschel's words about the prophet have astonishing resonances. Certainly O'Connor's single-minded insistence that following Christ is the only possible antidote to her hostile audience's spiritual illness makes her seem to some an "unbearable extremist." She ardently resisted the reasonable, middle-of-the-road responses of the modern rationalism, seeing those analyses as simply a mask for unbelief. Perhaps even more striking is the resemblance between the first section of Heschel's comments and O'Connor's most famous description of her method, written in 1957:

> When you can assume that your audience holds the same beliefs you do, you can relax a little and use more normal means of talking to it; when you have to assume that it does not, then you have to make your vision apparent by shock—to the hard of hearing you shout, and for the almost-blind you draw large and startling figures"

> (*Mystery* 34)

To the prophet O'Connor, her unbelieving audience appeared indeed deaf and blind, and she spent her writing career attempting to penetrate their limited understanding. For as a prophet, O'Connor could imagine no more important task for her fiction than to have it shock a reader into believing.

Gautreaux's view of his audience as companion leads him to a different tone and approach. Gautreaux's deep understanding of the people with whom he grew up and about whom he writes is made clear in a brief essay, "How Sweet It Was," that focuses on Louisiana's sugar mills. As he draws us into the web of connections that make up the community, he describes how the mill locomotive was also used to haul children to school and to Mass. Thus, Gautreaux explains, the old engineer says that when the railroad was shut down, "he felt as if a relative had died. His reaction was an emotional connection not with a machine but with the life the machine provided. Such was the mill community's relationship with the factory itself" (25). These kinds of profound relationships that Gautreaux formed when he was growing up seem to have fed into his sense of story writing and of audience. For in his fiction, his imagined audience is composed of people who share a common set of values, of a community that needs only to be called back to its best conception of itself. As such, Gautreaux's fiction does not have the prophetic ring of O'Connor's stories, for he is not trying to convert his readers. In this context, Wayne Booth's comment is instructive: "The reader whom the implied author writes to can be found as much in the text's silence as in its overt appeals. What the author felt no need to mention tells us who he thinks we'll be—or hopes we'll be" (423). Gautreaux feels no need to make a case for Catholic beliefs and values or the importance of community because they have become ingrained in him and, he assumes, in his audience, his companions on the journey.

Notes

1. O'Connor's willingness to speak about her stories is very different, for example, from her contemporary writer, Bernard Malamud, whose fiction she much admired. Malamud was reticent about seeming to explicate his writing, telling an interviewer, "You know one thing that I don't like about what we're doing is that I have begun to explain my fiction, and I don't like to do that" (*Conversations with Bernard Malamud* 143).

2. Katherine Hemple Prown views O'Connor as being especially negative toward female characters, citing as evidence that O'Connor said she admired only three characters, all male: Hazel Motes and both Tarwaters. Young girls could occasionally escape O'Connor's wrath, but for O'Connor, "ladyhood was a comical state at best, a perilous and cursed state at worse [sic]. Women who embraced it deserved their fate" (6). Christina Bieber Lake reasonably points out, in response to Prown, that few of O'Connor's characters—male or female—escape unharmed, so it seems difficult to draw conclusions about her views of women from her treatment of characters (121).

3. In focusing on O'Connor's desire to preach, Brinkmeyer notes that she is not as explicit as an evangelist, yet "her underlying strategies of shock and distortion are very similar to the evangelist's in terms of technique and intention" (7). Ralph Wood focuses on the connection between her tone and the Old Testament: "The narrative voice that speaks in her work is akin to the Old Testament in its unapologetic directness of approach to the reader" (81). The critic who most directly touches on my current point is John May:

   > O'Connor understood that the prophet interprets events in the light of the covenant, announcing God's judgment of the people's sins and His call to fidelity. An action or gesture of the prophet . . . often accompanies or replaces his words

(e.g., Jeremiah's yoke and Isaiah's nakedness), a mode of prophetic symbolism that O'Connor frequently employed.

(17)

However, May does not explore this connection more fully.

4. Vawter writes, "The symbolic act, whether accompanied by words or not, is a dramatized prophecy. Jeremiah's yoke, Isaiah's nakedness, Ezekiel's dumbness, Hosea's marriage, are all symbolic acts" (51).

5. To offer just one example: One summer, I participated in a summer seminar focusing on the public theology of our students, with participants drawn from across the disciplines. As my contribution to the seminar's reading, I requested "A Good Man Is Hard To Find," since I see it as a form of public theology for O'Connor. Although the theology professor leading the seminar never spoke with me directly, I learned from another participant that she refused to have this story discussed because she was appalled by its gore.

6. When critics focus too fully on the characters as real people, they can be led to make odd assertions. For instance, Sally Fitzgerald finds this story to have a "happy ending," for the grandmother is in death child-like,

   > echoing the requisite for entering the cloudless kingdom of heaven, which was for Flannery O'Connor the only happy ending to be sought, or for that matter to be hoped for, by any of us. The grandmother has accepted the grace offered to her; she has passed the test of real charity and been transformed by her realization.

(76)

Fitzgerald's reading of the story is generally sound, but her insistence of seeing the positive impact of the story as a "happy ending" results from a misplaced need to evaluate how a *character* experienced the story rather than reader.

7. O'Connor does offer some speculative hope about the Misfit:

   > I prefer to think that, however unlikely this may seem, the old lady's gesture, like the mustard-seed, will grow to be a great crow-filled tree in the Misfit's heart, and will be enough of a pain to him there to turn him into the prophet he was meant to become. But that's another story.

(*Mystery* 112-13)

Works Cited

Booth, Wayne C. *The Rhetoric of Fiction.* Second ed. Chicago: U of Chicago P, 1983.

Brinkmeyer, Robert H., Jr. "A Closer Walk with Thee: Flannery O'Connor and Southern Fundamentalists." *The Southern Literary Journal* 18.2 (Spring 1986): 3-13.

Callanan, Liam. "La. Stories." *New York Times Book Review* 3 Oct. 1999: 31.

Cash, Jean. *Flannery O'Connor: A Life.* Knoxville: U of Tennessee P, 2000.

Enjolras, Laurence. *Flannery O'Connor's Characters.* New York: UP of America, 1998.

Feeley, Kathleen, S. S. N. D. *Flannery O'Connor: Voice of the Peacock.* New York: Fordham UP, 1982.

Fitzgerald, Sally. "Happy Endings." *Image* 16 (Summer 1997): 73-80.

Fodor, Sarah J. *"No Literary Orthodoxy": Flannery O'Connor and the New Critics.* Diss. U of Chicago, 1994.

Gautreaux, Tim. "Behind The Great Stories there are Great Sentences." *Boston Globe* 19 Oct. 1997: P4. NewsBank.

———. Contributors' Notes. *The Best American Short Stories 1998.* Ed. Garrison Keillor. New York: Houghton Mifflin, 1998.

———. "How Sweet It Was." *Preservation* May/June 2005: 24-25.

———. Interview with Christopher Scanlan. *Creative Loafing.* 9 May 2005. <http://charlotte.creative loafing.com/2004-06-16/news_cover3.html> printout 1-4.

———. Interview with Darlene Meyering. Calvin College Festival of Faith & Writing. Grand Rapids, MI. 22 April 2004.

———. Interview with Jennifer Levasseur and Kevin Rabalais. *Mississippi Review* 27.3 (1999): 19-40.

———. Interview with Julie Kane. "A Postmodern Southern Moralist and Storyteller: Tim Gautreaux." *Voces de America, American Voices.* Ed. Laura P. Alonso Gallo. Cadiz, Spain: Aduana Vieja, 2004. 123-45.

———. Interview with Maria Hebert-Leiter. "An Interview with Tim Gautreaux." *The Carolina Quarterly* 57.2 (Summer 2005). Bluffton U Literature Resource Center. 18 Jan. 2006. printout 1-9.

———. *Same Place, Same Things.* New York: Picador USA, 1996.

———. *Welding with Children.* New York: Picador USA, 1999.

Giannone, Richard. *Flannery O'Connor and the Mystery of Love.* Urbana: U of Illinois P, 1989.

———. *Flannery O'Connor, Hermit Novelist.* Urbana: U of Illinois P, 2000.

Giles, Paul. *American Catholic Arts and Fiction: Culture, Ideology, Aesthetics.* Cambridge Studies in American Literature and Culture. New York: Cambridge UP, 1992.

Gordon, Sarah. *Flannery O'Connor: The Obedient Imagination.* Athens: U of Georgia P, 2000.

Heaton, E. W. *The Old Testament Prophets.* Atlanta: John Knox P, 1977.

Heschel, Abraham. *The Prophets.* New York: Harper & Row, 1962.

Kirkland, William. "Flannery O'Connor, the Person and the Writer." *The East-West Review* 3 (1967): 159-63.

Kuhl, Curt. *The Prophets of Israel.* Trans. Rudolf Ehrlich and J. P. Smith. Richmond, VA: John Knox, 1963.

Lake, Christina Bieber. *The Incarnational Art of Flannery O'Connor.* Macon: Mercer UP, 2005.

Larson, Susan. "The Writer Next Door." *Times-Picayune* 15 March 1998: El. Lexis-Nexis Academic Universe. Bluffton U. 20 June 2001. printout 1-3.

Malamud, Bernard. *Conversations with Bernard Malamud.* Ed. Lawrence M. Lasher. Jackson: UP of Mississippi, 1991.

May, John R. *The Pruning Word: The Parables of Flannery O'Connor.* Notre Dame: U of Notre Dame P, 1976.

McGraw, Erin. "Authoritative Voice." Review. *Georgia Review* 54 (2000): 727-37.

McMullen, Joanne Halleran. *Writing against God: Language as Message in the Literature of Flannery O'Connor.* Macon: Mercer UP, 1996.

O'Connor, Flannery. *Collected Works.* New York: Library of America, 1988.

———. *Conversations with Flannery O'Connor.* Ed. Rosemary M. Magee. Jackson: UP of Mississippi, 1987.

———. *The Habit of Being.* Ed. Sally Fitzgerald. New York: Farrar, Straus and Giroux, 1979.

———. *Mystery and Manners.* Ed. Sally Fitzgerald. New York: Farrar, Straus and Giroux, 1961.

———. *The Presence of Grace and Other Book Reviews.* Comp. Leo J. Zuber. Ed. Cart W. Martin. Athens: U of Georgia P, 1983.

Oliver, Bill. "Flannery O'Connor's Compassion." *The Flannery O'Connor Bulletin* 15 (1986): 1-15.

Piacentino, Ed. "Second Chances: Patterns of Failure and Redemption in Tim Gautreaux's *Same Place, Same Things.*" *The Southern Literary Journal* 38.1 (Fall 2005). Bluffton U Literature Resource Center. 18 Jan. 2006. printout 1-12.

Prown, Katherine Hemple. *Revising Flannery O'Connor: Southern Literary Culture and the Problem of Female Authorship.* Charlottesville: UP of Virginia, 2001.

Rabinowitz, Peter J. *Before Reading: Narrative Conventions and the Politics of Interpretation.* Ithaca: Cornell UP, 1987.

———. "Where We Are When We Read." *Authorizing Readers: Resistance and Respect in the Teaching of Literature.* Peter J. Rabinowitz and Michael W. Smith. New York: Teachers College P, 1998. 1-28.

Sawyer, John F. A. *Prophecy and the Biblical Prophets.* New York: Oxford UP, 1993.

Stephens, Martha. *The Question of Flannery O'Connor.* Baton Rouge: Louisiana State UP, 1973.

Vawter, Bruce. *The Conscience of Israel: Pre-exilic Prophets and Prophecy.* New York: Sheed & Ward, 1961.

Wood, Ralph C. *Flannery O'Connor and the Christ-Haunted South.* Grand Rapids: Eerdmans, 2004.

FURTHER READING

Criticism

Berne, Suzanne. Review of *Same Place, Same Things.* *The New York Times* (22 September 1996): n.p.

> Asserts that Gautreaux's *Same Place, Same Things* is populated with emotionally stagnant people who live in a swamp of recurring mistakes and disappointments.

Gautreaux, Tim, and Julie Kane. "A Postmodern Southern Moralist and Storyteller: Tim Gautreaux." In *Voces de América/American Voices: Interviews with American Writers,* edited by Laura P. Alonso Gallo, pp. 123-45. Cadiz, Spain: Colección de Estudios Culturales, 2004.

> Interview in which Gautreaux discusses the sense of place and autobiographical impulses demonstrated in his work.

L. P. Hartley
1895-1972

(Full name Leslie Poles Hartley) English novelist, short story writer, and critic.

INTRODUCTION

Highly lauded for his short stories and novels, Hartley was a prolific author whose writing was influenced by the nineteenth-century Gothic tradition, containing elements of darkness, horror, and romance. Although he is better known for his novels, Hartley's short fiction is often studied in relationship to his longer works. His first published collection of stories, *Night Fears and Other Stories,* was published in 1924 and received favorable critical attention but was not commercially successful. His novels, one of which (*The Go-Between,* 1953) was later made into a film, were well received among critics and readers. Yet Hartley continued to write in both genres, in addition to working as a literary critic himself. In his fiction, he often depicts characters that are morally sick, or evil, and eager for revenge and retribution. His tone is ironic and his settings characteristically domestic, lending an air of lightness to writing that is often undercut by Hartley's darker themes.

BIOGRAPHICAL INFORMATION

Born in the small town of Whittlesea, in England, in 1895, to H. B. and Mary Elizabeth Thompson Hartley, Hartley grew up near the city of Peterbourough, where his family moved when he was a young boy. His father was a solicitor and later the chairman and director of a brickworks, which provided the family a substantial income. Schooled at Harrow as a youth and later at Balliol College, Oxford, Hartley left Balliol to enlist in the army in April of 1916. He served as a second lieutenant in World War I. Following a medical discharge in 1918, he returned to Balliol to complete his studies. He published his first collection of short stories in 1924. At the same time that he was pursuing a career as an author, Hartley also worked as a fiction reviewer, beginning in 1923, for periodicals such as the *Spectator* and the *Saturday Review*. He continued in his work as a critic for thirty years, and along the way, he garnered his own critical and popular success as both a novelist and short story writer. This success

dwindled toward the end of Hartley's career and he lamented never having found an American publisher for his works. Plagued by heart trouble in his later years, he died in his London home of heart failure in 1972.

MAJOR WORKS OF SHORT FICTION

Hartley's short fiction is infused with elements of suspense and fear. For example, the title story of his first anthology, *Night Fears and Other Stories,* features a night watchman who is gripped by a growing sense of dread as he talks with a mysterious stranger. By the story's end the watchman is murdered with his own knife. This first volume of stories was followed in 1932 by *The Killing Bottle* and some years later by *The Travelling Grave and Other Stories* (1948). Hartley uses his short fiction to expand the margins of reality, often incorporating elements of the supernatural in order to present larger themes, such as malevolence and immorality, in a stylized manner. His short fiction also explores the relationship between the artist and everyday life; in *The White Wand and Other Stories* (1954), a volume that included some works from previous collections, Hartley wrote a story about an author and his fictional creation, highlighting their conflict via a series of letters. This anthology was followed by *Two for the River and Other Stories* (1961), in which Hartley includes Christmas horror stories reminiscent of Charles Dickens's *A Christmas Carol*. The last collection of short fiction Hartley published in his lifetime was *Mrs. Carteret Receives and Other Stories* (1971). This collection includes selections featuring light satire, which are similar to the social observations Hartley makes in his longer novels of manners. The stories in this volume also feature Hartley's dark humor, in pieces such as "Paradise Paddock," in which a cursed artifact leaves a trail of death and injury, and in "Please Do Not Touch," in which a London bachelor, determined to catch a burglar, leaves out poisoned liquor and finds the next morning that he has inadvertently murdered an old acquaintance. The character of the wealthy, often snobbish bachelor is featured in other tales as well, and Hartley renders such individuals with humor and sometimes even affection.

CRITICAL RECEPTION

The critical response to Hartley's short fiction was initially favorable, but reviewers often showed preference for his novels once he began writing longer works. Toward the end of his career, Hartley began to receive less enthusiastic critical attention for both his short stories and novels. In the 1960s, critics of Hartley's work often focused on the relationship between his shorter works and his novels. John Athos, in his assessment of Hartley's work through 1962, explores the way Hartley's works of short fiction, as well as his novella *Simonetta Perkins* (1925), provide both inspiration and material from which Hartley drew for his novels. In particular, Athos points to the connection between Hartley's conception of evil and use of Gothic images in his shorter stories and the development of such concepts in his novels. Giorgio Melchiori takes another approach to Hartley's fiction, finding evidence of American influence on Hartley's work, in particular the works of Nathaniel Hawthorne. Following Hartley's death in 1972, critics began to examine the full scope of his work, concluding that his short fiction was mostly a vessel that contained kernels of ideas that were fully explored only in his longer works. Edward T. Jones finds deep connections between the themes and symbols of Hartley's short stories and his novels. John Atkins approaches Hartley's fiction through the lens of the author's world view; Atkins maintains that Hartley's work reflects his disapproval of post-World War I society and its emphasis on class distinctions. At the same time, Atkins points out that Hartley's fascination with the aristocratic class was evident throughout the author's career.

PRINCIPAL WORKS

Short Fiction

Night Fears and Other Stories 1924
Simonetta Perkins (novella) 1925
The Killing Bottle 1932
The Travelling Grave and Other Stories 1948
The White Wand and Other Stories 1954
Two for the River and Other Stories 1961
The Collected Short Stories of L. P. Hartley 1968
Mrs. Carteret Receives and Other Stories 1971
The Complete Short Stories of L. P. Hartley 1973
Night Fears and Other Supernatural Tales 1993
The Collected Macabre Stories of L. P. Hartley 2001

Other Major Works

*The Shrimp and the Anemone (novel) 1944; republished as *The West Window* in 1945
†The Sixth Heaven (novel) 1946

‡Eustace and Hilda (novel) 1947
The Boat (novel) 1949
My Fellow Devils (novel) 1951
The Go-Between (novel) 1953
A Perfect Woman (novel) 1955
The Hireling (novel) 1957
Facial Justice (novel) 1960
The Brickfield (novel) 1964
The Betrayal (novel) 1966
The Novelist's Responsibility: Essays and Lectures (nonfiction) 1967
Poor Clare (novel) 1968
The Love-Adept: A Variation on a Theme (novel) 1969
My Sisters' Keeper (novel) 1970
The Harness Room (novel) 1971
The Collections: A Novel (novel) 1972
The Will and the Way (novel) 1973

*This is the first book in the *Eustace and Hilda* series.

†This is the second book in the *Eustace and Hilda* series.

‡This is the third book in the *Eustace and Hilda* series.

CRITICISM

Giorgio Melchiori (essay date 1955)

SOURCE: Melchiori, Giorgio. "The English Novelist and the American Tradition (1955)." *Sewanee Review* 68, no. 1 (January-March 1960): 502-15.

[*In the following essay, written in 1955, Melchiori traces the influence of Nathaniel Hawthorne's fiction on that of Hartley, arguing that through his use of traditional forms, Hartley offers a bridge between the past and the modern notion of the English narrative.*]

One of the most popular English novelists since the last war is undoubtedly L. P. Hartley. Perhaps too popular for the taste of many critics, who grant him only the single merit of being in the novel tradition. But which tradition? Tracing back his traditionalism to its source, to see which authors are most frequently echoed in his pages, it is not the great names of the English novel which occur to us. Take a passage like the following, from *The Go-Between* (London, 1953, p. 42):

> 'Wednesday 11th of July. Saw the Deadly Nightshade—Atropa Belladonna.' Marcus wasn't with me, I was alone, exploring some derelict outhouses which for me had obviously more attraction than the view of Brandham Hall from the S. W. In one, which was roofless as well as derelict, I suddenly came upon the plant. But it wasn't a plant, in my sense of the word, it was a

shrub, almost a tree, and as tall as I was. It looked the picture of evil, and also the picture of health, it was so glossy and strong and juicy-looking: I could almost see the sap rising to nourish it. It seemed to have found the place in all the world that suited it best.

I knew that every part of it was poisonous, I knew too that it was beautiful, for did not my mother's botany book say so? I stood on the threshold, not daring to go in, staring at the button-bright berries and the dull, pur-plish, heavy, bell shaped flowers reaching out towards me. I felt that the plant could poison me, even if I didn't touch it, and that if I didn't eat it, it would eat me, it looked so hungry in spite of all the nourishment it was getting.

Nothing in the English tradition comes so close to this as do the following passages, taken from the description of the garden in Hawthorne's "Rappaccini's Daughter":

The aspect of one and all of them [the plants] dissatis-fied him; their gorgeousness seemed fierce, passionate, and even unnatural. There was hardly an individual shrub which a wanderer, straying by himself through a forest, would not have been startled to find growing wild. . . . Giovanni recognized but two or three plants in the collection, and those of a kind that he well knew to be poisonous.

In the middle of this garden of poisonous plants there is a ruined marble fountain, in which the water still flows:

All about the pool into which the water subsided grew various plants, that seemed to require a plentiful supply of moisture for the nourishment of gigantic leaves, and in some instances, flowers gorgeously magnificent. There was one shrub in particular, set in a marble vase in the midst of the pool, that bore a profusion of purple blossoms, each of which had the lustre and richness of a gem; and the whole together made a show so resplen-dent that it seemed enough to illuminate the garden, even had there been no sunshine.

The plant with the purple blossoms is the most poi-sonous of all, so that Doctor Rappaccini approaches it with the greatest caution:

When, in his walk through the garden he came to the magnificent plant that hung its purple gems beside the marble fountain, he placed a kind of mask over his mouth and nostrils, as if all this beauty did but conceal a deadlier malice.

This plant sparkling with gems, evil and fascinating, is the central symbol of Hawthorne's story, in the same way as the belladonna plant is the central symbol of Hartley's novel. There is more here than analogy—it is a case of derivation, for Hawthorne's influence is to be felt in method (the concentration of the narrative around certain emblematic symbols), in atmosphere (a sunny scene pervaded by a mysterious evil), and in

the moral concern (the tragedy of innocence opposed by evil, which is also the tragedy of original sin). In *The Go-Between* a boy, only obscurely aware of sin, causes a tragedy by involuntarily revealing a guilty re-lation between two adults. In "Rappaccini's Daughter" a young man causes the death of the girl he loves by administering an antidote against the deadly exhala-tions to which she had been accustomed since child-hood. In both cases the catastrophe is brought about by the very forces which were acting in the name of goodness and innocence against the evil or guilt which is part of the very nature of those they mean to save; evil and guilt which clearly represent original sin.

Hawthorne's influence over Hartley is unquestionable, and Hartley himself has paid a tribute to the American writer, coming openly to his defence against those who consider him second-rate. The letter he wrote to the *Times Literary Supplement* (June 11, 1954) de-serves ample quotation for the light it throws on Hart-ley himself:

. . . Not all great novelists have written good prose, but Hawthorne was an exquisite stylist, and *The Scarlet Letter* is the only novel I know that is a complete work of art in the sense that a poem is. It has a unity of mood and feeling that no other novel of comparable complexity possesses, and a quality of timelessness that liberates it from the contemporary and even from the temporary. And yet it is so deeply imbued with the atmosphere of history and legend, and has its roots so firmly implanted in the soil of New England, that it could not have been written about any other place. It is at once local and universal.

. . . No novelist, in my opinion, has written of the problems of evil and sin with such a complete sense of the issues involved as Hawthorne has. In addition to a far-reaching compassion for human frailty . . . he has a delicate but uncompromising sense of justice. Melville's treatment of these problems is more sensa-tional and catastrophic and as such recommends itself to our times; but Hawthorne's still small voice is to my mind far more satisfying.

What, in the first place, is the quality which for Hart-ley makes *The Scarlet Letter* "a complete work of art in the sense that a poem is"? Hartley is clearly not thinking of a poem as being the perfect expression of a world as feeling (in that case also *Emma* and *The Warden, Our Mutual Friend* and *Vanity Fair,* and many other novels would be poetry), but as a precise literary form. What then brings Hawthorne's work closer to the language and form of poetry than to the language and form of Dickens or Trollope? *The Scarlet Letter* is distinguished by at least one feature characteristic of poetry, which was completely absent from the English novel of the nineteenth century: the constant use of symbol, which turns the book into a sort of extended metaphor. It is curious at this point to recall Haw-thorne's opinion of Anthony Trollope, a typical En-glish novelist of the nineteenth century:

They precisely suit my taste—solid and substantial, written on the strength of beef and through the inspiration of ale, and just as real as if some giant had hewn a great lump out of the earth and put it under a glass case, with all its inhabitants going about their daily business, and not suspecting that they were being made a show of.

Hawthorne here recognizes the essential features of the English Victorian novel: its solid sense of reality, its minute observation of the surrounding world; and he declares his admiration for these qualities. Yet where are they to be found in his own work? Things themselves, the world around him, although observed in detail, are never objectively recorded in his stories and novels: instead every event, every character that he describes, suggests the possibility of an interpretation on a completely different plane, and becomes the living metaphor of something unexpressed. Behind every episode and every character there hides—inevitably—some hidden meaning, which can only be glimpsed and sensed, but which always remains ambiguous, even for the author himself. The most obvious example is the scarlet letter which Hester Prynne carries embroidered on her dress: a precise emblem, a mark of infamy; yet at the end of the novel, when the scarlet letter appears branded on Dimmesdale's flesh, its meaning becomes much more complex and polyvalent:

> Most of the spectators testified to having seen, on the breast of the unhappy minister, a *Scarlet Letter*—the very semblance of that worn by Hester Prynne—imprinted in the flesh. As regarded its origin, there were various explanations, all of which must necessarily have been conjectural. Some affirmed that the Rev. Mr. Dimmesdale, on the very day when Hester Prynne first wore her ignominious badge, had begun a course of penance . . . by inflicting a hideous torture on himself. Others contended that the stigma had not been produced until a long time subsequent, when old Roger Chillingworth, being a potent necromancer, had caused it to appear, through the agency of magic and poisonous drugs. Others, again, . . . whispered their belief, that the awful symbol was the effect of the ever-active tooth of remorse, gnawing from the inmost heart outwardly, and at last manifesting Heaven's dreadful judgment by the visible presence of the letter. The reader may choose among these theories. We have thrown all the light we could acquire upon the portent, and would gladly . . . erase its deep print out of our own brain, where long meditation has fixed it in very undesirable distinctness.

I have quoted this famous passage in full precisely because it reveals all the ambiguity of the symbol, which no longer stands unequivocally for the power of good or of evil, but which seems to have come alive for Hawthorne himself, to exist in its own right with obsessive intensity. A moment later, Hawthorne goes further and suggests that perhaps that ambiguous and obsessive sign was never really there at all:

> . . . certain persons, who were spectators of the whole scene . . . denied that there was any mark whatsoever on his breast, more than on a newborn infant's.

In this way, at the very moment when the symbol seems finally to become identified with original sin, the invisible mark which each one of us carries from his birth, it becomes more immaterial, complex and evasive: it is felt as a tortuous and insoluble problem, present but on a different level of consciousness from everyday reality. We have only to read Hawthorne's *American Notebooks* to realize how everything for him existed contemporaneously on two different levels of consciousness: everyday reality was only the "cipher," the "emblem," the "hieroglyph" (he uses all these words) of a world made up of ambiguous suggestions and intuitions. More than once, after noting down ideas for stories, he comments: "It might be made emblematical or something," or "It would be symbolical of something." It is the very indefiniteness of this *something* which characterizes Hawthorne's deepest inspiration: his capacity to jump from the plane of reality to an intuitive plane which was genuinely symbolical and not allegorical. In allegory precise correspondences are set up between facts and logically developed abstract conceptions; the symbol instead escapes from the hands of logic and appeals directly to the feelings: it exists outside the scope of reason: it seems rich in meanings, nevertheless, no sooner are they subjected to analysis by reason, than they conflict with each other. Hawthorne himself had vaguely realized this when, for example, in the remarkable introductory chapter to *The Scarlet Letter* he wrote in connection with the mysterious letter A:

> Certainly there was some deep meaning in it, most worthy of interpretation, and which, as it were, streamed forth from the mystic symbol, subtly communicating itself to my sensibilities, but evading the analysis of my mind.

Hawthorne set out consciously on the one hand to build up real allegories, capable of being rationally interpreted, and on the other to model his work on the solid English tradition of realistic narrative that he so much admired. But the results he reached, almost in spite of himself, and without realizing it, were of an entirely different nature, and were much more important than those at which he was aiming. In his hands the English novel of the eighteenth and nineteenth centuries underwent a sort of transformation from within: the description of the real, the lump of the earth put under a glass case, becomes something very different:

> Nothing is too small or too trifling to undergo this change, and acquire dignity thereby. A child's shoe; the doll, seated in her little wicker carriage; the hobby-

horse—whatever, in a word, has been used or played with, is now invested with a quality of strangeness and remoteness, though still almost as vividly present as by daylight. Thus, therefore, the floor of our familiar room has become a neutral territory, somewhere between the real world and fairyland, where the Actual and the Imaginary may meet, and each imbue itself with the nature of the other.

We seem to hear Ariel's song once more, with its subtle intuition of the transfiguring power of poetry:

> Nothing of him that doth fade,
> But doth suffer a sea-change
> Into something rich and strange.

It is this instinctive and irresistible capacity for transposition from the realistic to the symbolic plane, which prevented Hawthorne from following in the tracks of the English novelists he admired. And it is this same quality of symbolism which prevents him from constructing those logical allegories which he had set out to write. Or rather I should say that it is just those stories where he is really writing allegorically which are weakest and most mechanical, while the tales where his symbolic world kept all its ambiguities, such as "Ethan Brand," were much more forceful. An anecdote related by Hawthorne's son, Julian, in connection with "Rappaccini's Daughter," seems very significant:

> When Hawthorne was writing "Rappaccini's Daughter" . . . he read the as yet unfinished manuscript to his wife. "But how is it to end?" she asked him, when he laid down the paper; "is Beatrice to be a demon, or an angel?" "I have no idea!" was Hawthorne's reply, spoken with some emotion.

These uncertainties of the author as to the interpretation of his character reveal just how far his original allegorical intention had been transformed in the creation of ambiguous symbols, which, while they live for him, evade rational analysis.

It has been noted before how the constant presence of this symbolic level, which so profoundly distinguishes Hawthorne's novels from those of his English contemporaries, is characteristic of all the major American writing of his time; it is more than obvious in Melville, and has been generally acknowledged in Poe. Matthiessen, and more recently Feidelson, have made a wide study of this tendency towards symbolism in American literature, recognizing it as a truly native element: a constant moral concern due to its Puritan origins. I do not wish to go over their arguments here: what I want to emphasize is simply that this instinctive symbolism of American authors introduces a new dimension into the narrative, a dimension which in the past had seemed proper rather to poetry. This is why Hartley refers to *The Scarlet Letter* as a work of art

"in the sense that a poem is." Hawthorne and Melville—and perhaps I should add Thoreau and Emerson—introduced into prose the plurality of levels of significance which has characterized the poetry of all ages.

The symbolist tendency of American letters (the "second" level of meaning) accounts also for the second point raised by Hartley in connection with *The Scarlet Letter,* its quality of timelessness. And this in spite of the novel's deep roots in New England history. Indeed, the other basic element in the American intellectual makeup (from the nineteenth century till today) could hardly fail to make itself felt: the sense of the land, of contemporary reality. This continual shifting from reality to symbol is typical of poetic expression. The influence of American writers on the origins of the symbolist movement itself has long been explored: the Poe-Baudelaire-Symbolist relation needs no further comment. What I should like to note here, instead, is the fundamental influence which the new narrative method of Hawthorne and Melville has had on the twentieth century novel. This is not merely a question of language (to which Feidelson's book restricts itself) but of a much more far-reaching revolution in narrative form, the revolution which some thirty years ago was talked of as the "crisis of the novel." The names most generally connected with this crisis are Joyce, Proust, and Virginia Woolf. These are the writers who radically changed both the tempo of the narrative and its centre of interest, annulling the time sequence and directing attention to levels of perception existing below the normal plane of consciousness. They investigated the secret world in which objective reality seemed to sink, giving rise to the ambiguous symbols of the unconscious; and in this way they often reached results which are closer to poetry (as has been noted a number of times) than to traditional prose. I do not wish to put forward an exaggerated claim for the novels of Hawthorne and Melville, but I do wish to state that they were the first to introduce into narrative that continual interchange between reality and symbol which was to underlie the works not only of the writers I have mentioned, but also (to name two other major writers who yet differ profoundly from each other), of Lawrence and Gide. It is in the two American novelists that we find for the first time in prose the methods which hitherto belonged exclusively to poetry; I am referring here to the imaginative approach, and not to the language which enables us, for example, to recognize long sequences of Shakespearian blank verse in certain passages of *Moby Dick.*

The objection could be raised at this point that a deep distinction exists between the analysis of the subliminal psychological processes on which the symbolism of recent English authors is based, and the motivation of the symbolism of the American novelists, which is essentially and almost exclusively moral. The American novelists, it is true, were building their world of symbols on the old puritan way of thinking, which interpreted every happening as a manifestation of the divine will: which was constantly concerned with evil and sin. These considerations bring us to Hartley's third point in relation to Hawthorne, which is precisely his treatment of these problems. Certainly Hawthorne handled them with "a complete sense of the issues involved" and also with compassion and justice. This does not mean, however, that he ceased to be troubled by these problems, unsolved and ambiguous, expressible only through the indefiniteness of symbols, which find their deepest poetic truth just in their rational imprecision. The twentieth-century English novelists, living in a different moral setting, set out rather from aesthetics than ethics; but nevertheless they transferred from poetry to prose what we can call the "symbolist method," though without drawing directly on Hawthorne or Melville.

The fact is that another writer more or less consciously acted as go-between for the two traditions of the novel, the American and the English. Henry James had come very deeply under Hawthorne's influence, and had also absorbed the doctrines of the English aesthetic movement. James succeeded in reaching a very delicate balance between these two currents of thought, and, on the level of narrative technique, between the two novel traditions. It is perhaps for this reason that his style, in his major works, gives the impression of being dangerously poised, constantly on the verge of the "false." The problem of evil, the use of symbols and ambiguities, are coupled in his work with an exquisite perception of the problems of aesthetics and even of literary technique, which were sweeping through the European art of his day. In this way he built up a personal form of expression which was capable of introducing into European literature the problems and way of expressing them which until that time had been the exclusive property of American letters. He was a forerunner of the revolution in European fiction, and the American symbolist method of narrative was one of the elements which contributed to this revolution. Walter Allen wrote of D. H. Lawrence, Dorothy Richardson, James Joyce and Virginia Woolf:

> At the same time, no later writers can afford to neglect the discoveries of these novelists. The problem is how to marry these discoveries to an adequate conception of structure. No one has yet succeeded in solving the problem on a large scale, but it is because they have solved it, or partly solved it, within the limits they have set themselves that we can consider Graham Greene, Joyce

Cary, Elizabeth Bowen, Henry Green, Anthony Powell, L. P. Hartley, James Hanley, and P. H. Newby as among the most significant English novelists at present writing.

These comments of Allen's bring us back to L. P. Hartley, who is one of the "post-revolutionary" novelists, one of those who have attempted, after the radical overturning of the narrative form, to find a *modus vivendi* between past and present, and to create a compromise narrative structure. Hartley, it seems to me, is a clear proof of the existence of an American element in the new conception of English narrative. Like other English novelists, once the acute phase of the crisis of the novel had passed, he was anxious to link back to the traditional forms, to bridge the gap between present and past. So, although he is a fundamentally English writer, and although he is engaged in portraying an authentically English scene, the narrative tradition by which he was inspired was not that of the great nineteenth century English novel, but the American tradition.

Born in 1895 and educated at Harrow and Oxford, Hartley must have come in his youth under the influence of the aesthetic movement of the early years of this century: his first long story or short novel *Simonetta Perkins* (1925) reflects, in fact, even in its title, this literary movement, though he treats it with a certain irony. From the first sentence the tone recalls Firbank (a less brilliant and, as the story shows, much less perverse Firbank):

> "Love is the greatest of all passions", Miss Johnstone read, "the first and the last". She lifted her eyes from the book, and they rested on the grey dome of Santa Maria della Salute, rising like a blister on the inflamed and suppurating stonework below. . . .

Even the plot recalls Firbank: the daughter of a good and wealthy American family who falls in love with a Venetian gondolier. But it does not take long to discover that Hartley's real model, chosen perhaps with the intent of irony, is Henry James. Miss Johnstone in *Simonetta Perkins* is a Daisy Miller devoid of drama and deprived of her pathetic halo. The story has the same dimension as James' *nouvelles,* and the heroine is a faithful, though somewhat toned-down copy of James's innocents abroad. From its beginning in *Simonetta Perkins* James's influence became constant in Hartley's work stylistically—one quite often comes across such sentences as these:

> "No, you don't", he said. I didn't, nor as he might have seen, was I in any condition to; but the formulation of this magnificent comprehensive negative riveted, so to speak, my fetters.

The same influence is to be seen in his psychological treatment of his character: the child heroes of both his major novels, *The Shrimp and the Anemone* and *The*

Go-Between are very close to those described by Henry James (it is enough to cite *The Turn of the Screw*). Hartley, indeed, seems to have followed James' development through an ever-growing symbolic concentration. Just as the American, in his last novels, moved the narrative more and more onto the second level, the level of symbolism, so Hartley, after having employed symbols only occasionally for emotive emphasis in his early works, built up a whole novel around a group of symbols in *The Boat* and *The Go-Between*. In this way he went back beyond James himself, back to the complex symbolism of Hawthorne.

Hartley little by little absorbed not only the "method" typical of American (not English) novelists of the mid-nineteenth century, but also their moral problems. The problems of sin and evil became his own, though in *Simonetta Perkins* he could still smile at them, attributing them to the puritan mentality of Miss Johnstone, to whom he ascribes the following meditation:

> "If Hester Prynne had lived in Venice", she thought, "she needn't have stood in the pillory". For a moment she wished that Hawthorne's heroine could have found a country more congenial to her temperament.

In spite of the jocose tone of the quotation, it is worth noticing that *The Scarlet Letter* is the only book Hartley refers to in his first novel. And perhaps another sentence in *Simonetta Perkins* is worthy of comment:

> in her ears, perhaps, defunctive music, the leave-taking of the gods she loved.

The echo is so clear that it seems to be almost a deliberate allusion to T. S. Eliot's:

> Defunctive music under sea
>   Passed seaward with the passing bell
> Slowly: the God Hercules
>   Had left him, that had loved him well.

In spite of the generous treatment of Venice in English literature, Hartley recalls an author who is English only by choice: the only poem on Venice by T. S. Eliot: "Burbank with a Baedeker: Bleistein with a Cigar."

Hartley, a thoroughly English writer, goes back in narrative method, style, textual analogy and even moral problems to a typically American tradition. It is easy to realize how this could come about by glancing at the bridge thrown by writers like James and Eliot between the two continents and the two traditions. The same two writers, for instance, are among the most obvious stylistic influences on the prose of another novelist, Henry Green. The problem of evil and sin, on the other hand, the puritan heritage so vigorously

expressed by Hawthorne and Melville, reacquired British citizenship in the last twenty or thirty years (perhaps from the moment when in 1927 Eliot became a British subject) and found new expression in the Catholic novelist, Graham Greene, often based on the realistic and "tough" style of yet other American writers.

While little more than a century ago many American writers, though keeping in their writings a local flavor and tone, drew on English literature for themes and narrative processes, today, when the completely autonomous characteristics of the American literary tradition are acknowledged also in England, typically English writers are using styles and themes which date back to mid-nineteenth century America.

John Athos (essay date January 1962)

SOURCE: Athos, John. "L. P. Hartley and the Gothic Infatuation." *Twentieth Century Literature* 7, no. 4 (January 1962): 172-79.

[*In the essay that follows, Athos asserts that Hartley's short fiction inspired his longer works and provided source material from which he often drew. Athos focuses in particular on Hartley's use of Gothic motifs and on his concept of evil in both genres.*]

L. P. Hartley's achievement is now substantial. *The Go-Between* and *The Boat* are frequently spoken of as among the best novels in recent years but there are others that challenge them, and indeed all his work is notable for its integrity and finish.

His sophistication, his knowledge of contemporary society, his intimacy with cosmopolitan life, all give him an appeal as a writer who is genuinely contemporary. His experiments in form and technique, however, are limited, and it is not unfair, I think, to speak of him in these respects as an Edwardian writer, although his main inspiration goes back still farther. His impetus from the beginning has been romantic, and in particular he has always been drawn to the substance as well as the devices of the "Gothic" writers. It is in the light of this, I think, that one can usefully view an important aspect of his work.

Hartley published a volume of short stories in 1924, and a novelette, *Miss Simonetta Perkins,* in 1925. There were a few other stories after that but there was no novel until 1944. The eleven novels of these last seventeen or eighteen years are remarkably finished works, and it seems indeed that a long period of the most intelligent apprenticeship had prepared for them.

I think we can observe in the first works—*Miss Simonetta Perkins* and the stories—the substantial material and inspiration he was to continue to draw on when the time came for the more sustained efforts.

It all centers, I think, in the way he conceives of evil. In one of the cruelest of the short stories, **"Podolo,"** an Englishman, resident in Venice, takes the wife of a friend of his for a picnic lunch to Podolo, a small island in the Venetian lagoon. "Except for perhaps a rat or two it was quite uninhabited." While they were idling pleasantly off the shore the Englishwoman noticed a cat on the island, scrawny, starving, and crying for food. She was shocked at the sight of such suffering, so she went ashore to take the animal some food. She tried to catch hold of it, but the cat snarled at her and ran away. She wanted to rescue it so she pursued it while her friend and the gondolier napped in the boat, and when they woke, near dark, surprisingly Angela was nowhere to be seen. When at last the gondolier found her, she was, we are to suppose, mangled almost beyond recognition, and able in her suffering only to ask him to kill her before "it" came back. "It's starving, too, and it won't wait."

That is all we ever learn of the monstrous creature inhabiting the island. The Englishman and the gondolier return to the city, stunned and silent.

The reader is apparently supposed to be satisfiied with the shock and with conjuring up his own horrible invention to account for the catastrophe. As for the pleasure the story is designed to give, it can only be, in addition to the titillation of horror, admiration for the economy and cleverness by which the conclusion takes hold of us.

This kind of mere imagining, and only that, without the extensions of thought or the beginning of commitments, is an effort to create a fragmentary sensation at once interesting for its intensity and for its limits in sensation. Because it stops short of meaning it claims a dignity as it were free from irresponsibility or morbidity. It makes no claims other than as a fragment, a shock. Its value is in the brilliance of the effect, a sudden glare.

This is a special capacity of the modern short story, to provide the narrator with a role he can keep to the end, the role of someone imagining something for its own sake. In his novels Hartley takes that same trick, the flash lost in the darkness, and the purpose, in the first of them, almost remains the same—to exclude the context, to elaborate endlessly but still keep everything within itself, and to absolve the reader from thought. But as time goes on, elaborations extend the vista, and meaning forces itself inevitably upon us—

the flash in the dark by the very constancy of its limits comes inescapably to signify the absolute and irredeemable tyranny of evil. In the conventional "Gothic" way these images of horror are developed into symbols, not merely as comments upon the events in the narrative but as active forces in the lives of the characters. In the trilogy that tells of the lives of a brother and sister from their earliest childhood, the first book, *The Shrimp and the Anemone,* takes its name from an incident both children once witnessed, a sight that turned out to be the expression of what was forming and was to destroy their own lives.

"Eustace bent over the pool. His feet sank in its soggy edge, so he drew back, for he must not get them wet. But he could still see the anemone. Its base was fastened to a boulder, just above the waterline. From the middle of the other end, which was below, something stuck out, quivering. It was a shrimp, Eustace decided, and the anemone was eating it, sucking it in. A tumult arose in Eustace's breast. His heart bled for the shrimp, he longed to rescue it; but, on the other hand, how could he bear to rob the anemone of its dinner? The anemone was more beautiful than the shrimp, more interesting, and much rarer."

What the boy was seeing turns out to be the key to his own and his sister's life—at the moment, for the boy, a merely hideous and almost mesmeric sight, but for the novelist and the reader it comes to be the evidence of a mysterious way the universe has of foretelling the boy's victimization by his sister, and of outlining his capitulation to something he acknowledged as "more interesting and rarer" than himself. Here the shock goes beyond that of **"Podolo,"** although I think they are the same in kind—a transfixing horror for which there is no saving justification, and to the degree that it is different it may have lost something of its force. In *The Mill on the Floss* George Eliot also shows how the lives of a brother and sister may be fatally intertwined from an early date, but with her the emphasis is on the power of fate through devices that reward our most curious speculation; in Hartley the emphasis is more upon a striking parallel in the exterior world, and the rewards of speculating upon an incident regarded superstitiously are much more limited. Hartley's technique here, developing more than the merely sensational, is yet not deeply enough conceived—there is a more judicious than imaginative combining of images and ideas, and the ideas themselves are too much limited by a view of evil that is itself limited by obsession.

In *The Go-Between* the symbol of a deadly night-shade encompasses innumerable aspects of the story. A small boy, already disposed to see magic in everything, comes upon the plant: " . . . it wasn't a plant, in my sense of the word, it was a shrub, almost a tree, and as tall as I was. It looked the picture of evil and also the picture of health, it was so glossy and strong and juicy-looking . . . staring at the button-bright berries and the dull, purplish, hairy, bell-shaped flowers reaching out towards me, even if I didn't touch it, . . . I knew that if I didn't eat it, it would eat me."

This time the image is not merely a stage-symbol, some hallucinatory sight containing a picture in little of the future, it is also something of a parable. The boy this time is older, and however mysterious the occasion and the presence of the plant and what it seemed to tell him, he is also less naively reporting its mythical and demonic force. To a certain extent he is outside its influence: he is not so completely enslaved because so much more of his life has already taken its own direction before this monstrous being appeared to capture the rest. All the same, his destruction is certain.

"At first I was afraid of hurting the plant, then in my terror I began to tear at it, and heard its branches ripping and crackling. Soon I cleared a space around my head, but that was not enough, it must all be clear. The plant was much less strong than I supposed: I fought with it: I got hold of its main stem and snapped it off. There was a swish; a soft, sighing fall of leaf on leaf, a swirl, a debris of upturned leaves, knee-deep all round me: and standing up among them, the torn stem. I seized it and pulled with all my might, and as I pulled the words of the missing spell floated into my mind out of some history lesson—'delenda est belladonna! delenda est belladonna!'"

What follows in the novel, however, almost justifies the hideousness and even preposterousness of this incident, for the way in which Hartley shows how life breaks the spirit of this boy is as profound and vivid a presentation of a dying-in-life as one can expect of fiction. It almost justifies the use of Gothic artifice as a device to show how moments of hysteria may indeed reveal the pattern of what is foreordained, but here the technique finally does the writer a disservice—Hartley's conception of the way the boy's loss of faith in life cripples him is so much more profound and sensitively accurate than the trick and the superstition comprehend. But in the effect of the novel as a whole, the image maintains a dominating and limiting darkness. It was meant to show that the boy—an innocent go-between for illicit lovers—was to be destroyed by being put to an evil use, but what it does affirm goes beyond this—that all human passion is evil and, inescapably, totally destructive.

The significances we attach to the scenes in *The Go-Between* we are confident of from what we know of all such Gothic imaginings, and, were it not for that,

we might be disposed to take Hartley's treatment of such an image here as another explanation of co-ordinate patterns in the ways of the universe and the lives of individuals. But in this instance, at least, it is difficult to take the incident so seriously. Even if one were to grant it the weight and power Hartley seems to want it to embody, we still feel that it is false and stale, because the whole Gothic way was forced, from its beginnings with Walpole—the dedication to horror and evil and meaninglessness was the initial assumption. The game was rigged, and this was in fact the source of the determining satisfaction of such works. When writers used the Gothic devices for serious references to actuality, they took the risk of mistaking the limited terms of the initially preposterous conventions as legitimate means for interpreting life. More particularly, the temptation was to make the horrors they dealt in bear reference to the realities of sin and evil in circumstances when the reasoning supporting the use of the conventions might not be adequate or valid. This was the temptation of Hawthorne, whom Giorgio Melchiori has shown to be Hartley's original, but in Hawthorne, as Henry James saw it, there was a saving power:

"The conscience, by no fault of its own, in every genuine offshoot of that sombre lineage [of Puritanism], lay under the shadow of the sense of *sin*. This darkening cloud was no essential part of the nature of the individual; it stood fixed in the general moral heaven under which he grew up and looked at life. It projected from above, from outside, a black patch over his spirit, and it was for him to do what he could with the black patch. . . . Hawthorne's way was the best; for he contrived, by an exquisite process, best known to himself, to transmute this heavy moral burden into the very substance of his imagination, to make it evaporate in the light and changing forms of artistic production."

Hartley's mind in a systematic elaboration of the chances of life plays back and forth over the way Eustace or Leo or Marian seem at one moment to escape, at the next to throw themselves into the arms of the anemone or the night shade. The images are frightful, as limitlessly deep in horror, we are meant to see, as death itself. And it is the ambitiousness of the pretension that accounts for one of the chief faults of this kind of writing—the lack of humor. The stupidity of superstition necessarily limits its exploitation. Hartley evidently came to understand this, and in a manner not unlike Faulkner's he came to employ humor to dignify the Gothic techniques with intelligence, perhaps meaning in this way also to lighten the darkness.

In *My Fellow Devils* he takes a monster for his hero, the Devil himself. He is as serious about this being and his power as he is about the deadly night-shade, but this time the characters in the story are adults and he cannot exploit the humorless seriousness of children as a way of effecting horror. Instead, he tricks us by making us think, at first, that the Devil is not too bad a fellow—a movie actor, in fact, attractive, glamorous, and the dupe of his profession.

And this gives his intelligence its chance, to match the obsessive images of evil and horror with the observation of the endless capriciousness of life, to match horror with the most sophisticated humor.

In *My Fellow Devils* the humor is brilliant. And although this may not "transmute the heavy moral burden," may not finally emancipate the novelist from the intolerable Puritan gloom, it gives the mind of the narrator at least the semblance of freedom.

A film star has become a matinee idol through his portrayal of criminal roles, tough, brutal, clever, but with the look of a misguided boy. And this is his true character—the films in their characteristic way have made the fictional character out of the real one. But Colin MacInnes goes his films one better—he is in fact a thief, a second-story man. He burgles houses wherever he is, London or Venice. He steals from his own possessions and collects the insurance. He steals his wife's jewels, and a longtime girl-friend helps him unload the stuff. A final prank all but gets him tried for manslaughter and theft, but by a succession of tricks and lies, his own and of those who love him, he is exonerated and the tables are turned again—the film star who was about to lose his public as a condemned criminal becomes more popular than ever, persecuted, his audience now thinks, because the law hates the charm of the tough, wayward little boy.

The film that comes out at this very time, called "The Devil is Distinguished," had a premiere like no other, it was a tremendous success, and at the banquet following the first night the toast that everyone—or almost everyone—gave with the hysteria of teenagers was, "To the Devil! May he live forever!" The only one who refused to join in the toast was a priest who smelled the brimstone—the others are happy, if that is the word, to recognize the Devil as their fellow.

Colin, as Hartley shows him, is miraculously self-possessed and joyless, and the evil he embodies triumphs through a thousand conspiracies with chance, so that finally we come to accept these as the tricks of life itself. The presentation of these countless involutions is paralleled by the coincidences that draw his wife to him and then finally take her away. The success of the Devil is interwoven with perfect integrity into the flight of Colin's wife from and towards God.

But even here Hartley takes the fatal chance of leaving us with nothing else than this "black patch" James wrote of, fixed and all-encompassing. Where, sometimes, Hawthorne brings us out of this to some self-awareness and to a criticism of the limits of the world of total sin, Hartley even with his humor and with his Catholic faith does not quite break free, nor in this book does he want to. God's rescue of Colin's wife, beautifully convincing as it is in its portrayal of a religious experience, is presented foremost as a joke on the devil, and under the circumstances this is a dusty answer for so sustained and serious a presentation of the resources of evil.

In a more recent book, *The Hireling*, Hartley shifts his point of view. He takes the capriciousness of life and the arbitrariness of humor into a realm where it manifests the intervention of grace and the humor becomes irony, and tragic. Which is to say that he is again following the progress of Hawthorne, this time into allegory. Those original merely meaningless horrors are now more than hallucinatory and more than parables or symbols—although they continue to share something of the nature of the earlier devices—but by the method of making the narrator a metaphysician the incidents themselves take on the status of occurring in two different realms of existence at one time. By such a means I suppose a writer can free himself from some, at least, of the initially arbitrary and narrow limitations of the Gothic techniques. At any rate, this seems to be Hartley's intention here, and the results are in many respects as admirable as they are extraordinary.

A man and a woman, corrupt in one way or another but wanting deeply to make peace with themselves and with love, are caught in a kind of suspended existence, prey to various fantasies, hardly knowing from time to time what is reality and what isn't. As the lines of fate entangle them there is a smash-up, and the man is killed, pierced by a strut from the steering wheel. His death, it turns out, has the effect of sacrifice, and a letter he sent before his death is the means of bringing the woman to religion and under the protection of the saints. Ideas of death, sacrifice, redemption, salvation, and the Crucifixion, all participate in the image of the dead man at the steering wheel.

The full impact of the powerful ending is apparent only as the very culmination of all that has gone before. There is no weight of doctrine or improbability intruding here, for the movement from fantasy to illumination advances integrally. The transformation is represented by acts of extraordinary clarity, and in which mystification takes on the status of mystery. Leadbetter interrupted the conversation of his passengers on that last ride to tell them what they thought no person on earth could have told them, that only God would have known: that the woman on the back seat had not betrayed her lover to Lady Franklin, whom her lover was about to marry, although he believed she had, for who else but his mistress could know he had promised to keep on with her? And as the lovers quarrel over their supposed treason to each other, Leadbetter interrupts to free them of their trouble. They had forgotten the chauffeur while they were confiding with each other. In this symbolical development, in the voice of the driver whose presence they had ignored, that came to them now as the voice of the omniscient God, the effect upon the reader has the surprise and felicity of poetry.

All the same, I think the book as a whole does not quite succeed. At the beginning there was the quotation,

> Trop de perversités règne au siècle où
>   nous sommes,
> Et je veux me tirer du commerce des
>   hommes,

and I suppose as we come to the end and see the illumination offered Lady Franklin, we are to take it that this means something like

> O come quickly, sweetest Lord, and
> take my soul to rest.

But I think one cannot avoid viewing the conclusion, moving as it is, by the light of the initial preoccupation with "perversities," the nature of the world now claimed to be transmuted, not the evil alone but the perfection of perversity. Overshadowing all, we feel, is the same imagination that comprehended the whole of life in the nightshade, where even childhood is corrupt—Lady Franklin is saved by an anonymous letter—the emphasis even in the resolution is upon the meanness of the way of saving her.

As we begin to take in the magnitude of Hartley's work, the genius of it, the brilliance and integrity, the modern exploitation of the Edwardian novel forms and the new life he may succeed in giving them, one comes back to the thought of the uselessness of art in such a service as this. The exploitation of horror and cruelty always raises questions about the value of literature when it concentrates on such effects. The questions keep returning to the idea that sensations of this nature may not be sufficient either for the enlightenment or the satisfaction of a reader. On one side, there is the answer that it is quite enough for art to present us with the abysses that surround us, and on the other, that what shocks us serves reflection finally, and indeed the reader needs to be shocked in order to know what, or how, to think.

In *My Fellow Devils* and *The Hireling*, however, the advances into thought are there for all to see. It is true, as I have heard it said, that *My Fellow Devils* is a reconstruction of what the *Spiritual Exercises* of Saint Ignatius present as the logic of a back-slider, and the extraordinary humor of the book is in the suspense—each step is made to appear to us as anything but inevitable although the heroine is forced to think it is inevitable, and each step that she thought was bringing her back to God was also always another selfishness and betrayal. The complexity and the sum of the sequences is perfectly schematic, and the humor of the book is in just that, the schematization of a person struggling with the devil in herself. And the irony and humor lead us from one complexity of thought to another, for we do not know if, as in the ways of the emancipated, we are to shrug and wink, like those Hollywood stars in Venice she has come to live with; or if we are to be horrified by the implacable ways of fate; or whether we are to regard this furious enslavement as the scourge of God.

But it is not only the brilliance that attracts us. In the manipulation of words and techniques Hartley is the master of his art, and he re-creates as the best fiction does the very force of life. There are times when the heroine turns her face to the light in some instinctive question and we see the light strike her, and at such moments we know that we never ask more of art than this, to catch such light and shadow, such a gesture, such a significance in passion and interest in the flesh of the girl's face about the bones of her brow and chin, in the glance through which her thought and feeling pour into her eyes and across what is before her.

Hartley's work is at its best in the creation of sights like this, and in verifying the complexities of dream and passion. If such were his main aims, his achievement would be of the highest order. His special limiting of the ways of evil, however, too often spoils our enjoyment of the beauty and vitality and complexity of his work. The meaninglessness of the horrors he exploits in the end discourages our attention.

John Atkins (essay date 1977)

SOURCE: Atkins, John. "L. P. Hartley: Tarnished Glamour." In *Six Novelists Look at Society: An Enquiry into the Social Views of Elizabeth Bowen, L. P. Hartley, Rosamund Lehman, Christopher Isherwood, Nancy Mitford, C. P. Snow,* pp. 77-111. London: John Calder, 1977.

[*In this essay, Atkins contends that Hartley's short fiction is often an expression of the author's disapproval of the modern age; the critic also discusses the historical context of Hartley's writing, his social commentary, and his abiding interest in the aristocracy.*]

THE MODERN WORLD

Hartley doesn't like it. There is no equivocation, no attempt to be 'fair', to look at things from other angles, as with Elizabeth Bowen. The world is going from bad to worse. The distaste is increasingly implicit in his work, and when things become unbearable there is the occasional explicit statement. Hartley begins his story, **'Mrs Carteret Receives',** in the collection of that name, 1971, with a brief essay, almost in the manner of Arnold Bennett, on the social change that has taken place in England since the turn of the century. The motor-car, he says, has corroded the 'democracy of place and local habitations.'

To begin with, ours is an ugly world. The English part of it is worse than many other parts. In **'Three, or Four, for Dinner'** (in the collection, *The Travelling Grave,* 1948) two Englishmen see a couple of tramp-steamers moored in a Venetian canal. One says, 'This reminds me of Hull. Good old Hull! Civilization at last! Nothing picturesque and old-world. Two ugly, useful old ships, nice oily water, and lots of foreign bodies floating about in it.'

The distaste increases with Hartley's maturity. He finds life sufficiently enjoyable during the early years to ignore its worst manifestations. But the war inevitably drags things down. By the time he wrote *The Boat,* 1949, he was quite disgruntled. The epigraph from Emily Brontë prepares us:

> Gaze on the wretch, recall to mind
> His golden days left long behind.

It will be useful to consider this novel in some detail.

It could be viewed as a subtle Right Wing apologia if one felt that Hartley were at all interested in making such a thing—which he never was, or not in such crude terms. If the Conservative Party had been more aware they would have adopted it as a cultural mascot, just as other political groups have adopted *Animal Farm* and *Lord of the Flies.* It is a protest against the idiotic class attitudes which became so prominent during the war. The dominant symbol (Hartley being very partial to such devices) is a flood. The flood overwhelms and brings everyone to their senses and destroys evil. Timothy Casson, like the more famous Eustace, has it easy and lives on a legacy. This is the ideal situation, and its social implications are never considered. Also like Eustace he cannot resist fantasies of grandeur, tremendous self-dramatizations, accompanied by a wretched sense of personal inadequacy. That such a character should be presented in such detail in four consecutive books suggests that Hartley feels these qualities in himself.

We are in the Age of the Common Man but, if we take sides with our author, we don't feel at home in it. The period is the early stages of the war, but is set in an English village (West Country, with a view of the Welsh hills), among retired and evacuated populations. Timothy is always trying to adjust himself to new circumstances, although he has no understanding of social structures. The village of Upton is divided into two nations, but they are not Disraeli's: they are the old stagers and the newcomers. It is war within the middle class. The working class form a comic chorus in traditional English literary style, and they are also beyond communication. No sooner does Timothy feel that he is beginning to understand them than something begins to baffle him anew. His gardener tells him that there is a similar cleavage among the working people. Some of the lower classes realize that things have changed and that their labour is in short supply. When Beattie, his cook, phones a friend, she says: 'The tables are turned now, they can't talk to us like they used to, they know they can't get anyone in our place.'

The class war, however, is within the traditional middle class (between Orwellian sub-groups) rather than between the major social divisions. Miss Vera Cross, who turns out to be a Communist Party agent, dedicated to causing social unrest (this is a bit hard to take, because her field of operations seems so petty and remote from the real struggle, and one wonders what Stalin's agents are doing there), wants to enlist Timothy with the newcomers (mostly business wives from the towns) against the retired colonels: 'We're tired of being high-hatted by all these stuffed shirts'. Edgell Purbright, the rector's son, says the retired gentry are finished. Symbolically, he and Vera fall in love. The rector himself disapproves of the new trend because the local landowner (Mrs Lampard) has done up dilapidated cottages for weekend businessmen, leaving several labouring families homeless. She has unwittingly hastened the process. She goes mad, which is symbolically unobjectionable.

Much of this is satire on Left Wing romanticism. Timothy's socialite friend, Magda, writes of a Russian girl's deep-chested laughter 'which no European corrupted by centuries of bourgeois culture, can hope to understand.' This is typical of the idiotic kind of statement one heard during the war when thousands of people, including many rich and even of aristocratic background, were emotionally stampeded into acceptance of communism as the complete answer to everything. One of the paradoxes of our time has been that the first scientific approach to politics, Marxism, gave rise to one of the most irresponsibly romantic political movements in history. Timothy is infected. He is a sitting target because his intelligence is undeveloped, his notivations are luxurious and aesthetic, he has nothing to do and the devil finds work for idle hands. When we left Eustace at the end of the famous trilogy, he was already going that way. Timothy becomes impressed by the uselessness of the fishermen (that is to say, the retired gentry) who, he imagines, will not let him use the river for boating. 'Almost for the first time Timothy felt himself warmly proletarian, a champion of the have-nots against the high-ups.'

Urged to take action by Vera, lectured in letters from Magda, Timothy came to appreciate the virtues inherent in the proletariat. 'It might not be such a bad thing after all, he said, if we were governed by them, for their feelings were still direct and natural, not vitiated by theories of behaviour.' In another letter he writes: 'I don't approve of people being allowed to hand on their money, of course . . . ', but while the law is what it is he must (fortunately) act within its framework. Timothy owes everything to a legacy, and he is here telling his friend Tyro that he is leaving his estate to him and two other friends. In a letter to Esther he asks if she can find him servants, for he has given his own servant notice. He doesn't mind what sins they may have committed—'in any case, it's society's fault, not theirs.' Timothy is an excellent example of the willy-nilly and absolutely superficial embracement of socialist belief encountered during the war. It wasn't socialism and it wasn't sincere. A puff of wind could have blown it away.

In a way this book comes closer to social commentary than most books of the period, even those which adopted a socialist philosophy and were intended as criticism. It is about social fantasy which, in its results, is as real as social reality. (What people think is as important as what people do.) Vera was no fool, though. After the River Revolution (in itself an absurd, though tragic affair) 'the labourers would be less willing to touch their caps and the bosses would not get out their fishing tackle with the same confidence as before. The two nations would be conscious of their apartness, their irreconcilability; and the rift would widen in preparation for the final struggle.' Water will wear away a stone. And Vera was right, for the change has come. But Timothy was a mere fool. Miss Chadwick, his landlord, advises him not to make friends with his servants. 'Their outlook is so very different from ours. Kindness is so often constructed as weakness or worse, and familiarity is always a mistake.' This is a basic tenet of the English social creed. The policeman says the same thing about the evacuees, for the police are a bridge between classes, in the pay of the upper and middle. Hartley gives this philosophy a cruel twist when Timothy makes his blow for equality by rowing his boat on the river and giving two little boys a ride. All the mothers want him to take their

own children. When he is compelled to refuse, one says: 'I didn't think you'd descend to favouritism. What's the good of gassing about the freedom of the river, when you've packed your boat with your friends?' Timothy's friend Esther does not sympathize with his betrayal of the group, though she does not put it so crudely. It is necessary for them to stick together, for people need an example to look up to. This, in its halting way, is the crux of the matter: there must be an élite.

The war is definitely seen as a watershed: on one side lay the Land of Cockayne, on the other it sloped away to the Bad Lands. **'The White Wand',** a story which gave its name to a collection in 1954, pressed the point home. C.F. is telling his story:

> All through the war, in England, stopping in strange hotels up and down the country, and not only at hotels, I had been the victim of innumerable acts of pilfering—don't tell me, Arthur, please don't tell me, that the war has done our morals any good. All the little trinkets I possessed—yes, and necessities, too—were pinched from me—watches, watchchains, cuff-links, travelling clocks—even the shirt off my back, when it was new enough. The war turned us into a nation of thieves. . . .

It will be recalled that economists and sociologists often claimed that the war had had an excellent effect on morality—it had reduced privilege and introduced a remarkable degree of solidarity. But C.F. didn't agree. Originally he had tried to cultivate his responses to the variety of life but since the war he had stopped. What was the point of trying to maintain civilized behaviour when those who were loudest in defending it were the first to abandon it? He flatly contradicted the solidarity theory, asking 'for how many people the steady warmth of personal relationships perished in the burning heat of September 1939? Certainly with me it did; I felt I had nothing to give out or to take in . . . The blight of political hatred was on everything.' And when the war was over he felt that people were always waiting for some specific event to take place (for example, the hydrogen bomb to be perfected or the Korean war to come to an end) before they would attempt to return to a post-war habit of life. Such references to current political events are extremely rare in Hartley's work.

But his feelings about society led him to write the kind of novel that it is certain he is least fitted to write, and that one of his admirers would never have foreseen. This was *Facial Justice,* 1960, an essay in science fiction. In it he presents the Uniform State, which is the characteristic Dystopia of the English liberal. In this society it was unwise to show a marked Personal Preference, for it led to inflammation of the ego. Citizens were graded into Alphas, Betas and Gammas. 'Alphas are anti-social.' In fact, like other egalitarian states, it was governed by an élite, who were the Alphas. But these were 'pure' Alphas, the Inspectors, specially chosen by the Dictator. Those who did not quite come up to standard were called Failed Alphas, and were encouraged to merge with the Betas. The women were even Betafied, which involved a facial operation which reduced them to the mediocrity of the middle rank. Gammas, who were unattractive, gained by the operation. For women were graded according to beauty, and it was anti-social to be more beautiful than your neighbour.

The social poles were Equality and Envy, Good E and Bad E, Good Egg and Bad Egg, as the jargon had it. Mention of either involved the speaker in a ritual dance: 'a few jerky, gymnastic capers for Envy, a long intricate, ecstatic exercise for Equality.' There were time-saving concessions: a curtsey for Equality and a token spit for Envy. It followed that one must not mention 'bad luck' for luck is a leveller, therefore good. You should always look your own height for there is nothing higher. The Horizontal View of Life (On the Level) was generally accepted. At eleven o'clock the population ate pastilles, coloured violet, with an E engraved on them. Laughter was discouraged, but was permitted for five minutes a day to get it out of your system. Cinemas showed films of the horrors of war twice a week and attendance was compulsory unless a doctor's certificate could be produced. Everyone had the same income and money could only be transferred in return for an official receipt. There were no such things as tastes, only taste—the *reductio absurdum* of Good Taste. By the time Jael, the heroine, was Betafied (against her will) four-fifths of all women had the same Government-approved face. The remainder were Gammas, ugly by comparison. When Jael attacked the regime she used ridicule based on the regime's own principles. She suggested it was unfair and an abuse of privilege for some to enjoy better health than others, and suggested the injection of the healthy with some form of not necessarily serious illness, 'so that the level of physical and mental wellbeing in the New State should be roughly regularized—no one too ill, no one too well.'

This state was a juvenilocracy. Citizens were treated as if they were children. Slogans regulated every aspect of life (as in *Brave New World*) and were usually alliterative. The method was even applied to foreign countries, all foreign relations being excellent. The adjectives varied but were always favourable—Belgium was beautiful one day, brave the next, bountiful the next, and so on. If anyone called Belgium beastly he was fined, as he was if he didn't know the adjective of the day, if challenged. This seems so pointless the

childishness of the regime rubs off on the book. At times it irritates through its perverse lack of perceptiveness, its uncritical criticality. Paradoxically, few children were seen on the streets. Radioactivity had caused a high degree of male impotence and the children were carefully segregated. A stranger might have thought it an exclusively adult community. This is one of Hartley's keener insights, for in fact the adults were mentally immature.

The Dictator was never seen but was occasionally heard when he addressed the nation in a broadcast, which could be heard throughout the country. The automatic reaction to any mention of him was the exclamation, 'Dear Dictator'. This is clearly a variant on Big Brother. A daily dose of bromide maintained obedience. The Dictator called his subjects Patients and Delinquents to remind them of their fallen state. This is after the Third World War when the people have emerged from their underground shelters. Each person was obliged to take the name of a murderer or a murderess. (This theme is from *Ape and Essence*.) They wore sackcloth and had ashes in their hair. A confirmed Delinquent wore PS (Permanent Sackcloth). As always, the organization of this totalitarian state involved opposition to home and family. 'Families were still permitted but they were very much frowned on, and the majority of children were brought up in crèches . . . ' Homes were still on trial but were considered a hotbed of bad influences, especially Bad E (like personal beauty). They were as uniform as possible but each had something particular to itself—an ornament, or the arrangement of the furniture—which made it individual and therefore a standard of comparison. Individualism was naturally abhorred. Private Motoring was not allowed, being considered dangerous, decivilizing, egotistical and ideologically unsound. The Motor Expeditions (Country) Service was for the benefit of a few backsliders. And here is a hospital sister praising organization:

> ' . . . making them do all the right things at the right time! If I listened to every moan and groan and squawk and squeak, do you think I should get *anywhere?* Discipline, discipline is what matters. . . . There isn't a single one (i.e., of her patients) that hasn't wanted something special doing for her—more food or less food or different food, more light or less light or no light, more wireless or less wireless or louder wireless or softer wireless or no wireless, they simply have no idea of collective action, they think that being ill (and it's their own fault they are, in most cases) entitles them to special consideration.'

Life was planned, everything was made as pleasant and easy as possible, to inhibit the need for personal effort. The result was a suggestion of liberty that was entirely specious. It is here that Hartley does put his finger on one of the crucial aspects of our time. In one of his addresses the Dictator managed to oppose the Voluntary Principle to Free Will. 'Has not the motto of our régime always been Free Will? Would any of you, standing, sitting or lying (alas, you are all of you fond of lying), who hear these words, dare to say that since the time our envoy led you from the Shades, into this unpromising land, you have ever acted under compulsion? That we have ever forced you, our dear subjects, to do anything you did not want to do?' Of course not; before any of them acted, they were always first persuaded that they wished to do what they would be compelled to do. Jael's revolt eventually takes the form of demanding the right not to be equal. She puts this to her committee, formed to discover and destroy the Dictator. In the Bad Old Days people accepted variations in liberty and a lack of equality because they considered them to be the consequences of luck: 'it hadn't been earned, it hadn't even been stolen.' Jael wrote of the Dictator, sarcastically: 'Long may he live to make the New State safe for mediocrity!' There was no conflict between the generations, but sex conflict flourished. It was one of the foundations of the state. Beautiful women were Betafied to reduce the tensions of Envy. Men were not touched. Jael revolted against this and became a man-hater. She wanted men's looks to be Betafied but they were horrified at the suggestion. But this aspect is poorly integrated with the main theme.

What a surprise! That Hartley, the least political of my six novelists, should write such a book! The reason is that he was the unhappiest of my six. Unlike Waugh (who admired his work), he could not enjoy his blustering. There is a certain amount of band-wagon in Hartley's choice of theme but it enabled him to express his abhorrence of modern trends of uniformity, standardization, statistical administration and communalization. His talent is not suited to this kind of theme—most of his ideas seem to come from Huxley, Orwell and Heard, he has nothing to say about the modern state that has not been said before, and what he does say is clumsily expressed. The rebel, from the liberal-individual standpoint, is Jael, but all her plans go astray and usually lead to bloodshed and chaos. In the end she even replaces the dead Dictator, who had also been a woman. What does Hartley mean? That a Dictator is inevitable? That his rule will be better for us in the last resort than one of freedom and personal choice? No clear message comes through, and much of the detail remains obscure. I think the most likely interpretation is that dictators and leaders of revolt belong to the same category of political man. Revolutionary Djugashvili is Dictator Stalin.

Hartley is much more successful when he is dealing with the minor aspects of life. In *Poor Clare,* 1968, he makes a comment on freedom, but domesticates it. He says that Italy is a freer country, in some ways, than England. This point is repeated in the story, **'Mrs Carteret Receives'**, in the collection of that name, 1971: 'it must be said that most Latin countries, if not so democratically governed, are socially more democratically-minded, than we are, and this is true of all ranks of society.' This has nothing to do with the polls or leading articles. It sounds like heresy to an English patriot, who regards freedom as his personal property, but the remark contains a whole philosophy, that of the Edwardian man of leisure. In England attempts have been made to safeguard freedom by legislation. The rich safeguard their freedom by bribes, but the rich are disappearing. The poor need the paraphernalia of Bureaucracy, which appears to some to be the major enemy of personal freedom. Again in *Poor Clare* Hartley refers to the fascination that ugliness has for modern man. Is this part of the same complex? Possibly—Hartley is not an analytical writer. The inspiration of Gilbert's ugly music was conflict. He used his friends as sparring partners as well as sounding boards. As a result he composed *Sinfonia Disorientate*. His music was modern and dissonant—in Edwards's opinion (which is Hartley's) ugly. 'It didn't appeal to me but it did, no doubt, appeal to people who were at odds with themselves and with the world.' He refers to Gilbert's music as 'all that chaotic, life-destroying stuff, which is about as much like art as a town hit by an atom-bomb!' How can you expect people who demand conflict and thrive on it to understand and appreciate nineteenth century freedoms?

In *The Love-Adept* 1969 we are given another picture of The World We Live In which is more successful because it is contained in Hartley's familiar manner: the personal and the domestic. It is about a novelist who is writing a novel, and corresponding with four ladies all named Elizabeth. He asks one how he should finish his novel and adds, it could be murder, as 'they could all, with the approval of the permissive society, plead that they were suffering from "diminished responsibility"'. Hartley's distaste for the permissive society is so pronounced I am leaving it to another section, along with his most bitter denunciation in *The Betrayal.*

Hartley likes to present himself (often as a first person narrator) as an elderly man of rather pliable character who is never quite at ease in his environment. One of the ladies in *The Love-Adept* (his strongest critic) accuses him of bending over backwards to be a man of his day! She tells him what people are like and it is probably a list of the things Hartley dislikes most about the contemporary world.

> You don't realize that people of today don't want to step out of the ruck; they want to be in it and *with* it, in all senses of the term. They want to keep up with the

Joneses, they don't want to outstrip them, they just want to be with them, they are ruled by *fashion*, a factor you never seem to take into account, but fashion is the ruling passion, and of course it doesn't encourage individualism, or eccentricity, how could it? . . . (Teenagers) only want the emotions that are within their range and by which they can be communicably excited, such as train-wrecking, telephone-kiosk breaking, throwing bottles at football matches, fighting with each other at the seaside, here or abroad, or battling with the police and then accusing them of brutality. Apart from these stimulants, this release for their egos, their ideal, which they will never realize, is to bask semi-nude on a deck-chair or some ocean-going cruise, or to bask, still semi-nude, on the beach of some West Indian island, ready for a bathe or just returned from a bathe, with a sub-tropical sun beating down on their nicely tanned or badly blistered bodies, and a white-coated black-faced waiter hovering by, handing out dry martinis.

She goes on to say that the only kind of humour that will draw people together is sick humour, perhaps a joke about the atom bomb, because they feel a common calamity is threatening them. There is no happiness or reasonableness today, so you must not try to get your effect from pretending there is a background of it, and making a contrast. We are all aware that the future is going to be very unpleasant, and our humour consists in making brief comments on that unpleasantness. Being *with* it is the key, people today don't want contrasts, they are only interested in intensifications of the horrid fact.

She also finds fault with his treatment of children, especially the way they talk to each other ('they talk like little grown-ups, each aware of the other's identity . . . '). Children today probably regard their elders as enemies or potential enemies, who frown on their proper pastimes of bottle-throwing, etc. She explains that she uses 'proper' in the original sense—pastimes that are natural, inevitable, even desirable. 'I don't use the word as you would, ironically or sarcastically, to denigrate our youngsters aged between twelve and twenty. They are only acting according to their natures, relieved from, or rebelling against, parental control.' How should they feel or act differently? If there is to be blame, it should be of their elders whose nationalism and submissiveness to *their* elders have made two world wars possible. That we are already on the road to the society of *Facial Justice* is illustrated by the little boy who talks to Granny Kirkwood. He said that all did well at school but none did best and when asked how this was possible, he replied, 'Because it would make the others jealous.' This negativism seems to be the natural end of democracy to Hartley.

His dislike of the age, which makes itself felt in his post-war fiction, receives emphasis in his best-known essay, 'The Novelist's Responsibility', which is not only printed in his own book of essays, bearing the same title, but also in *Essays by Divers Hands,* Vol. XXXIV, 1966. These are the Transactions of the Royal Society of Literature, and are edited by himself. In his Introduction to this volume he calls our period a 'drab age'. The essay, which he read on 17 March 1963 stresses this impression. Three writers, he says, have helped to undermine the individual's sense of responsibility: Dostoevsky, Marx and Freud. Behind their dogmas lay another, more insidious idea, that of the Little Man: 'a poor, puzzled creature, pushed around by everyone', who has become almost a symbol of man in the modern world. He is nondescript, essentially *little,* from whom nothing much, either good or bad, could be expected. He became the hero of the modern novel, but he had no heroic qualities, so the heroic qualities became unfashionable and to have them was to be anti-social.

In fiction the individual has been devalued and his stature has shrunk. One cause was the enormous amount of suffering and inconvenience endured during the war, so that people ceased to expect a happy, easy or even physically safe life. 'What was one broken heart when so many millions of hearts had been broken?' People today suffer from a state of 'diminished responsibility'—the excuse for breaking your word or your appointment is now 'enshrined in the Statute Book'—and you can literally get away with murder. Compassion is now fashionable but it is for the criminal, not the victim. 'If the question "Whither Fiction?" is raised, the novelist will have to make up his mind which side he is on. Is he to write: "She was a beautiful woman, witty, clever, cultivated, sympathetic, charming, *but,* alas, she was a murderess?" Or is he to write: "She was a beautiful woman, witty, clever, etc., *and* to crown it all, she was a murderess"?'

In a letter to Peter Bien he wrote:

> My great enemy was the State. . . . When I was at Oxford for a short time in 1915 and 1916, and again in 1919. . . . Herbert Spencer, Mill, all the individualist and *laissez-faire* writers, were utterly out of fashion—I suppose they still are. Not only had socialism triumphed over them, but 'political science' was against them. The political philosophers we were told to admire were Hobbes, Locke, Rousseau, Bosanquet (even possibly Macchiavelli), because they all exalted some form of human *association* (usually the State) at the expense of the individual. As I thought that all our troubles came from the State, I was infuriated by this—and the idea of the State having a sort of entity of its own, to which we must sacrifice ourselves, drove me nearly frantic. . . .

> (Printed as a footnote in *L. P. Hartley,* by Peter Bien, 1963)

Bien says that in *Facial Justice* Hartley took Vera, the immoral communist of *The Boat,* 1949, and magnified her into an impersonal government system. But he does not attribute this to implacable economic or historic forces. A people gets the government it deserves and a tyranny comes when individuals show themselves incapable of the moral alertness necessary to a free society.

When a novelist writes out of conviction, as Hartley does, his meaning will often be revealed in oblique ways. Bolshevism is not a subject that crops up often in his work, but when it does in *The Sixth Heaven* Hilda said that at least it stood for something. Hilda could not bear sloppiness or pretentiousness, she loathed the idea of living beyond your income, or trying to adopt a style you were not accustomed to. She is also very domineering. W. W. Robson, discussing William Golding in *Modern English Literature,* 1970, said that a more profound study of 'the impulse to dominate' might be found in Hartley's trilogy. If Vera is a preview of an impersonal system, Hilda prepares us for the earnest commissar, longing out of love to compel us to do what is right.

THE WONDERFUL WORLD OF THE ARISTOCRATS

Hartley was not an aristocrat, nor are his heroes, but they all love the aristocrats. Like his heroes, he has always lived in close proximity to the most privileged section of our population and he has shared some of their privileges. He was educated at Harrow and went to Oxford, where he got to know the Oxford and Asquith family. Many of his stories and novels take us into homes of the nobility. In the stories in particular, castles are in vogue, e.g. **'The Killing Bottle'** and **'Conrad and the Dragon'**, which is a fairy tale and reflects the childlike obsession that is so strong in Hartley's work. Substitute castles (country houses) are even more in evidence—in **'Feet Foremost'**, **'The Travelling Grave'**, **'Cotillon'** and **'Monkshood Manor'** and several of the novels. Valentine in **'Home, Sweet Home'** has a nightmare in which he discovers his old home has become a home for disturbed children (*Mrs Carteret Receives*, 1971). The U/Non-U polarity has always interested Hartley, long before Professor Ross and Nancy Mitford turned it into a game, and scattered through Hartley's work are many examples which did not appear in their *Noblesse Oblige.* For example, in **'The Corner Cupboard'** (*Two For the River,* 1961) Philip Holroyd engages a cook and is saddened when she calls the sitting-room the lounge. In the same collection (**'The Pampas Clump'**) two men, aged forty-one and thirty-eight, entertain two women to dinner. The women leave the men to their port and later the men 'join the ladies', a desperate attempt to maintain a tradition in miniature. Hartley seems to be fascinated by the ephemera of upper-class behaviour. Long before he bewailed modern manners he celebrated the fancies of the rich. One could have forecast his post-war reactions.

His first book, a collection of stories called *Night Fears,* appeared in 1924 and is undergraduate in tone. It is largely concerned with a world of privilege. The leading story, and one of the best, **'The Island'**, is a spine-chiller and is set in a fantastic Usher-like house, with a maze of corridors, jutting into a furious sea. **'The New Prime Minister'** is marked by allusive conversation between the new man of the hour and an old school friend, and reflects the kind of society where all important men (and most of their women) come from a tiny social group, all known to each other. **'A Portrait'** begins with a house party but moves to a tedious discussion betwen a lady and an artist, who is painting her (for the Academy) for the second time in ten years. Here is a sample of the conversation, from the lady, replying to the artist who said he slept like a log. 'The simile is unworthy of you. Why use it in preference to the better and truer one? We sleep like tops. It is only when the day comes that we begin to flag, to wobble and throw ourselves about, hither and thither, in ludicrous and ungainly movement. No wonder such a pitiable spectacle induces Providence to chastise us into uprightness.' One thanks God for Hemingway, Bennett having apparently failed. This is aristocratic literature with a vengeance.

The only exception is to be found in the title story, **'Night Fears'.** An untypical class angle is introduced by a stranger who reminds a night-watchman of his sorry lot. One has a suspicion that he is the Stranger from the Third-Floor Back out for a walk.

> 'Do you like this job?'
>
> 'Oh, not so bad', said the man carelessly; 'good money, you know.'
>
> 'Good money', repeated the stranger scornfully. 'How much do you get?'
>
> The night-watchman named the sum.
>
> 'Are you married and have you got any children?' the stranger persisted.
>
> The night-watchman said 'Yes' without any enthusiasm.
>
> 'Well, that won't go very far when the children are a bit older', declared the stranger. 'Have you any prospect of a rise?' The man said no, he had just had one.
>
> 'Prices going up, too', the stranger commented.

An unusual tone for Hartley. But the motive of the stranger is neither economic nor social reform; it is part of a dramatic plot, a fiendish one in the event.

It is in the Eustace trilogy, particularly the two latter volumes, that the enthusiasm for the aristocracy reaches its peak. *The Shrimp and the Anemone,* 1944 is an extremely sensitive and beautifully controlled study of childhood. The urge to know the aristocracy has its seeds here but is barely recognized. But there is an entirely different atmosphere in *The Sixth Heaven,* 1946. The period of events is fixed. The Cherringtons left Anchorstone, first for Wolverhampton and then for Willesden, in 1907 when Eustace was eleven. The action of the novel takes place in 1919. Eustace is now at Oxford. He has a private income and aristocratic, wealthy friends. All his friends 'tended to be rather well off', like Stephen Hilliard, whose rooms had been redecorated in black, scarlet and lilac, with valuable pieces of furniture and *objets d'art.* Eustace used to look down on to Carfax, black with people, none of whom seemed to realize that a few feet above them was a summit of social eminence to which they could never attain. It is only fair to add that Hartley's treatment of Eustace's social climbing is pleasantly ironical.

Eustace is terribly excited when he realizes his boyhood dream and is invited to spend the weekend at Anchorstone Hall. He imagines himself showing Stephen the window of his bedroom. Stephen was even slightly jealous of Eustace because he numbered among his friends a very minor foreign royalty. Then there was Antony Lachish, 'a freshman of ancient family and winning manners who went through Oxford like a ball of quicksilver.' When Eustace went to church during the Anchorstone weekend the church was filled with fishermen and farm labourers, or more often their wives. 'They looked so conscious of their collars that you could tell that they wore them but once a week. Eustace felt like a first-class passenger whom circumstances had obliged to travel third.' It was here that Eustace met Lady Eleanor (Nelly), who was to have such a great influence on his life. She took a great interest in local events, used to get up plays and entertainments for the village people, and helped with charities. 'She was adored there', said Lady Staveley. Eustace, a sucker for the feudal virtues, believed it.

But Eustace was by no means sure of himself. He had mastered the intricacies of upper-class speech, and when a workman, asking the time, called him 'mate', he feared his own accent would militate against matehood. This was, of course, really a matter for congratulation. But he wasn't nearly so sure of 'correct behaviour'. When staying at a country house he wanted to go into his sister Hilda's room to see how she was getting on, but was afraid it might not be done. He had given her a wristwatch and now worried about whether she ought to wear it at dinner or take it off. The responsibility for this momentous decision was all his, for she wouldn't know. Did one leave one's shoes outside the bedroom door in a private house? (The answer, given many years later in **'The**

Shadow on the Wall', *Mrs Carteret Receives,* is that you do not.) In one of his self-accusing dramatic fantasies, a servant wonders where he was brought up—obviously not in a gentleman's house. (It is the judgment of the servant that is the cruellest of all—remember poor Eddie in Elizabeth Bowen's *Death of the Heart.*)

Then there is what one says, as against how one says it. Here, perhaps fortunately, the upper class is not completely united. Stephen would indulge in arty talk of the kind that would appal Dick Staveley of Anchorstone Hall. But then Stephen was not really class, coming from a family of solicitors. He talks about music in a way that, according to Simon Raven, causes the hackles of the lower classes to bristle. Beethoven: 'gigantic gestures against a hostile sky'. Brahms: 'those steamy wallowings—let him stew in his own undergrowth'. Boccherini: 'that sugared eighteenth century chit-chat of "Haydn's wife", as they called him', etc., etc.[1]

Eustace, a delightful but anxious little boy, develops into a young man who deliberately destroys his own personality in favour of an aristocratic similitude. In *Eustace and Hilda,* 1952, the third book of the trilogy, we see him in Venice, the guest of a female member of the English aristocracy; he is almost a gigolo, 'dancing attendance'. It would appear that he has reached his haven, but we learn from a letter from Lady Staveley at Anchorstone Hall that Venice is not what it used to be. Rather queer people go there now. There used to be some really nice English people who had houses there, and one or two Americans ('half English, of course'). One old lady used to make enquiries about the people she 'received'. Hilda, too, is getting on. She is seen at the Ritz with Dick Staveley—what's more, seen and reported by Lord Morecambe. Eustace is photographed with Lady Nelly in *Gossip* and Barbara (his younger sister) writes to say how *thrilled* they all are (even Aunt Sarah, though she won't admit it) to think of him in such *exalted* circles.

The wonderful thing about the aristocrats is that they needed no excuse to exist, unlike other people. Eustace, for example, had to be explained as a writer, another guest as an Olympic hurdler. Count Andrea di Monfalcone might not be important but he fitted in and 'no doubt there were countless fine shades of understanding that she had with him that she could not have with Eustace.' He became positively abject in his admiration of the aristocracy. They wore their clothes so gracefully, something he could never do. He used to stuff so much in his pockets Lady Nelly said he looked like the Michelin man. 'All situations could be met and on their own terms, if only one knew how. But he would never master the gradations between a bathing-suit and an overcoat.' The aristocracy was like a hermetic society. At the most one could enjoy reflected prestige, as when the bank clerks were deferential to him. This was only partly because he had money, even more because he moved in the right circles.

Some of the mysteries of Establishment behaviour were revealed to him. Eustace always felt that other people's principles were better founded than his own. Lady Staveley was conventional, which meant doing things in a certain way, a known way. 'It's the technique of living, as practised by the experts', said Lady Nelly. 'It may not take you very far, but you'll always feel you are on the right road, and in good company.' You can still get into trouble but people will be on your side so long as they know that in spirit you still toe the line. (This was the mistake made by Timothy Casson in *The Boat*.) You can do an immense number of things so long as you do them in a certain way. Here is an example of aristocratic ruling, from Contessa Loredan, about ladies: *On peut coucher avec un gondolier, si on le désire; mais on ne danse pas avec lui*. This shocked Eustace greatly. But the rules of sex did not apply to marriage. Aristocrats didn't like mixed marriages, i.e., cross-class. For instance, Hilda had not been brought up in the same world as Dick. They would never find the right things to say to each other. At a party Miss Cherrington wore a red dress. Lady Staveley wrote in a letter to Lady Nelly: 'my dear, there was nothing really *against* it, it would have looked all right on the stage, I dare say, but it wasn't right for Anchorstone.' Aunt Sarah shared this view of social climbing, but from the other end: 'no good ever comes of trying to climb out of the class of society into which you are born.'

Hartley's fascination with the aristocracy gets a new twist in *The Brickfield*, 1964 and its sequel, *The Betrayal*, 1965 because here the tables are turned and Denys Aspin, a young aristocrat, works for the first-person narrator as his secretary and companion. Denys's forebears would not have deigned to speak to Richard's! Richard sometimes wonders if he would have found Denys attractive without the background of Aspin Castle. In fact, Denys is not aristocratic at all—he was adopted by an impoverished branch of the family and he turned out to be rather wild. As soon as Richard learns this he not only begins to have a lower opinion of Denys but Denys actually begins to behave badly. Richard has to fight against what he feels is disloyalty in himself: 'the fact that Denys was or might not be a true Aspin, made no difference, indeed, it only served to show up Richard's snobbishness, as if he had valued his friend for his name, not for himself. My secretary, Mr Denys Aspin of Aspin Castle! I pay him, it is true, but he lends me the lustre of his ancient lineage, so we are quits.' Richard's lack of reality where aristocracy is concerned becomes apparent when he discovers how Denys has been cheating him. 'The dishonesty, the calculated cheating, landing him in for hundreds—it was rather much. No Aspin would have done it. But Denys wasn't a real Aspin, he was only a nominal one . . .' Richard had previously gloated over the romantic probability that the original Aspins had been border cattle thieves and gangsters. Now the likelihood was revealed that Denys's biological origin had been proletarian, and Richard understood that the proletariat had quite different moral standards from the middle and upper middle classes.

The pronounced social changes that have occurred since the war have brought home to Hartley the possibility that a new kind of aristocracy may be forming. *My Fellow Devils*, 1951, treats the tensions between this new group and the conventional old English squirearchy. Margaret Pennefather comes of a well-heeled family that lives in considerable style (they employ a chauffeur) in a small town not far from London. She becomes associated in an unexpected way with Colum MacInnes, a leading film star, and eventually marries him. Although Colum went to a minor public school he is not considered a 'gentleman' by acquaintances such as Margaret's father or Stuart, her best friend's husband. In fact, his vocation would proscribe this. Margaret is a magistrate and is known for her good works. She has a strong desire to do good and is convinced that Colum suffers from a poor background. She hopes she can save him from himself and his friends. Her desire to serve others is linked with a fascination with the opposite, the romantic and the glamorous. This is her fantasy of Colum MacInnes:

> . . . a rough little boy with ragged clothes and pleading eyes, a juvenile delinquent with a bad home background, who had never had a chance, but who had been brought up before her and to whom she was now going to lend a helping hand. No, he should not go to an Approved School if she could help it; she was going to try what kindness could do. She would, in a sense, adopt him; take him into her comfortable, pretty house; and there, with Nick and her father helping, she would reform him, teach him to be clean, orderly, affectionate and honest; and after years, many years, of good food, good example and good treatment and good education, he would emerge into the world, a good citizen.

This was before she married him—while she was still engaged to another man, in fact. It represents a decent, upper class view of the less fortunate (in traditional terms, that is, not financial) and exhibits great social optimism.

The new aristocracy (in this case, the film world) lived in much greater style than the decaying remnants of the old. Party-going was the favourite activity. Colum had a staff of three: Richards (the butler), the cook and the resident house-parlour-maid. 'Colum never had the smallest difficulty in getting servants, indeed he had difficulty in keeping them away, for nearly every day some beglamoured girl wrote offering him her services—sometimes free. Thus the servant problem, the modern housekeeper's supreme concern, did not exist for Margaret.' But this sort of relationship was disturbing to her. 'To Margaret service was a blessed word.' She came from that solid, rural, squirearchy-J.P. belt that accepted the existence of social duties in return for privilege. Nothing could be further removed from the world of the film star-pop-trendy executive.

LIMBO

If Hartley's work aspires towards aristocratic harmonies it is rooted in the class that used to be called 'the backbone of England': a class that is no longer sure of itself, is often intensely miserable, filled with envy, engrossed in self-pity. We see all these states in Hartley's work, but we also see aspects of an earlier phase, when the middle class was content with its lot and convinced of its usefulness. *The Brickfield* is largely about a period that has passed away. It is the kind of novel that makes a small impact on reading it but stays to ruffle the mind. It is heavy (at times, turgid) with nostalgia. It evokes the late Victorian and Edwardian provincial life lovingly. Changes in social feeling are stressed, for example, the attitude towards money. Mr Soames was a gentleman farmer, and not a very efficient one—but why should he be, when it wasn't necessary? His possession of independent means set him apart from the other farmers. 'It would now, but in a different way. There was no socialistic feeling that they had no right to their wealth, but it put them in another category.' They were 'living upright', which meant they had private means.

The chief character, Richard Mardick, comes as usual from a respectable but not wealthy middle class family. His father was a bank manager and he had an interest in a brick works, more as a hobby than a source of income. It brought in about £500 a year, which in fact doubled his salary (at the beginning of the century). Richard went to the grammar school, along with the farmers' sons. His grandfather, himself a farmer, had many servants (groom, shepherd, carpenter, gardener, two house servants and a charwoman, a foreman at each farm, farm labourers, grooms and horses) but he didn't have an easy time. The servant question was not acute then, as it is now. 'With my grandfather it wasn't a status symbol, still less a sign of wealth, to have a certain number of dependants. For a man in his position they were necessities, not luxuries. The farm and the farmhouse couldn't do without them. It was an inelastic, semi-feudal system; he *had*

to live in that way, it didn't mean that he was well off.' In those days farmers could only just make both ends meet, even in South Lincolnshire, where things were easier.

The aristocracy in this novel is represented by Denys Aspin (already referred to), who was Richard's secretary. Denys pretends to be apologetic about his ancestors, saying they were probably 'a shady lot'. They were Border chieftains, the Aspins of Aspin Castle, and the ruin was still in the family's keeping. There are still a few advantages accruing to the aristocrat—he is addressed as Honourable which is useful in shops and for getting things on tick.

The Perfect Woman, 1955, is set in another sector of the middle class. It is rooted deep in suburbia and for once there is no bourgeois-aristocratic tension.[2] There is a marked sense of restlessness and ephemerality compared with the world of the Lincolnshire farmers. Isabel's husband, Harold, is an accountant for whom assessing a person's income is a routine enquiry. He mistrusted Alex Goodrich, a novelist, especially his tendency to joke about money. In the end, he felt, everything went back to income. We are not really so far away from Eustace, who was ruled by monetary considerations. And like Eustace he was impressed by those in a higher social position but in his case the gulfs to cross are minute. They are between grades within a class, not between distinct classes. Poor Isabel was much more aware of her class situation because she was secretly ashamed of it. When she knew that Goodrich was coming to stay she felt she would have to apologize for 'our suburban home'. She was sufficiently realistic to know that, however superior she felt towards Harold (as a clergyman's daughter), times had changed and in fact it was Harold who was conferring the favour when they married. There had been a reversal of fortune within the social grouping. She is a romantic, longing to belong to a cultured society, aching to express her sensitivity, scorning the brute cash that kept her comfortable. She despised her own milieu and believed herself superior to it. One of the most prolific sources of modern romantic sentiment derives from the revulsion from suburbia. She goes for a walk outside her home town, on the cliffs, and identifies her lover, Alec, with the ocean.[3] But what a difference on the other side! 'Low hills rose behind the town, green hills already fledged with autumn yellow, and pimpled over by a rash of villas. One of those red roofs, nestling so snugly and smugly in the foliage, was hers . . . ', and she turned her eyes back to the sea.

Three middle-class approaches to life are contrasted, and Isabel is their battle-ground. Harold's plans for the children's future are unflinchingly bourgeois and solid. 'I'm all for them getting on in the world, as you know, but I haven't got extravagant ideas for them. I want them to develop on the lines that we have—and be safe, reliable sort of people with a stake in the place and in the country. People you can look up to, but no frills, no sob-stuff—solid, you know, and just above the average.' In comparison Alec was pretentious. He said he had a feudal relationship with the country people, although he didn't really 'belong'. 'Anyone they look on as gentry they treat as such. Before the war they did, at any rate. Everyone seemed in their right place and not spilling into someone else's . . . ' Alec benefited from his discovery that most people are prepared to take you at your own valuation. And then finally, a minor strand, the progressives Isabel had mingled with during the war when she had roomed with another girl in London. They had been left behind but occasionally she remembered them, occasionally she felt guilty because she had not always measured up to their ideals. Their ideals were of classlessness (on the whole, a middle class emotion, as they are the people who get squeezed, but even so, they form a small minority of their class), a society where all should be equal, where no-one should be 'just above the average'. They preached the end of the individual. 'We don't want tragedy or catastrophe or any high-powered emotion, because the individual doesn't count any more.' Modern fiction (they might be discussing the work of Alexander Goodrich) 'mustn't be about people wanting to get on, in any sense, because (a) there's no where to get to, and (b) we don't *want* to get ahead of other people now, we don't *want* to jump the queue!'

But there weren't many who thought like that. Most of them, in this minutely graded hierarchy, were intent on social climbing. The situation was rather like the one provided by football pools—a small win will bring a better car or even a small yacht, while a large one opens the way to the public schools and (who knows?) a peerage if the money is used discreetly. Talking about Lady Ditchworth and her dead husband, Eileen Faulkner says tartly: 'When he made his pile out of whatever it was—something slightly shady—which he did in an incredibly short space of time, they were wafted into spheres far, far above ours, and mixed with people in the same income bracket with themselves. I don't know whether they ever quite made the grade, socially, I mean' (*Poor Clare*, 1968). Lady Ditchworth was well aware of her situation. She was said to have replied to a titled woman who had been rude to her: 'My name may not be as good as yours, but it's better at the bottom of a cheque.' In a sense, this is Hartley's version of the class war. The other war he recognizes (referred to in an earlier section) is psychological and grounded in generational differences.

Now we can see Eustace, Hartley's most famous creation, in his true setting. He is lovable in his innocence, his concern for truth and his determination not to hurt others. He is also a disgusting little crawler whenever wealth or rank are concerned. His own accession to wealth enables him to become the intimate of aristocrats and to squander his personal gifts of character. Money is revealed as an evil—it permits the worst characteristics (which need it) to triumph over the better (which don't).

Eustace is only too willing to use his elder sister Hilda to further his social ambitions, that is, to become a guest at Anchorstone Hall. Stephen Hilliard sees it as a sacrifice, leading to tragedy, and writes to Eustace: 'I see now that you meant her to marry Staveley. But perhaps I'm wrong, perhaps you only wanted to use her as a rung in the social ladder. How cleverly you contrived that visit to Anchorstone . . . ' When his younger sister Barbara and her husband Jimmy discuss what to do with Hilda after she is paralysed, various alternatives are mentioned—and now Eustace is going to stay with them. This is all a burden but Barbara points out to Jimmy that he likes Eustace, 'in spite of his being rather a toady'. She adds, 'I wish he wouldn't speak about his friends in that low, respectful voice.' Eustace tries to persuade himself that his mistakes were not due to wickedness (or the modern equivalent, a flaw in the character) but to his habit of turning all experience into fantasy. 'The temptation to see things larger than life, to invest them with grandeur and glamour and glory—that had been his downfall. Everything, he told himself, could be traced to that; above all, his wish to aggrandise Hilda and make her the Lady of Anchorstone Hall.'

The Lady of Anchorstone Hall! Hilda was in fact intended to be a governess and the misery of this state, as illustrated by a score of Victorian novels, seemed to have eaten its way into her soul already. Her attitude to the future is one of acquiescent helplessness. In the end, Eustace is compelled to face reality. In the third book of the trilogy he returns to Anchorstone, where he had spent his childhood and nourished the dreams which so nearly destroyed himself and his sister, and now he has to acquire a new conception of reality. In Venice he had bought his way out of trouble and into people's regard. He had treasured a piece of masonry from Anchorstone Hall which Dick Staveley had given him. It was a worthless talisman and eventually he knows he must get rid of it. He needed a substitute (but Anchorstone had no antique shop) and anyway, such objects were useless and dust-collecting and static, and he could no longer afford such indulgences. So he bought a bicycle—it had high practical utility, it was a vital part of industry, essential to the proletariat. He began to feel the joy of intimate association. Eustace was really unregenerate, passing from the influence of one symbol to that of another. This is the first instance of the attraction of proletarian associations, later developed so crazily in Timothy Casson in *The Boat*. The world was changing, Eustace realized that his dreams were not the stuff of life. While Eustace dutifully pedalled his bicycle, exulting in his developing social conscience, Bert Craddock, the old cab-driver's grandson, got a scholarship to St Joseph's. To revert to sporting allusions (and none are more apt for our time) Bert was winning promotion, Eustace suffering relegation.

Eustace and his type, living through their symbols, felt that machinery created a kind of social watershed. The aristocracy, even when its position was grounded on industrial wealth, centred their interests on land, horses and foreign travel. Their fortunes came from the use of machinery, but their pose was to reject it. When Eustace uses the phrase, 'throw a spanner in the works', Stephen protests, 'What unpleasant metaphors you use. I don't think machinery's a fit subject for ordinary conversation. . . . ' He then lists a series of mechanical objects which suggest he knows far more about their existence, if not their use, than he would have us believe. Ignorance of machinery is a pose much appreciated in certain quarters. Barbara, who had no time for poses, married Jimmy, 'a representative of the Better Sort rather than of the Finer Grain'. Jimmy treated life like a machine that would go if set up properly and given plenty of oil and power. 'These both existed in his own nature; the power was steam rather than electricity, the oil was crude, but not sticky or glutinous. Messy Jimmy might be, but it was the messiness of the engine-room or the garage, a creative messiness inseparable from energy and movement. . . . ' Eustace felt left out of it. He was aspiring to the horse culture, Barbara was content to accept the internal combustion machine.

Barbara and Jimmy Crankshaw represent the traditionless but vital class that is setting the pace in contemporary society, challenging and replacing the exhausted older stock. Peter Bien, in his book on L. P. Hartley, writes: 'In the Eustace series, the union of Barbara and Jimmy, though not central to the plot, is the only positive, creative, happy outcome of the events therein. . . . ' They are the kind of people we like to call 'Americanized'. (In fact, the only book of Hartley's where both the ambience and the characters, and hence the social comment, are American is the early *Simonetta Perkins*, 1925). Hartley devotes most of his literary energies, within the middle class framework, to marginal characters such as writers, film stars, well-to-do expatriates, or dilettantes such as Alexey, one of the leading characters in the novel-within-a-novel of *The Love-Adept*, 1969. He wasn't an artist but he had

done well enough in business to retire in his late forties. Such men are becoming increasingly rare because few have the leisure to pursue joint vocations. Too often Hartley's work is marred by triviality; insignificant people are given as much attention as more noteworthy ones; all are treated with equal respect. *The Boat* in particular fails through this lack of discrimination. A story like **'Mr Blandfoot's Picture'** (*The White Wand*, 1954) is much too kind to the society of Settlemarsh. The vein of satire, which is all it deserves, is, if existent, extremely thin. This is odd because elsewhere Hartley claims that one of the requirements of good fiction is that the leading characters should be interesting. In itself, such a dictum begs a lot of questions. One wonders to whom and from what standpoint, and at times one feels it is position in the class hierarchy that determines the quality of the treatment.

SERVANTS AND OTHERS

'Foreigners refer to distinctions of class more openly than we do', comments L. P. Hartley in **'Three, or Four, for Dinner'** (*The Travelling Grave*, 1948). Lurking behind the paraphernalia of what is called Society are the workers. In writers like Hartley these are as untypical as many of his middle class characters: servants, chauffeurs, yeomen farmers barely distinguishable from labourers. Trouble with retainers is a perennial subject in the post-war novels—it crops up in *The Boat, The Betrayal* and stories in **The White Wand**. Servants are so touchy. You have to be so careful. 'Unless he kept watch on his tongue he might lose both his retainers' (**'The Corner Cupboard'**, *Two for the River*, 1961). The trouble is 'they're all so class-conscious nowadays', says Mrs Marriner in **'The Waits'** (same collection). She is talking not specifically about servants but of the class they come from.

There are certain types of behaviour that belong to the working class only, and one is puzzled to find them cropping up elsewhere. For example, Richard in *The Brickfield* knew that his aunt had got into some sort of trouble connected with love. 'I knew, by hearsay, that servant-girls and suchlike did, but never imagined that love could lead anyone of our sort into "trouble"'. Actually, she was not in that sort of trouble. 'Trouble connected with love' is the theme of this novel, the tragedy of ignorance, no matter what the class. Nevertheless, Hartley does seem to regard the middle class (the solid, traditional middle class of farmers and professional men) as beleaguered, and slowly yielding to influences from below. The 'proletarianization' of English life is a favourite theme of his. One finds it in his description of 'Restbourne', an unidentifiable coastal resort, with its 'appalling vulgarity'. Having used the term 'proletarianization', he continues: 'It is the apotheosis of the synthetic. I dreaded it, and when

I got there it was worse than I remembered—an exhibition of what was, to my middle class mind, a substitute for every form of pleasure.' (**'The Face'**, *Two for the River*). Hartley believes in class and fears the destruction of the class structure. According to Paul Bloomfield, author of the British Council and National Book League pamphlet on Hartley, *Facial Justice*, 1960 is about the abolition of class. The motive is envy.

Working class characters play an important part in two of Hartley's novels, a strong auxiliary part in a third, and in a fourth one of the leading characters is a yeoman farmer whose way of life is much closer to that of one of his labourers than it is to that of, say, a novelist or a retired business man, This is *The Go-Between*, 1953, one of the finest novels of our time. It describes the events of a very hot summer at the turn of the century, with the Boer War in the background. Leo Colston celebrates his thirteenth birthday during the course of the period. The story is told by him looking back from his sixties, an old and empty man. Leo is from a small village near Salisbury, grandly called Court Place. He stays with his schoolfriend Marcus at their Norfolk mansion, Brandham Hall. Of the two, Marcus (who is a snob) is the more impressed, but entirely on a comparison of names. Court Place was very old and the bishops of Salisbury once held court there, but it was an ordinary house, set back in the village street behind looped chains. The child-hero is immune from the more pressing cares of life because his father had been a book-collector, although the proceeds of the business supported him in later life, not now. His father was dead, and he lived with his mother on her money and a pension.

As with Eustace, it is the story of a boy who is fascinated by his social superiors, and who apes them whenever he can. When he is invited to stay with Marcus, the latter's mother writes grandly that although it is the Season neither she nor her husband have been well. . . . The house belongs to the ancient Trimingham family, but the tenants are the Maudsleys, in business. The ninth Viscount Trimingham is a guest in his own house—he hopes to marry Marian Maudsley. Half a century later his grandson is living in a small wing of the house and the rest is let to a girls' school. The story centres on the ill-starred attempt to break through the very pronounced class barriers, for Marian is having an affair with a local farmer. How this extraordinary though possible relationship began we are never told. It ends in disaster. Leo was 'acutely aware of social inferiority'. He himself felt out of place among rich people, a misfit. Marcus makes unflattering references to 'the plebs', and identifies his mother with the same feelings. After the cricket concert in the village hall (where Leo had had a singing triumph), Marcus

said, 'Anyhow, we've said goodbye to the village for a year. Did you notice the stink in the hall?' Ted Burgess, the farmer-lover, is a solidly attractive character. When he catches Leo sliding down his rick he bawls at him first, but his tone changes when he discovers that Leo is from the hall. Leo is delighted. He had felt a similar change of attitude in himself when he discovered Trimingham was a Viscount. 'I did not despise him for changing his tune when he knew where I came from: it seemed to me right, natural and proper that he should, just as it had seemed right and proper for me to change my tune with Trimingham when I realized he was a Viscount.'

Marcus is a constant fund of information about class behaviour. Leo asks him how long engagements last. 'In the case of grooms, gardeners, skivvies and suchlike scum, it may go on for ever. With people like ourselves it generally doesn't go on very long.' (The violence of his language can be partly discounted because it was part of a game he played with Leo, but the content was sincere enough.) Leo was puzzled when Marcus said his mother was a hysterical type because he thought hysteria was something only servants had. When Leo started to cry in front of Ted he didn't feel ashamed: 'I had an instinct that, unlike the people of my own class, he wouldn't think the worse of me for crying.' Then there were the things that were done and not done. Very frequently these marked the border line between middle and upper classes rather than between upper and lower. Only cads wore school clothes in the holidays. It was wrong to go to breakfast in slippers, that's what bank clerks do. You can put them on after tea. (This was hard for Leo, though he didn't let on; his father had worked in a bank and always came to breakfast in slippers.) You shouldn't fold your clothes when you undressed and put them on a chair. 'You must leave them lying where they happen to fall—the servants will pick them up—that's what they're there for.' When hot, you shouldn't mop your face with a handkerchief, but dab it. At breakfast, men ate their porridge walking about but not the women—who were, incidentally, never called ladies. As for a made-up tie, it was the mark of a cad. In his more recent work Hartley has reacted to another type of inhibition, originating at a different social level. 'You mustn't use the word "servants" in these days', says Ralph in *My Sister's Keeper*, 1970. In **'The Prayer'** (*Mrs Carteret Receives*, 1971) we are told that the word 'staff' has replaced it.

The Hireling, 1957, actually has a working man (a car-hire driver) for its hero. Leadbitter is not a pure proletarian, out of the industrial melting pot. His family background is 'shortage of money' but no details are given. His status is a marginal one, virtually a servant of the rich, and eventually he sets up for himself.

He becomes his own man and is no longer a working chap. Even when he was an employee he was always striving to rise socially. His customers had something he was hoping to acquire. In telling his story Hartley has picked up the We/They jargon. 'No wonder that his customers were "they" to him, beings of an alien, if not hostile race, idle, capricious. . . . ' He was just as unreal to those who employed him. 'To "them" Leadbitter was just part of the car's furniture, with as little personal feeling as the car had, whereas Leadbitter had no moods, or was supposed to have none, and couldn't break down, he couldn't afford to. For at least half his customers, Leadbitter didn't exist as a man.'

This novel contains Hartley's expression of the alienation effect in modern society. Leadbitter had very little to thank his patrons for.

> In the nature of things they treated him with less consideration than he treated them. Many a time they kept him waiting till the small hours, at a night club or a dance, without the offer of a sandwich or a cup of tea; many a time they cancelled a good job at the last moment, without apology or the promise of redress; sometimes they forgot about him altogether. They took his patience under their thoughtlessness for granted; they didn't seem aware that he had feelings to hurt or interests to injure, and some of them talked together as freely in his presence as if he wasn't there.

Lady Franklin feels the difference in their positions, though not as keenly as he does. On one occasion she felt she had been talking down to him and tried to make amends. 'It's the difference in our social positions, she thought, that makes me use this artificial tone—that, and the effort to be more articulate than I am normally, or have grown to be.'

The Love-Adept, 1969, has another chauffeur-hero, Jock, who resembles Leadbitter in being physically strong, unimaginative and humourless. The author of the novel-within-a-novel imagines Jock's first meeting with the actress, Pauline, who becomes his mistress, as embarrassing, 'with Jock oily and greasy and dirty in his workingclothes, and perhaps unshaven.' She liked him better that way than when he had smartened himself up. James Golightly's chief critic reminds him that he has used the Lady Chatterley situation in a previous novel, which implies he must be fond of it. As the same can be said of Hartley himself, it is impossible to avoid identification. My impression is that Hartley has a slightly pathetic desire to make himself more familiar with working class conditions and attitudes. I am led to say this not only because of this recurring situation but also because of a scattering of comments and asides which appear throughout his fiction. In the post-war work they become more frequent,

paralleling the greater confidence of the working class which appears to affect Hartley in two ways: he recognizes it and he hates it.

In an imaginary reply to his critic James defends his use of his trio of characters, especially in their social aspect: actress-business man-chauffeur.

> It happens . . . quite often, and more often than it used to, because the changing structure of society makes such irregular relationships more possible and more probable, and more permissible. They weren't probable, though they weren't impossible, fifty or sixty years ago, when Strindberg wrote *Mademoiselle Julie.* Then it shocked people that a well-born girl should fall in love with a footman: it wouldn't shock people now. Footmen may be a dying race, but they have their counterparts in other walks of life.

In the chapters of the novel that are quoted Jock's plebeian nature is stressed. In the restaurant with Pauline and Alexey he munches his chop (he eats much more than they do) 'with his knife and fork spread facing each way on his plate'. He had too much white shirt-cuff showing above his thick wrists, and pulled his sleeves down when no-one was looking. He had a simple way of finishing an argument. If it happened in a bar, he would take the fellow outside and thump him.[4]

The normal class relationship in Hartley's novels is between an embattled employer and his domestic servants. Leadbitter and Jock represent attempts to get outside the circle of the home, and in each case they are portrayed as individuals. In *The Betrayal* Richard is everybody's victim. We are immediately reminded of his place in the social structure when he answers the telephone and hears 'quite a cultivated voice—the voice of someone you might know.' Lower middle and working class harpies feed on him. All the time he is aware of the gap between them and him but can do nothing about it. 'Oh dear', he thought, 'these people! Their ways are past finding out.' Just as the ruling class is 'Them' to the working class, so the servants are 'They' to Richard. He discovers you can't have domestics without domestic troubles.[5] He wants to make people happy, but as soon as they grasp this they take advantage of him. They would probably like it better if he were a martinet. The two daily helps, Mrs Cuddesdon and Mrs Stonegappe, didn't like Denys presumably because he was a gentleman. But Mrs Stonegappe wouldn't accept this and said to the doctor: 'he's no more a gentleman than you or I are'—a text on which a fascinating study in social relationships might be written. The servants tell tales about each other, but pretend all the time to be the souls of righteousness. 'You know what those people are—they cannot admit they are in the wrong, or they lose face, and, among each other, never hear the last of it. They *have* to be in the right.' A new mood had come over the working people. They were determined to assert their equality, even their superiority. Class battles raged incessantly.

Hartley returns to this theme in **'The Prayer'** *(Mrs Carteret Receives)*: 'if Anthony wasn't easy-going with them, indeed if he criticized them—their cooking, their driving, the friends of both sexes, or any sex, that they brought into the flat from time to time, their unwarrantable absences or their sometimes more disturbing presences—at the faintest hint of criticism they departed, almost before the offending words were out of his mouth.' The exploitation of the classes was being stood on its head.

THE MONEY OBSESSION

I have assumed all along that the reader is acquainted with Eustace, Hartley's most famous hero. Eustace is a beautiful study in growing up: a boy who is kind-hearted, generous, always worried, given to fantasy—and obsessed with money. He is also determined to become the familiar of aristocrats, and underlying the claims of tradition, breeding and vast estates there is an unsentimental concern for wealth. A title brings credit, even in a democratic age, as Denys Aspin admitted. One is reminded of Lady Brett Ashley in Hemingway's *Fiesta*. When the count says a title does him no good, it only costs a lot of money, she replies, 'Oh, I don't know. It's damned useful sometimes.' She tells him he hasn't used his title properly and adds, 'I've had hell's own amount of credit on mine.' Now Eustace is not so crude as to want entry into the charmed circle of the aristocracy for mercenary reasons, but he is convinced that the possession of wealth is one of the mainsprings of social life.

The Shrimp and the Anemone appeared in 1944. One of the main themes of this very fine novel is the corruption that follows on wealth reflected in the mind of innocence. One is tempted to see it as a complex of symbolism, in the manner of the modern literary don, but that would be no more than a transcription. Most of what passes for symbolism debases: the novel should be a revelation, not a piece of spiritual algebra, which is the balm of the inferior mind. It would of course be easy to make out a heavy symbolic argument that, let us say, Eustace's legacy brought him at one and the same time wealth and a conviction that he was going to die, and therefore that money and death are qualitatively alike—but this is the kind of half-baked use of symbolic equivalences which has nothing to do with the writing of fiction. In fact, *The Shrimp and the Anemone* would be a better book if its author had not opened with the imagery from which the book

gets its title. Nearly all the book is intensely living but it starts in the lecture hall.

From the first page onwards we know that Eustace is agonized by an over-active conscience, which includes the social conscience. His heart bled for the shrimp, he longed to rescue it—but how could he rob the anemone? And then, shouldn't he be helping Hilda build up the bank? And so on, right through to the time when he's planning his will and thinks that some poor boy might like his sponge, toothbrush and flannel—once they'd been well dried, of course.

We are always aware of the social hierarchy. Eustace is convinced that most of his acquaintances are higher up the ladder than he is and that he is lucky to know them. He is surprised that the Steptoes invite him to a picnic for they are the kind of people who probably have one every day, whereas for him it is an exciting rarity. Nevertheless, Eustace is proud that his father is a chartered accountant with an office in Ousemouth. There are plenty of unfortunates below them. Although he stood in considerable awe of Mr Craddock, who hired out the horse and carriage, for Aunt Sarah the old man belonged to the category of things that had not been properly washed. The Steptoes had a very clear view of life in general. They knew that Mr Johnson's was 'a potty little school' for tradesmen's sons, that the South of England was socially superior to other parts, that there is a world of difference between Cliftonville and Margate, where trippers go, and that Anchorstone should be pronounced Anxton. (This is an important part of the upper class code: Wiveliscombe-Wilscombe, Cirencester-Sister, Cholmondeley-Chumley, Beauchamp-Beecham.)

The period is about 1906. Though relatively poor (Mr Cherrington speaks in some awe of a colleague who is in the thousand-a-year bracket) they feel obliged to have a nanny for the baby and also a daily help. Families were judged by the number of servants they employed. Minney saw three different ones while she was at Miss Fothergill's. The behaviour of the rich towards their servants and the poor in general was baffling but had to be learnt. Eustace was alarmed to think that the coachman would have to wait for Dick when the latter called to see him. (Eustace would have dashed off immediately.) On the other hand, Minney was surprised to find Dick pouring tea for himself, yet in some way it was understood that this confirmed his rank. Dick spoke easily of 'family retainers' and had to translate the term for Eustace.

The Cherringtons had their full share of bourgeois narrowness, particularly Aunt Sarah, Mr Cherrington's sister, who looked after his family after the death of his wife when Barbara, the third child, was born. She had a fierce dislike of all gambling and games of chance, which even extended to making a decision by tossing a coin. She was irritated when her brother relaxed after the day's work—it was something she felt he had to stop and so she used to bring up awkward family matters. (Hilda adopted her aunt's view without resistance—cards, for instance, were a waste of time.) Aunt Sarah didn't want to accept Miss Fothergill's legacy, and certainly was against telling Eustace about it. It would spoil him. Hilda told Eustace it wouldn't be *good* for children to be rich. In the sequel, *The Sixth Heaven,* Aunt Sarah shows a poor opinion of Eustace. He has always had it too easy.

Mr Cherrington was not rich enough to send Eustace to a feepaying school, therefore he did not go to school. A state school was out of the question. One day, if Mr Cherrington could afford it, he might go to the Rev Johnson's prep school, but we all know what Nancy Steptoe (greatly admired by Eustace) thought of that: not much. Miss Fothergill commented that he ought to be at school. As she says it he is conscious of the darn in his blue jersey and tells her he has lessons at home. Eustace puts the position beautifully: 'Daddy can't afford to send me to a good school and Aunt Sarah won't let me go to a bad one.' As for Hilda, it is generally accepted that she will become a governess. It is not a fate to look forward to, but their poverty seems to make it inevitable. An aura of hopelessness hangs around Hilda, and we find it repeated in *My Sister's Keeper,* 1970, which again has childhood lack of means (one can hardly call it poverty) as a background. 'Daddy isn't rich enough to give any of us a pony', wails Gwendolen. She never expects to eat asparagus again as there are so many of them to bring up and educate.

In absolute terms the Cherringtons are not poor. In the framework of the English social system they scarcely count. Money is the key. Money and its power and the corruption that can emanate from it are never absent long, as a pervading threat. Eustace naively says to the driver on the way to the picnic, 'It's very hard to make money, isn't it?' At times Hilda makes a virtue of the family poverty—just as there is a hole in Eustace's jersey, so there is a ladder in her stocking when Dick calls, and she hopes he sees it. She refused to learn to ride a horse because she knew she would never be able to afford one of her own.

Mr Cherrington is not above using the family poverty as a threat. Because of Eustace's irresponsible behaviour he fell ill and there were heavy doctor's bills and a nurse, which meant that Hilda had to have a room outside. It was suggested that they might have to leave Cambo because they had no money left. Eustace feels

that his father will never be able to spend much time with him again because he will be so busy earning money to make up what it cost him to pay for the illness.

Then Miss Fothergill's legacy changes the situation completely. Mr Cherrington immediately begins to live in a more expansive way, and we learn from *The Sixth Heaven,* 1946 that he was drinking too much in his later years. 'Who would have thought the old lady had all that money!' he mused, echoing Lady Macbeth, and thus equating money in the mind with blood, life itself. His sister Sarah can see nothing but danger coming from the new wealth: how could he control Eustace, who would be getting £700 a year, much more than himself? And what would be the position of Hilda and Barbara, penniless sisters of a well-to-do young man? (In fact, these dread forecasts were not realized.) When Eustace becomes rich, everyone's attitude towards him changes. He notices this (they are kinder, more considerate), but he doesn't know the cause. Mr Craddock now finds it possible to bring the carriage down the rutted track to Cambo—in the past he had waited at the end of the lane. Nancy tells Eustace he won't ever have to work, he'll be like Dick, live at home, play golf, shoot, hunt and go to Homburg or Carlsbad. But probably most important of all, from Eustace's point of view, he will able to enjoy himself more in the bath. He had a game (flooding cities) but he used to suffer from fears such as having his leg sucked down the plughole by escaping water or, a more rational one, that the water might overflow, sink into the floor and dissolve it, and let him down into the drawing room, costing his father several pounds. Now he would be able to cover any such disaster.

We see what Miss Fothergill's legacy really did to Eustace in the second book of the trilogy, *The Sixth Heaven.* It took away his initiative. He is aware of this, tries to wish he hadn't had it, but cannot quite manage it. Aunt Sarah is convinced that he has received no benefit at all from the legacy; it has removed the circumstances that might have strengthened an already weak character. Stephen, a more positive man than Eustace, despite his precious way of speaking, tells Hilda (who has Aunt Sarah's distrust of money) that it is not 'just an extension of one's emotions: it has a reality of its own which one ought to respect'. He says that Eustace is not to be trusted with money: 'he thinks it is just a natural adjunct of benevolence.' In fact, Eustace hovers on the edge of a different world but never quite belongs to it. Lady Nelly tells him that when she married Freddie 'he hadn't a penny—I mean, about a thousand a year.' Eustace's father had once spoken in some awe of a colleague who earned that amount. Now he betrays his background and says, 'It doesn't seem very much.' Mr Cherrington was a nine-to-five man, who regarded one evening drink as a luxury. The Staveleys got their money from a coal-mine in Derbyshire, which is mentioned as frequently as the unnamed product that supported the wealth of the Newsomes in James's *The Ambassadors.*

In the third volume, *Eustace and Hilda,* 1952, Eustace discovers that money can buy anything—except, of course, happiness. Temporary depression can easily be put right by a visit to the bank. Hilda is in trouble with the governors of the clinic she works at—he will send her a thousand pounds to carry out repairs. He wires the money. 'He left the post office lighter in step, lighter in heart, lighter by a thousand pounds.' In fact his sister is passing through a grave psychological crisis but he makes no effort to understand it because it would disturb his personal idyll. Without the money he might have been forced to help Hilda in the way she needed. But Eustace was getting accustomed to buying his way out of difficulties or into personal favour. By overpaying the boatman on the ferry he won special smiles, even a return to fetch him after the ferry had left, and considerable pains to see that he was safely disembarked. 'Such attentions pleased Eustace very much.' And yet his money is not inexhaustible and even Eustace is finally compelled to adopt a higher degree of realism towards money, exactly what it can do and what it cannot. When he returns to Cambo he has an altercation with the cab driver and is heard to say, 'I'm sorry, but I think sixpence is quite enough.' In a later edition this was changed to, 'Sixpence over the fare is quite enough.' Hartley explained to Peter Bien that he wanted to convey that Eustace has become more realistic about money matters. Previously he would have given two or three shillings and thought nothing of it. He is being reborn.

It is natural that money should never be far from the consciousness of Leadbitter, the working class hero of *The Hireling,* 1957. He is always striving to improve his position and this requires money. His greatest step forward is made when Lady Franklin gives him a cheque that enables him to pay off the instalments on his car. His concern with money is contrasted with her indifference, as a wealthy widow. He did not envy her indifference but took it as a fact of life. She warns him that money is not everything and says that when he gets rich he may find that money will lock the door on his prison—or at least, fail to unlock it. ('It would take a good deal of money to lock the door on me', thought Leadbitter). When he buys a powerful new car he feels he will now impel recognition, and it will be through the power of money. Sometimes he takes a young couple in his car. The girl, Constance, says rich people never seem quite real: 'Their problems are not

the same as ours, and all that freedom of action—it's like a fairy tale. They float around, they don't belong—there are not enough of them, now, to make a social unit. They are an anachronism, a vestigial survival. . . . ' This is rather over Leadbitter's head. What he notices when he has some money to his name (in his case, a flourishing business) is exactly what Eustace noticed in Venice—the banks behave differently. Before, if the clerks even raised their heads, it was only to show blank faces. But now he was welcomed by smiles and even the manager put on a friendly air: 'Of course, old chap, of course', and practically bowed him out.

Money still provides the ground-bass for *The Betrayal,* 1966. Superficially Richard should have no money worries, but he is constantly cheated by his employees and he becomes worried about his security, as Eustace used to be. Richard could recall times when his parents were anxious but when he asked his mother what was the matter, she used to say, 'It's about something you wouldn't understand, my darling—something to do with money.' When they passed the Abbey his mother always told him to look away so that he would not see the ugly buttresses in the form of an M. The ugly M, she called it. On one occasion he thought of ugly words starting with M, and one was Money. Richard owed his material prosperity to the Brickworks, left him by his father. His novels had brought in only marginal wealth. 'His first novel had come out in the twenties, when it was still possible for an author, or anyone else, to keep the bulk of his earnings from the clutches of the Inland Revenue. It was only his first novel that had brought in money—it had been filmed and dramatized. But when his earnings from authorship fell off he still had the Brickworks and it was not necessary for him to ask: 'How can I please the public better?'

I doubt if there is a contemporary writer who has illustrated more emphatically the fundamental role played by money in our society than L. P. Hartley, nor the subtle changes in its value relative to human service or the consequent erosion in the morality of its use. In 'The White Wand' we read that CF had come to stay in Venice for a month. He lost the services of his gondolier after a quarrel, and did not replace him. By saving this money he was able to stay a little longer—and yet it must have been so little! It is always embarrassing to see someone trying to play the role of the cosmopolitan and at the same time having to count the pennies. As Richard's financial situation became more and more difficult *(The Betrayal),* his solicitor advised him to sell his shares in the Fosdyke Fundamental Brick Company, and to buy shares in Juvenile and General Hair Stylists. It was the traditional remedy, realising capital on stock. But there is a new tone in this transaction, a symbolic change from solid values to something more frivolous. Immediately the Fosdyke shares soar and the J. & G.H.S. fall to a quarter. So much for values. As for morality, it was his solicitor who bought his Fosdykes. It is the end of an era for Richard. Money still counts, but you have to have it. Hartley's characters are usually without it, or enough of it, or if they have it they are likely to lose it. But the marginal men, like Alexey in *The Love-Adept,* 1969, are all right. This is the story of a trio, two men and a woman, who are emotionally and sexually implicated. They break up and go their own ways with their own desires. 'Alexey was the luckiest, because besides having money. . . . '

Notes

1. We are given a different picture of university life in *My Sister's Keeper,* 1970. Here the tone is more earthy, less pretentious. Instead of art, literature and music, the young men discuss society and morality. A later period is intended ('those days', when long hair was becoming fashionable) so a clearcut comparison is not possible.

2. The same can be said about the Hancock family in *My Sister's Keeper,* 1970. At the back of the house is a gravel path with a herbaceous border on one side and a lawn on the other, both separated from next door by black split-wood palings.

3. Hartley's work is full of symbolism, usually well handled. One of the weaknesses of modern criticism is its compulsive search for the symbol and its uncritical admiration of it, just for existing, no matter whether it is well or badly integrated. Hartley's use is often subtle, though occasionally heavy-handed (as in the prominence given to the shrimp-anemone tension) and one feels that he has perhaps been pushed into this by undue attention to the academic critics. On the other hand, the misuse of symbolism is one of Eustace's worst mental disorders, and Hartley admits this after Eustace has returned to his old haunts and is compelled to face the wreckage of all his high hopes. When Isabel identifies the sea with her lover she is avoiding reality in typical Eustace fashion. 'He turned from the lighthouse and looked over the cliff. The sea was far out, and straight in front of him, beyond old Anchorstone, the mussel-bed, the great black sandbank, extended its giant strength like a stranded whale. No, not like a whale— Hamlet had laid that trap for Polonius: it was a sandbank, and like a sandbank, and no good would come of seeing it as something else'. (*Eustace and Hilda,* 1952) In an interview with Francis King held at Glebe House, the P.E.N. H.Q., on 12th November 1970, Hartley denied that the shrimp-anemone symbolism was conscious. 'I had written half the book before I saw that the eating of the shrimp by the anemone was a symbol of the relationship. . . . '

4. This novel is dedicated to Elizabeth Bowen, who must have been working on *Eva Trout* at about the same time. In her novel there is also a working man whose would-be mistress, a rich girl, helps invest in a garage. Pauline does the same for Jock. At one stage in their careers both girls drove Jags. Is it possible that Hartley and Bowen were both inspired by the same relationship which was known to each of them? In other ways, the novels are vastly different, including the major themes.

5. Hartley's approach to servants is quite different from Snow's. They always cheat Hartley and he knows it. It seems very likely that they cheat Snow's well-meaning characters, but the latter would not admit it. It was necessary to maintain a fiction of trust, democracy and mutual respect.

Edward T. Jones (essay date 1978)

SOURCE: Jones, Edward T. "L. P. Hartley and Short Fiction." In *L. P. Hartley,* pp. 35-58. Boston: Twayne Publishers, 1978.

[*In the following essay, Jones provides an overview of Hartley's short fiction, exploring the relationship between the author's short stories and novels, and emphasizing his use of similar symbols, metaphors, and themes across his short and long fiction.*]

Hartley's earliest successes in imaginative literature were with short stories, beginning with his first volume, **Night Fears** (1924); and his interest in this genre continued throughout his life, with additional volumes appearing at regular intervals: **The Killing Bottle** (1932), **The Travelling Grave** (1951), **The White Wand** (1954), **Two for the River** (1961), and **Mrs. Carteret Receives** (1971). **The Collected Stories of L. P. Hartley** appeared in 1968, and a revised volume including the stories from **Mrs. Carteret Receives** appeared posthumously in 1973 under the title, **The Complete Short Stories of L. P. Hartley,** which is the edition used here.[1]

By far the largest number of these stories is in the Gothic mode which Hartley derived from his beloved forbears, Poe, Hawthorne, James, and the Brontës. Hartley's point presumably was to write the kind of story that these great predecessors might have written had they lived in the twentieth century. If Hartley demonstrates that he occasionally possesses what T. S. Eliot called in Hawthorne, "the ghost sense," in a larger measure his tales of the supernatural are examples of craft rather than art, an *amusette,* as Henry James rather erroneously termed the deceptive child's play of his own *The Turn of the Screw.*

Admittedly some other commentators have regarded these productions more highly, as manifestations of Hartley's genius rather than of his powers to mimic his favorite antecedents. Lord David Cecil, for example, asserts,

> Mr. Hartley's moral preoccupations also have their place in his tales of terror. His ghosts are never inexplicable elementals, but the spirit of vengeance or manifestations of spiritual evil. This moral element in his tales gives them a disturbing seriousness not to be found in the ordinary ghost story. Like those of Henry James and Walter De LaMare, they are parables of their authors' profounder beliefs.
>
> ("Introduction to *The Collected Short Stories* of L. P. Hartley," 1968, *The Complete Short Stories,* p. viii)

One's approach to the Hartley canon may well determine the thematic emphasis and evaluation accorded the short stories. Thus Anne Mary Mulkeen, who sees as the center of Hartley's art his exploitation of new artistic forms to reveal and illuminate the spiritual crisis in contemporary civilization, finds that his "ghost stories give us intimations of the apocalyptic universe which moves in the background of his novels." In her view of Hartley, "the visible world we live in is surrounded by, in touch with a greater and more frightening invisible one of spirits, forces, connections, and consequences." (Mulkeen, p. 26)

I CROSSCURRENTS BETWEEN SHORT STORIES AND NOVELS

Students of Hartley's fiction should be grateful to Miss Mulkeen and to Paul Bloomfield before her (in his Hartley monograph for the British Council's Writers and Their Work series) for initiating the pleasure of making and marking connections between the short stories and the novels, a task which earlier interpreters had not attempted. These crosscurrents may be as casual as a shared image or symbolic description or the germ of a theme begun in a short story and amplified in a novel.

An example of a shared image or metaphor in **"The Island"** from the earliest collection, *Night Fears,* appears when Mrs. Santander's island is described "as some crustacean, swallowed by an ill-turned starfish, but unassimilated." (p. 210) Another image derived from marine biology comes to the mind of someone familiar with Hartley's canon—the shrimp and the anemone of the *Eustace and Hilda* trilogy, the first volume of which was probably begun about the same time as "The Island." Although the Santanders in this

story have constructed their island home without sharp angles and edges—an architectural feature which Hartley will return to in *Facial Justice*—their marriage develops its own "edges" as Mrs. Santander in her husband's absence takes on a series of lovers. To the narrator, the latest, if least, of the lovers, Mr. Santander explains how he acquired his torn fingernail, "a jagged rent revealing the quick, moist and gelatinous." (p. 221) The description again suggests a similar slimy, sea provenance. Santander's injury was incurred in the act of strangling his wife. He, in turn, kills himself by leaping sixty feet onto the rocks below, and the primordial ooze reclaims a sophisticated specimen. Meanwhile, the corpse of Mrs. Santander remains in its place in the easy chair.

The genesis of *Poor Clare* (1968) would seem to be two stories from **The White Wand** collection, **"Witheling End"** and **"Up the Garden Path."** In the former story, Oswald Clayton signals the end of a friendship by inviting guests to spend a weekend with him at his home in Witheling End. The narrator of the story assumes he has been given the *coup de grâce* as a result of his weekend visit; but a mutual friend, a painter named Ponting, explains the basis of Oswald's dilemma, which he succeeded in extracting from him in the course of another weekend visit:

> He said it made him nervous and shy, looking after people in his own house, especially when he felt he had got on their nerves. He did everything he could, he went out of his way to give them a jolly time; but it was killing work, he said, like trying to warm up an icicle; they just moped and drooped and dripped. What he really meant was, they were like warmed-up death. But he didn't blame them; he said it was all his fault. Then we laughed over the whole affair.
>
> (pp. 343-344)

The air cleared, **"Witheling End"** closes with reconciliation and friendships intact as Ponting whistles for Oswald to join him and the narrator upstairs in the latter's flat.

"Up the Garden Path," on the other hand, catches the tragic tone and the insuperable misunderstanding and betrayal of friendship which characterizes *Poor Clare.* The story examines a love triangle which pits a man of aesthetic sensibility against a callous realist for the affections of a woman named, ironically, Constantia. Christopher Fenton, away in Rome, asks his barrister friend, Ernest Gretton, to visit his country home and at a designated hour to inspect his beloved garden as if through the eyes of his absent host. Yielding to his friend's request, Ernest journeys to New Forest and discovers Constantia already there with the same commission. Christopher's absence being almost more potent than his presence, Constantia refuses to submit to Ernest's suggestion that since they have been put into the position of an illicit couple, they should accept the challenge. Ernest ruminates with distaste on what Christopher's flowers represent:

> The flowers, I felt, represented that part of Christopher with which I was least in sympathy; his instinct to substitute for life something that was apart from life—something that would prettify it, aromatize it, falsify it, enervate and finally destroy it.
>
> (p. 420)

Hartley exposes a contest of wills played out against an alternating sinister Hawthornian garden and a Lawrentian garden of pastoral fulfillment, the backdrop emblematic of Hartley's recurring ambivalence toward his literary predecessors. Ernest insists that Christopher has kept Constantia trapped in the unreality of what he terms a "eunuch's paradise" (p. 422), thereby denying himself and Constantia the opportunity to become man and wife. When the time comes for the couple to view the garden according to their promise to Christopher, Ernest manages to lock Constantia in the house and then proceeds to fall asleep outside her door until the sound of a shot wakes him. He finds her uninjured, and silently they repair to the garden to follow the promenades outlined for them in Christopher's letters. Their absent host, in the shadow of a towering rhododendron bush, is found shot:

> Something or someone—perhaps Christopher, perhaps Constantia in the shock of her discovery, had shaken the bush, for the body was covered with rose-pink petals, and his forehead, his damaged forehead, was adrift with them. Even the revolver in his hand had petals on it, softening its steely gleam. But for that, and for something in his attitude that suggested he was defying Nature, not obeying her, one might have supposed that he had fallen asleep under his own flowers.
>
> (p. 427)

In his final letter dated Sunday 4:30, Christopher explains that he had meant to join his two friends at the garden-party, but their tardiness in keeping their promise has led him to alternative action, suicide. "Was it too much to ask, that you should keep your promise to me, or too little? All my life I have been asking myself this question, in one form or another, and perhaps this is the only answer. Bless you, my children, be happy—Christopher." (p. 427) The benediction anticipatory also of the ending of *Facial Justice* renders impossible Christopher's injunction to happiness. As in *Poor Clare*, Constantia is unable to forgive either herself or Ernest for having failed their friend; and after the inquest, Ernest reports they never met again.

Seen from Ernest's point of view, Christopher was a failure who deserved to die because he was unable to come to terms with life; but **"Up the Garden Path"** is more complex (or at least more equivocal) than Ernest's interpretation of events in the story. Christopher is a lover of beauty, and as his garden shows, a careful cultivator of art. But the artist needs appreciators of his handiwork—an audience. His art, however, is too remote from human life to be intelligible to realists like Ernest. Men of action scarcely ever credit their counterparts who cultivate imagination and sensibility with anything more than sentimentality. Ernest assumes Christopher must have some ulterior motive which, in fact, he probably does not have. However, Christopher's innocence and ingenuousness hold danger both for himself and others in a corrupt world; his suicide note tacitly acknowledges the guilt which accompanies innocence, especially when one indulges in the typically Hartleian go-between role of experiencing life vicariously through friends.

Less covertly, Hartley in the same collection, explores the relationship of the literary artist to his life and work which prefigures *The Love-Adept*. In "A Rewarding Experience," writer Henry Tarrant is unable to write a short story he has been commissioned to produce. Despite precedents like *The Golden Bowl*, Tarrant cannot write any longer about objects nor can he evoke Nature in the manner of Hardy or Conrad. While he had written often in the past about the human race, nothing new on the species stirs his consciousness. Hartley's description of Tarrant and his dilemma approaches droll self-reference, even self-parody:

> Harry Tarrant was a bachelor and fiction-writing had confirmed him in the single state. The more he wrote about human beings the less he wanted to have anything to do with them. He got them where he wanted them, and that was outside. Outside, they obeyed the rules—his rules. Critics had remarked on his aloofness, but it was perfectly in order for an artist to be aloof.
>
> (p. 379)

Later, he reminisces that he had kept "illness at bay, the war at bay, marriage at bay: he had kept life itself at bay. Only art had he welcomed; and now art had gone back on him." (p. 379)

Into this life comes a lady and her dog who bring, much to Tarrant's relief, blood and dirt into his fastidious house and too well-ordered rooms. On a walk he encounters a dog-fight; separating the two dogs and returning a pet to its mistress, Tarrant sustains a bloody hand. The woman is solicitous about him and accompanies him to his home. Proud of the evidence of his own blood shed in defense of another, even a spaniel, Tarrant enjoys the nursing attention given his hand by his new acquaintance. The spaniel, understandably nervous after his ordeal, wets the rug, but Tarrant is inexplicably happier because his house has now been fouled and blood-stained, although he cannot articulate his feelings to the woman who elects to leave without the sherry he has offered. But once outside the lady and her spaniel discover again their original attacker. Triumphantly Henry Tarrant shuts his gate, exclaiming, "Now you simply *must* come back." (p. 381) The implied consequence is that the writer will find his art less desiccated because of this renewed contact with life.

A less fortunate portrait of the artist is on display in "W.S." In this story Hartley examines the relationship between the author and his creation, somewhat along the lines of epistemological hide and seek. Walter Streeter keeps getting postcards from a "W.S." who, sounding like a critic, accuses him of moral ambiguity and spiritual drifting in his character delineation. When "W.S." finally appears in the "flesh," he turns out to be the one completely evil character Streeter created in his youth before he graduated to "ambiguity." Streeter realizes that his characters are largely projections of himself or else diametric opposites to him. Hartley once more includes some amusing self-reference. "W.S.", for example, sends Streeter postcards showing towers of famous cathedrals because the author, like Hartley himself, is known to admire cathedrals. However, the ominous tone is more reminiscent of cathedrals in M. R. James perhaps than in L. P. Hartley. The character goes by the eponym, William Stainsforth, and he claims his author made him a scapegoat, unloading all his self-dislike on a helpless character. The author is given one chance to soften his portrayal of Stainsforth. All Streeter must do is find one virtue with which he ever credited his character— "just one kind thought—just one redeeming feature." (p. 390) Faced with a moral and aesthetic choice, Streeter tries desperately to think of something or to fabricate something within the two minutes alloted him, but his moral rigor and the cause of goodness prevent him from asserting good where there is only evil. Of necessity he submits to the literally iron hand of his character, and he is strangled mercilessly. Streeter has come face to face with his own unpardonable sin, and he deals with it without extenuation or ambiguity. "W.S." is a disturbing fable, given Hartley's usual component of "realistic" plausibility, of the artist submitting to the perilous limitations of his own former creations—the identification turns inward without sympathy, and with fatal results.

Hartley offers a range of statements in the short stories on the uses and value of possessions and art objects, a perennial theme in his fiction and the subject of *The Collections* (1972). Three stories, in particular, illuminate his somewhat ambivalent feelings about objects and possessions.

"Two for the River," the title story of another collection, is a very beguiling tale, narrated in first-person by Mr. Minchin, a bachelor writer who debates with himself the advisability of selling his river home to a young couple:

> My beautiful things! They had seemed so once, when one by one I had collected them: but how seldom had the glow of acquisition lasted from one side of the counter to the other! How soon one took them all for granted! Whereas the possessions of the mind!—It was the onset of old age, no doubt: once I hadn't felt that way. Nor would a young couple coming fresh to a place, with eyes and hearts alive to pretty things, feel that way either.
>
> (p. 469)

The *genius loci* of his house accuses Mr. Minchin of fickleness; as the writer once had fallen in love with the house, now he was transferring his affections to the young couple—"'Their youth shall be my youth, their happiness my happiness, their children my children, their future mine!' Yes, grey-haired Mr. Minchin, you thought you could renew yourself in them, and lead vicariously the life you never led!" (p. 471) Paradise Paddock seems ill-suited to the sounds of squalling children whose din will forever drown out the voice of the house. Mr. Minchin himself fears that the house will be altered, broken up into flats, and that he will be left homeless.

His interior monologue is interrupted by the sounds of a swan attack on the river. The Marchmonts, the house-hunting couple, have taken their canoe on the river to give Mr. Minchin time to reach his decision about selling his house. Although he has decided to sell, Minchin's announcement is stifled by the couple's story of how they were attacked on the river. Marchmont has destroyed the male swan with his canoe paddle, and thus saved his wife from drowning, when the swan had jumped on her back. Wanting no more swansongs, the honeymooning Marchmonts decide Paradise Paddock is not for them. In gratitude for his hospitality, they offer Minchin their canoe, and he accepts. The canoe signifies the true ownership of the river and the house.

Minchin apostrophizes the river, claiming it has let him down. But, in truth, it has saved him through the intervention of the swans. He spies the female swan anxiously seeking her fallen mate and thinks, "She never had to call him before, . . . and now he will not hear her." (p. 476) Minchin's identity with the house and river are once more indivisible; he is his own *genius loci*:

> There was nothing more to wait for; the air was turning cool; I had an irrational feeling that my clothes were wet. Stiffly I got up and climbed back to the house—my

house, for it was mine after all: the swan had saved it for me. A moment's doubt remained: would the switch work? It did, and showed me what was still my own.

(p. 476)

Hartley's **"Two for the River"** embodies his best manner, method, and tone. The interior monologues and dream narrations succeed in penetrating beyond consciousness into the privacy of the interior self which Hartley values and seeks methods to explore. In his evocation of the house and the swans used as symbolic reminders of Mr. Minchin, Hartley resembles the late Elizabeth Bowen. The outer, external world becomes a character itself as well as the symbol of the narrator's inner self. Hartley's animation of inert matter clarifies the special human relationship with the universe of objects, often with both affection and some chagrin, as in the instance of Mr. Minchin. The undertone of self-deprecation and the pathos he feels for the bereft swan make Minchin even more ingratiating.

Inanimate objects, though aesthetically satisfying, are not always held by Hartley in such high esteem apart from the human value affixed to them. In **"The Price of the Absolute,"** for example, Timothy Carswell goes off with his over-priced Celadon Vase utterly elated because he feels he is the possessor (having been told so by the salesman) of Absolute Beauty incarnate. Lord David Cecil thinks that Hartley is endorsing art over life in the following description of the art object:

> Suddenly he stopped, for on a shelf above his head was a vase that arrested his attention as sharply as if it had spoken to him. Who can describe perfection? I shall not attempt to, nor even indicate the colour; for, like a pearl, the vase had its own colour, which floated on its surface more lightly than morning mist hangs on a river. . . .
>
> "Turn on the light!" commanded the proprietor. So illuminated, the vase shone as if brightness had been poured over it. It might have been floating in its own essence, so insubstantial did it look. Through layer on layer of soft transparency you seemed to see right into the heart of the vase.
>
> (pp. ix-x)

Cecil notes of the foregoing: "This passage is memorable not only for the light it throws on Mr. Hartley's beliefs, but also as an example of his art in its beautiful best; the precise and exquisite expression of an exquisitely refined sensibility." (p. x)

But in the context of the story Carswell's faith in his art object is largely vitiated, although he does not admit this fact to himself, by his overhearing the salesman deliver a similar endorsement to another customer about another *objet d'art.* To Carswell, his vase may well be *sui generis,* but Hartley has dramatized

the situational absurdity of purchasing Absolute Beauty in the marketplace. If art is absolute, life remains distressingly relative, and survival requires continual attention. The inherent comedy of the claim, **"The Price of the Absolute,"** surely is the best incarnation in the story.

The ultimate *reductio ad absurdum* of any claim regarding the superiority of art over life is sketched in **"Mr. Blandfoot's Picture,"** where all the fashionable ladies in Settlemarsh contrive to get a glimpse of Mr. Blandfoot's reputed masterpiece. The redoubtable Mrs. Marling succeeds in getting Mr. Blandfoot to accept an invitation to her salon to exhibit his picture. She discovers to her shame that the picture is tattooed on her guest's chest. Social snobbery and the pretension to elegance are of little avail before such an exhibition. Poor Blandfoot collapses in the middle of his display, to be revived shortly. The Lawrentian Blandfoot thrusts his physicality into the rarefied atmosphere of the drawing-room, to rebuke through his own selfhood the Settlemarsh culture vultures. The Jamesian Hartley again shows another visage (or a bared chest), and Lawrentian life takes precedent over disembodied art.

Lastly, the resources of deliberate fantasy wherein the settings are enchanted or imaginary and the plots point to magical themes of an archetypal life-giving quality appear in Hartley prior to his adult fantasy, *Facial Justice* (1960) in **"Conrad and the Dragon"** and **"The Crossways."** Conrad is a most unlikely dragon-slayer, as might be expected in a fairytale devised by L. P. Hartley. His older brother has died earlier in a futile attempt to free the Princess Hermione from the dragon, and since then Conrad's indifference to the Princess "had deepened into positive dislike." Yet the only way to get at the dragon is to utter words of love about the Princess:

> [Conrad] could not bring himself to say he loved her, even without meaning it. So he set himself to devise a form of words which would sound to the greedy, stupid Dragon sufficiently like praise, but to him, the speaker, would mean something quite different.
>
> (p. 204)

His novel approach to the dragon is successful; and he slays the beast only to discover, as does the kingdom to its horror, that the Princess and the dragon are one and the same. His address to the dragon is a masterpiece of equivocation:

> But when I remember what you have done for me: rescued me from the dull round of woodland life; raised me from obscurity into fame; transformed me from a dreamer into a warrior, an idler into a hunter of Dragons; deigned to make yourself the limit of my hopes and the end of my endeavors—I have no words to thank you, and I cannot love you more than I do now!

The conquering hero is transformed instantly into a social pariah, paralleling somewhat the duality of the Princess herself. Conrad is given the opportunity to leave the country, in secret. With Charlotte, his deceased brother's sweetheart, Conrad makes his way to a Republic where the couple marry and live happily ever after.

The import of **"Conrad and the Dragon"** is appropriately mysterious. At one level it provides a nightmare projection of the nascent sexual fears that Hartleian men frequently manifest toward women. Or possibly it is a parable of the dragons women become, because their lovers and admirers will them to be so, a variation on Hartley's perverse teleology where the promised adult end is frustrated by the inner child. When Hartley turns again to a wildly imaginative fable in *Facial Justice,* he wisely concentrates his moral vision on political rather than sexual issues; but, in passing, **"Conrad and the Dragon"** compels attention as much for what it does not say as what it does.

"The Crossways" fulfills the expectations for an ideal fairy-tale by suggesting the conditions necessary for a happy marriage; therefore it serves as a harbinger of Hartley's happy-ending novels like *My Sisters' Keeper* (1970). Lucindra, a stranger in a strange land, marries the strong and handsome woodsman, Michael, whose only blemish is an enormous scar from a previous encounter with a bear. A peddler from her native country one day entices Lucindra with stories of the road to the Land of Heart's Desire, which is to be found at the Crossways deep in the forest. In time, Lucindra leaves her husband and two typically Hartleian children, Olga and Peter, in search of her heart's desire. Finally, despite their father's warning, the children penetrate the forest, and they find Lucindra injured in a ditch by the Crossways. But all the road signs are blank. When Michael appears, he insists he has been unkind to his wife, for she must have the freedom to go where she likes. With this reaffirmation of her free will, she desires only to return home. Dependent now on her husband to carry her, Lucindra expresses the renewed love she feels for all her family. The signpost suddenly becomes clear. The Land of Heart's Desire is the homeward path they must follow. This parable of wedded love is a little too clear; the blond dreamer Lucindra takes the realist woodsman Michael hereafter to love and to cherish. The supernaturally unclosed world of fairy-tale loses something in translation to the more problematic and realistic milieu of the novel, as the deceptively sanguine L. P. Hartley at this juncture fully understands. The trembling balance which D. H. Lawrence saw as the necessary play of opposites requires not a fairy-tale but another genre—the novel.

II HARTLEY AND THE UNCANNY: GHOSTS, EVIL, AND PUNISHMENT

The macabre tales in Hartley's *Complete Short Stories* represent explorations in fantasy different in kind from the near allegories of **"Conrad and the Dragon"** and **"The Crossways."** Hartley here concerns himself less with right and wrong, as he does in the novels, than with evil and its effects. His conception of the horror story seems closely allied to H. P. Lovecraft's definition:

> The true weird tale has something more than secret murder, bloody bones, or a sheeted form clanking chains according to rule. A certain atmosphere of breathless and unexplainable dread of outer, unknown forces must be present; and there must be a hint, expressed with a seriousness and portentousness becoming its subject, of that most terrible conception of the human brain—a malign and particular suspension or defeat of those fixed laws of Nature which are our only safeguard against the assaults of chaos and the daemons of unplumbed space.[2]

And insofar as can be determined, his intended effect upon the reader likewise suggests Lovecraft's standard:

> The one test of the really weird is simply this—whether or not there be excited in the reader a profound sense of dread, and of contact with unknown spheres and powers; a subtle attitude of awed listening, as if for the beating of black wings or the scratching of outside shapes and entities on the known universe's utmost rim. And of course, the more completely and unifiedly a story conveys this atmosphere, the better it is as a work of art in a given medium.

> (Lovecraft, p. 16)

Withal, though, Hartley's climaxes in these stories are often predictable, and strangely flat, because they have not been made to matter very much. When Hartley attaches fear to what Freud calls the "uncanny," i.e., "nothing else than a hidden, familiar thing that has undergone repression and then emerged from it,"[3] his macabre stories can be genuinely chilling as in **"Night Fears"** and **"A Visitor from Down Under."** Otherwise, fear becomes merely decorative.

In **"Night Fears,"** a newly-hired nightwatchman who has been fabricating incidents of trial and stress to impress his wife finds himself sharing his brazier with a stranger. In conversation with the stranger the watchman articulates the anxiety-producing circumstances of his life, as the stranger, Iago-like, stimulates his most submerged fears—of his wife's fidelity, the loss of his children's affection, the real possibility of his own mental breakdown as a result of his inability to sleep during the day. In desperation, the watchman pulls a knife and, in turn, is murdered with it. And the stranger steps over the dead body, disappearing into a blind alley with only a track of dark, irregular footprints left behind. The watchman's previous fictions of peril and threats have become gruesome reality for him. The imagination, of course, has the power to terrify without any external correlative. The watchman could be a victim of his own dark mind. But there was a stranger, uncannily not feeling the cold which grips and finally destroys the watchman.

The tell-tale icicle on the window-sill in **"A Visitor from Down Under,"** a "thin claw of ice curved like a Chinaman's nail, with a bit of flesh sticking to it" (p. 73), similarly makes palpably real the visitation of the ghost which carries off Mr. Rumbold, who back in Australia had killed Mr. James Hagberg. Rubold had been forwarned that vengeance was imminent, when he listened to a children's program on the radio where innocent rhymes suddenly were transformed into ominous threats from beyond the grave.

Hartley is fond of symbolic retributions as the villain in **"The Travelling Grave"** is trapped by his own trick coffin which he would have used on his guest; or symbolic substitution as in "Feet Foremost" where the curse and ghost of Low Threshold Hall spare the ailing Antony, preferring the recently crashed aviator. Thus the apparition is subject to its own law: "to abandon her Victim and seeking another tenement enter into it and transfer her vengenace, should its path be crossed by a Body yet nearer Dissolution. . . . " (p. 142) Both retribution and substitution figure dramatically in **"The Killing Bottle"** where the would-be victim, Jimmy Rintoul, amateur lepidopterist, survives the plot of Rollo Verdew against him. Rollo's brother, the insane Randolph, takes homicidal action against people and animals who are unnecessarily cruel to living things. When Jimmy appears at Verdew Castle with his killing bottle of cyanide to collect butterflies and moths, Rollo has a perfect set-up to contrive murder. Once Randolph is arrested for killing Jimmy, the family estate and fortune will devolve to Rollo.

At Randolph's insistence Jimmy Rintoul gives a demonstration of how the killing bottle works, using as victim the rather unworthy Large Tortoiseshell butterfly. Randolph expresses disappointment that the bottle is not larger, possibly large enough to admit a man. Hartley's description of the butterfly's death is appropriately grisly and lends ironic suspense in the context of the story:

> Alas, alas, for the experiment in humane slaughter! The butterfly must have been stronger than it looked; the power of the killing bottle had no doubt declined with frequent usage. Up and down, round and round flew the butterfly; its frantic flutterings could be heard

through the thick walls of its glass prison. It clung to the cotton-wool, pressed itself into corners, its straining, delicate tongue coiling and uncoiling in the effort to suck in a breath of living air. Now it was weakening. It fell from the cotton-wool and lay with its back on the plaster slab. It jolted itself up and down and, when strength for this movement failed, it clawed the air with its thin legs as though pedalling an imaginary bicycle. Suddenly, with a violent spasm, it gave birth to a thick cluster of yellowish eggs. Its body twitched once or twice and at last lay still.

(p. 251)

The last fillip to the foregoing comes when Rintoul blithely tells Randolph that this particular butterfly is not a parasite of any flower or vegetable, because it is too scarce to be a pest but is fond of gardens and frequented places, a rather sociable specimen like a robin.

Predictably, with what he considers a patent betrayal of natural piety having been committed, Randolph murderously takes after Jimmy Rintoul. The latter manages with great effort to escape, only to find vengeance fall upon Rollo, who is unable to remonstrate against the intent of his crazed brother. Once more abrogation of the age-old sanction to protect one's guest results in disaster for the villainous host.

In the best and most provocative of these horror stories, Hartley seems to be saying that man, the sick animal, bears within him an appetite for evil, revenge, and retribution which is inexorable. The more familiar masochism of Hartley's novels is transformed here in to something closer to sadism. Hartley can be not only cold to life but actively punishing to it. Of course, the figure in Hartley's carpet may well be a Rorschach inkblot of considerable psychological unpleasantness. As a character observes in **"Podolo,"** "We loved her and so we had to kill her." (p. 79) Admittedly, this statement is made in a dream sequence, yet for that very reason its relevance might be greater than a waking insight. Perhaps Hartley is using the horror story as a kind of little theatre of submerged passions, transforming hidden desires for punishment into freedom, play, and pleasure. Playfully Hartley presents the ubiquity of guilt and corruption in tales of elegant literary spookery through the implication that everyone is latently a killer.

Two stories from Hartley's last collection, *Mrs. Carteret Receives,* record that the wages of thievery is death, as typically Hartleian protagonists devise ingenious retributions for theft. In **"Paradise Paddock,"** Marcus Foster very much wants to have his turquoise-colored beetle, possibly an Egyptian scarab, stolen. A friend who has traveled extensively in the Near East informs him the object may be cursed. As no person is wholly innocent in Hartley, perhaps no object is either.

Because a series of fairly trivial misfortunes have befallen members of the household at Paradise Paddock, credence is lent to the friend's warning about the scarab's potential evil. Marcus, consequently, removes the beetle from the drawer and places it on the mantel to see what will happen. Mrs. Crumble, his daily help, shortly confesses she has accidently knocked the insect off the mantel and, according to her, it broke into dozens of unmendable pieces. Greatly relieved to be rid of the jinx on his house, Marcus learns from his factotum, Henry, that Mrs. Crumble slipped the scarab into her bag. The unfortunate Mrs. Crumble becomes mortally ill; and upon her death, her daughter comes to return the scarab to its rightful owner, as requested by her dying mother:

> For once Marcus was able to make up his mind quickly. Never, never would he accept, above all from a dead woman's hand, a gift which had given his subconscious mind, however misguided it might be, so much anxiety.
>
> (p. 689)

Expressing desire it may bring the child luck, Marcus forces the scarab upon her. Later, when the friend who had originally alerted him to the potential danger of the art object returns for a visit, Marcus proudly tells him the evil has been exorcised from Paradise Paddock. He jokingly relates that the local people refer to his home as the House of Death. As the two men take an evening stroll after dinner, Marcus's friend catches his foot on the curb and falls headlong. He sustains a broken leg:

> Writhing a little, he turned his screwed face towards the street-lamp overhead, which invested it with a yellowish pallor and gasped, between broken breaths, 'Thank you for only breaking my leg—you might have killed me. Did no one ever tell you you had the Evil Eye?'
>
> (p. 691)

Vivian Vosper, yet another Hartleian bachelor living alone in a small mews house in "a burglarious part of London," devises a clever retaliatory scheme against thieves in **"Please Do Not Touch"**:

> He survived, however, and he hadn't lost much of value for he hadn't much of value to lose; chiefly the drinks he kept on the sideboard, to which the thieves had liberally helped themselves, before relieving themselves, as is the habit of burglars, all over his sitting room floor. With the help of his daily help . . . he cleared up the mess; but the material stink of it, no less than the indescribable smell of violation that any burglary brings, remained with him for several days.
>
> (p. 723)

He breaks out a bottle of Amontillado sherry and doctors the wine with potassium cyanide left over from his youthful days of butterfly and moth collecting. He

reflects on his lack of malice toward the poor creatures which he as a naturalist used to collect as opposed to the very real animus he feels against the burglars who have "robbed him and beaten him and pinioned him as if he were a moth on a stretching-board." (p. 725)

Rationalizing about his diabolical scheme, Vivian Vosper notes that experts now claim violence is inherent in human nature and that any retaliation he might take would merely illustrate the well-known law of every action having an equal and consequent reaction. Still his fundamental decency triumphs, and he resolves to empty the poisonous bottles down the drain in the morning with a measure of precaution taken for that evening:

> Having written on a stick-on label, in the largest capital letters, 'PLEASE DO NOT TOUCH' he affixed it to the sherry bottle, which he placed in a prominent position on his drink-table so that neither by day nor night could its warning notice be ignored.
>
> (p. 726)

The following morning, Ethel, his daily help, reports that more rats have infiltrated his home, and Vivian decides to set the poisoned sherry as bait for them. This extermination maneuver works surprisingly well; his solution to the rat problem becomes the envy of his mews' neighbors. Meanwhile, Vivian takes additional precautions against future burglaries by installing ornamental iron over his front door and lower windows. Hartley at this point includes special comment on one of his favorite topics in the later novels—the fact that the permissive society often places the victim in the wrong: "Permissiveness was the password to today's society; and little as he agreed with it he felt slightly guilty for trying to stand in its way." (p. 732)

Despite the laws of probability, Vivian Vosper finds burglary striking again, but this time he discovers one of the three burglars dead in his sitting-room, looking like a butterfly on a stretching-board. To Vivian's shock, he perceives the deceased burglar to have been an acquaintance he had met at parties. During the subsequent police investigation, the possibility that the burglars were there as a result of a homosexual invitation is subtly intimated: "You'd be surprised, Mr. Vosper, if you knew how many men living alone as you do, complain of burglars who aren't really burglars, but burglars by invitation, so to speak." (p. 735)

"Please Do Not Touch" depicts a world in which anything can happen, and seemingly innocent things are threats, including casual acquaintances and bottles of sherry. Distinctions and priorities become ever more elusive. Vivian Vosper, however, finds his new emotion, revenge, enthralling. While revenge may stand as the historical fallout of a violent age, it gives him a renewed sense of ironic union with his fellows:

> Revenge, revenge. It was an emotion as old as jealousy, from which it so often sprang. It was a classic emotion, coeval with the human race, and to profess oneself to be free of it was as dehumanizing, almost as much, and perhaps more, as if one professed oneself to be free of love—of which, as of jealousy, it was an offspring.
>
> (pp. 736-737)

Thus, with the disappearance of the original cyanide sherry taken by the police as evidence, Vivian repairs to the basement for another bottle of sherry in which he mixes a portion of cyanide neglected by the police. He puts his warning on the bottle in red ink this time; and cautiously sniffing the almond-breathing perfume, "he had a sensation of ineffable, blissful sweetness." (p. 738)

At once humorous and frightening, **"Please Do Not Touch"** distills Hartley's special variety of macabre comedy and displays his mastery of emotional rhythm in short fiction. The story illustrates Hartley's endorsement of Bacon's sentiment that revenge is a kind of wild justice, an idea which propels a number of the short stories. Moreover, **"Please Do Not Touch"** confirms Hartley's understanding of the Poesque principle that the short, highly unified literary work is ideal as a vehicle for producing a pronounced emotional effect. This story is probably the best achieved tale in *Mrs. Carteret Receives,* proving that the elderly Hartley has not lost his "touch."

Unfortunately, Hartley exhibits the greatest tendency to repeat himself in the stories of terror and the supernatural, which appear sometimes more than twice-told. While some repetition may be inevitable in works which depend on similar plot devices, Hartley's imagination does seem to fail him when he ascribes virtually the same unfulfilled goals to thirty-three-year old Jimmy Rintoul in **"The Killing Bottle"** and seventy-year old Henry Kitson in **"Pains and Pleasures"**: to play the Moonlight Sonata quite perfectly, climb the Matterhorn, read the *Critique of Pure Reason,* in the case of Rintoul, and write a book that would be classic, in the instance of Kitson. Otherwise, the recurring wet footprints, *Doppelgängers,* masks, and games of hide-and-seek proliferating in Hartley's stories with slight variation from one to another have some charm even in their predictability. As James Hall has noted about the evolution of Hartley's novelistic technique from his suspense stories, human relations in the novels are seen "as absurdly dangerous games of hide-

and-seek, though he no longer deals in mystery." (Hall, pp. 111-112) What is supernaturally explicable in the tales of terror becomes ironically more oblique in the presumed reality of the novels where revenants are generally excluded. The writer of horror stories can reduce both evil and adversaries to size by stylizing the situation to suit his abstract purposes. Supernaturalism gives the writer the means of controlling reality, if not necessarily understanding it, for magic deals in feints, ambiguities, distractions, and illusions.

III STUDIES IN HUMAN PSYCHOLOGY AND DOMESTIC RELATIONS

Among the more interesting stories are those in which Hartley examines imaginatively the by-ways of human psychology. An especially incisive portrayal of a Hartleian fearful self is found in **"A Tonic,"** a tenderly destructive vignette of hypochondriacal Mr. Amber's visit to the specialist who inexorably confirms the patient's worst suspicions:

> "I read about diseases for pleasure!" said Mr. Amber simply. "But of course it is hard when you have so many of the symptoms, not to feel that you must have at any rate one or two of the diseases."
>
> (p. 322)

Mr. Amber's heart is, indeed, badly damaged, as Sir Sigismund Keen discovers during the examination which he is able to conduct only after his patient has fainted. No disguising of symptoms and requests for a tonic can obviate the painful future for Amber.

In a related vein, the first-person protagonist of **"A Summons"** awakened shortly after midnight lets his morbid imagination roam as he listens to a bluebottle fly in his room:

> Flies have a *flair* for putrefaction; what had brought this one to my bedside, what strange prescience had inspired its sharp, virulent rushes and brought that note of deadly exultation into its buzz? It had been all I could do to keep the creature off my face. Now it was biding its time, but my ears were apprehensive for the renewal of its message of mortality, its monotonous *memento mori.* That spray of virginia creeper, too, had apparently given up its desultory, stealthy, importunate attack upon the window. . . . I seemed to see its shrivelled, upturned leaves, its pathetic, strained curve of a creature that curls up to die. . . .
>
> (p. 315)

Indulging in these associations, he refuses to answer the summons of his little sister in the next room who hitherto has informed him she has recurring dreams about being murdered, doubtless inspired by vivid recitals of his own thoughts and dreams:

> For my sister knew, or would know now at any rate, that I was a heavy sleeper; and if she referred to the matter at breakfast I would use a little pious dissimula-

tion—children are so easily put off. Probably she would be ashamed to mention it. After all it wasn't my fault; I couldn't direct people's dreams; at her age, too, I slept like a top. Dreaming about murders . . . not very nice in a child. I would have to talk to her alone about it some time.

(p. 317)

Such self-righteousness coupled with surprising lack of self-knowledge produces a wry character sketch.

"Someone in the Lift" relates a grisly Oedipal accident at Christmastime. The Maldons with their son, Peter, are spending Christmas at Brompton Court Hotel. Peter is fascinated by the hotel lift which he imagines has an occupant who disappears as soon as the elevator comes to rest. Peter's mother tells him to ask his father whether someone is truly there each time, but the son hesitates to risk his father's ridicule:

Like all well-regulated modern fathers, Mr. Maldon was aware of the danger of offending a son of tender years: the psychological results might be regrettable. But Freud or no Freud, fathers are still fathers, and sometimes when Peter irritated him Mr. Maldon would let fly. Although he was fond of him, Peter's private vision of his father was of someone more authoritative and awe-inspiring than a stranger, seeing them together, would have guessed.

(p. 478)

When his father is with him, Peter never sees the figure in the lift. Hence Peter theorizes that the "someone" in the lift must be his father.

Two days before Christmas Day the lift breaks down, and Peter is forbidden to touch the button during the period of repair. On Christmas Eve, however, as he waits for the appearance of Father-Christmas whom he knows is really his father, he surreptitiously pushes the button and activates the lift:

The lift was coming up from below, not down from above, and there was something wrong with its roof—a jagged hole that let the light through. But the figure was there in its accustomed corner, and this time it hadn't disappeared, it was still there, he could see it through the mazy criss-cross of the bars, a figure in a red robe with white fur edges, and wearing a red cowl on its head: his father, Father Christmas, Daddy in the lift. But why didn't he look at Peter, and why was his white beard streaked with red?

(p. 481)

The final image in the story is of toys covered with blood at the feet of Peter's father, "red as the jag of lightning that tore through his brain. . . ." (p. 481) Although Peter never manifested any conscious desire to harm his father, circumstances have contrived to bring the unconscious Freudian struggle to hideous re-

ality. **"Someone in the Lift"** and **"The Waits,"** in which ghostly carolers turn assailants, introduce psychological terror to the silent night of Christmas Eve.

Another story illuminating father-son relationships and jealousies is **"The Pylon."** Laurie identifies himself with a large electrical transformer symbolized by a great steel pylon:

One day his short, plump body would shoot upwards, tall and straight as the pylon was; one day his mind, that was so dense in some ways, and so full of darkness, would fine down to an aery structure that let the light in everywhere and hardly cast a shadow. He would be the bearer of an electric current, thousands of volts strong, bringing light and power to countless homes.

The pylon, then, had served him as a symbol of angelic strength. But in other moods it stood for something different, this grey-white skeleton. In meaner moods, rebellious moods, destructive moods, he had but to look at it to realize how remote it was from everything that grew, that took its nourishment from the earth and was conditioned by this common limitation. It was self-sufficient, it owed nothing to anyone.

(pp. 611-612)

The adult masculine presence of Laurie's father produces additional ambivalence for his son, threatening, in particular, the child's imaginative identification with the pylon. The father who is delighted when the pylon is dismantled contrasts with the son who at that point feels he has lost some standard by which to measure himself. Subsequently Laurie has a bad dream where the pylon becomes equated with his father and both frustrate his desires. At the end of the story a bigger and better pylon is about to be erected, the father's denial to the contrary; but Laurie finds himself overwhelmed by his own violent and discordant emotions regarding the pylon, his father, and himself. The Freudian bruise which the father hoped not to inflict seems only too patent.

In **"Per Far l'Amore"** a father in Venice between the wars worries about his daughter's too ready availability to young men who buzz around Annette like the omnipresent August mosquitoes Mr. Elkington equally deplores. A party is organized where guests may find respite from the heat and mosquitoes in tent of netting. Here they may indulge their fancy—for conversation, cards, even for misanthropy, and especially per far l'amore, for making love. In one of the latter the misanthropic father discovers his young daughter strangled with the tent's scarlet fork-tailed pennon. Hartley once more suggests the pain and mortal risk implicit in love and passion when the wild blood is stirring.

A number of Hartley's last stories and some of the earlier ones concern the relationship of master to servant and vice versa. In most of them the Hartleian employer is desperately trying to keep domestics happy, because the servant, having learned well the tasks of his trade, has acquired a mastery over the immediate environment that his employer usually lacks. Hartley adroitly develops with humor and some pathos contemporary stresses which put strain on the historic master-servant relationship. He delineates especially well the servant's power over his master, born of the latter's dependency upon the person who competently deals with the trivial details of daily life.

In **"The Prayer,"** for example, Anthony Easterfield loses his expert chauffeur, because Copperthwaite's ambition has always been to drive a Roland-Rex, which an American employer makes available to him. Easterfield's aging, temperamental automobile offers no contest against the Roland-Rex. Indeed, Anthony had previously prayed that Copperthwaite might be granted the gift of a Roland-Rex motor-car, but his prayer's answer proves disadvantageous to the original petitioner who then is without a chauffeur. But before long Copperthwaite writes to his former employer, asking to be rehired:

> Never take a servant back again was the advice of our forebears. The word "servant" was now out of date, it was archaic; it could never be used in polite or impolite society. A "servant" was "staff": even one "servant" was "staff". One envisaged a bundle of staves, of fasces (infamous word) once used as a symbol of their office by Roman Lictors, and then by Mussolini.

> Copperthwaite a staff? The staff of life? Thinking of the dreary days and weeks that had passed since his departure, thinking of his forerunners, so much less helpful and hopeful than he, looking to the future, which seemed to hold in store nothing more alluring than an Old People's Home, Anthony began to think more favourably of Copperthwaite's return.

> (p. 676)

Easterfield fears that the returning Copperthwaite might become even more bossy than he had been previously, deciding "for Anthony many small problems of food, wine, and so on, that Anthony had been too tired, or too old, or too uninterested, to decide for himself." (p. 676) The chauffeur informs his old employer of the reason for his return to him: he found the Roland-Rex such a perfect car that he had nothing to do. With Easterfield and his car, Copperthwaite explains, "I *am* the car, sir." (p. 682) The story closes with the chauffeur asking his employer to say a big prayer for the car, and Anthony Easterfield speculates that an answer to his own prayer has perhaps been given to the mutual satisfaction of both himself and Copperthwaite.

In **"Fall in at the Double,"** like **"The Prayer"** included in Hartley's last collection, *Mrs. Carteret Receives,* Philip Osgood finds himself haunted in his

West Country house by ghosts from the Army occupation of the dwelling during the Second World War. He discovers beneath the coat of thick paint on his bedroom door that Lieut.-Col. Alexander McCreeth had formerly occupied the room, which the officer had marked *private*. His factotum, Alfred, claims to be psychic and familiar with poltergeists, and he relates to his employer what he has learned about the house's past history at the local pub. The men of Col. McCreeth's command staged an incident during which their commander was drowned at the weir below the house. The Colonel was purportedly checking on a suspicious person, possibly a German spy, whom his men claimed was down by the river.

A few nights later Philip awakes to knocking on his bedroom door and hears the thrice-given order, "Fall in at the double." As if seized by an irresistible compulsion, Philip obligingly falls in and follows the apparitions to the riverside where he sees re-enacted the original plot against McCreeth. The Colonel, however, directs his mutinous men to transfer their hate to his double, Philip:

> Their strong hands were round him and Philip, hardly struggling, felt himself being hoisted over the garden wall, to where, a few feet below, he could see his own face mirrored in the water.

> "Let's get rid of the bastard!"

> (p. 666)

The psychic Alfred intervenes to save his employer from the fates:

> "A hot bath, a hot bottle, a whisky perhaps, and then bed for you, sir. And don't pay any attention to that lot, they're up to no good."

> (p. 667)

The story celebrates the faithful servant who fully anticipates and meets the needs of his employer, to a truly life-saving extent.

In **"Pains and Pleasures"** the well-ordered miniaturized universe of Henry Kitson and his general factotum, "Bill," who cleaned his cottage, cooked his meals, and drove his car, is disrupted by the behavior of Kitson's old tomcat, Ginger. Objecting to his ritual banishment from the house at night, Ginger claws and bites whoever performs this task. When the cat is permitted to spend the night comfortably inside, his forgotten house-training results in a mess each morning for Bill to clean up. Henry Kitson feels guilty about subjecting Bill to this ordeal, especially out of fear that he must choose between the cat and his employee. Bill suggests providing Ginger with a box of sawdust for bathroom purposes, but the cat prefers to use its new box for a bed. When Bill finally gives notice of his imminent departure, saying he will look for a job where there are no animals, Kitson offers to clean up any future messes. Bill explains rather that he minds putting the cat out at night:

> "It isn't his scratching and mauling I mind, it's when he purrs and tries to pretend I'm doing him a kindness. I'm not that tender-hearted, but I know what it's like to spend a night in the open," the ex-policeman added.
>
> (p. 720)

Shortly thereafter Ginger dies, and Bill elects, much to Kitson's delight, to remain with his old employer. The "master" is temporarily disturbed at the end of the story when the cutlets which Bill offers for lunch sound like "catlets," but as Bill accepts a drink from his employer, their mutual dependency and affection are shown to be secure. The story may be trivial, yet its tribute to Bill seems genuine and heartfelt, although like Hartley himself Kitson has difficulty thinking about others without serving his own psychological needs:

> With the advent of Bill, "a soundless calm", in Emily Brontë's words, descended on Henry. Domestic troubles were over; nothing to resent; nothing to fight against; no sense of Sisyphus bearing an unbearable weight uphill. No grievance at all. Had he lived by his grievances, was a question that Henry sometimes asked himself. Had his resistance to them, his instinct to fight back and assert himself and show what he was made of, somehow strengthened his hold on life and prolonged it?
>
> (p. 714)

In the highly personal genre of the short story, Hartley sometimes reveals more about himself, as the foregoing suggests, than he does elsewhere in his fiction. Little broken bits of the author's life and habits of mind help to substantiate some rather negligible stories like **"Pains and Pleasures"** with that imaginative reality which, when applied to Hartley's subjective self, seems intuitively and emotionally right. The fifty stories of *The Complete Short Stories* vary considerably in quality. This chapter has sought to focus on the representative majority of Hartley's better stories where his contrived manipulation of plots and the general sameness of characterization are yet somewhat redeemed by intuitive perceptions which, at their best, transcend authorial wishfulness, a besetting vice in Hartley's short stories. His evocation of feeling is usually richer than his assertion of strangeness and mystery. Hence the supernatural tales seem appreciably less significant than those stories where Hartley looks more attentively at character interaction and the inner life of his characters. On these latter occasions, he invests characters with his own special brand of self-knowledge—that which is carried along, sometimes acted well upon, but knowledge which, in general, issues no clarion call to action. Hartley masters such knowledge as a clue to being with quiet grace and occasionally lyric intensity. Understandably, Hartley achieves his most convincing character portrayals with people, like Henry Kitson, who most resemble their author.

While Hartley's short stories manifest the restrictiveness and limitations which are equally a part of his longer, more sustained narratives, the further narrowness of the short story genre itself points up, to a greater disadvantage than the novels, the limitation inherent in the author's viewpoint and preoccupations. Nevertheless, any claim for excellence in Hartley's short fiction must rest with these restrictive character sketches and not, I suspect, in the more wildly imaginative Gothic tales which appear unduly derivative. In variations on the Hartleian personae the short fiction holds its interest and authenticity. These short stories are best seen, according to Anne Mulkeen's suggestion, as studies, sketches, experiments for the larger canvasses of the novels (Mulkeen, p. 17). The cumulative effect of *The Complete Short Stories* is that the quantitative largess of the collection far outstrips its qualitative richness; such a result may be the price of completeness. Yet the sameness of Hartley's oeuvre in short fiction bespeaks a high level of consistency which should be respected and not ignored. Hartley's symbols and metaphors, situations and moral stringency in the short stories become ghosts which haunt, often to good effect, his larger fictions.

Notes

1. All references to Hartley's short stories in this chapter are to the following edition with page references included in parentheses within the text: *L. P. Hartley, The Complete Short Stories*, with an Introduction by Lord David Cecil (London: Hamish Hamilton, 1973).

2. Howard Phillips Lovecraft, *Supernatural Horror in Literature* (New York: Dover Publications, Inc., 1973), p. 15. Subsequent references to this work are included in the text with page numbers in parentheses.

3. Sigmund Freud, "The 'Uncanny,' *Collected Papers*, Vol. 4 (New York: Basic Books, Inc., 1959), p. 399.

Selected Bibliography

Primary Sources

Night Fears and Other Stories. London and New York: G. P. Putnam's Sons, 1924.

The Killing Bottle. London and New York: G. P. Putnam's Sons, 1932.

The Traveling Grave and Other Stories. Sauk City, Wisconsin: Arkham House, 1948; London: James Barrie, 1951; London: Hamish Hamilton, 1957.

The White Wand and Other Stories. London: Hamish Hamilton, 1954.

Two for the River. London: Hamish Hamilton, 1961; Toronto: Collins, 1961.

The Collected Stories of L. P. Hartley. London: Hamish Hamilton, 1968.

Mrs. Carteret Receives and Other Stories. London: Hamish Hamilton, 1971.

SECONDARY SOURCES

Hall, James. "Games of Apprehension: L. P. Hartley," *The Tragic Comedians: Seven Modern British Novelists.* Bloomington: Indiana University Press, 1963, pp. 111-128.

Mulkeen, Anne. *Wild Thyme, Winter Lightning: The Symbolic Novels of L. P. Hartley.* Detroit: Wayne State University Press, 1974.

FURTHER READING

Criticism

Paul Bloomfield. "L. P. Hartley," 6-23. In *L. P. Hartley / Anthony Powell,* by Bernard Bergonzi and Paul Bloomfield. London: Longmans Green & Co., 1962.

Examines the theme of social commentary present in Hartley's novels, finding that his short stories are of the same high quality as the longer works.

Cecil, David. "Foreword." In *The Collected Short Stories of L. P. Hartley,* pp. v-viii. London: Hamish Hamilton, 1968.

Assesses Hartley's short fiction, observing that the author explored Gothicism in his short stories more completely than in his novels, expertly balancing elements of terror with reality.

Mulkeen, Anne. "Crystallizations: Hartley's Shorter Fiction." In *Wild Thyme, Winter Lightning: The Symbolic Novels of L. P. Hartley,* pp. 16-41. Detroit, Mich.: Wayne State University Press, 1974.

Identifies three main groups of Hartley short fiction (the psychological short story, the Gothic short story, and the short story dealing with contemporary social issues), emphasizing that an interest in the human mind and psychology permeates all of Hartley's short stories.

Wright, Adrian. "A Place at the Fireside." In *Foreign Country: The Life of L. P. Hartley,* pp. 57-87. London: Tauris Parke Paperbacks, 2001.

Comments on Hartley's short fiction within the context of his career as a whole and explores the themes of pessimism and the dangerous nature of love in *Night Fears and Other Stories.* This essay was first published in 1996.

Additional coverage of Hartley's life and career is contained in the following sources published by Gale: *British Writers Supplement,* **Vol. 7;** *Contemporary Authors,* **Vols. 45-48;** *Contemporary Authors—Obiturary,* **Vols. 37-40R;** *Contemporary Authors New Revision Series,* **Vol. 33;** *Contemporary Literary Criticism,* **Vols. 2, 22;** *Contemporary Novelists,* **Ed. 1.;** *Dictionary of Literary Biography,* **Vols. 15, 139;** *Encyclopedia of World Literature in the 20th Century,* **Ed. 3;** *Literature Resource Center;* *Major 20th-Century Writers,* **Eds. 1, 2;** *Major 21st-Century Writers,* **(eBook), Ed. 2005;** *Modern British Literature,* **Ed. 2;** *Reference Guide to English Literature,* **Ed. 2;** *Reference Guide to Short Fiction,* **Ed. 2;** *St. James Guide to Horror, Ghost & Gothic Writers,;* **and** *Supernatural Fiction Writers,* **Ed. 1.**

How to Use This Index

CDALBS = Concise Dictionary of American Literary Biography Supplement
CDBLB = Concise Dictionary of British Literary Biography
CMW = St. James Guide to Crime & Mystery Writers
CN = Contemporary Novelists
CP = Contemporary Poets
CPW = Contemporary Popular Writers
CSW = Contemporary Southern Writers
CWD = Contemporary Women Dramatists
CWP = Contemporary Women Poets
CWRI = St. James Guide to Children's Writers
CWW = Contemporary World Writers
DA = DISCovering Authors
DA3 = DISCovering Authors 3.0
DAB = DISCovering Authors: British Edition
DAC = DISCovering Authors: Canadian Edition
DAM = DISCovering Authors: Modules
   DRAM: Dramatists Module; **MST:** Most-studied Authors Module;
   MULT: Multicultural Authors Module; **NOV:** Novelists Module;
   POET: Poets Module; **POP:** Popular Fiction and Genre Authors Module
DFS = Drama for Students
DLB = Dictionary of Literary Biography
DLBD = Dictionary of Literary Biography Documentary Series
DLBY = Dictionary of Literary Biography Yearbook
DNFS = Literature of Developing Nations for Students
EFS = Epics for Students
EW = European Writers
EWL = Encyclopedia of World Literature in the 20th Century
EXPN = Exploring Novels
EXPP = Exploring Poetry
EXPS = Exploring Short Stories
FANT = St. James Guide to Fantasy Writers
FW = Feminist Writers
GFL = Guide to French Literature, Beginnings to 1789, 1798 to the Present
GLL = Gay and Lesbian Literature
HGG = St. James Guide to Horror, Ghost & Gothic Writers
HW = Hispanic Writers
IDFW = International Dictionary of Films and Filmmakers: Writers and Production Artists
IDTP = International Dictionary of Theatre: Playwrights
LAIT = Literature and Its Times
LAW = Latin American Writers
JRDA = Junior DISCovering Authors
MAICYA = Major Authors and Illustrators for Children and Young Adults
MAICYAS = Major Authors and Illustrators for Children and Young Adults Supplement
MAWW = Modern American Women Writers
MJW = Modern Japanese Writers
MTCW = Major 20th-Century Writers
NCFS = Nonfiction Classics for Students
NFS = Novels for Students
PAB = Poets: American and British
PFS = Poetry for Students
RGAL = Reference Guide to American Literature
RGEL = Reference Guide to English Literature
RGSF = Reference Guide to Short Fiction
RGWL = Reference Guide to World Literature
RHW = Twentieth-Century Romance and Historical Writers
SAAS = Something about the Author Autobiography Series
SATA = Something about the Author
SFW = St. James Guide to Science Fiction Writers
SSFS = Short Stories for Students
TCWW = Twentieth-Century Western Writers
WLIT = World Literature and Its Times
WP = World Poets
YABC = Yesterday's Authors of Books for Children
YAW = St. James Guide to Young Adult Writers

Literary Criticism Series
Cumulative Author Index

Ammons, A.R. 1926-2001 .. **CLC 2, 3, 5, 8, 9, 25, 57, 108; PC 16**
See also AITN 1; AMWS 7; CA 9-12R; 193; CANR 6, 36, 51, 73, 107, 156; CP 1, 2, 3, 4, 5, 6, 7; CSW; DAM POET; DLB 5, 165, 342; EWL 3; MAL 5; MTCW 1, 2; PFS 19; RGAL 4; TCLE 1:1

Ammons, Archie Randolph
See Ammons, A.R.

Amo, Tauraatua i
See Adams, Henry (Brooks)

Amory, Thomas 1691(?)-1788 .... **LC 48**
See also DLB 39

Anand, Mulk Raj 1905-2004 ..... **CLC 23, 93, 237**
See also CA 65-68; 231; CANR 32, 64; CN 1, 2, 3, 4, 5, 6, 7; DAM NOV; DLB 323; EWL 3; MTCW 1, 2; MTFW 2005; RGSF 2

Anatol
See Schnitzler, Arthur

Anaximander c. 611B.C.-c. 546B.C. .... **CMLC 22**

Anaya, Rudolfo A. 1937- . **CLC 23, 148, 255; HLC 1**
See also AAYA 20; BYA 13; CA 45-48; CAAS 4; CANR 1, 32, 51, 124, 169; CLR 129; CN 4, 5, 6, 7; DAM MULT, NOV; DLB 82, 206, 278; HW 1; LAIT 4; LLW; MAL 5; MTCW 1, 2; MTFW 2005; NFS 12; RGAL 4; RGSF 2; TCWW 2; WLIT 1

Anaya, Rudolpho Alfonso
See Anaya, Rudolfo A.

Andersen, Hans Christian
1805-1875 ...... **NCLC 7, 79, 214; SSC 6, 56; WLC 1**
See also AAYA 57; CLR 6, 113; DA; DA3; DAB; DAC; DAM MST, POP; EW 6; MAICYA 1, 2; RGSF 2; RGWL 2, 3; SATA 100; TWA; WCH; YABC 1

Anderson, C. Farley
See Mencken, H(enry) L(ouis); Nathan, George Jean

Anderson, Jessica (Margaret) Queale
1916- .... **CLC 37**
See also CA 9-12R; CANR 4, 62; CN 4, 5, 6, 7; DLB 325

Anderson, Jon (Victor) 1940- .... **CLC 9**
See also CA 25-28R; CANR 20; CP 1, 3, 4, 5; DAM POET

Anderson, Lindsay (Gordon)
1923-1994 .... **CLC 20**
See also CA 125; 128; 146; CANR 77

Anderson, Maxwell 1888-1959 .... **TCLC 2, 144**
See also CA 105; 152; DAM DRAM; DFS 16, 20; DLB 7, 228; MAL 5; MTCW 2; MTFW 2005; RGAL 4

Anderson, Poul 1926-2001 .... **CLC 15**
See also AAYA 5, 34; BPFB 1; BYA 6, 8, 9; CA 1-4R, 181; 199; CAAE 181; CAAS 2; CANR 2, 15, 34, 64, 110; CLR 58; DLB 8; FANT; INT CANR-15; MTCW 1, 2; MTFW 2005; SATA 90; SATA-Brief 39; SATA-Essay 106; SCFW 1, 2; SFW 4; SUFW 1, 2

Anderson, Robert 1917-2009 .... **CLC 23**
See also AITN 1; CA 21-24R; CANR 32; CD 6; DAM DRAM; DLB 7; LAIT 5

Anderson, Robert Woodruff
See Anderson, Robert

Anderson, Roberta Joan
See Mitchell, Joni

Anderson, Sherwood 1876-1941 ... **SSC 1, 46, 91; TCLC 1, 10, 24, 123; WLC 1**
See also AAYA 30; AMW; AMWC 2; BPFB 1; CA 104; 121; CANR 61; CDALB 1917-1929; DA; DA3; DAB; DAC; DAM MST, NOV; DLB 4, 9, 86; DLBD 1; EWL 3; EXPS; GLL 2; MAL 5; MTCW 1, 2; MTFW 2005; NFS 4; RGAL 4; RGSF 2; SSFS 4, 10, 11; TUS

Anderson, Wes 1969- .... **CLC 227**
See also CA 214

Andier, Pierre
See Desnos, Robert

Andouard
See Giraudoux, Jean(-Hippolyte)

Andrade, Carlos Drummond de
See Drummond de Andrade, Carlos

Andrade, Mario de
See de Andrade, Mario

Andreae, Johann V(alentin)
1586-1654 .... **LC 32**
See also DLB 164

Andreas Capellanus fl. c. 1185- .... **CMLC 45**
See also DLB 208

Andreas-Salome, Lou 1861-1937 ... **TCLC 56**
See also CA 178; DLB 66

Andreev, Leonid
See Andreyev, Leonid (Nikolaevich)

Andress, Lesley
See Sanders, Lawrence

Andrew, Joseph Maree
See Occomy, Marita (Odette) Bonner

Andrewes, Lancelot 1555-1626 .... **LC 5**
See also DLB 151, 172

Andrews, Cicily Fairfield
See West, Rebecca

Andrews, Elton V.
See Pohl, Frederik

Andrews, Peter
See Soderbergh, Steven

Andrews, Raymond 1934-1991 .... **BLC 2:1**
See also BW 2; CA 81-84; 136; CANR 15, 42

Andreyev, Leonid (Nikolaevich)
1871-1919 .... **TCLC 3**
See also CA 104; 185; DLB 295; EWL 3

Andrezel, Pierre
See Blixen, Karen (Christentze Dinesen)

Andric, Ivo 1892-1975 .... **CLC 8; SSC 36; TCLC 135**
See also CA 81-84; 57-60; CANR 43, 60; CDWLB 4; DLB 147, 329; EW 11; EWL 3; MTCW 1; RGSF 2; RGWL 2, 3

Androvar
See Prado (Calvo), Pedro

Angela of Foligno 1248(?)-1309 .... **CMLC 76**

Angelique, Pierre
See Bataille, Georges

Angell, Judie
See Angell, Judie

Angell, Judie 1937- .... **CLC 30**
See also AAYA 11, 71; BYA 6; CA 77-80; CANR 49; CLR 33; JRDA; SATA 22, 78; WYA; YAW

Angell, Roger 1920- .... **CLC 26**
See also CA 57-60; CANR 13, 44, 70, 144; DLB 171, 185

Angelou, Maya 1928- ...... **BLC 1:1; CLC 12, 35, 64, 77, 155; PC 32; WLCS**
See also AAYA 7, 20; AMWS 4; BPFB 1; BW 2, 3; BYA 2; CA 65-68; CANR 19, 42, 65, 111, 133; CDALBS; CLR 53; CP 4, 5, 6, 7; CPW; CSW; CWP; DA; DA3; DAB; DAC; DAM MST, MULT, POET, POP; DLB 38; EWL 3; EXPN; EXPP; FL 1:5; LAIT 4; MAICYA 2; MAICYAS 1; MAL 5; MBL; MTCW 1, 2; MTFW 2005; NCFS 2; NFS 2; PFS 2, 3; RGAL 4; SATA 49, 136; TCLE 1:1; WYA; YAW

Angouleme, Marguerite d'
See de Navarre, Marguerite

Anna Comnena 1083-1153 .... **CMLC 25**

Annensky, Innokentii Fedorovich
See Annensky, Innokenty (Fyodorovich)

Annensky, Innokenty (Fyodorovich)
1856-1909 .... **TCLC 14**
See also CA 110; 155; DLB 295; EWL 3

Annunzio, Gabriele d'
See D'Annunzio, Gabriele

Anodos
See Coleridge, Mary E(lizabeth)

Anon, Charles Robert
See Pessoa, Fernando

Anouilh, Jean 1910-1987 ..... **CLC 1, 3, 8, 13, 40, 50; DC 8, 21; TCLC 195**
See also AAYA 67; CA 17-20R; 123; CANR 32; DAM DRAM; DFS 9, 10, 19; DLB 321; EW 13; EWL 3; GFL 1789 to the Present; MTCW 1, 2; MTFW 2005; RGWL 2, 3; TWA

Ansa, Tina McElroy 1949- .... **BLC 2:1**
See also BW 2; CA 142; CANR 143; CSW

Anselm of Canterbury
1033(?)-1109 .... **CMLC 67**
See also DLB 115

Anthony, Florence
See Ai

Anthony, John
See Ciardi, John (Anthony)

Anthony, Peter
See Shaffer, Anthony; Shaffer, Peter

Anthony, Piers 1934- .... **CLC 35**
See also AAYA 11, 48; BYA 7; CA 200; CAAE 200; CANR 28, 56, 73, 102, 133; CLR 118; CPW; DAM POP; DLB 8; FANT; MAICYA 2; MAICYAS 1; MTCW 1, 2; MTFW 2005; SAAS 22; SATA 84, 129; SATA-Essay 129; SFW 4; SUFW 1, 2; YAW

Anthony, Susan B(rownell)
1820-1906 .... **TCLC 84**
See also CA 211; FW

Antiphon c. 480B.C.-c. 411B.C. .... **CMLC 55**

Antoine, Marc
See Proust, (Valentin-Louis-George-Eugene) Marcel

Antoninus, Brother
See Everson, William (Oliver)

Antonioni, Michelangelo
1912-2007 .... **CLC 20, 144, 259**
See also CA 73-76; 262; CANR 45, 77

Antschel, Paul 1920-1970 .... **CLC 10, 19, 53, 82; PC 10**
See also CA 85-88; CANR 33, 61; CDWLB 2; DLB 69; EWL 3; MTCW 1; PFS 21; RGHL; RGWL 2, 3

Anwar, Chairil 1922-1949 .... **TCLC 22**
See also CA 121; 219; EWL 3; RGWL 3

Anyidoho, Kofi 1947- .... **BLC 2:1**
See also BW 3; CA 178; CP 5, 6, 7; DLB 157; EWL 3

Anzaldua, Gloria (Evanjelina)
1942-2004 .... **CLC 200; HLCS 1**
See also CA 175; 227; CSW; CWP; DLB 122; FW; LLW; RGAL 4; SATA-Obit 154

Apess, William 1798-1839(?) .... **NCLC 73; NNAL**
See also DAM MULT; DLB 175, 243

Apollinaire, Guillaume 1880-1918 .... **PC 7; TCLC 3, 8, 51**
See also CA 104; 152; DAM POET; DLB 258, 321; EW 9; EWL 3; GFL 1789 to the Present; MTCW 2; PFS 24; RGWL 2, 3; TWA; WP

Apollonius of Rhodes
See Apollonius Rhodius

Apollonius Rhodius c. 300B.C.-c. 220B.C. .... **CMLC 28**
See also AW 1; DLB 176; RGWL 2, 3

Appelfeld, Aharon 1932- ... **CLC 23, 47; SSC 42**
See also CA 112; 133; CANR 86, 160; CWW 2; DLB 299; EWL 3; RGHL; RGSF 2; WLIT 6

Appelfeld, Aron
See Appelfeld, Aharon

Apple, Max (Isaac) 1941- .... **CLC 9, 33; SSC 50**
See also AMWS 17; CA 81-84; CANR 19, 54; DLB 130

Appleman, Philip (Dean) 1926- .... **CLC 51**
See also CA 13-16R; CAAS 18; CANR 6, 29, 56

Appleton, Lawrence
See Lovecraft, H. P.

Apteryx
See Eliot, T(homas) S(tearns)

Apuleius, (Lucius Madaurensis) c. 125-c. 164 .... **CMLC 1, 84**
See also AW 2; CDWLB 1; DLB 211; RGWL 2, 3; SUFW; WLIT 8

Aquin, Hubert 1929-1977 .... **CLC 15**
See also CA 105; DLB 53; EWL 3

Aquinas, Thomas 1224(?)-1274 ..... **CMLC 33**
See also DLB 115; EW 1; TWA

Aragon, Louis 1897-1982 .... **CLC 3, 22; TCLC 123**
See also CA 69-72; 108; CANR 28, 71; DAM NOV, POET; DLB 72, 258; EW 11; EWL 3; GFL 1789 to the Present; GLL 2; LMFS 2; MTCW 1, 2; RGWL 2, 3

Arany, Janos 1817-1882 .... **NCLC 34**

Aranyos, Kakay 1847-1910
See Mikszath, Kalman

Aratus of Soli c. 315B.C.-c. 240B.C. .... **CMLC 64**
See also DLB 176

Arbuthnot, John 1667-1735 .... **LC 1**
See also DLB 101

Archer, Herbert Winslow
See Mencken, H(enry) L(ouis)

Archer, Jeffrey 1940- .... **CLC 28**
See also AAYA 16; BEST 89:3; BPFB 1; CA 77-80; CANR 22, 52, 95, 136; CPW; DA3; DAM POP; INT CANR-22; MTFW 2005

Archer, Jeffrey Howard
See Archer, Jeffrey

Archer, Jules 1915- .... **CLC 12**
See also CA 9-12R; CANR 6, 69; SAAS 5; SATA 4, 85

Archer, Lee
See Ellison, Harlan

Archilochus c. 7th cent. B.C.- .... **CMLC 44**
See also DLB 176

Ard, William
See Jakes, John

Arden, John 1930- .... **CLC 6, 13, 15**
See also BRWS 2; CA 13-16R; CAAS 4; CANR 31, 65, 67, 124; CBD; CD 5, 6; DAM DRAM; DFS 9; DLB 13, 245; EWL 3; MTCW 1

Arenas, Reinaldo 1943-1990 .. **CLC 41; HLC 1; TCLC 191**
See also CA 124; 128; 133; CANR 73, 106; DAM MULT; DLB 145; EWL 3; GLL 2; HW 1; LAW; LAWS 1; MTCW 2; MTFW 2005; RGSF 2; RGWL 3; WLIT 1

Arendt, Hannah 1906-1975 .... **CLC 66, 98; TCLC 193**
See also CA 17-20R; 61-64; CANR 26, 60, 172; DLB 242; MTCW 1, 2

Aretino, Pietro 1492-1556 .... **LC 12, 165**
See also RGWL 2, 3

Arghezi, Tudor
See Theodorescu, Ion N.

Arguedas, Jose Maria 1911-1969 .... **CLC 10, 18; HLCS 1; TCLC 147**
See also CA 89-92; CANR 73; DLB 113; EWL 3; HW 1; LAW; RGWL 2, 3; WLIT 1

Argueta, Manlio 1936- .... **CLC 31**
See also CA 131; CANR 73; CWW 2; DLB 145; EWL 3; HW 1; RGWL 3

Arias, Ron 1941- .... **HLC 1**
See also CA 131; CANR 81, 136; DAM MULT; DLB 82; HW 1, 2; MTCW 2; MTFW 2005

Ariosto, Lodovico
See Ariosto, Ludovico

Ariosto, Ludovico 1474-1533 ... **LC 6, 87; PC 42**
See also EW 2; RGWL 2, 3; WLIT 7

Aristides
See Epstein, Joseph

Aristophanes 450B.C.-385B.C. .... **CMLC 4, 51; DC 2; WLCS**
See also AW 1; CDWLB 1; DA; DA3; DAB; DAC; DAM DRAM, MST; DFS 10; DLB 176; LMFS 1; RGWL 2, 3; TWA; WLIT 8

Aristotle 384B.C.-322B.C. .... **CMLC 31; WLCS**
See also AW 1; CDWLB 1; DA; DA3; DAB; DAC; DAM MST; DLB 176; RGWL 2, 3; TWA; WLIT 8

Arlt, Roberto (Godofredo Christophersen) 1900-1942 .... **HLC 1; TCLC 29**
See also CA 123; 131; CANR 67; DAM MULT; DLB 305; EWL 3; HW 1, 2; IDTP; LAW

Armah, Ayi Kwei 1939- . **BLC 1:1, 2:1; CLC 5, 33, 136**
See also AFW; BRWS 10; BW 1; CA 61-64; CANR 21, 64; CDWLB 3; CN 1, 2, 3, 4, 5, 6, 7; DAM MULT, POET; DLB 117; EWL 3; MTCW 1; WLIT 2

Armatrading, Joan 1950- .... **CLC 17**
See also CA 114; 186

Armin, Robert 1568(?)-1615(?) .... **LC 120**

Armitage, Frank
See Carpenter, John (Howard)

Armstrong, Jeannette (C.) 1948- .... **NNAL**
See also CA 149; CCA 1; CN 6, 7; DAC; DLB 334; SATA 102

Arnette, Robert
See Silverberg, Robert

Arnim, Achim von (Ludwig Joachim von Arnim) 1781-1831 .. **NCLC 5, 159; SSC 29**
See also DLB 90

Arnim, Bettina von 1785-1859 ...... **NCLC 38, 123**
See also DLB 90; RGWL 2, 3

Arnold, Matthew 1822-1888 ..... **NCLC 6, 29, 89, 126; PC 5, 94; WLC 1**
See also BRW 5; CDBLB 1832-1890; DA; DAB; DAC; DAM MST, POET; DLB 32, 57; EXPP; PAB; PFS 2; TEA; WP

Arnold, Thomas 1795-1842 .... **NCLC 18**
See also DLB 55

Arnow, Harriette (Louisa) Simpson 1908-1986 ...... **CLC 2, 7, 18; TCLC 196**
See also BPFB 1; CA 9-12R; 118; CANR 14; CN 2, 3, 4; DLB 6; FW; MTCW 1, 2; RHW; SATA 42; SATA-Obit 47

Arouet, Francois-Marie
See Voltaire

Arp, Hans
See Arp, Jean

Arp, Jean 1887-1966 .... **CLC 5; TCLC 115**
See also CA 81-84; 25-28R; CANR 42, 77; EW 10

Arrabal
See Arrabal, Fernando

Arrabal (Teran), Fernando
See Arrabal, Fernando

Arrabal, Fernando 1932- ... **CLC 2, 9, 18, 58**
See also CA 9-12R; CANR 15; CWW 2; DLB 321; EWL 3; LMFS 2

Arreola, Juan Jose 1918-2001 .... **CLC 147; HLC 1; SSC 38**
See also CA 113; 131; 200; CANR 81; CWW 2; DAM MULT; DLB 113; DNFS 2; EWL 3; HW 1, 2; LAW; RGSF 2

Arrian c. 89(?)-c. 155(?) .... **CMLC 43**
See also DLB 176

Arrick, Fran
See Angell, Judie

Arrley, Richmond
See Delany, Samuel R., Jr.

Artaud, Antonin (Marie Joseph) 1896-1948 .... **DC 14; TCLC 3, 36**
See also CA 104; 149; DA3; DAM DRAM; DFS 22; DLB 258, 321; EW 11; EWL 3; GFL 1789 to the Present; MTCW 2; MTFW 2005; RGWL 2, 3

Arthur, Ruth M(abel) 1905-1979 ..... **CLC 12**
See also CA 9-12R; 85-88; CANR 4; CWRI 5; SATA 7, 26

Artsybashev, Mikhail (Petrovich) 1878-1927 .... **TCLC 31**
See also CA 170; DLB 295

Arundel, Honor (Morfydd) 1919-1973 .... **CLC 17**
See also CA 21-22; 41-44R; CAP 2; CLR 35; CWRI 5; SATA 4; SATA-Obit 24

Arzner, Dorothy 1900-1979 .... **CLC 98**

Asch, Sholem 1880-1957 .... **TCLC 3**
See also CA 105; DLB 333; EWL 3; GLL 2; RGHL

Ascham, Roger 1516(?)-1568 .... **LC 101**
See also DLB 236

Ash, Shalom
See Asch, Sholem

Ashbery, John 1927- ... **CLC 2, 3, 4, 6, 9, 13, 15, 25, 41, 77, 125, 221; PC 26**
See also AMWS 3; CA 5-8R; CANR 9, 37, 66, 102, 132, 170; CP 1, 2, 3, 4, 5, 6, 7; DA3; DAM POET; DLB 5, 165; DLBY 1981; EWL 3; GLL 1; INT CANR-9; MAL 5; MTCW 1, 2; MTFW 2005; PAB; PFS 11, 28; RGAL 4; TCLE 1:1; WP

Ashbery, John Lawrence
See Ashbery, John

Ashbridge, Elizabeth 1713-1755 .... **LC 147**
See also DLB 200

Ashdown, Clifford
See Freeman, R(ichard) Austin

Ashe, Gordon
See Creasey, John

Ashton-Warner, Sylvia (Constance) 1908-1984 .... **CLC 19**
See also CA 69-72; 112; CANR 29; CN 1, 2, 3; MTCW 1, 2

Asimov, Isaac 1920-1992 ..... **CLC 1, 3, 9, 19, 26, 76, 92**
See also AAYA 13; BEST 90:2; BPFB 1; BYA 4, 6, 7, 9; CA 1-4R; 137; CANR 2, 19, 36, 60, 125; CLR 12, 79; CMW 4; CN 1, 2, 3, 4, 5; CPW; DA3; DAM POP; DLB 8; DLBY 1992; INT CANR-19; JRDA; LAIT 5; LMFS 2; MAICYA 1, 2; MAL 5; MTCW 1, 2; MTFW 2005; NFS 29; RGAL 4; SATA 1, 26, 74; SCFW 1, 2; SFW 4; SSFS 17; TUS; YAW

Askew, Anne 1521(?)-1546 .... **LC 81**
See also DLB 136

Assis, Joaquim Maria Machado de
See Machado de Assis, Joaquim Maria

Astell, Mary 1666-1731 .... **LC 68**
See also DLB 252, 336; FW

Beardsley, Aubrey 1872-1898 .... **NCLC 6**

Beattie, Ann 1947- ..... **CLC 8, 13, 18, 40, 63, 146; SSC 11**
    See also AMWS 5; BEST 90:2; BPFB 1; CA 81-84; CANR 53, 73, 128; CN 4, 5, 6, 7; CPW; DA3; DAM NOV, POP; DLB 218, 278; DLBY 1982; EWL 3; MAL 5; MTCW 1, 2; MTFW 2005; RGAL 4; RGSF 2; SSFS 9; TUS

Beattie, James 1735-1803 .... **NCLC 25**
    See also DLB 109

Beauchamp, Kathleen Mansfield 1888-1923 . **SSC 9, 23, 38, 81; TCLC 2, 8, 39, 164; WLC 4**
    See also BPFB 2; BRW 7; CA 104; 134; DA; DA3; DAB; DAC; DAM MST; DLB 162; EWL 3; EXPS; FW; GLL 1; MTCW 2; RGEL 2; RGSF 2; SSFS 2, 8, 10, 11; TEA; WWE 1

Beaumarchais, Pierre-Augustin Caron de 1732-1799 .... **DC 4; LC 61**
    See also DAM DRAM; DFS 14, 16; DLB 313; EW 4; GFL Beginnings to 1789; RGWL 2, 3

Beaumont, Francis 1584(?)-1616 .. **DC 6; LC 33**
    See also BRW 2; CDBLB Before 1660; DLB 58; TEA

Beauvoir, Simone de 1908-1986 .... **CLC 1, 2, 4, 8, 14, 31, 44, 50, 71, 124; SSC 35; WLC 1**
    See also BPFB 1; CA 9-12R; 118; CANR 28, 61; DA; DA3; DAB; DAC; DAM MST, NOV; DLB 72; DLBY 1986; EW 12; EWL 3; FL 1:5; FW; GFL 1789 to the Present; LMFS 2; MTCW 1, 2; MTFW 2005; RGSF 2; RGWL 2, 3; TWA

Beauvoir, Simone Lucie Ernestine Marie Bertrand de
    See Beauvoir, Simone de

Becker, Carl (Lotus) 1873-1945 ..... **TCLC 63**
    See also CA 157; DLB 17

Becker, Jurek 1937-1997 .... **CLC 7, 19**
    See also CA 85-88; 157; CANR 60, 117; CWW 2; DLB 75, 299; EWL 3; RGHL

Becker, Walter 1950- .... **CLC 26**

Becket, Thomas a 1118(?)-1170 .... **CMLC 83**

Beckett, Samuel 1906-1989 .... **CLC 1, 2, 3, 4, 6, 9, 10, 11, 14, 18, 29, 57, 59, 83; DC 22; SSC 16, 74; TCLC 145; WLC 1**
    See also BRWC 2; BRWR 1; BRWS 1; CA 5-8R; 130; CANR 33, 61; CBD; CDBLB 1945-1960; CN 1, 2, 3, 4; CP 1, 2, 3, 4; DA; DA3; DAB; DAC; DAM DRAM, MST, NOV; DFS 2, 7, 18; DLB 13, 15, 233, 319, 321, 329; DLBY 1990; EWL 3; GFL 1789 to the Present; LATS 1:2; LMFS 2; MTCW 1, 2; MTFW 2005; RGSF 2; RGWL 2, 3; SSFS 15; TEA; WLIT 4

Beckford, William 1760-1844 .... **NCLC 16, 214**
    See also BRW 3; DLB 39, 213; GL 2; HGG; LMFS 1; SUFW

Beckham, Barry (Earl) 1944- .... **BLC 1:1**
    See also BW 1; CA 29-32R; CANR 26, 62; CN 1, 2, 3, 4, 5, 6; DAM MULT; DLB 33

Beckman, Gunnel 1910- .... **CLC 26**
    See also CA 33-36R; CANR 15, 114; CLR 25; MAICYA 1, 2; SAAS 9; SATA 6

Becque, Henri 1837-1899 .... **DC 21; NCLC 3**
    See also DLB 192; GFL 1789 to the Present

Becquer, Gustavo Adolfo 1836-1870 .... **HLCS 1; NCLC 106**
    See also DAM MULT

Beddoes, Thomas Lovell 1803-1849 .. **DC 15; NCLC 3, 154**
    See also BRWS 11; DLB 96

Bede c. 673-735 .... **CMLC 20**
    See also DLB 146; TEA

Bedford, Denton R. 1907-(?) .... **NNAL**

Bedford, Donald F.
    See Fearing, Kenneth (Flexner)

Beecher, Catharine Esther 1800-1878 .... **NCLC 30**
    See also DLB 1, 243

Beecher, John 1904-1980 .... **CLC 6**
    See also AITN 1; CA 5-8R; 105; CANR 8; CP 1, 2, 3

Beer, Johann 1655-1700 .... **LC 5**
    See also DLB 168

Beer, Patricia 1924- .... **CLC 58**
    See also BRWS 14; CA 61-64; 183; CANR 13, 46; CP 1, 2, 3, 4, 5, 6; CWP; DLB 40; FW

Beerbohm, Max
    See Beerbohm, (Henry) Max(imilian)

Beerbohm, (Henry) Max(imilian) 1872-1956 .... **TCLC 1, 24**
    See also BRWS 2; CA 104; 154; CANR 79; DLB 34, 100; FANT; MTCW 2

Beer-Hofmann, Richard 1866-1945 .... **TCLC 60**
    See also CA 160; DLB 81

Beg, Shemus
    See Stephens, James

Begiebing, Robert J(ohn) 1946- .... **CLC 70**
    See also CA 122; CANR 40, 88

Begley, Louis 1933- .... **CLC 197**
    See also CA 140; CANR 98, 176; DLB 299; RGHL; TCLE 1:1

Behan, Brendan (Francis) 1923-1964 .... **CLC 1, 8, 11, 15, 79**
    See also BRWS 2; CA 73-76; CANR 33, 121; CBD; CDBLB 1945-1960; DAM DRAM; DFS 7; DLB 13, 233; EWL 3; MTCW 1, 2

Behn, Aphra 1640(?)-1689 .. **DC 4; LC 1, 30, 42, 135; PC 13, 88; WLC 1**
    See also BRWS 3; DA; DA3; DAB; DAC; DAM DRAM, MST, NOV, POET; DFS 16, 24; DLB 39, 80, 131; FW; TEA; WLIT 3

Behrman, S(amuel) N(athaniel) 1893-1973 .... **CLC 40**
    See also CA 13-16; 45-48; CAD; CAP 1; DLB 7, 44; IDFW 3; MAL 5; RGAL 4

Bekederemo, J. P. Clark
    See Clark Bekederemo, J.P.

Belasco, David 1853-1931 .... **TCLC 3**
    See also CA 104; 168; DLB 7; MAL 5; RGAL 4

Belcheva, Elisaveta Lyubomirova 1893-1991 .... **CLC 10**
    See also CA 178; CDWLB 4; DLB 147; EWL 3

Beldone, Phil "Cheech"
    See Ellison, Harlan

Beleno
    See Azuela, Mariano

Belinski, Vissarion Grigoryevich 1811-1848 .... **NCLC 5**
    See also DLB 198

Belitt, Ben 1911- .... **CLC 22**
    See also CA 13-16R; CAAS 4; CANR 7, 77; CP 1, 2, 3, 4, 5, 6; DLB 5

Belknap, Jeremy 1744-1798 .... **LC 115**
    See also DLB 30, 37

Bell, Gertrude (Margaret Lowthian) 1868-1926 .... **TCLC 67**
    See also CA 167; CANR 110; DLB 174

Bell, J. Freeman
    See Zangwill, Israel

Bell, James Madison 1826-1902 ..... **BLC 1:1; TCLC 43**
    See also BW 1; CA 122; 124; DAM MULT; DLB 50

Bell, Madison Smartt 1957- ..... **CLC 41, 102, 223**
    See also AMWS 10; BPFB 1; CA 111, 183; CAAE 183; CANR 28, 54, 73, 134, 176; CN 5, 6, 7; CSW; DLB 218, 278; MTCW 2; MTFW 2005

Bell, Marvin (Hartley) 1937- ...... **CLC 8, 31; PC 79**
    See also CA 21-24R; CAAS 14; CANR 59, 102; CP 1, 2, 3, 4, 5, 6, 7; DAM POET; DLB 5; MAL 5; MTCW 1; PFS 25

Bell, W. L. D.
    See Mencken, H(enry) L(ouis)

Bellamy, Atwood C.
    See Mencken, H(enry) L(ouis)

Bellamy, Edward 1850-1898 ..... **NCLC 4, 86, 147**
    See also DLB 12; NFS 15; RGAL 4; SFW 4

Belli, Gioconda 1948- .... **HLCS 1**
    See also CA 152; CANR 143; CWW 2; DLB 290; EWL 3; RGWL 3

Bellin, Edward J.
    See Kuttner, Henry

Bello, Andres 1781-1865 .... **NCLC 131**
    See also LAW

Belloc, (Joseph) Hilaire (Pierre Sebastien Rene Swanton) 1870-1953 .... **PC 24; TCLC 7, 18**
    See also CA 106; 152; CLR 102; CWRI 5; DAM POET; DLB 19, 100, 141, 174; EWL 3; MTCW 1; MTFW 2005; SATA 112; WCH; YABC 1

Belloc, Joseph Peter Rene Hilaire
    See Belloc, (Joseph) Hilaire (Pierre Sebastien Rene Swanton)

Belloc, Joseph Pierre Hilaire
    See Belloc, (Joseph) Hilaire (Pierre Sebastien Rene Swanton)

Belloc, M. A.
    See Lowndes, Marie Adelaide (Belloc)

Belloc-Lowndes, Mrs.
    See Lowndes, Marie Adelaide (Belloc)

Bellow, Saul 1915-2005 ...... **CLC 1, 2, 3, 6, 8, 10, 13, 15, 25, 33, 34, 63, 79, 190, 200; SSC 14, 101; WLC 1**
    See also AITN 2; AMW; AMWC 2; AMWR 2; BEST 89:3; BPFB 1; CA 5-8R; 238; CABS 1; CANR 29, 53, 95, 132; CDALB 1941-1968; CN 1, 2, 3, 4, 5, 6, 7; DA; DA3; DAB; DAC; DAM MST, NOV, POP; DLB 2, 28, 299, 329; DLBD 3; DLBY 1982; EWL 3; MAL 5; MTCW 1, 2; MTFW 2005; NFS 4, 14, 26; RGAL 4; RGHL; RGSF 2; SSFS 12, 22; TUS

Belser, Reimond Karel Maria de 1929- .... **CLC 14**
    See also CA 152

Bely, Andrey
    See Bugayev, Boris Nikolayevich

Belyi, Andrei
    See Bugayev, Boris Nikolayevich

Bembo, Pietro 1470-1547 .... **LC 79**
    See also RGWL 2, 3

Benary, Margot
    See Benary-Isbert, Margot

Benary-Isbert, Margot 1889-1979 .... **CLC 12**
    See also CA 5-8R; 89-92; CANR 4, 72; CLR 12; MAICYA 1, 2; SATA 2; SATA-Obit 21

Benavente (y Martinez), Jacinto 1866-1954 .... **DC 26; HLCS 1; TCLC 3**
    See also CA 106; 131; CANR 81; DAM DRAM, MULT; DLB 329; EWL 3; GLL 2; HW 1, 2; MTCW 1, 2

Benchley, Peter 1940-2006 .... **CLC 4, 8**
See also AAYA 14; AITN 2; BPFB 1; CA 17-20R; 248; CANR 12, 35, 66, 115; CPW; DAM NOV, POP; HGG; MTCW 1, 2; MTFW 2005; SATA 3, 89, 164

Benchley, Peter Bradford
See Benchley, Peter

Benchley, Robert (Charles)
1889-1945 .... **TCLC 1, 55**
See also CA 105; 153; DLB 11; MAL 5; RGAL 4

Benda, Julien 1867-1956 .... **TCLC 60**
See also CA 120; 154; GFL 1789 to the Present

Benedict, Ruth 1887-1948 .... **TCLC 60**
See also CA 158; CANR 146; DLB 246

Benedict, Ruth Fulton
See Benedict, Ruth

Benedikt, Michael 1935- .... **CLC 4, 14**
See also CA 13-16R; CANR 7; CP 1, 2, 3, 4, 5, 6, 7; DLB 5

Benet, Juan 1927-1993 .... **CLC 28**
See also CA 143; EWL 3

Benet, Stephen Vincent 1898-1943 ..... **PC 64; SSC 10, 86; TCLC 7**
See also AMWS 11; CA 104; 152; DA3; DAM POET; DLB 4, 48, 102, 249, 284; DLBY 1997; EWL 3; HGG; MAL 5; MTCW 2; MTFW 2005; RGAL 4; RGSF 2; SSFS 22; SUFW; WP; YABC 1

Benet, William Rose 1886-1950 ..... **TCLC 28**
See also CA 118; 152; DAM POET; DLB 45; RGAL 4

Benford, Gregory 1941- .... **CLC 52**
See also BPFB 1; CA 69-72, 175, 268; CAAE 175, 268; CAAS 27; CANR 12, 24, 49, 95, 134; CN 7; CSW; DLBY 1982; MTFW 2005; SCFW 2; SFW 4

Benford, Gregory Albert
See Benford, Gregory

Bengtsson, Frans (Gunnar)
1894-1954 .... **TCLC 48**
See also CA 170; EWL 3

Benjamin, David
See Slavitt, David R.

Benjamin, Lois
See Gould, Lois

Benjamin, Walter 1892-1940 .... **TCLC 39**
See also CA 164; CANR 181; DLB 242; EW 11; EWL 3

Ben Jelloun, Tahar 1944- .... **CLC 180**
See also CA 135, 162; CANR 100, 166; CWW 2; EWL 3; RGWL 3; WLIT 2

Benn, Gottfried 1886-1956 .. **PC 35; TCLC 3**
See also CA 106; 153; DLB 56; EWL 3; RGWL 2, 3

Bennett, Alan 1934- .... **CLC 45, 77**
See also BRWS 8; CA 103; CANR 35, 55, 106, 157; CBD; CD 5, 6; DAB; DAM MST; DLB 310; MTCW 1, 2; MTFW 2005

Bennett, (Enoch) Arnold
1867-1931 .... **TCLC 5, 20, 197**
See also BRW 6; CA 106; 155; CDBLB 1890-1914; DLB 10, 34, 98, 135; EWL 3; MTCW 2

Bennett, Elizabeth
See Mitchell, Margaret (Munnerlyn)

Bennett, George Harold 1930- .... **CLC 5**
See also BW 1; CA 97-100; CAAS 13; CANR 87; DLB 33

Bennett, Gwendolyn B. 1902-1981 .... **HR 1:2**
See also BW 1; CA 125; DLB 51; WP

Bennett, Hal
See Bennett, George Harold

Bennett, Jay 1912- .... **CLC 35**
See also AAYA 10, 73; CA 69-72; CANR 11, 42, 79; JRDA; SAAS 4; SATA 41, 87; SATA-Brief 27; WYA; YAW

Bennett, Louise 1919-2006 .... **BLC 1:1; CLC 28**
See also BW 2, 3; CA 151; 252; CDWLB 3; CP 1, 2, 3, 4, 5, 6, 7; DAM MULT; DLB 117; EWL 3

Bennett, Louise Simone
See Bennett, Louise

Bennett-Coverley, Louise
See Bennett, Louise

Benoit de Sainte-Maure fl. 12th cent.
- .... **CMLC 90**

Benson, A. C. 1862-1925 .... **TCLC 123**
See also DLB 98

Benson, E(dward) F(rederic)
1867-1940 .... **TCLC 27**
See also CA 114; 157; DLB 135, 153; HGG; SUFW 1

Benson, Jackson J. 1930- .... **CLC 34**
See also CA 25-28R; DLB 111

Benson, Sally 1900-1972 .... **CLC 17**
See also CA 19-20; 37-40R; CAP 1; SATA 1, 35; SATA-Obit 27

Benson, Stella 1892-1933 .... **TCLC 17**
See also CA 117; 154, 155; DLB 36, 162; FANT; TEA

Bentham, Jeremy 1748-1832 .... **NCLC 38**
See also DLB 107, 158, 252

Bentley, E(dmund) C(lerihew)
1875-1956 .... **TCLC 12**
See also CA 108; 232; DLB 70; MSW

Bentley, Eric 1916- .... **CLC 24**
See also CA 5-8R; CAD; CANR 6, 67; CBD; CD 5, 6; INT CANR-6

Bentley, Eric Russell
See Bentley, Eric

ben Uzair, Salem
See Horne, Richard Henry Hengist

Beolco, Angelo 1496-1542 .... **LC 139**

Beranger, Pierre Jean de
1780-1857 .... **NCLC 34**

Berdyaev, Nicolas
See Berdyaev, Nikolai (Aleksandrovich)

Berdyaev, Nikolai (Aleksandrovich)
1874-1948 .... **TCLC 67**
See also CA 120; 157

Berdyayev, Nikolai (Aleksandrovich)
See Berdyaev, Nikolai (Aleksandrovich)

Berendt, John 1939- .... **CLC 86**
See also CA 146; CANR 75, 83, 151

Berendt, John Lawrence
See Berendt, John

Beresford, J(ohn) D(avys)
1873-1947 .... **TCLC 81**
See also CA 112; 155; DLB 162, 178, 197; SFW 4; SUFW 1

Bergelson, David (Rafailovich)
1884-1952 .... **TCLC 81**
See also CA 220; DLB 333; EWL 3

Bergelson, Dovid
See Bergelson, David (Rafailovich)

Berger, Colonel
See Malraux, (Georges-)Andre

Berger, John 1926- .... **CLC 2, 19**
See also BRWS 4; CA 81-84; CANR 51, 78, 117, 163; CN 1, 2, 3, 4, 5, 6, 7; DLB 14, 207, 319, 326

Berger, John Peter
See Berger, John

Berger, Melvin H. 1927- .... **CLC 12**
See also CA 5-8R; CANR 4, 142; CLR 32; SAAS 2; SATA 5, 88, 158; SATA-Essay 124

Berger, Thomas 1924- .... **CLC 3, 5, 8, 11, 18, 38, 259**
See also BPFB 1; CA 1-4R; CANR 5, 28, 51, 128; CN 1, 2, 3, 4, 5, 6, 7; DAM NOV; DLB 2; DLBY 1980; EWL 3; FANT; INT CANR-28; MAL 5; MTCW 1, 2; MTFW 2005; RHW; TCLE 1:1; TCWW 1, 2

Bergman, Ernst Ingmar
See Bergman, Ingmar

Bergman, Ingmar 1918-2007 ..... **CLC 16, 72, 210**
See also AAYA 61; CA 81-84; 262; CANR 33, 70; CWW 2; DLB 257; MTCW 2; MTFW 2005

Bergson, Henri(-Louis) 1859-1941 . **TCLC 32**
See also CA 164; DLB 329; EW 8; EWL 3; GFL 1789 to the Present

Bergstein, Eleanor 1938- .... **CLC 4**
See also CA 53-56; CANR 5

Berkeley, George 1685-1753 .... **LC 65**
See also DLB 31, 101, 252

Berkoff, Steven 1937- .... **CLC 56**
See also CA 104; CANR 72; CBD; CD 5, 6

Berlin, Isaiah 1909-1997 .... **TCLC 105**
See also CA 85-88; 162

Bermant, Chaim (Icyk) 1929-1998 ... **CLC 40**
See also CA 57-60; CANR 6, 31, 57, 105; CN 2, 3, 4, 5, 6

Bern, Victoria
See Fisher, M(ary) F(rances) K(ennedy)

Bernanos, (Paul Louis) Georges
1888-1948 .... **TCLC 3**
See also CA 104; 130; CANR 94; DLB 72; EWL 3; GFL 1789 to the Present; RGWL 2, 3

Bernard, April 1956- .... **CLC 59**
See also CA 131; CANR 144

Bernard, Mary Ann
See Soderbergh, Steven

Bernard of Clairvaux 1090-1153 .. **CMLC 71**
See also DLB 208

Bernard Silvestris fl. c. 1130-fl. c.
1160 .... **CMLC 87**
See also DLB 208

Bernart de Ventadorn c. 1130-c.
1190 .... **CMLC 98**

Berne, Victoria
See Fisher, M(ary) F(rances) K(ennedy)

Bernhard, Thomas 1931-1989 ..... **CLC 3, 32, 61; DC 14; TCLC 165**
See also CA 85-88; 127; CANR 32, 57; CD-WLB 2; DLB 85, 124; EWL 3; MTCW 1; RGHL; RGWL 2, 3

Bernhardt, Sarah (Henriette Rosine)
1844-1923 .... **TCLC 75**
See also CA 157

Bernstein, Charles 1950- .... **CLC 142**
See also CA 129; CAAS 24; CANR 90; CP 4, 5, 6, 7; DLB 169

Bernstein, Ingrid
See Kirsch, Sarah

Beroul fl. c. 12th cent. - .... **CMLC 75**

Berriault, Gina 1926-1999 .... **CLC 54, 109; SSC 30**
See also CA 116; 129; 185; CANR 66; DLB 130; SSFS 7,11

Berrigan, Daniel 1921- .... **CLC 4**
See also CA 33-36R; 187; CAAE 187; CAAS 1; CANR 11, 43, 78; CP 1, 2, 3, 4, 5, 6, 7; DLB 5

Berrigan, Edmund Joseph Michael, Jr.
1934-1983 .... **CLC 37**
See also CA 61-64; 110; CANR 14, 102; CP 1, 2, 3; DLB 5, 169; WP

Berrigan, Ted
See Berrigan, Edmund Joseph Michael, Jr.

Berry, Charles Edward Anderson
1931- .... **CLC 17**
See also CA 115

Berry, Chuck
See Berry, Charles Edward Anderson

Berry, Jonas
See Ashbery, John

Berry, Wendell 1934- .... **CLC 4, 6, 8, 27, 46; PC 28**
See also AITN 1; AMWS 10; ANW; CA 73-76; CANR 50, 73, 101, 132, 174; CP 1, 2, 3, 4, 5, 6, 7; CSW; DAM POET; DLB 5, 6, 234, 275, 342; MTCW 2; MTFW 2005; PFS 30; TCLE 1:1

Berryman, John 1914-1972 ... **CLC 1, 2, 3, 4, 6, 8, 10, 13, 25, 62; PC 64**
See also AMW; CA 13-16; 33-36R; CABS 2; CANR 35; CAP 1; CDALB 1941-1968; CP 1; DAM POET; DLB 48; EWL 3; MAL 5; MTCW 1, 2; MTFW 2005; PAB; PFS 27; RGAL 4; WP

Bertolucci, Bernardo 1940- ...... **CLC 16, 157**
See also CA 106; CANR 125

Berton, Pierre (Francis de Marigny) 1920-2004 .... **CLC 104**
See also CA 1-4R; 233; CANR 2, 56, 144; CPW; DLB 68; SATA 99; SATA-Obit 158

Bertrand, Aloysius 1807-1841 .... **NCLC 31**
See also DLB 217

Bertrand, Louis oAloysiusc
See Bertrand, Aloysius

Bertran de Born c. 1140-1215 .... **CMLC 5**

Besant, Annie (Wood) 1847-1933 ..... **TCLC 9**
See also CA 105; 185

Bessie, Alvah 1904-1985 .... **CLC 23**
See also CA 5-8R; 116; CANR 2, 80; DLB 26

Bestuzhev, Aleksandr Aleksandrovich 1797-1837 .... **NCLC 131**
See also DLB 198

Bethlen, T.D.
See Silverberg, Robert

Beti, Mongo
See Biyidi, Alexandre

Betjeman, John 1906-1984 ...... **CLC 2, 6, 10, 34, 43; PC 75**
See also BRW 7; CA 9-12R; 112; CANR 33, 56; CDBLB 1945-1960; CP 1, 2, 3; DA3; DAB; DAM MST, POET; DLB 20; DLBY 1984; EWL 3; MTCW 1, 2

Bettelheim, Bruno 1903-1990 .... **CLC 79; TCLC 143**
See also CA 81-84; 131; CANR 23, 61; DA3; MTCW 1, 2; RGHL

Betti, Ugo 1892-1953 .... **TCLC 5**
See also CA 104; 155; EWL 3; RGWL 2, 3

Betts, Doris (Waugh) 1932- ..... **CLC 3, 6, 28, 275; SSC 45**
See also CA 13-16R; CANR 9, 66, 77; CN 6, 7; CSW; DLB 218; DLBY 1982; INT CANR-9; RGAL 4

Bevan, Alistair
See Roberts, Keith (John Kingston)

Bey, Pilaff
See Douglas, (George) Norman

Beyala, Calixthe 1961- .... **BLC 2:1**
See also EWL 3

Beynon, John
See Harris, John (Wyndham Parkes Lucas) Beynon

Bialik, Chaim Nachman 1873-1934 .... **TCLC 25, 201**
See also CA 170; EWL 3; WLIT 6

Bialik, Hayyim Nahman
See Bialik, Chaim Nachman

Bickerstaff, Isaac
See Swift, Jonathan

Bidart, Frank 1939- .... **CLC 33**
See also AMWS 15; CA 140; CANR 106; CP 5, 6, 7; PFS 26

Bienek, Horst 1930- .... **CLC 7, 11**
See also CA 73-76; DLB 75

Bierce, Ambrose (Gwinett) 1842-1914(?) . **SSC 9, 72, 124; TCLC 1, 7, 44; WLC 1**
See also AAYA 55; AMW; BYA 11; CA 104; 139; CANR 78; CDALB 1865-1917; DA; DA3; DAC; DAM MST; DLB 11, 12, 23, 71, 74, 186; EWL 3; EXPS; HGG; LAIT 2; MAL 5; RGAL 4; RGSF 2; SSFS 9, 27; SUFW 1

Biggers, Earl Derr 1884-1933 .... **TCLC 65**
See also CA 108; 153; DLB 306

Billiken, Bud
See Motley, Willard (Francis)

Billings, Josh
See Shaw, Henry Wheeler

Billington, (Lady) Rachel (Mary) 1942- .... **CLC 43**
See also AITN 2; CA 33-36R; CANR 44; CN 4, 5, 6, 7

Binchy, Maeve 1940- .... **CLC 153**
See also BEST 90:1; BPFB 1; CA 127; 134; CANR 50, 96, 134; CN 5, 6, 7; CPW; DA3; DAM POP; DLB 319; INT CA-134; MTCW 2; MTFW 2005; RHW

Binyon, T(imothy) J(ohn) 1936-2004 .... **CLC 34**
See also CA 111; 232; CANR 28, 140

Bion 335B.C.-245B.C. .... **CMLC 39**

Bioy Casares, Adolfo 1914-1999 ... **CLC 4, 8, 13, 88; HLC 1; SSC 17, 102**
See also CA 29-32R; 177; CANR 19, 43, 66; CWW 2; DAM MULT; DLB 113; EWL 3; HW 1, 2; LAW; MTCW 1, 2; MTFW 2005; RGSF 2

Birch, Allison CLC 65

Bird, Cordwainer
See Ellison, Harlan

Bird, Robert Montgomery 1806-1854 .... **NCLC 1, 197**
See also DLB 202; RGAL 4

Birdwell, Cleo
See DeLillo, Don

Birkerts, Sven 1951- .... **CLC 116**
See also CA 128; 133, 176; CAAE 176; CAAS 29; CANR 151; INT CA-133

Birney, (Alfred) Earle 1904-1995 .. **CLC 1, 4, 6, 11; PC 52**
See also CA 1-4R; CANR 5, 20; CN 1, 2, 3, 4; CP 1, 2, 3, 4, 5, 6; DAC; DAM MST, POET; DLB 88; MTCW 1; PFS 8; RGEL 2

Biruni, al 973-1048(?) .... **CMLC 28**

Bishop, Elizabeth 1911-1979 ..... **CLC 1, 4, 9, 13, 15, 32; PC 3, 34; TCLC 121**
See also AMWR 2; AMWS 1; CA 5-8R; 89-92; CABS 2; CANR 26, 61, 108; CDALB 1968-1988; CP 1, 2, 3; DA; DA3; DAC; DAM MST; EWL 3; GLL 2; MAL 5; MBL; MTCW 1, 2; PAB; PFS 6, 12, 27; RGAL 4; SATA-Obit 24; TUS; WP

Bishop, George Archibald
See Crowley, Edward Alexander

Bishop, John 1935- .... **CLC 10**
See also CA 105

Bishop, John Peale 1892-1944 ..... **TCLC 103**
See also CA 107; 155; DLB 4, 9, 45; MAL 5; RGAL 4

Bissett, Bill 1939- .... **CLC 18; PC 14**
See also CA 69-72; CAAS 19; CANR 15; CCA 1; CP 1, 2, 3, 4, 5, 6, 7; DLB 53; MTCW 1

Bissoondath, Neil 1955- .... **CLC 120**
See also CA 136; CANR 123, 165; CN 6, 7; DAC

Bissoondath, Neil Devindra
See Bissoondath, Neil

Bitov, Andrei (Georgievich) 1937- ... **CLC 57**
See also CA 142; DLB 302

Biyidi, Alexandre 1932- ... **BLC 1:1; CLC 27**
See also AFW; BW 1, 3; CA 114; 124; CANR 81; DA3; DAM MULT; EWL 3; MTCW 1, 2

Bjarme, Brynjolf
See Ibsen, Henrik (Johan)

Bjoernson, Bjoernstjerne (Martinius) 1832-1910 .... **TCLC 7, 37**
See also CA 104

Black, Benjamin
See Banville, John

Black, Robert
See Holdstock, Robert

Blackburn, Paul 1926-1971 .... **CLC 9, 43**
See also BG 1:2; CA 81-84; 33-36R; CANR 34; CP 1; DLB 16; DLBY 1981

Black Elk 1863-1950 .... **NNAL; TCLC 33**
See also CA 144; DAM MULT; MTCW 2; MTFW 2005; WP

Black Hawk 1767-1838 .... **NNAL**

Black Hobart
See Sanders, (James) Ed(ward)

Blacklin, Malcolm
See Chambers, Aidan

Blackmore, R(ichard) D(oddridge) 1825-1900 .... **TCLC 27**
See also CA 120; DLB 18; RGEL 2

Blackmur, R(ichard) P(almer) 1904-1965 .... **CLC 2, 24**
See also AMWS 2; CA 11-12; 25-28R; CANR 71; CAP 1; DLB 63; EWL 3; MAL 5

Black Tarantula
See Acker, Kathy

Blackwood, Algernon 1869-1951 .... **SSC 107; TCLC 5**
See also AAYA 78; CA 105; 150; CANR 169; DLB 153, 156, 178; HGG; SUFW 1

Blackwood, Algernon Henry
See Blackwood, Algernon

Blackwood, Caroline (Maureen) 1931-1996 .... **CLC 6, 9, 100**
See also BRWS 9; CA 85-88; 151; CANR 32, 61, 65; CN 3, 4, 5, 6; DLB 14, 207; HGG; MTCW 1

Blade, Alexander
See Hamilton, Edmond; Silverberg, Robert

Blaga, Lucian 1895-1961 .... **CLC 75**
See also CA 157; DLB 220; EWL 3

Blair, Eric (Arthur) 1903-1950 .... **SSC 68; TCLC 2, 6, 15, 31, 51, 123, 128, 129; WLC 4**
See also BPFB 3; BRW 7; BYA 5; CA 104; 132; CDBLB 1945-1960; CLR 68; DA; DA3; DAB; DAC; DAM MST, NOV; DLB 15, 98, 195, 255; EWL 3; EXPN; LAIT 4, 5; LATS 1:1; MTCW 1, 2; MTFW 2005; NFS 3, 7; RGEL 2; SATA 29; SCFW 1, 2; SFW 4; SSFS 4; TEA; WLIT 4; YAW X

Blair, Hugh 1718-1800 .... **NCLC 75**

Blais, Marie-Claire 1939- .... **CLC 2, 4, 6, 13, 22**
See also CA 21-24R; CAAS 4; CANR 38, 75, 93; CWW 2; DAC; DAM MST; DLB 53; EWL 3; FW; MTCW 1, 2; MTFW 2005; TWA

Blaise, Clark 1940- .... **CLC 29, 261**
See also AITN 2; CA 53-56, 231; CAAE 231; CAAS 3; CANR 5, 66, 106; CN 4, 5, 6, 7; DLB 53; RGSF 2

Blake, Fairley
See De Voto, Bernard (Augustine)

Blake, Nicholas
See Day Lewis, C(ecil)

Blake, Sterling
See Benford, Gregory

Brady, Joan 1939- .... **CLC 86**
See also CA 141

Bragg, Melvyn 1939- .... **CLC 10**
See also BEST 89:3; CA 57-60; CANR 10, 48, 89, 158; CN 1, 2, 3, 4, 5, 6, 7; DLB 14, 271; RHW

Brahe, Tycho 1546-1601 .... **LC 45**
See also DLB 300

Braine, John (Gerard) 1922-1986 . **CLC 1, 3, 41**
See also CA 1-4R; 120; CANR 1, 33; CD-BLB 1945-1960; CN 1, 2, 3, 4; DLB 15; DLBY 1986; EWL 3; MTCW 1

Braithwaite, William Stanley (Beaumont) 1878-1962 ...... **BLC 1:1; HR 1:2; PC 52**
See also BW 1; CA 125; DAM MULT; DLB 50, 54; MAL 5

Bramah, Ernest 1868-1942 .... **TCLC 72**
See also CA 156; CMW 4; DLB 70; FANT

Brammer, Billy Lee
See Brammer, William

Brammer, William 1929-1978 .... **CLC 31**
See also CA 235; 77-80

Brancati, Vitaliano 1907-1954 .... **TCLC 12**
See also CA 109; DLB 264; EWL 3

Brancato, Robin F(idler) 1936- .... **CLC 35**
See also AAYA 9, 68; BYA 6; CA 69-72; CANR 11, 45; CLR 32; JRDA; MAICYA 2; MAICYAS 1; SAAS 9; SATA 97; WYA; YAW

Brand, Dionne 1953- .... **CLC 192**
See also BW 2; CA 143; CANR 143; CWP; DLB 334

Brand, Max
See Faust, Frederick (Schiller)

Brand, Millen 1906-1980 .... **CLC 7**
See also CA 21-24R; 97-100; CANR 72

Branden, Barbara 1929- .... **CLC 44**
See also CA 148

Brandes, Georg (Morris Cohen) 1842-1927 .... **TCLC 10**
See also CA 105; 189; DLB 300

Brandys, Kazimierz 1916-2000 .... **CLC 62**
See also CA 239; EWL 3

Branley, Franklyn M(ansfield) 1915-2002 .... **CLC 21**
See also CA 33-36R; 207; CANR 14, 39; CLR 13; MAICYA 1, 2; SAAS 16; SATA 4, 68, 136

Brant, Beth (E.) 1941- .... **NNAL**
See also CA 144; FW

Brant, Sebastian 1457-1521 .... **LC 112**
See also DLB 179; RGWL 2, 3

Brathwaite, Edward Kamau 1930- ..... **BLC 2:1; BLCS; CLC 11; PC 56**
See also BRWS 12; BW 2, 3; CA 25-28R; CANR 11, 26, 47, 107; CDWLB 3; CP 1, 2, 3, 4, 5, 6, 7; DAM POET; DLB 125; EWL 3

Brathwaite, Kamau
See Brathwaite, Edward Kamau

Brautigan, Richard (Gary) 1935-1984 .... **CLC 1, 3, 5, 9, 12, 34, 42; PC 94; TCLC 133**
See also BPFB 1; CA 53-56; 113; CANR 34; CN 1, 2, 3; CP 1, 2, 3, 4; DA3; DAM NOV; DLB 2, 5, 206; DLBY 1980, 1984; FANT; MAL 5; MTCW 1; RGAL 4; SATA 56

Brave Bird, Mary
See Crow Dog, Mary

Braverman, Kate 1950- .... **CLC 67**
See also CA 89-92; CANR 141; DLB 335

Brecht, (Eugen) Bertolt (Friedrich) 1898-1956 ..... **DC 3; TCLC 1, 6, 13, 35, 169; WLC 1**
See also CA 104; 133; CANR 62; CDWLB 2; DA; DA3; DAB; DAC; DAM DRAM, MST; DFS 4, 5, 9; DLB 56, 124; EW 11; EWL 3; IDTP; MTCW 1, 2; MTFW 2005; RGHL; RGWL 2, 3; TWA

Brecht, Eugen Berthold Friedrich
See Brecht, (Eugen) Bertolt (Friedrich)

Bremer, Fredrika 1801-1865 .... **NCLC 11**
See also DLB 254

Brennan, Christopher John 1870-1932 .... **TCLC 17**
See also CA 117; 188; DLB 230; EWL 3

Brennan, Maeve 1917-1993 ... **CLC 5; TCLC 124**
See also CA 81-84; CANR 72, 100

Brenner, Jozef 1887-1919 .... **TCLC 13**
See also CA 111; 240

Brent, Linda
See Jacobs, Harriet A(nn)

Brentano, Clemens (Maria) 1778-1842 .... **NCLC 1, 191; SSC 115**
See also DLB 90; RGWL 2, 3

Brent of Bin Bin
See Franklin, (Stella Maria Sarah) Miles (Lampe)

Brenton, Howard 1942- .... **CLC 31**
See also CA 69-72; CANR 33, 67; CBD; CD 5, 6; DLB 13; MTCW 1

Breslin, James
See Breslin, Jimmy

Breslin, Jimmy 1930- .... **CLC 4, 43**
See also CA 73-76; CANR 31, 75, 139, 187; DAM NOV; DLB 185; MTCW 2; MTFW 2005

Bresson, Robert 1901(?)-1999 .... **CLC 16**
See also CA 110; 187; CANR 49

Breton, Andre 1896-1966 .. **CLC 2, 9, 15, 54; PC 15**
See also CA 19-20; 25-28R; CANR 40, 60; CAP 2; DLB 65, 258; EW 11; EWL 3; GFL 1789 to the Present; LMFS 2; MTCW 1, 2; MTFW 2005; RGWL 2, 3; TWA; WP

Breton, Nicholas c. 1554-c. 1626 .... **LC 133**
See also DLB 136

Breytenbach, Breyten 1939(?)- .. **CLC 23, 37, 126**
See also CA 113; 129; CANR 61, 122; CWW 2; DAM POET; DLB 225; EWL 3

Bridgers, Sue Ellen 1942- .... **CLC 26**
See also AAYA 8, 49; BYA 7, 8; CA 65-68; CANR 11, 36; CLR 18; DLB 52; JRDA; MAICYA 1, 2; SAAS 1; SATA 22, 90; SATA-Essay 109; WYA; YAW

Bridges, Robert (Seymour) 1844-1930 .... **PC 28; TCLC 1**
See also BRW 6; CA 104; 152; CDBLB 1890-1914; DAM POET; DLB 19, 98

Bridie, James
See Mavor, Osborne Henry

Brin, David 1950- .... **CLC 34**
See also AAYA 21; CA 102; CANR 24, 70, 125, 127; INT CANR-24; SATA 65; SCFW 2; SFW 4

Brink, Andre 1935- .... **CLC 18, 36, 106**
See also AFW; BRWS 6; CA 104; CANR 39, 62, 109, 133, 182; CN 4, 5, 6, 7; DLB 225; EWL 3; INT CA-103; LATS 1:2; MTCW 1, 2; MTFW 2005; WLIT 2

Brinsmead, H. F.
See Brinsmead, H(esba) F(ay)

Brinsmead, H. F(ay)
See Brinsmead, H(esba) F(ay)

Brinsmead, H(esba) F(ay) 1922- ...... **CLC 21**
See also CA 21-24R; CANR 10; CLR 47; CWRI 5; MAICYA 1, 2; SAAS 5; SATA 18, 78

Brittain, Vera (Mary) 1893(?)-1970 . **CLC 23**
See also BRWS 10; CA 13-16; 25-28R; CANR 58; CAP 1; DLB 191; FW; MTCW 1, 2

Broch, Hermann 1886-1951 ... **TCLC 20, 204**
See also CA 117; 211; CDWLB 2; DLB 85, 124; EW 10; EWL 3; RGWL 2, 3

Brock, Rose
See Hansen, Joseph

Brod, Max 1884-1968 .... **TCLC 115**
See also CA 5-8R; 25-28R; CANR 7; DLB 81; EWL 3

Brodkey, Harold (Roy) 1930-1996 .. **CLC 56; TCLC 123**
See also CA 111; 151; CANR 71; CN 4, 5, 6; DLB 130

Brodsky, Iosif Alexandrovich 1940-1996
See Brodsky, Joseph
See also AAYA 71; AITN 1; AMWS 8; CA 41-44R; 151; CANR 37, 106; CWW 2; DA3; DAM POET; DLB 285, 329; EWL 3; MTCW 1, 2; MTFW 2005; RGWL 2, 3

Brodsky, Joseph **CLC 4, 6, 13, 36, 100; PC 9; TCLC 219**
See Brodsky, Iosif Alexandrovich

Brodsky, Michael 1948- .... **CLC 19**
See also CA 102; CANR 18, 41, 58, 147; DLB 244

Brodsky, Michael Mark
See Brodsky, Michael

Brodzki, Bella **CLC 65**

Brome, Richard 1590(?)-1652 .... **LC 61**
See also BRWS 10; DLB 58

Bromell, Henry 1947- .... **CLC 5**
See also CA 53-56; CANR 9, 115, 116

Bromfield, Louis (Brucker) 1896-1956 .... **TCLC 11**
See also CA 107; 155; DLB 4, 9, 86; RGAL 4; RHW

Broner, E(sther) M(asserman) 1930- .... **CLC 19**
See also CA 17-20R; CANR 8, 25, 72; CN 4, 5, 6; DLB 28

Bronk, William (M.) 1918-1999 .... **CLC 10**
See also CA 89-92; 177; CANR 23; CP 3, 4, 5, 6, 7; DLB 165

Bronstein, Lev Davidovich
See Trotsky, Leon

Bronte, Anne
See Bronte, Anne

Bronte, Anne 1820-1849 ..... **NCLC 4, 71, 102**
See also BRW 5; BRWR 1; DA3; DLB 21, 199, 340; NFS 26; TEA

Bronte, (Patrick) Branwell 1817-1848 .... **NCLC 109**
See also DLB 340

Bronte, Charlotte
See Bronte, Charlotte

Bronte, Charlotte 1816-1855 ...... **NCLC 3, 8, 33, 58, 105, 155; WLC 1**
See also AAYA 17; BRW 5; BRWC 2; BRWR 1; BYA 2; CDBLB 1832-1890; DA; DA3; DAB; DAC; DAM MST, NOV; DLB 21, 159, 199, 340; EXPN; FL 1:2; GL 2; LAIT 2; NFS 4; TEA; WLIT 4

Bronte, Emily
See Bronte, Emily (Jane)

Bronte, Emily (Jane) 1818-1848 ... **NCLC 16, 35, 165; PC 8; WLC 1**
See also AAYA 17; BPFB 1; BRW 5; BRWC 1; BRWR 1; BYA 3; CDBLB 1832-1890; DA; DA3; DAB; DAC; DAM MST, NOV, POET; DLB 21, 32, 199, 340; EXPN; FL 1:2; GL 2; LAIT 1; TEA; WLIT 3

Author Index

Buchanan, George 1506-1582 .... **LC 4**
See also DLB 132
Buchanan, Robert 1841-1901 .... **TCLC 107**
See also CA 179; DLB 18, 35
Buchheim, Lothar-Guenther
1918-2007 .... **CLC 6**
See also CA 85-88; 257
Buchner, (Karl) Georg
1813-1837 .... **NCLC 26, 146**
See also CDWLB 2; DLB 133; EW 6;
RGSF 2; RGWL 2, 3; TWA
Buchwald, Art 1925-2007 .... **CLC 33**
See also AITN 1; CA 5-8R; 256; CANR 21,
67, 107; MTCW 1, 2; SATA 10
Buchwald, Arthur
See Buchwald, Art
Buck, Pearl S(ydenstricker)
1892-1973 .... **CLC 7, 11, 18, 127**
See also AAYA 42; AITN 1; AMWS 2;
BPFB 1; CA 1-4R; 41-44R; CANR 1, 34;
CDALBS; CN 1; DA; DA3; DAB; DAC;
DAM MST, NOV; DLB 9, 102, 329; EWL
3; LAIT 3; MAL 5; MTCW 1, 2; MTFW
2005; NFS 25; RGAL 4; RHW; SATA 1,
25; TUS
Buckler, Ernest 1908-1984 .... **CLC 13**
See also CA 11-12; 114; CAP 1; CCA 1;
CN 1, 2, 3; DAC; DAM MST; DLB 68;
SATA 47
Buckley, Christopher 1952- .... **CLC 165**
See also CA 139; CANR 119, 180
Buckley, Christopher Taylor
See Buckley, Christopher
Buckley, Vincent (Thomas)
1925-1988 .... **CLC 57**
See also CA 101; CP 1, 2, 3, 4; DLB 289
Buckley, William F., Jr. 1925-2008 ... **CLC 7,
18, 37**
See also AITN 1; BPFB 1; CA 1-4R; 269;
CANR 1, 24, 53, 93, 133, 185; CMW 4;
CPW; DA3; DAM POP; DLB 137; DLBY
1980; INT CANR-24; MTCW 1, 2;
MTFW 2005; TUS
Buckley, William Frank
See Buckley, William F., Jr.
Buckley, William Frank, Jr.
See Buckley, William F., Jr.
Buechner, Frederick 1926- ..... **CLC 2, 4, 6, 9**
See also AMWS 12; BPFB 1; CA 13-16R;
CANR 11, 39, 64, 114, 138; CN 1, 2, 3,
4, 5, 6, 7; DAM NOV; DLBY 1980; INT
CANR-11; MAL 5; MTCW 1, 2; MTFW
2005; TCLE 1:1
Buell, John (Edward) 1927- .... **CLC 10**
See also CA 1-4R; CANR 71; DLB 53
Buero Vallejo, Antonio 1916-2000 ... **CLC 15,
46, 139, 226; DC 18**
See also CA 106; 189; CANR 24, 49, 75;
CWW 2; DFS 11; EWL 3; HW 1; MTCW
1, 2
Bufalino, Gesualdo 1920-1996 .... **CLC 74**
See also CA 209; CWW 2; DLB 196
Bugayev, Boris Nikolayevich
1880-1934 .... **PC 11; TCLC 7**
See also CA 104; 165; DLB 295; EW 9;
EWL 3; MTCW 2; MTFW 2005; RGWL
2, 3
Bukowski, Charles 1920-1994 ... **CLC 2, 5, 9,
41, 82, 108; PC 18; SSC 45**
See also CA 17-20R; 144; CANR 40, 62,
105, 180; CN 4, 5; CP 1, 2, 3, 4, 5; CPW;
DA3; DAM NOV, POET; DLB 5, 130,
169; EWL 3; MAL 5; MTCW 1, 2;
MTFW 2005; PFS 28
Bulgakov, Mikhail 1891-1940 .... **SSC 18;
TCLC 2, 16, 159**
See also AAYA 74; BPFB 1; CA 105; 152;
DAM DRAM, NOV; DLB 272; EWL 3;
MTCW 2; MTFW 2005; NFS 8; RGSF 2;
RGWL 2, 3; SFW 4; TWA

Bulgakov, Mikhail Afanasevich
See Bulgakov, Mikhail
Bulgya, Alexander Alexandrovich
1901-1956 .... **TCLC 53**
See also CA 117; 181; DLB 272; EWL 3
Bullins, Ed 1935- ...... **BLC 1:1; CLC 1, 5, 7;
DC 6**
See also BW 2, 3; CA 49-52; CAAS 16;
CAD; CANR 24, 46, 73, 134; CD 5, 6;
DAM DRAM, MULT; DLB 7, 38, 249;
EWL 3; MAL 5; MTCW 1, 2; MTFW
2005; RGAL 4
Bulosan, Carlos 1911-1956 .... **AAL**
See also CA 216; DLB 312; RGAL 4
**Bulwer-Lytton, Edward (George Earle
Lytton)** 1803-1873 .... **NCLC 1, 45**
See also DLB 21; RGEL 2; SFW 4; SUFW
1; TEA
Bunin, Ivan
See Bunin, Ivan Alexeyevich
Bunin, Ivan Alekseevich
See Bunin, Ivan Alexeyevich
Bunin, Ivan Alexeyevich 1870-1953 ... **SSC 5;
TCLC 6**
See also CA 104; DLB 317, 329; EWL 3;
RGSF 2; RGWL 2, 3; TWA
Bunting, Basil 1900-1985 ...... **CLC 10, 39, 47**
See also BRWS 7; CA 53-56; 115; CANR
7; CP 1, 2, 3, 4; DAM POET; DLB 20;
EWL 3; RGEL 2
Bunuel, Luis 1900-1983 ... **CLC 16, 80; HLC
1**
See also CA 101; 110; CANR 32, 77; DAM
MULT; HW 1
Bunyan, John 1628-1688 .. **LC 4, 69; WLC 1**
See also BRW 2; BYA 5; CDBLB 1660-
1789; CLR 124; DA; DAB; DAC; DAM
MST; DLB 39; RGEL 2; TEA; WCH;
WLIT 3
Buravsky, Alexandr CLC 59
Burchill, Julie 1959- .... **CLC 238**
See also CA 135; CANR 115, 116
Burckhardt, Jacob (Christoph)
1818-1897 .... **NCLC 49**
See also EW 6
Burford, Eleanor
See Hibbert, Eleanor Alice Burford
Burgess, Anthony 1917-1993 . **CLC 1, 2, 4, 5,
8, 10, 13, 15, 22, 40, 62, 81, 94**
See also AAYA 25; AITN 1; BRWS 1; CA
1-4R; 143; CANR 2, 46; CDBLB 1960 to
Present; CN 1, 2, 3, 4, 5; DA3; DAB;
DAC; DAM NOV; DLB 14, 194, 261;
DLBY 1998; EWL 3; MTCW 1, 2; MTFW
2005; NFS 15; RGEL 2; RHW; SFW 4;
TEA; YAW
Buridan, John c. 1295-c. 1358 ...... **CMLC 97**
Burke, Edmund 1729(?)-1797 .... **LC 7, 36,
146; WLC 1**
See also BRW 3; DA; DA3; DAB; DAC;
DAM MST; DLB 104, 252, 336; RGEL
2; TEA
Burke, Kenneth (Duva) 1897-1993 ... **CLC 2,
24**
See also AMW; CA 5-8R; 143; CANR 39,
74, 136; CN 1, 2; CP 1, 2, 3, 4, 5; DLB
45, 63; EWL 3; MAL 5; MTCW 1, 2;
MTFW 2005; RGAL 4
Burke, Leda
See Garnett, David
Burke, Ralph
See Silverberg, Robert
Burke, Thomas 1886-1945 .... **TCLC 63**
See also CA 113; 155; CMW 4; DLB 197
Burney, Fanny 1752-1840 .... **NCLC 12, 54,
107**
See also BRWS 3; DLB 39; FL 1:2; NFS
16; RGEL 2; TEA

Burney, Frances
See Burney, Fanny
Burns, Robert 1759-1796 ... **LC 3, 29, 40; PC
6; WLC 1**
See also AAYA 51; BRW 3; CDBLB 1789-
1832; DA; DA3; DAB; DAC; DAM MST,
POET; DLB 109; EXPP; PAB; RGEL 2;
TEA; WP
Burns, Tex
See L'Amour, Louis
Burnshaw, Stanley 1906-2005 ..... **CLC 3, 13,
44**
See also CA 9-12R; 243; CP 1, 2, 3, 4, 5, 6,
7; DLB 48; DLBY 1997
Burr, Anne 1937- .... **CLC 6**
See also CA 25-28R
Burroughs, Edgar Rice 1875-1950 . **TCLC 2,
32**
See also AAYA 11; BPFB 1; BYA 4, 9; CA
104; 132; CANR 131; DA3; DAM NOV;
DLB 8; FANT; MTCW 1, 2; MTFW
2005; RGAL 4; SATA 41; SCFW 1, 2;
SFW 4; TCWW 1, 2; TUS; YAW
Burroughs, William S. 1914-1997 . **CLC 1, 2,
5, 15, 22, 42, 75, 109; TCLC 121; WLC
1**
See also AAYA 60; AITN 2; AMWS 3; BG
1:2; BPFB 1; CA 9-12R; 160; CANR 20,
52, 104; CN 1, 2, 3, 4, 5, 6; CPW; DA;
DA3; DAB; DAC; DAM MST, NOV;
POP; DLB 2, 8, 16, 152, 237; DLBY
1981, 1997; EWL 3; GLL 1; HGG; LMFS
2; MAL 5; MTCW 1, 2; MTFW 2005;
RGAL 4; SFW 4
Burroughs, William Seward
See Burroughs, William S.
Burton, Sir Richard F(rancis)
1821-1890 .... **NCLC 42**
See also DLB 55, 166, 184; SSFS 21
Burton, Robert 1577-1640 .... **LC 74**
See also DLB 151; RGEL 2
Buruma, Ian 1951- .... **CLC 163**
See also CA 128; CANR 65, 141
Busch, Frederick 1941-2006 .. **CLC 7, 10, 18,
47, 166**
See also CA 33-36R; 248; CAAS 1; CANR
45, 73, 92, 157; CN 1, 2, 3, 4, 5, 6, 7;
DLB 6, 218
Busch, Frederick Matthew
See Busch, Frederick
Bush, Barney (Furman) 1946- .... **NNAL**
See also CA 145
Bush, Ronald 1946- .... **CLC 34**
See also CA 136
Busia, Abena, P. A. 1953- .... **BLC 2:1**
Bustos, F(rancisco)
See Borges, Jorge Luis
Bustos Domecq, H(onorio)
See Bioy Casares, Adolfo; Borges, Jorge
Luis
Butler, Octavia E. 1947-2006 .... **BLC 2:1;
BLCS; CLC 38, 121, 230, 240**
See also AAYA 18, 48; AFAW 2; AMWS
13; BPFB 1; BW 2, 3; CA 73-76; 248;
CANR 12, 24, 38, 73, 145, 240; CLR 65;
CN 7; CPW; DA3; DAM MULT, POP;
DLB 33; LATS 1:2; MTCW 1, 2; MTFW
2005; NFS 8, 21; SATA 84; SCFW 2;
SFW 4; SSFS 6; TCLE 1:1; YAW
Butler, Octavia Estelle
See Butler, Octavia E.
Butler, Robert Olen, (Jr.) 1945- ...... **CLC 81,
162; SSC 117**
See also AMWS 12; BPFB 1; CA 112;
CANR 66, 138; CN 7; CSW; DAM POP;
DLB 173, 335; INT CA-112; MAL 5;
MTCW 2; MTFW 2005; SSFS 11, 22
Butler, Samuel 1612-1680 . **LC 16, 43; PC 94**
See also DLB 101, 126; RGEL 2

Butler, Samuel 1835-1902 .... **TCLC 1, 33; WLC 1**
　　See also BRWS 2; CA 143; CDBLB 1890-1914; DA; DA3; DAB; DAC; DAM MST, NOV; DLB 18, 57, 174; RGEL 2; SFW 4; TEA

Butler, Walter C.
　　See Faust, Frederick (Schiller)

Butor, Michel (Marie Francois) 1926- .... **CLC 1, 3, 8, 11, 15, 161**
　　See also CA 9-12R; CANR 33, 66; CWW 2; DLB 83; EW 13; EWL 3; GFL 1789 to the Present; MTCW 1, 2; MTFW 2005

Butts, Mary 1890(?)-1937 ... **SSC 124; TCLC 77**
　　See also CA 148; DLB 240

Buxton, Ralph
　　See Silverstein, Alvin; Silverstein, Virginia B(arbara Opshelor)

Buzo, Alex
　　See Buzo, Alexander (John)

Buzo, Alexander (John) 1944- .... **CLC 61**
　　See also CA 97-100; CANR 17, 39, 69; CD 5, 6; DLB 289

Buzzati, Dino 1906-1972 .... **CLC 36**
　　See also CA 160; 33-36R; DLB 177; RGWL 2, 3; SFW 4

Byars, Betsy 1928- .... **CLC 35**
　　See also AAYA 19; BYA 3; CA 33-36R, 183; CAAE 183; CANR 18, 36, 57, 102, 148; CLR 1, 16, 72; DLB 52; INT CANR-18; JRDA; MAICYA 1, 2; MAICYAS 1; MTCW 1; SAAS 1; SATA 4, 46, 80, 163; SATA-Essay 108; WYA; YAW

Byars, Betsy Cromer
　　See Byars, Betsy

Byatt, Antonia Susan Drabble
　　See Byatt, A.S.

Byatt, A.S. 1936- .... **CLC 19, 65, 136, 223; SSC 91**
　　See also BPFB 1; BRWC 2; BRWS 4; CA 13-16R; CANR 13, 33, 50, 75, 96, 133; CN 1, 2, 3, 4, 5, 6; DA3; DAM NOV, POP; DLB 14, 194, 319, 326; EWL 3; MTCW 1, 2; MTFW 2005; RGSF 2; RHW; SSFS 26; TEA

Byrd, William II 1674-1744 .... **LC 112**
　　See also DLB 24, 140; RGAL 4

Byrne, David 1952- .... **CLC 26**
　　See also CA 127

Byrne, John Keyes 1926-2009 .... **CLC 19**
　　See also CA 102; CANR 78, 140; CBD; CD 5, 6; DFS 13, 24; DLB 13; INT CA-102

Byron, George Gordon (Noel) 1788-1824 ..... **DC 24; NCLC 2, 12, 109, 149; PC 16, 95; WLC 1**
　　See also AAYA 64; BRW 4; BRWC 2; CD-BLB 1789-1832; DA; DA3; DAB; DAC; DAM MST, POET; DLB 96, 110; EXPP; LMFS 1; PAB; PFS 1, 14, 29; RGEL 2; TEA; WLIT 3; WP

Byron, Robert 1905-1941 .... **TCLC 67**
　　See also CA 160; DLB 195

C. 3. 3.
　　See Wilde, Oscar

Caballero, Fernan 1796-1877 .... **NCLC 10**

Cabell, Branch
　　See Cabell, James Branch

Cabell, James Branch 1879-1958 .... **TCLC 6**
　　See also CA 105; 152; DLB 9, 78; FANT; MAL 5; MTCW 2; RGAL 4; SUFW 1

Cabeza de Vaca, Alvar Nunez 1490-1557(?) .... **LC 61**

Cable, George Washington 1844-1925 .... **SSC 4; TCLC 4**
　　See also CA 104; 155; DLB 12, 74; DLBD 13; RGAL 4; TUS

Cabral de Melo Neto, Joao 1920-1999 .... **CLC 76**
　　See also CA 151; CWW 2; DAM MULT; DLB 307; EWL 3; LAW; LAWS 1

Cabrera Infante, G. 1929-2005 ... **CLC 5, 25, 45, 120; HLC 1; SSC 39**
　　See also CA 85-88; 236; CANR 29, 65, 110; CDWLB 3; CWW 2; DA3; DAM MULT; DLB 113; EWL 3; HW 1, 2; LAW; LAWS 1; MTCW 1, 2; MTFW 2005; RGSF 2; WLIT 1

Cabrera Infante, Guillermo
　　See Cabrera Infante, G.

Cade, Toni
　　See Bambara, Toni Cade

Cadmus and Harmonia
　　See Buchan, John

Caedmon fl. 658-680 .... **CMLC 7**
　　See also DLB 146

Caeiro, Alberto
　　See Pessoa, Fernando

Caesar, Julius
　　See Julius Caesar

Cage, John (Milton), (Jr.) 1912-1992 .... **CLC 41; PC 58**
　　See also CA 13-16R; 169; CANR 9, 78; DLB 193; INT CANR-9; TCLE 1:1

Cahan, Abraham 1860-1951 .... **TCLC 71**
　　See also CA 108; 154; DLB 9, 25, 28; MAL 5; RGAL 4

Cain, Christopher
　　See Fleming, Thomas

Cain, G.
　　See Cabrera Infante, G.

Cain, Guillermo
　　See Cabrera Infante, G.

Cain, James M(allahan) 1892-1977 .. **CLC 3, 11, 28**
　　See also AITN 1; BPFB 1; CA 17-20R; 73-76; CANR 8, 34, 61; CMW 4; CN 1, 2; DLB 226; EWL 3; MAL 5; MSW; MTCW 1; RGAL 4

Caine, Hall 1853-1931 .... **TCLC 97**
　　See also RHW

Caine, Mark
　　See Raphael, Frederic (Michael)

Calasso, Roberto 1941- .... **CLC 81**
　　See also CA 143; CANR 89

Calderon de la Barca, Pedro 1600-1681 . **DC 3; HLCS 1; LC 23, 136**
　　See also DFS 23; EW 2; RGWL 2, 3; TWA

Caldwell, Erskine 1903-1987 ... **CLC 1, 8, 14, 50, 60; SSC 19; TCLC 117**
　　See also AITN 1; AMW; BPFB 1; CA 1-4R; 121; CAAS 1; CANR 2, 33; CN 1, 2, 3, 4; DA3; DAM NOV; DLB 9, 86; EWL 3; MAL 5; MTCW 1, 2; MTFW 2005; RGAL 4; RGSF 2; TUS

Caldwell, (Janet Miriam) Taylor (Holland) 1900-1985 .... **CLC 2, 28, 39**
　　See also BPFB 1; CA 5-8R; 116; CANR 5; DA3; DAM NOV, POP; DLBD 17; MTCW 2; RHW

Calhoun, John Caldwell 1782-1850 .... **NCLC 15**
　　See also DLB 3, 248

Calisher, Hortense 1911-2009 .... **CLC 2, 4, 8, 38, 134; SSC 15**
　　See also CA 1-4R; CANR 1, 22, 117; CN 1, 2, 3, 4, 5, 6, 7; DA3; DAM NOV; DLB 2, 218; INT CANR-22; MAL 5; MTCW 1, 2; MTFW 2005; RGAL 4; RGSF 2

Callaghan, Morley Edward 1903-1990 ..... **CLC 3, 14, 41, 65; TCLC 145**
　　See also CA 9-12R; 132; CANR 33, 73; CN 1, 2, 3, 4; DAC; DAM MST; DLB 68; EWL 3; MTCW 1, 2; MTFW 2005; RGEL 2; RGSF 2; SSFS 19

Callimachus c. 305B.C.-c. 240B.C. .... **CMLC 18**
　　See also AW 1; DLB 176; RGWL 2, 3

Calvin, Jean
　　See Calvin, John

Calvin, John 1509-1564 .... **LC 37**
　　See also DLB 327; GFL Beginnings to 1789

Calvino, Italo 1923-1985 .... **CLC 5, 8, 11, 22, 33, 39, 73; SSC 3, 48; TCLC 183**
　　See also AAYA 58; CA 85-88; 116; CANR 23, 61, 132; DAM NOV; DLB 196; EW 13; EWL 3; MTCW 1, 2; MTFW 2005; RGHL; RGSF 2; RGWL 2, 3; SFW 4; SSFS 12; WLIT 7

Camara Laye
　　See Laye, Camara

Cambridge, A Gentleman of the University of
　　See Crowley, Edward Alexander

Camden, William 1551-1623 .... **LC 77**
　　See also DLB 172

Cameron, Carey 1952- .... **CLC 59**
　　See also CA 135

Cameron, Peter 1959- .... **CLC 44**
　　See also AMWS 12; CA 125; CANR 50, 117, 188; DLB 234; GLL 2

Camoens, Luis Vaz de 1524(?)-1580
　　See Camoes, Luis de

Camoes, Luis de 1524(?)-1580 . **HLCS 1; LC 62; PC 31**
　　See also DLB 287; EW 2; RGWL 2, 3

Camp, Madeleine L'Engle
　　See L'Engle, Madeleine

Campana, Dino 1885-1932 .... **TCLC 20**
　　See also CA 117; 246; DLB 114; EWL 3

Campanella, Tommaso 1568-1639 .... **LC 32**
　　See also RGWL 2, 3

Campbell, Bebe Moore 1950-2006 . **BLC 2:1; CLC 246**
　　See also AAYA 26; BW 2, 3; CA 139; 254; CANR 81, 134; DLB 227; MTCW 2; MTFW 2005

Campbell, John Ramsey
　　See Campbell, Ramsey

Campbell, John W(ood, Jr.) 1910-1971 .... **CLC 32**
　　See also CA 21-22; 29-32R; CANR 34; CAP 2; DLB 8; MTCW 1; SCFW 1, 2; SFW 4

Campbell, Joseph 1904-1987 .... **CLC 69; TCLC 140**
　　See also AAYA 3, 66; BEST 89:2; CA 1-4R; 124; CANR 3, 28, 61, 107; DA3; MTCW 1, 2

Campbell, Maria 1940- .... **CLC 85; NNAL**
　　See also CA 102; CANR 54; CCA 1; DAC

Campbell, Ramsey 1946- ... **CLC 42; SSC 19**
　　See also AAYA 51; CA 57-60; 228; CAAE 228; CANR 7, 102, 171; DLB 261; HGG; INT CANR-7; SUFW 1, 2

Campbell, (Ignatius) Roy (Dunnachie) 1901-1957 .... **TCLC 5**
　　See also AFW; CA 104; 155; DLB 20, 225; EWL 3; MTCW 2; RGEL 2

Campbell, Thomas 1777-1844 .... **NCLC 19**
　　See also DLB 93, 144; RGEL 2

Campbell, Wilfred
　　See Campbell, William

Campbell, William 1858(?)-1918 ..... **TCLC 9**
　　See also CA 106; DLB 92

Campbell, William Edward March 1893-1954 .... **TCLC 96**
　　See also CA 108; 216; DLB 9, 86, 316; MAL 5

Campion, Jane 1954- .... **CLC 95, 229**
　　See also AAYA 33; CA 138; CANR 87

Campion, Thomas 1567-1620 . **LC 78; PC 87**
　　See also CDBLB Before 1660; DAM POET; DLB 58, 172; RGEL 2

Author Index

Corso, Gregory 1930-2001 .... **CLC 1, 11; PC 33**
See also AMWS 12; BG 1:2; CA 5-8R; 193; CANR 41, 76, 132; CP 1, 2, 3, 4, 5, 6, 7; DA3; DLB 5, 16, 237; LMFS 2; MAL 5; MTCW 1, 2; MTFW 2005; WP

Cortazar, Julio 1914-1984 ... **CLC 2, 3, 5, 10, 13, 15, 33, 34, 92; HLC 1; SSC 7, 76**
See also BPFB 1; CA 21-24R; CANR 12, 32, 81; CDWLB 3; DA3; DAM MULT, NOV; DLB 113; EWL 3; EXPS; HW 1, 2; LAW; MTCW 1, 2; MTFW 2005; RGSF 2; RGWL 2, 3; SSFS 3, 20; TWA; WLIT 1

Cortes, Hernan 1485-1547 .... **LC 31**

Cortez, Jayne 1936- .... **BLC 2:1**
See also BW 2, 3; CA 73-76; CANR 13, 31, 68, 126; CWP; DLB 41; EWL 3

Corvinus, Jakob
See Raabe, Wilhelm (Karl)

Corwin, Cecil
See Kornbluth, C(yril) M.

Cosic, Dobrica 1921- .... **CLC 14**
See also CA 122; 138; CDWLB 4; CWW 2; DLB 181; EWL 3

Costain, Thomas B(ertram)
1885-1965 .... **CLC 30**
See also BYA 3; CA 5-8R; 25-28R; DLB 9; RHW

Costantini, Humberto 1924(?)-1987 . **CLC 49**
See also CA 131; 122; EWL 3; HW 1

Costello, Elvis 1954- .... **CLC 21**
See also CA 204

Costenoble, Philostene
See Ghelderode, Michel de

Cotes, Cecil V.
See Duncan, Sara Jeannette

Cotter, Joseph Seamon Sr.
1861-1949 .... **BLC 1:1; TCLC 28**
See also BW 1; CA 124; DAM MULT; DLB 50

Couch, Arthur Thomas Quiller
See Quiller-Couch, Sir Arthur (Thomas)

Coulton, James
See Hansen, Joseph

Couperus, Louis (Marie Anne)
1863-1923 .... **TCLC 15**
See also CA 115; EWL 3; RGWL 2, 3

Coupland, Douglas 1961- .... **CLC 85, 133**
See also AAYA 34; CA 142; CANR 57, 90, 130, 172; CCA 1; CN 7; CPW; DAC; DAM POP; DLB 334

Coupland, Douglas Campbell
See Coupland, Douglas

Court, Wesli
See Turco, Lewis

Courtenay, Bryce 1933- .... **CLC 59**
See also CA 138; CPW

Courtney, Robert
See Ellison, Harlan

Cousteau, Jacques-Yves 1910-1997 .. **CLC 30**
See also CA 65-68; 159; CANR 15, 67; MTCW 1; SATA 38, 98

Coventry, Francis 1725-1754 .... **LC 46**
See also DLB 39

Coverdale, Miles c. 1487-1569 .... **LC 77**
See also DLB 167

Cowan, Peter (Walkinshaw)
1914-2002 .... **SSC 28**
See also CA 21-24R; CANR 9, 25, 50, 83; CN 1, 2, 3, 4, 5, 6, 7; DLB 260; RGSF 2

Coward, Noel (Peirce) 1899-1973 . **CLC 1, 9, 29, 51**
See also AITN 1; BRWS 2; CA 17-18; 41-44R; CANR 35, 132; CAP 2; CBD; CD-BLB 1914-1945; DA3; DAM DRAM; DFS 3, 6; DLB 10, 245; EWL 3; IDFW 3, 4; MTCW 1, 2; MTFW 2005; RGEL 2; TEA

Cowley, Abraham 1618-1667 .. **LC 43; PC 90**
See also BRW 2; DLB 131, 151; PAB; RGEL 2

Cowley, Malcolm 1898-1989 .... **CLC 39**
See also AMWS 2; CA 5-8R; 128; CANR 3, 55; CP 1, 2, 3, 4; DLB 4, 48; DLBY 1981, 1989; EWL 3; MAL 5; MTCW 1, 2; MTFW 2005

Cowper, William 1731-1800 ..... **NCLC 8, 94; PC 40**
See also BRW 3; DA3; DAM POET; DLB 104, 109; RGEL 2

Cox, William Trevor
See Trevor, William

Coyne, P. J.
See Masters, Hilary

Coyne, P.J.
See Masters, Hilary

Cozzens, James Gould 1903-1978 . **CLC 1, 4, 11, 92**
See also AMW; BPFB 1; CA 9-12R; 81-84; CANR 19; CDALB 1941-1968; CN 1, 2; DLB 9, 294; DLBD 2; DLBY 1984, 1997; EWL 3; MAL 5; MTCW 1, 2; MTFW 2005; RGAL 4

Crabbe, George 1754-1832 ... **NCLC 26, 121; PC 97**
See also BRW 3; DLB 93; RGEL 2

Crace, Jim 1946- .... **CLC 157; SSC 61**
See also BRWS 14; CA 128; 135; CANR 55, 70, 123, 180; CN 5, 6, 7; DLB 231; INT CA-135

Craddock, Charles Egbert
See Murfree, Mary Noailles

Craig, A. A.
See Anderson, Poul

Craik, Mrs.
See Craik, Dinah Maria (Mulock)

Craik, Dinah Maria (Mulock)
1826-1887 .... **NCLC 38**
See also DLB 35, 163; MAICYA 1, 2; RGEL 2; SATA 34

Cram, Ralph Adams 1863-1942 ..... **TCLC 45**
See also CA 160

Cranch, Christopher Pearse
1813-1892 .... **NCLC 115**
See also DLB 1, 42, 243

Crane, (Harold) Hart 1899-1932 .... **PC 3; TCLC 2, 5, 80; WLC 2**
See also AMW; AMWR 2; CA 104; 127; CDALB 1917-1929; DA; DA3; DAB; DAC; DAM MST, POET; DLB 4, 48; EWL 3; MAL 5; MTCW 1, 2; MTFW 2005; RGAL 4; TUS

Crane, R(onald) S(almon)
1886-1967 .... **CLC 27**
See also CA 85-88; DLB 63

Crane, Stephen (Townley)
1871-1900 .... **PC 80; SSC 7, 56, 70; TCLC 11, 17, 32, 216; WLC 2**
See also AAYA 21; AMW; AMWC 1; BPFB 1; BYA 3; CA 109; 140; CANR 84; CDALB 1865-1917; CLR 132; DA; DA3; DAB; DAC; DAM MST, NOV, POET; DLB 12, 54, 78; EXPN; EXPS; LAIT 2; LMFS 2; MAL 5; NFS 4, 20; PFS 9; RGAL 4; RGSF 2; SSFS 4; TUS; WYA; YABC 2

Cranmer, Thomas 1489-1556 .... **LC 95**
See also DLB 132, 213

Cranshaw, Stanley
See Fisher, Dorothy (Frances) Canfield

Crase, Douglas 1944- .... **CLC 58**
See also CA 106

Crashaw, Richard 1612(?)-1649 .. **LC 24; PC 84**
See also BRW 2; DLB 126; PAB; RGEL 2

Cratinus c. 519B.C.-c. 422B.C. ..... **CMLC 54**
See also LMFS 1

Craven, Margaret 1901-1980 .... **CLC 17**
See also BYA 2; CA 103; CCA 1; DAC; LAIT 5

Crawford, F(rancis) Marion
1854-1909 .... **TCLC 10**
See also CA 107; 168; DLB 71; HGG; RGAL 4; SUFW 1

Crawford, Isabella Valancy
1850-1887 .... **NCLC 12, 127**
See also DLB 92; RGEL 2

Crayon, Geoffrey
See Irving, Washington

Creasey, John 1908-1973 .... **CLC 11**
See also CA 5-8R; 41-44R; CANR 8, 59; CMW 4; DLB 77; MTCW 1

Crebillon, Claude Prosper Jolyot de (fils)
1707-1777 .... **LC 1, 28**
See also DLB 313; GFL Beginnings to 1789

Credo
See Creasey, John

Credo, Alvaro J. de
See Prado (Calvo), Pedro

Creeley, Robert 1926-2005 .... **CLC 1, 2, 4, 8, 11, 15, 36, 78, 266; PC 73**
See also AMWS 4; CA 1-4R; 237; CAAS 10; CANR 23, 43, 89, 137; CP 1, 2, 3, 4, 5, 6, 7; DA3; DAM POET; DLB 5, 16, 169; DLBD 17; EWL 3; MAL 5; MTCW 1, 2; MTFW 2005; PFS 21; RGAL 4; WP

Creeley, Robert White
See Creeley, Robert

Crenne, Helisenne de 1510-1560 .... **LC 113**
See also DLB 327

Crevecoeur, Hector St. John de
See Crevecoeur, Michel Guillaume Jean de

Crevecoeur, Michel Guillaume Jean de
1735-1813 .... **NCLC 105**
See also AMWS 1; ANW; DLB 37

Crevel, Rene 1900-1935 .... **TCLC 112**
See also GLL 2

Crews, Harry 1935- .... **CLC 6, 23, 49**
See also AITN 1; AMWS 11; BPFB 1; CA 25-28R; CANR 20, 57; CN 3, 4, 5, 6, 7; CSW; DA3; DLB 6, 143, 185; MTCW 1, 2; MTFW 2005; RGAL 4

Crichton, John Michael
See Crichton, Michael

Crichton, Michael 1942-2008 .. **CLC 2, 6, 54, 90, 242**
See also AAYA 10, 49; AITN 2; BPFB 1; CA 25-28R; 279; CANR 13, 40, 54, 76, 127, 179; CMW 4; CN 2, 3, 6, 7; CPW; DA3; DAM NOV, POP; DLB 292; DLBY 1981; INT CANR-13; JRDA; MTCW 1, 2; MTFW 2005; SATA 9, 88; SATA-Obit 199; SFW 4; YAW

Crispin, Edmund
See Montgomery, (Robert) Bruce

Cristina of Sweden 1626-1689 .... **LC 124**

Cristofer, Michael 1945(?)- .... **CLC 28**
See also CA 110; 152; CAD; CANR 150; CD 5, 6; DAM DRAM; DFS 15; DLB 7

Cristofer, Michael Ivan
See Cristofer, Michael

Criton
See Alain

Croce, Benedetto 1866-1952 .... **TCLC 37**
See also CA 120; 155; EW 8; EWL 3; WLIT 7

Crockett, David 1786-1836 .... **NCLC 8**
See also DLB 3, 11, 183, 248

Crockett, Davy
See Crockett, David

Crofts, Freeman Wills 1879-1957 .. **TCLC 55**
See also CA 115; 195; CMW 4; DLB 77; MSW

Croker, John Wilson 1780-1857 .... **NCLC 10**
See also DLB 110

Deighton, Leonard Cyril 1929- ..... **CLC 4, 7, 22, 46**
See also AAYA 57, 6; BEST 89:2; BPFB 1; CA 9-12R; CANR 19, 33, 68; CDBLB 1960- Present; CMW 4; CN 1, 2, 3, 4, 5, 6, 7; CPW; DA3; DAM NOV, POP; DLB 87; MTCW 1, 2; MTFW 2005

Dekker, Thomas 1572(?)-1632 ..... **DC 12; LC 22, 159**
See also CDBLB Before 1660; DAM DRAM; DLB 62, 172; LMFS 1; RGEL 2

de Laclos, Pierre Ambroise Franois
See Laclos, Pierre-Ambroise Francois

Delacroix, (Ferdinand-Victor-)Eugene 1798-1863 .... **NCLC 133**
See also EW 5

Delafield, E. M.
See Dashwood, Edmee Elizabeth Monica de la Pasture

de la Mare, Walter (John) 1873-1956 ..... **PC 77; SSC 14; TCLC 4, 53; WLC 2**
See also CA 163; CDBLB 1914-1945; CLR 23; CWRI 5; DA3; DAB; DAC; DAM MST, POET; DLB 19, 153, 162, 255, 284; EWL 3; EXPP; HGG; MAICYA 1, 2; MTCW 2; MTFW 2005; RGEL 2; RGSF 2; SATA 16; SUFW 1; TEA; WCH

de Lamartine, Alphonse (Marie Louis Prat)
See Lamartine, Alphonse (Marie Louis Prat) de

Delaney, Franey
See O'Hara, John (Henry)

Delaney, Shelagh 1939- .... **CLC 29**
See also CA 17-20R; CANR 30, 67; CBD; CD 5, 6; CDBLB 1960 to Present; CWD; DAM DRAM; DFS 7; DLB 13; MTCW 1

Delany, Martin Robison 1812-1885 .... **NCLC 93**
See also DLB 50; RGAL 4

Delany, Mary (Granville Pendarves) 1700-1788 .... **LC 12**

Delany, Samuel R., Jr. 1942- .... **BLC 1:1; CLC 8, 14, 38, 141**
See also AAYA 24; AFAW 2; BPFB 1; BW 2, 3; CA 81-84; CANR 27, 43, 116, 172; CN 2, 3, 4, 5, 6, 7; DAM MULT; DLB 8, 33; FANT; MAL 5; MTCW 1, 2; RGAL 4; SATA 92; SCFW 1, 2; SFW 4; SUFW 2

Delany, Samuel Ray
See Delany, Samuel R., Jr.

de la Parra, (Ana) Teresa (Sonojo) 1890(?)-1936 .... **HLCS 2; TCLC 185**
See also CA 178; HW 2; LAW

Delaporte, Theophile
See Green, Julien (Hartridge)

De La Ramee, Marie Louise 1839-1908 .... **TCLC 43**
See also CA 204; DLB 18, 156; RGEL 2; SATA 20

de la Roche, Mazo 1879-1961 .... **CLC 14**
See also CA 85-88; CANR 30; DLB 68; RGEL 2; RHW; SATA 64

De La Salle, Innocent
See Hartmann, Sadakichi

de Laureamont, Comte
See Lautreamont

Delbanco, Nicholas 1942- ..... **CLC 6, 13, 167**
See also CA 17-20R, 189; CAAE 189; CAAS 2; CANR 29, 55, 116, 150; CN 7; DLB 6, 234

Delbanco, Nicholas Franklin
See Delbanco, Nicholas

del Castillo, Michel 1933- .... **CLC 38**
See also CA 109; CANR 77

Deledda, Grazia (Cosima) 1875(?)-1936 .... **TCLC 23**
See also CA 123; 205; DLB 264, 329; EWL 3; RGWL 2, 3; WLIT 7

Deleuze, Gilles 1925-1995 .... **TCLC 116**
See also DLB 296

Delgado, Abelardo (Lalo) B(arrientos) 1930-2004 .... **HLC 1**
See also CA 131; 230; CAAS 15; CANR 90; DAM MST, MULT; DLB 82; HW 1, 2

Delibes, Miguel
See Delibes Setien, Miguel

Delibes Setien, Miguel 1920- .... **CLC 8, 18**
See also CA 45-48; CANR 1, 32; CWW 2; DLB 322; EWL 3; HW 1; MTCW 1

DeLillo, Don 1936- ..... **CLC 8, 10, 13, 27, 39, 54, 76, 143, 210, 213**
See also AMWC 2; AMWS 6; BEST 89:1; BPFB 1; CA 81-84; CANR 21, 76, 92, 133, 173; CN 3, 4, 5, 6, 7; CPW; DA3; DAM NOV, POP; DLB 6, 173; EWL 3; MAL 5; MTCW 1, 2; MTFW 2005; NFS 28; RGAL 4; TUS

de Lisser, H. G.
See De Lisser, H(erbert) G(eorge)

De Lisser, H(erbert) G(eorge) 1878-1944 .... **TCLC 12**
See also BW 2; CA 109; 152; DLB 117

Deloire, Pierre
See Peguy, Charles (Pierre)

Deloney, Thomas 1543(?)-1600 .... **LC 41; PC 79**
See also DLB 167; RGEL 2

Deloria, Ella (Cara) 1889-1971(?) ..... **NNAL**
See also CA 152; DAM MULT; DLB 175

Deloria, Vine, Jr. 1933-2005 .... **CLC 21, 122; NNAL**
See also CA 53-56; 245; CANR 5, 20, 48, 98; DAM MULT; DLB 175; MTCW 1; SATA 21; SATA-Obit 171

Deloria, Vine Victor, Jr.
See Deloria, Vine, Jr.

del Valle-Inclan, Ramon (Maria)
See Valle-Inclan, Ramon (Maria) del

Del Vecchio, John M(ichael) 1947- .. **CLC 29**
See also CA 110; DLBD 9

de Man, Paul (Adolph Michel) 1919-1983 .... **CLC 55**
See also CA 128; 111; CANR 61; DLB 67; MTCW 1, 2

de Mandiargues, Andre Pieyre
See Pieyre de Mandiargues, Andre

DeMarinis, Rick 1934- .... **CLC 54**
See also CA 57-60, 184; CAAE 184; CAAS 24; CANR 9, 25, 50, 160; DLB 218; TCWW 2

de Maupassant, (Henri Rene Albert) Guy
See Maupassant, (Henri Rene Albert) Guy de

Dembry, R. Emmet
See Murfree, Mary Noailles

Demby, William 1922- ...... **BLC 1:1; CLC 53**
See also BW 1, 3; CA 81-84; CANR 81; DAM MULT; DLB 33

de Menton, Francisco
See Chin, Frank (Chew, Jr.)

Demetrius of Phalerum c. 307B.C.- .... **CMLC 34**

Demijohn, Thom
See Disch, Thomas M.

De Mille, James 1833-1880 .... **NCLC 123**
See also DLB 99, 251

Democritus c. 460B.C.-c. 370B.C. . **CMLC 47**

de Montaigne, Michel (Eyquem)
See Montaigne, Michel (Eyquem) de

de Montherlant, Henry (Milon)
See Montherlant, Henry (Milon) de

Demosthenes 384B.C.-322B.C. ...... **CMLC 13**
See also AW 1; DLB 176; RGWL 2, 3; WLIT 8

de Musset, (Louis Charles) Alfred
See Musset, Alfred de

de Natale, Francine
See Malzberg, Barry N(athaniel)

de Navarre, Marguerite 1492-1549 .... **LC 61, 167; SSC 85**
See also DLB 327; GFL Beginnings to 1789; RGWL 2, 3

Denby, Edwin (Orr) 1903-1983 .... **CLC 48**
See also CA 138; 110; CP 1

de Nerval, Gerard
See Nerval, Gerard de

Denham, John 1615-1669 .... **LC 73**
See also DLB 58, 126; RGEL 2

Denis, Julio
See Cortazar, Julio

Denmark, Harrison
See Zelazny, Roger

Dennis, John 1658-1734 .... **LC 11, 154**
See also DLB 101; RGEL 2

Dennis, Nigel (Forbes) 1912-1989 ...... **CLC 8**
See also CA 25-28R; 129; CN 1, 2, 3, 4; DLB 13, 15, 233; EWL 3; MTCW 1

Dent, Lester 1904-1959 .... **TCLC 72**
See also CA 112; 161; CMW 4; DLB 306; SFW 4

Dentinger, Stephen
See Hoch, Edward D.

De Palma, Brian 1940- .... **CLC 20, 247**
See also CA 109

De Palma, Brian Russell
See De Palma, Brian

de Pizan, Christine
See Christine de Pizan

De Quincey, Thomas 1785-1859 ..... **NCLC 4, 87, 198**
See also BRW 4; CDBLB 1789-1832; DLB 110, 144; RGEL 2

De Ray, Jill
See Moore, Alan

Deren, Eleanora 1908(?)-1961 .. **CLC 16, 102**
See also CA 192; 111

Deren, Maya
See Deren, Eleanora

Derleth, August (William) 1909-1971 .... **CLC 31**
See also BPFB 1; BYA 9, 10; CA 1-4R; 29-32R; CANR 4; CMW 4; CN 1; DLB 9; DLBD 17; HGG; SATA 5; SUFW 1

Der Nister 1884-1950 .... **TCLC 56**
See also DLB 333; EWL 3

de Routisie, Albert
See Aragon, Louis

Derrida, Jacques 1930-2004 ...... **CLC 24, 87, 225**
See also CA 124; 127; 232; CANR 76, 98, 133; DLB 242; EWL 3; LMFS 2; MTCW 2; TWA

Derry Down Derry
See Lear, Edward

Dersonnes, Jacques
See Simenon, Georges (Jacques Christian)

Der Stricker c. 1190-c. 1250 .... **CMLC 75**
See also DLB 138

Derzhavin, Gavrila Romanovich NCLC 215
See also DLB 150

Desai, Anita 1937- . **CLC 19, 37, 97, 175, 271**
See also BRWS 5; CA 81-84; CANR 33, 53, 95, 133; CN 1, 2, 3, 4, 5, 6, 7; CWRI 5; DA3; DAB; DAM NOV; DLB 271, 323; DNFS 2; EWL 3; FW; MTCW 1, 2; MTFW 2005; SATA 63, 126

Desai, Kiran 1971- .... **CLC 119**
See also BYA 16; CA 171; CANR 127; NFS 28

de Saint-Luc, Jean
See Glassco, John
de Saint Roman, Arnaud
See Aragon, Louis
Desbordes-Valmore, Marceline
1786-1859 .... **NCLC 97**
See also DLB 217
Descartes, Rene 1596-1650 .... **LC 20, 35, 150**
See also DLB 268; EW 3; GFL Beginnings
to 1789
Deschamps, Eustache 1340(?)-1404 .. **LC 103**
See also DLB 208
De Sica, Vittorio 1901(?)-1974 .... **CLC 20**
See also CA 117
Desnos, Robert 1900-1945 .... **TCLC 22**
See also CA 121; 151; CANR 107; DLB
258; EWL 3; LMFS 2
Destouches, Louis-Ferdinand
1894-1961 .... **CLC 1, 3, 4, 7, 47, 124**
See also CA 85-88; CANR 28; DLB 72;
EW 11; EWL 3; GFL 1789 to the Present;
MTCW 1; RGWL 2, 3
de Teran, Lisa St. Aubin
See St. Aubin de Teran, Lisa
de Tolignac, Gaston
See Griffith, D.W.
Deutsch, Babette 1895-1982 .... **CLC 18**
See also BYA 3; CA 1-4R; 108; CANR 4,
79; CP 1, 2, 3; DLB 45; SATA 1; SATA-
Obit 33
Devenant, William 1606-1649 .... **LC 13**
Deville, Rene
See Kacew, Romain
Devkota, Laxmiprasad 1909-1959 . **TCLC 23**
See also CA 123
De Voto, Bernard (Augustine)
1897-1955 .... **TCLC 29**
See also CA 113; 160; DLB 9, 256; MAL
5; TCWW 1, 2
De Vries, Peter 1910-1993 ..... **CLC 1, 2, 3, 7,**
10, 28, 46
See also CA 17-20R; 142; CANR 41; CN
1, 2, 3, 4, 5; DAM NOV; DLB 6; DLBY
1982; MAL 5; MTCW 1, 2; MTFW 2005
Dewey, John 1859-1952 .... **TCLC 95**
See also CA 114; 170; CANR 144; DLB
246, 270; RGAL 4
Dexter, John
See Bradley, Marion Zimmer
Dexter, Martin
See Faust, Frederick (Schiller)
Dexter, Pete 1943- .... **CLC 34, 55**
See also BEST 89:2; CA 127; 131; CANR
129; CPW; DAM POP; INT CA-131;
MAL 5; MTCW 1; MTFW 2005
Diamano, Silmang
See Senghor, Leopold Sedar
Diamant, Anita 1951- .... **CLC 239**
See also CA 145; CANR 126
Diamond, Neil 1941- .... **CLC 30**
See also CA 108
Diaz, Junot 1968- .... **CLC 258**
See also BYA 12; CA 161; CANR 119, 183;
LLW; SSFS 20
Diaz del Castillo, Bernal c.
1496-1584 .... **HLCS 1; LC 31**
See also DLB 318; LAW
di Bassetto, Corno
See Shaw, George Bernard
Dick, Philip K. 1928-1982 ... **CLC 10, 30, 72;**
SSC 57
See also AAYA 24; BPFB 1; BYA 11; CA
49-52; 106; CANR 2, 16, 132; CN 2, 3;
CPW; DA3; DAM NOV, POP; DLB 8;
MTCW 1, 2; MTFW 2005; NFS 5, 26;
SCFW 1, 2; SFW 4
Dick, Philip Kindred
See Dick, Philip K.

Dickens, Charles (John Huffam)
1812-1870 .... **NCLC 3, 8, 18, 26, 37, 50,**
86, 105, 113, 161, 187, 203, 206, 211;
SSC 17, 49, 88; WLC 2
See also AAYA 23; BRW 5; BRWC 1, 2;
BYA 1, 2, 3, 13, 14; CDBLB 1832-1890;
CLR 95; CMW 4; DA; DA3; DAB; DAC;
DAM MST, NOV; DLB 21, 55, 70, 159,
166; EXPN; GL 2; HGG; JRDA; LAIT 1,
2; LATS 1:1; LMFS 1; MAICYA 1, 2;
NFS 4, 5, 10, 14, 20, 25; RGEL 2; RGSF
2; SATA 15; SUFW 1; TEA; WCH; WLIT
4; WYA
Dickey, James (Lafayette)
1923-1997 .... **CLC 1, 2, 4, 7, 10, 15, 47,**
109; PC 40; TCLC 151
See also AAYA 50; AITN 1, 2; AMWS 4;
BPFB 1; CA 9-12R; 156; CABS 2; CANR
10, 48, 61, 105; CDALB 1968-1988; CP
1, 2, 3, 4, 5, 6; CPW; CSW; DA3; DAM
NOV, POET, POP; DLB 5, 193, 342;
DLBD 7; DLBY 1982, 1993, 1996, 1997,
1998; EWL 3; INT CANR-10; MAL 5;
MTCW 1, 2; NFS 9; PFS 6, 11; RGAL 4;
TUS
Dickey, William 1928-1994 .... **CLC 3, 28**
See also CA 9-12R; 145; CANR 24, 79; CP
1, 2, 3, 4; DLB 5
Dickinson, Charles 1951- .... **CLC 49**
See also CA 128; CANR 141
Dickinson, Emily (Elizabeth)
1830-1886 ..... **NCLC 21, 77, 171; PC 1;**
WLC 2
See also AAYA 22; AMW; AMWR 1;
CDALB 1865-1917; DA; DA3; DAB;
DAC; DAM MST, POET; DLB 1, 243;
EXPP; FL 1:3; MBL; PAB; PFS 1, 2, 3,
4, 5, 6, 8, 10, 11, 13, 16, 28; RGAL 4;
SATA 29; TUS; WP; WYA
Dickinson, Mrs. Herbert Ward
See Phelps, Elizabeth Stuart
Dickinson, Peter (Malcolm de Brissac)
1927- .... **CLC 12, 35**
See also AAYA 9, 49; BYA 5; CA 41-44R;
CANR 31, 58, 88, 134; CLR 29, 125;
CMW 4; DLB 87, 161, 276; JRDA; MAI-
CYA 1, 2; SATA 5, 62, 95, 150; SFW 4;
WYA; YAW
Dickson, Carr
See Carr, John Dickson
Dickson, Carter
See Carr, John Dickson
Diderot, Denis 1713-1784 .... **LC 26, 126**
See also DLB 313; EW 4; GFL Beginnings
to 1789; LMFS 1; RGWL 2, 3
Didion, Joan 1934- . **CLC 1, 3, 8, 14, 32, 129**
See also AITN 1; AMWS 4; CA 5-8R;
CANR 14, 52, 76, 125, 174; CDALB
1968-1988; CN 2, 3, 4, 5, 6, 7; DA3;
DAM NOV; DLB 2, 173, 185; DLBY
1981, 1986; EWL 3; MAL 5; MBL;
MTCW 1, 2; MTFW 2005; NFS 3; RGAL
4; TCLE 1:1; TCWW 2; TUS
di Donato, Pietro 1911-1992 .... **TCLC 159**
See also CA 101; 136; DLB 9
Dietrich, Robert
See Hunt, E. Howard
Difusa, Pati
See Almodovar, Pedro
di Lampedusa, Giuseppe Tomasi
See Tomasi di Lampedusa, Giuseppe
Dillard, Annie 1945- ...... **CLC 9, 60, 115, 216**
See also AAYA 6, 43; AMWS 6; ANW; CA
49-52; CANR 3, 43, 62, 90, 125; DA3;
DAM NOV; DLB 275, 278; DLBY 1980;
LAIT 4, 5; MAL 5; MTCW 1, 2; MTFW
2005; NCFS 1; RGAL 4; SATA 10, 140;
TCLE 1:1; TUS

Dillard, R(ichard) H(enry) W(ilde)
1937- .... **CLC 5**
See also CA 21-24R; CAAS 7; CANR 10;
CP 2, 3, 4, 5, 6, 7; CSW; DLB 5, 244
Dillon, Eilis 1920-1994 .... **CLC 17**
See also CA 9-12R, 182; 147; CAAE 182;
CAAS 3; CANR 4, 38, 78; CLR 26; MAI-
CYA 1, 2; MAICYAS 1; SATA 2, 74;
SATA-Essay 105; SATA-Obit 83; YAW
Dimont, Penelope
See Mortimer, Penelope (Ruth)
Dinesen, Isak
See Blixen, Karen (Christentze Dinesen)
Ding Ling
See Chiang, Pin-chin
Diodorus Siculus c. 90B.C.-c.
31B.C. .... **CMLC 88**
Diphusa, Patty
See Almodovar, Pedro
Disch, Thomas M. 1940-2008 .... **CLC 7, 36**
See also CA 17; BPFB 1; CA 21-24R;
274; CAAS 4; CANR 17, 36, 54, 89; CLR
18; CP 5, 6, 7; DA3; DLB 8, 282; HGG;
MAICYA 1, 2; MTCW 1, 2; MTFW 2005;
SAAS 15; SATA 92; SATA-Obit 195;
SCFW 1, 2; SFW 4; SUFW 2
Disch, Thomas Michael
See Disch, Thomas M.
Disch, Tom
See Disch, Thomas M.
d'Isly, Georges
See Simenon, Georges (Jacques Christian)
Disraeli, Benjamin 1804-1881 ... **NCLC 2, 39,**
79
See also BRW 4; DLB 21, 55; RGEL 2
Ditcum, Steve
See Crumb, R.
Dixon, Paige
See Corcoran, Barbara (Asenath)
Dixon, Stephen 1936- .... **CLC 52; SSC 16**
See also AMWS 12; CA 89-92; CANR 17,
40, 54, 91, 175; CN 4, 5, 6, 7; DLB 130;
MAL 5
Dixon, Thomas, Jr. 1864-1946 ..... **TCLC 163**
See also RHW
Djebar, Assia 1936- .... **BLC 2:1; CLC 182;**
SSC 114
See also CA 188; CANR 169; DLB 346;
EWL 3; RGWL 3; WLIT 2
Doak, Annie
See Dillard, Annie
Dobell, Sydney Thompson
1824-1874 .... **NCLC 43**
See also DLB 32; RGEL 2
Doblin, Alfred
See Doeblin, Alfred
Dobroliubov, Nikolai Aleksandrovich
See Dobrolyubov, Nikolai Alexandrovich
Dobrolyubov, Nikolai Alexandrovich
1836-1861 .... **NCLC 5**
See also DLB 277
Dobson, Austin 1840-1921 .... **TCLC 79**
See also DLB 35, 144
Dobyns, Stephen 1941- .... **CLC 37, 233**
See also AMWS 13; CA 45-48; CANR 2,
18, 99; CMW 4; CP 4, 5, 6, 7; PFS 23
Doctorow, Cory 1971- .... **CLC 273**
See also CA 221
Doctorow, Edgar Laurence
See Doctorow, E.L.
Doctorow, E.L. 1931- . **CLC 6, 11, 15, 18, 37,**
44, 65, 113, 214
See also AAYA 22; AITN 2; AMWS 4;
BEST 89:3; BPFB 1; CA 45-48; CANR
2, 33, 51, 76, 97, 133, 170; CDALB 1968-
1988; CN 3, 4, 5, 6, 7; CPW; DA3; DAM
NOV, POP; DLB 2, 28, 173; DLBY 1980;

EWL 3; LAIT 3; MAL 5; MTCW 1, 2; MTFW 2005; NFS 6; RGAL 4; RGHL; RHW; SSFS 27; TCLE 1:1; TCWW 1, 2; TUS

Dodgson, Charles Lutwidge
See Carroll, Lewis

Dodsley, Robert 1703-1764 .... **LC 97**
See also DLB 95; RGEL 2

Dodson, Owen (Vincent)
1914-1983 .... **BLC 1:1; CLC 79**
See also BW 1; CA 65-68; 110; CANR 24; DAM MULT; DLB 76

Doeblin, Alfred 1878-1957 .... **TCLC 13**
See also CA 110; 141; CDWLB 2; DLB 66; EWL 3; RGWL 2, 3

Doerr, Harriet 1910-2002 .... **CLC 34**
See also CA 117; 122; 213; CANR 47; INT CA-122; LATS 1:2

Domecq, H(onorio) Bustos
See Bioy Casares, Adolfo; Borges, Jorge Luis

Domini, Rey
See Lorde, Audre

Dominic, R. B.
See Hennissart, Martha

Dominique
See Proust, (Valentin-Louis-George-Eugene) Marcel

Don, A
See Stephen, Sir Leslie

Donaldson, Stephen R. 1947- ... **CLC 46, 138**
See also AAYA 36; BPFB 1; CA 89-92; CANR 13, 55, 99; CPW; DAM POP; FANT; INT CANR-13; SATA 121; SFW 4; SUFW 1, 2

Donleavy, J(ames) P(atrick) 1926- .... **CLC 1, 4, 6, 10, 45**
See also AITN 2; BPFB 1; CA 9-12R; CANR 24, 49, 62, 80, 124; CBD; CD 5, 6; CN 1, 2, 3, 4, 5, 6, 7; DLB 6, 173; INT CANR-24; MAL 5; MTCW 1, 2; MTFW 2005; RGAL 4

Donnadieu, Marguerite
See Duras, Marguerite

Donne, John 1572-1631 ... **LC 10, 24, 91; PC 1, 43; WLC 2**
See also AAYA 67; BRW 1; BRWC 1; BRWR 2; CDBLB Before 1660; DA; DAB; DAC; DAM MST, POET; DLB 121, 151; EXPP; PAB; PFS 2, 11; RGEL 3; TEA; WLIT 3; WP

Donnell, David 1939(?)- .... **CLC 34**
See also CA 197

Donoghue, Denis 1928- .... **CLC 209**
See also CA 17-20R; CANR 16, 102

Donoghue, Emma 1969- .... **CLC 239**
See also CA 155; CANR 103, 152; DLB 267; GLL 2; SATA 101

Donoghue, P.S.
See Hunt, E. Howard

Donoso (Yanez), Jose 1924-1996 ... **CLC 4, 8, 11, 32, 99; HLC 1; SSC 34; TCLC 133**
See also CA 81-84; 155; CANR 32, 73; CD-WLB 3; CWW 2; DAM MULT; DLB 113; EWL 3; HW 1, 2; LAW; LAWS 1; MTCW 1, 2; MTFW 2005; RGSF 2; WLIT 1

Donovan, John 1928-1992 .... **CLC 35**
See also AAYA 20; CA 97-100; 137; CLR 3; MAICYA 1, 2; SATA 72; SATA-Brief 29; YAW

Don Roberto
See Cunninghame Graham, Robert (Gallnigad) Bontine

Doolittle, Hilda 1886-1961 . **CLC 3, 8, 14, 31, 34, 73; PC 5; WLC 3**
See also AAYA 66; AMWS 1; CA 97-100; CANR 35, 131; DA; DAC; DAM MST, POET; DLB 4, 45; EWL 3; FL 1:5; FW; GLL 1; LMFS 2; MAL 5; MBL; MTCW 1, 2; MTFW 2005; PFS 6, 28; RGAL 4

Doppo
See Kunikida Doppo

Doppo, Kunikida
See Kunikida Doppo

Dorfman, Ariel 1942- .... **CLC 48, 77, 189; HLC 1**
See also CA 124; 130; CANR 67, 70, 135; CWW 2; DAM MULT; DFS 4; EWL 3; HW 1, 2; INT CA-130; WLIT 1

Dorn, Edward (Merton)
1929-1999 .... **CLC 10, 18**
See also CA 93-96; 187; CANR 42, 79; CP 1, 2, 3, 4, 5, 6, 7; DLB 5; INT CA-93-96; WP

Dor-Ner, Zvi CLC 70

Dorris, Michael 1945-1997 .... **CLC 109; NNAL**
See also AAYA 20; BEST 90:1; BYA 12; CA 102; 157; CANR 19, 46, 75; CLR 58; DA3; DAM MULT, NOV; DLB 175; LAIT 5; MTCW 2; MTFW 2005; NFS 3; RGAL 4; SATA 75; SATA-Obit 94; TCWW 2; YAW

Dorris, Michael A.
See Dorris, Michael

Dorsan, Luc
See Simenon, Georges (Jacques Christian)

Dorsange, Jean
See Simenon, Georges (Jacques Christian)

Dorset
See Sackville, Thomas

Dos Passos, John (Roderigo)
1896-1970 ... **CLC 1, 4, 8, 11, 15, 25, 34, 82; WLC 2**
See also AMW; BPFB 1; CA 1-4R; 29-32R; CANR 3; CDALB 1929-1941; DA; DA3; DAB; DAC; DAM MST, NOV; DLB 4, 9, 274, 316; DLBD 1, 15; DLBY 1996; EWL 3; MAL 5; MTCW 1, 2; MTFW 2005; NFS 14; RGAL 4; TUS

Dossage, Jean
See Simenon, Georges (Jacques Christian)

Dostoevsky, Fedor Mikhailovich
1821-1881 .. **NCLC 2, 7, 21, 33, 43, 119, 167, 202; SSC 2, 33, 44; WLC 2**
See also AAYA 40; DA; DA3; DAB; DAC; DAM MST, NOV; DLB 238; EW 7; EXPN; LATS 1:1; LMFS 1, 2; NFS 28; RGSF 2; RGWL 2, 3; SSFS 8; TWA

Dostoevsky, Fyodor
See Dostoevsky, Fedor Mikhailovich

Doty, Mark 1953(?)- .... **CLC 176; PC 53**
See also AMWS 11; CA 161, 183; CAAE 183; CANR 110, 173; CP 7; PFS 28

Doty, Mark A.
See Doty, Mark

Doty, Mark Alan
See Doty, Mark

Doty, M.R.
See Doty, Mark

Doughty, Charles M(ontagu)
1843-1926 .... **TCLC 27**
See also CA 115; 178; DLB 19, 57, 174

Douglas, Ellen 1921- .... **CLC 73**
See also CA 115; CANR 41, 83; CN 5, 6, 7; CSW; DLB 292

Douglas, Gavin 1475(?)-1522 .... **LC 20**
See also DLB 132; RGEL 2

Douglas, George
See Brown, George Douglas

Douglas, Keith (Castellain)
1920-1944 .... **TCLC 40**
See also BRW 7; CA 160; DLB 27; EWL 3; PAB; RGEL 2

Douglas, Leonard
See Bradbury, Ray

Douglas, Michael
See Crichton, Michael

Douglas, Michael
See Crichton, Michael

Douglas, (George) Norman
1868-1952 .... **TCLC 68**
See also BRW 6; CA 119; 157; DLB 34, 195; RGEL 2

Douglas, William
See Brown, George Douglas

Douglass, Frederick 1817(?)-1895 .. **BLC 1:1; NCLC 7, 55, 141; WLC 2**
See also AAYA 48; AFAW 1, 2; AMWC 1; AMWS 3; CDALB 1640-1865; DA; DA3; DAC; DAM MST, MULT; DLB 1, 43, 50, 79, 243; FW; LAIT 2; NCFS 2; RGAL 4; SATA 29

Dourado, (Waldomiro Freitas) Autran
1926- .... **CLC 23, 60**
See also CA 25-28R; 179; CANR 34, 81; DLB 145, 307; HW 2

Dourado, Waldomiro Freitas Autran
See Dourado, (Waldomiro Freitas) Autran

Dove, Rita 1952- . **BLC 2:1; BLCS; CLC 50, 81; PC 6**
See also AAYA 46; AMWS 4; BW 2; CA 109; CAAS 19; CANR 27, 42, 68, 76, 97, 132; CDALBS; CP 5, 6, 7; CSW; CWP; DA3; DAM MULT, POET; DLB 120; EWL 3; EXPP; MAL 5; MTCW 2; MTFW 2005; PFS 1, 15; RGAL 4

Dove, Rita Frances
See Dove, Rita

Doveglion
See Villa, Jose Garcia

Dowell, Coleman 1925-1985 .... **CLC 60**
See also CA 25-28R; 117; CANR 10; DLB 130; GLL 2

Downing, Major Jack
See Smith, Seba

Dowson, Ernest (Christopher)
1867-1900 .... **TCLC 4**
See also CA 105; 150; DLB 19, 135; RGEL 2

Doyle, A. Conan
See Doyle, Sir Arthur Conan

Doyle, Sir Arthur Conan
1859-1930 ..... **SSC 12, 83, 95; TCLC 7; WLC 2**
See also AAYA 14; BPFB 1; BRWS 2; BYA 4, 5, 11; CA 104; 122; CANR 131; CD-BLB 1890-1914; CLR 106; CMW 4; DA; DA3; DAB; DAC; DAM MST, NOV; DLB 18, 70, 156, 178; EXPS; HGG; LAIT 2; MSW; MTCW 1, 2; MTFW 2005; NFS 28; RGEL 2; RGSF 2; RHW; SATA 24; SCFW 1, 2; SFW 4; SSFS 2; TEA; WCH; WLIT 4; WYA; YAW

Doyle, Conan
See Doyle, Sir Arthur Conan

Doyle, John
See Graves, Robert

Doyle, Roddy 1958- .... **CLC 81, 178**
See also AAYA 14; BRWS 5; CA 143; CANR 73, 128, 168; CN 6, 7; DA3; DLB 194, 326; MTCW 2; MTFW 2005

Doyle, Sir A. Conan
See Doyle, Sir Arthur Conan

Dr. A
See Asimov, Isaac; Silverstein, Alvin; Silverstein, Virginia B(arbara Opshelor)

Drabble, Margaret 1939- ...... **CLC 2, 3, 5, 8, 10, 22, 53, 129**
See also BRWS 4; CA 13-16R; CANR 18, 35, 63, 112, 131, 174; CDBLB 1960 to Present; CN 1, 2, 3, 4, 5, 6, 7; CPW; DA3; DAB; DAC; DAM MST, NOV, POP; DLB 14, 155, 231; EWL 3; FW; MTCW 1, 2; MTFW 2005; RGEL 2; SATA 48; TEA

Drakulic, Slavenka 1949- .... **CLC 173**
See also CA 144; CANR 92

Engelhardt, Frederick
See Hubbard, L. Ron
Engels, Friedrich 1820-1895 .. NCLC **85, 114**
See also DLB 129; LATS 1:1
Enquist, Per Olov 1934- .... CLC **257**
See also CA 109; 193; CANR 155; CWW
2; DLB 257; EWL 3
Enright, D(ennis) J(oseph)
1920-2002 .... CLC **4, 8, 31; PC 93**
See also CA 1-4R; 211; CANR 1, 42, 83;
CN 1, 2; CP 1, 2, 3, 4, 5, 6, 7; DLB 27;
EWL 3; SATA 25; SATA-Obit 140
Ensler, Eve 1953- .... CLC **212**
See also CA 172; CANR 126, 163; DFS 23
Enzensberger, Hans Magnus
1929- .... CLC **43; PC 28**
See also CA 116; 119; CANR 103; CWW
2; EWL 3
Ephron, Nora 1941- .... CLC **17, 31**
See also AAYA 35; AITN 2; CA 65-68;
CANR 12, 39, 83, 161; DFS 22
Epicurus 341B.C.-270B.C. .... CMLC **21**
See also DLB 176
Epinay, Louise d' 1726-1783 .... LC **138**
See also DLB 313
Epsilon
See Betjeman, John
Epstein, Daniel Mark 1948- .... CLC **7**
See also CA 49-52; CANR 2, 53, 90
Epstein, Jacob 1956- .... CLC **19**
See also CA 114
Epstein, Jean 1897-1953 .... TCLC **92**
Epstein, Joseph 1937- .... CLC **39, 204**
See also AMWS 14; CA 112; 119; CANR
50, 65, 117, 164
Epstein, Leslie 1938- .... CLC **27**
See also AMWS 12; CA 73-76, 215; CAAE
215; CAAS 12; CANR 23, 69, 162; DLB
299; RGHL
Equiano, Olaudah 1745(?)-1797 ..... BLC **1:2;**
LC **16, 143**
See also AFAW 1, 2; CDWLB 3; DAM
MULT; DLB 37, 50; WLIT 2
Erasmus, Desiderius 1469(?)-1536 ..... LC **16,**
93
See also DLB 136; EW 2; LMFS 1; RGWL
2, 3; TWA
Erdman, Paul E. 1932-2007 .... CLC **25**
See also AITN 1; CA 61-64; 259; CANR
13, 43, 84
Erdman, Paul Emil
See Erdman, Paul E.
Erdrich, Karen Louise
See Erdrich, Louise
Erdrich, Louise 1954- .... CLC **39, 54, 120,**
176; NNAL; PC 52; SSC 121
See also AAYA 10, 47; AMWS 4; BEST
89:1; BPFB 1; CA 114; CANR 41, 62,
118, 138; CDALBS; CN 5, 6, 7; CP 6, 7;
CPW; CWP; DA3; DAM MULT, NOV,
POP; DLB 152, 175, 206; EWL 3; EXPP;
FL 1:5; LAIT 5; LATS 1:2; MAL 5;
MTCW 1, 2; MTFW 2005; NFS 5; PFS
14; RGAL 4; SATA 94, 141; SSFS 14,
22; TCWW 2
Erenburg, Ilya (Grigoryevich)
See Ehrenburg, Ilya (Grigoryevich)
See also DLB 272
Erickson, Stephen Michael
See Erickson, Steve
Erickson, Steve 1950- .... CLC **64**
See also CA 129; CANR 60, 68, 136;
MTFW 2005; SFW 4; SUFW 2
Erickson, Walter
See Fast, Howard
Ericson, Walter
See Fast, Howard
Eriksson, Buntel
See Bergman, Ingmar

Eriugena, John Scottus c.
810-877 .... CMLC **65**
See also DLB 115
Ernaux, Annie 1940- .... CLC **88, 184**
See also CA 147; CANR 93; MTFW 2005;
NCFS 3, 5
Erskine, John 1879-1951 .... TCLC **84**
See also CA 112; 159; DLB 9, 102; FANT
Erwin, Will
See Eisner, Will
Eschenbach, Wolfram von
See von Eschenbach, Wolfram
Eseki, Bruno
See Mphahlele, Es'kia
Esekie, Bruno
See Mphahlele, Es'kia
Esenin, S.A.
See Esenin, Sergei
Esenin, Sergei 1895-1925 .... TCLC **4**
See also CA 104; EWL 3; RGWL 2, 3
Esenin, Sergei Aleksandrovich
See Esenin, Sergei
Eshleman, Clayton 1935- .... CLC **7**
See also CA 33-36R, 212; CAAE 212;
CAAS 6; CANR 93; CP 1, 2, 3, 4, 5, 6,
7; DLB 5
Espada, Martin 1957- .... PC **74**
See also CA 159; CANR 80; CP 7; EXPP;
LLW; MAL 5; PFS 13, 16
Espriella, Don Manuel Alvarez
See Southey, Robert
Espriu, Salvador 1913-1985 .... CLC **9**
See also CA 154; 115; DLB 134; EWL 3
Espronceda, Jose de 1808-1842 ..... NCLC **39**
Esquivel, Laura 1950(?)- ... CLC **141; HLCS**
1
See also AAYA 29; CA 143; CANR 68, 113,
161; DA3; DNFS 2; LAIT 3; LMFS 2;
MTCW 2; MTFW 2005; NFS 5; WLIT 1
Esse, James
See Stephens, James
Esterbrook, Tom
See Hubbard, L. Ron
Esterhazy, Peter 1950- .... CLC **251**
See also CA 140; CANR 137; CDWLB 4;
CWW 2; DLB 232; EWL 3; RGWL 3
Estleman, Loren D. 1952- .... CLC **48**
See also AAYA 27; CA 85-88; CANR 27,
74, 139, 177; CMW 4; CPW; DA3; DAM
NOV, POP; DLB 226; INT CANR-27;
MTCW 1, 2; MTFW 2005; TCWW 1, 2
Etherege, Sir George 1636-1692 . DC **23; LC**
78
See also BRW 2; DAM DRAM; DLB 80;
PAB; RGEL 2
Euclid 306B.C.-283B.C. .... CMLC **25**
Eugenides, Jeffrey 1960- .... CLC **81, 212**
See also AAYA 51; CA 144; CANR 120;
MTFW 2005; NFS 24
Euripides c. 484B.C.-406B.C. .... CMLC **23,**
51; DC 4; WLCS
See also AW 1; CDWLB 1; DA; DA3;
DAB; DAC; DAM DRAM, MST; DFS 1,
4, 6, 25; DLB 176; LAIT 1; LMFS 1;
RGWL 2, 3; WLIT 8
Eusebius c. 263-c. 339 .... CMLC **103**
Evan, Evin
See Faust, Frederick (Schiller)
Evans, Caradoc 1878-1945 ... SSC **43; TCLC**
85
See also DLB 162
Evans, Evan
See Faust, Frederick (Schiller)
Evans, Marian
See Eliot, George
Evans, Mary Ann
See Eliot, George

Evarts, Esther
See Benson, Sally
Evelyn, John 1620-1706 .... LC **144**
See also BRW 2; RGEL 2
Everett, Percival 1956- .... CLC **57**
See Everett, Percival L.
See also AMWS 18; BW 2; CA 129; CANR
94, 134, 179; CN 7; MTFW 2005
Everett, Percival L.
See Everett, Percival
See also CSW
Everson, R(onald) G(ilmour)
1903-1992 .... CLC **27**
See also CA 17-20R; CP 1, 2, 3, 4; DLB 88
Everson, William (Oliver)
1912-1994 .... CLC **1, 5, 14**
See also BG 1:2; CA 9-12R; 145; CANR
20; CP 1; DLB 5, 16, 212; MTCW 1
Evtushenko, Evgenii Aleksandrovich
See Yevtushenko, Yevgeny (Alexandrovich)
Ewart, Gavin (Buchanan)
1916-1995 .... CLC **13, 46**
See also BRWS 7; CA 89-92; 150; CANR
17, 46; CP 1, 2, 3, 4, 5, 6; DLB 40;
MTCW 1
Ewers, Hanns Heinz 1871-1943 ..... TCLC **12**
See also CA 109; 149
Ewing, Frederick R.
See Sturgeon, Theodore (Hamilton)
Exley, Frederick (Earl) 1929-1992 .... CLC **6,**
11
See also AITN 2; BPFB 1; CA 81-84; 138;
CANR 117; DLB 143; DLBY 1981
Eynhardt, Guillermo
See Quiroga, Horacio (Sylvestre)
Ezekiel, Nissim (Moses) 1924-2004 .. CLC **61**
See also CA 61-64; 223; CP 1, 2, 3, 4, 5, 6,
7; DLB 323; EWL 3
Ezekiel, Tish O'Dowd 1943- .... CLC **34**
See also CA 129
Fadeev, Aleksandr Aleksandrovich
See Bulgya, Alexander Alexandrovich
Fadeev, Alexandr Alexandrovich
See Bulgya, Alexander Alexandrovich
Fadeyev, A.
See Bulgya, Alexander Alexandrovich
Fadeyev, Alexander
See Bulgya, Alexander Alexandrovich
Fagen, Donald 1948- .... CLC **26**
Fainzil'berg, Il'ia Arnol'dovich
See Fainzilberg, Ilya Arnoldovich
Fainzilberg, Ilya Arnoldovich
1897-1937 .... TCLC **21**
See also CA 120; 165; DLB 272; EWL 3
Fair, Ronald L. 1932- .... CLC **18**
See also BW 1; CA 69-72; CANR 25; DLB
33
Fairbairn, Roger
See Carr, John Dickson
Fairbairns, Zoe (Ann) 1948- .... CLC **32**
See also CA 103; CANR 21, 85; CN 4, 5,
6, 7
Fairfield, Flora
See Alcott, Louisa May
Falco, Gian
See Papini, Giovanni
Falconer, James
See Kirkup, James
Falconer, Kenneth
See Kornbluth, C(yril) M.
Falkland, Samuel
See Heijermans, Herman
Fallaci, Oriana 1930-2006 .... CLC **11, 110**
See also CA 77-80; 253; CANR 15, 58, 134;
FW; MTCW 1
Faludi, Susan 1959- .... CLC **140**
See also CA 138; CANR 126; FW; MTCW
2; MTFW 2005; NCFS 3

Faludy, George 1913- .... **CLC 42**
See also CA 21-24R
Faludy, Gyoergy
See Faludy, George
Fanon, Frantz 1925-1961 ...... **BLC 1:2; CLC 74; TCLC 188**
See also BW 1; CA 116; 89-92; DAM MULT; DLB 296; LMFS 2; WLIT 2
Fanshawe, Ann 1625-1680 .... **LC 11**
Fante, John (Thomas) 1911-1983 .... **CLC 60; SSC 65**
See also AMWS 11; CA 69-72; 109; CANR 23, 104; DLB 130; DLBY 1983
Farah, Nuruddin 1945- .. **BLC 1:2, 2:2; CLC 53, 137**
See also AFW; BW 2, 3; CA 106; CANR 81, 148; CDWLB 3; CN 4, 5, 6, 7; DAM MULT; DLB 125; EWL 3; WLIT 2
Fardusi
See Ferdowsi, Abu'l Qasem
Fargue, Leon-Paul 1876(?)-1947 .... **TCLC 11**
See also CA 109; CANR 107; DLB 258; EWL 3
Farigoule, Louis
See Romains, Jules
Farina, Richard 1936(?)-1966 .... **CLC 9**
See also CA 81-84; 25-28R
Farley, Walter (Lorimer)
1915-1989 .... **CLC 17**
See also AAYA 58; BYA 14; CA 17-20R; CANR 8, 29, 84; DLB 22; JRDA; MAICYA 1, 2; SATA 2, 43, 132; YAW
Farmer, Philip Jose 1918-2009 ..... **CLC 1, 19**
See also AAYA 28; BPFB 1; CA 1-4R; CANR 4, 35, 111; DLB 8; MTCW 1; SATA 93; SCFW 1, 2; SFW 4
Farquhar, George 1677-1707 .... **LC 21**
See also BRW 2; DAM DRAM; DLB 84; RGEL 2
Farrell, J(ames) G(ordon)
1935-1979 .... **CLC 6**
See also CA 73-76; 89-92; CANR 36; CN 1, 2; DLB 14, 271, 326; MTCW 1; RGEL 2; RHW; WLIT 4
Farrell, James T(homas) 1904-1979 . **CLC 1, 4, 8, 11, 66; SSC 28**
See also AMW; BPFB 1; CA 5-8R; 89-92; CANR 9, 61; CN 1, 2; DLB 4, 9, 86; DLBD 2; EWL 3; MAL 5; MTCW 1, 2; MTFW 2005; RGAL 4
Farrell, M. J.
See Keane, Mary Nesta (Skrine)
Farrell, Warren (Thomas) 1943- ...... **CLC 70**
See also CA 146; CANR 120
Farren, Richard J.
See Betjeman, John
Farren, Richard M.
See Betjeman, John
Fassbinder, Rainer Werner
1946-1982 .... **CLC 20**
See also CA 93-96; 106; CANR 31
Fast, Howard 1914-2003 .... **CLC 23, 131**
See also AAYA 16; BPFB 1; CA 1-4R; 181; 214; CAAE 181; CAAS 18; CANR 1, 33, 54, 75, 98, 140; CMW 4; CN 1, 2, 3, 4, 5, 6, 7; CPW; DAM NOV; DLB 9; INT CANR-33; LATS 1:1; MAL 5; MTCW 2; MTFW 2005; RHW; SATA 7; SATA-Essay 107; TCWW 1, 2; YAW
Faulcon, Robert
See Holdstock, Robert
Faulkner, William (Cuthbert)
1897-1962 .... **CLC 1, 3, 6, 8, 9, 11, 14, 18, 28, 52, 68; SSC 1, 35, 42, 92, 97; TCLC 141; WLC 2**
See also AAYA 7; AMW; AMWR 1; BPFB 1; BYA 5, 15; CA 81-84; CANR 33; CDALB 1929-1941; DA; DA3; DAB; DAC; DAM MST, NOV; DLB 9, 11, 44,

102, 316, 330; DLBD 2; DLBY 1986, 1997; EWL 3; EXPN; EXPS; GL 2; LAIT 2; LATS 1:1; LMFS 2; MAL 5; MTCW 1, 2; MTFW 2005; NFS 4, 8, 13, 24; RGAL 4; RGSF 2; SSFS 2, 5, 6, 12, 27; TUS
Fauset, Jessie Redmon
1882(?)-1961 ...... **BLC 1:2; CLC 19, 54; HR 1:2**
See also AFAW 2; BW 1; CA 109; CANR 83; DAM MULT; DLB 51; FW; LMFS 2; MAL 5; MBL
Faust, Frederick (Schiller)
1892-1944 .... **TCLC 49**
See also BPFB 1; CA 108; 152; CANR 143; DAM POP; DLB 256; TCWW 1, 2; TUS
Faust, Irvin 1924- .... **CLC 8**
See also CA 33-36R; CANR 28, 67; CN 1, 2, 3, 4, 5, 6, 7; DLB 2, 28, 218, 278; DLBY 1980
Fawkes, Guy
See Benchley, Robert (Charles)
Fearing, Kenneth (Flexner)
1902-1961 .... **CLC 51**
See also CA 93-96; CANR 59; CMW 4; DLB 9; MAL 5; RGAL 4
Fecamps, Elise
See Creasey, John
Federman, Raymond 1928- .... **CLC 6, 47**
See also CA 17-20R, 208; CAAE 208; CAAS 8; CANR 10, 43, 83, 108; CN 3, 4, 5, 6; DLBY 1980
Federspiel, J.F. 1931-2007 .... **CLC 42**
See also CA 146; 257
Federspiel, Juerg F.
See Federspiel, J.F.
Federspiel, Jurg F.
See Federspiel, J.F.
Feiffer, Jules 1929- .... **CLC 2, 8, 64**
See also AAYA 3, 62; CA 17-20R; CAD; CANR 30, 59, 129, 161; CD 5, 6; DAM DRAM; DLB 7, 44; INT CANR-30; MTCW 1; SATA 8, 61, 111, 157
Feiffer, Jules Ralph
See Feiffer, Jules
Feige, Hermann Albert Otto Maximilian
See Traven, B.
Fei-Kan, Li
See Jin, Ba
Feinberg, David B. 1956-1994 .... **CLC 59**
See also CA 135; 147
Feinstein, Elaine 1930- .... **CLC 36**
See also CA 69-72; CAAS 1; CANR 31, 68, 121, 162; CN 3, 4, 5, 6, 7; CP 2, 3, 4, 5, 6, 7; CWP; DLB 14, 40; MTCW 1
Feke, Gilbert David CLC 65
Feldman, Irving (Mordecai) 1928- ..... **CLC 7**
See also CA 1-4R; CANR 1; CP 1, 2, 3, 4, 5, 6, 7; DLB 169; TCLE 1:1
Felix-Tchicaya, Gerald
See Tchicaya, Gerald Felix
Fellini, Federico 1920-1993 .... **CLC 16, 85**
See also CA 65-68; 143; CANR 33
Felltham, Owen 1602(?)-1668 .... **LC 92**
See also DLB 126, 151
Felsen, Henry Gregor 1916-1995 ..... **CLC 17**
See also CA 1-4R; 180; CANR 1; SAAS 2; SATA 1
Felski, Rita CLC 65
Fenelon, Francois de Pons de Salignac de la Mothe- 1651-1715 .... **LC 134**
See also DLB 268; EW 3; GFL Beginnings to 1789
Fenno, Jack
See Calisher, Hortense

Fenollosa, Ernest (Francisco)
1853-1908 .... **TCLC 91**
Fenton, James 1949- .... **CLC 32, 209**
See also CA 102; CANR 108, 160; CP 2, 3, 4, 5, 6, 7; DLB 40; PFS 11
Fenton, James Martin
See Fenton, James
Ferber, Edna 1887-1968 .... **CLC 18, 93**
See also AITN 1; CA 5-8R; 25-28R; CANR 68, 105; DLB 9, 28, 86, 266; MAL 5; MTCW 1, 2; MTFW 2005; RGAL 4; RHW; SATA 7; TCWW 1, 2
Ferdousi
See Ferdowsi, Abu'l Qasem
Ferdovsi
See Ferdowsi, Abu'l Qasem
Ferdowsi
See Ferdowsi, Abu'l Qasem
Ferdowsi, Abolghasem Mansour
See Ferdowsi, Abu'l Qasem
Ferdowsi, Abolqasem
See Ferdowsi, Abu'l Qasem
Ferdowsi, Abol-Qasem
See Ferdowsi, Abu'l Qasem
Ferdowsi, Abu'l Qasem
940-1020(?) .... **CMLC 43**
See also CA 276; RGWL 2, 3; WLIT 6
Ferdowsi, A.M.
See Ferdowsi, Abu'l Qasem
Ferdowsi, Hakim Abolghasem
See Ferdowsi, Abu'l Qasem
Ferguson, Helen
See Kavan, Anna
Ferguson, Niall 1964- .... **CLC 134, 250**
See also CA 190; CANR 154
Ferguson, Niall Campbell
See Ferguson, Niall
Ferguson, Samuel 1810-1886 .... **NCLC 33**
See also DLB 32; RGEL 2
Fergusson, Robert 1750-1774 .... **LC 29**
See also DLB 109; RGEL 2
Ferling, Lawrence
See Ferlinghetti, Lawrence
Ferlinghetti, Lawrence 1919(?)- .... **CLC 2, 6, 10, 27, 111; PC 1**
See also AAYA 74; BG 1:2; CA 5-8R; CAD; CANR 3, 41, 73, 125, 172; CDALB 1941-1968; CP 1, 2, 3, 4, 5, 6, 7; DA3; DAM POET; DLB 5, 16; MAL 5; MTCW 1, 2; MTFW 2005; PFS 28; RGAL 4; WP
Ferlinghetti, Lawrence Monsanto
See Ferlinghetti, Lawrence
Fern, Fanny
See Parton, Sara Payson Willis
Fernandez, Vicente Garcia Huidobro
See Huidobro Fernandez, Vicente Garcia
Fernandez-Armesto, Felipe CLC 70
See also CA 142; CANR 93, 153, 189
Fernandez-Armesto, Felipe Fermin Ricardo
1950-
See Fernandez-Armesto, Felipe
Fernandez de Lizardi, Jose Joaquin
See Lizardi, Jose Joaquin Fernandez de
Ferre, Rosario 1938- ...... **CLC 139; HLCS 1; SSC 36, 106**
See also CA 131; CANR 55, 81, 134; CWW 2; DLB 145; EWL 3; HW 1, 2; LAWS 1; MTCW 2; MTFW 2005; WLIT 1
Ferrer, Gabriel (Francisco Victor) Miro
See Miro (Ferrer), Gabriel (Francisco Victor)
Ferrier, Susan (Edmonstone)
1782-1854 .... **NCLC 8**
See also DLB 116; RGEL 2
Ferrigno, Robert 1947- .... **CLC 65**
See also CA 140; CANR 125, 161

Franklin, (Stella Maria Sarah) Miles (Lampe) 1879-1954 .... **TCLC 7**
See also CA 104; 164; DLB 230; FW; MTCW 2; RGEL 2; TWA

Franzen, Jonathan 1959- .... **CLC 202**
See also AAYA 65; CA 129; CANR 105, 166

Fraser, Antonia 1932- .... **CLC 32, 107**
See also AAYA 57; CA 85-88; CANR 44, 65, 119, 164; CMW; DLB 276; MTCW 1, 2; MTFW 2005; SATA-Brief 32

Fraser, George MacDonald 1925-2008 .... **CLC 7**
See also AAYA 48; CA 45-48, 180; 268; CAAE 180; CANR 2, 48, 74; MTCW 2; RHW

Fraser, Sylvia 1935- .... **CLC 64**
See also CA 45-48; CANR 1, 16, 60; CCA 1

Frater Perdurabo
See Crowley, Edward Alexander

Frayn, Michael 1933- .... **CLC 3, 7, 31, 47, 176; DC 27**
See also AAYA 69; BRWC 2; BRWS 7; CA 5-8R; CANR 30, 69, 114, 133, 166; CBD; CD 5, 6; CN 1, 2, 3, 4, 5, 6, 7; DAM DRAM, NOV; DFS 22; DLB 13, 14, 194, 245; FANT; MTCW 1, 2; MTFW 2005; SFW 4

Fraze, Candida (Merrill) 1945- .... **CLC 50**
See also CA 126

Frazer, Andrew
See Marlowe, Stephen

Frazer, J(ames) G(eorge) 1854-1941 .... **TCLC 32**
See also BRWS 3; CA 118; NCFS 5

Frazer, Robert Caine
See Creasey, John

Frazer, Sir James George
See Frazer, J(ames) G(eorge)

Frazier, Charles 1950- .... **CLC 109, 224**
See also AAYA 34; CA 161; CANR 126, 170; CSW; DLB 292; MTFW 2005; NFS 25

Frazier, Charles R.
See Frazier, Charles

Frazier, Charles Robinson
See Frazier, Charles

Frazier, Ian 1951- .... **CLC 46**
See also CA 130; CANR 54, 93

Frederic, Harold 1856-1898 ... **NCLC 10, 175**
See also AMW; DLB 12, 23; DLBD 13; MAL 5; NFS 22; RGAL 4

Frederick, John
See Faust, Frederick (Schiller)

Frederick the Great 1712-1786 .... **LC 14**

Fredro, Aleksander 1793-1876 .... **NCLC 8**

Freeling, Nicolas 1927-2003 .... **CLC 38**
See also CA 49-52; 218; CAAS 12; CANR 1, 17, 50, 84; CMW 4; CN 1, 2, 3, 4, 5, 6; DLB 87

Freeman, Douglas Southall 1886-1953 .... **TCLC 11**
See also CA 109; 195; DLB 17; DLBD 17

Freeman, Judith 1946- .... **CLC 55**
See also CA 148; CANR 120, 179; DLB 256

Freeman, Mary E(leanor) Wilkins 1852-1930 .... **SSC 1, 47, 113; TCLC 9**
See also CA 106; 177; DLB 12, 78, 221; EXPS; FW; HGG; MBL; RGAL 4; RGSF 2; SSFS 4, 8, 26; SUFW 1; TUS

Freeman, R(ichard) Austin 1862-1943 .... **TCLC 21**
See also CA 113; CANR 84; CMW 4; DLB 70

French, Albert 1943- .... **CLC 86**
See also BW 3; CA 167

French, Antonia
See Kureishi, Hanif

French, Marilyn 1929- .. **CLC 10, 18, 60, 177**
See also BPFB 1; CA 69-72; CANR 3, 31, 134, 163; CN 5, 6, 7; CPW; DAM DRAM, NOV, POP; FL 1:5; FW; INT CANR-31; MTCW 1, 2; MTFW 2005

French, Paul
See Asimov, Isaac

Freneau, Philip Morin 1752-1832 .. **NCLC 1, 111**
See also AMWS 2; DLB 37, 43; RGAL 4

Freud, Sigmund 1856-1939 .... **TCLC 52**
See also CA 115; 133; CANR 69; DLB 296; EW 8; EWL 3; LATS 1:1; MTCW 1, 2; MTFW 2005; NCFS 3; TWA

Freytag, Gustav 1816-1895 .... **NCLC 109**
See also DLB 129

Friedan, Betty 1921-2006 .... **CLC 74**
See also CA 65-68; 248; CANR 18, 45, 74; DLB 246; FW; MTCW 1, 2; MTFW 2005; NCFS 5

Friedan, Betty Naomi
See Friedan, Betty

Friedlander, Saul 1932- .... **CLC 90**
See also CA 117; 130; CANR 72; RGHL

Friedman, B(ernard) H(arper) 1926- .... **CLC 7**
See also CA 1-4R; CANR 3, 48

Friedman, Bruce Jay 1930- ...... **CLC 3, 5, 56**
See also CA 9-12R; CAD; CANR 25, 52, 101; CD 5, 6; CN 1, 2, 3, 4, 5, 6, 7; DLB 2, 28, 244; INT CANR-25; MAL 5; SSFS 18

Friel, Brian 1929- .. **CLC 5, 42, 59, 115, 253; DC 8; SSC 76**
See also BRWS 5; CA 21-24R; CANR 33, 69, 131; CBD; CD 5, 6; DFS 11; DLB 13, 319; EWL 3; MTCW 1; RGEL 2; TEA

Friis-Baastad, Babbis Ellinor 1921-1970 .... **CLC 12**
See also CA 17-20R; 134; SATA 7

Frisch, Max 1911-1991 ...... **CLC 3, 9, 14, 18, 32, 44; TCLC 121**
See also CA 85-88; 134; CANR 32, 74; CD-WLB 2; DAM DRAM, NOV; DFS 25; DLB 69, 124; EW 13; EWL 3; MTCW 1, 2; MTFW 2005; RGHL; RGWL 2, 3

Fromentin, Eugene (Samuel Auguste) 1820-1876 .... **NCLC 10, 125**
See also DLB 123; GFL 1789 to the Present

Frost, Frederick
See Faust, Frederick (Schiller)

Frost, Robert 1874-1963 . **CLC 1, 3, 4, 9, 10, 13, 15, 26, 34, 44; PC 1, 39, 71; WLC 2**
See also AAYA 21; AMW; AMWR 1; CA 89-92; CANR 33; CDALB 1917-1929; CLR 67; DA; DA3; DAB; DAC; DAM MST, POET; DLB 54, 284, 342; DLBD 7; EWL 3; EXPP; MAL 5; MTCW 1, 2; MTFW 2005; PAB; PFS 1, 2, 3, 4, 5, 6, 7, 10, 13; RGAL 4; SATA 14; TUS; WP; WYA

Frost, Robert Lee
See Frost, Robert

Froude, James Anthony 1818-1894 .... **NCLC 43**
See also DLB 18, 57, 144

Froy, Herald
See Waterhouse, Keith (Spencer)

Fry, Christopher 1907-2005 ... **CLC 2, 10, 14**
See also BRWS 3; CA 17-20R; 240; CAAS 23; CANR 9, 30, 74, 132; CBD; CD 5, 6; CP 1, 2, 3, 4, 5, 6, 7; DAM DRAM; DLB 13; EWL 3; MTCW 1, 2; MTFW 2005; RGEL 2; SATA 66; TEA

Frye, (Herman) Northrop 1912-1991 .... **CLC 24, 70; TCLC 165**
See also CA 5-8R; 133; CANR 8, 37; DLB 67, 68, 246; EWL 3; MTCW 1, 2; MTFW 2005; RGAL 4; TWA

Fuchs, Daniel 1909-1993 .... **CLC 8, 22**
See also CA 81-84; 142; CAAS 5; CANR 40; CN 1, 2, 3, 4, 5; DLB 9, 26, 28; DLBY 1993; MAL 5

Fuchs, Daniel 1934- .... **CLC 34**
See also CA 37-40R; CANR 14, 48

Fuentes, Carlos 1928- .. **CLC 3, 8, 10, 13, 22, 41, 60, 113; HLC 1; SSC 24, 125; WLC 2**
See also AAYA 4, 45; AITN 2; BPFB 1; CA 69-72; CANR 10, 32, 68, 104, 138; CDWLB 3; CWW 2; DA; DA3; DAB; DAC; DAM MST, MULT, NOV; DLB 113; DNFS 2; EWL 3; HW 1, 2; LAIT 3; LATS 1:2; LAW; LAWS 1; LMFS 2; MTCW 1, 2; MTFW 2005; NFS 8; RGSF 2; RGWL 2, 3; TWA; WLIT 1

Fuentes, Gregorio Lopez y
See Lopez y Fuentes, Gregorio

Fuertes, Gloria 1918-1998 .... **PC 27**
See also CA 178; 180; DLB 108; HW 2; SATA 115

Fugard, (Harold) Athol 1932- . **CLC 5, 9, 14, 25, 40, 80, 211; DC 3**
See also AAYA 17; AFW; CA 85-88; CANR 32, 54, 118; CD 5, 6; DAM DRAM; DFS 3, 6, 10, 24; DLB 225; DNFS 1, 2; EWL 3; LATS 1:2; MTCW 1; MTFW 2005; RGEL 2; WLIT 2

Fugard, Sheila 1932- .... **CLC 48**
See also CA 125

Fujiwara no Teika 1162-1241 .... **CMLC 73**
See also DLB 203

Fukuyama, Francis 1952- .... **CLC 131**
See also CA 140; CANR 72, 125, 170

Fuller, Charles (H.), (Jr.) 1939- ..... **BLC 1:2; CLC 25; DC 1**
See also BW 2; CA 108; 112; CAD; CANR 87; CD 5, 6; DAM DRAM, MULT; DFS 8; DLB 38, 266; EWL 3; INT CA-112; MAL 5; MTCW 1

Fuller, Henry Blake 1857-1929 .... **TCLC 103**
See also CA 108; 177; DLB 12; RGAL 4

Fuller, John (Leopold) 1937- .... **CLC 62**
See also CA 21-24R; CANR 9, 44; CP 1, 2, 3, 4, 5, 6, 7; DLB 40

Fuller, Margaret
See Ossoli, Sarah Margaret (Fuller)

Fuller, Roy (Broadbent) 1912-1991 ... **CLC 4, 28**
See also BRWS 7; CA 5-8R; 135; CAAS 10; CANR 53, 83; CN 1, 2, 3, 4, 5; CP 1, 2, 3, 4, 5; CWRI 5; DLB 15, 20; EWL 3; RGEL 2; SATA 87

Fuller, Sarah Margaret
See Ossoli, Sarah Margaret (Fuller)

Fuller, Thomas 1608-1661 .... **LC 111**
See also DLB 151

Fulton, Alice 1952- .... **CLC 52**
See also CA 116; CANR 57, 88; CP 5, 6, 7; CWP; DLB 193; PFS 25

Furey, Michael
See Ward, Arthur Henry Sarsfield

Furphy, Joseph 1843-1912 .... **TCLC 25**
See also CA 163; DLB 230; EWL 3; RGEL 2

Furst, Alan 1941- .... **CLC 255**
See also CA 69-72; CANR 12, 34, 59, 102, 159; DLBY 01

Fuson, Robert H(enderson) 1927- .... **CLC 70**
See also CA 89-92; CANR 103

Fussell, Paul 1924- .... **CLC 74**
See also BEST 90:1; CA 17-20R; CANR 8,
21, 35, 69, 135; INT CANR-21; MTCW
1, 2; MTFW 2005

Futabatei, Shimei 1864-1909 .... **TCLC 44**
See also CA 162; DLB 180; EWL 3; MJW

Futabatei Shimei
See Futabatei, Shimei

Futrelle, Jacques 1875-1912 .... **TCLC 19**
See also CA 113; 155; CMW 4

GAB
See Russell, George William

Gaberman, Judie Angell
See Angell, Judie

Gaboriau, Emile 1835-1873 .... **NCLC 14**
See also CMW 4; MSW

Gadda, Carlo Emilio 1893-1973 ...... **CLC 11;**
TCLC 144
See also CA 89-92; DLB 177; EWL 3;
WLIT 7

Gaddis, William 1922-1998 ... **CLC 1, 3, 6, 8,**
10, 19, 43, 86
See also AMWS 4; BPFB 1; CA 17-20R;
172; CANR 21, 48, 148; CN 1, 2, 3, 4, 5,
6; DLB 2, 278; EWL 3; MAL 5; MTCW
1, 2; MTFW 2005; RGAL 4

Gage, Walter
See Inge, William (Motter)

Gaiman, Neil 1960- .... **CLC 195**
See also AAYA 19, 42; CA 133; CANR 81,
129, 188; CLR 109; DLB 261; HGG;
MTFW 2005; SATA 85, 146, 197; SFW
4; SUFW 2

Gaiman, Neil Richard
See Gaiman, Neil

Gaines, Ernest J. 1933- ..... **BLC 1:2; CLC 3,**
11, 18, 86, 181; SSC 68
See also AAYA 18; AFAW 1, 2; AITN 1;
BPFB 2; BW 2, 3; BYA 6; CA 9-12R;
CANR 6, 24, 42, 75, 126; CDALB 1968-
1988; CLR 62; CN 1, 2, 3, 4, 5, 6, 7;
CSW; DA3; DAM MULT; DLB 2, 33,
152; DLBY 1980; EWL 3; EXPN; LAIT
5; LATS 1:2; MAL 5; MTCW 1, 2;
MTFW 2005; NFS 5, 7, 16; RGAL 4;
RGSF 2; RHW; SATA 86; SSFS 5; YAW

Gaitskill, Mary 1954- .... **CLC 69**
See also CA 128; CANR 61, 152; DLB 244;
TCLE 1:1

Gaitskill, Mary Lawrence
See Gaitskill, Mary

Gaius Suetonius Tranquillus
See Suetonius

Galdos, Benito Perez
See Perez Galdos, Benito

Gale, Zona 1874-1938 .... **DC 30; TCLC 7**
See also CA 105; 153; CANR 84; DAM
DRAM; DFS 17; DLB 9, 78, 228; RGAL
4

Galeano, Eduardo 1940- ... **CLC 72; HLCS 1**
See also CA 29-32R; CANR 13, 32, 100,
163; HW 1

Galeano, Eduardo Hughes
See Galeano, Eduardo

Galiano, Juan Valera y Alcala
See Valera y Alcala-Galiano, Juan

Galilei, Galileo 1564-1642 .... **LC 45**

Gallagher, Tess 1943- .... **CLC 18, 63; PC 9**
See also CA 106; CP 3, 4, 5, 6, 7; CWP;
DAM POET; DLB 120, 212, 244; PFS 16

Gallant, Mavis 1922- ..... **CLC 7, 18, 38, 172;**
SSC 5, 78
See also CA 69-72; CANR 29, 69, 117;
CCA 1; CN 1, 2, 3, 4, 5, 6, 7; DAC; DAM
MST; DLB 53; EWL 3; MTCW 1, 2;
MTFW 2005; RGEL 2; RGSF 2

Gallant, Roy A(rthur) 1924- .... **CLC 17**
See also CA 5-8R; CANR 4, 29, 54, 117;
CLR 30; MAICYA 1, 2; SATA 4, 68, 110

Gallico, Paul (William) 1897-1976 ..... **CLC 2**
See also AITN 1; CA 5-8R; 69-72; CANR
23; CN 1, 2; DLB 9, 171; FANT; MAI-
CYA 1, 2; SATA 13

Gallo, Max Louis 1932- .... **CLC 95**
See also CA 85-88

Gallois, Lucien
See Desnos, Robert

Gallup, Ralph
See Whitemore, Hugh (John)

Galsworthy, John 1867-1933 .... **SSC 22;**
TCLC 1, 45; WLC 2
See also BRW 6; CA 104; 141; CANR 75;
CDBLB 1890-1914; DA; DA3; DAB;
DAC; DAM DRAM, MST, NOV; DLB
10, 34, 98, 162, 330; DLBD 16; EWL 3;
MTCW 2; RGEL 2; SSFS 3; TEA

Galt, John 1779-1839 .... **NCLC 1, 110**
See also DLB 99, 116, 159; RGEL 2; RGSF
2

Galvin, James 1951- .... **CLC 38**
See also CA 108; CANR 26

Gamboa, Federico 1864-1939 .... **TCLC 36**
See also CA 167; HW 2; LAW

Gandhi, M. K.
See Gandhi, Mohandas Karamchand

Gandhi, Mahatma
See Gandhi, Mohandas Karamchand

Gandhi, Mohandas Karamchand
1869-1948 .... **TCLC 59**
See also CA 121; 132; DA3; DAM MULT;
DLB 323; MTCW 1, 2

Gann, Ernest Kellogg 1910-1991 ..... **CLC 23**
See also AITN 1; BPFB 2; CA 1-4R; 136;
CANR 1, 83; RHW

Gao Xingjian 1940-
See Xingjian, Gao

Garber, Eric 1943(?)- .... **CLC 38**
See also CA 144; CANR 89, 162; GLL 1

Garber, Esther
See Lee, Tanith

Garcia, Cristina 1958- .... **CLC 76**
See also AMWS 11; CA 141; CANR 73,
130, 172; CN 7; DLB 292; DNFS 1; EWL
3; HW 2; LLW; MTFW 2005

Garcia Lorca, Federico 1898-1936 ...... **DC 2;**
HLC 2; PC 3; TCLC 1, 7, 49, 181,
197; WLC 2
See also AAYA 46; CA 104; 131; CANR
81; DA; DA3; DAB; DAC; DAM DRAM,
MST, MULT, POET; DFS 4; DLB 108;
EW 11; EWL 3; HW 1, 2; LATS 1:2;
MTCW 1, 2; MTFW 2005; PFS 20;
RGWL 2, 3; TWA; WP

Garcia Marquez, Gabriel 1928- .... **CLC 2, 3,**
8, 10, 15, 27, 47, 55, 68, 170, 254; HLC
1; SSC 8, 83; WLC 3
See also AAYA 3, 33; BEST 89:1, 90:4;
BPFB 2; BYA 12, 16; CA 33-36R; CANR
10, 28, 50, 75, 82, 128; CDWLB 3; CPW;
CWW 2; DA; DA3; DAB; DAC; DAM
MST, MULT, NOV, POP; DLB 113, 330;
DNFS 1, 2; EWL 3; EXPN; EXPS; HW
1, 2; LAIT 2; LATS 1:2; LAW; LAWS 1;
LMFS 2; MTCW 1, 2; MTFW 2005;
NCFS 3; NFS 1, 5, 10; RGSF 2; RGWL
2, 3; SSFS 1, 6, 16, 21; TWA; WLIT 1

Garcia Marquez, Gabriel Jose
See Garcia Marquez, Gabriel

Garcilaso de la Vega, El Inca
1539-1616 .... **HLCS 1; LC 127**
See also DLB 318; LAW

Gard, Janice
See Latham, Jean Lee

Gard, Roger Martin du
See Martin du Gard, Roger

Gardam, Jane 1928- .... **CLC 43**
See also CA 49-52; CANR 2, 18, 33, 54,
106, 167; CLR 12; DLB 14, 161, 231;
MAICYA 1, 2; MTCW 1; SAAS 9; SATA
39, 76, 130; SATA-Brief 28; YAW

Gardam, Jane Mary
See Gardam, Jane

Gardner, Herb(ert George)
1934-2003 .... **CLC 44**
See also CA 149; 220; CAD; CANR 119;
CD 5, 6; DFS 18, 20

Gardner, John, Jr. 1933-1982 ... **CLC 2, 3, 5,**
7, 8, 10, 18, 28, 34; SSC 7; TCLC 195
See also AAYA 45; AITN 1; AMWS 6;
BPFB 2; CA 65-68; 107; CANR 33, 73;
CDALBS; CN 2, 3; CPW; DA3; DAM
NOV, POP; DLB 2; DLBY 1982; EWL 3;
FANT; LATS 1:2; MAL 5; MTCW 1, 2;
MTFW 2005; NFS 3; RGAL 4; RGSF 2;
SATA 40; SATA-Obit 31; SSFS 8

Gardner, John 1926-2007 .... **CLC 30**
See also CA 103; 263; CANR 15, 69, 127,
183; CMW 4; CPW; DAM POP; MTCW
1

Gardner, John Edmund
See Gardner, John

Gardner, Miriam
See Bradley, Marion Zimmer

Gardner, Noel
See Kuttner, Henry

Gardons, S.S.
See Snodgrass, W. D.

Garfield, Leon 1921-1996 .... **CLC 12**
See also AAYA 8, 69; BYA 1, 3; CA 17-
20R; 152; CANR 38, 41, 78; CLR 21;
DLB 161; JRDA; MAICYA 1, 2; MAIC-
YAS 1; SATA 1, 32, 76; SATA-Obit 90;
TEA; WYA; YAW

Garland, (Hannibal) Hamlin
1860-1940 .... **SSC 18, 117; TCLC 3**
See also CA 104; DLB 12, 71, 78, 186;
MAL 5; RGAL 4; RGSF 2; TCWW 1, 2

Garneau, (Hector de) Saint-Denys
1912-1943 .... **TCLC 13**
See also CA 111; DLB 88

Garner, Alan 1934- .... **CLC 17**
See also AAYA 18; BYA 3, 5; CA 73-76;
178; CAAE 178; CANR 15, 64, 134; CLR
20, 130; CPW; DAB; DAM POP; DLB
161, 261; FANT; MAICYA 1, 2; MTCW
1, 2; MTFW 2005; SATA 18, 69; SATA-
Essay 108; SUFW 1, 2; YAW

Garner, Hugh 1913-1979 .... **CLC 13**
See also CA 69-72; CANR 31; CCA 1; CN
1, 2; DLB 68

Garnett, David 1892-1981 .... **CLC 3**
See also CA 5-8R; 103; CANR 17, 79; CN
1, 2; DLB 34; FANT; MTCW 2; RGEL 2;
SFW 4; SUFW 1

Garnier, Robert c. 1545-1590 .... **LC 119**
See also DLB 327; GFL Beginnings to 1789

Garrett, George 1929-2008 ... **CLC 3, 11, 51;**
SSC 30
See also AMWS 7; BPFB 2; CA 1-4R; 202;
272; CAAE 202; CAAS 5; CANR 1, 42,
67, 109; CN 1, 2, 3, 4, 5, 6, 7; CP 1, 2, 3,
4, 5, 6, 7; CSW; DLB 2, 5, 130, 152;
DLBY 1983

Garrett, George P.
See Garrett, George

Garrett, George Palmer
See Garrett, George

Garrett, George Palmer, Jr.
See Garrett, George

Garrick, David 1717-1779 .... **LC 15, 156**
See also DAM DRAM; DLB 84, 213;
RGEL 2

Garrigue, Jean 1914-1972 .... **CLC 2, 8**
 See also CA 5-8R; 37-40R; CANR 20; CP
 1; MAL 5
Garrison, Frederick
 See Sinclair, Upton
Garrison, William Lloyd
 1805-1879 .... **NCLC 149**
 See also CDALB 1640-1865; DLB 1, 43,
 235
Garro, Elena 1920(?)-1998 .. **HLCS 1; TCLC
 153**
 See also CA 131; 169; CWW 2; DLB 145;
 EWL 3; HW 1; LAWS 1; WLIT 1
Garth, Will
 See Hamilton, Edmond; Kuttner, Henry
Garvey, Marcus (Moziah, Jr.)
 1887-1940 ..... **BLC 1:2; HR 1:2; TCLC
 41**
 See also BW 1; CA 120; 124; CANR 79;
 DAM MULT; DLB 345
Gary, Romain
 See Kacew, Romain
Gascar, Pierre
 See Fournier, Pierre
Gascoigne, George 1539-1577 .... **LC 108**
 See also DLB 136; RGEL 2
Gascoyne, David (Emery)
 1916-2001 .... **CLC 45**
 See also CA 65-68; 200; CANR 10, 28, 54;
 CP 1, 2, 3, 4, 5, 6, 7; DLB 20; MTCW 1;
 RGEL 2
Gaskell, Elizabeth Cleghorn
 1810-1865 .... **NCLC 5, 70, 97, 137, 214;
 SSC 25, 97**
 See also BRW 5; CDBLB 1832-1890; DAB;
 DAM MST; DLB 21, 144, 159; RGEL 2;
 RGSF 2; TEA
Gass, William H. 1924- . **CLC 1, 2, 8, 11, 15,
 39, 132; SSC 12**
 See also AMWS 6; CA 17-20R; CANR 30,
 71, 100; CN 1, 2, 3, 4, 5, 6, 7; DLB 2,
 227; EWL 3; MAL 5; MTCW 1, 2;
 MTFW 2005; RGAL 4
Gassendi, Pierre 1592-1655 .... **LC 54**
 See also GFL Beginnings to 1789
Gasset, Jose Ortega y
 See Ortega y Gasset, Jose
Gates, Henry Louis, Jr. 1950- ... **BLCS; CLC
 65**
 See also BW 2, 3; CA 109; CANR 25, 53,
 75, 125; CSW; DA3; DAM MULT; DLB
 67; EWL 3; MAL 5; MTCW 2; MTFW
 2005; RGAL 4
Gatos, Stephanie
 See Katz, Steve
Gautier, Theophile 1811-1872 .. **NCLC 1, 59;
 PC 18; SSC 20**
 See also DAM POET; DLB 119; EW 6;
 GFL 1789 to the Present; RGWL 2, 3;
 SUFW; TWA
Gautreaux, Tim 1947- .... **CLC 270; SSC 125**
 See also CA 187; CSW; DLB 292
Gay, John 1685-1732 .... **LC 49**
 See also BRW 3; DAM DRAM; DLB 84,
 95; RGEL 2; WLIT 3
Gay, Oliver
 See Gogarty, Oliver St. John
Gay, Peter 1923- .... **CLC 158**
 See also CA 13-16R; CANR 18, 41, 77,
 147; INT CANR-18; RGHL
Gay, Peter Jack
 See Gay, Peter
Gaye, Marvin (Pentz, Jr.)
 1939-1984 .... **CLC 26**
 See also CA 195; 112
Gebler, Carlo 1954- .... **CLC 39**
 See also CA 119; 133; CANR 96, 186; DLB
 271

Gebler, Carlo Ernest
 See Gebler, Carlo
Gee, Maggie 1948- .... **CLC 57**
 See also CA 130; CANR 125; CN 4, 5, 6,
 7; DLB 207; MTFW 2005
Gee, Maurice 1931- .... **CLC 29**
 See also AAYA 42; CA 97-100; CANR 67,
 123; CLR 56; CN 2, 3, 4, 5, 6, 7; CWRI
 5; EWL 3; MAICYA 2; RGSF 2; SATA
 46, 101
Gee, Maurice Gough
 See Gee, Maurice
Geiogamah, Hanay 1945- .... **NNAL**
 See also CA 153; DAM MULT; DLB 175
Gelbart, Larry
 See Gelbart, Larry (Simon)
Gelbart, Larry (Simon) 1928- .... **CLC 21, 61**
 See also CA 73-76; CAD; CANR 45, 94;
 CD 5, 6
Gelber, Jack 1932-2003 ...... **CLC 1, 6, 14, 79**
 See also CA 1-4R; 216; CAD; CANR 2;
 DLB 7, 228; MAL 5
Gellhorn, Martha (Ellis)
 1908-1998 .... **CLC 14, 60**
 See also CA 77-80; 164; CANR 44; CN 1,
 2, 3, 4, 5, 6, 7; DLBY 1982, 1998
Genet, Jean 1910-1986 .. **CLC 1, 2, 5, 10, 14,
 44, 46; DC 25; TCLC 128**
 See also CA 13-16R; CANR 18; DA3;
 DAM DRAM; DFS 10; DLB 72, 321;
 DLBY 1986; EW 13; EWL 3; GFL 1789
 to the Present; GLL 1; LMFS 2; MTCW
 1, 2; MTFW 2005; RGWL 2, 3; TWA
Genlis, Stephanie-Felicite Ducrest
 1746-1830 .... **NCLC 166**
 See also DLB 313
Gent, Peter 1942- .... **CLC 29**
 See also AITN 1; CA 89-92; DLBY 1982
Gentile, Giovanni 1875-1944 .... **TCLC 96**
 See also CA 119
Geoffrey of Monmouth c.
 1100-1155 .... **CMLC 44**
 See also DLB 146; TEA
George, Jean
 See George, Jean Craighead
George, Jean Craighead 1919- .... **CLC 35**
 See also AAYA 8, 69; BYA 2, 4; CA 5-8R;
 CANR 25; CLR 1, 80, 136; DLB 52;
 JRDA; MAICYA 1, 2; SATA 2, 68, 124,
 170; WYA; YAW
George, Stefan (Anton) 1868-1933 . **TCLC 2,
 14**
 See also CA 104; 193; EW 8; EWL 3
Georges, Georges Martin
 See Simenon, Georges (Jacques Christian)
Gerald of Wales c. 1146-c. 1223 ... **CMLC 60**
Gerhardi, William Alexander
 See Gerhardie, William Alexander
Gerhardie, William Alexander
 1895-1977 .... **CLC 5**
 See also CA 25-28R; 73-76; CANR 18; CN
 1, 2; DLB 36; RGEL 2
Gerome
 See Thibault, Jacques Anatole Francois
Gerson, Jean 1363-1429 .... **LC 77**
 See also DLB 208
Gersonides 1288-1344 .... **CMLC 49**
 See also DLB 115
Gerstler, Amy 1956- .... **CLC 70**
 See also CA 146; CANR 99
Gertler, T. **CLC 34**
 See also CA 116; 121
Gertrude of Helfta c. 1256-c.
 1301 .... **CMLC 105**
Gertsen, Aleksandr Ivanovich
 See Herzen, Aleksandr Ivanovich
Ghalib
 See Ghalib, Asadullah Khan

Ghalib, Asadullah Khan
 1797-1869 .... **NCLC 39, 78**
 See also DAM POET; RGWL 2, 3
Ghelderode, Michel de 1898-1962 ..... **CLC 6,
 11; DC 15; TCLC 187**
 See also CA 85-88; CANR 40, 77; DAM
 DRAM; DLB 321; EW 11; EWL 3; TWA
Ghiselin, Brewster 1903-2001 .... **CLC 23**
 See also CA 13-16R; CAAS 10; CANR 13;
 CP 1, 2, 3, 4, 5, 6, 7
Ghose, Aurabinda 1872-1950 .... **TCLC 63**
 See also CA 163; EWL 3
Ghose, Aurobindo
 See Ghose, Aurabinda
Ghose, Zulfikar 1935- .... **CLC 42, 200**
 See also CA 65-68; CANR 67; CN 1, 2, 3,
 4, 5, 6, 7; CP 1, 2, 3, 4, 5, 6, 7; DLB 323;
 EWL 3
Ghosh, Amitav 1956- .... **CLC 44, 153**
 See also CA 147; CANR 80, 158; CN 6, 7;
 DLB 323; WWE 1
Giacosa, Giuseppe 1847-1906 .... **TCLC 7**
 See also CA 104
Gibb, Lee
 See Waterhouse, Keith (Spencer)
Gibbon, Edward 1737-1794 .... **LC 97**
 See also BRW 3; DLB 104, 336; RGEL 2
Gibbon, Lewis Grassic
 See Mitchell, James Leslie
Gibbons, Kaye 1960- .... **CLC 50, 88, 145**
 See also AAYA 34; AMWS 10; CA 151;
 CANR 75, 127; CN 7; CSW; DA3; DAM
 POP; DLB 292; MTCW 2; MTFW 2005;
 NFS 3; RGAL 4; SATA 117
Gibran, Kahlil 1883-1931 ..... **PC 9; TCLC 1,
 9, 205**
 See also CA 104; 150; DA3; DAM POET,
 POP; DLB 346; EWL 3; MTCW 2; WLIT
 6
Gibran, Khalil
 See Gibran, Kahlil
Gibson, Mel 1956- .... **CLC 215**
Gibson, William 1914-2008 .... **CLC 23**
 See also CA 9-12R; 279; CAD; CANR 9,
 42, 75, 125; CD 5, 6; DA; DAB; DAC;
 DAM DRAM, MST; DFS 2; DLB 7;
 LAIT 2; MAL 5; MTCW 2; MTFW 2005;
 SATA 66; SATA-Obit 199; YAW
Gibson, William 1948- .... **CLC 39, 63, 186,
 192; SSC 52**
 See also AAYA 12, 59; AMWS 16; BPFB
 2; CA 126; 133; CANR 52, 90, 106, 172;
 CN 6, 7; CPW; DA3; DAM POP; DLB
 251; MTCW 2; MTFW 2005; SCFW 2;
 SFW 4; SSFS 26
Gibson, William Ford
 See Gibson, William
Gide, Andre (Paul Guillaume)
 1869-1951 ...... **SSC 13; TCLC 5, 12, 36,
 177; WLC 3**
 See also CA 104; 124; DA; DA3; DAB;
 DAC; DAM MST, NOV; DLB 65, 321,
 330; EW 8; EWL 3; GFL 1789 to the
 Present; MTCW 1, 2; MTFW 2005; NFS
 21; RGSF 2; RGWL 2, 3; TWA
Gifford, Barry 1946- .... **CLC 34**
 See also CA 65-68; CANR 9, 30, 40, 90,
 180
Gifford, Barry Colby
 See Gifford, Barry
Gilbert, Frank
 See De Voto, Bernard (Augustine)
Gilbert, W(illiam) S(chwenck)
 1836-1911 .... **TCLC 3**
 See also CA 104; 173; DAM DRAM, POET;
 DLB 344; RGEL 2; SATA 36

Greve, Felix Paul (Berthold Friedrich)
   1879-1948 .... **TCLC 4**
   See also CA 104; 141, 175; CANR 79;
   DAC; DAM MST; DLB 92; RGEL 2;
   TCWW 1, 2
Greville, Fulke 1554-1628 .... **LC 79**
   See also BRWS 11; DLB 62, 172; RGEL 2
Grey, Lady Jane 1537-1554 .... **LC 93**
   See also DLB 132
Grey, Zane 1872-1939 .... **TCLC 6**
   See also BPFB 2; CA 104; 132; DA3; DAM
   POP; DLB 9, 212; MTCW 1, 2; MTFW
   2005; RGAL 4; TCWW 1, 2; TUS
Griboedov, Aleksandr Sergeevich
   1795(?)-1829 .... **NCLC 129**
   See also DLB 205; RGWL 2, 3
Grieg, (Johan) Nordahl (Brun)
   1902-1943 .... **TCLC 10**
   See also CA 107; 189; EWL 3
Grieve, C(hristopher) M(urray)
   1892-1978 ... **CLC 2, 4, 11, 19, 63; PC 9**
   See also BRWS 12; CA 5-8R; 85-88; CANR
   33, 107; CDBLB 1945-1960; CP 1, 2;
   DAM POET; DLB 20; EWL 3; MTCW 1;
   RGEL 2
Griffin, Gerald 1803-1840 .... **NCLC 7**
   See also DLB 159; RGEL 2
Griffin, John Howard 1920-1980 ..... **CLC 68**
   See also AITN 1; CA 1-4R; 101; CANR 2
Griffin, Peter 1942- .... **CLC 39**
   See also CA 136
Griffith, David Lewelyn Wark
   See Griffith, D.W.
Griffith, D.W. 1875(?)-1948 .... **TCLC 68**
   See also AAYA 78; CA 119; 150; CANR 80
Griffith, Lawrence
   See Griffith, D.W.
Griffiths, Trevor 1935- .... **CLC 13, 52**
   See also CA 97-100; CANR 45; CBD; CD
   5, 6; DLB 13, 245
Griggs, Sutton (Elbert)
   1872-1930 .... **TCLC 77**
   See also CA 123; 186; DLB 50
Grigson, Geoffrey (Edward Harvey)
   1905-1985 .... **CLC 7, 39**
   See also CA 25-28R; 118; CANR 20, 33;
   CP 1, 2, 3, 4; DLB 27; MTCW 1, 2
Grile, Dod
   See Bierce, Ambrose (Gwinett)
Grillparzer, Franz 1791-1872 .... **DC 14;
   NCLC 1, 102; SSC 37**
   See also CDWLB 2; DLB 133; EW 5;
   RGWL 2, 3; TWA
Grimble, Reverend Charles James
   See Eliot, T(homas) S(tearns)
Grimke, Angelina (Emily) Weld
   1880-1958 .... **HR 1:2**
   See also BW 1; CA 124; DAM POET; DLB
   50, 54; FW
Grimke, Charlotte L(ottie) Forten
   1837(?)-1914 .... **BLC 1:2; TCLC 16**
   See also BW 1; CA 117; 124; DAM MULT,
   POET; DLB 50, 239
Grimm, Jacob Ludwig Karl
   1785-1863 .... **NCLC 3, 77; SSC 36, 88**
   See also CLR 112; DLB 90; MAICYA 1, 2;
   RGSF 2; RGWL 2, 3; SATA 22; WCH
Grimm, Wilhelm Karl 1786-1859 .. **NCLC 3,
   77; SSC 36**
   See also CDWLB 2; CLR 112; DLB 90;
   MAICYA 1, 2; RGSF 2; RGWL 2, 3;
   SATA 22; WCH
Grimm and Grim
   See Grimm, Jacob Ludwig Karl; Grimm,
   Wilhelm Karl
Grimm Brothers
   See Grimm, Jacob Ludwig Karl; Grimm,
   Wilhelm Karl

**Grimmelshausen, Hans Jakob Christoffel
   von**
   See Grimmelshausen, Johann Jakob Christ-
   offel von
**Grimmelshausen, Johann Jakob Christoffel
   von** 1621-1676 .... **LC 6**
   See also CDWLB 2; DLB 168; RGWL 2, 3
Grindel, Eugene 1895-1952 .... **PC 38; TCLC
   7, 41**
   See also CA 104; 193; EWL 3; GFL 1789
   to the Present; LMFS 2; RGWL 2, 3
Grisham, John 1955- .... **CLC 84, 273**
   See also AAYA 14, 47; BPFB 2; CA 138;
   CANR 47, 69, 114, 133; CMW 4; CN 6,
   7; CPW; CSW; DA3; DAM POP; MSW;
   MTCW 2; MTFW 2005
Grosseteste, Robert 1175(?)-1253 . **CMLC 62**
   See also DLB 115
Grossman, David 1954- .... **CLC 67, 231**
   See also CA 138; CANR 114, 175; CWW
   2; DLB 299; EWL 3; RGHL; WLIT 6
Grossman, Vasilii Semenovich
   See Grossman, Vasily (Semenovich)
Grossman, Vasily (Semenovich)
   1905-1964 .... **CLC 41**
   See also CA 124; 130; DLB 272; MTCW 1;
   RGHL
Grove, Frederick Philip
   See Greve, Felix Paul (Berthold Friedrich)
Grubb
   See Crumb, R.
Grumbach, Doris 1918- .... **CLC 13, 22, 64**
   See also CA 5-8R; CAAS 2; CANR 9, 42,
   70, 127; CN 6, 7; INT CANR-9; MTCW
   2; MTFW 2005
Grundtvig, Nikolai Frederik Severin
   1783-1872 .... **NCLC 1, 158**
   See also DLB 300
Grunge
   See Crumb, R.
Grunwald, Lisa 1959- .... **CLC 44**
   See also CA 120; CANR 148
Gryphius, Andreas 1616-1664 .... **LC 89**
   See also CDWLB 2; DLB 164; RGWL 2, 3
Guare, John 1938- .... **CLC 8, 14, 29, 67; DC
   20**
   See also CA 73-76; CAD; CANR 21, 69,
   118; CD 5, 6; DAM DRAM; DFS 8, 13;
   DLB 7, 249; EWL 3; MAL 5; MTCW 1,
   2; RGAL 4
Guarini, Battista 1538-1612 .... **LC 102**
   See also DLB 339
Gubar, Susan 1944- .... **CLC 145**
   See also CA 108; CANR 45, 70, 139, 179;
   FW; MTCW 1; RGAL 4
Gubar, Susan David
   See Gubar, Susan
Gudjonsson, Halldor Kiljan
   1902-1998 .... **CLC 25**
   See also CA 103; 164; CWW 2; DLB 293,
   331; EW 12; EWL 3; RGWL 2, 3
Guedes, Vincente
   See Pessoa, Fernando
Guenter, Erich
   See Eich, Gunter
Guest, Barbara 1920-2006 ... **CLC 34; PC 55**
   See also BG 1:2; CA 25-28R; 248; CANR
   11, 44, 84; CP 1, 2, 3, 4, 5, 6, 7; CWP;
   DLB 5, 193
Guest, Edgar A(lbert) 1881-1959 ... **TCLC 95**
   See also CA 112; 168
Guest, Judith 1936- .... **CLC 8, 30**
   See also AAYA 7, 66; CA 77-80; CANR
   15, 75, 138; DA3; DAM NOV, POP;
   EXPN; INT CANR-15; LAIT 5; MTCW
   1, 2; MTFW 2005; NFS 1
Guevara, Che
   See Guevara (Serna), Ernesto

Guevara (Serna), Ernesto
   1928-1967 .... **CLC 87; HLC 1**
   See also CA 127; 111; CANR 56; DAM
   MULT; HW 1
Guicciardini, Francesco 1483-1540 ..... **LC 49**
Guido delle Colonne c. 1215-c.
   1290 .... **CMLC 90**
Guild, Nicholas M. 1944- .... **CLC 33**
   See also CA 93-96
Guillemin, Jacques
   See Sartre, Jean-Paul
Guillen, Jorge 1893-1984 . **CLC 11; HLCS 1;
   PC 35**
   See also CA 89-92; 112; DAM MULT,
   POET; DLB 108; EWL 3; HW 1; RGWL
   2, 3
Guillen, Nicolas (Cristobal)
   1902-1989 .... **BLC 1:2; CLC 48, 79;
   HLC 1; PC 23**
   See also BW 2; CA 116; 125; 129; CANR
   84; DAM MST, MULT, POET; DLB 283;
   EWL 3; HW 1; LAW; RGWL 2, 3; WP
Guillen y Alvarez, Jorge
   See Guillen, Jorge
Guillevic, (Eugene) 1907-1997 .... **CLC 33**
   See also CA 93-96; CWW 2
Guillois
   See Desnos, Robert
Guillois, Valentin
   See Desnos, Robert
Guimaraes Rosa, Joao 1908-1967 ... **CLC 23;
   HLCS 1**
   See also CA 175; 89-92; DLB 113, 307;
   EWL 3; LAW; RGSF 2; RGWL 2, 3;
   WLIT 1
Guiney, Louise Imogen
   1861-1920 .... **TCLC 41**
   See also CA 160; DLB 54; RGAL 4
Guinizelli, Guido c. 1230-1276 ...... **CMLC 49**
   See also WLIT 7
Guinizzelli, Guido
   See Guinizelli, Guido
Guiraldes, Ricardo (Guillermo)
   1886-1927 .... **TCLC 39**
   See also CA 131; EWL 3; HW 1; LAW;
   MTCW 1
Gumilev, Nikolai (Stepanovich)
   1886-1921 .... **TCLC 60**
   See also CA 165; DLB 295; EWL 3
Gumilyov, Nikolay Stepanovich
   See Gumilev, Nikolai (Stepanovich)
Gump, P. Q.
   See Card, Orson Scott
Gump, P.Q.
   See Card, Orson Scott
Gunesekera, Romesh 1954- .... **CLC 91**
   See also BRWS 10; CA 159; CANR 140,
   172; CN 6, 7; DLB 267, 323
Gunn, Bill
   See Gunn, William Harrison
Gunn, Thom(son William)
   1929-2004 . **CLC 3, 6, 18, 32, 81; PC 26**
   See also BRWS 4; CA 17-20R; 227; CANR
   9, 33, 116; CDBLB 1960 to Present; CP
   1, 2, 3, 4, 5, 6, 7; DAM POET; DLB 27;
   INT CANR-33; MTCW 1; PFS 9; RGEL
   2
Gunn, William Harrison
   1934(?)-1989 .... **CLC 5**
   See also AITN 1; BW 1, 3; CA 13-16R;
   128; CANR 12, 25, 76; DLB 38
Gunn Allen, Paula
   See Allen, Paula Gunn
Gunnars, Kristjana 1948- .... **CLC 69**
   See also CA 113; CCA 1; CP 6, 7; CWP;
   DLB 60
Gunter, Erich
   See Eich, Gunter

Gurdjieff, G(eorgei) I(vanovich)
1877(?)-1949 .... **TCLC 71**
See also CA 157

Gurganus, Allan 1947- .... **CLC 70**
See also BEST 90:1; CA 135; CANR 114;
CN 6, 7; CPW; CSW; DAM POP; GLL 1

Gurney, A. R.
See Gurney, A(lbert) R(amsdell), Jr.

Gurney, A(lbert) R(amsdell), Jr.
1930- .... **CLC 32, 50, 54**
See also AMWS 5; CA 77-80; CAD; CANR
32, 64, 121; CD 5, 6; DAM DRAM; DLB
266; EWL 3

Gurney, Ivor (Bertie) 1890-1937 ... **TCLC 33**
See also BRW 6; CA 167; DLBY 2002;
PAB; RGEL 2

Gurney, Peter
See Gurney, A(lbert) R(amsdell), Jr.

Guro, Elena (Genrikhovna)
1877-1913 .... **TCLC 56**
See also DLB 295

Gustafson, James M(oody) 1925- ... **CLC 100**
See also CA 25-28R; CANR 37

Gustafson, Ralph (Barker)
1909-1995 .... **CLC 36**
See also CA 21-24R; CANR 8, 45, 84; CP
1, 2, 3, 4, 5, 6; DLB 88; RGEL 2

Gut, Gom
See Simenon, Georges (Jacques Christian)

Guterson, David 1956- .... **CLC 91**
See also CA 132; CANR 73, 126; CN 7;
DLB 292; MTCW 2; MTFW 2005; NFS
13

Guthrie, A(lfred) B(ertram), Jr.
1901-1991 .... **CLC 23**
See also CA 57-60; 134; CANR 24; CN 1,
2, 3; DLB 6, 212; MAL 5; SATA 62;
SATA-Obit 67; TCWW 1, 2

Guthrie, Isobel
See Grieve, C(hristopher) M(urray)

Gutierrez Najera, Manuel
1859-1895 .... **HLCS 2; NCLC 133**
See also DLB 290; LAW

Guy, Rosa (Cuthbert) 1925- .... **CLC 26**
See also AAYA 4, 37; BW 2; CA 17-20R;
CANR 14, 34, 83; CLR 13, 137; DLB 33;
DNFS 1; JRDA; MAICYA 1, 2; SATA 14,
62, 122; YAW

Gwendolyn
See Bennett, (Enoch) Arnold

H. D.
See Doolittle, Hilda

H. de V.
See Buchan, John

Haavikko, Paavo Juhani 1931- .. **CLC 18, 34**
See also CA 106; CWW 2; EWL 3

Habbema, Koos
See Heijermans, Herman

Habermas, Juergen 1929- .... **CLC 104**
See also CA 109; CANR 85, 162; DLB 242

Habermas, Jurgen
See Habermas, Juergen

Hacker, Marilyn 1942- ...... **CLC 5, 9, 23, 72,
91; PC 47**
See also CA 77-80; CANR 68, 129; CP 3,
4, 5, 6, 7; CWP; DAM POET; DLB 120,
282; FW; GLL 2; MAL 5; PFS 19

Hadewijch of Antwerp fl. 1250- ... **CMLC 61**
See also RGWL 3

Hadrian 76-138 .... **CMLC 52**

Haeckel, Ernst Heinrich (Philipp August)
1834-1919 .... **TCLC 83**
See also CA 157

Hafiz c. 1326-1389(?) .... **CMLC 34**
See also RGWL 2, 3; WLIT 6

Hagedorn, Jessica T(arahata)
1949- .... **CLC 185**
See also CA 139; CANR 69; CWP; DLB
312; RGAL 4

Haggard, H(enry) Rider
1856-1925 .... **TCLC 11**
See also BRWS 3; BYA 4, 5; CA 108; 148;
CANR 112; DLB 70, 156, 174, 178;
FANT; LMFS 1; MTCW 2; RGEL 2;
RHW; SATA 16; SCFW 1, 2; SFW 4;
SUFW 1; WLIT 4

Hagiosy, L.
See Larbaud, Valery (Nicolas)

Hagiwara, Sakutaro 1886-1942 .... **PC 18;
TCLC 60**
See also CA 154; EWL 3; RGWL 3

Hagiwara Sakutaro
See Hagiwara, Sakutaro

Haig, Fenil
See Ford, Ford Madox

Haig-Brown, Roderick (Langmere)
1908-1976 .... **CLC 21**
See also CA 5-8R; 69-72; CANR 4, 38, 83;
CLR 31; CWRI 5; DLB 88; MAICYA 1,
2; SATA 12; TCWW 2

Haight, Rip
See Carpenter, John (Howard)

Haij, Vera
See Jansson, Tove (Marika)

Hailey, Arthur 1920-2004 .... **CLC 5**
See also AITN 2; BEST 90:3; BPFB 2; CA
1-4R; 233; CANR 2, 36, 75; CCA 1; CN
1, 2, 3, 4, 5, 6, 7; CPW; DAM NOV, POP;
DLB 88; DLBY 1982; MTCW 1, 2;
MTFW 2005

Hailey, Elizabeth Forsythe 1938- ..... **CLC 40**
See also CA 93-96; 188; CAAE 188; CAAS
1; CANR 15, 48; INT CANR-15

Haines, John (Meade) 1924- .... **CLC 58**
See also AMWS 12; CA 17-20R; CANR
13, 34; CP 1, 2, 3, 4, 5; CSW; DLB 5,
212; TCLE 1:1

Ha Jin
See Jin, Xuefei

Hakluyt, Richard 1552-1616 .... **LC 31**
See also DLB 136; RGEL 2

Haldeman, Joe 1943- .... **CLC 61**
See also AAYA 38; CA 53-56; 179; CAAE
179; CAAS 25; CANR 6, 70, 72, 130,
171; DLB 8; INT CANR-6; SCFW 2;
SFW 4

Haldeman, Joe William
See Haldeman, Joe

Hale, Janet Campbell 1947- .... **NNAL**
See also CA 49-52; CANR 45, 75; DAM
MULT; DLB 175; MTCW 2; MTFW 2005

Hale, Sarah Josepha (Buell)
1788-1879 .... **NCLC 75**
See also DLB 1, 42, 73, 243

Halevy, Elie 1870-1937 .... **TCLC 104**

Haley, Alex(ander Murray Palmer)
1921-1992 ...... **BLC 1:2; CLC 8, 12, 76;
TCLC 147**
See also AAYA 26; BPFB 2; BW 2, 3; CA
77-80; 136; CANR 61; CDALBS; CPW;
CSW; DA; DA3; DAB; DAC; DAM MST,
MULT, POP; DLB 38; LAIT 5; MTCW
1, 2; NFS 9

Haliburton, Thomas Chandler
1796-1865 .... **NCLC 15, 149**
See also DLB 11, 99; RGEL 2; RGSF 2

Hall, Donald 1928- ... **CLC 1, 13, 37, 59, 151,
240; PC 70**
See also AAYA 63; CA 5-8R; CAAS 7;
CANR 2, 44, 64, 106, 133; CP 1, 2, 3, 4,
5, 6, 7; DAM POET; DLB 5, 342; MAL
5; MTCW 2; MTFW 2005; RGAL 4;
SATA 23, 97

Hall, Donald Andrew, Jr.
See Hall, Donald

Hall, Frederic Sauser
See Sauser-Hall, Frederic

Hall, James
See Kuttner, Henry

Hall, James Norman 1887-1951 ..... **TCLC 23**
See also CA 123; 173; LAIT 1; RHW 1;
SATA 21

Hall, Joseph 1574-1656 .... **LC 91**
See also DLB 121, 151; RGEL 2

Hall, Marguerite Radclyffe
See Hall, Radclyffe

Hall, Radclyffe 1880-1943 ...... **TCLC 12, 215**
See also BRWS 6; CA 110; 150; CANR 83;
DLB 191; MTCW 2; MTFW 2005; RGEL
2; RHW

Hall, Rodney 1935- .... **CLC 51**
See also CA 109; CANR 69; CN 6, 7; CP
1, 2, 3, 4, 5, 6, 7; DLB 289

Hallam, Arthur Henry
1811-1833 .... **NCLC 110**
See also DLB 32

Halldor Laxness
See Gudjonsson, Halldor Kiljan

Halleck, Fitz-Greene 1790-1867 .... **NCLC 47**
See also DLB 3, 250; RGAL 4

Halliday, Michael
See Creasey, John

Halpern, Daniel 1945- .... **CLC 14**
See also CA 33-36R; CANR 93, 174; CP 3,
4, 5, 6, 7

Hamburger, Michael 1924-2007 ... **CLC 5, 14**
See also CA 5-8R; 196; 261; CAAE 196;
CAAS 4; CANR 2, 47; CP 1, 2, 3, 4, 5, 6,
7; DLB 27

Hamburger, Michael Peter Leopold
See Hamburger, Michael

Hamill, Pete 1935- .... **CLC 10, 261**
See also CA 25-28R; CANR 18, 71, 127,
180

Hamill, William Peter
See Hamill, Pete

Hamilton, Alexander 1712-1756 .... **LC 150**
See also DLB 31

Hamilton, Alexander
1755(?)-1804 .... **NCLC 49**
See also DLB 37

Hamilton, Clive
See Lewis, C.S.

Hamilton, Edmond 1904-1977 .... **CLC 1**
See also CA 1-4R; CANR 3, 84; DLB 8;
SATA 118; SFW 4

Hamilton, Elizabeth 1758-1816 ... **NCLC 153**
See also DLB 116, 158

Hamilton, Eugene (Jacob) Lee
See Lee-Hamilton, Eugene (Jacob)

Hamilton, Franklin
See Silverberg, Robert

Hamilton, Gail
See Corcoran, Barbara (Asenath)

Hamilton, (Robert) Ian 1938-2001 . **CLC 191**
See also CA 106; 203; CANR 41, 67; CP 1,
2, 3, 4, 5, 6, 7; DLB 40, 155

Hamilton, Jane 1957- .... **CLC 179**
See also CA 147; CANR 85, 128; CN 7;
MTFW 2005

Hamilton, Mollie
See Kaye, M.M.

Hamilton, (Anthony Walter) Patrick
1904-1962 .... **CLC 51**
See also CA 176; 113; DLB 10, 191

Hamilton, Virginia 1936-2002 .... **CLC 26**
See also AAYA 2, 21; BW 2, 3; BYA 1, 2,
8; CA 25-28R; 206; CANR 20, 37, 73,
126; CLR 1, 11, 40, 127; DAM MULT;
DLB 33, 52; DLBY 2001; INT CANR-
20; JRDA; LAIT 5; MAICYAS 1; MAI-
CYAS 1; MTCW 1, 2; MTFW 2005;
SATA 4, 56, 79, 123; SATA-Obit 132;
WYA; YAW

Hammett, (Samuel) Dashiell
　1894-1961 .... **CLC 3, 5, 10, 19, 47; SSC 17; TCLC 187**
　See also AAYA 59; AITN 1; AMWS 4; BPFB 2; CA 81-84; CANR 42; CDALB 1929-1941; CMW 4; DA3; DLB 226, 280; DLBD 6; DLBY 1996; EWL 3; LAIT 3; MAL 5; MSW; MTCW 1, 2; MTFW 2005; NFS 21; RGAL 4; RGSF 2; TUS

Hammon, Jupiter 1720(?)-1800(?) . **BLC 1:2; NCLC 5; PC 16**
　See also DAM MULT, POET; DLB 31, 50

Hammond, Keith
　See Kuttner, Henry

Hamner, Earl (Henry), Jr. 1923- ...... **CLC 12**
　See also AITN 2; CA 73-76; DLB 6

Hampton, Christopher 1946- .... **CLC 4**
　See also CA 25-28R; CD 5, 6; DLB 13; MTCW 1

Hampton, Christopher James
　See Hampton, Christopher

Hamsun, Knut
　See Pedersen, Knut

Hamsund, Knut Pedersen
　See Pedersen, Knut

Handke, Peter 1942- .... **CLC 5, 8, 10, 15, 38, 134; DC 17**
　See also CA 77-80; CANR 33, 75, 104, 133, 180; CWW 2; DAM DRAM, NOV; DLB 85, 124; EWL 3; MTCW 1, 2; MTFW 2005; TWA

Handler, Chelsea 1976(?)- .... **CLC 269**
　See also CA 243

Handy, W(illiam) C(hristopher)
　1873-1958 .... **TCLC 97**
　See also BW 3; CA 121; 167

Hanley, James 1901-1985 ..... **CLC 3, 5, 8, 13**
　See also CA 73-76; 117; CANR 36; CBD; CN 1, 2, 3; DLB 191; EWL 3; MTCW 1; RGEL 2

Hannah, Barry 1942- .. **CLC 23, 38, 90, 270; SSC 94**
　See also BPFB 2; CA 108; 110; CANR 43, 68, 113; CN 4, 5, 6, 7; CSW; DLB 6, 234; INT CA-110; MTCW 1; RGSF 2

Hannon, Ezra
　See Hunter, Evan

Hanrahan, Barbara 1939-1991 .... **TCLC 219**
　See also CA 121; 127; CN 4, 5; DLB 289

Hansberry, Lorraine (Vivian)
　1930-1965 ... **BLC 1:2, 2:2; CLC 17, 62; DC 2; TCLC 192**
　See also AAYA 25; AFAW 1, 2; AMWS 4; BW 1, 3; CA 109; 25-28R; CABS 3; CAD; CANR 58; CDALB 1941-1968; CWD; DA; DA3; DAB; DAC; DAM DRAM, MST, MULT; DFS 2; DLB 7, 38; EWL 3; FL 1:6; FW; LAIT 4; MAL 5; MTCW 1, 2; MTFW 2005; RGAL 4; TUS

Hansen, Joseph 1923-2004 .... **CLC 38**
　See also BPFB 2; CA 29-32R; 233; CAAS 17; CANR 16, 44, 66, 125; CMW 4; DLB 226; GLL 1; INT CANR-16

Hansen, Karen V. 1955- .... **CLC 65**
　See also CA 149; CANR 102

Hansen, Martin A(lfred)
　1909-1955 .... **TCLC 32**
　See also CA 167; DLB 214; EWL 3

Hanson, Kenneth O(stlin) 1922- .... **CLC 13**
　See also CA 53-56; CANR 7; CP 1, 2, 3, 4, 5

Hardwick, Elizabeth 1916-2007 .... **CLC 13**
　See also AMWS 3; CA 5-8R; 267; CANR 3, 32, 70, 100, 139; CN 4, 5, 6; CSW; DA3; DAM NOV; DLB 6; MBL; MTCW 1, 2; MTFW 2005; TCLE 1:1

Hardwick, Elizabeth Bruce
　See Hardwick, Elizabeth

Hardwick, Elizabeth Bruce
　See Hardwick, Elizabeth

Hardy, Thomas 1840-1928 . **PC 8, 92; SSC 2, 60, 113; TCLC 4, 10, 18, 32, 48, 53, 72, 143, 153; WLC 3**
　See also AAYA 69; BRW 6; BRWC 1, 2; BRWR 1, 2; CA 104; 123; CDBLB 1890-1914; DA; DA3; DAB; DAC; DAM MST, NOV, POET; DLB 18, 19, 135, 284; EWL 3; EXPN; EXPP; LAIT 2; MTCW 1, 2; MTFW 2005; NFS 3, 11, 15, 19; PFS 3, 4, 18; RGEL 2; RGSF 2; TEA; WLIT 4

Hare, David 1947- . **CLC 29, 58, 136; DC 26**
　See also BRWS 4; CA 97-100; CANR 39, 91; CBD; CD 5, 6; DFS 4, 7, 16; DLB 13, 310; MTCW 1; TEA

Harewood, John
　See Van Druten, John (William)

Harford, Henry
　See Hudson, W(illiam) H(enry)

Hargrave, Leonie
　See Disch, Thomas M.

Hariri, Al- al-Qasim ibn 'Ali Abu Muhammad al-Basri
　See al-Hariri, al-Qasim ibn 'Ali Abu Muhammad al-Basri

Harjo, Joy 1951- ..... **CLC 83; NNAL; PC 27**
　See also AMWS 12; CA 114; CANR 35, 67, 91, 129; CP 6, 7; CWP; DAM MULT; DLB 120, 175, 342; EWL 3; MTCW 2; MTFW 2005; PFS 15; RGAL 4

Harlan, Louis R(udolph) 1922- .... **CLC 34**
　See also CA 21-24R; CANR 25, 55, 80

Harling, Robert 1951(?)- .... **CLC 53**
　See also CA 147

Harmon, William (Ruth) 1938- .... **CLC 38**
　See also CA 33-36R; CANR 14, 32, 35; SATA 65

Harper, F. E. W.
　See Harper, Frances Ellen Watkins

Harper, E. W.
　See Harper, Frances Ellen Watkins

Harper, Frances E. Watkins
　See Harper, Frances Ellen Watkins

Harper, Frances Ellen
　See Harper, Frances Ellen Watkins

Harper, Frances Ellen Watkins
　1825-1911 . **BLC 1:2; PC 21; TCLC 14, 217**
　See also AFAW 1, 2; BW 1, 3; CA 111; 125; CANR 79; DAM MULT, POET; DLB 50, 221; MBL; RGAL 4

Harper, Michael S(teven) 1938- ..... **BLC 2:2; CLC 7, 22**
　See also AFAW 2; BW 1; CA 33-36R, 224; CAAE 224; CANR 24, 108; CP 2, 3, 4, 5, 6, 7; DLB 41; RGAL 4; TCLE 1:1

Harper, Mrs. F. E. W.
　See Harper, Frances Ellen Watkins

Harpur, Charles 1813-1868 .... **NCLC 114**
　See also DLB 230; RGEL 2

Harris, Christie
　See Harris, Christie (Lucy) Irwin

Harris, Christie (Lucy) Irwin
　1907-2002 .... **CLC 12**
　See also CA 5-8R; CANR 6, 83; CLR 47; DLB 88; JRDA; MAICYA 1, 2; SAAS 10; SATA 6, 74; SATA-Essay 116

Harris, Frank 1856-1931 .... **TCLC 24**
　See also CA 109; 150; CANR 80; DLB 156, 197; RGEL 2

Harris, George Washington
　1814-1869 .... **NCLC 23, 165**
　See also DLB 3, 11, 248; RGAL 4

Harris, Joel Chandler 1848-1908 ..... **SSC 19, 103; TCLC 2**
　See also CA 104; 137; CANR 80; CLR 49, 128; DLB 11, 23, 42, 78, 91; LAIT 2; MAICYA 1, 2; RGSF 2; SATA 100; WCH; YABC 1

Harris, John (Wyndham Parkes Lucas)
　Beynon 1903-1969 .... **CLC 19**
　See also BRWS 13; CA 102; 89-92; CANR 84; DLB 255; SATA 118; SCFW 1, 2; SFW 4

Harris, MacDonald
　See Heiney, Donald (William)

Harris, Mark 1922-2007 .... **CLC 19**
　See also CA 5-8R; 260; CAAS 3; CANR 2, 55, 83; CN 1, 2, 3, 4, 5, 6, 7; DLB 2; DLBY 1980

Harris, Norman CLC 65

Harris, (Theodore) Wilson 1921- ... **BLC 2:2; CLC 25, 159**
　See also BRWS 5; BW 2, 3; CA 65-68; CAAS 16; CANR 11, 27, 69, 114; CD-WLB 3; CN 1, 2, 3, 4, 5, 6, 7; CP 1, 2, 3, 4, 5, 6, 7; DLB 117; EWL 3; MTCW 1; RGEL 2

Harrison, Barbara Grizzuti
　1934-2002 .... **CLC 144**
　See also CA 77-80; 205; CANR 15, 48; INT CANR-15

Harrison, Elizabeth (Allen) Cavanna
　1909-2001 .... **CLC 12**
　See also CA 9-12R; 200; CANR 6, 27, 85, 104, 121; JRDA; MAICYA 1; SAAS 4; SATA 1, 30; YAW

Harrison, Harry 1925- .... **CLC 42**
　See also CA 1-4R; CANR 5, 21, 84; DLB 8; SATA 4; SCFW 2; SFW 4

Harrison, Harry Max
　See Harrison, Harry

Harrison, James
　See Harrison, Jim

Harrison, James Thomas
　See Harrison, Jim

Harrison, Jim 1937- .... **CLC 6, 14, 33, 66, 143; SSC 19**
　See also AMWS 8; CA 13-16R; CANR 8, 51, 79, 142; CN 5, 6; CP 1, 2, 3, 4, 5, 6; DLBY 1982; INT CANR-8; RGAL 4; TCWW 2; TUS

Harrison, Kathryn 1961- .... **CLC 70, 151**
　See also CA 144; CANR 68, 122

Harrison, Tony 1937- .... **CLC 43, 129**
　See also BRWS 5; CA 65-68; CANR 44, 98; CBD; CD 5, 6; CP 2, 3, 4, 5, 6, 7; DLB 40, 245; MTCW 1; RGEL 2

Harriss, Will(ard Irvin) 1922- .... **CLC 34**
　See also CA 111

Hart, Ellis
　See Ellison, Harlan

Hart, Josephine 1942(?)- .... **CLC 70**
　See also CA 138; CANR 70, 149; CPW; DAM POP

Hart, Moss 1904-1961 .... **CLC 66**
　See also CA 109; 89-92; CANR 84; DAM DRAM; DFS 1; DLB 7, 266; RGAL 4

Harte, (Francis) Bret(t)
　1836(?)-1902 ... **SSC 8, 59; TCLC 1, 25; WLC 3**
　See also AMWS 2; CA 104; 140; CANR 80; CDALB 1865-1917; DA; DA3; DAC; DAM MST; DLB 12, 64, 74, 79, 186; EXPS; LAIT 2; RGAL 4; RGSF 2; SATA 26; SSFS 3; TUS

Hartley, L(eslie) P(oles) 1895-1972 ... **CLC 2, 22; SSC 125**
　See also BRWS 7; CA 45-48; 37-40R; CANR 33; CN 1; DLB 15, 139; EWL 3; HGG; MTCW 1, 2; MTFW 2005; RGEL 2; RGSF 2; SUFW 1

Hartman, Geoffrey H. 1929- .... **CLC 27**
　See also CA 117; 125; CANR 79; DLB 67

Hartmann, Sadakichi 1869-1944 ... **TCLC 73**
　See also CA 157; DLB 54

Hartmann von Aue c. 1170-c. 1210 .... **CMLC 15**
See also CDWLB 2; DLB 138; RGWL 2, 3

Hartog, Jan de
See de Hartog, Jan

Haruf, Kent 1943- .... **CLC 34**
See also AAYA 44; CA 149; CANR 91, 131

Harvey, Caroline
See Trollope, Joanna

Harvey, Gabriel 1550(?)-1631 .... **LC 88**
See also DLB 167, 213, 281

Harvey, Jack
See Rankin, Ian

Harwood, Ronald 1934- .... **CLC 32**
See also CA 1-4R; CANR 4, 55, 150; CBD; CD 5, 6; DAM DRAM, MST; DLB 13

Hasegawa Tatsunosuke
See Futabatei, Shimei

Hasek, Jaroslav (Matej Frantisek) 1883-1923 .... **SSC 69; TCLC 4**
See also CA 104; 129; CDWLB 4; DLB 215; EW 9; EWL 3; MTCW 1, 2; RGSF 2; RGWL 2, 3

Hass, Robert 1941- ... **CLC 18, 39, 99; PC 16**
See also AMWS 6; CA 111; CANR 30, 50, 71, 187; CP 3, 4, 5, 6, 7; DLB 105, 206; EWL 3; MAL 5; MTFW 2005; RGAL 4; SATA 94; TCLE 1:1

Hassler, Jon 1933-2008 .... **CLC 263**
See also CA 73-76; 270; CANR 21, 80, 161; CN 6, 7; INT CANR-21; SATA 19; SATA-Obit 191

Hassler, Jon Francis
See Hassler, Jon

Hastings, Hudson
See Kuttner, Henry

Hastings, Selina **CLC 44**
See also CA 257

Hastings, Selina Shirley
See Hastings, Selina

Hastings, Victor
See Disch, Thomas M.

Hathorne, John 1641-1717 .... **LC 38**

Hatteras, Amelia
See Mencken, H(enry) L(ouis)

Hatteras, Owen
See Mencken, H(enry) L(ouis); Nathan, George Jean

Hauff, Wilhelm 1802-1827 .... **NCLC 185**
See also DLB 90; SUFW 1

Hauptmann, Gerhart (Johann Robert) 1862-1946 ...... **DC 34; SSC 37; TCLC 4**
See also CA 104; 153; CDWLB 2; DAM DRAM; DLB 66, 118, 330; EW 8; EWL 3; RGSF 2; RGWL 2, 3; TWA

Havel, Vaclav 1936- ..... **CLC 25, 58, 65, 123; DC 6**
See also CA 104; CANR 36, 63, 124, 175; CDWLB 4; CWW 2; DA3; DAM DRAM; DFS 10; DLB 232; EWL 3; LMFS 2; MTCW 1, 2; MTFW 2005; RGWL 3

Haviaras, Stratis
See Chaviaras, Strates

Hawes, Stephen 1475(?)-1529(?) .... **LC 17**
See also DLB 132; RGEL 2

Hawkes, John 1925-1998 .. **CLC 1, 2, 3, 4, 7, 9, 14, 15, 27, 49**
See also BPFB 2; CA 1-4R; 167; CANR 2, 47, 64; CN 1, 2, 3, 4, 5, 6; DLB 2, 7, 227; DLBY 1980, 1998; EWL 3; MAL 5; MTCW 1, 2; MTFW 2005; RGAL 4

Hawking, S. W.
See Hawking, Stephen W.

Hawking, Stephen W. 1942- ..... **CLC 63, 105**
See also AAYA 13; BEST 89:1; CA 126; 129; CANR 48, 115; CPW; DA3; MTCW 2; MTFW 2005

Hawking, Stephen William
See Hawking, Stephen W.

Hawkins, Anthony Hope
See Hope, Anthony

Hawthorne, Julian 1846-1934 .... **TCLC 25**
See also CA 165; HGG

Hawthorne, Nathaniel 1804-1864 ... **NCLC 2, 10, 17, 23, 39, 79, 95, 158, 171, 191; SSC 3, 29, 39, 89; WLC 3**
See also AAYA 18; AMW; AMWC 1; AMWR 1; BPFB 2; BYA 3; CDALB 1640-1865; CLR 103; DA; DA3; DAB; DAC; DAM MST, NOV; DLB 1, 74, 183, 223, 269; EXPN; EXPS; GL 2; HGG; LAIT 1; NFS 1, 20; RGAL 4; RGSF 2; SSFS 1, 7, 11, 15; SUFW 1; TUS; WCH; YABC 2

Hawthorne, Sophia Peabody 1809-1871 .... **NCLC 150**
See also DLB 183, 239

Haxton, Josephine Ayres
See Douglas, Ellen

Hayaseca y Eizaguirre, Jorge
See Echegaray (y Eizaguirre), Jose (Maria Waldo)

Hayashi, Fumiko 1904-1951 .... **TCLC 27**
See also CA 161; DLB 180; EWL 3

Hayashi Fumiko
See Hayashi, Fumiko

Haycraft, Anna 1932-2005 .... **CLC 40**
See also CA 122; 237; CANR 90, 141; CN 4, 5, 6; DLB 194; MTCW 2; MTFW 2005

Haycraft, Anna Margaret
See Haycraft, Anna

Hayden, Robert E(arl) 1913-1980 . **BLC 1:2; CLC 5, 9, 14, 37; PC 6**
See also AFAW 1, 2; AMWS 2; BW 1, 3; CA 69-72; 97-100; CABS 2; CANR 24, 75, 82; CDALB 1941-1968; CP 1, 2, 3; DA; DAC; DAM MST, MULT, POET; DLB 5, 76; EWL 3; EXPP; MAL 5; MTCW 1, 2; PFS 1; RGAL 4; SATA 19; SATA-Obit 26; WP

Haydon, Benjamin Robert 1786-1846 .... **NCLC 146**
See also DLB 110

Hayek, F(riedrich) A(ugust von) 1899-1992 .... **TCLC 109**
See also CA 93-96; 137; CANR 20; MTCW 1, 2

Hayford, J(oseph) E(phraim) Casely
See Casely-Hayford, J(oseph) E(phraim)

Hayman, Ronald 1932- .... **CLC 44**
See also CA 25-28R; CANR 18, 50, 88; CD 5, 6; DLB 155

Hayne, Paul Hamilton 1830-1886 . **NCLC 94**
See also DLB 3, 64, 79, 248; RGAL 4

Hays, Mary 1760-1843 .... **NCLC 114**
See also DLB 142, 158; RGEL 2

Haywood, Eliza (Fowler) 1693(?)-1756 .... **LC 1, 44**
See also BRWS 12; DLB 39; RGEL 2

Hazlitt, William 1778-1830 ...... **NCLC 29, 82**
See also BRW 4; DLB 110, 158; RGEL 2; TEA

Hazzard, Shirley 1931- .... **CLC 18, 218**
See also CA 9-12R; CANR 4, 70, 127; CN 1, 2, 3, 4, 5, 6, 7; DLB 289; DLBY 1982; MTCW 1

Head, Bessie 1937-1986 . **BLC 1:2, 2:2; CLC 25, 67; SSC 52**
See also AFW; BW 2, 3; CA 29-32R; 119; CANR 25, 82; CDWLB 3; CN 1, 2, 3, 4; DA3; DAM MULT; DLB 117, 225; EWL 3; EXPS; FL 1:6; FW; MTCW 1, 2; MTFW 2005; RGSF 2; SSFS 5, 13; WLIT 2; WWE 1

Headley, Elizabeth
See Harrison, Elizabeth (Allen) Cavanna

Headon, (Nicky) Topper 1956(?)- ..... **CLC 30**

Heaney, Seamus 1939- . **CLC 5, 7, 14, 25, 37, 74, 91, 171, 225; PC 18; WLCS**
See also AAYA 61; BRWR 1; BRWS 2; CA 85-88; CANR 25, 48, 75, 91, 128, 184; CDBLB 1960 to Present; CP 1, 2, 3, 4, 5, 6, 7; DA3; DAB; DAM POET; DLB 40, 330; DLBY 1995; EWL 3; EXPP; MTCW 1, 2; MTFW 2005; PAB; PFS 2, 5, 8, 17, 30; RGEL 2; TEA; WLIT 4

Hearn, (Patricio) Lafcadio (Tessima Carlos) 1850-1904 .... **TCLC 9**
See also CA 105; 166; DLB 12, 78, 189; HGG; MAL 5; RGAL 4

Hearne, Samuel 1745-1792 .... **LC 95**
See also DLB 99

Hearne, Vicki 1946-2001 .... **CLC 56**
See also CA 139; 201

Hearon, Shelby 1931- .... **CLC 63**
See also AITN 2; AMWS 8; CA 25-28R; CAAS 11; CANR 18, 48, 103, 146; CSW

Heat-Moon, William Least
See Trogdon, William (Lewis)

Hebbel, Friedrich 1813-1863 . **DC 21; NCLC 43**
See also CDWLB 2; DAM DRAM; DLB 129; EW 6; RGWL 2, 3

Hebert, Anne 1916-2000 . **CLC 4, 13, 29, 246**
See also CA 85-88; 187; CANR 69, 126; CCA 1; CWP; CWW 2; DA3; DAC; DAM MST, POET; DLB 68; EWL 3; GFL 1789 to the Present; MTCW 1, 2; MTFW 2005; PFS 20

Hecht, Anthony (Evan) 1923-2004 .... **CLC 8, 13, 19; PC 70**
See also AMWS 10; CA 9-12R; 232; CANR 6, 108; CP 1, 2, 3, 4, 5, 6, 7; DAM POET; DLB 5, 169; EWL 3; PFS 6; WP

Hecht, Ben 1894-1964 ..... **CLC 8; TCLC 101**
See also CA 85-88; DFS 9; DLB 7, 9, 25, 26, 28, 86; FANT; IDFW 3, 4; RGAL 4

Hedayat, Sadeq 1903-1951 .... **TCLC 21**
See also CA 120; EWL 3; RGSF 2

Hegel, Georg Wilhelm Friedrich 1770-1831 .... **NCLC 46, 151**
See also DLB 90; TWA

Heidegger, Martin 1889-1976 .... **CLC 24**
See also CA 81-84; 65-68; CANR 34; DLB 296; MTCW 1, 2; MTFW 2005

Heidenstam, (Carl Gustaf) Verner von 1859-1940 .... **TCLC 5**
See also CA 104; DLB 330

Heidi Louise
See Erdrich, Louise

Heifner, Jack 1946- .... **CLC 11**
See also CA 105; CANR 47

Heijermans, Herman 1864-1924 .... **TCLC 24**
See also CA 123; EWL 3

Heilbrun, Carolyn G(old) 1926-2003 .... **CLC 25, 173**
See also BPFB 1; CA 45-48; 220; CANR 1, 28, 58, 94; CMW; CPW; DLB 306; FW; MSW

Hein, Christoph 1944- .... **CLC 154**
See also CA 158; CANR 108; CDWLB 2; CWW 2; DLB 124

Heine, Heinrich 1797-1856 .... **NCLC 4, 54, 147; PC 25**
See also CDWLB 2; DLB 90; EW 5; RGWL 2, 3; TWA

Heinemann, Larry 1944- .... **CLC 50**
See also CA 110; CAAS 21; CANR 31, 81, 156; DLBD 9; INT CANR-31

Heinemann, Larry Curtiss
See Heinemann, Larry

Heiney, Donald (William) 1921-1993 . **CLC 9**
See also CA 1-4R; 142; CANR 3, 58; FANT

Heinlein, Robert A. 1907-1988 .. **CLC 1, 3, 8, 14, 26, 55; SSC 55**
See also AAYA 17; BPFB 2; BYA 4, 13; CA 1-4R; 125; CANR 1, 20, 53; CLR 75; CN 1, 2, 3, 4; CPW; DA3; DAM POP; DLB 8; EXPS; JRDA; LAIT 5; LMFS 2; MAICYA 1, 2; MTCW 1, 2; MTFW 2005; RGAL 4; SATA 9, 69; SATA-Obit 56; SCFW 1, 2; SFW 4; SSFS 7; YAW

Held, Peter
See Vance, Jack

Heldris of Cornwall fl. 13th cent.
- .... **CMLC 97**

Helforth, John
See Doolittle, Hilda

Heliodorus fl. 3rd cent. - .... **CMLC 52**
See also WLIT 8

Hellenhofferu, Vojtech Kapristian z
See Hasek, Jaroslav (Matej Frantisek)

Heller, Joseph 1923-1999 . **CLC 1, 3, 5, 8, 11, 36, 63; TCLC 131, 151; WLC 3**
See also AAYA 24; AITN 1; AMWS 4; BPFB 2; BYA 1; CA 5-8R; 187; CABS 1; CANR 8, 42, 66, 126; CN 1, 2, 3, 4, 5, 6; CPW; DA; DA3; DAB; DAC; DAM MST, NOV, POP; DLB 2, 28, 227; DLBY 1980, 2002; EWL 3; EXPN; INT CANR-8; LAIT 4; MAL 5; MTCW 1, 2; MTFW 2005; NFS 1; RGAL 4; TUS; YAW

Hellman, Lillian 1905-1984 . **CLC 2, 4, 8, 14, 18, 34, 44, 52; DC 1; TCLC 119**
See also AAYA 47; AITN 1, 2; AMWS 1; CA 13-16R; 112; CAD; CANR 33; CWD; DA3; DAM DRAM; DFS 1, 3, 14; DLB 7, 228; DLBY 1984; EWL 3; FL 1:6; FW; LAIT 3; MAL 5; MBL; MTCW 1, 2; MTFW 2005; RGAL 4; TUS

Helprin, Mark 1947- .... **CLC 7, 10, 22, 32**
See also CA 81-84; CANR 47, 64, 124; CDALBS; CN 7; CPW; DA3; DAM NOV, POP; DLB 335; DLBY 1985; FANT; MAL 5; MTCW 1, 2; MTFW 2005; SSFS 25; SUFW 2

Helvetius, Claude-Adrien 1715-1771 .. **LC 26**
See also DLB 313

Helyar, Jane Penelope Josephine
1933- .... **CLC 17**
See also CA 21-24R; CANR 10, 26; CWRI 5; SAAS 2; SATA 5; SATA-Essay 138

Hemans, Felicia 1793-1835 ...... **NCLC 29, 71**
See also DLB 96; RGEL 2

Hemingway, Ernest (Miller)
1899-1961 .... **CLC 1, 3, 6, 8, 10, 13, 19, 30, 34, 39, 41, 44, 50, 61, 80; SSC 1, 25, 36, 40, 63, 117; TCLC 115, 203; WLC 3**
See also AAYA 19; AMW; AMWC 1; AMWR 1; BPFB 2; BYA 2, 3, 13, 15; CA 77-80; CANR 34; CDALB 1917-1929; DA; DA3; DAB; DAC; DAM MST, NOV; DLB 4, 9, 102, 210, 308, 316, 330; DLBD 1, 15, 16; DLBY 1981, 1987, 1996, 1998; EWL 3; EXPN; EXPS; LAIT 3, 4; LATS 1:1; MAL 5; MTCW 1, 2; MTFW 2005; NFS 1, 5, 6, 14; RGAL 4; RGSF 2; SSFS 17; TUS; WYA

Hempel, Amy 1951- .... **CLC 39**
See also CA 118; 137; CANR 70, 166; DA3; DLB 218; EXPS; MTCW 2; MTFW 2005; SSFS 2

Henderson, F. C.
See Mencken, H(enry) L(ouis)

Henderson, Mary
See Mavor, Osborne Henry

Henderson, Sylvia
See Ashton-Warner, Sylvia (Constance)

Henderson, Zenna (Chlarson)
1917-1983 .... **SSC 29**
See also CA 1-4R; 133; CANR 1, 84; DLB 8; SATA 5; SFW 4

Henkin, Joshua 1964- .... **CLC 119**
See also CA 161; CANR 186

Henley, Beth CLC 23, 255; DC 6, 14
See Henley, Elizabeth Becker
See also CABS 3; CAD; CD 5, 6; CSW; CWD; DFS 2, 21, 26; DLBY 1986; FW

Henley, Elizabeth Becker 1952- ...... **CLC 23, 255; DC 6, 14**
See Henley, Beth
See also AAYA 70; CA 107; CABS 3; CAD; CANR 32, 73, 140; CD 5, 6; CSW; DA3; DAM DRAM, MST; DFS 2, 21; DLBY 1986; FW; MTCW 1, 2; MTFW 2005

Henley, William Ernest 1849-1903 .. **TCLC 8**
See also CA 105; 234; DLB 19; RGEL 2

Hennissart, Martha 1929- .... **CLC 2**
See also BPFB 2; CA 85-88; CANR 64; CMW 4; DLB 306

Henry VIII 1491-1547 .... **LC 10**
See also DLB 132

Henry, O. 1862-1910 . **SSC 5, 49, 117; TCLC 1, 19; WLC 3**
See also AAYA 41; AMWS 2; CA 104; 131; CDALB 1865-1917; DA; DA3; DAB; DAC; DAM MST; DLB 12, 78, 79; EXPS; MAL 5; MTCW 1, 2; MTFW 2005; RGAL 4; RGSF 2; SSFS 2, 18, 27; TCWW 1, 2; TUS; YABC 2

Henry, Oliver
See Henry, O.

Henry, Patrick 1736-1799 .... **LC 25**
See also LAIT 1

Henryson, Robert 1430(?)-1506(?) ..... **LC 20, 110; PC 65**
See also BRWS 7; DLB 146; RGEL 2

Henschke, Alfred
See Klabund

Henson, Lance 1944- .... **NNAL**
See also CA 146; DLB 175

Hentoff, Nat(han Irving) 1925- .... **CLC 26**
See also AAYA 4, 42; BYA 6; CA 1-4R; CAAS 6; CANR 5, 25, 77, 114; CLR 1, 52; DLB 345; INT CANR-25; JRDA; MAICYA 1, 2; SATA 42, 69, 133; SATA-Brief 27; WYA; YAW

Heppenstall, (John) Rayner
1911-1981 .... **CLC 10**
See also CA 1-4R; 103; CANR 29; CN 1, 2; CP 1, 2, 3; EWL 3

Heraclitus c. 540B.C.-c. 450B.C. ... **CMLC 22**
See also DLB 176

Herbert, Frank 1920-1986 ... **CLC 12, 23, 35, 44, 85**
See also AAYA 21; BPFB 2; BYA 4, 14; CA 53-56; 118; CANR 5, 43; CDALBS; CPW; DAM POP; DLB 8; INT CANR-5; LAIT 5; MTCW 1, 2; MTFW 2005; NFS 17; SATA 9, 37; SATA-Obit 47; SCFW 1, 2; SFW 4; YAW

Herbert, George 1593-1633 . **LC 24, 121; PC 4**
See also BRW 2; BRWR 2; CDBLB Before 1660; DAB; DAM POET; DLB 126; EXPP; PFS 25; RGEL 2; TEA; WP

Herbert, Zbigniew 1924-1998 ..... **CLC 9, 43; PC 50; TCLC 168**
See also CA 89-92; 169; CANR 36, 74, 177; CDWLB 4; CWW 2; DAM POET; DLB 232; EWL 3; MTCW 1; PFS 22

Herbst, Josephine (Frey)
1897-1969 .... **CLC 34**
See also CA 5-8R; 25-28R; DLB 9

Herder, Johann Gottfried von
1744-1803 .... **NCLC 8, 186**
See also DLB 97; EW 4; TWA

Heredia, Jose Maria 1803-1839 ...... **HLCS 2; NCLC 209**
See also LAW

Hergesheimer, Joseph 1880-1954 ... **TCLC 11**
See also CA 109; 194; DLB 102, 9; RGAL 4

Herlihy, James Leo 1927-1993 .... **CLC 6**
See also CA 1-4R; 143; CAD; CANR 2; CN 1, 2, 3, 4, 5

Herman, William
See Bierce, Ambrose (Gwinett)

Hermogenes fl. c. 175- .... **CMLC 6**

Hernandez, Jose 1834-1886 .... **NCLC 17**
See also LAW; RGWL 2, 3; WLIT 1

Herodotus c. 484B.C.-c. 420B.C. ... **CMLC 17**
See also AW 1; CDWLB 1; DLB 176; RGWL 2, 3; TWA; WLIT 8

Herr, Michael 1940(?)- .... **CLC 231**
See also CA 89-92; CANR 68, 142; DLB 185; MTCW 1

Herrick, Robert 1591-1674 .. **LC 13, 145; PC 9**
See also BRW 2; BRWC 2; DA; DAB; DAC; DAM MST, POP; DLB 126; EXPP; PFS 13, 29; RGAL 4; RGEL 2; TEA; WP

Herring, Guilles
See Somerville, Edith Oenone

Herriot, James 1916-1995
See Wight, James Alfred

Herris, Violet
See Hunt, Violet

Herrmann, Dorothy 1941- .... **CLC 44**
See also CA 107

Herrmann, Taffy
See Herrmann, Dorothy

Hersey, John 1914-1993 .. **CLC 1, 2, 7, 9, 40, 81, 97**
See also AAYA 29; BPFB 2; CA 17-20R; 140; CANR 33; CDALBS; CN 1, 2, 3, 4, 5; CPW; DAM POP; DLB 6, 185, 278, 299; MAL 5; MTCW 1, 2; MTFW 2005; RGHL; SATA 25; SATA-Obit 76; TUS

Hervent, Maurice
See Grindel, Eugene

Herzen, Aleksandr Ivanovich
1812-1870 .... **NCLC 10, 61**
See also DLB 277

Herzen, Alexander
See Herzen, Aleksandr Ivanovich

Herzl, Theodor 1860-1904 .... **TCLC 36**
See also CA 168

Herzog, Werner 1942- .... **CLC 16, 236**
See also CA 89-92

Hesiod fl. 8th cent. B.C.- .... **CMLC 5, 102**
See also AW 1; DLB 176; RGWL 2, 3; WLIT 8

Hesse, Hermann 1877-1962 ... **CLC 1, 2, 3, 6, 11, 17, 25, 69; SSC 9, 49; TCLC 148, 196; WLC 3**
See also AAYA 43; BPFB 2; CA 17-18; CAP 2; CDWLB 2; DA; DA3; DAB; DAC; DAM MST, NOV; DLB 66, 330; EW 9; EWL 3; EXPN; LAIT 1; MTCW 1, 2; MTFW 2005; NFS 6, 15, 24; RGWL 2, 3; SATA 50; TWA

Hewes, Cady
See De Voto, Bernard (Augustine)

Heyen, William 1940- .... **CLC 13, 18**
See also CA 33-36R; 220; CAAE 220; CAAS 9; CANR 98, 188; CP 3, 4, 5, 6, 7; DLB 5; RGHL

Heyerdahl, Thor 1914-2002 .... **CLC 26**
See also CA 5-8R; 207; CANR 5, 22, 66, 73; LAIT 4; MTCW 1, 2; MTFW 2005; SATA 2, 52

Heym, Georg (Theodor Franz Arthur)
1887-1912 .... **TCLC 9**
See also CA 106; 181

Heym, Stefan 1913-2001 .... **CLC 41**
See also CA 9-12R; 203; CANR 4; CWW 2; DLB 69; EWL 3

Hoffman, Eva 1945- .... **CLC 182**
See also AMWS 16; CA 132; CANR 146

Hoffman, Stanley 1944- .... **CLC 5**
See also CA 77-80

Hoffman, William 1925- .... **CLC 141**
See also AMWS 18; CA 21-24R; CANR 9, 103; CSW; DLB 234; TCLE 1:1

Hoffman, William M.
See Hoffman, William M(oses)

Hoffman, William M(oses) 1939- ..... **CLC 40**
See also CA 57-60; CAD; CANR 11, 71; CD 5, 6

Hoffmann, E(rnst) T(heodor) A(madeus) 1776-1822 ..... **NCLC 2, 183; SSC 13, 92**
See also CDWLB 2; CLR 133; DLB 90; EW 5; GL 2; RGSF 2; RGWL 2, 3; SATA 27; SUFW 1; WCH

Hofmann, Gert 1931-1993 .... **CLC 54**
See also CA 128; CANR 145; EWL 3; RGHL

Hofmannsthal, Hugo von 1874-1929 ... **DC 4; TCLC 11**
See also CA 106; 153; CDWLB 2; DAM DRAM; DFS 17; DLB 81, 118; EW 9; EWL 3; RGWL 2, 3

Hogan, Linda 1947- ..... **CLC 73; NNAL; PC 35**
See also AMWS 4; ANW; BYA 12; CA 120, 226; CAAE 226; CANR 45, 73, 129; CWP; DAM MULT; DLB 175; SATA 132; TCWW 2

Hogarth, Charles
See Creasey, John

Hogarth, Emmett
See Polonsky, Abraham (Lincoln)

Hogarth, William 1697-1764 .... **LC 112**
See also AAYA 56

Hogg, James 1770-1835 .... **NCLC 4, 109**
See also BRWS 10; DLB 93, 116, 159; GL 2; HGG; RGEL 2; SUFW 1

Holbach, Paul-Henri Thiry 1723-1789 .... **LC 14**
See also DLB 313

Holberg, Ludvig 1684-1754 .... **LC 6**
See also DLB 300; RGWL 2, 3

Holbrook, John
See Vance, Jack

Holcroft, Thomas 1745-1809 .... **NCLC 85**
See also DLB 39, 89, 158; RGEL 2

Holden, Ursula 1921- .... **CLC 18**
See also CA 101; CAAS 8; CANR 22

Holderlin, (Johann Christian) Friedrich 1770-1843 .... **NCLC 16, 187; PC 4**
See also CDWLB 2; DLB 90; EW 5; RGWL 2, 3

Holdstock, Robert 1948- .... **CLC 39**
See also CA 131; CANR 81; DLB 261; FANT; HGG; SFW 4; SUFW 2

Holdstock, Robert P.
See Holdstock, Robert

Holinshed, Raphael fl. 1580- .... **LC 69**
See also DLB 167; RGEL 2

Holland, Isabelle (Christian) 1920-2002 .... **CLC 21**
See also AAYA 11, 64; CA 21-24R; 205; CAAE 181; CANR 10, 25, 47; CLR 57; CWRI 5; JRDA; LAIT 4; MAICYA 1, 2; SATA 8, 70; SATA-Essay 103; SATA-Obit 132; WYA

Holland, Marcus
See Caldwell, (Janet Miriam) Taylor (Holland)

Hollander, John 1929- .... **CLC 2, 5, 8, 14**
See also CA 1-4R; CANR 1, 52, 136; CP 1, 2, 3, 4, 5, 6, 7; DLB 5; MAL 5; SATA 13

Hollander, Paul
See Silverberg, Robert

Holleran, Andrew
See Garber, Eric

Holley, Marietta 1836(?)-1926 .... **TCLC 99**
See also CA 118; DLB 11; FL 1:3

Hollinghurst, Alan 1954- .... **CLC 55, 91**
See also BRWS 10; CA 114; CN 5, 6, 7; DLB 207, 326; GLL 1

Hollis, Jim
See Summers, Hollis (Spurgeon, Jr.)

Holly, Buddy 1936-1959 .... **TCLC 65**
See also CA 213

Holmes, Gordon
See Shiel, M(atthew) P(hipps)

Holmes, John
See Souster, (Holmes) Raymond

Holmes, John Clellon 1926-1988 ...... **CLC 56**
See also BG 1:2; CA 9-12R; 125; CANR 4; CN 1, 2, 3, 4; DLB 16, 237

Holmes, Oliver Wendell, Jr. 1841-1935 .... **TCLC 77**
See also CA 114; 186

Holmes, Oliver Wendell 1809-1894 .... **NCLC 14, 81; PC 71**
See also AMWS 1; CDALB 1640-1865; DLB 1, 189, 235; EXPP; PFS 24; RGAL 4; SATA 34

Holmes, Raymond
See Souster, (Holmes) Raymond

Holt, Samuel
See Westlake, Donald E.

Holt, Victoria
See Hibbert, Eleanor Alice Burford

Holub, Miroslav 1923-1998 .... **CLC 4**
See also CA 21-24R; 169; CANR 10; CD-WLB 4; CWW 2; DLB 232; EWL 3; RGWL 3

Holz, Detlev
See Benjamin, Walter

Homer c. 8th cent. B.C.- .... **CMLC 1, 16, 61; PC 23; WLCS**
See also AW 1; CDWLB 1; DA; DA3; DAB; DAC; DAM MST, POET; DLB 176; EFS 1; LAIT 1; LMFS 1; RGWL 2, 3; TWA; WLIT 8; WP

Hong, Maxine Ting Ting
See Kingston, Maxine Hong

Hongo, Garrett Kaoru 1951- .... **PC 23**
See also CA 133; CAAS 22; CP 5, 6, 7; DLB 120, 312; EWL 3; EXPP; PFS 25; RGAL 4

Honig, Edwin 1919- .... **CLC 33**
See also CA 5-8R; CAAS 8; CANR 4, 45, 144; CP 1, 2, 3, 4, 5, 6, 7; DLB 5

Hood, Hugh (John Blagdon) 1928- . **CLC 15, 28, 273; SSC 42**
See also CA 49-52; CAAS 17; CANR 1, 33, 87; CN 1, 2, 3, 4, 5, 6, 7; DLB 53; RGSF 2

Hood, Thomas 1799-1845 . **NCLC 16; PC 93**
See also BRW 4; DLB 96; RGEL 2

Hooker, (Peter) Jeremy 1941- .... **CLC 43**
See also CA 77-80; CANR 22; CP 2, 3, 4, 5, 6, 7; DLB 40

Hooker, Richard 1554-1600 .... **LC 95**
See also BRW 1; DLB 132; RGEL 2

Hooker, Thomas 1586-1647 .... **LC 137**
See also DLB 24

hooks, bell 1952(?)- .... **BLCS; CLC 94**
See also BW 2; CA 143; CANR 87, 126; DLB 246; MTCW 2; MTFW 2005; SATA 115, 170

Hooper, Johnson Jones 1815-1862 .... **NCLC 177**
See also DLB 3, 11, 248; RGAL 4

Hope, A(lec) D(erwent) 1907-2000 .... **CLC 3, 51; PC 56**
See also BRWS 7; CA 21-24R; 188; CANR 33, 74; CP 1, 2, 3, 4, 5; DLB 289; EWL 3; MTCW 1, 2; MTFW 2005; PFS 8; RGEL 2

Hope, Anthony 1863-1933 .... **TCLC 83**
See also CA 157; DLB 153, 156; RGEL 2; RHW

Hope, Brian
See Creasey, John

Hope, Christopher 1944- .... **CLC 52**
See also AFW; CA 106; CANR 47, 101, 177; CN 4, 5, 6, 7; DLB 225; SATA 62

Hope, Christopher David Tully
See Hope, Christopher

Hopkins, Gerard Manley 1844-1889 .... **NCLC 17, 189; PC 15; WLC 3**
See also BRW 5; BRWR 2; CDBLB 1890-1914; DA; DA3; DAB; DAC; DAM MST, POET; DLB 35, 57; EXPP; PAB; PFS 26; RGEL 2; TEA; WP

Hopkins, John (Richard) 1931-1998 .. **CLC 4**
See also CA 85-88; 169; CBD; CD 5, 6

Hopkins, Pauline Elizabeth 1859-1930 .... **BLC 1:2; TCLC 28**
See also AFAW 2; BW 2, 3; CA 141; CANR 82; DAM MULT; DLB 50

Hopkinson, Francis 1737-1791 .... **LC 25**
See also DLB 31; RGAL 4

Hopley, George
See Hopley-Woolrich, Cornell George

Hopley-Woolrich, Cornell George 1903-1968 .... **CLC 77**
See also CA 13-14; CANR 58, 156; CAP 1; CMW 4; DLB 226; MSW; MTCW 2

Horace 65B.C.-8B.C. .... **CMLC 39; PC 46**
See also AW 2; CDWLB 1; DLB 211; RGWL 2, 3; WLIT 8

Horatio
See Proust, (Valentin-Louis-George-Eugene) Marcel

Horgan, Paul (George Vincent O'Shaughnessy) 1903-1995 .. **CLC 9, 53**
See also BPFB 2; CA 13-16R; 147; CANR 9, 35; CN 1, 2, 3, 4, 5; DAM NOV; DLB 102, 212; DLBY 1985; INT CANR-9; MTCW 1, 2; MTFW 2005; SATA 13; SATA-Obit 84; TCWW 1, 2

Horkheimer, Max 1895-1973 .... **TCLC 132**
See also CA 216; 41-44R; DLB 296

Horn, Peter
See Kuttner, Henry

Hornby, Nick 1957(?)- .... **CLC 243**
See also AAYA 74; CA 151; CANR 104, 151; CN 7; DLB 207

Horne, Frank (Smith) 1899-1974 ...... **HR 1:2**
See also BW 1; CA 125; 53-56; DLB 51; WP

Horne, Richard Henry Hengist 1802(?)-1884 .... **NCLC 127**
See also DLB 32; SATA 29

Hornem, Horace Esq.
See Byron, George Gordon (Noel)

Horne Tooke, John 1736-1812 ..... **NCLC 195**

Horney, Karen (Clementine Theodore Danielsen) 1885-1952 .... **TCLC 71**
See also CA 114; 165; DLB 246; FW

Hornung, E(rnest) W(illiam) 1866-1921 .... **TCLC 59**
See also CA 108; 160; CMW 4; DLB 70

Horovitz, Israel 1939- .... **CLC 56**
See also CA 33-36R; CAD; CANR 46, 59; CD 5, 6; DAM DRAM; DLB 7, 341; MAL 5

Horton, George Moses 1797(?)-1883(?) .... **NCLC 87**
See also DLB 50

Horvath, odon von 1901-1938
See von Horvath, Odon
See also EWL 3

Horvath, Oedoen von -1938
See von Horvath, Odon

Author Index

Hunt, Everette Howard, Jr.
See Hunt, E. Howard
Hunt, Francesca
See Holland, Isabelle (Christian)
Hunt, Howard
See Hunt, E. Howard
Hunt, Kyle
See Creasey, John
Hunt, (James Henry) Leigh
1784-1859 .... **NCLC 1, 70; PC 73**
See also DAM POET; DLB 96, 110, 144;
RGEL 2; TEA
Hunt, Marsha 1946- .... **CLC 70**
See also BW 2, 3; CA 143; CANR 79
Hunt, Violet 1866(?)-1942 .... **TCLC 53**
See also CA 184; DLB 162, 197
Hunter, E. Waldo
See Sturgeon, Theodore (Hamilton)
Hunter, Evan 1926-2005 .... **CLC 11, 31**
See also AAYA 39; BPFB 2; CA 5-8R; 241;
CANR 5, 38, 62, 97, 149; CMW 4; CN 1,
2, 3, 4, 5, 6, 7; CPW; DAM POP; DLB
306; DLBY 1982; INT CANR-5; MSW;
MTCW 1; SATA 25; SATA-Obit 167;
SFW 4
Hunter, Kristin
See Lattany, Kristin (Elaine Eggleston)
Hunter
Hunter, Mary
See Austin, Mary (Hunter)
Hunter, Mollie 1922- .... **CLC 21**
See also AAYA 13, 71; BYA 6; CANR 37,
78; CLR 25; DLB 161; JRDA; MAICYA
1, 2; SAAS 7; SATA 2, 54, 106, 139;
SATA-Essay 139; WYA; YAW
Hunter, Robert (?)-1734 .... **LC 7**
Hurston, Zora Neale 1891-1960 ..... **BLC 1:2;**
CLC 7, 30, 61; DC 12; HR 1:2; SSC 4,
80; TCLC 121, 131; WLCS
See also AAYA 15, 71; AFAW 1, 2; AMWS
6; BW 1, 3; BYA 12; CA 85-88; CANR
61; CDALBS; DA; DA3; DAC; DAM
MST, MULT, NOV; DFS 6; DLB 51, 86;
EWL 3; EXPN; EXPS; FL 1:6; FW; LAIT
3; LATS 1:1; LMFS 2; MAL 5; MBL;
MTCW 1, 2; MTFW 2005; NFS 3; RGAL
4; RGSF 2; SSFS 1, 6, 11, 19, 21; TUS;
YAW
Husserl, E. G.
See Husserl, Edmund (Gustav Albrecht)
Husserl, Edmund (Gustav Albrecht)
1859-1938 .... **TCLC 100**
See also CA 116; 133; DLB 296
Huston, John (Marcellus)
1906-1987 .... **CLC 20**
See also CA 73-76; 123; CANR 34; DLB
26
Hustvedt, Siri 1955- .... **CLC 76**
See also CA 137; CANR 149
Hutcheson, Francis 1694-1746 .... **LC 157**
See also DLB 252
Hutchinson, Lucy 1620-1675 .... **LC 149**
Hutten, Ulrich von 1488-1523 .... **LC 16**
See also DLB 179
Huxley, Aldous (Leonard)
1894-1963 .... **CLC 1, 3, 4, 5, 8, 11, 18,**
35, 79; SSC 39; WLC 3
See also AAYA 11; BPFB 2; BRW 7; CA
85-88; CANR 44, 99; CDBLB 1914-1945;
DA; DA3; DAB; DAC; DAM MST, NOV;
DLB 36, 100, 162, 195, 255; EWL 3;
EXPN; LAIT 5; LMFS 2; MTCW 1, 2;
MTFW 2005; NFS 6; RGEL 2; SATA 63;
SCFW 1, 2; SFW 4; TEA; YAW
Huxley, T(homas) H(enry)
1825-1895 .... **NCLC 67**
See also DLB 57; TEA
Huygens, Constantijn 1596-1687 .... **LC 114**
See also RGWL 2, 3

Huysmans, Joris-Karl 1848-1907 ... **TCLC 7,**
69, 212
See also CA 104; 165; DLB 123; EW 7;
GFL 1789 to the Present; LMFS 2; RGWL
2, 3
Hwang, David Henry 1957- .... **CLC 55, 196;**
DC 4, 23
See also CA 127; 132; CAD; CANR 76,
124; CD 5, 6; DA3; DAM DRAM; DFS
11, 18; DLB 212, 228, 312; INT CA-132;
MAL 5; MTCW 2; MTFW 2005; RGAL
4
Hyatt, Daniel
See James, Daniel (Lewis)
Hyde, Anthony 1946- .... **CLC 42**
See also CA 136; CCA 1
Hyde, Margaret O. 1917- .... **CLC 21**
See also CA 1-4R; CANR 1, 36, 137, 181;
CLR 23; JRDA; MAICYA 1, 2; SAAS 8;
SATA 1, 42, 76, 139
Hyde, Margaret Oldroyd
See Hyde, Margaret O.
Hynes, James 1956(?)- .... **CLC 65**
See also CA 164; CANR 105
Hypatia c. 370-415 .... **CMLC 35**
Ian, Janis 1951- .... **CLC 21**
See also CA 105; 187
Ibanez, Vicente Blasco
See Blasco Ibanez, Vicente
Ibarbourou, Juana de
1895(?)-1979 .... **HLCS 2**
See also DLB 290; HW 1; LAW
Ibarguengoitia, Jorge 1928-1983 ..... **CLC 37;**
TCLC 148
See also CA 124; 113; EWL 3; HW 1
Ibn Arabi 1165-1240 .... **CMLC 105**
Ibn Battuta, Abu Abdalla
1304-1368(?) .... **CMLC 57**
See also WLIT 2
Ibn Hazm 994-1064 .... **CMLC 64**
Ibn Zaydun 1003-1070 .... **CMLC 89**
Ibsen, Henrik (Johan) 1828-1906 .. **DC 2, 30;**
TCLC 2, 8, 16, 37, 52; WLC 3
See also AAYA 46; CA 104; 141; DA; DA3;
DAB; DAC; DAM DRAM, MST; DFS 1,
6, 8, 10, 11, 15, 16, 25; EW 7; LAIT 2;
LATS 1:1; MTFW 2005; RGWL 2, 3
Ibuse, Masuji 1898-1993 .... **CLC 22**
See also CA 127; 141; CWW 2; DLB 180;
EWL 3; MJW; RGWL 3
Ibuse Masuji
See Ibuse, Masuji
Ichikawa, Kon 1915-2008 .... **CLC 20**
See also CA 121; 269
Ichiyo, Higuchi 1872-1896 .... **NCLC 49**
See also MJW
Idle, Eric 1943- .... **CLC 21**
See also CA 116; CANR 35, 91, 148
Idris, Yusuf 1927-1991 .... **SSC 74**
See also AFW; DLB 346; EWL 3; RGSF 2,
3; RGWL 3; WLIT 2
Ignatieff, Michael 1947- .... **CLC 236**
See also CA 144; CANR 88, 156; CN 6, 7;
DLB 267
Ignatieff, Michael Grant
See Ignatieff, Michael
Ignatow, David 1914-1997 .... **CLC 4, 7, 14,**
40; PC 34
See also CA 9-12R; 162; CAAS 3; CANR
31, 57, 96; CP 1, 2, 3, 4, 5, 6; DLB 5;
EWL 3; MAL 5
Ignotus
See Strachey, (Giles) Lytton
Ihimaera, Witi (Tame) 1944- .... **CLC 46**
See also CA 77-80; CANR 130; CN 2, 3, 4,
5, 6, 7; RGSF 2; SATA 148
Il'f, Il'ia
See Fainzilberg, Ilya Arnoldovich

Ilf, Ilya
See Fainzilberg, Ilya Arnoldovich
Illyes, Gyula 1902-1983 .... **PC 16**
See also CA 114; 109; CDWLB 4; DLB
215; EWL 3; RGWL 2, 3
Imalayen, Fatima-Zohra
See Djebar, Assia
Immermann, Karl (Lebrecht)
1796-1840 .... **NCLC 4, 49**
See also DLB 133
Ince, Thomas H. 1882-1924 .... **TCLC 89**
See also IDFW 3, 4
Inchbald, Elizabeth 1753-1821 ...... **NCLC 62**
See also DLB 39, 89; RGEL 2
Inclan, Ramon (Maria) del Valle
See Valle-Inclan, Ramon (Maria) del
Incogniteau, Jean-Louis
See Kerouac, Jack
Infante, G(uillermo) Cabrera
See Cabrera Infante, G.
Ingalls, Rachel 1940- .... **CLC 42**
See also CA 123; 127; CANR 154
Ingalls, Rachel Holmes
See Ingalls, Rachel
Ingamells, Reginald Charles
See Ingamells, Rex
Ingamells, Rex 1913-1955 .... **TCLC 35**
See also CA 167; DLB 260
Inge, William (Motter) 1913-1973 ..... **CLC 1,**
8, 19
See also CA 9-12R; CAD; CDALB 1941-
1968; DA3; DAM DRAM; DFS 1, 3, 5,
8; DLB 7, 249; EWL 3; MAL 5; MTCW
1, 2; MTFW 2005; RGAL 4; TUS
Ingelow, Jean 1820-1897 .... **NCLC 39, 107**
See also DLB 35, 163; FANT; SATA 33
Ingram, Willis J.
See Harris, Mark
Innaurato, Albert (F.) 1948(?)- ... **CLC 21, 60**
See also CA 115; 122; CAD; CANR 78;
CD 5, 6; INT CA-122
Innes, Michael
See Stewart, J(ohn) I(nnes) M(ackintosh)
Innis, Harold Adams 1894-1952 .... **TCLC 77**
See also CA 181; DLB 88
Insluis, Alanus de
See Alain de Lille
Iola
See Wells-Barnett, Ida B(ell)
Ionesco, Eugene 1912-1994 ... **CLC 1, 4, 6, 9,**
11, 15, 41, 86; DC 12; WLC 3
See also CA 9-12R; 144; CANR 55, 132;
CWW 2; DA; DA3; DAB; DAC; DAM
DRAM, MST; DFS 4, 9, 25; DLB 321;
EW 13; EWL 3; GFL 1789 to the Present;
LMFS 2; MTCW 1, 2; MTFW 2005;
RGWL 2, 3; SATA 7; SATA-Obit 79;
TWA
Iqbal, Muhammad 1877-1938 .... **TCLC 28**
See also CA 215; EWL 3
Ireland, Patrick
See O'Doherty, Brian
Irenaeus St. 130- .... **CMLC 42**
Irigaray, Luce 1930- .... **CLC 164**
See also CA 154; CANR 121; FW
Irish, William
See Hopley-Woolrich, Cornell George
Irland, David
See Green, Julien (Hartridge)
Iron, Ralph
See Schreiner, Olive (Emilie Albertina)
Irving, John 1942- . **CLC 13, 23, 38, 112, 175**
See also AAYA 8, 62; AMWS 6; BEST
89:3; BPFB 2; CA 25-28R; CANR 28, 73,
112, 133; CN 3, 4, 5, 6, 7; CPW; DA3;
DAM NOV, POP; DLB 6, 278; DLBY
1982; EWL 3; MAL 5; MTCW 1, 2;
MTFW 2005; NFS 12, 14; RGAL 4; TUS

Keneally, Thomas 1935- .... **CLC 5, 8, 10, 14, 19, 27, 43, 117**
See also BRWS 4; CA 85-88; CANR 10, 50, 74, 130, 165; CN 1, 2, 3, 4, 5, 6, 7; CPW; DA3; DAM NOV; DLB 289, 299, 326; EWL 3; MTCW 1, 2; MTFW 2005; NFS 17; RGEL 2; RGHL; RHW

Keneally, Thomas Michael
See Keneally, Thomas

Kennedy, A. L. 1965- .... **CLC 188**
See also CA 168, 213; CAAE 213; CANR 108; CD 5, 6; CN 6, 7; DLB 271; RGSF 2

Kennedy, Adrienne (Lita) 1931- .... **BLC 1:2; CLC 66; DC 5**
See also AFAW 2; BW 2, 3; CA 103; CAAS 20; CABS 3; CAD; CANR 26, 53, 82; CD 5, 6; DAM MULT; DFS 9; DLB 38, 341; FW; MAL 5

Kennedy, Alison Louise
See Kennedy, A. L.

Kennedy, John Pendleton
1795-1870 .... **NCLC 2**
See also DLB 3, 248, 254; RGAL 4

Kennedy, Joseph Charles 1929- .. **CLC 8, 42; PC 93**
See Kennedy, X. J.
See also AMWS 15; CA 1-4R, 201; CAAE 201; CAAS 9; CANR 4, 30, 40; CLR 27; CP 1, 2, 3, 4, 5, 6, 7; CWRI 5; DLB 5; MAICYA 2; MAICYAS 1; SAAS 22; SATA 14, 86, 130; SATA-Essay 130

Kennedy, William 1928- .. **CLC 6, 28, 34, 53, 239**
See also AAYA 1, 73; AMWS 7; BPFB 2; CA 85-88; CANR 14, 31, 76, 134; CN 4, 5, 6, 7; DA3; DAM NOV; DLB 143; DLBY 1985; EWL 3; INT CANR-31; MAL 5; MTCW 1, 2; MTFW 2005; SATA 57

Kennedy, X. J. CLC 8, 42
See Kennedy, Joseph Charles
See also CAAS 9; CLR 27; DLB 5; SAAS 22

Kenny, Maurice (Francis) 1929- ..... **CLC 87; NNAL**
See also CA 144; CAAS 22; CANR 143; DAM MULT; DLB 175

Kent, Kelvin
See Kuttner, Henry

Kenton, Maxwell
See Southern, Terry

Kenyon, Jane 1947-1995 .... **PC 57**
See also AAYA 63; AMWS 7; CA 118; 148; CANR 44, 69, 172; CP 6, 7; CWP; DLB 120; PFS 9, 17; RGAL 4

Kenyon, Robert O.
See Kuttner, Henry

Kepler, Johannes 1571-1630 .... **LC 45**

Ker, Jill
See Conway, Jill K.

Kerkow, H. C.
See Lewton, Val

Kerouac, Jack 1922-1969 ...... **CLC 1, 2, 3, 5, 14, 61; TCLC 117; WLC**
See also AAYA 25; AITN 1; AMWC 1; AMWS 3; BG 3; BPFB 2; CA 5-8R; 25-28R; CANR 26, 54, 95, 184; CDALB 1941-1968; CP 1; CPW; DA; DA3; DAB; DAC; DAM MST, NOV, POET, POP; DLB 2, 16, 237; DLBY 1995; EWL 3; GLL 1; LATS 1:2; LMFS 2; MAL 5; MTCW 1, 2; MTFW 2005; NFS 8; RGAL 4; TUS; WP

Kerouac, Jean-Louis le Brisde
See Kerouac, Jack

Kerouac, John
See Kerouac, Jack

Kerr, (Bridget) Jean (Collins)
1923(?)-2003 .... **CLC 22**
See also CA 5-8R; 212; CANR 7; INT CANR-7

Kerr, M. E.
See Meaker, Marijane

Kerr, Robert CLC 55

Kerrigan, (Thomas) Anthony 1918- .. **CLC 4, 6**
See also CA 49-52; CAAS 11; CANR 4

Kerry, Lois
See Duncan, Lois

Kesey, Ken 1935-2001 .... **CLC 1, 3, 6, 11, 46, 64, 184; WLC 3**
See also AAYA 25; BG 1:3; BPFB 2; CA 1-4R; 204; CANR 22, 38, 66, 124; CDALB 1968-1988; CN 1, 2, 3, 4, 5, 6, 7; CPW; DA; DA3; DAB; DAC; DAM MST, NOV, POP; DLB 2, 16, 206; EWL 3; EXPN; LAIT 4; MAL 5; MTCW 1, 2; MTFW 2005; NFS 2; RGAL 4; SATA 66; SATA-Obit 131; TUS; YAW

Kesselring, Joseph (Otto)
1902-1967 .... **CLC 45**
See also CA 150; DAM DRAM, MST; DFS 20

Kessler, Jascha (Frederick) 1929- ...... **CLC 4**
See also CA 17-20R; CANR 8, 48, 111; CP 1

Kettelkamp, Larry (Dale) 1933- .... **CLC 12**
See also CA 29-32R; CANR 16; SAAS 3; SATA 2

Key, Ellen (Karolina Sofia)
1849-1926 .... **TCLC 65**
See also DLB 259

Keyber, Conny
See Fielding, Henry

Keyes, Daniel 1927- .... **CLC 80**
See also AAYA 23; BYA 11; CA 17-20R, 181; CAAE 181; CANR 10, 26, 54, 74; DA; DA3; DAC; DAM MST, NOV; EXPN; LAIT 4; MTCW 2; MTFW 2005; NFS 2; SATA 37; SFW 4

Keynes, John Maynard
1883-1946 .... **TCLC 64**
See also CA 114; 162, 163; DLBD 10; MTCW 2; MTFW 2005

Khanshendel, Chiron
See Rose, Wendy

Khayyam, Omar 1048-1131 ... **CMLC 11; PC 8**
See also DA3; DAM POET; RGWL 2, 3; WLIT 6

Kherdian, David 1931- .... **CLC 6, 9**
See also AAYA 42; CA 21-24R, 192; CAAE 192; CAAS 2; CANR 39, 78; CLR 24; JRDA; LAIT 3; MAICYA 1, 2; SATA 16, 74; SATA-Essay 125

Khlebnikov, Velimir TCLC 20
See Khlebnikov, Viktor Vladimirovich
See also DLB 295; EW 10; EWL 3; RGWL 2, 3

Khlebnikov, Viktor Vladimirovich 1885-1922
See Khlebnikov, Velimir
See also CA 117; 217

Khodasevich, V.F.
See Khodasevich, Vladislav

Khodasevich, Vladislav
1886-1939 .... **TCLC 15**
See also CA 115; DLB 317; EWL 3

Khodasevich, Vladislav Felitsianovich
See Khodasevich, Vladislav

Kidd, Sue Monk 1948- .... **CLC 267**
See also AAYA 72; CA 202; MTFW 2005; NFS 27

Kielland, Alexander Lange
1849-1906 .... **TCLC 5**
See also CA 104

Kiely, Benedict 1919-2007 . **CLC 23, 43; SSC 58**
See also CA 1-4R; 257; CANR 2, 84; CN 1, 2, 3, 4, 5, 6, 7; DLB 15, 319; TCLE 1:1

Kienzle, William X. 1928-2001 .... **CLC 25**
See also CA 93-96; 203; CAAS 1; CANR 9, 31, 59, 111; CMW 4; DA3; DAM POP; INT CANR-31; MSW; MTCW 1, 2; MTFW 2005

Kierkegaard, Soren 1813-1855 ..... **NCLC 34, 78, 125**
See also DLB 300; EW 6; LMFS 2; RGWL 3; TWA

Kieslowski, Krzysztof 1941-1996 .... **CLC 120**
See also CA 147; 151

Killens, John Oliver 1916-1987 ...... **BLC 2:2; CLC 10**
See also BW 2; CA 77-80; 123; CAAS 2; CANR 26; CN 1, 2, 3, 4; DLB 33; EWL 3

Killigrew, Anne 1660-1685 .... **LC 4, 73**
See also DLB 131

Killigrew, Thomas 1612-1683 .... **LC 57**
See also DLB 58; RGEL 2

Kim
See Simenon, Georges (Jacques Christian)

Kincaid, Jamaica 1949- . **BLC 1:2, 2:2; CLC 43, 68, 137, 234; SSC 72**
See also AAYA 13, 56; AFAW 2; AMWS 7; BRWS 7; BW 2, 3; CA 125; CANR 47, 59, 95, 133; CDALBS; CDWLB 3; CLR 63; CN 4, 5, 6, 7; DA3; DAM MULT, NOV; DLB 157, 227; DNFS 1; EWL 3; EXPS; FW; LATS 1:2; LMFS 2; MAL 5; MTCW 2; MTFW 2005; NCFS 1; NFS 3; SSFS 5, 7; TUS; WWE 1; YAW

King, Francis (Henry) 1923- .... **CLC 8, 53, 145**
See also CA 1-4R; CANR 1, 33, 86; CN 1, 2, 3, 4, 5, 6, 7; DAM NOV; DLB 15, 139; MTCW 1

King, Kennedy
See Brown, George Douglas

King, Martin Luther, Jr.
1929-1968 ... **BLC 1:2; CLC 83; WLCS**
See also BW 2, 3; CA 25-28; CANR 27, 44; CAP 2; DA; DA3; DAB; DAC; DAM MST, MULT; LAIT 5; LATS 1:2; MTCW 1, 2; MTFW 2005; SATA 14

King, Stephen 1947- .... **CLC 12, 26, 37, 61, 113, 228, 244; SSC 17, 55**
See also AAYA 1, 17; AMWS 5; BEST 90:1; BPFB 2; CA 61-64; CANR 1, 30, 52, 76, 119, 134, 168; CLR 124; CN 7; CPW; DA3; DAM NOV, POP; DLB 143; DLBY 1980; HGG; JRDA; LAIT 5; MTCW 1, 2; MTFW 2005; RGAL 4; SATA 9, 55, 161; SUFW 1, 2; WYAS 1; YAW

King, Stephen Edwin
See King, Stephen

King, Steve
See King, Stephen

King, Thomas 1943- .... **CLC 89, 171; NNAL**
See also CA 144; CANR 95, 175; CCA 1; CN 6, 7; DAC; DAM MULT; DLB 175, 334; SATA 96

King, Thomas Hunt
See King, Thomas

Kingman, Lee
See Natti, (Mary) Lee

Kingsley, Charles 1819-1875 .... **NCLC 35**
See also CLR 77; DLB 21, 32, 163, 178, 190; FANT; MAICYA 2; MAICYAS 1; RGEL 2; WCH; YABC 2

Kingsley, Henry 1830-1876 .... **NCLC 107**
See also DLB 21, 230; RGEL 2

La Bruyere, Jean de 1645-1696 .... **LC 17**
See also DLB 268; EW 3; GFL Beginnings to 1789

LaBute, Neil 1963- .... **CLC 225**
See also CA 240

Lacan, Jacques (Marie Emile)
1901-1981 .... **CLC 75**
See also CA 121; 104; DLB 296; EWL 3; TWA

Laclos, Pierre-Ambroise Francois
1741-1803 .... **NCLC 4, 87**
See also DLB 313; EW 4; GFL Beginnings to 1789; RGWL 2, 3

Lacolere, Francois
See Aragon, Louis

La Colere, Francois
See Aragon, Louis

La Deshabilleuse
See Simenon, Georges (Jacques Christian)

Lady Gregory
See Gregory, Lady Isabella Augusta (Persse)

Lady of Quality, A
See Bagnold, Enid

La Fayette, Marie-(Madelaine Pioche de la Vergne) 1634-1693 .... **LC 2, 144**
See also DLB 268; GFL Beginnings to 1789; RGWL 2, 3

Lafayette, Marie-Madeleine
See La Fayette, Marie-(Madelaine Pioche de la Vergne)

Lafayette, Rene
See Hubbard, L. Ron

La Flesche, Francis 1857(?)-1932 ...... **NNAL**
See also CA 144; CANR 83; DLB 175

La Fontaine, Jean de 1621-1695 .... **LC 50**
See also DLB 268; EW 3; GFL Beginnings to 1789; MAICYA 1, 2; RGWL 2, 3; SATA 18

LaForet, Carmen 1921-2004 .... **CLC 219**
See also CA 246; CWW 2; DLB 322; EWL 3

LaForet Diaz, Carmen
See LaForet, Carmen

Laforgue, Jules 1860-1887 . **NCLC 5, 53; PC 14; SSC 20**
See also DLB 217; EW 7; GFL 1789 to the Present; RGWL 2, 3

Lagerkvist, Paer (Fabian)
1891-1974 .. **CLC 7, 10, 13, 54; SSC 12; TCLC 144**
See also CA 85-88; 49-52; DA3; DAM DRAM, NOV; DLB 259, 331; EW 10; EWL 3; MTCW 1, 2; MTFW 2005; RGSF 2; RGWL 2, 3; TWA

Lagerkvist, Par
See Lagerkvist, Paer (Fabian)

Lagerloef, Selma (Ottiliana Lovisa)
See Lagerlof, Selma (Ottiliana Lovisa)

Lagerlof, Selma (Ottiliana Lovisa)
1858-1940 .... **TCLC 4, 36**
See also CA 108; 188; CLR 7; DLB 259, 331; MTCW 2; RGWL 2, 3; SATA 15; SSFS 18

La Guma, Alex 1925-1985 .. **BLCS; CLC 19; TCLC 140**
See also AFW; BW 1, 3; CA 49-52; 118; CANR 25, 81; CDWLB 3; CN 1, 2, 3; CP 1; DAM NOV; DLB 117, 225; EWL 3; MTCW 1, 2; MTFW 2005; WLIT 2; WWE 1

Lahiri, Jhumpa 1967- .... **SSC 96**
See also AAYA 56; CA 193; CANR 134, 184; DLB 323; MTFW 2005; SSFS 19, 27

Laidlaw, A. K.
See Grieve, C(hristopher) M(urray)

Lainez, Manuel Mujica
See Mujica Lainez, Manuel

Laing, R(onald) D(avid) 1927-1989 . **CLC 95**
See also CA 107; 129; CANR 34; MTCW 1

Laishley, Alex
See Booth, Martin

Lamartine, Alphonse (Marie Louis Prat) de
1790-1869 .... **NCLC 11, 190; PC 16**
See also DAM POET; DLB 217; GFL 1789 to the Present; RGWL 2, 3

Lamb, Charles 1775-1834 ..... **NCLC 10, 113; SSC 112; WLC 3**
See also BRW 4; CDBLB 1789-1832; DA; DAB; DAC; DAM MST; DLB 93, 107, 163; RGEL 2; SATA 17; TEA

Lamb, Lady Caroline 1785-1828 ... **NCLC 38**
See also DLB 116

Lamb, Mary Ann 1764-1847 ...... **NCLC 125; SSC 112**
See also DLB 163; SATA 17

Lame Deer 1903(?)-1976 .... **NNAL**
See also CA 69-72

Lamming, George (William)
1927- . **BLC 1:2, 2:2; CLC 2, 4, 66, 144**
See also BW 2, 3; CA 85-88; CANR 26, 76; CDWLB 3; CN 1, 2, 3, 4, 5, 6, 7; CP 1; DAM MULT; DLB 125; EWL 3; MTCW 1, 2; MTFW 2005; NFS 15; RGEL 2

L'Amour, Louis 1908-1988 .... **CLC 25, 55**
See also AAYA 16; AITN 2; BEST 89:2; BPFB 2; CA 1-4R; 125; CANR 3, 25, 40; CPW; DA3; DAM NOV, POP; DLB 206; DLBY 1980; MTCW 1, 2; MTFW 2005; RGAL 4; TCWW 1, 2

Lampedusa, Giuseppe (Tomasi) di
See Tomasi di Lampedusa, Giuseppe

Lampman, Archibald 1861-1899 .. **NCLC 25, 194**
See also DLB 92; RGEL 2; TWA

Lancaster, Bruce 1896-1963 .... **CLC 36**
See also CA 9-10; CANR 70; CAP 1; SATA 9

Lanchester, John 1962- .... **CLC 99**
See also CA 194; DLB 267

Landau, Mark Alexandrovich
See Aldanov, Mark (Alexandrovich)

Landau-Aldanov, Mark Alexandrovich
See Aldanov, Mark (Alexandrovich)

Landis, Jerry
See Simon, Paul

Landis, John 1950- .... **CLC 26**
See also CA 112; 122; CANR 128

Landolfi, Tommaso 1908-1979 .... **CLC 11, 49**
See also CA 127; 117; DLB 177; EWL 3

Landon, Letitia Elizabeth
1802-1838 .... **NCLC 15**
See also DLB 96

Landor, Walter Savage
1775-1864 .... **NCLC 14**
See also BRW 4; DLB 93, 107; RGEL 2

Landwirth, Heinz
See Lind, Jakov

Lane, Patrick 1939- .... **CLC 25**
See also CA 97-100; CANR 54; CP 3, 4, 5, 6, 7; DAM POET; DLB 53; INT CA-97-100

Lane, Rose Wilder 1887-1968 ...... **TCLC 177**
See also CA 102; CANR 63; SATA 29; SATA-Brief 28; TCWW 2

Lang, Andrew 1844-1912 .... **TCLC 16**
See also CA 114; 137; CANR 85; CLR 101; DLB 98, 141, 184; FANT; MAICYA 1, 2; RGEL 2; SATA 16; WCH

Lang, Fritz 1890-1976 .... **CLC 20, 103**
See also AAYA 65; CA 77-80; 69-72; CANR 30

Lange, John
See Crichton, Michael

Langer, Elinor 1939- .... **CLC 34**
See also CA 121

Langland, William 1332(?)-1400(?) .... **LC 19, 120**
See also BRW 1; DA; DAB; DAC; DAM MST, POET; DLB 146; RGEL 2; TEA; WLIT 3

Langstaff, Launcelot
See Irving, Washington

Lanier, Sidney 1842-1881 . **NCLC 6, 118; PC 50**
See also AMWS 1; DAM POET; DLB 64; DLBD 13; EXPP; MAICYA 1; PFS 14; RGAL 4; SATA 18

Lanyer, Aemilia 1569-1645 .... **LC 10, 30, 83; PC 60**
See also DLB 121

Lao-Tzu
See Lao Tzu

Lao Tzu c. 6th cent. B.C.-3rd cent. B.C. .... **CMLC 7**

Lapine, James (Elliot) 1949- .... **CLC 39**
See also CA 123; 130; CANR 54, 128; DFS 25; DLB 341; INT CA-130

Larbaud, Valery (Nicolas)
1881-1957 .... **TCLC 9**
See also CA 106; 152; EWL 3; GFL 1789 to the Present

Larcom, Lucy 1824-1893 .... **NCLC 179**
See also AMWS 13; DLB 221, 243

Lardner, Ring
See Lardner, Ring(gold) W(ilmer)

Lardner, Ring W., Jr.
See Lardner, Ring(gold) W(ilmer)

Lardner, Ring(gold) W(ilmer)
1885-1933 ..... **SSC 32, 118; TCLC 2, 14**
See also AMW; BPFB 2; CA 104; 131; CDALB 1917-1929; DLB 11, 25, 86, 171; DLBD 16; MAL 5; MTCW 1, 2; MTFW 2005; RGAL 4; RGSF 2; TUS

Laredo, Betty
See Codrescu, Andrei

Larkin, Maia
See Wojciechowska, Maia (Teresa)

Larkin, Philip (Arthur) 1922-1985 ... **CLC 3, 5, 8, 9, 13, 18, 33, 39, 64; PC 21**
See also BRWS 1; CA 5-8R; 117; CANR 24, 62; CDBLB 1960 to Present; CP 1, 2, 3, 4; DA3; DAB; DAM MST, POET; DLB 27; EWL 3; MTCW 1, 2; MTFW 2005; PFS 3, 4, 12; RGEL 2

La Roche, Sophie von
1730-1807 .... **NCLC 121**
See also DLB 94

La Rochefoucauld, Francois
1613-1680 .... **LC 108**
See also DLB 268; EW 3; GFL Beginnings to 1789; RGWL 2, 3

Larra (y Sanchez de Castro), Mariano Jose de 1809-1837 ... **NCLC 17, 130**

Larsen, Eric 1941- .... **CLC 55**
See also CA 132

Larsen, Nella 1893(?)-1963 ... **BLC 1:2; CLC 37; HR 1:3; TCLC 200**
See also AFAW 1, 2; AMWS 18; BW 1; CA 125; CANR 83; DAM MULT; DLB 51; FW; LATS 1:1; LMFS 2

Larson, Charles R(aymond) 1938- ... **CLC 31**
See also CA 53-56; CANR 4, 121

Larson, Jonathan 1960-1996 .... **CLC 99**
See also AAYA 28; CA 156; DFS 23; MTFW 2005

La Sale, Antoine de c. 1386-1460(?) . **LC 104**
See also DLB 208

Las Casas, Bartolome de
1474-1566 .... **HLCS; LC 31**
See also DLB 318; LAW; WLIT 1

Lasch, Christopher 1932-1994 .... **CLC 102**
See also CA 73-76; 144; CANR 25, 118; DLB 246; MTCW 1, 2; MTFW 2005

MacDonald, John D. 1916-1986 .. **CLC 3, 27, 44**
See also BPFB 2; CA 1-4R; 121; CANR 1, 19, 60; CMW 4; CPW; DAM NOV, POP; DLB 8, 306; DLBY 1986; MSW; MTCW 1, 2; MTFW 2005; SFW 4

Macdonald, John Ross
See Millar, Kenneth

Macdonald, Ross
See Millar, Kenneth

MacDougal, John
See Blish, James (Benjamin)

MacDowell, John
See Parks, Tim(othy Harold)

MacEwen, Gwendolyn (Margaret) 1941-1987 .... **CLC 13, 55**
See also CA 9-12R; 124; CANR 7, 22; CP 1, 2, 3, 4; DLB 53, 251; SATA 50; SATA-Obit 55

MacGreevy, Thomas 1893-1967 .... **PC 82**
See also CA 262

Macha, Karel Hynek 1810-1846 .... **NCLC 46**

Machado (y Ruiz), Antonio 1875-1939 .... **TCLC 3**
See also CA 104; 174; DLB 108; EW 9; EWL 3; HW 2; PFS 23; RGWL 2, 3

Machado de Assis, Joaquim Maria 1839-1908 . **BLC 1:2; HLCS 2; SSC 24, 118; TCLC 10**
See also CA 107; 153; CANR 91; DLB 307; LAW; RGSF 2; RGWL 2, 3; TWA; WLIT 1

Machaut, Guillaume de c. 1300-1377 .... **CMLC 64**
See also DLB 208

Machen, Arthur SSC 20; TCLC 4
See Jones, Arthur Llewellyn
See also CA 179; DLB 156, 178; RGEL 2

Machen, Arthur Llewelyn Jones
See Jones, Arthur Llewellyn

Machiavelli, Niccolo 1469-1527 ... **DC 16; LC 8, 36, 140; WLCS**
See also AAYA 58; DA; DAB; DAC; DAM MST; EW 2; LAIT 1; LMFS 1; NFS 9; RGWL 2, 3; TWA; WLIT 7

MacInnes, Colin 1914-1976 .... **CLC 4, 23**
See also CA 69-72; 65-68; CANR 21; CN 1, 2; DLB 14; MTCW 1, 2; RGEL 2; RHW

MacInnes, Helen (Clark) 1907-1985 .... **CLC 27, 39**
See also BPFB 2; CA 1-4R; 117; CANR 1, 28, 58; CMW 4; CN 1, 2; CPW; DAM POP; DLB 87; MSW; MTCW 1, 2; MTFW 2005; SATA 22; SATA-Obit 44

Mackay, Mary 1855-1924 .... **TCLC 51**
See also CA 118; 177; DLB 34, 156; FANT; RGEL 2; RHW; SUFW 1

Mackay, Shena 1944- .... **CLC 195**
See also CA 104; CANR 88, 139; DLB 231, 319; MTFW 2005

Mackenzie, Compton (Edward Montague) 1883-1972 .... **CLC 18; TCLC 116**
See also CA 21-22; 37-40R; CAP 2; CN 1; DLB 34, 100; RGEL 2

Mackenzie, Henry 1745-1831 .... **NCLC 41**
See also DLB 39; RGEL 2

Mackey, Nathaniel 1947- .... **BLC 2:3; PC 49**
See also CA 153; CANR 114; CP 6, 7; DLB 169

Mackey, Nathaniel Ernest
See Mackey, Nathaniel

MacKinnon, Catharine A. 1946- .... **CLC 181**
See also CA 128; 132; CANR 73, 140, 189; FW; MTCW 2; MTFW 2005

Mackintosh, Elizabeth 1896(?)-1952 .... **TCLC 14**
See also CA 110; CMW 4; DLB 10, 77; MSW

Macklin, Charles 1699-1797 .... **LC 132**
See also DLB 89; RGEL 2

MacLaren, James
See Grieve, C(hristopher) M(urray)

MacLaverty, Bernard 1942- ..... **CLC 31, 243**
See also CA 116; 118; CANR 43, 88, 168; CN 5, 6, 7; DLB 267; INT CA-118; RGSF 2

MacLean, Alistair (Stuart) 1922(?)-1987 .... **CLC 3, 13, 50, 63**
See also CA 57-60; 121; CANR 28, 61; CMW 4; CP 2, 3, 4, 5, 6, 7; CPW; DAM POP; DLB 276; MTCW 1; SATA 23; SATA-Obit 50; TCWW 2

Maclean, Norman (Fitzroy) 1902-1990 .... **CLC 78; SSC 13**
See also AMWS 14; CA 102; 132; CANR 49; CPW; DAM POP; DLB 206; TCWW 2

MacLeish, Archibald 1892-1982 ... **CLC 3, 8, 14, 68; PC 47**
See also AMW; CA 9-12R; 106; CAD; CANR 33, 63; CDALBS; CP 1, 2; DAM POET; DFS 15; DLB 4, 7, 45; DLBY 1982; EWL 3; EXPP; MAL 5; MTCW 1, 2; MTFW 2005; PAB; PFS 5; RGAL 4; TUS

MacLennan, (John) Hugh 1907-1990 .... **CLC 2, 14, 92**
See also CA 5-8R; 142; CANR 33; CN 1, 2, 3, 4; DAC; DAM MST; DLB 68; EWL 3; MTCW 1, 2; MTFW 2005; RGEL 2; TWA

MacLeod, Alistair 1936- .. **CLC 56, 165; SSC 90**
See also CA 123; CCA 1; DAC; DAM MST; DLB 60; MTCW 2; MTFW 2005; RGSF 2; TCLE 1:2

Macleod, Fiona
See Sharp, William

MacNeice, (Frederick) Louis 1907-1963 .... **CLC 1, 4, 10, 53; PC 61**
See also BRW 7; CA 85-88; CANR 61; DAB; DAM POET; DLB 10, 20; EWL 3; MTCW 1, 2; MTFW 2005; RGEL 2

MacNeill, Dand
See Fraser, George MacDonald

Macpherson, James 1736-1796 .... **CMLC 28; LC 29; PC 97**
See also BRWS 8; DLB 109, 336; RGEL 2

Macpherson, (Jean) Jay 1931- .... **CLC 14**
See also CA 5-8R; CANR 90; CP 1, 2, 3, 4, 6, 7; CWP; DLB 53

Macrobius fl. 430- .... **CMLC 48**

MacShane, Frank 1927-1999 .... **CLC 39**
See also CA 9-12R; 186; CANR 3, 33; DLB 111

Macumber, Mari
See Sandoz, Mari(e Susette)

Madach, Imre 1823-1864 .... **NCLC 19**

Madden, (Jerry) David 1933- .... **CLC 5, 15**
See also CA 1-4R; CAAS 3; CANR 4, 45; CN 3, 4, 5, 6, 7; CSW; DLB 6; MTCW 1

Maddern, Al(an)
See Ellison, Harlan

Madhubuti, Haki R. 1942- .... **BLC 1:2; CLC 2; PC 5**
See also BW 2, 3; CA 73-76; CANR 24, 51, 73, 139; CP 2, 3, 4, 5, 6, 7; CSW; DAM MULT, POET; DLB 5, 41; DLBD 8; EWL 3; MAL 5; MTCW 2; MTFW 2005; RGAL 4

Madison, James 1751-1836 .... **NCLC 126**
See also DLB 37

Maepenn, Hugh
See Kuttner, Henry

Maepenn, K. H.
See Kuttner, Henry

Maeterlinck, Maurice 1862-1949 .... **DC 32; TCLC 3**
See also CA 104; 136; CANR 80; DAM DRAM; DLB 192, 331; EW 8; EWL 3; GFL 1789 to the Present; LMFS 2; RGWL 2, 3; SATA 66; TWA

Maginn, William 1794-1842 .... **NCLC 8**
See also DLB 110, 159

Mahapatra, Jayanta 1928- .... **CLC 33**
See also CA 73-76; CAAS 9; CANR 15, 33, 66, 87; CP 4, 5, 6, 7; DAM MULT; DLB 323

Mahfouz, Nagib
See Mahfouz, Naguib

Mahfouz, Naguib 1911(?)-2006 . **CLC 52, 55, 153; SSC 66**
See also AAYA 49; AFW; BEST 89:2; CA 128; 253; CANR 55, 101; DA3; DAM NOV; DLB 346; DLBY 1988; MTCW 1, 2; MTFW 2005; RGSF 2; RGWL 2, 3; SSFS 9; WLIT 2

Mahfouz, Naguib Abdel Aziz Al-Sabilgi
See Mahfouz, Naguib

Mahfouz, Najib
See Mahfouz, Naguib

Mahfuz, Najib
See Mahfouz, Naguib

Mahon, Derek 1941- .... **CLC 27; PC 60**
See also BRWS 6; CA 113; 128; CANR 88; CP 1, 2, 3, 4, 5, 6, 7; DLB 40; EWL 3

Maiakovskii, Vladimir
See Mayakovski, Vladimir (Vladimirovich)

Mailer, Norman 1923-2007 ... **CLC 1, 2, 3, 4, 5, 8, 11, 14, 28, 39, 74, 111, 234**
See also AAYA 31; AITN 2; AMW; AMWC 2; AMWR 2; BPFB 2; CA 9-12R; 266; CABS 1; CANR 28, 74, 77, 130; CDALB 1968-1988; CN 1, 2, 3, 4, 5, 6, 7; CPW; DA; DA3; DAB; DAC; DAM MST, NOV, POP; DLB 2, 16, 28, 185, 278; DLBD 3; DLBY 1980, 1983; EWL 3; MAL 5; MTCW 1, 2; MTFW 2005; NFS 10; RGAL 4; TUS

Mailer, Norman Kingsley
See Mailer, Norman

Maillet, Antonine 1929- .... **CLC 54, 118**
See also CA 115; 120; CANR 46, 74, 77, 134; CCA 1; CWW 2; DAC; DLB 60; INT CA-120; MTCW 2; MTFW 2005

Maimonides, Moses 1135-1204 ..... **CMLC 76**
See also DLB 115

Mais, Roger 1905-1955 .... **TCLC 8**
See also BW 1, 3; CA 105; 124; CANR 82; CDWLB 3; DLB 125; EWL 3; MTCW 1; RGEL 2

Maistre, Joseph 1753-1821 .... **NCLC 37**
See also GFL 1789 to the Present

Maitland, Frederic William 1850-1906 .... **TCLC 65**

Maitland, Sara (Louise) 1950- .... **CLC 49**
See also BRWS 11; CA 69-72; CANR 13, 59; DLB 271; FW

Major, Clarence 1936- ...... **BLC 1:2; CLC 3, 19, 48**
See also AFAW 2; BW 2, 3; CA 21-24R; CAAS 6; CANR 13, 25, 53, 82; CN 3, 4, 5, 6, 7; CP 2, 3, 4, 5, 6, 7; CSW; DAM MULT; DLB 33; EWL 3; MAL 5; MSW

Major, Kevin (Gerald) 1949- .... **CLC 26**
See also AAYA 16; CA 97-100; CANR 21, 38, 112; CLR 11; DAC; DLB 60; INT CANR-21; JRDA; MAICYA 1, 2; MAIC-YAS 1; SATA 32, 82, 134; WYA; YAW

Maki, James
See Ozu, Yasujiro

Makin, Bathsua 1600-1675(?) .... **LC 137**

Makine, Andrei 1957-
See Makine, Andrei

Marks, J.
See Highwater, Jamake (Mamake)

Marks-Highwater, J.
See Highwater, Jamake (Mamake)

Markson, David M. 1927- .... **CLC 67**
See also AMWS 17; CA 49-52; CANR 1, 91, 158; CN 5, 6

Markson, David Merrill
See Markson, David M.

Marlatt, Daphne (Buckle) 1942- .... **CLC 168**
See also CA 25-28R; CANR 17, 39; CN 6, 7; CP 4, 5, 6, 7; CWP; DLB 60; FW

Marley, Bob
See Marley, Robert Nesta

Marley, Robert Nesta 1945-1981 ...... **CLC 17**
See also CA 107; 103

Marlowe, Christopher 1564-1593 . **DC 1; LC 22, 47, 117; PC 57; WLC 4**
See also BRW 1; BRWR 1; CDBLB Before 1660; DA; DA3; DAB; DAC; DAM DRAM, MST; DFS 1, 5, 13, 21; DLB 62; EXPP; LMFS 1; PFS 22; RGEL 2; TEA; WLIT 3

Marlowe, Stephen 1928-2008 .... **CLC 70**
See also CA 13-16R; 269; CANR 6, 55; CMW 4; SFW 4

Marmion, Shakerley 1603-1639 .... **LC 89**
See also DLB 58; RGEL 2

Marmontel, Jean-Francois 1723-1799 .. **LC 2**
See also DLB 314

Maron, Monika 1941- .... **CLC 165**
See also CA 201

Marot, Clement c. 1496-1544 .... **LC 133**
See also DLB 327; GFL Beginnings to 1789

Marquand, John P(hillips)
1893-1960 .... **CLC 2, 10**
See also AMW; BPFB 2; CA 85-88; CANR 73; CMW 4; DLB 9, 102; EWL 3; MAL 5; MTCW 2; RGAL 4

Marques, Rene 1919-1979 .. **CLC 96; HLC 2**
See also CA 97-100; 85-88; CANR 78; DAM MULT; DLB 305; EWL 3; HW 1, 2; LAW; RGSF 2

Marquez, Gabriel Garcia
See Garcia Marquez, Gabriel

Marquis, Don(ald Robert Perry)
1878-1937 .... **TCLC 7**
See also CA 104; 166; DLB 11, 25; MAL 5; RGAL 4

Marquis de Sade
See Sade, Donatien Alphonse Francois

Marric, J. J.
See Creasey, John

Marryat, Frederick 1792-1848 .... **NCLC 3**
See also DLB 21, 163; RGEL 2; WCH

Marsden, James
See Creasey, John

Marsh, Edward 1872-1953 .... **TCLC 99**

Marsh, (Edith) Ngaio 1895-1982 .. **CLC 7, 53**
See also CA 9-12R; CANR 6, 58; CMW 4; CN 1, 2, 3; CPW; DAM POP; DLB 77; MSW; MTCW 1, 2; RGEL 2; TEA

Marshall, Alan
See Westlake, Donald E.

Marshall, Allen
See Westlake, Donald E.

Marshall, Garry 1934- .... **CLC 17**
See also AAYA 3; CA 111; SATA 60

Marshall, Paule 1929- .... **BLC 1:3, 2:3; CLC 27, 72, 253; SSC 3**
See also AFAW 1, 2; AMWS 11; BPFB 2; BW 2, 3; CA 77-80; CANR 25, 73, 129; CN 1, 2, 3, 4, 5, 6, 7; DA3; DAM MULT; DLB 33, 157, 227; EWL 3; LATS 1:2; MAL 5; MTCW 1, 2; MTFW 2005; RGAL 4; SSFS 15

Marshallik
See Zangwill, Israel

Marsilius of Inghen c.
1340-1396 .... **CMLC 106**

Marsten, Richard
See Hunter, Evan

Marston, John 1576-1634 .... **LC 33**
See also BRW 2; DAM DRAM; DLB 58, 172; RGEL 2

Martel, Yann 1963- .... **CLC 192**
See also AAYA 67; CA 146; CANR 114; DLB 326, 334; MTFW 2005; NFS 27

Martens, Adolphe-Adhemar
See Ghelderode, Michel de

Martha, Henry
See Harris, Mark

Marti, Jose
See Marti (y Perez), Jose (Julian)

Marti (y Perez), Jose (Julian)
1853-1895 ..... **HLC 2; NCLC 63; PC 76**
See also DAM MULT; DLB 290; HW 2; LAW; RGWL 2, 3; WLIT 1

Martial c. 40-c. 104 .... **CMLC 35; PC 10**
See also AW 2; CDWLB 1; DLB 211; RGWL 2, 3

Martin, Ken
See Hubbard, L. Ron

Martin, Richard
See Creasey, John

Martin, Steve 1945- .... **CLC 30, 217**
See also AAYA 53; CA 97-100; CANR 30, 100, 140; DFS 19; MTCW 1; MTFW 2005

Martin, Valerie 1948- .... **CLC 89**
See also BEST 90:2; CA 85-88; CANR 49, 89, 165

Martin, Violet Florence 1862-1915 .. **SSC 56; TCLC 51**

Martin, Webber
See Silverberg, Robert

Martindale, Patrick Victor
See White, Patrick (Victor Martindale)

Martin du Gard, Roger
1881-1958 .... **TCLC 24**
See also CA 118; CANR 94; DLB 65, 331; EWL 3; GFL 1789 to the Present; RGWL 2, 3

Martineau, Harriet 1802-1876 ...... **NCLC 26, 137**
See also DLB 21, 55, 159, 163, 166, 190; FW; RGEL 2; YABC 2

Martines, Julia
See O'Faolain, Julia

Martinez, Enrique Gonzalez
See Gonzalez Martinez, Enrique

Martinez, Jacinto Benavente y
See Benavente (y Martinez), Jacinto

Martinez de la Rosa, Francisco de Paula
1787-1862 .... **NCLC 102**
See also TWA

Martinez Ruiz, Jose 1873-1967 .... **CLC 11**
See also CA 93-96; DLB 322; EW 3; EWL 3; HW 1

Martinez Sierra, Gregorio
See Martinez Sierra, Maria

Martinez Sierra, Gregorio
1881-1947 .... **TCLC 6**
See also CA 115; EWL 3

Martinez Sierra, Maria 1874-1974 .. **TCLC 6**
See also CA 250; 115; EWL 3

Martinsen, Martin
See Follett, Ken

Martinson, Harry (Edmund)
1904-1978 .... **CLC 14**
See also CA 77-80; CANR 34, 130; DLB 259, 331; EWL 3

Martyn, Edward 1859-1923 .... **TCLC 131**
See also CA 179; DLB 10; RGEL 2

Marut, Ret
See Traven, B.

Marut, Robert
See Traven, B.

Marvell, Andrew 1621-1678 .... **LC 4, 43; PC 10, 86; WLC 4**
See also BRW 2; BRWR 2; CDBLB 1660-1789; DA; DAB; DAC; DAM MST, POET; DLB 131; EXPP; PFS 5; RGEL 2; TEA; WP

Marx, Karl (Heinrich)
1818-1883 .... **NCLC 17, 114**
See also DLB 129; LATS 1:1; TWA

Masaoka, Shiki -1902
See Masaoka, Tsunenori

Masaoka, Tsunenori 1867-1902 ..... **TCLC 18**
See also CA 117; 191; EWL 3; RGWL 3; TWA

Masaoka Shiki
See Masaoka, Tsunenori

Masefield, John (Edward)
1878-1967 .... **CLC 11, 47; PC 78**
See also CA 19-20; 25-28R; CANR 33; CAP 2; CDBLB 1890-1914; DAM POET; DLB 10, 19, 153, 160; EWL 3; EXPP; FANT; MTCW 1, 2; PFS 5; RGEL 2; SATA 19

Maso, Carole 1955(?)- .... **CLC 44**
See also CA 170; CANR 148; CN 7; GLL 2; RGAL 4

Mason, Bobbie Ann 1940- ... **CLC 28, 43, 82, 154; SSC 4, 101**
See also AAYA 5, 42; AMWS 8; BPFB 2; CA 53-56; CANR 11, 31, 58, 83, 125, 169; CDALBS; CN 5, 6, 7; CSW; DA3; DLB 173; DLBY 1987; EWL 3; EXPS; INT CANR-31; MAL 5; MTCW 1, 2; MTFW 2005; NFS 4; RGAL 4; RGSF 2; SSFS 3, 8, 20; TCLE 1:2; YAW

Mason, Ernst
See Pohl, Frederik

Mason, Hunni B.
See Sternheim, (William Adolf) Carl

Mason, Lee W.
See Malzberg, Barry N(athaniel)

Mason, Nick 1945- .... **CLC 35**

Mason, Tally
See Derleth, August (William)

Mass, Anna **CLC 59**

Mass, William
See Gibson, William

Massinger, Philip 1583-1640 .... **LC 70**
See also BRWS 11; DLB 58; RGEL 2

Master Lao
See Lao Tzu

Masters, Edgar Lee 1868-1950 ...... **PC 1, 36; TCLC 2, 25; WLCS**
See also AMWS 1; CA 104; 133; CDALB 1865-1917; DA; DAC; DAM MST, POET; DLB 54; EWL 3; EXPP; MAL 5; MTCW 1, 2; MTFW 2005; RGAL 4; TUS; WP

Masters, Hilary 1928- .... **CLC 48**
See also CA 25-28R; 217; CAAE 217; CANR 13, 47, 97, 171; CN 6, 7; DLB 244

Masters, Hilary Thomas
See Masters, Hilary

Mastrosimone, William 1947- .... **CLC 36**
See also CA 186; CAD; CD 5, 6

Mathe, Albert
See Camus, Albert

Mather, Cotton 1663-1728 .... **LC 38**
See also AMWS 2; CDALB 1640-1865; DLB 24, 30, 140; RGAL 4; TUS

Mather, Increase 1639-1723 .... **LC 38, 161**
See also DLB 24

Mathers, Marshall
See Eminem

Mathers, Marshall Bruce
See Eminem

Mehta, Ved 1934- .... **CLC 37**
See also CA 1-4R, 212; CAAE 212; CANR 2, 23, 69; DLB 323; MTCW 1; MTFW 2005

Melanchthon, Philipp 1497-1560 .... **LC 90**
See also DLB 179

Melanter
See Blackmore, R(ichard) D(oddridge)

Meleager c. 140B.C.-c. 70B.C. ...... **CMLC 53**

Melies, Georges 1861-1938 .... **TCLC 81**

Melikow, Loris
See Hofmannsthal, Hugo von

Melmoth, Sebastian
See Wilde, Oscar

Melo Neto, Joao Cabral de
See Cabral de Melo Neto, Joao

Meltzer, Milton 1915- .... **CLC 26**
See also AAYA 8, 45; BYA 2, 6; CA 13-16R; CANR 38, 92, 107; CLR 13; DLB 61; JRDA; MAICYA 1, 2; SAAS 1; SATA 1, 50, 80, 128; SATA-Essay 124; WYA; YAW

Melville, Herman 1819-1891 ..... **NCLC 3, 12, 29, 45, 49, 91, 93, 123, 157, 181, 193; PC 82; SSC 1, 17, 46, 95; WLC 4**
See also AMW; AMWR 1; CDALB 1640-1865; DA; DA3; DAB; DAC; DAM MST, NOV; DLB 3, 74, 250, 254; EXPN; EXPS; GL 3; LAIT 1, 2; NFS 7, 9; RGAL 4; RGSF 2; SATA 59; SSFS 3; TUS

Members, Mark
See Powell, Anthony

Membreno, Alejandro CLC 59

Menand, Louis 1952- .... **CLC 208**
See also CA 200

Menander c. 342B.C.-c. 293B.C. .... **CMLC 9, 51, 101; DC 3**
See also AW 1; CDWLB 1; DAM DRAM; DLB 176; LMFS 1; RGWL 2, 3

Menchu, Rigoberta 1959- .. **CLC 160; HLCS 2**
See also CA 175; CANR 135; DNFS 1; WLIT 1

Mencken, H(enry) L(ouis)
1880-1956 .... **TCLC 13, 18**
See also AMW; CA 105; 125; CDALB 1917-1929; DLB 11, 29, 63, 137, 222; EWL 3; MAL 5; MTCW 1, 2; MTFW 2005; NCFS 4; RGAL 4; TUS

Mendelsohn, Jane 1965- .... **CLC 99**
See also CA 154; CANR 94

Mendelssohn, Moses 1729-1786 .... **LC 142**
See also DLB 97

Mendoza, Inigo Lopez de
See Santillana, Inigo Lopez de Mendoza, Marques de

Menton, Francisco de
See Chin, Frank (Chew, Jr.)

Mercer, David 1928-1980 .... **CLC 5**
See also CA 9-12R; 102; CANR 23; CBD; DAM DRAM; DLB 13, 310; MTCW 1; RGEL 2

Merchant, Paul
See Ellison, Harlan

Meredith, George 1828-1909 .. **PC 60; TCLC 17, 43**
See also CA 117; 153; CANR 80; CDBLB 1832-1890; DAM POET; DLB 18, 35, 57, 159; RGEL 2; TEA

Meredith, William 1919-2007 ...... **CLC 4, 13, 22, 55; PC 28**
See also CA 9-12R; 260; CAAS 14; CANR 6, 40, 129; CP 1, 2, 3, 4, 5, 6, 7; DAM POET; DLB 5; MAL 5

Meredith, William Morris
See Meredith, William

Merezhkovsky, Dmitrii Sergeevich
See Merezhkovsky, Dmitry Sergeyevich

Merezhkovsky, Dmitry Sergeevich
See Merezhkovsky, Dmitry Sergeyevich

Merezhkovsky, Dmitry Sergeyevich
1865-1941 .... **TCLC 29**
See also CA 169; DLB 295; EWL 3

Merezhkovsky, Zinaida
See Gippius, Zinaida (Nikolaevna)

Merimee, Prosper 1803-1870 . **DC 33; NCLC 6, 65; SSC 7, 77**
See also DLB 119, 192; EW 6; EXPS; GFL 1789 to the Present; RGSF 2; RGWL 2, 3; SSFS 8; SUFW

Merkin, Daphne 1954- .... **CLC 44**
See also CA 123

Merleau-Ponty, Maurice
1908-1961 .... **TCLC 156**
See also CA 114; 89-92; DLB 296; GFL 1789 to the Present

Merlin, Arthur
See Blish, James (Benjamin)

Mernissi, Fatima 1940- .... **CLC 171**
See also CA 152; DLB 346; FW

Merrill, James 1926-1995 ...... **CLC 2, 3, 6, 8, 13, 18, 34, 91; PC 28; TCLC 173**
See also AMWS 3; CA 13-16R; 147; CANR 10, 49, 63, 108; CP 1, 2, 3, 4; DA3; DAM POET; DLB 5, 165; DLBY 1985; EWL 3; INT CANR-10; MAL 5; MTCW 1, 2; MTFW 2005; PAB; PFS 23; RGAL 4

Merrill, James Ingram
See Merrill, James

Merriman, Alex
See Silverberg, Robert

Merriman, Brian 1747-1805 .... **NCLC 70**

Merritt, E. B.
See Waddington, Miriam

Merton, Thomas (James)
1915-1968 . **CLC 1, 3, 11, 34, 83; PC 10**
See also AAYA 61; AMWS 8; CA 5-8R; 25-28R; CANR 22, 53, 111, 131; DA3; DLB 48; DLBY 1981; MAL 5; MTCW 1, 2; MTFW 2005

Merwin, W.S. 1927- ..... **CLC 1, 2, 3, 5, 8, 13, 18, 45, 88; PC 45**
See also AMWS 3; CA 13-16R; CANR 15, 51, 112, 140; CP 1, 2, 3, 4, 5, 6, 7; DA3; DAM POET; DLB 5, 169, 342; EWL 3; INT CANR-15; MAL 5; MTCW 1, 2; MTFW 2005; PAB; PFS 5, 15; RGAL 4

Metastasio, Pietro 1698-1782 .... **LC 115**
See also RGWL 2, 3

Metcalf, John 1938- .... **CLC 37; SSC 43**
See also CA 113; CN 4, 5, 6, 7; DLB 60; RGSF 2; TWA

Metcalf, Suzanne
See Baum, L(yman) Frank

Mew, Charlotte (Mary) 1870-1928 .. **TCLC 8**
See also CA 105; 189; DLB 19, 135; RGEL 2

Mewshaw, Michael 1943- .... **CLC 9**
See also CA 53-56; CANR 7, 47, 147; DLBY 1980

Meyer, Conrad Ferdinand
1825-1898 .... **NCLC 81; SSC 30**
See also DLB 129; EW; RGWL 2, 3

Meyer, Gustav 1868-1932 .... **TCLC 21**
See also CA 117; 190; DLB 81; EWL 3

Meyer, June
See Jordan, June

Meyer, Lynn
See Slavitt, David R.

Meyer-Meyrink, Gustav
See Meyer, Gustav

Meyers, Jeffrey 1939- .... **CLC 39**
See also CA 73-76, 186; CAAE 186; CANR 54, 102, 159; DLB 111

Meynell, Alice (Christina Gertrude Thompson) 1847-1922 .... **TCLC 6**
See also CA 104; 177; DLB 19, 98; RGEL 2

Meyrink, Gustav
See Meyer, Gustav

Mhlophe, Gcina 1960- .... **BLC 2:3**

Michaels, Leonard 1933-2003 ..... **CLC 6, 25; SSC 16**
See also AMWS 16; CA 61-64; 216; CANR 21, 62, 119, 179; CN 3, 45, 6, 7; DLB 130; MTCW 1; TCLE 1:2

Michaux, Henri 1899-1984 .... **CLC 8, 19**
See also CA 85-88; 114; DLB 258; EWL 3; GFL 1789 to the Present; RGWL 2, 3

Micheaux, Oscar (Devereaux)
1884-1951 .... **TCLC 76**
See also BW 3; CA 174; DLB 50; TCWW 2

Michelangelo 1475-1564 .... **LC 12**
See also AAYA 43

Michelet, Jules 1798-1874 .... **NCLC 31**
See also EW 5; GFL 1789 to the Present

Michels, Robert 1876-1936 .... **TCLC 88**
See also CA 212

Michener, James A. 1907(?)-1997 . **CLC 1, 5, 11, 29, 60, 109**
See also AAYA 27; AITN 1; BEST 90:1; BPFB 2; CA 5-8R; 161; CANR 21, 45, 68; CN 1, 2, 3, 4, 5, 6; CPW; DA3; DAM NOV, POP; DLB 6; MAL 5; MTCW 1, 2; MTFW 2005; RHW; TCWW 1, 2

Mickiewicz, Adam 1798-1855 . **NCLC 3, 101; PC 38**
See also EW 5; RGWL 2, 3

Middleton, (John) Christopher
1926- .... **CLC 13**
See also CA 13-16R; CANR 29, 54, 117; CP 1, 2, 3, 4, 5, 6, 7; DLB 40

Middleton, Richard (Barham)
1882-1911 .... **TCLC 56**
See also CA 187; DLB 156; HGG

Middleton, Stanley 1919- .... **CLC 7, 38**
See also CA 25-28R; CAAS 23; CANR 21, 46, 81, 157; CN 1, 2, 3, 4, 5, 6, 7; DLB 14, 326

Middleton, Thomas 1580-1627 ...... **DC 5; LC 33, 123**
See also BRW 2; DAM DRAM, MST; DFS 18, 22; DLB 58; RGEL 2

Mieville, China 1972(?)- .... **CLC 235**
See also AAYA 52; CA 196; CANR 138; MTFW 2005

Migueis, Jose Rodrigues 1901-1980 . **CLC 10**
See also DLB 287

Mihura, Miguel 1905-1977 .... **DC 34**
See also CA 214

Mikszath, Kalman 1847-1910 .... **TCLC 31**
See also CA 170

Miles, Jack CLC 100
See also CA 200

Miles, John Russiano
See Miles, Jack

Miles, Josephine (Louise)
1911-1985 .... **CLC 1, 2, 14, 34, 39**
See also CA 1-4R; 116; CANR 2, 55; CP 1, 2, 3, 4; DAM POET; DLB 48; MAL 5; TCLE 1:2

Militant
See Sandburg, Carl (August)

Mill, Harriet (Hardy) Taylor
1807-1858 .... **NCLC 102**
See also FW

Mill, John Stuart 1806-1873 ... **NCLC 11, 58, 179**
See also CDBLB 1832-1890; DLB 55, 190, 262; FW 1; RGEL 2; TEA

Nervo, (Jose) Amado (Ruiz de)
1870-1919 .... HLCS 2; TCLC 11
See also CA 109; 131; DLB 290; EWL 3;
HW 1; LAW

Nesbit, Malcolm
See Chester, Alfred

Nessi, Pio Baroja y
See Baroja, Pio

Nestroy, Johann 1801-1862 .... NCLC 42
See also DLB 133; RGWL 2, 3

Netterville, Luke
See O'Grady, Standish (James)

Neufeld, John (Arthur) 1938- .... CLC 17
See also AAYA 11; CA 25-28R; CANR 11,
37, 56; CLR 52; MAICYA 1, 2; SAAS 3;
SATA 6, 81, 131; SATA-Essay 131; YAW

Neumann, Alfred 1895-1952 .... TCLC 100
See also CA 183; DLB 56

Neumann, Ferenc
See Molnar, Ferenc

Neville, Emily Cheney 1919- .... CLC 12
See also BYA 2; CA 5-8R; CANR 3, 37,
85; JRDA; MAICYA 1, 2; SAAS 2; SATA
1; YAW

Newbound, Bernard Slade 1930- .... CLC 11,
46
See also CA 81-84; CAAS 9; CANR 49;
CCA 1; CD 5, 6; DAM DRAM; DLB 53

Newby, P(ercy) H(oward)
1918-1997 .... CLC 2, 13
See also CA 5-8R; CANR 32, 67; CN
1, 2, 3, 4, 5, 6; DAM NOV; DLB 15, 326;
MTCW 1; RGEL 2

Newcastle
See Cavendish, Margaret Lucas

Newlove, Donald 1928- .... CLC 6
See also CA 29-32R; CANR 25

Newlove, John (Herbert) 1938- .... CLC 14
See also CA 21-24R; CANR 9, 25; CP 1, 2,
3, 4, 5, 6, 7

Newman, Charles 1938-2006 .... CLC 2, 8
See also CA 21-24R; 249; CANR 84; CN
3, 4, 5, 6

Newman, Charles Hamilton
See Newman, Charles

Newman, Edwin (Harold) 1919- ...... CLC 14
See also AITN 1; CA 69-72; CANR 5

Newman, John Henry 1801-1890 . NCLC 38,
99
See also BRWS 7; DLB 18, 32, 55; RGEL
2

Newton, (Sir) Isaac 1642-1727 ...... LC 35, 53
See also DLB 252

Newton, Suzanne 1936- .... CLC 35
See also BYA 7; CA 41-44R; CANR 14;
JRDA; SATA 5, 77

New York Dept. of Ed. CLC 70

Nexo, Martin Andersen
1869-1954 .... TCLC 43
See also CA 202; DLB 214; EWL 3

Nezval, Vitezslav 1900-1958 .... TCLC 44
See also CA 123; CDWLB 4; DLB 215;
EWL 3

Ng, Fae Myenne 1956- .... CLC 81
See also BYA 11; CA 146

Ngcobo, Lauretta 1931- .... BLC 2:3
See also CA 165

Ngema, Mbongeni 1955- .... CLC 57
See also BW 2; CA 143; CANR 84; CD 5,
6

Ngugi, James T.
See Ngugi wa Thiong'o

Ngugi, James Thiong'o
See Ngugi wa Thiong'o

Ngugi wa Thiong'o 1938- .... BLC 1:3, 2:3;
CLC 3, 7, 13, 36, 182, 275
See also AFW; BRWS 8; BW 2; CA 81-84;
CANR 27, 58, 164; CD 3, 4, 5, 6, 7; CD-
WLB 3; CN 1, 2; DAM MULT, NOV;
DLB 125; DNFS 2; EWL 3; MTCW 1, 2;
MTFW 2005; RGEL 2; WWE 1

Niatum, Duane 1938- .... NNAL
See also CA 41-44R; CANR 21, 45, 83;
DLB 175

Nichol, B(arrie) P(hillip) 1944-1988 . CLC 18
See also CA 53-56; CP 1, 2, 3, 4; DLB 53;
SATA 66

Nicholas of Autrecourt c.
1298-1369 .... CMLC 108

Nicholas of Cusa 1401-1464 .... LC 80
See also DLB 115

Nichols, John 1940- .... CLC 38
See also AMWS 13; CA 9-12R, 190; CAAE
190; CAAS 2; CANR 6, 70, 121, 185;
DLBY 1982; LATS 1:2; MTFW 2005;
TCWW 1, 2

Nichols, Leigh
See Koontz, Dean R.

Nichols, Peter (Richard) 1927- .... CLC 5, 36,
65
See also CA 104; CANR 33, 86; CBD; CD
5, 6; DLB 13, 245; MTCW 1

Nicholson, Linda CLC 65

Ni Chuilleanain, Eilean 1942- .... PC 34
See also CA 126; CANR 53, 83; CP 5, 6, 7;
CWP; DLB 40

Nicolas, F. R. E.
See Freeling, Nicolas

Niedecker, Lorine 1903-1970 ..... CLC 10, 42;
PC 42
See also CA 25-28; CAP 2; DAM POET;
DLB 48

Nietzsche, Friedrich (Wilhelm)
1844-1900 .... TCLC 10, 18, 55
See also CA 107; 121; CDWLB 2; DLB
129; EW 7; RGWL 2, 3; TWA

Nievo, Ippolito 1831-1861 .... NCLC 22

Nightingale, Anne Redmon 1943- .... CLC 22
See also CA 103; DLBY 1986

Nightingale, Florence 1820-1910 ... TCLC 85
See also CA 188; DLB 166

Nijo Yoshimoto 1320-1388 .... CMLC 49
See also DLB 203

Nik. T. O.
See Annensky, Innokenty (Fyodorovich)

Nin, Anais 1903-1977 ..... CLC 1, 4, 8, 11, 14,
60, 127; SSC 10
See also AITN 2; AMWS 10; BPFB 2; CA
13-16R; 69-72; CANR 22, 53; CN 1, 2;
DAM NOV, POP; DLB 2, 4, 152; EWL
3; GLL 2; MAL 5; MBL; MTCW 1, 2;
MTFW 2005; RGAL 4; RGSF 2

Nisbet, Robert A(lexander)
1913-1996 .... TCLC 117
See also CA 25-28R; 153; CANR 17; INT
CANR-17

Nishida, Kitaro 1870-1945 .... TCLC 83

Nishiwaki, Junzaburo 1894-1982 .... PC 15
See also CA 194; 107; EWL 3; MJW;
RGWL 3

Nissenson, Hugh 1933- .... CLC 4, 9
See also CA 17-20R; CANR 27, 108, 151;
CN 5, 6; DLB 28, 335

Nister, Der
See Der Nister

Niven, Larry 1938- .... CLC 8
See also AAYA 27; BPFB 2; BYA 10; CA
21-24R, 207; CAAE 207; CAAS 12;
CANR 14, 44, 66, 113, 155; CPW; DAM
POP; DLB 8; MTCW 1, 2; SATA 95, 171;
SCFW 1, 2; SFW 4

Niven, Laurence VanCott
See Niven, Larry

Nixon, Agnes Eckhardt 1927- .... CLC 21
See also CA 110

Nizan, Paul 1905-1940 .... TCLC 40
See also CA 161; DLB 72; EWL 3; GFL
1789 to the Present

Nkosi, Lewis 1936- .... BLC 1:3; CLC 45
See also BW 1, 3; CA 65-68; CANR 27,
81; CBD; CD 5, 6; DAM MULT; DLB
157, 225; WWE 1

Nodier, (Jean) Charles (Emmanuel)
1780-1844 .... NCLC 19
See also DLB 119; GFL 1789 to the Present

Noguchi, Yone 1875-1947 .... TCLC 80

Nolan, Brian
See O Nuallain, Brian

Nolan, Christopher 1965-2009 .... CLC 58
See also CA 111; CANR 88

Noon, Jeff 1957- .... CLC 91
See also CA 148; CANR 83; DLB 267;
SFW 4

Norden, Charles
See Durrell, Lawrence (George)

Nordhoff, Charles Bernard
1887-1947 .... TCLC 23
See also CA 108; 211; DLB 9; LAIT 1;
RHW 1; SATA 23

Norfolk, Lawrence 1963- .... CLC 76
See also CA 144; CANR 85; CN 6, 7; DLB
267

Norman, Marsha (Williams) 1947- . CLC 28,
186; DC 8
See also CA 105; CABS 3; CAD; CANR
41, 131; CD 5, 6; CSW; CWD; DAM
DRAM; DFS 2; DLB 266; DLBY 1984;
FW; MAL 5

Normyx
See Douglas, (George) Norman

Norris, (Benjamin) Frank(lin, Jr.)
1870-1902 . SSC 28; TCLC 24, 155, 211
See also AAYA 57; AMW; AMWC 2; BPFB
2; CA 110; 160; CDALB 1865-1917; DLB
12, 71, 186; LMFS 2; MAL 5; NFS 12;
RGAL 4; TCWW 1, 2; TUS

Norris, Kathleen 1947- .... CLC 248
See also CA 160; CANR 113

Norris, Leslie 1921-2006 .... CLC 14
See also CA 11-12; 251; CANR 14, 117;
CAP 1; CP 1, 2, 3, 4, 5, 6, 7; DLB 27,
256

North, Andrew
See Norton, Andre

North, Anthony
See Koontz, Dean R.

North, Captain George
See Stevenson, Robert Louis (Balfour)

North, Captain George
See Stevenson, Robert Louis (Balfour)

North, Milou
See Erdrich, Louise

Northrup, B. A.
See Hubbard, L. Ron

North Staffs
See Hulme, T(homas) E(rnest)

Northup, Solomon 1808-1863 ...... NCLC 105

Norton, Alice Mary
See Norton, Andre

Norton, Andre 1912-2005 .... CLC 12
See also AAYA 14; BPFB 2; BYA 4, 10,
12; CA 1-4R; 237; CANR 2, 31, 68, 108,
149; CLR 50; DLB 8, 52; JRDA; MAI-
CYA 1, 2; MTCW 1; SATA 1, 43, 91;
SUFW 1, 2; YAW

Norton, Caroline 1808-1877 .. NCLC 47, 205
See also DLB 21, 159, 199

Norway, Nevil Shute 1899-1960 .... CLC 30
See also BPFB 3; CA 102; 93-96; CANR
85; DLB 255; MTCW 2; NFS 9; RHW 4;
SFW 4

Private 19022
    See Manning, Frederic
Probst, Mark 1925- .... **CLC 59**
    See also CA 130
Procaccino, Michael
    See Cristofer, Michael
Proclus c. 412-c. 485 .... **CMLC 81**
Prokosch, Frederic 1908-1989 ...... **CLC 4, 48**
    See also CA 73-76; 128; CANR 82; CN 1,
    2, 3, 4; CP 1, 2, 3, 4; DLB 48; MTCW 2
Propertius, Sextus c. 50B.C.-c.
    16B.C. .... **CMLC 32**
    See also AW 2; CDWLB 1; DLB 211;
    RGWL 2, 3; WLIT 8
Prophet, The
    See Dreiser, Theodore
Prose, Francine 1947- .... **CLC 45, 231**
    See also AMWS 16; CA 109; 112; CANR
    46, 95, 132, 175; DLB 234; MTFW 2005;
    SATA 101, 149, 198
Protagoras c. 490B.C.-420B.C. ...... **CMLC 85**
    See also DLB 176
Proudhon
    See Cunha, Euclides (Rodrigues Pimenta)
    da
Proulx, Annie
    See Proulx, E. Annie
Proulx, E. Annie 1935- ...... **CLC 81, 158, 250**
    See also AMWS 7; BPFB 3; CA 145;
    CANR 65, 110; CN 6, 7; CPW 1; DA3;
    DAM POP; DLB 335; MAL 5; MTCW 2;
    MTFW 2005; SSFS 18, 23
Proulx, Edna Annie
    See Proulx, E. Annie
**Proust, (Valentin-Louis-George-Eugene)
    Marcel** 1871-1922 ..... **SSC 75; TCLC 7,
    13, 33, 220; WLC 5**
    See also AAYA 58; BPFB 3; CA 104; 120;
    CANR 110; DA; DA3; DAB; DAC; DAM
    MST, NOV; DLB 65; EW 8; EWL 3; GFL
    1789 to the Present; MTCW 1, 2; MTFW
    2005; RGWL 2, 3; TWA
Prowler, Harley
    See Masters, Edgar Lee
Prudentius, Aurelius Clemens 348-c.
    405 .... **CMLC 78**
    See also EW 1; RGWL 2, 3
Prudhomme, Rene Francois Armand
    1839-1907
    See Sully Prudhomme, Rene-Francois-
    Armand
Prus, Boleslaw 1845-1912 .... **TCLC 48**
    See also RGWL 2, 3
Prynne, William 1600-1669 .... **LC 148**
Prynne, Xavier
    See Hardwick, Elizabeth
Pryor, Aaron Richard
    See Pryor, Richard
Pryor, Richard 1940-2005 .... **CLC 26**
    See also CA 122; 152; 246
Pryor, Richard Franklin Lenox Thomas
    See Pryor, Richard
Przybyszewski, Stanislaw
    1868-1927 .... **TCLC 36**
    See also CA 160; DLB 66; EWL 3
Pseudo-Dionysius the Areopagite fl. c. 5th
    cent. - .... **CMLC 89**
    See also DLB 115
Pteleon
    See Grieve, C(hristopher) M(urray)
Puckett, Lute
    See Masters, Edgar Lee
Puig, Manuel 1932-1990 .... **CLC 3, 5, 10, 28,
    65, 133; HLC 2**
    See also BPFB 3; CA 45-48; CANR 2, 32,
    63; CDWLB 3; DA3; DAM MULT; DLB
    113; DNFS 1; EWL 3; GLL 1; HW 1, 2;
    LAW; MTCW 1, 2; MTFW 2005; RGWL
    2, 3; TWA; WLIT 1

Pulitzer, Joseph 1847-1911 .... **TCLC 76**
    See also CA 114; DLB 23
Pullman, Philip 1946- .... **CLC 245**
    See also AAYA 15, 41; BRWS 13; BYA 8,
    13; CA 127; CANR 50, 77, 105, 134;
    CLR 20, 62, 84; JRDA; MAICYA 1, 2;
    MAICYAS 1; MTFW 2005; SAAS 17;
    SATA 65, 103, 150, 198; SUFW 2; WYAS
    1; YAW
Purchas, Samuel 1577(?)-1626 .... **LC 70**
    See also DLB 151
Purdy, A(lfred) W(ellington)
    1918-2000 .... **CLC 3, 6, 14, 50**
    See also CA 81-84; 189; CAAS 17; CANR
    42, 66; CP 1, 2, 3, 4, 5, 6, 7; DAC; DAM
    MST, POET; DLB 88; PFS 5; RGEL 2
Purdy, James 1923-2009 .... **CLC 2, 4, 10, 28,
    52**
    See also AMWS 7; CA 33-36R; CAAS 1;
    CANR 19, 51, 132; CN 1, 2, 3, 4, 5, 6, 7;
    DLB 2, 218; EWL 3; INT CANR-19;
    MAL 5; MTCW 1; RGAL 4
Purdy, James Amos
    See Purdy, James
Pure, Simon
    See Swinnerton, Frank Arthur
Pushkin, Aleksandr Sergeevich
    See Pushkin, Alexander (Sergeyevich)
Pushkin, Alexander (Sergeyevich)
    1799-1837 .... **NCLC 3, 27, 83; PC 10;
    SSC 27, 55, 99; WLC 5**
    See also DA; DA3; DAB; DAC; DAM
    DRAM, MST, POET; DLB 205; EW 5;
    EXPS; PFS 28; RGSF 2; RGWL 2, 3;
    SATA 61; SSFS 9; TWA
P'u Sung-ling 1640-1715 .... **LC 49; SSC 31**
Putnam, Arthur Lee
    See Alger, Horatio, Jr.
Puttenham, George 1529(?)-1590 ...... **LC 116**
    See also DLB 281
Puzo, Mario 1920-1999 .... **CLC 1, 2, 6, 36,
    107**
    See also BPFB 3; CA 65-68; 185; CANR 4,
    42, 65, 99, 131; CN 1, 2, 3, 4, 5, 6; CPW;
    DA3; DAM NOV, POP; DLB 6; MTCW
    1, 2; MTFW 2005; NFS 16; RGAL 4
Pygge, Edward
    See Barnes, Julian
Pyle, Ernest Taylor 1900-1945 .... **TCLC 75**
    See also CA 115; 160; DLB 29; MTCW 2
Pyle, Ernie
    See Pyle, Ernest Taylor
Pyle, Howard 1853-1911 .... **TCLC 81**
    See also AAYA 57; BYA 2, 4; CA 109; 137;
    CLR 22, 117; DLB 42, 188; DLBD 13;
    LAIT 1; MAICYA 1, 2; SATA 16, 100;
    WCH; YAW
Pym, Barbara (Mary Crampton)
    1913-1980 .... **CLC 13, 19, 37, 111**
    See also BPFB 3; BRWS 2; CA 13-14; 97-
    100; CANR 13, 34; CAP 1; DLB 14, 207;
    DLBY 1987; EWL 3; MTCW 1, 2; MTFW
    2005; RGEL 2; TEA
Pynchon, Thomas 1937- .. **CLC 2, 3, 6, 9, 11,
    18, 33, 62, 72, 123, 192, 213; SSC 14,
    84; WLC 5**
    See also AMWS 2; BEST 90:2; BPFB 3;
    CA 17-20R; CANR 22, 46, 73, 142; CN
    1, 2, 3, 4, 5, 6, 7; CPW 1; DA; DA3;
    DAB; DAC; DAM MST, NOV, POP;
    DLB 2, 173; EWL 3; MAL 5; MTCW 1,
    2; MTFW 2005; NFS 23; RGAL 4; SFW
    4; TCLE 1:2; TUS
Pythagoras c. 582B.C.-c. 507B.C. . **CMLC 22**
    See also DLB 176

Q
    See Quiller-Couch, Sir Arthur (Thomas)
Qian, Chongzhu
    See Ch'ien, Chung-shu

Qian, Sima 145B.C.-c. 89B.C. .... **CMLC 72**
Qian Zhongshu
    See Ch'ien, Chung-shu
Qroll
    See Dagerman, Stig (Halvard)
Quarles, Francis 1592-1644 .... **LC 117**
    See also DLB 126; RGEL 2
Quarrington, Paul 1953- .... **CLC 65**
    See also CA 129; CANR 62, 95
Quarrington, Paul Lewis
    See Quarrington, Paul
Quasimodo, Salvatore 1901-1968 .... **CLC 10;
    PC 47**
    See also CA 13-16; 25-28R; CAP 1; DLB
    114, 332; EW 12; EWL 3; MTCW 1;
    RGWL 2, 3
Quatermass, Martin
    See Carpenter, John (Howard)
Quay, Stephen 1947- .... **CLC 95**
    See also CA 189
Quay, Timothy 1947- .... **CLC 95**
    See also CA 189
Queen, Ellery
    See Dannay, Frederic; Hoch, Edward D.;
    Lee, Manfred B.; Marlowe, Stephen; Stur-
    geon, Theodore (Hamilton); Vance, Jack
Queneau, Raymond 1903-1976 ..... **CLC 2, 5,
    10, 42**
    See also CA 77-80; 69-72; CANR 32; DLB
    72, 258; EW 12; EWL 3; GFL 1789 to
    the Present; MTCW 1, 2; RGWL 2, 3
Quevedo, Francisco de 1580-1645 ...... **LC 23,
    160**
Quiller-Couch, Sir Arthur (Thomas)
    1863-1944 .... **TCLC 53**
    See also CA 118; 166; DLB 135, 153, 190;
    HGG; RGEL 2; SUFW 1
Quin, Ann 1936-1973 .... **CLC 6**
    See also CA 9-12R; 45-48; CANR 148; CN
    1; DLB 14, 231
Quin, Ann Marie
    See Quin, Ann
Quincey, Thomas de
    See De Quincey, Thomas
Quindlen, Anna 1953- .... **CLC 191**
    See also AAYA 35; AMWS 17; CA 138;
    CANR 73, 126; DA3; DLB 292; MTCW
    2; MTFW 2005
Quinn, Martin
    See Smith, Martin Cruz
Quinn, Peter 1947- .... **CLC 91**
    See also CA 197; CANR 147
Quinn, Peter A.
    See Quinn, Peter
Quinn, Simon
    See Smith, Martin Cruz
Quintana, Leroy V. 1944- ...... **HLC 2; PC 36**
    See also CA 131; CANR 65, 139; DAM
    MULT; DLB 82; HW 1, 2
Quintilian c. 40-c. 100 .... **CMLC 77**
    See also AW 2; DLB 211; RGWL 2, 3
Quiroga, Horacio (Sylvestre)
    1878-1937 ... **HLC 2; SSC 89; TCLC 20**
    See also CA 117; 131; DAM MULT; EWL
    3; HW 1; LAW; MTCW 1; RGSF 2;
    WLIT 1
Quoirez, Francoise 1935-2004 ... **CLC 3, 6, 9,
    17, 36**
    See also CA 49-52; 231; CANR 6, 39, 73;
    CWW 2; DLB 83; EWL 3; GFL 1789 to
    the Present; MTCW 1, 2; MTFW 2005;
    TWA
Raabe, Wilhelm (Karl) 1831-1910 . **TCLC 45**
    See also CA 167; DLB 129
Rabe, David (William) 1940- .. **CLC 4, 8, 33,
    200; DC 16**
    See also CA 85-88; CABS 3; CAD; CANR
    59, 129; CD 5, 6; DAM DRAM; DFS 3,
    8, 13; DLB 7, 228; EWL 3; MAL 5

Saint-Exupery, Antoine Jean Baptiste Marie Roger de
See Saint-Exupery, Antoine de

St. John, David
See Hunt, E. Howard

St. John, J. Hector
See Crevecoeur, Michel Guillaume Jean de

Saint-John Perse
See Leger, (Marie-Rene Auguste) Alexis Saint-Leger

Saintsbury, George (Edward Bateman)
1845-1933 .... **TCLC 31**
See also CA 160; DLB 57, 149

Sait Faik
See Abasiyanik, Sait Faik

Saki
See Munro, H(ector) H(ugh)

Sala, George Augustus 1828-1895 . **NCLC 46**

Saladin 1138-1193 .... **CMLC 38**

Salama, Hannu 1936- .... **CLC 18**
See also CA 244; EWL 3

Salamanca, J(ack) R(ichard) 1922- .. **CLC 4, 15**
See also CA 25-28R, 193; CAAE 193

Salas, Floyd Francis 1931- .... **HLC 2**
See also CA 119; CAAS 27; CANR 44, 75, 93; DAM MULT; DLB 82; HW 1, 2; MTCW 2; MTFW 2005

Sale, J. Kirkpatrick
See Sale, Kirkpatrick

Sale, John Kirkpatrick
See Sale, Kirkpatrick

Sale, Kirkpatrick 1937- .... **CLC 68**
See also CA 13-16R; CANR 10, 147

Salinas, Luis Omar 1937- ... **CLC 90; HLC 2**
See also AMWS 13; CA 131; CANR 81, 153; DAM MULT; DLB 82; HW 1, 2

Salinas (y Serrano), Pedro
1891(?)-1951 .... **TCLC 17, 212**
See also CA 117; DLB 134; EWL 3

Salinger, J.D. 1919- . **CLC 1, 3, 8, 12, 55, 56, 138, 243; SSC 2, 28, 65; WLC 5**
See also AAYA 2, 36; AMW; AMWC 1; BPFB 3; CA 5-8R; CANR 39, 129; CDALB 1941-1968; CLR 18; CN 1, 2, 3, 4, 5, 6, 7; CPW 1; DA; DA3; DAB; DAC; DAM MST, NOV, POP; DLB 2, 102, 173; EWL 3; EXPN; LAIT 4; MAICYA 1, 2; MAL 5; MTCW 1, 2; MTFW 2005; NFS 1; RGAL 4; RGSF 2; SATA 67; SSFS 17; TUS; WYA; YAW

Salisbury, John
See Caute, (John) David

Sallust c. 86B.C.-35B.C. .... **CMLC 68**
See also AW 2; CDWLB 1; DLB 211; RGWL 2, 3

Salter, James 1925- .... **CLC 7, 52, 59, 275; SSC 58**
See also AMWS 9; CA 73-76; CANR 107, 160; DLB 130; SSFS 25

Saltus, Edgar (Everton) 1855-1921 . **TCLC 8**
See also CA 105; DLB 202; RGAL 4

Saltykov, Mikhail Evgrafovich
1826-1889 .... **NCLC 16**
See also DLB 238:

Saltykov-Shchedrin, N.
See Saltykov, Mikhail Evgrafovich

Samarakis, Andonis
See Samarakis, Antonis

Samarakis, Antonis 1919-2003 .... **CLC 5**
See also CA 25-28R; 224; CAAS 16; CANR 36; EWL 3

Samigli, E.
See Schmitz, Aron Hector

Sanchez, Florencio 1875-1910 .... **TCLC 37**
See also CA 153; DLB 305; EWL 3; HW 1; LAW

Sanchez, Luis Rafael 1936- .... **CLC 23**
See also CA 128; DLB 305; EWL 3; HW 1; WLIT 1

Sanchez, Sonia 1934- . **BLC 1:3, 2:3; CLC 5, 116, 215; PC 9**
See also BW 2, 3; CA 33-36R; CANR 24, 49, 74, 115; CLR 18; CP 2, 3, 4, 5, 6, 7; CSW; CWP; DA3; DAM MULT; DLB 41; DLBD 8; EWL 3; MAICYA 1, 2; MAL 5; MTCW 1, 2; MTFW 2005; PFS 26; SATA 22, 136; WP

Sancho, Ignatius 1729-1780 .... **LC 84**

Sand, George 1804-1876 .... **DC 29; NCLC 2, 42, 57, 174; WLC 5**
See also DA; DA3; DAB; DAC; DAM MST, NOV; DLB 119, 192; EW 6; FL 1:3; FW; GFL 1789 to the Present; RGWL 2, 3; TWA

Sandburg, Carl (August) 1878-1967 . **CLC 1, 4, 10, 15, 35; PC 2, 41; WLC 5**
See also AAYA 24; AMW; BYA 1, 3; CA 5-8R; 25-28R; CANR 35; CDALB 1865-1917; CLR 67; DA; DA3; DAB; DAC; DAM MST, POET; DLB 17, 54, 284; EWL 3; EXPP; LAIT 2; MAICYA 1, 2; MAL 5; MTCW 1, 2; MTFW 2005; PAB; PFS 3, 6, 12; RGAL 4; SATA 8; TUS; WCH; WP; WYA

Sandburg, Charles
See Sandburg, Carl (August)

Sandburg, Charles A.
See Sandburg, Carl (August)

Sanders, (James) Ed(ward) 1939- .... **CLC 53**
See also BG 1:3; CA 13-16R; CAAS 21; CANR 13, 44, 78; CP 1, 2, 3, 4, 5, 6, 7; DAM POET; DLB 16, 244

Sanders, Edward
See Sanders, (James) Ed(ward)

Sanders, Lawrence 1920-1998 .... **CLC 41**
See also BEST 89:4; BPFB 3; CA 81-84; 165; CANR 33, 62; CMW 4; CPW; DA3; DAM POP; MTCW 1

Sanders, Noah
See Blount, Roy, Jr.

Sanders, Winston P.
See Anderson, Poul

Sandoz, Mari(e Susette) 1900-1966 .. **CLC 28**
See also CA 1-4R; 25-28R; CANR 17, 64; DLB 9, 212; LAIT 2; MTCW 1, 2; SATA 5; TCWW 1, 2

Sandys, George 1578-1644 .... **LC 80**
See also DLB 24, 121

Saner, Reg(inald Anthony) 1931- .... **CLC 9**
See also CA 65-68; CP 3, 4, 5, 6, 7

Sankara 788-820 .... **CMLC 32**

Sannazaro, Jacopo 1456(?)-1530 .... **LC 8**
See also RGWL 2, 3; WLIT 7

Sansom, William 1912-1976 . **CLC 2, 6; SSC 21**
See also CA 5-8R; 65-68; CANR 42; CN 1, 2; DAM NOV; DLB 139; EWL 3; MTCW 1; RGEL 2; RGSF 2

Santayana, George 1863-1952 .... **TCLC 40**
See also AMW; CA 115; 194; DLB 54, 71, 246, 270; DLBD 13; EWL 3; MAL 5; RGAL 4; TUS

Santiago, Danny
See James, Daniel (Lewis)

Santillana, Inigo Lopez de Mendoza, Marques de 1398-1458 .... **LC 111**
See also DLB 286

Santmyer, Helen Hooven
1895-1986 .... **CLC 33; TCLC 133**
See also CA 1-4R; 118; CANR 15, 33; DLBY 1984; MTCW 1; RHW

Santoka, Taneda 1882-1940 .... **TCLC 72**

Santos, Bienvenido N(uqui)
1911-1996 ... **AAL; CLC 22; TCLC 156**
See also CA 101; 151; CANR 19, 46; CP 1; DAM MULT; DLB 312, 348; EWL; RGAL 4; SSFS 19

Santos, Miguel
See Mihura, Miguel

Sapir, Edward 1884-1939 .... **TCLC 108**
See also CA 211; DLB 92

Sapper
See McNeile, Herman Cyril

Sapphire 1950- .... **CLC 99**
See also CA 262

Sapphire, Brenda
See Sapphire

Sappho fl. 6th cent. B.C.- ... **CMLC 3, 67; PC 5**
See also CDWLB 1; DA3; DAM POET; DLB 176; FL 1:1; PFS 20; RGWL 2, 3; WLIT 8; WP

Saramago, Jose 1922- .... **CLC 119, 275; HLCS 1**
See also CA 153; CANR 96, 164; CWW 2; DLB 287, 332; EWL 3; LATS 1:2; NFS 27; SSFS 23

Sarduy, Severo 1937-1993 .... **CLC 6, 97; HLCS 2; TCLC 167**
See also CA 89-92; 142; CANR 58, 81; CWW 2; DLB 113; EWL 3; HW 1, 2; LAW

Sargeson, Frank 1903-1982 ..... **CLC 31; SSC 99**
See also CA 25-28R; 106; CANR 38, 79; CN 1, 2, 3; EWL 3; GLL 2; RGEL 2; RGSF 2; SSFS 20

Sarmiento, Domingo Faustino
1811-1888 .... **HLCS 2; NCLC 123**
See also LAW; WLIT 1

Sarmiento, Felix Ruben Garcia
See Dario, Ruben

Saro-Wiwa, Ken(ule Beeson)
1941-1995 .... **CLC 114; TCLC 200**
See also BW 2; CA 142; 150; CANR 60; DLB 157

Saroyan, William 1908-1981 ... **CLC 1, 8, 10, 29, 34, 56; DC 28; SSC 21; TCLC 137; WLC 5**
See also AAYA 66; CA 5-8R; 103; CAD; CANR 30; CDALBS; CN 1, 2; DA; DA3; DAB; DAC; DAM DRAM, MST, NOV; DFS 17; DLB 7, 9, 86; DLBY 1981; EWL 3; LAIT 4; MAL 5; MTCW 1, 2; MTFW 2005; RGAL 4; RGSF 2; SATA 23; SATA-Obit 24; SSFS 14; TUS

Sarraute, Nathalie 1900-1999 .... **CLC 1, 2, 4, 8, 10, 31, 80; TCLC 145**
See also BPFB 3; CA 9-12R; 187; CANR 23, 66, 134; CWW 2; DLB 83, 321; EW 12; EWL 3; GFL 1789 to the Present; MTCW 1, 2; MTFW 2005; RGWL 2, 3

Sarton, May 1912-1995 ... **CLC 4, 14, 49, 91; PC 39; TCLC 120**
See also AMWS 8; CA 1-4R; 149; CANR 1, 34, 55, 116; CN 1, 2, 3, 4, 5, 6; CP 1, 2, 3, 4, 5, 6; DAM POET; DLB 48; DLBY 1981; EWL 3; FW; INT CANR-34; MAL 5; MTCW 1, 2; MTFW 2005; RGAL 4; SATA 36; SATA-Obit 86; TUS

Sartre, Jean-Paul 1905-1980 . **CLC 1, 4, 7, 9, 13, 18, 24, 44, 50, 52; DC 3; SSC 32; WLC 5**
See also AAYA 62; CA 9-12R; 97-100; CANR 21; DA; DA3; DAB; DAC; DAM DRAM, MST, NOV; DFS 5, 26; DLB 72, 296, 321, 332; EW 12; EWL 3; GFL 1789 to the Present; LMFS 2; MTCW 1, 2; MTFW 2005; NFS 21; RGHL; RGSF 2; RGWL 2, 3; SSFS 9; TWA

Sassoon, Siegfried (Lorraine)
1886-1967 .... **CLC 36, 130; PC 12**
See also BRW 6; CA 104; 25-28R; CANR
36; DAB; DAM MST, NOV, POET; DLB
20, 191; DLBD 18; EWL 3; MTCW 1, 2;
MTFW 2005; PAB; PFS 28; RGEL 2;
TEA

Satterfield, Charles
See Pohl, Frederik

Satyremont
See Peret, Benjamin

Saul, John III
See Saul, John

Saul, John 1942- .... **CLC 46**
See also AAYA 10, 62; BEST 90:4; CA 81-
84; CANR 16, 40, 81, 176; CPW; DAM
NOV, POP; HGG; SATA 98

Saul, John W.
See Saul, John

Saul, John W. III
See Saul, John

Saul, John Woodruff III
See Saul, John

Saunders, Caleb
See Heinlein, Robert A.

Saura (Atares), Carlos 1932-1998 .... **CLC 20**
See also CA 114; 131; CANR 79; HW 1

Sauser, Frederic Louis
See Sauser-Hall, Frederic

Sauser-Hall, Frederic 1887-1961 ..... **CLC 18, 106**
See also CA 102; 93-96; CANR 36, 62;
DLB 258; EWL 3; GFL 1789 to the
Present; MTCW 1; WP

Saussure, Ferdinand de
1857-1913 .... **TCLC 49**
See also DLB 242

Savage, Catharine
See Brosman, Catharine Savage

Savage, Richard 1697(?)-1743 .... **LC 96**
See also DLB 95; RGEL 2

Savage, Thomas 1915-2003 .... **CLC 40**
See also CA 126; 132; 218; CAAS 15; CN
6, 7; INT CA-132; SATA-Obit 147;
TCWW 2

Savan, Glenn 1953-2003 .... **CLC 50**
See also CA 225

Savonarola, Girolamo 1452-1498 ...... **LC 152**
See also LMFS 1

Sax, Robert
See Johnson, Robert

Saxo Grammaticus c. 1150-c.
1222 .... **CMLC 58**

Saxton, Robert
See Johnson, Robert

Sayers, Dorothy L(eigh) 1893-1957 . **SSC 71; TCLC 2, 15**
See also BPFB 3; BRWS 3; CA 104; 119;
CANR 60; CDBLB 1914-1945; CMW 4;
DAM POP; DLB 10, 36, 77, 100; MSW;
MTCW 1, 2; MTFW 2005; RGEL 2;
SSFS 12; TEA

Sayers, Valerie 1952- .... **CLC 50, 122**
See also CA 134; CANR 61; CSW

Sayles, John (Thomas) 1950- .... **CLC 7, 10, 14, 198**
See also CA 57-60; CANR 41, 84; DLB 44

Scamander, Newt
See Rowling, J.K.

Scammell, Michael 1935- .... **CLC 34**
See also CA 156

Scannel, John Vernon
See Scannell, Vernon

Scannell, Vernon 1922-2007 .... **CLC 49**
See also CA 5-8R; 266; CANR 8, 24, 57,
143; CN 1, 2; CP 1, 2, 3, 4, 5, 6, 7; CWRI
5; DLB 27; SATA 59; SATA-Obit 188

Scarlett, Susan
See Streatfeild, Noel

Scarron 1847-1910
See Mikszath, Kalman

Scarron, Paul 1610-1660 .... **LC 116**
See also GFL Beginnings to 1789; RGWL
2, 3

Schaeffer, Susan Fromberg 1941- ..... **CLC 6, 11, 22**
See also CA 49-52; CANR 18, 65, 160; CN
4, 5, 6, 7; DLB 28, 299; MTCW 1, 2;
MTFW 2005; SATA 22

Schama, Simon 1945- .... **CLC 150**
See also BEST 89:4; CA 105; CANR 39,
91, 168

Schama, Simon Michael
See Schama, Simon

Schary, Jill
See Robinson, Jill

Schell, Jonathan 1943- .... **CLC 35**
See also CA 73-76; CANR 12, 117, 187

Schelling, Friedrich Wilhelm Joseph von
1775-1854 .... **NCLC 30**
See also DLB 90

Scherer, Jean-Marie Maurice
1920- .... **CLC 16**
See also CA 110

Schevill, James (Erwin) 1920- .... **CLC 7**
See also CA 5-8R; CAAS 12; CAD; CD 5,
6; CP 1, 2, 3, 4, 5

Schiller, Friedrich von 1759-1805 ...... **DC 12; NCLC 39, 69, 166**
See also CDWLB 2; DAM DRAM; DLB
94; EW 5; RGWL 2, 3; TWA

Schisgal, Murray (Joseph) 1926- .... **CLC 6**
See also CA 21-24R; CAD; CANR 48, 86;
CD 5, 6; MAL 5

Schlee, Ann 1934- .... **CLC 35**
See also CA 101; CANR 29, 88; SATA 44;
SATA-Brief 36

Schlegel, August Wilhelm von
1767-1845 .... **NCLC 15, 142**
See also DLB 94; RGWL 2, 3

Schlegel, Friedrich 1772-1829 .... **NCLC 45**
See also DLB 90; EW 5; RGWL 2, 3; TWA

Schlegel, Johann Elias (von)
1719(?)-1749 .... **LC 5**

Schleiermacher, Friedrich
1768-1834 .... **NCLC 107**
See also DLB 90

Schlesinger, Arthur M., Jr.
1917-2007 .... **CLC 84**
See Schlesinger, Arthur Meier
See also AITN 1; CA 1-4R; 257; CANR 1,
28, 58, 105, 187; DLB 17; INT CANR-
28; MTCW 1, 2; SATA 61; SATA-Obit
181

Schlink, Bernhard 1944- .... **CLC 174**
See also CA 163; CANR 116, 175; RGHL

Schmidt, Arno (Otto) 1914-1979 ...... **CLC 56**
See also CA 128; 109; DLB 69; EWL 3

Schmitz, Aron Hector 1861-1928 ..... **SSC 25; TCLC 2, 35**
See also CA 104; 122; DLB 264; EW 8;
EWL 3; MTCW 1; RGWL 2, 3; WLIT 7

Schnackenberg, Gjertrud 1953- ...... **CLC 40; PC 45**
See also AMWS 15; CA 116; CANR 100;
CP 5, 6, 7; CWP; DLB 120, 282; PFS 13,
25

Schnackenberg, Gjertrud Cecelia
See Schnackenberg, Gjertrud

Schneider, Leonard Alfred
1925-1966 .... **CLC 21**
See also CA 89-92

Schnitzler, Arthur 1862-1931 ..... **DC 17; SSC 15, 61; TCLC 4**
See also CA 104; CDWLB 2; DLB 81, 118;
EW 8; EWL 3; RGSF 2; RGWL 2, 3

Schoenberg, Arnold Franz Walter
1874-1951 .... **TCLC 75**
See also CA 109; 188

Schonberg, Arnold
See Schoenberg, Arnold Franz Walter

Schopenhauer, Arthur 1788-1860 . **NCLC 51, 157**
See also DLB 90; EW 5

Schor, Sandra (M.) 1932(?)-1990 ..... **CLC 65**
See also CA 132

Schorer, Mark 1908-1977 .... **CLC 9**
See also CA 5-8R; 73-76; CANR 7; CN 1,
2; DLB 103

Schrader, Paul (Joseph) 1946- . **CLC 26, 212**
See also CA 37-40R; CANR 41; DLB 44

Schreber, Daniel 1842-1911 .... **TCLC 123**

Schreiner, Olive (Emilie Albertina)
1855-1920 .... **TCLC 9**
See also AFW; BRWS 2; CA 105; 154;
DLB 18, 156, 190, 225; EWL 3; FW;
RGEL 2; TWA; WLIT 2; WWE 1

Schulberg, Budd 1914- .... **CLC 7, 48**
See also AMWS 18; BPFB 3; CA 25-28R;
CANR 19, 87, 178; CN 1, 2, 3, 4, 5, 6, 7;
DLB 6, 26, 28; DLBY 1981, 2001; MAL
5

Schulberg, Budd Wilson
See Schulberg, Budd

Schulman, Arnold
See Trumbo, Dalton

Schulz, Bruno 1892-1942 .. **SSC 13; TCLC 5, 51**
See also CA 115; 123; CANR 86; CDWLB
4; DLB 215; EWL 3; MTCW 2; MTFW
2005; RGSF 2; RGWL 2, 3

Schulz, Charles M. 1922-2000 .... **CLC 12**
See also AAYA 39; CA 9-12R; 187; CANR
6, 132; INT CANR-6; MTFW 2005;
SATA 10; SATA-Obit 118

Schulz, Charles Monroe
See Schulz, Charles M.

Schumacher, E(rnst) F(riedrich)
1911-1977 .... **CLC 80**
See also CA 81-84; 73-76; CANR 34, 85

Schumann, Robert 1810-1856 ...... **NCLC 143**

Schuyler, George Samuel 1895-1977 . **HR 1:3**
See also BW 2; CA 81-84; 73-76; CANR
42; DLB 29, 51

Schuyler, James Marcus 1923-1991 .. **CLC 5, 23; PC 88**
See also CA 101; 134; CP 1, 2, 3, 4, 5;
DAM POET; DLB 5, 169; EWL 3; INT
CA-101; MAL 5; WP

Schwartz, Delmore (David)
1913-1966 . **CLC 2, 4, 10, 45, 87; PC 8; SSC 105**
See also AMWS 2; CA 17-18; 25-28R;
CANR 35; CAP 2; DLB 28, 48; EWL 3;
MAL 5; MTCW 1, 2; MTFW 2005; PAB;
RGAL 4; TUS

Schwartz, Ernst
See Ozu, Yasujiro

Schwartz, John Burnham 1965- .... **CLC 59**
See also CA 132; CANR 116, 188

Schwartz, Lynne Sharon 1939- .... **CLC 31**
See also CA 103; CANR 44, 89, 160; DLB
218; MTCW 2; MTFW 2005

Schwartz, Muriel A.
See Eliot, T(homas) S(tearns)

Schwarz-Bart, Andre 1928-2006 .... **CLC 2, 4**
See also CA 89-92; 253; CANR 109; DLB
299; RGHL

Schwarz-Bart, Simone 1938- . **BLCS; CLC 7**
See also BW 2; CA 97-100; CANR 117;
EWL 3

Schwerner, Armand 1927-1999 .... **PC 42**
See also CA 9-12R; 179; CANR 50, 85; CP
2, 3, 4, 5, 6; DLB 165

Shimazaki Toson
See Shimazaki, Haruki
Shirley, James 1596-1666 .... **DC 25; LC 96**
See also DLB 58; RGEL 2
Shirley Hastings, Selina
See Hastings, Selina
Sholem Aleykhem
See Rabinovitch, Sholem
Sholokhov, Mikhail (Aleksandrovich)
1905-1984 .... **CLC 7, 15**
See also CA 101; 112; DLB 272, 332; EWL
3; MTCW 1, 2; MTFW 2005; RGWL 2,
3; SATA-Obit 36
Sholom Aleichem 1859-1916
See Rabinovitch, Sholem
Shone, Patric
See Hanley, James
Showalter, Elaine 1941- .... **CLC 169**
See also CA 57-60; CANR 58, 106; DLB
67; FW; GLL 2
Shreve, Susan
See Shreve, Susan Richards
Shreve, Susan Richards 1939- .... **CLC 23**
See also CA 49-52; CAAS 5; CANR 5, 38,
69, 100, 159; MAICYA 1, 2; SATA 46,
95, 152; SATA-Brief 41
Shue, Larry 1946-1985 .... **CLC 52**
See also CA 145; 117; DAM DRAM; DFS
7
Shu-Jen, Chou 1881-1936 . **SSC 20; TCLC 3**
See also CA 104; EWL 3
Shulman, Alix Kates 1932- .... **CLC 2, 10**
See also CA 29-32R; CANR 43; FW; SATA
7
Shuster, Joe 1914-1992 .... **CLC 21**
See also AAYA 50
Shute, Nevil
See Norway, Nevil Shute
Shuttle, Penelope (Diane) 1947- .... **CLC 7**
See also CA 93-96; CANR 39, 84, 92, 108;
CP 3, 4, 5, 6, 7; CWP; DLB 14, 40
Shvarts, Elena 1948- .... **PC 50**
See also CA 147
Sidhwa, Bapsi 1939-
See Sidhwa, Bapsy (N.)
Sidhwa, Bapsy (N.) 1938- .... **CLC 168**
See also CA 108; CANR 25, 57; CN 6, 7;
DLB 323; FW
Sidney, Mary 1561-1621 .... **LC 19, 39**
See also DLB 167
Sidney, Sir Philip 1554-1586 .... **LC 19, 39,
131; PC 32**
See also BRW 1; BRWR 2; CDBLB Before
1660; DA; DA3; DAB; DAC; DAM MST,
POET; DLB 167; EXPP; PAB; PFS 30;
RGEL 2; TEA; WP
Sidney Herbert, Mary
See Sidney, Mary
Siegel, Jerome 1914-1996 .... **CLC 21**
See also AAYA 50; CA 116; 169; 151
Siegel, Jerry
See Siegel, Jerome
Sienkiewicz, Henryk (Adam Alexander Pius)
1846-1916 .... **TCLC 3**
See also CA 104; 134; CANR 84; DLB 332;
EWL 3; RGSF 2; RGWL 2, 3
Sierra, Gregorio Martinez
See Martinez Sierra, Gregorio
Sierra, Maria de la O'LeJarraga Martinez
See Martinez Sierra, Maria
Sigal, Clancy 1926- .... **CLC 7**
See also CA 1-4R; CANR 85, 184; CN 1,
2, 3, 4, 5, 6, 7
Siger of Brabant 1240(?)-1284(?) . **CMLC 69**
See also DLB 115
Sigourney, Lydia H.
See Sigourney, Lydia Howard (Huntley)
See also DLB 73, 183

Sigourney, Lydia Howard (Huntley)
1791-1865 .... **NCLC 21, 87**
See Sigourney, Lydia H.
See also DLB 1, 42, 239, 243
Sigourney, Lydia Huntley
See Sigourney, Lydia Howard (Huntley)
Siguenza y Gongora, Carlos de
1645-1700 .... **HLCS 2; LC 8**
See also LAW
Sigurjonsson, Johann
See Sigurjonsson, Johann
Sigurjonsson, Johann 1880-1919 ... **TCLC 27**
See also CA 170; DLB 293; EWL 3
Sikelianos, Angelos 1884-1951 .... **PC 29;
TCLC 39**
See also EWL 3; RGWL 2, 3
Silkin, Jon 1930-1997 .... **CLC 2, 6, 43**
See also CA 5-8R; CAAS 5; CANR 89; CP
1, 2, 3, 4, 5, 6; DLB 27
Silko, Leslie 1948- ...... **CLC 23, 74, 114, 211;
NNAL; SSC 37, 66; WLCS**
See also AAYA 14; AMWS 4; ANW; BYA
12; CA 115; 122; CANR 45, 65, 118; CN
4, 5, 6, 7; CP 4, 5, 6, 7; CPW 1; CWP;
DA; DA3; DAC; DAM MST, MULT,
POP; DLB 143, 175, 256, 275; EWL 3;
EXPP; EXPS; LAIT 4; MAL 5; MTCW
2; MTFW 2005; NFS 4; PFS 9, 16; RGAL
4; RGSF 2; SSFS 4, 8, 10, 11; TCWW 1,
2
Sillanpaa, Frans Eemil 1888-1964 ... **CLC 19**
See also CA 129; 93-96; DLB 332; EWL 3;
MTCW 1
Sillitoe, Alan 1928- .. **CLC 1, 3, 6, 10, 19, 57,
148**
See also AITN 1; BRWS 5; CA 9-12R, 191;
CAAE 191; CAAS 2; CANR 8, 26, 55,
139; CDBLB 1960 to Present; CN 1, 2, 3,
4, 5, 6; CP 1, 2, 3, 4, 5; DLB 14, 139;
EWL 3; MTCW 1, 2; MTFW 2005; RGEL
2; RGSF 2; SATA 61
Silone, Ignazio 1900-1978 .... **CLC 4**
See also CA 25-28; 81-84; CANR 34; CAP
2; DLB 264; EW 12; EWL 3; MTCW 1;
RGSF 2; RGWL 2, 3
Silone, Ignazione
See Silone, Ignazio
Siluriensis, Leolinus
See Jones, Arthur Llewellyn
Silver, Joan Micklin 1935- .... **CLC 20**
See also CA 114; 121; INT CA-121
Silver, Nicholas
See Faust, Frederick (Schiller)
Silverberg, Robert 1935- .... **CLC 7, 140**
See also AAYA 24; BPFB 3; BYA 7, 9; CA
1-4R, 186; CAAE 186; CAAS 3; CANR
1, 20, 36, 85, 140, 175; CLR 59; CN 6, 7;
CPW; DAM POP; DLB 8; INT CANR-
20; MAICYA 1, 2; MTCW 1, 2; MTFW
2005; SATA 13, 91; SATA-Essay 104;
SCFW 1, 2; SFW 4; SUFW 2
Silverstein, Alvin 1933- .... **CLC 17**
See also CA 49-52; CANR 2; CLR 25;
JRDA; MAICYA 1, 2; SATA 8, 69, 124
Silverstein, Shel 1932-1999 .... **PC 49**
See also AAYA 40; BW 3; CA 107; 179;
CANR 47, 74, 81; CLR 5, 96; CWRI 5;
JRDA; MAICYA 1, 2; MTCW 2; MTFW
2005; SATA 33, 92; SATA-Brief 27;
SATA-Obit 116
Silverstein, Virginia B(arbara Opshelor)
1937- .... **CLC 17**
See also CA 49-52; CANR 2; CLR 25;
JRDA; MAICYA 1, 2; SATA 8, 69, 124
Sim, Georges
See Simenon, Georges (Jacques Christian)

Simak, Clifford D(onald) 1904-1988 . **CLC 1,
55**
See also CA 1-4R; 125; CANR 1, 35; DLB
8; MTCW 1; SATA-Obit 56; SCFW 1, 2;
SFW 4
Simenon, Georges (Jacques Christian)
1903-1989 .... **CLC 1, 2, 3, 8, 18, 47**
See also BPFB 3; CA 85-88; 129; CANR
35; CMW 4; DA3; DAM POP; DLB 72;
DLBY 1989; EW 12; EWL 3; GFL 1789
to the Present; MSW; MTCW 1, 2; MTFW
2005; RGWL 2, 3
Simic, Charles 1938- .... **CLC 6, 9, 22, 49, 68,
130, 256; PC 69**
See also AAYA 78; AMWS 8; CA 29-32R;
CAAS 4; CANR 12, 33, 52, 61, 96, 140;
CP 2, 3, 4, 5, 6, 7; DA3; DAM POET;
DLB 105; MAL 5; MTCW 2; MTFW
2005; PFS 7; RGAL 4; WP
Simmel, Georg 1858-1918 .... **TCLC 64**
See also CA 157; DLB 296
Simmons, Charles (Paul) 1924- .... **CLC 57**
See also CA 89-92; INT CA-89-92
Simmons, Dan 1948- .... **CLC 44**
See also AAYA 16, 54; CA 138; CANR 53,
81, 126, 174; CPW; DAM POP; HGG;
SUFW 2
Simmons, James (Stewart Alexander)
1933- .... **CLC 43**
See also CA 105; CAAS 21; CP 1, 2, 3, 4,
5, 6, 7; DLB 40
Simmons, Richard
See Simmons, Dan
Simms, William Gilmore
1806-1870 .... **NCLC 3**
See also DLB 3, 30, 59, 73, 248, 254;
RGAL 4
Simon, Carly 1945- .... **CLC 26**
See also CA 105
Simon, Claude 1913-2005 ... **CLC 4, 9, 15, 39**
See also CA 89-92; 241; CANR 33, 117;
CWW 2; DAM NOV; DLB 83, 332; EW
13; EWL 3; GFL 1789 to the Present;
MTCW 1
Simon, Claude Eugene Henri
See Simon, Claude
Simon, Claude Henri Eugene
See Simon, Claude
Simon, Marvin Neil
See Simon, Neil
Simon, Myles
See Follett, Ken
Simon, Neil 1927- .... **CLC 6, 11, 31, 39, 70,
233; DC 14**
See also AAYA 32; AITN 1; AMWS 4; CA
21-24R; CAD; CANR 26, 54, 87, 126;
CD 5, 6; DA3; DAM DRAM; DFS 2, 6,
12, 18,, 24; DLB 7, 266; LAIT 4; MAL 5;
MTCW 1, 2; MTFW 2005; RGAL 4; TUS
Simon, Paul 1941(?)- .... **CLC 17**
See also CA 116; 153; CANR 152
Simon, Paul Frederick
See Simon, Paul
Simonon, Paul 1956(?)- .... **CLC 30**
Simonson, Rick CLC 70
Simpson, Harriette
See Arnow, Harriette (Louisa) Simpson
Simpson, Louis 1923- ... **CLC 4, 7, 9, 32, 149**
See also AMWS 9; CA 1-4R; CAAS 4;
CANR 1, 61, 140; CP 1, 2, 3, 4, 5, 6, 7;
DAM POET; DLB 5; MAL 5; MTCW 1,
2; MTFW 2005; PFS 7, 11, 14; RGAL 4
Simpson, Mona 1957- .... **CLC 44, 146**
See also CA 122; 135; CANR 68, 103; CN
6, 7; EWL 3
Simpson, Mona Elizabeth
See Simpson, Mona

Smith, William Jay 1918- .... **CLC 6**
 See also AMWS 13; CA 5-8R; CANR 44,
 106; CP 1, 2, 3, 4, 5, 6, 7; CSW; CWRI
 5; DLB 5; MAICYA 1, 2; SAAS 22;
 SATA 2, 68, 154; SATA-Essay 154; TCLE
 1:2

Smith, Woodrow Wilson
 See Kuttner, Henry

Smith, Zadie 1975- .... **CLC 158**
 See also AAYA 50; CA 193; DLB 347;
 MTFW 2005

Smolenskin, Peretz 1842-1885 .... **NCLC 30**

Smollett, Tobias (George) 1721-1771 ... **LC 2,
 46**
 See also BRW 3; CDBLB 1660-1789; DLB
 39, 104; RGEL 2; TEA

Snodgrass, Quentin Curtius
 See Twain, Mark

Snodgrass, Thomas Jefferson
 See Twain, Mark

Snodgrass, W. D. 1926-2009 .... **CLC 2, 6, 10,
 18, 68; PC 74**
 See also AMWS 6; CA 1-4R; CANR 6, 36,
 65, 85, 185; CP 1, 2, 3, 4, 5, 6, 7; DAM
 POET; DLB 5; MAL 5; MTCW 1, 2;
 MTFW 2005; PFS 29; RGAL 4; TCLE
 1:2

Snodgrass, William De Witt
 See Snodgrass, W. D.

Snorri Sturluson 1179-1241 .... **CMLC 56**
 See also RGWL 2, 3

Snow, C(harles) P(ercy) 1905-1980 ... **CLC 1,
 4, 6, 9, 13, 19**
 See also BRW 7; CA 5-8R; 101; CANR 28;
 CDBLB 1945-1960; CN 1, 2; DAM NOV;
 DLB 15, 77; DLBD 17; EWL 3; MTCW
 1, 2; MTFW 2005; RGEL 2; TEA

Snow, Frances Compton
 See Adams, Henry (Brooks)

Snyder, Gary 1930- . **CLC 1, 2, 5, 9, 32, 120;
 PC 21**
 See also AAYA 72; AMWS 8; ANW; BG
 1:3; CA 17-20R; CANR 30, 60, 125; CP
 1, 2, 3, 4, 5, 6, 7; DA3; DAM POET; DLB
 5, 16, 165, 212, 237, 275, 342; EWL 3;
 MAL 5; MTCW 2; MTFW 2005; PFS 9,
 19; RGAL 4; WP

Snyder, Zilpha Keatley 1927- .... **CLC 17**
 See also AAYA 15; BYA 1; CA 9-12R, 252;
 CAAE 252; CANR 38; CLR 31, 121;
 JRDA; MAICYA 1, 2; SAAS 2; SATA 1,
 28, 75, 110, 163; SATA-Essay 112, 163;
 YAW

Soares, Bernardo
 See Pessoa, Fernando

Sobh, A.
 See Shamlu, Ahmad

Sobh, Alef
 See Shamlu, Ahmad

Sobol, Joshua 1939- .... **CLC 60**
 See also CA 200; CWW 2; RGHL

Sobol, Yehoshua 1939-
 See Sobol, Joshua

Socrates 470B.C.-399B.C. .... **CMLC 27**

Soderberg, Hjalmar 1869-1941 ...... **TCLC 39**
 See also DLB 259; EWL 3; RGSF 2

Soderbergh, Steven 1963- .... **CLC 154**
 See also AAYA 43; CA 243

Soderbergh, Steven Andrew
 See Soderbergh, Steven

Sodergran, Edith (Irene) 1892-1923
 See Soedergran, Edith (Irene)

Soedergran, Edith (Irene)
 1892-1923 .... **TCLC 31**
 See also CA 202; DLB 259; EW 11; EWL
 3; RGWL 2, 3

Softly, Edgar
 See Lovecraft, H. P.

Softly, Edward
 See Lovecraft, H. P.

Sokolov, Alexander V(sevolodovich)
 1943- .... **CLC 59**
 See also CA 73-76; CWW 2; DLB 285;
 EWL 3; RGWL 2, 3

Sokolov, Raymond 1941- .... **CLC 7**
 See also CA 85-88

Sokolov, Sasha
 See Sokolov, Alexander V(sevolodovich)

Solo, Jay
 See Ellison, Harlan

Sologub, Fedor
 See Teternikov, Fyodor Kuzmich

Sologub, Feodor
 See Teternikov, Fyodor Kuzmich

Sologub, Fyodor
 See Teternikov, Fyodor Kuzmich

Solomons, Ikey Esquir
 See Thackeray, William Makepeace

Solomos, Dionysios 1798-1857 .... **NCLC 15**

Solwoska, Mara
 See French, Marilyn

Solzhenitsyn, Aleksandr 1918-2008 ... **CLC 1,
 2, 4, 7, 9, 10, 18, 26, 34, 78, 134, 235;
 SSC 32, 105; WLC 5**
 See also AAYA 49; AITN 1; BPFB 3; CA
 69-72; CANR 40, 65, 116; CWW 2; DA;
 DA3; DAB; DAC; DAM MST, NOV;
 DLB 302, 332; EW 13; EWL 3; EXPS;
 LAIT 4; MTCW 1, 2; MTFW 2005; NFS
 6; RGSF 2; RGWL 2, 3; SSFS 9; TWA

Solzhenitsyn, Aleksandr I.
 See Solzhenitsyn, Aleksandr

Solzhenitsyn, Aleksandr Isayevich
 See Solzhenitsyn, Aleksandr

Somers, Jane
 See Lessing, Doris

Somerville, Edith Oenone
 1858-1949 .... **SSC 56; TCLC 51**
 See also CA 196; DLB 135; RGEL 2; RGSF
 2

Somerville & Ross
 See Martin, Violet Florence; Somerville,
 Edith Oenone

Sommer, Scott 1951- .... **CLC 25**
 See also CA 106

Sommers, Christina Hoff 1950- ...... **CLC 197**
 See also CA 153; CANR 95

Sondheim, Stephen 1930- .. **CLC 30, 39, 147;
 DC 22**
 See also AAYA 11, 66; CA 103; CANR 47,
 67, 125; DAM DRAM; DFS 25; LAIT 4

Sondheim, Stephen Joshua
 See Sondheim, Stephen

Sone, Monica 1919- .... **AAL**
 See also DLB 312

Song, Cathy 1955- .... **AAL; PC 21**
 See also CA 154; CANR 118; CWP; DLB
 169, 312; EXPP; FW; PFS 5

Sontag, Susan 1933-2004 ... **CLC 1, 2, 10, 13,
 31, 105, 195**
 See also AMWS 3; CA 17-20R; 234; CANR
 25, 51, 74, 97, 184; CN 1, 2, 3, 4, 5, 6, 7;
 CPW; DA3; DAM POP; DLB 2, 67; EWL
 3; MAL 5; MBL; MTCW 1, 2; MTFW
 2005; RGAL 4; RHW; SSFS 10

Sophocles 496(?)B.C.-406(?)B.C. .... **CMLC 2,
 47, 51, 86; DC 1; WLCS**
 See also AW 1; CDWLB 1; DA; DA3;
 DAB; DAC; DAM DRAM, MST; DFS 1,
 4, 8, 24; DLB 176; LAIT 1; LATS 1:1;
 LMFS 1; RGWL 2, 3; TWA; WLIT 8

Sordello 1189-1269 .... **CMLC 15**

Sorel, Georges 1847-1922 .... **TCLC 91**
 See also CA 118; 188

Sorel, Julia
 See Drexler, Rosalyn

Sorokin, Vladimir CLC 59
 See also CA 258; DLB 285

Sorokin, Vladimir Georgievich
 See Sorokin, Vladimir

Sorrentino, Gilbert 1929-2006 .... **CLC 3, 7,
 14, 22, 40, 247**
 See also CA 77-80; 250; CANR 14, 33, 115,
 157; CN 3, 4, 5, 6, 7; CP 1, 2, 3, 4, 5, 6,
 7; DLB 5, 173; DLBY 1980; INT
 CANR-14

Soseki
 See Natsume, Soseki

Soto, Gary 1952- ... **CLC 32, 80; HLC 2; PC
 28**
 See also AAYA 10, 37; BYA 11; CA 119;
 125; CANR 50, 74, 107, 157; CLR 38;
 CP 4, 5, 6, 7; DAM MULT; DFS 26; DLB
 82; EWL 3; EXPP; HW 1, 2; INT CA-
 125; JRDA; LLW; MAICYA 2; MAIC-
 YAS 1; MAL 5; MTCW 2; MTFW 2005;
 PFS 7, 30; RGAL 4; SATA 80, 120, 174;
 WYA; YAW

Soupault, Philippe 1897-1990 .... **CLC 68**
 See also CA 116; 147; EWL 3; GFL
 1789 to the Present; LMFS 2

Souster, (Holmes) Raymond 1921- .... **CLC 5,
 14**
 See also CA 13-16R; CAAS 14; CANR 13,
 29, 53; CP 1, 2, 3, 4, 5, 6, 7; DA3; DAC;
 DAM POET; DLB 88; RGEL 2; SATA 63

Southern, Terry 1924(?)-1995 .... **CLC 7**
 See also AMWS 11; BPFB 3; CA 1-4R;
 150; CANR 1, 55, 107; CN 1, 2, 3, 4, 5,
 6; DLB 2; IDFW 3, 4

Southerne, Thomas 1660-1746 .... **LC 99**
 See also DLB 80; RGEL 2

Southey, Robert 1774-1843 .... **NCLC 8, 97**
 See also BRW 4; DLB 93, 107, 142; RGEL
 2; SATA 54

Southwell, Robert 1561(?)-1595 .... **LC 108**
 See also DLB 167; RGEL 2; TEA

Southworth, Emma Dorothy Eliza Nevitte
 1819-1899 .... **NCLC 26**
 See also DLB 239

Souza, Ernest
 See Scott, Evelyn

Soyinka, Wole 1934- .. **BLC 1:3, 2:3; CLC 3,
 5, 14, 36, 44, 179; DC 2; WLC 5**
 See also AFW; BW 2, 3; CA 13-16R;
 CANR 27, 39, 82, 136; CD 5, 6; CDWLB
 3; CN 6, 7; CP 1, 2, 3, 4, 5, 6 ,7; DA;
 DA3; DAB; DAC; DAM DRAM, MST,
 MULT; DFS 10, 26; DLB 125, 332; EWL
 3; MTCW 1, 2; MTFW 2005; PFS 27;
 RGEL 2; TWA; WLIT 2; WWE 1

Spackman, W(illiam) M(ode)
 1905-1990 .... **CLC 46**
 See also CA 81-84; 132

Spacks, Barry (Bernard) 1931- .... **CLC 14**
 See also CA 154; CANR 33, 109; CP 3, 4,
 5, 6, 7; DLB 105

Spanidou, Irini 1946- .... **CLC 44**
 See also CA 185; CANR 179

Spark, Muriel 1918-2006 .... **CLC 2, 3, 5, 8,
 13, 18, 40, 94, 242; PC 72; SSC 10, 115**
 See also BRWS 1; CA 5-8R; 251; CANR
 12, 36, 76, 89, 131; CDBLB 1945-1960;
 CN 1, 2, 3, 4, 5, 6, 7; CP 1, 2, 3, 4, 5, 6,
 7; DA3; DAB; DAC; DAM MST, NOV;
 DLB 15, 139; EWL 3; FW; INT CANR-
 12; LAIT 4; MTCW 1, 2; MTFW 2005;
 NFS 22; RGEL 2; TEA; WLIT 4; YAW

Spark, Muriel Sarah
 See Spark, Muriel

Spaulding, Douglas
 See Bradbury, Ray

Steiner, George 1929- .... **CLC 24, 221**
See also CA 73-76; CANR 31, 67, 108; DAM NOV; DLB 67, 299; EWL 3; MTCW 1, 2; MTFW 2005; RGHL; SATA 62

Steiner, K. Leslie
See Delany, Samuel R., Jr.

Steiner, Rudolf 1861-1925 .... **TCLC 13**
See also CA 107

Stendhal 1783-1842 .... **NCLC 23, 46, 178; SSC 27; WLC 5**
See also DA; DA3; DAB; DAC; DAM MST, NOV; DLB 119; EW 5; GFL 1789 to the Present; RGWL 2, 3; TWA

Stephen, Adeline Virginia
See Woolf, (Adeline) Virginia

Stephen, Sir Leslie 1832-1904 .... **TCLC 23**
See also BRW 5; CA 123; DLB 57, 144, 190

Stephen, Sir Leslie
See Stephen, Sir Leslie

Stephen, Virginia
See Woolf, (Adeline) Virginia

Stephens, James 1882(?)-1950 .... **SSC 50; TCLC 4**
See also CA 104; 192; DLB 19, 153, 162; EWL 3; FANT; RGEL 2; SUFW

Stephens, Reed
See Donaldson, Stephen R.

Stephenson, Neal 1959- .... **CLC 220**
See also AAYA 38; CA 122; CANR 88, 138; CN 7; MTFW 2005; SFW 4

Steptoe, Lydia
See Barnes, Djuna

Sterchi, Beat 1949- .... **CLC 65**
See also CA 203

Sterling, Brett
See Bradbury, Ray; Hamilton, Edmond

Sterling, Bruce 1954- .... **CLC 72**
See also AAYA 78; CA 119; CANR 44, 135, 184; CN 7; MTFW 2005; SCFW 2; SFW 4

Sterling, George 1869-1926 .... **TCLC 20**
See also CA 117; 165; DLB 54

Stern, Gerald 1925- .... **CLC 40, 100**
See also AMWS 9; CA 81-84; CANR 28, 94; CP 3, 4, 5, 6, 7; DLB 105; PFS 26; RGAL 4

Stern, Richard (Gustave) 1928- ... **CLC 4, 39**
See also CA 1-4R; CANR 1, 25, 52, 120; CN 1, 2, 3, 4, 5, 6, 7; DLB 218; DLBY 1987; INT CANR-25

Sternberg, Josef von 1894-1969 .... **CLC 20**
See also CA 81-84

Sterne, Laurence 1713-1768 .. **LC 2, 48, 156; WLC 5**
See also BRW 3; BRWC 1; CDBLB 1660-1789; DA; DAB; DAC; DAM MST, NOV; DLB 39; RGEL 2; TEA

Sternheim, (William Adolf) Carl
1878-1942 .... **TCLC 8**
See also CA 105; 193; DLB 56, 118; EWL 3; IDTP; RGWL 2, 3

Stevens, Margaret Dean
See Aldrich, Bess Streeter

Stevens, Mark 1951- .... **CLC 34**
See also CA 122

Stevens, R. L.
See Hoch, Edward D.

Stevens, Wallace 1879-1955 . **PC 6; TCLC 3, 12, 45; WLC 5**
See also AMW; AMWR 1; CA 104; 124; CANR 181; CDALB 1929-1941; DA; DA3; DAB; DAC; DAM MST, POET; DLB 54, 342; EWL 3; EXPP; MAL 5; MTCW 1, 2; PAB; PFS 13, 16; RGAL 4; TUS; WP

Stevenson, Anne (Katharine) 1933- .. **CLC 7, 33**
See also BRWS 6; CA 17-20R; CAAS 9; CANR 9, 33, 123; CP 3, 4, 5, 6, 7; CWP; DLB 40; MTCW 1; RHW

Stevenson, Robert Louis (Balfour)
1850-1894 ...... **NCLC 5, 14, 63, 193; PC 84; SSC 11, 51; WLC 5**
See also AAYA 24; BPFB 3; BRW 5; BRWC 1; BRWR 1; BYA 1, 2, 4, 13; CD-BLB 1890-1914; CLR 10, 11, 107; DA; DA3; DAB; DAC; DAM MST, NOV; DLB 18, 57, 141, 156, 174; DLBD 13; GL 3; HGG; JRDA; LAIT 1, 3; MAICYA 1, 2; NFS 11, 20; RGEL 2; RGSF 2; SATA 100; SUFW; TEA; WCH; WLIT 4; WYA; YABC 2; YAW

Stewart, J(ohn) I(nnes) M(ackintosh)
1906-1994 .... **CLC 7, 14, 32**
See also CA 85-88; 147; CAAS 3; CANR 47; CMW 4; CN 1, 2, 3, 4, 5; DLB 276; MSW; MTCW 1, 2

Stewart, Mary (Florence Elinor)
1916- .... **CLC 7, 35, 117**
See also AAYA 29, 73; BPFB 3; CA 1-4R; CANR 1, 59, 130; CMW 4; CPW; DAB; FANT; RHW; SATA 12; YAW

Stewart, Mary Rainbow
See Stewart, Mary (Florence Elinor)

Stewart, Will
See Williamson, John Stewart

Stifle, June
See Campbell, Maria

Stifter, Adalbert 1805-1868 ... **NCLC 41, 198; SSC 28**
See also CDWLB 2; DLB 133; RGSF 2; RGWL 2, 3

Still, James 1906-2001 .... **CLC 49**
See also CA 65-68; 195; CAAS 17; CANR 10, 26; CSW; DLB 9; DLBY 01; SATA 29; SATA-Obit 127

Sting 1951- .... **CLC 26**
See also CA 167

Stirling, Arthur
See Sinclair, Upton

Stitt, Milan 1941-2009 .... **CLC 29**
See also CA 69-72

Stockton, Francis Richard
1834-1902 .... **TCLC 47**
See also AAYA 68; BYA 4, 13; CA 108; 137; DLB 42, 74; DLBD 13; EXPS; MAICYA 1, 2; SATA 44; SATA-Brief 32; SFW 4; SSFS 3; SUFW; WCH

Stockton, Frank R.
See Stockton, Francis Richard

Stoddard, Charles
See Kuttner, Henry

Stoker, Abraham 1847-1912 . **SSC 62; TCLC 8, 144; WLC 6**
See also AAYA 23; BPFB 3; BRWS 3; BYA 5; CA 105; 150; CDBLB 1890-1914; DA; DA3; DAB; DAC; DAM MST, NOV; DLB 304; GL 3; HGG; LATS 1:1; MTFW 2005; NFS 18; RGEL 2; SATA 29; SUFW; TEA; WLIT 4

Stoker, Bram
See Stoker, Abraham

Stolz, Mary 1920-2006 .... **CLC 12**
See also AAYA 8, 73; AITN 1; CA 5-8R; 255; CANR 13, 41, 112; JRDA; MAICYA 1, 2; SAAS 3; SATA 10, 71, 133; SATA-Obit 180; YAW

Stolz, Mary Slattery
See Stolz, Mary

Stone, Irving 1903-1989 .... **CLC 7**
See also AITN 1; BPFB 3; CA 1-4R; 129; CAAS 3; CANR 1, 23; CN 1, 2, 3, 4; CPW; DA3; DAM POP; INT CANR-23; MTCW 1, 2; MTFW 2005; RHW; SATA 3; SATA-Obit 64

Stone, Oliver 1946- .... **CLC 73**
See also AAYA 15, 64; CA 110; CANR 55, 125

Stone, Oliver William
See Stone, Oliver

Stone, Robert 1937- .... **CLC 5, 23, 42, 175**
See also AMWS 5; BPFB 3; CA 85-88; CANR 23, 66, 95, 173; CN 4, 5, 6, 7; DLB 152; EWL 3; INT CANR-23; MAL 5; MTCW 1; MTFW 2005

Stone, Robert Anthony
See Stone, Robert

Stone, Ruth 1915- .... **PC 53**
See also CA 45-48; CANR 2, 91; CP 5, 6, 7; CSW; DLB 105; PFS 19

Stone, Zachary
See Follett, Ken

Stoppard, Tom 1937- ... **CLC 1, 3, 4, 5, 8, 15, 29, 34, 63, 91; DC 6, 30; WLC 6**
See also AAYA 63; BRWC 1; BRWR 2; BRWS 1; CA 81-84; CANR 39, 67, 125; CBD; CD 5, 6; CDBLB 1960 to Present; DA; DA3; DAB; DAC; DAM DRAM, MST; DFS 2, 5, 8, 11, 13, 16; DLB 13, 233; DLBY 1985; EWL 3; LATS 1:2; MTCW 1, 2; MTFW 2005; RGEL 2; TEA; WLIT 4

Storey, David (Malcolm) 1933- . **CLC 2, 4, 5, 8**
See also BRWS 1; CA 81-84; CANR 36; CBD; CD 5, 6; CN 1, 2, 3, 4, 5, 6; DAM DRAM; DLB 13, 14, 207, 245, 326; EWL 3; MTCW 1; RGEL 2

Storm, Hyemeyohsts 1935- ... **CLC 3; NNAL**
See also CA 81-84; CANR 45; DAM MULT

Storm, (Hans) Theodor (Woldsen)
1817-1888 ... **NCLC 1, 195; SSC 27, 106**
See also CDWLB 2; DLB 129; EW; RGSF 2; RGWL 2, 3

Storni, Alfonsina 1892-1938 . **HLC 2; PC 33; TCLC 5**
See also CA 104; 131; DAM MULT; DLB 283; HW 1; LAW

Stoughton, William 1631-1701 .... **LC 38**
See also DLB 24

Stout, Rex (Todhunter) 1886-1975 ..... **CLC 3**
See also AAYA 79; AITN 2; BPFB 3; CA 61-64; CANR 71; CMW 4; CN 2; DLB 306; MSW; RGAL 4

Stow, (Julian) Randolph 1935- ... **CLC 23, 48**
See also CA 13-16R; CANR 33; CN 1, 2, 3, 4, 5, 6, 7; CP 1, 2, 3, 4; DLB 260; MTCW 1; RGEL 2

Stowe, Harriet (Elizabeth) Beecher
1811-1896 .... **NCLC 3, 50, 133, 195; WLC 6**
See also AAYA 53; AMWS 1; CDALB 1865-1917; CLR 131; DA; DA3; DAB; DAC; DAM MST, NOV; DLB 1, 12, 42, 74, 189, 239, 243; EXPN; FL 1:3; JRDA; LAIT 2; MAICYA 1, 2; NFS 6; RGAL 4; TUS; YABC 1

Strabo c. 64B.C.-c. 25 .... **CMLC 37**
See also DLB 176

Strachey, (Giles) Lytton
1880-1932 .... **TCLC 12**
See also BRWS 2; CA 110; 178; DLB 149; DLBD 10; EWL 3; MTCW 2; NCFS 4

Stramm, August 1874-1915 .... **PC 50**
See also CA 195; EWL 3

Strand, Mark 1934- .. **CLC 6, 18, 41, 71; PC 63**
See also AMWS 4; CA 21-24R; CANR 40, 65, 100; CP 1, 2, 3, 4, 5, 6, 7; DAM POET; DLB 5; EWL 3; MAL 5; PAB; PFS 9, 18; RGAL 4; SATA 41; TCLE 1:2

Thorpe, Thomas Bangs
1815-1878 .... **NCLC 183**
See also DLB 3, 11, 248; RGAL 4
Thubron, Colin 1939- .... **CLC 163**
See also CA 25-28R; CANR 12, 29, 59, 95, 171; CN 5, 6, 7; DLB 204, 231
Thubron, Colin Gerald Dryden
See Thubron, Colin
Thucydides c. 455B.C.-c. 395B.C. . **CMLC 17**
See also AW 1; DLB 176; RGWL 2, 3; WLIT 8
Thumboo, Edwin Nadason 1933- .... **PC 30**
See also CA 194; CP 1
Thurber, James (Grover)
1894-1961 .. **CLC 5, 11, 25, 125; SSC 1, 47**
See also AAYA 56; AMWS 1; BPFB 3; BYA 5; CA 73-76; CANR 17, 39; CDALB 1929-1941; CWRI 5; DA; DA3; DAB; DAC; DAM DRAM, MST, NOV; DLB 4, 11, 22, 102; EWL 3; EXPS; FANT; LAIT 3; MAICYA 1, 2; MAL 5; MTCW 1, 2; MTFW 2005; RGAL 4; RGSF 2; SATA 13; SSFS 1, 10, 19; SUFW; TUS
Thurman, Wallace (Henry)
1902-1934 .. **BLC 1:3; HR 1:3; TCLC 6**
See also BW 1, 3; CA 104; 124; CANR 81; DAM MULT; DLB 51
Tibullus c. 54B.C.-c. 18B.C. .... **CMLC 36**
See also AW 2; DLB 211; RGWL 2, 3; WLIT 8
Ticheburn, Cheviot
See Ainsworth, William Harrison
Tieck, (Johann) Ludwig
1773-1853 ..... **NCLC 5, 46; SSC 31, 100**
See also CDWLB 2; DLB 90; EW 5; IDTP; RGSF 2; RGWL 2, 3; SUFW
Tiger, Derry
See Ellison, Harlan
Tilghman, Christopher 1946- .... **CLC 65**
See also CA 159; CANR 135, 151; CSW; DLB 244
Tillich, Paul (Johannes)
1886-1965 .... **CLC 131**
See also CA 5-8R; 25-28R; CANR 33; MTCW 1, 2
Tillinghast, Richard (Williford)
1940- .... **CLC 29**
See also CA 29-32R; CAAS 23; CANR 26, 51, 96; CP 2, 3, 4, 5, 6, 7; CSW
Tillman, Lynne (?)- .... **CLC 231**
See also CA 173; CANR 144, 172
Timrod, Henry 1828-1867 .... **NCLC 25**
See also DLB 3, 248; RGAL 4
Tindall, Gillian (Elizabeth) 1938- ...... **CLC 7**
See also CA 21-24R; CANR 11, 65, 107; CN 1, 2, 3, 4, 5, 6, 7
Ting Ling
See Chiang, Pin-chin
Tiptree, James, Jr.
See Sheldon, Alice Hastings Bradley
Tirone Smith, Mary-Ann 1944- .... **CLC 39**
See also CA 118; 136; CANR 113; SATA 143
Tirso de Molina 1580(?)-1648 .... **DC 13; HLCS 2; LC 73**
See also RGWL 2, 3
Titmarsh, Michael Angelo
See Thackeray, William Makepeace
Tocqueville, Alexis (Charles Henri Maurice Clerel Comte) de 1805-1859 .. **NCLC 7, 63**
See also EW 6; GFL 1789 to the Present; TWA
Toe, Tucker
See Westlake, Donald E.

Toer, Pramoedya Ananta
1925-2006 .... **CLC 186**
See also CA 197; 251; CANR 170; DLB 348; RGWL 3
Toffler, Alvin 1928- .... **CLC 168**
See also CA 13-16R; CANR 15, 46, 67, 183; CPW; DAM POP; MTCW 1, 2
Toibin, Colm 1955- .... **CLC 162**
See also CA 142; CANR 81, 149; CN 7; DLB 271
Tolkien, John Ronald Reuel
See Tolkien, J.R.R
Tolkien, J.R.R 1892-1973 ...... **CLC 1, 2, 3, 8, 12, 38; TCLC 137; WLC 6**
See also AAYA 10; AITN 1; BPFB 3; BRWC 2; BRWS 2; CA 17-18; 45-48; CANR 36, 134; CAP 2; CDBLB 1914-1945; CLR 56; CN 1; CPW 1; CWRI 5; DA; DA3; DAB; DAC; DAM MST, NOV, POP; DLB 15, 160, 255; EFS 2; EWL 3; FANT; JRDA; LAIT 1; LATS 1:2; LMFS 2; MAICYA 1, 2; MTCW 1, 2; MTFW 2005; NFS 8, 26; RGEL 2; SATA 2, 32, 100; SATA-Obit 24; SFW 4; SUFW; TEA; WCH; WYA; YAW
Toller, Ernst 1893-1939 .... **TCLC 10**
See also CA 107; 186; DLB 124; EWL 3; RGWL 2, 3
Tolson, M. B.
See Tolson, Melvin B(eaunorus)
Tolson, Melvin B(eaunorus)
1898(?)-1966 .... **BLC 1:3; CLC 36, 105; PC 88**
See also AFAW 1, 2; BW 1, 3; CA 124; 89-92; CANR 80; DAM MULT, POET; DLB 48, 76; MAL 5; RGAL 4
Tolstoi, Aleksei Nikolaevich
See Tolstoy, Alexey Nikolaevich
Tolstoi, Lev
See Tolstoy, Leo (Nikolaevich)
Tolstoy, Aleksei Nikolaevich
See Tolstoy, Alexey Nikolaevich
Tolstoy, Alexey Nikolaevich
1882-1945 .... **TCLC 18**
See also CA 107; 158; DLB 272; EWL 3; SFW 4
Tolstoy, Leo (Nikolaevich)
1828-1910 . **SSC 9, 30, 45, 54; TCLC 4, 11, 17, 28, 44, 79, 173; WLC 6**
See also AAYA 56; CA 104; 123; DA; DA3; DAB; DAC; DAM MST, NOV; DLB 238; EFS 2; EW 7; EXPS; IDTP; LAIT 2; LATS 1:1; LMFS 1; NFS 10, 28; RGSF 2; RGWL 2, 3; SATA 26; SSFS 5; TWA
Tolstoy, Count Leo
See Tolstoy, Leo (Nikolaevich)
Tomalin, Claire 1933- .... **CLC 166**
See also CA 89-92; CANR 52, 88, 165; DLB 155
Tomasi di Lampedusa, Giuseppe
1896-1957 .... **TCLC 13**
See also CA 111; 164; DLB 177; EW 11; EWL 3; MTCW 2; MTFW 2005; RGWL 2, 3; WLIT 7
Tomlin, Lily 1939(?)- .... **CLC 17**
See also CA 117
Tomlin, Mary Jane
See Tomlin, Lily
Tomlin, Mary Jean
See Tomlin, Lily
Tomline, F. Latour
See Gilbert, W(illiam) S(chwenck)
Tomlinson, (Alfred) Charles 1927- .... **CLC 2, 4, 6, 13, 45; PC 17**
See also CA 5-8R; CANR 33; CP 1, 2, 3, 4, 5, 6, 7; DAM POET; DLB 40; TCLE 1:2
Tomlinson, H(enry) M(ajor)
1873-1958 .... **TCLC 71**
See also CA 118; 161; DLB 36, 100, 195

Tomlinson, Mary Jane
See Tomlin, Lily
Tonna, Charlotte Elizabeth
1790-1846 .... **NCLC 135**
See also DLB 163
Tonson, Jacob fl. 1655(?)-1736 .... **LC 86**
See also DLB 170
Toole, John Kennedy 1937-1969 ..... **CLC 19, 64**
See also BPFB 3; CA 104; DLBY 1981; MTCW 2; MTFW 2005
Toomer, Eugene
See Toomer, Jean
Toomer, Eugene Pinchback
See Toomer, Jean
Toomer, Jean 1894-1967 ... **BLC 1:3; CLC 1, 4, 13, 22; HR 1:3; PC 7; SSC 1, 45; TCLC 172; WLCS**
See also AFAW 1, 2; AMWS 3, 9; BW 1; CA 85-88; CDALB 1917-1929; DA3; DAM MULT; DLB 45, 51; EWL 3; EXPP; EXPS; LMFS 2; MAL 5; MTCW 1, 2; MTFW 2005; NFS 11; RGAL 4; RGSF 2; SSFS 5
Toomer, Nathan Jean
See Toomer, Jean
Toomer, Nathan Pinchback
See Toomer, Jean
Torley, Luke
See Blish, James (Benjamin)
Tornimparte, Alessandra
See Ginzburg, Natalia
Torre, Raoul della
See Mencken, H(enry) L(ouis)
Torrence, Ridgely 1874-1950 .... **TCLC 97**
See also DLB 54, 249; MAL 5
Torrey, E. Fuller 1937- .... **CLC 34**
See also CA 119; CANR 71, 158
Torrey, Edwin Fuller
See Torrey, E. Fuller
Torsvan, Ben Traven
See Traven, B.
Torsvan, Benno Traven
See Traven, B.
Torsvan, Berick Traven
See Traven, B.
Torsvan, Berwick Traven
See Traven, B.
Torsvan, Bruno Traven
See Traven, B.
Torsvan, Traven
See Traven, B.
Toson
See Shimazaki, Haruki
Tourneur, Cyril 1575(?)-1626 .... **LC 66**
See also BRW 2; DAM DRAM; DLB 58; RGEL 2
Tournier, Michel 1924- .... **CLC 6, 23, 36, 95, 249; SSC 88**
See also CA 49-52; CANR 3, 36, 74, 149; CWW 2; DLB 83; EWL 3; GFL 1789 to the Present; MTCW 1, 2; SATA 23
Tournier, Michel Edouard
See Tournier, Michel
Tournimparte, Alessandra
See Ginzburg, Natalia
Towers, Ivar
See Kornbluth, C(yril) M.
Towne, Robert (Burton) 1936(?)- ..... **CLC 87**
See also CA 108; DLB 44; IDFW 3, 4
Townsend, Sue
See Townsend, Susan Lilian
Townsend, Susan Lilian 1946- .... **CLC 61**
See also AAYA 28; CA 119; 127; CANR 65, 107; CBD; CD 5, 6; CPW; CWD; DAB; DAC; DAM MST; DLB 271; INT CA-127; SATA 55, 93; SATA-Brief 48; YAW

Van Druten, John (William)
1901-1957 .... **TCLC 2**
See also CA 104; 161; DLB 10; MAL 5;
RGAL 4

Van Duyn, Mona 1921-2004 .... **CLC 3, 7, 63,
116**
See also CA 9-12R; 234; CANR 7, 38, 60,
116; CP 1, 2, 3, 4, 5, 6, 7; CWP; DAM
POET; DLB 5; MAL 5; MTFW 2005;
PFS 20

Van Dyne, Edith
See Baum, L(yman) Frank

van Herk, Aritha 1954- .... **CLC 249**
See also CA 101; CANR 94; DLB 334

van Itallie, Jean-Claude 1936- .... **CLC 3**
See also CA 45-48; CAAS 2; CAD; CANR
1, 48; CD 5, 6; DLB 7

Van Loot, Cornelius Obenchain
See Roberts, Kenneth (Lewis)

van Ostaijen, Paul 1896-1928 .... **TCLC 33**
See also CA 163

Van Peebles, Melvin 1932- .... **CLC 2, 20**
See also BW 2, 3; CA 85-88; CANR 27,
67, 82; DAM MULT

van Schendel, Arthur(-Francois-Emile)
1874-1946 .... **TCLC 56**
See also EWL 3

Van See, John
See Vance, Jack

Vansittart, Peter 1920-2008 .... **CLC 42**
See also CA 1-4R; 278; CANR 3, 49, 90;
CN 4, 5, 6, 7; RHW

Van Vechten, Carl 1880-1964 ... **CLC 33; HR
1:3**
See also AMWS 2; CA 183; 89-92; DLB 4,
9, 51; RGAL 4

van Vogt, A(lfred) E(lton) 1912-2000 . **CLC 1**
See also BPFB 3; BYA 13, 14; CA 21-24R;
190; CANR 28; DLB 8, 251; SATA 14;
SATA-Obit 124; SCFW 1, 2; SFW 4

Vara, Madeleine
See Jackson, Laura (Riding)

Varda, Agnes 1928- .... **CLC 16**
See also CA 116; 122

Vargas Llosa, Jorge Mario Pedro
See Vargas Llosa, Mario

Vargas Llosa, Mario 1936- .. **CLC 3, 6, 9, 10,
15, 31, 42, 85, 181; HLC 2**
See also BPFB 3; CA 73-76; CANR 18, 32,
42, 67, 116, 140, 173; CDWLB 3; CWW
2; DA; DA3; DAB; DAC; DAM MST,
MULT, NOV; DLB 145; DNFS 2; EWL
3; HW 1, 2; LAIT 5; LATS 1:2; LAW;
LAWS 1; MTCW 1, 2; MTFW 2005;
RGWL 2, 3; SSFS 14; TWA; WLIT 1

Varnhagen von Ense, Rahel
1771-1833 .... **NCLC 130**
See also DLB 90

Vasari, Giorgio 1511-1574 .... **LC 114**

Vasilikos, Vasiles
See Vassilikos, Vassilis

Vasiliu, George
See Bacovia, George

Vasiliu, Gheorghe
See Bacovia, George

Vassa, Gustavus
See Equiano, Olaudah

Vassilikos, Vassilis 1933- .... **CLC 4, 8**
See also CA 81-84; CANR 75, 149; EWL 3

Vaughan, Henry 1621-1695 .... **LC 27; PC 81**
See also BRW 2; DLB 131; PAB; RGEL 2

Vaughn, Stephanie CLC 62

Vazov, Ivan (Minchov) 1850-1921 . **TCLC 25**
See also CA 121; 167; CDWLB 4; DLB
147

Veblen, Thorstein B(unde)
1857-1929 .... **TCLC 31**
See also AMWS 1; CA 115; 165; DLB 246;
MAL 5

Vega, Lope de 1562-1635 ... **HLCS 2; LC 23,
119**
See also EW 2; RGWL 2, 3

Veldeke, Heinrich von c. 1145-c.
1190 .... **CMLC 85**

Vendler, Helen (Hennessy) 1933- ... **CLC 138**
See also CA 41-44R; CANR 25, 72, 136;
MTCW 1, 2; MTFW 2005

Venison, Alfred
See Pound, Ezra (Weston Loomis)

Ventsel, Elena Sergeevna
1907-2002 .... **CLC 59**
See also CA 154; CWW 2; DLB 302

Venttsel', Elena Sergeevna
See Ventsel, Elena Sergeevna

Verdi, Marie de
See Mencken, H(enry) L(ouis)

Verdu, Matilde
See Cela, Camilo Jose

Verga, Giovanni (Carmelo)
1840-1922 .... **SSC 21, 87; TCLC 3**
See also CA 104; 123; CANR 101; EW 7;
EWL 3; RGSF 2; RGWL 2, 3; WLIT 7

Vergil 70B.C.-19B.C. .. **CMLC 9, 40, 101; PC
12; WLCS**
See also AW 2; CDWLB 1; DA; DA3;
DAB; DAC; DAM MST, POET; DLB
211; EFS 1; LAIT 1; LMFS 1; RGWL 2,
3; WLIT 8; WP

Vergil, Polydore c. 1470-1555 .... **LC 108**
See also DLB 132

Verhaeren, Emile (Adolphe Gustave)
1855-1916 .... **TCLC 12**
See also CA 109; EWL 3; GFL 1789 to the
Present

Verlaine, Paul (Marie) 1844-1896 .. **NCLC 2,
51; PC 2, 32**
See also DAM POET; DLB 217; EW 7;
GFL 1789 to the Present; LMFS 2; RGWL
2, 3; TWA

Verne, Jules (Gabriel) 1828-1905 ... **TCLC 6,
52**
See also AAYA 16; BYA 4; CA 110; 131;
CLR 88; DA3; DLB 123; GFL 1789 to
the Present; JRDA; LAIT 2; LMFS 2;
MAICYA 1, 2; MTFW 2005; RGWL 2, 3;
SATA 21; SCFW 1, 2; SFW 4; TWA;
WCH

Verus, Marcus Annius
See Aurelius, Marcus

Very, Jones 1813-1880 .... **NCLC 9; PC 86**
See also DLB 1, 243; RGAL 4

Very, Rev. C.
See Crowley, Edward Alexander

Vesaas, Tarjei 1897-1970 .... **CLC 48**
See also CA 190; 29-32R; DLB 297; EW
11; EWL 3; RGWL 3

Vialis, Gaston
See Simenon, Georges (Jacques Christian)

Vian, Boris 1920-1959(?) .... **TCLC 9**
See also CA 106; 164; CANR 111; DLB
72, 321; EWL 3; GFL 1789 to the Present;
MTCW 2; RGWL 2, 3

Viator, Vacuus
See Hughes, Thomas

Viaud, (Louis Marie) Julien
1850-1923 .... **TCLC 11**
See also CA 107; DLB 123; GFL 1789 to
the Present

Vicar, Henry
See Felsen, Henry Gregor

Vicente, Gil 1465-c. 1536 .... **LC 99**
See also DLB 318; IDTP; RGWL 2, 3

Vicker, Angus
See Felsen, Henry Gregor

Vico, Giambattista
See Vico, Giovanni Battista

Vico, Giovanni Battista 1668-1744 .... **LC 138**
See also EW 3; WLIT 7

Vidal, Eugene Luther Gore
See Vidal, Gore

Vidal, Gore 1925- ...... **CLC 2, 4, 6, 8, 10, 22,
33, 72, 142**
See also AAYA 64; AITN 1; AMWS 4;
BEST 90:2; BPFB 3; CA 5-8R; CAD;
CANR 13, 45, 65, 100, 132, 167; CD 5,
6; CDALBS; CN 1, 2, 3, 4, 5, 6, 7; CPW;
DA3; DAM NOV, POP; DFS 2; DLB 6,
152; EWL 3; GLL 1; INT CANR-13;
MAL 5; MTCW 1, 2; MTFW 2005;
RGAL 4; RHW; TUS

Viereck, Peter 1916-2006 .... **CLC 4; PC 27**
See also CA 1-4R; 250; CANR 1, 47; CP 1,
2, 3, 4, 5, 6, 7; DLB 5; MAL 5; PFS 9,
14

Viereck, Peter Robert Edwin
See Viereck, Peter

Vigny, Alfred (Victor) de
1797-1863 .... **NCLC 7, 102; PC 26**
See also DAM POET; DLB 119, 192, 217;
EW 5; GFL 1789 to the Present; RGWL
2, 3

Vilakazi, Benedict Wallet
1906-1947 .... **TCLC 37**
See also CA 168

Vile, Curt
See Moore, Alan

Villa, Jose Garcia 1914-1997 ... **AAL; PC 22;
TCLC 176**
See also CA 25-28R; CANR 12, 118; CP 1,
2, 3, 4; DLB 312; EWL 3; EXPP

Villard, Oswald Garrison
1872-1949 .... **TCLC 160**
See also CA 113; 162; DLB 25, 91

Villarreal, Jose Antonio 1924- .... **HLC 2**
See also CA 133; CANR 93; DAM MULT;
DLB 82; HW 1; LAIT 4; RGAL 4

Villaurrutia, Xavier 1903-1950 ...... **TCLC 80**
See also CA 192; EWL 3; HW 1; LAW

Villaverde, Cirilo 1812-1894 .... **NCLC 121**
See also LAW

Villehardouin, Geoffroi de
1150(?)-1218(?) .... **CMLC 38**

Villiers, George 1628-1687 .... **LC 107**
See also DLB 80; RGEL 2

**Villiers de l'Isle Adam, Jean Marie Mathias
Philippe Auguste** 1838-1889 ... **NCLC 3;
SSC 14**
See also DLB 123, 192; GFL 1789 to the
Present; RGSF 2

Villon, Francois 1431-1463(?) .... **LC 62, 166;
PC 13**
See also DLB 208; EW 2; RGWL 2, 3;
TWA

Vine, Barbara
See Rendell, Ruth

Vinge, Joan (Carol) D(ennison)
1948- .... **CLC 30; SSC 24**
See also AAYA 32; BPFB 3; CA 93-96;
CANR 72; SATA 36, 113; SFW 4; YAW

Viola, Herman J(oseph) 1938- .... **CLC 70**
See also CA 61-64; CANR 8, 23, 48, 91;
SATA 126

Violis, G.
See Simenon, Georges (Jacques Christian)

Viramontes, Helena Maria 1954- .... **HLCS 2**
See also CA 159; CANR 182; DLB 122;
HW 2; LLW

Virgil
See Vergil

Visconti, Luchino 1906-1976 .... **CLC 16**
See also CA 81-84; 65-68; CANR 39

Vitry, Jacques de
See Jacques de Vitry

Vittorini, Elio 1908-1966 .... **CLC 6, 9, 14**
See also CA 133; 25-28R; DLB 264; EW
12; EWL 3; RGWL 2, 3

Vivekananda, Swami 1863-1902 .... **TCLC 88**

Vizenor, Gerald Robert 1934- .... **CLC 103, 263; NNAL**
    See also CA 13-16R, 205; CAAE 205; CAAS 22; CANR 5, 21, 44, 67; DAM MULT; DLB 175, 227; MTCW 2; MTFW 2005; TCWW 2

Vizinczey, Stephen 1933- .... **CLC 40**
    See also CA 128; CCA 1; INT CA-128

Vliet, R(ussell) G(ordon) 1929-1984 .... **CLC 22**
    See also CA 37-40R; 112; CANR 18; CP 2, 3

Vogau, Boris Andreevich
    See Vogau, Boris Andreyevich

Vogau, Boris Andreyevich 1894-1938 .... **SSC 48; TCLC 23**
    See also CA 123; 218; DLB 272; EWL 3; RGSF 2; RGWL 2, 3

Vogel, Paula A. 1951- .... **CLC 76; DC 19**
    See also CA 108; CAD; CANR 119, 140; CD 5, 6; CWD; DFS 14; DLB 341; MTFW 2005; RGAL 4

Voigt, Cynthia 1942- .... **CLC 30**
    See also AAYA 3, 30; BYA 1, 3, 6, 7, 8; CA 106; CANR 18, 37, 40, 94, 145; CLR 13, 48, 141; INT CANR-18; JRDA; LAIT 5; MAICYA 1, 2; MAICYAS 1; MTFW 2005; SATA 48, 79, 116, 160; SATA-Brief 33; WYA; YAW

Voigt, Ellen Bryant 1943- .... **CLC 54**
    See also CA 69-72; CANR 11, 29, 55, 115, 171; CP 5, 6, 7; CSW; CWP; DLB 120; PFS 23

Voinovich, Vladimir 1932- .. **CLC 10, 49, 147**
    See also CA 81-84; CAAS 12; CANR 33, 67, 150; CWW 2; DLB 302; MTCW 1

Voinovich, Vladimir Nikolaevich
    See Voinovich, Vladimir

Vollmann, William T. 1959- ...... **CLC 89, 227**
    See also AMWS 17; CA 134; CANR 67, 116, 185; CN 7; CPW; DA3; DAM NOV, POP; MTCW 2; MTFW 2005

Voloshinov, V. N.
    See Bakhtin, Mikhail Mikhailovich

Voltaire 1694-1778 .. **LC 14, 79, 110; SSC 12, 112; WLC 6**
    See also BYA 13; DA; DA3; DAB; DAC; DAM DRAM, MST; DLB 314; EW 4; GFL Beginnings to 1789; LATS 1:1; LMFS 1; NFS 7; RGWL 2, 3; TWA

von Aschendrof, Baron Ignatz
    See Ford, Ford Madox

von Chamisso, Adelbert
    See Chamisso, Adelbert von

von Daeniken, Erich 1935- .... **CLC 30**
    See also AITN 1; CA 37-40R; CANR 17, 44

von Daniken, Erich
    See von Daeniken, Erich

von Eschenbach, Wolfram c. 1170-c. 1220 .... **CMLC 5**
    See also CDWLB 2; DLB 138; EW 1; RGWL 2, 3

von Hartmann, Eduard 1842-1906 .... **TCLC 96**

von Hayek, Friedrich August
    See Hayek, F(riedrich) A(ugust von)

von Heidenstam, (Carl Gustaf) Verner
    See Heidenstam, (Carl Gustaf) Verner von

von Heyse, Paul (Johann Ludwig)
    See Heyse, Paul (Johann Ludwig von)

von Hofmannsthal, Hugo
    See Hofmannsthal, Hugo von

von Horvath, Odon
    See von Horvath, Odon

von Horvath, Odon
    See von Horvath, Odon

von Horvath, Odon 1901-1938 .... **TCLC 45**
    See also CA 118; 184, 194; DLB 85, 124; RGWL 2, 3

von Horvath, Oedoen
    See von Horvath, Odon

von Kleist, Heinrich
    See Kleist, Heinrich von

Vonnegut, Kurt, Jr.
    See Vonnegut, Kurt

Vonnegut, Kurt 1922-2007 .... **CLC 1, 2, 3, 4, 5, 8, 12, 22, 40, 60, 111, 212, 254; SSC 8; WLC 6**
    See also AAYA 6, 44; AITN 1; AMWS 2; BEST 90:4; BPFB 3; BYA 3, 14; CA 1-4R; 259; CANR 1, 25, 49, 75, 92; CDALB 1968-1988; CN 1, 2, 3, 4, 5, 6, 7; CPW 1; DA; DA3; DAB; DAC; DAM MST, NOV, POP; DLB 2, 8, 152; DLBD 3; DLBY 1980; EWL 3; EXPN; EXPS; LAIT 4; LMFS 2; MAL 5; MTCW 1, 2; MTFW 2005; NFS 3, 28; RGAL 4; SCFW; SFW 4; SSFS 5; TUS; YAW

Von Rachen, Kurt
    See Hubbard, L. Ron

von Sternberg, Josef
    See Sternberg, Josef von

Vorster, Gordon 1924- .... **CLC 34**
    See also CA 133

Vosce, Trudie
    See Ozick, Cynthia

Voznesensky, Andrei (Andreievich) 1933- .... **CLC 1, 15, 57**
    See also CA 89-92; CANR 37; CWW 2; DAM POET; EWL 3; MTCW 1

Voznesensky, Andrey
    See Voznesensky, Andrei (Andreievich)

Wace, Robert c. 1100-c. 1175 .... **CMLC 55**
    See also DLB 146

Waddington, Miriam 1917-2004 .... **CLC 28**
    See also CA 21-24R; 225; CANR 12, 30; CCA 1; CP 1, 2, 3, 4, 5, 6, 7; DLB 68

Wade, Alan
    See Vance, Jack

Wagman, Fredrica 1937- .... **CLC 7**
    See also CA 97-100; CANR 166; INT CA-97-100

Wagner, Linda W.
    See Wagner-Martin, Linda (C.)

Wagner, Linda Welshimer
    See Wagner-Martin, Linda (C.)

Wagner, Richard 1813-1883 ..... **NCLC 9, 119**
    See also DLB 129; EW 6

Wagner-Martin, Linda (C.) 1936- .... **CLC 50**
    See also CA 159; CANR 135

Wagoner, David (Russell) 1926- .... **CLC 3, 5, 15; PC 33**
    See also AMWS 9; CA 1-4R; CAAS 3; CANR 2, 71; CN 1, 2, 3, 4, 5, 6, 7; CP 1, 2, 3, 4, 5, 6, 7; DLB 5, 256; SATA 14; TCWW 1, 2

Wah, Fred(erick James) 1939- .... **CLC 44**
    See also CA 107; 141; CP 1, 6, 7; DLB 60

Wahloo, Per 1926-1975 .... **CLC 7**
    See also BPFB 3; CA 61-64; CANR 73; CMW 4; MSW

Wahloo, Peter
    See Wahloo, Per

Wain, John (Barrington) 1925-1994 . **CLC 2, 11, 15, 46**
    See also CA 5-8R; 145; CAAS 4; CANR 23, 54; CDBLB 1960 to Present; CN 1, 2, 3, 4, 5; CP 1, 2, 3, 4, 5; DLB 15, 27, 139, 155; EWL 3; MTCW 1, 2; MTFW 2005

Wajda, Andrzej 1926- .... **CLC 16, 219**
    See also CA 102

Wakefield, Dan 1932- .... **CLC 7**
    See also CA 21-24R, 211; CAAE 211; CAAS 7; CN 4, 5, 6, 7

Wakefield, Herbert Russell 1888-1965 .... **TCLC 120**
    See also CA 5-8R; CANR 77; HGG; SUFW

Wakoski, Diane 1937- ...... **CLC 2, 4, 7, 9, 11, 40; PC 15**
    See also CA 13-16R, 216; CAAE 216; CAAS 1; CANR 9, 60, 106; CP 1, 2, 3, 4, 5, 6, 7; CWP; DAM POET; DLB 5; INT CANR-9; MAL 5; MTCW 2; MTFW 2005

Wakoski-Sherbell, Diane
    See Wakoski, Diane

Walcott, Derek 1930- . **BLC 1:3, 2:3; CLC 2, 4, 9, 14, 25, 42, 67, 76, 160; DC 7; PC 46**
    See also BW 2; CA 89-92; CANR 26, 47, 75, 80, 130; CBD; CD 5, 6; CDWLB 3; CP 1, 2, 3, 4, 5, 6, 7; DA3; DAB; DAC; DAM MST, MULT, POET; DLB 117, 332; DLBY 1981; DNFS 1; EFS 1; EWL 3; LMFS 2; MTCW 1, 2; MTFW 2005; PFS 6; RGEL 2; TWA; WWE 1

Waldman, Anne (Lesley) 1945- .... **CLC 7**
    See also BG 1:3; CA 37-40R; CAAS 17; CANR 34, 69, 116; CP 1, 2, 3, 4, 5, 6, 7; CWP; DLB 16

Waldo, E. Hunter
    See Sturgeon, Theodore (Hamilton)

Waldo, Edward Hamilton
    See Sturgeon, Theodore (Hamilton)

Walker, Alice 1944- .... **BLC 1:3, 2:3; CLC 5, 6, 9, 19, 27, 46, 58, 103, 167; PC 30; SSC 5; WLCS**
    See also AAYA 3, 33; AFAW 1, 2; AMWS 3; BEST 89:4; BPFB 3; BW 2, 3; CA 37-40R; CANR 9, 27, 49, 66, 82, 131; CDALB 1968-1988; CN 4, 5, 6, 7; CPW; CSW; DA; DA3; DAB; DAC; DAM MST, MULT, NOV, POET, POP; DLB 6, 33, 143; EWL 3; EXPN; EXPS; FL 1:6; FW; INT CANR-27; LAIT 3; MAL 5; MBL; MTCW 1, 2; MTFW 2005; NFS 5; PFS 30; RGAL 4; RGSF 2; SATA 31; SSFS 2, 11; TUS; YAW

Walker, Alice Malsenior
    See Walker, Alice

Walker, David Harry 1911-1992 ...... **CLC 14**
    See also CA 1-4R; 137; CANR 1; CN 1, 2; CWRI 5; SATA 8; SATA-Obit 71

Walker, Edward Joseph 1934-2004 .. **CLC 13**
    See also CA 21-24R; 226; CANR 12, 28, 53; CP 1, 2, 3, 4, 5, 6, 7; DLB 40

Walker, George F(rederick) 1947- .. **CLC 44, 61**
    See also CA 103; CANR 21, 43, 59; CD 5, 6; DAB; DAC; DAM MST; DLB 60

Walker, Joseph A. 1935-2003 .... **CLC 19**
    See also BW 1, 3; CA 89-92; CAD; CANR 26, 143; CD 5, 6; DAM DRAM, MST; DFS 12; DLB 38

Walker, Margaret 1915-1998 .... **BLC 1:3; CLC 1, 6; PC 20; TCLC 129**
    See also AFAW 1, 2; BW 2, 3; CA 73-76; 172; CANR 26, 54, 76, 136; CN 1, 2, 3, 4, 5, 6; CP 1, 2, 3, 4, 5, 6; CSW; DAM MULT; DLB 76, 152; EXPP; FW; MAL 5; MTCW 1, 2; MTFW 2005; RGAL 4; RHW

Walker, Ted
    See Walker, Edward Joseph

Wallace, David Foster 1962-2008 .... **CLC 50, 114, 271; SSC 68**
    See also AAYA 50; AMWS 10; CA 132; 277; CANR 59, 133; CN 7; DA3; MTCW 2; MTFW 2005

Wallace, Dexter
    See Masters, Edgar Lee

Wallace, (Richard Horatio) Edgar
1875-1932 .... **TCLC 57**
See also CA 115; 218; CMW 4; DLB 70;
MSW; RGEL 2

Wallace, Irving 1916-1990 .... **CLC 7, 13**
See also AITN 1; BPFB 3; CA 1-4R; 132;
CAAS 1; CANR 1, 27; CPW; DAM NOV,
POP; INT CANR-27; MTCW 1, 2

Wallant, Edward Lewis 1926-1962 ... **CLC 5,
10**
See also CA 1-4R; CANR 22; DLB 2, 28,
143, 299; EWL 3; MAL 5; MTCW 1, 2;
RGAL 4; RGHL

Wallas, Graham 1858-1932 .... **TCLC 91**

Waller, Edmund 1606-1687 .... **LC 86; PC 72**
See also BRW 2; DAM POET; DLB 126;
PAB; RGEL 2

Walley, Byron
See Card, Orson Scott

Walpole, Horace 1717-1797 ..... **LC 2, 49, 152**
See also BRW 3; DLB 39, 104, 213; GL 3;
HGG; LMFS 1; RGEL 2; SUFW 1; TEA

Walpole, Hugh (Seymour)
1884-1941 .... **TCLC 5**
See also CA 104; 165; DLB 34; HGG;
MTCW 2; RGEL 2; RHW

Walrond, Eric (Derwent) 1898-1966 . **HR 1:3**
See also BW 1; CA 125; DLB 51

Walser, Martin 1927- .... **CLC 27, 183**
See also CA 57-60; CANR 8, 46, 145;
CWW 2; DLB 75, 124; EWL 3

Walser, Robert 1878-1956 ..... **SSC 20; TCLC
18**
See also CA 118; 165; CANR 100; DLB
66; EWL 3

Walsh, Gillian Paton
See Paton Walsh, Jill

Walsh, Jill Paton
See Paton Walsh, Jill

Walter, Villiam Christian
See Andersen, Hans Christian

Walter of Chatillon c. 1135-c.
1202 .... **CMLC 111**

Walters, Anna L(ee) 1946- .... **NNAL**
See also CA 73-76

Walther von der Vogelweide c.
1170-1228 .... **CMLC 56**

Walton, Izaak 1593-1683 .... **LC 72**
See also BRW 2; CDBLB Before 1660;
DLB 151, 213; RGEL 2

Walzer, Michael (Laban) 1935- ...... **CLC 238**
See also CA 37-40R; CANR 15, 48, 127

Wambaugh, Joseph, Jr. 1937- ...... **CLC 3, 18**
See also AITN 1; BEST 89:3; BPFB 3; CA
33-36R; CANR 42, 65, 115, 167; CMW
4; CPW 1; DA3; DAM NOV, POP; DLB
6; DLBY 1983; MSW; MTCW 1, 2

Wambaugh, Joseph Aloysius
See Wambaugh, Joseph, Jr.

Wang Wei 699(?)-761(?) . **CMLC 100; PC 18**
See also TWA

Warburton, William 1698-1779 .... **LC 97**
See also DLB 104

Ward, Arthur Henry Sarsfield
1883-1959 .... **TCLC 28**
See also CA 108; 173; CMW 4; DLB 70;
HGG; MSW; SUFW

Ward, Douglas Turner 1930- .... **CLC 19**
See also BW 1; CA 81-84; CAD; CANR
27; CD 5, 6; DLB 7, 38

Ward, E. D.
See Lucas, E(dward) V(errall)

Ward, Mrs. Humphry 1851-1920
See Ward, Mary Augusta
See also RGEL 2

Ward, Mary Augusta 1851-1920 ... **TCLC 55**
See Ward, Mrs. Humphry
See also DLB 18

Ward, Nathaniel 1578(?)-1652 .... **LC 114**
See also DLB 24

Ward, Peter
See Faust, Frederick (Schiller)

Warhol, Andy 1928(?)-1987 .... **CLC 20**
See also AAYA 12; BEST 89:4; CA 89-92;
121; CANR 34

Warner, Francis (Robert Le Plastrier)
1937- .... **CLC 14**
See also CA 53-56; CANR 11; CP 1, 2, 3, 4

Warner, Marina 1946- .... **CLC 59, 231**
See also CA 65-68; CANR 21, 55, 118; CN
5, 6, 7; DLB 194; MTFW 2005

Warner, Rex (Ernest) 1905-1986 ...... **CLC 45**
See also CA 89-92; 119; CN 1, 2, 3, 4; CP
1, 2, 3, 4; DLB 15; RGEL 2; RHW

Warner, Susan (Bogert)
1819-1885 .... **NCLC 31, 146**
See also AMWS 18; DLB 3, 42, 239, 250,
254

Warner, Sylvia (Constance) Ashton
See Ashton-Warner, Sylvia (Constance)

Warner, Sylvia Townsend
1893-1978 .. **CLC 7, 19; SSC 23; TCLC
131**
See also BRWS 7; CA 61-64; 77-80; CANR
16, 60, 104; CN 1, 2; DLB 34, 139; EWL
3; FANT; FW; MTCW 1, 2; RGEL 2;
RGSF 2; RHW

Warren, Mercy Otis 1728-1814 ..... **NCLC 13**
See also DLB 31, 200; RGAL 4; TUS

Warren, Robert Penn 1905-1989 .. **CLC 1, 4,
6, 8, 10, 13, 18, 39, 53, 59; PC 37; SSC
4, 58; WLC 6**
See also AITN 1; AMW; AMWC 2; BPFB
3; BYA 1; CA 13-16R; 129; CANR 10,
47; CDALB 1968-1988; CN 1, 2, 3, 4;
CP 1, 2, 3, 4; DA; DA3; DAB; DAC;
DAM MST, NOV, POET; DLB 2, 48, 152,
320; DLBY 1980, 1989; EWL 3; INT
CANR-10; MAL 5; MTCW 1, 2; MTFW
2005; NFS 13; RGAL 4; RGSF 2; RHW;
SATA 46; SATA-Obit 63; SSFS 8; TUS

Warrigal, Jack
See Furphy, Joseph

Warshofsky, Isaac
See Singer, Isaac Bashevis

Warton, Joseph 1722-1800 ... **LC 128; NCLC
118**
See also DLB 104, 109; RGEL 2

Warton, Thomas 1728-1790 .... **LC 15, 82**
See also DAM POET; DLB 104, 109, 336;
RGEL 2

Waruk, Kona
See Harris, (Theodore) Wilson

Warung, Price
See Astley, William

Warwick, Jarvis
See Garner, Hugh

Washington, Alex
See Harris, Mark

Washington, Booker T(aliaferro)
1856-1915 .... **BLC 1:3; TCLC 10**
See also BW 1; CA 114; 125; DA3; DAM
MULT; DLB 345; LAIT 2; RGAL 4;
SATA 28

Washington, George 1732-1799 .... **LC 25**
See also DLB 31

Wassermann, (Karl) Jakob
1873-1934 .... **TCLC 6**
See also CA 104; 163; DLB 66; EWL 3

Wasserstein, Wendy 1950-2006 . **CLC 32, 59,
90, 183; DC 4**
See also AAYA 73; AMWS 15; CA 121;
129; 247; CABS 3; CAD; CANR 53, 75,
128; CD 5, 6; CWD; DA3; DAM DRAM;
DFS 5, 17; DLB 228; EWL 3; FW; INT
CA-129; MAL 5; MTCW 2; MTFW 2005;
SATA 94; SATA-Obit 174

Waterhouse, Keith (Spencer) 1929- . **CLC 47**
See also BRWS 13; CA 5-8R; CANR 38,
67, 109; CBD; CD 6; CN 1, 2, 3, 4, 5, 6,
7; DLB 13, 15; MTCW 1, 2; MTFW 2005

Waters, Frank (Joseph) 1902-1995 .. **CLC 88**
See also CA 5-8R; 149; CAAS 13; CANR
3, 18, 63, 121; DLB 212; DLBY 1986;
RGAL 4; TCWW 1, 2

Waters, Mary C. CLC 70

Waters, Roger 1944- .... **CLC 35**

Watkins, Frances Ellen
See Harper, Frances Ellen Watkins

Watkins, Gerrold
See Malzberg, Barry N(athaniel)

Watkins, Gloria Jean
See hooks, bell

Watkins, Paul 1964- .... **CLC 55**
See also CA 132; CANR 62, 98

Watkins, Vernon Phillips
1906-1967 .... **CLC 43**
See also CA 9-10; 25-28R; CAP 1; DLB
20; EWL 3; RGEL 2

Watson, Irving S.
See Mencken, H(enry) L(ouis)

Watson, John H.
See Farmer, Philip Jose

Watson, Richard F.
See Silverberg, Robert

Watts, Ephraim
See Horne, Richard Henry Hengist

Watts, Isaac 1674-1748 .... **LC 98**
See also DLB 95; RGEL 2; SATA 52

Waugh, Auberon (Alexander)
1939-2001 .... **CLC 7**
See also CA 45-48; 192; CANR 6, 22, 92;
CN 1, 2, 3; DLB 14, 194

Waugh, Evelyn 1903-1966 ... **CLC 1, 3, 8, 13,
19, 27, 44, 107; SSC 41; WLC 6**
See also AAYA 78; BPFB 3; BRW 7; CA
85-88; 25-28R; CANR 22; CDBLB 1914-
1945; DA; DA3; DAB; DAC; DAM MST,
NOV, POP; DLB 15, 162, 195; EWL 3;
MTCW 1, 2; MTFW 2005; NFS 13, 17;
RGEL 2; RGSF 2; TEA; WLIT 4

Waugh, Evelyn Arthur St. John
See Waugh, Evelyn

Waugh, Harriet 1944- .... **CLC 6**
See also CA 85-88; CANR 22

Ways, C.R.
See Blount, Roy, Jr.

Waystaff, Simon
See Swift, Jonathan

Webb, Beatrice (Martha Potter)
1858-1943 .... **TCLC 22**
See also CA 117; 162; DLB 190; FW

Webb, Charles 1939- .... **CLC 7**
See also CA 25-28R; CANR 114, 188

Webb, Charles Richard
See Webb, Charles

Webb, Frank J. NCLC 143
See also DLB 50

Webb, James, Jr.
See Webb, James

Webb, James 1946- .... **CLC 22**
See also CA 81-84; CANR 156

Webb, James H.
See Webb, James

Webb, James Henry
See Webb, James

Webb, Mary Gladys (Meredith)
1881-1927 .... **TCLC 24**
See also CA 182; 123; DLB 34; FW; RGEL
2

Webb, Mrs. Sidney
See Webb, Beatrice (Martha Potter)

Webb, Phyllis 1927- .... **CLC 18**
See also CA 104; CANR 23; CCA 1; CP 1,
2, 3, 4, 5, 6, 7; CWP; DLB 53

Wilson, (Thomas) Woodrow
1856-1924 .... **TCLC 79**
See also CA 166; DLB 47

Winchester, Simon 1944- .... **CLC 257**
See also AAYA 66; CA 107; CANR 90, 130

Winchilsea, Anne (Kingsmill) Finch
1661-1720
See Finch, Anne
See also RGEL 2

Winckelmann, Johann Joachim
1717-1768 .... **LC 129**
See also DLB 97

Windham, Basil
See Wodehouse, P(elham) G(renville)

Wingrove, David 1954- .... **CLC 68**
See also CA 133; SFW 4

Winnemucca, Sarah 1844-1891 .... **NCLC 79; NNAL**
See also DAM MULT; DLB 175; RGAL 4

Winstanley, Gerrard 1609-1676 .... **LC 52**

Wintergreen, Jane
See Duncan, Sara Jeannette

Winters, Arthur Yvor
See Winters, Yvor

Winters, Janet Lewis
See Lewis, Janet

Winters, Yvor 1900-1968 .. **CLC 4, 8, 32; PC 82**
See also AMWS 2; CA 11-12; 25-28R; CAP 1; DLB 48; EWL 3; MAL 5; MTCW 1; RGAL 4

Winterson, Jeanette 1959- .... **CLC 64, 158**
See also BRWS 4; CA 136; CANR 58, 116, 181; CN 5, 6, 7; CPW; DA3; DAM POP; DLB 207, 261; FANT; FW; GLL 1; MTCW 2; MTFW 2005; RHW; SATA 190

Winthrop, John 1588-1649 .... **LC 31, 107**
See also DLB 24, 30

Winthrop, Theodore 1828-1861 ... **NCLC 210**
See also DLB 202

Winton, Tim 1960- .... **CLC 251; SSC 119**
See also AAYA 34; CA 152; CANR 118; CN 6, 7; DLB 325; SATA 98

Wirth, Louis 1897-1952 .... **TCLC 92**
See also CA 210

Wiseman, Frederick 1930- .... **CLC 20**
See also CA 159

Wister, Owen 1860-1938 ..... **SSC 100; TCLC 21**
See also BPFB 3; CA 108; 162; DLB 9, 78, 186; RGAL 4; SATA 62; TCWW 1, 2

Wither, George 1588-1667 .... **LC 96**
See also DLB 121; RGEL 2

Witkacy
See Witkiewicz, Stanislaw Ignacy

Witkiewicz, Stanislaw Ignacy
1885-1939 .... **TCLC 8**
See also CA 105; 162; CDWLB 4; DLB 215; EW 10; EWL 3; RGWL 2, 3; SFW 4

Wittgenstein, Ludwig (Josef Johann)
1889-1951 .... **TCLC 59**
See also CA 113; 164; DLB 262; MTCW 2

Wittig, Monique 1935-2003 .... **CLC 22**
See also CA 116; 135; 212; CANR 143; CWW 2; DLB 83; EWL 3; FW; GLL 1

Wittlin, Jozef 1896-1976 .... **CLC 25**
See also CA 49-52; 65-68; CANR 3; EWL 3

Wodehouse, P(elham) G(renville)
1881-1975 .. **CLC 1, 2, 5, 10, 22; SSC 2, 115; TCLC 108**
See also AAYA 65; AITN 2; BRWS 3; CA 45-48; 57-60; CANR 3, 33; CDBLB 1914-1945; CN 1, 2; CPW 1; DA3; DAB; DAC; DAM NOV; DLB 34, 162; MTCW 1, 2; MTFW 2005; RGEL 2; RGSF 2; SATA 22; SSFS 10

Woiwode, L.
See Woiwode, Larry (Alfred)

Woiwode, Larry (Alfred) 1941- ... **CLC 6, 10**
See also CA 73-76; CANR 16, 94; CN 3, 4, 5, 6, 7; DLB 6; INT CANR-16

Wojciechowska, Maia (Teresa)
1927-2002 .... **CLC 26**
See also AAYA 8, 46; BYA 3; CA 9-12R, 183; 209; CAAE 183; CANR 4, 41; CLR 1; JRDA; MAICYA 1, 2; SAAS 1; SATA 1, 28, 83; SATA-Essay 104; SATA-Obit 134; YAW

Wojtyla, Karol (Jozef)
See John Paul II, Pope

Wojtyla, Karol (Josef)
See John Paul II, Pope

Wolf, Christa 1929- ...... **CLC 14, 29, 58, 150, 261**
See also CA 85-88; CANR 45, 123; CDWLB 2; CWW 2; DLB 75; EWL 3; FW; MTCW 1; RGWL 2, 3; SSFS 14

Wolf, Naomi 1962- .... **CLC 157**
See also CA 141; CANR 110; FW; MTFW 2005

Wolfe, Gene 1931- .... **CLC 25**
See also AAYA 35; CA 57-60; CAAS 9; CANR 6, 32, 60, 152; CPW; DAM POP; DLB 8; FANT; MTCW 2; MTFW 2005; SATA 118, 165; SCFW 2; SFW 4; SUFW 2

Wolfe, Gene Rodman
See Wolfe, Gene

Wolfe, George C. 1954- .... **BLCS; CLC 49**
See also CA 149; CAD; CD 5, 6

Wolfe, Thomas (Clayton)
1900-1938 .... **SSC 33, 113; TCLC 4, 13, 29, 61; WLC 6**
See also AMW; BPFB 3; CA 104; 132; CANR 102; CDALB 1929-1941; DA; DA3; DAB; DAC; DAM MST, NOV; DLB 9, 102, 229; DLBD 2, 16; DLBY 1985, 1997; EWL 3; MAL 5; MTCW 1, 2; NFS 18; RGAL 4; SSFS 18; TUS

Wolfe, Thomas Kennerly, Jr. 1931- .. **CLC 1, 2, 9, 15, 35, 51, 147**
See also AAYA 8, 67; AITN 2; AMWS 3; BEST 89:1; BPFB 3; CA 13-16R; CANR 9, 33, 70, 104; CN 5, 6, 7; CPW; CSW; DA3; DAM POP; DLB 152, 185 185; EWL 3; INT CANR-9; LAIT 5; MTCW 1, 2; MTFW 2005; RGAL 4; TUS

Wolfe, Tom
See Wolfe, Thomas Kennerly, Jr.

Wolff, Geoffrey 1937- .... **CLC 41**
See also CA 29-32R; CANR 29, 43, 78, 154

Wolff, Geoffrey Ansell
See Wolff, Geoffrey

Wolff, Sonia
See Levitin, Sonia

Wolff, Tobias 1945- .... **CLC 39, 64, 172; SSC 63**
See also AAYA 16; AMWS 7; BEST 90:2; BYA 12; CA 114; 117; CAAS 22; CANR 54, 76, 96; CN 5, 6, 7; CSW; DA3; DLB 130; EWL 3; INT CA-117; MTCW 2; MTFW 2005; RGAL 4; RGSF 2; SSFS 4, 11

Wolitzer, Hilma 1930- .... **CLC 17**
See also CA 65-68; CANR 18, 40, 172; INT CANR-18; SATA 31; YAW

Wollstonecraft, Mary 1759-1797 .... **LC 5, 50, 90, 147**
See also BRWS 3; CDBLB 1789-1832; DLB 39, 104, 158, 252; FL 1:1; FW; LAIT 1; RGEL 2; TEA; WLIT 3

Wonder, Stevie 1950- .... **CLC 12**
See also CA 111

Wong, Jade Snow 1922-2006 .... **CLC 17**
See also CA 109; 249; CANR 91; SATA 112; SATA-Obit 175

Wood, Ellen Price
See Wood, Mrs. Henry

Wood, Mrs. Henry 1814-1887 ...... **NCLC 178**
See also CMW 4; DLB 18; SUFW

Wood, James 1965- .... **CLC 238**
See also CA 235

Woodberry, George Edward
1855-1930 .... **TCLC 73**
See also CA 165; DLB 71, 103

Woodcott, Keith
See Brunner, John (Kilian Houston)

Woodruff, Robert W.
See Mencken, H(enry) L(ouis)

Woodward, Bob 1943- .... **CLC 240**
See also CA 69-72; CANR 31, 67, 107, 176; MTCW 1

Woodward, Robert Upshur
See Woodward, Bob

Woolf, (Adeline) Virginia 1882-1941 .. **SSC 7, 79; TCLC 1, 5, 20, 43, 56, 101, 123, 128; WLC 6**
See also AAYA 44; BPFB 3; BRW 7; BRWC 2; BRWR 1; CA 104; 130; CANR 64, 132; CDBLB 1914-1945; DA; DA3; DAB; DAC; DAM MST, NOV; DLB 36, 100, 162; DLBD 10; EWL 3; EXPS; FL 1:6; FW; LAIT 3; LATS 1:1; LMFS 2; MTCW 1, 2; MTFW 2005; NCFS 2; NFS 8, 12, 28; RGEL 2; RGSF 2; SSFS 4, 12; TEA; WLIT 4

Woollcott, Alexander (Humphreys)
1887-1943 .... **TCLC 5**
See also CA 105; 161; DLB 29

Woolman, John 1720-1772 .... **LC 155**
See also DLB 31

Woolrich, Cornell
See Hopley-Woolrich, Cornell George

Woolson, Constance Fenimore
1840-1894 .... **NCLC 82; SSC 90**
See also DLB 12, 74, 189, 221; RGAL 4

Wordsworth, Dorothy 1771-1855 . **NCLC 25, 138**
See also DLB 107

Wordsworth, William 1770-1850 .. **NCLC 12, 38, 111, 166, 206; PC 4, 67; WLC 6**
See also AAYA 70; BRW 4; BRWC 1; CD-BLB 1789-1832; DA; DA3; DAB; DAC; DAM MST, POET; DLB 93, 107; EXPP; LATS 1:1; LMFS 1; PAB; PFS 2; RGEL 2; TEA; WLIT 2; WP

Wotton, Sir Henry 1568-1639 .... **LC 68**
See also DLB 121; RGEL 2

Wouk, Herman 1915- .... **CLC 1, 9, 38**
See also BPFB 2, 3; CA 5-8R; CANR 6, 33, 67, 146; CDALBS; CN 1, 2, 3, 4, 5, 6; CPW; DA3; DAM NOV, POP; DLBY 1982; INT CANR-6; LAIT 4; MAL 5; MTCW 1, 2; MTFW 2005; NFS 7; TUS

Wright, Charles 1932-2008 ... **BLC 1:3; CLC 49**
See also BW 1; CA 9-12R; 278; CANR 26; CN 1, 2, 3, 4, 5, 6, 7; DAM MULT; POET; DLB 33

Wright, Charles 1935- ... **CLC 6, 13, 28, 119, 146**
See also AMWS 5; CA 29-32R; CAAS 7; CANR 23, 36, 62, 88, 135, 180; CP 3, 4, 5, 6, 7; DLB 165; DLBY 1982; EWL 3; MTCW 1, 2; MTFW 2005; PFS 10

Wright, Charles Penzel, Jr.
See Wright, Charles

Wright, Charles Stevenson
See Wright, Charles

Wright, Frances 1795-1852 .... **NCLC 74**
See also DLB 73

Wright, Frank Lloyd 1867-1959 .... **TCLC 95**
See also AAYA 33; CA 174

Wright, Harold Bell 1872-1944 .... **TCLC 183**
See also BPFB 3; CA 110; DLB 9; TCWW 2

Wright, Jack R.
See Harris, Mark
Wright, James (Arlington)
1927-1980 .... **CLC 3, 5, 10, 28; PC 36**
See also AITN 2; AMWS 3; CA 49-52; 97-100; CANR 4, 34, 64; CDALBS; CP 1, 2; DAM POET; DLB 5, 169, 342; EWL 3; EXPP; MAL 5; MTCW 1, 2; MTFW 2005; PFS 7, 8; RGAL 4; TUS; WP
Wright, Judith 1915-2000 ... **CLC 11, 53; PC 14**
See also CA 13-16R; 188; CANR 31, 76, 93; CP 1, 2, 3, 4, 5, 6, 7; CWP; DLB 260; EWL 3; MTCW 1, 2; MTFW 2005; PFS 8; RGEL 2; SATA 14; SATA-Obit 121
Wright, L(aurali) R. 1939- .... **CLC 44**
See also CA 138; CMW 4
Wright, Richard 1908-1960 .. **BLC 1:3; CLC 1, 3, 4, 9, 14, 21, 48, 74; SSC 2, 109; TCLC 136, 180; WLC 6**
See also AAYA 5, 42; AFAW 1, 2; AMW; BPFB 3; BW 1; BYA 2; CA 108; CANR 64; CDALB 1929-1941; DA; DA3; DAB; DAC; DAM MST, MULT, NOV; DLB 76, 102; DLBD 2; EWL 3; EXPN; LAIT 3, 4; MAL 5; MTCW 1, 2; MTFW 2005; NCFS 1; NFS 1, 7; RGAL 4; RGSF 2; SSFS 3, 9, 15, 20; TUS; YAW
Wright, Richard B. 1937- .... **CLC 6**
See also CA 85-88; CANR 120; DLB 53
Wright, Richard Bruce
See Wright, Richard B.
Wright, Richard Nathaniel
See Wright, Richard
Wright, Rick 1945- .... **CLC 35**
Wright, Rowland
See Wells, Carolyn
Wright, Stephen 1946- .... **CLC 33**
See also CA 237
Wright, Willard Huntington
1888-1939 .... **TCLC 23**
See also CA 115; 189; CMW 4; DLB 306; DLBD 16; MSW
Wright, William 1930- .... **CLC 44**
See also CA 53-56; CANR 7, 23, 154
Wroth, Lady Mary 1587-1653(?) .... **LC 30, 139; PC 38**
See also DLB 121
Wu Ch'eng-en 1500(?)-1582(?) .... **LC 7**
Wu Ching-tzu 1701-1754 .... **LC 2**
Wulfstan c. 10th cent. -1023 .... **CMLC 59**
Wurlitzer, Rudolph 1938(?)- .... **CLC 2, 4, 15**
See also CA 85-88; CN 4, 5, 6, 7; DLB 173
Wyatt, Sir Thomas c. 1503-1542 . **LC 70; PC 27**
See also BRW 1; DLB 132; EXPP; PFS 25; RGEL 2; TEA
Wycherley, William 1640-1716 .... **LC 8, 21, 102, 136**
See also BRW 2; CDBLB 1660-1789; DAM DRAM; DLB 80; RGEL 2
Wyclif, John c. 1330-1384 .... **CMLC 70**
See also DLB 146
Wylie, Elinor (Morton Hoyt)
1885-1928 .... **PC 23; TCLC 8**
See also AMWS 1; CA 105; 162; DLB 9, 45; EXPP; MAL 5; RGAL 4
Wylie, Philip (Gordon) 1902-1971 ... **CLC 43**
See also CA 21-22; 33-36R; CAP 2; CN 1; DLB 9; SFW 4
Wyndham, John
See Harris, John (Wyndham Parkes Lucas) Beynon
Wyss, Johann David Von
1743-1818 .... **NCLC 10**
See also CLR 92; JRDA; MAICYA 1, 2; SATA 29; SATA-Brief 27

Xenophon c. 430B.C.-c. 354B.C. ... **CMLC 17**
See also AW 1; DLB 176; RGWL 2, 3; WLIT 8
Xingjian, Gao 1940- .... **CLC 167**
See also CA 193; DFS 21; DLB 330; MTFW 2005; RGWL 3
Yakamochi 718-785 .... **CMLC 45; PC 48**
Yakumo Koizumi
See Hearn, (Patricio) Lafcadio (Tessima Carlos)
Yamada, Mitsuye (May) 1923- .... **PC 44**
See also CA 77-80
Yamamoto, Hisaye 1921- .... **AAL; SSC 34**
See also CA 214; DAM MULT; DLB 312; LAIT 4; SSFS 14
Yamauchi, Wakako 1924- .... **AAL**
See also CA 214; DLB 312
Yan, Mo
See Moye, Guan
Yanez, Jose Donoso
See Donoso (Yanez), Jose
Yanovsky, Basile S.
See Yanovsky, V(assily) S(emenovich)
Yanovsky, V(assily) S(emenovich)
1906-1989 .... **CLC 2, 18**
See also CA 97-100; 129
Yates, Richard 1926-1992 .... **CLC 7, 8, 23**
See also AMWS 11; CA 5-8R; 139; CANR 10, 43; CN 1, 2, 3, 4, 5; DLB 2, 234; DLBY 1981, 1992; INT CANR-10; SSFS 24
Yau, John 1950- .... **PC 61**
See also CA 154; CANR 89; CP 4, 5, 6, 7; DLB 234, 312; PFS 26
Yearsley, Ann 1753-1806 .... **NCLC 174**
See also DLB 109
Yeats, W. B.
See Yeats, William Butler
Yeats, William Butler 1865-1939 . **DC 33; PC 20, 51; TCLC 1, 11, 18, 31, 93, 116; WLC 6**
See also AAYA 48; BRW 6; BRWR 1; CA 104; 127; CANR 45; CDBLB 1890-1914; DA; DA3; DAB; DAC; DAM DRAM, MST, POET; DLB 10, 19, 98, 156, 332; EWL 3; EXPP; MTCW 1, 2; MTFW 2005; NCFS 3; PAB; PFS 1, 2, 5, 7, 13, 15; RGEL 2; TEA; WLIT 4; WP
Yehoshua, A.B. 1936- .... **CLC 13, 31, 243**
See also CA 33-36R; CANR 43, 90, 145; CWW 2; EWL 3; RGHL; RGSF 2; RGWL 3; WLIT 6
Yehoshua, Abraham B.
See Yehoshua, A.B.
Yellow Bird
See Ridge, John Rollin
Yep, Laurence 1948- .... **CLC 35**
See also AAYA 5, 31; BYA 7; CA 49-52; CANR 1, 46, 92, 161; CLR 3, 17, 54, 132; DLB 52, 312; FANT; JRDA; MAICYA 1, 2; MAICYAS 1; SATA 7, 69, 123, 176; WYA; YAW
Yep, Laurence Michael
See Yep, Laurence
Yerby, Frank G(arvin) 1916-1991 . **BLC 1:3; CLC 1, 7, 22**
See also BPFB 3; BW 1, 3; CA 9-12R; 136; CANR 16, 52; CN 1, 2, 3, 4, 5; DAM MULT; DLB 76; INT CANR-16; MTCW 1; RGAL 4; RHW
Yesenin, Sergei Aleksandrovich
See Esenin, Sergei
Yevtushenko, Yevgeny (Alexandrovich)
1933- ...... **CLC 1, 3, 13, 26, 51, 126; PC 40**
See also CA 81-84; CANR 33, 54; CWW 2; DAM POET; EWL 3; MTCW 1; PFS 29; RGHL; RGWL 2, 3

Yezierska, Anzia 1885(?)-1970 .... **CLC 46; TCLC 205**
See also CA 126; 89-92; DLB 28, 221; FW; MTCW 1; NFS 29; RGAL 4; SSFS 15
Yglesias, Helen 1915-2008 .... **CLC 7, 22**
See also CA 37-40R; 272; CAAS 20; CANR 15, 65, 95; CN 4, 5, 6, 7; INT CANR-15; MTCW 1
Y.O.
See Russell, George William
Yokomitsu, Riichi 1898-1947 .... **TCLC 47**
See also CA 170; EWL 3
Yolen, Jane 1939- .... **CLC 256**
See also AAYA 4, 22; BPFB 3; BYA 9, 10, 11, 14, 16; CA 13-16R; CANR 11, 29, 56, 91, 126, 185; CLR 4, 44; CWRI 5; DLB 52; FANT; INT CANR-29; JRDA; MAICYA 1, 2; MTFW 2005; SAAS 1; SATA 4, 40, 75, 112, 158, 194; SATA-Essay 111; SFW 4; SUFW 2; WYA; YAW
Yonge, Charlotte (Mary)
1823-1901 .... **TCLC 48**
See also CA 109; 163; DLB 18, 163; RGEL 2; SATA 17; WCH
York, Jeremy
See Creasey, John
York, Simon
See Heinlein, Robert A.
Yorke, Henry Vincent 1905-1974 ...... **CLC 2, 13, 97**
See also BRWS 2; CA 85-88; 175; 49-52; DLB 15; EWL 3; RGEL 2
Yosano, Akiko 1878-1942 ... **PC 11; TCLC 59**
See also CA 161; EWL 3; RGWL 3
Yoshimoto, Banana
See Yoshimoto, Mahoko
Yoshimoto, Mahoko 1964- .... **CLC 84**
See also AAYA 50; CA 144; CANR 98, 160; NFS 7; SSFS 16
Young, Al(bert James) 1939- .... **BLC 1:3; CLC 19**
See also BW 2, 3; CA 29-32R; CANR 26, 65, 109; CN 2, 3, 4, 5, 6, 7; CP 1, 2, 3, 4, 5, 6, 7; DAM MULT; DLB 33
Young, Andrew (John) 1885-1971 ...... **CLC 5**
See also CA 5-8R; CANR 7, 29; CP 1; RGEL 2
Young, Collier
See Bloch, Robert (Albert)
Young, Edward 1683-1765 .... **LC 3, 40**
See also DLB 95; RGEL 2
Young, Marguerite (Vivian)
1909-1995 .... **CLC 82**
See also CA 13-16; 150; CAP 1; CN 1, 2, 3, 4, 5, 6
Young, Neil 1945- .... **CLC 17**
See also CA 110; CCA 1
Young Bear, Ray A. 1950- ... **CLC 94; NNAL**
See also CA 146; DAM MULT; DLB 175; MAL 5
Yourcenar, Marguerite 1903-1987 ... **CLC 19, 38, 50, 87; TCLC 193**
See also BPFB 3; CA 69-72; CANR 23, 60, 93; DAM NOV; DLB 72; DLBY 1988; EW 12; EWL 3; GFL 1789 to the Present; GLL 1; MTCW 1, 2; MTFW 2005; RGWL 2, 3
Yuan, Chu 340(?)B.C.-278(?)B.C. . **CMLC 36**
Yu Dafu 1896-1945 .... **SSC 122**
See also DLB 328; RGSF 2
Yurick, Sol 1925- .... **CLC 6**
See also CA 13-16R; CANR 25; CN 1, 2, 3, 4, 5, 6, 7; MAL 5
Zabolotsky, Nikolai Alekseevich
1903-1958 .... **TCLC 52**
See also CA 116; 164; EWL 3
Zabolotsky, Nikolay Alekseevich
See Zabolotsky, Nikolai Alekseevich

Literary Criticism Series
Cumulative Topic Index

This index lists all topic entries in Gale's *Children's Literature Review* (CLR), *Classical and Medieval Literature Criticism* (CMLC), *Contemporary Literary Criticism* (CLC), *Drama Criticism* (DC), *Literature Criticism from 1400 to 1800* (LC), *Nineteenth-Century Literature Criticism* (NCLC), *Short Story Criticism* (SSC), and *Twentieth-Century Literary Criticism* (TCLC). The index also lists topic entries in the Gale Critical Companion Collection, which includes the following publications: *The Beat Generation* (BG), *Feminism in Literature* (FL), *Gothic Literature* (GL), and *Harlem Renaissance* (HR).

Topic Index

Topic Index

SSC Cumulative Nationality Index

Nationality Index

SSC-125 Title Index

ISBN-13: 978-1-4144-4204-4
ISBN-10: 1-4144-4204-1

90000

9 781414 442044